EDITORIAL ADVISORS

ASPEN PUBLISHERS

INFORMATION PRIVACY LAW

Third Edition

Daniel J. Solove
Professor of Law
George Washington University Law School

Paul M. Schwartz
Professor of Law
U.C. Berkeley Law School

AUSTIN BOSTON CHICAGO NEW YORK THE NETHERLANDS

Aspen Publishers
Attn: Permissions Department
76 Ninth Avenue, 7th Floor
New York, NY 10011-5201

To contact Customer Care, e-mail customer.care@aspenpublishers.com, call 1-800-234-1660, fax 1-800-901-9075, or mail correspondence to:

Aspen Publishers
Attn: Order Department
PO Box 990
Frederick, MD 21705

Printed in the United States of America.

1 2 3 4 5 6 7 8 9 0

ISBN 978-0-7355-7641-4

Library of Congress Cataloging-in-Publication Data

Solove, Daniel J., 1972-
Information privacy law / Daniel J. Solove, Paul M. Schwartz. — 3rd ed.
p. cm.
Includes index.
ISBN 978-0-7355-7641-4
1. Privacy, Right of — United States. 2. Data protection — Law and legislation — United States. 3. Confidential communications — United States. 4. Personality (Law) — United States. I. Schwartz, Paul M., 1959- II. Title.

KF1262.S66 2008
342.7308'58—dc22

2008034854

PREFACE

The rapid growth of the Internet, coupled with new business practices and new efforts by government to deploy technology for law enforcement and the administration of programs, has raised far-reaching questions about the future of privacy.

The role of law is central to many of these debates. To what extent can the law safeguard the right of privacy in an era of rapidly evolving technology? What competing interests must be considered? What is the appropriate role of the courts and the legislatures? These questions are not new, but they have acquired greater urgency as the law is asked to evaluate an increasingly complex array of privacy matters.

For lawyers, these developments have raised both new challenges and new opportunities. In the private sector, attorneys now routinely advise business clients about the development of privacy policies, compliance with privacy statutes, and privacy regulations in new markets. Attorneys litigate on behalf of clients who believe that their privacy has been violated, while others defend against these allegations. State attorneys general have become leading champions of privacy rights. Policymakers in government evaluate new legislative proposals both to expand and to limit privacy claims. Legal advisors on trade policy, technology development, consumer protection, and national security all consider privacy issues in the course of their work.

Clearly, privacy has emerged as one of the critical legal subjects in the modern era. Since the first edition of this book was published in 2003, the field of information privacy has grown tremendously. Many new laws have been passed, countless cases have been decided, and a litany of fascinating new issues has arisen. Courses in information privacy law are being offered at law schools around the country, and many lawyers devote their practice to information privacy issues.

This text provides a cornerstone for the study of information privacy law. Our goal is to provide a comprehensive and accessible introduction for the student and an authoritative reference for the practitioner. We have organized the book around the general topics and themes of this area of law. Information privacy law is a complicated and vast body of different types of legal protections, and our organizational choices reflect our aim of producing a clear and coherent synthesis of the field. When selecting cases, we have included the leading cases as well as endeavored to provide a solid historical background and a timely and fresh perspective on the major privacy issues facing lawyers in the twenty-first century. Important majority opinions are followed by equally important dissents. The text includes extensive notes and commentary, and it integrates cases and statutes with policy and jurisprudential perspectives. To facilitate discussion and debate, we have included excerpts from commentators with a wide range of viewpoints. Technical terms are clearly explained.

Information Privacy Law also draws heavily on recent developments in the high-tech field as well as international law. We anticipate that these factors will contribute significantly to the development of privacy law in the near future. The text also explores the major themes in the development of the field — the meaning of privacy, the reasonable expectation of privacy, the application of constitutional principles to new technologies, and the transformation of norms into legal frameworks. We hope that this text provides a useful introduction to the challenges of the field of information privacy now and in the future.

A Note on the Casebook Website. We strive to keep the book up to date between editions, and we maintain a web page for the book with downloadable updates and other useful information. We invite you to visit the website:

http://informationprivacylaw.com

The website contains links to useful news sites, blogs, and online resources pertaining to information privacy law issues. We also provide a list of recommended books that can be read in conjunction with this book.

A Note on the Statutory Supplement. For those who want to examine the full text of information privacy statutes and regulations, we recommend our statutory supplement, *Information Privacy: Statues and Regulations*, published separately. More information about this volume can be found at http://informationprivacylaw.com.

A Note on New Changes to the Book. We made many changes and updates to the book but have retained its basic organizational structure and pedagogical style. We added extensive new material on national security, data mining, NSA surveillance, data security breaches, online gossip and social network sites, and much more.

We have also improved the statutory coverage in many parts by adding more cases to illustrate the ways in which the statutes are interpreted and applied. We believe that this change will improve understanding of the statutes and provide for interesting classroom discussions. In particular, we added several cases for the Privacy Act (Chapter 6) and the Fair Credit Reporting Act (Chapter 7).

We added a short section on decisional privacy in Chapter 4. Some instructors commented to us that they wanted to spend more time covering the decisional privacy cases and their relationship to information privacy. We therefore added a section that covers the substantive due process privacy cases. Our focus is on the relationship between decisional and information privacy.

We reorganized Chapter 7 in a more thematic way, and we enhanced our coverage of data security and identity theft. We hope that these changes will make Chapter 7 even more lively, concrete, and accessible.

A Note on the Editing. We have deleted many citations and footnotes from the cases to facilitate readability. The footnotes that have been retained in the cases have been renumbered. When discussing books, articles, and other materials in the notes and commentary, we have included full citations in footnotes in order to make the text easier to read. We have also included many citations to additional works in the footnotes that may be of interest to the reader.

Daniel J. Solove
Paul M. Schwartz

September 2008

ACKNOWLEDGMENTS

Daniel J. Solove: I would like to thank Carl Coleman, Scott Forbes, Susan Freiwald, Tomás Gómez-Arostegui, Stephen Gottlieb, Marcia Hofmann, Chris Hoofnagle, John Jacobi, Orin Kerr, Raymond Ku, Peter Raven-Hansen, Joel Reidenberg, Neil Richards, Michael Risinger, Lior Strahilevitz, Peter Swire, William Thompson, and Peter Winn for helpful comments and suggestions. Charlie Sullivan and Jake Barnes provided indispensable advice about how to bring this project to fruition. Special thanks to Richard Mixter at Aspen Publishers for his encouragement and faith in this project. Thanks as well to the other folks at Aspen who have contributed greatly to the editing and development of this book: John Devins, Christine Hannan, Carmen Reid, Jessica Barmack, John Burdeaux, and Sandra Doherty. I would like to thank my research assistants Peter Choy, Monica Contreras, Carly Grey, Maeve Miller, James Murphy, Poornima Ravishankar, Sheerin Shahinpoor, John Spaccarotella, Tiffany Stedman, Eli Weiss, and Kate Yannitte. I would also like to thank Dean Fred Lawrence for providing the resources I needed.

Paul M. Schwartz: For their suggestions, encouragement, and insights into information privacy law, I would like to thank Ken Bamberger, Fred Cate, Malcolm Crompton, Chris Gulotta, Andrew Guzman, Chris Hoofnagle, Ted Janger, Ronald D. Lee, Lance Liebman, Steven McDonald, Deirdre Mulligan, Joel Reidenberg, Ira Rubinstein, Pam Samuelson, Lior Strahilevitz, Viktor Mayer-Schönberger, Peter Swire, Peter Winn, and William M. Treanor. I benefited as well from the help of my talented research assistants: Cesar Alvarez, Kai-Dieter Classen, Alpa Patel, Karl Saddlemire, and Laura Sullivan. Many thanks to my co-author, Daniel Solove. Many thanks as well to my mother, Nancy Schwartz, and to Laura Schwartz and Ed Holden; David Schwartz and Kathy Smith; and Daniel Schwartz.

A profound debt is owed Spiros Simitis. My interest in the subject of information privacy began in 1985 with his suggestion that I visit his office of the Hessian Data Protection Commissioner in Wiesbaden and sit in on meetings there. Through his scholarship, example, and friendship, Professor Simitis has provided essential guidance during the decades since that initial trip to Wiesbaden. My portion of the book is dedicated to Steffie, Clara, and Leo, with my gratitude and love.

Finally, both of us would like to thank Marc Rotenberg, who helped us shape the book in its first two editions and provided invaluable input.

We are grateful to the following sources for their permission to reprint excerpts of their scholarship:

Anita L. Allen, *Coercing Privacy*, 40 William & Mary L. Rev. 723 (1999). Used by permission. © 1999 by William & Mary Law Review and Anita L. Allen.

William C. Banks & M.E. Bowman, *Executive Authority For National Security Surveillance,* 50 Am. U. L. Rev. 1 (2000). Reprinted with permission.

Fred H. Cate, *The Privacy Problem: A Broader View of Information Privacy and the Costs and Consequences of Protecting It*, 4 First Reports 1 (March 2003). Reprinted with permission.

Julie E. Cohen, *Examined Lives: Informational Privacy*, 52 Stan. L. Rev. 1371 (2000). © 2000. Reprinted by permission of the Stanford Law Review in the format textbook via Copyright Clearance Center and Julie Cohen.

Mary DeRosa, *Data Mining and Data Analysis for Counterterrorism,* Center for Strategic and International Studies 6-8 (CSIS) (2004). Reprinted with permission.

Richard Epstein, *The Legal Regulation of Genetic Discrimination: Old Responses to New Technology,* 74 B.U. L. Rev. 1, 2-4, 8-13, 18-19 (1994). Reprinted with permission of Richard Epstein.

Amitai Etzioni, The Limits of Privacy 2-3, 213-214 (1999). © 1999 by Amitai Etzioni. Reprinted by permission of Basic Books, a member of Perseus Books, LLC and Amitai Etzioni.

Eric Goldman, *The Privacy Hoax,* Forbes (Oct. 14, 2002) available at http://www.ericgoldman.org/Articles/privacyhoax.htm. Reprinted with permission.

Lawrence O. Gostin, Health Information Privacy, 80 Cornell L. Rev. 451 (1995). Reprinted with permission.

Steven Hetcher, *The FTC as Internet Privacy Norm Entrepreneur*, 53 Vand. L. Rev. 2041 (2000). Reprinted with the permission of Steven Hetcher.

Orin S. Kerr, *A User's Guide to the Stored Communications Act — and a Legislator's Guide to Amending It,* 72 Geo. Wash. L. Rev. 1208 (2004). Reprinted with permission.

Orin S. Kerr, *The Fourth Amendment and New Technologies: Constitutional Myths and the Case for Caution*, 102 Mich. L. Rev. 801 (2004). © 2004 by the Michigan Law Review Association. Reprinted with permission.

Pauline T. Kim, *Privacy Rights, Public Policy, and the Employment Relationship*, 57 Ohio St. L.J. 671 (1996). Reprinted with permission.

Catharine A. MacKinnon, Toward a Feminist Theory of the State 190-193 (1989). © 1989 by Harvard University Press. Reprinted with permission.

Richard A. Posner, *The Right of Privacy,* 12 Ga. L. Rev. 393 (1978). Reprinted with permission.

Radhika Rao, *Property, Privacy and the Human Body,* 80 B.U. L Rev. 359 (2000). Reprinted with permission of the Boston University Law Review and Radhika Rao.

Joel Reidenberg, *E-Commerce and Trans-Atlantic Privacy,* 38 Hous. L. Rev. 717 (2001). Reprinted with permission.

Marc Rotenberg, *Fair Information Practices and the Architecture of Privacy (What Larry Doesn't Get)*, 2001 Stan. Tech. L. Rev. 1, 43 (2001). Reprinted with permission.

Paul M. Schwartz, *Privacy and Democracy in Cyberspace*, 52 Vand. L. Rev. 1609 (1999). Reprinted with the permission of Paul Schwartz.

Paul M. Schwartz, *Privacy and the Economics of Health Care Information*, 76 Tex. L. Rev. 1 (1997). © 1997 the Texas Law Review. Reprinted with permission.

Reva B. Seigel, *The Rule of Love: Wife Beating as Prerogative of Privacy*, 105 Yale L.J. 2117 (1996). Reprinted by permission of the *Yale Law Journal* Company and the William S. Hein Company, from the *Yale Law Journal,* vol. 105, pages 2117-2207.

Spiros Simitis, *Reviewing Privacy in an Informational Society*, 135 U. Pa. L. Rev. 707, 709-710, 724-726, 732-738, 746 (1987). © 1987 by the University of Pennsylvania Law Review. Reprinted by permission of the University of Pennsylvania Law Review and Spiros Simitis.

Richard Sobel, *The Degradation of the Moral Economy of Political Identity Under a Computerized National Identification System*, 8 B.U. J. Sci. & Tech. L. 37 (2002). Reprinted with permission.

Daniel J. Solove, *Conceptualizing Privacy,* 90 California Law Review 1087 (2002). © 2002 by the California Law Review.

Daniel J. Solove, *Reconstructing Electronic Surveillance Law*, 72 George Washington Law Review 1264 (2004). © 2004 by Daniel J. Solove.

Jeff Sovern, *Opting In, Opting Out, or No Options at All: The Fight for Control of Personal Information,* 74 Wash. L. Rev. 1033 (1999). Reprinted with permission.

Michael E. Staten & Fred H. Cate, *The Impact of Opt-In Privacy Rules on Retail Markets: A Case Study of MBNA*, 52 Duke L.J. 745 (2003). Reprinted with permission.

Alan Westin, Privacy and Freedom 7, 31-38 (1967). A study sponsored by the Association of the Bar of the City of New York. Reprinted with permission.

James Q. Whitman, *The Two Western Cultures of Privacy: Dignity Versus Liberty,* 113 Yale L.J. 1151 (2004). Reprinted with permission.

Peter A. Winn, *Online Court Records: Balancing Judicial Accountability and Privacy in an Age of Electronic Information*, 79 Wash. L. Rev. 307 (2004). Reprinted with permission.

INFORMATION PRIVACY LAW

CHAPTER 1

INTRODUCTION

A. INFORMATION PRIVACY, TECHNOLOGY, AND THE LAW

We live in a world shaped by technology and fueled by information. Technological devices — such as telephones, video and audio recording devices, computers, and the Internet — have revolutionized our ability to capture information about the world and to communicate with each other. Information is the lifeblood of today's society. Increasingly, our everyday activities involve the transfer and recording of information. The government collects vast quantities of personal information in records pertaining to an individual's birth, marriage, divorce, property, court proceedings, motor vehicles, voting activities, criminal transgressions, professional licensing, and other activities. Private sector entities also amass gigantic databases of personal information for marketing purposes or to prepare credit histories. Wherever we go, whatever we do, we could easily leave behind a trail of data that is recorded and gathered together.

These new technologies, coupled with the increasing use of personal information by business and government, pose new challenges for the protection of privacy. This book is about the law's response to new challenges to privacy. A significant amount of law regulates information privacy in the United States and around the world. Is this law responsive to the present and future dangers to privacy? Can information privacy itself endanger other important values? What duties and responsibilities must corporations, government agencies, and other private and public sector entities have with regard to personal data? What rights do individuals have to prevent and redress invasions to their privacy? When and how should privacy rights be limited? Does the war on terrorism require less privacy and more sharing of information? These are some of the questions that this text will address.

This book's topic is information privacy law. Information privacy concerns the collection, use, and disclosure of personal information. Information privacy is often contrasted with "decisional privacy," which concerns the freedom to make decisions about one's body and family. Decisional privacy involves matters such as contraception, procreation, abortion, and child rearing, and is at the center of a series of Supreme Court cases often referred to as "substantive due process" or "the constitutional right to privacy." But information privacy increasingly incorporates elements of decisional privacy as the use of data both expands and limits individual autonomy.

Information privacy law is an interrelated web of tort law, federal and state constitutional law, federal and state statutory law, evidentiary privileges, property law, contract law, and criminal law. Information privacy law is relatively new, although its roots reach far back. It is developing coherence as privacy doctrines in one area are being used to inform and structure legal responses in other areas. Information privacy law raises a related set of political, policy, and philosophical questions: What is privacy? Why is privacy important? What is the impact of technology on privacy? How does privacy affect the efforts of law enforcement and national security agencies to protect the public? What is the role of the courts, the legislatures, and the law in safeguarding, or in placing limits on, privacy?

Furthermore, one might wonder: Why study information privacy law? There are a number of answers to this question. First, in today's Information Age, privacy is an issue of paramount significance for freedom, democracy, and security. One of the central issues of information privacy concerns the power of commercial and government entities over individual autonomy and decision making. Privacy also concerns the drawing of rules that may limit this autonomy and decision making by necessarily permitting commercial and government entities access to personal information. Understood broadly, information privacy plays an important role in the society we are constructing in today's Information Age.

Second, information privacy is an issue of growing public concern. Information privacy has become a priority on the legislative agenda of Congress and many state legislatures. Information privacy problems are also timely, frequently in the news, and often the subject of litigation.

Third, there are many new laws and legal developments regarding information privacy. It is a growth area in the law. Increased litigation, legislation, regulation, as well as public concern over privacy are spurring corporations in a variety of businesses to address privacy. Lawyers are drafting privacy policies, litigating privacy issues, and developing ways for dot-com companies, corporations, hospitals, insurers, and banks to conform to privacy regulations. A new position, the Chief Privacy Officer, is a mainstay at most corporations. The leading organization of these officers, the International Association of Privacy Professionals (IAPP), boasts thousands of members. Attorneys increasingly are grappling with privacy issues — either through litigation of privacy violations or through measures to comply with privacy regulations and to prevent litigation. All of these developments demand lawyers who are well-versed in the grand scheme and subtle nuances of information privacy law.

Fourth, information privacy law is an engaging and fascinating topic. The issues are controversial, complex, relevant, and current. Few areas of law are more closely intertwined with our world of rapid technological innovation. Moreover, concerns regarding information privacy play an important role in debates regarding security in post 9-11 America. The study of privacy law also helps us understand how our legal institutions respond to change and may help prepare us for other challenges ahead.

SIDIS V. F-R PUBLISHING CORP.

113 F.2d 806 (2d Cir. 1940)

[William James Sidis (1898–1944) was perhaps the most famous child prodigy of his day. According to Amy Wallace's biography of Sidis, *The Prodigy*, he was able to read the *New York Times* at the age of 18 months.[1] By the time he was three, William had learned to operate a typewriter and used it to compose a letter to Macy's to order toys. At that age, he also learned Latin "as a birthday present for his father." That year, after his father taught him the Greek alphabet, he taught himself to read Homer with the aid of a Greek primer. By the time he started elementary school, at the age of six, he could speak and read at least eight languages. At the age of five, he had already devised a method for calculating the day of the week on which any given date occurred, and when he was seven years old, he wrote a book about calendars. At that time, he had already prepared manuscripts about anatomy, astronomy, grammar, linguistics, and mathematics. At the age of eight, he created a new table of logarithms, which used a base of twelve instead of the conventional ten. From early childhood on, Sidis was also passionately interested in politics and world events. According to Wallace, Sidis was one of the few child prodigies in world history whose talents were not limited to a single field.

In 1909, Harvard University permitted Sidis to enroll in it; he was 11 years old and the youngest student in the history of Harvard. Sidis also made the front pages of newspapers around the nation when on January 5, 1910, he delivered a two-hour lecture to the Harvard Mathematics Club. The *New York Times* featured Sidis on its front page of October 11, 1909, as "Harvard's Child Prodigy."[2]

Boris Sidis, William's father, was a distinguished physician, early pioneer of American psychology (and opponent of Sigmund Freud), and prolific author. In 1911, Boris published a book about his educational theories and his virulent opposition to the educational institutions of the day. At the time of the publication of this book, *Philistine and Genius*, William was 13, and in Wallace's description, "teetering on the edge of his endurance to public exposure." Although the book did not mention his son by name, it did discuss him and his accomplishments, which brought William additional publicity. Sarah Sidis, William's mother and herself a physician, had a domineering and deeply troubled relationship with her son. Neither she nor Boris did anything to shelter William from the great publicity that followed him from an early age and the tremendous stress that it created in his life.

When he graduated from Harvard at age 16, William told reporters: "I want to live the perfect life. The only way to live the perfect life is to live it in seclusion. I have always hated crowds." After graduating from college, Sidis accepted a teaching position at the Rice University in Houston. After a difficult eight months as a professor of mathematics there, William returned to Boston

---

[1] Amy Wallace, *The Prodigy* (1986).

[2] *Harvard's Child Prodigy: All Amazed at Mathematical Grasp of Youngest Matriculate, Aged 13 Years*, N.Y. Times (Oct. 10, 1909), at A1.

and enrolled in Harvard Law School in 1916. He left the law school in his last semester there without taking a degree.

From 1918 until a *New Yorker* article about him in 1937, Sidis engaged in socialist and other radical politics, published numerous newsletters, lived an active social life, addressed a monthly study group, wrote a treatise about the classification of streetcar transfers, and financed his life through a series of modest clerical jobs and sales of his patented "perpetual calendar." During this period, in 1925, Sidis also published *The Animate and the Inanimate.* In Wallace's view, this book is the first work on the subject of "black holes" in space as well as an extraordinary work in the field of cosmogony, or the study of the origins of the universe. The book did not receive a single review at the time and was ignored by academia.

Before 1937, Sidis had done an excellent job of avoiding publicity for a decade. In that year, however, a local paper, the *Boston Sunday Advertiser*, published an article about him. This was followed by the August 14, 1937, issue of the *New Yorker*, which contained a brief biographical sketch about Sidis, his life following his graduation from Harvard, and the subsequent decades during which he lived in obscurity.[3] The article was part of a regular feature of the magazine called "Where Are They Now?," which provided brief updates on the lives of famous figures of the past. The article was printed under the subtitle *April Fool*, a reference to the fact that Sidis was born on April Fool's Day. The article recounted the history of Sidis's life and his current whereabouts: "William James Sidis lives today, at the age of thirty-nine, in a hall bedroom of Boston's shabby south end." The article also contained numerous errors about Sidis's life.

A mystery still exists regarding the interview at the basis of this article. According to Wallace, Sidis's contemporary biographer, a member of the monthly study group, whom she refers to only as "John," had brought along a friend to one meeting. Several members of this group suspected that this woman, who was the daughter of a publisher at a large company, served as the basis for the *New Yorker*'s report. Yet, the mystery remains as this individual did not interview Sidis at the time of the monthly meeting. Wallace writes: "William always maintained that the entire article was a combination of imagination and old stories about him, and no strangers had gained access to his room." Another possibility is that Sidis spoke to someone without knowing that she was a reporter, which seems unlikely due to his aversion to publicity.

The *New Yorker* article described Sidis's famous childhood and then recounted his subsequent career as an insignificant clerk: "He seems to get a great and ironic enjoyment out of leading a life of wandering irresponsibility after a childhood of scrupulous regimentation." Sidis never remained at one job for too long because "his employers or fellow-workers [would] soon find out that he is the famous boy wonder, and he can't tolerate a position after that." According to Sidis: "The every sight of a mathematical formula makes me physically ill. . . . All I want to do is run an adding machine, but they won't let me alone." The article also described Sidis's dwelling, a small bedroom in a poor part of Boston and his personal activities, interests, and habits.

---

[3] J.L. Manley, *Where Are They Now?: April Fool!*, New Yorker 22 (Aug. 14, 1937).

In his legal action against the *Boston Sunday Advertiser*, Sidis won a settlement of $375. Sidis also sued F-R Publishing Corporation, the publisher of the *New Yorker*. Among his claims were a violation of his privacy rights under §§ 50-51 of the N.Y. Civil Rights Law.]

CLARK, C. J. . . . It is not contended that any of the matter printed is untrue. Nor is the manner of the author unfriendly; Sidis today is described as having "a certain childlike charm." But the article is merciless in its dissection of intimate details of its subject's personal life, and this in company with elaborate accounts of Sidis' passion for privacy and the pitiable lengths to which he has gone in order to avoid public scrutiny. The work possesses great reader interest, for it is both amusing and instructive; but it may be fairly described as a ruthless exposure of a once public character, who has since sought and has now been deprived of the seclusion of private life.

The article of December 25, 1937, was a biographical sketch of another former child prodigy, in the course of which William James Sidis and the recent account of him were mentioned. The advertisement published in the New York World-Telegram of August 13, 1937, read: "Out Today. Harvard Prodigy. Biography of the man who astonished Harvard at age 11. Where are they now? by J.L. Manley. Page 22. The New Yorker."

The complaint contains a general allegation, repeated for all the claims, of publication by the defendant of *The New Yorker*, "a weekly magazine of wide circulation throughout the United States." Then each separate "cause" contains an allegation that the defendant publicly circulated the articles or caused them to be circulated in the particular states upon whose law that cause is assumed to be founded. Circulation of the New York World-Telegram advertisement is, however, alleged only with respect to the second "cause," for asserted violation of New York law.

Under the first "cause of action" we are asked to declare that this exposure transgresses upon plaintiff's right of privacy, as recognized in California, Georgia, Kansas, Kentucky, and Missouri. Each of these states except California grants to the individual a common law right, and California a constitutional right, to be let alone to a certain extent. The decisions have been carefully analyzed by the court below, and we need not examine them further. None of the cited rulings goes so far as to prevent a newspaper or magazine from publishing the truth about a person, however intimate, revealing, or harmful the truth may be. Nor are there any decided cases that confer such a privilege upon the press. . . .

It must be conceded that under the strict standards suggested by [Warren and Brandeis in their article, *The Right to Privacy*] plaintiff's right of privacy has been invaded. Sidis today is neither politician, public administrator, nor statesman. Even if he were, some of the personal details revealed were of the sort that Warren and Brandeis believed "all men alike are entitled to keep from popular curiosity."

But despite eminent opinion to the contrary, we are not yet disposed to afford to all of the intimate details of private life an absolute immunity from the prying of the press. Everyone will agree that at some point the public interest in obtaining information becomes dominant over the individual's desire for privacy. Warren and Brandeis were willing to lift the veil somewhat in the case of public officers. We would go further, though we are not yet prepared to say how far. At least we would permit limited scrutiny of the "private" life of any person who has achieved, or has had thrust upon him, the questionable and indefinable status of a "public figure."

William James Sidis was once a public figure. As a child prodigy, he excited both admiration and curiosity. Of him great deeds were expected. In 1910, he was a person about whom the newspapers might display a legitimate intellectual interest, in the sense meant by Warren and Brandeis, as distinguished from a trivial and unseemly curiosity. But the precise motives of the press we regard as unimportant. And even if Sidis had loathed public attention at that time, we think his uncommon achievements and personality would have made the attention permissible. Since then Sidis has cloaked himself in obscurity, but his subsequent history, containing as it did the answer to the question of whether or not he had fulfilled his early promise, was still a matter of public concern. The article in *The New Yorker* sketched the life of an unusual personality, and it possessed considerable popular news interest.

We express no comment on whether or not the newsworthiness of the matter printed will always constitute a complete defense. Revelations may be so intimate and so unwarranted in view of the victim's position as to outrage the community's notions of decency. But when focused upon public characters, truthful comments upon dress, speech, habits, and the ordinary aspects of personality will usually not transgress this line. Regrettably or not, the misfortunes and frailties of neighbors and "public figures" are subjects of considerable interest and discussion to the rest of the population. And when such are the mores of the community, it would be unwise for a court to bar their expression in the newspapers, books, and magazines of the day.

Plaintiff in his first "cause of action" charged actual malice in the publication, and now claims that an order of dismissal was improper in the face of such an allegation. We cannot agree. If plaintiff's right of privacy was not invaded by the article, the existence of actual malice in its publication would not change that result. Unless made so by statute, a truthful and therefore non-libelous statement will not become libelous when uttered maliciously. A similar rule should prevail on invasions of the right of privacy. "Personal ill-will is not an ingredient of the offence, any more than in an ordinary case of trespass to person or to property." Warren and Brandeis, supra at page 218. Nor does the malice give rise to an independent wrong based on an intentional invasion of the plaintiff's interest in mental and emotional tranquility.

If the article appearing in the issue of August 14, 1937, does not furnish grounds for action, then it is clear that the brief and incidental reference to it contained in the article of December 25, 1937, is not actionable. . . .

[The court concluded that the second cause of action under N.Y. Civil Rights Law was properly dismissed as well. The second cause of action charged invasion of the rights conferred on plaintiff by §§ 50 and 51 of the N.Y. Civil Rights Law. Section 50 states: "A person, firm or corporation that uses for advertising purposes, or for the purposes of trade, the name, portrait or picture of any living person without having first obtained the written consent of such person, or if a minor of his or her parent or guardian, is guilty of a misdemeanor." Section 51 gives the injured person an injunction remedy and damages. The court found: "Though a publisher sells a commodity, and expects to profit from the sale of his product, he is immune from the interdict of Secs. 50 and 51 so long as he confines himself to the unembroidered dissemination of facts. . . . *The New Yorker* articles limit themselves to the unvarnished, unfictionalized truth."]

NOTES & QUESTIONS

1. ***Involuntary Public Figures.*** After losing his privacy suit against the *New Yorker,* Sidis sued it for libel for the false information in the story. Among his charges, he claimed that a reader of the article would think that he was a reprehensible character, disloyal to his country, a loathsome and filthy person in personal habits, suffered a mental breakdown, and was a fool, who lived in misery and poverty. The *New Yorker* settled this case out of court for a small amount of money, which Wallace estimates in her biography of Sidis at between $500 and $600.

   Sidis suffered from high blood pressure, and, approximately three months after receiving the settlement from the *New Yorker*, on July 17, 1944, he died from a cerebral hemorrhage and pneumonia. He was 46 years old and had $652.81 in his bank account.

   The life of William Sidis illustrates a man profoundly disturbed by being thrust by his parents into the limelight as a child and by the media hounding him. He tried to spend his adult life fleeing from being the focus of any public attention. If he had been an involuntary public figure in the past, should this affect whether he should be able to retreat from the public eye in the future? Does it matter that he became a public figure as a child, that is, that he did not voluntarily choose this status as an adult?

   The *Sidis* case suggests the principle that once one is a public figure, one is always a public figure. Can people who were once famous ever retreat into obscurity?

2. ***Who Was J.L. Manley? What Did He Try to Convey in His Article?*** The Sidis article was written by a "J.L. Manley." In a biography of James Thurber, the famous American humorist, Burton Bernstein reveals that Thurber used Jared L. Manley as a pseudonym.[4] Under this signature, Thurber wrote 24 profiles of onetime celebrities, including the Sidis piece. All pieces were based on the research of other reporters at the *New Yorker*, including the unnamed reporter who actually interviewed Sidis.

---

[4] *See* Burton Bernstein, *Thurber* 261 (1975). Bernstein writes:

> For all the distractions of city life and his sleepless schedule, Thurber was getting a lot of good work done. In early 1936, he began to write (really rewrite, since some of the New Yorker's best reporters, like Eugene Kinkead, were doing the research) a number of short, retrospective Profiles. His nonfiction craft rose to a new high in these excellent pieces, which lent themselves to his human approach.

Id. Bernstein also reveals that Jared L. Manley was a name that Thurber cobbled together when writing his first piece about an old boxer based on the initials of the boxer John L. Sullivan and "Manley" based on "the manly art of self-defense."

In Thurber's own account of his time at the *New Yorker*, he faulted the *Sidis* court on one matter: "[N]owhere was there any indication of what I thought had stood out all through my story, implicit though it was — my feeling that the piece would help to curb the great American thrusting of talented children into the glare of fame or notoriety, a procedure in so many cases disastrous to the later career and happiness of the exploited youngsters."[5]

3. ***J.D. Salinger's Letters.*** In 1998, Joyce Maynard wrote an autobiography, *At Home in the World*, that describes her romance with J.D. Salinger in the 1970s. J.D. Salinger, an acclaimed author who wrote *The Catcher in the Rye*, had long ago completely retreated from public life and adopted a highly secluded existence in New Hampshire. In 1999, Maynard auctioned the letters J.D. Salinger wrote to her. She received $156,500 for the letters from the auction at Sotheby's. CNN reported at that time, "California philanthropist Peter Norton, who bought the letters, said he plans to return them to Salinger." Should Salinger have a right to privacy in the disclosure of the letters? Copyright law does create a copyright interest in unpublished letters — which prevents not only the publication of the entire contents of the letters, but a paraphrase of the letters that is too close to the actual text of the letters. *See Salinger v. Random House, Inc.*, 811 F.2d 90 (2d Cir. 1987). Should privacy law provide Salinger with the right to sue over the writing of Maynard's book?
4. ***Girls Gone Wild.*** A company markets videotapes of young college women at spring break or Mardi Gras flashing and undressing. The women, often intoxicated, reveal their nudity in public and give their permission to use the video footage on the company's videotapes, which are called "Girls Gone Wild." Later on, when sober, some of the women regret their decision to be in the video. Have they waived all privacy rights to their nude images on the video if they sign a consent form? Or should they be entitled to have some time to reconsider? Should they not be able to sign away these rights even when sober? Others have sued claiming that they were just filmed in public without signing a consent form. Do they have a valid privacy claim even when they exposed themselves in public?
5. ***Privacy Inalienability.*** Do we care whether or not Sidis knew he was talking to a reporter as opposed to a new neighbor? Can we assume that anyone who talks to a reporter has abandoned a privacy interest in the information that she shares with the journalist? More broadly, to what extent should privacy interests be tradable, waiveable, or otherwise alienable?[6]
6. ***Googleization.*** The Internet makes the preservation and dissemination of information much easier. Information about a person can be easily discovered by "Googling" them — running a search on their name with the Internet search engine Google. Google will pull up dozens, sometimes hundreds of

[5] James Thurber, *My Years with Ross* (1959).

[6] Paul M. Schwartz, *Property, Privacy, and Personal Data*, 117 Harv. L. Rev. 2055, 2074 (2004).

thousands, of information fragments about a person. It is becoming increasingly difficult for people to hide their personal information, which used to fade into obscurity but is now preserved forever on the Internet. Youthful indiscretions become permanent baggage. Consider the plight of one Michael, who was briefly imprisoned as a minor. The information comes up on a Google search, and Michael finds that it is inhibiting his ability to date, since many of the women he dates inquire about his time in prison. They have obviously Googled him:

> "When you meet someone," Michael says, "you don't say, 'I had an affair one time,' or 'I was arrested for DUI once,' or 'I cheated on my taxes in 1984.'"... [W]hat Michael finds most disturbing are the sudden silences. "Instead of thinking, 'Was I curt last week?' or 'Did I insult this political party or that belief?' I have to think about what happened when I was 17."[7]

Is Sidis's claim to privacy quaint by today's standards? How do we protect privacy in a post-Google world?

7. ***The* Star Wars *Kid and the Numa Numa Dance.*** An overweight, awkward 15-year-old kid videotaped himself pretending to be a character from a *Star Wars* movie.[8] He swung around a golf ball retriever pretending that it was a light saber and made his own sound effects. Somebody found the video, digitized it, and posted it on the Internet. The video created a buzz on the Internet, and it was downloaded millions of times around the world. Versions of the video with music and special effects were soon posted. People made fun of the kid in various discussions throughout the Internet.

In December 2005, Gary Brolsma placed on the Internet a clip of himself lip-synching and dancing in a chair to a Romanian pop song.[9] He called his performance the "Numa Numa Dance." The video was featured on newsgrounds.com, a web site devoted to animation and videos, as well as elsewhere on the Internet. Newsgrounds.com alone soon received almost two million hits for the "Numa Numa Dance." Brolsma appeared on Good Morning America, and CNN and VHI showed his clip.

Suddenly, however, he decided that he disliked the attention. The *New York Times* reported that Brolsma "has now sought refuge from his fame in his family's small house on a gritty street in Saddle Brook." The article added: "According to his relatives, he mopes around the house. . . . He is distraught, embarrassed." His grandmother quoted him as saying: "I just want this to end."

Is this simply life in the Internet Age? Does it matter that the parents of the "*Star Wars* kid" alleged that the clip of their son was placed online without his permission? In contrast, Brolsma posted the video of his dance himself. Is

---

[7] Neil Swidey, *A Nation of Voyeurs: How the Internet Search Engine Google Is Changing What We Can Find Out About Each Other and Raising Questions About Whether We Should,* Boston Globe Mag., Feb. 2, 2003, at 10.

[8] Amy Harmon, *Fame Is No Laughing Matter for the "Star Wars" Kid,* N.Y. Times, May 19, 2003, at C3.

[9] Alan Feuer & Jason George, *Internet Fame Is Cruel Mistress for Dancer of the Numa Numa,* N.Y. Times, Feb. 26, 2005, at A1.

there something that the law can do to protect people like the *Star Wars* kid or Numa Numa dancer? If so, what?

As an update to the story of the Numa Numa Dance, Brolsma had gotten over his anguish at his fame. In September 2006, he released a second video, "New Numa" with corporate sponsorship at newnuma.com. The new video features Brolsma and members of a rock band, the Nowadays, and a new song. The video was released along a promotion that allowed the public to submit their own videos and win a share of $45,000 in prizes. Brolsma also offered a selection of t-shirts and a coffee mug for sale to the public.

B. INFORMATION PRIVACY LAW: ORIGINS AND TYPES

Information privacy law is a wide-ranging body of law, encompassing common law, constitutional law, statutory law, and international law. This section will provide a brief introduction to the various strands of information privacy law that will be covered throughout this book. It begins by looking in detail at the most important article ever written about privacy.

1. COMMON LAW

(a) The Warren and Brandeis Article

The common law's development of tort remedies to protect privacy is one of the most significant chapters in the history of privacy law. In the late nineteenth century, considerable concerns about privacy captured the public's attention, ultimately resulting in the 1890 publication of Samuel Warren and Louis Brandeis's pathbreaking article, *The Right to Privacy*.[10] According to Roscoe Pound, the article did "nothing less than add a chapter to our law."[11] Harry Kalven even hailed it as the "most influential law review article of all."[12] The clearest indication of the article's ongoing vitality can be found in the Supreme Court's decision *Kyllo v. United States*, 533 U.S. 27 (2001). The Brandeis and Warren article is cited by the majority, those in concurrence, and even those in dissent.

Several developments in the late nineteenth century created a growing interest in privacy. First, the press became increasingly sensationalistic. Prior to the Civil War, wide-circulation newspapers were rare. However, the development of a new form of sensationalistic journalism, known as "yellow journalism," made newspapers wildly successful. In 1833, Benjamin Day began publishing a newspaper called the *Sun* patterned after the "penny presses" in London (so named because they sold for a penny). The *Sun* contained news of scandals, such as family squabbles, public drunkenness, and petty crimes. In about four months,

---

[10] Samuel Warren & Louis Brandeis, *The Right to Privacy*, 4 Harv. L. Rev. 193 (1890).

[11] Quoted in Alpheus Mason, *Brandeis: A Free Man's Life* 70 (1946).

[12] Harry Kalven, Jr., *Privacy in Tort Law — Were Warren and Brandeis Wrong?*, 31 L. & Contemp. Probs. 326, 327 (1966).

the *Sun* had a circulation of 4,000, almost the same as the existing New York daily papers. Just two months later, the *Sun* was reaching 8,000 in circulation. Other penny press papers soon followed. In reporting on his travels in America, Charles Dickens observed that New York newspapers were "pulling off the roofs of private houses."[13] In his great novel of 1844, *The Life and Adventures of Martin Chuzzlewit*, he listed (imaginary) New York newspapers called *The Sewer, The Stabber, The Family Spy, The Private Listener, The Peeper, The Plunderer,* and *The Keyhole Reporter*.[14]

Between 1850 and 1890, newspaper circulation increased about 1,000 percent — from 100 papers with 800,000 readers to 900 papers with more than 8 million readers. Joseph Pulitzer and William Randolph Hearst became the leading rivals in the newspaper business, each amassing newspaper empires. Their highly sensationalistic journalism became the paradigm for yellow journalism.[15]

Second, technological developments caused great alarm for privacy. In their article, Warren and Brandeis pointed to the invention of "instantaneous photography" as a new challenge to privacy. Photography had been around for many years before Warren and Brandeis penned their article. However, the equipment was expensive, cumbersome, and complicated to use. In 1884, the Eastman Kodak Company introduced the "snap camera," a handheld camera that was small and cheap enough for use by the general public. The snap camera allowed people to take candid photographs in public places for the first time. In the late nineteenth century, few daily newspapers even printed drawings, let alone photographs. Warren and Brandeis, however, astutely recognized the potential for the new technology of cameras to be used by the sensationalistic press.

The question of the origin of Warren and Brandeis's article has led to considerable debate. Some scholars suggest that Warren and Brandeis were strongly influenced by an article written in 1890 by E.L. Godkin, a famous social commentator in his day.[16] In the article, Godkin observed:

> . . . Privacy is a distinctly modern product, one of the luxuries of civilization, which is not only unsought for but unknown in primitive or barbarous societies. . . .
>
> The chief enemy of privacy in modern life is that interest in other people and their affairs known as curiosity, which in the days before newspapers created personal gossip. . . . [A]s long as gossip was oral, it spread, as regarded any one individual, over a very small area, and was confined to the immediate circle of his acquaintances. It did not reach, or but rarely reached, those who knew nothing of him. It did not make his name, or his walk, or his

---

[13] Charles Dickens, *American Notes* (1842).

[14] Charles Dickens, *The Life and Adventures of Martin Chuzzlewit* (1844).

[15] For more information about yellow journalism, *see generally* Gini Graham Scott, *Mind Your Own Business: The Battle for Personal Privacy* 37-38 (1995); Robert Ellis Smith, *Ben Franklin's Web Site: Privacy and Curiosity from Plymouth Rock to the Internet* 102-20 (2000).

[16] *See* Elbridge L. Adams, *The Right to Privacy and Its Relation to the Law of Libel*, 39 Am. L. Rev. 37 (1905); Dorothy J. Glancy, *The Invention of the Right to Privacy*, 21 Ariz. L. Rev. 1 (1979).

> conversation familiar to strangers. . . . [G]ossip about private individuals is now printed, and makes its victim, with all his imperfections on his head, known to hundreds or thousands miles away from his place of abode; and, what is worst of all, brings to his knowledge exactly what is said about him, with all its details. It thus inflicts what is, to many men, the great pain of believing that everybody he meets in the street is perfectly familiar with some folly, or misfortune, or indiscretion, or weakness, which he had previously supposed had never got beyond his domestic circle. . . .
>
> In truth, there is only one remedy for the violations of the right to privacy within the reach of the American public, and that is but an imperfect one. It is to be found in attaching social discredit to invasions of it on the part of conductors of the press. At present this check can hardly be said to exist. It is to a large extent nullified by the fact that the offence is often pecuniarily profitable.[17]

Warren and Brandeis referred to Godkin's essay, and their article does bear some similarities to his work. One difference is that Godkin, although recognizing the growing threats to privacy, remained cynical about the possibility of a solution, expressing only the hope that attitudes would change to be more respectful of privacy. Warren and Brandeis had a different view. In their judgment, the law could and should provide protection for privacy.

Another theory suggests that incursions by journalists into the privacy of Samuel Warren inspired the article. Warren, a wealthy and powerful attorney in Boston, practiced law with Louis Brandeis, who later went on to become a U.S. Supreme Court Justice. In 1883, Samuel Warren married Mabel Bayard, the daughter of a prominent senator from Delaware, and set up house in Boston's Back Bay. The Warrens were among the Boston elite and were frequently reported on in the *Saturday Evening Gazette*, "which specialized in 'blue blood items,'" and "reported their activities in lurid detail."[18]

According to William Prosser, Warren was motivated to write the article because reporters intruded upon his daughter's wedding. However, this certainly could not have been the reason because in 1890, Warren's oldest daughter was not even ten years old![19] Most likely, the impetus for writing the article was Warren's displeasure about a number of stories in the *Gazette* about his dinner parties.[20]

Whatever inspired them to write, Warren and Brandeis published an article that profoundly shaped the development of the law of privacy.

---

[17] E.L. Godkin, *The Rights of the Citizen: To His Own Reputation*, Scribner's Mag. (1890); *see also* E.L. Godkin, *The Right to Privacy*, The Nation (Dec. 25, 1890).

[18] Mason, *Brandeis, supra*, at 46.

[19] *See* James H. Barron, *Warren and Brandeis*, The Right to Privacy, 4 Harv. L. Rev. 193 (1890): *Demystifying a Landmark Citation*, 13 Suffolk L. Rev. 875 (1979).

[20] *See* Smith, *Ben Franklin's Web Site, supra*, at 118-19. For further discussion of the circumstances surrounding the publication of the article, see Martin Burgess Green, *The Mount Vernon Street Warrens: A Boston Story, 1860–1910* (1989); Morris L. Ernst & Alan U. Schwartz, *Privacy: The Right to Be Let Alone* 45-46 (1962); Philippa Strum, *Brandeis: Beyond Progressivism* (1993); Lewis J. Paper, *Brandeis* (1983); Irwin R. Kramer, *The Birth of Privacy Law: A Century Since Warren and Brandeis*, 39 Cath. U. L. Rev. 703 (1990); Dorothy Glancy, *The Invention of the Right to Privacy*, 21 Ariz. L. Rev. 1, 25-27 (1979); Symposium, *The Right to Privacy One Hundred Years Later*, 41 Case W. Res. L. Rev. 643-928 (1991).

SAMUEL D. WARREN AND LOUIS D. BRANDEIS, *THE RIGHT TO PRIVACY*

4 Harv. L. Rev. 193 (1890)

> It could be done only on principles of private justice, moral fitness, and public convenience, which, when applied to a new subject, make common law without a precedent; much more when received and approved by usage.
>
> — Willes, J., in *Millar v. Taylor,* 4 Burr. 2303, 2312

That the individual shall have full protection in person and in property is a principle as old as the common law; but it has been found necessary from time to time to define anew the exact nature and extent of such protection. Political, social, and economic changes entail the recognition of new rights, and the common law, in its eternal youth, grows to meet the demands of society. Thus, in very early times, the law gave a remedy only for physical interference with life and property, for trespasses *vi et armis.*[21] Then the "right to life" served only to protect the subject from battery in its various forms; liberty meant freedom from actual restraint; and the right to property secured to the individual his lands and his cattle. Later, there came a recognition of man's spiritual nature, of his feelings and his intellect. Gradually the scope of these legal rights broadened; and now the right to life has come to mean the right to enjoy life, — the right to be let alone; the right to liberty secures the exercise of extensive civil privileges; and the term "property" has grown to comprise every form of possession — intangible, as well as tangible.

Thus, with the recognition of the legal value of sensations, the protection against actual bodily injury was extended to prohibit mere attempts to do such injury; that is, the putting another in fear of such injury. From the action of battery grew that of assault. Much later there came a qualified protection of the individual against offensive noises and odors, against dust and smoke, and excessive vibration. The law of nuisance was developed. So regard for human emotions soon extended the scope of personal immunity beyond the body of the individual. His reputation, the standing among his fellow-men, was considered, and the law of slander and libel arose. Man's family relations became a part of the legal conception of his life, and the alienation of a wife's affections was held remediable. Occasionally the law halted, — as in its refusal to recognize the intrusion by seduction upon the honor of the family. But even here the demands of society were met. A mean fiction, the action *per quod servitium amisit,*[22] was resorted to, and by allowing damages for injury to the parents' feelings, an adequate remedy was ordinarily afforded. Similar to the expansion of the right to life was the growth of the legal conception of property. From corporeal property arose the incorporeal rights issuing out of it; and then there opened the wide realm of intangible property, in the products and processes of the mind, as works of literature and art, goodwill, trade secrets, and trademarks.

This development of the law was inevitable. The intense intellectual and emotional life, and the heightening of sensations which came with the advance of

---

[21] Editors' Note: Latin — By or with force and arms.

[22] Editors' Note: Latin — Whereby he lost the services (of his servant).

civilization, made it clear to men that only a part of the pain, pleasure, and profit of life lay in physical things. Thoughts, emotions, and sensations demanded legal recognition, and the beautiful capacity for growth which characterizes the common law enabled the judges to afford the requisite protection, without the interposition of the legislature.

Recent inventions and business methods call attention to the next step which must be taken for the protection of the person, and for securing to the individual what Judge Cooley calls the right "to be let alone."[23] Instantaneous photographs and newspaper enterprise have invaded the sacred precincts of private and domestic life; and numerous mechanical devices threaten to make good the prediction that "what is whispered in the closet shall be proclaimed from the house-tops." For years there has been a feeling that the law must afford some remedy for the unauthorized circulation of portraits of private persons; and the evil of invasion of privacy by the newspapers, long keenly felt, has been but recently discussed by an able writer. The alleged facts of a somewhat notorious case brought before an inferior tribunal in New York a few months ago, directly involved the consideration of the right of circulating portraits; and the question whether our law will recognize and protect the right to privacy in this and in other respects must soon come before our courts for consideration.

Of the desirability — indeed of the necessity — of some such protection, there can, it is believed, be no doubt. The press is overstepping in every direction the obvious bounds of propriety and of decency. Gossip is no longer the resource of the idle and of the vicious, but has become a trade, which is pursued with industry as well as effrontery. To satisfy a prurient taste the details of sexual relations are spread broadcast in the columns of the daily papers. To occupy the indolent, column upon column is filled with idle gossip, which can only be procured by intrusion upon the domestic circle. The intensity and complexity of life, attendant upon advancing civilization, have rendered necessary some retreat from the world, and man, under the refining influence of culture, has become more sensitive to publicity, so that solitude and privacy have become more essential to the individual; but modern enterprise and invention have, through invasions upon his privacy, subjected him to mental pain and distress, far greater than could be inflicted by mere bodily injury. Nor is the harm wrought by such invasions confined to the suffering of those who may be made the subjects of journalistic or other enterprise. In this, as in other branches of commerce, the supply creates the demand. Each crop of unseemly gossip, thus harvested, becomes the seed of more, and, in direct proportion to its circulation, results in a lowering of social standards and of morality. Even gossip apparently harmless, when widely and persistently circulated, is potent for evil. It both belittles and perverts. It belittles by inverting the relative importance of things, thus dwarfing the thoughts and aspirations of a people. When personal gossip attains the dignity of print, and crowds the space available for matters of real interest to the community, what wonder that the ignorant and thoughtless mistake its relative importance. Easy of comprehension, appealing to that weak side of human nature which is never wholly cast down by the misfortunes and frailties of our neighbors, no one can be surprised that it usurps the place of interest in brains

[23] Cooley on Torts, 2d ed., p. 29.

capable of other things. Triviality destroys at once robustness of thought and delicacy of feeling. No enthusiasm can flourish, no generous impulse can survive under its blighting influence.

It is our purpose to consider whether the existing law affords a principle which can properly be invoked to protect the privacy of the individual; and, if it does, what the nature and extent of such protection is.

Owing to the nature of the instruments by which privacy is invaded, the injury inflicted bears a superficial resemblance to the wrongs dealt with by the law of slander and of libel, while a legal remedy for such injury seems to involve the treatment of mere wounded feelings, as a substantive cause of action. The principle on which the law of defamation rests, covers, however, a radically different class of effects from those for which attention is now asked. It deals only with damage to reputation, with the injury done to the individual in his external relations to the community, by lowering him in the estimation of his fellows. The matter published of him, however widely circulated, and however unsuited to publicity, must, in order to be actionable, have a direct tendency to injure him in his intercourse with others, and even if in writing or in print, must subject him to the hatred, ridicule, or contempt of his fellow-men, — the effect of the publication upon his estimate of himself and upon his own feelings not forming an essential element in the cause of action. In short, the wrongs and correlative rights recognized by the law of slander and libel are in their nature material rather than spiritual. That branch of the law simply extends the protection surrounding physical property to certain of the conditions necessary or helpful to worldly prosperity. On the other hand, our law recognizes no principle upon which compensation can be granted for mere injury to the feelings. However painful the mental effects upon another of an act, though purely wanton or even malicious, yet if the act itself is otherwise lawful, the suffering inflicted is *damnum absque injuria*.[24] Injury of feelings may indeed be taken account of in ascertaining the amount of damages when attending what is recognized as a legal injury; but our system, unlike the Roman law, does not afford a remedy even for mental suffering which results from mere contumely and insult, from an intentional and unwarranted violation of the "honor" of another.

It is not however necessary, in order to sustain the view that the common law recognizes and upholds a principle applicable to cases of invasion of privacy, to invoke the analogy, which is but superficial, to injuries sustained, either by an attack upon reputation or by what the civilians called a violation of honor; for the legal doctrines relating to infractions of what is ordinarily termed the common-law right to intellectual and artistic property are, it is believed, but instances and applications of a general right to privacy, which properly understood afford a remedy for the evils under consideration.

The common law secures to each individual the right of determining, ordinarily, to what extent his thoughts, sentiments, and emotions shall be communicated to others. Under our system of government, he can never be compelled to express them (except when upon the witness-stand); and even if he has chosen to give them expression, he generally retains the power to fix the

---

[24] Editors' Note: Latin — Loss or harm from something other than a wrongful act and which occasions no legal remedy.

limits of the publicity which shall be given them. The existence of this right does not depend upon the particular method of expression adopted. It is immaterial whether it be by word or by signs, in painting, by sculpture, or in music. Neither does the existence of the right depend upon the nature or value of the thought or emotion, nor upon the excellence of the means of expression. The same protection is accorded to a casual letter or an entry in a diary and to the most valuable poem or essay, to a botch or daub and to a masterpiece. In every such case the individual is entitled to decide whether that which is his shall be given to the public. No other has the right to publish his productions in any form, without his consent. This right is wholly independent of the material on which, or the means by which, the thought, sentiment, or emotion is expressed. It may exist independently of any corporeal being, as in words spoken, a song sung, a drama acted. Or if expressed on any material, as in a poem in writing, the author may have parted with the paper, without forfeiting any proprietary right in the composition itself. The right is lost only when the author himself communicates his production to the public, — in other words, publishes it. It is entirely independent of the copyright laws, and their extension into the domain of art. The aim of those statutes is to secure to the author, composer, or artist the entire profits arising from publication; but the common-law protection enables him to control absolutely the act of publication, and in the exercise of his own discretion, to decide whether there shall be any publication at all. The statutory right is of no value, *unless* there is a publication; the common-law right is lost *as soon as* there is a publication.

What is the nature, the basis, of this right to prevent the publication of manuscripts or works of art? It is stated to be the enforcement of a right of property; and no difficulty arises in accepting this view, so long as we have only to deal with the reproduction of literary and artistic compositions. They certainly possess many of the attributes of ordinary property: they are transferable; they have a value; and publication or reproduction is a use by which that value is realized. But where the value of the production is found not in the right to take the profits arising from publication, but in the peace of mind or the relief afforded by the ability to prevent any publication at all, it is difficult to regard the right as one of property, in the common acceptation of that term. A man records in a letter to his son, or in his diary, that he did not dine with his wife on a certain day. No one into whose hands those papers fall could publish them to the world, even if possession of the documents had been obtained rightfully; and the prohibition would not be confined to the publication of a copy of the letter itself, or of the diary entry; the restraint extends also to a publication of the contents. What is the thing which is protected? Surely, not the intellectual act of recording the fact that the husband did not dine with his wife, but that fact itself. It is not the intellectual product, but the domestic occurrence. A man writes a dozen letters to different people. No person would be permitted to publish a list of the letters written. If the letters or the contents of the diary were protected as literary compositions, the scope of the protection afforded should be the same secured to a published writing under the copyright law. But the copyright law would not prevent an enumeration of the letters, or the publication of some of the facts contained therein. The copyright of a series of paintings or etchings would prevent a reproduction of the paintings as pictures; but it would not prevent a publication of list or even a description of them. Yet in the famous case of *Prince Albert v. Strange*, the court held that the common-law rule prohibited not merely the reproduction of the etchings which the plaintiff and Queen Victoria had made for their own pleasure, but also "the publishing (at least by printing or writing), though not by copy or resemblance, a description of them, whether more or less limited or summary, whether in the form of a catalogue or otherwise." Likewise, an unpublished collection of news possessing no element of a literary nature is protected from piracy.

That this protection cannot rest upon the right to literary or artistic property in any exact sense, appears the more clearly when the subject-matter for which protection is invoked is not even in the form of intellectual property, but has the attributes of ordinary tangible property. Suppose a man has a collection of gems or curiosities which he keeps private: it would hardly be contended that any person could publish a catalogue of them, and yet the articles enumerated are certainly not intellectual property in the legal sense, any more than a collection of stoves or of chairs.

The belief that the idea of property in its narrow sense was the basis of the protection of unpublished manuscripts led an able court to refuse, in several cases, injunctions against the publication of private letters, on the ground that "letters not possessing the attributes of literary compositions are not property entitled to protection;" and that it was "evident the plaintiff could not have considered the letters as of any value whatever as literary productions, for a letter cannot be considered of value to the author which he never would consent to have published." But those decisions have not been followed, and it may now be considered settled that the protection afforded by the common law to the author of any writing is entirely independent of its pecuniary value, its intrinsic merits, or of any intention to publish the same and, of course, also, wholly independent of the material, if any, upon which, or the mode in which, the thought or sentiment was expressed.

Although the courts have asserted that they rested their decisions on the narrow grounds of protection to property, yet there are recognitions of a more liberal doctrine. Thus in the case of *Prince Albert v. Strange*, already referred to, the opinions both of the Vice-Chancellor and of the Lord Chancellor, on appeal, show a more or less clearly defined perception of a principle broader than those which were mainly discussed, and on which they both placed their chief reliance. Vice-Chancellor Knight Bruce referred to publishing of a man that he had "written to particular persons or on particular subjects" as an instance of possibly injurious disclosures as to private matters, that the courts would in a proper case prevent; yet it is difficult to perceive how, in such a case, any right of privacy, in the narrow sense, would be drawn in question, or why, if such a publication would be restrained when it threatened to expose the victim not merely to sarcasm, but to ruin, it should not equally be enjoined, if it threatened to embitter his life. To deprive a man of the potential profits to be realized by publishing a catalogue of his gems cannot *per se* be a wrong to him. The possibility of future profits is not a right of property which the law ordinarily recognizes; it must, therefore, be an infraction of other rights which constitutes the wrongful act, and that infraction is equally wrongful, whether its results are to forestall the profits that the individual himself might secure by giving the matter a publicity obnoxious to him, or to gain an advantage at the expense of his mental pain and suffering. . . .

These considerations lead to the conclusion that the protection afforded to thoughts, sentiments, and emotions, expressed through the medium of writing or of the arts, so far as it consists in preventing publication, is merely an instance of the enforcement of the more general right of the individual to be let alone. It is like the right not be assaulted or beaten, the right not be imprisoned, the right not to be maliciously prosecuted, the right not to be defamed. In each of these rights, as indeed in all other rights recognized by the law, there inheres the quality of being owned or possessed — and (as that is the distinguishing attribute of property) there may be some propriety in speaking of those rights as property. But, obviously, they bear little resemblance to what is ordinarily comprehended under that term. The principle which protects personal writings and all other personal productions, not against theft and physical appropriation, but against publication in any form, is in reality not the principle of private property, but that of an inviolate personality.

If we are correct in this conclusion, the existing law affords a principle which may be invoked to protect the privacy of the individual from invasion either by the too enterprising press, the photographer, or the possessor of any other modern device for recording or reproducing scenes or sounds. For the protection afforded is not confined by the authorities to those cases where any particular medium or form of expression has been adopted, not to products of the intellect. The same protection is afforded to emotions and sensations expressed in a musical composition or other work of art as to a literary composition; and words spoken, a pantomime acted, a sonata performed, is no less entitled to protection than if each had been reduced to writing. The circumstance that a thought or emotion has been recorded in a permanent form renders its identification easier, and hence may be important from the point of view of evidence, but it has no significance as a matter of substantive right. If, then, the decisions indicate a general right to privacy for thoughts, emotions, and sensations, these should receive the same protection, whether expressed in writing, or in conduct, in conversation, in attitudes, or in facial expression.

It may be urged that a distinction should be taken between the deliberate expression of thoughts and emotions in literary or artistic compositions and the casual and often involuntary expression given to them in the ordinary conduct of life. In other words, it may be contended that the protection afforded is granted to the conscious products of labor, perhaps as an encouragement to effort. This contention, however plausible, has, in fact, little to recommend it. If the amount of labor involved be adopted as the test, we might well find that the effort to conduct one's self properly in business and in domestic relations had been far greater than that involved in painting a picture or writing a book; one would find that it was far easier to express lofty sentiments in a diary than in the conduct of a noble life. If the test of deliberateness of the act be adopted, much casual correspondence which is now accorded full protection would be excluded from the beneficent operation of existing rules. After the decisions denying the distinction attempted to be made between those literary productions which it was intended to publish and those which it was not, all considerations of the amount of labor involved, the degree of deliberation, the value of the product, and the intention of publishing must be abandoned, and no basis is discerned upon which the right to restrain publication and reproduction of such so-called literary and artistic works can be rested, except the right to privacy, as a part of the more general right to the immunity of the person, — the right to one's personality.

It should be stated that, in some instances where protection has been afforded against wrongful publication, the jurisdiction has been asserted, not on the ground of property, or at least not wholly on that ground, but upon the ground of an alleged breach of an implied contract or of a trust or confidence. . . .

This process of implying a term in a contract, or of implying a trust (particularly where the contract is written, and where there is no established usage or custom), is nothing more nor less than a judicial declaration that public morality, private justice, and general convenience demand the recognition of such a rule, and that the publication under similar circumstances would be considered an intolerable abuse. So long as these circumstances happen to present a contract upon which such a term can be engrafted by the judicial mind, or to supply relations upon which a trust or confidence can be erected, there may be no objection to working out the desired protection through the doctrines of contract or of trust. But the court can hardly stop there. The narrower doctrine may have satisfied the demands of society at a time when the abuse to be guarded against could rarely have arisen without violating a contract or a special confidence; but now that modern devices afford abundant opportunities for the perpetration of such wrongs without any participation by the injured party, the protection granted by the law must be placed upon a broader foundation. While, for instance, the state of the photographic art was such that one's picture could seldom be taken without his consciously "sitting" for the purpose, the law of contract or of trust might afford the prudent man sufficient safeguards against the improper circulation of his portrait; but since the latest advances in photographic art have rendered it possible to take pictures surreptitiously, the doctrines of contract and of trust are inadequate to support the required protection, and the law of tort must be resorted to. The right of property in its widest sense, including all possession, including all rights and privileges, and hence embracing the right to an inviolate personality, affords alone that broad basis upon which the protection which the individual demands can be rested.

Thus, the courts, in searching for some principle upon which the publication of private letters could be enjoined, naturally came upon the ideas of a breach of confidence, and of an implied contract; but it required little consideration to discern that this doctrine could not afford all the protection required, since it would not support the court in granting a remedy against a stranger; and so the theory of property in the contents of letters was adopted. Indeed, it is difficult to conceive on what theory of the law the casual recipient of a letter, who proceeds to publish it, is guilty of a breach of contract, express or implied, or of any breach of trust, in the ordinary acceptation of that term. Suppose a letter has been addressed to him without his solicitation. He opens it, and reads. Surely, he has not made any contract; he has not accepted any trust. He cannot, by opening and reading the letter, have come under any obligation save what the law declares; and, however expressed, that obligation is simply to observe the legal right of the sender, whatever it may be, and whether it be called his right or property in the contents of the letter, or his right to privacy. . . .

We must therefore conclude that the rights, so protected, whatever their exact nature, are not rights arising from contract or from special trust, but are rights as against the world; and, as above stated, the principle which has been applied to protect these rights is in reality not the principle of private property, unless that word be used in an extended and unusual sense. The principle which protects personal writings and any other productions of the intellect of or the emotions, is the right to privacy, and the law has no new principle to formulate when it extends this protection to the personal appearance, sayings, acts, and to personal relation, domestic or otherwise.

If the invasion of privacy constitutes a legal *injuria*, the elements for demanding redress exist, since already the value of mental suffering, caused by an act wrongful in itself, is recognized as a basis for compensation.

The right of one who has remained a private individual, to prevent his public portraiture, presents the simplest case for such extension; the right to protect one's self from pen portraiture, from a discussion by the press of one's private affairs, would be a more important and far-reaching one. If casual and unimportant statements in a letter, if handiwork, however inartistic and valueless, if possessions of all sorts are protected not only against reproduction, but against description and enumeration, how much more should the acts and sayings of a man in his social and domestic relations be guarded from ruthless publicity. If you may not reproduce a woman's face photographically without her consent, how much less should be tolerated the reproduction of her face, her form, and her actions, by graphic descriptions colored to suit a gross and depraved imagination.

The right to privacy, limited as such right must necessarily be, has already found expression in the law of France.

It remains to consider what are the limitations of this right to privacy, and what remedies may be granted for the enforcement of the right. To determine in advance of experience the exact line at which the dignity and convenience of the individual must yield to the demands of the public welfare or of private justice would be a difficult task; but the more general rules are furnished by the legal analogies already developed in the law of slander and libel, and in the law of literary and artistic property.

1. The right to privacy does not prohibit any publication of matter which is of public or general interest.

In determining the scope of this rule, aid would be afforded by the analogy, in the law of libel and slander, of cases which deal with the qualified privilege of comment and criticism on matters of public and general interest. There are of course difficulties in applying such a rule; but they are inherent in the subject-matter, and are certainly no greater than those which exist in many other branches of the law, — for instance, in that large class of cases in which the reasonableness or unreasonableness of an act is made the test of liability. The design of the law must be to protect those persons with whose affairs the community has no legitimate concern, from being dragged into an undesirable and undesired publicity and to protect all persons, whatsoever; their position or station, from having matters which they may properly prefer to keep private, made public against their will. It is the unwarranted invasion of individual privacy which is reprehended, and to be, so far as possible, prevented. The distinction, however, noted in the above statement is obvious and fundamental.

There are persons who may reasonably claim as a right, protection from the notoriety entailed by being made the victims of journalistic enterprise. There are others who, in varying degrees, have renounced the right to live their lives screened from public observation. Matters which men of the first class may justly contend, concern themselves alone, may in those of the second be the subject of legitimate interest to their fellow-citizens. Peculiarities of manner and person, which in the ordinary individual should be free from comment, may acquire a public importance, if found in a candidate for public office. Some further discrimination is necessary, therefore, than to class facts or deeds as public or private according to a standard to be applied to the fact or deed *per se*. To publish of a modest and retiring individual that he suffers from an impediment in his speech or that he cannot spell correctly, is an unwarranted, if not an unexampled, infringement of his rights, while to state and comment on the same characteristics found in a would-be congressman could not be regarded as beyond the pale of propriety.

The general object in view is to protect the privacy of private life, and to whatever degree and in whatever connection a man's life has ceased to be private, before the publication under consideration has been made, to that extent the protection is to be withdrawn. Since, then, the propriety of publishing the very same facts may depend wholly upon the person concerning whom they are published, no fixed formula can be used to prohibit obnoxious publications. Any rule of liability adopted must have in it an elasticity which shall take account of the varying circumstances of each case, — a necessity which unfortunately renders such a doctrine not only more difficult of application, but also to a certain extent uncertain in its operation and easily rendered abortive. Besides, it is only the more flagrant breaches of decency and propriety that could in practice be reached, and it is not perhaps desirable even to attempt to repress everything which the nicest taste and keenest sense of the respect due to private life would condemn.

In general, then, the matters of which the publication should be repressed may be described as those which concern the private life, habits, acts, and relations of an individual, and have no legitimate connection with his fitness for a public office which he seeks or for which he is suggested, or for any public or quasi public position which he seeks or for which he is suggested, and have no legitimate relation to or bearing upon any act done by him in a public or quasi public capacity. The foregoing is not designed as a wholly accurate or exhaustive definition, since that which must ultimately in a vast number of cases become a question of individual judgment and opinion is incapable of such definition; but it is an attempt to indicate broadly the class of matters referred to. Some things all men alike are entitled to keep from popular curiosity, whether in public life or not, while others are only private because the persons concerned have not assumed a position which makes their doings legitimate matters of public investigation.

2. The right to privacy does not prohibit the communication of any matter, though in its nature private, when the publication is made under circumstances which would render it a privileged communication according to the law of slander and libel.

Under this rule, the right to privacy is not invaded by any publication made in a court of justice, in legislative bodies, or the committees of those bodies; in municipal assemblies, or the committees of such assemblies, or practically by any communication made in any other public body, municipal or parochial, or in any body quasi public, like the large voluntary associations formed for almost every purpose of benevolence, business, or other general interest; and (at least in many jurisdictions) reports of any such proceedings would in some measure be accorded a like privilege. Nor would the rule prohibit any publication made by one in the discharge of some public or private duty, whether legal or moral, or in conduct of one's own affairs, in matters where his own interest is concerned.

3. The law would probably not grant any redress for the invasion of privacy by oral publication in the absence of special damage.

The same reasons exist for distinguishing between oral and written publications of private matters, as is afforded in the law of defamation by the restricted liability for slander as compared with the liability for libel. The injury resulting from such oral communications would ordinarily be so trifling that the law might well, in the interest of free speech, disregard it altogether.

4. The right to privacy ceases upon the publication of the facts by the individual, or with his consent.

This is but another application of the rule which has become familiar in the law of literary and artistic property. The cases there decided establish also what should be deemed a publication, — the important principle in this connection being that a private communication of circulation for a restricted purpose is not a publication within the meaning of the law.

5. The truth of the matter published does not afford a defence. Obviously this branch of the law should have no concern with the truth or falsehood of the matters published. It is not for injury to the individual's character that redress or prevention is sought, but for injury to the right of privacy. For the former, the law of slander and libel provides perhaps a sufficient safeguard. The latter implies the right not merely to prevent inaccurate portrayal of private life, but to prevent its being depicted at all.

6. The absence of "malice" in the publisher does not afford a defence.

Personal ill-will is not an ingredient of the offence, any more than in an ordinary case of trespass to person or to property. Such malice is never necessary to be shown in an action for libel or slander at common law, except in rebuttal of some defence, *e.g.*, that the occasion rendered the communication privileged, or, under the statutes in this State and elsewhere, that the statement complained of was true. The invasion of the privacy that is to be protected is equally complete and equally injurious, whether the motives by which the speaker or writer was actuated are, taken by themselves, culpable or not; just as the damage to character, and to some extent the tendency to provoke a breach of the peace, is equally the result of defamation without regard to the motives leading to its publication. Viewed as a wrong to the individual, this rule is the same pervading the whole law of torts, by which one is held responsible for his intentional acts, even though they are committed with no sinister intent; and viewed as a wrong to society, it is the same principle adopted in a large category of statutory offences.

The remedies for an invasion of the right of privacy are also suggested by those administered in the law of defamation, and in the law of literary and artistic property, namely: —

1. An action of tort for damages in all cases. Even in the absence of special damages, substantial compensation could be allowed for injury to feelings as in the action of slander and libel.

2. An injunction, in perhaps a very limited class of cases.

It would doubtless be desirable that the privacy of the individual should receive the added protection of the criminal law, but for this, legislation would be required. Perhaps it would be deemed proper to bring the criminal liability for such publication within narrower limits; but that the community has an interest in preventing such invasions of privacy, sufficiently strong to justify the introduction of such a remedy, cannot be doubted. Still, the protection of society must come mainly through a recognition of the rights of the individual. Each man is responsible for his own acts and omissions only. If he condones what he reprobates, with a weapon at hand equal to his defence, he is responsible for the results. If he resists, public opinion will rally to his support. Has he then such a weapon? It is believed that the common law provides him with one, forged in the slow fire of the centuries, and to-day fitly tempered to his hand. The common law has always recognized a man's house as his castle, impregnable, often, even to its own officers engaged in the execution of its command. Shall the courts thus close the front entrance to constituted authority, and open wide the back door to idle or prurient curiosity?

NOTES & QUESTIONS

1. ***The Need for a New Right.*** The article argued for the creation of a new right — the right to privacy. Why did the authors believe that other legal claims were inadequate? For example, why does the law of defamation or the law of contracts not provide a sufficient remedy for the harm described by the authors? Why do Warren and Brandeis reject property rights and copyright as tools to protect privacy?

2. ***Deriving a Right to Privacy in the Common Law.*** How do Warren and Brandeis derive a right to privacy from the common law? Under what principle do they locate this right? In a footnote in the article, Warren and Brandeis observe:

> The application of an existing principle to a new state of facts is not judicial legislation. To call it such is to assert that the existing body of law consists practically of the statutes and decided cases, and to deny that the principles (of which these cases are ordinarily said to be evidence) exist at all. It is not the application of an existing principle to new cases, but the introduction of a new principle, which is properly termed judicial legislation.
>
> But even the fact that a certain decision would involve judicial legislation should not be taken against the property of making it. This power has been commonly exercised by our judges, when applying to a new subject principles of private justice, moral fitness, and public convenience. Indeed, the elasticity of our law, its adaptability to new conditions, the capacity for

> growth, which has enabled it to meet the wants of an ever changing society and to apply immediate relief for every recognized wrong, have been its greatest boast. . . .

Why do they include this footnote? Do you agree with their argument?

3. ***Inviolate Personality.*** The authors describe privacy as not "the principle of private property but that of inviolate personality." What does that mean? James Whitman traces the idea of the personality right from Warren and Brandeis back to nineteenth-century German legal philosophy:

> . . . [N]ineteenth-century Germans often thought of "freedom" as opposed primarily to determinism. To be free was, in the first instance, not to be free from government control, nor to be free to engage in market transactions. Instead, to be free was to exercise free will, and the defining characteristic of creatures with free will was that they were unpredictably individual, creatures whom no science of mechanics or biology could ever capture in their full richness. For Germans who thought of things in this way, the purpose of "freedom" was to allow each individual fully to realize his potential as an individual: to give full expression to his peculiar capacities and powers.[25]

What interests are protected by this right? Is this a unified view of privacy, or are there differing interests?

4. ***"The Right to Be Let Alone."*** Warren and Brandeis refer to privacy as "the right to be let alone." This phrase was coined by Judge Thomas Cooley earlier in his famous treatise on torts.[26] Do Warren and Brandeis define what privacy is or elaborate upon what being "let alone" consists of? If so, what do they say privacy is? Is this a good account of what constitutes privacy?
5. ***The Scope of the Right to Privacy.*** Brandeis and Warren were careful not to describe privacy as an absolute right. They set out six limitations on the right to privacy. Consider the first limitation and the relationship between the right to privacy and the need for publication on matters of public concern. What conclusions do the authors reach about these competing claims? According to Warren and Brandeis, would the reporting that a public official engaged in illegal business practices be protected by a right to privacy? What about illicit sexual activity? Consider the holding of the *Sidis* court regarding a person who was once of public interest due to his great achievements. Do you think that Warren and Brandeis would agree with the conclusion of *Sidis*?
6. ***The Nature of the Injury Caused by Privacy Invasions.*** Warren and Brandeis argue that privacy invasions are more harmful than bodily injuries. Do you agree? Warren and Brandeis characterize the injury caused by the violation of privacy as an injury to the feelings. Do you agree? Or do you think that the injury extends beyond an injury to the feelings?
7. ***Remedies.*** Brandeis and Warren suggest two remedies for an invasion of privacy — an action in tort and injunction. These remedies are similar to

---

[25] James Q. Whitman, *The Two Western Cultures of Privacy: Dignity Versus Liberty*, 113 Yale L.J. 1151, 1181 (2004).

[26] Thomas C. Cooley, *Law of Torts* 29 (2d ed. 1888).

those in defamation and copyright. What do the authors say about a criminal remedy?

8. ***Criticisms.*** Some have argued that the article is a defense of bourgeois values, i.e., the freedom of an elite group to avoid public scrutiny.[27] Which aspects of the article support this view? Do parts of the article suggest otherwise? Is privacy, as described in the Warren and Brandeis article, a class-based right?

(b) The Recognition of Warren and Brandeis's Privacy Torts

Warren and Brandeis's 1890 article suggested that the existing causes of action under the common law did not adequately protect privacy but that the legal concepts in the common law could be modified to achieve the task. As early as 1903, courts and legislatures responded to the Warren and Brandeis article by creating a number of privacy torts to redress the harms that Warren and Brandeis had noted. In *Roberson v. Rochester Folding Box Co.*, 64 N.E. 442 (N.Y. 1902), the New York Court of Appeals refused to recognize a common law tort action for privacy invasions. Franklin Mills Flour displayed a lithograph of Abigail Roberson (a teenager) on 25,000 advertisement flyers without her consent. The lithograph printed her photograph with the advertising pun: "Flour of the Family." Roberson claimed that the use of her image on the flyer caused her great humiliation and resulted in illness requiring medical help. The court, however, concluded:

> . . . There is no precedent for such an action to be found in the decisions of this court. . . . Mention of such a right is not to be found in Blackstone, Kent, or any other of the great commentators upon the law; nor, so far as the learning of counsel or the courts in this case have been able to discover, does its existence seem to have been asserted prior to about the year 1890. . . .
>
> The legislative body could very well interfere and arbitrarily provide that no one should be permitted for his own selfish purpose to use the picture or the name of another for advertising purposes without his general consent. In such event no embarrassment would result to the general body of law, for the law would be applicable only to cases provided for by statute. The courts, however, being without authority to legislate, are required to decide cases upon principle, and so are necessarily embarrassed by precedents created by an extreme, and therefore unjustifiable, application of an old principle. . . . [W]hile justice in a given case may be worked out by a decision of the court according to the notions of right which govern the individual judge or body of judges comprising the court, the mischief which will finally result may be almost incalculable under our system, which makes a decision in one case a precedent for decisions in all future cases which are akin to it in the essential facts. . . .

Shortly after the decision, a note in the *Yale Law Journal* criticized the *Roberson* decision because it enabled the press "to pry into and grossly display

---

[27] *See* Donald R. Pember, *Privacy and the Press* (1972).

before the public matters of the most private and personal concern."[28] One of the judges in the majority defended the opinion in the *Columbia Law Review*.[29]

In 1903, the New York legislature responded to the explicit invitation in *Roberson* to legislate by creating a privacy tort action by statute. *See* N.Y. Civ. Rights Act § 51. This statute is still in use today. As you will see again later on in this text, courts are frequently engaged in a dialogue with legislatures about the scope of privacy rights.

In the 1905 case *Pavesich v. New England Life Insurance Co.*, 50 S.E. 68 (Ga. 1905), Georgia became the first state to recognize a common law tort action for privacy invasions. There, a newspaper published a life insurance advertisement with a photograph of the plaintiff without the plaintiff's consent. The court held:

> . . . The right of privacy has its foundation in the instincts of nature. It is recognized intuitively, consciousness being the witness that can be called to establish its existence. Any person whose intellect is in a normal condition recognizes at once that as to each individual member of society there are matters private, and there are matters public so far as the individual is concerned. Each individual as instinctively resents any encroachment by the public upon his rights which are of a private nature as he does the withdrawal of those of his rights which are of a public nature. A right of privacy in matters purely private is therefore derived from natural law. . . .
>
> One who desires to live a life of partial seclusion has a right to choose the times, places, and manner in which and at which he will submit himself to the public gaze. Subject to the limitation above referred to, the body of a person cannot be put on exhibition at any time or at any place without his consent. . . .
>
> It therefore follows from what has been said that a violation of the right of privacy is a direct invasion of a legal right of the individual. . . .

In 1960, Dean William Prosser wrote his famous article, *Privacy*, examining the over 300 privacy tort cases decided in the 70 years since the Warren and Brandeis article.

WILLIAM PROSSER, *PRIVACY*
48 Cal. L. Rev. 383 (1960)

. . . The law of privacy comprises four distinct kinds of invasion of four different interests of the plaintiff, which are tied together by the common name, but otherwise have almost nothing in common except that each represents an interference with the right of the plaintiff, in the phrase coined by Judge Cooley, "to be let alone." Without any attempt at exact definition, these four torts may be described as follows:

1. Intrusion upon the plaintiff's seclusion or solitude, or into his private affairs.
2. Public disclosure of embarrassing private facts about the plaintiff.

---

[28] *An Actionable Right to Privacy?*, 12 Yale L.J. 34 (1902).
[29] Denis O'Brien, *The Right to Privacy*, 2 Colum. L. Rev. 486 (1902).

3. Publicity which places the plaintiff in a false light in the public eye.
4. Appropriation, for the defendant's advantage, of the plaintiff's name or likeness. . . .

Judge Briggs has described the present state of the law of privacy as "still that of a haystack in a hurricane." Disarray there certainly is; but almost all of the confusion is due to a failure to separate and distinguish these four forms of invasion and to realize that they call for different things. . . .

Taking them in order — intrusion, disclosure, false light, and appropriation — the first and second require the invasion of something secret, secluded or private pertaining to the plaintiff; the third and fourth do not. The second and third depend upon publicity, while the first does not, nor does the fourth, although it usually involves it. The third requires falsity or fiction; the other three do not. The fourth involves a use for the defendant's advantage, which is not true of the rest. Obviously this is an area in which one must tread warily and be on the lookout for bogs. Nor is the difficulty decreased by the fact that quite often two or more of these forms of invasion may be found in the same case, and quite conceivably in all four.

NOTES & QUESTIONS

1. ***The Restatement of Torts.*** Prosser's analytical framework imposed order and clarity on the jumbled line of cases that followed the Warren and Brandeis article. The Restatement of Torts recognizes the four torts Prosser described in his article. These torts are known collectively as "invasion of privacy." The torts include (1) intrusion upon seclusion, (2) public disclosure of private facts, (3) false light, and (4) appropriation.
2. ***The Interests Protected by the Privacy Torts.*** In response to Prosser's assertion that the privacy torts have almost "nothing in common," Edward Bloustein replied that "what provoked Warren and Brandeis to write their article was a fear that a rampant press feeding on the stuff of private life would destroy individual dignity and integrity and emasculate individual freedom and independence." This underlying principle is a protection of "human dignity" and "personality."[30]

   In contrast to Bloustein, Robert Post contends that the privacy torts do "not simply uphold the interests of individuals against the demands of the community, but instead safeguard[ ] rules of civility that in some significant measure constitute both individuals and community." Post argues that the torts establish boundaries between people, which when violated create strife. The privacy torts promote "forms of respect [for other people] by which we maintain a community."[31]

---

[30] Edward J. Bloustein, *Privacy as an Aspect of Human Dignity: An Answer to Dean Prosser*, 39 N.Y.U. L. Rev. 962, 974, 1000-01 (1964).

[31] Robert C. Post, *The Social Foundations of Privacy: Community and Self in the Common Law Tort*, 77 Cal. L. Rev. 957 (1989).

LAKE V. WAL-MART STORES, INC.

582 N.W.2d 231 (Minn. 1998)

BLATZ, C. J. . . . Elli Lake and Melissa Weber appeal from a dismissal of their complaint for failure to state a claim upon which relief may be granted. The district court and court of appeals held that Lake and Weber's complaint alleging intrusion upon seclusion, appropriation, publication of private facts, and false light publicity could not proceed because Minnesota does not recognize a common law tort action for invasion of privacy. We reverse as to the claims of intrusion upon seclusion, appropriation, and publication of private facts, but affirm as to false light publicity.

Nineteen-year-old Elli Lake and 20-year-old Melissa Weber vacationed in Mexico in March 1995 with Weber's sister. During the vacation, Weber's sister took a photograph of Lake and Weber naked in the shower together. After their vacation, Lake and Weber brought five rolls of film to the Dilworth, Minnesota Wal-Mart store and photo lab. When they received their developed photographs along with the negatives, an enclosed written notice stated that one or more of the photographs had not been printed because of their "nature."

In July 1995, an acquaintance of Lake and Weber alluded to the photograph and questioned their sexual orientation. Again, in December 1995, another friend told Lake and Weber that a Wal-Mart employee had shown her a copy of the photograph. By February 1996, Lake was informed that one or more copies of the photograph were circulating in the community.

Lake and Weber filed a complaint against Wal-Mart Stores, Inc. and one or more as-yet unidentified Wal-Mart employees on February 23, 1996, alleging the four traditional invasion of privacy torts — intrusion upon seclusion, appropriation, publication of private facts, and false light publicity. . . . The district court granted Wal-Mart's motion to dismiss, explaining that Minnesota has not recognized any of the four invasion of privacy torts. The court of appeals affirmed.

Whether Minnesota should recognize any or all of the invasion of privacy causes of action is a question of first impression in Minnesota. . . .

This court has the power to recognize and abolish common law doctrines. The common law is not composed of firmly fixed rules. Rather, as we have long recognized, the common law:

> is the embodiment of broad and comprehensive unwritten principles, inspired by natural reason, an innate sense of justice, adopted by common consent for the regulation and government of the affairs of men. It is the growth of ages, and an examination of many of its principles, as enunciated and discussed in the books, discloses a constant improvement and development in keeping with advancing civilization and new conditions of society. Its guiding star has always been the rule of right and wrong, and in this country its principles demonstrate that there is in fact, as well as in theory, a remedy for all wrongs.

As society changes over time, the common law must also evolve:

> It must be remembered that the common law is the result of growth, and that its development has been determined by the social needs of the community which it governs. It is the resultant of conflicting social forces, and those forces which

> are for the time dominant leave their impress upon the law. It is of judicial origin, and seeks to establish doctrines and rules for the determination, protection, and enforcement of legal rights. Manifestly it must change as society changes and new rights are recognized. To be an efficient instrument, and not a mere abstraction, it must gradually adapt itself to changed conditions.

To determine the common law, we look to other states as well as to England.

The tort of invasion of privacy is rooted in a common law right to privacy first described in an 1890 law review article by Samuel Warren and Louis Brandeis. The article posited that the common law has always protected an individual's person and property, with the extent and nature of that protection changing over time. The fundamental right to privacy is both reflected in those protections and grows out of them:

> Thus, in the very early times, the law gave a remedy only for physical interference with life and property, for trespass vi et armis. Then the "right to life" served only to protect the subject from battery in its various forms; liberty meant freedom from actual restraint; and the right to property secured to the individual his lands and his cattle. Later, there came a recognition of a man's spiritual nature, of his feelings and his intellect. Gradually the scope of these legal rights broadened; and now the right to life has come to mean the right to enjoy life, — the right to be let alone; the right to liberty secures the exercise of extensive civil privileges; and the term "property" has grown to comprise every form of possession — intangible, as well as tangible.

Although no English cases explicitly articulated a "right to privacy," several cases decided under theories of property, contract, or breach of confidence also included invasion of privacy as a basis for protecting personal violations. The article encouraged recognition of the common law right to privacy, as the strength of our legal system lies in its elasticity, adaptability, capacity for growth, and ability "to meet the wants of an ever changing society and to apply immediate relief for every recognized wrong.". . .

Today, the vast majority of jurisdictions now recognize some form of the right to privacy. Only Minnesota, North Dakota, and Wyoming have not yet recognized any of the four privacy torts. Although New York and Nebraska courts have declined to recognize a common law basis for the right to privacy and instead provide statutory protection, we reject the proposition that only the legislature may establish new causes of action. The right to privacy is inherent in the English protections of individual property and contract rights and the "right to be let alone" is recognized as part of the common law across this country. Thus, it is within the province of the judiciary to establish privacy torts in this jurisdiction.

Today we join the majority of jurisdictions and recognize the tort of invasion of privacy. The right to privacy is an integral part of our humanity; one has a public persona, exposed and active, and a private persona, guarded and preserved. The heart of our liberty is choosing which parts of our lives shall become public and which parts we shall hold close.

We decline to recognize the tort of false light publicity at this time. We are concerned that claims under false light are similar to claims of defamation, and to the extent that false light is more expansive than defamation, tension between this tort and the First Amendment is increased.

False light is the most widely criticized of the four privacy torts and has been rejected by several jurisdictions. . . .

Thus we recognize a right to privacy present in the common law of Minnesota, including causes of action in tort for intrusion upon seclusion, appropriation, and publication of private facts, but we decline to recognize the tort of false light publicity. . . .

TOMLJANOVICH, J. dissenting. I would not recognize a cause of action for intrusion upon seclusion, appropriation or publication of private facts. . . .

An action for an invasion of the right to privacy is not rooted in the Constitution. "[T]he Fourth Amendment cannot be translated into a general constitutional 'right to privacy.'" *Katz v. United States*, 389 U.S. 347, 350 (1967). Those privacy rights that have their origin in the Constitution are much more fundamental rights of privacy — marriage and reproduction. *See Griswold v. Connecticut*, 381 U.S. 479, 485 (1965) (penumbral rights of privacy and repose protect notions of privacy surrounding the marriage relationship and reproduction).

We have become a much more litigious society since 1975 when we acknowledged that we have never recognized a cause of action for invasion of privacy. We should be even more reluctant now to recognize a new tort.

In the absence of a constitutional basis, I would leave to the legislature the decision to create a new tort for invasion of privacy.

NOTES & QUESTIONS

1. ***Other Remedies?*** If the Minnesota Supreme Court had rejected the privacy tort, what other legal remedies might be available to Elli Lake?
2. ***Postscript.*** What happened in *Lake* after the Minnesota Supreme Court's decision? In response to a query from the casebook authors, the lead attorney for the *Lake* plaintiff, Keith L. Miller of Miller, Norman & Associates, Ltd., explained that his client lost at the trial that followed the remand. He writes: "The jury found that an invasion of Ms. Lake's privacy had occurred, but that it did not happen 'in the course and scope' of a Wal-Mart worker's employment." In other words, tort notions of agency were found to apply, and a privacy tort violation could be attributed to Wal-Mart only if the employee had carried out the tort in the course and scope of employment. Miller added: "Our proof was problematic because, expectedly, no employee could specifically be identified as the culprit. It was all circumstantial." Finally, he summarized his experience litigating this case: "Gratifying? Certainly. Remunerative? Not so much."
3. ***Legislatures vs. Courts.*** The dissent in *Lake* contends, in a similar way as *Roberson*, that it should be the legislature, not the courts, that recognize new tort actions to protect privacy. In New York, the statute passed in response to *Roberson* remains the state's source for privacy tort remedies. Like New York, some states have recognized the privacy torts legislatively; other states,

like Georgia in *Pavesich* and Minnesota in *Lake*, have recognized them judicially. Which means of recognizing the torts do you believe to be most justifiable? Why? Does the legislature have expertise that courts lack? Are courts more or less sensitive to civil rights issues, such as privacy?

(c) Privacy Protection in Tort Law

The Privacy Torts. Prosser's classification of these torts survives to this day. The Restatement (Second) of Torts recognizes four privacy torts:

(1) *Public Disclosure of Private Facts.* This tort creates a cause of action for one who publicly discloses a private matter that is "highly offensive to a reasonable person" and "is not of legitimate concern to the public." Restatement (Second) of Torts § 652D (1977).

(2) *Intrusion upon Seclusion.* This tort provides a remedy when one intrudes "upon the solitude or seclusion of another or his private affairs or concerns" if the intrusion is "highly offensive to a reasonable person." Restatement (Second) of Torts § 652B (1977).

(3) *False Light.* This tort creates a cause of action when one publicly discloses a matter that places a person "in a false light" that is "highly offensive to a reasonable person." Restatement (Second) of Torts § 652E (1977).

(4) *Appropriation.* Under this tort, a plaintiff has a remedy against one "who appropriates to his own use or benefit the name or likeness" of the plaintiff. Restatement (Second) of Torts § 652C (1977).

Today, most states recognize some or all of these torts.

Breach of Confidentiality. The tort of breach of confidentiality provides a remedy when a professional (i.e., doctor, lawyer, banker) divulges a patient or client's confidential information.

Defamation. The law of defamation existed long before Warren and Brandeis's article. Defamation law, consisting of the torts of libel and slander, creates liability when one makes a false statement about a person that harms the person's reputation. The Supreme Court has held that the First Amendment places certain limits on defamation law.

Infliction of Emotional Distress. The tort of intentional infliction of emotional distress can also serve as a remedy for certain privacy invasions. This tort provides a remedy when one "by extreme and outrageous conduct intentionally or recklessly causes severe emotional distress to another." Restatement (Second) of Torts § 46 (1977). Since privacy invasions can often result in severe emotional distress, this tort may provide a remedy. However, it is limited by the requirement of "extreme and outrageous conduct."

(d) Privacy Protection in Evidence Law

The law of evidence has long recognized privacy as an important goal that can override the truth-seeking function of the trial. Under the common law, certain communications are privileged, and hence cannot be inquired into during a legal proceeding. The law of evidence has recognized the importance of protecting the privacy of communications between attorney and client, priest and penitent, husband and wife, physician and patient, and psychotherapist and patient.

(e) Privacy Protection via Property Rights

Property Rights. Although there are few property laws specifically governing privacy, these laws often implicate privacy. The appropriation tort is akin to a property right, and some commentators suggest that personal information should be viewed as a form of property.[32] If personal information is understood as a form of property, the tort of conversion might apply to those who collect and use a person's private data. Take a look at the *Moore* case in the section on genetic privacy in Chapter 4. Recall, however, that Warren and Brandeis rejected property as an adequate protection for privacy. What kind of market structures might be needed if personal data is to be traded or sold?

Trespass. The law of trespass, which provides tort remedies and criminal penalties for the unauthorized entry onto another's land, can protect privacy. There is some overlap between the torts of intrusion and trespass, as many forms of intrusion involve a trespass as well.

(f) Privacy Protection in Contract Law

Sometimes specific contractual provisions protect against the collection, use, or disclosure of personal information. In certain contexts, courts have entertained actions for breach of implied contract or tort actions based on implicit duties once certain relationships are established, such as physician-patient relationships, which have been analogized to fiduciary relationships. Privacy policies as well as terms of service containing privacy provisions can sometimes be analogized to a contract.

Contract often functions as a way of sidestepping state and federal privacy laws. Many employers make employees consent to drug testing as well as e-mail and workplace surveillance in their employment contracts.

Some commentators advocate a contractual approach to privacy, such as Jerry Kang, who suggests a contractual default rule that limits the way personal information can be used but that can be contracted around by parties who do not desire to be governed by the rule.[33]

(g) Privacy Protection in Criminal Law

Warren and Brandeis noted that under certain circumstances, criminal law would be appropriate to protect privacy. The criminal law protects bodily

---

[32] *See, e.g.*, Alan Westin, *Privacy and Freedom* 324 (1967); *see also* Richard S. Murphy, *Property Rights in Personal Information: An Economic Defense of Privacy*, 84 Geo. L.J. 2381 (1996); Richard A. Posner, *The Economics of Justice* (1981); Lawrence Lessig, *Code and Other Laws of Cyberspace* 154-62 (1999).

[33] *See* Jerry Kang, *Information Privacy in Cyberspace Transactions*, 50 Stan. L. Rev. 1193 (1998).

invasions, such as assault, battery, and rape. The privacy of one's home is also protected by criminal sanctions for trespass. Stalking and harassing can give rise to criminal culpability. The crime of blackmail prohibits coercing an individual by threatening to expose her personal secrets. Many of the statutes protecting privacy also contain criminal penalties, such as the statutes pertaining to wiretapping and identity theft.

2. CONSTITUTIONAL LAW

Federal Constitutional Law. Although the United States Constitution does not specifically mention privacy, it has a number of provisions that protect privacy, and it has been interpreted as providing a right to privacy. In some instances the First Amendment serves to safeguard privacy. For example, the First Amendment protects the right to speak anonymously. *See McIntyre v. Ohio Election Comm'n*, 514 U.S. 334 (1995). The First Amendment's freedom of association clause protects individuals from being compelled to disclose the groups to which they belong or contribute. Under the First Amendment "Congress shall make no law . . . abridging . . . the right of the people peaceably to assemble. . . ." For example, the Court has struck down the compulsory disclosure of the names and addresses of an organization's members, *see NAACP v. Alabama*, 357 U.S. 449 (1958), as well as a law requiring public teachers to list all organizations to which they belong or contribute. *See Shelton v. Tucker*, 364 U.S. 479 (1960).

The Third Amendment protects the privacy of the home by preventing the government from requiring soldiers to reside in people's homes: "No Soldier shall, in time of peace be quartered in any house, without the consent of the Owner, nor in time of war, but in a manner to be prescribed by law."

The Fourth Amendment provides that people have the right "to be secure in their persons, houses, papers, and effects, against unreasonable searches and seizures. . . ." Almost 40 years after writing *The Right to Privacy*, Brandeis, then a Supreme Court Justice, wrote a dissent that has had a significant influence on Fourth Amendment law. The case was *Olmstead v. United States*, 277 U.S. 438 (1928), where the Court held that wiretapping was not an invasion of privacy under the Fourth Amendment because it was not a physical trespass into the home. Justice Brandeis dissented, contending that the central interest protected by the Fourth Amendment was not property but the "right to be let alone":

> The protection guaranteed by the amendments is much broader in scope. The makers of our Constitution undertook to secure conditions favorable to the pursuit of happiness. They recognized the significance of man's spiritual nature, of his feelings and of his intellect. They knew that only a part of the pain, pleasure and satisfactions of life are to be found in material things. They sought to protect Americans in their beliefs, their thoughts, their emotions and their sensations. They conferred, as against the government, the right to be let alone — the most comprehensive of rights and the right most valued by civilized men. To protect that right, every unjustifiable intrusion by the government upon the privacy of the individual, whatever the means employed, must be deemed a violation of the Fourth Amendment.

Brandeis's dissent demonstrated that the "right to be let alone" did not merely have common law roots (as he had argued in *The Right to Privacy*) but also had constitutional roots as well in the Fourth Amendment.

Modern Fourth Amendment law incorporates much of Brandeis's view. In *Katz v. United States*, 389 U.S. 347 (1967), the Court held that the Fourth Amendment "protects people, not places" and said that the police must obtain a warrant when a search takes place in a public pay phone on a public street. The Court currently determines a person's right to privacy by the "reasonable expectations of privacy" test, a standard articulated in Justice Harlan's concurrence to *Katz*. First, a person must "have exhibited an actual (subjective) expectation of privacy" and, second, "the expectation [must] be one that society is prepared to recognize as 'reasonable.' "

The Fifth Amendment guarantees that: "No person . . . shall be compelled in any criminal case to be a witness against himself. . . ." This right, commonly referred to as the "privilege against self-incrimination," protects privacy by restricting the ability of the government to force individuals to divulge certain information about themselves.

In the landmark 1965 case *Griswold v. Connecticut*, 318 U.S. 479 (1965), the Court declared that an individual has a constitutional right to privacy. The Court located this right within the "penumbras" or "zones" of freedom created by an expansive interpretation of the Bill of Rights. Subsequently, the Court has handed down a line of cases protecting certain fundamental life choices such as abortion and aspects of one's intimate sexual life.

In *Whalen v. Roe*, 433 U.S. 425 (1977), the Court extended its substantive due process privacy protection to information privacy, holding that the "zone of privacy" protected by the Constitution encompasses the "individual interest in avoiding disclosure of personal matters." This offshoot of the right to privacy has become known as the "constitutional right to information privacy."

State Constitutional Law. A number of states have directly provided for the protection of privacy in their constitutions. For example, the Alaska Constitution provides: "The right of the people to privacy is recognized and shall not be infringed." Alaska Const. art. I, § 22. According to the California Constitution: "All people are by their nature free and independent and have inalienable rights. Among these are enjoying and defending life and liberty, acquiring, possessing, and protecting property, and pursuing and obtaining safety, happiness, and privacy." Cal. Const. art. I, § 1. Unlike most state constitutional provisions, the California constitutional right to privacy applies not only to state actors but also to private parties. *See, e.g.*, *Hill v. NCAA*, 865 P.2d 638 (Cal. 1994). The Florida Constitution provides: "Every natural person has the right to be let alone and free from governmental intrusion into his private life except as otherwise provided herein." Fla. Const. art. I, § 23.[34]

---

[34] For more examples, see Ariz. Const. art. II, § 8; Mont. Const. art. II, § 10; Haw. Const. art. I, § 6; Ill. Const. art. I, §§ 6, 12; La. Const. art. I, § 5; S.C. Const. art. I, § 10; Wash. Const. art. I, § 7. For a further discussion of state constitutional protections of privacy, see Timothy O. Lenz, *"Rights Talk" about Privacy in State Courts*, 60 Alb. L. Rev. 1613 (1997); Mark Silverstein, Note, *Privacy Rights in State Constitutions: Models for Illinois?*, 1989 U. Ill. L. Rev. 215.

3. STATUTORY LAW

Federal Statutory Law. From the mid-1960s to the mid-1970s, privacy emerged as a central political and social concern. In tune with the heightened attention to privacy, philosophers, legal scholars, and others turned their focus on privacy, raising public awareness about the growing threats to privacy from technology.[35]

In the mid-1960s electronic eavesdropping erupted into a substantial public issue, spawning numerous television news documentaries as well as receiving significant attention in major newspapers. A proposal for a National Data Center in 1965 triggered public protest and congressional hearings. At this time, the computer was a new and unexplored technological tool that raised risks of unprecedented data collection about individuals, with potentially devastating effects on privacy. Indeed, toward the end of the 1960s, the issue of the collection of personal information in databases had become one of the defining social issues of American society.

During this time the Supreme Court announced landmark decisions regarding the right to privacy, including *Griswold v. Connecticut* in 1965 and *Roe v. Wade* in 1973, which were landmark decisions regarding the right to decisional/reproductive privacy and autonomy. The famous reasonable expectations of privacy test in Fourth Amendment jurisprudence emerged in 1967 with *Katz v. United States*.

Due to growing fears about the ability of computers to store and search personal information, Congress devoted increasing attention to the issue of privacy. As Priscilla Regan observes:

> In 1965, a new problem was placed on the congressional agenda by subcommittee chairs in both the House and the Senate. The problem was defined as the invasion of privacy by computers and evoked images of *1984*, the "Computerized Man," and a dossier society. Press interest was high, public concern was generated and resulted in numerous letters being sent to members of Congress, and almost thirty days of congressional hearings were held in the late 1960s and early 1970s.[36]

In 1973, in a highly influential report, the United States Department of Health, Education, and Welfare (HEW) undertook an extensive review of data processing in the United States. Among many recommendations, the HEW report proposed that a Code of Fair Information Practices be established. The Fair Information Practices consist of a number of basic information privacy principles that allocate rights and responsibilities in the collection and use of personal information:

---

[35] *See, e.g.*, Vance Packard, *The Naked Society* (1964); Myron Brenton, *The Privacy Invaders* (1964); Alan Westin, *Privacy and Freedom* (1967); Arthur Miller, *The Assault on Privacy* (1971); *Nomos XII: Privacy* (J. Ronald Pennock & J.W. Chapman eds., 1971); Alan Westin & Michael A. Baker, *Databanks in a Free Society: Computers, Record-Keeping and Privacy* (1972); Aryeh Neier, *The Secret Files They Keep on You* (1975); Kenneth L. Karst, *"The Files": Legal Controls over the Accuracy and Accessibility of Stored Personal Data*, 31 L. & Contemp. Probs. 342 (1966); Symposium, *Computers, Data Banks, and Individual Privacy*, 53 Minn. L. Rev. 211-45 (1968); Symposium, *Privacy*, 31 L. & Contemp. Probs. 251-435 (1966).

[36] Priscilla M. Regan, *Legislating Privacy: Technology, Social Values, and Public Policy* 82 (1995).

- There must be no personal-data record-keeping systems whose very existence is secret.
- There must be a way for an individual to find out what information about him is in a record and how it is used.
- There must be a way for an individual to prevent information about him obtained for one purpose from being used or made available for other purposes without his consent.
- There must be a way for an individual to correct or amend a record of identifiable information about him.
- Any organization creating, maintaining, using, or disseminating records of identifiable personal data must ensure the reliability of the data for their intended use and must take reasonable precautions to prevent misuse of the data.[37]

As Marc Rotenberg observes, the Fair Information Practices have "played a significant role in framing privacy laws in the United States."[38]

Beginning in the 1970s, Congress has passed a number of laws protecting privacy in various sectors of the information economy:

- Fair Credit Reporting Act of 1970, Pub. L. No. 90-32, 15 U.S.C. §§ 1681 et seq. — provides citizens with rights regarding the use and disclosure of their personal information by credit reporting agencies.
- Privacy Act of 1974, Pub. L. No. 93-579, 5 U.S.C. § 552a — provides individuals with a number of rights concerning their personal information maintained in government record systems, such as the right to see one's records and to ensure that the information in them is accurate.
- Family Educational Rights and Privacy Act of 1974, Pub. L. No. 93-380, 20 U.S.C. §§ 1221 note, 1232g — protects the privacy of school records.
- Right to Financial Privacy Act of 1978, Pub. L. No. 95-630, 12 U.S.C. §§ 3401–3422 — requires a subpoena or search warrant for law enforcement officials to obtain financial records.
- Foreign Intelligence Surveillance Act of 1978, Pub. L. No. 95-511, 15 U.S.C. §§ 1801-1811 — regulates foreign intelligence gathering within the U.S.
- Privacy Protection Act of 1980, Pub. L. No. 96-440, 42 U.S.C. § 2000aa — restricts the government's ability to search and seize the work product of the press and the media.
- Cable Communications Policy Act of 1984, Pub. L. No. 98-549, 47 U.S.C. § 551 — mandates privacy protection for records maintained by cable companies.

---

[37] *See* U.S. Dep't of Health, Education, and Welfare, *Secretary's Advisory Committee on Automated Personal Data Systems, Records, Computers, and Rights of Citizens* viii (1973).

[38] Marc Rotenberg, *Fair Information Practices and the Architecture of Privacy (What Larry Doesn't Get)*, Stan. Tech. L. Rev. 1, 44 (2001).

- Electronic Communications Privacy Act of 1986, Pub. L. No. 99-508 and Pub. L. No. 103-414, 18 U.S.C §§ 2510–2522, 2701–2709 — updates federal electronic surveillance law to respond to the new developments in technology.
- Computer Matching and Privacy Protection Act of 1988, Pub. L. No. 100-503, 5 U.S.C. §§ 552a — regulates automated investigations conducted by government agencies comparing computer files.
- Employee Polygraph Protection Act of 1988, Pub. L. No. 100-347, 29 U.S.C. §§ 2001–2009 — governs the use of polygraphs by employers.
- Video Privacy Protection Act of 1988, Pub. L. No. 100-618, 18 U.S.C. §§ 2710–2711 — protects the privacy of videotape rental information.
- Telephone Consumer Protection Act of 1991, Pub. L. No. 102-243, 47 U.S.C. § 227 — provides certain remedies from repeat telephone calls by telemarketers.
- Driver's Privacy Protection Act of 1994, Pub. L. No. 103-322, 18 U.S.C. §§ 2721–2725 — restricts the states from disclosing or selling personal information in their motor vehicle records.
- Health Insurance Portability and Accountability Act of 1996, Pub. L. No. 104-191 — gives the Department of Health and Human Services (HHS) the authority to promulgate regulations governing the privacy of medical records.
- Identity Theft and Assumption Deterrence Act of 1998, Pub. L. No. 105-318, 18 U.S.C. § 1028 — criminalizes the transfer or use of fraudulent identification with the intent to commit unlawful activity.
- Children's Online Privacy Protection Act of 1998, Pub. L. No. 106-170, 15 U.S.C. §§ 6501–6506 — restricts the use of information gathered from children under age 13 by Internet websites.
- Gramm-Leach-Bliley Act of 1999, Pub. L. No. 106-102, 15 U.S.C. §§ 6801–6809 — requires privacy notices and provides opt-out rights when financial institutions seek to disclose personal data to other companies.
- CAN-SPAM Act of 2003, Pub. L. No. 108-187 — provides penalties for the transmission of unsolicited e-mail.
- Fair and Accurate Credit Transactions Act of 2003, Pub. L. No. 108-159 — amends and updates the Fair Credit Reporting Act, providing (among other things) additional protections against identity theft.
- Video Voyeurism Prevention Act of 2004, Pub. L. No. 108-495, 18 U.S.C. § 1801 — criminalizes the capturing of nude images of people (when on federal property) under circumstances where they have a reasonable expectation of privacy.

Not all of Congress's legislation regarding privacy has been protective of privacy. A number of statutes have mandated the government collection of sensitive personal data or facilitated government investigation techniques:

- Bank Secrecy Act of 1970, Pub. L. No. 91-508 — requires banks to maintain reports of people's financial transactions to assist in government white collar investigations.

- Communications Assistance for Law Enforcement Act of 1994, Pub. L. No. 103-414 — requires telecommunication providers to help facilitate government interceptions of communications and surveillance.
- Personal Responsibility and Work Opportunity Reconciliation Act of 1996, Pub. L. No. 104-193 — requires the collection of personal information (including Social Security numbers, addresses, and wages) of all people who obtain a new job anywhere in the nation, which will be placed into a national database to help track down deadbeat parents.
- USA-PATRIOT Act of 2001, Pub. L. No. 107-56 — amends a number of electronic surveillance statutes and other statutes to facilitate law enforcement investigations and access to information.

State Statutory Law. The states have passed statutes protecting privacy in many contexts, regulating both the public and private sectors. These laws cover a wide range of subjects, from employment records and medical records to library records and student records. However, fewer than a third have enacted a general privacy law akin to the Privacy Act.[39] As Paul Schwartz observes, most states lack "omnibus data protection laws."[40]

4. INTERNATIONAL LAW

Privacy is a global concern. International law, and more precisely, the privacy laws of other countries and international privacy norms, implicate privacy interests in the United States. For example, commercial firms in the United States must comply with the various standards for global commerce. The Organization of Economic Cooperation and Development (OECD) developed an extensive series of privacy guidelines in 1980 that formed the basis for privacy laws in North America, Europe, and East Asia. In 1995, the European Union issued the *European Community Directive on Data Protection*, which outlines the basic principles for privacy legislation for European Union member countries.[41] The Directive became effective on October 25, 1998. In November 2004, an Asian-Pacific Economic Cooperative (APEC) Privacy Framework was endorsed by the ministers of the APEC countries. The APEC countries are more than 20 nations, mostly in Asia, but also including the United States.

---

[39] *See* Smith, *Ben Franklin's Web Site*, *supra*, at 333. For a compilation of state privacy laws, see Robert Ellis Smith, *Compilation of State and Federal Privacy Laws* (2002).

[40] Paul M. Schwartz, *Privacy and Participation: Personal Information and Public Sector Regulation in the United States*, 80 Iowa L. Rev. 553, 605 (1995).

[41] *See* Directive of the European Parliament and the Council of Europe on the Protection of Individuals with Regard to the Processing of Personal Data and on the Free Movement of Such Data (1996). For more information about the EU Data Directive, see Paul M. Schwartz & Joel R. Reidenberg, *Data Privacy Law* (1996); Peter P. Swire & Robert E. Litan, *None of Your Business: World Data Flows, Electronic Commerce, and the European Privacy Directive* (1998); Colin J. Bennett, *Regulating Privacy: Data Protection of Public Policy in Europe and the United States* (1992); David H. Flaherty, *Protecting Privacy in Surveillance Societies* (1989).

C. PERSPECTIVES ON PRIVACY

1. THE PHILOSOPHICAL DISCOURSE ABOUT PRIVACY

(a) The Concept of Privacy and the Right to Privacy

At the outset, it is important to distinguish between the concept of privacy and the right of privacy. As Hyman Gross observed, "[t]he law does not determine what privacy is, but only what situations of privacy will be afforded legal protection."[42] Privacy as a concept involves what privacy entails and how it is to be valued. Privacy as a right involves the extent to which privacy is (and should be) legally protected.

While instructive and illuminative, law cannot be the exclusive material for constructing a concept of privacy. Law is the product of the weighing of competing values, and it sometimes embodies difficult trade-offs. In order to determine what the law *should* protect, we cannot merely look to what the law *does* protect.

(b) The Public and Private Spheres

A long-standing distinction in philosophical discourse is between the public and private spheres. Some form of boundary between public and private has been maintained throughout the history of Western civilization.[43]

Generally, the public sphere is the realm of life experienced in the open, in the community, and in the world of politics. The private sphere is the realm of life where one retreats to isolation or to one's family. At its core is the world of the home. The private sphere, observes Edward Shils, is a realm where the individual "is not bound by the rules that govern public life. . . . The 'private life' is a secluded life, a life separated from the compelling burdens of public authority."[44]

According to Hannah Arendt, both spheres are essential dimensions of human life:

> . . . In ancient feeling, the privative trait of privacy, indicated in the word itself, was all-important; it meant literally a state of being deprived of something, and even of the highest and most human of man's capacities. A man who lived only a private life, who like the slave was not permitted to enter the public realm, or like the barbarian had chosen not to establish such a realm, was not fully human. We no longer think primarily of deprivation when we use the word "privacy," and this is partly due to the enormous enrichment of the private sphere through modern individualism. . . .
>
> To live an entirely private life means above all to be deprived of things essential to a truly human life: to be deprived of the reality that comes from being seen and heard by others, to be deprived of an "objective" relationship

---

[42] Hyman Gross, *The Concept of Privacy*, 42 N.Y.U. L. Rev. 34, 36 (1967).

[43] *See* Georges Duby, *Foreword*, in *A History of the Private Life I: From Pagan Rome to Byzantium* viii (Paul Veyne ed. & Arthur Goldhammer trans., 1987); *see also* Jürgen Habermas, *The Structural Transformation of the Public Sphere* (Thomas Burger trans., 1991).

[44] Edward Shils, *Privacy: Its Constitution and Vicissitudes*, 31 L. & Contemp. Probs. 281, 283 (1966).

> with them that comes from being related to and separated from them through the intermediary of a common world of things, to be deprived of the possibility of achieving something more permanent than life itself. . . .
>
> . . . [T]he four walls of one's private property offer the only reliable hiding place from the common public world, not only from everything that goes on in it but also from its very publicity, from being seen and being heard. A life spent entirely in public, in the presence of others, becomes, as we would say, shallow. While it retains visibility, it loses the quality of rising into sight from some darker ground which must remain hidden if it is not to lose its depth in a very real, non-subjective sense. . . .[45]

John Stuart Mill relied upon a notion of the public/private dichotomy to determine when society should regulate individual conduct. Mill contended that there was a realm where people had social responsibilities and where society could properly restrain people from acting or punish them for their deeds. This realm consisted in acts that were hurtful to others or to which people "may rightfully be compelled to perform; such as to give evidence in a court of justice; to bear his fair share in the common defence, or in any other joint work necessary to the interest of the society of which he enjoys the protection." However, "there is a sphere of action in which society, as distinguished from the individual, has, if any, only an indirect interest; comprehending all that portion of a person's life and conduct which affects only himself, or if it also affects others, only with their free, voluntary, and undeceived consent and participation." Conduct within this sphere consists of "self-regarding" acts, and society should not interfere with such acts. As Mill further elaborated:

> . . . I fully admit that the mischief which a person does to himself may seriously affect, both through their sympathies and their interests, those nearly connected with him and, in a minor degree, society at large. When, by conduct of this sort, a person is led to violate a distinct and assignable obligation to any other person or persons, the case is taken out of the self-regarding class, and becomes amenable to moral disapprobation in the proper sense of the term. . . . Whenever, in short, there is a definite damage, or a definite risk of damage, either to an individual or to the public, the case is taken out of the province of liberty, and placed in that of morality or law.
>
> But with regard to the merely contingent, or, as it may be called, constructive injury which a person causes to society, by conduct which neither violates any specific duty to the public, nor occasions perceptible hurt to any assignable individual except himself; the inconvenience is one which society can afford to bear, for the sake of the greater good of human freedom. . . .[46]

2. THE DEFINITION AND THE VALUE OF PRIVACY

The following excerpts explore the definition and value of privacy. Those who attempt to define privacy seek to describe what privacy constitutes. Over the past four decades, academics have defined privacy as a right of personhood, intimacy, secrecy, limited access to the self, and control over information. However, defining privacy has proven to be quite complicated, and many commenta-

---

[45] Hannah Arendt, *The Human Condition* (1958).

[46] John Stuart Mill, *On Liberty* 12, 13, 74-75 (1859).

tors have expressed great difficulty in defining precisely what privacy is. In the words of one commentator, "even the most strenuous advocate of a right to privacy must confess that there are serious problems of defining the essence and scope of this right."[47] According to Robert Post, "[p]rivacy is a value so complex, so entangled in competing and contradictory dimensions, so engorged with various and distinct meanings, that I sometimes despair whether it can be usefully addressed at all."[48]

Conceptualizing privacy not only involves defining privacy but articulating the value of privacy. The value of privacy concerns its importance — how privacy is to be weighed relative to other interests and values. The excerpts that follow attempt to grapple with the complicated task of defining privacy and explaining why privacy is worth protecting.

ALAN WESTIN, *PRIVACY AND FREEDOM*

(1967)

. . . Privacy is the claim of individuals, groups, or institutions to determine for themselves when, how, and to what extent information about them is communicated to others. Viewed in terms of the relation of the individual to social participation, privacy is the voluntary and temporary withdrawal of a person from the general society through physical or psychological means, either in a state of solitude or small-group intimacy or, when among larger groups, in a condition of anonymity or reserve. The individual's desire for privacy is never absolute, since participation in society is an equally powerful desire. Thus each individual is continually engaged in a personal adjustment process in which he balances the desire for privacy with the desire for disclosure and communication of himself to others, in light of the environmental conditions and social norms set by the society in which he lives. The individual does so in the face of pressures from the curiosity of others and from the processes of surveillance that every society sets in order to enforce its social norms. . . .

Recognizing the differences that political and sensory cultures make in setting norms of privacy among modern societies, it is still possible to describe the general functions that privacy performs for individuals and groups in Western democratic nations. Before describing these, it is helpful to explain in somewhat greater detail the four basic states of individual privacy [which are solitude, intimacy, anonymity, and reserve.] . . .

The first state of privacy is solitude; here the individual is separated from the group and freed from the observation of other persons. He may be subjected to jarring physical stimuli, such as noise, odors, and vibrations. His peace of mind may continue to be disturbed by physical sensations of heat, cold, itching, and pain. He may believe that he is being observed by God or some supernatural force, or fear that some authority is secretly watching him. Finally, in solitude he will be especially subject to that familiar dialogue with the mind or conscience.

---

[47] William M. Beaney, *The Right to Privacy and American Law*, 31 L. & Contemp. Probs. 253, 255 (1966).

[48] Robert C. Post, *Three Concepts of Privacy*, 89 Geo. L.J. 2087, 2087 (2001).

But, despite all these physical or psychological intrusions, solitude is the most complete state of privacy that individuals can achieve.

In the second state of privacy, the individual is acting as part of a small unit that claims and is allowed to exercise corporate seclusion so that it may achieve a close, relaxed, and frank relationship between two or more individuals. Typical units of intimacy are husband and wife, the family, a friendship circle, or a work clique. Whether close contact brings relaxed relations or abrasive hostility depends on the personal interaction of the members, but without intimacy a basic need of human contact would not be met.

The third state of privacy, anonymity, occurs when the individual is in public places or performing public acts but still seeks, and finds, freedom from identification and surveillance. He may be riding a subway, attending a ball game, or walking the streets; he is among people and knows that he is being observed; but unless he is a well-known celebrity, he does not expect to be personally identified and held to the full rules of behavior and role that would operate if he were known to those observing him. In this state the individual is able to merge into the "situational landscape." Knowledge or fear that one is under systematic observation in public places destroys the sense of relaxation and freedom that men seek in open spaces and public arenas. . . .

Still another kind of anonymity is the publication of ideas anonymously. Here the individual wants to present some idea publicly to the community or to a segment of it, but does not want to be universally identified at once as the author — especially not by the authorities, who may be forced to take action if they "know" the perpetrator. The core of each of these types of anonymous action is the desire of individuals for times of "public privacy."

Reserve, the fourth and most subtle state of privacy, is the creation of a psychological barrier against unwanted intrusion; this occurs when the individual's need to limit communication about himself is protected by the willing discretion of those surrounding him. Most of our lives are spent not in solitude or anonymity but in situations of intimacy and in group settings where we are known to others. Even in the most intimate relations, communication of self to others is always incomplete and is based on the need to hold back some parts of one's self as either too personal and sacred or too shameful and profane to express. This circumstance gives rise to what Simmel called "reciprocal reserve and indifference," the relation that creates "mental distance" to protect the personality. This creation of mental distance—a variant of the concept of "social distance" — takes place in every sort of relationship under rules of social etiquette; it expresses the individual's choice to withhold or disclose information — the choice that is the dynamic aspect of privacy in daily interpersonal relations. . . .

This analysis of the various states of privacy is useful in discussing the basic question of the functions privacy performs for individuals in democratic societies. These can also be grouped conveniently under four headings — personal autonomy, emotional release, self-evaluation, and limited and protected communication. . . .

Personal Autonomy. . . . Each person is aware of the gap between what he wants to be and what he actually is, between what the world sees of him and what he knows to be his much more complex reality. In addition, there are aspects of himself that the individual does not fully understand but is slowly exploring and shaping as he develops. Every individual lives behind a mask in this manner; indeed, the first etymological meaning of the word "person" was "mask," indicating both the conscious and expressive presentation of the self to a social audience. If this mask is torn off and the individual's real self bared to a world in which everyone else still wears his mask and believes in masked performances, the individual can be seared by the hot light of selective, forced exposure. . . .

The autonomy that privacy protects is also vital to the development of individuality and consciousness of individual choice in life. . . . This development of individuality is particularly important in democratic societies, since qualities of independent thought, diversity of views, and non-conformity are considered desirable traits for individuals. Such independence requires time for sheltered experimentation and testing of ideas, for preparation and practice in thought and conduct, without fear of ridicule or penalty, and for the opportunity to alter opinions before making them public. The individual's sense that it is he who decides when to "go public" is a crucial aspect of his feeling of autonomy. Without such time for incubation and growth, through privacy, many ideas and positions would be launched into the world with dangerous prematurity. . . .

Emotional Release. Life in society generates such tensions for the individual that both physical and psychological health demand periods of privacy for various types of emotional release. At one level, such relaxation is required from the pressure of playing social roles. Social scientists agree that each person constantly plays a series of varied and multiple roles, depending on his audience and behavioral situation. On any given day a man may move through the roles of stern father, loving husband, car-pool comedian, skilled lathe operator, union steward, water-cooler flirt, and American Legion committee chairman — all psychologically different roles that he adopts as he moves from scene to scene on the social stage. Like actors on the dramatic stage, Goffman has noted, individuals can sustain roles only for reasonable periods of time, and no individual can play indefinitely, without relief, the variety of roles that life demands. There have to be moments "off stage" when the individual can be "himself": tender, angry, irritable, lustful, or dream-filled. . . .

Another form of emotional release is provided by the protection privacy gives to minor non-compliance with social norms. Some norms are formally adopted — perhaps as law — which society really expects many persons to break. This ambivalence produces a situation in which almost everyone does break some social or institutional norms — for example, violating traffic laws, breaking sexual mores, cheating on expense accounts, overstating income-tax deductions, or smoking in rest rooms when this is prohibited. Although society will usually punish the most flagrant abuses, it tolerates the great bulk of the violations as "permissible" deviations. If there were no privacy to permit society to ignore these deviations — if all transgressions were known — most persons in society would be under organizational discipline or in jail, or could be manipulated by threats of such action. The firm expectation of having privacy for permissible deviations is a distinguishing characteristic of life in a free society. At a lesser but still important level, privacy also allows individuals to deviate temporarily from social etiquette when alone or among intimates, as by putting feet on desks, cursing, letting one's face go slack, or scratching wherever one itches.

Another aspect of release is the "safety-valve" function afforded by privacy. Most persons need to give vent to their anger at "the system," "city hall," "the boss," and various others who exercise authority over them, and to do this in the intimacy of family or friendship circles, or in private papers, without fear of being held responsible for such comments. . . . Without the aid of such release in accommodating the daily abrasions with authorities, most people would experience serious emotional pressure. . . .

Limited and Protected Communication. The greatest threat to civilized social life would be a situation in which each individual was utterly candid in his communications with others, saying exactly what he knew or felt at all times. The havoc done to interpersonal relations by children, saints, mental patients, and adult "innocents" is legendary. . . .

Privacy for limited and protected communication has two general aspects. First, it provides the individual with the opportunities he needs for sharing confidences and intimacies with those he trusts — spouse, "the family," personal friends, and close associates at work. The individual discloses because he knows that his confidences will be held, and because he knows that breach of confidence violates social norms in a civilized society. "A friend," said Emerson, "is someone before . . . [whom] I can think aloud." In addition, the individual often wants to secure counsel from persons with whom he does not have to live daily after disclosing his confidences. He seeks professionally objective advice from persons whose status in society promises that they will not later use his distress to take advantage of him. To protect freedom of limited communication, such relationships — with doctors, lawyers, ministers, psychiatrists, psychologists, and others — are given varying but important degrees of legal privilege against forced disclosure. . . .

NOTES & QUESTIONS

1. ***Privacy as Control over Information.*** A number of theorists, including Westin, conceive of privacy as a form of control over personal information.[49] Consider Charles Fried's definition of privacy:

> At first approximation, privacy seems to be related to secrecy, to limiting the knowledge of others about oneself. This notion must be refined. It is not true, for instance, that the less that is known about us the more privacy we have. Privacy is not simply an absence of information about what is in the minds of others; rather it is the *control* we have over information about ourselves.
>
> To refer for instance to the privacy of a lonely man on a desert island would be to engage in irony. The person who enjoys privacy is able to grant or deny access to others. . . .

[49] *See* Adam Carlyle Breckenridge, *The Right to Privacy* 1 (1970); Randall P. Bezanson, *The Right to Privacy Revisited: Privacy, News, and Social Change, 1810–1990*, 80 Cal. L. Rev. 1133 (1992). For a critique of privacy as control, see Anita L. Allen, *Privacy as Data Control: Conceptual, Practical, and Moral Limits of the Paradigm*, 32 Conn. L. Rev. 861 (2000).

> Privacy, thus, is control over knowledge about oneself. But it is not simply control over the quantity of information abroad; there are modulations in the quality of the knowledge as well. We may not mind that a person knows a general fact about us, and yet feel our privacy invaded if he knows the details.[50]

Is this a compelling definition of privacy?

2. ***Privacy as Limited Access to the Self.*** Another group of theorists view privacy as a form of limited access to the self. Consider Ruth Gavison:

> . . . Our interest in privacy . . . is related to our concern over our accessibility to others: the extent to which we are known to others, the extent to which others have physical access to us, and the extent to which we are the subject of others' attention. This concept of privacy as concern for limited accessibility enables us to identify when losses of privacy occur. Furthermore, the reasons for which we claim privacy in different situations are similar. They are related to the functions privacy has in our lives: the promotion of liberty, autonomy, selfhood, and human relations, and furthering the existence of a free society. . . .
>
> The concept of privacy suggested here is a complex of these three independent and irreducible elements: secrecy, anonymity, and solitude. Each is independent in the sense that a loss of privacy may occur through a change in any one of the three, without a necessary loss in either of the other two. The concept is nevertheless coherent because the three elements are all part of the same notion of accessibility, and are related in many important ways.[51]

How does this theory of privacy differ from the notion of privacy as "the right to be let alone"? How does it differ from privacy as control over information? How much control should individuals have over access to themselves? Should the decision depend upon each particular person's desires? Or should there be an objective standard — a reasonable degree of control over access?

3. ***Privacy as Intimacy.*** A number of theorists argue that "intimacy" appropriately defines what information or matters are private. For example, Julie Inness argues that "intimacy" is the common denominator in all the matters that people claim to be private. Privacy is "the state of the agent having control over decisions concerning matters that draw their meaning and value from the agent's love, caring, or liking. These decisions cover choices on the agent's part about access to herself, the dissemination of information about herself, and her actions."[52]

---

[50] Charles Fried, *Privacy*, 77 Yale L.J. 475 (1968).

[51] Ruth Gavison, *Privacy and the Limits of Law*, 89 Yale L.J. 421 (1980); *see also* Edward Shils, *Privacy: Its Constitution and Vicissitudes*, 31 L. & Contemp. Probs. 281, 281 (1996); Sissela Bok, *Secrets: On the Ethics of Concealment and Revelation* 10-11 (1982); Ernest Van Den Haag, *On Privacy*, in *Nomos XII: Privacy* 149 (J. Ronald Pennock & J.W. Chapman eds., 1971); Sidney M. Jourard, *Some Psychological Aspects of Privacy*, 31 L. & Contemp. Probs. 307, 307 (1966); David O'Brien, *Privacy, Law, and Public Policy* 16 (1979); Hyman Gross, *The Concept of Privacy*, 42 N.Y.U. L. Rev. 34 (1967).

[52] Julie C. Inness, *Privacy, Intimacy, and Isolation* 56, 58, 63, 64, 67 (1992). For other proponents of privacy as intimacy, see Robert S. Gerstein, *Intimacy and Privacy*, in *Philosophical Dimensions of Privacy: An Anthology* 265, 265 (Ferdinand David Schoeman ed., 1984); James Rachels, *Why Privacy Is Important*, in *Philosophical Dimensions of Privacy: An Anthology* 290,

Jeffrey Rosen adopts a similar view when he writes:

> . . . Privacy protects us from being misdefined and judged out of context in a world of short attention spans, a world in which information can easily be confused with knowledge. True knowledge of another person is the culmination of a slow process of mutual revelation. It requires the gradual setting aside of social masks, the incremental building of trust, which leads to the exchange of personal disclosures. It cannot be rushed; this is why, after intemperate self-revelation in the heat of passion, one may feel something close to self-betrayal. True knowledge of another person, in all of his or her complexity, can be achieved only with a handful of friends, lovers, or family members. In order to flourish, the intimate relationships on which true knowledge of another person depends need space as well as time: sanctuaries from the gaze of the crowd in which slow mutual self-disclosure is possible.
>
> When intimate personal information circulates among a small group of people who know us well, its significance can be weighed against other aspects of our personality and character. By contrast, when intimate information is removed from its original context and revealed to strangers, we are vulnerable to being misjudged on the basis of our most embarrassing, and therefore most memorable, tastes and preferences. . . . In a world in which citizens are bombarded with information, people form impressions quickly, based on sound bites, and these impressions are likely to oversimplify and misrepresent our complicated and often contradictory characters.[53]

Does "intimacy" adequately separate private matters from public ones? Can something be private but not intimate? Can something be intimate but not private?

In reaction to Rosen's views on privacy, Lawrence Lessig restates the problem of short attention spans in this fashion: "Privacy, the argument goes, would remedy such a problem by concealing those things that would not be understood with the given attention span. Privacy's function . . . is not to protect the presumptively innocent from true but damaging information, but rather to protect the actually innocent from damaging conclusions drawn from misunderstood information."[54] Lessig notes his skepticism regarding this approach: privacy will not alone solve the problem with the information market. Moreover, there "are possible solutions to this problem of attention span. But what should be clear is that there is no guarantee that a particular problem of attention span will have any solution at all."

JULIE E. COHEN, *EXAMINED LIVES: INFORMATIONAL PRIVACY AND THE SUBJECT AS OBJECT*

52 Stan. L. Rev. 1373 (2000)

Prevailing market-based approaches to data privacy policy — including "solutions" in the form of tradable privacy rights or heightened disclosure require-

---

292 (Ferdinand David Schoeman ed., 1984); Tom Gerety, *Redefining Privacy*, 12 Harv. C.R.-C.L. L. Rev. 233 (1977).

[53] Jeffrey Rosen, *The Unwanted Gaze: The Destruction of Privacy in America* 8-9 (2000).

[54] Lawrence Lessig, *Privacy and Attention Span*, 89 Geo. L. J. 2063, 2065 (2001).

ments before consent — treat preferences for informational privacy as a matter of individual taste, entitled to no more (and often much less) weight than preferences for black shoes over brown or red wine over white. But the values of informational privacy are far more fundamental. A degree of freedom from scrutiny and categorization by others promotes important noninstrumental values, and serves vital individual and collective ends.

First, informational autonomy comports with important values concerning the fair and just treatment of individuals within society. From Kant to Rawls, a central strand of Western philosophical tradition emphasizes respect for the fundamental dignity of persons, and a concomitant commitment to egalitarianism in both principle and practice. Advocates of strong data privacy protection argue that these principles have clear and very specific implications for the treatment of personally-identified data: They require that we forbid data-processing practices that treat individuals as mere conglomerations of transactional data, or that rank people as prospective customers, tenants, neighbors, employees, or insureds based on their financial or genetic desirability. . . .

Autonomous individuals do not spring full-blown from the womb. We must learn to process information and to draw our own conclusions about the world around us. We must learn to choose, and must learn something before we can choose anything. Here, though, information theory suggests a paradox: "Autonomy" connotes an essential independence of critical faculty and an imperviousness to influence. But to the extent that information shapes behavior, autonomy is radically contingent upon environment and circumstance. . . . Autonomy in a contingent world requires a zone of relative insulation from outside scrutiny and interference — a field of operation within which to engage in the conscious construction of self. The solution to the paradox of contingent autonomy, in other words, lies in a second paradox: To exist in fact as well as in theory, autonomy must be nurtured.

A realm of autonomous, unmonitored choice, in turn, promotes a vital diversity of speech and behavior. The recognition that anonymity shelters constitutionally-protected decisions about speech, belief, and political and intellectual association — decisions that otherwise might be chilled by unpopularity or simple difference — is part of our constitutional tradition. . . .

The benefits of informational privacy are related to, but distinct from, those afforded by seclusion from visual monitoring. It is well-recognized that respite from visual scrutiny affords individuals an important measure of psychological repose. Within our society, at least, we are accustomed to physical spaces within which we can be unobserved, and intrusion into those spaces is experienced as violating the boundaries of self. But the scrutiny, and the repose, can be informational as well as visual, and this does not depend entirely on whether the behavior takes place "in private." The injury, here, does not lie in the exposure of formerly private behaviors to public view, but in the dissolution of the boundaries that insulate different spheres of behavior from one another. The universe of all information about all record-generating behaviors generates a "picture" that, in some respects, is more detailed and intimate than that produced by visual observation, and that picture is accessible, in theory and often in reality, to just about anyone who wants to see it. In such a world, we all may be more cautious.

The point is not that people will not learn under conditions of no-privacy, but that they will learn differently, and that the experience of being watched will constrain, ex ante, the acceptable spectrum of belief and behavior. Pervasive monitoring of every first move or false start will, at the margin, incline choices toward the bland and the mainstream. The result will be a subtle yet fundamental shift in the content of our character, a blunting and blurring of rough edges and sharp lines. . . . The condition of no-privacy threatens not only to chill the expression of eccentric individuality, but also, gradually, to dampen the force of our aspirations to it. . . .

. . . [T]he insulation provided by informational privacy also plays a subtler, more conservative role in reinforcing the existing social fabric. Sociologist Erving Goffman demonstrated that the construction of social facades to mediate between self and community is both instinctive and expected. Alan Westin describes this social dimension of privacy as "reserve." This characterization, though, seems incomplete. On Goffman's account, the construction of social personae isn't just about withholding information that we don't want others to have. It is about defining the parameters of social interaction in ways that maximize social ease, and thus is about collective as well as individual comfort. We do not need, or even want, to know each other that well. Less information makes routine interactions easier; we are then free to choose, consensually and without embarrassment, the interactions that we wish to treat as less routine. Informational privacy, in short, is a constitutive element of a civil society in the broadest sense of that term. . . .

NOTES & QUESTIONS

1. ***Privacy and Respect for Persons.*** Julie Cohen's theory locates the purpose of privacy as promoting the development of autonomous individuals and, more broadly, civil society. Compare her theory to the following theory by Stanley Benn:

> Finding oneself an object of scrutiny, as the focus of another's attention, brings one to a new consciousness of oneself, as something seen through another's eyes. According to [Jean-Paul] Sartre, indeed, it is a necessary condition for knowing oneself as anything at all that one should conceive oneself as an object of scrutiny. It is only through the regard of the other that the observed becomes aware of himself as an object, knowable, having a determinate character, in principle predictable. His consciousness of pure freedom as subject, as originator and chooser, is at once assailed by it; he is fixed as *something* — with limited probabilities rather than infinite, indeterminate possibilities. . . .
>
> The underpinning of a claim not to be watched without leave will be more general if it can be grounded in this way on the principle of respect for persons than on a utilitarian duty to avoid inflicting suffering. . . . But respect for persons will sustain an objection even to secret watching, which may do no actual harm at all. Covert observation — spying — is objectionable because it deliberately deceives a person about his world, thwarting, for reasons that *cannot* be his reasons, his attempts to make a rational choice. One cannot be said to respect a man as engaged on an enterprise worthy of consideration if

one knowingly and deliberately alters his conditions of action, concealing the fact from him. . . .[55]

How is Cohen's theory similar to and/or different from Benn's?

Benn argues that privacy is a form of respect for persons. By being watched, Benn contends, the observed becomes "fixed as *something* — with limited probabilities rather than infinite indeterminate possibilities." Does Benn adequately capture why surveillance is harmful? Is Benn really concerned about the negative consequences of surveillance on a person's behavior? Or is Benn more concerned about the violation of respect for another?

DANIEL J. SOLOVE, *CONCEPTUALIZING PRIVACY*

90 Cal. L. Rev. 1087 (2002)

Despite what appears to be a welter of different conceptions of privacy, I argue that they can be dealt with under six general headings, which capture the recurrent ideas in the discourse. These headings include: (1) the right to be let alone — Samuel Warren and Louis Brandeis's famous formulation for the right to privacy; (2) limited access to the self — the ability to shield oneself from unwanted access by others; (3) secrecy — the concealment of certain matters from others; (4) control over personal information — the ability to exercise control over information about oneself; (5) personhood — the protection of one's personality, individuality, and dignity; and (6) intimacy — control over, or limited access to, one's intimate relationships or aspects of life. Some of the conceptions concentrate on means to achieve privacy; others focus on the ends or goals of privacy. Further, there is overlap between conceptions, and the conceptions discussed under different headings are by no means independent from each other. For example, control over personal information can be seen as a subset of limited access to the self, which in turn bears significant similarities to the right to be let alone. . . .

The most prevalent problem with the conceptions is that they are either too narrow or too broad. The conceptions are often too narrow because they fail to include the aspects of life that we typically view as private, and are often too broad because they fail to exclude matters that we do not deem private. Often, the same conceptions can suffer from being both too narrow and too broad. I contend that these problems stem from the way that the discourse goes about the task of conceptualizing privacy. . . .

Most attempts to conceptualize privacy thus far have followed the traditional method of conceptualizing. The majority of theorists conceptualize privacy by defining it *per genus et differentiam*. In other words, theorists look for a common set of necessary and sufficient elements that single out privacy as unique from other conceptions. . . .

[Philosopher Ludwig] Wittgenstein suggests that certain concepts might not share one common characteristic; rather they draw from a common pool of simi-

---

[55] Stanley I. Benn, *Privacy, Freedom, and Respect for Persons*, from *Nomos XIII: Privacy* (J. Ronald Pennock & J.W. Chapman eds., 1971).

lar characteristics, "a complicated network of similarities overlapping and criss-crossing: sometimes overall similarities, sometimes similarities of detail." . . . Wittgenstein uses the term "family resemblances," analogizing to the overlapping and crisscrossing characteristics that exist between members of a family, such as "build, features, colour of eyes, gait, temperament, etc." For example, in a family, each child has certain features similar to each parent; and the children share similar features with each other; but they may not all resemble each other in the same way. Nevertheless, they all bear a resemblance to each other. . . .

When we state that we are protecting "privacy," we are claiming to guard against disruptions to certain practices. Privacy invasions disrupt and sometimes completely annihilate certain practices. Practices can be disrupted in certain ways, such as interference with peace of mind and tranquility, invasion of solitude, breach of confidentiality, loss of control over facts about oneself, searches of one's person and property, threats to or violations of personal security, destruction of reputation, surveillance, and so on.

There are certain similarities in particular types of disruptions as well as in the practices that they disrupt; but there are differences as well. We should conceptualize privacy by focusing on the specific types of disruption and the specific practices disrupted rather than looking for the common denominator that links all of them. If privacy is conceptualized as a web of interconnected types of disruption of specific practices, then the act of conceptualizing privacy should consist of mapping the typography of the web. . . .

It is reductive to carve the world of social practices into two spheres, public and private, and then attempt to determine what matters belong in each sphere. First, the matters we consider private change over time. While some form of dichotomy between public and private has been maintained throughout the history of Western civilization, the matters that have been considered public and private have metamorphosed throughout history due to changing attitudes, institutions, living conditions, and technology. The matters we consider to be private are shaped by culture and history, and have differed across cultures and historical epochs.

Second, although certain matters have moved from being public to being private and vice versa, the change often has been more subtle than a complete transformation from public to private. Particular matters have long remained private but in different ways; they have been understood as private but because of different attributes; or they have been regarded as private for some people or groups but not for others. In other words, to say simply that something is public or private is to make a rather general claim; what it means for something to be private is the central question. We consider our Social Security number, our sexual behavior, our diary, and our home private, but we do not consider them private in the same way. A number of aspects of life have commonly been viewed as private: the family, body, and home to name a few. To say simply that these things are private is imprecise because what it means for them to be private is different today than it was in the past. . . .

. . . [P]rivacy is not simply an empirical and historical question that measures the collective sense in any given society of what is and has long been considered to be private. Without a normative component, a conception of privacy can only provide a status report on existing privacy norms rather than guide us toward shaping privacy law and policy in the future. If we focus simply on people's current expectations of privacy, our conception of privacy would continually shrink given the increasing surveillance in the modern world. Similarly, the government could gradually condition people to accept wiretapping or other privacy incursions, thus altering society's expectations of privacy. On the other hand, if we merely seek to preserve those activities and matters that have historically been considered private, then we fail to adapt to the changing realities of the modern world. . .

NOTES & QUESTIONS

1. ***Core Characteristics vs. Family Resemblances.*** Is there a core characteristic common in all the things we understand as being "private"? If so, what do you think it is? Can privacy be more adequately conceptualized by shifting away from the quest to find the common core characteristics of privacy?
2. ***Context.*** Solove contends that the meaning of privacy depends upon context, that there is no common denominator to all things we refer to as "privacy." Does this make privacy too amorphous a concept?

   Consider Helen Nissenbaum:

   > Specifically, whether a particular action is determined a violation of privacy is a function of several variables, including the nature of the situation, or context; the nature of the information in relation to that context; the roles of agents receiving information; their relationships to information subjects; on what terms the information is shared by the subject; and the terms of further dissemination. . . .
   >
   > [N]orms of privacy in fact vary considerably from place to place, culture to culture, period to period; this theory not only incorporates this reality but systematically pinpoints the sources of variation. A second consequence is that, because questions about whether particular restrictions on flow are acceptable call for investigation into the relevant contextual details, protecting privacy will be a messy task, requiring a grasp of concepts and social institutions as well as knowledge of facts of the matter.[56]

3. ***Revising the Prosser Taxonomy.*** Daniel Solove contends that the taxonomy of four privacy interests identified by William Prosser, *supra,* must be revised as well as expanded beyond tort law. Solove identifies 16 different kinds of activity that create privacy harms or problems:

   > The first group of activities that affect privacy involve information collection. *Surveillance* is the watching, listening to, or recording of an individual's activities. *Interrogation* consists of various forms of questioning or probing for information.
   >
   > A second group of activities involves the way information is stored, manipulated, and used — what I refer to collectively as "information processing." *Aggregation* involves the combination of various pieces of data about a person. *Identification* is linking information to particular individuals. *Insecurity* involves carelessness in protecting stored information from being leaked or

[56] Helen Nissenbaum, *Privacy as Contextual Integrity,* 79 Wash. L. Rev. 119, 155-56 (2004).

improperly accessed. *Secondary use* is the use of information collected for one purpose for a different purpose without a person's consent. *Exclusion* concerns the failure to allow people to know about the data that others have about them and participate in its handling and use. These activities do not involve the gathering of data, since it has already been collected. Instead, these activities involve the way data is maintained and used.

The third group of activities involves the dissemination of information. *Breach of confidentiality* is breaking the promise to keep a person's information confidential. *Disclosure* involves the revelation of truthful information about a person which impacts the way others judge that person's character. *Exposure* involves revealing another's nudity, grief, or bodily functions. *Increased accessibility* is amplifying the accessibility of information. *Blackmail* is the threat to disclose personal information. *Appropriation* involves the use of another's identity to serve the aims and interests of another. *Distortion* consists of the dissemination of false or misleading information about individuals. Information dissemination activities all involve the spreading or transfer of personal data — or the threat to do so.

The fourth and final group of activities involves invasions into people's private affairs. Invasion, unlike the other groupings, need not involve personal information (although in numerous instances, it does). *Intrusion* concerns invasive acts that disturb one's tranquility or solitude. *Decisional interference* involves the government's incursion into people's decisions regarding their private affairs.[57]

4. ***Reductionists.*** Some theorists, referred to as "reductionists," assert that privacy can be reduced to other concepts and rights. For example, Judith Jarvis Thomson contends that there is nothing particularly distinctive about privacy and to talk about things as violating the "right to privacy" is not all that useful. Privacy is really a cluster of other rights, such as the right to liberty, property rights, and the right not to be injured: "[T]he right to privacy is everywhere overlapped by other rights."[58] Is there something distinctive about privacy? Or can privacy be explained in terms of other, more primary rights and interests? What does privacy capture that these other rights and interests (autonomy, property, liberty, etc.) do not?

ANITA L. ALLEN, *COERCING PRIVACY*

40 Wm. & Mary L. Rev. 723 (1999)

. . . The final decades of the twentieth century could be remembered for the rapid erosion of expectations of personal privacy and of the taste for personal privacy in the United States. . . . I sense that people expect increasingly little physical, informational, and proprietary privacy, and that people seem to prefer less of these types of privacy relative to other goods. . . .

One way to address the erosion would be to stop the avalanche of technology and commercial opportunity responsible for the erosion. We could stop the

---

[57] Daniel J. Solove, *A Taxonomy of Privacy,* 154 U. Pa. L. Rev. 477 (2006). For a more complete account of Solove's theory, see Daniel J. Solove, *Understanding Privacy* (2008).

[58] Judith Jarvis Thomson, *The Right to Privacy*, 4 Phil. & Pub. Aff. 295 (1975).

avalanche of technology, but we will not, if the past is any indication. . . . In the United States, with a few exceptions like government-funded human cloning and fetal tissue research, the rule is that technology marches on.

We could stop the avalanche of commercial opportunity by intervening in the market for privacy; that is, we could (some way or another) increase the costs of consuming other people's privacy and lower the profits of voluntarily giving up one's own privacy. The problem with this suggested strategy is that, even without the details of implementation, it raises the specter of censorship, repression, paternalism, and bureaucracy. Privacy is something we think people are supposed to want; if it turns out that they do not, perhaps third parties should not force it on them, decreasing both their utility and that of those who enjoy disclosure, revelation, and exposure.

Of course, we force privacy on people all the time. Our elected officials criminalize public nudity, even to the point of discouraging breastfeeding. . . . It is one thing, the argument might go, to force privacy on someone by criminalizing nude sun-bathing and topless dancing. These activities have pernicious third-party effects and attract vice. It would be wrong, the argument might continue, to force privacy on someone, in the absence of harm to others, solely on the grounds that one ought not say too much about one's thoughts, feelings, and experiences; one ought not reveal in detail how one spends one's time at home; and one ought not live constantly on display. Paternalistic laws against extremes of factual and physical self-revelation seem utterly inconsistent with liberal self-expression, and yet such laws are suggested by the strong claims liberal theorists make about the value of privacy. Liberal theorists claim that we need privacy to be persons, independent thinkers, free political actors, and citizens of a tolerant democracy. . . .

For people under forty-five who understand that they do not, and cannot, expect to have many secrets, informational privacy may now seem less important. As a culture, we seem to be learning how to be happy and productive — even spiritual — knowing that we are like open books, our houses made of glass. Our parents may appear on the television shows of Oprah Winfrey or Jerry Springer to discuss incest, homosexuality, miscegenation, adultery, transvestitism, and cruelty in the family. Our adopted children may go on television to be reunited with their birth parents. Our law students may compete with their peers for a spot on the MTV program The Real World, and a chance to live with television cameras for months on end and be viewed by mass audiences. Our ten-year-olds may aspire to have their summer camp experiences — snits, fights, fun, and all — chronicled by camera crews and broadcast as entertainment for others on the Disney Channel.

Should we worry about any of this? What values are at stake? Scholars and other commentators associate privacy with several important clusters of value. Privacy has value relative to normative conceptions of spiritual personality, political freedom, health and welfare, human dignity, and autonomy. . . .

To speak of "coercing" privacy is to call attention to privacy as a foundation, a precondition of a liberal egalitarian society. Privacy is not an optional good, like a second home or an investment account. . . .

A hard task seems to lay before us — namely, deciding which forms of privacy are so critical that they should become matters of coercion. . . .

As liberals, we should not want people to sell all their freedom, and, as liberals, we should not want people to sell all their privacy and capacities for private choices. This is, in part, because the liberal conceptions of private choice as freedom from governmental and other outside interference with decisionmaking closely link privacy and freedom. The liberal conception of privacy as freedom from unwanted disclosures, publicity, and loss of control of personality also closely links privacy to freedom. . . .

Government will have to intervene in private lives for the sake of privacy and values associated with it. . . . The threat to liberalism is not that individuals sometimes expose their naked bodies in public places, display affection with same-sex partners in public, or broadcast personal information on national television. The threat to liberalism is that in an increasing variety of ways our lives are being emptied of privacy on a daily basis, especially physical and informational privacy. . . .

NOTES & QUESTIONS

1. ***Should Privacy Be an Inalienable Right?*** Allen argues that people regularly surrender their privacy and that we should "coerce" privacy. In other words, privacy must be seen as an inalienable right, one that people cannot give away. What if a person wants to live in the spotlight or to give away her personal information? Why shouldn't she be allowed to do so? Recall those who defined privacy as control over information. One aspect of control is that an individual can decide for herself how much privacy she desires. What would Allen say about such a definition of privacy?
2. ***Privacy and Publicity.*** Consider also whether a desire for publicity and a desire for privacy can coexist. Does the person who "tells it all" on the Jerry Springer talk show have any less expectation of privacy when she returns home to be with her family and friends or picks up the telephone to make a private call?
3. ***Eroding Expectations of Privacy.*** Allen contends that our society is changing by becoming more exhibitionistic and voyeuristic. The result is that expectations of privacy are eroding. If people no longer expect privacy in many situations, then why should we continue to protect it?

PAUL M. SCHWARTZ, *PRIVACY AND DEMOCRACY IN CYBERSPACE*

52 Vand. L. Rev. 1609 (1999)

. . . Self-determination is a capacity that is embodied and developed through social forms and practices. The threat to this quality arises when private or government action interferes with a person's control of her reasoning process. . . . [P]erfected surveillance of naked thought's digital expression short-circuits the individual's own process of decisionmaking. . . .

The maintenance of a democratic order requires both deliberative democracy and an individual capacity for self-determination. . . . [T]he emerging pattern of information use in cyberspace poses a risk to these two essential values. Our task now is to develop privacy standards that are capable of structuring the right kind of information use. . . .

Most scholars, and much of the law in this area, work around a liberal paradigm that we can term "privacy-control." From the age of computer mainframes in the 1960s to the current reign of the Internet's decentralized networks, academics and the law have gravitated towards the idea of privacy as a personal right to control the use of one's data. . . .

. . . [One flaw with the "privacy-control" paradigm is the "autonomy trap."] [T]he organization of information privacy through individual control of personal data rests on a view of autonomy as a given, preexisting quality. . . .

As a policy cornerstone, however, the idea of privacy-control falls straight into the "autonomy trap." The difficulty with privacy-control in the Information Age is that individual self-determination is itself shaped by the processing of personal data. . . .

To give an example of an autonomy trap in cyberspace, the act of clicking through a "consent" screen on a Web site may be considered by some observers to be an exercise of self-reliant choice. Yet, this screen can contain boilerplate language that permits all further processing and transmission of one's personal data. Even without a consent screen, some Web sites place consent boilerplate within a "privacy statement" on their home page or elsewhere on their site. For example, the online version of one New York newspaper states, "By using this site, you agree to the Privacy Policy of the New York Post." This language presents the conditions for data processing on a take-it-or-leave-it basis. It seeks to create the legal fiction that all who visit this Web site have expressed informed consent to its data processing practices. An even more extreme manifestation of the "consent trap" is a belief that an initial decision to surf the Web itself is a self-reliant choice to accept all further use of one's personal data generated by this activity. . . .

The liberal ideal views autonomous individuals as able to interact freely and equally so long as the government or public does not interfere. The reality is, however, that individuals can be trapped when such glorification of freedom of action neglects the actual conditions of choice. Here, another problem arises with self-governance through information-control: the "data seclusion deception." The idea of privacy as data seclusion is easy to explain: unless the individual wishes to surrender her personal information, she is to be free to use her privacy right as a trump to keep it confidential or to subject its release to conditions that she alone wishes to set. The individual is to be at the center of shaping data anonymity. Yet, this right to keep data isolated quickly proves illusory because of the demands of the Information Age. . . .

NOTES & QUESTIONS

1. ***Privacy and Personhood.*** Like Schwartz, a number of theorists argue that privacy is essential for self-development. According to Jeffrey Reiman, privacy "protects the individual's interest in becoming, being, and remaining

a person."[59] The notion that privacy protects personhood or identity is captured in Warren and Brandeis's notion of "inviolate personality." How does privacy promote self-development?

Consider the following: "Every acceptance of a public role entails the repression, channelizing, and deflection of 'private' or personal attention, motives, and demands upon the self in order to address oneself to the expectations of others."[60] Can we really be ourselves in the public sphere? Is our "public self" any less part of our persona than our "private self"?

2. ***Privacy and Democracy.*** Schwartz views privacy as essential for a democratic society. Why is privacy important for political participation?
3. ***Privacy and Role Playing.*** Recall Westin's view of selfhood:

> Each person is aware of the gap between what he wants to be and what he actually is, between what the world sees of him and what he knows to be his much more complex reality. In addition, there are aspects of himself that the individual does not fully understand but is slowly exploring and shaping as he develops. Every individual lives behind a mask in this manner; indeed, the first etymological meaning of the word "person" was "mask," indicating both the conscious and expressive presentation of the self to a social audience. If this mask is torn off and the individual's real self bared to a world in which everyone else still wears his mask and believes in masked performances, the individual can be seared by the hot light of selective, forced exposure.

Is there a "true" or "core" or "authentic" self? Or do we perform many roles and perhaps have multiple selves? Is there a self beneath the roles that we play?

Daniel Solove contends that "[s]ociety accepts that public reputations will be groomed to some degree. . . . Society protects privacy because it wants to provide individuals with some degree of influence over how they are judged in the public arena."[61] To what extent should the law allow people to promote a polished public image and hide the dirt in private?

4. ***Control over Information.*** Schwartz criticizes the conception of privacy as control over information. Why? What are the problems of viewing privacy as a right to control personal information?

SPIROS SIMITIS, *REVIEWING PRIVACY IN AN INFORMATION SOCIETY*

135 U. Pa. L. Rev. 707 (1987)

. . . The increased access to personal information resulting from modern, sophisticated techniques of automated processing has sharpened the need to abandon the search for a "neutral" concept in favor of an understanding free of abstractions and fully aware of the political and societal background of all

[59] Jeffrey H. Reiman, *Privacy, Intimacy, and Personhood*, in *Philosophical Dimensions of Privacy: An Anthology* 300, 308 (Ferdinand David Schoeman ed., 1984).

[60] Joseph Bensman & Robert Lilienfeld, *Between Public and Private: Lost Boundaries of the Self* 174 (1979).

[61] Daniel J. Solove, *The Virtues of Knowing Less: Justifying Privacy Protections Against Disclosure,* 53 Duke L.J. 957 (2003).

privacy debates. Modern forms of data collection have altered the privacy discussion in three principal ways. First, privacy considerations no longer arise out of particular individual problems; rather, they express conflicts affecting everyone. The course of the privacy debate is neither determined by the caricature of a prominent golfer with a chocolate packet protruding out of his pocket, nor by the hints at the use of a sexual stimulant by a respected university professor, but by the intensive retrieval of personal data of virtually every employee, taxpayer, patient, bank customer, welfare recipient, or car driver. Second, smart cards and videotex make it possible to record and reconstruct individual activities in minute detail.[62] Surveillance has thereby lost its exceptional character and has become a more and more routine practice. Finally, personal information is increasingly used to enforce standards of behavior. Information processing is developing, therefore, into an essential element of long-term strategies of manipulation intended to mold and adjust individual conduct. . . .

. . . [B]ecause of both the broad availability of personal data and the elaborate matching procedures, individual activities can be accurately reconstructed through automated processing. Surveillance becomes the order of the day. Significantly enough, security agencies were among the first to discover the advantages of automated retrieval. They not only quickly computerized their own data collections but also sought and obtained access to state and private data banks. Entirely new investigation techniques, such as computer profiling, were developed, enabling the agencies to trace wanted persons by matching a presumptive pattern of consumption habits against, for instance, the records of utility companies. The successful attempts at computer-based voice and picture identification will probably influence the work of security agencies even more. . . .

Both the quest for greater transparency and the defense of free speech are legitimated by the goal of allowing the individual to understand social reality better and thus to form a personal opinion on its decisive factors as well as on possible changes. The citizen's right to be "a participator in the government of affairs," to use Jefferson's terms, reflects a profoundly rational process. It presupposes individuals who not only disperse the necessary information but also have the capacity to transform the accessible data into policy expectations. Transparency is, in other words, a basic element of competent communicative action and consequently remains indispensable as long as social discourse is to be promoted, not inhibited.

Inhibition, however, tends to be the rule once automated processing of personal data becomes a normal tool of both government and private enterprises. The price for an undoubted improvement in transparency is a no less evident loss in competence of communication. Habits, activities, and preferences are compiled, registered, and retrieved to facilitate better adjustment, not to improve the individual's capacity to act and to decide. Whatever the original incentive for

[62] Editors' Note: Smart cards are also known as "chip cards" or "integrated circuit cards." These devices, generally the size of a credit card, feature an embedded circuit for the processing of data. A precursor of the Internet, Videotex enjoyed its heyday from the late 1970s to mid-1980s. Videotex was typically deployed through a centralized system with one provider of information and involved the display of text on a television screen or dedicated terminal. France Telecom's Minitel was the most successful videotext system in the world.

computerization may have been, processing increasingly appears as the ideal means to adapt an individual to a predetermined, standardized behavior that aims at the highest possible degree of compliance with the model patient, consumer, taxpayer, employee, or citizen. Furthermore, interactive systems do not, despite all contrary assertions, restore a long lost individuality by correcting the effects of mass production in a mass society. On the contrary, the telematic integration forces the individual once more into a preset scheme. The media supplier dictates the conditions under which communication takes place, fixes the possible subjects of the dialogue, and, due to the personal data collected, is in an increasingly better position to influence the subscriber's behavior. Interactive systems, therefore, suggest individual activity where in fact no more than stereotyped reactions occur.

In short, the transparency achieved through automated processing creates possibly the best conditions for colonization of the individual's lifeworld.[63] Accurate, constantly updated knowledge of her personal history is systematically incorporated into policies that deliberately structure her behavior. The more routinized automated processing augments the transparency, however, the more privacy proves to be a prerequisite to the capacity to participate in social discourse. Where privacy is dismantled, both the chance for personal assessment of the political and societal process and the opportunity to develop and maintain a particular style of life fade. . . .

The processing of personal data is not unique to a particular society. On the contrary, the attractiveness of information technology transcends political boundaries, particularly because of the opportunity to guide the individual's behavior. For a democratic society, however, the risks are high: labeling of individuals, manipulative tendencies, magnification of errors, and strengthening of social control threaten the very fabric of democracy. Yet, despite the incontestable importance of its technical aspects, informatization, like industrialization, is primarily a political and social challenge. When the relationship between information processing and democracy is understood, it becomes clear that the protection of privacy is the price necessary to secure the individual's ability to communicate and participate. Regulations that create precisely specified conditions for personal data processing are the decisive test for discerning whether society is aware of this price and willing to pay it. If the signs of experience are correct, this payment can be delayed no further. There is, in fact, no alternative to the advice of Horace: Seize the day, put not trust in the morrow. . . .

NOTES & QUESTIONS

1. ***Privacy and Democracy.*** As Simitis and other authors in this section observe, privacy is an issue about social structure. What is the relationship between privacy and democracy according to Simitis?

---

[63] For both the colonization process and the impact of the individual's lifeworld on communicative action, see Jürgen Habermas, 1 *The Theory of Communicative Action* 70-71 (1983) (defining "lifeworld" as shared understandings about what will be treated as a fact, valid norms, and subjective experience). . . .

2. ***Privacy Law and Information Flow.*** Generally, one would assume that greater information flow facilitates democracy — it enables more expression, more political discourse, more information about the workings of government. Simitis, however, contends that privacy is "necessary to secure the individual's ability to communicate and participate." How are these two notions about information flow to be reconciled? Consider Joel Reidenberg:

> Data privacy rules are often cast as a balance between two basic liberties: fundamental human rights on one side and the free flow of information on the other side. Yet, because societies differ on how and when personal information should be available for private and public sector needs, the treatment and interaction of these liberties will express a specific delineation between the state, civil society, and the citizen.[64]

Privacy, according to Reidenberg, involves establishing a balance between protecting the rights of individuals and enabling information flow. Do you think these interests always exist in opposition? Consider financial services, communications networks, and medical care. Does privacy impair or enable information flow?[65]

3. CRITICS OF PRIVACY

AMITAI ETZIONI, *THE LIMITS OF PRIVACY*
(1999)

. . . Although we cherish privacy in a free society, we also value other goods. Hence, we must address the moral, legal, and social issues that arise when serving the common good entails violating privacy.

When I mentioned the subject of this book to audiences of friends, students in my classes, and members of the public, initially they were all taken aback. Privacy, they pointed out, is under siege, if not already overrun. Given privacy's great importance to a free people, my listeners stressed, one should seek new ways to shore it up, not cast more aspersions on it.

To begin a new dialogue about privacy, I have asked these and similar audiences if they would like to know whether the person entrusted with their child care is a convicted child molester. I mention that when such screening is done, thousands are found to have criminal records, ones that include pedophilia. I further ask: Would they want to know whether the staff of a nursing home in which their mother now lives have criminal records that include abusing the elderly? I note that 14 percent of such employees are found to have criminal records, some of which include violent acts against senior citizens. And should

---

[64] Joel R. Reidenberg, *Resolving Conflicting International Data Privacy Rules in Cyberspace,* 52 Stan. L. Rev. 1315 (2000).

[65] For additional reading about philosophical theories of privacy, see Judith W. DeCew, *In Pursuit of Privacy: Law, Ethics, and the Rise of Technology* (1997) (surveying and critiquing various theories of privacy); Anita L. Allen, *Uneasy Access: Privacy for Women in a Free Society* (1988) (same); Ferdinand David Schoeman, ed., *Philosophical Dimensions of Privacy* (1984) (anthology of articles about the concept of privacy).

public authorities be entitled to determine whether drivers of school buses, pilots, or police officers are under the influence of illegal drugs? Should the FBI be in a position to crack the encryption messages employed by terrorists before they use them to orchestrate the next Oklahoma City bombing? Addressing such concerns raises the question of if and when we are justified in implementing measures that diminish privacy in the service of the common good. . . .

Communitarianism holds that a good society seeks a carefully crafted balance between individual rights and social responsibilities, between liberty and the common good. . . .

. . . [T]he next step is to apply this principle to actual societies. We can then ask whether a particular society, in a given period, leans too far in one direction or the other. In a society that strongly enforces social duties but neglects individual rights (as does Japan, for instance, when it comes to the rights of women, minorities, and the disabled), strenuously fostering the other side in order to achieve balance would entail the expansion of autonomy. Indeed, even in the West, when John Locke, Adam Smith, and John Stuart Mill wrote their influential works, and for roughly the first 190 years of the American republic, the struggle to expand the realm of individual liberty was extremely justified, and there was little reason to be concerned that social responsibilities would be neglected. However, as communitarians have repeatedly noted, the relationship between rights and responsibilities drastically shifted in American society between 1960 and 1990 as a new emphasis on personal autonomy and individualism gradually overwhelmed other societal considerations. . . .

. . . *[T]he best way to curtail the need for governmental control and intrusion is to have somewhat less privacy*. This point requires some elaboration.

The key to understanding this notion lies in the importance, especially to communitarians, of the "third realm." This realm is not the state or the market (or individual choices), but rather the community, which relies on subtle social fostering of prosocial conduct by such means as communal recognition, approbation, and censure. These processes require the scrutiny of some behavior, not by police or secret agents, but by friends, neighbors, and fellow members of voluntary associations. . . .

. . . [P]ublicness reduces the need for public control, while excessive privacy often necessitates state-imposed limits on private choices. . . .

NOTES & QUESTIONS

1. ***Privacy and the Common Good.*** Is Etzioni correct in viewing privacy as in tension with the common good? In what ways might privacy serve the common good? Consider the following argument from Priscilla Regan:

> . . . The philosophical basis of privacy policy overemphasizes the importance of privacy to the individual and fails to recognize the broader social importance of privacy. This emphasis of privacy as an individual right or an individual interest provides a weak basis for formulating policy to protect privacy. When privacy is defined as an individual right, policy formulation entails a balancing of the individual right to privacy against a competing interest or right. In general, the competing interest is recognized as a social

> interest. For example, the police interest in law enforcement, the government interest in detecting fraud, and an employer's interest in securing an honest work force are discussed and defined as societal interests. It is also assumed that the individual has a stake in these societal interests. As a result, privacy has been on the defensive, with those alleging a privacy invasion bearing the burden of proving that a certain activity does indeed invade privacy and that the "social" benefit to be gained from the privacy invasion is less important than the individual harm incurred. . . .
>
> Privacy is a *common value* in that all individuals value some degree of privacy and have some common perceptions about privacy. Privacy is also a *public value* in that it has value not just to the individual as an individual or to all individuals in common but also to the democratic political system. . .
>
> A public value of privacy derives not only from its protection of the individual as an individual but also from its usefulness as a restraint on the government or on the use of power. . . .[66]

2. ***Communities and Privacy Norms.*** Paul Schwartz has criticized Etzioni's approach to privacy on a number of grounds.[67] First, groups that act as intermediaries between the individual and the State have often proven oppressive of their members, and this intolerance undercuts Etzioni's belief that strengthening the community will further privacy. Second, communities, as norm theorists have pointed out, often generate inefficient norms. The standard examples of such inefficient norms are the overfishing of New England waters by whalers and dueling, which long persisted as a means of resolving disputes in the antebellum South. Beyond inefficiency, communities may generate privacy norms that are wrong for other reasons.
3. ***Warren and Brandeis.*** Consider once again the characterization of privacy set out by Brandeis and Warren. Does this strengthen or undermine the various communal interests described by Etzioni?

RICHARD A. POSNER, *THE RIGHT OF PRIVACY*

12 Ga. L. Rev. 393 (1978)

People invariably possess information, including facts about themselves and contents of communications, that they will incur costs to conceal. Sometimes such information is of value to others: that is, others will incur costs to discover it. Thus we have two economic goods, "privacy" and "prying." . . .

[M]uch of the casual prying (a term used her without any pejorative connotation) into the private lives of friends and colleagues that is so common a feature of social life is also motivated, to a greater extent than we may realize, by rational considerations of self-interest. Prying enables one to form a more accurate picture of a friend or colleague, and the knowledge gained is useful in one's social or professional dealings with him. For example, in choosing a friend one legitimately wants to know whether he will be discreet or indiscreet, selfish

---

[66] Priscilla M. Regan, *Legislating Privacy: Technology, Social Values, and Public Policy* 213, 225 (1995).

[67] Paul M. Schwartz, *Internet Privacy and the State*, 32 Conn L. Rev. 815, 838-43 (2000).

or generous, and these qualities are not always apparent on initial acquaintance. Even a pure altruist needs to know the (approximate) wealth of any prospective beneficiary of his altruism in order to be able to gauge the value of a transfer to him.

The other side of the coin is that social, like business, dealings present opportunities for exploitation through misrepresentation. Psychologists and sociologists have pointed out that even in every day life people try to manipulate by misrepresentation other people's opinion of them. As one psychologist has written, the "wish for privacy expresses a desire . . . to control others' perceptions and beliefs vis-à-vis the self-concealing person." Even the strongest defenders of privacy describe the individual's right to privacy as the right to "control the flow of information about him." A seldom remarked corollary to a right to misrepresent one's character is that others have a legitimate interest in unmasking the deception.

Yet some of the demand for private information about other people is not self-protection in the foregoing sense but seems mysteriously disinterested — for example, that of the readers of newspaper gossip columns, whose "idle curiosity" Warren and Brandeis deplored, groundlessly in my opinion. Gossip columns recount the personal lives of wealthy and successful people whose tastes and habits offer models — that is, yield information — to the ordinary person in making consumption, career, and other decisions. . . . Gossip columns open people's eyes to opportunities and dangers; they are genuinely informational. . . .

Warren and Brandeis attributed the rise of curiosity about people's lives to the excesses of the press. The economist does not believe, however, that supply creates demand. A more persuasive explanation for the rise of the gossip column is the secular increase in personal incomes. There is apparently very little privacy in poor societies, where, consequently, people can easily observe at first hand the intimate lives of others. Personal surveillance is costlier in wealthier societies both because people live in conditions that give them greater privacy from such observation and because the value (and hence opportunity cost) of time is greater—too great to make a generous allotment of time to watching neighbors worthwhile. People in wealthier societies sought an alternative method of informing themselves about how others live and the press provided it. A legitimate and important function of the press is to provide specialization in prying in societies where the costs of obtaining information have become too great for the Nosey Parker. . . .

Transaction-cost considerations may also militate against the assignment of a property right to the possessor of a secret. . . . Consider, for example, . . . whether the law should allow a magazine to sell its subscriber list to another magazine without obtaining the subscribers' consent. . . . [T]he costs of obtaining subscriber approval would be high relative to the value of the list. If, therefore, we believe that these lists are generally worth more to the purchasers than being shielded from possible unwanted solicitations is worth to the subscribers, we should assign the property right to the magazine; and the law does this. . . .

Much of the demand for privacy . . . concerns discreditable information, often information concerning past or present criminal activity or moral conduct at variance with a person's professed moral standards. And often the motive for concealment is, as suggested earlier, to mislead those with whom he transacts.

Other private information that people wish to conceal, while not strictly discreditable, would if revealed correct misapprehensions that the individual is trying to exploit, as when a worker conceals a serious health problem from his employer or a prospective husband conceals his sterility from his fiancée. It is not clear why society should assign the property right in such information to the individual to whom it pertains; and the common law, as we shall see, generally does not. . . .

We think it wrong (and inefficient) that the law should permit a seller in hawking his wares to make false or incomplete representations as to their quality. But people "sell" themselves as well as their goods. They profess high standards of behavior in order to induce others to engage in social or business dealings with them from which they derive an advantage but at the same time they conceal some of the facts that these acquaintances would find useful in forming an accurate picture of their character. There are practical reasons for not imposing a general legal duty of full and frank disclosure of one's material. . . .

. . . [E]veryone should be allowed to protect himself from disadvantageous transactions by ferreting out concealed facts about individuals which are material to the representations (implicit or explicit) that those individuals make concerning their moral qualities.

It is no answer that such individuals have "the right to be let alone." Very few people want to be let alone. They want to manipulate the world around them by selective disclosure of facts about themselves. Why should others be asked to take their self-serving claims at face value and be prevented from obtaining the information necessary to verify or disprove these claims?

NOTES & QUESTIONS

1. ***Posner's Conception of Privacy.*** What is Posner's definition of privacy? How does Posner determine the value of privacy (i.e., how it should be weighed relative to other interests and values)? In what circumstances is Posner likely to defend a privacy claim?
2. ***Irrational Judgments.*** One economic argument for privacy is that sometimes people form irrational judgments based upon learning certain information about others. For example, an employer may not hire certain people based on their political views or associations, sexual orientation, mental illness, and prior criminal convictions — even though these facts may have no relevance to a potential employee's abilities to do the job. These judgments decrease efficiency. In *The Economics of Justice*, Posner offers a response:

   > This objection overlooks the opportunity costs of shunning people for stupid reasons, or, stated otherwise, the gains from dealing with someone whom others shun irrationally. If ex-convicts are good workers but most employers do not know this, employers who do know will be able to hire them at a below-average wage because of their depressed job opportunities and will thereby obtain a competitive advantage over the bigots. In a diverse,

> decentralized, and competitive society, irrational shunning will be weeded out over time. . .[68]

Will the market be able to eradicate irrational judgments?

3. ***The Dangers of the "Masquerade Ball."*** Consider Dennis Bailey:

> . . . [I]t is interesting to consider the ways in which the world has become like a giant masquerade ball. Far removed from the tight knit social fabric of the village of the past, we've lost the ability to recognize the people we pass on the street. People might as well be wearing masks because we are likely to know very little about them. In other words, these strangers are anonymous to us, anonymous in the sense that not only their names, but their entire identities, are unknown to us — the intimate details of who they are, where they have come from, and how they have lived their lives. . . .
>
> [A]nonymity has become one of the central vulnerabilities of an open society. Freedom may have allowed [9/11 terrorists] al-Mihdhar and al-Hamzi to rent an apartment, use a cell phone, meet with terrorists overseas, and take flying lessons in preparation for 9/11, but anonymity kept hidden the manner in which these individual actions fit together into a larger mosaic of death.[69]

Are we living in a "masquerade ball"? Businesses and the government have unprecedented new technologies to engage in surveillance and gather information. Should the law facilitate or restrict anonymity?

Also consider Steven Nock:

> Any method of social control depends, immediately, on information about individuals. . . . There can be no social control without such information. . . .
>
> Modern Americans enjoy vastly more privacy than did their forebears because ever and ever larger numbers of strangers in our lives are legitimately denied access to our personal affairs. . . . Privacy, however, makes it difficult to form reliable opinions of one another. Legitimately shielded from other's regular scrutiny, we are thereby more immune to the routine monitoring that once formed the basis of our individual reputations.[70]

Does too much privacy erode trust and lessen social control in detrimental ways?

4. ***Information Dissemination and Economic Efficiency.*** Does economic theory necessarily lead to the conclusion that more personal information is generally preferable? Consider the following critique of Posner by Edward Bloustein:

> We must remember that Posner stated in *Economic Analysis of Law* that economics "cannot prescribe social change"; it can only tell us about the economic costs of managing it one way or another. . . . [Posner's] characterization of the privacy of personal information as a species of commercial fraud . . . [is an] extension[ ] of a social value judgment rather than implications or conclusions of economic theory. . . .Our society, in fact,

---

[68] Richard A. Posner, *The Economics of Justice* (1981). Posner further develops his theories about privacy in Richard A. Posner, *Overcoming Law* 531-51 (1995). Posner first set out his views on privacy in Richard A. Posner, *An Economic Theory of Privacy*, Regulations (May/June 1978).

[69] Dennis Bailey, *The Open Society Paradox* 26-27 (2004).

[70] Steven L. Nock, *The Costs of Privacy: Surveillance and Reputation in America* (1993).

> places a very high value on maintaining individual privacy, even to the extent of concealing "discreditable" information. . . .[71]

Also consider Richard Murphy's critique of Posner:

> [D]emarcating a relatively large sphere for the private self creates an opportunity for discovery or actualization of a "true" nature, which may have a value beyond the utility of satisfying preferences. . . . As Roger Rosenblatt put it, "Out of our private gropings and self-inspections grow our imaginative values — private language, imagery, memory. In the caves of the mind one bats about to discover a light entirely of one's own which, though it should turn out to be dim, is still worth a life." Unless a person can investigate without risk of reproach what his own preferences are, he will not be able to maximize his own happiness.[72]

When can the circulation of less personal information be more economically efficient than greater information flow?

5. ***Why Don't Individuals Protect Their Privacy?*** Empirical studies frequently report on growing privacy concerns across the United States. Yet, individuals seem willing to exchange privacy for services or small rewards and generally fail to adopt technologies and techniques that would protect their privacy. If people are willing to sell their privacy for very little in return, isn't this evidence that they do not really value privacy as much as they say they do?

Alessandro Acqusiti and Jens Grossklags have pointed to a number of reasons for this divergence between stated privacy preferences and actual behavior:

> First, incomplete information affects privacy decision making because of externalities (when third parties share personal information about an individual, they might affect that individual without his being part of the transaction between those parties), information asymmetries (information relevant to the privacy decision process — for example, how personal information will be used — might be known only to a subset of the parties making decisions), risk (most privacy related payoffs are not deterministic), and uncertainties (payoffs might not only be stochastic, but dependent on unknown random distributions). Benefits and costs associated with privacy intrusions and protection are complex, multifaceted, and context-specific. They are frequently bundled with other products and services (for example, a search engine query can prompt the desired result but can also give observers information about the searcher's interests), and they are often recognized only after privacy violations have taken place. They can be monetary but also immaterial and, thus, difficult to quantify.
>
> Second, even if individuals had access to complete information, they would be unable to process and act optimally on vast amounts of data. Especially in the presence of complex, ramified consequences associated with the protection or release of personal information, our innate bounded rationality limits our ability to acquire, memorize and process all relevant information,

[71] Edward J. Bloustein, *Privacy Is Dear at Any Price: A Response to Professor Posner's Economic Theory*, 12 Ga. L. Rev. 429, 441 (1978). For another critique of Posner's approach, see Kim Lane Scheppele, *Legal Secrets: Equality and Efficiency in the Common Law* (1988).

[72] Richard S. Murphy, *Property Rights in Personal Information: An Economic Defense of Privacy,* 84 Geo. L.J. 2381 (1996).

and it makes us rely on simplified mental models, approximate strategies, and heuristics. These strategies replace theoretical quantitative approaches with qualitative evaluations and "aspirational" solutions that stop short of perfect (numerical) optimization. Bounded problem solving is usually neither unreasonable nor irrational, and it needs not be inferior to rational utility maximization. However, even marginal deviations by several individuals from their optimal strategies can substantially impact the market outcome.

Third, even if individuals had access to complete information and could successfully calculate optimization strategies for their privacy sensitive decisions, they might still deviate from the rational strategy. A vast body of economic and psychological literature has revealed several forms of systematic psychological deviations from rationality that affect individual decision making. . . . Research in psychology . . . documents how individuals mispredict their own future preferences or draw inaccurate conclusions from past choices. In addition, individuals often suffer from self-control problems — in particular, the tendency to trade off costs and benefits in ways that damage their future utility in favor of immediate gratification. Individuals' behavior can also be guided by social preferences or norms, such as fairness or altruism. Many of these deviations apply naturally to privacy-sensitive scenarios.[73]

FRED H. CATE, *PRINCIPLES OF INTERNET PRIVACY*

32 Conn. L. Rev. 877 (2000)

Perhaps the most important consideration when balancing restrictions on information is the historical importance of the free flow of information. The free flow concept is one that is not only enshrined in the First Amendment, but frankly in any form of democratic or market economy. In the United States, we have placed extraordinary importance on the open flow of information. As the Federal Reserve Board noted in its report to Congress on data protection in financial institutions, "it is the freedom to speak, supported by the availability of information and the free-flow of data, that is the cornerstone of a democratic society and market economy."

The significance of open data flows is reflected in the constitutional provisions not only for freedom of expression, but for copyrights — to promote the creation and dissemination of expression, and for a post office — to deliver the mail and the news. Federal regulations demonstrate a sweeping preference for openness, reflected in the Freedom of Information Act, Government in the Sunshine Act, and dozens of other laws applicable to the government. There are even more laws requiring disclosure by private industry, such as the regulatory disclosures required by securities and commodities laws, banking and insurance laws, and many others. This is a very basic tenet of the society in which we live. Laws that restrict that free flow almost always conflict with this basic principle. That does not mean that such laws are never upheld, but merely that they face a considerable constitutional hurdle.

---

[73] Alessandro Acquisti & Jens Grossklags, *Privacy and Rationality in Decision Making*, IEEE, Security and Privacy 24 (2005).

This is done with good reason. Open information flows are not only essential to self-governance; they have also generated significant, practical benefits. The ready availability of personal information helps businesses "deliver the right products and services to the right customers, at the right time, more effectively and at lower cost," Fred Smith, founder and President of the Competitive Enterprise Institute, has written. Federal Reserve Board Governor Edward Gramlich testified before Congress in July 1999 that "[i]nformation about individuals' needs and preferences is the cornerstone of any system that allocates goods and services within an economy." The more such information is available, he continued, "the more accurately and efficiently will the economy meet those needs and preferences."

Federal Reserve Board Chairman Alan Greenspan has been perhaps the most articulate spokesperson for the extraordinary value of accessible personal information. In 1998, he wrote to Congressman Ed Markey (D-Mass.):

> A critical component of our ever more finely hewn competitive market system has been the plethora of information on the characteristics of customers both businesses and individuals. Such information has enabled producers and marketers to fine tune production schedules to the ever greater demands of our consuming public for diversity and individuality of products and services. Newly devised derivative products, for example, have enabled financial institutions to unbundle risk in a manner that enables those desirous of taking on that risk (and potential reward) to do so, and those that chose otherwise, to be risk averse. It has enabled financial institutions to offer a wide variety of customized insurance and other products.
>
> Detailed data obtained from consumers as they seek credit or make product choices help engender the whole set of sensitive price signals that are so essential to the functioning of an advanced information based economy such as ours. . . .

In a recent report on public record information, Richard Varn, Chief Information Officer of the State of Iowa, and I examined the critical roles played by public record information in our economy and society. We concluded that such information constitutes part of this nation's "essential infrastructure," the benefits of which are "so numerous and diverse that they impact virtually every facet of American life. . . ." The ready availability of public record data "facilitates a vibrant economy, improves efficiency, reduces costs, creates jobs, and provides valuable products and services that people want."

Perhaps most importantly, widely accessible personal information has helped to create a democratization of opportunity in the United States. Anyone can go almost anywhere, make purchases from vendors they will never see, maintain accounts with banks they will never visit, and obtain credit far from home all because of open information flows. Americans can take advantage of opportunities based on their records, on what they have done rather than who they know, because access to consumer information makes it possible for distant companies and creditors to make rational decisions about doing business with individuals. The open flow of information gives consumers real choice. This is what the open flow of information principle reflects, not just the constitutional importance of information flows, but their significant economic and social benefits as well.

NOTES & QUESTIONS

1. ***The Pros and Cons of the Free Flow of Information.*** In a striking passage, Cate points out that free flows of information create a "democratization of opportunity in the United States." With this phrase, he reminds us that part of the equality at the basis of American life concerns economic opportunity, and that, in his view, a certain kind of flow of personal information will contribute to this goal. While privacy can be problematic, can open access to information also raise difficulties? How should one establish a baseline for open access or restricted access to personal information?
2. ***The Costs of Privacy.*** Can you think of some of the other important values with which privacy might conflict and the costs that privacy can impose? What should the baseline be in measuring costs?
3. ***The Business of Data Trade.*** The trade in personal information is now a valuable part of the U.S. economy. As a single example, Google reached an agreement on April 14, 2007, to purchase DoubleClick, an online advertising company, for $3.1 billion. The deal was driven by Google's interest in behavioral advertising, in which companies use digital data collection techniques to track individuals around the Internet and serve them targeted ads. Should consumers be allowed to sign up for a National Do Not Track List?
4. ***The Benefits of Information Collection and Use.*** Consider Kent Walker:

> Having some information about yourself out there in the world offers real convenience that goes beyond dollars and cents. Many people benefit from warehousing information — billing and shipping addresses, credit card numbers, individual preferences, and the like — with trustworthy third parties. Such storage of information can dramatically simplify the purchasing experience, ensure that you get a nonsmoking room, or automate the task of ordering a kiddie meal every time your child boards a plane. Likewise, most people prefer to use a credit card rather than a debit card, trading confidentiality of purchases for the convenience of deferred payment. . . .
>
> While there's often little individual incentive to participate in the aggregation of information about people, a great collective good results from the default participation of most people. The aggregation of information often requires a critical mass to be worth doing, or for the results to be worth using. (A phone book with only one out of ten numbers would hardly be worth using, let alone printing.) . . .
>
> Another example is Caller ID, which pits different privacy claims against one another. Many people like the notion of an electronic peephole, letting them know who's at the electronic door before they decide whether to pick up the phone. Yet many people block transmission of their own numbers, valuing protection of their privacy. Neither choice is necessarily right, but it's worth recognizing that the assertion of the privacy claim affects the contending desires of others. The classic Tragedy of the Commons aspects are clear. From my selfish perspective, I want access to information about everyone else — the identity of who's calling me, their listed phone number, etc. I want to be able to intrude on others without their knowing who I am (which I can accomplish by blocking Caller ID), and don't want others to be able to intrude

> on me unbidden (which I can accomplish by unlisting my phone number). The gain in privacy makes it harder to find the people you want to reach, and harder to know who's calling you.[74]

5. ***Privacy as the "Cheshire Cat of Values"?*** Many commentators have noted that although people express concern over privacy, their behavior indicates that they do not care very much about privacy. As Jonathan Franzen, the novelist, writes:

> The panic about privacy has all the finger-pointing and paranoia of a good old American scare, but it's missing one vital ingredient: a genuinely alarmed public. Americans care about privacy in the abstract. . . .
>
> On closer examination . . . privacy proves to be the Cheshire cat of values: not much substance, but a very winning smile.
>
> Legally, the concept is a mess. Privacy violation is the emotional core of many crimes, from stalking and rape to Peeping Tommery and trespass, but no criminal statute forbids it in the abstract. . . .
>
> When Americans do genuinely sacrifice privacy . . . they do so for tangible gains in health or safety or efficiency. Most legalized infringements — HIV notification, airport X-rays, Megan's Law, Breathalyzer roadblocks, the drug-testing of student athletes, . . . remote monitoring of automobile emissions . . . are essentially public health measures. I resent the security cameras in Washington Square, but I appreciate the ones on a subway platform. The risk that someone is abusing my E-ZPass toll records seems to me comfortably low in comparison with my gain in convenience. Ditto the risk that some gossip rag will make me a victim of the First Amendment; with two hundred and seventy million people in the country, any individual's chances of being nationally exposed are next to nil.[75]

Do arguments about bounded rationality, as developed in the earlier section, answer Franzen's concerns?

4. THE FEMINIST PERSPECTIVE ON PRIVACY

Has the legal concept of privacy hurt or helped women throughout history? What is the impact of privacy on women today?

STATE V. RHODES

1868 WL 1278 (N.C. 1868)

[The defendant was indicted for an assault and battery upon his wife, Elizabeth Rhodes. The jury returned the following special verdict: "We find that the defendant struck Elizabeth Rhodes, his wife, three licks, with a switch about the size of one of his fingers (but not as large as a man's thumb) without any provocation except some words uttered by her and not recollected by the witness." The lower court found that the defendant "had a right to whip his wife

---

[74] Kent Walker, *Where Everybody Knows Your Name: A Pragmatic Look at the Costs of Privacy and the Benefits of Information Exchange,* 2000 Stan. Tech. L. Rev. 2, 39, 46, 48 (2000).

[75] Jonathan Franzen, *How to Be Alone: Essays* 42, 45-46 (2003).

with a switch no larger than his thumb, and that upon the facts found in the special verdict he was not guilty in law." Judgment in favor of the defendant was entered from which the State appealed.]

The laws of this State do not recognize *the right of the husband to whip his wife,* but our Courts will not interfere to punish him for moderate correction of her, even if there had been no provocation for it.

Family government being in its nature as complete in itself as the State government is in itself, the Courts will not attempt to control, or interfere with it, in favor of either party, except in cases where permanent or malicious injury is inflicted or threatened, or the condition of the party is intolerable.

In determining whether the husband has been guilty of an indictable assault and battery upon his wife, the criterion is the *effect produced,* and not the manner of producing it or the instrument used. . . .

READE J. The violence complained of would without question have constituted a battery if the subject of it had not been the defendant's wife. The question is how far that fact affects the case.

The courts have been loath to take cognizance of trivial complaints arising out of the domestic relations — such as master and apprentice, teacher and pupil, parent and child, husband and wife. Not because those relations are not subject to the law, but because the evil of publicity would be greater than the evil involved in the trifles complained of; and because they ought to be left to family government. . . .

In this case no provocation worth the name was proved. The fact found was that it was "without any provocation except some words which were not recollected by the witness." The words must have been of the slightest import to have made no impression on the memory. We must therefore, consider the violence as unprovoked. The question is therefore plainly presented, whether the court will allow a conviction of the husband for moderate correction of the wife without provocation.

Our divorce laws do not compel a separation of husband and wife, unless the conduct of the husband be so cruel as to render the wife's condition intolerable, or her life burdensome. What sort of conduct on the part of the husband, would be allowed to have that effect, has been repeatedly considered. And it has not been found easy to lay down any iron rule upon the subject. In some cases it has been held that actual and repeated violence to the person, was not sufficient. In others that insults, indignities and neglect without any actual violence, were quite sufficient. So much does each case depend upon its peculiar surroundings.

We have sought the aid of the experience and wisdom of other times, and of other countries.

Blackstone says "that the husband, by the old law, might give the wife moderate correction, for as he was to answer for her misbehavior, he ought to have the power to control her; but that in the polite reign of Charles the Second, this power of correction began to be doubted." . . . The old law of moderate correction has been questioned even in England, and has been repudiated in Ireland and Scotland. The old rule is approved in Mississippi, but it has met with but little favor elsewhere in the United States. In looking into the discussions of the other States we find but little uniformity. . . .

Our conclusion is that family government is recognized by law as being as complete in itself as the State government is in itself, and yet subordinate to it; and that we will not interfere with or attempt to control it, in favor of either husband or wife, unless in cases where permanent or malicious injury is inflicted or threatened, or the condition of the party is intolerable. For, however great are the evils of ill temper, quarrels, and even personal conflicts inflicting only temporary pain, they are not comparable with the evils which would result from raising the curtain, and exposing to public curiosity and criticism, the nursery and the bed chamber. Every household has and must have, a government of its own, modeled to suit the temper, disposition and condition of its inmates. Mere ebullitions of passion, impulsive violence, and temporary pain, affection will soon forget and forgive; and each member will find excuse for the other in his own frailties. But when trifles are taken hold of by the public, and the parties are exposed and disgraced, and each endeavors to justify himself or herself by criminating the other, that which ought to be forgotten in a day, will be remembered for life.

It is urged in this case, that as there was no provocation the violence was of course excessive and malicious; that every one in whatever relation of life should be able to purchase immunity from pain, by obedience to authority and faithfulness in duty. . . . Take the case before us. The witness said, there was no provocation except some slight words. But then who can tell what significance the trifling words may have had to the husband? Who can tell what had happened an hour before, and every hour for a week? To him they may have been sharper than a sword. And so in every case, it might be impossible for the court to appreciate what might be offered as an excuse, or no excuse might appear at all, when a complete justification exists. Or, suppose the provocation could in every case be known, and the court should undertake to weigh the provocation in every trifling family broil, what would be the standard? Suppose a case coming up to us from a hovel, where neither delicacy of sentiment nor refinement of manners is appreciated or known. The parties themselves would be amazed, if they were to be held responsible for rudeness or trifling violence. What do they care for insults and indignities? In such cases what end would be gained by investigation or punishment? Take a case from the middle class, where modesty and purity have their abode but nevertheless have not immunity from the frailties of nature, and are sometimes moved by the mysteries of passion. What could be more harassing to them, or injurious to society, than to draw a crowd around their seclusion. Or take a case from the higher ranks, where education and culture have so refined nature, that a look cuts like a knife, and a word strikes like a hammer; where the most delicate attention gives pleasure, and the slightest neglect pain; where an indignity is disgrace and exposure is ruin. Bring all these cases into court side by side, with the same offence charged and the same proof made; and what conceivable charge of the court to the jury would be alike appropriate to all the cases, except, That they all have domestic government, which they have formed for themselves, suited to their own peculiar conditions, and that those governments are supreme, and from them there is no appeal except in cases of great importance requiring the strong arm of the law, and that to those governments they must submit themselves.

It will be observed that the ground upon which we have put this decision, is not, that the husband has the *right* to whip his wife much or little; but that we will not interfere with family government in trifling cases. We will no more interfere where the husband whips the wife, than where the wife whips the husband; and yet we would hardly be supposed to hold, that a wife has a *right* to whip her husband. We will not inflict upon society the greater evil of raising the curtain upon domestic privacy, to punish the lesser evil of trifling violence. Two boys under fourteen years of age fight upon the play-ground, and yet the courts will take no notice of it, not for the reason that boys have the *right* to fight, but because the interests of society require that they should be left to the more appropriate discipline of the school room and of home. . . . The standard is the *effect produced,* and not the manner of producing it, or the instrument used.

Because our opinion is not in unison with the decisions of some of the sister States, or with the philosophy of some very respectable law writers, and could not be in unison with all, because of their contrariety, — a decent respect for the opinions of others has induced us to be very full in stating the reasons for our conclusion.

REVA B. SIEGEL, *"THE RULE OF LOVE": WIFE BEATING AS PREROGATIVE AND PRIVACY*

105 Yale L.J. 2117 (1996)

. . . The Anglo-American common law originally provided that a husband, as master of his household, could subject his wife to corporal punishment or "chastisement" so long as he did not inflict permanent injury upon her. During the nineteenth century, an era of feminist agitation for reform of marriage law, authorities in England and the United States declared that a husband no longer had the right to chastise his wife. Yet, for a century after courts repudiated the right of chastisement, the American legal system continued to treat wife beating differently from other cases of assault and battery. While authorities denied that a husband had the right to beat his wife, they intervened only intermittently in cases of marital violence: Men who assaulted their wives were often granted formal and informal immunities from prosecution, in order to protect the privacy of the family and to promote "domestic harmony." In the late 1970s, the feminist movement began to challenge the concept of family privacy that shielded wife abuse, and since then, it has secured many reforms designed to protect women from marital violence. . . .

Until the late nineteenth century, Anglo-American common law structured marriage to give a husband superiority over his wife in most aspects of the relationship. By law, a husband acquired rights to his wife's person, the value of her paid and unpaid labor, and most property she brought into the marriage. A wife was obliged to obey and serve her husband, and the husband was subject to a reciprocal duty to support his wife and represent her within the legal system. . . .

As master of the household, a husband could command his wife's obedience, and subject her to corporal punishment or "chastisement" if she defied his authority. In his treatise on the English common law, Blackstone explained that a husband could "give his wife moderate correction." . . .

During the 1850s, woman's rights advocates organized numerous conventions throughout the Northeast and Midwest, published newspapers, and conducted petition campaigns seeking for women the right to vote and demanding various reforms of marriage law. And in time the movement did elicit a response. Legislatures and courts began to modify the common law of marital status — first giving wives the right to hold property in marriage, and then the right to their earnings and the rudiments of legal agency: the right to file suit in their own names and to claim contract and tort damages. . . .

. . . By the 1880s, prominent members of the American Bar Association advocated punishing wife beaters at the whipping post, and campaigned vigorously for legislation authorizing the penalty. Between 1876 and 1906, twelve states and the District of Columbia considered enacting legislation that provided for the punishment of wife beaters at the whipping post. The bills were enacted in Maryland (1882), Delaware (1901), and Oregon (1906). . . .

We are left with a striking portrait of legal change. Jurists and lawmakers emphatically repudiated the doctrine of marital chastisement, yet responded to marital violence erratically — often condoning it, and condemning it in circumstances suggesting little interest in the plight of battered wives. Given this record, how are we to make sense of chastisement's demise? . . .

A key concept in the doctrinal regime that emerged from chastisement's demise was the notion of marital privacy. During the antebellum era, courts began to invoke marital privacy as a supplementary rationale for chastisement, in order to justify the common law doctrine within the discourse of companionate marriage, when rationales rooted in authority-based discourses of marriage had begun to lose their persuasive power. . . .

To quote a North Carolina chastisement opinion:

> We know that a slap on the cheek, let it be as light as it may, indeed any touching of the person of another in a rude or angry manner — is in law an assault and battery. In the nature of things it cannot apply to persons in the marriage state, it would break down the great principle of mutual confidence and dependence; throw open the bedroom to the gaze of the public; and spread discord and misery, contention and strife, where peace and concord ought to reign. It must be remembered that rules of law are intended to act in all classes of society. . . .

In *Rhodes*, the defendant whipped his wife "three licks, with a switch about the size of one of his fingers (but not as large as a man's thumb)"; the trial court ruled that a husband had the right to chastise his wife and so was not guilty of assault and battery. On appeal, the North Carolina Supreme Court upheld the verdict but justified it on different grounds. Opening its opinion with the blunt observation that "[t]he violence complained of would without question have constituted a battery if the subject of it had not been the defendant's wife," the court explained why it would not find the defendant guilty:

> The courts have been loath to take cognizance of trivial complaints arising out of the domestic relations — such as master and apprentice, teacher and pupil, parent and child, husband and wife. Not because those relations are not subject to law, but because the evil of publicity would be greater than the evil involved

in the trifles complained of; and because they ought to be left to family government. . . .

. . . By now it should be clear enough how privacy talk was deployed in the domestic violence context to enforce and preserve authority relations between man and wife. . . .

. . . By the early twentieth century, numerous state supreme courts had barred wives from suing their husbands for intentional torts — typically on the grounds that "the tranquility of family relations" would be "disturb[ed]." . . .

It was not until the late 1970s that the contemporary women's rights movement mounted an effective challenge to this regime. Today, after numerous protest activities and law suits, there are shelters for battered women and their children, new arrest procedures for police departments across the country, and even federal legislation making gender-motivated assaults a civil rights violation. . .

There is remarkably little scholarship on the social history of privacy discourses; consequently, we know very little about the ways in which conceptions of privacy shaped popular understandings of marriage, or marital violence, in the nineteenth century. But there is no reason to assume that, before demise of the chastisement prerogative, married persons understood a traditional prerogative of marriage, rooted in notions of a husband's authority as master and head of his household, in a framework of "privacy" and "domestic harmony." It seems just as likely that legal elites devised the story linking "privacy" and "domestic harmony" to wife beating in the wake of chastisement's demise (or in anticipation of it). . . .

CATHARINE A. MACKINNON, *TOWARD A FEMINIST THEORY OF THE STATE* (1989)

The liberal ideal of the private holds that, as long as the public does not interfere, autonomous individuals interact freely and equally. Privacy is the ultimate value of the negative state. Conceptually, this private is hermetic. It means that which is inaccessible to, unaccountable to, unconstructed by, anything beyond itself. By definition, it is not part of or conditioned by anything systematic outside it. It is personal, intimate, autonomous, particular, individual, the original source and final outpost of the self, gender neutral. It is defined by everything that feminism reveals women have never been allowed to be or to have, and by everything that women have been equated with and defined in terms of men's ability to have. To complain in public of inequality within the private contradicts the liberal definition of the private. . . . Its inviolability by the state, framed as an individual right, presupposes that the private is not already an arm of the state. In this scheme, intimacy is implicitly thought to guarantee symmetry of power. Injuries arise through violation of the private sphere, not within and by and because of it.

In private, consent tends to be presumed. Showing coercion is supposed to avoid this presumption. But the problem is getting anything private to be perceived as coercive. This is an epistemic problem of major dimensions and explains why privacy doctrine is most at home at home, the place women experience the most force, in the family, and why it centers on sex. Why a person would "allow" force in private (the "why doesn't she leave" question raised to battered women) is a question given its insult by the social meaning of the private as a sphere of choice. For women the measure of the intimacy has been the measure of oppression. This is why feminism has seen the personal as the political. The private is public for those for whom the personal is political. In this sense, for women there is no private, either normatively or empirically. Feminism confronts the fact that women have no privacy to lose or to guarantee. Women are not inviolable. Women's sexuality is not only violable, it is — hence, women are — seen in and as their violation. To confront the fact that women have no privacy is to confront the intimate degradation of women as the public order. . . .

When the law of privacy restricts intrusions into intimacy, it bars changes in control over that intimacy through law. The existing distribution of power and resources within the private sphere are precisely what the law of privacy exists to protect. . . . [T]he legal concept of privacy can and has shielded the place of battery, marital rape, and women's exploited domestic labor. It has preserved the central institutions whereby women are deprived of identity, autonomy, control, and self-definition. It has protected a primary activity through which male supremacy is expressed and enforced. . . .

This right to privacy is a right of men "to be let alone" to oppress women one at a time. . . .

ANITA L. ALLEN, *UNEASY ACCESS: PRIVACY FOR WOMEN IN A FREE SOCIETY* (1988)

Critiques of privacy such as MacKinnon's go wrong at the point where the historic unequal treatment of women and the misuse of the private household to further women's domination is taken as grounds for rejecting either the condition of privacy itself or the long-overdue legal rights to effective decisionmaking that promote and protect that condition. Privacy, here broadly defined as the inaccessibility of persons, their mental states, or information about them to the senses and surveillance devices of others . . . does not pose an inherent threat to women. Nor do sex, love, marriage, and children any longer presume the total abrogation of the forms of privacy a woman might otherwise enjoy. On the contrary, women today are finally in a position to expect, experience, and exploit real privacy within the home and within heterosexual relationships. The women's movement, education, access to affordable birth control, liberalized divorce laws, and the larger role for women in politics, government, and the economy have expanded women's opinions and contributed to the erosion of oppressively nonegalitarian styles of home life. These advances have enhanced the capacity of American men and women, but especially and for the first time women, to secure conditions of adequate and meaningful privacy at home paramount to moral personhood and responsible participation in families and larger segments of society. Instead of rejecting privacy as "male ideology" and subjugation, women can and ought to embrace opportunities for privacy and the exercise of reproductive liberty in their private lives.

NOTES & QUESTIONS

1. ***Privacy and Gender.*** As the *Rhodes* court stated in 1868: "We will not interfere with family government in trifling cases. We will no more interfere where the husband whips the wife, than where the wife whips the husband; and yet we would hardly be supposed to hold, that a wife has a *right* to whip her husband." Is this decision really a neutral one? Does the right to privacy described by Warren and Brandeis apply equally to men and women?[76]
2. ***The Uses of the Public/Private Distinction.*** Reva Siegel points out the troubling use of privacy to protect the oppression of women in the home, which Catharine MacKinnon has discussed at length elsewhere. Is MacKinnon's negative response to the public/private distinction justifiable given the prior uses of this distinction? Or do you agree with Anita Allen that privacy can and should not be abandoned as a value despite its checkered past?[77]
3. ***To What Extent Can Law Change Social Practices?*** According to Frances Olsen, "The notion of noninterference in the family depends upon some shared conception of proper family roles, and 'neutrality' [of the State] can be understood only with reference to such roles."[78] This idea suggests that privacy, within or without the family, might also depend on shared views as to proper social roles. Do you agree?

   Olsen also notes: "The theory of the private family, like free market theory, includes the assertion that particularized adjustments of seemingly unfair or inhumane results will not actually serve anybody's long run interests." Specifically, "it is claimed that state intervention to protect the weaker family members from abuse by the stronger is ineffective because powerful, underlying 'real' relations between family members will inevitably reassert themselves." This argument, which one might term the argument from futility, was rejected in the course of the twentieth century by the powerful social movement to stop spousal abuse and mistreatment of children. Are similar arguments from futility being made today about the "inevitable" erosion of privacy?

---

[76] For a feminist critique of the Warren and Brandeis article, see Anita L. Allen & Erin Mack, *How Privacy Got Its Gender*, 10 N. Ill. U. L. Rev. 441 (1990).

[77] For an overview of the feminist critique of privacy, see generally Judith W. DeCew, *In Pursuit of Privacy: Law, Ethics, and the Rise of Technology* 81-94 (1997); Patricia Boling, *Privacy and the Politics of Intimate Life* (1996); Frances Olsen, *Constitutional Law: Feminist Critiques of the Public/Private Distinction*, 10 Const. Commentary 327 (1993); Ruth Gavison, *Feminism and the Public/Private Distinction,* 45 Stan. L. Rev. 21 (1992).

[78] Frances Olsen, *The Family and the Market: A Study of Ideology and Legal Reform*, 96 Harv. L. Rev. 1497, 1506 (1983).

CHAPTER 2

PRIVACY AND THE MEDIA

In 1890, Samuel Warren and Louis Brandeis wrote about the increasing proliferation of gossip in newspapers.[1] Today, the problems Warren and Brandeis were concerned about are dramatically magnified by the vast expansion of the media. In addition to newspapers, there are magazines, movies, television, and the Internet. From marketers to moviemakers, from tabloids to 24-hour news channels, from talk shows to reality TV, we are witnessing an explosion in the demand for images, video, and stories about the personal lives of individuals, both famous and obscure. Further, anybody with a website can now disseminate information instantly around the world.

Warren and Brandeis were also concerned with photography, a new technology that had the potential to greatly facilitate information gathering by the media. Today, technologies of gathering data are significantly more sophisticated. Video cameras are in widespread use and exist in miniature forms for easy concealment; high-powered telephoto lenses can enable one to film or photograph from large distances. Moreover, almost every cell phone now contains a small built-in camera.

This chapter focuses on legal remedies for the gathering and dissemination of personal information by media entities. "Media" is understood broadly in this chapter to include people and businesses that gather and disseminate information to inform, advertise, or entertain. The chapter then explores four general types of privacy incursion by the media: (1) intrusions and harassment in the course of gathering information; (2) the disclosure of truthful information, (3) the dissemination of misleading or false information; and (4) the appropriation of name or likeness. The principal remedies for media incursions into privacy are the four privacy torts inspired by Warren and Brandeis's article. The privacy torts are not the only remedies for privacy invasions. The tort of defamation, discussed at length in this chapter, is an older remedy for a particular type of privacy intrusion — the dissemination of false information. Another remedy is the tort of infliction of emotional distress, which is discussed briefly in section C. Additionally, a number of states have enacted statutes that protect against particular forms of disclosure.

---

[1] Samuel D. Warren & Louis D. Brandeis, *The Right to Privacy,* 4 Harv. L. Rev. 193 (1890).

A. INFORMATION GATHERING

In order to report the news, journalists must gather information. This task often involves being nosy, inquisitive, and aggressive. Given the vast proliferation of media and the tremendous competition to get breaking information and live video or photographs, there is great potential for media information gathering to become intrusive and harassing, especially when a person becomes the subject of a prominent story. In response to such intrusions by information gatherers, an injured party has available a number of remedies. The primary remedy is the tort of intrusion upon seclusion. Some states, such as California, have passed statutes providing remedies from aggressive photographers, known as "paparazzi." These two types of remedies will be the focus of this section. Other remedies include trespass (if the newsgatherer wrongfully entered one's home or property) and fraud (if the newsgatherer lied or used deceitful methods to obtain information). Additionally, the electronic surveillance laws of many states provide remedies when one records the conversations of others without their consent. In a number of states, consent is required from all participants to a conversation. In some states and under federal electronic surveillance law, consent is only required from one of the parties. As a consequence of such one-party consent statutes, a journalist can secretly record a conversation in which she participates.

1. INTRUSION UPON SECLUSION

INTRUSION UPON SECLUSION

Restatement (Second) of Torts § 652B

One who intentionally intrudes, physically or otherwise, upon the solitude or seclusion of another or his private affairs or concerns, is subject to liability to the other for invasion of his privacy, if the intrusion would be highly offensive to a reasonable person.

NOTES & QUESTIONS

1. ***Intrusion Upon Seclusion vs. Public Disclosure of Private Facts.*** The tort of intrusion concerns the way that the information is obtained. In contrast, for the tort of public disclosure of private facts, liability does not depend upon how the information is obtained. Consider the following commentary to the Restatement:

   Comment (a): Intrusion "does not depend upon any publicity given to the person whose interest is invaded or to his affairs."

   Comment (b): "The intrusion itself makes the defendant subject to liability, even though there is no publication or other use of any kind of the photograph or information outlined."

NADER V. GENERAL MOTORS CORP.

255 N.E.2d 765 (N.Y. Ct. App. 1970)

FULD, C. J. . . . The plaintiff [Ralph Nader], an author and lecturer on automotive safety, has, for some years, been an articulate and severe critic of General Motors' products from the standpoint of safety and design. According to the complaint — which, for present purposes, we must assume to be true — the appellant [General Motors Corporation], having learned of the imminent publication of the plaintiff's book "Unsafe at Any Speed," decided to conduct a campaign of intimidation against him in order to "suppress plaintiff's criticism of and prevent his disclosure of information" about its products. To that end, the appellant authorized and directed the other defendants to engage in a series of activities which, the plaintiff claims in his first two causes of action, violated his right to privacy.

Specifically, the plaintiff alleges that the appellant's agents (1) conducted a series of interviews with acquaintances of the plaintiff, "questioning them about, and casting aspersions upon (his) political . . . racial and religious views. . . ; his integrity; his sexual proclivities and inclinations; and his personal habits"; (2) kept him under surveillance in public places for an unreasonable length of time; (3) caused him to be accosted by girls for the purpose of entrapping him into illicit relationships; (4) made threatening, harassing and obnoxious telephone calls to him; (5) tapped his telephone and eavesdropped, by means of mechanical and electronic equipment, on his private conversations with others; and (6) conducted a "continuing" and harassing investigation of him. [Nader's complaint, among other things, contained a cause of action for intrusion.]

. . . It should be emphasized that the mere gathering of information about a particular individual does not give rise to a cause of action under [the intrusion tort]. Privacy is invaded only if the information sought is of a confidential nature and the defendant's conduct was unreasonably intrusive. Just as a common-law copyright is lost when material is published, so, too, there can be no invasion of privacy where the information sought is open to public view or has been voluntarily revealed to others. In order to sustain a cause of action for invasion of privacy, therefore, the plaintiff must show that the appellant's conduct was truly "intrusive" and that it was designed to elicit information which would not be available through normal inquiry or observation. . . .

. . . At most, only two of the activities charged to the appellant are, in our view, actionable as invasions of privacy under the law of the District of Columbia. . . .

Turning, then, to the particular acts charged in the complaint, we cannot find any basis for a claim of invasion of privacy, under District of Columbia law, in the allegations that the appellant, through its agents or employees, interviewed many persons who knew the plaintiff, asking questions about him and casting aspersions on his character. Although those inquiries may have uncovered information of a personal nature, it is difficult to see how they may be said to have invaded the plaintiff's privacy. Information about the plaintiff which was already known to others could hardly be regarded as private to the plaintiff. Presumably, the plaintiff had previously revealed the information to such other persons, and he would necessarily assume the risk that a friend or acquaintance in whom he had confided might breach the confidence. If, as alleged, the questions tended to disparage the plaintiff's character, his remedy would seem to be by way of an action for defamation, not for breach of his right to privacy.

Nor can we find any actionable invasion of privacy in the allegations that the appellant caused the plaintiff to be accosted by girls with illicit proposals, or that it was responsible for the making of a large number of threatening and harassing telephone calls to the plaintiff's home at odd hours. Neither of these activities, howsoever offensive and disturbing, involved intrusion for the purpose of gathering information of a private and confidential nature. . . .

Apart, however, from the foregoing allegations which we find inadequate to spell out a cause of action for invasion of privacy under District of Columbia law, the complaint contains allegations concerning other activities by the appellant or its agents which do satisfy the requirements for such a cause of action. The one which most clearly meets those requirements is the charge that the appellant and its codefendants engaged in unauthorized wiretapping and eavesdropping by mechanical and electronic means. . . .

There are additional allegations that the appellant hired people to shadow the plaintiff and keep him under surveillance. In particular, he claims that, on one occasion, one of its agents followed him into a bank, getting sufficiently close to him to see the denomination of the bills he was withdrawing from his account. From what we have already said, it is manifest that the mere observation of the plaintiff in a public place does not amount to an invasion of his privacy. But, under certain circumstances, surveillance may be so "overzealous" as to render it actionable. Whether or not the surveillance in the present case falls into this latter category will depend on the nature of the proof. A person does not automatically make public everything he does merely by being in a public place, and the mere fact that Nader was in a bank did not give anyone the right to try to discover the amount of money he was withdrawing. On the other hand, if the plaintiff acted in such a way as to reveal that fact to any casual observer, then, it may not be said that the appellant intruded into his private sphere. In any event, though, it is enough for present purposes to say that the surveillance allegation is not insufficient as a matter of law. . . .

BRIETEL, J. concurring in the result. . . . [S]cholars, in trying to define the elusive concept of the right of privacy, have, as of the present, subdivided the common law right into separate classifications, most significantly distinguishing between unreasonable intrusion and unreasonable publicity. This does not mean, however, that the classifications are either frozen or exhausted, or that several of the classifications may not overlap.

Concretely applied to this case, it is suggested, for example, that it is premature to hold that the attempted entrapment of plaintiff in a public place by seemingly promiscuous ladies is no invasion of any of the categories of the right to privacy and is restricted to a much more limited cause of action for intentional infliction of mental distress. Moreover, it does not strain credulity or imagination to conceive of the systematic "public" surveillance of another as being the implementation of a plan to intrude on the privacy of another. Although acts performed in "public," especially if taken singly or in small numbers, may not be confidential, at least arguably a right to privacy may nevertheless be invaded through extensive or exhaustive monitoring and cataloguing of acts normally disconnected and anonymous.

These are but illustrations of the problems raised in attempting to determine issues of relevancy and allocability of evidence in advance of a trial record. The other allegations so treated involve harassing telephone calls, and investigatory interviews. It is just as important that while allegations treated singly may not constitute a cause of action, they may do so in combination, or serve to enhance other violations of the right to privacy.

It is not unimportant that plaintiff contends that a giant corporation had allegedly sought by surreptitious and unusual methods to silence an unusually effective critic. If there was such a plan, and only a trial would show that, it is unduly restrictive of the future trial to allocate the evidence beforehand based only on a pleader's specification of overt acts on the bold assumption that they are not connected causally or do not bear on intent and motive.

It should be observed, too, that the right to privacy, even as thus far developed, does not always refer to that which is not known to the public or is confidential. Indeed, the statutory right of privacy in this State and perhaps the most traditional right of privacy in the "common law sense" relates to the commercialized publicity of one's face or name, perhaps the two most public aspects of an individual. . . .

Accordingly, because of the prematurity of ruling on any other question but the sufficiency of the causes of action, I concur in result only.

NOTES & QUESTIONS

1. ***Postscript.*** General Motors eventually settled the case with Nader for $425,000. It also made a public apology to Nader.[2]
2. ***Intrusion Liability Only for Confidential Information?*** The *Nader* court finds that mere information gathering is not actionable under the intrusion tort. It states: "Privacy is invaded only if the information sought is of a confidential nature and the defendant's conduct was unreasonably intrusive." Hence, GM's interviewing of Nader's acquaintances, harassing phone calls, and use of "girls with illicit proposals" did not constitute an intrusion on his privacy. Note, however, the text of Restatement (Second) Torts, § 652B. Does this text require the court's holding in this regard? Is the text consistent with this holding?
3. ***Surveillance in Public Places.*** The Restatement of Torts adopts a similar approach to the majority in *Nader*:

> The defendant is subject to liability under the rule stated in this Section only when he has intruded into a private place, or has otherwise invaded a private seclusion that the plaintiff has thrown about his person or affairs. Thus there is no liability for the examination of a public record concerning the plaintiff, or of documents that the plaintiff is required to keep and make available for public inspection. Nor is there liability for observing him or even taking his

[2] For more background about case, see Stuart M. Speiser, *Lawsuit* (1980).

> photograph while he is walking on the public highway, since he is not then in seclusion, and his appearance is public and open to the public eye. Even in a public place, however, there may be some matters about the plaintiff, such as his underwear or lack of it, that are not exhibited to the public gaze; and there may still be invasion of privacy when there is intrusion upon these matters. Restatement (Second) of Torts § 652B comment(c).

Judge Breitel's concurrence goes even further than the majority: "Although acts performed in 'public,' especially if taken singly or in small numbers, may not be confidential, at least arguably a right to privacy may nevertheless be invaded through extensive or exhaustive monitoring and cataloguing of acts normally disconnected and anonymous." How does Breitel's approach differ from the majority's approach and that of the Restatement?

Also consider *Summers v. Bailey*, 55 F.3d 1564 (11th Cir. 1995), where the court held:

> Traditionally, watching or observing a person in a public place is not an intrusion upon one's privacy. However, Georgia courts have held that surveillance of an individual on public thoroughfares, where such surveillance aims to frighten or torment a person, is an unreasonable intrusion upon a person's privacy.

4. ***Wiretapping and Electronic Surveillance.*** In *Hamberger v. Eastman*, 206 A.2d 239 (N.H. 1964), a husband and wife brought an intrusion action against their landlord for installing a secret recording device in their bedroom. The device had wires going into the landlord's residence. The court sided with the plaintiffs:

> The defendant contends that the right of privacy should not be recognized on the facts of the present case as they appear in the pleadings because there are no allegations that anyone listened or overheard any sounds or voices originating from the plaintiffs' bedroom. The tort of intrusion on the plaintiffs' solitude or seclusion does not require publicity and communication to third persons although this would affect the amount of damages, as Prosser makes clear. The defendant also contends that the right of privacy is not violated unless something has been published, written or printed and that oral publicity is not sufficient. Recent cases make it clear that this is not a requirement.
>
> If the peeping Tom, the big ear and the electronic eavesdropper (whether ingenious or ingenuous) have a place in the hierarchy of social values, it ought not to be at the expense of a married couple minding their own business in the seclusion of their bedroom who have never asked for or by their conduct deserved a potential projection of their private conversations and actions to their landlord or to others. Whether actual or potential such "publicity with respect to private matters of purely personal concern is an injury to personality. It impairs the mental peace and comfort of the individual and may produce suffering more acute than that produced by a mere bodily injury." III Pound, Jurisprudence 58 (1959). The use of parabolic microphones and sonic wave devices designed to pick up conversations in a room without entering it and at a considerable distance away makes the problem far from fanciful.

5. ***The Highly Offensive Requirement.*** What intrusions are "highly offensive to a reasonable person" as required by the tort? Courts have held that trespasses into places where people have reasonable expectations of privacy are actionable, as are unjustified searches. *See, e.g., Gerard v. Parish of Jefferson*, 424 So. 2d 440 (La. App. 1982) (dog catcher entered plaintiff's property without authorization); *K-Mart Corp. v. Trotti*, 677 S.W.2d 632 (Tex. App. 1984) (unauthorized search of employee's personal locker). In *Klebanoff v. McMongale,* 552 A.2d 677 (Pa. Super. 1988), about 20 to 30 pro-life demonstrators picketed noisily on the public street directly outside of an abortion doctor's home. This had a "devastating effect . . . on the [doctor and his family's] quiet enjoyment of their home," and the family was "figuratively, and perhaps literally, trapped within the home, and held captive." The court held that the protestors could be enjoined.

   As illustrated by *Hamburger* and *Nader,* non-physical activities such as wiretapping and overzealous surveillance can amount to highly offensive intrusions. Peering into a person's home windows can be actionable according to the court in *Pinkerton Nat'l Detective Agency, Inc. v. Stevens,* 132 S.E.2d 119 (Ga. App. 1963). In *Pulla v. Amoco Oil Co.*, 882 F. Supp. 836 (S.D. Iowa 1994), the court held that it was actionable when the defendant illegally accessed the plaintiff's credit card records to determine if he abused his sick leave at work. Harassing a person by telephone can also constitute a highly offensive intrusion. In *Donnel v. Lara*, 703 S.W.2d 257 (Tex. App. 1985), the court held that excessive telephone harassment "by placing repeated phone calls to [a person's] residence at unreasonable hours" can be actionable. In *Harms v. Miami Daily News, Inc.,* 127 So. 2d 715 (Fla. App. 1961), the defendant published in the newspaper the following statement: "Wanna hear a sexy telephone voice? Call [number] and ask for Louise." As a result, the plaintiff was "flooded with hundreds of telephone calls by various and sundry persons." The court concluded that the plaintiff had an actionable claim against the defendant, and that there was sufficient evidence for the jury to decide whether it was highly offensive. With regard to this issue, the Restatement provides that "there is no liability for knocking at the plaintiff's door, or calling him to the telephone on one occasion or even two or three, to demand payment of a debt. It is only when the telephone calls are repeated with such persistence and frequency as to amount to a course of hounding the plaintiff, that becomes a substantial burden to his existence, that his privacy is invaded." Restatement (Second) of Torts § 652B comment (d).

6. ***Collective Actions by Different Journalists.*** Suppose a person is accosted by throngs of reporters. At any moment, there is always one or more reporters on her trail. Groups of reporters camp outside her home. The impact from the collective actions of all the reporters is extremely disruptive to the person's life. Can she sue the reporters collectively? Bruce Sanford argues that each reporter should only be liable for his or her own behavior: "A stake-out by a group of unrelated reporters should be viewed as no more than the sum of its separate parts."[3]

---

[3] Bruce W. Sanford, *Libel and Privacy* § 11.2, at 541 (2d ed. 1991).

DIETEMANN V. TIME, INC.

449 F.2d 245 (9th Cir. 1971)

HUFSTEDLER, C. J. . . . Plaintiff, a disabled veteran with little education, was engaged in the practice of healing with clay, minerals, and herbs — as practiced, simple quackery.

Defendant, Time, Incorporated, a New York corporation, publishes Life Magazine. Its November 1, 1963 edition carried an article entitled "Crackdown on Quackery." The article depicted plaintiff as a quack and included two pictures of him. One picture was taken at plaintiff's home on September 20, 1963, previous to his arrest on a charge of practicing medicine without a license, and the other taken at the time of his arrest.

Life Magazine entered into an arrangement with the District Attorney's Office of Los Angeles County whereby Life's employees would visit plaintiff and obtain facts and pictures concerning his activities. Two employees of Life, Mrs. Jackie Metcalf and Mr. William Ray, went to plaintiff's home on September 20, 1963. When they arrived at a locked gate, they rang a bell and plaintiff came out of his house and was told by Mrs. Metcalf and Ray that they had been sent there by a friend, a Mr. Johnson. The use of Johnson's name was a ruse to gain entrance. Plaintiff admitted them and all three went into the house and into plaintiff's den.

The plaintiff had some equipment which could at best be described as gadgets, not equipment which had anything to do with the practice of medicine. Plaintiff, while examining Mrs. Metcalf, was photographed by Ray with a hidden camera without the consent of plaintiff. One of the pictures taken by him appeared in Life Magazine showing plaintiff with his hand on the upper portion of Mrs. Metcalf's breast while he was looking at some gadgets and holding what appeared to be a wand in his right hand. Mrs. Metcalf had told plaintiff that she had a lump in her breast. Plaintiff concluded that she had eaten some rancid butter 11 years, 9 months, and 7 days prior to that time. Other persons were seated in the room during this time.

The conversation between Mrs. Metcalf and plaintiff was transmitted by radio transmitter hidden in Mrs. Metcalf's purse to a tape recorder in a parked automobile occupied by Joseph Bride, Life employee, John Miner of the District Attorney's Office, and Grant Leake, an investigator of the State Department of Public Health. While the recorded conversation was not quoted in the article in Life, it was mentioned that Life correspondent Bride was making notes of what was being received via the radio transmitter, and such information was at least referred to in the article.

The foregoing events were photographed and recorded by an arrangement among Miner of the District Attorney's Office, Leake of the State Department of Public Health, and Bride, a representative of Life. It had been agreed that Life would obtain pictures and information for use as evidence, and later could be used by Life for publication. . . .

Plaintiff, although a journeyman plumber, claims to be a scientist. Plaintiff had no listings and his home had no sign of any kind. He did not advertise, nor did he have a telephone. He made no charges when he attempted to diagnose or to prescribe herbs and minerals. He did accept contributions.

[The plaintiff was arrested at his home on a charge of practicing medicine without a license. After the plaintiff entered a plea of nolo contendere to the charges, *Life*'s article was published. The plaintiff sued *Life* in federal district court. The district court concluded that the defendant had invaded the plaintiff's privacy and awarded $1,000 in damages.]

. . . In jurisdictions other than California in which a common law tort for invasion of privacy is recognized, it has been consistently held that surreptitious electronic recording of a plaintiff's conversation causing him emotional distress is actionable. Despite some variations in the description and the labels applied to the tort, there is agreement that publication is not a necessary element of the tort, that the existence of a technical trespass is immaterial, and that proof of special damages is not required. . . .[4]

. . . [W]e have little difficulty in concluding that clandestine photography of the plaintiff in his den and the recordation and transmission of his conversation without his consent resulting in his emotional distress warrants recovery for invasion of privacy in California. . . .

Plaintiff's den was a sphere from which he could reasonably expect to exclude eavesdropping newsmen. He invited two of defendant's employees to the den. One who invites another to his home or office takes a risk that the visitor may not be what he seems, and that the visitor may repeat all he hears and observes when he leaves. But he does not and should not be required to take the risk that what is heard and seen will be transmitted by photograph or recording, or in our modern world, in full living color and hi-fi to the public at large or to any segment of it that the visitor may select. A different rule could have a most pernicious effect upon the dignity of man and it would surely lead to guarded conversations and conduct where candor is most valued, e.g., in the case of doctors and lawyers.

The defendant claims that the First Amendment immunizes it from liability for invading plaintiff's den with a hidden camera and its concealed electronic instruments because its employees were gathering news and its instrumentalities "are indispensable tools of investigative reporting." We agree that newsgathering is an integral part of news dissemination. We strongly disagree, however, that the hidden mechanical contrivances are "indispensable tools" of newsgathering. Investigative reporting is an ancient art; its successful practice long antecedes the invention of miniature cameras and electronic devices. The First Amendment has never been construed to accord newsmen immunity from torts or crimes committed during the course of newsgathering. The First Amendment is not a license to trespass, to steal, or to intrude by electronic means into the precincts of another's home or office. It does not become such a license simply because the person subjected to the intrusion is reasonably suspected of committing a crime.

Defendant relies upon the line of cases commencing with *New York Times Co. v. Sullivan* and extending through *Rosenbloom v. Metromedia, Inc.* to sustain

[4] Editors' Note: Special damages, or "consequential" damages, are damages that follow from the initial harm. They include lost profits and other diminishments of the plaintiff's income, such as increased expenses.

its contentions that (1) publication of news, however tortiously gathered, insulates defendant from liability for the antecedent tort, and (2) even if it is not thus shielded from liability, those cases prevent consideration of publication as an element in computing damages. . . .

No interest protected by the First Amendment is adversely affected by permitting damages for intrusion to be enhanced by the fact of later publication of the information that the publisher improperly acquired. Assessing damages for the additional emotional distress suffered by a plaintiff when the wrongfully acquired data are purveyed to the multitude chills intrusive acts. It does not chill freedom of expression guaranteed by the First Amendment. A rule forbidding the use of publication as an ingredient of damages would deny to the injured plaintiff recovery for real harm done to him without any countervailing benefit to the legitimate interest of the public in being informed. The same rule would encourage conduct by news media that grossly offends ordinary men. . . .

DESNICK V. AMERICAN BROADCASTING CO., INC.

44 F.3d 1345 (7th Cir. 1995)

[Dr. Desnick owned an ophthalmic clinic known as the Desnick Eye Center. The Eye Center had 25 offices in four states and performed over 10,000 cataract operations each year, mainly on elderly persons under Medicare. In 1993, Entine, the producer of ABC's news program *Primetime Live*, telephoned Dr. Desnick and told him that the show wanted to do a segment on cataract practices. Entine told Desnick that the segment would be "fair and balanced" and that it would not include undercover surveillance. Desnick permitted an ABC crew to videotape the Eye Center's Chicago office, to film a cataract operation, and to interview doctors and patients. However, unknown to Desnick, Entine sent seven people with concealed cameras to the Eye Center's Wisconsin and Indiana offices. These seven people posed as patients and requested eye operations. Glazer and Simon are among the employees who were secretly videotaped examining these "test patients."

When the program aired, it was introduced by Sam Donaldson, who began by stating: "We begin tonight with the story of a so-called 'big cutter,' Dr. James Desnick. . . . [I]n our undercover investigation of the big cutter you'll meet tonight, we turned up evidence that he may also be a big charger, doing unnecessary cataract surgery for the money." As part of the segment, brief interviews with four patients of the Desnick Eye Center were shown. While one of the patients was satisfied ("I was blessed"), the other three were not. Indeed, one of them commented, "If you got three eyes, he'll get three eyes." Donaldson then reported on the experiences of the seven test patients. The two who were under 65 and therefore ineligible for Medicare reimbursement were found by the clinic not to need cataract surgery. The Desnick eye clinic told four of the other five that they did need this operation.

Donaldson told the viewer that *Primetime Live* hired a professor of ophthalmology to examine the test patients who had been told they needed cataract surgery. The professor not only said that these patients did not need it, but with regard to one, he stated, "I think it would be near malpractice to do surgery on him." Later in the segment he denies that this could just be an honest difference of opinion between professionals. The show also mentioned that the Illinois Medical Board had charged Dr. Desnick with malpractice and deception. Additionally, the show contained an "ambush interview" of Dr. Desnick while he was at an airport, with Donaldson shouting out allegations of fraud to Desnick.

Among a number of causes of action raised by the plaintiffs, who included Desnick, Simon, and Glazer, is an action for intrusion upon seclusion.]

POSNER, C. J. . . . To enter upon another's land without consent is a trespass. The force of this rule has, it is true, been diluted somewhat by concepts of privilege and of implied consent. But there is no journalists' privilege to trespass. And there can be no implied consent in any nonfictitious sense of the term when express consent is procured by a misrepresentation or a misleading omission. The Desnick Eye Center would not have agreed to the entry of the test patients into its offices had it known they wanted eye examinations only in order to gather material for a television expose of the Center and that they were going to make secret videotapes of the examinations. Yet some cases, illustrated by *Martin v. Fidelity & Casualty Co.*, 421 So. 2d 109, 111 (Ala. 1982), deem consent effective even though it was procured by fraud. There must be *something* to this surprising result. Without it a restaurant critic could not conceal his identity when he ordered a meal, or a browser pretend to be interested in merchandise that he could not afford to buy. Dinner guests would be trespassers if they were false friends who never would have been invited had the host known their true character, and a consumer who in an effort to bargain down an automobile dealer falsely claimed to be able to buy the same car elsewhere at a lower price would be a trespasser in the dealer's showroom. Some of these might be classified as privileged trespasses, designed to promote competition. Others might be thought justified by some kind of implied consent — the restaurant critic for example might point by way of analogy to the use of the "fair use" defense by book reviewers charged with copyright infringement and argue that the restaurant industry as a whole would be injured if restaurants could exclude critics. But most such efforts at rationalization would be little better than evasions. The fact is that consent to an entry is often given legal effect even though the entrant has intentions that if known to the owner of the property would cause him for perfectly understandable and generally ethical or at least lawful reasons to revoke his consent.

The law's willingness to give effect to consent procured by fraud is not limited to the tort of trespass. The *Restatement* gives the example of a man who obtains consent to sexual intercourse by promising a woman $100, yet (unbeknownst to her, of course) he pays her with a counterfeit bill and intended to do so from the start. The man is not guilty of battery, even though unconsented-to sexual intercourse is a battery. Yet we know that to conceal the fact that one has a venereal disease transforms "consensual" intercourse into battery. Seduction, standardly effected by false promises of love, is not rape; intercourse under the pretense of rendering medical or psychiatric treatment is, at least in most states. It certainly is battery. Trespass presents close parallels. If a homeowner opens his door to a purported meter reader who is in fact nothing of the sort — just a busybody curious about the interior of the home — the homeowner's consent to his entry is not a defense to a suit for trespass. And likewise if a competitor gained entry to a business firm's premises posing as a customer but in fact hoping to steal the firm's trade secrets.

How to distinguish the two classes of case — the seducer from the medical impersonator, the restaurant critic from the meter-reader impersonator? The answer can have nothing to do with fraud; there is fraud in all the cases. It has to do with the interest that the torts in question, battery and trespass, protect. The one protects the inviolability of the person, the other the inviolability of the person's property. The woman who is seduced wants to have sex with her seducer, and the restaurant owner wants to have customers. The woman who is victimized by the medical impersonator has no desire to have sex with her doctor; she wants medical treatment. And the homeowner victimized by the phony meter reader does not want strangers in his house unless they have authorized service functions. The dealer's objection to the customer who claims falsely to have a lower price from a competing dealer is not to the physical presence of the customer, but to the fraud that he is trying to perpetuate. The lines are not bright — they are not even inevitable. They are the traces of the old forms of action, which have resulted in a multitude of artificial distinctions in modern law. But that is nothing new.

There was no invasion in the present case of any of the specific interests that the tort of trespass seeks to protect. The test patients entered offices that were open to anyone expressing a desire for ophthalmic services and videotaped physicians engaged in professional, not personal, communications with strangers (the testers themselves). The activities of the offices were not disrupted. . . . Nor was there any "inva[sion of] a person's private space," as in our hypothetical meter-reader case, as in the famous case of *De May v. Roberts*, 9 N.W. 146 (Mich. 1881) (where a doctor, called to the plaintiff's home to deliver her baby, brought along with him a friend who was curious to see a birth but was not a medical doctor, and represented the friend to be his medical assistant), as in one of its numerous modern counterparts, . . . and as in *Dietemann v. Time, Inc.*, 449 F.2d 245 (9th Cir. 1971), on which the plaintiffs in our case rely. *Dietemann* involved a home. True, the portion invaded was an office, where the plaintiff performed quack healing of nonexistent ailments. The parallel to this case is plain enough, but there is a difference. Dietemann was not in business, and did not advertise his services or charge for them. His quackery was private.

No embarrassingly intimate details of anybody's life were publicized in the present case. There was no eavesdropping on a private conversation; the testers recorded their own conversations with the Desnick Eye Center's physicians. There was no violation of the doctor-patient privilege. There was no theft, or intent to steal, trade secrets; no disruption of decorum, of peace and quiet; no noisy or distracting demonstrations. Had the testers been undercover FBI agents, there would have been no violation of the Fourth Amendment, because there would have been no invasion of a legally protected interest in property or privacy. . . .

NOTES & QUESTIONS

1. ***Investigative Reporting.*** As is illustrated by *Dietemann* and *Desnick*, investigative reporting often depends upon deception. Those cases are split on

the issue of whether such investigative techniques can give rise to intrusion. Recall the *Dietemann* court's statement:

> Investigative reporting is an ancient art; its successful practice long antecedes the invention of miniature cameras and electronic devices. The First Amendment has never been construed to accord newsmen immunity from torts or crimes committed during the course of newsgathering. The First Amendment is not a license to trespass, to steal, or to intrude by electronic means into the precincts of another's home or office. It does not become such a license simply because the person subjected to the intrusion is reasonably suspected of committing a crime.

However, investigative reporting has served an important function throughout history. In 1887, a reporter named Nellie Bly pretended to be mentally ill to gain access to a mental asylum. Her portrayal of the brutal conditions led to significant reforms. Upton Sinclair went undercover as a meatpacker to expose conditions in slaughterhouses for his book *The Jungle* in 1904. C. Thomas Dienes argues:

> . . . Undercover journalism often serves the public interest. In the public sector, it allows the media to perform its role as the eyes and ears of the people, to perform a checking function on government. Especially at a time when citizens are often unable or unwilling to supervise government, this media role is critical to self-government. In the private sector, when the government fails in its responsibility to protect the public against fraudulent and unethical business and professional practices, whether because of lack of resources or unwillingness, media exposure of such practices can and often does provide the spur forcing government action.
>
> Nevertheless, the techniques of investigative reporting generally, and undercover journalism in particular, are controversial even within journalism. Many editors and journalists condemn the use of confidential sources, any misrepresentation or lying to get information, and the use of the new snooping technology to probe where eyes and ears cannot go.
>
> Undercover reporting has sometimes been called "stunt journalism." But it is difficult to believe that many of the stories of public importance of the kind that I have noted could have been published without the use of undercover reporting.[5]

2. ***Posner's Analogies in* Desnick.** Judge Posner draws an analogy between (1) seduction with false promises of love in order to have sexual intercourse and (2) the deceitful trespass in *Desnick*. Are these situations really analogous?
3. ***Trespass: The* Food Lion *Case.*** The tort of trespass is related to the tort of intrusion. To commit a trespass, one must enter upon another's land without consent. To what extent does trespass overlap with intrusion? In many respects, it has fewer requirements — no requirement that solitude or seclusion be invaded, that a private matter be involved, or that the invasion be

[5] C. Thomas Dienes, *Protecting Investigative Journalism*, 67 Geo. Wash. L. Rev. 1139, 1141, 1143 (1999). For further background about investigative journalism and the use of deception, see Bernard W. Bell, *Secrets and Lies: News Media and Law Enforcement Use of Deception as an Investigative Tool*, 60 U. Pitt. L. Rev. 745 (1999).

highly offensive. On the other hand, intrusion can be committed without entering upon another's land.

Can one trespass if one obtains consent through deception? And can a person trespass if she is present upon another's land with consent but secretly engages in activities that the landowner would likely not authorize? Consider *Food Lion, Inc. v. ABC*, 194 F.3d 505 (4th Cir. 2001). ABC reporters investigated allegations of unsanitary food-handling practices at supermarkets operated by Food Lion, Inc. According to the allegations, "Food Lion employees ground out-of-date beef together with new beef, bleached rank meat to remove its odor, and re-dated (and offered for sale) products not sold before their printed expiration date." Two reporters submitted fake resumes to obtain jobs at Food Lion supermarkets. The reporters secretly videotaped the food-handling practices at the stores. The reporters quit their jobs within a few weeks. The video was broadcast on the show *Primetime Live*. "The broadcast included, for example, videotape that appeared to show Food Lion employees repackaging and redating fish that had passed the expiration date, grinding expired beef with fresh beef, and applying barbeque sauce to chicken past its expiration date in order to mask the smell and sell it as fresh in the gourmet food section." Food Lion sued for fraud, breach of duty of loyalty, trespass, and unfair trade practices. Food Lion won at trial — $1,400 on the fraud claim, $1 each for the duty of loyalty and trespass claims, and $1,500 on the unfair trade practices claim. The jury awarded approximately $5.5 million in punitive damages on the fraud claim, which the court reduced to $315,000.

On appeal, the court dismissed the fraud and unfair trade practices claims because, although the reporters submitted false employment applications, they made no false promises as to the duration of their employment.

The court affirmed the duty of loyalty and trespass claims: "[I]t is possible to perform the assigned tasks of a job adequately and still breach the duty of loyalty. For fraud damages Food Lion still had to prove reliance on the misrepresentations." The court reasoned that "the reporters — in promoting the interests of one master, ABC, to the detriment of a second, Food Lion — committed the tort of disloyalty against Food Lion."

Regarding the trespass claim, the court held:

> [I]t is a trespass to enter upon another's land without consent. Accordingly, consent is a defense to a claim of trespass. Even consent gained by misrepresentation is sometimes sufficient. *See Desnick v. American Broad. Cos.*, 44 F.3d 1345 (7th Cir. 1995). The consent to enter is canceled out, however, "if a wrongful act is done in excess of and in abuse of authorized entry."
>
> We turn first to whether Dale and Barnett's consent to be in non-public areas of Food Lion property was void from the outset because of the resume misrepresentations. "[C]onsent to an entry is often given legal effect" even though it was obtained by misrepresentation or concealed intentions. *Desnick*, 44 F.3d at 1351. . . .
>
> We like *Desnick*'s thoughtful analysis about when a consent to enter that is based on misrepresentation may be given effect. . . .

> [W]e have not found any case suggesting that consent based on a resume misrepresentation turns a successful job applicant into a trespasser the moment she enters the employer's premises to begin work. . . .
>
> There is a problem, however, with what Dale and Barnett did after they entered Food Lion's property. The jury also found that the reporters committed trespass by breaching their duty of loyalty to Food Lion "as a result of pursuing [their] investigation for ABC." We affirm the finding of trespass on this ground because the breach of duty of loyalty — triggered by the filming in non-public areas, which was adverse to Food Lion — was a wrongful act in excess of Dale and Barnett's authority to enter Food Lion's premises as employees. . . .
>
> [S]ecretly installing a video camera in someone's private home can be a wrongful act in excess of consent given to enter. In the trespass case of *Miller v. Brooks* the (defendant) wife, who claimed she had consent to enter her estranged husband's (the plaintiff's) house, had a private detective place a video camera in the ceiling of her husband's bedroom. The court noted that "[e]ven an authorized entry can be trespass if a wrongful act is done in excess of and in abuse of authorized entry." . . . We recognize that *Miller* involved a private home, not a grocery store, and that it involved some physical alteration to the plaintiff's property (installation of a camera). Still, we believe the general principle is applicable here, at least in the case of Dale, who worked in a Food Lion store in North Carolina. Although Food Lion consented to Dale's entry to do her job, she exceeded that consent when she videotaped in non-public areas of the store and worked against the interests of her second employer, Food Lion, in doing so. . . .
>
> ABC argues that even if state tort law covers some of Dale and Barnett's conduct, the district court erred in refusing to subject Food Lion's claims to any level of First Amendment scrutiny. ABC makes this argument because Dale and Barnett were engaged in newsgathering for *Primetime Live.* It is true that there are "First Amendment interests in newsgathering." However, the Supreme Court has said in no uncertain terms that "generally applicable laws do not offend the First Amendment simply because their enforcement against the press has incidental effects on its ability to gather and report the news." *Cohen v. Cowles Media Co.,* 501 U.S. 663 (1991). . . .
>
> The torts Dale and Barnett committed, breach of the duty of loyalty and trespass, fit neatly into the *Cowles* framework. Neither tort targets or singles out the press. . . . Nor do we believe that applying these laws against the media will have more than an "incidental effect" on newsgathering. We are convinced that the media can do its important job effectively without resort to the commission of run-of-the-mill torts.

The court only affirmed the duty of loyalty and trespass claims. As a result, *Food Lion* could only collect $2 in damages because the punitive damages were based on the fraud claim. Although *Food Lion* did not involve the tort of intrusion, to what extent is its holding regarding the tort of trespass applicable to intrusion cases? Is its holding consistent with *Dietemann* and *Desnick*?

4. ***Intrusion Liability for the Receipt of Data Obtained by Intrusion.*** In *Pearson v. Dodd*, 410 F.2d 701 (D.C. Cir. 1969), two former employees of Senator Thomas Dodd of Connecticut, with the assistance of two of Dodd's active staff members, entered Dodd's office without authorization and surreptitiously made copies of many documents in his files. These documents

related to Dodd's relationship to lobbyists for foreign interests. Newspaper columnists Drew Pearson and Jack Anderson published articles containing information from these documents. Pearson and Anderson did not participate in or order the illegal copying; they only received copies of the documents knowing that they had been copied without authorization. Dodd sued Pearson and Anderson for invasion of privacy. The court held that intrusion could not extend to those who merely received the information:

> If we were to hold appellants liable for invasion of privacy on these facts, we would establish the proposition that one who receives information from an intruder, knowing it has been obtained by improper intrusion, is guilty of a tort. In an untried and developing area of tort law, we are not prepared to go so far. A person approached by an eavesdropper with an offer to share in the information gathered through the eavesdropping would perhaps play the nobler part should he spurn the offer and shut his ears. However, it seems to us that at this point it would place too great a strain on human weakness to hold one liable in damages who merely succumbs to temptation and listens.

SHULMAN V. GROUP W PRODUCTIONS, INC.

955 P.2d 469 (Cal. 1998)

WERDEGAR, J. . . . On June 24, 1990, plaintiffs Ruth and Wayne Shulman, mother and son, were injured when the car in which they and two other family members were riding on interstate 10 in Riverside County flew off the highway and tumbled down an embankment into a drainage ditch on state-owned property, coming to rest upside down. Ruth, the most seriously injured of the two, was pinned under the car. Ruth and Wayne both had to be cut free from the vehicle by the device known as "the jaws of life."

A rescue helicopter operated by Mercy Air was dispatched to the scene. The flight nurse, who would perform the medical care at the scene and on the way to the hospital, was Laura Carnahan. Also on board were the pilot, a medic and Joel Cooke, a video camera operator employed by defendants Group W Productions, Inc., and 4MN Productions. Cooke was recording the rescue operation for later broadcast.

Cooke roamed the accident scene, videotaping the rescue. Nurse Carnahan wore a wireless microphone that picked up her conversations with both Ruth and the other rescue personnel. Cooke's tape was edited into a piece approximately nine minutes long, which, with the addition of narrative voice-over, was broadcast on September 29, 1990, as a segment of *On Scene: Emergency Response*.

The segment begins with the Mercy Air helicopter shown on its way to the accident site. The narrator's voice is heard in the background, setting the scene and describing in general terms what has happened. . . .

The videotape shows only a glimpse of Wayne, and his voice is never heard. Ruth is shown several times, either by brief shots of a limb or her torso, or with her features blocked by others or obscured by an oxygen mask. She is also heard speaking several times. Carnahan calls her "Ruth" and her last name is not mentioned on the broadcast.

While Ruth is still trapped under the car, Carnahan asks Ruth's age. Ruth responds, "I'm old." On further questioning, Ruth reveals she is 47, and Carnahan observes that "it's all relative. You're not that old." During her extrication from the car, Ruth asks at least twice if she is dreaming. At one point she asks Carnahan, who has told her she will be taken to the hospital in a helicopter: "Are you teasing?" At another point she says: "This is terrible. Am I dreaming?" She also asks what happened and where the rest of her family is, repeating the questions even after being told she was in an accident and the other family members are being cared for. While being loaded into the helicopter on a stretcher, Ruth says: "I just want to die." Carnahan reassures her that she is "going to do real well," but Ruth repeats: "I just want to die. I don't want to go through this."

Ruth and Wayne are placed in the helicopter, and its door is closed. The narrator states: "Once airborne, Laura and [the flight medic] will update their patients' vital signs and establish communications with the waiting trauma teams at Loma Linda." Carnahan, speaking into what appears to be a radio microphone, transmits some of Ruth's vital signs and states that Ruth cannot move her feet and has no sensation. The video footage during the helicopter ride includes a few seconds of Ruth's face, covered by an oxygen mask. Wayne is neither shown nor heard.

The helicopter lands on the hospital roof. With the door open, Ruth states while being taken out: "My upper back hurts." Carnahan replies: "Your upper back hurts. That's what you were saying up there." Ruth states: "I don't feel that great." Carnahan responds: "You probably don't."

Finally, Ruth is shown being moved from the helicopter into the hospital. . . .

The accident left Ruth a paraplegic. When the segment was broadcast, Wayne phoned Ruth in her hospital room and told her to turn on the television because "Channel 4 is showing our accident now." Shortly afterward, several hospital workers came into the room to mention that a videotaped segment of her accident was being shown. Ruth was "shocked, so to speak, that this would be run and I would be exploited, have my privacy invaded, which is what I felt had happened." She did not know her rescue had been recorded in this manner and had never consented to the recording or broadcast. Ruth had the impression from the broadcast "that I was kind of talking non-stop, and I remember hearing some of the things I said, which were not very pleasant." Asked at deposition what part of the broadcast material she considered private, Ruth explained: "I think the whole scene was pretty private. It was pretty gruesome, the parts that I saw, my knee sticking out of the car. I certainly did not look my best, and I don't feel it's for the public to see. I was not at my best in what I was thinking and what I was saying and what was being shown, and it's not for the public to see this trauma that I was going through."

Ruth and Wayne sued the producers of *On Scene: Emergency Response*, as well as others. The first amended complaint included two causes of action for invasion of privacy, one based on defendants' unlawful intrusion by videotaping the rescue in the first instance and the other based on the public disclosure of private facts, i.e., the broadcast. . . .

The trial court granted the media defendants' summary judgment motion, basing its ruling on plaintiffs' admissions that the accident and rescue were matters of public interest and public affairs. Those admissions, in the trial court's view, showed as a matter of law that the broadcast material was newsworthy, thereby vesting the media defendants' conduct with First Amendment protection. The court entered judgment for defendants on all causes of action. . . .

[T]he action for intrusion has two elements: (1) intrusion into a private place, conversation or matter, (2) in a manner highly offensive to a reasonable person. We consider the elements in that order.

We ask first whether defendants "intentionally intrude[d], physically or otherwise, upon the solitude or seclusion of another," that is, into a place or conversation private to Wayne or Ruth. . . .

Cameraman Cooke's mere presence at the accident scene and filming of the events occurring there cannot be deemed either a physical or sensory intrusion on plaintiffs' seclusion. Plaintiffs had no right of ownership or possession of the property where the rescue took place, nor any actual control of the premises. Nor could they have had a reasonable expectation that members of the media would be excluded or prevented from photographing the scene; for journalists to attend and record the scenes of accidents and rescues is in no way unusual or unexpected.

Two aspects of defendants' conduct, however, raise triable issues of intrusion on seclusion. First, a triable issue exists as to whether both plaintiffs had an objectively reasonable expectation of privacy in the interior of the rescue helicopter, which served as an ambulance. Although the attendance of reporters and photographers at the scene of an accident is to be expected, we are aware of no law or custom permitting the press to ride in ambulances or enter hospital rooms during treatment without the patient's consent. Other than the two patients and Cooke, only three people were present in the helicopter, all Mercy Air staff. As the Court of Appeal observed, "[i]t is neither the custom nor the habit of our society that any member of the public at large or its media representatives may hitch a ride in an ambulance and ogle as paramedics care for an injured stranger."

Second, Ruth was entitled to a degree of privacy in her conversations with Carnahan and other medical rescuers at the accident scene, and in Carnahan's conversations conveying medical information regarding Ruth to the hospital base. Cooke, perhaps, did not intrude into that zone of privacy merely by being present at a place where he could hear such conversations with unaided ears. But by placing a microphone on Carnahan's person, amplifying and recording what she said and heard, defendants may have listened in on conversations the parties could reasonably have expected to be private. . . .

We turn to the second element of the intrusion tort, offensiveness. . . .

On this summary judgment record, we believe a jury could find defendants' recording of Ruth's communications to Carnahan and other rescuers, and filming in the air ambulance, to be "'highly offensive to a reasonable person.'" With regard to the depth of the intrusion, a reasonable jury could find highly offensive the placement of a microphone on a medical rescuer in order to intercept what would otherwise be private conversations with an injured patient. In that setting, as defendants could and should have foreseen, the patient would not know her words were being recorded and would not have occasion to ask about, and object or consent to, recording. Defendants, it could reasonably be said, took calculated advantage of the patient's "vulnerability and confusion." Arguably, the last thing an injured accident victim should have to worry about while being pried from her wrecked car is that a television producer may be recording everything she says to medical personnel for the possible edification and entertainment of casual television viewers.

For much the same reason, a jury could reasonably regard entering and riding in an ambulance — whether on the ground or in the air — with two seriously injured patients to be an egregious intrusion on a place of expected seclusion. Again, the patients, at least in this case, were hardly in a position to keep careful watch on who was riding with them, or to inquire as to everyone's business and consent or object to their presence. A jury could reasonably believe that fundamental respect for human dignity requires the patients' anxious journey be taken only with those whose care is solely for them and out of sight of the prying eyes (or cameras) of others.

Nor can we say as a matter of law that defendants' motive — to gather usable material for a potentially newsworthy story — necessarily privileged their intrusive conduct as a matter of common law tort liability. A reasonable jury could conclude the producers' desire to get footage that would convey the "feel" of the event — the real sights and sounds of a difficult rescue — did not justify either placing a microphone on Nurse Carnahan or filming inside the rescue helicopter. Although defendants' purposes could scarcely be regarded as evil or malicious (in the colloquial sense), their behavior could, even in light of their motives, be thought to show a highly offensive lack of sensitivity and respect for plaintiffs' privacy. A reasonable jury could find that defendants, in placing a microphone on an emergency treatment nurse and recording her conversation with a distressed, disoriented and severely injured patient, without the patient's knowledge or consent, acted with highly offensive disrespect for the patient's personal privacy. . . .

Turning to the question of constitutional protection for newsgathering, one finds the decisional law reflects a general rule of *nonprotection*: the press in its newsgathering activities enjoys no immunity or exemption from generally applicable laws. . . .

As should be apparent from the above discussion, the constitutional protection accorded newsgathering, if any, is far narrower than the protection surrounding the publication of truthful material; consequently, the fact that a reporter may be seeking "newsworthy" material does not in itself privilege the investigatory activity. The reason for the difference is simple: the intrusion tort, unlike that for publication of private facts, does not subject the press to liability for the contents of its publications. Newsworthiness . . . is a complete bar to liability for publication of private facts and is evaluated with a high degree of deference to editorial judgment. The same deference is not due, however, when the issue is not the media's right to publish or broadcast what they choose, but their right to intrude into secluded areas or conversations in pursuit of publishable material. At most, the Constitution may preclude tort liability that would "place an impermissible burden on newsgatherers" by depriving them of their "'indispensable tools'". . .

NOTES & QUESTIONS

1. ***Intrusion in Public Places.*** Consider *Sanders v. ABC*, 978 P.2d 67 (Cal. 1999), decided by the same court one year after *Shulman*. In *Sanders*, a reporter obtained a job with a telephone psychics company that gave "readings" to callers for a fee. The psychics worked in a large room with rows of cubicles. The reporter secretly videotaped conversations of the plaintiff, an employee, with others at his cubicle or other cubicles. The plaintiff sued for intrusion upon seclusion. The defendants argued that the employee lacked a reasonable expectation of privacy in his conversations because they could be seen and overheard by co-workers. The court sided with the plaintiff:

> . . . [W]e adhere to the view suggested in *Shulman*: privacy, for purposes of the intrusion tort, is not a binary, all-or-nothing characteristic. There are degrees and nuances to societal recognition of our expectations of privacy: the fact that the privacy one expects in a given setting is not complete or absolute does not render the expectation unreasonable as a matter of law. Although the intrusion tort is often defined in terms of "seclusion" the seclusion referred to need not be absolute. "Like 'privacy,' the concept of 'seclusion' is relative. The mere fact that a person can be seen by someone does not automatically mean that he or she can legally be forced to be subject to being seen by everyone."

2. PAPARAZZI

Paparazzi are aggressive photographers who often harass celebrities to take candid photographs to sell to newspapers, tabloids, and magazines. Fueling the behavior of the paparazzi are the exorbitant prices that photographs of celebrities command. For example, a photo of Princess Diana embracing Dodi Al-Fayed was sold for over $3 million. Paparazzi have a reputation for being very invasive into the privacy of celebrities. For example, paparazzi flew over Michael J. Fox's wedding in helicopters to take photographs. Disguised photographers took photographs of Paul Reiser's baby in the hospital. Paparazzi also camped outside Reiser's backyard taking photographs with telephoto lenses. Paparazzi chased Arnold Schwarzenegger and Maria Shriver off the road to take the first photos of him leaving the hospital after heart surgery. In 2005, paparazzi followed Lindsey Lohan as she drove onto a dead end street. When she tried to make a U-turn, one photographer drove his automobile into her vehicle. Lohan suffered cuts and bruises from the accident. To what extent does the law of privacy restrict the behavior of paparazzi?

GALELLA V. ONASSIS

487 F.2d 986 (2d Cir. 1973)

SMITH, J. . . . Galella is a free-lance photographer specializing in the making and sale of photographs of well-known persons. Defendant Onassis is the widow of the late President, John F. Kennedy, mother of the two Kennedy children, John and Caroline, and is the wife of Aristotle Onassis, widely known shipping figure and reputed multimillionaire. John Walsh, James Kalafatis and John Connelly are U.S. Secret Service agents assigned to the duty of protecting the Kennedy children under 18 U.S.C. § 3056, which provides for protection of the children of deceased presidents up to the age of 16.

Galella fancies himself as a "paparazzo" (literally a kind of annoying insect, perhaps roughly equivalent to the English "gadfly.") Paparazzi make themselves as visible to the public and obnoxious to their photographic subjects as possible to aid in the advertisement and wide sale of their works.[6]

Some examples of Galella's conduct brought out at trial are illustrative. Galella took pictures of John Kennedy riding his bicycle in Central Park across the way from his home. He jumped out into the boy's path, causing the agents concern for John's safety. The agents' reaction and interrogation of Galella led to Galella's arrest and his action against the agents; Galella on other occasions interrupted Caroline at tennis, and invaded the children's private schools. At one time he came uncomfortably close in a power boat to Mrs. Onassis swimming. He often jumped and postured around while taking pictures of her party notably at a theater opening but also on numerous other occasions. He followed a practice of bribing apartment house, restaurant and nightclub doormen as well as romancing a family servant to keep him advised of the movements of the family.

After detention and arrest following complaint by the Secret Service agents protecting Mrs. Onassis' son and his acquittal in the state court, Galella filed suit in state court against the agents and Mrs. Onassis. Galella claimed that under orders from Mrs. Onassis, the three agents had falsely arrested and maliciously prosecuted him, and that this incident in addition to several others described in the complaint constituted an unlawful interference with his trade.

Mrs. Onassis answered denying any role in the arrest or any part in the claimed interference with his attempts to photograph her, and counterclaimed for damages and injunctive relief, charging that Galella had invaded her privacy, assaulted and battered her, intentionally inflicted emotional distress and engaged in a campaign of harassment. . .

After a six-week trial the court dismissed Galella's claim and granted relief to both the defendant and the intervenor. Galella was enjoined from (1) keeping the defendant and her children under surveillance or following any of them; (2) approaching within 100 yards of the home of defendant or her children, or within 100 yards of either child's school or within 75 yards of either child or 50 yards of defendant; (3) using the name, portrait or picture of defendant or her children for advertising; (4) attempting to communicate with defendant or her children except through her attorney.

We conclude that grant of summary judgment and dismissal of Galella's claim against the Secret Service agents was proper. . . .

Evidence offered by the defense showed that Galella had on occasion intentionally physically touched Mrs. Onassis and her daughter, caused fear of physical contact in his frenzied attempts to get their pictures, followed defendant and her children too closely in an automobile, endangered the safety of the

---

[6] The newspapers report a recent incident in which one Marlon Brando, annoyed by Galella, punched Galella, breaking Galella's jaw and infecting Brando's hand.

children while they were swimming, water skiing and horseback riding. Galella cannot successfully challenge the court's finding of tortious conduct.

Finding that Galella had "insinuated himself into the very fabric of Mrs. Onassis' life . . ." the court framed its relief in part on the need to prevent further invasion of the defendant's privacy. Whether or not this accords with present New York law, there is no doubt that it is sustainable under New York's proscription of harassment.

Of course legitimate countervailing social needs may warrant some intrusion despite an individual's reasonable expectation of privacy and freedom from harassment. However the interference allowed may be no greater than that necessary to protect the overriding public interest. Mrs. Onassis was properly found to be a public figure and thus subject to news coverage. Nonetheless, Galella's action went far beyond the reasonable bounds of news gathering. When weighed against the de minimis public importance of the daily activities of the defendant, Galella's constant surveillance, his obtrusive and intruding presence, was unwarranted and unreasonable. If there were any doubt in our minds, Galella's inexcusable conduct toward defendant's minor children would resolve it.

Galella does not seriously dispute the court's finding of tortious conduct. Rather, he sets up the First Amendment as a wall of immunity protecting newsmen from any liability for their conduct while gathering news. There is no such scope to the First Amendment right. Crimes and torts committed in news gathering are not protected. There is no threat to a free press in requiring its agents to act within the law. . . .

CALIFORNIA ANTI-PAPARAZZI ACT

Cal. Civ. Code § 1708.8

Princess Diana's death in 1997 precipitated calls for anti-paparazzi legislation in the United States. On the evening of August 30, Princess Diana and Dodi Al-Fayed were being chauffeured in a Mercedes from the Ritz Hotel in Paris. Paparazzi followed the Mercedes on motorcycles and in cars. A chase developed, and according to eyewitnesses, the motorcycles were swarming around the Mercedes as it entered a tunnel. The Mercedes crashed in the tunnel, killing both Princess Diana and Dodi Al-Fayed. About 10 to 15 photographers gathered around the Mercedes after the crash and continued to take pictures at the scene of the accident. Seven photographers were arrested by French police at the scene of the accident.

In the United States, anti-paparazzi legislation was introduced in Congress but failed to be passed. In 1998, California became the first state to adopt anti-paparazzi legislation. The legislative history for the Anti-Paparazzi Act discusses the need "to reduce aggressive and often dangerous paparazzi-like behavior against private individuals to feed the public's apparently insatiable appetite for sensationalized reporting." It also quotes the actor Billy Crystal in support of the then proposed Bill: "The combination of technology, bounties and intrusive, dangerous and often illegal behavior has now become such a national problem that SB 262 is needed." The Directors Guild of America advocated the bill "as a necessary step towards restoring the notion of common decency to media coverage of those who find themselves in the spotlight." In 2005, California amended the existing statute to add enhanced penalties for violations of the statute by paparazzi who engage in an "assault" to capture a photograph.

California's Anti-Paparazzi Act does not supplant the state's existing privacy torts. Rather, it provides rights and remedies "in addition to any other rights and remedies provided by law." § 1708.8(h).

The Act recognizes two forms of invasion of privacy. First, it defines liability for "physical invasion of privacy":

> (a) A person is liable for physical invasion of privacy when the defendant knowingly enters onto the land of another without permission or otherwise committed a trespass, in order to physically invade the privacy of the plaintiff with the intent to capture any type of visual image, sound recording, or other physical impression of the plaintiff engaging in a personal or familial activity and the physical invasion occurs in a manner that is offensive to a reasonable person.

"Personal or familial activity" is defined as including, but not limited to "intimate details of the plaintiff's personal life, interactions with the plaintiff's family or significant others, or other aspects of plaintiff's private affairs or concerns." § 1708.8(k).

Second, the Act defines liability for "constructive invasion of privacy":

> (b) A person is liable for constructive invasion of privacy when the defendant attempts to capture, in a manner that is offensive to a reasonable person, any type of visual image, sound recording, or other physical impression of the plaintiff engaging in a personal or familial activity under circumstances in which the plaintiff had a reasonable expectation of privacy, through the use of a visual or auditory enhancing device, regardless of whether there is a physical trespass, if this image, sound recording, or other physical impression could not have been achieved without a trespass unless the visual or auditory enhancing device was used.

The Act provides for increased damages for the two types of privacy violations defined above:

> (c) A person who commits physical invasion of privacy or constructive invasion of privacy, or both, is liable for up to three times the amount of any general and special damages that are proximately caused by the violation of this section. This person may also be liable for punitive damages, subject to proof according to Section 3294. If the plaintiff proves that the invasion of privacy was committed for a commercial purpose, the defendant shall also be subject to disgorgement to the plaintiff of any proceeds or other consideration obtained as a result of the violation of this section.

Equitable relief is also available. § 1708.8(g).

Further, the Act punishes a person who "directs, solicits, actually induces, or actually causes" a person to violate the law. § 1708.8(d). However, the Act does not punish the sale or dissemination of images or recordings in violation of the Act. § 1708.8(e).

Since the Act is aimed at limiting the intrusive activities of paparazzi, not merely the invasion of privacy caused by having one's photograph taken or voice recorded, the Act applies even if no image or recording is ever captured or sold. § 1708.8(i).

The Act exempts the activities of law enforcement personnel or government employees who "in the course and scope of their employment, and supported by an articulable suspicion, attempt to capture any type of visual image, sound recording, or other physical impression of a person during an investigation, surveillance, or monitoring of any conduct to obtain evidence of suspected illegal activity, the suspected violation of any administrative rule or regulation, a suspected fraudulent insurance claim, or any other suspected fraudulent conduct or activity involving a violation of law or pattern of business practices adversely affecting the public health or safety." § 1708.8(f).

As noted above, the California legislature amended the Act in 2005 by enacting Assembly Bill 381. As amended, the law now prohibits an "assault committed with the intent to capture any type of visual image, sound recording, or other physical impression of the plaintiff." According to the legislative history, the purpose of the bill was to respond to a trend in which paparazzi are "assaulting the celebrity in order to either capture the victim's reaction to the assault on film or tape, or to use the threat of assault in order to impede the mobility of a celebrity so that an image may be taken." The legislative history cited incidents involving Lindsey Lohan, Reese Witherspoon, Jennifer Lopez, and Nicole Kidman. The bill sought to create civil liability to prevent such aggressive behavior. In opposition to the bill, the Newspaper Publisher's Association warned: "Under AB 381, newsworthy persons with a bone to pick with the press will file frivolous lawsuits against journalists and the newspapers that employ them in an attempt to chill the public's right to know. . . . Essentially, AB 381 would create liability whenever a reporter gets too close to a news subject and appears to have the present ability to get even closer."

NOTES & QUESTIONS

1. ***The Anti-Paparazzi Act vs. the Intrusion Tort.*** How does California's Anti-Paparazzi Act differ from the ordinary intrusion upon seclusion tort?
2. ***Chasing Celebrities.*** Does California's Anti-Paparazzi Act prevent the kind of paparazzi behavior that caused or contributed to Princess Diana's death? Consider the 2005 amendments that prohibit an assault created with the intent to capture a photograph or video. If photographers swarm around a celebrity driving on Hollywood Boulevard or Mulholland Drive, is there recourse under the California Act? According to Lisa Vance, this amendment to the statute is flawed because "[a]ssault is an intentional tort and the actor must have intended to inflict harmful or offensive contact upon the other person." In Vance's analysis, the law only prohibits situations in which a defendant acts with the intention to inflict harmful or offensive contact upon the other person. She proposes that the law be further amended to cover situations in

which a paparazzo negligently causes apprehension of contact.[7] This new language would, therefore, also cover situations where a photographer is driving carelessly in pursuit of a subject and collides with a victim's car.

In January 2008, the police in Los Angeles arrested four paparazzi for reckless driving. The photographers were following Britney Spears's car very closely, travelling at high speed, and changing lanes in an unsafe manner. Would the laws against reckless driving adequately protect against this conduct? What does the anti-paparazzi statute add? Is the anti-paparazzi law necessary?

3. ***Jurisdictional Limits?*** Where does the forbidden behavior have to take place under the Act? Imagine a photograph taken of a movie star in Sydney, Australia, under circumstances that violate California's Anti-Paparazzi Act. This photograph is then published in a magazine in San Francisco. Does this behavior violate California's Anti-Paparazzi Act?
4. ***The Anti-Paparazzi Act and the First Amendment.*** Is California's Anti-Paparazzi Act constitutional? Rodney Smolla argues that this law is content based because it looks to the perpetrator's intent to sell or transfer communicative material. Smolla also argues that the First Amendment should prohibit liability for intrusion when a plaintiff is in a public place.[8] However, much paparazzi activity occurs in public. Would an anti-paparazzi law be viable if it were limited only to instances where plaintiffs were in private places? Do you agree with Smolla that the Act violates the First Amendment?

Erwin Chemerinsky contends that newsgathering, although currently not protected by the First Amendment, should be protected by intermediate scrutiny:

> Speech is protected because it matters in people's lives, and aggressive newsgathering is often crucial to obtaining the information. The very notion of a marketplace of ideas rests on the availability of information. Aggressive newsgathering, such as by undercover reporters, is often the key to gathering the information. People on their own cannot expose unhealthy practices in supermarkets or fraud by telemarketers or unnecessary surgery by doctors. But the media can expose this, if it is allowed the tools to do so, and the public directly benefits from the reporting.

However, Chemerinsky goes on to argue that the California Anti-Paparazzi Act would survive intermediate scrutiny:

> Despite strongly believing in First Amendment protection for newsgathering, I believe that this law is constitutional. The government has an important interest in protecting the privacy of the home. Fourth Amendment cases have recognized the special privacy interests surrounding the home. Additionally, in the First Amendment area, the Court has expressly protected the privacy of the home. In *Frisby v. Schultz*, the Court sustained an ordinance that prohibited picketing "before or about" any residence. Although the law was

---

[7] Lisa Vance, *Amending Its Anti-Paparazzi Statute: California's Latest Baby Step in Its Attempt to Curb the Aggressive Paparazzi*, 29 Hastings Comm. & Ent. L.J. 99 (2006).

[8] *See* Rodney A. Smolla, *Privacy and the First Amendment Right to Gather News*, 67 Geo. Wash. L. Rev. 1097, 1113, 1127 (1999).

adopted in response to targeted picketing by antiabortion protestors of a doctor's home, the Court concluded that the law was permissible because it was content neutral and narrowly tailored to protect people's tranquility and repose in their homes. . . .

The California Privacy Protection Act says that people, no matter how famous, should be able to shut their door and close out the media and the world. If the image could not have been gained except through a trespass, the media should not be able to obtain it through technological enhancement equipment. Simply put, the law is constitutional because it substantially advances the government's interest in safeguarding privacy in the home.[9]

Consider the following argument by C. Thomas Dienes:

While it is well established that the media are subject to neutral tort, contract, and criminal laws of general applicability, the First Amendment still prohibits laws that are not neutral. Laws that discriminate against particular forms of expressive activity or against the press are presumptively unconstitutional. As the Supreme Court warned: "Laws that single out the press, or certain elements thereof, for special treatment 'pose a particular danger of abuse by the State.'"

The antipaparazzi laws, by focusing only on taking photographs and making sound recordings when done for commercial purposes and on the defendant photographer's profits, clearly target the press. Liability for photographing or recording the same event will depend on whether the photographer is a private individual or a for-profit photojournalist whose work is intended for public distribution. Statements made at legislative hearings by proponents of these laws leave no doubt that the press is the focus of the antipaparazzi legislation.

The taking of photographs or the making of sound recordings is not itself speech. . . . [T]he sale or trade of a photo or recording is probably not a form of expression. . . .

Nevertheless the antipaparazzi legislation singles out press photography and sound recording for significant and discriminatory burdens. Even if such acts do not themselves constitute speech, they are protected means of newsgathering vital to press publication. If the photographs and sound recordings cannot be made, they cannot be published. As the Supreme Court said in *Arcara v. Cloud Books, Inc.*, laws are subject to heightened scrutiny "although directed at activity with no expressive component, [if they] impose a disproportionate burden upon those engaged in protected First Amendment activities." Because media speech-related activity is significantly and disproportionately burdened, the antipaparazzi laws should be treated as presumptively unconstitutional, subject to strict scrutiny review.[10]

3. VIDEO VOYEURISM

Cameras are everywhere today. Warren and Brandeis wrote about the perils of small accessible cameras; one wonders what they would have thought about

---

[9] Erwin Chemerinsky, *Protect the Press: A First Amendment Standard for Safeguarding Aggressive Newsgathering*, 33 U. Rich. L. Rev. 1143, 1159, 1163-64 (2000).

[10] C. Thomas Dienes, *Protecting Investigative Journalism,* 67 Geo. Wash. L. Rev. 1139 (1999).

the proliferation of cell phone cameras, which millions of people now carry around with them at all times. Some people are posting their cell phone snapshots on the Web. The dark underbelly of these practices is the rise of what is referred to as "video voyeurism," the use of video or photography to capture people naked without their consent. Websites have been popping up with "upskirt" photos — pictures taken up women's skirts. There are more than 100 websites with images of unsuspecting people who are caught in the act of showering or undressing.[11] Indeed, it is relatively easy to snap photos in locker rooms with a cell phone camera. Several states have passed video voyeurism laws, some with criminal penalties. *See, e.g.,* La. Rev. Stat. Ann. § 14:283; N.J. Stat. Ann. § 2C:18-3; N.Y. Penal Law § 250.45.

The state of Washington passed a video voyeurism law that provided that

> [a] person commits the crime of voyeurism if, for the purpose of arousing or gratifying the sexual desire of any person, he or she knowingly views, photographs, or films another person, without that person's knowledge and consent, while the person being viewed, photographed, or filmed is in a place where he or she would have a reasonable expectation of privacy.

RCW 9A.44.115. The statute defined the place where people have a reasonable expectation of privacy as:

> (i) A place where a reasonable person would believe that he or she could disrobe in privacy, without being concerned that his or her undressing was being photographed or filmed by another; *or*
>
> (ii) A place where one may reasonably expect to be safe from casual or hostile intrusion or surveillance. . . .

Id. In *Washington v. Glas,* 54 P.3d 147 (Wash. 2002), Sean Glas was convicted under the statute for taking photos up women's skirts in a shopping mall without their consent. The court dismissed Glas's conviction because "although the Legislature may have intended to cover intrusions of privacy in public places, the plain language of the statute does not accomplish this goal." The court reasoned that "[c]asual surveillance frequently occurs in public. Therefore, public places could not logically constitute locations where a person could reasonably expect to be safe from casual or hostile intrusion or surveillance."

Shortly after this opinion, in 2003, Washington revised its statute to include "intimate areas of another person without that person's knowledge and consent and under circumstances where the person has a reasonable expectation of privacy, whether in a public or private place." RCW 9A.44.115.

Consider the following law enacted by the U.S. Congress in 2004:

VIDEO VOYEURISM PREVENTION ACT

18 U.S.C. § 1801

(a) Whoever, in the special maritime and territorial jurisdiction of the United States, having the intent to capture an improper image of an individual, knowingly

[11] Clay Calvert, *Voyeur Nation: Media, Privacy, and Peering in Modern Culture* (2000).

does so and that individual's naked or undergarment clad genitals, pubic area, buttocks, or female breast is depicted in the improper image under circumstances in which that individual has a reasonable expectation of privacy regarding such body part or parts, shall be fined under this title or imprisoned not more than one year, or both.

(b) In this section —

(1) the term "captures," with respect to an image, means videotapes, photographs, films, or records by any means or broadcasts;

(2) the term "female breast" means any portion of the female breast below the top of the areola;

(3) the term "improper image," with respect to an individual, means an image, captured without the consent of that individual, of the naked or undergarment clad genitals, pubic area, buttocks, or female breast of that individual; and

(4) the term "under circumstances in which that individual has a reasonable expectation of privacy" means —

(A) circumstances in which a reasonable person would believe that he or she could disrobe in privacy, without being concerned that his or her image was being videotaped, photographed, filmed, broadcast, or otherwise recorded by any means; or

(B) circumstances in which a reasonable person would believe that his or her naked or undergarment-clad pubic area, buttocks, genitals, or female breast would not be visible to the public, regardless of whether that person is in a public or private area.

(c) This section shall not apply to any person engaged in lawful law enforcement or intelligence activities.

NOTES & QUESTIONS

1. ***The Washington Statute vs. the Video Voyeurism Protection Act.*** How does the federal statute compare with the Washington statute? Does the federal statute violate the First Amendment?
2. ***Privacy in Public.*** Clay Calvert contends that because the Act "applies in public areas, not merely those that are private . . . [t]his would be a radical change for the legal system's conception of privacy, but surely one that is necessary to preserve human dignity from offensive intrusions."[12] Consider again *Nader v. General Motors,* where the court held that "a person does not automatically make public everything he does merely by being in a public place." In what circumstances might a person have an expectation of privacy in a public place?
3. ***The Burning Man Festival Video.*** The Burning Man Festival, held annually in the Nevada desert, has nearly 25,000 participants, including a large contingent of technology professionals. There is significant nudity at the

[12] Clay Calvert, *Revisiting the Voyeurism Value in the First Amendment: From the Sexually Sordid to the Details of Death,* 27 Seattle U. L. Rev. 721, 731 (2004); *see also* Helen Nissenbaum, *Protecting Privacy in the Information Age: The Problem of Privacy in Public*, 17 Law & Phil. 559 (1998) (arguing that being in public should not eliminate one's privacy interest).

festival, as people are encouraged to engage in "radical self-expression." Videos for personal use are permitted with prior approval by the festival organizers. In 2002, 12 videos of nude participants at the festival appeared for sale on a pornographic website called Video Voyeur. Video Voyeur had sought permission to videotape the event, but was denied.[13] Does Video Voyeur's videotaping, which captures naked people, including breasts and genitals, violate the Video Voyeurism Prevention Act?

B. DISCLOSURE OF TRUTHFUL INFORMATION

In certain circumstances, the law provides remedies for individuals who suffer harm as a result of the disclosure of their personal information. One of the primary remedies is the tort of public disclosure of private facts. Other remedies include statutes passed by states and the federal government that restrict the disclosure of specific information. For example, a number of states have laws prohibiting the disclosure of the identities of sexual offense victims. *See, e.g.*, N.Y. Civ. Rights L. § 50-b; 42 Pa. Comp. Stat. § 5988. States have also provided statutory remedies for the disclosure that a person has AIDS. *See, e.g.*, 410 Ill. Comp. Stat. 305/9; Fla. Stat. § 381.004. Federal wiretap law prohibits the disclosure of a communication that one has reason to know was obtained through an illegal wiretap. *See* 18 U.S.C. § 2511(1)(c). This provision of federal wiretap law is the subject of *Bartnicki v. Vopper*, discussed below. What types of disclosures of personal information can and should give rise to civil liability? How can liability for the disclosure of true information coexist with the First Amendment's protection of free speech?

1. PUBLIC DISCLOSURE OF PRIVATE FACTS

(a) Introduction

PUBLICITY GIVEN TO PRIVATE LIFE

Restatement (Second) of Torts § 652D

One who gives publicity to a matter concerning the private life of another is subject to liability to the other for invasion of his privacy, if the matter publicized is of a kind that

(a) would be highly offensive to a reasonable person, and
(b) is not of legitimate concern to the public

---

[13] Evelyn Nieves, *A Festival With Nudity Sues a Sex Web Site,* N.Y. Times, July 5, 2002. The Burning Man Festival's suit was filed prior to the Video Voyeurism Prevention Act. Among the claims were intrusion, appropriation, public disclosure, breach of contract, and trespass. The suit was settled when Video Voyeur agreed to stop selling the videos, to turn them over to the festival organizers, and to cease from videotaping the event in the future.

NOTES & QUESTIONS

1. ***Publicity.*** "Publicity" means that the matter is communicated to the "public at large" or "to so many persons that the matter must be regarded as substantially certain to become one of public knowledge."
2. ***Highly Offensive.*** The disclosure must be highly offensive. According to the Restatement (comment c):

   > Complete privacy does not exist in this world except in a desert, and anyone who is not a hermit must expect and endure the ordinary incidents of the community life of which he is a part. Thus he must expect the more or less casual observation of his neighbors as to what he does, and that his comings and goings and his ordinary daily activities, will be described in the press as a matter of casual interest to others. The ordinary reasonable man does not take offense at a report in a newspaper that he has returned from a visit, gone camping in the woods or given a party at his house for his friends. Even minor and moderate annoyance, as for example through public disclosure of the fact that the plaintiff has clumsily fallen downstairs and broken his ankle, is not sufficient to give him a cause of action under the rule stated in this Section. It is only when the publicity given to him is such that a reasonable person would feel justified in feeling seriously aggrieved by it, that the cause of action arises.

   Note the irony. The Restatement commentary suggests that the ordinary person does not take offense of a newspaper report that he has "given a party at his house for his friends." Indeed, it was such a newspaper report that some suggest inspired Samuel Warren to write the law review article with Louis Brandeis that gave rise to this very tort.
3. ***Newsworthiness.*** As stated by Restatement (comment f): "When the subject-matter of the publicity is of legitimate public concern, there is no invasion of privacy." Recall that the first exception to the right to privacy proposed by Brandeis and Warren was for "any publication of matter which is of general public interest."
4. ***Recognition of the Tort by the States.*** Most states recognize the public disclosure tort.[14] There are some states that have not recognized the tort: Nebraska, New York, North Carolina, North Dakota, Rhode Island, Utah, and Virginia.[15] As you read in *Lake v. Wal-Mart*, Minnesota, a long time holdout on recognizing the public disclosure tort, finally recognized the tort in 1998.

---

[14] For more background about the public disclosure tort, see Jonathan B. Mintz, *The Remains of Privacy's Disclosure Tort: An Exploration of the Private Domain,* 55 Md. L. Rev. 425 (1996); Robert C. Post, *The Social Foundations of Privacy: Community and Self in the Common Law Tort,* 77 Cal. L. Rev. 957 (1989); Peter L. Felcher & Edward L. Rubin, *Privacy, Publicity, and the Portrayal of Real People by the Media,* 88 Yale L.J. 1577 (1979); Dorsey D. Ellis, Jr., *Damages and the Privacy Tort: Sketching a "Legal Profile,"* 64 Iowa L. Rev. 1111 (1979); Randall Bezanson, *Public Disclosure as News: Injunctive Relief and Newsworthiness in Privacy Actions Involving the Press*, 64 Iowa L. Rev. 1061 (1979); John W. Wade, *Defamation and the Right to Privacy*, 15 Vand. L. Rev. 1093 (1962).

[15] *See* Geoff Dendy, Note, *The Newsworthiness Defense to the Public Disclosure Tort*, 85 Ky. L.J. 147, 158 (1997).

(b) Private Matters

GILL V. HEARST PUBLISHING CO.

253 P.2d 441 (Cal. 1953)

SPENCE, J. . . . [P]laintiffs, husband and wife, sought damages for an alleged invasion of their right of privacy. . . . Plaintiffs' original complaint was predicated solely on the charge that in the October, 1947, issue of Harper's Bazaar, a magazine published and distributed by the corporate defendants, there appeared an unauthorized photograph of plaintiffs taken by defendants' employee while plaintiffs were seated in an affectionate pose at their place of business, a confectionery and ice cream concession in the Farmers' Market in Los Angeles. This photograph was used to illustrate an article entitled "And So the World Goes Round," a short commentary reaffirming "the poet's conviction that the world could not revolve without love," despite "vulgarization" of the sentiment by some, and that ballads may still be written about everyday people in love. . . .

Plaintiffs . . . amended their complaint to allege that the same photograph was republished with defendants' consent in the May, 1949, issue of the Ladies' Home Journal, a monthly magazine published and distributed by the Curtis Publishing Company. . . . Specifically, it is here alleged that the "picture" was republished with the "knowledge, permission and consent" of defendants and that "credit" for the publication was given to and required by defendants; that the published photograph depicts plaintiffs in an "uncomplimentary" pose; that plaintiffs' right of privacy was thereby invaded and plaintiffs were subjected to humiliation and annoyance to their damage in the sum of $25,000. . . .

. . . [M]ere publication of the photograph standing alone does not constitute an actionable invasion of plaintiffs' right of privacy. The right "to be let alone" and to be protected from undesired publicity is not absolute but must be balanced against the public interest in the dissemination of news and information consistent with the democratic processes under the constitutional guaranties of freedom of speech and of the press. The right of privacy may not be extended to prohibit any publication of matter which may be of public or general interest, but rather the "general object in view is to protect the privacy of private life, and to whatever degree and in whatever connection a man's life has ceased to be private, before the publication under consideration has been made, to that extent the protection is to be withdrawn." Brandeis-Warren Essay, 4 Harvard Law Rev., 193, 215. Moreover, the right of privacy is determined by the norm of the ordinary man; that is to say, the alleged objectionable publication must appear offensive in the light of "ordinary sensibilities." . . .

The picture allegedly was taken at plaintiffs' "place of business," a confectionery and ice cream concession in the Farmers' Market, Los Angeles. It shows plaintiffs, a young man and young woman, seated at a counter near a cash register, the young woman apparently in intent thought, with a notebook and pencil in her hands, which rest on the counter. Plaintiffs are dressed informally and are in a romantic pose, the young man having one arm about the young woman. There are at least five other persons plainly visible in the photograph in positions in close proximity to plaintiffs as the central figures. Apparently the picture has no particular news value but is designed to serve the function of entertainment as a matter of legitimate public interest. However, the constitution guaranties of freedom of expression apply with equal force to the publication whether it be a news report or an entertainment feature, and defendants' liability accrues only in the event that it can be said that there has been a wrongful invasion of plaintiffs' right of privacy.

In considering the nature of the picture in question, it is significant that it was not surreptitiously snapped on private grounds, but rather was taken of plaintiffs in a pose voluntarily assumed in a public market place. . . . Here plaintiffs, photographed at their concession allegedly "well known to persons and travelers throughout the world" as conducted for "many years" in the "world-famed" Farmers' Market, had voluntarily exposed themselves to public gaze in a pose open to the view of any persons who might then be at or near their place of business. By their own voluntary action plaintiffs waived their right of privacy so far as this particular public pose was assumed, for "There can be no privacy in that which is already public." *Melvin v. Reid*, 297 P. 91, 93. The photograph of plaintiffs merely permitted other members of the public, who were not at plaintiffs' place of business at the time it was taken, to see them as they had voluntarily exhibited themselves. Consistent which their own voluntary assumption of this particular pose in a public place, plaintiffs' right to privacy as to this photographed incident ceased and it in effect became a part of the public domain, as to which they could not later rescind their waiver in an attempt to assert a right of privacy. In short, the photograph did not disclose anything which until then had been private, but rather only extended knowledge of the particular incident to a somewhat larger public then had actually witnessed it at the time of occurrence.

Nor does there appear to be anything "uncomplimentary" or discreditable in the photograph itself, so that its publication might be objectionable as going "beyond the limits of decency" and reasonably indicate defendants' conduct to be such that they "should have realized it would be offensive to persons of ordinary sensibilities." Here the picture of plaintiffs, sitting romantically close to one another, the man with his arm around the woman, depicts no more than a portrayal of an incident which may be seen almost daily in ordinary life couples in a sentimental mood on public park benches, in railroad depots or hotel lobbies, at public games, the beaches, the theatres. Such situation is readily distinguishable from cases where the right of privacy has been enforced with regard to the publication of a picture which was shocking, revolting or indecent in its portrayal of the human body. In fact, here the photograph may very well be said to be complimentary and pleasing in its pictorial representation of plaintiffs.

Plaintiffs have failed to cite, and independent research has failed to reveal, any case where the publication of a mere photograph under the circumstances here prevailing a picture (1) taken in a pose voluntarily assumed in a public place and (2) portraying nothing to shock the ordinary sense of decency or propriety has been held an actionable invasion of the right of privacy. To so hold would mean that plaintiffs "under all conceivable circumstances had an absolute legal right to (prevent publication of) any photograph of them taken without their permission. If every person has such a right, no (periodical) could lawfully publish a photograph of a parade or a street scene. We are not prepared to sustain the assertion of such a right." . . .

CARTER, J. DISSENTING. I dissent, however, from the holding that the publication of the photograph alone did not violate plaintiffs' right of privacy. . . .

[F]irst, it should be quite obvious that there is no news or educational value whatsoever in the photograph alone. It depicts two persons (plaintiffs) in an amorous pose. There is nothing to show whether they are or are not married. While some remote news significance might be attached to persons in such a pose on the theory that the public likes and is entitled to see persons in such a pose, there is no reason why the publisher need invade the privacy of John and Jane Doe for his purpose. He can employ models for that purpose and the portion of the public interested will never know the difference but its maudlin curiosity will be appeased.

For the same reasons the discussion in the majority opinion to the effect that plaintiffs consented to the publication because they assumed the pose in a public place is fallacious. But in addition, such a theory is completely at odds with the violation of the right of privacy. By plaintiffs doing what they did in view of a tiny fraction of the public, does not mean that they consented to observation by the millions of readers of the defendant's magazine. In effect, the majority holding means that anything anyone does outside of his own home is with consent to the publication thereof, because, under those circumstances he waives his right of privacy even though there is no news value in the event. If such were the case, the blameless exposure of a portion of the naked body of a man or woman in a public place as the result of inefficient buttons, hooks or other clothes-holding devices could be freely photographed and widely published with complete immunity. The majority opinion confuses the situation, as have some of the other cases, with the question of newsworthiness. It has been said that when a person is involved in either a public or private event, voluntarily or involuntarily, of news value, that he has waived his right of privacy. Plainly such is not the case where the event is involuntary such as the victim of a holdup. . . . There is no basis for the conclusion that the second a person leaves the portals of his home he consents to have his photograph taken under all circumstances thereafter. There being no legitimate public interest, there is no excuse for the publication.

The [argument] that the picture would not offend the senses of an ordinary person is equally untenable. It is alleged in plaintiffs' complaint, and admitted by the demurrer that it so offended them. It is then a matter of proof at the trial. Certainly reasonable men could view the picture as showing plaintiffs in a sultry or sensual pose. For this Court to say as a matter of law that such portrayal would not seriously offend the feelings of an ordinary man is to take an extreme view to say the least. The question is one for the trier of fact. If it is in part a question of law it is so only to the extent that the right does not extend to "supersensitiveness or agoraphobia." An examination of the photograph shows that it would offend the feelings of persons other than oversensitive ones. . . .

In announcing a rule of law defining the right of a private citizen to be left alone, and not have his photograph published to the four winds, especially when he is depicted in an uncomplimentary pose, courts should consider the effect of such publication upon the sensibility of the ordinary private citizen, and not upon the sensibility of those persons who seek and enjoy publicity and notoriety and seeing their pictures on public display, or those who are in the "public eye" such as public officials, clergymen, lecturers, actors and others whose professional career brings them in constant contact with the public and in whom the public or some segment thereof is interested. Obviously anything the latter group may do or say has news or educational value such cannot be said of the persons engaged in private business or employment who constitute more that 90% of our population. These private citizens, who desire to be left alone, should have and enjoy a right of privacy so long as they do nothing which can reasonably be said to have news value. Certainly this right is entitled to protection. It seems to me that the law should be so molded as to protect the right of the 90% who do not desire publicity or notoriety and who may be offended by publications such as that here involved. . . .

NOTES & QUESTIONS

1. ***Privacy in Public.*** Similar to *Gill,* many courts hold that matters cease to be "private" when occurring in public. Appearing in public "necessarily involves doffing the cloak of privacy which the law protects." *Cefalu v. Globe Newspaper Co.*, 391 N.E.2d 935, 939 (Mass. App. 1979). In *Penwell v. Taft Broadcasting*, 469 N.E.2d 1025 (Ohio App. 1984), a husband and wife were arrested in a bar, handcuffed, and taken to the police station, where it was discovered that they had been arrested due to mistaken identity. A television film crew that arrived at the bar with the police filmed the plaintiff's arrest and removal from the bar, and the footage was later broadcast by the television station. The court dismissed the plaintiff's public disclosure action because the arrest was filmed in public and was "left open to the public eye." Does appearing in public extinguish a person's claim to privacy?
2. ***Photography of Public Scenes.*** Judge Carter, in dissent, argues that there is a difference between engaging in public displays of affection "in view of a tiny fraction of the public" and being observed by millions of magazine readers. Thus, the prior public exposure of the plaintiffs did not extinguish their privacy claim. How is the law to draw the appropriate line? At what point does the public exposure of the plaintiff's activities become too great to sustain a claim that the activities are private? Suppose, for example, a photographer is taking photos of people in the park. How is that photographer to know if she can publish the photos? Should she obtain the consent of everyone captured in the photos? According to the majority opinion, if Judge Carter's view were the law, this "would mean that plaintiffs under all conceivable circumstances had an absolute legal right to (prevent publication of) any photograph of them taken without their permission. If every person has such a right, no (periodical) could lawfully publish a photograph of a parade or a street scene." How would Judge Carter respond?

DAILY TIMES DEMOCRAT V. GRAHAM

162 So. 2d 474 (Ala. 1964)

HARWOOD, J. This is an appeal from a judgment in favor of the plaintiff in an action charging an invasion by the defendant of the plaintiff's right of privacy. Damages were assessed by the jury at $4,166.00. . . .

Appellee is a woman 44 years of age who has lived in Cullman County, Alabama her entire life. She is married and has two sons, ages 10 and 8. The family resides in a rural community where her husband is engaged in the business of raising chickens. . . .

On 9 October 1961, the Cullman County Fair was in progress. On that day the appellee took her two children to the Fair. After going on some of the rides, the boys expressed a wish to go through what is called in the record the "Fun House." The boys were afraid to enter alone so the appellee accompanied them. She testified she had never been through a Fun House before and had no knowledge that there was a device that blew jets of air up from the platform of the Fun House upon which one exited therefrom.

The appellee entered the Fun House with her two boys and as she was leaving her dress was blown up by the air jets and her body was exposed from the waist down, with the exception of that portion covered by her "panties."

At this moment the appellant's photographer snapped a picture of the appellee in this situation. This was done without the appellee's knowledge or consent. Four days later the appellant published this picture on the front page of its newspaper.

The appellant publishes about five thousand newspapers daily which are delivered to homes, mailed to subscribers, and displayed on racks in various locations in the city of Cullman and elsewhere.

On the Sunday following the publication of the picture, the appellee went into the city of Cullman. There she saw the appellant's newspaper display with her picture on the front page in one of the appellant's newspaper racks, and she also saw copies of the said newspaper in other places.

While the appellee's back was largely towards the camera in the picture, her two sons are in the picture, and the photograph was recognized as being of her by other people with whom she was acquainted. The matter of her photograph was mentioned to the appellee by others on several occasions. Evidence offered by the appellee during the trial tended to show that the appellee, as a result of the publication of the picture, became embarrassed, self-conscious, upset and was known to cry on occasions. . . .

. . . Counsel contends that as a matter of law the publication of the photograph was a matter of legitimate news of interest to the public; that the publishing of the picture was in connection with a write-up of the Fair, which was a matter of legitimate news. If this be so, then of course the appellant would have been privileged to have published the picture.

Counsel has quoted from an array of cases as to what constitutes news. We see no need to refer to these cases in that their applicability to the facts now before us is negligible. We can see nothing of legitimate news value in the photograph. Certainly it discloses nothing as to which the public is entitled to be informed. . . .

Not only was this photograph embarrassing to one of normal sensibilities, we think it could properly be classified as obscene, in that "obscene" means "offensive to modesty or decency"; or expressing to the mind or view something which delicacy, purity, or decency forbid to be expressed.

The appellant's insistence of error in this aspect is therefore without merit.

Counsel further argues that the court erred in refusal of appellant's requested affirmative charges in that appellee's picture was taken at the time she was a part of a public scene, and the publication of the photograph could not therefore be deemed an invasion of her privacy as a matter of law.

The proposition for which appellant contends is probably best illustrated by the following quotation from *Forster v. Manchester*, 410 Pa. 192, 189 A.2d 147:

> On the public street, or in any other public place, the plaintiff has no right to be alone, and it is no invasion of his privacy to do no more than follow him about. Neither is it such an invasion to take his photograph in such a place, since this amounts to nothing more than making a record, not differing essentially from a full written description of a public sight which anyone present would be free to see.

Admittedly this principle is established by the cases. As well stated in *Hinish v. Meir & Frank Co., Inc.*, 113 P.2d 438:

> When a legal principle is pushed to an absurdity, the principle is not abandoned, but the absurdity avoided.

In other words, a purely mechanical application of legal principles should not be permitted to create an illogical conclusion.

To hold that one who is involuntarily and instantaneously enmeshed in an embarrassing pose forfeits her right of privacy merely because she happened at the moment to be part of a public scene would be illogical, wrong, and unjust.

One who is a part of a public scene may be lawfully photographed as an incidental part of that scene in his ordinary status. Where the status he expects to occupy is changed without his volition to a status embarrassing to an ordinary person of reasonable sensitivity, then he should not be deemed to have forfeited his right to be protected from an indecent and vulgar intrusion of his right of privacy merely because misfortune overtakes him in a public place. . . .

NOTES & QUESTIONS

1. ***The Focus of the News Article.*** Would a change in the focus of the news article change the outcome? What if the article appeared in a journal devoted to amusement parks, the (hypothetical) *Fun House Journal*?
2. ***Voluntary vs. Involuntary Exposure.*** The court holds that although Graham was in public, the exposure of her body was involuntary, and hence a private matter. Does whether a matter is public or private depend upon voluntary or involuntary disclosure or upon one's expectation? Is *Graham* consistent with *Gill v. Hearst Publishing Co.*? Can these cases be reconciled?

Also consider *McNamara v. Freedom Newspapers, Inc.*, 802 S.W.2d 901 (Tex. Ct. App. 1991). A newspaper published a photo of a high school soccer player's inadvertently exposed genitalia while running on a soccer field. The plaintiff, McNamara, relied on *Daily Times Democrat v. Graham*, but the court found *Graham* unpersuasive and concluded:

> The uncontroverted facts in this case establish that the photograph of McNamara was taken by a newspaper photographer for media purposes. The picture accurately depicted a public event and was published as part of a newspaper article describing the game. At the time the photograph was taken, McNamara was voluntarily participating in a spectator sport at a public place. None of the persons involved in the publishing procedure actually noticed that McNamara's genitals were exposed.

Can *McNamara* be reconciled with *Graham*?

3. ***Privacy and Communication to Other People.*** Generally, a fact widely known about a person is not considered private; however, certain limited disclosures of information do not destroy its private nature. In *Times Mirror Co. v. Superior Court*, 244 Cal. Rptr. 556 (Cal. Ct. App. 1988), the plaintiff (Doe) discovered the murdered body of her roommate lying on the floor of her apartment and saw the perpetrator before she fled the apartment. Doe's identity was withheld from the public by the police to protect her safety (since the murderer was still at large), but her identity was leaked to a reporter and published in a newspaper article about the incident. Doe sued for public disclosure, and the newspaper argued that the matter was not private because Doe revealed it to certain neighbors, friends, family members, and investigating officials. The court, however, concluded that Doe had not "rendered otherwise private information public by cooperating in the criminal investigation and seeking solace from friends and relatives."

   How many people must a person tell a secret to before it ceases to become private? In *Y.G. v. Jewish Hospital,* 795 S.W.2d 488 (Mo. Ct. App. 1990), a couple used in vitro fertilization at a hospital to become pregnant. While people at the hospital knew about their use of in vitro fertilization, the couple kept this hidden from others because it was against the teachings of their church. At a party in this hospital for in vitro couples, a camera crew from a television station filmed the plaintiffs (despite their making reasonable efforts to not be filmed). The court held that the plaintiffs retained an expectation of privacy because "attending this limited gathering . . . did not waive their right to keep their condition and the process of in vitro private, in respect to the general public." In *Multimedia WMAZ, Inc. v. Kubach*, 443 S.E.2d 491 (Ga. 1994), an HIV-positive plaintiff disclosed that he had the disease to about 60 people — family, friends, doctors, and members of an HIV support group. The plaintiff agreed to appear on a television show with his face obscured, but the obscuring process was botched, and the plaintiff was identifiable. He sued, and the court concluded that his telling his HIV-positive status to 60 people did not extinguish his privacy interest because these people "cared about him . . . or because they also had AIDS."

In contrast, consider *Duran v. Detroit News, Inc.*, 504 N.W.2d 715 (Mich. Ct. App. 1993). A Colombian judge, who indicted the violent drug lord Pablo Escobar, fled to Detroit after receiving death threats. She told a few people about her identity. Reporters, however, revealed her address and discussed the million-dollar bounty on her head. The court rejected Duran's public disclosure claim because she had exposed her identity "to the public eye." In *Fisher v. Ohio Dep't of Rehabilitation and Correction*, 578 N.E.2d 901 (Ohio Ct. Cl. 1988), the plaintiff told just four co-workers about encounters with her child that had "sexual overtones." The court concluded that the information was no longer private because the plaintiff "publicly and openly" told it to her co-workers.

Lior Strahilevitz concludes that "courts are not being terribly explicit or precise about why particular disclosures waive privacy expectations and others do not. Certainly, a simple head-counting approach does not reconcile the precedents. After all, Kubach's disclosure of facts to sixty people did not render them public, but Fisher's disclosure to three people did." Strahilevitz suggests that looking to the number of people who are exposed to a secret is not the right approach. Instead, he uses social network theory.

Network theory describes how information flows between people. In particular, network theory seeks to assess the probability that information disclosed to one member of a particular group or community will be disseminated to others outside of that realm. According to Strahilevitz, the analysis should not focus on how many people already know a person's secret but how likely the secret is to be widely disseminated beyond the group of people who already know it. Information should be deemed private so long as it remains within a confined group — even if that group is rather large. The law should recognize that a particular person expects information to stay within these boundaries.

Strahilevitz identifies three key factors that affect the likelihood of data staying within a particular group: (1) how interesting the information is (the more interesting, the more likely it is to spread beyond the group); (2) the norms that a particular group has with regard to spreading the kind of information at issue; and (3) the way the group is structured and how information generally flows within and beyond the group. Strahilevtiz agrees with the *Kubach* court's decision that the plaintiff still retained a privacy interest in his HIV positive status even though 60 others knew about it:

> [An empirical] study of HIV disclosure suggests that information about HIV status is frequently shared with some parts of an individual's social network, while other members, who might know the HIV positive person well and be interested in her health status, remain in the dark. Information about HIV status, therefore, seems not to flow through social networks readily, at least in the case of private figures. . . . Kubach had a reasonable expectation that his disclosure to some people who knew him would not result in the information being revealed to others who knew him, let alone thousands of people in his local community.

Strahilevitz argues that the holding in *Duran* "cannot be squared with social network theory":

According to the court, Duran used her real name when shopping in stores or eating in restaurants, which waived an expectation of privacy in her identity. Under a network theory approach, these acts, combined with her notoriety in Colombia, would not have eliminated her reasonable expectation of privacy in her identity. . . . [When shopping or at a restaurant, at] most, Duran would have come into fleeting contact with other customers or service sector employees. There was nothing interesting about Duran's shopping or eating out. In order to generate interest in the story, the defendant had to connect Duran's presence in Detroit to her past notoriety in Colombia and the bounty that had been placed on her head. Such information was quite unlikely to be aggregated through the kinds of weak ties that Duran established in Detroit's public spaces. Perhaps a Colombian waiter put two-and-two together, but this would have been a highly improbable turn of events. Duran's general obscurity in Detroit properly engendered a reasonable expectation of privacy with respect to her shopping and visiting restaurants.[16]

4. ***Retracting Statements Made to the Media.*** In *Virgil v. Time, Inc.*, 527 F.2d 1122 (9th Cir. 1975), a well-known body surfer was interviewed by *Sports Illustrated*, and photographs of the surfer were taken for the story. The surfer revoked his consent to publishing the story when he discovered that the article was not going to be exclusively about his surfing but was also going to discuss some of his personal eccentricities and incidents about his life in order to explain the psychological profile of those who engage in such a dangerous sport. The story was published, and the surfer sued for public disclosure. The court held that the information about the surfer's life was private:

It is not the manner in which information has been obtained that determines whether it is public or private. Here it is undisputed that the information was obtained without commission of a tort and in a manner wholly unobjectionable. However, that is not determinative as to this particular tort. The offense with which we are here involved is not the intrusion by means of which information is obtained; it is the publicizing of that which is private in character. The question, then, is whether the information disclosed was public rather than private — whether it was generally known and, if not, whether the disclosure by appellant can be said to have been to the public at large.

Talking freely to someone is not in itself . . . making public the substance of the talk. There is an obvious and substantial difference between the disclosure of private facts to an individual — a disclosure that is selective and based on a judgment as to whether knowledge by that person would be felt to be objectionable — and the disclosure of the same facts to the public at large. . . .

Talking freely to a member of the press, knowing the listener to be a member of the press, is not then in itself making public. Such communication can be said to anticipate that what is said will be made public since making public is the function of the press, and accordingly such communication can be construed as a consent to publicize. Thus if publicity results it can be said to have been consented to. However, if consent is withdrawn prior to the act of publicizing, the consequent publicity is without consent. . . .

---

[16] Lior Jacob Strahilevitz, *A Social Networks Theory of Privacy,* 72 U. Chi. L. Rev. 919 (2005).

5. ***Further Dissemination of Previously Disclosed Information.*** Media entities that further disseminate information already disclosed by another media entity are not liable for public disclosure. *Ritzmann v. Weekly World News*, 614 F. Supp. 1336 (N.D. Tex. 1985) (giving further publicity to information contained in news stories already published is not actionable because the information is no longer private); *Heath v. Playboy Enterprises, Inc.*, 732 F. Supp. 1145 (S.D. Fla. 1990) ("Republication of facts already publicized elsewhere cannot provide a basis for an invasion of privacy claim.").

However, when only partial facts are revealed, the disclosure of more information can give rise to a viable action for public disclosure. For example, in *Michaels v. Internet Entertainment Group, Inc.*, 5 F. Supp. 2d 823 (C.D. Cal. 1998), Bret Michaels, the former lead singer for the rock band Poison, and Pamela Anderson Lee, a celebrity, sought a preliminary injunction to prevent the defendant from making a videotape of the two having sex available on the Internet. The defendant argued that the plaintiffs lacked a privacy interest in the tape because a part of the tape had already been released by a foreign Internet source. The court, however, concluded that "plaintiffs' privacy interest in the unreleased portions of the Tape is undiminished." Further, another videotape depicting Lee having sex with her husband, Tommy Lee, had been widely distributed, and the defendant contended that this negated Lee's privacy interest. The court rejected the defendant's argument: "The Court is not prepared to conclude that public exposure of one sexual encounter forever removes a person's privacy interest in all subsequent and previous sexual encounters." The defendant also contended that Lee lacked a privacy interest because she had previously appeared nude in magazines and on video, but the court concluded that the defendant's "contention unreasonably blurs the line between fiction and reality. Lee is a professional actor. She has played roles involving sex and sexual appeal. The fact that she has performed a role involving sex does not, however, make her real sex life open to the public."

(c) Publicity

MILLER V. MOTOROLA, INC.

560 N.E.2d 900 (Ill. App. 1990)

BUCKLEY, J. Joy V. Miller (plaintiff) filed an action in the circuit court of Cook County against her employer, Motorola, Inc. (defendant), seeking recovery for damages resulting from defendant's disclosure of her mastectomy surgery to plaintiff's co-employees. Plaintiff appeals from the circuit court's order dismissing her complaint with prejudice. . . .

Considering first plaintiff's public disclosure claim, this cause of action is defined by the Restatement (Second) of Torts as follows:

> One who gives publicity to a matter concerning the private life of another is subject to liability to the other for invasion of privacy, if the matter publicized is

> of a kind that (a) would be highly offensive to a reasonable person, and (b) is not of a legitimate concern to the public. . . .

Plaintiff's complaint alleges that she consulted with defendant's resident nurse, Felicia Masters, relative to three leaves of absence taken by plaintiff from 1984 to 1986 to undergo mastectomy and reconstructive surgeries and that Masters advised her during those consultations that her medical information would be confidential. The complaint further alleges that plaintiff, who did not consent to the release of any of her medical information which was maintained at defendant's place of business, was told by a co-employee on or about October 1, 1987, that she had been informed of plaintiff's mastectomy. As a result of defendant's disclosure and plaintiff's belief of the awareness by numerous other employees of her condition, the complaint alleges that plaintiff suffered severe physical, mental and emotional distress and took an early retirement from her 23-year employment with defendant.

Defendant argues that these allegations are insufficient to show that any private facts were publicized because Illinois law requires the disclosure be widespread and that the communication be written. . . .

. . . The Restatement indicates that the required communication must be more than that made to a small group; rather, the communication must be made to the public at large. In acknowledging this general requirement, however, some courts have recognized the need for flexibility in the application of the Restatement's theory to permit recovery for egregious conduct. These courts have realized that in circumstances where a special relationship exists between the plaintiff and the "public" to whom the information has been disclosed, the disclosure may be just as devastating to the person even though the disclosure was made to a limited number of people. The court in *Beaumont* [*v. Brown*, 257 N.W.2d 522 (Mich. 1977),] explained:

> Communication of embarrassing facts about an individual to a public not concerned with that individual and with whom the individual is not concerned obviously is not a "serious interference" with plaintiff's right to privacy, although it might be "unnecessary" or "unreasonable." An invasion of a plaintiff's right to privacy is important if it exposes private facts to a public whose knowledge of those facts would be embarrassing to the plaintiff. Such a public might be the general public, if the person were a public figure, or a particular public such as fellow employees, club members, church members, family, or neighbors, if the person were not a public figure.

We adopt the position of the above authorities that the public disclosure requirement may be satisfied by proof that the plaintiff has a special relationship with the "public" to whom the information is disclosed. Plaintiff's allegation that her medical condition was disclosed to her fellow employees sufficiently satisfies the requirement that publicity be given to the private fact. . . .

NOTES & QUESTIONS

1. ***The Restatement and Publicity.*** Consider the Restatement (comment b):

> Thus it is not an invasion of the right of privacy, within the rule stated in this Section, to communicate a fact concerning the plaintiff's private life to a single person or even to a small group of persons. On the other hand, any publication in a newspaper or a magazine, even of small circulation, or in a handbill distributed to a large number of persons, or any broadcast over the radio, or statement made in an address to a large audience, is sufficient to give publicity within the meaning of the term as it is used in this Section. The distinction, in other words, is one between private and public communication.

Is *Miller v. Motorola* at odds with the commentary of the Restatement?

2. ***The Publicity Element and the Extent of the Disclosure.*** Many courts have held that disclosure to a small group of individuals does not constitute publicity. In *Yoder v. Smith*, 112 N.W.2d 862 (Iowa 1962), the court held that the publicity element was not satisfied when the defendant disclosed the plaintiff's debts to the plaintiff's employer. In *Vogel v. W.T. Grant Co.*, 327 A.2d 133 (Pa. 1974), the court held that the publicity element was not satisfied when the defendant contacted the plaintiff's employer and mother in an attempt to collect a debt owed by the plaintiff because the "notification of two or four third parties is not sufficient to constitute publication" of the debt. Likewise, in *Wells v. Thomas*, 569 F. Supp. 426 (E.D. Pa. 1983), the court held that disclosure to "the community of employees at [hospital] staff meetings and discussions between defendants and other employees" was not sufficient to establish the requisite publicity for a viable public disclosure action.

In contrast, consider *Brents v. Morgan*, 299 S.W. 967 (Ky. 1927), where the court held that there was sufficient publicity when the owner of an automobile garage posted a large sign on a show window of his garage stating that the plaintiff owed him a debt. Also consider *Biederman's of Springfield, Inc. v. Wright*, 322 S.W.2d 892 (Mo. 1959), where the defendant, attempting to collect a debt owed by the plaintiff, made "loud, overbearing, tough, degrading and embarrassing demands that she pay [the debt]" in a café while she was working as a waitress. This behavior occurred in front of numerous customers. The court concluded: "We believe that the oral publication over the three-day period in a public restaurant with numerous customers present satisfies any reasonable requirement as to publicity." How do *Brents* and *Biederman's* differ from *Yoder*, *Vogel*, and *Wells*?

A few courts have applied the publicity requirement in a similar manner as *Miller v. Motorola*. Consider the following statement in *Beaumont v. Brown*, 257 N.W.2d 522 (Mich. 1977):

> To begin with "communication to the general public" is somewhat ambiguous, because a communication rarely, if ever, reaches everyone. . . . Communication of embarrassing facts about an individual to a public not concerned with that individual and with whom the individual is not concerned obviously is not a "serious interference" with plaintiff's right to privacy, although it might be "unnecessary" or "unreasonable." An invasion of a

plaintiff's right to privacy is important if it exposes private facts to a public whose knowledge of those facts would be embarrassing to the plaintiff. Such a public might be the general public, if the person were a public figure, or a particular public such as fellow employees, club members, church members, family, or neighbors, if the person were not a public figure.

Here we have developed the criterion of a particular public, whose knowledge of the private facts would be embarrassing to the plaintiff. . . [W]e do not engage in a numbers game. . . .

3. ***Criticism of the Publicity Requirement.*** As one court observed, the requirement of widespread publicity "singles out the print, film, and broadcast media for legal restraints that will not be applied to gossip-mongers in neighborhood taverns or card-parties, to letter writers or telephone tattlers." *Anderson v. Fisher Broadcasting Co.*, 712 P.2d 803, 805 (Or. 1986). Consider Jonathan Mintz's criticism of the publicity requirement:

> This hair-splitting rationale seems plainly flawed. It facilitates the conservation of judicial resources far more than the dignity interests deemed worthy of protection by tort law. The difference in the injury to a person's dignity between five persons' and fifty persons' access to a private fact is merely one of degree, not of nature. A person loses some sense of privacy the moment a second person divulges a private fact to a third person, particularly when the third person is a member of the same community as the first person. Thus, the degree of publicity, and the corresponding degree of injury to a person's dignity, is a factor better addressed in damage calculations than in summary judgments or motions to dismiss.[17]

Also consider Robert Post:

> We often care more about what those within our "group" think of us than we do about our reputation among the strangers who comprise the general public. Yet the publicity requirement, as defined by the Restatement, would impose sanctions for the disclosure of a husband's marital infidelity to the general public, but not for its disclosure to his wife.[18]

(d) The Newsworthiness Test

SIPPLE V. CHRONICLE PUBLISHING CO.

201 Cal. Rptr. 665 (Cal. Ct. App. 1984)

CALDECOTT, J. On September 22, 1975, Sara Jane Moore attempted to assassinate President Gerald R. Ford while the latter was visiting San Francisco, California. Plaintiff Oliver W. Sipple (hereafter appellant or Sipple) who was in the crowd at Union Square, San Francisco, grabbed or struck Moore's arm as the latter was about to fire the gun and shoot at the President. Although no one can be certain whether or not Sipple actually saved the President's life, the

---

[17] Jonathan B. Mintz, *The Remains of Privacy's Disclosure Tort: An Exploration of the Private Domain*, 55 Md. L. Rev. 425, 438 (1996).

[18] Robert C. Post, *The Social Foundations of Privacy: Community and Self in the Common Law Tort*, 77 Cal. L. Rev. 957, 992 (1989).

assassination attempt did not succeed and Sipple was considered a hero for his selfless action and was subject to significant publicity throughout the nation following the assassination attempt.

Among the many articles concerning the event was a column, written by Herb Caen and published by the San Francisco Chronicle on September 24, 1975. The article read in part as follows: "One of the heroes of the day, Oliver 'Bill' Sipple, the ex-Marine who grabbed Sara Jane Moore's arm just as her gun was fired and thereby may have saved the President's life, was the center of midnight attention at the Red Lantern, a Golden Gate Ave. bar he favors. The Rev. Ray Broshears, head of Helping Hands, and Gay Politico, Harvey Milk, who claim to be among Sipple's close friends, describe themselves as 'proud — maybe this will help break the stereotype'. Sipple is among the workers in Milk's campaign for Supervisor."

Thereafter, the Los Angeles Times and numerous out-of-state newspapers published articles which referring to the primary source, (i.e., the story published in the San Francisco Chronicle) mentioned both the heroic act shown by Sipple and the fact that he was a prominent member of the San Francisco gay community. Some of those articles speculated that President Ford's failure to promptly thank Sipple for his heroic act was a result of Sipple's sexual orientation.[19]

. . . Sipple filed an action against the [newspapers]. The complaint was predicated upon the theory of invasion of privacy and alleged in essence that defendants without authorization and consent published private facts about plaintiff's life by disclosing that plaintiff was homosexual in his personal and private sexual orientation; that said publications were highly offensive to plaintiff inasmuch as his parents, brothers and sisters learned for the first time of his homosexual orientation; and that as a consequence of disclosure of private facts about his life plaintiff was abandoned by his family, exposed to contempt and ridicule causing him great mental anguish, embarrassment and humiliation. Plaintiff finally alleged that defendants' conduct amounted to malice and oppression calling for both compensatory and punitive damages.

Appellant's principal contention on appeal is that the trial court prejudicially erred in granting summary judgment in favor of respondents. More precisely, appellant argues that the individual elements of the invasion of privacy (i.e., public disclosure of private facts; the offensiveness of the public disclosure; and the newsworthiness of the publication as an exception to tort liability) constituted a factual determination which could not be resolved or adjudicated by way of summary procedure.

---

[19] For example, the September 25, 1975, issue of the *Los Angeles Times* wrote inter alia as follows: "A husky ex-marine who was a hero in the attempted assassination of President Ford emerged Wednesday as a prominent figure in the gay community. And questions were raised in the gay community if Oliver (Bill) Sipple, 32, was being shunned by the White House because of his associations. Sipple, who lunged at Sara Jane Moore and deflected her revolver as she fired at the President, conceded that he is a member of the 'court' of Mike Caringi, who was elected 'emperor of San Francisco' by the gay community. A column item in a morning newspaper here strongly implied Wednesday that Sipple is gay. . . . Harvey Milk, a prominent member of this city's large homosexual community and a longtime friend of Sipple, speculated Wednesday that the absence of a phone call or telegram of gratitude from the White House might not be just an oversight."

Before discussing appellant's contentions on the merits, as an initial matter we set out the legal principles governing the case. It is well settled that there are three elements of a cause of action predicated on tortious invasion of privacy. First, the disclosure of the private facts must be a public disclosure. Second, the facts disclosed must be private facts, and not public ones. Third, the matter made public must be one which would be offensive and objectionable to a reasonable person of ordinary sensibilities. It is likewise recognized, however, that due to the supreme mandate of the constitutional protection of freedom of the press even a tortious invasion of one's privacy is exempt from liability if the publication of private facts is truthful and newsworthy. . . .

When viewed in light of the aforegoing principles, the summary judgment in this case must be upheld on two grounds. First, as appears from the record properly considered for the purposes of summary judgment, the facts disclosed by the articles were not private facts within the meaning of the law. Second, the record likewise reveals on its face that the publications in dispute were newsworthy and thus constituted a protective shield from liability based upon invasion of privacy. . . .

[Regarding the first ground,] the cases explain that there can be no privacy with respect to a matter which is already public or which has previously become part of the "public domain." Moreover, it is equally underlined that there is no liability when the defendant merely gives further publicity to information about the plaintiff which is already public or when the further publicity relates to matters which the plaintiff leaves open to the public eye.

The case at bench falls within the aforestated rules. The undisputed facts reveal that prior to the publication of the newspaper articles in question appellant's homosexual orientation and participation in gay community activities had been known by hundreds of people in a variety of cities, including New York, Dallas, Houston, San Diego, Los Angeles and San Francisco. Thus, appellant's deposition shows that prior to the assassination attempt appellant spent a lot of time in "Tenderloin" and "Castro," the well-known gay sections of San Francisco; that he frequented gay bars and other homosexual gatherings in both San Francisco and other cities; that he marched in gay parades on several occasions; that he supported the campaign of Mike Caringi for the election of "Emperor"; that he participated in the coronation of the "Emperor" and sat at Caringi's table on that occasion; that his friendship with Harvey Milk, another prominent gay, was well-known and publicized in gay newspapers; and that his homosexual association and name had been reported in gay magazines (such as Data Boy, Pacific Coast Times, Male Express, etc.) several times before the publications in question. In fact, appellant quite candidly conceded that he did not make a secret of his being a homosexual and that if anyone would ask, he would frankly admit that he was gay. In short, since appellant's sexual orientation was already in public domain and since the articles in question did no more than to give further publicity to matters which appellant left open to the eye of the public, a vital element of the tort was missing rendering it vulnerable to summary disposal. . . .

[Turning to the second ground — newsworthiness,] our courts have recognized a broad privilege cloaking the truthful publication of all newsworthy matters. . . . [T]he cases and authorities further explain that the paramount test of newsworthiness is whether the matter is of legitimate public interest which in turn must be determined according to the community mores. As pointed out in *Virgil v. Time, Inc.*, "In determining what is a matter of legitimate public interest, account must be taken of the customs and conventions of the community; and in the last analysis what is proper becomes a matter of the community mores. The line is to be drawn when the publicity ceases to be the giving of information to which the public is entitled, and becomes a morbid and sensational prying into private lives for its own sake, with which a reasonable member of the public, with decent standards, would say that he had no concern."

In the case at bench the publication of appellant's homosexual orientation which had already been widely known by many people in a number of communities was not so offensive even at the time of the publication as to shock the community notions of decency. Moreover, and perhaps even more to the point, the record shows that the publications were not motivated by a morbid and sensational prying into appellant's private life but rather were prompted by legitimate political considerations, i.e., to dispel the false public opinion that gays were timid, weak and unheroic figures and to raise the equally important political question whether the President of the United States entertained a discriminatory attitude or bias against a minority group such as homosexuals. . . .

Appellant's contention that by saving the President's life he did not intend to enter into the limelight and become a public figure, can be easily answered. In elaborating on involuntary public figures, Restatement Second of Torts section 625D, comment f, sets out in part as follows: "There are other individuals who have not sought publicity or consented to it, but through their own conduct or otherwise have become a legitimate subject of public interest. They have, in other words, become 'news.'"

NOTES & QUESTIONS

1. ***The Sad Fate of a Hero.*** Sipple passed away in January 1989, alone in a cluttered apartment with half-gallon bottles of bourbon within reach of his bed. A story in the *Los Angeles Times* almost a month after he passed away detailed the sad circumstances of his death and filled in some details of his life. Sipple had been wounded twice in Vietnam, lived on a veteran's disability pension, and, despite his lack of funds and poor health, was remembered by friends as a generous person who would readily give money to charity or to help a derelict.

   The *L.A. Times* also noted that a framed letter hung in the apartment where Sipple had died — it was a letter of "heartfelt appreciation," signed "Jerry Ford," which thanked Sipple for his "selfless actions" in acting quickly and without fear and averting danger to the President and the crowd. The letter was sent three days after Sipple had knocked away the gun of the would-be assassin in San Francisco.

   The *L.A. Times* article also stressed how much Sipple had suffered after the press outed him. It quoted George Sipple, Bill's brother: "His personal life never should have made it back to Detroit" (his hometown). Sipple's parents were shocked by the revelation of their son's sexual orientation; as the *L.A.*

Times states: "The estrangement between Sipple and his father was so deep that when his mother died in 1979, his father made it clear that he was not welcome."[20] Sipple remained in San Francisco and did not attend his mother's funeral.

Taking a break from cleaning his brother's apartment, George Sipple noted that his brother was pleased that he left a mark and remembered that his brother once said that long after he died, "somebody will pick up a book and see Oliver Sipple saved President Ford's life."

2. ***Group Privacy.*** The court rejects Sipple's claim in part because Sipple's homosexuality and participation in the gay community were known by hundreds of people in many cities. But Sipple's argument is that he wanted to keep his homosexuality a secret from certain people — namely his parents and siblings. Can Sipple legitimately claim that something known widely to many people can still remain private?
3. ***President Ford's Prejudice.*** In *Sipple*, the newsworthiness of the story did not just turn on exposing the background of a hero who prevented an assassination. The story also exposed President Ford's possible prejudice against homosexuals. Does this fact alone establish that the story was newsworthy?
4. ***Outing.*** There has been extensive debate about the propriety of outing gays. Is the fact that a prominent individual is gay newsworthy? John Elwood observes that there are three rationales advanced for outing gays:

   > According to its advocates, outing serves three basic purposes: (1) to expose the illogic of governmental policies that discriminate against homosexuals and of the hypocrisy of gay public officials who publicly support such policies; (2) to provide positive examples of gays, as role models to other gays and as ambassadors to mainstream America; and (3) to break down the stigma surrounding homosexuality by making it commonplace.

   Elwood contends: "Even under the best of circumstances, the relationship between outing a particular figure and effecting a societal change is simply too attenuated to override the outing target's privacy rights." However, "a closeted government official who made disparaging public remarks about homosexuals or who enforced discriminatory programs might be a valid target for outing. Her hypocrisy calls into question her honesty and motivation, and thus information about her sexuality is relevant to the question of her fitness for office."[21] How would this argument apply in the *Sipple* case?

   In contrast to Elwood, Kathleen Guzman disagrees with the hypocrisy justification for outing:

   > . . . [T]his justification presupposes two potentially invalid assumptions. Presuming that the outers are even correct in asserting someone's orientation, one wonders whether there is such a thing as a "gay viewpoint." While abstract generalization may be made regarding the tendency of a group

---

[20] Dean Morain, *Sorrow Trailed a Veteran Who Saved a President's Life and Then Was Cast in an Unwanted Spotlight*, L.A. Times, Feb. 13, 1989, at Part 5, 1.

[21] John P. Elwood, Note, *Outing, Privacy, and the First Amendment*, 102 Yale L.J. 747, 748-49, 773-74 (1992).

> member to sympathize with in-group concerns, it is absurd to attribute to an individual a pre-packaged set of opinions merely because that individual is gay. One's views should no more be determined by sexual orientation than by being Caucasian or agnostic or underweight or female. . . .
>
> Second, what is orientation hypocrisy and at what level of conduct should it be penalized? Hypocrisy is a broad term which can encompass a range of activity: merely keeping same-sex orientation a secret; actively asserting heterosexuality; failing to vote for or affirmatively and publicly support pro-gay legislation; actively opposing similar legislation. The (non)actor whose conduct contravenes the mythical "gay viewpoint" need not necessarily be driven by "hypocrisy," but is equally likely to act through privacy, self-preservation, cowardice, or merely a different belief. A smoker who supports legislation restricting cigarette sales to minors is no more a hypocrite than a non-smoker who does so. A woman who votes against equal rights legislation is no more a hypocrite than a man who does so. To assert that she or he must be a hypocrite anathematizes individuality and accords insufficient weight to the myriad reasons that impel behavior or decision making.[22]

After Sipple's death, Fred Friendly, a journalism professor and former head of CBS News, wrote that journalists did not act fairly in Sipple's case and should not have written about his sexuality.[23] Friendly argued that the right to privacy should prevail unless the "individual's private conduct becomes relevant in assessing his integrity or validity in a public role." Do you agree with this approach? Does it resolve the *Sipple* case?

5. ***Newsworthiness Tests.*** Courts use at least three newsworthiness tests.[24] First is the "leave it to the press" approach, where courts defer to editorial judgment and do not attempt to distinguish between what is news and what is entertainment. Second, the Restatement looks to the "customs and conventions of the community" and draws a line between the "giving of information to which the public is entitled" and "morbid and sensational prying into private lives for its own sake." A third approach is the "nexus test," which involves the Restatement approach but also requires a "logical nexus (or relationship) . . . between the complaining individual and the matter of legitimate public interest." Which test do you find most appropriate?

6. ***What Is Newsworthy?*** Many of the cases applying the newsworthiness test do so to avoid First Amendment problems. Keep in mind that the newsworthiness test is an element of the tort of public disclosure. Applications of the tort — involving possibly even non-newsworthy facts — can still be subject to an independent First Amendment challenge. This issue will be discussed later in this chapter.

How are courts to determine what is newsworthy? According to the Restatement of Torts § 652D (comment h), adopting language from *Virgil v.*

---

[22] Kathleen Guzman, *About Outing: Public Discourse, Private Lives*, 73 Wash. U. L.Q. 1531, 1536-37, 1555-56 (1995). For further arguments against outing, see Jean L. Cohen, *Is Privacy a Legal Duty?*, in *Public and Private: Legal, Political, and Philosophical Perspectives* 117, 125 (Maurizio Passerin d'Entreves & Ursula Vogel eds., 2000).

[23] Fred W. Friendly, *Gays, Privacy and a Free Press*, Wash. Post, Apr. 8, 1990, at B7.

[24] *See* Geoff Dendy, Note, *The Newsworthiness Defense to the Public Disclosure Tort*, 85 Ky. L.J. 147 (1997).

Time, 527 F.2d 1122, 1129 (9th Cir. 1975), courts are to look to the "customs and conventions of the community."

Consider the case of *Diaz v. Oakland Tribune*, 188 Cal. Rptr. 762 (Ct. App. 1983). Diaz was the first woman student body president elected at a community college. The *Oakland Tribune* published the fact that Diaz was a transsexual. Diaz sued for public disclosure, and the court held that the suit could proceed to the jury, which would determine whether the fact that Diaz was a transsexual was newsworthy. The court noted: "[W]e find little if any connection between the information disclosed and Diaz's fitness for office. The fact that she is a transsexual does not adversely reflect on her honesty or judgment." Eugene Volokh, who opposes the tort of public disclosure altogether, argues:

> Now I agree with the [*Diaz*] court's factual conclusion; people's gender identity strikes me as irrelevant to their fitness for office. But other voters take a different view. Transsexuality, in their opinion, may say various things about politicians (even student body politicians): It may say that they lack attachment to traditional values, that they are morally corrupt, or even just that they have undergone an unnatural procedure and therefore are somehow tainted by it. These views may be wrong and even immoral, but surely it is not for government agents — whether judges or jurors — to dictate the relevant criteria for people's political choices, and to use the coercive force of law to keep others from informing them of things that they may consider relevant to those choices. I may disagree with what you base your vote on, but I must defend your right to base your vote on it, and the right of others to tell you about it.[25]

If Volokh is right, then what isn't relevant for fitness for office? Do public figures have any claim to privacy, or is everything about them newsworthy?

In *Neff v. Time, Inc.*, 406 F. Supp. 858 (W.D. Pa. 1976), a *Sports Illustrated* photographer printed a photograph of John W. Neff, a teacher, with the front zipper of his pants open in *Sports Illustrated*. The photograph was used in a story about Pittsburgh Steelers fans, and the article was entitled: "A Strange Kind of Love." The photograph was taken while Neff was with a group of fans at a football game between the Cleveland Browns and Pittsburgh Steelers. The fans were waving Steeler banners, drinking beer, and appeared slightly intoxicated. When the *Sports Illustrated* photographer approached them and the group found out that the photographer was covering the game for *Sports Illustrated*, the group "hammed it up" while the photographer snapped the pictures. Of the 30 pictures of the group that were taken, a committee of five employees at *Sports Illustrated* selected the photograph of Neff with his fly open for inclusion in the issue. According to the court, "[a]lthough Neff's fly was not open to the point of being revealing, the selection was deliberate and surely in utmost bad taste; subjectively, as to Neff, the published picture could have been embarrassing, humiliating and offensive to his sensibilities." According to Neff, the photograph implied "that he is a 'crazy, drunken slob,' and combined with the title of the article, 'a sexual deviate.'" Neff asserted that the article invaded his right to privacy,

---

[25] Eugene Volokh, *Freedom of Speech and Information Privacy: The Troubling Implications of a Right to Stop People from Speaking About You*, 52 Stan. L. Rev. 1049, 1090 (2000).

caused him reputational injury, subjected him to public ridicule, destroyed his peace of mind, and caused him severe emotional distress. The court, however, rejected Neff's claim:

> . . . It seems to us that art directors and editors should hesitate to deliberately publish a picture which most likely would be offensive and cause embarrassment to the subject when many other pictures of the same variety are available. Notwithstanding, "(t)he courts are not concerned with establishing canons of good taste for the press or the public." . . .
>
> The article about Pittsburgh Steeler fans was of legitimate public interest; the football game in Cleveland was of legitimate public interest; Neff's picture was taken in a public place with his knowledge and with his encouragement; he was catapulted into the news by his own actions; nothing was falsified; a photograph taken at a public event which everyone present could see, with the knowledge and implied consent of the subject, is not a matter concerning a private fact. A factually accurate public disclosure is not tortious when connected with a newsworthy event even though offensive to ordinary sensibilities. The constitutional privilege protects all truthful publications relevant to matters of public interest. . . .

Graham involved a photograph taken of a woman who was in an embarrassing position in public. How does the situation in *Neff* differ from that in *Graham*? *Graham* did not focus much on newsworthiness, but suppose that the case were being decided by the *Neff* court — would the photograph in *Graham* be newsworthy?

7. ***The Privacy of Public Figures.*** Consider the Restatement of Torts (Second) § 652D (comment h):

> Permissible publicity to information concerning either voluntary or involuntary public figures is not limited to the particular events that arouse the interest of the public. That interest, once aroused by the event, may legitimately extend, to some reasonable degree, to further information concerning the individual and to facts about him, which are not public and which, in the case of one who had not become a public figure, would be regarded as an invasion of his purely private life. Thus the life history of one accused of murder, together with such heretofore private facts as may throw some light upon what kind of person he is, his possible guilt or innocence, or his reasons for committing the crime, are a matter of legitimate public interest. On the same basis the home life and daily habits of a motion picture actress may be of legitimate and reasonable interest to the public that sees her on the screen.

To what extent can a public figure's life be private? The Restatement goes on to say:

> The extent of the authority to make public private facts is not, however, unlimited. There may be some intimate details of her life, such as sexual relations, which even the actress is entitled to keep to herself. In determining what is a matter of legitimate public interest, account must be taken of the customs and conventions of the community; and in the last analysis what is proper becomes a matter of the community mores. The line is to be drawn when the publicity ceases to be the giving of information to which the public is entitled, and becomes a morbid and sensational prying into private lives for

its own sake, with which a reasonable member of the public, with decent standards, would say that he had no concern. The limitations, in other words, are those of common decency, having due regard to the freedom of the press and its reasonable leeway to choose what it will tell the public, but also due regard to the feelings of the individual and the harm that will be done to him by the exposure. Some reasonable proportion is also to be maintained between the event or activity that makes the individual a public figure and the private facts to which publicity is given. Revelations that may properly be made concerning a murderer or the President of the United States would not be privileged if they were to be made concerning one who is merely injured in an automobile accident.

Are all "intimate details" private? J.M. Balkin argues that by creating media events that show the politician "with his or her family, participating in casual activities or in a seemingly unguarded and intimate moment," politicians have been "willing accomplices in the creation of a new political culture that sees private aspects of a person's life as politically relevant, that collapses older boundaries between public and private."

Who decides what is in the public and private spheres? Balkin argues that these spheres are dynamic, in constant flux, and that the media is actively shaping their contours:

> . . . [B]y making these new forms of knowledge part of democratic decisionmaking, journalists change the contours of public discourse and the definition of a "public issue." Journalists do not simply respect the existing boundaries of the public and the private but actively reshape them: Merely by talking about sexual scandal and encouraging others to do so journalists make these topics part of public discourse and public comment. . . .
>
> Some journalists can even convince themselves that they are empowering the public through these revelations. But instead of empowering their audiences or increasing information, journalists may in fact simply be altering the mix of stories presented to the public; the practical effect may be a contraction of the scope of public discourse.[26]

8. ***Public Figures and the Lapse of Time.*** If a person is a public figure, can she ever retreat from the public glare? Recall *Sidis v. F-R Publishing Corp.,* 113 F.2d 806 (2d Cir. 1940) (Chapter 1). There, a child prodigy, famous when he was young, had subsequently retreated from the public spotlight for many decades. An article then revealed details of his life in a column called "Where Are They Now?" The court concluded that "Sidis has cloaked himself in obscurity, but his subsequent history, containing as it did the answer to the question of whether or not he had fulfilled his early promise, was still a matter of public concern." Consider the comment k from the Restatement (Second) of Torts § 652D:

> The fact that there has been a lapse of time, even of considerable length, since the event that has made the plaintiff a public figure, does not of itself defeat

[26] J.M. Balkin, *How Mass Media Stimulate Political Transparency*, 3 Cultural Values 393 (1999). For a discussion of when public figures should be entitled to privacy, see Anita L. Allen, *Lying to Protect Privacy*, 44 Vill. L. Rev. 161, 177 (1999); Anita L. Allen, *Privacy and the Public Official: Talking About Sex as a Dilemma for Democracy*, 67 Geo. Wash. L. Rev. 1165 (1999).

> the authority to give him publicity or to renew publicity when it has formerly been given. Past events and activities may still be of legitimate interest to the public, and a narrative reviving recollection of what has happened even many years ago may be both interesting and valuable for purposes of information and education. Such a lapse of time is, however, a factor to be considered, with other facts, in determining whether the publicity goes to unreasonable lengths in revealing facts about one who has resumed the private, lawful and unexciting life led by the great bulk of the community.

9. ***The Disclosure of Identifying Information.*** In *Barber v. Time, Inc.*, 159 S.W.2d 291 (Mo. 1942), the plaintiff's photograph taken in a hospital was published in a *Time* magazine article about the plaintiff's unusual disease. The article, "Starving Glutton," described the plaintiff's rare disorder where no matter how much she ate, she continued to lose weight. The photograph showed the plaintiff in her hospital bed. The court held that "[w]hile plaintiff's ailment may have been a matter of some public interest because unusual, certainly the identity of the person who suffered this ailment was not." In other words, the matter about the rare disorder was newsworthy, but the plaintiff's identity was not of public concern.

In contrast, consider *Haynes v. Alfred A. Knopf, Inc.*, 8 F.3d 1222 (7th Cir. 1993). In 1991, Alfred A. Knopf, Inc. published Nicholas Lemann's best-selling historical book entitled *The Promised Land: The Great Black Migration and How It Changed America*. The book chronicled the migration of five million African-Americans from the rural areas in the South to urban areas in the North from 1940 to 1970. The book focuses centrally around the story of one individual, Ruby Lee Daniels. The book recounts Ruby's troubled marriage to Luther Haynes. Luther had a well-paying factory job but began to drink too much, waste money, and get into bitter fights with Ruby. The book recounts the couple's financial struggles, Luther's squandering of their money, their spiral into poverty, and their difficulties in providing for their children. When the couple was finally able to buy a home, Luther purchased a new car, and as a result, they couldn't meet their house payments and lost the home. Luther would frequently lose jobs and would often fail to come home. Luther then began to have an affair with their neighbor Dorothy Johnson, which was discovered by the children. Ruby and Luther got a divorce.

Subsequently, Luther married Dorothy. He turned his life around and began acting more responsibly. In their new community, nobody knew of Luther's past behavior toward Ruby. As Judge Posner writing for the Seventh Circuit summarizes:

> Luther's alcohol problem is behind him. He has steady employment as a doorman. His wife is a nurse, and in 1990 he told Lemann that the couple's combined income was $60,000 a year. He is not in trouble with the domestic relations court. He is a deacon of his church. He has come a long way from sharecropping in Mississippi and public housing in Chicago and he and his wife want to bury their past. . . . In Luther Haynes's own words, from his deposition, "I know I haven't been no angel, but since almost 30 years ago I have turned my life completely around. I stopped the drinking and all this bad

> habits and stuff like that, which I deny, some of [it] I didn't deny, because I have changed my life. It take me almost 30 years to change it and I am deeply in my church. I look good in the eyes of my church members and my community. Now, what is going to happen now when this public reads this garbage which I didn't tell Mr. Lemann to write? Then all this is going to go down the drain. And I worked like a son of a gun to build myself up in a good reputation and he has torn it down."

Luther and Dorothy Haynes sued Lemann and his publisher Knopf under the public disclosure tort. Their claim was that the book threatened to destroy the new life Luther had built.

Judge Posner rejected their claim:

> The two criteria, offensiveness and newsworthiness, are related. An individual, and more pertinently perhaps the community, is most offended by the publication of intimate personal facts when the community has no interest in them beyond the voyeuristic thrill of penetrating the wall of privacy that surrounds a stranger. The reader of a book about the black migration to the North would have no legitimate interest in the details of Luther Haynes's sex life; but no such details are disclosed. Such a reader does have a legitimate interest in the aspects of Luther's conduct that the book reveals. . . . No detail in the book claimed to invade the Hayneses' privacy is not germane to the story that the author wanted to tell, a story not only of legitimate but of transcendent public interest. . . .

Was Luther Haynes's actual name really necessary for telling the story? Judge Posner argues that changing his name would not have been enough to avoid legal liability:

> Well, argue the Hayneses, at least Lemann could have changed their names. But the use of pseudonyms would not have gotten Lemann and Knopf off the legal hook. The details of the Hayneses' lives recounted in the book would identify them unmistakably to anyone who has known the Hayneses well for a long time (members of their families, for example), or who knew them before they got married; and no more is required for liability either in defamation law or in privacy law. Lemann would have had to change some, perhaps many, of the details. But then he would no longer have been writing history. He would have been writing fiction. The nonquantitative study of living persons would be abolished as a category of scholarship, to be replaced by the sociological novel. That is a genre with a distinguished history punctuated by famous names, such as Dickens, Zola, Stowe, Dreiser, Sinclair, Steinbeck, and Wolfe, but we do not think that the law of privacy makes it (or that the First Amendment would permit the law of privacy to make it) the exclusive format for a social history of living persons that tells their story rather than treating them as data points in a statistical study. Reporting the true facts about real people is necessary to "obviate any impression that the problems raised in the [book] are remote or hypothetical."

Also consider *Gilbert v. Medical Economics Co.*, 665 F.2d 305 (10th Cir. 1981). An article describing a doctor's malpractice and arguing that hospitals and other physicians were not adequately self-policing included the doctor's name and photograph and discussed her psychiatric and marital problems. The doctor sued, contending that her photo, name, and personal life "add[ed] nothing to the concededly newsworthy topic of policing failures in the medical profession." The court disagreed, concluding:

> . . . [T]hese truthful representations are substantially relevant to a newsworthy topic because they strengthen the impact and credibility of the article. They obviate any impression that the problems raised in the article are remote or hypothetical, thus providing an aura of immediacy and even urgency that might not exist had plaintiff's name and photograph been suppressed. Similarly, we find the publication of plaintiff's psychiatric and marital problems to be substantially relevant to the newsworthy topic [because] . . . they are connected to the newsworthy topic by the rational inference that plaintiff's personal problems were the underlying cause of the acts of alleged malpractice.

When is identifying information newsworthy?

In *Howard v. Des Moines Register & Tribune Co.*, 870 F.2d 271 (5th Cir. 1989), the identities of victims of involuntary sterilization were disclosed in a report about abuses by a mental institution. The court rejected the argument that the identities were unnecessarily disclosed because they were needed to "strengthen the accuracy of the public perception of the merits of the controversy." *See also Ross v. Midwest Communications, Inc.*, 870 F.2d 271 (5th Cir. 1989) (holding that the disclosure of a rape victim's name in an article about the potential innocence of the man convicted of the rape was of "unique importance to the credibility and persuasive force of the story.").

Daniel Solove argues in favor of the approach taken in *Barber*. He contends that the use of initials or pseudonyms is a workable compromise between the interests of reporting the news and of protecting privacy: "Journalists generally do not include the names of rape victims or whistleblowers in their stories. On television, the media sometimes obscures the faces of particular people in video footage. With minimal effort, the media can report stories and also protect privacy."[27]

However, the cost of not using people's real names is that stories become harder to verify. Reporters from major newspapers and magazines have been caught making up false stories. How are news stories to be verified if the public cannot have necessary information to investigate further the individuals involved in the story? Solove replies:

> [S]tories of paramount importance have not identified the critical parties; for example, in exposing Watergate, Bob Woodward and Carl Bernstein relied on the well-known pseudonymous source "Deep Throat." Certainly, it affects verifiability when a story does not identify a party. However, when the journalists protect confidential sources, they engage in a balancing determination, sacrificing the public's ability to verity for the importance of protecting confidentiality. Public verifiability is not sacrosanct, but can be outweighed by privacy interests.[28]

---

[27] Daniel J. Solove, *The Virtues of Knowing Less: Justifying Privacy Protections Against Disclosure*, 53 Duke L.J. 967, 1018-19 (2003).

[28] *Id.* at 1018.

Currently, however, the media reluctantly uses pseudonyms. If the media were to do this with more regularity, it might create a culture where more journalists would create fictional stories because they could more readily get away with it. And if Solove is right, who should conduct the balance between public verifiability and privacy?

10. ***Who Decides What Is Newsworthy?*** Who ought to determine the proper subject for news? Courts? Journalists? The market? Juries? A number of courts defer to the judgment of the press for newsworthiness: "[W]hat is newsworthy is primarily a function of the publisher, not the courts." *Heath v. Playboy Enterprises, Inc.*, 732 F. Supp. 1145, 1149 (S.D. Fla. 1990); *see also Jenkins v. Dell Publishing Co.*, 251 F.2d 447, 451-52 (3d Cir. 1958); *Wagner v. Fawcett Publications*, 307 F.2d 409, 410 (7th Cir. 1962). If courts are not to second guess the judgment of the press, how are courts to determine newsworthiness? Is anything not newsworthy?

Daniel Solove contends that the deference to the media approach is a poor one. He argues that although the media might be a capable decision maker for assessing public interest in a story, "[w]hat is of interest to most of society is not the same question as what is of legitimate public concern. . . . [Public] interest can stem from a desire for entertainment or sexual pleasure just as much as it can from wanting to learn about the news and current events." Therefore, Solove concludes, "the media should not have a monopoly on determining what is of public concern."[29] In contrast, consider Eugene Volokh, who contends: "Under the First Amendment, it's generally not the government's job to decide what subjects speakers and listeners should concern themselves with."[30]

SHULMAN V. GROUP W PRODUCTIONS, INC.

955 P.2d 469 (Cal. 1998)

[Recall the facts of this case earlier in this chapter. The plaintiffs, Ruth and Wayne Shulman, mother and son, were injured in a car accident. A medical transport and rescue helicopter crew came to their assistance along with a video camera operator, who filmed the plaintiffs' rescue from the car, the flight nurse and medic's medical aid during the rescue, as well as their medical aid in the helicopter en route to the hospital. The flight nurse wore a small microphone that picked up her conversations with Ruth and other rescue workers. The segment was broadcast on a television show called *On Scene: Emergency Response*. Ruth, a paraplegic from the accident, watched the episode in her hospital room in shock. Neither Ruth nor Wayne Shulman consented to the filming or broadcasting. They sued the producers of the show, and their complaint included causes of action for public disclosure of private facts and intrusion upon

---

[29] Daniel J. Solove, *The Virtues of Knowing Less: Justifying Privacy Protections Against Disclosure*, 53 Duke L.J. 967, 1001, 1006 (2003).

[30] Eugene Volokh, *Freedom of Speech and Information Privacy: The Troubling Implications of a Right to Stop People from Speaking About You,* 52 Stan. L. Rev. 1049, 1089 (2000).

seclusion. The trial court granted the defendants' motion for summary judgment on all causes of action.

On the intrusion claim, the California Supreme Court held that the activities of the defendants in recording the events in the helicopter constituted a valid cause of action for intrusion upon seclusion. The court's decision on the public disclosure claim is excerpted below.]

WERDEGAR, J. . . . [U]nder California common law the dissemination of truthful, newsworthy material is not actionable as a publication of private facts. If the contents of a broadcast or publication are of legitimate public concern, the plaintiff cannot establish a necessary element of the tort action, the lack of newsworthiness. . . .

Although we speak of the lack of newsworthiness as an element of the private facts tort, newsworthiness is at the same time a constitutional defense to, or privilege against, liability for publication of truthful information. . . . Tort liability, obviously, can extend no further than the First Amendment allows; conversely, we see no reason or authority for fashioning the newsworthiness element of the private facts tort to *preclude* liability where the Constitution would allow it. . . .

Newsworthiness — constitutional or common law — is also difficult to define because it may be used as either a descriptive or a normative term. "Is the term 'newsworthy' a descriptive predicate, intended to refer to the fact there is widespread public interest? Or is it a value predicate, intended to indicate that the publication is a meritorious contribution and that the public's interest is praiseworthy?" A position at either extreme has unpalatable consequences. If "newsworthiness" is completely descriptive — if all coverage that sells papers or boosts ratings is deemed newsworthy — it would seem to swallow the publication of private facts tort, for "it would be difficult to suppose that publishers were in the habit of reporting occurrences of little interest." At the other extreme, if newsworthiness is viewed as a purely normative concept, the courts could become to an unacceptable degree editors of the news and self-appointed guardians of public taste. . . .

Courts balancing these interests in cases similar to this have recognized that, when a person is involuntarily involved in a newsworthy incident, not all aspects of the person's life, and not everything the person says or does, is thereby rendered newsworthy. . . . This principle is illustrated in the decisions holding that, while a particular event was newsworthy, identification of the plaintiff as the person involved, or use of the plaintiff's identifiable image, added nothing of significance to the story and was therefore an unnecessary invasion of privacy. . .

Consistent with the above, courts have generally protected the privacy of otherwise private individuals involved in events of public interest "by requiring that a logical nexus exist between the complaining individual and the matter of legitimate public interest." . . .

Intensely personal or intimate revelations might not, in a given case, be considered newsworthy, especially where they bear only slight relevance to a topic of legitimate public concern. . . .

Turning now to the case at bar, we consider whether the possibly private facts complained of here — broadly speaking, Ruth's appearance and words during the rescue and evacuation — were of legitimate public interest. If so, summary judgment was properly entered. . . .

We agree at the outset with defendants that the subject matter of the broadcast as a whole was of legitimate public concern. Automobile accidents are by their nature of interest to that great portion of the public that travels frequently by automobile. The rescue and medical treatment of accident victims is also of legitimate concern to much of the public, involving as it does a critical service that any member of the public may someday need. The story of Ruth's difficult extrication from the crushed car, the medical attention given her at the scene, and her evacuation by helicopter was of particular interest because it highlighted some of the challenges facing emergency workers dealing with serious accidents.

The more difficult question is whether Ruth's appearance and words as she was extricated from the overturned car, placed in the helicopter and transported to the hospital were of legitimate public concern. Pursuant to the analysis outlined earlier, we conclude the disputed material was newsworthy as a matter of law. One of the dramatic and interesting aspects of the story as a whole is its focus on flight nurse Carnahan, who appears to be in charge of communications with other emergency workers, the hospital base and Ruth, and who leads the medical assistance to Ruth at the scene. Her work is portrayed as demanding and important and as involving a measure of personal risk (e.g., in crawling under the car to aid Ruth despite warnings that gasoline may be dripping from the car). The broadcast segment makes apparent that this type of emergency care requires not only medical knowledge, concentration and courage, but an ability to talk and listen to severely traumatized patients. One of the challenges Carnahan faces in assisting Ruth is the confusion, pain and fear that Ruth understandably feels in the aftermath of the accident. For that reason the broadcast video depicting Ruth's injured physical state (which was not luridly shown) and audio showing her disorientation and despair were substantially relevant to the segment's newsworthy subject matter.

Plaintiffs argue that showing Ruth's "intimate private, medical facts and her suffering was not *necessary* to enable the public to understand the significance of the accident or the rescue as a public event." The standard, however, is not necessity. That the broadcast *could* have been edited to exclude some of Ruth's words and images and still excite a minimum degree of viewer interest is not determinative. Nor is the possibility that the members of this or another court, or a jury, might find a differently edited broadcast more to their taste or even more interesting. The courts do not, and constitutionally could not, sit as superior editors of the press. . . .

BROWN, J. concurring and dissenting. . . . I respectfully dissent . . . from the conclusion that summary judgment was proper as to plaintiff Ruth Shulman's cause of action for publication of private facts. . . .

. . . The private facts broadcast had little, if any, social value. The public has no legitimate interest in witnessing Ruth's disorientation and despair. Nor does it have any legitimate interest in knowing Ruth's personal and innermost thoughts immediately after sustaining injuries that rendered her a paraplegic and left her hospitalized for months — "I just want to die. I don't want to go through this." The depth of the broadcast's intrusion into ostensibly private affairs was substantial. . . . There was nothing voluntary about Ruth's position of public notoriety. She was involuntarily caught up in events of public interest, all the more so because defendants appear to have surreptitiously and unlawfully recorded her private conversations with nurse Laura Carnahan. . . .

NOTES & QUESTIONS

1. ***Voluntariness and Public Exposure.*** Is this case consistent with *Graham*?
2. ***Grief and Newsworthiness.*** Reality television shows and "caught on film" docudramas frequently capture people in moments of profound trauma and grief. Is it newsworthy to display footage of grieving relatives after a disaster or personal tragedy occurs?
3. ***Autopsy Photographs.*** Should autopsy photographs be published by the media? This question arose in a case involving the famous race car driver Dale Earnhardt, who died tragically when his car collided with a barrier. Would it be significant if the photos accompanied an article on auto racing safety? What if they were posted on a website of "famous dead people"?

BONOME V. KAYSEN

32 Media L. Rep. 1520 (2004)

MUSE, J. Joseph Bonome filed this action alleging invasion of privacy against Susana Kaysen, the author of a memoir at the center of this case, and Random House, Inc., the publisher. . . .

In the early 1990s, Bonome owned and operated a tree surgery and landscaping business primarily in the Cambridge, Massachusetts area. At the time, he was living in New Hampshire and was married with step-children. Kaysen was an author living in Cambridge. She had gained success and notoriety for her book *Girl, Interrupted* which was made into what has been described to be a critically acclaimed film. In 1994, Bonome met Kaysen and the two began having an affair, including a physical relationship. Kaysen pressured Bonome to leave his wife, and Bonome ultimately succumbed to that pressure. Bonome divorced his wife in 1996 and shortly thereafter moved into Kaysen's home, where they continued the relationship.

Within six months or a year into the relationship, Kaysen began to experience severe vaginal pain. She began to regularly see doctors for her problem, but over the course of several years was unable to receive sufficient curative treatment. During this time period, she began working on a new book, which book is the subject of this case. Despite Bonome's inquiries, Kaysen would not reveal the subject of the book to him.

The fact of their relationship was well-known to Bonome's family, friends, and clientele. However, the details of their physical relationship were private. Bonome's parents and three brothers all spent time, including some holidays, with the couple. However, in July 1998, the relationship "ended" when Kaysen asked Bonome to move out, which he did. Despite the breakup, their physical relationship continued for at least three months longer.

In 2001, Random House published the book [*The Camera My Mother Gave Me*]. The book only refers to Bonome as Kaysen's "boyfriend" and alters details about his life — such as where he was from, and his occupation. The book is an autobiographical memoir chronicling the effects of Kaysen's seemingly undiagnosable vaginal pain in a series of ruminations about the condition's effects on many aspects of her life, including her overall physical and emotional state, friendships, and her relationship with her boyfriend. It details her intense pain and discomfort and her many fruitless attempts to obtain an accurate medical diagnosis and effective treatment.

One of the central themes of the book concerns the impact of her chronic pain on the emotional and physical relationship with Kaysen's boyfriend. To that end, the book details, graphically on a few occasions, several sexual encounters between them. It portrays the boyfriend as becoming increasingly frustrated and impatient with Kaysen's condition and her reluctance and/or refusal to engage in physical intimacy. The boyfriend is described as "always bugging [her] for sex" and "whining and pleading" for sex, as well as being ignorant and insensitive to her emotional and physical state. In this vein, it attributes many aggressive and overtly offensive sexual quotes to him. Ultimately, the development of this theme culminates in a scene where the boyfriend is physically forceful in an attempt to engage her in sex. This scene is followed by ruminations about whether the relationship had exceeded the bounds of consensual sexual relations into the realm of coerced non-consensual sex. . . .

After publication of the book, Bonome learned that many local friends and family had read the book and understood the portrayal of the "boyfriend" to be a depiction of him. In addition, Bonome's business clientele included friends of Kaysen who also understood that Bonome was the "boyfriend." As a result of the publication, Bonome has suffered severe personal humiliation, and his reputation has been severely damaged among a substantial percentage of his clients and acquaintances. . . .

General Laws chapter 214 Section 1B provides that: "[a] person shall have a right against unreasonable, substantial or serious interference with his privacy." Section 1B has been interpreted to include the common-law tort of "public disclosure of private facts" as articulated in the Restatement (Second) of Torts. . . .

[T]his case presents an additional challenge in that it pits Kaysen's right of publicity — her own right to disclose intimate facts about herself — directly in conflict Bonome's right to control the dissemination of private information about himself. . . .

Undoubtedly, the information revealed was of an intensely intimate and personal nature. Indeed, commentators and courts have almost universally recognized one's sexual affairs as falling squarely within the sphere of private life. . . .

[O]therwise private information may properly be published when it is sufficiently related to a broader topic of legitimate public concern. In this case, a critical issue is whether the personal information concerning Bonome is in the book for its relevance to issues of legitimate public concern or is merely "morbid and sensational plying into [Bonome's] private [life] for its own sake."

After examining the statements concerning the boyfriend and their relevance to the broader themes of the book, it is clear that the details are included to develop and explore those themes. Specifically, the book explores the way in which Kaysen's undiagnosed physical condition impacted her physical and emotional relationship with "her boyfriend." Moreover, it explores the issue of when undesired physical intimacy crosses the line into non-consensual sexual relations in the context of her condition. These broader topics are all matters of legitimate public concern, and it is within this specific context that the explicit and highly personal details of the relationship are discussed. Thus, the defendants had a legitimate and protected interest to publish these facts.

As noted above, there is an additional interest in this case: Kaysen's right to disclose her own intimate affairs. In this case, it is critical that Kaysen was not a disinterested third party telling Bonome's personal story in order to develop the themes in her book. Rather, she is telling *her own* personal story — which inextricably involves Bonome in an intimate way. In this regard, several courts have held that where an autobiographical account related to a matter of legitimate public interest reveals private information concerning a third party, the disclosure is protected so long as there is a sufficient nexus between those private details and the issue of public concern.

Where one's own personal story involves issues of legitimate public concern, it is often difficult, if not impossible, to separate one's intimate and personal experiences from the people with whom those experiences are shared. Thus, it is within the context of Bonome and Kaysen's lives being inextricably bound together by their intimate relationship that the disclosures in this case must be viewed. Because the First Amendment protects Kaysen's ability to contribute *her own* personal experiences to the public discourse on important and legitimate issues of public concern, disclosing Bonome's involvement in those experiences is a necessary incident thereto.

. . . [T]he privilege to disclose private information is limited by the requirement that the disclosure bear the necessary nexus (both logical and proportional) to the issue of legitimate public concern. In this regard, it is of importance that Kaysen did not use Bonome's name in the book. The defendants did not subject Bonome to unnecessary publicity or attention. The realm of people that could identify Bonome as the boyfriend are those close personal friends, family, and business clients that knew of the relationship. This is not to overlook or discount the impact this disclosure may have had on Bonome, or his substantial claim that Kaysen breached a fundamental trust of their relationship. However arguably odious, the defendants did not exercise the right of disclosure in a manner offensive to the balance of those interests. See Restatement (Second) Torts § 652D, comment a ("Publicity . . . means that the matter is made public, by communicating it to the public at large, or to so many persons that the matter must be regarded as substantially certain to become one of public knowledge"). . . .

This court is not unmindful of the injury claimed by Bonome, who alleges to have suffered personal humiliation within his familial circle, as well as with friends and business clientele as a result of the book's publication. Nonetheless, Kaysen's own personal story — insofar as it relates to matters of legitimate public concern — is hers to contribute to the public discourse. This right is protected by the First Amendment. Inasmuch as the book does not exceed the bounds of that constitutional privilege, Bonome's claim for invasion of privacy under G.L.c. 214, § 1B is *DISMISSED*.

NOTES & QUESTIONS

1. ***The Right to Tell One's Story.*** The newsworthiness test examines whether a disclosure is of "legitimate concern to the public." It does not matter who is making the disclosure for the purposes of the test. However, the court suggests that "there is an additional interest in this case: Kaysen's right to disclose her own intimate affairs." The court states that "it is critical that Kaysen was not a disinterested third party telling Bonome's personal story in order to develop the themes in her book. Rather, she is telling *her own* personal story — which inextricably involves Bonome in an intimate way." Does the autobiographical nature of the disclosure change the newsworthiness analysis? Should it?

   Sonja West contends that when autobiographical speech is involved, courts should not look to whether it is of legitimate public interest: "The power to decide what is of consequence in a person's life story should ultimately lie with that person alone. As long as the content and intention of the speech is truly autobiographical, its perceived importance by others should not affect its constitutional protection."[31] Should a person have increased latitude when revealing private information about others when it also involves her own autobiographical details?

   Suppose Kaysen told her story to a journalist, who wrote about it in an article. Should the journalist receive less protection for making the disclosure than Kaysen would receive for revealing the same facts?

2. ***Blogs, Social Network Websites, and Gossip.*** In *Steinbuch v. Cutler*, 463 F. Supp. 2d 1 (D.D.C. 2006), Jessica Cutler, a staff member for a U.S. senator, wrote a blog about her relationships with several men, including a man she was dating who also worked for the senator. In her blog, The Washingtonienne, she recounted in vivid detail their budding romance. Specifically, Cutler described their sexual practices, personal conversations, and other intimate details. Cutler did not identify Steinbuch directly, but she used his real initials and disclosed other personally identifiable information that made it possible for him to be identified. For a few weeks, only a handful of people knew about Cutler's blog. Then Wonkette, a very popular political gossip blog, linked to her blog and tens of thousands began flocking to the site. The story was written about in many major newspapers, and Cutler wrote a book based on the blog and posed for *Playboy* magazine. Robert Steinbuch, the attorney who worked for the same senator as Cutler, sued her for violating his privacy. The case never proceeded to trial because Cutler declared bankruptcy. Had the case proceeded further, how should it have been resolved? Should *Bonome v. Kaysen* control? Can it be distinguished, and if so, how?

   One of Cutler's arguments was that the blog was only read by a handful of her friends until Wonkette linked to it. Cutler contended that she never gave widespread publicity to the information — Wonkette did. When information

---

[31] Sonja West, *The Story of Me: The Underprotection of Autobiographical Speech,* 84 Wash. U. L. Rev. 905, 966 (2006).

is disclosed on the Internet, but only a few people read it, is disclosure sufficiently widespread for the publicity element to be satisfied?

Cutler also argued that her account of her relationships was newsworthy. According to her motion to dismiss: "Cutler's Blog makes a shocking and disturbing portrayal of casual and even reckless sexual encounters between young, entry-level Capitol Hill staffers like Cutler and more senior staffers like Steinbuch. . . . The interrelationship between youth, beauty, sex, money, and power in Washington has long been a matter of legitimate and sometimes *pressing* public interest." Is Cutler's blog newsworthy? What are the best arguments on each side of the issue?

In his book, *The Future of Reputation,* Daniel Solove observes that people are increasingly expressing themselves in blogs and social network websites such as MySpace and Facebook. People are revealing information about their private lives as well as gossip and rumors about their friends, family, co-workers, and others. Solove notes:

> In the past, gossip occurred backstage; it was fleeting and localized. The anthropologist Sally Engle Merry observes: "Gossip flourishes in close-knit, highly connected social networks but atrophies in loose-knit, unconnected ones." Before the rise of the blogosphere, Jessica Cutler's gossip about her sexual experiences with Robert would probably have remained within her small circle of friends. But today details about people's private lives are increasingly migrating to the Internet. Jessica's blog was read by hundreds of thousands of people—perhaps millions. It is becoming harder and harder for people to escape their pasts. . . . Moreover, traditional gossip occurs in a context, among people who know the person being gossiped about. But the Internet strips away that context, and this can make gossip even more pernicious.
>
> The Internet is transforming the nature and effects of gossip. It is making gossip more permanent and widespread, but less discriminating in the appropriateness of audience. . . . The problem with Internet gossip is that it can so readily be untethered from its context.

More broadly, Solove observes, the transformation of gossip from the fleeting and forgettable to the permanent and searchable might have significant social effects:

> The Internet allows information to flow more freely than ever before. We can communicate and share ideas in unprecedented ways. These developments are revolutionizing our self-expression and enhancing our freedom.
>
> But there's a problem. We're heading toward a world where an extensive trail of information fragments about us will be forever preserved on the Internet, displayed instantly in a Google search. We will be forced to live with a detailed record beginning with childhood that will stay with us for life wherever we go, searchable and accessible from anywhere in the world. This data can often be of dubious reliability; it can be false and defamatory; or it can be true but deeply humiliating or discrediting. We may find it increasingly difficult to have a fresh start, a second chance, or a clean slate. We might find it harder to engage in self-exploration if every false step and foolish act is chronicled forever in a permanent record. This record will affect our ability to define our identities, to obtain jobs, to participate in public life, and more.

> Ironically, the unconstrained flow of information on the Internet might impede our freedom.[32]

Are the privacy torts a viable way to protect people from having their personal lives written about online?

3. ***The Breach of Confidentiality Tort.*** The breach of confidentiality tort protects against the nonconsensual disclosures of confidential information. To establish liability under the tort, a plaintiff must prove that the defendant owed the plaintiff a duty of confidentiality and that the defendant breached that duty.[33] Unlike the tort of public disclosure, the breach of confidentiality tort does not have the elements of highly offensive, publicity, or the newsworthiness test. In America, the breach of confidentiality tort has been applied to doctors and other professionals. In contrast, in England, which rejects the Warren and Brandeis privacy torts, including the public disclosure tort, has a robust breach of confidentiality tort. As Neil Richards and Daniel Solove observe:

> The law of confidentiality in England also has attributes that the American privacy torts lack. In America, the prevailing belief is that people assume the risk of betrayal when they share secrets with each other. But in England, spouses, ex-spouses, friends, and nearly anyone else can be liable for divulging confidences. As one English court noted: "The fact is that when people kiss and later one of them tells, that second person is almost certainly breaking a confidential arrangement." Confidentiality thus recognizes that nondisclosure expectations emerge not just from norms of individual dignity, but also from norms of relationships, trust, and reliance on promises. American privacy law has never fully embraced privacy within relationships; it typically views information exposed to others as no longer private. Although a tort remedying breach of confidence would emerge later on in American law, it has developed slowly in comparison to the Warren and Brandeis privacy torts.[34]

Should a person accept the risk of betrayal when sharing confidential information with another?

Suppose the breach of confidentiality tort were applied more broadly to situations where friends, spouses, and others disclosed the secrets of others. Andrew McClurg notes that the First Amendment implications of the breach of confidentiality tort are different from those of the public disclosure tort:

> If one accepts the proposition that a party to an intimate relationship impliedly agrees not the breach the other party's confidence by publishing private,

[32] Daniel J. Solove, *The Future of Reputation: Gossip, Rumor, and Privacy on the Internet* (2007). For more background about applying the privacy torts to blogs and social network sites, see Patricia Sánchez Abril, *Recasting Privacy Torts in a Spaceless World,* 21 Harv. J.L. & Tech. 1 (2007).

[33] For more background about the tort, see Alan B. Vickery, Note, *Breach of Confidence: An Emerging Tort,* 82 Colum. L. Rev. 1426 (1982); G. Michael Harvey, Comment, *Confidentiality: A Measured Response to the Failure of Privacy,* 140 U. Pa. L. Rev. 2385 (1992); Susan M. Gilles, *Promises Betrayed: Breach of Confidence as a Remedy for Invasion of Privacy,* 43 Buff. L. Rev. 1 (1995).

[34] Neil M. Richards & Daniel J. Solove, *Privacy's Other Path: Recovering the Law of Confidentiality,* 96 Geo. L.J. 123 (2007).

> embarrassing information about them via an instrument of mass communication, the speech restriction is one that is self-imposed, rather than state-imposed.[35]

How might a broader application of the breach of confidentiality tort impact bloggers like Jessica Cutler who write about their sexual activities with others? Would the tort impair free speech too much? Note that there is no newsworthiness test under the tort, so information of public concern is not protected. On the other hand, as McClurg notes, the breach of confidentiality tort understands that parties have made an implicit contract of confidentiality. Is it a violation of free speech to enforce a person's explicit or implicit promise not to speak about something?

4. ***Reputation-Tracking Technologies.*** Lior Strahilevitz argues that reputation-tracking technologies can yield beneficial results. He points to programs such as "How's My Driving?" (HMD) programs in which some commercial vehicles have stickers with a number to call to complain about bad driving. Insurance company statistics reveal significant reductions in crash costs and accidents (declines of well over 30 percent) following the implementation of HMD programs. Strahilevitz argues that the reason for the effectiveness of HMD programs is that they reduce driver anonymity:

> The problems associated with urban and suburban driving are, by and large, creatures of motorist anonymity. That statement may seem too bold to readers accustomed to hearing about drunken driving, drowsy driving, and road rage. But a review of the literature on driving suggests that these problems largely stem from roadway anonymity. If society were able to monitor its roadways around the clock and to analyze this data immediately to identify and punish problematic motorists, many of the traffic accident deaths that occur every year would be averted. A dangerous driving environment is the almost inevitable consequence of sporadic traffic law enforcement by the police combined with rare traffic norm enforcement by motorists.[36]

Strahilevitz points out that various websites such as Amazon.com, Tripadvisor.com, and eBay.com harness user feedback, where people can leave comments about a particular merchant or individual: "Though eBay's reputation system is admittedly imperfect, it has been extraordinarily successful at preventing fraud among auction participants." He proposes that more measures like HMD programs in other contexts might be beneficial. In what other situations would reputation-tracking technologies be useful? What are the potential problems with such technologies? Is there a way to implement these technologies that minimize these problems?

---

[35] Andrew J. McClurg, *Kiss and Tell: Protecting Intimate Relationship Privacy Through Implied Contracts of Confidentiality*, 74 U. Cin. L. Rev. 887, 938 (2006).

[36] Lior Strahilevitz, *"How's* My *Driving?" For Everyone (and Everything?)*, 81 N.Y.U. L. Rev. 1699, 1706 (2006).

2. FIRST AMENDMENT LIMITATIONS

The First Amendment has a complex relationship to privacy. In many instances, the First Amendment and privacy are mutually reinforcing. Privacy is often essential to freedom of assembly. The Supreme Court has noted that there is a "vital relationship between freedom to associate and privacy in one's associations." *NAACP v. Alabama*, 357 U.S. 449 (1958). Privacy is also essential for freedom of speech, as the Supreme Court has recognized the importance of protecting the anonymity of speakers. *See McIntyre v. Ohio Elections Commission*, 514 U.S. 334 (1995). Additionally, freedom of speech is in harmony with privacy in the context of protecting encryption technology. *See Junger v. Daley*, 209 F.3d 481 (6th Cir. 2000).

However, privacy can come into conflict with the First Amendment. The privacy torts exist in an uneasy tension with the First Amendment. Indeed, Warren and Brandeis's article was aimed at the excesses of the press. Recall the authors' strong criticism of the press: "The press is overstepping in every direction the obvious bounds of propriety and of decency. Gossip is no longer the resource of the idle and of the vicious, but has become a trade, which is pursued with industry as well as effrontery."[37]

It is interesting to note that as a Supreme Court Justice, Louis Brandeis was one of the champions of free speech. Consider Brandeis's concurrence in *Whitney v. California*, 274 U.S. 357, 375 (1927):

> Those who won our independence believed that the final end of the state was to make men free to develop their faculties, and that in its government the deliberative forces should prevail over the arbitrary. They valued liberty both as an end and as a means. They believed liberty to be the secret of happiness and courage to be the secret of liberty. They believed that freedom to think as you will and to speak as you think are means indispensable to the discovery and spread of political truth; that without free speech and assembly discussion would be futile; that with them, discussion affords ordinarily adequate protection against the dissemination of noxious doctrine; that the greatest menace to freedom is an inert people; that public discussion is a political duty; and that this should be a fundamental principle of the American government. They recognized the risks to which all human institutions are subject. But they knew that order cannot be secured merely through fear of punishment for its infraction; that it is hazardous to discourage thought, hope and imagination; that fear breeds repression; that repression breeds hate; that hate menaces stable government; that the path of safety lies in the opportunity to discuss freely supposed grievances and proposed remedies; and that the fitting remedy for evil counsels is good ones. Believing in the power of reason as applied through public discussion, they eschewed silence coerced by law — the argument of force in its worst form. Recognizing the occasional tyrannies of governing majorities, they amended the Constitution so that free speech and assembly should be guaranteed.

Although the privacy torts are litigated by private parties, they employ the machinery of the state (its tort law and legal system) to impose costs on the press for gathering, producing, and disseminating news. The danger is that the threat of

---

[37] Samuel D. Warren & Louis D. Brandeis, *The Right to Privacy*, 4 Harv. L. Rev. 193 (1890).

lawsuits will chill the press from running certain stories. Further, the threat of lawsuits alone might chill the press, because even if the press ultimately prevails in such suits, the lawsuits cost money to defend.

The public disclosure tort raises complicated tensions with the First Amendment, for it permits liability for the publication of truthful information. Built into the tort, however, is the newsworthiness test, which a number of courts have stated is required to square the tort with the First Amendment. The newsworthiness test, however, is a limitation *within* the tort. Does the First Amendment provide any additional limitations upon the tort?[38] The cases in this section address this question. In order to understand the cases, some basic background about First Amendment analysis is necessary.

Unprotected Forms of Expression. The Court has held that certain forms of expression receive no First Amendment protection. Such categories include obscenity, *Miller v. California,* 413 U.S. 15 (1973); fighting words, *Chaplinsky v. New Hampshire,* 315 U.S. 568 (1942); and child pornography, *New York v. Ferber,* 458 U.S. 747 (1982).

Strict and Intermediate Scrutiny. Most restrictions on speech are reviewed under either strict or intermediate scrutiny. Under strict scrutiny, a law must be the "least restrictive means" to achieve a "compelling" government interest. *Sable Communications, Inc. v. FCC,* 492 U.S. 115, 116 (1989). Strict scrutiny is very difficult to withstand, and most laws subject to it are struck down. In contrast, under intermediate scrutiny, a law must be narrowly tailored to a "substantial government interest." *United States v. O'Brien,* 391 U.S. 467, 377 (1968).

Content-Based vs. Content-Neutral Regulation. Under First Amendment analysis, the Court first analyzes whether a speech restriction is content-based or content-neutral. A content-based regulation targets particular messages. Content-neutral regulation restricts speech regardless of its message, such as regulating the time, place, or manner of the speech. If a speech restriction is content-based, then strict scrutiny is generally applied. There are some exceptions. For example, the Court has held that the government may single out content if the purpose is to

---

[38] For more background on the First Amendment and the privacy torts, see Peter B. Edelman, *Free Press v. Privacy: Haunted by the Ghost of Justice Black*, 68 Tex. L. Rev. 1195 (1990); Diane Leenheer Zimmerman, *Real People in Fiction: Cautionary Words About Troublesome Old Torts Poured into New Jugs*, 51 Brook. L. Rev. 355 (1985); Thomas I. Emerson, *The Right of Privacy and Freedom of Press*, 14 Harv. CR-CL L. Rev. 329 (1979); Alfred Hill, *Defamation and Privacy Under the First Amendment*, 76 Colum. L. Rev. 1205 (1976); Edward Bloustein, *The First Amendment and Privacy: The Supreme Court Justice and the Philosopher*, 28 Rutgers L. Rev. 41 (1974); Melville B. Nimmer, *The Right to Speak from Times to Time: First Amendment Theory Applied to Libel and Misapplied to Privacy*, 56 Calif. L. Rev. 935 (1968); Harry Kalven, Jr., *Privacy in Tort Law — Were Warren and Brandeis Wrong?*, 31 Law & Contemp. Probs. 326 (1966); Marc A. Franklin, *A Constitutional Problem in Privacy Protection: Legal Inhibitions on Reporting of Fact*, 16 Stan. L. Rev. 107 (1963); William K. Jones, *Insult to Injury: Libel, Slander, and Invasions of Privacy* (2003); Bruce W. Sanford, *Don't Shoot the Messenger: How Our Growing Hatred of the Media Threatens Free Speech for All of Us* (1999); Robert M. O'Neil, *The First Amendment and Civil Liability* (2001); Rodney A. Smolla, *Accounting for the Slow Growth of American Privacy Law,* 27 Nova L. Rev. 289 (2002).

prevent certain secondary effects caused by such speech. In *City of Renton v. Playtime Theatres,* 475 U.S. 41 (1986), the Court did not apply strict scrutiny to an ordinance restricting the location of adult movie theaters because the purpose was to prevent crime — a secondary effect. Content-neutral speech regulation is generally subject to intermediate scrutiny.

In *R.A.V. v. City of St. Paul,* 505 U.S. 377 (1992), the Court held that a content-based regulation of expression that falls in an unprotected category will be subject to strict scrutiny. The Court struck down a hate speech law because it regulated the content of "fighting words" — it applied to fighting words based on "race, color, creed, religion, or gender." Unprotected categories of expression, such as fighting words, may be regulated so long as they are not "made the vehicle for content discrimination unrelated to their distinctively proscribable content. Thus, the government may proscribe libel; but it may not make the further content discrimination of proscribing only libel critical of the government." Content-based regulation on an unprotected category of expression is permissible if "based on the very reasons why the particular class of speech . . . is proscribable."

COX BROADCASTING CORP. V. COHN

420 U.S. 469 (1975)

WHITE, J. . . . In August 1971, appellee's 17-year-old daughter was the victim of a rape and did not survive the incident. Six youths were soon indicted for murder and rape. Although there was substantial press coverage of the crime and of subsequent developments, the identity of the victim was not disclosed pending trial, perhaps because of Ga. Code Ann. § 26-9901 (1972),[39] which makes it a misdemeanor to publish or broadcast the name or identity of a rape victim. In April 1972, some eight months later, the six defendants appeared in court. Five pleaded guilty to rape or attempted rape, the charge of murder having been dropped. The guilty pleas were accepted by the court, and the trial of the defendant pleading not guilty was set for a later date.

In the course of the proceedings that day, appellant Wasell, a reporter covering the incident for his employer, learned the name of the victim from an examination of the indictments which were made available for his inspection in the courtroom. That the name of the victim appears in the indictments and that the indictments were public records available for inspection are not disputed. Later that day, Wassell broadcast over the facilities of station WSB-TV, a television station owned by appellant Cox Broadcasting Corp., a news report concerning the court proceedings. The report named the victim of the crime and was repeated the following day.

---

[39] "It shall be unlawful for any news media or any other person to print and publish, broadcast, televise, or disseminate through any other medium of public dissemination or cause to be printed and published, broadcast, televised, or disseminated in any newspaper, magazine, periodical or other publication published in this State or through any radio or television broadcast originating in the State the name or identity of any female who may have been raped or upon whom an assault with intent to commit rape may have been made. Any person or corporation violating the provisions of this section shall, upon conviction, be punished as for a misdemeanor." Three other States have similar statutes. . . .

In May 1972, appellee brought an action for money damages against appellants, relying on § 26-9901 and claiming that his right to privacy had been invaded by the television broadcasts giving the name of his deceased daughter. . . .

Georgia stoutly defends both § 26-9901 and the State's common-law privacy action challenged here. Its claims are not without force, for powerful arguments can be made, and have been made, that however it may be ultimately defined, there is a zone of privacy surrounding every individual, a zone within which the State may protect him from intrusion by the press, with all its attendant publicity. Indeed, the central thesis of the root article by Warren and Brandeis, *The Right to Privacy*, 4 Harv. L. Rev. 193 (1890), was that the press was overstepping its prerogatives by publishing essentially private information and that there should be a remedy for the alleged abuses.

More compellingly, the century has experienced a strong tide running in favor of the so-called right of privacy. In 1967, we noted that "[it] has been said that a 'right of privacy' has been recognized at common law in 30 States plus the District of Columbia and by statute in four States." *Time, Inc. v. Hill*, 385 U.S. 374, 383 n.7. We there cited the 1964 edition of Prosser's *Law of Torts*. The 1971 edition of that same source states that "[in] one form or another, the right of privacy is by this time recognized and accepted in all but a very few jurisdictions." . . .

These are impressive credentials for a right of privacy, but we should recognize that we do not have at issue here an action for the invasion of privacy involving the appropriation of one's name or photograph, a physical or other tangible intrusion into a private area, or a publication of otherwise private information that is also false although perhaps not defamatory. The version of the privacy tort now before us — termed in Georgia "the tort of public disclosure," — is that in which the plaintiff claims the right to be free from unwanted publicity about his private affairs, which, although wholly true, would be offensive to a person of ordinary sensibilities. Because the gravamen of the claimed injury is the publication of information, whether true or not, the dissemination of which is embarrassing or otherwise painful to an individual, it is here that claims of privacy most directly confront the constitutional freedoms of speech and press. The face-off is apparent, and the appellants urge upon us the broad holding that the press may not be made criminally or civilly liable for publishing information that is neither false nor misleading but absolutely accurate, however damaging it may be to reputation or individual sensibilities. . . .

It is true that in defamation actions, where the protected interest is personal reputation, the prevailing view is that truth is a defense. . . .

The Court has nevertheless carefully left open the question whether the First and Fourteenth Amendments require that truth be recognized as a defense in a defamation action brought by a private person as distinguished from a public official or public figure. . . . In similar fashion, *Time, Inc. v. Hill*, expressly saved the question whether truthful publication of very private matters unrelated to public affairs could be constitutionally proscribed. . . .

Those precedents, as well as other considerations, counsel similar caution here. In this sphere of collision between claims of privacy and those of the free press, the interests on both sides are plainly rooted in the traditions and significant concerns of our society. Rather than address the broader question whether truthful publications may ever be subjected to civil or criminal liability consistently with the First and Fourteenth Amendments, or to put it another way, whether the State may ever define and protect an area of privacy free from unwanted publicity in the press, it is appropriate to focus on the narrower interface between press and privacy that this case presents, namely, whether the State may impose sanctions on the accurate publication of the name of a rape victim obtained from public records — more specifically, from judicial records which are maintained in connection with a public prosecution and which themselves are open to public inspection. We are convinced that the State may not do so.

In the first place, in a society in which each individual has but limited time and resources with which to observe at first hand the operations of his government, he relies necessarily upon the press to bring to him in convenient form the facts of those operations. Great responsibility is accordingly placed upon the news media to report fully and accurately the proceedings of government, and official records and documents open to the public are the basic data of governmental operations. Without the information provided by the press most of us and many of our representatives would be unable to vote intelligently or to register opinions on the administration of government generally. With respect to judicial proceedings in particular, the function of the press serves to guarantee the fairness of trials and to bring to bear the beneficial effects of public scrutiny upon the administration of justice. . . .

. . . By placing the information in the public domain on official court records, the State must be presumed to have concluded that the public interest was thereby being served. Public records by their very nature are of interest to those concerned with the administration of government, and a public benefit is performed by the reporting of the true contents of the records by the media. The freedom of the press to publish that information appears to us to be of critical importance to our type of government in which the citizenry is the final judge of the proper conduct of public business. In preserving that form of government the First and Fourteenth Amendments command nothing less than that the States may not impose sanctions on the publication of truthful information contained in official court records open to public inspection.

We are reluctant to embark on a course that would make public records generally available to the media but forbid their publication if offensive to the sensibilities of the supposed reasonable man. Such a rule would make it very difficult for the media to inform citizens about the public business and yet stay within the law. The rule would invite timidity and self-censorship and very likely lead to the suppression of many items that would otherwise be published and that should be made available to the public. At the very least, the First and Fourteenth Amendments will not allow exposing the press to liability for truthfully publishing information released to the public in official court records. If there are privacy interests to be protected in judicial proceedings, the States must respond by means which avoid public documentation or other exposure of private information. Their political institutions must weigh the interests in privacy with the interests of the public to know and of the press to publish. Once true information is disclosed in public court documents open to public inspection, the press cannot be sanctioned for publishing it. In this instance as in others reliance must rest upon the judgment of those who decide what to publish or broadcast.

NOTES & QUESTIONS

1. ***Justifications for the* Cox *Holding.*** There are two potential justifications for the rule in *Cox*. The first is that the information in public records is not private because it is in the public domain, and once that information falls into the public domain, the First Amendment prohibits restrictions on speaking about it. The other justification is that the press must be able to report on public records dealing with the criminal justice system to permit greater accountability and transparency in government. Which justification does the Court's opinion rely upon most heavily? Under the second justification, would the state be permitted to keep rape victims' names confidential?
2. ***The* Oklahoma Publishing *and* Daily Mail *Cases.*** After *Cox*, the Supreme Court held in *Oklahoma Publishing Co. v. Oklahoma County District Court*, 430 U.S. 308 (1977), that a state court violated the First Amendment by prohibiting the media from publishing the name or photograph of an 11-year-old boy in a juvenile proceeding which members of the media attended. A few years later, the Court confronted the issue of whether a state could prohibit the press from publishing the name of a juvenile offender. In *Smith v. Daily Mail Publishing Co.*, 443 U.S. 97 (1979), two newspapers published the name and photograph of a 15-year-old who had shot and killed his 14-year-old classmate. The newspapers were indicted with the misdemeanor offense of publishing the name of a juvenile offender without a court order. The Court stated: "At issue is simply the power of a state to punish the truthful publication of an alleged juvenile delinquent's name lawfully obtained by a newspaper. The asserted state interest [to protect the anonymity of juvenile offenders] cannot justify the statute's imposition of criminal sanctions on this type of publication."
3. **Melvin v. Reid.** One of the earliest cases to recognize the tort of public disclosure is *Melvin v. Reid,* 297 P. 91 (Cal. 1931). Gabrielle Darley was a prostitute who was tried for murder but was acquitted. She abandoned her life as a prostitute, married Bernard Melvin, and became a housewife. In 1925, *The Red Kimono,* a motion picture based on her past life, was released. The film used her maiden name of Darley. As a result, some of her friends learned "for the first time of the unsavory incidents of her early life." Gabrielle sued. The California Supreme Court concluded that she had a cause of action:

> One of the major objectives of society as it is now constituted, and of the administration of our penal system, is the rehabilitation of the fallen and the reformation of the criminal. Under these theories of sociology, it is our object to lift up and sustain the unfortunate rather than tear him down. Where a person has by his own efforts rehabilitated himself, we, as right-thinking members of society, should permit him to continue in the path of rectitude rather than throw him back into a life of shame or crime. Even the thief on the cross was permitted to repent during the hours of his final agony.

According to Lawrence Friedman, who has examined the history of the case, the facts surrounding Gabrielle's murder trial were sensational. Gabrielle was on trial for murdering her lover, who was also her pimp. Gabrielle had given him money to buy her a wedding ring, but instead he used the money to buy a ring to wed another woman. Gabrielle confronted him in the street with a gun and shot him dead. Gabrielle was charged with murder. Friedman writes:

> The trial was fairly spectacular. Earl Rogers, a flamboyant criminal defense lawyer, represented Gabrielle. He put on a fantastic show. Gabrielle took the stand, and she told a pitiful story of love, abandonment, and betrayal. She said nothing about her career as a prostitute. When the prosecution tried to bring out certain nasty details, Gabrielle burst into tears. Rogers furiously condemned the prosecution and its "contemptible effort to influence the jury at the price of humiliating a pitiful young woman already bowed down by the weight of a terrible load of misfortune." Gabrielle claimed the revolver went off accidentally.

Gabrielle was acquitted. But the lurid details surrounding the incident attracted attention:

> Rogers's daughter, Adela Rogers St. John, a writer, covered the trial. Later, she wrote a short story based on the case and called it "The Red Kimono." It used incidents from Gabrielle's life, and it used her actual name. Dorothy Reid bought the story and produced a movie based on it. The film also was called *The Red Kimono*. It was shown in theaters in 1927. The movie identified the heroine as Gabrielle Darley. The next year, Gabrielle, now calling herself Gabrielle Darley Melvin, brought suit against Reid and Reid's motion picture company.

Friedman believes that Gabrielle's claim that she had reformed herself was fake:

> There is good evidence that she was, in fact, as phony as a three dollar bill. A journalist in Arizona argues that she was still working as a prostitute and madam at the time of the trial in a town in Arizona. During her lifetime she had several husbands, but they had the distressing habit of turning up dead.[40]

After Gabrielle won in the California Supreme Court, she moved to dismiss the case in 1933 prior to trial, presumably because she either settled the case or because Reid went bankrupt. Are the facts about Gabrielle in *The Red Kimono* newsworthy? Should the interest in allowing people like Gabrielle to start a new life trump people like Reid's right to make her movie or the public's right to know about a person's past?

4. ***Information About Past Crimes.*** In *Briscoe v. Reader's Digest*, 483 P.2d 34 (Cal. 1971), a magazine article about hijacking discussed the plaintiff's hijacking of a truck 11 years earlier. Since then, the plaintiff had rehabilitated himself, and many people did not know of his previous crime. Similar to

---

[40] Lawrence M. Friedman, *Guarding Life's Dark Secrets: Legal and Social Controls over Reputation, Propriety, and Privacy* 216-18 (2007).

Melvin v. Reid, the court held that the article was newsworthy, but that the use of the plaintiff's real name had no relevance to the article.

> We have no doubt that reports of the facts of past crimes are newsworthy. . . . However, identification of the Actor in reports of long past crimes usually serves little independent public purpose. Once legal proceedings have terminated, and a suspect or offender has been released, identification of the individual will not usually aid the administration of justice. Identification will no longer serve to bring forth witnesses or obtain succor for victims. Unless the individual has reattracted the public eye to himself in some independent fashion, the only public "interest" that would usually be served is that of curiosity. . . .
>
> Another factor militating in favor of protecting the individual's privacy here is the state's interest in the integrity of the rehabilitative process. . . .
>
> One of the premises of the rehabilitative process is that the rehabilitated offender can rejoin that great bulk of the community from which he has been ostracized for his anti-social acts. In return for becoming a "new man," he is allowed to melt into the shadows of obscurity. . . .
>
> Plaintiff is a man whose last offense took place 11 years before, who has paid his debt to society, who has friends and an 11-year-old daughter who were unaware of his early life—a man who assumed a position in "respectable" society. Ideally, his neighbors should recognize his present worth and forget his past life of shame. But men are not so divine as to forgive the past trespasses of others, and plaintiff therefore endeavored to reveal as little as possible of his past life. Yet, as if in some bizarre canyon of echoes, petitioner's past life pursues him through the pages of Reader's Digest, now published in 13 languages and distributed in 100 nations, with a circulation in California alone of almost 2,000,000 copies. . . .

Consider Eugene Volokh's criticism of the *Briscoe* case:

> [S]ome people do take a view that differs from that of the *Briscoe* judges: While criminals can change their character, this view asserts, they often don't. Someone who was willing to fight a gun battle with the police eleven years ago may be more willing than the average person to do something bad today, even if he has led a blameless life since then. . . .
>
> Under this ideology, it's perfectly proper to keep this possibility in mind in one's dealings with the supposedly "reformed" felon. While the government may want to give him a second chance by releasing him from prison, restoring his right to vote and possess firearms, and even erasing its publicly accessible records related to the conviction, his friends, acquaintances, and business associates are entitled to adopt a different attitude. Most presumably wouldn't treat him as a total pariah, but they might use extra caution in dealing with him, especially when it comes to trusting their business welfare or even their physical safety (or that of their children) to his care. . . .[41]

According to Richard Posner, the *Briscoe* case improperly assumes that people will behave irrationally toward rehabilitated people:

---

[41] Eugene Volokh, *Freedom of Speech and Information Privacy: The Troubling Implications of a Right to Stop People from Speaking About You*, 52 Stan. L. Rev. 1049, 1091-92 (2000). For another critique, see T. Markus Funk, *The Dangers of Hiding Criminal Pasts*, 66 Tenn. L. Rev. 287 (1998).

> Remote past criminal activity is less relevant to a prediction of future misconduct than recent — and those who learn of it will discount it accordingly — but such information is hardly irrelevant to people considering whether to enter into or continue social or business relations with the individual; if it were irrelevant, publicizing it would not injure the individual. People conceal past criminal acts not out of bashfulness but because potential acquaintances quite sensibly regard a criminal past as negative evidence of the value of associating with a person.[42]

In *Gates v. Discovery Communications, Inc.*, 101 P.3d 552 (Cal. 2004), the California Supreme Court held that the U.S. Supreme Court's "decision in *Cox* and its subsequent pronouncements . . . have fatally undermined *Briscoe*'s holding that a media defendant may be held liable in tort for recklessly publishing true but not newsworthy facts concerning a rehabilitated former criminal, insofar as that holding applies to facts obtained from public official court records."

To what extent does *Gates* overturn *Melvin* or *Briscoe*? In both cases, the information about them was available in public records. But do *Cox* and its progeny turn on the *availability* of the information in public records or whether the media actually *obtained* the information from public records? In other words, if the information was obtained elsewhere, would plaintiffs in *Melvin* and *Briscoe* still have a cause of action?

THE FLORIDA STAR V. B.J.F.

491 U.S. 524 (1989)

MARSHALL, J. Florida Stat. § 794.03 (1987) makes it unlawful to "print, publish, or broadcast . . . in any instrument of mass communication" the name of the victim of a sexual offense. Pursuant to this statute, appellant The Florida Star was found civilly liable for publishing the name of a rape victim which it had obtained from a publicly released police report. The issue presented here is whether this result comports with the First Amendment. We hold that it does not. . . .

The Florida Star is a weekly newspaper which serves the community of Jacksonville, Florida, and which has an average circulation of approximately 18,000 copies. A regular feature of the newspaper is its "Police Reports" section. That section, typically two to three pages in length, contains brief articles describing local criminal incidents under police investigation.

On October 20, 1983, appellee B.J.F.[43] reported to the Duval County, Florida, Sheriff's Department (Department) that she had been robbed and sexually assaulted by an unknown assailant. The Department prepared a report on the incident which identified B.J.F. by her full name. The Department then

---

[42] Richard A. Posner, *The Economics of Justice* 260-61 (1983).

[43] In filing this lawsuit, appellee used her full name in the caption of the case. On appeal, the Florida District Court of Appeal sua sponte revised the caption, stating that it would refer to the appellee by her initials, "in order to preserve [her] privacy interests." Respecting those interests, we, too, refer to appellee by her initials, both in the caption and in our discussion.

placed the report in its pressroom. The Department does not restrict access either to the pressroom or to the reports made available therein.

A Florida Star reporter-trainee sent to the pressroom copied the police report verbatim, including B.J.F.'s full name, on a blank duplicate of the Department's forms. A Florida Star reporter then prepared a one-paragraph article about the crime, derived entirely from the trainee's copy of the police report. The article included B.J.F.'s full name. It appeared in the "Robberies" subsection of the "Police Reports" section on October 29, 1983, one of 54 police blotter stories in that day's edition. . . .

In printing B.J.F.'s full name, The Florida Star violated its internal policy of not publishing the names of sexual offense victims.

On September 26, 1984, B.J.F. filed suit in the Circuit Court of Duval County against the Department and The Florida Star, alleging that these parties negligently violated § 794.03. Before trial, the Department settled with B.J.F. for $2,500. The Florida Star moved to dismiss, claiming, inter alia, that imposing civil sanctions on the newspaper pursuant to § 794.03 violated the First Amendment. The trial judge rejected the motion.

At the ensuing daylong trial, B.J.F. testified that she had suffered emotional distress from the publication of her name. She stated that she had heard about the article from fellow workers and acquaintances; that her mother had received several threatening phone calls from a man who stated that he would rape B.J.F. again; and that these events had forced B.J.F. to change her phone number and residence, to seek police protection, and to obtain mental health counseling. In defense, The Florida Star put forth evidence indicating that the newspaper had learned B.J.F.'s name from the incident report released by the Department, and that the newspaper's violation of its internal rule against publishing the names of sexual offense victims was inadvertent.

At the close of B.J.F.'s case, and again at the close of its defense, The Florida Star moved for a directed verdict. On both occasions, the trial judge denied these motions. He ruled from the bench that § 794.03 was constitutional because it reflected a proper balance between the First Amendment and privacy rights, as it applied only to a narrow set of "rather sensitive . . . criminal offenses." . . . The jury awarded B.J.F. $75,000 in compensatory damages and $25,000 in punitive damages. . . .

Appellant takes the position that this case is indistinguishable from *Cox Broadcasting*. Alternatively, it urges that our decisions . . . can be distilled to yield a broader First Amendment principle that the press may never be punished, civilly or criminally, for publishing the truth. . . .

We conclude that imposing damages on appellant for publishing B.J.F.'s name violates the First Amendment, although not for either of the reasons appellant urges. Despite the strong resemblance this case bears to *Cox Broadcasting*, that case cannot fairly be read as controlling here. The name of the rape victim in that case was obtained from courthouse records that were open to public inspection. . . . Significantly, one of the reasons we gave in *Cox Broadcasting* for invalidating the challenged damages award was the important role the press plays in subjecting trials to public scrutiny and thereby helping guarantee their fairness. That role is not directly compromised where, as here, the information in question comes from a police report prepared and disseminated at a time at which not only had no adversarial criminal proceedings begun, but no suspect had been identified.

Nor need we accept appellant's invitation to hold broadly that truthful publication may never be punished consistent with the First Amendment. Our cases have carefully eschewed reaching this ultimate question, mindful that the future may bring scenarios which prudence counsels our not resolving anticipatorily. . . . We continue to believe that the sensitivity and significance of the interests presented in clashes between First Amendment and privacy rights counsel relying on limited principles that sweep no more broadly than the appropriate context of the instant case.

In our view, this case is appropriately analyzed with reference to such a limited First Amendment principle. It is the one, in fact, which we articulated in *Daily Mail* in our synthesis of prior cases involving attempts to punish truthful publication: "[I]f a newspaper lawfully obtains truthful information about a matter of public significance then state officials may not constitutionally punish publication of the information, absent a need to further a state interest of the highest order." According the press the ample protection provided by that principle is supported by at least three separate considerations, in addition to, of course, the overarching "'public interest, secured by the Constitution, in the dissemination of truth.'" . . .

First, because the *Daily Mail* formulation only protects the publication of information which a newspaper has "lawfully obtain[ed]," the government retains ample means of safeguarding significant interests upon which publication may impinge, including protecting a rape victim's anonymity. . . . Where information is entrusted to the government, a less drastic means than punishing truthful publication almost always exists for guarding against the dissemination of private facts.[44]

A second consideration undergirding the *Daily Mail* principle is the fact that punishing the press for its dissemination of information which is already publicly available is relatively unlikely to advance the interests in the service of which the State seeks to act. . . . [W]here the government has made certain information publicly available, it is highly anomalous to sanction persons other than the source of its release. . . . As *Daily Mail* observed in its summary of Oklahoma Publishing, "once the truthful information was 'publicly revealed' or 'in the public domain' the court could not constitutionally restrain its dissemination."

A third and final consideration is the "timidity and self-censorship" which may result from allowing the media to be punished for publishing certain truthful information. . . . A contrary rule, depriving protection to those who rely on the government's implied representations of the lawfulness of dissemination, would force upon the media the onerous obligation of sifting through government press releases, reports, and pronouncements to prune out material arguably unlawful for publication. . . .

---

[44] The *Daily Mail* principle does not settle the issue whether, in cases where information has been acquired unlawfully by a newspaper or by a source, government may ever punish not only the unlawful acquisition, but the ensuing publication as well. This issue was raised but not definitively resolved in *New York Times Co. v. United States*, 403 U.S. 713 (1971), and reserved in *Landmark Communications*, 435 U.S., at 837. We have no occasion to address it here.

Applied to the instant case, the *Daily Mail* principle clearly commands reversal. The first inquiry is whether the newspaper "lawfully obtain[ed] truthful information about a matter of public significance." It is undisputed that the news article describing the assault on B.J.F. was accurate. In addition, appellant lawfully obtained B.J.F.'s name. Appellee's argument to the contrary is based on the fact that under Florida law, police reports which reveal the identity of the victim of a sexual offense are not among the matters of "public record" which the public, by law, is entitled to inspect. But the fact that state officials are not required to disclose such reports does not make it unlawful for a newspaper to receive them when furnished by the government. . . . It is, clear, furthermore, that the news article concerned "a matter of public significance," in the sense in which the *Daily Mail* synthesis of prior cases used that term. That is, the article generally, as opposed to the specific identity contained within it, involved a matter of paramount public import: the commission, and investigation, of a violent crime which had been reported to authorities.

The second inquiry is whether imposing liability on appellant pursuant to § 794.03 serves "a need to further a state interest of the highest order." Appellee argues that a rule punishing publication furthers three closely related interests: the privacy of victims of sexual offenses; the physical safety of such victims, who may be targeted for retaliation if their names become known to their assailants; and the goal of encouraging victims of such crimes to report these offenses without fear of exposure.

At a time in which we are daily reminded of the tragic reality of rape, it is undeniable that these are highly significant interests. . . . For three independent reasons, however, imposing liability for publication under the circumstances of this case is too precipitous a means of advancing these interests to convince us that there is a "need" within the meaning of the *Daily Mail* formulation for Florida to take this extreme step.

First is the manner in which appellant obtained the identifying information in question. As we have noted, where the government itself provides information to the media, it is most appropriate to assume that the government had, but failed to utilize, far more limited means of guarding against dissemination than the extreme step of punishing truthful speech. That assumption is richly borne out in this case. B.J.F.'s identity would never have come to light were it not for the erroneous, if inadvertent, inclusion by the Department of her full name in an incident report made available in a pressroom open to the public. Florida's policy against disclosure of rape victims' identities, reflected in § 794.03, was undercut by the Department's failure to abide by this policy. Where, as here, the government has failed to police itself in disseminating information, it is clear under *Cox Broadcasting*, *Oklahoma Publishing*, and *Landmark Communications* that the imposition of damages against the press for its subsequent publication can hardly be said to be a narrowly tailored means of safeguarding anonymity. . . .

A second problem with Florida's imposition of liability for publication is the broad sweep of the negligence per se standard applied under the civil cause of action implied from § 794.03. Unlike claims based on the common law tort of invasion of privacy, civil actions based on § 794.03 require no case-by-case findings that the disclosure of a fact about a person's private life was one that a reasonable person would find highly offensive. On the contrary, under the per se theory of negligence adopted by the courts below, liability follows automatically from publication. This is so regardless of whether the identity of the victim is already known throughout the community; whether the victim has voluntarily called public attention to the offense; or whether the identity of the victim has otherwise become a reasonable subject of public concern — because, perhaps, questions have arisen whether the victim fabricated an assault by a particular person. Nor is there a scienter requirement of any kind under § 794.03, engendering the perverse result that truthful publications challenged pursuant to this cause of action are less protected by the First Amendment than even the least protected defamatory falsehoods. . . .

Third, and finally, the facial underinclusiveness of § 794.03 raises serious doubts about whether Florida is, in fact, serving, with this statute, the significant interests which appellee invokes in support of affirmance. Section 794.03 prohibits the publication of identifying information only if this information appears in an "instrument of mass communication," a term the statute does not define. Section 794.03 does not prohibit the spread by other means of the identities of victims of sexual offenses. An individual who maliciously spreads word of the identity of a rape victim is thus not covered, despite the fact that the communication of such information to persons who live near, or work with, the victim may have consequences as devastating as the exposure of her name to large numbers of strangers.

When a State attempts the extraordinary measure of punishing truthful publication in the name of privacy, it must demonstrate its commitment to advancing this interest by applying its prohibition evenhandedly, to the smalltime disseminator as well as the media giant. Where important First Amendment interests are at stake, the mass scope of disclosure is not an acceptable surrogate for injury. . . .

Our holding today is limited. We do not hold that truthful publication is automatically constitutionally protected, or that there is no zone of personal privacy within which the State may protect the individual from intrusion by the press, or even that a State may never punish publication of the name of a victim of a sexual offense. We hold only that where a newspaper publishes truthful information which it has lawfully obtained, punishment may lawfully be imposed, if at all, only when narrowly tailored to a state interest of the highest order, and that no such interest is satisfactorily served by imposing liability under § 794.03 to appellant under the facts of this case. . . .

WHITE, J. joined by REHNQUIST, C. J. and O'CONNOR, J. dissenting. . . . *Cox Broadcasting* reversed a damages award entered against a television station, which had obtained a rape victim's name from public records maintained in connection with the judicial proceedings brought against her assailants. While there are similarities, critical aspects of that case make it wholly distinguishable from this one. First, in *Cox Broadcasting*, the victim's name had been disclosed in the hearing where her assailants pleaded guilty; and, as we recognized, judicial records have always been considered public information in this country. . . . Second, unlike the incident report at issue here, which was meant by state law to be withheld from public release, the judicial proceedings at issue in *Cox Broadcasting* were open as a matter of state law. . . .

Cox Broadcasting stands for the proposition that the State cannot make the press its first line of defense in withholding private information from the public — it cannot ask the press to secrete private facts that the State makes no effort to safeguard in the first place. In this case, however, the State has undertaken "means which avoid [but obviously, not altogether prevent] public documentation or other exposure of private information." . . .

More importantly, at issue in *Daily Mail* was the disclosure of the name of the perpetrator of an infamous murder of a 15-year-old student. Surely the rights of those accused of crimes and those who are their victims must differ with respect to privacy concerns. That is, whatever rights alleged criminals have to maintain their anonymity pending an adjudication of guilt — and after *Daily Mail*, those rights would seem to be minimal — the rights of crime victims to stay shielded from public view must be infinitely more substantial. . . .

Consequently, I cannot agree that *Cox Broadcasting*, or *Oklahoma Publishing*, or *Daily Mail* requires — or even substantially supports — the result reached by the Court today. . . .

We are left, then, to wonder whether the . . . "independent reasons" the Court cites for reversing the judgment for B.J.F. support its result.

The first of these reasons relied on by the Court is the fact "appellant gained access to [B.J.F.'s name] through a government news release." "The government's issuance of such a release, without qualification, can only convey to recipients that the government considered dissemination lawful," the Court suggests. So described, this case begins to look like the situation in *Oklahoma Publishing*, where a judge invited reporters into his courtroom, but then tried to prohibit them from reporting on the proceedings they observed. But this case is profoundly different. Here, the "release" of information provided by the government was not, as the Court says, "without qualification." As the Star's own reporter conceded at trial, the crime incident report that inadvertently included B.J.F.'s name was posted in a room that contained signs making it clear that the names of rape victims were not matters of public record, and were not to be published. The Star's reporter indicated that she understood that she "[was not] allowed to take down that information" (i.e., B.J.F.'s name) and that she "[was] not supposed to take the information from the police department." Thus, by her own admission the posting of the incident report did not convey to the Star's reporter the idea that "the government considered dissemination lawful"; the Court's suggestion to the contrary is inapt. . . .

. . . By amending its public records statute to exempt rape victims names from disclosure, and forbidding its officials to release such information, the State has taken virtually every step imaginable to prevent what happened here. This case presents a far cry, then, from *Cox Broadcasting* or *Oklahoma Publishing*, where the State asked the news media not to publish information it had made generally available to the public: here, the State is not asking the media to do the State's job in the first instance. Unfortunately, as this case illustrates, mistakes happen: even when States take measures to "avoid" disclosure, sometimes rape victims' names are found out. As I see it, it is not too much to ask the press, in instances such as this, to respect simple standards of decency and refrain from publishing a victims' name, address, and/or phone number. . . .

. . . By holding that only "a state interest of the highest order" permits the State to penalize the publication of truthful information, and by holding that protecting a rape victim's right to privacy is not among those state interests of the highest order, the Court accepts appellant's invitation to obliterate one of the most noteworthy legal inventions of the 20th century: the tort of the publication of private facts. Even if the Court's opinion does not say as much today, such obliteration will follow inevitably from the Court's conclusion here. . . .

NOTES & QUESTIONS

1. ***The Government's Responsibility for Leaking the Information.*** What more could the state have done to protect the information? Florida made it a crime to disseminate the information. The state recognized that the police might make a mistake in certain cases and accidentally fail to redact a rape victim's name from the report. To protect against this, signs were put up outside the room notifying the press not to record a rape victim's name that was inadvertently left on the report. The Court did not dispute that the government could refuse to divulge the rape victim's name. If the government is not required to divulge the name, what is the problem with the government making it available and then punishing its further disclosure?
2. ***The Legality of How the Information Was Obtained.*** The Court relies in part on the fact that the information was "legally available." If the journalist had stolen a confidential police report and published the information, would the Court's holding have been different? Since the Florida law proscribed both the government dissemination of the information and the press publication of it, was the information "legally available"?
3. ***The Future of the Public Disclosure Tort After* Florida Star.** What effect does *Florida Star* have on the public disclosure tort? Rodney Smolla writes that the public disclosure tort exists "more 'in the books' than in practice."[45] Commentators describe the tort as "alive, but on life support"[46] and as "a phantom tort."[47] According to Jacqueline Rolfs: "Given the narrow class of information that fulfills the *Florida Star* requirements, the tort can no longer be an effective tool for protecting individual privacy."[48] Peter Edelman contends: "The Court paid lip service to the possibility that a private fact plaintiff may recover in some cases, but its decisions leave little hope for

---

[45] Rodney A. Smolla, *Privacy and the First Amendment Right to Gather News*, 67 Geo. Wash. L. Rev. 1097 (1999).

[46] Richard S. Murphy, *Property Rights in Personal Information: An Economic Defense of Privacy*, 84 Geo. L.J. 2381, 2388 (1996). *But see* John A. Jurata, Jr., *Comment, The Tort That Refuses to Go Away: The Subtle Reemergence of Public Disclosure of Private Facts*, 36 San Diego L. Rev. 489 (1999).

[47] Phillip E. DeLaTorre, *Resurrecting a Sunken Ship: An Analysis of Current Judicial Attitudes Toward Public Disclosure Claims*, 38 Sw. L.J. 1151, 1184 (1985).

[48] Jacqueline K. Rolfs, The Florida Star v. B.J.F.: *The Beginning of the End for the Tort of Public Disclosure*, 1990 Wis. L. Rev. 1107, 1128.

vindication of such a plaintiff's rights."[49] Do you agree with these characterizations?

Consider Daniel Solove:

> Many have read *Florida Star* as a broad indication that restrictions on the disclosure of true information are unconstitutional. Nevertheless, this case can be read very narrowly. The Court suggested that the Florida statute was far too broad. The statute applied "regardless of whether the identity of the victim is already known throughout the community; whether the victim has voluntarily called public attention to the offense; or whether the identity of the victim [had] otherwise become a reasonable subject of public concern." The law focused only on the nature of the information, rather than on whether each particular use of a rape victim's name in a specific context would be of public or private concern. *Florida Star* can be construed to suggest that a law adopting a less categorical approach—by addressing the use of the identifying data more contextually—might not be subject to strict scrutiny under the First Amendment.[50]

Under this analysis, how could the Florida statute be rewritten to pass constitutional muster?

4. ***Free Speech and Privacy: Weighing the Values.*** Eugene Volokh argues that both normatively and doctrinally, free speech considerations outweigh privacy:

> . . . [T]he speech vs. privacy and speech vs. speech tensions are not tensions between constitutional rights on both sides. The Constitution presumptively prohibits government restrictions on speech and perhaps some government revelation of personal information, but it says nothing about interference with speech or revelation of personal information by nongovernmental speakers. . .
>
> [I]s it constitutional for the government to suppress certain kinds of speech in order to protect dignity, prevent disrespectful behavior, prevent emotional distress, or to protect a supposed civil right not to be talked about? Under current constitutional doctrine, the answer seems to be no. . . . Even offensive, outrageous, disrespectful, and dignity-assaulting speech is constitutionally protected.
>
> And there is good reason for this approach. All of us can imagine some speech that is so offensive and at the same time so valueless that we would feel no loss if it were restricted, but the trouble is that each of us has a somewhat different vision of which speech should qualify. . . .
>
> . . . [A] good deal of speech that reveals information about people, including speech that some describe as being of merely "private concern," is actually of eminently legitimate interest. Some of it is directly relevant to the formation of general social and political opinions; most of it is of interest to people deciding how to behave in their daily lives, whether daily business or daily personal lives — whom to approach to do business, whom to trust with their money, and the like.[51]

---

[49] Peter B. Edelman, *Free Press v. Privacy: Haunted by the Ghost of Justice Black*, 68 Tex. L. Rev. 1195, 1207 (1990).

[50] Solove, *Virtues of Knowing Less, supra.*

[51] Eugene Volokh, *Freedom of Speech and Information Privacy: The Troubling Implications of a Right to Stop People from Speaking About You,* 52 Stan. L. Rev. 1049, 1089, 1092-93, 1107,

In contrast to Volokh, Daniel Solove argues that privacy fares quite well when balanced against free speech. Solove argues that "speech of private concern does not strongly further the interests justifying free speech. If society wants to promote the interests justifying free speech, a vigorous protection of speech at the expense of privacy can, in fact, impair these interests." Free speech is often justified as essential for individual autonomy, but Solove contends that "[t]here is no clear reason why the autonomy of speakers or listeners should prevail over that of the harmed individuals." Regarding the theory that free speech is valued because it promotes democratic self-governance, Solove argues:

> [S]peech of private concern often does not promote democratic self-governance. For example, it is difficult to justify how the sale from one company to another of mailing lists about people's hobbies and incomes promotes democratic self-governance. Additionally, the reporting of one's personal secrets often does not illuminate the sphere of politics. In fact, privacy protections against disclosure strongly promote democratic self-governance. . . .
>
> Privacy encourages uninhibited speech by enabling individuals to direct frank communication to those people they trust and who will not cause them harm because of what they say. Important discourse, especially communication essential for democratic participation, often takes place in microlevel contexts (between two people or in small groups) rather than in macrolevel contexts (public rallies or nationwide television broadcasts). Indeed, a significant amount of political discussion occurs not on soapboxes or street corners, but within private conversations. . . . Therefore, privacy protections do not just inhibit free speech; they can promote it as well.

Solove argues that the value of speech of private concern is significantly less than that of public concern: "Privacy regulations that promote speech should not simply be viewed in terms of their speech-restrictive elements; they should be understood holistically, in terms of their overall purpose in the protection of free speech. We protect free speech to promote certain ends. Volokh loses sight of the ends of the First Amendment by focusing too heavily on the means."[52]

5. ***The First Amendment and Threats to People's Private Lives.*** In *Planned Parenthood v. American Coalition of Life Activists*, 290 F.3d 1058 (9th Cir. 2002) (en banc), the American Coalition of Life Activists (ACLA), an antiabortion advocacy group, provided a series of dossiers it assembled on doctors, clinic employees, politicians, judges, and other abortion rights supporters to Neal Horsley, an antiabortion activist, who posted the information on his website entitled the "Nuremberg Files." The "Nuremberg

1112-15 (2000). For other free speech critiques of privacy protections, see Thomas I. Emerson, *The System of Freedom of Expression* (1970); Solveig Singleton, *Privacy Versus the First Amendment: A Skeptical Approach,* 11 Fordham Intell. Prop. Media & Ent. L.J. 97 (2000); Harry Kalven, Jr., *Privacy in Tort Law — Were Warren and Brandeis Wrong?*, 31 Law & Contemp. Probs. 326 (1966); Diane L. Zimmerman, *Requiem for a Heavyweight: A Farewell to Warren and Brandeis's Privacy Tort*, 68 Cornell L. Rev. 291 (1983).

[52] Daniel J. Solove, *The Virtues of Knowing Less: Justifying Privacy Protections Against Disclosure*, 53 Duke L.J. 967, 988-98 (2003).

Files" dossiers included doctors' names, photos, Social Security numbers, home addresses, descriptions of their cars, and information about their families. The website marked the names of doctors who had been killed with a black line through them and the names of wounded doctors shaded in gray. The website did not contain any explicit threats against the doctors. The website caused the doctors great fear, and several protected themselves by wearing bulletproof vests, closing all the curtains to the windows of their homes, and even asking for the protection of the U.S. Marshals. Some of the doctors sued ACLA alleging a variety of causes of action including the Freedom of Access to Clinic Entrances Act of 1994 (FACE), 18 U.S.C. § 248.

A jury awarded the doctors $107 million in actual and punitive damages. The Ninth Circuit, en banc, affirmed the actual damages and reversed on punitive damages. The court held that the "Nuremberg Files" (in combination with "wanted" posters of various doctors) constituted a "true threat" to the doctors' lives under FACE, and such true threats were not protected under the First Amendment. Although speech advocating violence is protected, speech "directed to inciting or producing imminent lawless action" is not. "Violence is not a protected value. Nor is a *true threat* of violence *with intent to intimidate*. . . . ACLA was not staking out a position of debate but of threatened demise." According to a dissent by Judge Kozinski: "The Nuremberg Files website is clearly an expression of a political point of view. . . . [S]peech, including the intimidating message, does not constitute a direct threat because there is no evidence other than the speech itself that the speakers intend to resort to physical violence if their threat is not heeded." Would the doctors have a cause of action for public disclosure of private facts? Would the First Amendment prohibit liability on this basis?

Recently, antiabortion protesters have begun to photograph individuals entering abortion clinics. A loose network of activists across the country photographs women and places the photos on websites. Sometimes personal information, such as license plate numbers or medical records, is posted next to the photograph. Should these activities be actionable? What does the Restatement suggest? Based on the *American Coalition of Life Activists* case above, would liability for this activity run afoul of the First Amendment?

6. ***The Value of Gossip.*** Diane Zimmerman questions the very existence of the public disclosure tort. She argues that the tort should be "scuttled" as inconsistent with the First Amendment. According to Zimmerman, the "idle gossip" Warren and Brandeis complained about is highly valuable speech, entitled to no less protection than any other form of speech:

> . . . [F]rom the perspective of the anthropologist and sociologist, gossip is a basic form of information exchange that teaches about other lifestyles and attitudes, and through which community values are changed or reinforced. This description is a far cry from that of Warren and Brandeis, which characterized gossip as a trivializing influence that destroys "robustness of thought and delicacy of feeling" and serves the interests primarily of the "prurient" and the "indolent."
>
> Gossip thus appears to be a normal and necessary part of life for all but the rare hermit among us. Perceived in this way, gossip contributes directly to the

first amendment "marketplace of ideas," and the comparative weight assigned to an interest in its limitation merits careful consideration.[53]

Do you agree with Zimmerman about the high value of gossip? Does the value of gossip outweigh the harms it causes?

7. ***The Value of the Truth.*** Frederick Schauer argues that many commentators discussing the tension between free speech and privacy are too quick to assume that "truth is an ultimate, irreducible, and noninstrumental value." According to Schauer, we should be concerned with issues of power, and sometimes truth is outweighed by protecting those who lack power (i.e., private figures) from those who have it (i.e., media entities).[54] Likewise, Anita Allen contends:

> Judicial ascription of privacy rights is an allocation of power. Those who have license to say what they please about others without fear of criminal penalty or civil liability enjoy a brand of power. . . . Professor Schauer correctly concludes that the media should not always win: the mere fact that the media is the media and has published the truth should not automatically bar actions for invasion of privacy premised on the publication of private facts. The reason that the media and other defendants should not have legal immunity is that immunity gives them more power than the Constitution requires and fairness permits.[55]

On the other hand, Susan Gilles responds that if Schauer and Allen are correct and some truths have less value, then it "would require empowering the courts to decide what truths are of value to the public." This would embroil courts in making content-based discriminations about speech, and the "power to determine which truths are acceptable has been abused in the past."[56]

Do we really want speech to be so unfettered that it is subsidized by the harming of people — the destruction of their lives and reputations? The rise of television newsmagazines such as *Dateline*, *60 Minutes*, *20/20*, and so on create a great demand for human interest stories, which often involve examining the private lives of individuals. These newsmagazines often earn high ratings and make a significant profit for television networks. Volokh argues, in defense of the media, that "[t]he essence of news is precisely the reporting of things done or discovered by others; the essence of the news business is profiting from reporting on things done or discovered by others."[57]

---

[53] Diane L. Zimmerman, *Requiem for a Heavyweight: A Farewell to Warren and Brandeis's Privacy Tort*, 68 Cornell L. Rev. 291, 333-34, 340 (1983). Katherine Strandburg contends that society does not exalt unfettered gossip and that it is regulated by norms of restraint (which she calls "willpower norms"). Katherine J. Strandburg, *Privacy, Rationality, and Temptation: A Theory of Willpower Norms*, 57 Rutgers L. Rev. 1235 (2005).

[54] Frederick Schauer, *Reflections on the Value of Truth*, 41 Case W. Res. L. Rev. 699 (1991). For a critique of Schauer's position, see Erwin Chemerinsky, *In Defense of Truth*, 41 Case W. Res. L. Rev. 745 (1991).

[55] Anita L. Allen, *The Power of Private Facts*, 41 Case W. Res. L. Rev. 757 (1991).

[56] Susan M. Gilles, *All Truths Are Equal, But Are Some Truths More Equal Than Others?*, 41 Case W. Res. L. Rev. 725 (1991).

[57] Eugene Volokh, *Freedom of Speech and Information Privacy: The Troubling Implications of a Right to Stop People from Speaking About You*, 52 Stan. L. Rev. 1049 (2000).

Shouldn't the press bear some of the costs for its invasions into private lives? Do "reality shows," where individuals consent to have their privacy invaded, raise different issues?

8. ***The Press, Contracts, Promises, and the First Amendment.*** Does the enforcement of a contract of confidentiality against a media entity trigger First Amendment scrutiny? In *Cohen v. Cowles Media Co.*, 501 U.S. 663 (1991), a journalist had promised a source confidentiality but nevertheless published the source's name. The source sued and obtained a promissory estoppel damage award. According to the Court, *Florida Star* did not control because "generally applicable laws do not offend the First Amendment simply because their enforcement against the press has incidental effects on its ability to gather and report the news." Why is a suit under contract or promissory estoppel different from a suit under tort, such as public disclosure of private facts?

9. ***Prior Restraints.*** In *In re People v. Bryant*, 94 P.3d 624 (Colo. 2004), basketball star Kobe Byrant was accused of sexually assaulting a woman. Before the trial, the court held in camera proceedings regarding the relevance of the victim's prior sexual conduct under Colorado's rape shield law. Only if the judge deems the evidence relevant will it be allowed to be admitted in open court. However, the court reporter mistakenly e-mailed the in camera transcripts to seven media entities. When the court discovered the error, it ordered that the media entities "delete and destroy any copies and not reveal any contents thereof, or be subject to contempt of Court." The media entities challenged the order as a violation of the First Amendment. The case made it up to the Colorado Supreme Court, which determined that although the court's order was a prior restraint, it was nevertheless constitutional.

Prior restraints on speech have typically been reviewed much more stringently than after-the-fact regulation of speech, such as civil liability or criminal penalties once the speech has been made. The most famous case involving prior restraints was the Pentagon Papers case, *New York Times Co. v. United States,* 403 U.S. 713 (1971). Newspapers sought to publish classified documents concerning U.S. activities leading up to the Vietnam War. The government argued that publication of the papers would jeopardize national security. The Court held that the government failed to justify the imposition of the prior restraint. Indeed, prior restraints are so disfavored by courts that they are deemed presumptively unconstitutional. *See Nebraska Press Ass'n v. Stuart,* 427 U.S. 539 (1976).

The Colorado Supreme Court, however, concluded that the court's order was justified because protecting the privacy of rape victims is a state interest of the highest order and the restraint was narrowly tailored to protect that interest. Rape shield laws protect against "exposing the victim's most intimate life history to public view" that results in victims being "deterred from reporting the crime, or having reported it, from following through in the role of complaining witness."

The media entities argued that "the moment the transcript arrived at their computers, they lawfully acquired the information and were entitled to publish it." The media entities pointed to the *Florida Star* case. The court, however, distinguished *Florida Star:*

> . . . [I]n contrast to *Florida Star*, the contents of the *in camera* transcribed proceedings were not publicly available, there was no burden on the press to determine whether it should risk publication and sanctions in light of the District Court's prior restraint order, and the specter of the press having to impose self-censorship was not an issue, as the transcripts were clearly marked private by the "In Camera" notation. . . .
>
> The court reporter's mistake handed to only a few media entities contains material that was plainly marked and intended to be kept private. . . . [T]he confidentiality markings served to notify the non-authorized readers . . . that this document remained under seal. . . .

In dissent, Justice Bender argued that the privacy of a rape victim was not sufficient to justify a prior restraint, which is "meant to be issued only to prevent great, grave, and certain harm." Furthermore, the dissent argued: "It is the responsibility of the government, not the media, to protect information that lies within its control."

The criminal case against Bryant was ultimately dropped. Did the majority adequately distinguish the case from *Florida Star*? In light of the Pentagon Papers case, is the holding in *Bryant* justifiable? Should privacy justify a prior restraint on speech? Or should privacy be remedied exclusively with after-the-fact civil liability, such as the public disclosure tort?

BARTNICKI V. VOPPER

532 U.S. 514 (2001)

STEVENS, J. These cases raise an important question concerning what degree of protection, if any, the First Amendment provides to speech that discloses the contents of an illegally intercepted communication. That question is both novel and narrow. Despite the fact that federal law has prohibited such disclosures since 1934, this is the first time that we have confronted such an issue. . . .

During 1992 and most of 1993, the Pennsylvania State Education Association, a union representing the teachers at the Wyoming Valley West High School, engaged in collective-bargaining negotiations with the school board. Petitioner Kane, then the president of the local union, testified that the negotiations were "'contentious'" and received "a lot of media attention." In May 1993, petitioner Bartnicki, who was acting as the union's "chief negotiator," used the cellular phone in her car to call Kane and engage in a lengthy conversation about the status of the negotiations. An unidentified person intercepted and recorded that call.

In their conversation, Kane and Bartnicki discussed the timing of a proposed strike, difficulties created by public comment on the negotiations, and the need for a dramatic response to the board's intransigence. At one point, Kane said: "'If they're not gonna move for three percent, we're gonna have to go to their, their homes. . . . To blow off their front porches, we'll have to do some work on some of those guys. (PAUSES). Really, uh, really and truthfully because this is, you know, this is bad news. (UNDECIPHERABLE).'"

In the early fall of 1993, the parties accepted a non-binding arbitration proposal that was generally favorable to the teachers. In connection with news reports about the settlement, respondent Vopper, a radio commentator who had been critical of the union in the past, played a tape of the intercepted conversation on his public affairs talk show. Another station also broadcast the tape, and local newspapers published its contents. After filing suit against Vopper and other representatives of the media, Bartnicki and Kane (hereinafter petitioners) learned through discovery that Vopper had obtained the tape from Jack Yocum, the head of a local taxpayers' organization that had opposed the union's demands throughout the negotiations. Yocum, who was added as a defendant, testified that he had found the tape in his mailbox shortly after the interception and recognized the voices of Bartnicki and Kane. Yocum played the tape for some members of the school board, and later delivered the tape itself to Vopper. . . .

In their amended complaint, petitioners alleged that their telephone conversation had been surreptitiously intercepted by an unknown person using an electronic device, that Yocum had obtained a tape of that conversation, and that he intentionally disclosed it to Vopper, as well as other individuals and media representatives. Thereafter, Vopper and other members of the media repeatedly published the contents of that conversation. The amended complaint alleged that each of the defendants "knew or had reason to know" that the recording of the private telephone conversation had been obtained by means of an illegal interception. Relying on both federal and Pennsylvania statutory provisions, petitioners sought actual damages, statutory damages, punitive damages, and attorney's fees and costs. . . .

[Title 18 U.S.C. § 2511(1)(c) provides that any person who "intentionally discloses, or endeavors to disclose, to any other person the contents of any wire, oral, or electronic communication, knowing or having reason to know that the information was obtained through the interception of a wire, oral, or electronic communication in violation of this subsection; . . . shall be punished. . . ." The Pennsylvania Act contains a similar provision.]

. . . [W]e accept respondents' submission on three factual matters that serve to distinguish most of the cases that have arisen under § 2511. First, respondents played no part in the illegal interception. Rather, they found out about the interception only after it occurred, and in fact never learned the identity of the person or persons who made the interception. Second, their access to the information on the tapes was obtained lawfully, even though the information itself was intercepted unlawfully by someone else. Third, the subject matter of the conversation was a matter of public concern. If the statements about the labor negotiations had been made in a public arena — during a bargaining session, for example — they would have been newsworthy. This would also be true if a third party had inadvertently overheard Bartnicki making the same statements to Kane when the two thought they were alone.

We agree with petitioners that § 2511(1)(c), as well as its Pennsylvania analog, is in fact a content-neutral law of general applicability. . . . In this case, the basic purpose of the statute at issue is to "protec[t] the privacy of wire[, electronic,] and oral communications." S. Rep. No. 1097, 90th Cong., 2d Sess., 66 (1968). The statute does not distinguish based on the content of the intercepted conversations, nor is it justified by reference to the content of those conversations. Rather, the communications at issue are singled out by virtue of the fact that they were illegally intercepted — by virtue of the source, rather than the subject matter.

On the other hand, the naked prohibition against disclosures is fairly characterized as a regulation of pure speech. . . .

As a general matter, "state action to punish the publication of truthful information seldom can satisfy constitutional standards." *Smith v. Daily Mail Publishing Co.*, 443 U.S. 97, 102 (1979). More specifically, this Court has repeatedly held that "if a newspaper lawfully obtains truthful information about a matter of public significance then state officials may not constitutionally punish publication of the information, absent a need . . . of the highest order." *Id.*, at 103; *see also Florida Star v. B.J.F.*; *Landmark Communications, Inc. v. Virginia*. . . .

. . . [T]he issue here is this: "Where the punished publisher of information has obtained the information in question in a manner lawful in itself but from a source who has obtained it unlawfully, may the government punish the ensuing publication of that information based on the defect in a chain?" . . .

The Government identifies two interests served by the statute — first, the interest in removing an incentive for parties to intercept private conversations, and second, the interest in minimizing the harm to persons whose conversations have been illegally intercepted. . . .

The normal method of deterring unlawful conduct is to impose an appropriate punishment on the person who engages in it. If the sanctions that presently attach to a violation of § 2511(1)(a) do not provide sufficient deterrence, perhaps those sanctions should be made more severe. But it would be quite remarkable to hold that speech by a law-abiding possessor of information can be suppressed in order to deter conduct by a non-law-abiding third party. . . .

The Government's second argument, however, is considerably stronger. Privacy of communication is an important interest, and Title III's restrictions are intended to protect that interest, thereby "encouraging the uninhibited exchange of ideas and information among private parties. . . ." Moreover, the fear of public disclosure of private conversations might well have a chilling effect on private speech. . . .

Accordingly, it seems to us that there are important interests to be considered on both sides of the constitutional calculus. . . .

In this case, privacy concerns give way when balanced against the interest in publishing matters of public importance. As Warren and Brandeis stated in their classic law review article: "The right of privacy does not prohibit any publication of matter which is of public or general interest." *The Right to Privacy*, 4 Harv. L. Rev. 193, 214 (1890). One of the costs associated with participation in public affairs is an attendant loss of privacy. . . .

Our opinion in *New York Times Co. v. Sullivan*, 376 U.S. 254 (1964), reviewed many of the decisions that settled the "general proposition that freedom of expression upon public questions is secured by the First Amendment." . . .

We think it clear that parallel reasoning requires the conclusion that a stranger's illegal conduct does not suffice to remove the First Amendment shield from speech about a matter of public concern. The months of negotiations over the proper level of compensation for teachers at the Wyoming Valley West High School were unquestionably a matter of public concern, and respondents were clearly engaged in debate about that concern. . . .

BREYER, J. joined by O'CONNOR, J. concurring. I join the Court's opinion because I agree with its "narrow" holding, limited to the special circumstances present here: (1) the radio broadcasters acted lawfully (up to the time of final public disclosure); and (2) the information publicized involved a matter of unusual public concern, namely a threat of potential physical harm to others. I write separately to explain why, in my view, the Court's holding does not imply a significantly broader constitutional immunity for the media. . . .

As the Court recognizes, the question before us—a question of immunity from statutorily imposed civil liability—implicates competing constitutional concerns. The statutes directly interfere with free expression in that they prevent the media from publishing information. At the same time, they help to protect personal privacy—an interest here that includes not only the "right to be let alone." Given these competing interests "on both sides of the equation, the key question becomes one of proper fit."

I would ask whether the statutes strike a reasonable balance between their speech-restricting and speech-enhancing consequences. Or do they instead impose restrictions on speech that are disproportionate when measured against their corresponding privacy and speech-related benefits, taking into account the kind, the importance, and the extent of these benefits, as well as the need for the restrictions in order to secure those benefits? What this Court has called "strict scrutiny"—with its strong presumption against constitutionality—is normally out of place where, as here, important competing constitutional interests are implicated. The statutory restrictions before us directly enhance private speech. The statutes ensure the privacy of telephone conversations much as a trespass statute ensures privacy within the home. That assurance of privacy helps to overcome our natural reluctance to discuss private matters when we fear that our private conversations may become public. And the statutory restrictions consequently encourage conversations that otherwise might not take place.

At the same time, these statutes restrict public speech directly, deliberately, and of necessity. They include media publication within their scope not simply as a means, say, to deter interception, but also as an end. Media dissemination of an intimate conversation to an entire community will often cause the speakers serious harm over and above the harm caused by an initial disclosure to the person who intercepted the phone call. . . .

As a general matter, despite the statutes' direct restrictions on speech, the Federal Constitution must tolerate laws of this kind because of the importance of these privacy and speech-related objectives. . . . Rather than broadly forbid this kind of legislative enactment, the Constitution demands legislative efforts to tailor the laws in order reasonably to reconcile media freedom with personal, speech-related privacy.

Nonetheless, looked at more specifically, the statutes, as applied in these circumstances, do not reasonably reconcile the competing constitutional objectives. Rather, they disproportionately interfere with media freedom. For one thing, the broadcasters here engaged in no unlawful activity other than the ultimate publication of the information another had previously obtained. They "neither encouraged nor participated directly or indirectly in the interception." No one claims that they ordered, counselled, encouraged, or otherwise aided or abetted the interception, the later delivery of the tape by the interceptor to an intermediary, or the tape's still later delivery by the intermediary to the media. . . .

For another thing, the speakers had little or no *legitimate* interest in maintaining the privacy of the particular conversation. That conversation involved a suggestion about "blow[ing] off . . . front porches" and "do[ing] some work on some of those guys," thereby raising a significant concern for the safety of others. Where publication of private information constitutes a wrongful act, the law recognizes a privilege allowing the reporting of threats to public safety. . . .

Further, the speakers themselves, the president of a teacher's union and the union's chief negotiator, were "limited public figures," for they voluntarily engaged in a public controversy. They thereby subjected themselves to somewhat greater public scrutiny and had a lesser interest in privacy than an individual engaged in purely private affairs. . . .

This is not to say that the Constitution requires anyone, including public figures, to give up entirely the right to private communication, *i.e.,* communication free from telephone taps or interceptions. But the subject matter of the conversation at issue here is far removed from that in situations where the media publicizes truly private matters.

Thus, in finding a constitutional privilege to publish unlawfully intercepted conversations of the kind here at issue, the Court does not create a "public interest" exception that swallows up the statutes' privacy-protecting general rule. Rather, it finds constitutional protection for publication of intercepted information of a special kind. Here, the speakers' legitimate privacy expectations are unusually low, and the public interest in defeating those expectations is unusually high. Given these circumstances, along with the lawful nature of respondents' behavior, the statutes' enforcement would disproportionately harm media freedom.

I emphasize the particular circumstances before us because, in my view, the Constitution permits legislatures to respond flexibly to the challenges future technology may pose to the individual's interest in basic personal privacy. . . .

For these reasons, we should avoid adopting overly broad or rigid constitutional rules, which would unnecessarily restrict legislative flexibility. I consequently agree with the Court's holding that the statutes as applied here violate the Constitution, but I would not extend that holding beyond these present circumstances.

REHNQUIST, C. J., joined by SCALIA and THOMAS, J.J., dissenting. Technology now permits millions of important and confidential conversations to occur through a vast system of electronic networks. These advances, however, raise significant privacy concerns. We are placed in the uncomfortable position of not knowing who might have access to our personal and business e-mails, our medical and financial records, or our cordless and cellular telephone conversations. In an attempt to prevent some of the most egregious violations of privacy, the United States, the District of Columbia, and 40 States have enacted laws prohibiting the intentional interception and knowing disclosure of electronic communications. The Court holds that all of these statutes violate the First Amendment insofar as the illegally intercepted conversation touches upon a matter of "public concern," an amorphous concept that the Court does not even attempt to define. But the Court's decision diminishes, rather than enhances, the purposes of the First Amendment: chilling the speech of the millions of Americans who rely upon electronic technology to communicate each day. . . .

The Court correctly observes that these are "content-neutral law[s] of general applicability" which serve recognized interests of the "highest order": "the interest in individual privacy and . . . in fostering private speech." It nonetheless subjects these laws to the strict scrutiny normally reserved for governmental attempts to censor different viewpoints or ideas. There is scant support, either in precedent or in reason, for the Court's tacit application of strict scrutiny.

A content-neutral regulation will be sustained if

> "'it furthers an important or substantial governmental interest; if the governmental interest is unrelated to the suppression of free expression; and if the incidental restriction on alleged First Amendment freedoms is no greater than is essential to the furtherance of that interest.'" *Turner Broadcasting System, Inc. v. FCC*, 512 U.S. 622, 662 (1994). . . .

The Court's attempt to avoid these precedents by reliance upon the *Daily Mail* string of newspaper cases is unpersuasive. In these cases, we held that statutes prohibiting the media from publishing certain truthful information — the name of a rape victim, *Florida Star v. B. J. F.*; *Cox Broadcasting Corp. v. Cohn*, the confidential proceedings before a state judicial review commission, *Landmark Communications, Inc. v. Virginia*, and the name of a juvenile defendant, *Daily Mail* — violated the First Amendment. In so doing, we stated that "if a newspaper lawfully obtains truthful information about a matter of public significance then state officials may not constitutionally punish publication of the information, absent a need to further a state interest of the highest order." *Daily Mail*. Neither this *Daily Mail* principle nor any other aspect of these cases, however, justifies the Court's imposition of strict scrutiny here. . . .

First, the information published by the newspapers had been lawfully obtained from the government itself. . . . This factor has no relevance in the present cases, where we deal with private conversations that have been intentionally kept out of the public domain.

Second, the information in each case was already "publicly available," and punishing further dissemination would not have advanced the purported government interests of confidentiality. . . . These laws thus do not fall under the axiom that "the interests in privacy fade when the information involved already appears on the public record."

Third, these cases were concerned with "the 'timidity and self-censorship' which may result from allowing the media to be punished for publishing certain truthful information." But fear of "timidity and self-censorship" is a basis for upholding, not striking down, these antidisclosure provisions: They allow private conversations to transpire without inhibition. And unlike the statute at issue in *Florida Star*, which had no scienter requirement, these statutes only address those who knowingly disclose an illegally intercepted conversation. They do not impose a duty to inquire into the source of the information and one could negligently disclose the contents of an illegally intercepted communication without liability.

In sum, it is obvious that the *Daily Mail* cases upon which the Court relies do not address the question presented here. . . .

These laws are content neutral; they only regulate information that was illegally obtained; they do not restrict republication of what is already in the public domain; they impose no special burdens upon the media; they have a scienter requirement to provide fair warning; and they promote the privacy and free speech of those using cellular telephones. It is hard to imagine a more narrowly tailored prohibition of the disclosure of illegally intercepted communications, and it distorts our precedents to review these statutes under the often fatal standard of strict scrutiny. These laws therefore should be upheld if they further a substantial governmental interest unrelated to the suppression of free speech, and they do. . .

The "dry up the market" theory, which posits that it is possible to deter an illegal act that is difficult to police by preventing the wrongdoer from enjoying the fruits of the crime, is neither novel nor implausible. It is a time-tested theory that undergirds numerous laws, such as the prohibition of the knowing possession of stolen goods. We ourselves adopted the exclusionary rule based upon similar reasoning, believing that it would "deter unreasonable searches," by removing an officer's "incentive to disregard [the Fourth Amendment]."

The same logic applies here and demonstrates that the incidental restriction on alleged First Amendment freedoms is no greater than essential to further the interest of protecting the privacy of individual communications. Were there no prohibition on disclosure, an unlawful eavesdropper who wanted to disclose the conversation could anonymously launder the interception through a third party and thereby avoid detection. Indeed, demand for illegally obtained private information would only increase if it could be disclosed without repercussion. The law against interceptions, which the Court agrees is valid, would be utterly ineffectual without these antidisclosure provisions. . . .

These statutes also protect the important interests of deterring clandestine invasions of privacy and preventing the involuntary broadcast of private communications. Over a century ago, Samuel Warren and Louis Brandeis recognized that "[t]he intensity and complexity of life, attendant upon advancing civilization, have rendered necessary some retreat from the world, and man, under the refining influence of culture, has become more sensitive to publicity, so that solitude and privacy have become more essential to the individual." *The Right to Privacy*, 4 Harv. L. Rev. 193, 196 (1890). . . .

These statutes undeniably protect this venerable right of privacy. Concomitantly, they further the First Amendment rights of the parties to the conversation. "At the heart of the First Amendment lies the principle that each person should decide for himself or herself the ideas and beliefs deserving of expression, consideration, and adherence." *Turner Broadcasting System, Inc. v. FCC,* 512 U.S. 622 (1994). By "protecting the privacy of individual thought and expression," these statutes further the "uninhibited, robust, and wide-open" speech of the private parties, *New York Times Co. v. Sullivan,* 376 U.S. 254 (1964). Unlike the laws at issue in the *Daily Mail* cases, which served only to protect the identities and actions of a select group of individuals, these laws protect millions of people who communicate electronically on a daily basis. The chilling effect of the Court's decision upon these private conversations will surely be great. . . .

Perhaps the Court is correct that "[i]f the statements about the labor negotiations had been made in a public arena—during a bargaining session, for example—they would have been newsworthy." The point, however, is that Bartnicki and Kane had no intention of contributing to a public "debate" at all, and it is perverse to hold that another's unlawful interception and knowing disclosure of their conversation is speech "worthy of constitutional protection." Cf. *Hurley v. Irish-American Gay, Lesbian and Bisexual Group of Boston, Inc.*, 515 U.S. 557 (1995) ("[O]ne important manifestation of the principle of free speech is that one who chooses to speak may also decide 'what not to say'"). The Constitution should not protect the involuntary broadcast of personal conversations. Even where the communications involve public figures or concern public matters, the conversations are nonetheless private and worthy of protection. Although public persons may have forgone the right to live their lives screened from public scrutiny in some areas, it does not and should not follow that they also have abandoned their right to have a private conversation without fear of it being intentionally intercepted and knowingly disclosed. . . .

NOTES & QUESTIONS

1. ***Privacy and Free Speech.*** The concurrence and dissent both recognize that the statutory provisions of federal wiretap law serve to protect, rather than merely infringe, First Amendment values. According to the concurrence, the statutory provisions "directly enhance private speech," and in the words of the dissent, the statutory provisions serve to protect against "chilling the speech of millions of Americans who rely upon electronic technology to communicate each day." How should the Court analyze statutes that restrict some speech in order to promote more speech? Should such statutes be treated like laws that exclusively restrict speech?

   Consider Paul Gewirtz's critique of the majority opinion in *Bartnicki*:

   > But there is a more basic problem with Justice Stevens's approach: He looks to the content of the broadcast communication to decide whether the Constitution protects it, rather than to the circumstances under which the conversation took place. . . . [Instead, o]ne could look to whether the original communication takes place within a protected zone. If a zone is deemed a protected private zone — which can be either a place or a kind of situation — then the content of what is communicated within that zone would be irrelevant in deciding whether the First Amendment protects the media in reporting on it. The press could be sanctioned for publishing information about conversations within that zone, regardless of content. In Title III, Congress sought to protect privacy by creating such a protected zone, and made intrusions on that zone illegal. . . . Put another way, speech acts must be understood in terms of audiences as well as content. In our daily narrative transactions, we are always negotiating our relationship to an audience. Privacy is ultimately about our power to choose our audience. When privacy is invaded, we are compelled to have an audience we do not want. The Court in *Bartnicki* says that publishing

> the intercepted conversation contributed to public debate — but the two people speaking on their cell phones did not wish to contribute to a public debate before a public audience. Their words were taken from them by stealth and put into public debate against their will. If every private statement on a public subject may be forcibly disclosed because it contributes to public debate, then privacy is a dead letter. We cannot have it both ways.[58]

Would this hold true no matter what was said or who was saying it? In *Bartnicki,* it is safe to assume the comment about the bomb was not meant literally. Suppose the conversation was between two terrorists who were really planning to set off a bomb. Or suppose the conversation was the President talking to a chief advisor about covering up major corruption. Should these conversations also be protected because they are within the "protected private zone"?

2. ***The Effect of* Bartnicki *on the Public Disclosure Tort.*** According to Rodney Smolla, "*Bartnicki* accepted the premise that the conflict posed between speech and privacy is a conflict between two rights of constitutional stature. By this important measure, all nine Justices in *Bartnicki* were in agreement." Smolla reads *Bartnicki* to be "inviting the importation into First Amendment jurisprudence of the 'newsworthiness' analysis as it has developed so far in common-law cases."[59] The Court has yet to confront whether the tort of public disclosure is constitutional. As Daniel Solove observes:

> In numerous cases, the Court has articulated a public and private concern distinction, and it has applied the First Amendment to curtail restrictions on speech of public concern without answering questions about limiting speech of private concern. . . . The Court appears to view the public and private concern distinction as having significance because it has used this distinction to limit the application of heightened scrutiny to restrictions on speech of public concern. Although it has yet to address the private concern side of the distinction, the Court appears to be heading in the direction [of requiring less First Amendment protection to speech of private concern].[60]

Eugene Volokh takes issue with this conclusion:

> Though the Court has often said in dictum that political speech or public-issue speech is on the "highest rung" of constitutional protection, it has never held that there's any general exception for speech on matters of "private concern." Political speech, scientific speech, art, entertainment, consumer product reviews, and speech on matters of private concern are thus all doctrinally entitled to the same level of high constitutional protection, restrictable only through laws that pass strict scrutiny.[61]

---

[58] Paul Gewirtz, *Privacy and Speech,* 2001 Sup. Ct. Rev. 139, 154-55 (2001).

[59] Rodney A. Smolla, *Information as Contraband: The First Amendment and Liability for Trafficking in Speech,* 96 Nw. U. L. Rev. 1099, 1150, 1153 (2002).

[60] Solove, *Virtues of Knowing Less, supra,* at 987.

[61] Eugene Volokh, *Freedom of Speech and Information Privacy: The Troubling Implications of a Right to Stop People from Speaking About You,* 52 Stan. L. Rev. 1049, 1089, 1092-95 (2000). For other free speech critiques of privacy protections, see Thomas I. Emerson, *The System of Freedom of Expression* (1970); Solveig Singleton, *Privacy Versus the First Amendment: A Skeptical Approach,* 11 Fordham Intell. Prop. Media & Ent. L.J. 97 (2000); Harry Kalven, Jr.,

Does the newsworthiness test adequately deal with the First Amendment concerns of the public disclosure tort?

3. ***Protections Against the Disclosure of Leaked Information.*** In *Landmark Communications v. Virginia*, 435 U.S. 829 (1978), a newspaper was indicted for violating a Virginia law making it a misdemeanor to disclose the identity of a state judge whose conduct was being investigated by the Virginia Judicial Inquiry and Review Commission. The law was designed to ensure that judicial disciplinary proceedings would remain confidential (until such proceedings were concluded) to protect judges from the publication of frivolous and unwarranted complaints. The newspaper did not challenge the requirement of confidentiality, only the prohibition of disclosing the identities of judges if the newspaper happened to find out that a judge was the subject of a disciplinary proceeding. The Supreme Court held that such prohibition violated the First Amendment. Although the interest in confidentiality of disciplinary proceedings was legitimate, it was not sufficient to justify the encroachment on the First Amendment because "[t]he operations of the courts and the judicial conduct of judges are matters of utmost public concern." Further, the statutory scheme could remain effective by restricting the improper leaking of such information rather than criminalizing the disclosure of that information by parties that did not participate in the illegal obtaining of such information.

4. ***Interpreting the Scope of* Bartnicki.** In *Boehner v. McDermott*, 484 F.3d 573 (D.C. Cir. 2007), U.S. Representative James McDermott was provided with a tape of a conference call between U.S. Representative John Boehner, then-Speaker of the House Newt Gingrich, and other Republican Party members. Boeher participated via a cell phone, and John and Alice Martin intercepted the call with a police radio scanner. They gave the tape to another member of the U.S. House, and the tape was eventually forwarded on to McDermott, the ranking Democrat on the Ethics Committee. Along with the tape was a letter from the Martins stating that the call was "heard over a scanner" and that they understood that they would be granted immunity. McDermott contacted reporters at the *Atlanta Journal-Constitution* and the *New York Times*. He played the tape to the *New York Times* reporter, who wrote a story about the tape. The Martins were prosecuted for a violation of the Wiretap Act, 18 U.S.C. § 2511(1)(a), prohibiting the interception of wire, oral, or electronic communications. They pled guilty and paid a $500 fine.

   Boehner sued McDermott for violating 18 U.S.C. § 2511(1)(c), which prohibits disclosing a communication that one knows or has reason to know is acquired in violation of the Wiretap Act. The D.C. Circuit, en banc, concluded that *Bartnicki* could be distinguished:

   > Whatever the *Bartnicki* majority meant by "lawfully obtain," the decision does not stand for the proposition that anyone who has lawfully obtained truthful

---

Privacy in Tort Law — Were Warren and Brandeis Wrong?, 31 Law & Contemp. Probs. 326 (1966); Diane L. Zimmerman, *Requiem for a Heavyweight: A Farewell to Warren and Brandeis's Privacy Tort*, 68 Cornell L. Rev. 291 (1983).

information of public importance has a First Amendment right to disclose that information. *Bartnicki* avoided laying down such a broad rule of law, and for good reason. There are many federal provisions that forbid individuals from disclosing information they have lawfully obtained. The validity of these provisions has long been assumed. Grand jurors, court reporters, and prosecutors, for instance, may "not disclose a matter occurring before the grand jury." Fed. R. Crim. P. 6(e)(2)(B). The Privacy Act imposes criminal penalties on government employees who disclose agency records containing information about identifiable individuals to unauthorized persons. *See* 5 U.S.C. § 552a(i)(1). The Espionage Act punishes officials who willfully disclose sensitive national defense information to persons not entitled to receive it. *See* 18 U.S.C. § 793(d). The Intelligence Identities Protection Act prohibits the disclosure of a covert intelligence agent's identity. *See* 50 U.S.C. § 421. Employees of the Internal Revenue Service, among others, may not disclose tax return information. *See* 26 U.S.C. § 6103(a). State motor vehicle department employees may not make public information about an individual's driver's license or registration. *See* 18 U.S.C. § 2721. Employees of the Social Security Administration, as well as other government employees, may not reveal social security numbers or records. *See* 42 U.S.C. § 405(c)(2)(C)(viii)(I), (III). Judicial employees may not reveal confidential information received in the course of their official duties. *See* Code of Conduct for Judicial Employees Canon 3D. And so forth.

In analogous contexts the Supreme Court has sustained restrictions on disclosure of information even though the information was lawfully obtained. The First Amendment did not shield a television station from liability under the common law right of publicity when it filmed a plaintiff's "human cannonball" act and broadcast the film without his permission. *Zacchini v. Scripps-Howard Broad. Co.,* 433 U.S. 562 (1977). When a newspaper divulged the identity of an individual who provided information to it under a promise of confidentiality, the First Amendment did not provide the paper with a defense to a breach of contract claim. *Cohen v. Cowles Media Co.,* 501 U.S. 663 (1991). The First Amendment did not prevent the government from enforcing reasonable confidentiality restrictions on former employees of the CIA. *See Snepp v. United States,* 444 U.S. 507 (1980). Parties to civil litigation did not "have a First Amendment right to disseminate, in advance of trial, information gained through the pretrial discovery process." *Seattle Times Co. v. Rhinehart,* 467 U.S. 20 (1984).

In *United States v. Aguilar,* 515 U.S. 593 (1995), a case closely analogous to this one, the Supreme Court held that the First Amendment did not give a federal judge, who obtained information about an investigative wiretap from another judge, the right to disclose that information to the subject of the wiretap. The judge challenged his conviction for violating 18 U.S.C. § 2232(c), which prohibits the improper disclosure of an investigative wiretap. In rejecting his First Amendment claim, the Court wrote that the judge was not "simply a member of the general public who happened to lawfully acquire possession of information about the wiretap; he was a Federal District Court Judge who learned of a confidential wiretap application from the judge who had authorized the interception, and who wished to preserve the integrity of the court. Government officials in sensitive confidential positions may have special duties of non-disclosure."

Aguilar stands for the principle that those who accept positions of trust involving a duty not to disclose information they lawfully acquire while performing their responsibilities have no First Amendment right to disclose that information. The question thus becomes whether, in the words of *Aguilar,* Representative McDermott's position on the Ethics Committee imposed a "special" duty on him not to disclose this tape in these circumstances. *Bartnicki* has little to say about that issue. The individuals who disclosed the tape in that case were private citizens who did not occupy positions of trust.

All members of the Ethics Committee, including Representative McDermott, were subject to Committee Rule 9, which stated that "Committee members and staff shall not disclose any evidence relating to an investigation to any person or organization outside the Committee unless authorized by the Committee." . . .

There is no question that the rules themselves are reasonable and raise no First Amendment concerns. . . .

If the First Amendment does not protect Representative McDermott from House disciplinary proceedings, it is hard to see why it should protect him from liability in this civil suit. Either he had a First Amendment right to disclose the tape to the media or he did not. If he had the right, neither the House nor the courts could impose sanctions on him for exercising it. If he did not have the right, he has no shield from civil liability or from discipline imposed by the House. In that event, his civil liability would rest not on his breach of some ethical duty, but on his violation of a federal statute for which he had no First Amendment defense. The situation is the same as that in *Aguilar.* There the defendant-judge was punished not for violating his ethical duty to maintain judicial secrecy, but for violating the general prohibition on disclosing investigative searches. . . .

When Representative McDermott became a member of the Ethics Committee, he voluntarily accepted a duty of confidentiality that covered his receipt and handling of the Martins' illegal recording. He therefore had no First Amendment right to disclose the tape to the media.

Judge Sentelle, along with several others, dissented:

There is no distinction of legal, let alone constitutional, significance between our facts and those before the Court in *Bartnicki.* . . .

The Supreme Court has decided the first issue of this case, that is, whether the United States (or Florida) can constitutionally bar the publication of information originally obtained by unlawful interception but otherwise lawfully received by the communicator, in the negative. We venture to say that an opposite rule would be fraught with danger. Just as Representative McDermott knew that the information had been unlawfully intercepted, so did the newspapers to whom he passed the information. Representative Boehner has suggested no distinction between the constitutionality of regulating communication of the contents of the tape by McDermott or by *The Washington Post* or *The New York Times* or any other media resource. For that matter, every reader of the information in the newspapers also learned that it had been obtained by unlawful intercept. Under the rule proposed by Representative Boehner, no one in the United States could communicate on this topic of public interest because of the defect in the chain of title. We do not believe the First Amendment permits this interdiction of public information either at the stage of the newspaper-reading public, of the newspaper-publishing communicators, or at the stage of Representative McDermott's disclosure to the news media. Lest someone draw a distinction between the First Amendment rights of the press and the First Amendment speech rights of nonprofessional communicators, we would note that one of the communicators in *Bartnicki* was himself a news commentator, and the Supreme Court placed no reliance on that fact. . .

C. DISSEMINATION OF FALSE OR MISLEADING INFORMATION

1. DEFAMATION

(a) Introduction

At the most practical level, an understanding of defamation law is essential to understanding some of the aspects and issues related to the privacy torts. While the privacy torts are a relatively recent invention, a remedy for defamation extends far back in history. Since ancient times, one's reputation and character have been viewed as indispensable to one's ability to engage in public life. Accordingly, the importance of permitting people to protect their reputations has given rise to the law of defamation.[62]

Defamation goes way back to pre-Norman times. "Defamation" (*diffamatus*) was a technical term in church law. It signified a reputation bad enough to be put on trial in ecclesiastical court. Money awards for defamation were a way to prevent people from engaging in duels. Defamation law also served as a popular tool of the monarchy to prosecute its critics.[63]

According to modern defamation law:

> To create liability for defamation there must be:
>
> (a) a false and defamatory statement concerning another;
> (b) an unprivileged publication to a third party;
> (c) fault amounting at least to negligence on the part of the publisher; and
> (d) either actionability of the statement irrespective of special harm or the existence of special harm caused by the publication. Restatement (Second) of Torts § 558.

A "defamatory" statement "tends so to harm the reputation of another as to lower him in the estimation of the community or to deter third persons from associating or dealing with him." Restatement § 559.

A defamatory statement must also be "false." Therefore, a true statement that harms the reputation of another cannot give rise to liability for defamation.

"Publication" means that a defamatory statement is communicated "intentionally or by a negligent act to one other than the person defamed." Restatement § 577. If a person intentionally and unreasonably fails to remove defamatory matter that she knows is under her control, then that person is subject to liability

[62] For an excellent discussion of the rationales behind defamation law, see Robert C. Post, *The Social Foundations of Defamation Law: Reputation and the Constitution*, 74 Cal. L. Rev. 691 (1986).

[63] *See generally* Theodore F.T. Plucknett, *A Concise History of the Common Law* 484-87 (5th ed. 1956).

for its continued publication. *See* Restatement § 577. Further "one who repeats or otherwise republishes defamatory matter is subject to liability as if he had originally published it." Restatement § 578.

One who distributes, transmits, or broadcasts on television or radio defamatory material is also liable if she knows or would have reason to know of its defamatory character. *See* Restatement § 581.

Libel vs. Slander. There are two forms of defamation: libel, which consists of written defamatory statements, and slander, which consists of spoken defamatory statements. According to the Restatement:

> (1) Libel consists of the publication of defamatory matter by written or printed words, by its embodiment in physical form or by any other form of communication that has the potentially harmful qualities characteristic of written or printed words.
>
> (2) Slander consists of the publication of defamatory matter by spoken words, transitory gestures or by any form of communication other than those stated in Subsection (1). Restatement § 568.

As is demonstrated by the above definitions, the Restatement takes a rather broad view of what constitutes libel.

The classification of certain types of statements as either libel or slander has proven difficult. One example is a statement made over the radio or on television. According to the Restatement, all broadcasting is libel, see Restatement § 568A, but some states take a contrary view.

The distinction between libel and slander is important for the purposes of proving harm. To establish libel, a plaintiff does not need to show "special harm" (i.e., a particular harm or injury); damages are presumed. In contrast, for slander, a plaintiff must show actual pecuniary harm, with the exception of four types of slander known as "slander per se" for which damages are presumed. Slander per se consists of defamatory statements imputing to another (1) a criminal offense; (2) a loathsome disease; (3) a matter incompatible with one's business, trade, profession, or office; or (4) serious sexual misconduct. *See* Restatement §§ 570-574. The distinction between libel and slander is less important today, since, in the cases you will read below, the Supreme Court curtailed the availability of presumed damages in defamation law.

Why is libel treated more severely than slander? As then Judge Cardozo put it:

> The schism in the law of defamation between the older wrong of slander and the newer one of libel is not the product of mere accident. It has its genesis in evils which the years have not erased. Many things that are defamatory may be said with impunity through the medium of speech. Not so, however, when speech is caught upon the wing and transmuted into print. What gives the sting to writing is its permanence in form. The spoken word dissolves, but the written one abides and perpetuates the scandal. *Ostrowe v. Lee*, 175 N.E. 505, 506 (N.Y. Ct. App. 1931).

Defamation and Privacy. It might strike you that defamation does not have much to do with privacy. After all, defamation involves false information about individuals, whereas privacy seems to be about true information. This, however, is a limited view of privacy. Privacy involves more than finding out true things about individuals. If privacy is understood as an individual's ability to have some control over the self-image she projects to society, then the ability to prevent the spread of false information about oneself is essential for this sort of control. Indeed, one of the cornerstone principles of privacy law is the ability to correct errors in one's records.

(b) Defamation and the Internet

The Internet presents interesting problems for the application of defamation law and the privacy torts because the Internet enables the widespread publication of information by any individual. Typically, it was through the news media that defamatory or private information about individuals was communicated. As a result, it would be viable to sue such entities, since they would be able to pay any judgment a plaintiff might obtain. With the Internet, however, suppose an individual posts defamatory information about another person on her website. Most likely, that individual isn't wealthy enough to be sued. Further, information is sometimes posted anonymously. As a result of this difficulty, plaintiffs have attempted to advance theories upon which Internet Service Providers (ISPs) would be liable.

In defamation law, in addition to the one who makes a libelous statement, other parties who disseminate the libelous statement can also be found liable. Repeating or publishing the libelous statements of others can give rise to "publisher" liability. A newspaper is an example of a publisher because it exercises editorial control over its content. Merely disseminating a libelous statement can give rise to "distributor" liability. In contrast to a publisher, a distributor cannot be found liable unless it is found to be at fault — if it knew or had reason to know about the defamatory statement. Book stores and libraries are examples of distributors. When a person posts a statement on an ISP's electronic bulletin board or other online forum, is the ISP a "publisher," "distributor," or neither?

The first two courts to reach this issue reached contrary conclusions. In *Cubby, Inc. v. CompuServe, Inc.*, 776 F. Supp. 135 (S.D.N.Y. 1991), CompuServe, an Internet Service Provider, offered CompuServe Information Service (CIS), which was an online general information service that gave subscribers access to special interest forums. One publication available in such a forum was Rumorville USA, a newsletter published daily about journalism. CompuServe did not review Rumorville's contents before it was published in CompuServe's forums, available to subscribers. The plaintiffs developed Skuttlebut, a competing gossip service to Rumorville. The plaintiffs sued CompuServe, alleging that Rumorville published false and defamatory statements relating to Skuttlebut. CompuServe moved for summary judgment, arguing that even if the statements were defamatory, CompuServe could not be held liable for the statements because it didn't have knowledge or reason to know of the statements. The court held that CompuServe was a distributor rather than a publisher:

> With respect to the Rumorville publication, the undisputed facts are that DFA uploads the text of Rumorville into CompuServe's data banks and makes it

> available to approved CIS subscribers instantaneously. CompuServe has no more editorial control over such a publication than does a public library, book store, or newsstand, and it would be no more feasible for CompuServe to examine every publication it carries for potentially defamatory statements than it would be for any other distributor to do so. . . .

In *Stratton Oakmont, Inc. v. Prodigy Services Co.*, 23 Media L. Rep. 1794 (N.Y. Sup. 1995), the plaintiff brought a defamation action against Prodigy, the operator of the computer network. An unidentified user posted allegedly defamatory statements on one of Prodigy's electronic bulletin boards. The plaintiffs contended that Prodigy should be considered the "publisher" of the statements. Under Prodigy's stated policy, it was a family-oriented computer network:

> We make no apology for pursuing a value system that reflects the culture of the millions of American families we aspire to serve. Certainly no responsible newspaper does less when it chooses the type of advertising it publishes, the letters it prints, the degree of nudity and unsupported gossip its editors tolerate.

Prodigy, relying on *Cubby, Inc. v. CompuServe*, contended that it could not be liable as a publisher. Because of the great volume of messages posted daily on Prodigy bulletin boards — about 60,000 per day — it could not review each one. The court, however, concluded that Prodigy was liable as a publisher:

> The key distinction between CompuServe and Prodigy is two fold. First, Prodigy held itself out to the public and its members as controlling the content of its computer bulletin boards. Second, Prodigy implemented this control through its automatic software screening program, and the Guidelines which Board Leaders are required to enforce. By actively utilizing technology and manpower to delete notes from its computer bulletin boards on the basis of offensiveness and "bad taste," for example, Prodigy is clearly making decisions as to content, and such decisions constitute editorial control. That such control is not complete and is enforced both as early as the notes arrive and as late as a complaint is made, does not minimize or eviscerate the simple fact that Prodigy has uniquely arrogated to itself the role of determining what is proper for its members to post and read on its bulletin boards. Based on the foregoing, this Court is compelled to conclude that for the purposes of Plaintiffs' claims in this action, Prodigy is a publisher rather than a distributor. . . .

In response to these cases, Congress passed § 230 of the Communications Decency Act (CDA) of 1996, which provides in relevant part: "No provider or user of an interactive computer service shall be treated as the publisher or speaker of any information provided by another information content provider." 47 U.S.C. § 230(c)(1). Based on this provision, will ISPs that provide forums where defamatory statements are posted be treated as publishers, distributors, or neither?

ZERAN V. AMERICA ONLINE, INC.

129 F.3d 327 (4th Cir. 1997)

WILKINSON, C.J. . . . On April 25, 1995, an unidentified person posted a message on an [America Online (AOL)] bulletin board advertising "Naughty Oklahoma T-Shirts." The posting described the sale of shirts featuring offensive and tasteless slogans related to the April 19, 1995, bombing of the Alfred P. Murrah Federal Building in Oklahoma City. Those interested in purchasing the shirts were instructed to call "Ken" at [Kenneth] Zeran's home phone number in Seattle, Washington. As a result of this anonymously perpetrated prank, Zeran received a high volume of calls, comprised primarily of angry and derogatory messages, but also including death threats. Zeran could not change his phone number because he relied on its availability to the public in running his business out of his home. Later that day, Zeran called AOL and informed a company representative of his predicament. The employee assured Zeran that the posting would be removed from AOL's bulletin board but explained that as a matter of policy AOL would not post a retraction. The parties dispute the date that AOL removed this original posting from its bulletin board.

On April 26, the next day, an unknown person posted another message advertising additional shirts with new tasteless slogans related to the Oklahoma City bombing. Again, interested buyers were told to call Zeran's phone number, to ask for "Ken," and to "please call back if busy" due to high demand. The angry, threatening phone calls intensified. Over the next four days, an unidentified party continued to post messages on AOL's bulletin board, advertising additional items including bumper stickers and key chains with still more offensive slogans. During this time period, Zeran called AOL repeatedly and was told by company representatives that the individual account from which the messages were posted would soon be closed. Zeran also reported his case to Seattle FBI agents. By April 30, Zeran was receiving an abusive phone call approximately every two minutes.

Meanwhile, an announcer for Oklahoma City radio station KRXO received a copy of the first AOL posting. On May 1, the announcer related the message's contents on the air, attributed them to "Ken" at Zeran's phone number, and urged the listening audience to call the number. After this radio broadcast, Zeran was inundated with death threats and other violent calls from Oklahoma City residents. Over the next few days, Zeran talked to both KRXO and AOL representatives. He also spoke to his local police, who subsequently surveilled his home to protect his safety. By May 14, after an Oklahoma City newspaper published a story exposing the shirt advertisements as a hoax and after KRXO made an on-air apology, the number of calls to Zeran's residence finally subsided to fifteen per day.

Zeran first filed suit on January 4, 1996, against radio station KRXO in the United States District Court for the Western District of Oklahoma. On April 23, 1996, he filed this separate suit against AOL in the same court. Zeran did not bring any action against the party who posted the offensive messages.[64] . . . AOL answered Zeran's complaint and interposed [the Communications Decency Act,] 47 U.S.C. § 230 as an affirmative defense. AOL then moved for judgment on the pleadings pursuant to Fed. R. Civ. P. 12(c). The district court granted AOL's motion, and Zeran filed this appeal.

Because § 230 was successfully advanced by AOL in the district court as a defense to Zeran's claims, we shall briefly examine its operation here. Zeran seeks to hold AOL liable for defamatory speech initiated by a third party. He argued to the district court that once he notified AOL of the unidentified third party's hoax, AOL had a duty to remove the defamatory posting promptly, to notify its subscribers of the message's false nature, and to effectively screen future defamatory material. Section 230 entered this litigation as an affirmative defense pled by AOL. The company claimed that Congress immunized interactive computer service providers from claims based on information posted by a third party.

The relevant portion of § 230 states: "No provider or user of an interactive computer service shall be treated as the publisher or speaker of any information provided by another information content provider." 47 U.S.C. § 230(c)(1). By its plain language, § 230 creates a federal immunity to any cause of action that would make service providers liable for information originating with a third-party user of the service. Specifically, § 230 precludes courts from entertaining claims that would place a computer service provider in a publisher's role. Thus, lawsuits seeking to hold a service provider liable for its exercise of a publisher's traditional editorial functions — such as deciding whether to publish, withdraw, postpone or alter content — are barred.

The purpose of this statutory immunity is not difficult to discern. Congress recognized the threat that tort-based lawsuits pose to freedom of speech in the new and burgeoning Internet medium. The imposition of tort liability on service providers for the communications of others represented, for Congress, simply another form of intrusive government regulation of speech. . .

. . . Interactive computer services have millions of users. The amount of information communicated via interactive computer services is therefore staggering. The specter of tort liability in an area of such prolific speech would have an obvious chilling effect. It would be impossible for service providers to screen each of their millions of postings for possible problems. Faced with potential liability for each message republished by their services, interactive computer service providers might choose to severely restrict the number and type of messages posted. Congress considered the weight of the speech interests implicated and chose to immunize service providers to avoid any such restrictive effect.

Another important purpose of § 230 was to encourage service providers to self-regulate the dissemination of offensive material over their services. In this respect, § 230 responded to a New York state court decision, *Stratton Oakmont, Inc. v. Prodigy Servs. Co.* . . .

[64] Zeran maintains that AOL made it impossible to identify the original party by failing to maintain adequate records of its users. The issue of AOL's recordkeeping practices, however, is not presented by this appeal.

Congress enacted § 230 to remove the disincentives to self-regulation created by the *Stratton Oakmont* decision. Under that court's holding, computer service providers who regulated the dissemination of offensive material on their services risked subjecting themselves to liability, because such regulation cast the service provider in the role of a publisher. Fearing that the specter of liability would therefore deter service providers from blocking and screening offensive material, Congress enacted § 230's broad immunity "to remove disincentives for the development and utilization of blocking and filtering technologies that empower parents to restrict their children's access to objectionable or inappropriate online material." 47 U.S.C. § 230(b)(4). In line with this purpose, § 230 forbids the imposition of publisher liability on a service provider for the exercise of its editorial and self-regulatory functions.

Zeran argues, however, that the § 230 immunity eliminates only publisher liability, leaving distributor liability intact. Publishers can be held liable for defamatory statements contained in their works even absent proof that they had specific knowledge of the statement's inclusion. According to Zeran, interactive computer service providers like AOL are normally considered instead to be distributors, like traditional news vendors or book sellers. Distributors cannot be held liable for defamatory statements contained in the materials they distribute unless it is proven at a minimum that they have actual knowledge of the defamatory statements upon which liability is predicated. Zeran contends that he provided AOL with sufficient notice of the defamatory statements appearing on the company's bulletin board. This notice is significant, says Zeran, because AOL could be held liable as a distributor only if it acquired knowledge of the defamatory statements' existence.

Because of the difference between these two forms of liability, Zeran contends that the term "distributor" carries a legally distinct meaning from the term "publisher." Accordingly, he asserts that Congress' use of only the term "publisher" in § 230 indicates a purpose to immunize service providers only from publisher liability. He argues that distributors are left unprotected by § 230 and, therefore, his suit should be permitted to proceed against AOL. We disagree. Assuming arguendo that Zeran has satisfied the requirements for imposition of distributor liability, this theory of liability is merely a subset, or a species, of publisher liability, and is therefore also foreclosed by § 230. . . .

AOL falls squarely within this traditional definition of a publisher and, therefore, is clearly protected by § 230's immunity. . . .

Zeran simply attaches too much importance to the presence of the distinct notice element in distributor liability. The simple fact of notice surely cannot transform one from an original publisher to a distributor in the eyes of the law. . .

If computer service providers were subject to distributor liability, they would face potential liability each time they receive notice of a potentially defamatory statement — from any party, concerning any message. Each notification would require a careful yet rapid investigation of the circumstances surrounding the posted information, a legal judgment concerning the information's defamatory character, and an on-the-spot editorial decision whether to risk liability by allowing the continued publication of that information. Although this might be feasible for the traditional print publisher, the sheer number of postings on interactive computer services would create an impossible burden in the Internet context. Because service providers would be subject to liability only for the publication of information, and not for its removal, they would have a natural incentive simply to remove messages upon notification, whether the contents were defamatory or not. Thus, like strict liability, liability upon notice has a chilling effect on the freedom of Internet speech. . . .

More generally, notice-based liability for interactive computer service providers would provide third parties with a no-cost means to create the basis for future lawsuits. Whenever one was displeased with the speech of another party conducted over an interactive computer service, the offended party could simply "notify" the relevant service provider, claiming the information to be legally defamatory. In light of the vast amount of speech communicated through interactive computer services, these notices could produce an impossible burden for service providers, who would be faced with ceaseless choices of suppressing controversial speech or sustaining prohibitive liability. Because the probable effects of distributor liability on the vigor of Internet speech and on service provider self-regulation are directly contrary to § 230's statutory purposes, we will not assume that Congress intended to leave liability upon notice intact. . . .

BLUMENTHAL V. DRUDGE

992 F. Supp. 44 (D.D.C. 1998)

[A day before Sidney Blumenthal began his employment as an assistant to President Clinton on August 11, 1997, Matt Drudge, the creator of an Internet gossip publication called the Drudge Report, posted a story about Blumenthal having engaged in spousal abuse of his wife, Jacqueline Jordan Blumenthal, who also worked in the White House as director of White House fellowships. In addition to making its stories available on the Internet, the Drudge Report would be e-mailed to a list of regular readers. Since its creation in 1995, the Drudge Report grew from 1,000 e-mail subscribers to 85,000 by 1997. In 1997, Drudge and America Online (AOL), an Internet Service Provider, entered into a license agreement. Pursuant to the agreement, the Drudge Report would be made available to AOL members, and Drudge would receive a monthly royalty of $3,000 from AOL. The royalty was Drudge's only source of income. Under the agreement, Drudge would create the content of the Report, and AOL may "remove content that AOL reasonably determine[s] to violate AOL's then standard terms of service." The Blumenthals sued AOL and Drudge, contending that the statement was defamatory. Drudge later retracted the story and publicly apologized to the Blumenthals. AOL filed a motion for summary judgment, arguing that it was immune from suit by the Communications Decency Act.]

FRIEDMAN, J. . . . Section 230(c) of the Communications Decency Act of 1996 provides:

> No provider or user of an interactive computer service shall be treated as the publisher or speaker of any information provided by another information content provider.

47 U.S.C. § 230(c)(1). The statute goes on to define the term "information content provider" as "any person or entity that is responsible, in whole or in part, for the creation or development of information provided through the Internet or any other interactive computer service." 47 U.S.C. § 230(e)(3). In view of this statutory language, plaintiffs' argument that the Washington Post would be liable if it had done what AOL did here — "publish Drudge's story without doing anything whatsoever to edit, verify, or even read it (despite knowing what Drudge did for a living and how he did it)," — has been rendered irrelevant by Congress. . . .

Plaintiffs [argue] that Section 230 of the Communications Decency Act does not provide immunity to AOL in this case because Drudge was not just an anonymous person who sent a message over the Internet through AOL. He is a person with whom AOL contracted, whom AOL paid $3,000 a month — $36,000 a year, Drudge's sole, consistent source of income — and whom AOL promoted to its subscribers and potential subscribers as a reason to subscribe to AOL. Furthermore, the license agreement between AOL and Drudge by its terms contemplates more than a passive role for AOL. . . .

In addition, shortly after it entered into the licensing agreement with Drudge, AOL issued a press release making clear the kind of material Drudge would provide to AOL subscribers — gossip and rumor — and urged potential subscribers to sign onto AOL in order to get the benefit of the Drudge Report. The press release was captioned: "AOL Hires Runaway Gossip Success Matt Drudge." . . .

If it were writing on a clean slate, this Court would agree with plaintiffs. AOL has certain editorial rights with respect to the content provided by Drudge and disseminated by AOL, including the right to require changes in content and to remove it; and it has affirmatively promoted Drudge as a new source of unverified instant gossip on AOL. Yet it takes no responsibility for any damage he may cause. AOL is not a passive conduit like the telephone company, a common carrier with no control and therefore no responsibility for what is said over the telephone wires. Because it has the right to exercise editorial control over those with whom it contracts and whose words it disseminates, it would seem only fair to hold AOL to the liability standards applied to a publisher or, at least, like a book store owner or library, to the liability standards applied to a distributor. But Congress has made a different policy choice by providing immunity even where the interactive service provider has an active, even aggressive role in making available content prepared by others. In some sort of tacit quid pro quo arrangement with the service provider community, Congress has conferred immunity from tort liability as an incentive to Internet service providers to self-police the Internet for obscenity and other offensive material, even where the self-policing is unsuccessful or not even attempted. . . .

. . . While it appears to this Court that AOL in this case has taken advantage of all the benefits conferred by Congress in the Communications Decency Act, and then some, without accepting any of the burdens that Congress intended, the statutory language is clear: AOL is immune from suit, and the Court therefore must grant its motion for summary judgment.

NOTES & QUESTIONS

1. ***The Applicability of the CDA § 230 to the Privacy Torts.*** Is § 230 of the CDA applicable to the privacy torts? In *Barnes v. Yahoo!, Inc.*, 2005 WL 3005602 (D. Or. 2005) (not reported in F. Supp. 2d), a woman alleged that her former boyfriend created fake profiles under her name on Yahoo. He posted nude photos of her in the profiles and provided contact information for her. She also claimed that he was impersonating her in chatrooms and directing people to the profiles. She contacted Yahoo and asked them several times to try to put a stop to the boyfriend's misuse of Yahoo's services. She alleged that although Yahoo employees promised they would help her, they failed to stop the boyfriend's conduct. The court, in an unpublished opinion, concluded that Yahoo was immune under § 230.
2. ***Anonymity and Accountability for Harmful Internet Speech.*** Shouldn't plaintiffs sue the people who post defamatory or privacy-invasive statements rather than the ISPs or websites on which the statements appear? Recall in *Zeran* that the anonymous poster of the information could not be identified. Should the website be forced to maintain records of the identities of the individuals who post so that people can sue those individuals? What are the benefits and costs of such a solution?
3. ***Critiques of Zeran.*** Consider the following argument against *Zeran* from *Barrett v. Rosenthal*, 5 Cal. Rptr. 3d 416 (Cal. Ct. App. 2003):

   > . . . [W]e . . . think it debatable whether notice liability would actually have an unduly chilling effect on cyberspeech. Neither the record before us nor any other information brought to our attention provides an answer to that question. Moreover, the speculative conclusion of the *Zeran* court that exposing Internet intermediaries to knowledge-based liability would significantly chill online speech is disputed by the speculations of other authorities. . . .
   >
   > It is also asserted that by ignoring how difficult it is for a plaintiff to prevail on a defamation claim or receive significant money damages, the *Zeran* court overstated the danger such claims present to Internet intermediaries, and therefore also exaggerated the danger they would engage in excessive self-censorship.

   The California Supreme Court reversed the court of appeals in *Barrett v. Rosenthal*, 146 P.3d 510 (Cal. 2006):

   > We agree with the *Zeran* court, and others considering the question, that subjecting Internet service providers and users to defamation liability would tend to chill online speech. . . .
   >
   > We reject the argument that the difficulty of prevailing on a defamation claim mitigates the deterrent effect of potential liability. Defamation law is complex, requiring consideration of multiple factors. These include whether the statement at issue is true or false, factual or figurative, privileged or unprivileged, whether the matter is of public or private concern, and whether the plaintiff is a public or private figure. Any investigation of a potentially defamatory Internet posting is thus a daunting and expensive challenge. For that reason, we have observed that even when a defamation claim is "clearly

nonmeritorious," the threat of liability "ultimately chills the free exercise of expression."

Nor are we convinced by the observation that a "distributor" faces no liability without notice. Distributors are liable not merely upon receiving notice from a third party, but also if they independently "knew or had reason to know" of the defamatory statement. Thus, as the *Zeran* court pointed out, this aspect of distributor liability would discourage active monitoring of Internet postings. It could also motivate providers to insulate themselves from receiving complaints. Such responses would frustrate the goal of self-regulation.

The third practical implication noted in *Zeran* is no less compelling, and went unaddressed by the Court of Appeal. Notice-based liability for service providers would allow complaining parties to impose substantial burdens on the freedom of Internet speech by lodging complaints whenever they were displeased by an online posting. . . .

Requiring providers, users, and courts to account for the nuances of common law defamation, and all the various ways they might play out in the Internet environment, is a Herculean assignment that we are reluctant to impose. We conclude the *Zeran* court accurately diagnosed the problems that would attend notice-based liability for service providers.

Which opinion has the better argument as to the meaning and purpose of § 230?

Consider Daniel Solove:

Unfortunately, courts are interpreting Section 230 so broadly as to provide too much immunity, eliminating the incentive to foster a balance between speech and privacy. The way courts are using Section 230 exalts free speech to the detriment of privacy and reputation. As a result, a host of websites have arisen that encourage others to post gossip and rumors as well as to engage in online shaming. These websites thrive under Section 230's broad immunity.[65]

Solove contends that a notice and take-down system is preferable to a broader immunity that eliminates distributor liability. What are the benefits and problems of a notice and take-down regime? In copyright law, "one who distributes a device with the object of promoting its use to infringe copyright, as shown by clear expression or other affirmative steps taken to foster infringement, is liable for the resulting acts of infringement by third parties." *MGM Studios, Inc. v. Grokster, Ltd.* 545 U.S. 913 (2005). Examine the pros and cons of such a rule for defamation or privacy tort liability.

4. *Who Is the Content Provider?* In *Batzel v. Smith*, 333 F.3d 1018 (9th Cir. 2003), a handyman (Robert Smith) who worked at Ellen Batzel's home e-mailed Ton Cremers, the director of security at a museum in Amsterdam, who maintained an e-mail listserv about looted art. Smith said that several of Batzel's paintings were stolen from the Jews by the Nazis during World War II. Cremers made a few small changes to the text of Smith's e-mail and sent it out to his listserv. The paintings were not looted art from the Nazis, and

[65] Daniel J. Solove, *The Future of Reputation: Gossip, Rumor, and Privacy on the Internet* 159 (2007).

Batzel sued both Smith and Cremers. The court concluded that since Cremers was not the originator of the information, he was immune under § 230:

> Obviously, Cremers did not create Smith's e-mail. Smith composed the e-mail entirely on his own. . . . [T]he exclusion of "publisher" liability necessarily precludes liability for exercising the usual prerogative of publishers to choose among proffered material and to edit the material published while retaining its basic form and message.
>
> Because Cremers did no more than select and make minor alterations to Smith's e-mail, Cremers cannot be considered the content provider of Smith's e-mail for purposes of § 230. . . .
>
> We therefore hold that a service provider or user is immune from liability under § 230(c)(1) when a third person or entity that created or developed the information in question furnished it to the provider or user under circumstances in which a reasonable person in the position of the service provider or user would conclude that the information was provided for publication on the Internet or other "interactive computer service."

In dissent, Judge Gould wrote:

> Congress wanted to ensure that excessive government regulation did not slow America's expansion into the exciting new frontier of the Internet. But Congress did not want this new frontier to be like the Old West: a lawless zone governed by retribution and mob justice. The CDA does not license anarchy. A person's decision to disseminate the rankest rumor or most blatant falsehood should not escape legal redress merely because the person chose to disseminate it through the Internet rather than through some other medium. . . .
>
> In this case, I would hold that Cremers is *not* entitled to CDA immunity because Cremers actively selected Smith's e-mail message for publication.

Batzel demonstrates the difficulties in certain situations of determining whether a person is providing content or is merely disseminating the content of another. If a person is deemed the content provider, then § 230 immunity does not apply, as § 230 is designed to immunize a person from being liable for disseminating the content of others. In *Batzel,* is Cremers the content provider because he decided to forward the e-mail? Or is Smith the content provider because he wrote the e-mail? *Batzel* holds that if a person receives a communication sent by another for the purpose of having the person publish it online, then the person is immune under § 230 for publishing it. Few courts have adopted a rule like that in *Batzel* because few have explored situations where it is unclear who precisely is the content provider.

Suppose Cremers has a blog about stolen art. Smith is interested in spreading the rumor about the stolen art on Cremers's blog. Consider the following situations and examine whether Cremers would have § 230 immunity under the majority's rule and also under Judge Gould's:

(a) Cremers's blog allows anybody to post comments. Smith posts a comment about the rumor on Cremers's blog. Batzel wants Cremers to delete the comment, but Cremers refuses to do so.

(b) Cremers has a comment moderation system on his blog where he must approve comments before they are published on his blog. Smith posts the stolen art comment and Cremers approves it, whereupon it is published on the blog.

(c) Smith e-mails Cremers and tells him about the stolen art rumor. Instead of posting the e-mail itself, Cremers writes a blog post about the rumor in his own words and posts it.

(d) Smith calls Cremers and tells him the rumor about the stolen art. Cremers writes a post about the rumor.

Is there any meaningful difference between the above situations and the way that Cremers disseminated Smith's e-mail to the listserv? As a normative matter, should Cremers's liability be different in any of the above situations? How should the law determine when a person should be deemed the content provider and when a person should be deemed to merely be relaying the content of another?

5. *Wikipedia.* Wikipedia is an online encyclopedia that anybody can edit. It has millions of entries and is widely used and cited. What are the legal consequences when a Wikipedia entry is defamatory?

A notable case occurred in 2005 involving John Seigenthaler, a former assistant to Attorney General Bobby Kennedy during the Kennedy Administration. His Wikipedia entry falsely accused him of being involved in President John F. Kennedy's assassination. In an article in *USA Today,* Seigenthaler wrote:

> I have no idea whose sick mind conceived the false, malicious "biography" that appeared under my name for 132 days on Wikipedia, the popular, online, free encyclopedia whose authors are unknown and virtually untraceable.[66]

Eventually, the anonymous person who wrote the defamatory statement was identified, and he apologized. If Seigenthaler sued Wikipedia for defamation, would § 230 provide Wikipedia with immunity? Consider the views of Ken Myers on this topic:

> Because of the unique relationship between Wikipedia and its user-community, the question of whether an individual user-poster is a separate "information content provider," as opposed to somehow being a representative of Wikipedia, is unclear. If Wikipedia is determined to be the relevant "information content provider" then there is no immunity under § 230(c)(1), as Wikipedia itself will be held responsible for the defamatory content. Thus, the definition of "information content provider" raises an important threshold question in this case: what counts as the "person or entity" whose actions the court should analyze in determining whether Wikipedia is the "information content provider" under the third prong? . . .
>
> The Wikipedia community is self-consciously inclusive, designating all of its contributors as "Wikipedians." Presumably, this inclusiveness fosters the cooperative atmosphere critical to Wikipedia's success. However, if *all* members of the Wikipedia community — that is, all contributors — are considered part of the Wikipedia "entity," then it would, by definition and by operation of the third prong, not be eligible for § 230(c)(1) immunity because

---

[66] John Seigenthaler, *A False Wikipedia "Biography,"* USA Today, Nov. 29, 2005.

> Wikipedia would be the site's only contributor — there could be no "[]other information content provider." . . .
>
> Wikipedia would argue that, for purposes of § 230(f)(3), only employees of the Wikimedia Foundation should be considered as part of the Wikipedia "entity." However, "the fact that work is performed gratuitously does not relieve a principal of liability."[67]

To the extent that websites like Wikipedia create hierarchies of users, with some having greater editorial powers, does this alter immunity for the actions of the users at the top of the hierarchy?

(c) First Amendment Limitations

NEW YORK TIMES CO. V. SULLIVAN

376 U.S. 254 (1964)

[L.B. Sullivan, one of the three elected Commissioners of Montgomery, Alabama, sued four African-American clergymen and the *New York Times* for libel. Sullivan claimed that a full-page advertisement in the *New York Times* on March 29, 1960, entitled "Heed Their Rising Voices" defamed him. The advertisement discussed the civil rights movement and the wave of terror against the nonviolent protest. It was signed by various clergymen in Southern cities, including the four clergymen named in the lawsuit.

Two paragraphs of the ten in the advertisement were the basis of Sullivan's libel claim.

> . . . In Montgomery, Alabama, after students sang "My Country, 'Tis of Thee" on the State Capitol steps, their leaders were expelled from school, and truckloads of police armed with shotguns and tear-gas ringed the Alabama State College Campus. When the entire student body protested to state authorities by refusing to re-register, their dining hall was padlocked in an attempt to starve them into submission. . . .
>
> Again and again the Southern violators have answered Dr. King's peaceful protests with intimidation and violence. They have bombed his home almost killing his wife and child. They have assaulted his person. They have arrested him seven times — for "speeding," "loitering" and similar "offenses." And now they have charged him with "perjury" — a felony under which they could imprison him for ten years. . . .

Although Sullivan was never mentioned by name, he claimed that the word "police" implicated him because he supervised the police department. Although Sullivan made no effort to prove he suffered actual pecuniary loss as a result of the alleged libel, a Montgomery County jury awarded Sullivan damages of $500,000, the full amount claimed against all the petitioners, and the Supreme Court of Alabama affirmed.]

---

[67] Ken S. Myers, *Wikimmunity: Fitting the Communications Decency Act to Wikipedia*, 20 Harv. J.L. & Tech. 163, 188-90 (2006).

BRENNAN, J. . . . Under Alabama law as applied in this case, a publication is "libelous per se" if the words "tend to injure a person . . . in his reputation" or to "bring (him) into public contempt"; the trial court stated that the standard was met if the words are such as to "injure him in his public office, or impute misconduct to him in his office, or want of official integrity, or want of fidelity to a public trust. . . ." The jury must find that the words were published "of and concerning" the plaintiff, but where the plaintiff is a public official his place in the governmental hierarchy is sufficient evidence to support a finding that his reputation has been affected by statements that reflect upon the agency of which he is in charge. Once "libel per se" has been established, the defendant has no defense as to stated facts unless he can persuade the jury that they were true in all their particulars. His privilege of "fair comment" for expressions of opinion depends on the truth of the facts upon which the comment is based. Unless he can discharge the burden of proving truth, general damages are presumed, and may be awarded without proof of pecuniary injury. A showing of actual malice is apparently a prerequisite to recovery of punitive damages, and the defendant may in any event forestall a punitive award by a retraction meeting the statutory requirements. Good motives and belief in truth do not negate an inference of malice, but are relevant only in mitigation of punitive damages if the jury chooses to accord them weight.

The question before us is whether this rule of liability, as applied to an action brought by a public official against critics of his official conduct, abridges the freedom of speech and of the press that is guaranteed by the First and Fourteenth Amendments.

Respondent relies heavily, as did the Alabama courts, on statements of this Court to the effect that the Constitution does not protect libelous publications. . . . Like insurrection, contempt, advocacy of unlawful acts, breach of the peace, obscenity, solicitation of legal business, and the various other formulae for the repression of expression that have been challenged in this Court, libel can claim no talismanic immunity from constitutional limitations. It must be measured by standards that satisfy the First Amendment.

The general proposition that freedom of expression upon public questions is secured by the First Amendment has long been settled by our decisions. . . .

. . . [W]e consider this case against the background of a profound national commitment to the principle that debate on public issues should be uninhibited, robust, and wide-open, and that it may well include vehement, caustic, and sometimes unpleasantly sharp attacks on government and public officials. The present advertisement, as an expression of grievance and protest on one of the major public issues of our time, would seem clearly to qualify for the constitutional protection. The question is whether it forfeits that protection by the falsity of some of its factual statements and by its alleged defamation of respondent.

Authoritative interpretations of the First Amendment guarantees have consistently refused to recognize an exception for any test of truth — whether administered by judges, juries, or administrative officials — and especially one that puts the burden of proving truth on the speaker. The constitutional protection does not turn upon "the truth, popularity, or social utility of the ideas and beliefs which are offered." . . .

That erroneous statement is inevitable in free debate, and that it must be protected if the freedoms of expression are to have the "breathing space" that they "need to survive." . . .

A rule compelling the critic of official conduct to guarantee the truth of all his factual assertions — and to do so on pain of libel judgments virtually unlimited in amount — leads to a comparable "self-censorship." . . . Under such a rule, would-be critics of official conduct may be deterred from voicing their criticism, even though it is believed to be true and even though it is in fact true, because of doubt whether it can be proved in court or fear of the expense of having to do so. They tend to make only statements which "steer far wider of the unlawful zone." The rule thus dampens the vigor and limits the variety of public debate. It is inconsistent with the First and Fourteenth Amendments.

The constitutional guarantees require, we think, a federal rule that prohibits a public official from recovering damages for a defamatory falsehood relating to his official conduct unless he proves that the statement was made with "actual malice" — that is, with knowledge that it was false or with reckless disregard of whether it was false or not. . . .

We hold today that the Constitution delimits a State's power to award damages for libel in actions brought by public officials against critics of their official conduct. Since this is such an action, the rule requiring proof of actual malice is applicable. While Alabama law apparently requires proof of actual malice for an award of punitive damages, where general damages are concerned malice is "presumed." Such a presumption is inconsistent with the federal rule. Since the trial judge did not instruct the jury to differentiate between general and punitive damages, it may be that the verdict was wholly an award of one or the other. But it is impossible to know, in view of the general verdict returned. Because of this uncertainty, the judgment must be reversed and the case remanded. . . .

NOTES & QUESTIONS

1. ***Should Defamation Have Survived?*** Justices Black, Douglas, and Goldberg would have gone further, eliminating all defamation liability for public officials. In other words, public officials could not sue for defamation even if the defamatory statement were made with actual malice. As Justice Goldberg explained, the right to criticize public officials is unconditional and "should not depend upon a probing by the jury of the motivation of the citizen or press." Does Justice Brennan's logic lead to this result? Why not just bar all libel actions by public officials? Consider Justice Holmes's dissent in *Abrams v. United States*, 250 U.S. 616, 630 (1919):

> But when men have realized that time has upset many fighting faiths, they may come to believe even more than they believe the very foundations of their own conduct that the ultimate good desired is better reached by free trade in ideas — that the best test of truth is the power of the thought to get itself accepted in the competition of the market, and that truth is the only ground upon which their wishes safely can be carried out. That at any rate is the theory of our Constitution.

If Holmes is right, and the marketplace of ideas will result in the truth eventually winning out, then is defamation law even necessary?[68]

2. ***Actual Malice.*** The actual malice standard is a subjective one. As Randall Bezanson describes it:

> The actual malice inquiry is avowedly focused on the subjective state of mind of the publisher at the time of publication. It asks only whether falsity was calculated or whether the publisher's decision was sufficiently indifferent to likely falsity that the publication decision should not be respected under the First Amendment. Actual malice, in short, reveals a frame of mind, an animating intention for the publication, that belies any significant publisher concern for the audience or for the function being performed in the selection and presentation of information, or news. . . .

In practice, actual malice is very difficult for plaintiffs to establish. Bezanson observes:

> In making actual malice determinations, state courts attempt to determine the speaker's subjective state of mind by two primary means. First, courts examine the speaker's observable conduct at the time of the speech act, viewing such outward manifestations as a potential insight into the speaker's state of mind. . . . The second means by which courts attempt to determine the speaker's state of mind is through the personal testimony of the speaker. State courts grant considerable weight to the speaker's own reflective statements concerning his or her belief as to the truth of the speech at the time the speech judgment was made.[69]

3. ***Public Figures.*** Subsequently, the Court extended the approach in *New York Times* to persons who were not public officials but who were "'public figures' and involved in issues in which the public has a justified and important interest." *Curtis Publishing Co. v. Butts*, 388 U.S. 130 (1967).

In *Gertz v. Robert Welch, Inc.*, 418 U.S. 323 (1974), which is excerpted below, the Court turned to the issue of whether the *New York Times* approach should be extended to private figures.

GERTZ V. ROBERT WELCH, INC.

418 U.S. 323 (1974)

[In 1968, Nuccio, a Chicago policeman, shot and killed Nelson, a youth. Nuccio was prosecuted and convicted for murder in the second degree. The Nelson family retained petitioner Elmer Gertz, a reputable attorney, to represent them in civil litigation against Nuccio. Robert Welch, Inc. published *American Opinion*, a monthly magazine representing the views of the John Birch Society. The magazine had been warning of a national conspiracy to discredit local police forces and create a national police force as a step toward establishing a

---

[68] For more background about *New York Times v. Sullivan*, see Anthony Lewis, *Make No Law: The Sullivan Case and the First Amendment* (1991).

[69] Randall P. Bezanson, *The Developing Law of Editorial Judgment,* 78 Neb. L. Rev. 754, 774-75, 763-64 (1999).

Communist dictatorship. In 1969, the magazine published an article about the murder trial of Officer Nuccio, alleging that he was framed as part of the Communist campaign against the police. Among other things, the article portrayed Gertz as the mastermind of the frame-up. It stated that Gertz was a "Leninist" and a "Communist-fronter," that Gertz belonged to Marxist and Socialist organizations, and that Gertz had a criminal record. All of these statements were false. The managing editor made no effort to verify the charges; in fact, he wrote an editorial introduction stating that the author had conducted extensive research. Gertz sued for libel and won a jury verdict of $50,000. The district court, however, decided that the *New York Times* standard should apply and entered judgment for Robert Welch, Inc.]

POWELL, J. . . . The principal issue in this case is whether a newspaper or broadcaster that publishes defamatory falsehoods about an individual who is neither a public official nor a public figure may claim a constitutional privilege against liability for the injury inflicted by those statements. . . .

The legitimate state interest underlying the law of libel is the compensation of individuals for the harm inflicted on them by defamatory falsehood. We would not lightly require the State to abandon this purpose, for, as Mr. Justice Stewart has reminded us, the individual's right to the protection of his own good name

> reflects no more than our basic concept of the essential dignity and worth of every human being — a concept at the root of any decent system of ordered liberty. The protection of private personality, like the protection of life itself, is left primarily to the individual States under the Ninth and Tenth Amendments. But this does not mean that the right is entitled to any less recognition by this Court as a basic of our constitutional system. *Rosenblatt v. Baer*, 383 U.S. 75, 92 (1966) (concurring opinion). . . .

. . . [W]e have no difficulty in distinguishing among defamation plaintiffs. The first remedy of any victim of defamation is self-help — using available opportunities to contradict the lie or correct the error and thereby to minimize its adverse impact on reputation. Public officials and public figures usually enjoy significantly greater access to the channels of effective communication and hence have a more realistic opportunity to counteract false statements then private individuals normally enjoy. Private individuals are therefore more vulnerable to injury, and the state interest in protecting them is correspondingly greater.

More important than the likelihood that private individuals will lack effective opportunities for rebuttal, there is a compelling normative consideration underlying the distinction between public and private defamation plaintiffs. An individual who decides to seek governmental office must accept certain necessary consequences of that involvement in public affairs. He runs the risk of closer public scrutiny than might otherwise be the case. And society's interest in the officers of government is not strictly limited to the formal discharge of official duties. As the Court pointed out in *Garrison v. Louisiana*, the public's interest extends to "anything which might touch on an official's fitness for office. . . . Few personal attributes are more germane to fitness for office than dishonesty, malfeasance, or improper motivation, even though these characteristics may also affect the official's private character."

Those classed as public figures stand in a similar position. Hypothetically, it may be possible for someone to become a public figure through no purposeful action of his own, but the instances of truly involuntary public figures must be exceedingly rare. For the most part those who attain this status have assumed roles of especial prominence in the affairs of society. Some occupy positions of such persuasive power and influence that they are deemed public figures for all purposes. More commonly, those classed as public figures have thrust themselves to the forefront of particular public controversies in order to influence the resolution of the issues involved. In either event, they invite attention and comment.

Even if the foregoing generalities do not obtain in every instance, the communications media are entitled to act on the assumption that public officials and public figures have voluntarily exposed themselves to increased risk of injury from defamatory falsehood concerning them. No such assumption is justified with respect to a private individual. He has not accepted public office or assumed an "influential role in ordering society." He has relinquished no part of his interest in the protection of his own good name, and consequently he has a more compelling call on the courts for redress of injury inflicted by defamatory falsehood. Thus, private individuals are not only more vulnerable to injury than public officials and public figures; they are also more deserving of recovery.

For these reasons we conclude that the States should retain substantial latitude in their efforts to enforce a legal remedy for defamatory falsehood injurious to the reputation of a private individual. The extension of the *New York Times* test . . . would abridge this legitimate state interest to a degree that we find unacceptable. And it would occasion the additional difficulty of forcing state and federal judges to decide on an ad hoc basis which publications address issues of "general or public interest" and which do not — to determine, in the words of Mr. Justice Marshall, "what information is relevant to self-government." We doubt the wisdom of committing this task to the conscience of judges. . . .

We hold that, so long as they do not impose liability without fault, the States may define for themselves the appropriate standard of liability for a publisher or broadcaster of defamatory falsehood injurious to a private individual. . . .

. . . Under the traditional rules pertaining to actions for libel, the existence of injury is presumed from the fact of publication. Juries may award substantial sums as compensation for supposed damage to reputation without any proof that such harm actually occurred. The largely uncontrolled discretion of juries to award damages where there is no loss unnecessarily compounds the potential of any system of liability for defamatory falsehood to inhibit the vigorous exercise of First Amendment freedoms. Additionally, the doctrine of presumed damages invites juries to punish unpopular opinion rather than to compensate individuals for injury sustained by the publication of a false fact. More to the point, the States have no substantial interest in securing for plaintiffs such as this petitioner gratuitous awards of money damages far in excess of any actual injury. . . .

. . . It is necessary to restrict defamation plaintiffs who do not prove knowledge of falsity or reckless disregard for the truth to compensation for actual injury. . . . Suffice it to say that actual injury is not limited to out-of-pocket loss. Indeed, the more customary types of actual harm inflicted by defamatory falsehood include impairment of reputation and standing in the community, personal humiliation, and mental anguish and suffering. . . .

We also find no justification for allowing awards of punitive damages against publishers and broadcasters held liable under state-defined standards of liability for defamation. In most jurisdictions jury discretion over the amounts awarded is limited only by the gentle rule that they not be excessive. Consequently, juries assess punitive damages in wholly unpredictable amounts bearing no necessary relation to the actual harm caused. And they remain free to use their discretion selectively to punish expressions of unpopular views. Like the doctrine of presumed damages, jury discretion to award punitive damages unnecessarily exacerbates the danger of media self-censorship, but, unlike the former rule, punitive damages are wholly irrelevant to the state interest that justifies a negligence standard for private defamation actions. They are not compensation for injury. Instead, they are private fines levied by civil juries to punish reprehensible conduct and to deter its future occurrence. In short, the private defamation plaintiff who establishes liability under a less demanding standard than that stated by *New York Times* may recover only such damages as are sufficient to compensate him for actual injury.

Notwithstanding our refusal to extend the *New York Times* privilege to defamation of private individuals, respondent contends that we should affirm the judgment below on the ground that petitioner is either a public official or a public figure. . . .

. . . In some instances an individual may achieve such pervasive fame or notoriety that he becomes a public figure for all purposes and in all contexts. More commonly, an individual voluntarily injects himself or is drawn into a particular public controversy and thereby becomes a public figure for a limited range of issues. In either case such persons assume special prominence in the resolution of public questions.

Petitioner has long been active in community and professional affairs. He has served as an officer of local civic groups and of various professional organizations, and he has published several books and articles on legal subjects. Although petitioner was consequently well known in some circles, he had achieved no general fame or notoriety in the community. None of the prospective jurors called at the trial had ever heard of petitioner prior to this litigation, and respondent offered no proof that this response was atypical of the local population. We would not lightly assume that a citizen's participation in community and professional affairs rendered him a public figure for all purposes. Absent clear evidence of general fame or notoriety in the community, and pervasive involvement in the affairs of society, an individual should not be deemed a public personality for all aspects of his life. It is preferable to reduce the public-figure question to a more meaningful context by looking to the nature and extent of an individual's participation in the particular controversy giving rise to the defamation.

In this context it is plain that petitioner was not a public figure. He played a minimal role at the coroner's inquest, and his participation related solely to his representation of a private client. He took no part in the criminal prosecution of Officer Nuccio. Moreover, he never discussed either the criminal or civil litigation with the press and was never quoted as having done so. He plainly did not thrust himself into the vortex of this public issue, nor did he engage the public's attention in an attempt to influence its outcome. We are persuaded that the trial court did not err in refusing to characterize petitioner as a public figure for the purpose of this litigation. . . .

WHITE, J. dissenting. . . . The press today is vigorous and robust. To me, it is quite incredible to suggest that threats of libel suits from private citizens are causing the press to refrain from publishing the truth. I know of no hard facts to support that proposition, and the Court furnishes none.

The communications industry has increasingly become concentrated in a few powerful hands operating very lucrative businesses reaching across the Nation and into almost every home. Neither the industry as a whole nor its individual components are easily intimidated, and we are fortunate that they are not. Requiring them to pay for the occasional damage they do to private reputation will play no substantial part in their future performance or their existence. . . .

NOTES & QUESTIONS

1. ***Public vs. Private Figures.*** What distinguishes a public from a private figure? In *Time, Inc. v. Firestone*, 424 U.S. 448 (1976), Mary Alice Firestone and her husband had a messy divorce. The court issued a judgment granting the divorce, stating that according to the testimony of the husband, the wife's "extramarital escapades . . . were bizarre and of an amatory nature which would have made Dr. Freud's hair curl. Other testimony . . . would indicate that [the husband] was guilty of bounding from one bedpartner to another with the erotic zest of a satyr. The court is inclined to discount much of this testimony as unreliable." *Time* magazine published the following article in its "Milestones" section the following week:

> DIVORCED. By Russell A. Firestone Jr., 41, heir to the tire fortune: Mary Alice Sullivan Firestone, 32, his third wife; a onetime Palm Beach schoolteacher; on grounds of extreme cruelty and adultery; after six years of marriage, one son; in West Palm Beach, Fla. The 17-month intermittent trial produced enough testimony of extramarital adventures on both sides, said the judge, "to make Dr. Freud's hair curl."

Mary Firestone sued for libel. When the case ended up in the U.S. Supreme Court, the issue was whether Firestone was a public or private figure. According to the Court:

> Petitioner contends that because the Firestone divorce was characterized by the Florida Supreme Court as a "cause celebre," it must have been a public controversy and respondent must be considered a public figure. But in so doing petitioner seeks to equate "public controversy" with all controversies of interest to the public. . . .
>
> Dissolution of a marriage through judicial proceedings is not the sort of "public controversy" referred to in *Gertz*, even though the marital difficulties of extremely wealthy individuals may be of interest to some portion of the reading public. Nor did respondent freely choose to publicize issues as to the propriety of her married life. She was compelled to go to court by the State in

> order to obtain legal release from the bonds of matrimony. We have said that in such an instance "(r)esort to the judicial process . . . is no more voluntary in a realistic sense than that of the defendant called upon to defend his interests in court." . . . She assumed no "special prominence in the resolution of public questions." *Gertz*, 418 U.S., at 351. We hold respondent was not a "public figure" for the purpose of determining the constitutional protection afforded petitioner's report of the factual and legal basis for her divorce.

In *Wolston v. Readers Digest Ass'n, Inc.*, 443 U.S. 157 (1979), the plaintiff was summoned to appear before a grand jury in connection with an investigation into his aunt and uncle's spying for the Soviet Union in 1958. Due to mental depression, the plaintiff failed to appear before the grand jury and was held in contempt. In 1984, a book about Soviet agents stated that the plaintiff had been indicted for being such an agent. The district court and court of appeals held that the plaintiff was a limited purpose public figure (regarding Soviet espionage) — those who, under the language of *Gertz*, "thrust themselves to the forefront of particular public controversies in order to influence the resolution of the issues involved." The Supreme Court disagreed:

> . . . [T]he undisputed facts do not justify the conclusion of the District Court and Court of Appeals that petitioner "voluntarily thrust" or "injected" himself into the forefront of the public controversy surrounding the investigation of Soviet espionage in the United States. It would be more accurate to say that petitioner was dragged unwillingly into the controversy. The Government pursued him in its investigation. Petitioner did fail to respond to a grand jury subpoena, and this failure, as well as his subsequent citation for contempt, did attract media attention. But the mere fact that petitioner voluntarily chose not to appear before the grand jury, knowing that his action might be attended by publicity, is not decisive on the question of public-figure status. . . . It is clear that petitioner played only a minor role in whatever public controversy there may have been concerning the investigation of Soviet espionage. We decline to hold that his mere citation for contempt rendered him a public figure for purposes of comment on the investigation of Soviet espionage.
>
> Petitioner's failure to appear before the grand jury and citation for contempt no doubt were "newsworthy," but the simple fact that these events attracted media attention also is not conclusive of the public-figure issue. A private individual is not automatically transformed into a public figure just by becoming involved in or associated with a matter that attracts public attention. . . . A libel defendant must show more than mere newsworthiness to justify application of the demanding burden of *New York Times*. . . .

If being involved in newsworthy events is not the appropriate test for whether a person is a public figure, then what are the dispositive factors?

Consider *Atlanta Journal-Constitution v. Jewell,* 555 S.E.2d 175 (Ga. Ct. App. 2001). Richard Jewell, a security guard in Olympic Park during the 1996 Olympics in Atlanta, spotted a suspicious unattended package and helped to evacuate the area. The package contained a bomb, and Jewell was initially recognized as a hero for helping prevent the terrorist attack. The FBI, however, believed that Jewell might have planted the bomb to make himself into a hero, and the FBI's suspicions of Jewell were leaked to the press. The

Atlanta Journal-Constitution published an article entitled "FBI Suspects 'Hero' Guard May Have Planted Bomb." The FBI investigation eventually cleared Jewell. However, during the interim, Jewell's life was turned upside down, and he could not seek employment or even go out in public without being mobbed by reporters. Jewell sued the *Journal-Constitution* for defamation. The trial court held that Jewell was a "voluntary limited-purpose public figure." Jewell appealed, arguing that "he is not [such a public figure] because he did not assume a role of special prominence in the controversy over the safety of Olympic Park, he did not voluntarily thrust himself to the forefront of the controversy of the safety of Olympic Park, and he did not intentionally seek to influence the resolution or outcome of any public controversy surrounding the safety of Olympic Park." The court concluded that the trial court's designation of Jewell as a voluntary limited-purpose public figure was correct:

> In *Silvester v. American Broadcasting Cos.,* 839 F.2d 1491 (11th Cir. 1988), the Eleventh Circuit adopted a three-prong test to determine whether a person is a limited-purpose public figure. Under this test, the court must isolate the public controversy, examine the plaintiff's involvement in the controversy, and determine whether the alleged defamation was germane to the plaintiff's participation in the controversy. Whether a person is a public figure, general or limited, is a question of law for the court to resolve. . . .
>
> While we can envision situations in which news coverage alone would be insufficient to convert Jewell from private citizen to public figure, we agree with the trial court that Jewell's actions show that he voluntarily assumed a position of influence in the controversy. Jewell granted ten interviews and one photo shoot in the three days between the bombing and the reopening of the park, mostly to prominent members of the national press. While no magical number of media appearances is required to render a citizen a public figure, Jewell's participation in the public discussion of the bombing exceeds what has been deemed sufficient to render other citizens public figures. . . .
>
> Furthermore, the United States Supreme Court has held the actual malice rule is applicable whenever "an individual voluntarily injects himself *or is drawn into* a particular public controversy." The evidence in this case, at the very least, supports a finding that Jewell was initially drawn into the controversy unwillingly and thereafter assumed a prominent position as to its outcome. Jewell did not reject any role in the public controversy debate, was a prominent figure in the coverage of the controversy, and, whatever his reticence regarding his media appearances, encountered them voluntarily. . . .
>
> The third prong of the *Silvester* test requires the court to ascertain whether the allegedly defamatory statements were germane to Jewell's participation in the controversy. Anything which might touch on the controversy is relevant. Misstatements wholly unrelated to the controversy do not require a showing of actual malice to be actionable. . . .
>
> Certainly, the information reported regarding Jewell's character was germane to Jewell's participation in the controversy over the Olympic Park's safety. A public figure's talents, education, experience, and motives are relevant to the public's decision to listen to him. The articles and the challenged statements within them dealt with Jewell's status as a suspect in the bombing and his law enforcement background. . . .

> Whether he liked it or not, Jewell became a central figure in the specific public controversy with respect to which he was allegedly defamed: the controversy over park safety. . . .

2. ***Matters of Private Concern: The* Dun & Bradstreet *Case.*** Subsequent to *Gertz*, a plurality of the Court examined whether the *Gertz* rule would apply when, in contrast to the situation in Gertz, the alleged defamatory statements did not involve a matter of public concern. In *Dun & Bradstreet, Inc. v. Greenmoss Builders, Inc.*, 472 U.S. 749 (1985), Dun & Bradstreet, a credit reporting agency, provided an erroneous report about the financial condition of Greenmoss Builders. Upon learning of the defamatory report, the president of Greenmoss called Dun & Bradstreet and asked for a correction and a list of all those to whom Dun & Bradstreet had sent the report. Dun & Bradstreet corrected the report but did not inform Greenmoss of the list of recipients of the report. Greenmoss sued for defamation, winning $50,000 in compensatory or presumed damages and $300,000 in punitive damages. The Court held that this did not involve a matter of public concern and that therefore the *Gertz* rule should not apply:

> The First Amendment interest . . . is less important than the one weighed in Gertz. We have long recognized that not all speech is of equal First Amendment importance. It is speech on "'matters of public concern'" that is "at the heart of the First Amendment's protection." . . .
>
> In contrast, speech on matters of purely private concern is of less First Amendment concern. As a number of state courts, including the court below, have recognized, the role of the Constitution in regulating state libel law is far more limited when the concerns that activated *New York Times* and *Gertz* are absent. . . .
>
> While such speech is not totally unprotected by the First Amendment, its protections are less stringent. In *Gertz*, we found that the state interest in awarding presumed and punitive damages was not "substantial" in view of their effect on speech at the core of First Amendment concern. . . . In light of the reduced constitutional value of speech involving no matters of public concern, we hold that the state interest adequately supports awards of presumed and punitive damages — even absent a showing of "actual malice." . . .

2. FALSE LIGHT

(a) Introduction

PUBLICITY PLACING PERSON IN FALSE LIGHT

Restatement (Second) of Torts § 652E

One who gives publicity to a matter concerning another that places the other before the public in a false light is subject to liability to the other for invasion of his privacy, if

(a) the false light in which the other was placed would be highly offensive to a reasonable person, and

(b) the actor had knowledge of or acted in reckless disregard as to the falsity of the publicized matter and the false light in which the other would be placed.

NOTES & QUESTIONS

1. ***False Light vs. Defamation.*** False light is similar in many respects to defamation. Both torts protect against material false statements. However, defamation requires some form of reputational injury (although, once shown, one can collect for emotional distress). False light, on the other hand, can compensate exclusively for emotional distress. According to the Restatement: "It is enough that he is given unreasonable and highly objectionable publicity that attributes to him characteristics, conduct or beliefs that are false, and so is placed before the public in a false position. When this is the case and the matter attributed to the plaintiff is not defamatory, the rule here stated affords a different remedy, not available in an action for defamation." Comment (b). Since false light does not require reputational harm, a plaintiff can recover for false light that even improves her reputation.[70] While defamation concerns one's status in the community, false light concerns one's peace of mind. As Bryan Lasswell explains, the "false light tort, to the extent distinct from the tort of defamation . . . rests on an awareness that people who are made to seem pathetic or ridiculous may be shunned, and not just people who are thought to be dishonest or incompetent or immoral."[71]

   Another difference between false light and defamation is that false light requires a wider communication of the information. False light requires "publicity," which must be made to the public at large. Defamation requires "publication," which means that the communication merely requires communication to another person.
2. ***Damages for False Light and Defamation.*** In *Braun v. Flynt*, 726 F.2d 245 (5th Cir. 1984), Jeannie Braun worked at an amusement park and performed a routine with "Ralph the Diving Pig." The pig dove into the pool and was fed by Braun from a milk bottle. One of Larry Flynt's publications, *Chic*, a pornographic magazine, obtained a photograph of Braun's act. The picture appeared in a section of the magazine called "Chic Thrills," implying that something kinky was going on. When Braun saw the photograph, she was mortified. She could not return to work and suffered from depression. She sued Flynt for defamation and false light. A jury awarded her actual and punitive damages for both causes of action. Flynt appealed, arguing among other things that liability was barred by the First Amendment. The court, applying the *Gertz* rule, concluded that Braun was not a public figure and that the First Amendment did not bar her recovery. However, the court concluded that she could not recover damages for both false light and defamation. Accordingly, the case was remanded for a new trial on damages.

---

[70] *See, e.g.*, Nathan E. Ray, *Let There Be False Light: Resisting the Growing Trend Against an Important Tort*, 84 Minn. L. Rev. 713, 735 (2000).

[71] Bryan R. Lasswell, *In Defense of False Light: Why False Light Must Remain a Viable Cause of Action*, 34 S. Tex. L. Rev. 149, 176 (1993).

3. ***Critics of the False Light Tort.*** Diane Zimmerman argues: "Most injuries from untruths will, and should, be handled as defamation actions; of those that cannot be, many will either be too trivial to remedy or will not be actionable because the 'falsity' complained of will be constitutionally-protected opinion or ideas."[72] A number of courts agree. Recall *Lake v. Wal-Mart* from Chapter 1. There, the court recognized three of the four Warren and Brandeis privacy torts, declining to recognize false light: "We are concerned that claims under false light are similar to claims of defamation, and to the extent that false light is more expansive than defamation, tension between this tort and the First Amendment is increased." *See also Renwick v. News and Observer Publishing Co.*, 312 S.E.2d 405 (N.C. 1984) (declining to recognize false light tort). Does the false light tort serve a viable purpose?
4. ***Forms of False Light.*** An illustration of the type of misleading statement that can give rise to a false light action is when a mostly true story is somewhat embellished. *See Varnish v. Best Medium Publishing Co.*, 405 F.2d 608 (2d Cir. 1968) (viable false light action for false facts about the relationship between husband and wife who killed herself and their three children). Another example of a false light claim is when one's photograph is used out of context. *See, e.g., Thompson v. Close-up, Inc.*, 98 N.Y.S.2d 300 (1950) (article on drug dealing using the plaintiff's photo); *Holmes v. Curtis Publishing Co.*, 303 F. Supp. 522 (D.S.C. 1969) (use of plaintiff's photo with caption that plaintiff was a high-stakes gambler); *Morrell v. Forbes, Inc.*, 603 F. Supp. 1305 (D. Mass. 1985) (photo used in connection with article about organized crime). In *Wood v. Hustler Magazine*, 736 F.2d 1084 (5th Cir. 1984), a photograph of LaJuan Wood was stolen by another person, who sent it into *Hustler*, a pornographic magazine, along with a forged consent form. *Hustler* sent a mailgram to the address given on the forged consent form asking the sender to call *Hustler*. The sender did, and again lied that there was consent. *Hustler* published LaJuan's photo in its magazine stating: "LaJuan Wood is a 22-year old housewife and mother from Bryan, Texas, whose hobby is collecting arrowheads. Her fantasy is 'to be screwed by two bikers.'" LaJuan sued *Hustler*, and the court held that *Hustler* could be liable for false light because of the "publication of the false and highly offensive fantasy." The court reasoned that the magazine was negligent in making sure that the consent form was valid.
5. ***Obvious Fictions.*** Suppose a story is deliberately designed to be fictional and is so preposterous that a reasonable person could not possibly believe it to be true. Would there be a viable claim for false light? The answer is no, although it must be clear that the story is pure fiction. In *People's Bank and Trust Co. v. Globe International Publishing, Inc.*, 978 F.2d 1065 (8th Cir. 1992), a tabloid ran a story about a 97-year-old woman who became pregnant. The

---

[72] Diane Leehneer Zimmerman, *False Light Invasion of Privacy: The Light That Failed*, 64 N.Y.U. L. Rev. 364, 452 (1989). For a defense of the false light tort, see Ray, *Let There Be False Light, supra*; Lasswell, *In Defense of False Light, supra*; Gary T. Schwartz, *Explaining and Justifying a Limited Tort of False Light Invasion of Privacy*, 41 Case W. Res. L. Rev. 885 (1991).

story used the name of a real person, who sued. The tabloid contended that no reader could reasonably believe that the story was true. The court rejected the contention because the publisher of the tabloid "holds out the publication as factual and true," and it "mingles factual, fictional, and hybrid stories without overtly identifying one from the other."

(b) First Amendment Limitations

TIME, INC. V. HILL

385 U.S. 374 (1967)

[In 1952, the Hill family was held prisoner in their home for 19 hours by three escaped convicts. The family escaped unharmed and were treated courteously by the convicts. The convicts were later killed by police during their apprehension. The story made the front page news. The Hill family tried hard to remain out of the spotlight. Nevertheless, the Hill family's experience was written about in a novel by Joseph Hayes called *The Desperate Hours*. In contrast to the actual events, the book depicted the convicts beating the father and son and making a verbal sexual insult to the daughter. A Broadway play and a movie were made based on the book. In 1955, *Life* magazine published an article entitled "True Crime Inspires Tense Play." The article stated that "Americans all over the country read about the desperate ordeal of the James Hill family" and "read about it in Joseph Hayes's novel, *The Desperate Hours*, inspired by the family's experience." The article then stated: "Now they can see the story re-enacted in Hayes's Broadway play based on the book." Pictures accompanying the article displayed scenes from the play depicting the son being beaten and the daughter biting the hand of a convict. The *Life* magazine photographs were taken in the Hills' former home, where they had been held hostage. The Hills sued under §§ 50–51 of the New York Civil Rights Law, contending that the *Life* article gave the false impression that the play accurately depicted the Hills' experience. A jury awarded the Hills $50,000 compensatory and $25,000 punitive damages.]

BRENNAN, J. . . . The question in this case is whether appellant, publisher of Life Magazine, was denied constitutional protections of speech and press by the application by the New York courts of §§ 50–51 of the New York Civil Rights Law to award appellee damages on allegations that Life falsely reported that a new play portrayed an experience suffered by appellee and his family.

. . . In *New York Times Co. v. Sullivan*, we held that the Constitution delimits a State's power to award damages for libel in actions brought by public officials against critics of their official conduct. Factual error, content defamatory of official reputation, or both, are insufficient for an award of damages for false statements unless actual malice — knowledge that the statements are false or in reckless disregard of the truth — is alleged and proved. . . .

. . . We hold that the constitutional protections for speech and press preclude the application of the New York statute to redress false reports of matters of public interest in the absence of proof that the defendant published the report with knowledge of its falsity or in reckless disregard of the truth.

The guarantees for speech and press are not the preserve of political expression or comment upon public affairs, essential as those are to healthy government. One need only pick up any newspaper or magazine to comprehend the vast range of published matter which exposes persons to public view, both private citizens and public officials. Exposure of the self to others in varying degrees is a concomitant of life in a civilized community. The risk of this exposure is an essential incident of life in a society which places a primary value on freedom of speech and of press. "Freedom of discussion, if it would fulfill its historic function in this nation, must embrace all issues about which information is needed or appropriate to enable the members of society to cope with the exigencies of their period." . . . We have no doubt that the subject of the Life article, the opening of a new play linked to an actual incident, is a matter of public interest. "The line between the informing and the entertaining is too elusive for the protection of . . . (freedom of the press)." Erroneous statement is no less inevitable in such a case than in the case of comment upon public affairs, and in both, if innocent or merely negligent, ". . . it must be protected if the freedoms of expression are to have the 'breathing space' that they 'need . . . to survive' . . . ." *New York Times Co. v. Sullivan*. . . . We create a grave risk of serious impairment of the indispensable service of a free press in a free society if we saddle the press with the impossible burden of verifying to a certainty the facts associated in news articles with a person's name, picture or portrait, particularly as related to nondefamatory matter. Even negligence would be a most elusive standard, especially when the content of the speech itself affords no warning of prospective harm to another through falsity. A negligence test would place on the press the intolerable burden of guessing how a jury might assess the reasonableness of steps taken by it to verify the accuracy of every reference to a name, picture or portrait.

In this context, sanctions against either innocent or negligent misstatement would present a grave hazard of discouraging the press from exercising the constitutional guarantees. Those guarantees are not for the benefit of the press so much as for the benefit of all of us. A broadly defined freedom of the press assures the maintenance of our political system and an open society. Fear of large verdicts in damage suits for innocent or merely negligent misstatement, even fear of the expense involved in their defense, must inevitably cause publishers to "steer . . . wider of the unlawful zone," *New York Times Co. v. Sullivan*, and thus "create the danger that the legitimate utterance will be penalized."

But the constitutional guarantees can tolerate sanctions against calculated falsehood without significant impairment of their essential function. We held in *New York Times* that calculated falsehood enjoyed no immunity in the case of alleged defamation of a public official concerning his official conduct. Similarly, calculated falsehood should enjoy no immunity in the situation here presented us. . . .

. . . Turning to the facts of the present case, the proofs reasonably would support either a jury finding of innocent or merely negligent misstatement by Life, or a finding that Life portrayed the play as a reenactment of the Hill family's experience reckless of the truth or with actual knowledge that the portrayal was false. . . . [The jury instructions were thus defective because they did not instruct the jury that liability could only be found against *Life* if *Life* acted in reckless disregard for the truth or with actual knowledge that the play was false.]

The judgment of the Court of Appeals is set aside and the case is remanded for further proceedings not inconsistent with this opinion. . . .

NOTES & QUESTIONS

1. ***An Inside Look at* Time, Inc. v. Hill.** Before the Supreme Court, the Hills were represented by Richard Nixon, the future President, then in private practice. In a memoir, Leonard Garment, a long-time Nixon advisor, writes: "Nixon's main effort [as the Hills' attorney] was to demonstrate that the magazine had consciously presented the fictionalized play as a 're-enacted' account of the Hill incident." This depiction was, however, "a deliberate falsification," a gimmick "to justify the use of the former Hill home as a 'True Crime' site for the magazine's review of the play."

   Garment also observes that Nixon, in his first argument in any appellate court, "sounded like a polished professional of the bar — his footing confident, his language lawyer-like, his organization clear." Originally, the Court voted 6-3 in favor of the Hills, with Justice Abe Fortas to write the majority opinion. But after Fortas's memorandum was circulated, Justice Hugo Black circulated a pro-press memorandum and was able to convince a majority of the Court to join him in finding for Time.

   Elizabeth Hill committed suicide in August 1971. In Garment's opinion, the magazine article did not cause the suicide, but "troubled persons . . . suffer with special acuteness when they are forced into the spotlight of negative community attention."[73]
2. ***The Time Line of Leading Constitutional Law Cases.*** *Time, Inc. v. Hill* was decided after *New York Times v. Sullivan* but before *Gertz*. Do false light actions involving private figures also have to prove actual malice under *New York Times*? Although the Court never explicitly applied the *Gertz* rule to a false light case, courts are split in cases involving private figures as to whether *Gertz* applies to false light or whether all false light claims must satisfy the more stringent *New York Times* standard. *See, e.g., Braun v. Flynt*, 726 F.2d 245 (5th Cir. 1984) (applying *Gertz*); *Dietz v. Wometco West Michigan TV*, 407 N.W.2d 649 (Mich. App. 1987) (applying *Gertz*); *Dodrill v. Arkansas Democrat*, 590 S.W.2d 840 (Ark. 1979) (applying *New York Times*); *Schifano v. Greene County Greyhound Park, Inc.*, 624 So. 2d 178 (Ala. 1993) (applying *New York Times*). Consider Restatement (Second) of Torts § 652E comment d:

[73] Leonard Garment, *Crazy Rhythm: From Brooklyn and Jazz to Nixon's White House, Watergate, and Beyond* (1997).

> If *Time v. Hill* is modified along the lines of *Gertz v. Robert Welch*, then the reckless-disregard rule would apparently apply if the plaintiff is a public official or public figure and the negligence rule will apply to other plaintiffs.

3. INFLICTION OF EMOTIONAL DISTRESS

Another tort remedy for the dissemination of false or misleading information is the tort of infliction of emotional distress. This tort may also serve as a remedy to the disclosure of true information. As defined by the Restatement (Second) of Torts § 46, the tort requires:

> One who by extreme and outrageous conduct intentionally or recklessly causes severe emotional distress to another is subject to liability for such emotional distress, and if bodily harm to the other results from it, for such bodily harm.

The tort has some significant limitations as a remedy for privacy infringements. First, it requires "extreme and outrageous conduct," which is conduct significantly outside the bounds of propriety. This is quite a high bar for a plaintiff to leap over. Second, it requires "severe emotional distress," and many privacy violations may not be viewed by courts as causing such a high level of psychological turmoil. For example, in *DeGregario v. CBS*, 473 N.Y.S.2d 922 (N.Y. Sup. Ct. 1984), a news segment called "Couples in New York" included video of two construction workers, a male and a female, holding hands. Each was married or engaged to another person. After the video was shot, the workers asked the television crew not to include them in the segment, but they were included anyway. The court rejected their infliction of emotional distress claim because "broadcasting a film depicting unnamed couples engaging in romantic conduct on a public street . . . in a news report about romance cannot be said to be unusual conduct transcending the norms tolerated by a decent society."

In a similar fashion to the privacy torts, the tort of infliction of emotional distress is subject to First Amendment restrictions. Consider the following case:

HUSTLER MAGAZINE V. FALWELL

485 U.S. 46 (1988)

[A 1983 issue of *Hustler* magazine featured a parody using nationally known minister Jerry Falwell's name and photo. The parody, entitled "Jerry Falwell Talks About His First Time," was patterned after a series of ads for a brand of liquor which interviewed celebrities about their "first times" trying the liquor (but playing on the sexual double meaning). In a similar layout, *Hustler*'s parody interview with Falwell had him drunk and engaging in incest with his mother. In small print, the parody contained the disclaimer, "ad parody — not to be taken seriously." Falwell sued for, among other things, intentional infliction of emotional distress. This issue made it up to the U.S. Supreme Court, where the Court confronted the task of defining whether the First Amendment limitations that applied to defamation and false light also be applied to intentional infliction of emotional distress.]

REHNQUIST, C.J. . . . "Freedoms of expression require 'breathing space.'" This breathing space is provided by a constitutional rule that allows public figures to recover for libel or defamation only when they can prove *both* that the statement was false and that the statement was made with the requisite level of culpability.

Respondent argues, however, that a different standard should apply in this case because here the State seeks to prevent not reputational damage, but the severe emotional distress suffered by the person who is the subject of an offensive publication. *Cf. Zacchini v. Scripps-Howard Broadcasting Co.*, 433 U.S. 562 (ruling that the "actual malice" standard does not apply to the tort of appropriation of a right of publicity). In respondent's view, and in the view of the Court of Appeals, so long as the utterance was intended to inflict emotional distress, was outrageous, and did in fact inflict serious emotional distress, it is of no constitutional import whether the statement was a fact or an opinion, or whether it was true or false. It is the intent to cause injury that is the gravamen of the tort, and the State's interest in preventing emotional harm simply outweighs whatever interest a speaker may have in speech of this type.

Generally speaking the law does not regard the intent to inflict emotional distress as one which should receive much solicitude, and it is quite understandable that most if not all jurisdictions have chosen to make it civilly culpable where the conduct in question is sufficiently "outrageous." But in the world of debate about public affairs, many things done with motives that are less than admirable are protected by the First Amendment. . . .

Thus while such a bad motive may be deemed controlling for purposes of tort liability in other areas of the law, we think the First Amendment prohibits such a result in the area of public debate about public figures.

Were we to hold otherwise, there can be little doubt that political cartoonists and satirists would be subjected to damages awards without any showing that their work falsely defamed its subject. Webster's defines a caricature as "the deliberately distorted picturing or imitating of a person, literary style, etc. by exaggerating features or mannerisms for satirical effect." Webster's New Unabridged Twentieth Century Dictionary of the English Language 275 (2d ed. 1979). The appeal of the political cartoon or caricature is often based on exploitation of unfortunate physical traits or politically embarrassing events — an exploitation often calculated to injure the feelings of the subject of the portrayal. The art of the cartoonist is often not reasoned or evenhanded, but slashing and one-sided. . . .

Several famous examples of this type of intentionally injurious speech were drawn by Thomas Nast, probably the greatest American cartoonist to date, who was associated for many years during the post-Civil War era with Harper's Weekly. In the pages of that publication Nast conducted a graphic vendetta against William M. "Boss" Tweed and his corrupt associates in New York City's "Tweed Ring." . . .

Despite their sometimes caustic nature, from the early cartoon portraying George Washington as an ass down to the present day, graphic depictions and satirical cartoons have played a prominent role in public and political debate. Nast's castigation of the Tweed Ring, Walt McDougall's characterization of Presidential candidate James G. Blaine's banquet with the millionaires at

Delmonico's as "The Royal Feast of Belshazzar," and numerous other efforts have undoubtedly had an effect on the course and outcome of contemporaneous debate. Lincoln's tall, gangling posture, Teddy Roosevelt's glasses and teeth, and Franklin D. Roosevelt's jutting jaw and cigarette holder have been memorialized by political cartoons with an effect that could not have been obtained by the photographer or the portrait artist. From the viewpoint of history it is clear that our political discourse would have been considerably poorer without them. Respondent contends, however, that the caricature in question here was so "outrageous" as to distinguish it from more traditional political cartoons. There is no doubt that the caricature of respondent and his mother published in Hustler is at best a distant cousin of the political cartoons described above, and a rather poor relation at that. If it were possible by laying down a principled standard to separate the one from the other, public discourse would probably suffer little or no harm. But we doubt that there is any such standard, and we are quite sure that the pejorative description "outrageous" does not supply one. "Outrageousness" in the area of political and social discourse has an inherent subjectiveness about it which would allow a jury to impose liability on the basis of the jurors' tastes or views, or perhaps on the basis of their dislike of a particular expression. An "outrageousness" standard thus runs afoul of our longstanding refusal to allow damages to be awarded because the speech in question may have an adverse emotional impact on the audience. . . .

We conclude that public figures and public officials may not recover for the tort of intentional infliction of emotional distress by reason of publications such as the one here at issue without showing in addition that the publication contains a false statement of fact which was made with "actual malice," *i.e.*, with knowledge that the statement was false or with reckless disregard as to whether or not it was true. This is not merely a "blind application" of the *New York Times* standard, see *Time, Inc. v. Hill*, 385 U.S. 374 (1967), it reflects our considered judgment that such a standard is necessary to give adequate "breathing space" to the freedoms protected by the First Amendment.

Here it is clear that respondent Falwell is a "public figure" for purposes of First Amendment law. The jury found against respondent on his libel claim when it decided that the Hustler ad parody could not "reasonably be understood as describing actual facts about [respondent] or actual events in which [he] participated." The Court of Appeals interpreted the jury's finding to be that the ad parody "was not reasonably believable," and in accordance with our custom we accept this finding. Respondent is thus relegated to his claim for damages awarded by the jury for the intentional infliction of emotional distress by "outrageous" conduct. But for reasons heretofore stated this claim cannot, consistently with the First Amendment, form a basis for the award of damages when the conduct in question is the publication of a caricature such as the ad parody involved here. . . .

D. APPROPRIATION OF NAME OR LIKENESS

1. INTRODUCTION

APPROPRIATION OF NAME OR LIKENESS

Restatement (Second) of Torts § 652C

One who appropriates to his own use or benefit the name or likeness of another is subject to liability to the other for invasion of his privacy.

NOTES & QUESTIONS

1. ***The Development of the Appropriation Tort.*** The tort of appropriation protects "the interest of the individual in the exclusive use of his own identity, in so far as it is represented by his name or likeness, and in so far as the use may be of benefit to him or to others." Restatement § 652C, comment (a). To be liable for appropriation, "the defendant must have appropriated to his own use or benefit the reputation, prestige, social or commercial standing, public interest or other values of the plaintiff's name or likeness." *Id.*, comment (c).

   Recall from section A that two of the first cases to address the creation of new causes of action in response to the Warren and Brandeis article — *Roberson* and *Pavesich* — both involved appropriation claims.

   One of the most widely discussed state appropriation tort formulations is that of New York. New York's statute, passed in response to *Roberson*, which refused to recognize the tort in the common law, provides criminal and civil remedies for appropriation. Pursuant to New York Civil Rights Law § 50:

   > A person, firm or corporation that uses for advertising purposes, or for the purposes of trade, the name, portrait or picture of any living person without having first obtained the written consent of such person, or if a minor of his or her parent or guardian, is guilty of a misdemeanor.

   New York Civil Rights Law § 51 provides a civil remedy:

   > Any person whose name, portrait, picture or voice is used within this state for advertising purposes or for the purposes of trade without the written consent first obtained . . . may maintain an equitable action in the supreme court of this state against the person, firm or corporation so using his name, portrait, picture or voice, to prevent and restrain the use thereof; and may also sue and recover damages for any injuries sustained by reason of such use. . . .

   California has a similar statute, which provides: "Any person who knowingly uses another's name, photograph or likeness, in any manner, for purposes of advertising . . . or for purposes of solicitation of purchases of products . . . without . . . prior consent . . . shall be liable for any damages. . . ." Cal. Civ. Code § 3344. In many states, the tort of appropriation is recognized through the common law and is not statutory in nature.

2. ***Appropriation and the "Right of Publicity."*** The original rationale for the tort of appropriation was privacy-based, as a protection of one's dignity against the exploitation of her identity. However, another rationale for the tort has emerged, one that is property-based. Many courts and commentators refer to this alternative rationale as the "right of publicity."[74] The "right of publicity" was first referred to as such in *Haelan Laboratories v. Topps Chewing Gum, Inc.*, 202 F.2d 866 (2d Cir. 1953), where Judge Jerome Frank held that New York recognized a common law tort of "publicity" distinct from §§ 50–51's remedy for appropriation:

> We think that, in addition to and independent of that right of privacy (which in New York derives from statute), a man has a right in the publicity value of his photograph, i.e., the right to grant the exclusive privilege of publishing his picture, and that such a grant may validly be made "in gross," i.e., without an accompanying transfer of a business or of anything else. Whether it be labeled a "property" right is immaterial; for here, as often elsewhere, the tag "property" simply symbolizes the fact that courts enforce a claim which has pecuniary worth.
>
> This right might be called a "right of publicity." For it is common knowledge that many prominent persons (especially actors and ball-players), far from having their feelings bruised through public exposure of their likenesses, would feel sorely deprived if they no longer received money for authorizing advertisements, popularizing their countenances, displayed in newspapers, magazines, busses, trains and subways.

Subsequently, courts held that the publicity tort was subsumed under § 51 and was not a common law cause of action. *See Welch v. Group W Productions, Inc.*, 525 N.Y.S.2d 466, 468 n.1 (N.Y. Sup. Ct. 1987) ("In New York State the so-called 'right of publicity' is merely an aspect of the right of privacy and is not an independent common-law right.").

How is the "right of publicity" distinct from the privacy interests involved in appropriation? As one court describes the distinction:

> The privacy-based action is designed for individuals who have not placed themselves in the public eye. It shields such people from the embarrassment of having their faces plastered on billboards and cereal boxes without their permission. The interests protected are dignity and peace of mind, and damages are measured in terms of emotional distress. By contrast, a right of publicity action is designed for individuals who have placed themselves in the public eye. It secures for them the exclusive right to exploit the commercial value that attaches to their identities by virtue of their celebrity. The right to publicity protects that value as property, and its infringement is a commercial, rather than a personal tort. Damages stem not from embarrassment but from the unauthorized use of the plaintiffs' property. *Jim Henson Productions, Inc. v. John T. Brady & Associates, Inc.*, 687 F. Supp. 185, 188-89 (S.D.N.Y. 1994).

---

[74] J. Thomas McCarthy, *The Rights of Publicity and Privacy* (2000); Melville B. Nimmer, *The Right of Publicity*, 19 Law & Contemp. Probs. 203 (1954); Sheldon Halpern, *The Right of Publicity: Maturation of an Independent Right Protecting the Associative Value of Personality*, 46 Hastings L.J. 853 (1995); Oliver R. Goodenough, *Go Fish: Evaluating the Restatement's Formulation of the Law of Publicity*, 47 S.C. L. Rev. 709 (1996).

Thomas McCarthy articulates the distinction most succinctly: "Simplistically put, while the appropriation branch of the right of privacy is invaded by an injury to the psyche, the right of publicity is infringed by an injury to the pocket book."[75]

The Restatement (Third) of the Law of Unfair Competition § 46 provides for a distinct tort of "publicity":

> *Appropriation of the Commercial Value of a Person's Identity: The Right of Publicity.* One who appropriates the commercial value of a person's identity by using without consent the person's name, likeness, or other indicia of identity for purposes of trade is subject to liability for [monetary and injunctive] relief.

The commentary to the Restatement § 46 contrasts the "publicity" right in § 46 with the "appropriation tort" in the Restatement of Torts: "The 'appropriation' tort as described by Prosser and the Restatement, Second, of Torts, subsumes harm to both personal and commercial interests caused by an unauthorized exploitation of the plaintiff's identity." Restatement (Third) of the Law of Unfair Competition § 46 comment (b). A number of jurisdictions recognize a distinct tort of "publicity."

Although there is now a separate "right of publicity" to protect property interests, the tort of appropriation has shifted towards being a property protection similar to the right of publicity. William Prosser, in his 1960 article describing the torts spawned by Warren and Brandeis's article, did not recognize a distinct tort of publicity; it was merely a part of the appropriation tort. Likewise, the Restatement (Second) of Torts did not recognize a distinct tort of publicity. However, according to the Restatement, it appears that the central interest protected by appropriation is property rather than privacy: "Although the protection of [a person's] personal feelings against mental distress is an important factor leading to a recognition of the [appropriation tort], the right created by it is in the nature of a property right. . . ." Restatement (Second) of Torts § 652C, comment (a). A number of jurisdictions follow this approach. *See Ainsworth v. Century Supply Co.*, 693 N.E.2d 510 (Ill. App. 1998); *Candlebat v. Flanagan*, 487 So. 2d 207 (Miss. 1986). According to Jonathan Kahn:

> While publicity is grounded in property rights, appropriation of identity involves the personal right to privacy. Publicity rights implicate monetary interests. In contrast, privacy rights protect and vindicate less tangible personal interests in dignity and integrity of the self. However, both rights are clearly linked and find their common origin in American law around the turn of this century. Yet over the years, the privacy-based tort of appropriation has receded into the background as its flashier cousin, publicity, has risen to prominence. Such is perhaps to be expected in a world where seemingly everything has been turned into a saleable commodity.[76]

---

[75] J. Thomas McCarthy, *The Rights of Publicity and Privacy* § 5:61, at pp. 5-110 (2000).

[76] Jonathan Kahn, *Bringing Dignity Back to Light: Publicity Rights and the Eclipse of the Tort of Appropriation of Identity,* 17 Cardozo Arts & Ent. L.J. 213, 213-14 (1999); *see also* Jonathan Kahn, *What's in a Name? Law's Identity Under the Tort of Appropriation,* 74 Temp. L. Rev. 263 (2001).

Is privacy or property the central interest of appropriation? Or does the tort adequately redress both interests?

2. NAME OR LIKENESS

CARSON V. HERE'S JOHNNY PORTABLE TOILETS, INC.

698 F.2d 831 (6th Cir. 1983)

BROWN, J. . . . Appellant, John W. Carson (Carson), is the host and star of "The Tonight Show," a well-known television program broadcast five nights a week by the National Broadcasting Company. . . . From the time he began hosting "The Tonight Show" in 1962, he has been introduced [by Ed McMahon] on the show each night with the phrase "Here's Johnny." . . . The phrase "Here's Johnny" is generally associated with Carson by a substantial segment of the television viewing public. In 1967, Carson first authorized use of this phrase by an outside business venture, permitting it to be used by a chain of restaurants called "Here's Johnny Restaurants." . . .

. . . The phrase "Here's Johnny" has never been registered by appellants as a trademark or service mark.

Appellee, Here's Johnny Portable Toilets, Inc., is a Michigan corporation engaged in the business of renting and selling "Here's Johnny" portable toilets. Appellee's founder was aware at the time he formed the corporation that "Here's Johnny" was the introductory slogan for Carson on "The Tonight Show." He indicated that he coupled the phrase with a second one, "The World's Foremost Commodian," to make "a good play on a phrase."

[Carson brought an action for, among other things, invasion of privacy and the right to publicity.]

We do not believe that Carson's claim that his right of privacy has been invaded is supported by the law or the facts. Apparently, the gist of this claim is that Carson is embarrassed by and considers it odious to be associated with the appellee's product. Clearly, the association does not appeal to Carson's sense of humor. But the facts here presented do not, it appears to us, amount to an invasion of any of the interests protected by the right of privacy. . . .

The right of publicity has developed to protect the commercial interest of celebrities in their identities. The theory of the right is that a celebrity's identity can be valuable in the promotion of products, and the celebrity has an interest that may be protected from the unauthorized commercial exploitation of that identity. . . .

The district court dismissed appellants' claim based on the right of publicity because appellee does not use Carson's name or likeness. . . . We believe that, on the contrary, the district court's conception of the right of publicity is too narrow. The right of publicity, as we have stated, is that a celebrity has a protected pecuniary interest in the commercial exploitation of his identity. If the celebrity's identity is commercially exploited, there has been an invasion of his right whether or not his "name or likeness" is used. Carson's identity may be exploited even if his name, John W. Carson, or his picture is not used. . . .

In this case, Earl Braxton, president and owner of Here's Johnny Portable Toilets, Inc., admitted that he knew that the phrase "Here's Johnny" had been used for years to introduce Carson. Moreover, in the opening statement in the district court, appellee's counsel stated:

> Now, we've stipulated in this case that the public tends to associate the words "Johnny Carson," the words "Here's Johnny" with plaintiff, John Carson and, Mr. Braxton, in his deposition, admitted that he knew that and probably absent that identification, he would not have chosen it.

That the "Here's Johnny" name was selected by Braxton because of its identification with Carson was the clear inference from Braxton's testimony irrespective of such admission in the opening statement.

We therefore conclude that, applying the correct legal standards, appellants are entitled to judgment. The proof showed without question that appellee had appropriated Carson's identity in connection with its corporate name and its product. . . .

. . . It is not fatal to appellant's claim that appellee did not use his "name." Indeed, there would have been no violation of his right of publicity even if appellee had used his name, such as "J. William Carson Portable Toilet" or the "John William Carson Portable Toilet" or the "J. W. Carson Portable Toilet." The reason is that, though literally using appellant's "name," the appellee would not have appropriated Carson's identity as a celebrity. Here there was an appropriation of Carson's identity without using his "name.". . .

KENNEDY, J. dissenting. . . . The majority's extension of the right of publicity to include phrases or other things which are merely associated with the individual permits a popular entertainer or public figure, by associating himself or herself with a common phrase, to remove those words from the public domain. . . .

. . . [T]he majority is awarding Johnny Carson a windfall, rather than vindicating his economic interests, by protecting the phrase "Here's Johnny" which is merely associated with him. In *Zacchini*, the Supreme Court stated that a mechanism to vindicate an individual's economic rights is indicated where the appropriated thing is "the product of . . . [the individual's] own talents and energy, the end result of much time, effort and expense." There is nothing in the record to suggest that "Here's Johnny" has any nexus to Johnny Carson other than being the introduction to his personal appearances. The phrase is not part of an identity that he created. In its content "Here's Johnny" is a very simple and common introduction. The content of the phrase neither originated with Johnny Carson nor is it confined to the world of entertainment. The phrase is not said by Johnny Carson, but said of him. Its association with him is derived, in large part, by the context in which it is said — generally by Ed McMahon in a drawn out and distinctive voice after the theme music to "The Tonight Show" is played, and immediately prior to Johnny Carson's own entrance. Appellee's use of the content "Here's Johnny," in light of its value as a double entendre, written on its product and corporate name, and therefore outside of the context in which it is associated with Johnny Carson, does little to rob Johnny Carson of something which is unique to him or a product of his own efforts. . . .

Protection under the right of publicity confers a monopoly on the protected individual that is potentially broader, offers fewer protections and potentially competes with federal statutory monopolies. As an essential part of three federal monopoly rights, copyright, trademark and patents, notice to the public is required in the form of filing with the appropriate governmental office and use of an appropriate mark. This apprises members of the public of the nature and extent of what is being removed from the public domain and subject to claims of infringement. The right of publicity provides limited notice to the public of the extent of the monopoly right to be asserted, if one is to be asserted at all. As the right of privacy is expanded beyond protections of name, likeness and actual performances, which provide relatively objective notice to the public of the extent of an individual's rights, to more subjective attributes such as achievements and identifying characteristics, the public's ability to be on notice of a common law monopoly right, if one is even asserted by a given famous individual, is severely diminished. Protecting phrases and other things merely associated with an individual provides virtually no notice to the public at all of what is claimed to be protected. By ensuring the invocation of the adjudicative process whenever the commercial use of a phrase or other associated thing is considered to have been wrongfully appropriated, the public is left to act at their peril. The result is a chilling effect on commercial innovation and opportunity.

Also unlike the federal statutory monopolies, this common law monopoly right offers no protections against the monopoly existing for an indefinite time or even in perpetuity. . . .

NOTES & QUESTIONS

1. ***Privacy or Property?*** In *Carson*, Johnny Carson made two claims. First, he contended that a privacy interest was violated because his identity was being associated with toilets, which he found quite unflattering. The court appears to reject this claim. Carson's other claim is that a property interest was violated by his valuable identity being stolen and used for the commercial purposes of another. What do you think was the real reason Carson brought this suit? To vindicate his privacy interest, his property interest, or both? Suppose Carson were not famous and his name had little value. Would he be likely to succeed under the reasoning of the court?
2. ***What Constitutes "Name or Likeness"?*** The appropriation tort has been extended far beyond a person's actual name and likeness. Courts have held that the use of well-known nicknames can give rise to an appropriation action. In *Hirsch v. S.C. Johnson & Son, Inc.*, 280 N.W.2d 129 (Wis. 1979), the Supreme Court of Wisconsin found that an unauthorized commercial use of Elroy Hirsch's (a famous football player) nickname "Crazylegs" raised triable issues regarding violation of the appropriation tort. S.C. Johnson had used "Crazylegs" as the product name for a shaving gel for women. The court rejected the argument that an appropriation claim by Hirsch was not possible because Crazylegs was his nickname, not his actual name. It stated that to overcome the lower court's rejection of the cause of action, "[a]ll that is required is that the name clearly identify the wronged person." It also declared

that "[t]he question whether Crazylegs identifies Elroy Hirsch, however, is one of fact to be determined by the jury on remand. . . ."

Courts have also held that certain drawings depicting one's profession but otherwise with no distinctive facial characteristics can still give rise to an appropriation claim. In *Ali v. Playgirl, Inc.*, 447 F. Supp. 723 (S.D.N.Y. 1978), Muhammad Ali, former heavyweight boxing champion, sued *Playgirl* magazine for appropriation when the magazine published a drawing of a nude African-American male sitting on a stool in a corner of a boxing ring with hands taped. The drawing did not mention Ali's name and was entitled "Mystery Man," but accompanying text identified the man in the drawing as "The Greatest." Because "The Greatest" was Ali's nickname, the picture was sufficiently identifiable as Ali to constitute his likeness. The court emphasized the offensive nature of the full frontal nude of Ali; the fact that the portrait was clearly one of Ali; and that the publication was for "purposes of trade" within New York Civil Rights Law § 51. It stated, "the picture is a dramatization, an illustration falling somewhere between representational art and cartoon, and is accompanied by a plainly fictional and allegedly libelous bit of doggerel."

Appropriation has even been extended to identifying characteristics. In *Motschenbacher v. R.J. Reynolds Tobacco Co.*, 498 F.2d 821 (9th Cir. 1974), a famous race car driver alleged that a photograph of his distinctive racing car, which did not include a likeness of himself or use his name, was nevertheless an appropriation of his name or likeness. The court agreed. The photograph did use a "likeness" of the plaintiff because the "distinctive decorations" on his car "were not only peculiar to the plaintiff's cars but they caused some persons to think the car in question was plaintiff's and to infer that the person driving the car was the plaintiff."

Further, appropriation can also extend to use of a look-alike model. In *Onassis v. Christian Dior*, 472 N.Y.S. 2d 254 (N.Y. Supp. 1984), Jacqueline Kennedy Onassis won an injunction against use of a look-alike model in an advertisement. The *Onassis* court found a cause of action under the New York Civil Rights Law § 51, so long as the advertisement created an illusion that the plaintiff herself had appeared in the advertisement.

In *Zacchini v. Scripps-Howard Broadcasting Co.*, 433 U.S. 562 (1977), excerpted below, the plaintiff brought an appropriation action for his distinctive performance act.

Courts have extended appropriation to fictitious personas created by an individual. *See Groucho Marx Productions, Inc. v. Day & Night Co.*, 523 F. Supp. 485 (S.D.N.Y. 1981) (the characters of Groucho, Harpo, and Chico, also known as the Marx Brothers); *Price v. Hal Roach Studios, Inc.*, 400 F. Supp. 836 (S.D.N.Y. 1975) (Laurel & Hardy characters).

Courts have also recognized appropriation liability for the imitation of one's voice. In *Midler v. Ford Motor Co.*, 849 F.2d 460 (9th Cir. 1988), the Ninth Circuit held that singer Bette Midler had a viable cause of action for appropriation for the use of a singer to imitate her voice in a commercial. When a voice is a sufficient indication of the celebrity's identity, appropriation protects against a company hiring someone to imitate it for commercial purposes without the celebrity's consent.

In a later sound-alike case, the Ninth Circuit found for Tom Waits, a singer with a distinctive sound. *Waits v. Frito Lay*, 978 F. 2d 1093 (9th Cir. 1992). The court noted that Waits had "a distinctive gravelly singing voice, described by one fan as 'like how you'd sound if you drank a quart of bourbon, smoked a pack of cigarettes and swallowed a pack of razor blades. . . . Late at night. After not sleeping for three days.'" Like the *Midler* court, the *Waits* court upheld a jury verdict that found the celebrity plaintiff had a voice that was distinctive, widely known, and deliberately imitated by a defendant for a commercial purpose. The Ninth Circuit added that even if Tom Waits was not as well known as Bette Midler, "'[w]ell-known' is a relative term, and differences in the extent of celebrity are adequately reflected in the amount of damages recoverable."

In contrast, a court has rejected an appropriation actions for the "fictionalized version" of a celebrity's life story. *See, e.g., Guglielmi v. Spelling-Goldberg Productions*, 603 P.2d 454 (Cal. 1979). The celebrity in question in that case was Rudolf Valentino; his nephew had brought the action. At the time of this opinion, the applicable law in California held that publicity rights were not inheritable. This result is now different in California and other states; see the discussion in the note below. The *Guglielmi* court also found that the right of publicity did not outweigh freedom of expression in this context. Otherwise, "the creation of historical novels and other works inspired by actual events and people would be off limits to the fictional author."

3. ***Property Rights and Creativity.*** Consider the following argument against the propertization of identity by Judge Kozinski dissenting from the denial of a petition for rehearing en banc in *White v. Samsung Electronics America, Inc.*, 989 F.2d 1512 (9th Cir. 1993):

> . . . Saddam Hussein wants to keep advertisers from using his picture in unflattering contexts. Clint Eastwood doesn't want tabloids to write about him. Rudolf Valentino's heirs want to control his film biography. The Girl Scouts don't want their image soiled by association with certain activities. . . . And scads of copyright holders see purple when their creations are made fun of.
>
> Something very dangerous is going on here. . . .
>
> . . . Overprotecting intellectual property is as harmful as underprotecting it. Creativity is impossible without a rich public domain. . . .
>
> . . . Intellectual property rights aren't free. They're imposed at the expense of future creators and of the public at large. Where would we be if Charles Lindbergh had an exclusive right in the concept of a heroic solo aviator? If Arthur Conan Doyle had gotten a copyright in the idea of the detective story, or Albert Einstein had patented the theory of relativity? If every author and celebrity had been given the right to keep people from mocking them or their work? Surely this would have made the world poorer, not richer, culturally as well as economically. . . .

4. ***Property Rights, the Manufacturing of Identity, and Social Meanings.*** One of the predominant rationales for the right of publicity is that the celebrity,

through her labor, creates her persona. But, with regard to celebrities, does this rationale always hold true? According to Michael Madow, the identity of a celebrity is "the product of a complex social process in which the 'labor' of the celebrity is but one ingredient, and not always the main one."[77] In a similar argument, Rosemary Coombe observes: "Star images are authored by studios, the mass media, public relations agencies, fan clubs, gossip columnists, photographers, hairdressers, body-building coaches, athletic trainers, teachers, screenwriters, ghostwriters, directors, lawyers, and doctors."[78] Why should we afford celebrities property rights in their names and likenesses when frequently a celebrity's persona is manufactured by others?

Madow also argues that individuals and groups participating actively in the process of generating and circulating meanings that constitute "culture." Thus, "against-the-grain readings" of mainstream cultural products are possible. As an example, Madow points to the example of a card showing "John Wayne, wearing cowboy hat and bright red lipstick, above the caption, 'It's such a bitch being butch.'" Wayne's children, among others, objected to the card. Madow comments:

> Against-the-grain readings of John Wayne are also possible. For instance, in a course on how to survive as a prisoner of war, the U.S. Navy uses the term "John Wayning it" to mean trying foolishly to hold out against brutal torture. The particular greeting card that Wayne's children and others objected to so strenuously represents an even more subversive inflection of Wayne's image. The card uses his image to interrogate and challenge mainstream conceptions of masculinity and heterosexuality. It recodes Wayne's image so as to make it carry a cultural meaning that presumably works for gay men, among others, but which Wayne's children (and no doubt many of his fans) find deeply offensive. . . .
>
> What it comes down to, then, is that the power to license is the power to suppress. When the law gives a celebrity a right of publicity, it does more than funnel additional income her way. It gives her (or her assignee) a substantial measure of power over the production and circulation of meaning and identity in our society: power, if she so chooses, to suppress readings or appropriations of her persona that depart from, challenge, or subvert the meaning she prefers; power to deny to others the use of her persona in the construction and communication of alternative or oppositional identities and social relations; power, ultimately, to limit the expressive and communicative opportunities of the rest of us. The result is a potentially significant narrowing of the space available for alternative cultural and dialogic practice. Publicity rights, in other words, move us even further away from what John Fiske has called a "semiotic democracy" — a society in which all persons are free and able to participate actively, if not equally, in the generation and circulation of meanings and values.

---

[77] Michael T. Madow, *Private Ownership of Public Image: Popular Culture and Publicity Rights*, 81 Cal. L. Rev. 127, 195 (1993).

[78] Rosemary J. Coombe, *The Cultural Life of Intellectual Properties: Authorship, Appropriation, and the Law* 94 (1998).

Do you agree that the tort of appropriation and right of publicity threaten popular cultural production? Or will social debate about the meaning of John Wayne, Madonna, or Elvis continue, more or less unaffected, in spite of these legal interests?

5. ***Are Privacy and Property Rights Mutually Exclusive?*** According to Robert Post, the right of publicity views one's personality as "commodified," as an object separate from oneself that can be valued by the market. In his view, Warren and Brandeis's right to privacy, in contrast, "attaches personality firmly to the actual identity of a living individual." The right of publicity protects personality as detachable from individuals, as a commodity that can be bought and sold (and can persist after the death of the individual). The right to privacy, in contrast, protects personality as constitutive of the individual. Post suggests that perhaps we need both property rights and privacy rights to protect our personalities: "Personality can so effortlessly be legally embodied by either property or privacy rights precisely because it embraces both these aspects."[79]

3. FOR ONE'S OWN USE OR BENEFIT

The Restatement of Torts recognizes appropriation of another's name or likeness when it is used for the appropriator's "own use or benefit." Consider the Restatement § 652C comment (b):

> The common form of invasion of privacy under the rule here stated is the appropriation and use of the plaintiff's name or likeness to advertise the defendant's business or product, or for some similar commercial purpose. Apart from statute, however, the rule stated is not limited to commercial appropriation. It applies also when the defendant makes use of the plaintiff's name or likeness for his own purposes and benefit, even though the use is not a commercial one, and even though the benefit sought to be obtained is not a pecuniary one. Statutes in some states have, however, limited the liability to commercial uses of the name or likeness.

What does "use or benefit" mean? In many jurisdictions, appropriation occurs only when the use or benefit is commercial in nature — i.e., used to promote or endorse a service or product.

RAYMEN V. UNITED SENIOR ASSOCIATION, INC.

409 F. Supp. 2d 15 (D.D.C. 2006)

WALTON, J. On March 9, 2005, the plaintiffs filed this action seeking to prevent the defendants from further using their images in an advertising campaign which challenged various public policy positions taken by the American Association of Retired Persons ("AARP") regarding Social Security reform and the military.

[79] Robert C. Post, *Rereading Warren and Brandeis: Privacy, Property, and Appropriation*, 41 Case W. Res. L. Rev. 647 (1991).

Currently before the Court are the defendants' motions to dismiss, and the plaintiffs' opposition thereto. . . .

On March 3, 2004, the plaintiffs were among 300 citizens of Multnomah County, Oregon who were married pursuant to a newly established right to same-sex marriage in that county. While at City Hall awaiting their opportunity to marry, the plaintiffs, Steve Hansen and Richard Raymen, kissed. A photographer from a Portland, Oregon newspaper, the *Tribune,* captured the kiss in a photograph he took. The photograph was subsequently published in both the *Tribune* newspaper on March 4, 2004, and later on the *Tribune*'s website. At some later point in time, the *Tribune*'s website photograph was used without permission as part of an advertisement created by defendant Mark Montini. The advertising campaign was created for a nonprofit organization, United Senior Association, Inc., which does business under the name USA Next. The advertisement, which features the photograph of the plaintiffs kissing, was part of a campaign by USA Next challenging various public policy positions purportedly taken by the AARP. Specifically, the advertisement contains two pictures. The first is a picture of an American soldier, who presumably is in Iraq, with a red "X" superimposed over it, and the second is the photograph of the plaintiffs with a green checkmark superimposed over it. The caption under the advertisement reads: "The Real AARP Agenda," suggesting that the AARP opposes the United States military efforts abroad and supports the gay lifestyle. This advertisement ran on the website of *The American Spectator* magazine from February 15, 2005, to February 21, 2005.

According to the plaintiffs, the purpose of the advertising campaign was "to incite viewer passions against the AARP because of its alleged support of equal marriage rights for same-sex couples and its alleged lack of support of American troops." Moreover, the plaintiffs opine that the "advertisement also conveys the message that the plaintiffs . . . are against American troops . . . and are unpatriotic." The plaintiffs contend that the advertisement attracted media attention, which then caused an even wider distribution of the advertisement throughout the media. The plaintiffs assert that because of the advertisement, they "have suffered embarrassment, extreme emotional distress, and the invasion of their privacy." In addition, the plaintiffs represent that as a result of the false and misleading inference "communicated by the [a]dvertisement about [the] plaintiffs, their reputations as patriotic American citizens has been severely damaged." . . .

"'One who appropriates to his own use or benefit the name or likeness of another is subject to liability to the other for invasion of his privacy.'" *Martinez v. Democrat-Herald Publ'g Co., Inc.,* 669 P.2d 818, 820 (1983) (quoting Restatement (Second) of Torts § 652C (1976)). Under § 652C of the Restatement, plaintiffs can recover "damages when their names, pictures or other likenesses have been used without their consent to advertise a defendant's product, to accompany an article sold, to add luster to the name of a corporation or for some other business purpose." However, there is no actionable appropriation of a person's likeness claim "when a person's picture is used to illustrate a noncommercial, newsworthy article." . . . Whether a communication is commercial or noncommercial is a question of law. . . .

The photograph of the plaintiffs was used as part of USA Next's advertising campaign, which sought, at least in part, to engender opposition to AARP's policy position on social security reform. Presumably, the advertisement sought to vilify the AARP by conveying a message concerning AARP's alleged views on two hot button policy issues — support of same-sex marriage and opposition to the military. While the advertisement itself lacked any substantive discussion of these issues, it did convey AARP's purported position on both subjects. And someone who viewed the advertisement online could then access the USA Next's webpages which described the organization and its position on Social Security reform. Clearly the issues of same-sex marriage and support for the military are issues of public concern and both have been widely discussed in the media. In fact, the plaintiffs contend in their complaint that the purpose of the advertisement was to influence Congress.

The plaintiffs' argument that the advertisement is commercial in nature because it sought contributions and promoted USA Next's lobbying services, is unpersuasive. First, nothing in the advertisement itself seeks donations. Rather, only after using the advertisement (by clicking on it) to access the webpages were viewers exposed to the information about USA Next and the solicitation for financial contributions. This Court cannot conclude that this detached solicitation elevates the advertisement itself to a level where it can be deemed commercial in nature. *See, e.g., Martinez,* 669 P.2d at 820 ("The fact that the defendant is engaged in the business of publication, for example of a newspaper, out of which he makes or seeks to make a profit, is not enough to make the incidental publication of a commercial use of the name or likeness.") (quoting Restatement (Second) Torts § 652C, cmt. D (1976)). Moreover, contrary to the plaintiffs' assertion, this case is not analogous to . . . *Beverley v. Choices Women's Med. Ctr. Inc.,* 587 N.E.2d 275 (N.Y. 1991). . . .

In *Beverley,* the Court concluded that a calendar produced by a for-profit hospital was commercial in nature because it had the hospital's "name, logo, address, and telephone number on each page of the calendar," along with "glowing characterizations and endorsements concerning the services" provided by the hospital, and thus left no doubt that the calendar was created to preserve existing patronage and to solicit new patients. Here, the advertisement does not even associate itself with USA Next through the use of its address, telephone number, logo, or in any other manner. Moreover, the calendar in *Beverley* promoted the use of the hospital's services, while the advertisement here discusses public policy issues that are currently the subject of public debate. . . .

NOTES & QUESTIONS

1. ***The Fuzzy Line Between Commercial and Non-Commercial Uses.*** Is using a person's photograph to solicit donations a commercial use? In *Raymen,* the image of the plaintiffs kissing was used not as a positive endorsement but as a way to spark outrage in their readers and spur them to donate. Isn't this using their image for financial gain? On the other hand, the plaintiffs' anger at the use of their photograph stems from their outrage over the defendants' message. The defendant could argue that the image of the plaintiffs was a

popular iconic image representing gay marriage. Should the plaintiffs be able to control that image whenever they dislike the viewpoints of those that use it?

2. ***Girls Gone Wild.*** In *Lane v. MRA Holdings, LLC*, 242 F. Supp. 2d 1205 (M.D. Fla. 2002), the plaintiff was approached by a crew who produced the Girls Gone Wild video series, which featured clips of women stripping at various parties and events, such as spring break or Marti Gras. The plaintiff claimed that the crew promised that the footage would be for their personal use only, but it was used in a Girls Gone Wild video. Among many claims, the plaintiff argued that the makers of Girls Gone Wild appropriated her likeness. The court, however, rejected her appropriation claim:

> The Defendants first argue that they are not liable under Fla. Stat. § 540.08 because they did not use Lane's image for trade, commercial, or advertising purposes. Under Fla. Stat. § 540.08, the terms "trade", "commercial", or "advertising purpose" mean using a person's name or likeness to directly promote a product or service.
>
> As a matter of law, this Court finds that Lane's image and likeness were not used to directly promote a product or service. In coming to this conclusion, this Court relies upon Section 47 of the Restatement (Third) of Unfair Competition which defines "the purposes of trade" as follows:
>
>> The names, likeness, and other indicia of a person's identity are used "for the purposes of trade" . . . if they are used in advertising the user's goods or services, or are placed on merchandise marketed by the user, or are used in connection with services rendered by the user. However, use "for the purpose of trade" does not ordinarily include the use of a person's identity in news reporting, commentary, entertainment, works of fiction or nonfiction, or in advertising incidental to such uses.
>
> Therefore, under this definition, the "use of another's identity in a novel, play, or motion picture is . . . not ordinarily an infringement . . . [unless] the name or likeness is used solely to attract attention to a work that is not related to the identified person. . . ." *Id.* at comment c.
>
> In this case, it is irrefutable that the *Girls Gone Wild* video is an expressive work created solely for entertainment purposes. Similarly, it is also irrefutable that while Lane's image and likeness were used to sell copies of *Girls Gone Wild,* her image and likeness were never associated with a product or service unrelated to that work. Indeed, in both the video and its commercial advertisements, Lane is never shown endorsing or promoting a product, but rather, as part of an expressive work in which she voluntarily participated. Consequently, in accordance with Section 47 of the Restatement, the use of Lane's image or likeness in *Girls Gone Wild,* and in the marketing of that video cannot give rise to liability. . . .
>
> Upon reviewing Florida case law, it has come to this Court's attention that only one case has applied the provisions of Fla. Stat. § 540.08 to an expressive work. In *Gritzke v. M.R.A. Holding, LLC,* No. 4:01cv495-RH (N.D. Fla. Mar, 15, 2002), Judge Hinkle of the Northern District of Florida determined that the plaintiff stated a valid claim under § 540.08 by alleging that her half naked image was plastered on the front cover of the videotape *Girls Gone Wild* without her authorization. . . . [T]he plaintiff in *Gritzke* was complaining

> about the use of her image on the outside cover of a videotape package. In this case, Lane has not alleged that her image was plastered on a billboard or box cover advertising *Girls Gone Wild.* Rather, this cause of action arises from the Defendants truthful and accurate depiction of Lane voluntarily exposing her breasts to a camera, just as she did on Labor Day Weekend in Panama City Beach, Florida. Unlike in *Gritzke,* the Plaintiff's image in this case was never doctored. It has always remained in its original video format. Accordingly, the *Gritzke* case offers Lane little assistance. . . .
>
> Lane's lawsuit arose from an expressive work that has no purpose other than to entertain a segment of the general population. . . . [T]he Plaintiff in this case is not shown endorsing or promoting a product, but rather as participating in an expressive work. . . . [T]his Court finds that the publication of *Girls Gone Wild* is not actionable simply because it is sold for a profit.

The court's definition of commercial use in this case appears to be a use for "endorsing or promoting a product." Is this too limited a definition of commercial use? Would selling posters of a celebrity constitute a commercial use according to the *Lane* court?

4. CONNECTION TO MATTERS OF PUBLIC INTEREST

Unlike the tort of public disclosure, the lack of newsworthiness is not an element of the appropriation tort. However, appropriation protects against the "commercial" exploitation of one's name or likeness, not the use of one's name or likeness for news, art, literature, parody, satire, history, and biography. Otherwise, a newspaper would have to obtain the consent of every person it wrote about or photographed for use in a story. People could prevent others from writing their biographies or from criticizing them, making a parody of them, or using their names in a work of literature. In New York, for example, one's name or likeness must be used for "advertising purposes or for the uses of trade." N.Y. Civ. Rights L. §§ 50-51. Although not employing the same language, other states adopt a similar approach, requiring that the use of one's name or likeness be for "commercial" purposes. Some courts refer to this as a "First Amendment privilege" to use one's name or likeness in matters of legitimate public concern.

The quintessential instance where the use of one's name or likeness is newsworthy and not "commercial" is in connection with the reporting of the news. In *Time Inc. v. Sand Creek Partners*, 825 F. Supp. 210 (S.D. Ind. 1993), country singer Lyle Lovett and actress Julia Roberts were photographed together at a Lovett concert immediately prior to their marriage. Roberts was in her wedding gown. A photographer for *People* magazine snapped several rolls of film, but they were confiscated by security. The magazine's publisher sued to get the photos back, but Lovett claimed that they were his, because he had a property interest in his name or likeness. The court sided with the magazine:

> Lovett and Roberts are widely known celebrities and in that sense are public figures and, in addition, their appearance on stage before thousands of people on the day of their highly-publicized but theretofore unannounced and private wedding ceremony, with Roberts still wearing her wedding dress, was a newsworthy event of widespread public interest.

Beyond news, uses that are "commercial" or "for advertising or trade purposes" generally do not encompass works of fiction or nonfiction or artistic expression. In *Rosemont Enterprises, Inc. v. Random House, Inc.*, 294 N.Y.S.2d 122 (1968), the defendants published an unauthorized biography of the reclusive Howard Hughes. The court concluded that the biography "falls within those 'reports of newsworthy people or events'" and is therefore not subject to liability for appropriation. A sculpture of supermodel Cheryl Tiegs was not appropriation because "[w]orks of art, including sculptures, convey ideas, just as do literature, movies or theater." *Simeonov v. Tiegs*, 602 N.Y.S.2d 1014 (Civ. Ct. 1993). The use of a person's identity in a work of fiction generally cannot give rise to an appropriation action. *See, e.g., Maritote v. Desilu Productions, Inc.*, 345 F.2d 418 (7th Cir. 1965); *Loft v. Fuller*, 408 So. 2d 619 (Fla. Ct. App. 1981).

However, in New York and other states, the right of the media to use one's name or likeness for news purposes is not absolute. There must exist a "legitimate connection between the use of plaintiff's name and picture and the matter of public interest sought to be portrayed." *Delan by Delan v. CBS, Inc.*, 458 N.Y.S.2d 608 (N.Y. Ct. App. 1983). As another court articulated the test:

> A picture illustrating an article on a matter of public interest is not considered used for the purpose of trade or advertising within the prohibition of the statute unless it has no real relationship to the article, or unless the article is an advertisement in disguise. It makes no difference whether the article appears in a newspaper; a magazine; a newsreel; on television; in a motion picture; or in a book. The test of permissible use is not the currency of the publication in which the picture appears but whether it is illustrative of a matter of public interest. *Dallesandro v. Henry Holt & Co.*, 106 N.Y.S.2d 805 (1957).

This test has become known as the "real relationship" test. *See, e.g., Haskell v. Stauffer Communications, Inc.*, 990 P.2d 163 (Kan. App. 1999); *Lane v. Random House*, 985 F. Supp. 141 (D.D.C. 1995).

FINGER V. OMNI PUBLICATIONS INTERNATIONAL, LTD.

566 N.E.2d 141 (N.Y. Ct. App. 1990)

ALEXANDER, J. Plaintiffs Joseph and Ida Finger commenced this action on behalf of themselves and their six children against defendant Omni Publications International, Ltd. seeking damages for the publication, without their consent, of a photograph of plaintiffs in conjunction with an article in Omni magazine discussing a research project relating to caffeine-aided fertilization. . . .

. . . The June 1988 issue of Omni magazine included in its "Continuum" segment an article entitled "Caffeine and Fast Sperm," in which it was indicated that based on research conducted at the University of Pennsylvania School of Medicine, in vitro fertilization rates may be enhanced by exposing sperm to high concentrations of caffeine.

A photograph of plaintiffs depicting two adults surrounded by six attractive and apparently healthy children accompanied the article. The caption beneath the photograph read "Want a big family? Maybe your sperm needs a cup of Java in the morning. Tests reveal that caffeine-spritzed sperm swim faster, which may increase the chances for in vitro fertilization." Neither the article nor the caption mentioned plaintiffs' names or indicated in any fashion that the adult plaintiffs used caffeine or that the children were produced through in vitro fertilization.

Plaintiffs commenced this action alleging only violations of Civil Rights Law §§ 50 and 51. Defendant moved to dismiss the complaint, arguing that its use of the photograph in conjunction with the article did not violate Civil Rights Law §§ 50 and 51 because the picture was not used for trade or advertising but to illustrate a related news article on fertility. Defendant contended that because fertility is a topic of legitimate public interest, its use of the picture fit within the "newsworthiness exception" to the prohibitions of Civil Rights Law § 50. . . .

Plaintiffs contend that defendant violated Civil Rights Law §§ 50 and 51 by using their photograph without their consent "for advertising purposes or for the purposes of trade." . . .

Although the statute does not define "purposes of trade" or "advertising," courts have consistently refused to construe these terms as encompassing publications concerning newsworthy events or matters of public interest. Additionally, it is also well settled that "'[a] picture illustrating an article on a matter of public interest is not considered used for the purpose of trade or advertising within the prohibition of the statute . . . unless it has no real relationship to the article . . . or unless the article is an advertisement in disguise.'"

Plaintiffs do not contest the existence of this "newsworthiness exception" and concede that the discussion of in vitro fertilization and the use of caffeine to enhance sperm velocity and motility are newsworthy topics. They contend, however, that their photograph bears "no real relationship" to the article, that none of plaintiffs' children were conceived by in vitro fertilization or any other artificial means, and that they never participated in the caffeine-enhanced reproductive research conducted at the University of Pennsylvania.

Consequently, according to plaintiffs, there was no "real relationship" between their photograph and the article, and any relationship that may exist is too tenuous to be considered a relationship at all. They argue that there are no "external and objective" criteria . . . that would indicate that plaintiffs have any real or legitimate connection with the subject of caffeine-enhanced in vitro fertilization. . . .

Plaintiffs misperceive the "newsworthy" theme of the article, which is fertility or increased fertility. Indeed, the article, in its opening sentences, observes that caffeine "can increase a man's fertility by boosting the performance of his sperm" and further indicates that "those who are looking for a fertility tonic shouldn't head for the nearest coffee pot" because the concentrations of caffeine used in the experiment "were so high [as to] be toxic."

The theme of fertility is reasonably reflected both in the caption beneath the picture, "Want a big family?", and the images used — six healthy and attractive children with their parents to whom each child bears a striking resemblance. Clearly then, there is a "real relationship" between the fertility theme of the article and the large family depicted in the photograph. That the article also discusses in vitro fertilization as being enhanced by "caffeine-spritzed sperm" does no more than discuss a specific aspect of fertilization and does not detract from the relationship between the photograph and the article.

As we have noted, the "newsworthiness exception" should be liberally applied. . . . [Q]uestions of "newsworthiness" are better left to reasonable editorial judgment and discretion; judicial intervention should occur only in those instances where there is "no real relationship" between a photograph and an article or where the article is an "advertisement in disguise." . . .

NOTES & QUESTIONS

1. ***Levels of Generality in Applying the Real Relationship Test.*** Do you agree with the court's approach to the relationship between the photograph and the article? Does the court properly view the topic of the article broadly as about fertility in general? The Fingers' argument, however, is not that the picture has no relation to the subject matter of the article; rather, they contend that they have nothing to do with the article's specific topic. Is this relevant to the court?
2. ***What Injuries Does the Appropriation Tort Redress?*** What type of interest are the Fingers attempting to protect? Why doesn't the appropriation tort protect that interest?

   Consider *Arrington v. New York Times*, 434 N.E.2d 1319 (N.Y. Ct. App. 1982). The *New York Times Magazine* published an article called "The Black Middle Class: Making It." On the cover of the publication was the photograph of the plaintiff Clarence W. Arrington in a suit. The photograph was taken without Arrington's consent or knowledge as he was walking down the street. Arrington, a young African-American financial analyst, strongly disagreed with the views stated in the article, which criticized how the "expanding black middle/professional class in today's society" was growing more removed from its "less fortunate brethren." Arrington, along with many other readers, found the article to be "insulting, degrading, distorting and disparaging." Others, including his friends and acquaintances, thought that he had shared the ideas in the article because his picture was featured as the exemplar of the "black middle class." Arrington sued the publisher, the freelance photographer who took the picture, and the agency that arranged for the photo to be sold to the *Times* for appropriation and false light. With regard to appropriation, the New York law recognized the importance of protecting free speech values:

   > . . . [W]e not too long ago reiterated that "'[a] picture illustrating an article on a matter of public interest is not considered used for the purposes of trade or advertising within the prohibition of the statute . . . unless it has no real relationship to the article . . . or unless the article is an advertisement in disguise.'" And this holds true though the dissemination of news and views is carried on for a profit or that illustrations are added for the very purpose of encouraging sales of the publications.

   Arrington contended that his picture had no "real relationship" to the article, but the court disagreed:

   > Plaintiff's emphasis . . . is on the fact that, as he reads it, the article depicts the "black middle class" as one peopled by "materialistic, status-conscious and

> frivolous individuals without any sense of moral obligation to those of their race who are economically less fortunate," a conception of the "class" with which he disclaims any "legitimate connection." While the concededly innocuous title of the article is superimposed over part of the picture (as is the title of another on Christmas pleasures), nothing of the ideas with which he wishes to disassociate himself appear at this point. And, though the article itself gives the names and quotes the statements and opinions of persons whom the author interviewed, as indicated earlier, the plaintiff is neither mentioned, nor are any of the ideas or opinions it expresses attributed to him. The asserted lack of a "real relationship" boils down then, to his conviction that his views are not consonant with those of the author. . . . [However,] it would be unwise for us to assay the dangerous task of passing on value judgments based on the subjective happenstance of whether there is agreement with views expressed on a social issue.
>
> No more persuasive is plaintiff's perfectly understandable preference that his photograph not have been employed in this manner and in this connection. However, other than in the purely commercial setting covered by [New York's appropriation tort], an inability to vindicate a personal predilection for greater privacy may be part of the price every person must be prepared to pay for a society in which information and opinion flow freely.

However, as to the photographer and the agency that sold the photo, the court declared that Arrington's action could proceed because the sale of the photo "commercialized" it, and the other defendants were not protected in the same way by the statute as the publisher. Subsequent to *Arrington*, the New York legislature amended § 51 to protect photographers and agents.

How would you characterize Arrington's injury? Did it involve the commercial use of his photograph? Or did it involve his being associated with an article that he found distasteful? Should a person have legal recourse from having her image associated, without her consent, with views that she disagrees with?

Arrington also raised a false light claim, but the court rejected it because the use of the photo was not "highly offensive." Do you agree?

3. ***The Limits of the Real Relationship Test.*** In *Spahn v. Julian Messner, Inc.*, 233 N.E.2d 840 (N.Y. 1967), the defendants published a book about the famous baseball player, Warren Spahn. The book was largely a work of fiction, with imaginary events and dialogue. The defendants intended to create a fictitious biography, as they did not engage in research or interviews of Spahn or those who knew him. Spahn sued under New York's appropriation law (Civil Rights Law § 51) and won a jury verdict. The verdict was upheld on appeal:

> To hold that this research effort entitles the defendants to publish the kind of knowing fictionalization presented here would amount to granting a literary license which is not only unnecessary to the protection of free speech but destructive of an individual's right — albeit a limited one in the case of a public figure — to be free of the commercial exploitation of his name and personality.

In *Messenger v. Gruner + Jahr Printing and Publishing,* 208 F.3d 122 (2d Cir. 2000), photographs of a young woman were used to illustrate a story called "Love Crisis" in a magazine called *Young and Modern (YM)*:

> The column began with a letter to Sally Lee, *YM*'s editor-in-chief, from a 14-year-old girl identified only as "Mortified." Mortified writes that she got drunk at a party and then had sex with her 18-year-old boyfriend and two of his friends. Lee responds that Mortified should avoid similar situations in the future, and advises her to be tested for pregnancy and sexually transmitted diseases. Above the column, in bold type, is a pull-out quotation stating, "I got trashed and had sex with three guys." Three full-color photographs of plaintiff illustrate the column — one, for example, shows her hiding her face, with three young men gloating in the background. The captions are keyed to Lee's advice: "Wake up and face the facts: You made a pretty big mistake;" "Don't try to hide — just ditch him and his buds;" and "Afraid you're pregnant? See a doctor."

The court applied the real relationship test: "[W]here a photograph illustrates an article on a matter of public interest, the newsworthiness exception bars recovery unless there is no real relationship between the photograph and the article, or the article is an advertisement in disguise." The defendants cited *Finger* and *Arrington.* The plaintiff relied on *Spahn.* The court concluded that *Finger* and *Arrington* controlled, not *Spahn*. Like the photographs in *Young and Modern,* the photos used in *Finger* and *Arrington* were used to "illustrate newsworthy articles." In contrast, "*Spahn* concerned a strikingly different scenario from the one before us. . . . [D]efendants invented biographies of plaintiffs' lives. The courts concluded that the substantially fictional works at issue were nothing more than attempts to trade on the persona of Warren Spahn." The court also concluded that the tort of false light was not recognized in New York.

In dissent, Judge Bellacosa argued:

> [The holding of this case] justifies a too-facile escape valve from the operation of the [appropriation] statute, one that is also unilaterally within the control of the alleged wrongdoer. The paradigm for editors is a "newsworthy" homily to lovesick adolescents or any other audience; they then just have to use a journalistic conceit of tying the advice to a purported letter to the editor, with an inescapable first person identification of the letter as originating with any adolescent in the photo array. When an aggrieved person like Messenger reaches for the statutory lifeline, the newsworthiness notion dissipates it into a dry mirage. That is not fair or right.

Assess the strength of a potential defamation suit based on *Young and Modern*'s use of the photo.

5. FIRST AMENDMENT LIMITATIONS

ZACCHINI V. SCRIPPS-HOWARD BROADCASTING CO.

433 U.S. 562 (1977)

WHITE, J. Petitioner, Hugo Zacchini, is an entertainer. He performs a "human cannonball" act in which he is shot from a cannon into a net some 200 feet away. Each performance occupies some 15 seconds. In August and September 1972, petitioner was engaged to perform his act on a regular basis at the Geauga County Fair in Burton, Ohio. He performed in a fenced area, surrounded by grandstands, at the fair grounds. Members of the public attending the fair were not charged a separate admission fee to observe his act.

On August 30, a freelance reporter for Scripps-Howard Broadcasting Co., the operator of a television broadcasting station and respondent in this case, attended the fair. He carried a small movie camera. Petitioner noticed the reporter and asked him not to film the performance. The reporter did not do so on that day; but on the instructions of the producer of respondent's daily newscast, he returned the following day and videotaped the entire act. This film clip approximately 15 seconds in length, was shown on the 11 o'clock news program that night, together with favorable commentary.

Petitioner then brought this action for damages, alleging that he is "engaged in the entertainment business," that the act he performs is one "invented by his father and . . . performed only by his family for the last fifty years," that respondent "showed and commercialized the film of his act without his consent," and that such conduct was an "unlawful appropriation of plaintiff's professional property." Respondent answered and moved for summary judgment, which was granted by the trial court.

[The Ohio Supreme Court held that the broadcast was protected by the First Amendment because the press "must be accorded broad latitude in its choice of how much it presents of each story or incident, and of the emphasis to be given to such presentation." The United States Supreme Court granted certiorari to determine whether the First Amendment immunized the media broadcaster from damages under Ohio's "right of publicity" (appropriation tort).]

. . . The Ohio Supreme Court relied heavily on *Time, Inc. v. Hill*, 385 U.S. 374 (1967), but that case does not mandate a media privilege to televise a performer's entire act without his consent. Involved in *Time, Inc. v. Hill* was a claim under the New York "Right of Privacy" statute that Life Magazine, in the course of reviewing a new play, had connected the play with a long-past incident involving petitioner and his family and had falsely described their experience and conduct at that time. The complaint sought damages for humiliation and suffering flowing from these nondefamatory falsehoods that allegedly invaded Hill's privacy. The Court held, however, that the opening of a new play linked to an actual incident was a matter of public interest and that Hill could not recover without showing that the Life report was knowingly false or was published with reckless disregard for the truth the same rigorous standard that had been applied in *New York Times Co. v. Sullivan*.

Time, Inc. v. Hill, which was hotly contested and decided by a divided Court, involved an entirely different tort from the "right of publicity" recognized by the Ohio Supreme Court. As the opinion reveals in *Time, Inc. v. Hill*, the Court was steeped in the literature of privacy law and was aware of the developing distinctions and nuances in this branch of the law. . . . The Court was aware that it was adjudicating a "false light" privacy case involving a matter of public interest, not a case involving "intrusion," "appropriation" of a name or likeness for the purposes of trade, or "private details" about a non-newsworthy person or event. It is also abundantly clear that *Time, Inc. v. Hill* did not involve a performer, a person with a name having commercial value, or any claim to a "right of publicity." This discrete kind of "appropriation" case was plainly identified in the literature cited by the Court and had been adjudicated in the reported cases.

The differences between these two torts are important. First, the State's interests in providing a cause of action in each instance are different. "The interest protected" in permitting recovery for placing the plaintiff in a false light "is clearly that of reputation, with the same overtones of mental distress as in defamation." By contrast, the State's interest in permitting a "right of publicity" is in protecting the proprietary interest of the individual in his act in part to encourage such entertainment. As we later note, the State's interest is closely analogous to the goals of patent and copyright law, focusing on the right of the individual to reap the reward of his endeavors and having little to do with protecting feelings or reputation. Second, the two torts differ in the degree to which they intrude on dissemination of information to the public. In "false light" cases the only way to protect the interests involved is to attempt to minimize publication of the damaging matter, while in "right of publicity" cases the only question is who gets to do the publishing. An entertainer such as petitioner usually has no objection to the widespread publication of his act as long as he gets the commercial benefit of such publication. Indeed, in the present case petitioner did not seek to enjoin the broadcast of his act; he simply sought compensation for the broadcast in the form of damages. . . .

. . . *Time, Inc. v. Hill*, *New York Times*, *Metromedia*, *Gertz*, and *Firestone* all involved the reporting of events; in none of them was there an attempt to broadcast or publish an entire act for which the performer ordinarily gets paid. It is evident, and there is no claim here to the contrary, that petitioner's state-law right of publicity would not serve to prevent respondent from reporting the newsworthy facts about petitioner's act. Wherever the line in particular situations is to be drawn between media reports that are protected and those that are not, we are quite sure that the First and Fourteenth Amendments do not immunize the media when they broadcast a performer's entire act without his consent. The Constitution no more prevents a State from requiring respondent to compensate petitioner for broadcasting his act on television than it would privilege respondent to film and broadcast a copyrighted dramatic work without liability to the copyright owner, or to film and broadcast a prize fight, or a baseball game, where the promoters or the participants had other plans for publicizing the event. . . .

The broadcast of a film of petitioner's entire act poses a substantial threat to the economic value of that performance. . . . The effect of a public broadcast of the performance is similar to preventing petitioner from charging an admission fee. The rationale for (protecting the right of publicity) is the straightforward one of preventing unjust enrichment by the theft of good will. . . .

There is no doubt that entertainment, as well as news, enjoys First Amendment protection. It is also true that entertainment itself can be important news. But it is important to note that neither the public nor respondent will be deprived of the benefit of petitioner's performance as long as his commercial stake in his act is appropriately recognized. Petitioner does not seek to enjoin the broadcast of his performance; he simply wants to be paid for it. . . .

We conclude that although the State of Ohio may as a matter of its own law privilege the press in the circumstances of this case, the First and Fourteenth Amendments do not require it to do so. . . .

NOTES & QUESTIONS

1. ***Different First Amendment Treatment.*** Why does the *Zacchini* Court conclude that the First Amendment impacts the torts of appropriation and publicity differently than the other privacy torts? Do you agree with the distinction the Court makes?
2. ***Newsworthiness.*** Is Zacchini's human cannonball act newsworthy? The media frequently provides news about entertainment, such as sports and movies. If the act is newsworthy, then why shouldn't the First Amendment protect the broadcast of it? If Zacchini suffered an accident while performing his cannonball act, would a broadcast of it be newsworthy? Would this accident justify broadcast of the entire act?

ESTATE OF PRESLEY V. RUSSEN

513 F. Supp. 1339 (D.N.J. 1981)

During his lifetime, Elvis Presley established himself as one of the legends in the entertainment business. On August 16, 1977, Elvis Presley died, but his legend and worldwide popularity have survived. As Presley's popularity has subsisted and even grown, so has the capacity for generating financial rewards and legal disputes. Although the present case is another in this line, it presents questions not previously addressed. As a general proposition, this case is concerned with the rights and limitations of one who promotes and presents a theatrical production designed to imitate or simulate a stage performance of Elvis Presley. . . .

Plaintiff is the Estate of Elvis Presley (hereafter the Estate) located in Memphis, Tennessee, created by the Will of Elvis Presley and is, under the laws of the State of Tennessee, a legal entity with the power to sue and be sued. . . .

The Elvis Presley tours were billed as "Elvis in Concert," and his nightclub performances were billed as the Elvis Presley Show, while Elvis Presley shows in Las Vegas were billed simply as "Elvis." Most of Elvis Presley's record albums used the name ELVIS on the cover as part of the title. One of his albums was entitled ELVIS IN CONCERT. . . .

Although Elvis Presley exhibited a range of talents and degrees of change in his personality and physical make-up during his professional career, he, in association with his personal manager, Thomas A. (Col.) Parker, developed a certain, characteristic performing style, particularly as to his live stage shows. His voice, delivery, mannerisms (such as his hips and legs gyrations), appearance and dress (especially a certain type of jumpsuit and a ring), and actions accompanying a performance (such as handing out scarves to the audience), all contributed to this Elvis Presley style of performance. . . .

The plaintiff has asserted that the defendant's production, THE BIG EL SHOW, infringes on the right of publicity which plaintiff inherited from Elvis Presley.

The right of publicity is a concept which has evolved from the common law of privacy and its tort "of the appropriation, for the defendant's benefit or advantages, of the plaintiff's name or likeness." The term "right of publicity" has since come to signify the right of an individual, especially a public figure or a celebrity, to control the commercial value and exploitation of his name and picture or likeness and to prevent others from unfairly appropriating this value for their commercial benefit. The idea generally underlying an action for a right of privacy is that the individual has a right personal to him to be let alone and, thus, to prevent others from invading his privacy, injuring his feelings, or assaulting his peace of mind. In contrast, underlying the right of publicity concept is a desire to benefit from the commercial exploitation of one's name and likeness.

[The district court found that courts in New Jersey had long recognized an individual's right to prevent the unauthorized, commercial appropriation of his name or likeliness. The district court also found that Presley's right of publicity survived his death.]

Based on the current state of the record, the production can be described as a live theatrical presentation or concert designed to imitate a performance of the late Elvis Presley. The show stars an individual who closely resembles Presley and who imitates the appearance, dress, and characteristic performing style of Elvis Presley. The defendant has made no showing, nor attempted to show, that the production is intended to or acts as a parody, burlesque, satire, or criticism of Elvis Presley. As a matter of fact, the show is billed as "A TRIBUTE TO ELVIS PRESLEY." In essence, we confront the question of whether the use of the likeness of a famous deceased entertainer in a performance mainly designed to imitate that famous entertainer's own past stage performances is to be considered primarily as a commercial appropriation by the imitator or show's producer of the famous entertainer's likeness or as a valuable contribution of information or culture. After careful consideration of the activity, we have decided that although THE BIG EL SHOW contains an informational and entertainment element, the show serves primarily to commercially exploit the likeness of Elvis Presley without contributing anything of substantial value to society. In making this decision, the court recognizes that certain factors distinguish this situation from the pure commercial use of a picture of Elvis Presley to advertise a product. In the first place, the defendant uses Presley's likeness in an entertainment form . . . However, entertainment that is merely a copy or imitation, even if skillfully and accurately carried out, does not really have its own creative component and does not have a significant value as pure entertainment. As one authority has emphasized:

> The public interest in entertainment will support the sporadic, occasional and good-faith imitation of a famous person to achieve humor, to effect criticism or to season a particular episode, but it does not give a privilege to appropriate another's valuable attributes as one's own without the consent of the other. Neterville, *Copyright and Torts Aspects of Parody, Mimicry and Humorous Commentary*, 35 S. Cal. L. Rev. 225 (1962).

In the second place, the production does provide information in that it illustrates a performance of a legendary figure in the entertainment industry. Because of Presley's immense contribution to rock 'n roll, examples of him performing can be considered of public interest. However, in comparison to a biographical film or play of Elvis Presley or a production tracing the role of Elvis Presley in the development of rock 'n roll, the information about Presley which THE BIG EL SHOW provides is of limited value.

This recognition that defendant's production has some value does not diminish our conclusion that the primary purpose of defendant's activity is to appropriate the commercial value of the likeness of Elvis Presley.

In *Zacchini v. Scripps-Howard Broadcasting Co.* the Supreme Court addressed a situation which implicated both a performer's right of publicity and the First Amendment. The Court held that the First Amendment did not prevent a state from deciding that a television news show's unauthorized broadcast of a film showing plaintiff's "entire act," a fifteen second human cannonball performance, infringed plaintiff's right of publicity.

In the present case, although the defendant has not shown a film of an Elvis Presley performance, he has engaged in a similar form of behavior by presenting a live performance starring an imitator of Elvis Presley. To some degree, the defendant has appropriated the "very activity (live stage show) by which (Presley initially) acquired his reputation . . . ," and from which the value in his name and likeness developed. The death of Presley diminishes the impact of certain of the court's reasons, especially the one providing for an economic incentive to produce future performances. However, through receiving royalties, the heirs of Presley are the beneficiaries of the "right of the individual to reap the reward of his endeavors." *Zacchini*. Under the state's right of publicity, they are entitled to protect the commercial value of the name or likeness of Elvis Presley from activities such as defendant's which may diminish this value.

We thus find that the plaintiff has demonstrated a likelihood of success on the merits of its right of publicity claim with respect to the defendant's live stage production. In addition, we find this likelihood of success as to the defendant's unauthorized use of Elvis Presley's likeness on the cover or label of any records or on any pendants which are sold or distributed by the defendant.

Having found that the plaintiff is likely to succeed on the merits as to certain claims, we must next examine the second requirement for a plaintiff seeking a preliminary injunction. The plaintiff must demonstrate that irreparable injury will result if an injunction is not granted pendente lite.

Although the plaintiff has shown a likelihood of success on the merits of its right of publicity claim, the plaintiff has not made a sufficient showing that irreparable injury will result if the defendant's production is not preliminarily enjoined. In making this decision, we note that we are treating a right of publicity claim different than a service mark infringement or unfair competition claim.

Because the doctrine of the right of publicity emphasizes the protection of the commercial value of the celebrity's name or likeness, the plaintiff must demonstrate sufficiently that the defendant's use of the name and likeness of the celebrity has or is likely to result in an identifiable economic loss. In contrast, in the context of the service mark infringement, unfair competition, and § 43(a) of the Lanham Act claims, we found that irreparable injury could result even in the absence of economic harm per se. . . . As a result of such public deception or confusion as to source, the plaintiff is being harmed. The plaintiff is being unfairly compelled to place the control of the good will attached to its entertainment services in the hands of the defendant.

In addition, and perhaps even more importantly, the close relationship in this case between the right of publicity and the societal considerations of free expression supports the position that the plaintiff in seeking relief for an infringement of its rights of publicity should demonstrate an identifiable economic harm. . . . [T]he defendant's activity when viewed simply as a skilled, good faith imitation of an Elvis Presley performance, i.e., without the elements leading to a likelihood of confusion, is, in some measure, consistent with the goals of freedom of expression. Thus, before the harsh step of barring defendant's activity is undertaken, the plaintiff should have to make a showing of immediate, irreparable harm to the commercial value of the right of publicity and should not be able to rely on an intangible potentiality.

In light of these comments, we find that the plaintiff has not made a sufficient showing that the presentation of this particular production, THE BIG EL SHOW, has resulted in any loss of commercial benefits to the plaintiff or will result in an irreparable commercial harm in the near future. The plaintiff has not adequately demonstrated that the existence of defendant's activity has led to or is likely to lead to a diminished ability of the plaintiff to profit from the use of Elvis Presley's name or likeness. For example, there is insufficient evidence that plaintiff's (or its licensees') ability to enter into agreements licensing the use of Presley's name or likeness in connection with consumer products is seriously jeopardized by defendant's activity. As a matter of fact, it is even possible that defendant's production has stimulated the public's interest in buying Elvis Presley merchandise or in seeing films or hearing records embodying actual Elvis Presley performances. Thus, the defendant's show will not be preliminarily enjoined.

The considerations preventing the issuance of a preliminary injunction as to the show do not sufficiently apply to the sale of pendants or records even though the sales are limited. . . . We find that irreparable injury would result from the continued sale and distribution of pendants displaying Elvis Presley's likeness or of records whose covers or labels display pictures or artist's renderings which are or appear to be of Elvis Presley.

NOTES & QUESTIONS

1. ***Remedies for Elvis?*** In *Estate of Presley*, the court admits that a theatrical imitation of Elvis violates a right of publicity that survived his death. Yet, the remedies it permits are limited. Why did the court restrict its relief?

2. ***Elvis Imitators and the Right of Publicity***. In a footnote, the court in *Estate of Presley* acknowledges that a parody, burlesque, satire, or critical review of an Elvis's performance might be allowed. These kind of theatrical acts contribute to society in a way that a simple copying of an artist's performance does not. Do you agree with this distinction?

   Elvis, in particular, has attracted a legion of imitators of different stripes. The group Dread Zepplin combined an Elvis impersonator, Tortelvis (born Greg Tortell), with a repertoire heavy on reggae-influenced covers of Led Zeppelin songs. As another example, El Vez, the self-proclaimed "Mexican Elvis," uses the Elvis persona to engage in social satire and political commentary. As Allmusic.com reports, El Vez sings "Immigration Time" to the melody of Elvis's "Suspicious Minds," and uses new lyrics such as "I've got my green card. . . I want my gold card!" Do these acts violate Elvis's right of publicity?

3. ***Appropriation Forever?*** Should the publicity right and tort of appropriation create assignable and descendible rights? The question is a multi-million dollar issue. In 2006, Elvis Presley was the top earning dead celebrity. His estate generated $49 million that year; the bulk of that amount went to CKX Entertainment, a publicly traded firm that owned the majority of rights in Elvis. Other top earning deceased celebrities include John Lennon ($44 million), George Harrison ($22 million), Tupac Shakur ($9 million), Steve McQueen ($6 million), and James Brown ($5 million). Certain talent agencies now specialize in representing deceased celebrities. CMG Worldwide represents the interests of the Estates of Marilyn Monroe, Errol Flynn, Marlon Brando, Laurence Olivier, Rock Hudson, Jayne Mansfield, Bette Davis, Glen Miller, Christopher Wallace (Notorious B.I.G.), Babe Ruth, Lou Gehrig, and many others.

   Most courts have found assignable and descendible rights to be created by the publicity right and tort of appropriation. *See Martin Luther King, Jr., Center for Social Change, Inc. v. American Heritage Products*, 694 F.2d 674 (11th Cir. 1983); *Groucho Marx Productions v. Day and Night*, 523 F. Supp. 485 (S.D.N.Y. 1981); *Factors Etc., Inc. v. Pro Arts, Inc.*, 579 F.2d 215 (2d Cir. 1978); *Motschenbacher v. R.J. Reynolds Tobacco Co.*, 498 F.2d 821 (9th Cir. 1974).

   In some states, the right to use one's name, photograph, or likeness after death is permitted but also is limited to a statutorily defined period. In Tennessee, this period is ten years after the death of the individual. Tenn. Code § 47-24-1104(a). In California, this period is 50 years "from the death of the deceased personality." Cal. Civ. Code § 990(g).

   In 2007, California law was amended to state explicitly that the rights of a "deceased personality" were deemed "to have existed at the time of death of any deceased personality" — even if the person in question died prior to enactment of the California statute that recognized post mortem publicity rights. Cal. Civ. Code § 3344.1(b). But how can the will of such a celebrity have assigned a right that the law did not recognize at the time that the will was created?

4. ***The Endless (Virtual) Tour?*** The *Estate of Presley* court admitted that "the death of Presley diminishes the impact of certain of the [*Zacchini* Court's] reasons, especially the one providing for an economic reason to produce future performances." Note that the Presley Estate has found a way to have Elvis tour *after* his death. Its "Elvis Presley on Tour" production, which sadly was placed on hiatus in October 2007, featured state-of-the-art film projections of Elvis along with live accompaniment by members of his classic touring band. Does the possibility of such posthumous concerts mean that celebrity impersonators will substitute for an interest of the estate of the celebrity?
5. ***"Tribute Bands" and "Reverence Bands."*** Are similar issues or different issues raised by "tribute bands," which dress up in costumes and seek to imitate rock bands? In contrast, a "reverence band" only plays the songs popularized by one artist and does not seek to imitate the visual aspects of the original group.

   Should groups, as opposed to individuals, even have a right to publicity? In two cases, courts found that the Beatles had a group right of publicity. In *Apple Corps Limited v. Leber*, No. C 299149, 229 U.S.P.Q (BNA) 1015 (Cal. Sup. Ct., LA County 1986), a California court awarded $5.6 million to the Beatles and granted injunctive relief against further presentations by the defendants of the show "Beatlemania" as well as any further "exploitations of the Beatles persona in whatever form." In *Apple Corps Limited v. A.D.P.R.*, 843 F. Supp. 342 (M.D. Tenn. 1993) a federal district court found that a performing group known as "1964 as the Beatles" violated the Beatles' right of publicity under a Tennessee statute. It permanently enjoined the defendants from using the name "The Beatles," and the names and images of Beatles members in ads. Where does a group persona begin and end? Are there other problems with permitting groups to have publicity rights?
6. ***J.D. Salinger's Love Letters and the Privacy Torts.*** In 1999, 14 letters by the noted author J.D. Salinger (written 27 years prior) were auctioned at Sotheby's by his former lover Joyce Maynard. They sold for $156,500. The *New York Times* described the contents of the Salinger letters in general terms as "formal and avuncular at the outset," then "love-struck" and finally "brusque, chilly, and impersonal." As for the final letter, dated August 17, 1973, and written after Salinger broke off the relationship, the *Times* notes that it ended "the correspondence with a chilly thud." The *Times* states: "He responds clinically to her questions about ordering homeopathic publications and how to treat distemper in dogs and throws in a laundry list of favored remedies. Saying, 'it's late kiddo,' he complains that he is tired and has been answering letters all day and signs off."[80] Would any of the four privacy torts provide a successful basis for a lawsuit by Salinger against Maynard for auctioning off the letters?

---

[80] Peter Applebombe, *Love Letters in the Wind: A Private Affair of the Famously Private Salinger*, N.Y. Times, May 12, 1999, at E1.

CHAPTER 3

PRIVACY AND LAW ENFORCEMENT

A. THE FOURTH AMENDMENT AND EMERGING TECHNOLOGY

1. INTRODUCTION

(a) Privacy and Security

One of the central tensions in information privacy law is between privacy and security. Security involves society's interest in protecting its citizens from crimes, including physical and monetary threats. One way that government promotes security is by investigating and punishing crimes. To do this, law enforcement officials must gather information about suspected individuals. Monitoring and information gathering pose substantial threats to privacy. At the same time, however, monitoring and information gathering offer the potential of increasing security. Throughout the twentieth century, technology provided the government significantly greater ability to probe into the private lives of individuals.

The prevailing metaphor for the threat to privacy caused by law enforcement surveillance techniques is George Orwell's novel *Nineteen Eighty-Four*. Written in 1949, the novel depicted an all-powerful and omniscient government called "Big Brother" that monitored and controlled every facet of individuals' lives:

> Outside, even through the shut window-pane, the world looked cold. Down in the street little eddies of wind were whirling dust and torn paper into spirals, and though the sun was shining and the sky a harsh blue, there seemed to be no colour in anything, except the posters that were plastered everywhere. The black moustachio'd face gazed down from every commanding corner. There was one on the house-front immediately opposite. BIG BROTHER IS WATCHING YOU, the caption said, while the dark eyes looked deep into Winston's own. Down at streetlevel another poster, torn at one corner, flapped fitfully in the wind, alternately covering and uncovering the single word INGSOC. In the far distance a helicopter skimmed down between the roofs, hovered for an instant like a bluebottle, and darted away again with a curving flight. It was the police patrol, snooping into people's windows. The patrols did not matter, however. Only the Thought Police mattered.

> Behind Winston's back the voice from the telescreen was still babbling away about pig-iron and the overfulfilment of the Ninth Three-Year Plan. The telescreen received and transmitted simultaneously. Any sound that Winston made, above the level of a very low whisper, would be picked up by it, moreover, so long as he remained within the field of vision which the metal plaque commanded, he could be seen as well as heard. There was of course no way of knowing whether you were being watched at any given moment. How often, or on what system, the Thought Police plugged in on any individual wire was guesswork. It was even conceivable that they watched everybody all the time. But at any rate they could plug in your wire whenever they wanted to. You had to live — did live, from habit that became instinct — in the assumption that every sound you made was overheard, and, except in darkness, every movement scrutinized.[1]

Orwell's harrowing portrait of a police state illustrates the importance of limiting the power of the government to monitor its citizens. But consider the reverse as well: Will overly restrictive limitations on the power of the police restrict their ability to protect the public?

Although privacy and security may at times be viewed in conflict, consider the opening words of the Fourth Amendment: "The right of the people to be *secure* in their persons, houses, papers, and effects . . ." (emphasis added). Are the interests in public security and privacy fated to be always at odds? Are there times when the opposition between security and privacy proves a false dichotomy?

(b) The Fourth and Fifth Amendments

In the United States, policing is predominantly carried out by local governments. The Constitution, however, provides a national regulatory regime for police conduct. The Fourth and Fifth Amendments significantly limit the government's power to gather information. The Fourth Amendment provides:

> The right of the people to be secure in their persons, houses, papers, and effects, against unreasonable searches and seizures, shall not be violated, and no warrants shall issue, but upon probable cause, supported by oath or affirmation, and particularly describing the place to be searched, and the persons or things to be seized.

As the Supreme Court has recognized, "[t]he overriding function of the Fourth Amendment is to protect personal privacy and dignity against unwarranted intrusion by the State." *Schmerber v. California*, 384 U.S. 757 (1966).

The Fifth Amendment guarantees that "[n]o person . . . shall be compelled in any criminal case to be a witness against himself. . . ." The Fifth Amendment establishes a "privilege against self-incrimination," and it prohibits the government from compelling individuals to disclose inculpatory information about themselves.

The Fifth Amendment does not apply to all incriminating statements, but to information that is compelled. Further, the information must be "testimonial" in nature, and the Court has held that the Fifth Amendment does not apply to fin-

[1] George Orwell, *Nineteen Eighty-Four* 3-4 (1949).

gerprinting, photographing, taking measurements, writing or speaking for identification purposes, and having blood or bodily fluids drawn and tested. *See Schmerber v. California*, 384 U.S. 757 (1966). Finally, the Fifth Amendment does not protect broadly against prying into private secrets; it is limited to information that is incriminating.[2]

(c) Privacy of the Mail

In *Ex Parte Jackson,* 96 U.S. 727 (1877), one of its earliest Fourth Amendment cases, the Supreme Court held that the Fourth Amendment required a warrant to search sealed letters sent via the U.S. Postal Service:

> The constitutional guaranty of the right of the people to be secure in their persons against unreasonable searches and seizures extends to their papers, thus closed against inspection, wherever they may be. Whilst in the mail, they can only be opened and examined under like warrant, issued upon similar oath or affirmation, particularly describing the thing to be seized, as is required when papers are subjected to search in one's own household.

Although the Fourth Amendment protects the contents of a sealed letter, it does not protect the outside of letters, where addressing of information is typically located. As the Court noted in *Ex Parte Jackson,* "the outward form and weight" of letters and sealed packages are unprotected by the Fourth Amendment. Modern caselaw follows this distinction.

Today, federal law also restricts the government's ability to search people's mail. Pursuant to 39 U.S.C. §3623(d):

> No letter of such a class of domestic origin shall be opened except under authority of a search warrant authorized by law, or by an officer or employee of the Postal Service for the sole purpose of determining an address at which the letter can be delivered, or pursuant to the authorization of the addressee.

However, the government can search letters sent from abroad. *See United States v. Various Articles of Obscene Merchandise, Schedule No. 1213,* 395 F. Supp. 791 (S.D.N.Y. 1975), *aff'd,* 538 F.2d 317.

(d) Privacy of Papers and Documents

In *Boyd v. United States*, 116 U.S. 616 (1886), one of the foundational cases defining the meaning of the Fourth and Fifth Amendments, the government issued a subpoena to compel Boyd, a merchant, to produce invoices on cases of imported glass for use in a civil forfeiture proceeding. The Court held that the subpoena violated the Fourth and Fifth Amendments:

---

[2] For more background about the Fifth Amendment, see R. Kent Greenawalt, *Silence as a Moral and Constitutional Right*, 23 Wm. & Mary L. Rev. 15 (1981); Stephen J. Schulhofer, *Some Kind Words for the Privilege Against Self-Incrimination*, 26 Val. U. L. Rev. 311 (1991); William J. Stuntz, *Self-Incrimination and Excuse*, 99 Colum. L. Rev. 1227 (1988); David Donlinko, *Is There a Rationale for the Privilege Against Self-Incrimination?*, 33 UCLA L. Rev. 1063 (1986); Donald A. Dripps, *Self-Incrimination and Self-Preservation: A Skeptical View*, 1991 U. Ill. L. Rev. 329; Michael Dann, *The Fifth Amendment Privilege Against Self-Incrimination: Extorting Evidence from a Suspect*, 43 S. Cal. L. Rev. 597 (1970).

> . . . [B]y the proceeding now under consideration, the court attempts to extort from the party his private books and papers to make him liable for a penalty or to forfeit his property. . . .
>
> . . . It is not the breaking of his doors, and the rummaging of his drawers, that constitutes the essence of the offence; but it is the invasion of his indefeasible right to personal security, personal liberty and private property, where the right has never been forfeited by his conviction of some public offence. . . . Breaking into a house and opening boxes and drawers are circumstances of aggravation; but any forcible and compulsory extortion of a man's own testimony or of his private papers to be used as evidence to convict him of crime or to forfeit his goods, is within the condemnation of that judgment. In this regard the Fourth and Fifth Amendments run almost into each other.

In *Gouled v. United States*, 255 U.S. 298 (1921), the Court held that law enforcement officials could not use search warrants to search a person's "house or office or papers" to obtain evidence to use against her in a criminal proceeding. The holdings of *Boyd* and *Gouled* became known as the "mere evidence" rule — the government could only seize papers if they were instrumentalities of a crime, fruits of a crime, or illegal contraband.

The holding in *Boyd* has been significantly cut back. In *Warden v. Hayden*, 387 U.S. 294 (1967), the Court abolished the mere evidence rule. As the Court currently interprets the Fifth Amendment, the government can require a person to produce papers and records. *See Shapiro v. United States*, 335 U.S. 1 (1948). The Fifth Amendment also does not protect against subpoenas for a person's records and papers held by third parties. In *Couch v. United States*, 409 U.S. 322 (1973), the Court upheld a subpoena to a person's accountant for documents because "the Fifth Amendment privilege is a personal privilege: it adheres basically to the person, not to information that may incriminate him." The Fifth Amendment, the Court reasoned, only prevents "[i]nquisitorial pressure or coercion against a potentially accused person, compelling her, against her will, to utter self-condemning words or produce incriminating documents." Similarly, in *Fisher v. United States*, 425 U.S. 391 (1976), the Court upheld a subpoena to a person's attorney for documents pertaining to that person. The Fifth Amendment is not a "general protector of privacy" but protects against the "compelled self-incrimination."

(e) The Applicability of the Fourth Amendment

The Fourth Amendment governs the investigatory power of government officials. It applies every time a government official (not just police) conducts a "search" or the "seizure" of an object or document. Some examples of "searches" include peeking into one's pockets or searching one's person; entering into and looking around one's house, apartment, office, hotel room, or private property; and opening up and examining the contents of one's luggage or parcels. A "seizure" is a taking away of items by the police. A seizure can be of physical things or of persons (arrests). There must be a search or seizure to invoke the protection of the Fourth Amendment.

The Fourth Amendment does not apply simply when the police happen to observe something in "plain view." Whatever law enforcement officials see in plain view is not covered by the protection of the Fourth Amendment. Thus, the initial issue in Fourth Amendment analysis is whether the Amendment applies in the first place.[3]

(f) Reasonable Searches and Seizures

If the Fourth Amendment applies, then it requires that the search be "reasonable." Generally, a search is reasonable if the police have obtained a valid search warrant. To obtain a warrant, the police must go before a judge or magistrate and demonstrate that they have "probable cause" to conduct a search or seizure. Probable cause requires that government officials have "reasonably trustworthy information" that is sufficient to "warrant a man of reasonable caution in the belief that an offense has been or is being committed" or that evidence will be found in the place to be searched. *Brinegar v. United States*, 338 U.S. 160 (1949). Probable cause is more than "bare suspicion." Probable cause must be measured on a case-by-case basis, via the facts of particular cases. *See Wong Sun v. United States*, 371 U.S. 471 (1963). The purpose of a warrant is to have an independent party (judges) ensure that police really do have probable cause to conduct a search.

A search is valid if the warrant is supported by probable cause and the search is within the scope of the warrant. A warrantless search is generally considered to be per se unreasonable; however, there are a number of exceptions to this rule. Under these exceptions, a search is valid even if a warrant was not obtained as long as there was probable cause. For example, a search is not unreasonable if consent is obtained. When exigent circumstances make obtaining a warrant impractical, certain warrantless searches are reasonable.

Even with a warrant, certain searches are unreasonable. For example, in *Winston v. Lee*, 470 U.S. 753 (1985), the removal of a bullet lodged deep in the accused's chest was deemed unreasonable. However, the Court concluded that the taking of blood from a suspect constituted a reasonable search. *See Schmerber v. California*, 384 U.S. 757 (1966).[4]

(g) The "Special Needs" Doctrine

Under certain circumstances, the Fourth Amendment does not require government officials to have a warrant or probable cause to conduct a search. Pursuant to the "special needs" doctrine, searches and seizures are reasonable without a warrant or probable cause if "special needs, beyond the normal need for law enforcement, make the warrant and probable-cause requirement impracticable."

---

[3] There have been extensive writings about the Fourth Amendment's function of protecting privacy. For some background, see Christopher Slobogin, *The World Without a Fourth Amendment*, 39 UCLA L. Rev. 1 (1991); Silas J. Wasserstrom & Louis Michael Seidman, *The Fourth Amendment as Constitutional Theory*, 77 Geo. L.J. 19, 34 (1988); William J. Stuntz, *Privacy's Problem and the Law of Criminal Procedure*, 93 Mich. L. Rev. 1016 (1995); Scott E. Sundby, *"Everyman's" Fourth Amendment: Privacy or Mutual Trust Between Government and Citizen?*, 94 Colum. L. Rev. 1751 (1994); John Kent Walker, Jr., Note, *Covert Searches*, 39 Stan. L. Rev. 545 (1987).

[4] For more background about the Fourth Amendment's requirement of "reasonableness," see Sherry F. Colb, *The Qualitative Dimension of Fourth Amendment "Reasonableness,"* 98 Colum. L. Rev. 1642 (1998); Tracey Maclin, *Constructing Fourth Amendment Principles from the Government Perspective: Whose Amendment Is It, Anyway?*, 25 Am. Crim. L. Rev. 669 (1988).

Griffin v. Wisconsin, 483 U.S. 868 (1987). "The validity of a search is judged by the standard of 'reasonableness . . . under all the circumstances.'" *O'Connor v. Ortega*, 480 U.S. 709 (1987).

The special needs doctrine applies to searches in schools, government workplaces, and certain highly regulated businesses. As an example, the Supreme Court has upheld random drug tests for high school students participating in any competitive extracurricular activities, including academic extracurricular activities. *Board of Education v. Earls*, 536 U.S. 822 (2002). The special needs doctrine applies only when a search is not for a law enforcement purpose. Thus, in *New Jersey v. T.L.O.*, the Court upheld a search of a student's purse by school officials and noted that the search was "carried out by school authorities acting alone and on their own authority" as opposed to searches that might be conducted "in conjunction with or at the behest of law enforcement officials." *New Jersey v. T.L.O*, 469 U.S. 337 (1985).

(h) Administrative Searches

Generally, the need to inspect homes for health and safety violations is outweighed by the individual's privacy interest. *See Camara v. Municipal Court*, 387 U.S. 523 (1967) (holding that warrantless inspections of residences for housing code violations were unreasonable); *See v. City of Seattle*, 387 U.S. 541 (1967) (holding that search of a warehouse for fire code violations was unreasonable).

(i) Checkpoints

The police cannot randomly stop cars to check license and registration. *See Delaware v. Prouse*, 440 U.S. 648 (1979). However, fixed sobriety checkpoints are constitutional. *See Michigan Dep't of State Police v. Sitz*, 496 U.S. 444 (1990). Such a checkpoint search does not require "particularized suspicion." On the other hand, in *Indianapolis v. Edmond*, 531 U.S. 32 (2000), the Court held that checkpoints established to investigate possible drug violations were indistinguishable from a general purpose crime control search and were therefore unconstitutional:

> We have never approved a checkpoint program whose primary purpose was to detect evidence of ordinary criminal wrongdoing. Rather, our checkpoint cases have recognized only limited exceptions to the general rule that a seizure must be accompanied by some measure of individualized suspicion. We suggested in *Prouse* that we would not credit the "general interest in crime control" as justification for a regime of suspicionless stops. Consistent with this suggestion, each of the checkpoint programs that we have approved was designed primarily to serve purposes closely related to the problems of policing the border or the necessity of ensuring roadway safety. Because the primary purpose of the Indianapolis narcotics checkpoint program is to uncover evidence of ordinary criminal wrongdoing, the program contravenes the Fourth Amendment. . . .

The Supreme Court in *Illinois v. Lidster*, 540 U.S. 419 (2004), upheld the constitutionality of so-called "information-seeking highway stops." Following a hit-and-run accident that killed a 70-year-old bicyclist, the police in Lombard,

Illinois set up a checkpoint at the approximate scene of the accident. The po stopped vehicles, asked the occupants of the car whether they had seen anything the previous weekend, and gave each driver a flyer that described the fatal accident and asked for assistance in identifying the vehicle and driver in the accident. The Supreme Court found that "special law enforcement concerns will sometimes justify highway stops without individualized suspicion." It also found that the stop in question was reasonable as well as constitutional. First, the "relevant public concern was grave," involving police investigation of a human death. Second, the stop advanced the grave public concern to a significant degree. "The police appropriately tailored their checkpoint stops to fit important criminal investigatory needs." Third, and "[m]ost importantly, the stops interfered only minimally with liberty of the sort the Fourth Amendment seeks to protect." As the *Lidster* Court concluded: "Viewed objectively each stop required only a brief wait in line — a very few minutes at most. Contact with the police lasted only a few seconds. . . . Viewed subjectively, the contact provided little reason for anxiety or alarm."

In *MacWade v. Kelly*, 460 F.3d 260 (2d Cir. 2006), the New York Police Department instituted a random search program in the subways following a bombing on a subway in London. Police searched people's bags and other items as they entered subway stations. Those wishing not to be searched could leave the station. The court upheld the program under a Fourth Amendment challenge:

> Although a subway rider enjoys a full privacy expectation in the contents of his baggage, the kind of search at issue here minimally intrudes upon that interest. Several uncontested facts establish that the Program is narrowly tailored to achieve its purpose: (1) passengers receive notice of the searches and may decline to be searched so long as they leave the subway; (2) police search only those containers capable of concealing explosives, inspect eligible containers only to determine whether they contain explosives, inspect the containers visually unless it is necessary to manipulate their contents, and do not read printed or written material or request personal information; (3) a typical search lasts only for a matter of seconds; (4) uniformed personnel conduct the searches out in the open, which reduces the fear and stigma that removal to a hidden area can cause; and (5) police exercise no discretion in selecting whom to search, but rather employ a formula that ensures they do not arbitrarily exercise their authority. . . . .
>
> [W]e need only determine whether the Program is "a reasonably effective means of addressing" the government interest in deterring and detecting a terrorist attack on the subway system.
>
> We will not peruse, parse, or extrapolate four months' worth of data in an attempt to divine how many checkpoints the City ought to deploy in the exercise of its day-to-day police power. Counter-terrorism experts and politically accountable officials have undertaken the delicate and esoteric task of deciding how best to marshal their available resources in light of the conditions prevailing on any given day.

(j) *Terry* Stops

In *Terry v. Ohio,* 392 U.S. 1 (1968), the Court carved out another exception to warrants and probable cause. The Court held that a police officer can "stop" an cer has “reasonable suspicion” that criminal activity is afoot. on” is a standard that is lower than probable cause. A stop mporary. If it lasts too long, it becomes a seizure, which use. During the stop, the officer may “frisk” an individual for cer has reasonable suspicion that the person is armed and is not a full search. The officer cannot search the person for weapons. If, in the course of searching a person for weapons, the officer finds evidence of a crime, it will still be admissible if it was found within the scope of a valid frisk. For example, in *Minnesota v. Dickerson,* 508 U.S. 366 (1993), a police officer was searching a suspect for weapons and felt an object in the suspect’s pocket. The officer did not believe it to be a weapon, but continued to inspect it. The Court concluded that this was an invalid search that extended beyond the limited confines of a frisk.

(k) The Enforcement of the Fourth Amendment

When law enforcement officials violate an individual’s Fourth Amendment rights, the individual can seek at least two forms of redress. First, if the individual is a defendant in a criminal trial, she can move to have the evidence obtained in violation of the Fourth Amendment suppressed. This is known as the “exclusionary rule.” In *Weeks v. United States*, 232 U.S. 383 (1914), the Court established the exclusionary rule as the way to enforce the Fourth Amendment on federal officials. Later, in *Mapp v. Ohio*, 367 U.S. 643 (1961), the Court held that the exclusionary rule applies to all government searches, whether state or federal. The purpose of the exclusionary rule is to deter law enforcement officials from violating the Constitution.

If the police illegally search or seize evidence in violation of the Constitution, not only is that evidence suppressed but all other evidence derived from the illegally obtained evidence is also suppressed. This is known as the “fruit of the poisonous tree” doctrine. For example, suppose the police illegally search a person’s luggage and find evidence that the person is a drug trafficker. Armed with that evidence, the police obtain a warrant to search the person’s home, where they uncover new evidence of drug-trafficking along with a weapon used in a murder. The person is charged with drug trafficking and murder. Under the Fourth Amendment, the evidence found in the person’s luggage will be suppressed. Additionally, since the search warrant could not have been obtained but for the evidence turned up in the illegal search, the evidence found at the house, including the additional drug trafficking evidence as well as the murder evidence, will be suppressed. However, if the police obtained a warrant or located evidence by an “independent source,” then the fruit of the poisonous tree doctrine does not apply. *See Silverthorne Lumber Co. v. United States*, 251 U.S. 385 (1920). Returning to the example above, if the police had evidence supplied from the person’s cohort that the person was engaged in drug trafficking out of his home and had murdered somebody, this evidence may suffice to give the police probable cause to have a warrant issued to search the person’s house. This evidence is independent from the illegal search, and it is admissible.[5]

[5] The exclusionary rule has received significant scholarly attention. A number of scholars question its efficacy and advocate that the Fourth Amendment be enforced through other

The second form of redress for a violation of the Fourth Amendment is a civil remedy. A person, whether a criminal defendant or anybody else, can obtain civil damages for a Fourth Amendment violation by way of 42 U.S.C. § 1983.

2. WIRETAPPING, BUGGING, AND BEYOND

At common law, eavesdropping was considered a nuisance. "Eavesdropping" as William Blackstone defined it, meant to "listen under walls or window, or the eaves of a house, to hearken after discourse, and thereupon to frame slanderous and mischievous tales."[6] Before the advent of electronic communication, people could easily avoid eavesdroppers by ensuring that nobody else was around during their conversations.

The invention of the telegraph in 1844 followed by the telephone in 1876 substantially altered the way people communicated with each other. Today, the telephone has become an essential part of everyday communications. The advent of electronic communications was soon followed by the invention of recording and transmitting devices that enabled new and more sophisticated forms of eavesdropping than overhearing a conversation with the naked ear. One feature of electronic surveillance is that unlike the unsealing of letters, the interception of communications is undetectable. Some of the current forms of electronic surveillance technology include wiretaps, bugs, and parabolic microphones. New legal questions are raised by modern technology such as a cell phone, which can provide information about the physical location of the person using it.

A "wiretap" is a device used to intercept telephone (or telegraph) communications. Wiretapping began before the invention of the telephone. Wiretapping was used to intercept telegraph communications during the Civil War and became very prevalent after the invention of the telephone. The first police wiretap occurred in the early 1890s. In the first half of the twentieth century, wiretaps proliferated due to law enforcement attempts to monitor protests over bad industrial working conditions, social unrest caused by World War I, and the smuggling of alcohol during the Prohibition Years.[7]

A "bug" is a device, often quite miniature in size, that can be hidden on a person or in a place that can transmit conversations in a room to a remote receiving device, where the conversation can be listened to.

A "parabolic microphone" can pick up a conversation from a distance. Typically, a small dish behind the microphone enables the amplification of sound far away from the microphone itself.

---

mechanisms such as civil sanctions. *See* Akhil Reed Amar, *The Constitution and Criminal Procedure* 28 (1997); Christopher Slobogin, *Why Liberals Should Chuck the Exclusionary Rule*, 1999 U. Ill. L. Rev. 363, 400-01 (1999). Other commentators contend that civil sanctions will be ineffective. *See* Arnold H. Loewy, *The Fourth Amendment as a Device for Protecting the Innocent*, 81 Mich. L. Rev. 1229, 1266 (1983); Tracey Maclin, *When the Cure for the Fourth Amendment Is Worse Than the Disease*, 68 S. Cal. L. Rev. 1, 62 (1994).

[6] 4 Blackstone, *Commentaries* 168 (1769).

[7] For more background on the history of wiretapping, see generally Robert Ellis Smith, *Ben Franklin's Web Site: Privacy and Curiosity from Plymouth Rock to the Internet* (2000); Priscilla M. Regan, *Legislating Privacy: Technology, Social Values, and Public Policy* (1995); James G. Carr, *The Law of Electronic Surveillance* (1994); Whitfield Diffie & Susan Landau, *Privacy on the Line: The Politics of Wiretapping and Encryption* (1998).

Electronic surveillance devices were not in existence at the time that the Fourth Amendment was drafted. How, then, should the Fourth Amendment regulate these devices? In 1928, the Supreme Court attempted to answer this question in *Olmstead v. United States*, the first electronic surveillance case to come before the Court.

OLMSTEAD V. UNITED STATES

277 U.S. 438 (1928)

TAFT, C. J. The petitioners were convicted in the District Court for the Western District of Washington of a conspiracy to violate the National Prohibition Act by unlawfully possessing, transporting and importing intoxicating liquors and maintaining nuisances, and by selling intoxicating liquors. Seventy-two others, in addition to the petitioners, were indicted. Some were not apprehended, some were acquitted, and others pleaded guilty. . . .

The information which led to the discovery of the conspiracy and its nature and extent was largely obtained by intercepting messages on the telephones of the conspirators by four federal prohibition officers. Small wires were inserted along the ordinary telephone wires from the residences of four of the petitioners and those leading from the chief office. The insertions were made without trespass upon any property of the defendants. They were made in the basement of the large office building. The taps from house lines were made in the streets near the houses. . . .

The well-known historical purpose of the Fourth Amendment, directed against general warrants and writs of assistance, was to prevent the use of governmental force to search a man's house, his person, his papers, and his effects, and to prevent their seizure against his will. This phase of the misuse of governmental power of compulsion is the emphasis of the opinion of the court in the *Boyd* Case. . . .

. . . The Fourth Amendment may have proper application to a sealed letter in the mail, because of the constitutional provision for the Postoffice Department and the relations between the government and those who pay to secure protection of their sealed letters. . . . It is plainly within the words of the amendment to say that the unlawful rifling by a government agent of a sealed letter is a search and seizure of the sender's papers or effects. The letter is a paper, an effect, and in the custody of a government that forbids carriage, except under its protection.

The United States takes no such care of telegraph or telephone messages as of mailed sealed letters. The amendment does not forbid what was done here. There was no searching. There was no seizure. The evidence was secured by the use of the sense of hearing and that only. There was no entry of the houses or offices of the defendants. . . .

The language of the amendment cannot be extended and expanded to include telephone wires, reaching to the whole world from the defendant's house or office. The intervening wires are not part of his house or office, any more than are the highways along which they are stretched. . . .

Congress may, of course, protect the secrecy of telephone messages by making them, when intercepted, inadmissible in evidence in federal criminal trials, by direct legislation, and thus depart from the common law of evidence. But the courts may not adopt such a policy by attributing an enlarged and unusual meaning to the Fourth Amendment. The reasonable view is that one who installs in his house a telephone instrument with connecting wires intends to project his voice to those quite outside, and that the wires beyond his house, and messages while passing over them, are not within the protection of the Fourth Amendment. Here those who intercepted the projected voices were not in the house of either party to the conversation. . . .

BRANDEIS, J. dissenting. The government makes no attempt to defend the methods employed by its officers. Indeed, it concedes that, if wire tapping can be deemed a search and seizure within the Fourth Amendment, such wire tapping as was practiced in the case at bar was an unreasonable search and seizure, and that the evidence thus obtained was inadmissible. But it relies on the language of the amendment, and it claims that the protection given thereby cannot properly be held to include a telephone conversation.

"We must never forget," said Mr. Chief Justice Marshall in *McCulloch v. Maryland*, "that it is a Constitution we are expounding." Since then this court has repeatedly sustained the exercise of power by Congress, under various clauses of that instrument, over objects of which the fathers could not have dreamed. We have likewise held that general limitations on the powers of government, like those embodied in the due process clauses of the Fifth and Fourteenth Amendments, do not forbid the United States or the states from meeting modern conditions by regulations which "a century ago, or even half a century ago, probably would have been rejected as arbitrary and oppressive." Clauses guaranteeing to the individual protection against specific abuses of power, must have a similar capacity of adaptation to a changing world. It was with reference to such a clause that this court said in *Weems v. United States*, 217 U.S. 349, 373:

> Legislation, both statutory and constitutional, is enacted, it is true, from an experience of evils, but its general language should not, therefore, be necessarily confined to the form that evil had theretofore taken. Time works changes, brings into existence new conditions and purposes. Therefore a principle to be vital must be capable of wider application than the mischief which gave it birth. This is peculiarly true of Constitutions. They are not ephemeral enactments, designed to meet passing occasions. They are, to use the words of Chief Justice Marshall, "designed to approach immortality as nearly as human institutions can approach it." The future is their care and provision for events of good and bad tendencies of which no prophecy can be made. In the application of a Constitution, therefore, our contemplation cannot be only of what has been but of what may be. Under any other rule a Constitution would indeed be as easy of application as it would be deficient in efficacy and power. Its general principles would have little value and be converted by precedent into impotent and lifeless formulas. Rights declared in words might be lost in reality.

When the Fourth and Fifth Amendments were adopted, "the form that evil had theretofore taken" had been necessarily simple. Force and violence were then the only means known to man by which a government could directly effect self-incrimination. It could compel the individual to testify — a compulsion effected, if need be, by torture. It could secure possession of his papers and other articles incident to his private life — a seizure effected, if need be, by breaking and entry. Protection against such invasion of "the sanctities of a man's home and the privacies of life" was provided in the Fourth and Fifth Amendments by specific language. *Boyd v. United States*, 116 U.S. 616 (1886). But "time works changes, brings into existence new conditions and purposes." Subtler and more far-reaching means of invading privacy have become available to the government. Discovery and invention have made it possible for the government, by means far more effective than stretching upon the rack, to obtain disclosure in court of what is whispered in the closet.

Moreover, "in the application of a Constitution, our contemplation cannot be only of what has been, but of what may be." The progress of science in furnishing the government with means of espionage is not likely to stop with wire tapping. Ways may some day be developed by which the government, without removing papers from secret drawers, can reproduce them in court, and by which it will be enabled to expose to a jury the most intimate occurrences of the home. Advances in the psychic and related sciences may bring means of exploring unexpressed beliefs, thoughts and emotions. "That places the liberty of every man in the hands of every petty officer" was said by James Otis of much lesser intrusions than these. To Lord Camden a far slighter intrusion seemed "subversive of all the comforts of society." Can it be that the Constitution affords no protection against such invasions of individual security?

A sufficient answer is found in *Boyd v. United States*, 116 U.S. 616 (1886), a case that will be remembered as long as civil liberty lives in the United States. This court there reviewed the history that lay behind the Fourth and Fifth Amendments. We said with reference to Lord Camden's judgment in *Entick v. Carrington*, 19 Howell's State Trials, 1030:

> The principles laid down in this opinion affect the very essence of constitutional liberty and security. They reach farther than the concrete form of the case there before the court, with its adventitious circumstances; they apply to all invasions on the part of the government and its employees of the sanctities of a man's home and the privacies of life. It is not the breaking of his doors, and the rummaging of his drawers, that constitutes the essence of the offense; but it is the invasion of his indefeasible right of personal security, personal liberty and private property, where that right has never been forfeited by his conviction of some public offense — it is the invasion of this sacred right which underlies and constitutes the essence of Lord Camden's judgment. Breaking into a house and opening boxes and drawers are circumstances of aggravation; but any forcible and compulsory extortion of a man's own testimony or of his private papers to be used as evidence of a crime or to forfeit his goods, is within the condemnation of that judgment. In this regard the Fourth and Fifth Amendments run almost into each other.

In *Ex parte Jackson*, 96 U.S. 727 (1877), it was held that a sealed letter entrusted to the mail is protected by the amendments. The mail is a public service furnished by the government. The telephone is a public service furnished by its authority. There is, in essence, no difference between the sealed letter and the private telephone message. . . .

The evil incident to invasion of the privacy of the telephone is far greater than that involved in tampering with the mails. Whenever a telephone line is tapped, the privacy of the persons at both ends of the line is invaded, and all conversations between them upon any subject, and although proper, confidential, and privileged, may be overheard. Moreover, the tapping of one man's telephone line involves the tapping of the telephone of every other person whom he may call, or who may call him. As a means of espionage, writs of assistance and general warrants are but puny instruments of tyranny and oppression when compared with wire tapping.

Time and again this court, in giving effect to the principle underlying the Fourth Amendment, has refused to place an unduly literal construction upon it. . .

The protection guaranteed by the amendments is much broader in scope. The makers of our Constitution undertook to secure conditions favorable to the pursuit of happiness. They recognized the significance of man's spiritual nature, of his feelings and of his intellect. They knew that only a part of the pain, pleasure and satisfactions of life are to be found in material things. They sought to protect Americans in their beliefs, their thoughts, their emotions and their sensations. They conferred, as against the government, the right to be let alone — the most comprehensive of rights and the right most valued by civilized men. To protect that right, every unjustifiable intrusion by the government upon the privacy of the individual, whatever the means employed, must be deemed a violation of the Fourth Amendment. And the use, as evidence in a criminal proceeding, of facts ascertained by such intrusion must be deemed a violation of the Fifth.

Applying to the Fourth and Fifth Amendments the established rule of construction, the defendants' objections to the evidence obtained by wire tapping must, in my opinion, be sustained. It is, of course, immaterial where the physical connection with the telephone wires leading into the defendants' premises was made. And it is also immaterial that the intrusion was in aid of law enforcement. Experience should teach us to be most on our guard to protect liberty when the government's purposes are beneficent. Men born to freedom are naturally alert to repel invasion of their liberty by evil-minded rulers. The greatest dangers to liberty lurk in insidious encroachment by men of zeal, well-meaning but without understanding. . . .

NOTES & QUESTIONS

1. ***Background and Epilogue.*** Roy Olmstead, known as the "King of Bootleggers," ran a gigantic illegal alcohol distribution operation on the Pacific Coast during Prohibition. Formerly a police officer, Olmstead had long avoided trouble with state police by bribing them, but federal officials soon caught up with him. The federal investigators, led by Roy Lyle, Director of Prohibition, were wiretapping all of the telephones in Olmstead's home for around five months. The case was widely followed in the press, and it was dubbed "the case of the whispering wires." Olmstead was careful not to leave evidence in his very large home; when the agents searched it, they turned up no evidence. Most of the evidence in the case came from the wiretaps.

Olmstead knew he was being wiretapped; he had been tipped off by a freelance wiretapper the government had hired. But Olmstead believed that because wiretapping was illegal in the state of Washington, the wiretap evidence could not be used against him at trial. He was wrong. At trial, Olmstead was convicted and sentenced to four years in prison. He was later pardoned by President Roosevelt in 1935. In an ironic twist, while Olmstead was in prison, Roy Lyle was arrested for conspiring with rumrunners. Olmstead testified against Lyle at Lyle's trial. While in prison, Olmstead became a Christian Scientist, and after his release, he repudiated alcohol as one of the ills of society.[8]

2. ***The Physical Trespass Doctrine, Detectaphones, and "Spike Mikes."*** In *Olmstead,* the Supreme Court concluded that Fourth Amendment protections are triggered only when there is a physical trespass. The Court followed this approach for nearly 40 years. In *Goldman v. United States*, 316 U.S. 129 (1942), the police placed a device called a "detectaphone" next to a wall adjacent to a person's office. The device enabled the police to listen in on conversations inside the office. The Court concluded that since there was no trespass, there was no Fourth Amendment violation.

   In *Silverman v. United States*, 365 U.S. 505 (1961), the police used a device called a "spike mike" to listen in from a vacant row house to conversations in an adjoining row house. The device consisted of a microphone with a spike of about a foot in length attached to it. The spike was inserted into a baseboard of the vacant row house on the wall adjoining the row house next door. The spike hit the heating duct serving the next door row house, which transformed the heating system into a sound conductor. The Court held that the use of the "spike mike" violated the Fourth Amendment because it constituted an "unauthorized physical encroachment" into the adjoining row house. The Court distinguished *Olmstead* and *Goldman* because those cases did not involve any "physical invasion" or "trespass" onto the defendant's property, whereas the "spike mike" "usurp[ed] part of the [defendant's] house or office." Do you agree with the Court's distinction between *Goldman/Olmstead* and *Silverman* — between surveillance involving physical intrusion (however slight) and surveillance not involving any trespassing on the premises?

3. ***Brandeis's Dissent and the Warren and Brandeis Article.*** Justice Brandeis's dissent is one of the most famous dissents in Supreme Court history. Note the similarities between Brandeis's 1890 article, *The Right to Privacy*, and his dissent nearly 40 years later in *Olmstead.* What themes are repeated? Recall that *The Right to Privacy* concerned locating common law roots for privacy protection. What is Brandeis saying about the roots of constitutional protection of privacy?

---

[8] Samuel Dash, *The Intruders: Unreasonable Searches and Seizures from King John to John Ashcroft* 74-78 (2004); Robert C. Post, *Federalism, Positive Law, and the Emergence of the American Administrative State: Prohibition in the Taft Court Era,* 48 Wm. & Mary L. Rev. 1, 139-50 (2006).

4. ***Changing Technology and the Constitution.*** Brandeis contends that the Constitution should keep pace with changing technology. But given the rapid pace of technological change and the fact that the Constitution must serve as the stable foundation for our society, can the Constitution keep pace? How adaptable should the Constitution be?
5. ***Wiretapping vs. Mail Tampering.*** Brandeis contends that wiretapping is more insidious than tampering with the mail. Why? How would you compare wiretapping with intercepting e-mail or instant messages?
6. ***State Wiretapping Law.*** In the state of Washington, where the wiretapping in *Olmstead* took place, wiretapping was a criminal act, and the officers had thus violated the law. In a separate dissenting opinion, Justice Holmes noted that:

   > . . . [A]part from the Constitution the government ought not to use evidence obtained and only obtainable by a criminal act. . . . It is desirable that criminals should be detected, and to that end that all available evidence should be used. It also is desirable that the government should not itself foster and pay for other crimes, when they are the means by which the evidence is to be obtained. If it pays its officers for having got evidence by crime I do not see why it may not as well pay them for getting it in the same way, and I can attach no importance to protestations of disapproval if it knowingly accepts and pays and announces that in future it will pay for the fruits. We have to choose, and for my part I think it a less evil that some criminals should escape than that the government should play an ignoble part.

   Should it matter in Fourth Amendment analysis whether particular federal law enforcement surveillance tactics are illegal under state law?
7. ***The Birth of Federal Electronic Surveillance Law.*** The *Olmstead* decision was not well received by the public. In 1934, Congress responded to *Olmstead* by enacting § 605 of the Federal Communications Act, making wiretapping a federal crime. This statute will be discussed later in the part on electronic surveillance law.
8. ***Secret Agents and Misplaced Trust.*** In *Hoffa v. United States*, 385 U.S. 293 (1966), an undercover informant, Edward Partin, befriended James Hoffa and elicited statements from him about his plans to bribe jurors in a criminal trial in which Hoffa was a defendant. According to the Court:

   > In the present case . . . it is evident that no interest legitimately protected by the Fourth Amendment is involved. It is obvious that the petitioner was not relying on the security of his hotel suite when he made the incriminating statements to Partin or in Partin's presence. Partin did not enter the suite by force or by stealth. He was not a surreptitious eavesdropper. Partin was in the suite by invitation, and every conversation which he heard was either directed to him or knowingly carried on in his presence. The petitioner, in a word, was not relying on the security of the hotel room; he was relying upon his misplaced confidence that Partin would not reveal his wrongdoing.

   Likewise, in *Lewis v. United States*, 385 U.S. 206 (1966), the defendant sold drugs to an undercover agent in his house. The Court held:

> In the instant case . . . the petitioner invited the undercover agent to his home for the specific purpose of executing a felonious sale of narcotics. Petitioner's only concern was whether the agent was a willing purchaser who could pay the agreed price. . . . During neither of his visits to petitioner's home did the agent see, hear, or take anything that was not contemplated, and in fact intended, by petitioner as a necessary part of his illegal business. Were we to hold the deceptions of the agent in this case constitutionally prohibited, we would come near to a rule that the use of undercover agents in any manner is virtually unconstitutional per se. Such a rule would, for example, severely hamper the Government in ferreting out those organized criminal activities that are characterized by covert dealings with victims who either cannot or do not protest. A prime example is provided by the narcotics traffic. . . .

Hoffa and *Lewis* establish that a person does not have a privacy interest in the loyalty of her friends. The government may deceive a person by sending in secret agents to befriend her. Is it problematic that government is permitted to use spies and deception as a law enforcement technique? Consider the following observation by Anthony Amsterdam:

> I can see no significant difference between police spies . . . and electronic surveillance, either in their uses or abuses. Both have long been asserted by law enforcement officers to be indispensable tools in investigating crime, particularly victimless and political crime, precisely because they both search out privacies that government could not otherwise invade. Both tend to repress crime in the same way, by making people distrustful and unwilling to talk to one another. The only difference is that under electronic surveillance you are afraid to talk to anybody in your office or over the phone, while under a spy system you are afraid to talk to anybody at all.[9]

9. ***Bugs, Transmitters, and Recording Devices.*** In *On Lee v. United States*, 343 U.S. 747 (1952), Chin Poy, a government informant with a concealed transmitter, engaged On Lee in conversation for the purpose of eliciting that On Lee was a drug dealer. The conversation was transmitted to a law enforcement agent, who later testified at trial about the content of the conversation. The Court held that the Fourth Amendment did not apply:

> Petitioner was talking confidentially and indiscreetly with one he trusted, and he was overheard. This was due to aid from a transmitter and receiver, to be sure, but with the same effect on his privacy as if agent Lee had been eavesdropping outside an open window. The use of bifocals, field glasses or the telescope to magnify the object of a witness' vision is not a forbidden search or seizure, even if they focus without his knowledge or consent upon what one supposes to be private indiscretions. It would be a dubious service to the genuine liberties protected by the Fourth Amendment to make them bedfellows with spurious liberties improvised by farfetched analogies which would liken eavesdropping on a conversation, with the connivance of one of the parties, to an unreasonable search or seizure. We find no violation of the Fourth Amendment here.

---

[9] Anthony G. Amsterdam, *Perspectives on the Fourth Amendment*, 58 Minn. L. Rev. 349, 407 (1974). For a detailed analysis of undercover agents, see Gary T. Marx, *Under Cover: Police Surveillance in America* (1988).

Does the use of electronic devices distinguish *On Lee* from *Hoffa* and *Lewis* in a material way?

LOPEZ V. UNITED STATES

373 U.S. 427 (1963)

[The petitioner, German S. Lopez, was tried in a federal court on a four-count indictment charging him with attempted bribery of an Internal Revenue agent, Roger S. Davis. The evidence against him had been obtained by a series of meetings between him and Davis. The last meeting was recorded by Davis with a pocket wire recorder. Prior to trial, Lopez moved to suppress the recorded conversation.]

HARLAN, J. . . . [Petitioner's] argument is primarily addressed to the recording of the conversation, which he claims was obtained in violation of his rights under the Fourth Amendment. Recognizing the weakness of this position if Davis was properly permitted to testify about the same conversation, petitioner now challenges that testimony as well, although he failed to do so at the trial. . . .

Once it is plain that Davis could properly testify about his conversation with Lopez, the constitutional claim relating to the recording of that conversation emerges in proper perspective. The Court has in the past sustained instances of "electronic eavesdropping" against constitutional challenge, when devices have been used to enable government agents to overhear conversations which would have been beyond the reach of the human ear. *See, e.g.*, *Olmstead v. United States*. It has been insisted only that the electronic device not be planted by an unlawful physical invasion of a constitutionally protected area. . . . Indeed this case involves no "eavesdropping" whatever in any proper sense of that term. The Government did not use an electronic device to listen in on conversations it could not otherwise have heard. Instead, the device was used only to obtain the most reliable evidence possible of a conversation in which the Government's own agent was a participant and which that agent was fully entitled to disclose. And the device was not planted by means of an unlawful physical invasion of petitioner's premises under circumstances which would violate the Fourth Amendment. It was carried in and out by an agent who was there with petitioner's assent, and it neither saw nor heard more than the agent himself. . . .

Stripped to its essentials, petitioner's argument amounts to saying that he has a constitutional right to rely on possible flaws in the agent's memory, or to challenge the agent's credibility without being beset by corroborating evidence that is not susceptible of impeachment. For no other argument can justify excluding an accurate version of a conversation that the agent could testify to from memory. We think the risk that petitioner took in offering a bribe to Davis fairly included the risk that the offer would be accurately reproduced in court, whether by faultless memory or mechanical recording. . . .

WARREN, C.J. concurring. I also share the opinion of Mr. Justice Brennan that the fantastic advances in the field of electronic communication constitute a great danger to the privacy of the individual; that indiscriminate use of such devices in law enforcement raises grave constitutional questions under the Fourth and Fifth Amendments; and that these considerations impose a heavier responsibility on this Court in its supervision of the fairness of procedures in the federal court system. However, I do not believe that, as a result, all uses of such devices should be proscribed either as unconstitutional or as unfair law enforcement methods. One of the lines I would draw would be between this case and *On Lee*. . . .

The use and purpose of the transmitter in *On Lee* was substantially different from the use of the recorder here. Its advantage was not to corroborate the testimony of Chin Poy, but rather, to obviate the need to put him on the stand. The Court in *On Lee* itself stated:

> We can only speculate on the reasons why Chin Poy was not called. It seems a not unlikely assumption that the very defects of character and blemishes of record which made On Lee trust him with confidences would make a jury distrust his testimony. Chin Poy was close enough to the underworld to serve as bait, near enough the criminal design so that petitioner would embrace him as a confidante, but too close to it for the Government to vouch for him as a witness. Instead, the Government called agent Lee.

However, there were further advantages in not using Chin Poy. Had Chin Poy been available for cross-examination, counsel for On Lee could have explored the nature of Chin Poy's friendship with On Lee, the possibility of other unmonitored conversations and appeals to friendship, the possibility of entrapments, police pressure brought to bear to persuade Chin Poy to turn informer, and Chin Poy's own recollection of the contents of the conversation. . . .

Thus while I join the Court in permitting the use of electronic devices to corroborate an agent under the particular facts of this case, I cannot sanction by implication the use of these same devices to radically shift the pattern of presentation of evidence in the criminal trial, a shift that may be used to conceal substantial factual and legal issues concerning the rights of the accused and the administration of criminal justice.

BRENNAN, J. joined by DOUGLAS and GOLDBERG, J.J. dissenting. . . . [T]he Government's argument is that Lopez surrendered his right of privacy when he communicated his "secret thoughts" to Agent Davis. The assumption, manifestly untenable, is that the Fourth Amendment is only designed to protect secrecy. If a person commits his secret thoughts to paper, that is no license for the police to seize the paper; if a person communicates his secret thoughts verbally to another, that is no license for the police to record the words. *On Lee* certainly rested on no such theory of waiver. The right of privacy would mean little if it were limited to a person's solitary thoughts, and so fostered secretiveness. It must embrace a concept of the liberty of one's communications, and historically it has. "The common law secures to each individual the right of determining, ordinarily, to what extent his thoughts, sentiments, and emotions shall be communicated to others . . . and even if he has chosen to give them expression, he generally retains the power to fix the limits of the publicity which shall be given them." Warren and Brandeis, *The Right to Privacy*, 4 Harv. L. Rev. 193, 198 (1890).

That is not to say that all communications are privileged. On Lee assumed the risk that his acquaintance would divulge their conversation; Lopez assumed the same risk vis-à-vis Davis. The risk inheres in all communications which are not in the sight of the law privileged. It is not an undue risk to ask persons to assume, for it does no more than compel them to use discretion in choosing their auditors, to make damaging disclosures only to persons whose character and motives may be trusted. But the risk which both *On Lee* and today's decision impose is of a different order. It is the risk that third parties, whether mechanical auditors like the Minifon or human transcribers of mechanical transmissions as in *On Lee* — third parties who cannot be shut out of a conversation as conventional eavesdroppers can be, merely by a lowering of voices, or withdrawing to a private place — may give independent evidence of any conversation. There is only one way to guard against such a risk, and that is to keep one's mouth shut on all occasions. . . .

The risk of being overheard by an eavesdropper or betrayed by an informer or deceived as to the identity of one with whom one deals is probably inherent in the conditions of human society. It is the kind of risk we necessarily assume whenever we speak. But as soon as electronic surveillance comes into play, the risk changes crucially. There is no security from that kind of eavesdropping, no way of mitigating the risk, and so not even a residuum of true privacy. . . .

NOTES & QUESTIONS

1. ***Is Electronic Surveillance Different?*** Should electronic surveillance be treated similarly or differently than regular eavesdropping? Is it consistent to agree that Davis could testify as to what Lopez said via his memory but cannot introduce a recording of what Lopez said?

KATZ V. UNITED STATES

389 U.S. 347 (1967)

STEWART, J. The petitioner was convicted in the District Court for the Southern District of California under an eight-count indictment charging him with transmitting wagering information by telephone from Los Angeles to Miami and Boston in violation of a federal statute. At trial the Government was permitted, over the petitioner's objection, to introduce evidence of the petitioner's end of telephone conversations, overheard by FBI agents who had attached an electronic listening and recording device to the outside of the public telephone booth from which he had placed his calls. In affirming his conviction, the Court of Appeals rejected the contention that the recordings had been obtained in violation of the Fourth Amendment, because "[t]here was no physical entrance into the area occupied by, (the petitioner)." We granted certiorari in order to consider the constitutional questions thus presented.

The petitioner had phrased those questions as follows:

> A. Whether a public telephone booth is a constitutionally protected area so that evidence obtained by attaching an electronic listening recording device to the top of such a booth is obtained in violation of the right to privacy of the user of the booth.
> B. Whether physical penetration of a constitutionally protected area is necessary before a search and seizure can be said to be violative of the Fourth Amendment to the United States Constitution.

We decline to adopt this formulation of the issues. In the first place the correct solution of Fourth Amendment problems is not necessarily promoted by incantation of the phrase "constitutionally protected area." Secondly, the Fourth Amendment cannot be translated into a general constitutional "right to privacy." That Amendment protects individual privacy against certain kinds of governmental intrusion, but its protections go further, and often have nothing to do with privacy at all. Other provisions of the Constitution protect personal privacy from other forms of governmental invasion. But the protection of a person's general right to privacy — his right to be let alone by other people — is, like the protection of his property and of his very life, left largely to the law of the individual States.

Because of the misleading way the issues have been formulated, the parties have attached great significance to the characterization of the telephone booth from which the petitioner placed his calls. The petitioner has strenuously argued that the booth was a "constitutionally protected area." The Government has maintained with equal vigor that it was not. But this effort to decide whether or not a given "area," viewed in the abstract, is "constitutionally protected" deflects attention from the problem presented by this case. For the Fourth Amendment protects people, not places. What a person knowingly exposes to the public, even in his own home or office, is not a subject of Fourth Amendment protection. But what he seeks to preserve as private, even in an area accessible to the public, may be constitutionally protected.

The Government stresses the fact that the telephone booth from which the petitioner made his calls was constructed partly of glass, so that he was as visible after he entered it as he would have been if he had remained outside. But what he sought to exclude when he entered the booth was not the intruding eye — it was the uninvited ear. He did not shed his right to do so simply because he made his calls from a place where he might be seen. No less than an individual in a business office, in a friend's apartment, or in a taxicab, a person in a telephone booth may rely upon the protection of the Fourth Amendment. One who occupies it, shuts the door behind him, and pays the toll that permits him to place a call is surely entitled to assume that the words he utters into the mouthpiece will not be broadcast to the world. To read the Constitution more narrowly is to ignore the vital role that the public telephone has come to play in private communication.

The Government contends, however, that the activities of its agents in this case should not be tested by Fourth Amendment requirements, for the surveillance technique they employed involved no physical penetration of the telephone booth from which the petitioner placed his calls. It is true that the absence of such penetration was at one time thought to foreclose further Fourth Amendment inquiry, *Olmstead v. United States*, *Goldman v. United States*, for that Amendment was thought to limit only searches and seizures of tangible property. But "[t]he premise that property interests control the right of the Government to search and seize has been discredited." . . . [O]nce this much is acknowledged, and once it is recognized that the Fourth Amendment protects people — and not simply "areas" — against unreasonable searches and seizures it becomes clear that the reach of that Amendment cannot turn upon the presence or absence of a physical intrusion into any given enclosure.

We conclude that the underpinnings of *Olmstead* and *Goldman* have been so eroded by our subsequent decisions that the "trespass" doctrine there enunciated can no longer be regarded as controlling. . . .

The question remaining for decision, then, is whether the search and seizure conducted in this case complied with constitutional standards. In that regard, the Government's position is that its agents acted in an entirely defensible manner: They did not begin their electronic surveillance until investigation of the petitioner's activities had established a strong probability that he was using the telephone in question to transmit gambling information to persons in other States, in violation of federal law. Moreover, the surveillance was limited, both in scope and in duration, to the specific purpose of establishing the contents of the petitioner's unlawful telephonic communications. The agents confined their surveillance to the brief periods during which he used the telephone booth, and they took great care to overhear only the conversations of the petitioner himself. . . .

. . . It is apparent that the agents in this case acted with restraint. Yet the inescapable fact is that this restraint was imposed by the agents themselves, not by a judicial officer. They were not required, before commencing the search, to present their estimate of probable cause for detached scrutiny by a neutral magistrate. They were not compelled, during the conduct of the search itself, to observe precise limits established in advance by a specific court order. Nor were they directed, after the search had been completed, to notify the authorizing magistrate in detail of all that had been seized. In the absence of such safeguards, this Court has never sustained a search upon the sole ground that officers reasonably expected to find evidence of a particular crime and voluntarily confined their activities to the least intrusive means consistent with that end. Searches conducted without warrants have been held unlawful "notwithstanding facts unquestionably showing probable cause." . . . "Over and again this Court has emphasized that the mandate of the [Fourth] Amendment requires adherence to judicial processes," and that searches conducted outside the judicial process, without prior approval by judge or magistrate, are per se unreasonable under the Fourth Amendment — subject only to a few specifically established and well-delineated exceptions. . . .

HARLAN, J. concurring. . . . As the Court's opinion states, "the Fourth Amendment protects people, not places." The question, however, is what protection it affords to those people. Generally, as here, the answer to that question requires reference to a "place." My understanding of the rule that has emerged from prior decisions is that there is a twofold requirement, first that a person have exhibited an actual (subjective) expectation of privacy and, second, that the expectation be one that society is prepared to recognize as "reasonable." Thus a man's home is, for most purposes, a place where he expects privacy, but objects, activities, or statements that he exposes to the "plain view" of outsiders are not "protected" because no intention to keep them to himself has been exhibited. On the other hand, conversations in the open would not be protected against being overheard, for the expectation of privacy under the circumstances would be unreasonable.

The critical fact in this case is that "(o)ne who occupies it, (a telephone booth) shuts the door behind him, and pays the toll that permits him to place a call is surely entitled to assume" that his conversation is not being intercepted. The point is not that the booth is "accessible to the public" at other times, but that it is a temporarily private place whose momentary occupants' expectations of freedom from intrusion are recognized as reasonable.

BLACK, J. dissenting. . . . My basic objection is twofold: (1) I do not believe that the words of the Amendment will bear the meaning given them by today's decision, and (2) I do not believe that it is the proper role of this Court to rewrite the Amendment in order "to bring it into harmony with the times" and thus reach a result that many people believe to be desirable.

While I realize that an argument based on the meaning of words lacks the scope, and no doubt the appeal, of broad policy discussions and philosophical discourses on such nebulous subjects as privacy, for me the language of the Amendment is the crucial place to look in construing a written document such as our Constitution. The Fourth Amendment says that

> The right of the people to be secure in their persons, houses, papers, and effects, against unreasonable searches and seizures, shall not be violated, and no Warrants shall issue, but upon probable cause, supported by Oath or affirmation, and particularly describing the place to be searched, and the persons or things to be seized.

The first clause protects "persons, houses, papers, and effects, against unreasonable searches and seizures. . . ." These words connote the idea of tangible things with size, form, and weight, things capable of being searched, seized, or both. The second clause of the Amendment still further establishes its Framers' purpose to limit its protection to tangible things by providing that no warrants shall issue but those "particularly describing the place to be searched, and the persons or things to be seized." A conversation overheard by eavesdropping, whether by plain snooping or wiretapping, is not tangible and, under the normally accepted meanings of the words, can neither be searched nor seized. . . .

NOTES & QUESTIONS

1. ***Who Was Charlie Katz?*** David Skalansky describes the background to *Katz*:

> Charlie Katz was a Damon Runyon character plopped into 1960s Los Angeles. Katz was a professional bettor . . . Katz wagered on sports events, sometimes for himself and sometimes on commission for others. He specialized in basketball games, and he had his own, elaborate system for

ranking teams and predicting outcomes. In February 1965, he was living in a poolside hotel room on the Sunset Strip.[10]

Sklanksy describes how the FBI would observe Katz leaving his hotel to place his bets from the telephone booth. An agent stationed outside would radio the news to another agent near the booth. This second agent would turn on a tape recorder placed on top of the telephone booth, observe Katz making his calls, and once Katz was finished and left the telephone booth, turn the recorder off and take it down from the top of the booth.

2. ***The Reasonable Expectation of Privacy Test.*** The *Katz* decision established a widely cited test for whether the Fourth Amendment is applicable in a given situation. That test was articulated not in the majority opinion but in the concurring opinion by Justice Harlan. The rule as articulated in Justice Harlan's concurrence has become known as the "reasonable expectation of privacy test." Under the test, (1) a person must exhibit an "actual (subjective) expectation of privacy" and (2) "the expectation [must] be one that society is prepared to recognize as 'reasonable.'"

According to Christopher Slobogin and Joseph Schumacher:

> For the most part, the Court has been content with fleshing out the meaning of the phrase[] "reasonable expectations of privacy" . . . through [its] application to specific cases. But the Court has also provided two significant guidelines as to how [this phrase] should be interpreted. The first guideline came in *Rakas v. Illinois*, where the majority opinion, by then-Associate Justice Rehnquist, stated that "legitimation of expectations of privacy by law must have a source outside of the Fourth Amendment, either by reference to concepts of real or personal property law or to understandings that are recognized and permitted by society." Most important for present purposes is the last clause of this excerpt, which indicates the Court's willingness to rely on societal understandings in defining "reasonable expectations of privacy." Although this language appeared in a footnote, and was directed solely toward defining the standing concept, it has since been relied upon in the text of several other cases involving the "search" issue, often rephrased in terms of expectations of privacy "society is prepared to recognize as 'reasonable.'"
>
> The second guideline came from the same footnote in *Rakas*. According to the Court, the use of the word "legitimate" or "reasonable" before "expectations of privacy" is meant to convey "more than a subjective expectation of not being discovered." As the Court explained,
>
> > [a] burglar plying his trade in a summer cabin during the off season may have a thoroughly justified subjective expectation of privacy, but it is not one which the law recognizes as "legitimate." His presence . . . is "wrongful"; his expectation is not "one that society is prepared to recognize as 'reasonable.'"
>
> In short, the Fourth Amendment does not protect expectations of privacy that only a criminal would have.[11]

---

[10] David A. Sklansky, *Katz v. United States*, in *Criminal Procedure Stories* (Carol S. Steiker, ed., 2006).

[11] Christopher Slobogin & Joseph E. Schumacher, *Reasonable Expectations of Privacy and Autonomy in Fourth Amendment Cases: An Empirical Look at "Understandings Recognized and Permitted by Society,"* 42 Duke L.J. 727, 731-32 (1993).

3. ***Variations on* Katz.** What if the door to the telephone booth in *Katz* had been open? Would the Court still have concluded that the Fourth Amendment applied? What if the cop stood outside the booth, and Katz spoke loud enough for the cop to hear? Suppose the police placed a sound recording device outside the phone booth, and the device could pick up Katz's voice, which would be inaudible to the naked ear outside the phone booth. Would this be a violation of the Fourth Amendment?
4. ***"Conditioned" Expectations of Privacy.*** Before *Katz*, police sometimes tapped phones. How would this behavior affect a person's expectations of privacy when speaking on the phone? Consider the following observation by the Court in *Smith v. Maryland*, 442 U.S. 735, 741 n.5 (1979):

   > Situations can be imagined, of course, in which Katz' two-pronged inquiry would provide an inadequate index of Fourth Amendment protection. For example, if the Government were suddenly to announce on nationwide television that all homes henceforth would be subject to warrantless entry, individuals thereafter might not in fact entertain any actual expectation or privacy regarding their homes, papers, and effects. Similarly, if a refugee from a totalitarian country, unaware of this Nation's traditions, erroneously assumed that police were continuously monitoring his telephone conversations, a subjective expectation of privacy regarding the contents of his calls might be lacking as well. In such circumstances, where an individual's subjective expectations had been "conditioned" by influences alien to well-recognized Fourth Amendment freedoms, those subjective expectations obviously could play no meaningful role in ascertaining what the scope of Fourth Amendment protection was. In determining whether a "legitimate expectation of privacy" existed in such cases, a normative inquiry would be proper.

5. **Berger v. New York.** *Berger v. New York*, 388 U.S. 41 (1967), is an important Fourth Amendment case decided after the Supreme Court agreed to hear *Katz* but before it heard oral arguments in that case. In *Berger*, the Court struck down portions of New York's eavesdropping statute as violating the Fourth Amendment. The New York law authorized the installation of electronic surveillance devices for 60 days, and it allowed the surveillance to be extended beyond the 60 days without a showing of present probable cause to continue the eavesdrop. The Court held:

   > . . . The Fourth Amendment commands that a warrant issue not only upon probable cause supported by oath or affirmation, but also "particularly describing the place to be searched, and the persons or things to be seized." New York's statute lacks this particularization. It merely says that a warrant may issue on reasonable ground to believe that evidence of crime may be obtained by the eavesdrop. It lays down no requirement for particularity in the warrant as to what specific crime has been or is being committed, nor "the place to be searched," or "the persons or things to be seized" as specifically required by the Fourth Amendment. The need for particularity and evidence of reliability in the showing required when judicial authorization of a search is sought is especially great in the case of eavesdropping. By its very nature eavesdropping involves an intrusion on privacy that is broad in scope. . . .

> . . . New York's statute . . . lays down no . . . "precise and discriminate" requirements. . . . New York's broadside authorization rather than being "carefully circumscribed" so as to prevent unauthorized invasions of privacy actually permits general searches by electronic devices, the truly offensive character of which was first condemned in *Entick v. Carrington*, 19 How. St. Tr. 1029, and which were then known as "general warrants." The use of the latter was a motivating factor behind the Declaration of Independence. In view of the many cases commenting on the practice it is sufficient here to point out that under these "general warrants" customs officials were given blanket authority to conduct general searches for goods imported to the Colonies in violation of the tax laws of the Crown. The Fourth Amendment's requirement that a warrant "particularly describ(e) the place to be searched, and the persons or things to be seized," repudiated these general warrants and "makes general searches . . . impossible and prevents the seizure of one thing under a warrant describing another. As to what is to be taken, nothing is left to the discretion of the officer executing the warrant."
>
> We believe the statute here is equally offensive. First, as we have mentioned, eavesdropping is authorized without requiring belief that any particular offense has been or is being committed; nor that the "property" sought, the conversations, be particularly described. The purpose of the probable cause requirement of the Fourth Amendment, to keep the state out of constitutionally protected areas until it has reason to believe that a specific crime has been or is being committed, is thereby wholly aborted. Likewise the statute's failure to describe with particularity the conversations sought gives the officer a roving commission to "seize" any and all conversations. . . . As with general warrants this leaves too much to the discretion of the officer executing the order. Secondly, authorization of eavesdropping for a two-month period is the equivalent of a series of intrusions, searches, and seizures pursuant to a single showing of probable cause. Prompt execution is also avoided. During such a long and continuous (24 hours a day) period the conversations of any and all persons coming into the area covered by the device will be seized indiscriminately and without regard to their connection with the crime under investigation. Moreover, the statute permits, and there were authorized here, extensions of the original two-month period — presumably for two months each — on a mere showing that such extension is "in the public interest." Apparently the original grounds on which the eavesdrop order was initially issued also form the basis of the renewal. This we believe insufficient without a showing of present probable cause for the continuance of the eavesdrop. Third, the statute places no termination date on the eavesdrop once the conversation sought is seized. This is left entirely in the discretion of the officer. Finally, the statute's procedure, necessarily because its success depends on secrecy, has no requirement for notice as do conventional warrants, nor does it overcome this defect by requiring some showing of special facts. On the contrary, it permits uncontested entry without any showing of exigent circumstances. . . . In short, the statute's blanket grant of permission to eavesdrop is without adequate judicial supervision or protective procedures. . . .

As Sklansky points out, the effect of *Berger* combined with two other cases decided immediately before *Katz* — *Warren v. Hayden*, 387 U.S. 294 (1967) and *Camara v. Municipal Court*, 387 U.S. 523 (1967) — was to underscore the "centrality of the warrant requirement to the Fourth Amendment."[12]

UNITED STATES V. WHITE

401 U.S. 745 (1971)

WHITE, J. In 1966, respondent James A. White was tried and convicted under two consolidated indictments charging various illegal transactions in narcotics. . . . He was fined and sentenced as a second offender to 25-year concurrent sentences. The issue before us is whether the Fourth Amendment bars from evidence the testimony of governmental agents who related certain conversations which had occurred between defendant White and a government informant, Harvey Jackson, and which the agents overheard by monitoring the frequency of a radio transmitter carried by Jackson and concealed on his person. On four occasions the conversations took place in Jackson's home; each of these conversations was overheard by an agent concealed in a kitchen closet with Jackson's consent and by a second agent outside the house using a radio receiver. Four other conversations — one in respondent's home, one in a restaurant, and two in Jackson's car — were overheard by the use of radio equipment. The prosecution was unable to locate and produce Jackson at the trial and the trial court overruled objections to the testimony of the agents who conducted the electronic surveillance. The jury returned a guilty verdict and defendant appealed. . . .

Concededly a police agent who conceals his police connections may write down for official use his conversations with a defendant and testify concerning them, without a warrant authorizing his encounters with the defendant and without otherwise violating the latter's Fourth Amendment rights. For constitutional purposes, no different result is required if the agent instead of immediately reporting and transcribing his conversations with defendant, either (1) simultaneously records them with electronic equipment which he is carrying on his person, *Lopez v. United States*; (2) or carries radio equipment which simultaneously transmits the conversations either to recording equipment located elsewhere or to other agents monitoring the transmitting frequency. *On Lee v. United States*. If the conduct and revelations of an agent operating without electronic equipment do not invade the defendant's constitutionally justifiable expectations of privacy, neither does a simultaneous recording of the same conversations made by the agent or by others from transmissions received from the agent to whom the defendant is talking and whose trustworthiness the defendant necessarily risks.

Our problem is not what the privacy expectations of particular defendants in particular situations may be or the extent to which they may in fact have relied on the discretion of their companions. Very probably, individual defendants neither know nor suspect that their colleagues have gone or will go to the police or are

---

[12] David A. Sklansky, *Katz v. United States*, in *Criminal Procedure Stories* (Carol S. Steiker, ed., 2006).

carrying recorders or transmitters. Otherwise, conversation would cease and our problem with these encounters would be nonexistent or far different from those now before us. Our problem, in terms of the principles announced in *Katz*, is what expectations of privacy are constitutionally "justifiable" — what expectations the Fourth Amendment will protect in the absence of a warrant. So far, the law permits the frustration of actual expectations of privacy by permitting authorities to use the testimony of those associates who for one reason or another have determined to turn to the police, as well as by authorizing the use of informants in the manner exemplified by *Hoffa* and *Lewis*. If the law gives no protection to the wrongdoer whose trusted accomplice is or becomes a police agent, neither should it protect him when that same agent has recorded or transmitted the conversations which are later offered in evidence to prove the State's case.

Inescapably, one contemplating illegal activities must realize and risk that his companions may be reporting to the police. If he sufficiently doubts their trustworthiness, the association will very probably end or never materialize. But if he has no doubts, or allays them, or risks what doubt he has, the risk is his. In terms of what his course will be, what he will or will not do or say, we are unpersuaded that he would distinguish between probably informers on the one hand and probable informers with transmitters on the other. . . .

Nor should we be too ready to erect constitutional barriers to relevant and probative evidence which is also accurate and reliable. An electronic recording will many times produce a more reliable rendition of what a defendant has said than will the unaided memory of a police agent. It may also be that with the recording in existence it is less likely that the informant will change his mind, less chance that threat or injury will suppress unfavorable evidence and less chance that cross-examination will confound the testimony. Considerations like these obviously do not favor the defendant, but we are not prepared to hold that a defendant who has no constitutional right to exclude the informer's unaided testimony nevertheless has a Fourth Amendment privilege against a more accurate version of the events in question. . . .

HARLAN, J. dissenting. . . . Since it is the task of the law to form and project, as well as mirror and reflect, we should not, as judges, merely recite the expectations and risks without examining the desirability of saddling them upon society. The critical question, therefore, is whether under our system of government, as reflected in the Constitution, we should impose on our citizens the risks of the electronic listener or observer without at least the protection of a warrant requirement.

This question must, in my view, be answered by assessing the nature of a particular practice and the likely extent of its impact on the individual's sense of security balanced against the utility of the conduct as a technique of law enforcement. For those more extensive intrusions that significantly jeopardize the sense of security which is the paramount concern of Fourth Amendment liberties, I am of the view that more than self-restraint by law enforcement officials is required and at the least warrants should be necessary. The impact of the practice of third-party bugging, must, I think, be considered such as to undermine that confidence and sense of security in dealing with one another that is characteristic of individual relationships between citizens in a free society. It goes beyond the impact on privacy occasioned by the ordinary type of "informer" investigation upheld in *Lewis* and *Hoffa*. The argument of the plurality opinion, to the effect that it is irrelevant whether secrets are revealed by the mere tattletale or the transistor, ignores the differences occasioned by third-party monitoring and recording which insures full and accurate disclosure of all that is said, free of the possibility of error and oversight that inheres in human reporting.

Authority is hardly required to support the proposition that words would be measured a good deal more carefully and communication inhibited if one suspected his conversations were being transmitted and transcribed. Were third-party bugging a prevalent practice, it might well smother that spontaneity — reflected in frivolous, impetuous, sacrilegious, and defiant discourse — that liberates daily life. Much offhand exchange is easily forgotten and one may count on the obscurity of his remarks, protected by the very fact of a limited audience, and the likelihood that the listener will either overlook or forget what is said, as well as the listener's inability to reformulate a conversation without having to contend with a documented record. All these values are sacrificed by a rule of law that permits official monitoring of private discourse limited only by the need to locate a willing assistant. . . .

Interposition of a warrant requirement is designed not to shield "wrong-doers," but to secure a measure of privacy and a sense of personal security throughout our society. The Fourth Amendment does, of course, leave room for the employment of modern technology in criminal law enforcement, but in the stream of current developments in Fourth Amendment law I think it must be held that third-party electronic monitoring, subject only to the self-restraint of law enforcement officials, has no place in our society.

DOUGLAS, J. dissenting. . . . *On Lee* and *Lopez* are of a vintage opposed to *Berger* and *Katz*. However they may be explained, they are products of the old common-law notions of trespass. *Katz*, on the other hand, emphasized that with few exceptions "searches conducted outside the judicial process, without prior approval by judge or magistrate, are per se unreasonable under the Fourth Amendment." . .

Monitoring, if prevalent, certainly kills free discourse and spontaneous utterances. Free discourse — a First Amendment value — may be frivolous or serious, humble or defiant, reactionary or revolutionary, profane or in good taste; but it is not free if there is surveillance. . . .

Now that the discredited decisions in *On Lee* and *Lopez* are resuscitated and revived, must everyone live in fear that every word he speaks may be transmitted or recorded and later repeated to the entire world? I can imagine nothing that has a more chilling effect on people speaking their minds and expressing their views on important matters. The advocates of that regime should spend some time in totalitarian countries and learn firsthand the kind of regime they are creating here. . . .

NOTES & QUESTIONS

1. **White *vs.* Katz.** Is this case more akin to the bugging in *On Lee* and *Lopez* rather than the wiretapping of *Katz*? Does it matter whether the police heard the conversation simultaneously? Suppose the conversation had been recorded by a hidden recorder and then handed over later to the police.
2. ***Covert Agents and the Misplaced Trust Doctrine.*** *White* suggests that the misplaced trust doctrine in *Hoffa, Lewis, Lopez,* and *On Lee* survives after *Katz*. Under the misplaced trust doctrine, people place their trust in others at their own peril and must assume the risk of betrayal. But should the misplaced trust doctrine survive after *Katz*? Do we have a reasonable expectation that our friends aren't government agents in disguise?

   In a comparative study of how the United States and Germany regulate undercover policing, Jacqueline Ross identifies numerous differences in the two legal systems.[13] She argues:

   > In Germany, undercover policing is a necessary evil in that it harms targets by invading their constitutionally protected right to privacy, along with other fundamental rights. . . . German law responds to these concerns through legislation that carves out special limitations on the most intrusive covert tactics, namely long-term deep cover operations. Viewing covert policing as an invasion of privacy assimilates it to other police powers, like searches and seizures. While these tactics burden civil liberties, they do so permissibly, through police compliance with procedural constraints such as warrant requirements. Because civil liberties may lawfully be compromised in the name of security, thinking of covert surveillance as invasions of privacy allows the legal system to justify the burdens that covert policing imposes on rights. This regulatory approach also entails the use of procedural constraints on how covert tactics may be authorized, alongside substantive limits on what undercover operatives may do.
   >
   > German privacy law protects dignitary interests, while American conceptions of privacy emphasize physical privacy in the home along with decisional privacy or autonomy. Germany's concern with individual dignity is part of the German Constitution's concern with safeguarding the "free development of personality," in direct reaction to the totalitarian oppression and violations of personal dignity under the Nazi regime. Invasions of privacy also have special salience for residents of the five new eastern states who remember the encompassing surveillance practiced more recently in the GDR [German Democratic Republic, also known as East Germany]. Given these concerns, police infiltration is deeply problematic. It interferes with the rights of all persons to control the face they present to the world; it reveals too much about the intimate details of a person's life; and it disrupts personal relationships. Giving constitutional status to these harms means that the government must satisfy certain requirements before inflicting them. Constitutional protection entails a warrant procedure, a showing of need, and statutory limits on the crimes that the government may target in this way.
   >
   > By contrast, the United States legal system does not treat undercover policing as an intrinsic invasion of privacy rights. Undercover policing is not

---

[13] Jacqueline E. Ross, *The Place of Covert Surveillance in Democratic Societies: A Comparative Study of the United States and Germany*, 55 Am. J. Comp. L. 493 (2007).

recognized as a search or seizure under the Fourth Amendment. Because they have no Fourth Amendment significance, undercover investigations require no warrant and no showing of probable cause or even reasonable suspicion as a matter of constitutional law. . . .

Conceiving of covert policing as a threat to privacy creates other problems for the legitimacy of these tactics. Framing the discourse in terms of constitutional rights (like the right to privacy) invites critics to identify other constitutional rights that may be at risk. Accordingly, German courts (unlike their American counterparts) have accepted defense arguments that the use of jailhouse informers to squeeze admissions out of prisoners infringes on prisoners' autonomy, by taking advantage of targets' "psychological compulsion to unburden themselves." Critics also raise special objections to those sting operations by which undercover agents befriend and wring confessions from persons suspected of long-ago, unsolved crimes, arguing that these undercover contacts unfairly circumvent suspects' rights to counsel and their right not to incriminate themselves.

What would be the impact on law enforcement if *White* came out the other way after *Katz*? In other words, suppose that *Katz* eliminated the misplaced trust doctrine. How would the Fourth Amendment apply to covert agents or informers? Would this unduly hamper police investigations of drug rings, mafia activity, and terrorist cells?

3. ***Electronic Surveillance and the First Amendment.*** Justice Douglas contends that electronic surveillance impinges upon and chills freedom of expression for all individuals in society. Is electronic surveillance without a warrant consistent with the First Amendment? What kind of process should be required to make use of the warrant consistent with the First Amendment?

3. THE REASONABLE EXPECTATION OF PRIVACY TEST AND EMERGING TECHNOLOGY

(a) Applying the Reasonable Expectation of Privacy Test

SMITH V. MARYLAND

442 U.S. 735 (1979)

BLACKMUN, J. This case presents the question whether the installation and use of a pen register[14] constitutes a "search" within the meaning of the Fourth Amendment, made applicable to the States through the Fourteenth Amendment.

On March 5, 1976, in Baltimore, Md., Patricia McDonough was robbed. She gave the police a description of the robber and of a 1975 Monte Carlo automobile she had observed near the scene of the crime. After the robbery, McDonough began receiving threatening and obscene phone calls from a man identifying

---

[14] "A pen register is a mechanical device that records the numbers dialed on a telephone by monitoring the electrical impulses caused when the dial on the telephone is released. It does not overhear oral communications and does not indicate whether calls are actually completed." A pen register is "usually installed at a central telephone facility [and] records on a paper tape all numbers dialed from [the] line" to which it is attached.

himself as the robber. On one occasion, the caller asked that she step out on her front porch; she did so, and saw the 1975 Monte Carlo she had earlier described to police moving slowly past her home. On March 16, police spotted a man who met McDonough's description driving a 1975 Monte Carlo in her neighborhood. By tracing the license plate number, police learned that the car was registered in the name of petitioner, Michael Lee Smith.

The next day, the telephone company, at police request, installed a pen register at its central offices to record the numbers dialed from the telephone at petitioner's home. The police did not get a warrant or court order before having the pen register installed. The register revealed that on March 17 a call was placed from petitioner's home to McDonough's phone. On the basis of this and other evidence, the police obtained a warrant to search petitioner's residence. [A search of Smith's home revealed more evidence that Smith was the robber. Smith moved to suppress all evidence obtained from (and derived from) the pen register. The trial court denied his motion, and Smith was convicted and sentenced to six years' imprisonment.] . . .

The Fourth Amendment guarantees "[t]he right of the people to be secure in their persons, houses, papers, and effects, against unreasonable searches and seizures." In determining whether a particular form of government-initiated electronic surveillance is a "search" within the meaning of the Fourth Amendment,[15] our lodestar is *Katz v. United States*, 389 U.S. 347 (1967). . . .

Consistently with *Katz,* this Court uniformly has held that the application of the Fourth Amendment depends on whether the person invoking its protection can claim a "justifiable," a "reasonable," or a "legitimate expectation of privacy" that has been invaded by government action. This inquiry, as Mr. Justice Harlan aptly noted in his *Katz* concurrence, normally embraces two discrete questions. The first is whether the individual, by his conduct, has "exhibited an actual (subjective) expectation of privacy," — whether, in the words of the *Katz* majority, the individual has shown that "he seeks to preserve [something] as private." The second question is whether the individual's subjective expectation of privacy is "one that society is prepared to recognize as 'reasonable,' — whether, in the words of the *Katz* majority, the individual's expectation, viewed objectively, is "justifiable" under the circumstances.[16]

---

[15] In this case, the pen register was installed, and the numbers dialed were recorded, by the telephone company. The telephone company, however, acted at police request. In view of this, respondent appears to concede that the company is to be deemed an "agent" of the police for purposes of this case, so as to render the installation and use of the pen register "state action" under the Fourth and Fourteenth Amendments. We may assume that "state action" was present here.

[16] Situations can be imagined, of course, in which *Katz*'s two-pronged inquiry would provide an inadequate index of Fourth Amendment protection. For example, if the Government were suddenly to announce on nationwide television that all homes henceforth would be subject to warrantless entry, individuals thereafter might not in fact entertain any actual expectation or privacy regarding their homes, papers, and effects. Similarly, if a refugee from a totalitarian country, unaware of this Nation's traditions, erroneously assumed that police were continuously monitoring his telephone conversations, a subjective expectation of privacy regarding the contents of his calls might be lacking as well. In such circumstances, where an individual's subjective expectations had been "conditioned" by influences alien to well-recognized Fourth Amendment freedoms, those subjective expectations obviously could play no meaningful role in ascertaining what the scope of Fourth Amendment protection was. In determining whether a "legitimate expectation of privacy" existed in such cases, a normative inquiry would be proper.

In applying the *Katz* analysis to this case, it is important to begin by specifying precisely the nature of the state activity that is challenged. The activity here took the form of installing and using a pen register. Since the pen register was installed on telephone company property at the telephone company's central offices, petitioner obviously cannot claim that his "property" was invaded or that police intruded into a "constitutionally protected area." Petitioner's claim, rather, is that, notwithstanding the absence of a trespass, the State, as did the Government in *Katz*, infringed a "legitimate expectation of privacy" that petitioner held. Yet a pen register differs significantly from the listening device employed in *Katz*, for pen registers do not acquire the contents of communications. This Court recently noted:

> Indeed, a law enforcement official could not even determine from the use of a pen register whether a communication existed. These devices do not hear sound. They disclose only the telephone numbers that have been dialed — a means of establishing communication. Neither the purport of any communication between the caller and the recipient of the call, their identities, nor whether the call was even completed is disclosed by pen registers. *United States v. New York Tel. Co.*, 434 U.S. 159, 167 (1977).

Given a pen register's limited capabilities, therefore, petitioner's argument that its installation and use constituted a "search" necessarily rests upon a claim that he had a "legitimate expectation of privacy" regarding the numbers he dialed on his phone.

This claim must be rejected. First, we doubt that people in general entertain any actual expectation of privacy in the numbers they dial. All telephone users realize that they must "convey" phone numbers to the telephone company, since it is through telephone company switching equipment that their calls are completed. All subscribers realize, moreover, that the phone company has facilities for making permanent records of the numbers they dial, for they see a list of their long-distance (toll) calls on their monthly bills. In fact, pen registers and similar devices are routinely used by telephone companies "for the purposes of checking billing operations, detecting fraud and preventing violations of law." Electronic equipment is used not only to keep billing records of toll calls, but also "to keep a record of all calls dialed from a telephone which is subject to a special rate structure." Pen registers are regularly employed "to determine whether a home phone is being used to conduct a business, to check for a defective dial, or to check for overbilling." Although most people may be oblivious to a pen register's esoteric functions, they presumably have some awareness of one common use: to aid in the identification of persons making annoying or obscene calls. Most phone books tell subscribers, on a page entitled "Consumer Information," that the company "can frequently help in identifying to the authorities the origin of unwelcome and troublesome calls." Telephone users, in sum, typically know that they must convey numerical information to the phone company; that the phone company has facilities for recording this information; and that the phone company does in fact record this information for a variety of legitimate business purposes. Although subjective expectations cannot be scientifically gauged, it is too much to believe that telephone subscribers, under these circumstances, harbor any general expectation that the numbers they dial will remain secret.

Petitioner argues, however, that, whatever the expectations of telephone users in general, he demonstrated an expectation of privacy by his own conduct here, since he "us[ed] the telephone *in his house* to the exclusion of all others." But the site of the call is immaterial for purposes of analysis in this case. Although petitioner's conduct may have been calculated to keep the *contents* of his conversation private, his conduct was not and could not have been calculated to preserve the privacy of the number he dialed. Regardless of his location, petitioner had to convey that number to the telephone company in precisely the same way if he wished to complete his call. The fact that he dialed the number on his home phone rather than on some other phone could make no conceivable difference, nor could any subscriber rationally think that it would. Second, even if petitioner did harbor some subjective expectation that the phone numbers he dialed would remain private, this expectation is not "one that society is prepared to recognize as 'reasonable.'" This Court consistently has held that a person has no legitimate expectation of privacy in information he voluntarily turns over to third parties. In [*United States v.*] *Miller*, for example, the Court held that a bank depositor has no "legitimate 'expectation of privacy'" in financial information "voluntarily conveyed to . . . banks and exposed to their employees in the ordinary course of business." The Court explained:

> The depositor takes the risk, in revealing his affairs to another, that the information will be conveyed by that person to the Government. . . . This Court has held repeatedly that the Fourth Amendment does not prohibit the obtaining of information revealed to a third party and conveyed by him to Government authorities, even if the information is revealed on the assumption that it will be used only for a limited purpose and the confidence placed in the third party will not be betrayed.

Because the depositor "assumed the risk" of disclosure, the Court held that it would be unreasonable for him to expect his financial records to remain private.

This analysis dictates that petitioner can claim no legitimate expectation of privacy here. When he used his phone, petitioner voluntarily conveyed numerical information to the telephone company and "exposed" that information to its equipment in the ordinary course of business. In so doing, petitioner assumed the risk that the company would reveal to police the numbers he dialed. The switching equipment that processed those numbers is merely the modern counterpart of the operator who, in an earlier day, personally completed calls for the subscriber. Petitioner concedes that if he had placed his calls through an operator, he could claim no legitimate expectation of privacy. We are not inclined to hold that a different constitutional result is required because the telephone company has decided to automate.

Petitioner argues, however, that automatic switching equipment differs from a live operator in one pertinent respect. An operator, in theory at least, is capable of remembering every number that is conveyed to him by callers. Electronic equipment, by contrast can "remember" only those numbers it is programmed to record, and telephone companies, in view of their present billing practices, usually do not record local calls. Since petitioner, in calling McDonough, was making a local call, his expectation of privacy as to her number, on this theory, would be "legitimate."

This argument does not withstand scrutiny. The fortuity of whether or not the phone company in fact elects to make a quasi-permanent record of a particular number dialed does not in our view, make any constitutional difference. Regardless of the phone company's election, petitioner voluntarily conveyed to it information that it had facilities for recording and that it was free to record. In these circumstances, petitioner assumed the risk that the information would be divulged to police. . . .

STEWART, J. joined by BRENNAN, J. dissenting. . . . The numbers dialed from a private telephone — although certainly more prosaic than the conversation itself — are not without "content." Most private telephone subscribers may have their own numbers listed in a publicly distributed directory, but I doubt there are any who would be happy to have broadcast to the world a list of the local or long distance numbers they have called. This is not because such a list might in some sense be incriminating, but because it easily could reveal the identities of the persons and the places called, and thus reveal the most intimate details of a person's life.

MARSHALL J. joined by BRENNAN, J. dissenting. . . . Privacy is not a discrete commodity, possessed absolutely or not at all. Those who disclose certain facts to a bank or phone company for a limited business purpose need not assume that this information will be released to other persons for other purposes.

The crux of the Court's holding, however, is that whatever expectation of privacy petitioner may in fact have entertained regarding his calls, it is not one "society is prepared to recognize as 'reasonable.'" In so ruling, the Court determines that individuals who convey information to third parties have "assumed the risk" of disclosure to the government. This analysis is misconceived in two critical respects.

Implicit in the concept of assumption of risk is some notion of choice. At least in the third-party consensual surveillance cases, which first incorporated risk analysis into Fourth Amendment doctrine, the defendant presumably had exercised some discretion in deciding who should enjoy his confidential communications. By contrast here, unless a person is prepared to forgo use of what for many has become a personal or professional necessity, he cannot help but accept the risk of surveillance. It is idle to speak of "assuming" risks in contexts where, as a practical matter, individuals have no realistic alternative.

More fundamentally, to make risk analysis dispositive in assessing the reasonableness of privacy expectations would allow the government to define the scope of Fourth Amendment protections. For example, law enforcement officials, simply by announcing their intent to monitor the content of random samples of first-class mail or private phone conversations, could put the public on notice of the risks they would thereafter assume in such communications. . . .

In my view, whether privacy expectations are legitimate within the meaning of *Katz* depends not on the risks an individual can be presumed to accept when imparting information to third parties, but on the risks he should be forced to assume in a free and open society. . . .

The use of pen registers, I believe, constitutes such an extensive intrusion. To hold otherwise ignores the vital role telephonic communication plays in our personal and professional relationships, as well as the First and Fourth Amendment interests implicated by unfettered official surveillance. Privacy in placing calls is of value not only to those engaged in criminal activity. The prospect of unregulated governmental monitoring will undoubtedly prove disturbing even to those with nothing illicit to hide. Many individuals, including members of unpopular political organizations or journalists with confidential sources, may legitimately wish to avoid disclosure of their personal contacts. Permitting governmental access to telephone records on less than probable cause may thus impede certain forms of political affiliation and journalistic endeavor that are the hallmark of a truly free society. Particularly given the Government's previous reliance on warrantless telephonic surveillance to trace reporters' sources and monitor protected political activity, I am unwilling to insulate use of pen registers from independent judicial review. . . .

NOTES & QUESTIONS

1. ***Pen Registers and Trap and Trace Devices.*** A pen register records outgoing telephone calls. Another device, known as a trap and trace device, records all incoming calls. In *Smith v. Maryland*, the Supreme Court ruled that a use of pen registers or trap and trace devices was not a form of wiretap (akin to that in *Katz*). What are the critical differences between the pen register and trap and device, on the one hand, and the wiretap, on the other?
2. ***Critiques of the* Smith *Decision.*** Consider the following observation by Laurence Tribe about *Smith*:

> The "assumption of risk" — more aptly, "assumption of broadcast" — notion underling the holding in *Smith* . . . reveals alarming tendencies in the Supreme Court's understanding of what privacy means and ought to mean. The Court treats privacy almost as if it were "a discrete commodity, possessed absolutely or not at all" [quoting Justice Marshall's dissent]. Yet what could be more commonplace than the idea that it is up to the *individual* to *measure out information* about herself *selectively* — to whomever she chooses?[17]

Patricia Bellia contends that *Smith* conflicts with *Katz*: "In *Katz,* the phone company necessarily carried the defendant's telephone call, and the phone company no doubt had the technical ability to hear the contents of that call. That technical ability, however, was no impediment to the Court's conclusion that Katz had an expectation of privacy in the conversation."[18] Likewise, Susan Freiwald contends: "The *Smith* court ignored the lesson of *Katz*: We do not lose privacy in communications merely because they may be intercepted." She goes on to argue that the Court in *Smith* "avoided normative analysis and failed to consider how much privacy the law should actually grant to

---

[17] Laurence Tribe, *American Constitutional Law* 1391 (2d ed. 1988). For another critique of *Smith v. Maryland*, see Daniel J. Solove, *Digital Dossiers and the Dissipation*, 75 S. Cal. L. Rev. 1083 (2002).

[18] Patricia Bellia, *Surveillance Law Through Cyberlaw's Lens,* 72 Geo. Wash. L. Rev. 1375, 1405 (2004).

information. If the law treats information as private, then it will not be acceptable to acquire it, even when it possible to do so."[19]

Deirdre Mulligan explains that the Court addressed the discrepancies between *Katz* and *Smith* by discussing in *Smith* "at some length the limited information that can be gleaned from a phone number, contrasting it with what may be revealed from a telephone conversation."[20] Does the holding of *Smith* rest on the fact that the numbers were exposed to a third party or on the fact that the numbers revealed limited information about a person or on both of these factors?

3. ***State Constitutional Law.*** Some states have rejected the *Smith* holding under their constitutions. For example, in *State v. Hunt*, 450 A.2d 952 (N.J. 1982), the New Jersey Supreme Court rejected *Smith* and held that under the New Jersey Constitution, there is a reasonable expectation of privacy in telephone records:

> The telephone has become an essential instrument in carrying on our personal affairs. It has become part and parcel of the home. When a telephone call is made, it is as if two people are having a private conversation in the sanctity of their living room. . . .
>
> The telephone caller is . . . entitled to assume that the numbers he dials in the privacy of his home will be recorded solely for the telephone company's business purposes. From the viewpoint of the customer, all the information which he furnishes with respect to a particular call is private. The numbers dialed are private. . . .
>
> It is unrealistic to say that the cloak of privacy has been shed because the telephone company and some of its employees are aware of this information. Telephone calls cannot be made except through the telephone company's property and without payment to it for the service. This disclosure has been necessitated because of the nature of the instrumentality, but more significantly the disclosure has been made for a limited business purpose and not for release to other persons for other reasons. . . .

In an analysis of state constitutional law, Stephen Henderson concludes that 11 states have rejected the third party doctrine. Ten more states have not explicitly rejected the third party doctrine, but have case law suggesting that they might do so in the future.[21]

4. ***Federal Statutory Law.*** Sometimes when the Court fails to identify a privacy interest involving some aspect of the collection of personal information, Congress responds by enacting legislation that provides protection by statutory means. That happened after *Smith* with the Pen Register Act, 18 U.S.C. §§ 3121–3127. This statute requires that the government obtain a court order by certifying that the use of a pen register is "relevant to an ongoing

[19] Susan Freiwald, *Online Surveillance: Remembering the Lessons of the Wiretap Act,* 56 Ala. L. Rev. 9, 40, 66 (2004).

[20] Deirdre K. Mulligan, *Reasonable Expectations in Electronic Communications: A Critical Perspective on the Electronic Communications Privacy Act*, 72 Geo. Wash. L. Rev. 1557, 1581 (2004).

[21] Stephen E. Henderson, *Learning from All Fifty States: How to Apply the Fourth Amendment and Its State Analogs to Protect Third Party Information from Unreasonable Seizure*, 55 Cath. U. L. Rev. 373, 395 (2006).

investigation." This standard, however, is significantly less stringent than the probable cause required to obtain a Fourth Amendment warrant.

5. ***The First Amendment and Pen Register Information.*** Daniel Solove argues that the First Amendment should be understood as a source of criminal procedure and should protect pen register information:

> Although the Supreme Court has focused on the Fourth Amendment, obtaining pen register data without a warrant potentially violates the First Amendment. A log of incoming and outgoing calls can be used to trace channels of communication. It is relatively easy to link a phone number to a person or organization. Pen registers can reveal associational ties, since association in contemporary times often occurs by way of telephone or e-mail. As David Cole argues, modern communications technology has made association possible without physical assembly. For example, if the government scrutinized the phone logs of the main office of the Communist Party, it might discover many of the Party's members. The information would not be equivalent to a membership list, but it would probably include identifying data about countless individuals who would not want the government to discover their connection to the Communist Party. If the government were to examine the phone logs or e-mail headers of a particular individual, it might discover that the individual contacted particular organizations that the individual wants to keep private. The pen register information, therefore, implicates First Amendment values.[22]

Solove contends that government access to pen register information can violate the First Amendment, and he goes on to argue that the First Amendment should require a warrant before the government can obtain such information. Does pen register information implicate the First Amendment? If so, what kind of protections should the First Amendment require?

UNITED STATES V. PLACE

462 U.S. 696 (1983)

O'CONNOR, J. The Fourth Amendment "protects people from unreasonable government intrusions into their legitimate expectations of privacy." We have affirmed that a person possesses a privacy interest in the contents of personal luggage that is protected by the Fourth Amendment. A "canine sniff" by a well-trained narcotics detection dog, however, does not require opening the luggage. It does not expose noncontraband items that otherwise would remain hidden from public view, as does, for example, an officer's rummaging through the contents of the luggage. Thus, the manner in which information is obtained through this investigative technique is much less intrusive than a typical search. Moreover, the sniff discloses only the presence or absence of narcotics, a contraband item. Thus, despite the fact that the sniff tells the authorities something about the contents of the luggage, the information obtained is limited. This limited disclosure also ensures that the owner of the property is not subjected to the

---

[22] Daniel J. Solove, *The First Amendment as Criminal Procedure,* 82 N.Y.U. L. Rev. 112, 169 (2007).

embarrassment and inconvenience entailed in less discriminate and more intrusive investigative methods.

In these respects, the canine sniff is *sui generis*. We are aware of no other investigative procedure that is so limited both in the manner in which the information is obtained and in the content of the information revealed by the procedure. Therefore, we conclude that the particular course of investigation that the agents intended to pursue here — exposure of respondent's luggage, which was located in a public place, to a trained canine — did not constitute a "search" within the meaning of the Fourth Amendment. . . .

ILLINOIS V. CABALLES

543 U.S. 405 (2005)

STEVENS, J. Illinois State Trooper Daniel Gillette stopped respondent for speeding on an interstate highway. When Gillette radioed the police dispatcher to report the stop, a second trooper, Craig Graham, a member of the Illinois State Police Drug Interdiction Team, overheard the transmission and immediately headed for the scene with his narcotics-detection dog. When they arrived, respondent's car was on the shoulder of the road and respondent was in Gillette's vehicle. While Gillette was in the process of writing a warning ticket, Graham walked his dog around respondent's car. The dog alerted at the trunk. Based on that alert, the officers searched the trunk, found marijuana, and arrested respondent. The entire incident lasted less than 10 minutes.

Respondent was convicted of a narcotics offense and sentenced to 12 years' imprisonment and a $256,136 fine. . . .

The question on which we granted certiorari is narrow: "Whether the Fourth Amendment requires reasonable, articulable suspicion to justify using a drug-detection dog to sniff a vehicle during a legitimate traffic stop." Thus, we proceed on the assumption that the officer conducting the dog sniff had no information about respondent except that he had been stopped for speeding; accordingly, we have omitted any reference to facts about respondent that might have triggered a modicum of suspicion. . . .

In our view, conducting a dog sniff would not change the character of a traffic stop that is lawful at its inception and otherwise executed in a reasonable manner, unless the dog sniff itself infringed respondent's constitutionally protected interest in privacy. Our cases hold that it did not.

Official conduct that does not "compromise any legitimate interest in privacy" is not a search subject to the Fourth Amendment. We have held that any interest in possessing contraband cannot be deemed "legitimate," and thus, governmental conduct that *only* reveals the possession of contraband "compromises no legitimate privacy interest." This is because the expectation "that certain facts will not come to the attention of the authorities" is not the same as an interest in "privacy that society is prepared to consider reasonable." In *United States v. Place,* 462 U.S. 696 (1983), we treated a canine sniff by a well-trained narcotics-detection dog as "*sui generis*" because it "discloses only the presence or absence of narcotics, a contraband item." Respondent likewise concedes that "drug sniffs are designed, and if properly conducted are generally likely, to reveal only the presence of contraband." Although respondent argues that the error rates, particularly the existence of false positives, call into question the premise that drug-detection dogs alert only to contraband, the record contains no evidence or findings that support his argument. Moreover, respondent does not suggest that an erroneous alert, in and of itself, reveals any legitimate private information, and, in this case, the trial judge found that the dog sniff was sufficiently reliable to establish probable cause to conduct a full-blown search of the trunk.

Accordingly, the use of a well-trained narcotics-detection dog—one that "does not expose noncontraband items that otherwise would remain hidden from public view," *Place,* 462 U.S., at 707, during a lawful traffic stop, generally does not implicate legitimate privacy interests. In this case, the dog sniff was performed on the exterior of respondent's car while he was lawfully seized for a traffic violation. Any intrusion on respondent's privacy expectations does not rise to the level of a constitutionally cognizable infringement.

SOUTER, J., dissenting. I would hold that using the dog for the purposes of determining the presence of marijuana in the car's trunk was a search unauthorized as an incident of the speeding stop and unjustified on any other ground. I would accordingly affirm the judgment of the Supreme Court of Illinois, and I respectfully dissent.

At the heart both of *Place* and the Court's opinion today is the proposition that sniffs by a trained dog are *sui generis* because a reaction by the dog in going alert is a response to nothing but the presence of contraband.[23] Hence, the argument goes, because the sniff can only reveal the presence of items devoid of any legal use, the sniff "does not implicate legitimate privacy interests" and is not to be treated as a search.

The infallible dog, however, is a creature of legal fiction. Although the Supreme Court of Illinois did not get into the sniffing averages of drug dogs, their supposed infallibility is belied by judicial opinions describing well-trained animals sniffing and alerting with less than perfect accuracy, whether owing to errors by their handlers, the limitations of the dogs themselves, or even the pervasive contamination of currency by cocaine. *See, e.g., United States v. Kennedy,* 131 F.3d 1371, 1378 (C.A.10 1997) (describing a dog that had a 71% accuracy rate); *United States v. Scarborough,* 128 F.3d 1373, 1378, n. 3 (C.A.10 1997) (describing a dog that erroneously alerted 4 times out of 19 while working for the postal service and 8% of the time over its entire career); *United States v. Limares,* 269 F.3d 794, 797 (C.A.7 2001) (accepting as reliable a dog that gave false positives between 7 and 38% of the time); *Laime v. State,* 347 Ark. 142, 159, 60 S.W.3d 464, 476 (2001) (speaking of a dog that made between 10 and 50 errors); *United States v. $242,484.00,* 351 F.3d 499, 511 (C.A.11 2003) (noting that because as much as 80% of all currency in circulation contains drug residue,

---

[23] Another proffered justification for *sui generis* status is that a dog sniff is a particularly nonintrusive procedure. *United States v. Place,* 462 U.S. 696, 707 (1983). I agree with Justice Ginsburg that the introduction of a dog to a traffic stop (let alone an encounter with someone walking down the street) can in fact be quite intrusive.

a dog alert "is of little value"). . . . Indeed, a study cited by Illinois in this case for the proposition that dog sniffs are "generally reliable" shows that dogs in artificial testing situations return false positives anywhere from 12.5 to 60% of the time, depending on the length of the search. In practical terms, the evidence is clear that the dog that alerts hundreds of times will be wrong dozens of times.

Once the dog's fallibility is recognized, however, that ends the justification claimed in *Place* for treating the sniff as *sui generis* under the Fourth Amendment: the sniff alert does not necessarily signal hidden contraband, and opening the container or enclosed space whose emanations the dog has sensed will not necessarily reveal contraband or any other evidence of crime. This is not, of course, to deny that a dog's reaction may provide reasonable suspicion, or probable cause, to search the container or enclosure; the Fourth Amendment does not demand certainty of success to justify a search for evidence or contraband. The point is simply that the sniff and alert cannot claim the certainty that *Place* assumed, both in treating the deliberate use of sniffing dogs as *sui generis* and then taking that characterization as a reason to say they are not searches subject to Fourth Amendment scrutiny. And when that aura of uniqueness disappears, there is no basis in *Place*'s reasoning, and no good reason otherwise, to ignore the actual function that dog sniffs perform. They are conducted to obtain information about the contents of private spaces beyond anything that human senses could perceive, even when conventionally enhanced. The information is not provided by independent third parties beyond the reach of constitutional limitations, but gathered by the government's own officers in order to justify searches of the traditional sort, which may or may not reveal evidence of crime but will disclose anything meant to be kept private in the area searched. Thus in practice the government's use of a trained narcotics dog functions as a limited search to reveal undisclosed facts about private enclosures, to be used to justify a further and complete search of the enclosed area. And given the fallibility of the dog, the sniff is the first step in a process that may disclose "intimate details" without revealing contraband. . . .

GINSBURG & SOUTER, J.J., dissenting. . . . In *Terry v. Ohio,* the Court upheld the stop and subsequent frisk of an individual based on an officer's observation of suspicious behavior and his reasonable belief that the suspect was armed. . . . In a *Terry*-type investigatory stop, "the officer's action [must be] justified at its inception, and . . . reasonably related in scope to the circumstances which justified the interference in the first place." In applying *Terry,* the Court has several times indicated that the limitation on "scope" is not confined to the duration of the seizure; it also encompasses the manner in which the seizure is conducted. . . .

Terry, it merits repetition, instructs that any investigation must be "reasonably related in *scope* to the circumstances which justified the interference in the first place" (emphasis added). The unwarranted and nonconsensual expansion of the seizure here from a routine traffic stop to a drug investigation broadened the scope of the investigation in a manner that, in my judgment, runs afoul of the Fourth Amendment. . . .

A drug-detection dog is an intimidating animal. Injecting such an animal into a routine traffic stop changes the character of the encounter between the police and the motorist. The stop becomes broader, more adversarial, and (in at least some cases) longer. Caballes — who, as far as Troopers Gillette and Graham knew, was guilty solely of driving six miles per hour over the speed limit—was exposed to the embarrassment and intimidation of being investigated, on a public thoroughfare, for drugs.

NOTES & QUESTIONS

1. ***Detecting Only Illegal Contraband.*** Suppose the police had used a special x-ray machine to examine the contents of the bag. Would this be a Fourth Amendment violation under *Caballes*? Why or why not? Suppose that an x-ray device could be developed that would only detect illegal items, such as drugs, child pornography, weapons, or stolen items. Would the use of such a device to examine the contents of a person's bag or home constitute a search?
2. ***Is the Fourth Amendment Primarily Protective of the Individual or Society?*** Consider the following observation by Anthony Amsterdam:

   > [Should the Fourth Amendment] be viewed as a collection of protections of atomistic spheres of interest of individual citizens or as a regulation of governmental conduct[?] Does it safeguard *my* person and *your* house and *her* papers and *his* effects against unreasonable searches and seizures; or is it essentially a regulatory canon requiring government to order its law enforcement procedures in a fashion that keeps us collectively secure in our persons, houses, papers, and effects, against unreasonable searches and seizures?[24]

   Under what view does the Supreme Court seem to be operating? Which view do you think is the most appropriate?
3. ***Is Government Observation Different from Observation by Others?*** Amsterdam also argues that one's privacy may be violated by being observed by the police but may not be violated by the very same observation from others:

   > [I]f you live in a cheap hotel or in a ghetto flat, your neighbors can hear you breathing quietly even in temperate weather when it is possible to keep the windows and doors closed. For the tenement dweller, the difference between observation by neighbors and visitors who ordinarily use the common hallways and observation by policemen who come into hallways to "check up" or "look around" is the difference between all the privacy that his condition allows and none. Is that small difference too unimportant to claim [F]ourth [A]mendment protection?[25]

   Do you agree that our expectations of privacy turn on who is watching rather than simply whether we are being watched? Should the "reasonable

---

[24] Anthony G. Amsterdam, *Perspectives on the Fourth Amendment*, 58 Minn. L. Rev. 349, 367 (1974). For an additional critique of the reasonable expectation of privacy test, see Andrew E. Taslitz, *The Fourth Amendment in the Twenty-First Century: Technology, Privacy, and Human Emotions,* 65 Law & Contemp. Probs. 125 (2002).

[25] Amsterdam, *Fourth Amendment, supra*, at 404.

expectation of privacy" test be changed to the "reasonable expectation of what the police can observe or search" test?

4. ***Bomb Detection vs. Drug Detection?*** The dissents of both Justice Souter and Justice Ginsburg in *Caballes* distinguish a canine search for drugs from one for bombs. Justice Souter argued in a footnote of his dissent that he reserved judgment concerning "a possible case significantly unlike this one":

> All of us are concerned not to prejudge a claim of authority to detect explosives and dangerous chemical or biological weapons that might be carried by a terrorist who prompts no individualized suspicion. Suffice it to say here that what is a reasonable search depends in part on demonstrated risk. Unreasonable sniff searches for marijuana are not necessarily unreasonable sniff searches for destructive or deadly material if suicide bombs are a societal risk.

For Justice Ginsburg, the use of a bomb-detection dog to check vehicles would be closer to sobriety checkpoints that the Supreme Court has upheld. *Michigan Dep't of State Police v. Sitz*, 496 U.S. 444 (1990). Do you agree with these attempts to distinguish dogs that detect bombs from those that detect drugs?

CALIFORNIA V. GREENWOOD

486 U.S. 35 (1988)

[Police investigators searched the plastic garbage bags that Greenwood left on the curb in front of his house to be picked up by the trash collector. The officers found indications of drug use from the search of Greenwood's trash and obtained a warrant to search the house, where they uncovered more evidence of drug trafficking. Greenwood was arrested.]

WHITE, J. . . . The warrantless search and seizure of the garbage bags left at the curb outside the Greenwood house would violate the Fourth Amendment only if respondents manifested a subjective expectation of privacy in their garbage that society accepts as objectively reasonable.

. . . [The Greenwoods] assert . . . that they had, and exhibited, an expectation of privacy with respect to the trash that was searched by the police: The trash, which was placed on the street for collection at a fixed time, was contained in opaque plastic bags, which the garbage collector was expected to pick up, mingle with the trash of others, and deposit at the garbage dump. The trash was only temporarily on the street, and there was little likelihood that it would be inspected by anyone.

It may well be that respondents did not expect that the contents of their garbage bags would become known to the police or other members of the public. An expectation of privacy does not give rise to Fourth Amendment protection, however, unless society is prepared to accept that expectation as objectively reasonable.

Here, we conclude that respondents exposed their garbage to the public sufficiently to defeat their claim to Fourth Amendment protection. It is common knowledge that plastic garbage bags left on or at the side of a public street are readily accessible to animals, children, scavengers, snoops, and other members of the public. Moreover, respondents placed their refuse at the curb for the express purpose of conveying it to a third party, the trash collector, who might himself have sorted through respondents' trash or permitted others, such as the police, to do so. Accordingly, having deposited their garbage "in an area particularly suited for public inspection and, in a manner of speaking, public consumption, for the express purpose of having strangers take it," respondents could have had no reasonable expectation of privacy in the inculpatory items that they discarded. . .

BRENNAN, J. joined by MARSHALL, J. dissenting. . . . Scrutiny of another's trash is contrary to commonly accepted notions of civilized behavior. I suspect, therefore, that members of our society will be shocked to learn that the Court, the ultimate guarantor of liberty, deems unreasonable our expectation that the aspects of our private lives that are concealed safely in a trash bag will not become public.

"A container which can support a reasonable expectation of privacy may not be searched, even on probable cause, without a warrant." *United States v. Jacobsen*, 466 U.S. 109, 120, n.17 (1984) (citations omitted). Thus, as the Court observes, if Greenwood had a reasonable expectation that the contents of the bags that he placed on the curb would remain private, the warrantless search of those bags violated the Fourth Amendment. . . .

Our precedent, therefore, leaves no room to doubt that had respondents been carrying their personal effects in opaque, sealed plastic bags — identical to the ones they placed on the curb — their privacy would have been protected from warrantless police intrusion. . . .

Respondents deserve no less protection just because Greenwood used the bags to discard rather than to transport his personal effects. Their contents are not inherently any less private, and Greenwood's decision to discard them, at least in the manner in which he did, does not diminish his expectation of privacy.

A trash bag, like any of the above-mentioned containers, "is a common repository for one's personal effects" and, even more than many of them, is "therefore . . . inevitably associated with the expectation of privacy." "[A]lmost every human activity ultimately manifests itself in waste products. . . ." *Smith v. State*, 510 P.2d 793, 798 (Alaska 1973). A single bag of trash testifies eloquently to the eating, reading, and recreational habits of the person who produced it. A search of trash, like a search of the bedroom, can relate intimate details about sexual practices, health, and personal hygiene. Like rifling through desk drawers or intercepting phone calls, rummaging through trash can divulge the target's financial and professional status, political affiliations and inclinations, private thoughts, personal relationships, and romantic interests. It cannot be doubted that a sealed trash bag harbors telling evidence of the "intimate activity associated with the 'sanctity of a man's home and the privacies of life,'" which the Fourth Amendment is designed to protect. . . .

. . . Most of us, I believe, would be incensed to discover a meddler — whether a neighbor, a reporter, or a detective — scrutinizing our sealed trash containers to discover some detail of our personal lives. . . .

The mere possibility that unwelcome meddlers might open and rummage through the containers does not negate the expectation of privacy in their contents any more than the possibility of a burglary negates an expectation of privacy in the home; or the possibility of a private intrusion negates an expectation of privacy in an unopened package; or the possibility that an operator will listen in on a telephone conversation negates an expectation of privacy in the words spoken on the telephone. "What a person . . . seeks to preserve as private, even in an area accessible to the public, may be constitutionally protected." *Katz*, 389 U.S. at 351-52. . . .

NOTES & QUESTIONS

1. ***Recycling and Surveillance of Garbage.*** In dissent in *Greenwald*, a decision from 1988, Justice Brennan states, "Scrutiny of another's trash is contrary to commonly accepted notions of civilized behavior." In the twenty-first century, however, an increasing number of communities have imposed recycling obligations on its citizens. Sanitation departments sometimes oversee the recycling by routinely checking people's trash, and, in the case of noncompliance, imposing fines. Does this development alter the extent of any reasonable expectation of privacy in one's trash vis-à-vis the police?
2. ***Surveillance 24/7.*** In addition to searching through Greenwood's trash, the police were staking out his home, watching who came and went from his house. Does the Fourth Amendment protect against such surveillance? Imagine that for one year, the police were to stake out a person's home and follow the person wherever he or she went throughout the day. The person would be under 24-hour surveillance, seven days a week. Assume that the police would simply observe the person anytime he or she was in public. Is this more invasive to privacy than a one-time search of particular items, such as one's luggage? Does the Fourth Amendment provide any limitation on the police activities described above?

PLAIN VIEW, OPEN FIELDS, AND CURTILAGE

"[I]t has long been settled that objects falling in the plain view of an officer who has a right to be in the position to have that view are subject to seizure and may be introduced in evidence." *Harris v. United States*, 390 U.S. 234, 236 (1968). This has become known as the "plain view" doctrine. If it is possible for something to be seen or heard from a public vantage point, there can be no reasonable expectation of privacy.

An extension of the plain view rule is the "open fields" doctrine. An individual does not have a reasonable expectation of privacy in the open fields that she owns. In *Oliver v. United States*, 466 U.S. 170 (1984), the defendant placed "No Trespassing" signs throughout his farm and maintained a locked gate around the farm's entrance. The fields could not be seen from any public vantage point. The police trespassed onto the fields and found marijuana. The Court held, however, that there is no reasonable expectation of privacy in open fields, and the defendant's attempt to keep them secluded and shielded from public view was irrelevant.

An exception to the open fields doctrine is the legal treatment of a house's so-called "curtilage." Under the curtilage doctrine, parts of one's property immediately outside one's home do not fall within the open fields rule. This exception does not mean that the curtilage is automatically afforded Fourth Amendment protection; a reasonable expectation of privacy analysis still must be performed. The question of whether an area constitutes a curtilage depends upon "whether the area in question is so intimately tied to the home itself that it should be placed within the home's 'umbrella' of Fourth Amendment protection." *United States v. Dunn*, 480 U.S. 294, 301 (1987).

FLORIDA V. RILEY

488 U.S. 445 (1989)

WHITE, J. . . . Respondent Riley lived in a mobile home located on five acres of rural property. A greenhouse was located 10 to 20 feet behind the mobile home. Two sides of the greenhouse were enclosed. The other two sides were not enclosed but the contents of the greenhouse were obscured from view from surrounding property by trees, shrubs, and the mobile home. The greenhouse was covered by corrugated roofing panels, some translucent and some opaque. At the time relevant to this case, two of the panels, amounting to approximately 10% of the roof area, were missing. A wire fence surrounded the mobile home and the greenhouse, and the property was posted with a "DO NOT ENTER" sign.

This case originated with an anonymous tip to the Pasco County Sheriff's office that marijuana was being grown on respondent's property. When an investigating officer discovered that he could not see the contents of the greenhouse from the road, he circled twice over respondent's property in a helicopter at the height of 400 feet. With his naked eye, he was able to see through the openings in the roof and one or more of the open sides of the greenhouse and to identify what he thought was marijuana growing in the structure. A warrant was obtained based on these observations, and the ensuing search revealed marijuana growing in the greenhouse. Respondent was charged with possession of marijuana under Florida law. . . .

We agree with the State's submission that our decision in *California v. Ciraolo*, 476 U.S. 207 (1986), controls this case. There, acting on a tip, the police inspected the back-yard of a particular house while flying in a fixed-wing aircraft at 1,000 feet. With the naked eye the officers saw what they concluded was marijuana growing in the yard. A search warrant was obtained on the strength of this airborne inspection, and marijuana plants were found. The trial court refused to suppress this evidence, but a state appellate court held that the inspection violated the Fourth and Fourteenth Amendments to the United States Constitution, and that the warrant was therefore invalid. We in turn reversed, holding that the inspection was not a search subject to the Fourth Amendment. We recognized that the yard was within the curtilage of the house, that a fence shielded the yard from observation from the street, and that the occupant had a subjective expectation of privacy. We held, however, that such an expectation was not reasonable and not one "that society is prepared to honor." Our reasoning was that the home and its curtilage are not necessarily protected from inspection that involves no physical invasion. "'What a person knowingly exposes to the public, even in his own home or office, is not a subject of Fourth Amendment protection.'" As a general proposition, the police may see what may be seen "from a public vantage point where [they have] a right to be." Thus the police, like the public, would have been free to inspect the backyard garden from the street if their view had been unobstructed. They were likewise free to inspect the yard from the vantage point of an aircraft flying in the navigable airspace as this plane was. "In an age where private and commercial flight in the public airways is routine, it is unreasonable for respondent to expect that his marijuana plants were constitutionally protected from being observed with the naked eye from an altitude of 1,000 feet. The Fourth Amendment simply does not require the police traveling in the public airways at this altitude to obtain a warrant in order to observe what is visible to the naked eye."

We arrive at the same conclusion in the present case. In this case, as in *Ciraolo*, the property surveyed was within the curtilage of respondent's home. Riley no doubt intended and expected that his greenhouse would not be open to public inspection, and the precautions he took protected against ground-level observation. Because the sides and roof of his greenhouse were left partially open, however, what was growing in the greenhouse was subject to viewing from the air. Under the holding in *Ciraolo*, Riley could not reasonably have expected the contents of his greenhouse to be immune from examination by an officer seated in a fixed-wing aircraft flying in navigable airspace at an altitude of 1,000 feet or, as the Florida Supreme Court seemed to recognize, at an altitude of 500 feet, the lower limit of the navigable airspace for such an aircraft. Here, the inspection was made from a helicopter, but as is the case with fixed-wing planes, "private and commercial flight [by helicopter] in the public airways is routine" in this country, and there is no indication that such flights are unheard of in Pasco County, Florida. Riley could not reasonably have expected that his greenhouse was protected from public or official observation from a helicopter had it been flying within the navigable airspace for fixed-wing aircraft.

Nor on the facts before us, does it make a difference for Fourth Amendment purposes that the helicopter was flying at 400 feet when the officer saw what was growing in the greenhouse through the partially open roof and sides of the structure. We would have a different case if flying at that altitude had been contrary to law or regulation. But helicopters are not bound by the lower limits of the navigable airspace allowed to other aircraft.[26] Any member of the public could legally have been flying over Riley's property in a helicopter at the altitude of 400 feet and could have observed Riley's greenhouse. The police officer did no more. . . . As far as this record reveals, no intimate details connected with the use of the home or curtilage were observed, and there was no undue noise, and

---

[26] While Federal Aviation Administration regulations permit fixed-wing-aircraft to be operated at an altitude of 1,000 feet while flying over congested areas and at an altitude of 500 feet above the surface in other than congested areas, helicopters may be operated at less than the minimums for fixed-wing-aircraft "if the operation is conducted without hazard to persons or property on the surface. In addition, each person operating a helicopter shall comply with routes or altitudes specifically prescribed for helicopters by the [FAA] Administrator." 14 CFR § 91.79 (1988).

no wind, dust, or threat of injury. In these circumstances, there was no violation of the Fourth Amendment.

O'CONNOR, J. concurring in the judgment. Ciraolo's expectation of privacy was unreasonable not because the airplane was operating where it had a "right to be," but because public air travel at 1,000 feet is a sufficiently routine part of modern life that it is unreasonable for persons on the ground to expect that their curtilage will not be observed from the air at that altitude. Although "helicopters are not bound by the lower limits of the navigable airspace allowed to other aircraft,"there is no reason to assume that compliance with FAA regulations alone determines "'whether the government's intrusion infringes upon the personal and societal values protected by the Fourth Amendment.'" Because the FAA has decided that helicopters can lawfully operate at virtually any altitude so long as they pose no safety hazard, it does not follow that the expectations of privacy "society is prepared to recognize as 'reasonable'" simply mirror the FAA's safety concerns. . . .

BRENNAN, J. joined by MARSHALL and STEVENS, J.J. dissenting. Under the plurality's exceedingly grudging Fourth Amendment theory, the expectation of privacy is defeated if a single member of the public could conceivably position herself to see into the area in question without doing anything illegal. It is defeated whatever the difficulty a person would have in so positioning herself, and however infrequently anyone would in fact do so. In taking this view the plurality ignores the very essence of *Katz*. The reason why there is no reasonable expectation of privacy in an area that is exposed to the public is that little diminution in "the amount of privacy and freedom remaining to citizens" will result from police surveillance of something that any passerby readily sees. To pretend, as the plurality opinion does, that the same is true when the police use a helicopter to peer over high fences is, at best, disingenuous. . . .

It is a curious notion that the reach of the Fourth Amendment can be so largely defined by administrative regulations issued for purposes of flight safety.[27] It is more curious still that the plurality relies to such an extent on the legality of the officer's act, when we have consistently refused to equate police violation of the law with infringement of the Fourth Amendment.

The police officer positioned 400 feet above Riley's backyard was not, however, standing on a public road. The vantage point he enjoyed was not one any citizen could readily share. His ability to see over Riley's fence depended on his use of a very expensive and sophisticated piece of machinery to which few ordinary citizens have access. In such circumstances it makes no more sense to rely on the legality of the officer's position in the skies than it would to judge the constitutionality of the wiretap in *Katz* by the legality of the officer's position outside the telephone booth. The simple inquiry whether the police officer had

---

[27] The plurality's use of the FAA regulations as a means for determining whether Riley enjoyed a reasonable expectation of privacy produces an incredible result. Fixed-wing aircraft may not be operated below 500 feet (1,000 feet over congested areas), while helicopters may be operated below those levels. Therefore, whether Riley's expectation of privacy is reasonable turns on whether the police officer at 400 feet above his curtilage is seated in an airplane or a helicopter. This cannot be the law.

the legal right to be in the position from which he made his observations cannot suffice, for we cannot assume that Riley's curtilage was so open to the observations of passersby in the skies that he retained little privacy or personal security to be lost to police surveillance. The question before us must be not whether the police were where they had a right to be, but whether public observation of Riley's curtilage was so commonplace that Riley's expectation of privacy in his backyard could not be considered reasonable. . . .

. . . The Fourth Amendment demands that we temper our efforts to apprehend criminals with a concern for the impact on our fundamental liberties of the methods we use. I hope it will be a matter of concern to my colleagues that the police surveillance methods they would sanction were among those described 40 years ago in George Orwell's dread vision of life in the 1980's:

> The black-mustachio'd face gazed down from every commanding corner. There was one on the house front immediately opposite. BIG BROTHER IS WATCHING YOU, the caption said. . . . In the far distance a helicopter skimmed down between the roofs, hovered for an instant like a bluebottle, and darted away again with a curving flight. It was the Police Patrol, snooping into people's windows.

Who can read this passage without a shudder, and without the instinctive reaction that it depicts life in some country other than ours? I respectfully dissent.

NOTES & QUESTIONS

1. ***Privacy in Public.*** The court quotes from *Katz v. United States* that "[w]hat a person knowingly exposes to the public . . . is not a subject of Fourth Amendment protection." How far does this principle extend? Can there be situations where a person might have a reasonable expectation of privacy even when exposed in public? Recall the public disclosure tort cases in Chapter 2, which indicate that sometimes a person does have a privacy interest even in the event of public exposure or being in a public place.
2. ***Surveillance Cameras.*** The use of surveillance cameras is increasing. Since 1994, in response to terrorist bombings, Britain has been watching city streets through a system of surveillance cameras monitored by closed circuit television (CCTV).[28] In 2002, the National Park Service announced plans to set up a surveillance system at all major monuments on the National Mall in Washington, D.C. Given the frequent use of surveillance cameras, do we still have an expectation of privacy not to be filmed in our day-to-day activities? Consider Marc Blitz:

> People also need privacy and anonymity in many aspects of public life — for example, when they explore controversial films, books, or ideas, have conversations in public places, or seek aid or counsel of a sort they can only find by venturing into the public sphere. Although walls and windows do not shield these public activities from everyone's view, other features of physical

[28] For more background about CCTV, see Clive Norris & Gary Armstrong, *The Maximum Surveillance Society: The Rise of CCTV* (1999); Jeffrey Rosen, *A Cautionary Tale for a New Age of Surveillance*, N.Y. Times Mag. (Oct. 7, 2001).

> and social architecture, distinctive to public space, do shield them. Crowds and the diversity and separateness of the social circles that people move in allow people to find anonymity; the existence of isolated and unmonitored islands of public space allow them to find seclusion. . . . These privacy-enhancing features of public space cannot easily survive in a world of ubiquitous cameras, and the task of preserving them requires courts to do in a sense the opposite of what *Katz* recommends: They must abandon the task of identifying difficult-to-identify expectations of privacy . . . and instead return to the task of preserving the environment that makes privacy possible.[29]

What precisely are the harms of surveillance cameras? Consider Christopher Slobogin:

> Virtually all of us, no matter how innocent, feel somewhat unnerved when a police car pulls up behind us. Imagine now being watched by an officer, at a discreet distance and without any other intrusion, every time you walk through certain streets. Say you want to run (to catch a bus, for a brief bit of exercise or just for the hell of it). Will you? Or assume you want to obscure your face (because of the wind or a desire to avoid being seen by an officious acquaintance)? How about hanging out on the street corner (waiting for friends or because you have nothing else to do)?
>
> In all of these scenarios, you will probably feel and perhaps act differently than when the officer is not there. Perhaps your hesitancy comes from uncertainty as to the officer's likely reaction or simply from a desire to appear completely law-abiding; the important point is that it exists. Government-run cameras are a less tangible presence than the ubiquitous cop, but better at recording your actions. A police officer in Liverpool, England may have said it best: A camera is like having a cop "on duty 24 hours a day, constantly taking notes."[30]

Are there any other harms you can think of? What are the benefits of surveillance cameras? Should they not be permissible as a low-cost way to extend the reach of police? Do the benefits outweigh the harms? Regarding the benefits of surveillance cameras, consider Jeff Rosen:

> In 2000, Britain's violent-crime rates actually increased by 4.3 percent, even though the cameras continued to proliferate. But CCTV cameras have a mysterious knack for justifying themselves regardless of what happens to crime. When crime goes up, the cameras get the credit for detecting it, and when crime goes down, they get the credit for preventing it.[31]

Would it be possible to design an empirical study that would test the effectiveness of surveillance cameras in preventing crime?

3. ***Face Recognition Systems.*** In Tampa, a computer software program called "FaceIt" linked to 36 cameras attempts to scan the faces of individuals on public streets to match them against mug shots of wanted fugitives. A similar

---

[29] Marc Jonathan Blitz, *Video Surveillance and the Constitution of Public Space: Fitting the Fourth Amendment to a World that Tracks Image and Identity*, 82 Tex. L. Rev. 1349, 1481 (2004).

[30] Christopher Slobogin, *Public Privacy: Camera Surveillance of Public Places and the Right to Anonymity*, 72 Miss. L.J. 213, 247 (2002).

[31] Jeffrey Rosen, *The Naked Crowd: Reclaiming Security and Freedom in an Anxious Age* 49 (2004).

system was used to scan faces at Super Bowl XXXV in January 2001. The Tampa Police Department argues that "FaceIt" is analogous to a police officer standing on a street holding a mug shot. Philip Agre contends that face recognition systems are different:

> A human being who spots me in the park has the accountability that someone can spot them as well. Cameras are much more anonymous and easy to hide. More important is the question of scale. Most people understand the moral difference between a single chance observation in a park and an investigator who follows you everywhere you go.[32]

Further, contends Agre, the information used and collected by face recognition systems could fall into the wrong hands and be potentially abused by the government to exercise social control. Additionally, such systems can have errors, resulting in the tracking and potential arrest of innocent persons. As a policy matter, do the costs of facial recognition systems outweigh the benefits? Given the information privacy law you have learned so far, assess the legality and constitutionality of facial recognition systems.

The Tampa face recognition system was ultimately scrapped because of high errors and general ineffectiveness.

4. ***Who Decides What Constitutes a Reasonable Expectation of Privacy?*** Currently, judges decide whether a defendant has a reasonable expectation of privacy in a particular activity. Is this question appropriate for judges to decide? Or should juries decide it? In all of the cases so far, observe the sources that the Court cites to for support that there is no reasonable expectation of privacy. How is a reasonable expectation of privacy to be measured? Is it an empirical question about what most people in society would generally consider to be private? If so, why aren't polls taken? If you're an attorney arguing that there is a reasonable expectation of privacy in something, what do you cite to? How should courts measure what society as a whole thinks is private?

   Christopher Slobogin and Joseph Schumacher conducted a survey of individuals, asking them to rate on a scale of 0 to 100 the intrusiveness of certain types of searches or seizures, with 0 being nonintrusive and 100 being extremely intrusive. Several searches that the Court has concluded do not trigger a reasonable expectation of privacy rated in the middle of the scale. The flyover in *Florida v. Riley* rated at 40.32 on this scale; the dog sniff in *United States v. Place* rated at 58.33; the search of garbage in *California v. Greenwood* rated at 44.95; and the use of a beeper to track a car in *United States v. Knotts* rated at 54.46. Certain searches that the Court held do not involve a reasonable expectation of privacy rated highly on the scale, such as examining bank records in *United States v. Miller,* rated at 71.60. In other highly rated searches, the Court has concluded that the Fourth Amendment applies, such as monitoring a phone for 30 days, rating at 87.67 and a body cavity search at the border, rating at 90.14. The body cavity search was the

---

[32] Philip E. Agre, *Your Face Is Not a Bar Code: Arguments Against Automatic Face Recognition in Public Places* (Sept. 9, 2001), http://dlis.gseis.ucla.edu/people/pagre/bar-code.html.

highest rated search, and a search of foliage in a public park was the lowest rated at 6.48. Slobogin and Schumacher conclude that "the Supreme Court's conclusions about the scope of the Fourth Amendment are often not in tune with commonly held attitudes about police investigative techniques."[33]

To what extent should empirical evidence such as this study be used by courts in determining whether or not there is a reasonable expectation of privacy? If such evidence should be used, at what point in the scale should the line be drawn to establish the existence of a reasonable expectation of privacy?

5. ***Should the Reasonable Expectation of Privacy Test Be Empirical or Normative?*** There is an interesting paradox at the heart of the reasonable expectation of privacy test: Legal protection is triggered by people's expectations of privacy, but those expectations are, to a notable extent, shaped by the extent of the legal protection of privacy. Consider the following argument by Daniel Solove regarding the privacy of the postal letters:

> [I]n America, the privacy of letters was formed in significant part by a legal architecture that protected the confidentiality of letters from other people and government officials. In colonial America, mail was often insecure; it was difficult to seal letters; and the wax often used to keep letters sealed was not very effective. There was widespread suspicion of postal clerks reading letters; and a number of prominent individuals, such as Thomas Jefferson, Alexander Hamilton, and George Washington, decried the lack of privacy in their letters and would sometimes even write in code. . . . Despite these realities, and people's expectation that letters would not be confidential, the law evolved to provide strong protection of the privacy of letters. Benjamin Franklin, who was in charge of the colonial mails, required his employees to swear an oath not to open mail. In the late eighteenth and early nineteenth centuries, Congress passed several laws prohibiting the improper opening of mail. And the Supreme Court held in 1877 that despite the fact that people turned letters over to the government for delivery in the postal system, sealed parcels were protected from inspection by the Fourth Amendment. This example illustrates that privacy is not just found but constructed. By erecting a legal structure to protect the privacy of letters, our society shaped the practices of letter writing and using the postal system. It occurred because of the desire to make privacy an integral part of these practices rather than to preserve the status quo.[34]

Solove argues that societies seek to protect privacy with the law when they do not expect privacy but desire to have it. If Solove is right, then what should courts look to when applying the reasonable expectation of privacy test?

---

[33] Christopher Slobogin & Joseph E. Schumacher, *Reasonable Expectations of Privacy and Autonomy in Fourth Amendment Cases: An Empirical Look at "Understandings Recognized and Permitted by Society,"* 42 Duke L.J. 727 (1993).

[34] Daniel J. Solove, *Conceptualizing Privacy*, 90 Cal. L. Rev. 1087, 1142-43 (2002); *see also* Shaun Spencer, *Reasonable Expectations and the Erosion of Privacy,* 39 San Diego L. Rev. 843 (2002).

(b) Sensory Enhancement Technology

DOW CHEMICAL CO. V. UNITED STATES

476 U.S. 227 (1986)

BURGER, C. J. . . . Petitioner Dow Chemical Co. operates a 2,000-acre facility manufacturing chemicals at Midland, Michigan. The facility consists of numerous covered buildings, with manufacturing equipment and piping conduits located between the various buildings exposed to visual observation from the air. At all times, Dow has maintained elaborate security around the perimeter of the complex barring ground-level public views of these areas. It also investigates any low-level flights by aircraft over the facility. Dow has not undertaken, however, to conceal all manufacturing equipment within the complex from aerial views. Dow maintains that the cost of covering its exposed equipment would be prohibitive.

In early 1978, enforcement officials of EPA, with Dow's consent, made an on-site inspection of two power plants in this complex. A subsequent EPA request for a second inspection, however, was denied, and EPA did not thereafter seek an administrative search warrant. Instead, EPA employed a commercial aerial photographer, using a standard floor-mounted, precision aerial mapping camera, to take photographs of the facility from altitudes of 12,000, 3,000, and 1,200 feet. At all times the aircraft was lawfully within navigable airspace.

EPA did not inform Dow of this aerial photography, but when Dow became aware of it, Dow brought suit in the District Court alleging that EPA's action violated the Fourth Amendment and was beyond EPA's statutory investigative authority. The District Court granted Dow's motion for summary judgment on the ground that EPA had no authority to take aerial photographs and that doing so was a search violating the Fourth Amendment. EPA was permanently enjoined from taking aerial photographs of Dow's premises and from disseminating, releasing, or copying the photographs already taken. . . .

The photographs at issue in this case are essentially like those commonly used in mapmaking. Any person with an airplane and an aerial camera could readily duplicate them. In common with much else, the technology of photography has changed in this century. These developments have enhanced industrial processes, and indeed all areas of life; they have also enhanced law enforcement techniques. . . .

. . . Dow claims EPA's use of aerial photography was a "search" of an area that, notwithstanding the large size of the plant, was within an "industrial curtilage" rather than an "open field," and that it had a reasonable expectation of privacy from such photography protected by the Fourth Amendment. . . .

. . . Dow concedes that a simple flyover with naked-eye observation, or the taking of a photograph from a nearby hillside overlooking such a facility, would give rise to no Fourth Amendment problem.

In *California v. Ciraolo*, 476 U.S. 207 (1986), decided today, we hold that naked-eye aerial observation from an altitude of 1,000 feet of a backyard within the curtilage of a home does not constitute a search under the Fourth Amendment.

In the instant case, two additional Fourth Amendment claims are presented: whether the common-law "curtilage" doctrine encompasses a large industrial complex such as Dow's, and whether photography employing an aerial mapping camera is permissible in this context. Dow argues that an industrial plant, even one occupying 2,000 acres, does not fall within the "open fields" doctrine of *Oliver v. United States* but rather is an "industrial curtilage" having constitutional protection equivalent to that of the curtilage of a private home. Dow further contends that any aerial photography of this "industrial curtilage" intrudes upon its reasonable expectations of privacy. Plainly a business establishment or an industrial or commercial facility enjoys certain protections under the Fourth Amendment. . . .

. . . The curtilage area immediately surrounding a private house has long been given protection as a place where the occupants have a reasonable and legitimate expectation of privacy that society is prepared to accept. . . .

Dow plainly has a reasonable, legitimate, and objective expectation of privacy within the interior of its covered buildings, and it is equally clear that expectation is one society is prepared to observe. Moreover, it could hardly be expected that Dow would erect a huge cover over a 2,000-acre tract. In contending that its entire enclosed plant complex is an "industrial curtilage," Dow argues that its exposed manufacturing facilities are analogous to the curtilage surrounding a home because it has taken every possible step to bar access from ground level. . . .

. . . The intimate activities associated with family privacy and the home and its curtilage simply do not reach the outdoor areas or spaces between structures and buildings of a manufacturing plant. . . .

It may well be, as the Government concedes, that surveillance of private property by using highly sophisticated surveillance equipment not generally available to the public, such as satellite technology, might be constitutionally proscribed absent a warrant. But the photographs here are not so revealing of intimate details as to raise constitutional concerns. Although they undoubtedly give EPA more detailed information than naked-eye views, they remain limited to an outline of the facility's buildings and equipment. The mere fact that human vision is enhanced somewhat, at least to the degree here, does not give rise to constitutional problems. An electronic device to penetrate walls or windows so as to hear and record confidential discussions of chemical formulae or other trade secrets would raise very different and far more serious questions; other protections such as trade secret laws are available to protect commercial activities from private surveillance by competitors. . . .

We hold that the taking of aerial photographs of an industrial plant complex from navigable airspace is not a search prohibited by the Fourth Amendment. . . .

POWELL, J. joined by BRENNAN, MARSHALL, and BLACKMUN, J. J. concurring in part and dissenting in part. The Fourth Amendment protects private citizens from arbitrary surveillance by their Government. For nearly 20 years, this Court has adhered to a standard that ensured that Fourth Amendment rights would retain their vitality as technology expanded the Government's capacity to commit unsuspected intrusions into private areas and activities. Today, in the context of administrative aerial photography of commercial premises, the Court retreats from that standard. It holds that the photography was not a Fourth Amendment "search" because it was not accompanied by a physical trespass and because the equipment used was not the most highly sophisticated form of technology available to the Government. Under this holding, the existence of an asserted privacy interest apparently will be decided solely by reference to the manner of surveillance used to intrude on that interest. Such an inquiry will not protect Fourth Amendment rights, but rather will permit their gradual decay as technology advances. . . .

NOTES & QUESTIONS

1. ***New Surveillance Technologies.*** One of the rationales of *Dow Chemical* is that the device could have been acquired by a member of the general public. Does the case turn on this point? Suppose the police used a special camera that was developed exclusively for law enforcement purposes.

   The *Dow Chemical* Court stated: "It may well be, as the Government concedes, that surveillance of private property by using highly sophisticated surveillance equipment not generally available to the public, such as satellite technology, might be constitutionally proscribed absent a warrant." But does this sentence reflect contemporary technological reality? Mark Monmonier describes the rapid increase in the availability of commercial satellite capacities once the Cold War ended and the U.S. government lifted its restrictions in this area. The public now has cheaper and more detailed satellite images available to it than ever before.[35] As an example, look at maps.google.com, where free high-quality satellite imagery is available for most street maps.

   Recall that in *The Right to Privacy*, Warren and Brandeis complained in 1890 of the then new ability to take candid photographs of individuals. Before the invention of the snap camera, people did not expect to be photographed without their consent. Clearly today the ability to take pictures in public is greatly enhanced. There are video cameras, night-vision cameras, powerful zoom lenses, and satellite images available for sale. Are these new technologies eroding our reasonable expectation of privacy?[36] How should the law respond?

2. ***Flashlights.*** The use of a flashlight "to illuminate a darkened area simply does not constitute a search, and thus triggers no Fourth Amendment protection." *Texas v. Brown*, 460 U.S. 730 (1983). If this conclusion seems evident, how is a flashlight different from other devices that enhance human senses? Is any device that enhances the human senses merely an extension of ordinary senses? What factors should be considered in determining which sense enhancement devices trigger a search under the Fourth Amendment and which do not?

---

[35] Mark Monmonier, *Spying with Maps* (2002).

[36] For an argument that people do have reasonable expectations of privacy in public, see Helen Nissenbaum, *Protecting Privacy in an Information Age: The Problem of Privacy in Public*, 17 Law & Phil. 559 (1998).

3. ***Beepers and Tracking Devices.*** In *United States v. Knotts*, 460 U.S. 276 (1983), the police placed a beeper in a five-gallon drum of chloroform purchased by the defendants and placed in their car. The beeper transmitted signals that enabled the police to track the location of the defendants' vehicle. The Court held that the Fourth Amendment did not apply to the use of this device because a "person traveling in an automobile on public thoroughfares has no reasonable expectation of privacy in his movements from one place to another." Therefore, "[t]he governmental surveillance conducted by means of the beeper in this case amounted principally to the following of an automobile on public streets and highways." In *United States v. Karo*, 468 U.S. 705 (1984), law enforcement officials planted a beeper in a can of ether that the defendant bought from an informant. The officials tracked the movements of the can of ether through a variety of places, including within a residence. While the movements in *Knotts* were in public, the movements within the residence were not, and this amounted to an impermissible search of the residence:

> The monitoring of an electronic device such as a beeper is, of course, less intrusive than a full-scale search, but it does reveal a critical fact about the interior of the premises that the Government is extremely interested in knowing and that it could not have otherwise obtained without a warrant. The case is thus not like *Knotts*, for there the beeper told the authorities nothing about the interior of Knotts' cabin. The information obtained in *Knotts* was "voluntarily conveyed to anyone who wanted to look. . . ."

4. ***Global Positioning System (GPS).*** GPS is a radio navigation system, developed by the U.S. Department of Defense; it provides continuous worldwide positioning and timing information. GPS functions through use of 24 satellites in earth-based orbit, which are monitored by ground-based control stations. GPS devices raise technological issues similar to those at stake in *United States v. Karo* and *United States v. Knotts*. In interpreting the Washington State Constitution, the Washington Supreme Court in *State v. Jackson*, 76 P.3d 217 (Wash. 2003), concluded that the police need a warrant in order to attach a GPS device to a vehicle to track its movement — even in public:

> It is true that an officer standing at a distance in a lawful place may use binoculars to bring into closer view what he sees, or an officer may use a flashlight at night to see what is plainly there to be seen by day. However, when a GPS device is attached to a vehicle, law enforcement officers do not in fact follow the vehicle. Thus, unlike binoculars or a flashlight, the GPS device does not merely augment the officers' senses, but rather provides a technological substitute for traditional visual tracking. Further, the devices in this case were in place for approximately two and one-half weeks. It is unlikely that the sheriff's department could have successfully maintained uninterrupted 24-hour surveillance throughout this time by following Jackson. Even longer tracking periods might be undertaken, depending upon the circumstances of a case. We perceive a difference between the kind of uninterrupted, 24-hour a day surveillance possible through use of a GPS

device, which does not depend upon whether an officer could in fact have maintained visual contact over the tracking period, and an officer's use of binoculars or a flashlight to augment his or her senses.

Moreover, the intrusion into private affairs made possible with a GPS device is quite extensive as the information obtained can disclose a great deal about an individual's life. For example, the device can provide a detailed record of travel to doctors' offices, banks, gambling casinos, tanning salons, places of worship, political party meetings, bars, grocery stores, exercise gyms, places where children are dropped off for school, play, or day care, the upper scale restaurant and the fast food restaurant, the strip club, the opera, the baseball game, the "wrong" side of town, the family planning clinic, the labor rally. In this age, vehicles are used to take people to a vast number of places that can reveal preferences, alignments, associations, personal ails and foibles. The GPS tracking devices record all of these travels, and thus can provide a detailed picture of one's life.

Does the Washington Supreme Court's decision track the U.S. Supreme Court's reading of the Fourth Amendment in cases like *Karo* and *Knotts*?

KYLLO V. UNITED STATES

533 U.S. 27 (2001)

SCALIA, J. In 1991 Agent William Elliott of the United States Department of the Interior came to suspect that marijuana was being grown in the home belonging to petitioner Danny Kyllo, part of a triplex on Rhododendron Drive in Florence, Oregon. Indoor marijuana growth typically requires high-intensity lamps. In order to determine whether an amount of heat was emanating from petitioner's home consistent with the use of such lamps, at 3:20 A.M. on January 16, 1992, Agent Elliott and Dan Haas used an Agema Thermovision 210 thermal imager to scan the triplex. Thermal imagers detect infrared radiation, which virtually all objects emit but which is not visible to the naked eye. The imager converts radiation into images based on relative warmth — black is cool, white is hot, shades of gray connote relative differences; in that respect, it operates somewhat like a video camera showing heat images. The scan of Kyllo's home took only a few minutes and was performed from the passenger seat of Agent Elliott's vehicle across the street from the front of the house and also from the street in back of the house. The scan showed that the roof over the garage and a side wall of petitioner's home were relatively hot compared to the rest of the home and substantially warmer than neighboring homes in the triplex. Agent Elliott concluded that petitioner was using halide lights to grow marijuana in his house, which indeed he was. Based on tips from informants, utility bills, and the thermal imaging, a Federal Magistrate Judge issued a warrant authorizing a search of petitioner's home, and the agents found an indoor growing operation involving more than 100 plants. Petitioner was indicted on one count of manufacturing marijuana, in violation of 21 U.S.C. § 841(a)(1). He unsuccessfully moved to suppress the evidence seized from his home and then entered a conditional guilty plea. . . .

. . . "At the very core" of the Fourth Amendment "stands the right of a man to retreat into his own home and there be free from unreasonable governmental intrusion." With few exceptions, the question whether a warrantless search of a home is reasonable and hence constitutional must be answered no.

On the other hand, the antecedent question of whether or not a Fourth Amendment "search" has occurred is not so simple under our precedent. The permissibility of ordinary visual surveillance of a home used to be clear because, well into the 20th century, our Fourth Amendment jurisprudence was tied to common-law trespass. Visual surveillance was unquestionably lawful because "the eye cannot by the laws of England be guilty of a trespass." We have since decoupled violation of a person's Fourth Amendment rights from trespassory violation of his property, but the lawfulness of warrantless visual surveillance of a home has still been preserved. As we observed in *California v. Ciraolo*, 476 U.S. 207, (1986), "[t]he Fourth Amendment protection of the home has never been extended to require law enforcement officers to shield their eyes when passing by a home on public thoroughfares." . . .

The present case involves officers on a public street engaged in more than naked-eye surveillance of a home. We have previously reserved judgment as to how much technological enhancement of ordinary perception from such a vantage point, if any, is too much. While we upheld enhanced aerial photography of an industrial complex in *Dow Chemical*, we noted that we found "it important that this is not an area immediately adjacent to a private home, where privacy expectations are most heightened."

It would be foolish to contend that the degree of privacy secured to citizens by the Fourth Amendment has been entirely unaffected by the advance of technology. For example, as the cases discussed above make clear, the technology enabling human flight has exposed to public view (and hence, we have said, to official observation) uncovered portions of the house and its curtilage that once were private. The question we confront today is what limits there are upon this power of technology to shrink the realm of guaranteed privacy. . . .

. . . [I]n the case of the search of the interior of homes — the prototypical and hence most commonly litigated area of protected privacy — there is a ready criterion, with roots deep in the common law, of the minimal expectation of privacy that exists, and that is acknowledged to be reasonable. To withdraw protection of this minimum expectation would be to permit police technology to erode the privacy guaranteed by the Fourth Amendment. We think that obtaining by sense-enhancing technology any information regarding the interior of the home that could not otherwise have been obtained without physical "intrusion into a constitutionally protected area," *Silverman*, 365 U.S., at 512, constitutes a search — at least where (as here) the technology in question is not in general public use. This assures preservation of that degree of privacy against government that existed when the Fourth Amendment was adopted. On the basis of this criterion, the information obtained by the thermal imager in this case was the product of a search.[37]

---

[37] The dissent's repeated assertion that the thermal imaging did not obtain information regarding the interior of the home is simply inaccurate. A thermal imager reveals the relative heat

The Government maintains, however, that the thermal imaging must be upheld because it detected "only heat radiating from the external surface of the house." The dissent makes this its leading point, contending that there is a fundamental difference between what it calls "off-the-wall" observations and "through-the-wall surveillance." But just as a thermal imager captures only heat emanating from a house, so also a powerful directional microphone picks up only sound emanating from a house — and a satellite capable of scanning from many miles away would pick up only visible light emanating from a house. We rejected such a mechanical interpretation of the Fourth Amendment in *Katz*, where the eavesdropping device picked up only sound waves that reached the exterior of the phone booth. Reversing that approach would leave the homeowner at the mercy of advancing technology — including imaging technology that could discern all human activity in the home. While the technology used in the present case was relatively crude, the rule we adopt must take account of more sophisticated systems that are already in use or in development. The dissent's reliance on the distinction between "off-the-wall" and "through-the-wall" observation is entirely incompatible with the dissent's belief, which we discuss below, that thermal-imaging observations of the intimate details of a home are impermissible. The most sophisticated thermal imaging devices continue to measure heat "off-the-wall" rather than "through-the-wall"; the dissent's disapproval of those more sophisticated thermal-imaging devices, is an acknowledgement that there is no substance to this distinction. As for the dissent's extraordinary assertion that anything learned through "an inference" cannot be a search, that would validate even the "through-the-wall" technologies that the dissent purports to disapprove. Surely the dissent does not believe that the through-the-wall radar or ultrasound technology produces an 8-by-10 Kodak glossy that needs no analysis (i.e., the making of inferences). And, of course, the novel proposition that inference insulates a search is blatantly contrary to *United States v. Karo*, 468 U.S. 705 (1984), where the police "inferred" from the activation of a beeper that a certain can of ether was in the home. The police activity was held to be a search, and the search was held unlawful.

The Government also contends that the thermal imaging was constitutional because it did not "detect private activities occurring in private areas." . . . The Fourth Amendment's protection of the home has never been tied to measurement of the quality or quantity of information obtained. In *Silverman*, for example, we made clear that any physical invasion of the structure of the home, "by even a fraction of an inch," was too much, and there is certainly no exception to the warrant requirement for the officer who barely cracks open the front door and sees nothing but the nonintimate rug on the vestibule floor. . . .

---

of various rooms in the home. The dissent may not find that information particularly private or important, but there is no basis for saying it is not information regarding the interior of the home. The dissent's comparison of the thermal imaging to various circumstances in which outside observers might be able to perceive, without technology, the heat of the home — for example, by observing snowmelt on the roof — is quite irrelevant. The fact that equivalent information could sometimes be obtained by other means does not make lawful the use of means that violate the Fourth Amendment. The police might, for example, learn how many people are in a particular house by setting up year-round surveillance, but that does not make breaking and entering to find out the same information lawful. In any event, on the night of January 16, 1992, no outside observer could have discerned the relative heat of Kyllo's home without thermal imaging.

We have said that the Fourth Amendment draws "a firm line at the entrance to the house." That line, we think, must be not only firm but also bright — which requires clear specification of those methods of surveillance that require a warrant. While it is certainly possible to conclude from the videotape of the thermal imaging that occurred in this case that no "significant" compromise of the homeowner's privacy has occurred, we must take the long view, from the original meaning of the Fourth Amendment forward. . . .

Where, as here, the Government uses a device that is not in general public use, to explore details of the home that would previously have been unknowable without physical intrusion, the surveillance is a "search" and is presumptively unreasonable without a warrant. . . .

STEVENS, J. joined by REHNQUIST, C. J. and O'CONNOR and KENNEDY, J. dissenting. . . . [S]earches and seizures of property in plain view are presumptively reasonable. Whether that property is residential or commercial, the basic principle is the same: "What a person knowingly exposes to the public, even in his own home or office, is not a subject of Fourth Amendment protection." That is the principle implicated here.

While the Court "take[s] the long view" and decides this case based largely on the potential of yet-to-be-developed technology that might allow "through-the-wall surveillance," this case involves nothing more than off-the-wall surveillance by law enforcement officers to gather information exposed to the general public from the outside of petitioner's home. All that the infrared camera did in this case was passively measure heat emitted from the exterior surfaces of petitioner's home; all that those measurements showed were relative differences in emission levels, vaguely indicating that some areas of the roof and outside walls were warmer than others. As still images from the infrared scans show, no details regarding the interior of petitioner's home were revealed. . . .

. . . Heat waves, like aromas that are generated in a kitchen, or in a laboratory or opium den, enter the public domain if and when they leave a building. A subjective expectation that they would remain private is not only implausible but also surely not "one that society is prepared to recognize as 'reasonable.'" . . .

Despite the Court's attempt to draw a line that is "not only firm but also bright," the contours of its new rule are uncertain because its protection apparently dissipates as soon as the relevant technology is "in general public use." Yet how much use is general public use is not even hinted at by the Court's opinion, which makes the somewhat doubtful assumption that the thermal imager used in this case does not satisfy that criterion. In any event, putting aside its lack of clarity, this criterion is somewhat perverse because it seems likely that the threat to privacy will grow, rather than recede, as the use of intrusive equipment becomes more readily available. . . .

Because the new rule applies to information regarding the "interior" of the home, it is too narrow as well as too broad. Clearly, a rule that is designed to protect individuals from the overly intrusive use of sense-enhancing equipment should not be limited to a home. If such equipment did provide its user with the functional equivalent of access to a private place — such as, for example, the telephone booth involved in *Katz*, or an office building — then the rule should apply to such an area as well as to a home. . . .

NOTES & QUESTIONS

1. ***Thermal Imagers vs. Canine Sniffs.*** How does the Court distinguish the thermal imager in *Kyllo* from the camera in *Dow Chemical* and the dog sniff in *Place*? Does this distinction make sense?
2. ***Canine Sniffs Revisited.*** The Court decided *Illinois v. Caballes,* another dog sniff case, subsequent to *Kyllo*. In *Caballes*, the majority opinion and Justice Souter's dissent all revisited *Kyllo*. For the *Caballes* majority, the distinction between the two cases was that the thermal-imaging device in *Kyllo* was able to detect lawful activities, such as when an individual enjoyed a hot sauna or bath. The *Caballes* majority stated: "The legitimate expectation that information about perfectly lawful activity will remain private is categorically distinguishable from respondent's hopes or expectations concerning the nondetection of contraband in the trunk of his car." Justice Souter, dissenting, argued: "[G]iven the fallibility of the dog, the sniff is the first step in a process that may disclose 'intimate details' without revealing contraband, just as a thermal-imaging device might do, as described in *Kyllo v. United States*." Is the dog sniff like a thermal-imaging device? Or is it, as the *Caballes* majority argues, simply *sui generis*?
3. ***The Limits on Sense-Enhancing Technology.*** The *Kyllo* Court notes that there must be some limits on sense-enhancement technology. What is the limiting principle according to the Court? Do you think this is the appropriate limiting principle?[38]
4. ***Technology in General Public Use.*** The majority based its holding on the fact that a thermal sensor was *"a device not in general public use."* However, a search of eBay reveals different kinds of thermal-imaging devices for sale at a variety of prices. Hence, the thermal sensor device is one that is publicly available. Is this "eBay test" relevant? How should a court decide when a technology is "in general public use"?
5. ***The Home.*** Justice Stevens argues that "a rule that is designed to protect individuals from the overly intrusive use of sense-enhancing equipment should not be limited to a home." Do you agree? Given the reasoning of the majority, would the Court reach the same result if the thermal imager had been used outside a person's office rather than her home?
6. ***The Courts vs. Congress.*** Orin Kerr contends that when new technologies are involved, Congress, not the courts, should be the primary rulemaker. In particular, Kerr critiques the generally held view that "the Fourth Amendment should be interpreted broadly in response to technological change." According to Kerr:

> [C]ourts should place a thumb on the scale in favor of judicial caution when technology is in flux, and should consider allowing legislatures to provide the

[38] For background into sensory enhancement technology, see Christopher Slobogin, *Technologically-Assisted Physician Surveillance: The American Bar Association's Tentative Draft Standards*, 10 Harv. J.L. & Tech. 383 (1997); ABA Standards for Criminal Justice, Electronic Surveillance § B (3d ed. 1999) (technologically assisted physical surveillance), available at http://abanet.org/crimjust/standards/taps_toc.html.

> primary rules governing law enforcement investigations involving new technologies. . . . When technology is in flux, Fourth Amendment protections should remain relatively modest until the technology stabilizes.

Kerr justifies his conclusion by making an argument about the attributes of judicial versus legislative rulemaking:

> The first difference is that legislatures typically create generally applicable rules ex ante, while courts tend to create rules ex post in a case-by-case fashion. That is, legislatures enact generalized rules for the future, whereas courts resolve disputes settling the rights of parties arising from a past event. The difference leads to Fourth Amendment rules that tend to lag behind parallel statutory rules and current technologies by at least a decade, resulting in unsettled and then outdated rules that often make little sense given current technological facts. . . .
>
> A second difference between judicial and legislative rulemaking concerns their operative constraints. . . . Legislatures are up to the task [of adapting to technological change]; courts generally are not. Legislatures can experiment with different rules and make frequent amendments; they can place restrictions on both public and private actors; and they can even "sunset" rules so that they apply only for a particular period of time. The courts cannot. As a result, Fourth Amendment rules will tend to lack the flexibility that a regulatory response to new technologies may require. . . .
>
> The third important difference between judicial rules and legislative rules relates to the information environment in which rules are generated. Legislative rules tend to be the product of a wide range of inputs, ranging from legislative hearings and poll results to interest group advocacy and backroom compromises. Judicial rules tend to follow from a more formal and predictable presentation of written briefs and oral arguments by two parties. Once again, the difference offers significant advantages to legislative rulemaking. The task of generating balanced and nuanced rules requires a comprehensive understanding of technological facts. Legislatures are well-equipped to develop such understandings; courts generally are not.[39]

Peter Swire responds that Congress's privacy legislation was shaped by judicial decisions concerning the Fourth Amendment:

> At least four mutually reinforcing reasons underscore the importance of judicial decisions to how these privacy protections were enacted. First, the Supreme Court decision made the issue more salient, focusing attention on a topic that otherwise would not climb to the top of the legislative agenda. Second, the importance of the decision to the political process was greater because of what social scientists have called the "endowment effect" or "status quo bias." . . . [T]he concept is that individuals experience a loss as more important than a gain of equal size. . . . [T]he perceived "loss" of Fourth Amendment protections . . . would be a spur to legislative action. Third, the opinions of the Supreme Court shaped the legislative debates. Vigorous dissents in each case articulated reasons why privacy protections should be considered important. . . . Fourth, once the issue had moved high enough on

---

[39] Orin S. Kerr, *The Fourth Amendment and New Technologies: Constitutional Myths and the Case for Caution*, 102 Mich. L. Rev. 801, 803-05, 868, 871, 875 (2004).

> the agenda to warrant a vote, there were persuasive public-policy arguments that some privacy protections were appropriate.[40]

Daniel Solove also disagrees with Kerr's conclusions: "Where the courts have left open areas for legislative rules to fill in, Congress has created an uneven fabric of protections that is riddled with holes and that has weak protections in numerous places." Further, Solove contends, legislative ex ante rules are not necessarily preferable to judicial ex post rules:

> The problem with ex ante laws is that they cannot anticipate all of the new and changing factual situations that technology brings about. Ex post rules, in contrast, are often much better tailored to specific types of technology, because such rules arise as technology changes, rather than beforehand. . . .

Solove argues that the "historical record suggests that Congress is actually far worse than the courts in reacting to new technologies." In response to Kerr's argument that the legislature is better equipped to understand new technologies than the judiciary, Solove responds that "merely shifting to a statutory regime will not eliminate Kerr's concern with judges misunderstanding technology. In fact, many judicial misunderstandings stem from courts trying to fit new technologies into old statutory regimes built around old technologies."[41]

B. FEDERAL ELECTRONIC SURVEILLANCE LAW

1. SECTION 605 OF THE FEDERAL COMMUNICATIONS ACT

Recall that in 1928, the Court in *Olmstead* declared that wiretapping did not constitute a Fourth Amendment violation. By the time *Olmstead* was decided, more than 25 states had made wiretapping a crime.

Six years later, responding to significant criticism of the *Olmstead* decision, Congress enacted the Federal Communications Act (FCA) of 1934. Section 605 of the Act provided that "no person not being authorized by the sender shall intercept any communication and divulge or publish the existence, contents, substance, purport, effect, or meaning of such intercepted communications to any person." Although § 605 did not expressly provide for an exclusionary rule, the Court in *Nardone v. United States*, 302 U.S. 379 (1937), held that federal officers could not introduce evidence obtained by illegal wiretapping in federal court.

Section 605 had significant limitations. States could still use evidence in violation of § 605 in state prosecutions. Further, § 605 only applied to wire communications and wiretapping, not to eavesdropping on nonwire communications. Thus, bugging was not covered.

In the words of Attorney General Nicholas Katzenback, § 605 was the "worst of all possible solutions." It prevented law enforcement from using information

---

[40] Peter P. Swire, Katz *Is Dead. Long Live* Katz, 102 Mich. L. Rev. 904, 917 (2004).

[41] Daniel J. Solove, *Fourth Amendment Codification and Professor Kerr's Misguided Call for Judicial Deference*, 74 Fordham L. Rev. 747, 761-74 (2005).

gleaned from wiretaps in court — even if pursuant to a warrant supported by probable cause. And it did little to restrict government wiretapping since it was interpreted not to prohibit such activity so long as the evidence was not used in court.

With the absence of Fourth Amendment protections and the limited protections of § 605, the federal government engaged in extensive wiretapping. During World War II, J. Edgar Hoover, the director of the FBI, successfully urged President Franklin Roosevelt to allow FBI wiretapping to investigate subversive activities and threats to national security. During the Truman Administration, the justification for electronic surveillance expanded to include domestic security as well. In the 1950s, the FBI then expanded its electronic surveillance due to national concern about Communism and communist infiltration of government. During the Cold War Era and beyond, Hoover ordered wiretapping of hundreds of people, including political enemies, dissidents, Supreme Court Justices, professors, celebrities, writers, and others. Among Hoover's files were dossiers on John Steinbeck, Ernest Hemingway, Charlie Chaplin, Marlon Brando, Muhammad Ali, Albert Einstein, John Lennon, and numerous presidents and members of Congress.[42]

The FBI also placed Martin Luther King Jr. under extensive surveillance. Hoover believed King was a Communist (which he was not), and disliked him personally. When the FBI's electronic surveillance of King revealed King's extramarital affairs, the FBI sent copies of the tapes to King along with a letter insinuating that he should commit suicide or else the tapes would be leaked to the public. The FBI also sent the tapes to King's wife and played them to President Lyndon Johnson.[43] In reflecting on the FBI's campaign against King, Frederick Schwarz and Aziz Huq note that an important role was played by Hoover's "personal animus against King, and his profound distaste for the social changes pressed by the civil rights movement." Schwarz and Huq also observe: "But without an institutional underpinning, Hoover's bias would not have taken the form of a massive, multiyear surveillance and harassment campaign. The war against King highlights what happens when checks and balances are abandoned."[44]

During this time, state police also conducted wiretapping. To the extent that this wiretapping was regulated, this regulation was purely that of the individual states. Section 605 only applied at the federal level. In an influential study, Samuel Dash, Richard Schwartz, and Robert Knowlton revealed that regulation of wiretapping by the states was often ineffective. There were numerous unauthorized wiretaps and few checks against abuses.[45]

---

[42] Daniel J. Solove, *Reconstructing Electronic Surveillance Law,* 72 Geo. Wash. L. Rev. 1264, 1273-74 (2004).

[43] David J. Garrow, *The FBI and Martin Luther King, Jr.* (1980).

[44] Frederick A.O. Schwarz, Jr. & Aziz Z. Huq, *Unchecked and Unbalanced: Presidential Power in a Time of Terror* 23 (2007).

[45] *See* Samuel Dash, Richard Schwartz, & Robert Knowlton, *The Eavesdroppers* (1959).

2. TITLE III

In 1968, in response to *Katz v. United States* and *Berger v. New York*, Congress enacted Title III of the Omnibus Crime Control and Safe Streets Act of 1968, Pub. L. No. 90-351, codified at 18 U.S.C. §§ 2510–2520. This Act is commonly referred to as "Title III" or, subsequent to its amendment in 1986, as the "Wiretap Act."

Title III extended far beyond § 605; it applied to wiretaps by federal and state officials as well as by private parties. Title III required federal agents to apply for a warrant before wiretapping. The Act criminalized private wiretaps. However, if any party to the conversation consented to the tapping, then there was no violation of Title III.

Title III authorized the Attorney General to apply to a federal judge for an order authorizing the interception of a "wire or oral communication." A judge could not issue a court order unless there was probable cause. Many other procedural safeguards were established.

Title III excluded wiretaps for national security purposes from any restrictions at all. President Nixon frequently used the national security exception to place internal dissidents and radicals under surveillance. However, in *United States v. United States District Court* (the *Keith* case), 407 U.S. 297 (1972), the Court unanimously rejected Nixon's approach, stating that Title III's national security exception does not apply to internal threats but only to foreign threats.

3. THE ELECTRONIC COMMUNICATIONS PRIVACY ACT

(a) Statutory Structure

In 1986, Congress modernized federal wiretap law by passing the Electronic Communications Privacy Act (ECPA).[46] The ECPA amended Title III (the Wiretap Act), and it also included two new acts in response to developments in computer technology and communication networks. Hence, federal electronic surveillance law on the domestic side contains three parts: (1) the Wiretap Act (the updated version of Title III, which ECPA shifted to its first Title); (2) the Stored Communications Act (SCA); and (3) the Pen Register Act.

Many of the provisions of federal electronic surveillance law apply not only to government officials, but to private individuals and entities as well. In particular, cases involving the violation of federal electronic surveillance law by private parties often occur in the employment context when employers desire to use forms of electronic surveillance on their employees.

---

[46] For more background on electronic surveillance law, see Patricia L. Bellia, *Surveillance Law Through Cyberlaw's Lens,* 72 Geo. Wash. L. Rev. 1375 (2004); Deirdre K. Mulligan, *Reasonable Expectations in Electronic Communications: A Critical Perspective on the Electronic Communications Privacy Act,* 72 Geo. Wash. L. Rev. 1557 (2004); Paul K. Ohm, *Parallel-Effect Statutes and E-mail "Warrants": Reframing the Internet Surveillance Debate,* 72 Geo. Wash. L. Rev. 1599 (2004); Susan Freiwald, *Online Surveillance: Remembering the Lessons of the Wiretap Act,* 56 Ala. L. Rev. 9 (2004). *See generally* Symposium, *The Future of Internet Surveillance Law,* 72 Geo. Wash. L. Rev. 1139-1617 (2004).

TYPES OF COMMUNICATIONS

In order to comprehend how each of the three acts comprising ECPA works, it is important to know that ECPA classifies all communications into three types: (1) "wire communications"; (2) "oral communications"; and (3) "electronic communications." Each type of communication is protected differently. As a general matter, wire communications receive the most protection and electronic communications receive the least.

Wire Communications. A "wire communication," defined in § 2510(1), involves all "aural transfers" that travel through a wire or a similar medium:

> (1) "wire communication" means any aural transfer made in whole or in part through the use of facilities for the transmission of communications by the aid of wire, cable, or other like connection between the point of origin and the point of reception (including the use of such connection in a switching station) furnished or operated by any person engaged in providing or operating such facilities for the transmission of interstate or foreign communications or communications affecting interstate or foreign commerce.

An "aural transfer" is a communication containing the human voice at any point. § 2510(18). The human voice need only be a minor part of the communication. Further, the human voice need not always be present throughout the journey of the communication. Therefore, a communication that once consisted of the human voice that has been translated into code or tones still qualifies as an "aural transfer."

The aural transfer must travel through wire (i.e., telephone wires or cable wires) or a similar medium. The entire journey from origin to destination need not take place through wire, as many communications travel through a host of different mediums — wire, radio, satellite, and so on. Only part of the communication's journey must be through a wire.

Oral Communications. The second type of communication under federal wiretap law are "oral communications." Pursuant to § 2510(2), an "oral communication" is a communication "uttered by a person exhibiting an expectation that such communication is not subject to interception under circumstances justifying such expectation." Oral communications are typically intercepted through bugs and other recording or transmitting devices.

Electronic Communications. The final type of communication is an "electronic communication." Under § 2510(12), an electronic communication consists of all non-wire and non-oral communications:

> (12) "electronic communication" means any transfer of signs, signals, writing, images, sounds, data, or intelligence of any nature transmitted in whole or in part by a wire, radio, electromagnetic, photoelectronic or photooptical system that affects interstate or foreign commerce, but does not include —
>
> (A) any wire or oral communication. . . .

In other words, an electronic communication consists of all communications that do not constitute wire or oral communications. An example of an electronic communication is an e-mail — at least as long as it does not contain the human voice.

Although electronic communications are protected under the Stored Communications Act as well as the Wiretap Act, they are treated differently than wire and oral communications. The most notable difference is that the exclusionary rule in the Wiretap Act does not apply to electronic communications. Therefore, wire or oral communications that fall within the Wiretap Act are protected by the exclusionary rule, but not when they fall within the Stored Communications Act (which has no exclusionary rule). Electronic communications are not protected by the exclusionary rule in the Wiretap Act or the Stored Communications Act.

THE WIRETAP ACT

Interceptions. The Wiretap Act, which is codified at Title I of ECPA, 18 U.S.C. §§ 2510–2522, governs the interception of communications. In particular, § 2511 provides that:

> (1) Except as otherwise specifically provided in this chapter any person who —
>
> (a) intentionally intercepts, endeavors to intercept, or procures any other person to intercept or endeavor to intercept, any wire, oral, or electronic communication;
>
> (b) intentionally uses, endeavors to use, or procures any other person to use or endeavor to use any electronic, mechanical, or other device to intercept any oral communication when —
>
> (i) such device is affixed to, or otherwise transmits a signal through, a wire, cable, or other like connection used in wire communication; or
>
> (ii) such device transmits communications by radio, or interferes with the transmission of such communication; or
>
> (iii) such person knows, or has reason to know, that such device or any component thereof has been sent through the mail or transported in interstate or foreign commerce. . . .
>
> (c) intentionally discloses, or endeavors to disclose, to any other person the contents of any wire, oral, or electronic communication, knowing or having reason to know that the information was obtained through the interception of a wire, oral, or electronic communication in violation of this subsection;
>
> (d) intentionally uses, or endeavors to use, the contents of any wire, oral, or electronic communication, knowing or having reason to know that the information was obtained through the interception of a wire, oral, or electronic communication in violation of this subsection. . . .

As this provision indicates, the Wiretap Act applies to the intentional interception of a communication. To "intercept" a communication means to acquire its contents through the use of any "electronic, mechanical, or other device." § 2510(4). The classic example of an activity covered by the Act is the wiretapping of a phone conversation — a device is being used to listen to a conversation as it is occurring, as the words are moving through the wires. The

Wiretap Act applies when communications are intercepted contemporaneously with their transmission. Once the communication is completed and stored, then the Wiretap Act no longer applies.

In *Bartnicki v. Vopper*, 532 U.S. 514 (2001) (Chapter 2), the Court held that § 2511(1)(c) violated the First Amendment by restricting disclosures involving matters of public concern.

Exclusionary Rule. Under the Wiretap Act, "any aggrieved person . . . may move to suppress the contents of any wire or oral communication intercepted pursuant to this chapter, or evidence derived therefrom." § 2518 (10)(a).

Penalties. Violations of the Wiretap Act can result in fines of a minimum of $10,000 per violation as well as up to five years' imprisonment. *See* §§ 2511(4)(a); 2520(c)(2)(B).

Court Orders. Pursuant to § 2518, an application for a court wiretapping or electronic surveillance order must be made under oath and contain a variety of information, including details to justify the agent's belief that a crime has been, is being, or will be committed; specific description of place where communications will be intercepted; description of the type of communication; and period of time of interception. The judge may require the applicant to furnish additional testimony or documentary evidence in support of the application. The judge must find probable cause and that the particular communications concerning that offense will be obtained through the interception. Further, the court must find that alternatives to wiretapping were attempted and failed, or reasonably appear to be unlikely to succeed or to be too dangerous. The order can last for up to 30 days and can be renewed.

Under the Wiretap Act, only certain government officials are able to apply to a court for a wiretapping order — for federal law enforcement agencies, the relevant party is the attorney general, or a deputy or assistant attorney general; for state officials, the relevant party is the principal prosecuting attorney of a state or a local government, or any government attorney. In other words, the police themselves cannot obtain a wiretap order alone. The Wiretap Act also provides an exclusive list of crimes for which a wiretap order can be issued. The list is broad and includes most felonies. A wiretap order cannot be obtained, however, to investigate a misdemeanor.

Minimization. The Wiretap Act requires that interception must be minimized to avoid sweeping in communications beyond the purpose for which the order was sought. Pursuant to § 2518(6): "Every order and extension thereof shall contain a provision that the authorization to intercept shall be executed as soon as practicable, shall be conducted in such a way as to minimize the interception of communications not otherwise subject to interception under this chapter, and must terminate upon attainment of the authorized objective." For example, if law enforcement officials are wiretapping the home phone line of a person suspected of running an illegal gambling operation and the person's daughter is talking on the line to a friend about going to the movies, the officials should stop listening to the conversation.

Notice. After the surveillance is over, copies of the recorded conversations must be turned over to the court issuing the order. The court must notify the party that surveillance was undertaken within 90 days after the denial of a surveillance order or after the completion of the surveillance authorized by a granted surveillance order. § 2518(8)(d).

Exceptions. There are two notable exceptions under the Wiretap Act. First, the Act does not apply if one of the parties to the communication consents. § 2511(2)(c). For example, a person can secretly tap and record a communication to which that person is a party. Thus, secretly recording one's own phone conversations is not illegal under federal wiretap law. If they participate in the conversation, government agents and informants can record others without their knowledge. An exception to the consent exception is when an interception is carried out for the purpose of committing any criminal or tortious act. In that case, even when a party has consented, interception is illegal. § 2511(2)(d).

Second, a communications service provider is permitted "to intercept, disclose, or use that communication in the normal course of his employment while engaged in any activity which is a necessary incident to the rendition of his service or to the protection of the rights or property of the provider of that service." § 2511(2)(a). Also, a service provider may intentionally disclose intercepted communications to the proper authorities when criminal activity is afoot; with the consent of the originator, addressee, or intended recipient; or to any intermediary provider. § 2511(3).

THE STORED COMMUNICATIONS ACT

Stored Communications. Whereas communications in transmission are covered by the Wiretap Act, communications in storage are protected by the Stored Communications Act (SCA), codified at 18 U.S.C. §§ 2701–2711.[47] With many forms of modern communication, such as Internet service, communications and subscriber records are often maintained in storage by the electronic communications service provider. Pursuant to § 2701:

> (a) Offense. — Except as provided in subsection (c) of this section whoever —
>
> (1) intentionally accesses without authorization a facility through which an electronic communication service is provided; or
>
> (2) intentionally exceeds an authorization to access that facility; and thereby obtains, alters, or prevents authorized access to a wire or electronic communication while it is in electronic storage in such system shall be punished as provided in subsection (b) of this section.

The definition of "electronic storage" in the Wiretap Act also applies to the term as used in the SCA. "Electronic storage" means:

> (A) any temporary, intermediate storage of a wire or electronic communication incidental to the electronic transmission thereof; and

[47] For more background about the SCA, see Orin S. Kerr, *A User's Guide to the Stored Communications Act, and a Legislator's Guide to Amending It,* 72 Geo. Wash. L. Rev. 1208 (2004).

(B) any storage of such communication by an electronic communications service for purposes of backup protection of such communication. § 2510(17).

Section 2701(a) does not apply to "the person or entity providing a wire or electronic communications service" (such as Internet Service Providers) or to "a user of that service with respect to a communication of or intended for that user." § 2701(c).

The SCA also forbids the disclosure of the contents of stored communications by communications service providers. *See* § 2702(a). There are a number of exceptions, including disclosures to the intended recipient of the communication, disclosures with the consent of the creator or recipient of the communication, disclosures that are "necessarily incident to the rendition of the service or to the protection of the rights or property of the provider of that service," and disclosures to a law enforcement agency under certain circumstances. *See* § 2702(b).

Penalties. The SCA has less severe criminal penalties and civil liability than Title I. Under § 2701(b), violations can result in fines of a minimum of $1,000 per violation and up to six months imprisonment. If the wiretap is done for commercial advantage or gain, then a violation can result in up to one year of imprisonment.

Exclusionary Rule. The SCA does not provide for an exclusionary rule.

Judicial Authority for Obtaining Stored Communications. Under the SCA, the judicial process required for obtaining permission to access stored communications held by electronic communications service providers is much less rigorous than under the Wiretap Act. If the government seeks access to the contents of a communication that has been in storage for 180 days or less, then it must first obtain a warrant supported by probable cause. § 2703(a). If the government wants to access a communication that has been in storage for more than 180 days, the government must provide prior notice to the subscriber and obtain an administrative subpoena, a grand jury subpoena, a trial subpoena, or a court order. § 2703(b). The court order does not require probable cause, only "specific and articulable facts showing that there are reasonable grounds" to believe communications are relevant to the criminal investigation. 18 U.S.C. § 2703(d). However, if the government seeks to access a communication that has been in storage for more than 180 days and does not want to provide prior notice to the subscriber, it must obtain a warrant. § 2703(b). Notice to the subscriber that the government obtained her communications can be delayed for up to 90 days. § 2705.

Court Orders to Obtain Subscriber Records. According to § 2703(c)(1)(B), communication service providers must disclose subscriber information (i.e., identifying information, address, phone number, etc.) to the government under certain circumstances:

(B) A provider of electronic communication service or remote computing service shall disclose a record or other information pertaining to a subscriber to or customer of such service (not including the contents of communications

> covered by subsection (a) or (b) of this section) to a governmental entity only when the governmental entity —
>
> (i) obtains a warrant issued under the Federal Rules of Criminal Procedure or equivalent State warrant;
>
> (ii) obtains a court order for such disclosure under subsection (d) of this section;
>
> (iii) has the consent of the subscriber or customer to such disclosure

Communications service providers who disclose stored communications in accordance with any of the above orders or subpoenas cannot be held liable for that disclosure. *See* § 2703(e).

Exceptions. Similar to the Wiretap Act, the SCA also has a consent exception, see § 2702(b), and a service provider exception, see § 2701(c)(1). Unlike the service provider exception for the Wiretap Act, which allows interceptions on a limited basis (those necessary to provide the communications service), the SCA's exception is broader, entirely exempting "the person or entity providing a wire or electronic communications service." § 2701(c)(1).

THE PEN REGISTER ACT

The Pen Register Act, codified at 18 U.S.C. §§ 3121–3127, governs pen registers and trap and trace devices — and their modern analogues. Recall *Smith v. Maryland,* earlier in this chapter, where the Court held that the Fourth Amendment did not extend to pen register information. The Pen Register Act provides some limited protection for such information. Subject to certain exceptions, "no person may install or use a pen register or a trap and trace device without first obtaining a court order." § 3121(a). Traditionally, a pen register was a device that records the telephone numbers dialed from a particular telephone line (phone numbers of outgoing calls). A trap and trace device is the reverse of a pen register — it records the telephone numbers where incoming calls originate.

Definition of "Pen Register." The Pen Register Act defines pen registers more broadly than phone number information:

> [T]he term "pen register" means a device or process which records or decodes dialing, routing, addressing, or signaling information transmitted by an instrument or facility from which a wire or electronic communication is transmitted, provided, however, that such information shall not include the contents of any communication . . . 18 U.S.C. § 3127(3)

Court Orders. If the government certifies that "the information likely to be obtained by such installation and use is relevant to an ongoing investigation," § 3123(a), then courts "shall authorize the installation and use of a pen register or a trap and trace device for a period not to exceed sixty days." § 3123(c). This standard is a low threshold. As Susan Freiwald contends: "[T]he language of the [pen register] court order requirement raises doubt as to its efficacy as a guard against fishing expeditions. . . . The relevance standard in the transaction records provision allows law enforcement to obtain records of people who may be tangentially involved in a crime, even as innocent victims."[48]

Enforcement. There is no exclusionary rule for violations of the Pen Register Act. Rather than a suppression remedy, the Pen Register Act provides: "Whoever knowingly violates subsection (a) shall be fined under this title or imprisoned not more than one year, or both." § 3121(d).

VIDEO SURVEILLANCE

Prior to the enactment of the ECPA, video surveillance was not encompassed within the language of Title III. When it amended federal electronic surveillance law in 1986 by enacting the ECPA, Congress again failed to address video surveillance. Of course, if the government intercepts a *communication* consisting of video images (such as a transmission of a webcam image or an e-mail containing a video clip), then the Wiretap Act applies. If the government accesses an individual's stored video clip, then the SCA applies. However, being watched by video *surveillance* (such as a surveillance camera) does not involve an interception or an accessing of stored images. The video surveillance must be silent video surveillance, or else it could be an "oral" communication subject to the Wiretap Act. In sum, silent video surveillance is not covered under federal electronic surveillance law. *See, e.g.*, *United States v. Biasuci*, 786 F.2d 504 (2d Cir. 1986); *United States v. Koyomejian*, 970 F.2d 536 (9th Cir. 1992); *United States v. Falls*, 34 F.3d 674 (8th Cir. 1994).

In *United States v. Mesa-Rincon*, 911 F.2d 1433 (10th Cir. 1990), the court observed that although federal electronic surveillance law did not apply to video surveillance, the Fourth Amendment did:

> Unfortunately, Congress has not yet specifically defined the constitutional requirements for video surveillance. Nevertheless, the general fourth amendment requirements are still applicable to video surveillance; and suppression is required when the government fails to follow these requirements.
>
> Title III establishes elaborate warrant requirements for wiretapping and bugging. Unfortunately, Title III does not discuss television surveillance in any way. Thus, its requirements are not binding on this court in the context of video surveillance. However, the fact that Title III does not discuss television surveillance is no authority for the proposition that Congress meant to outlaw the practice.

ELECTRONIC SURVEILLANCE LAW AND THE FOURTH AMENDMENT

Electronic surveillance law operates independently of the Fourth Amendment. Even if a search is reasonable under the Fourth Amendment, electronic surveillance law may bar the evidence. Even if a search is authorized by a judge under federal electronic surveillance law, the Fourth Amendment could still prohibit the wiretap.

---

[48] Susan Freiwald, *Uncertain Privacy: Communications Attributes After the Digital Telephony Act,* 69 S. Cal. L. Rev. 949, 1005-06 (1996).

Moreover, procedures for obtaining a court order under the Wiretap Act are more stringent than those for obtaining a search warrant under the Fourth Amendment. As an example of how the Wiretap Act is stricter, under the Fourth Amendment, any law enforcement official can apply for a warrant. Under the Wiretap Act, in contrast, only certain officials (prosecuting attorneys) can apply.

In at least one significant way, federal electronic surveillance law is broader than the Fourth Amendment. Under the Fourth Amendment, search warrants generally authorize a single entry and prompt search. Warrants must be narrowly circumscribed. They are not a license for unlimited and continued investigation. Under the Wiretap Act, however, courts can authorize continuing surveillance — 24 hours a day for a 30-day period. This period can also be extended.

The Supreme Court has held that, pursuant to a warrant or an order under electronic surveillance law, the government can secretly enter one's residence or private property to install electronic surveillance devices, such as bugs. *See Dahlia v. United States*, 441 U.S. 238 (1979). The *Dahlia* Court further concluded that the Fourth Amendment does not require that an electronic surveillance order include a specific authorization to enter covertly the premises described in the order. In other words, the police need not request permission to make a covert entry when applying for an electronic surveillance order, and the order authorizing the use of electronic surveillance need not make any reference to a covert entry.

ELECTRONIC SURVEILLANCE ORDERS

The number of electronic surveillance orders issued under federal wiretap law has greatly expanded. In 1968, there were a total of 174 orders were approved. In 1980, 564 were approved; in 1990, 872 orders were approved; and in 1999, the number of approved orders was 1,350. In 2004, federal and state courts authorized 1,710 intercepts. In 2006, there was an increase to 1,839. The vast majority of requests for electronic surveillance orders have been granted. For example, from 1968 to 1996, about 20,000 requests for electronic surveillance orders were made, and only 28 have been denied.[49]

Wiretap orders over the last decade have increasingly become a phenomenon of state rather than federal courts. In 1997, there were 617 state orders and 569 federal orders. In 2001, the breakdown was 486 federal and 1,005 state orders. In 2006, there were 461 federal orders and 1,378 state orders.

States vary greatly based on the extent to which they wiretap. Indeed, wiretaps are primarily a phenomenon of a handful of jurisdictions. At the federal and state levels in 2006, four states, California (430 orders), New York (377), New Jersey (189), and Florida (98) accounted for 59 percent of all wiretap orders. This pattern of use is likely independent of crime patterns in the United States. Rather, it probably reflects local norms of law enforcement practice, including prosecutorial familiarity with the complex set of legal requirements for obtaining wiretap orders.

---

[49] *See* Title III Electronic Surveillance 1968-1999, http://www.epic.org/privacy/wiretap/stats/wiretap_stats.html.

In a comparative examination of statistics regarding electronic surveillance orders, Paul Schwartz examined trends in the United States and Germany. Schwartz found that in both countries, "law enforcement agencies in certain geographic areas generate a disproportionate amount of surveillance orders."[50] One German scholar, Johann Bizer, has observed that the differences between different German states cannot be explained by varying population structures or political orientation of state governments. Thus, in both Germany and the United States, requests for telecommunications surveillance are driven by local enforcement norms as well as the law. What factors are likely to shape local enforcement norms and encourage or discourage the use of telecommunications surveillance?

Returning to the U.S. wiretap statistics, 92 percent of all wiretaps in 2006 involved mobile devices, such as cell phones and pagers. In 2006, the average per interception order was 2,685 communications involving 122 persons. The average percentage of incriminating intercepts per wiretap order in 2006 was 20 percent, and this last statistic gives one pause. To be as clear as possible, this statistic is not inconsistent with each wiretap order leading to the collection of some incriminating intercepts. It means that on average 80 percent of the communications intercepted per order did not contain anything incriminating.

Is the glass 20 percent full or 80 percent empty? The Wiretap Act requires strict minimization of the collection of extraneous information once surveillance occurs. Are these statistics an indication that too much innocent communication is being monitored? Rarely will everything said by a particular person or on a particular phone line be incriminating. Is it practical to expect a much higher incriminating percentage than 20 percent?

Finally, the Wiretap Act Report details the results of wiretaps in terms of arrests as well as the number of motions made and granted to suppress with respect to interceptions.[51] Wiretaps terminated in 2006 led to the arrest of 4,376 persons and the conviction of 711 persons.[52] Regarding motions to suppress, the Administrative Office does not provide this information in its 2006 summary report, but it may be calculated from documents that prosecutors file with the Office. Of the 283 motions to suppress in 2006, 7 were granted and 61 were reported as pending.

STATE ELECTRONIC SURVEILLANCE LAW

A number of states have enacted their own versions of electronic surveillance law, some of which are more protective than federal electronic surveillance law. For example, several states require the consent of all parties to a conversation. Unless all parties consent, these states require a warrant for a wiretap. In contrast, federal wiretap law allows law enforcement to listen in to a conversation if any party to it consents to the surveillance.

---

[50] Paul M. Schwartz, *German and U.S. Telecommunications Privacy Law: Legal Regulation of Domestic Law Enforcement Surveillance*, 54 Hastings L.J. 751, 759-60 (2003); *see also* Paul M. Schwartz, *Evaluating Telecommunications Surveillance in Germany*, 72 Geo. Wash. L. Rev. 1244 (2004).

[51] 2006 Wiretap Act Report, p. 30 table 6, http://www.uscourts.gov/wiretap06/contents.html.

[52] *Id.* at 39 table 9.

One prominent example of a more protective state law was the indictment on July 30, 1999, of Linda Tripp on two counts of violating Maryland's wiretapping law. At the request of the Office of the Independent Counsel, Linda Tripp had secretly taped a phone conversation she had with Monica Lewinsky about Lewinsky's affair with President Clinton. Tripp then disclosed the contents of that conversation to a news magazine. Possible penalties under Maryland law included up to ten years' imprisonment and a $20,000 fine. Maryland's wiretapping law, in contrast to federal wiretap law, requires the consent of the other party to a communication. Tripp was indicted by a Maryland grand jury. Although Tripp was protected by a federal grant of immunity from prosecution, Maryland was not part of the immunity agreement and could prosecute Tripp. After a judicial ruling suppressing certain evidence, the case against Tripp was dropped.

Massachusetts also has an all-party-consent electronic surveillance law. Consider *Commonwealth v. Hyde,* 750 N.E.2d 963 (Mass. 2001). The defendant Michael Hyde was stopped by the police for a routine auto stop. The police searched the defendant, his passenger, and his car. No traffic citation was issued. Hyde filed a complaint at the police station about the stop, and he provided a hidden audio recording he had made of the encounter. The police subsequently charged Hyde with illegal electronic surveillance in violation of state law, G.L. c. 272, § 99, which provides that "any person who willfully commits an interception, attempts to commit an interception, or procures any other person to commit an interception or to attempt to commit an interception of any wire or oral communication shall be fined not more than ten thousand dollars, or imprisoned in the state prison for not more than five years, or imprisoned in a jail or house of correction for not more than two and one half years, or both so fined and given one such imprisonment." Hyde was convicted and sentenced to six months probation and a $500 fine.

The *Hyde* court concluded:

> We conclude that the Legislature intended G.L. c. 272, § 99, strictly to prohibit all secret recordings by members of the public, including recordings of police officers or other public officials interacting with members of the public, when made without their permission or knowledge. . . .
>
> We reject the defendant's argument that the statute is not applicable because the police officers were performing their public duties, and, therefore, had no reasonable expectation of privacy in their words. The statute's preamble expresses the Legislature's general concern that "the uncontrolled development and unrestricted use of modern electronic surveillance devices pose[d] grave dangers to the privacy of all citizens of the commonwealth" and this concern was relied on to justify the ban on the public's clandestine use of such devices. While we recognize that G.L. c. 272, § 99, was designed to prohibit the use of electronic surveillance devices by private individuals because of the serious threat they pose to the "privacy of all citizens," the plain language of the statute, which is the best indication of the Legislature's ultimate intent, contains nothing that would protect, on the basis of privacy rights, the recording that occurred here. In *Commonwealth v. Jackson, supra* at 506, 349 N.E.2d 337, this court rejected the argument that, because a kidnapper has no legitimate privacy interest in telephone calls made for ransom purposes, the secret electronic recording of that conversation by the victim's brother would not be prohibited under G.L. c.

> 272, § 99: "[W]e would render meaningless the Legislature's careful choice of words if we were to interpret 'secretly' as encompassing only those situations where an individual has a reasonable expectation of privacy." . . .
>
> Further, if the tape recording here is deemed proper on the ground that public officials are involved, then the door is opened even wider to electronic "bugging" or secret audio tape recording (both are prohibited by the statute and both are indistinguishable in the injury they inflict) of virtually every encounter or meeting between a person and a public official, whether the meeting or encounter is one that is stressful (like the one in this case or, perhaps, a session with a tax auditor) or nonstressful (like a routine meeting between a parent and a teacher in a public school to discuss a good student's progress). The door once opened would be hard to close, and the result would contravene the statute's broad purpose and the Legislature's clear prohibition of *all* secret interceptions and recordings by private citizens.

In dissent, Chief Justice Marshall wrote:

> The purpose of G.L. c. 272, § 99, is not to shield public officials from exposure of their wrongdoings. I have too great a respect for the Legislature to read any such meaning into a statute whose purpose is plain, and points in another direction entirely. Where the legislative intent is explicit, it violates a fundamental rule of statutory construction to reach a result that is plainly contrary to that objective. To hold that the Legislature intended to allow police officers to conceal possible misconduct behind a cloak of privacy requires a more affirmative showing than this statute allows.
>
> In our Republic the actions of public officials taken in their public capacities are not protected from exposure. Citizens have a particularly important role to play when the official conduct at issue is that of the police. Their role cannot be performed if citizens must fear criminal reprisals when they seek to hold government officials responsible by recording — secretly recording on occasion — an interaction between a citizen and a police officer. . . .
>
> The court's ruling today also threatens the ability of the press — print and electronic — to perform its constitutional role of watchdog. As the court construes the Massachusetts wiretapping statute, there is no principled distinction to explain why members of the media would not be held to the same standard as all other citizens.

A few years later, Hyde was convicted again of secretly recording a police officer who had pulled him over in a traffic stop. Are all-party electronic surveillance laws too broad? What kinds of exceptions, if any, should be made?

Note as well that these all-party-consent statutes will also regulate surveillance by private sector entities. In *Kearney v. Salomon Smith Barney*, 137 P.2d 914 (S. Ct. Cal. 2006), two California clients sued a financial institution because their telephone calls to brokers in the institution's Georgia office were recorded without their consent. A California statute prohibited recording a telephone conversation without consent of all parties to it. In contrast, a Georgia statute permitted recording a telephone conversation if consent of one party had been granted. The California Supreme Court concluded that "comparative impairment analysis supports the application of California law in this context." It reached this conclusion by assessing the relative harm suffered to each state due to this conflict of law:

> [I]n light of the substantial number of businesses operating in California that maintain out-of-state offices or telephone operators, a resolution of this conflict permitting all such businesses to regularly and routinely record telephone conversations made to or from California clients or consumers without the clients' or consumers' knowledge or consent would significantly impair the privacy policy guaranteed by California law, and potentially would place local California businesses (that would continue to be subject to California's protective privacy law) at an unfair competitive disadvantage vis-à-vis their out-of-state counterparts. At the same time, application of California law will not have a significant detrimental effect on Georgia's interests as embodied in the applicable Georgia law, because applying California law (1) will not adversely affect any privacy interest protected by Georgia law, (2) will affect only those business telephone calls in Georgia that are made to or are received from California clients, and (3) with respect to such calls, will not prevent a business located in Georgia from implementing or maintaining a practice of recording *all* such calls, but will require only that the business *inform* its clients or customers, at the outset of the call, of the company's policy of recording such calls. (. . . if a business informs a client or customer at the outset of a telephone call that the call is being recorded, the recording would not violate the applicable California statute.)

When state government officials are engaging in electronic surveillance, they are often subject to much less public scrutiny than their federal counterparts. Charles Kennedy and Peter Swire have concluded that there are likely to be significant differences between federal and state electronic surveillance because of differences in the respective "[i]nstitutions, procedures and training" of law enforcement personnel:

> Because state procedures are watched less systematically by the press and civil liberties organizations, abuses at the state level, whether deliberate or the result of inexperience, may not be detected. The under-reporting of state wiretaps . . . is both a symptom of and a contributing factor to this relative lack of oversight. The simple fact is that half of the states have wiretap powers, yet reported no wiretaps in 2001. The utter failure to file the annual wiretap report would be unthinkable at the federal level. In addition, the under-reporting of state wiretaps keeps the use and possible misuse of state wiretaps less visible.[53]

As noted above, moreover, wiretap orders over the last decade have increasingly become a phenomenon of state rather than federal courts. Yet, as Kennedy and Swire observe, we know far less about how state law enforcement agencies make use of their wiretap powers than federal ones. As for the lack of state wiretap reports from many states, the obligation to file a report with the Administrative Office of the U.S. Courts extends only to instances when the states actually make use of these powers. In other words, the Administrative Office does not require reports to be filed if no interception activity took place in the state during a given year.[54] As a simple, initial step at ending the ambiguity about the possible under-reporting of state wiretap orders, should states be

---

[53] Charles H. Kennedy & Peter P. Swire, *State Wiretaps and Electronic Surveillance After September 11,* 54 Hastings L.J. 971 (2003).

[54] Paul Schwartz, *German and U.S. Telecommunications Privacy Law*, 54 Hastings L.J. 751, 760 (2003).

required to file a report even if no surveillance activity takes place in it during a particular year?

4. THE COMMUNICATIONS ASSISTANCE FOR LAW ENFORCEMENT ACT

In *United States v. New York Telephone*, 434 U.S. 159 (1977), the Supreme Court held that 18 U.S.C. § 2518(4) required telecommunications providers to furnish "any assistance necessary to accomplish an electronic interception." However, the issue of whether a provider had to create and design its technology to facilitate authorized electronic surveillance remained an open question.

In the 1980s, new communications technology was developed to enable more wireless communications — cellular telephones, microwave, and satellite communications. As a result of fears that these new technologies would be harder to monitor, the law enforcement community successfully convinced Congress to force telecommunications providers to ensure that the government could continue to monitor electronic communications.[55]

The Communications Assistance for Law Enforcement Act (CALEA) of 1994, Pub. L. No. 103-414, (also known as the "Digital Telephony Act") requires telecommunication providers to help facilitate the government in executing legally authorized surveillance. The Act was passed against strong opposition from some civil liberties organizations. Congress appropriated federal funding of $500 million to telephone companies to make the proposed changes.

Requirements. CALEA requires all telecommunications providers to be able to isolate and intercept electronic communications and be able to deliver them to law enforcement personnel. If carriers provide an encryption service to users, then they must decrypt the communications. CALEA permits the telecommunications industry to develop the technology. Under a "safe harbor" provision, carriers that comply with accepted industry standards are in compliance with CALEA. 47 U.S.C. § 1006(a)(2).

Limits. CALEA contains some important limits. Carriers must "facilitat[e] authorized communications interceptions and access to call-identifying information . . . in a manner that protects . . . the privacy and security of communications and call-identifying information not authorized to be intercepted." § 1002(a)(4)(A). Further, CALEA is designed to provide "law enforcement no more and no less access to information than it had in the past." H.R. Rep. No. 103-827, pt. 1, at 22. Additionally, CALEA does not apply to "information services," such as e-mail and Internet access. §§ 1001(8)(C)(i), 1002(b)(2)(A).

The J-Standard. In *United States Telecom Ass'n v. FCC*, 227 F.3d 450 (D.C. Cir. 2000), the D.C. Circuit attempted to place certain limits on the FCC's interpretation of CALEA. This statute had set up a process by which the

[55] For a detailed analysis of CALEA, see Susan Freiwald, *Uncertain Privacy: Communication Attributes After the Digital Telephony Act*, 69 S. Cal. L. Rev. 949 (1996).

telecommunications industry "in consultation with law enforcement agencies, regulators, and consumers, [was] to develop its own technical standards for meeting the required surveillance capabilities." In 1995, the telecommunications industry started to develop this safe harbor standard, which was adopted by the industry in December 1997.

The standard is known as the Interim Standard/Trial Use Standard J-STD-025 (the "J-Standard"). The J-Standard sets forth the standards by which carriers can make communications and call-identifying information available to law enforcement officials. A group of industry associations as well as privacy organizations challenged the J-Standard and petitioned the Federal Communications Commission (FCC) to remove provisions that they argued extended beyond CALEA's authorization. In contrast, the Justice Department and FBI petitioned the FCC to add nine additional surveillance capabilities on its "punch list" to the J-Standard. The FCC refused the requests of the industry associations and privacy advocacy groups, but did add four of the nine items sought by the Justice Department and FBI to the J-Standard. The D.C. Circuit rejected the four challenged items added to the J-Standard and remanded to the FCC to demonstrate compliance with CALEA, including the statutory requirement of the use of "cost-effective means."

An item on the original J-Standard was a requirement that carriers inform law enforcement officials of the nearest antenna tower to a mobile telephone user, giving officials the ability to track the location of mobile telephones. The D.C. court held that the requirement was valid under CALEA:

> Not only did the Commission elucidate the textual basis for interpreting "call-identifying information" to include location information, but it also explained how that result comports with CALEA's goal of preserving the same surveillance capabilities that law enforcement agencies had in POTS (plain old telephone service). "[I]n the wireline environment," the Commission explained, law enforcement agencies "have generally been able to obtain location information routinely from the telephone number because the telephone number usually corresponds with location." In the wireless environment, "the equivalent location information" is "the location of the cell sites to which the mobile terminal or handset is connected at the beginning and at the termination of the call." Accordingly, the Commission concluded, "[p]rovision of this particular location information does not appear to expand or diminish law enforcement's surveillance authority under prior law applicable to the wireline environment."

On remand, the FCC returned the four items that it had earlier approved from the law enforcement "punch list" once again to the J-Standard. *In the Matter of Communications Assistance for Law Enforcement Act*, FCC 02-108 (Apr. 5, 2002). One of these items concerned "post-cut-through dialed digit extraction," which is a list of any digits that a person dials after a call has been connected. The FCC required that a telecommunications carrier "have the ability to turn on and off the dialed digit extraction capability." It therefore mandated a "toggle feature" that would allow a carrier to turn off the capability if it "had reservations about the legal basis for providing all post-cut through digits" while it was, at the same time, providing "other punch list capabilities included in the same software."

Voice over Internet Protocol (VoIP). A new way to make telephone calls is to use a broadband Internet connection to transmit the call. This technique, VoIP, converts a voice signal into a digital signal that travels over the Internet and connects to a phone number. On August 4, 2004, the FCC unanimously adopted a Notice of Proposed Rulemaking and Declaratory Ruling regarding VoIP and CALEA. *In the Matter of Communications Assistance for Law Enforcement Act and Broadband Access and Services*, FCC 04-187 (Aug. 4, 2004). It tentatively declared that CALEA applies to any facilities-based providers of any type of broadband Internet access service — including wireline, cable modem, satellite, wireless, and powerline — and to managed or mediated VoIP services. This conclusion was based on an FCC judgment that these services fall under CALEA statutory language as "a replacement for a substantial portion of the local telephone service." 47 U.S.C. § 1001(8)B)(ii).

The FCC continued its work in this area by issuing an Order in 2005 that built on its previous Notice of Proposed Rulemaking. This rulemaking, upheld by the D.C. Circuit in June 2006, established that broadband and VoIP are "hybrid telecommunications-information services" that fall under CALEA to the extent that they qualify as "telecommunications carriers." Communications Assistance for Law Enforcement and Broadband Access and Services, 20 F.C.C.R. 14989, at ¶ 18 (2005); *American Council on Education v. FCC*, 451 F.3d 266 (D.C. Cir. 2006).

In May 2006, the FCC issued an additional order to address remaining issues to achieve CALEA compliance. Second Report and Order and Memorandum Opinion and Order (Order), FCC 06-56 (May 12, 2006). The FCC's overarching policy perspective concerned giving law enforcement agencies all the resources that CALEA authorizes to combat crime and support homeland security. As FCC Chairman Kevin J. Martin observed in a statement issued as part of the Order, "Enabling law enforcement to ensure our safety and security is of paramount importance." The Order set a May 14, 2007, compliance date for both facilities-based broadband Internet access and interconnected VoIP providers. It also permitted entities covered by CALEA to have the option of using Trusted Third Parties (TTPs) to help meet their CALEA obligations. The role of the TTPs would include processing requests for intercepts, conducting electronic surveillance, and delivering relevant information to law enforcement agencies.

Susan Landau and Whitfield Diffie argue that extension of CALEA requirements to the Internet will ironically make it less secure and create a potential for cyber-terrorism. The problem is that CALEA has now been interpreted to require that modifications be made to Internet protocols, which present the risk of introducing vulnerabilities into the system. In their view, inserting wiretap requirements into Internet protocols will make the Internet less secure. A system that permits "legally authorized security breaches" (such as a wiretap by law enforcement officers) is also more open to unauthorized security breaches (such as hacking and other kinds of unlawful intrusions). They argue:

> On balance we are better off with a secure computer infrastructure than with one that builds surveillance into the network fabric. At times this may press law enforcement to exercise more initiative and imagination in its investigations. On the other hand, in a society completely dependent on computer-to-computer

communications, the alternative presents a hazard whose dimensions are as yet impossible to comprehend.[56]

5. THE USA PATRIOT ACT

On the morning of September 11, 2001, terrorists hijacked four planes and crashed three of them into the World Trade Center and the Pentagon, killing thousands of people. The nation was awakened into a world filled with new frightening dangers. Shortly after the September 11 attacks, a still unknown person or persons sent letters laced with the deadly bacteria anthrax through the mail to several prominent individuals in the news media and in politics. Acting with great haste, Congress passed a sweeping new law expanding the government's electronic surveillance powers in many significant ways.[57] Called the "Uniting and Strengthening America By Providing Appropriate Tools Required To Intercept and Obstruct Terrorism Act" (USA PATRIOT Act), the Act made a number of substantial changes to several statutes, including the federal electronic surveillance statutes.

Definition of Terrorism. Section 802 of the USA PATRIOT Act added to 18 U.S.C. § 2331 a new definition of "domestic terrorism." According to the Act, domestic terrorism involves "acts dangerous to human life that are a violation of the criminal laws of the United States or of any State" that "appear to be intended: (i) to intimidate or coerce a civilian population; (ii) to influence the policy of a government by intimidation or coercion; or (iii) to affect the conduct of a government by mass destruction, assassination, or kidnapping; and . . . occur primarily within the territorial jurisdiction of the United States." According to many proponents of civil liberties, this definition is very broad and could potentially encompass many forms of civil disobedience, which, although consisting of criminal conduct (minor violence, threats, property damage), includes conduct that has historically been present in many political protests and has never been considered to be terrorism.

Delayed Notice of Search Warrants. Under the Fourth Amendment, the government must obtain a warrant and provide notice to a person before conducting a search or seizure. Case law provided for certain limited exceptions. Section 213 of the USA PATRIOT Act adds a provision to 18 U.S.C. § 3103a, enabling the government to delay notice if the court concludes that there is "reasonable cause" that immediate notice will create an "adverse result" such as physical danger, the destruction of evidence, delayed trial, flight from prosecution, and other circumstances. § 3103a(b). Warrants enabling a covert search with delayed notice are often referred to as "sneak and peek" warrants. Civil libertarians consider "sneak and peek" warrants dangerous because they authorize covert searches, thus preventing individuals from safeguarding their rights during the search. Moreover, there is little supervision of the government's

[56] Susan Landau & Whitfield Diffie, *Privacy on the Line* 331, 328 (2d ed. 2007).

[57] For background about the passage of the USA PATRIOT Act, see Beryl A. Howell, *Seven Weeks: The Making of the USA Patriot Act,* 72 Geo. Wash. L. Rev. 1145 (2004).

carrying out of the search. Law enforcement officials argue that covert searches are necessary to avoid tipping off suspects that there is an investigation under way.

New Definition of Pen Registers and Trap and Trace Devices. Under the Pen Register Act of the ECPA, §§ 3121 *et seq.*, the definitions of pen registers and trap and trace devices focused primarily on telephone numbers. A pen register was defined under 18 U.S.C. § 3127(3) as

> a device which records or decodes electronic or other impulses which identify the numbers dialed or otherwise transmitted on the telephone line to which such device is attached. . . .

Section 216 of the USA PATRIOT Act changed the definition to read:

> a device *or process* which records or decodes *dialing, routing, addressing, or signaling information transmitted by an instrument or facility from which a wire or electronic communication is transmitted, provided, however, that such information shall not include the contents of any communication* is attached . . . (changes emphasized).

These changes altered the definition of a pen register from applying not only to telephone numbers but also to Internet addresses, e-mail addressing information (the "to" and "from" lines on e-mail), and the routing information of a wide spectrum of communications. The inclusion of "or process" after "device" enlarges the means by which such routing information can be intercepted beyond the use of a physical device. The definition of a trap and trace device was changed in a similar way. Recall that under the Pen Register Act, a court order to obtain such information does not require probable cause, but merely certification that "the information likely to be obtained by such installation and use is relevant to an ongoing criminal investigation." 18 U.S.C. § 3123. The person whose communications are subject to this order need not even be a criminal suspect; all that the government needs to certify is relevance to an investigation.

Recall *Smith v. Maryland* earlier in this chapter, where the Court held that pen registers were not protected under the Fourth Amendment. Does the new definition of pen register and trap and trace device under the USA PATRIOT Act go beyond *Smith v. Maryland*? Are Internet addresses and e-mail addressing information analogous to pen registers?

Private Right of Action for Government Disclosures. The USA PATRIOT Act adds a provision to the Stored Communications Act that provides for civil actions against the United States for any "willful" violations. 18 U.S.C. § 2712. The court may assess actual damages or $10,000 (whichever is greater) and litigation costs. Such an action must first be presented before the "appropriate department or agency under the procedures of the Federal Tort Claims Act."

Reauthorization. When the USA PATRIOT Act was passed, several provisions had sunset provisions and would expire on a particular date. On March 9, 2006, President George W. Bush signed the USA PATRIOT Reauthorization Act, which made permanent 14 of 16 expiring USA PATRIOT Act sections. It created a new sunset of December 31, 2009 for USA PATRIOT Act sections 205 and 215 (which concern "roving" FISA wiretaps and FISA orders for business records), and for FISA's "lone wolf" amendments. This law also expanded the list of predicate offenses for which law enforcement could obtain wiretap orders.

C. DIGITAL SEARCHES AND SEIZURES

1. SEARCHING THE CONTENTS OF COMPUTERS

The Scope of Warrants to Search Computers. In *United States v. Lacy,* 119 F.3d 742 (9th Cir. 1997), the defendant challenged a search warrant authorizing the seizure of his computer hard drive and disks. The defendant contended that the warrant was too general because it applied to his entire computer system. The court upheld the warrant because "this type of generic classification is acceptable when a more precise description is not possible." Several other courts have followed a similar approach as in *Lacy*, upholding generic warrants. In *United States v. Upham*, 168 F.3d 532 (1st Cir. 1999), the court reasoned: "A sufficient chance of finding some needles in the computer haystack was established by the probable-cause showing in the warrant application; and a search of a computer and co-located disks is not inherently more intrusive than the physical search of an entire house for a weapon or drugs." *See also United States v. Hay*, 231 F.3d 630 (9th Cir. 2000) (following *Lacy* and upholding a "generic" warrant application).[58]

However, there are limits to the scope of a search of a computer. In *United States v. Carey*, 172 F.3d 1268 (10th Cir. 1999), an officer obtained a warrant to search a computer for records about illegal drug distribution. When the officer stumbled upon a pornographic file, he began to search for similar files. The court concluded that these actions amounted to an expansion of the scope of the search and would require the obtaining of a second warrant.

In *United States v. Campos*, 221 F.3d 1143 (10th Cir. 2000), the defendant e-mailed two images of child pornography to a person he talked to in a chat room. The person informed the FBI, and the FBI obtained a warrant to search the defendant's home and computer. The agents seized the defendant's computer, and a search revealed the two images of child pornography as well as six other images of child pornography. The defendant challenged the search as beyond the scope of the warrant because the agents "had grounds to search only for the two images that had been sent." However, the court rejected the defendant's contention, quoting from the FBI's explanation why it is not feasible to search only for particular computer files in one's home:

> . . . Computer storage devices . . . can store the equivalent of thousands of pages of information. Especially when the user wants to conceal criminal evidence, he often stores it in random order with deceptive file names. This requires searching authorities to examine all the stored data to determine whether it is

[58] For more about computer searches, see Raphael Winnick, *Searches and Seizures of Computers and Computer Data*, 88 Harv. J.L. & Tech. 75 (1994).

included in the warrant. This sorting process can take weeks or months, depending on the volume of data stored, and it would be impractical to attempt this kind of data search on site. . . .

Searching computer systems for criminal evidence is a highly technical process requiring expert skill and a properly controlled environment. The wide variety of computer hardware and software available requires even computer experts to specialize in some systems and applications, so it is difficult to know before a search which expert should analyze the system and its data. . . . Since computer evidence is extremely vulnerable to tampering or destruction (both from external sources or from destructive code embedded into the system as "booby trap"), the controlled environment of a laboratory is essential to its complete analysis. . . .

Computer Searches and Seizures. Searches and seizures for digital information in computers present some unique conceptual puzzles for existing Fourth Amendment doctrine. Thomas Clancy contends:

> [C]omputers are containers. . . . They . . . contain electronic evidence, that is, a series of digitally stored 0s and 1s that, when combined with a computer program, yield such items as images, words, and spreadsheets. Accordingly, the traditional standards of the Fourth Amendment regulate obtaining the evidence in containers that happen to be computers.[59]

But is a computer a single container or is each computer file its own container? Orin Kerr argues:

> A single physical storage device can store the private files of thousands of different users. It would be quite odd if looking at one file on a server meant that the entire server had been searched, and that the police could then analyze everything on the server, perhaps belonging to thousands of different people, without any restriction.[60]

Is copying a computer file or other digital information a seizure under the Fourth Amendment? In *United States v. Gorshkov*, 2001 WL 1024026 (W.D. Wash. 2001), the FBI remotely copied the contents of the defendant's computer in Russia. The court held: "The agents' act of copying the data on the Russian computers was not a seizure under the Fourth Amendment because it did not interfere with Defendant's or anyone else's possessory interest in the data." However, as Susan Brenner and Barbara Frederiksen contend:

> [T]he information contained in computer files clearly belongs to the owner of the files. The ownership of information is similar to the contents of a private conversation in which the information belongs to the parties to the conversation. Copying computer data is analogous to recording a conversation. . . . Therefore, copying computer files should be treated as a seizure.[61]

---

[59] Thomas K. Clancy, *The Fourth Amendment Aspects of Computer Searches and Seizures: A Perspective and a Primer*, 75 Miss. L.J. 193, 196 (2005).

[60] Orin S. Kerr, *Searches and Seizures in a Digital World*, 119 Harv. L. Rev. 531, 556 (2005).

[61] Susan W. Brenner & Barbara A. Frederiksen, *Computer Searches and Seizures: Some Unresolved Issues*, 8 Mich. Telecomm. & Tech. L. Rev. 39, 111-12 (2002).

Password-Protected Files. In *Trulock v. Freeh*, 275 F.3d 391 (4th Cir. 2001), Notra Trulock and Linda Conrad shared a computer but maintained separate files protected by passwords. They did not know each other's password and could not access each other's files. When FBI officials, without a warrant, asked to search and seize the computer, Conrad consented. The court held that the FBI could not search Trulock's files since Trulock had not consented:

> Consent to search in the absence of a warrant may, in some circumstances, be given by a person other than the target of the search. Two criteria must be met in order for third party consent to be effective. First, the third party must have authority to consent to the search. Second, the third party's consent must be voluntary. . . .
>
> We conclude that, based on the facts in the complaint, Conrad lacked authority to consent to the search of Trulock's files. Conrad and Trulock both used a computer located in Conrad's bedroom and each had joint access to the hard drive. Conrad and Trulock, however, protected their personal files with passwords; Conrad did not have access to Trulock's passwords. Although Conrad had authority to consent to a general search of the computer, her authority did not extend to Trulock's password-protected files.

UNITED STATES V. ANDRUS

483 F.3d 711 (10th Cir. 2007)

[Federal authorities believed that Ray Andrus was downloading child pornography to his home computer. Ray Andrus resided at his parents' house. Federal officials obtained the consent of Dr. Andrus (Andrus's father) to search the home. He also consented to their searching any computers in the home. The officials went into Ray Andrus's bedroom and a forensic expert examined the contents of the computer's hard drive with forensic software. The software enabled direct access to the computer, bypassing any password protection the user put on it. The officials discovered child pornography on the computer. Later on, the officials learned that Ray Andrus had protected his computer with a password and that his father did not know the password. Is the father's consent to search the computer valid since he did not know the password?]

MURPHY, J. . . . Subject to limited exceptions, the Fourth Amendment prohibits warrantless searches of an individual's home or possessions. Voluntary consent to a police search, given by the individual under investigation or by a third party with authority over the subject property, is a well-established exception to the warrant requirement. Valid third party consent can arise either through the third party's actual authority or the third party's apparent authority. A third party has actual authority to consent to a search "if that third party has either (1) mutual use of the property by virtue of joint access, or (2) control for most purposes." Even where actual authority is lacking, however, a third party has apparent authority to consent to a search when an officer reasonably, even if erroneously, believes the third party possesses authority to consent. *See Georgia v. Randolph,* 547 U.S. 103 (2006).

Whether apparent authority exists is an objective, totality-of-the-circumstances inquiry into whether the facts available to the officers at the time they commenced the search would lead a reasonable officer to believe the third party had authority to consent to the search. When the property to be searched is an object or container, the relevant inquiry must address the third party's relationship to the object. In *Randolph,* the Court explained, "The constant element in assessing Fourth Amendment reasonableness in consent cases . . . is the great significance given to widely shared social expectations." For example, the Court said, "[W]hen it comes to searching through bureau drawers, there will be instances in which even a person clearly belonging on the premises as an occupant may lack any perceived authority to consent." . . .

It may be unreasonable for law enforcement to believe a third party has authority to consent to the search of an object typically associated with a high expectation of privacy, especially when the officers know or should know the owner has indicated the intent to exclude the third party from using or exerting control over the object.

Courts considering the issue have attempted to analogize computers to other items more commonly seen in Fourth Amendment jurisprudence. Individuals' expectations of privacy in computers have been likened to their expectations of privacy in "a suitcase or briefcase." Password-protected files have been compared to a "locked footlocker inside the bedroom." *Trulock v. Freeh,* 275 F.3d 391, 403 (4th Cir. 2001).

Given the pervasiveness of computers in American homes, this court must reach some, at least tentative, conclusion about the category into which personal computers fall. A personal computer is often a repository for private information the computer's owner does not intend to share with others. . . .

The inquiry into whether the owner of a highly personal object has indicated a subjective expectation of privacy traditionally focuses on whether the subject suitcase, footlocker, or other container is physically locked. Determining whether a computer is "locked," or whether a reasonable officer should know a computer may be locked, presents a challenge distinct from that associated with other types of closed containers. Unlike footlockers or suitcases, where the presence of a locking device is generally apparent by looking at the item, a "lock" on the data within a computer is not apparent from a visual inspection of the outside of the computer, especially when the computer is in the "off" position prior to the search. Data on an entire computer may be protected by a password, with the password functioning as a lock, or there may be multiple users of a computer, each of whom has an individual and personalized password-protected "user profile." . . .

Courts addressing the issue of third party consent in the context of computers, therefore, have examined officers' knowledge about password protection as an indication of whether a computer is "locked" in the way a footlocker would be. For example, in *Trulock,* the Fourth Circuit held a live-in girlfriend lacked actual authority to consent to a search of her boyfriend's computer files where the girlfriend told police she and her boyfriend shared the household computer but had separate password-protected files that were inaccessible to the other. The court in that case explained, "Although Conrad had authority to consent to a general search of the computer, her authority did not extend to Trulock's password-protected files." . . .

In addition to password protection, courts also consider the location of the computer within the house and other indicia of household members' access to the computer in assessing third party authority. Third party apparent authority to consent to a search has generally been upheld when the computer is located in a common area of the home that is accessible to other family members under circumstances indicating the other family members were not excluded from using the computer. In contrast, where the third party has affirmatively disclaimed access to or control over the computer or a portion of the computer's files, even when the computer is located in a common area of the house, courts have been unwilling to find third party authority.

Andrus' case presents facts that differ somewhat from those in other cases. Andrus' computer was located in a bedroom occupied by the homeowner's fifty-one year old son rather than in a true common area. Dr. Andrus, however, had unlimited access to the room. Law enforcement officers did not ask specific questions about Dr. Andrus' use of the computer, but Dr. Andrus said nothing indicating the need for such questions. *Cf. Trulock,* 275 F.3d at 398 (when law enforcement questioned third party girlfriend about computer, she indicated she and boyfriend had separate password-protected files). The resolution of this appeal turns on whether the officers' belief in Dr. Andrus' authority was reasonable, despite the lack of any affirmative assertion by Dr. Andrus that he used the computer and despite the existence of a user profile indicating Ray Andrus' intent to exclude other household members from using the computer. For the reasons articulated below, this court concludes the officers' belief in Dr. Andrus' authority was reasonable. . . .

First, the officers knew Dr. Andrus owned the house and lived there with family members. Second, the officers knew Dr. Andrus' house had internet access and that Dr. Andrus paid the Time Warner internet and cable bill. Third, the officers knew the email address bandrus@kc.rr.com had been activated and used to register on a website that provided access to child pornography. Fourth, although the officers knew Ray Andrus lived in the center bedroom, they also knew that Dr. Andrus had access to the room at will. Fifth, the officers saw the computer in plain view on the desk in Andrus' room and it appeared available for use by other household members. Furthermore, the record indicates Dr. Andrus did not say or do anything to indicate his lack of ownership or control over the computer when Cheatham asked for his consent to conduct a computer search. It is uncontested that Dr. Andrus led the officers to the bedroom in which the computer was located, and, even after he saw Kanatzar begin to work on the computer, Dr. Andrus remained silent about any lack of authority he had over the computer. Even if Ray Andrus' computer was protected with a user name and password, there is no indication in the record that the officers knew or had reason to believe such protections were in place.

Andrus argues his computer's password protection indicated his computer was "locked" to third parties, a fact the officers would have known had they asked questions of Dr. Andrus prior to searching the computer. Under our case law, however, officers are not obligated to ask questions unless the circumstances are ambiguous. In essence, by suggesting the onus was on the officers to ask about password protection prior to searching the computer, despite the absence of any indication that Dr. Andrus' access to the computer was limited by a password, Andrus necessarily submits there is inherent ambiguity whenever police want to search a household computer and a third party has not affirmatively provided information about his own use of the computer or about password protection. Andrus' argument presupposes, however, that password protection of home computers is so common that a reasonable officer ought to know password protection is likely. Andrus has neither made this argument directly nor proffered any evidence to demonstrate a high incidence of password protection among home computer users. . . .

Viewed under the requisite totality-of-the-circumstances analysis, the facts known to the officers at the time the computer search commenced created an objectively reasonable perception that Dr. Andrus was, at least, *one* user of the computer. That objectively reasonable belief would have been enough to give Dr. Andrus apparent authority to consent to a search. Even if Dr. Andrus had no actual ability to use the computer and the computer was password protected, these mistakes of fact do not negate a determination of Dr. Andrus' apparent authority. In this case, the district court found Agent Cheatham properly halted the search when further conversation with Dr. Andrus revealed he did not use the computer and that Andrus' computer was the only computer in the house. These later revelations, however, have no bearing on the reasonableness of the officers' belief in Dr. Andrus' authority at the outset of the computer search.

MCKAY, J., dissenting. This case concerns the reasonable expectation of privacy associated with password-protected computers. In examining the contours of a third party's apparent authority to consent to the search of a home computer, the majority correctly indicates that the extent to which law enforcement knows or should reasonably suspect that password protection is enabled is critical. . . . I take issue with the majority's implicit holding that law enforcement may use software deliberately designed to automatically bypass computer password protection based on third-party consent without the need to make a reasonable inquiry regarding the presence of password protection and the third party's access to that password.

The presence of security on Defendant's computer is undisputed. Yet, the majority curiously argues that Defendant's use of password protection is inconsequential because Defendant failed to argue that computer password protection is "commonplace." Of course, the decision provides no guidance on what would constitute sufficient proof of the prevalence of password protection, nor does it explain why the court could not take judicial notice that password protection is a standard feature of operating systems. Despite recognizing the "pervasiveness of computers in American homes," and the fact that the "personal computer is often a repository for private information the computer's owner does not intend to share with others," the majority requires the invocation of magical language in order to give effect to Defendant's subjective intent to exclude others from accessing the computer. . . .

The unconstrained ability of law enforcement to use forensic software such as the EnCase program to bypass password protection without first determining whether such passwords have been enabled does not "exacerbate[]" this difficulty; rather, it avoids it altogether, simultaneously and dangerously sidestepping the Fourth Amendment in the process. Indeed, the majority concedes that if such protection were "shown to be commonplace, law enforcement's use of forensic software like EnCase . . . may well be subject to question." But the fact that a computer password "lock" may not be *immediately* visible does not render it unlocked. I appreciate that unlike the locked file cabinet, computers have no handle to pull. But, like the padlocked footlocker, computers do exhibit outward signs of password protection: they display boot password screens, username/password log-in screens, and/or screen-saver reactivation passwords.

The fact remains that EnCase's ability to bypass security measures is well known to law enforcement. Here, ICE's forensic computer specialist found Defendant's computer turned off. Without turning it on, he hooked his laptop directly to the hard drive of Defendant's computer and ran the EnCase program. The agents made no effort to ascertain whether such security was enabled prior to initiating the search. . . .

The majority points out that law enforcement "did not ask specific questions" about Dr. Andrus' use of the computer or knowledge of Ray Andrus' use of password protection, but twice criticizes Dr. Andrus' failure to affirmatively disclaim ownership of, control over, or knowledge regarding the computer. Of course, the computer was located in Ray Andrus' very tiny bedroom, but the majority makes no effort to explain how this does not create an ambiguous situation as to ownership.

The burden on law enforcement to identify ownership of the computer was minimal. A simple question or two would have sufficed. Prior to the computer search, the agents questioned Dr. Andrus about Ray Andrus' status as a renter and Dr. Andrus' ability to enter his 51-year-old son's bedroom in order to determine Dr. Andrus' ability to consent to a search of the room, but the agents did not inquire whether Dr. Andrus used the computer, and if so, whether he had access to his son's password. At the suppression hearing, the agents testified that they were not immediately aware that Defendant's computer was the only one in the house, and they began to doubt Dr. Andrus' authority to consent when they learned this fact. The record reveals that, upon questioning, Dr. Andrus indicated that there was a computer in the house and led the agents to Defendant's room. The forensic specialist was then summoned. It took him approximately fifteen to twenty minutes to set up his equipment, yet, bizarrely, at no point during this period did the agents inquire about the presence of any other computers. . . .

Accordingly, in my view, given the case law indicating the importance of computer password protection, the common knowledge about the prevalence of password usage, and the design of EnCase or similar password bypass mechanisms, the Fourth Amendment and the reasonable inquiry rule, mandate that in consent-based, warrantless computer searches, law enforcement personnel inquire or otherwise check for the presence of password protection and, if a password is present, inquire about the consenter's knowledge of that password and joint access to the computer. . . .

NOTES & QUESTIONS

1. ***A Question of Perspective?*** Orin Kerr contends:

> From a virtual user's perspective, the child pornography was hidden to the father; it was behind a password-protected gate. Under these facts, the father couldn't consent to a search because he would lack common authority over it. From a physical perspective, however, the file was present on the hard drive just like all the other information. Under these facts, the father could consent to the search because he had access rights to the machine generally. . . .
>
> Viewed from the physical perspective, the investigators reasonably did not know about the user profile and reasonably believed that the father had rights to consent to that part of the hard drive.[62]

2. ***Checking for Password Protection.*** Was the investigators' belief about the father's authority over the computer reasonable? Should the investigators have asked the father more questions about his use of the computer first? Should they have turned on the machine to see if it was password-protected before hooking up the forensic software? What kinds of incentives does this decision engender for officers doing an investigation?

2. ENCRYPTION

Encryption includes the ability to keep communications secure by concealing the contents of a message. With encryption, even if a communication is intercepted, it still remains secure. Encryption works by translating a message into a code of letters or numbers called "cypher text." The parties to the communication hold a *key*, which consists of the information necessary to translate the code back to the original message, or "plain text." Since ancient times, code-makers have devised cryptographic systems to encode messages. But along with the code-makers arose code-breakers, who were able to figure out the keys to cryptographic systems by, for example, examining the patterns in the encoded messages and comparing them to patterns in a particular language and the frequency of use of certain letters in that language. Today, computers have vastly increased the complexity of encryption.

Encryption presents a difficult trade-off between privacy and surveillance. It is an essential technique to protect the privacy of electronic communications in an age when such communications can so easily be intercepted and monitored. On the other hand, it enables individuals to disguise their communications from detection by law enforcement officials.[63] As Whitfield Diffie and Susan Landau observe:

---

[62] Orin Kerr, *Virtual Analogies, Physical Searches, and the Fourth Amendment,* Volokh Conspiracy, Apr. 26, 2007, http://www.volokh.com/posts/1177562355.shtml.

[63] For more background on encryption, see Simon Singh, *The Code: The Evolution of Secrecy from Mary, Queen of Scots to Quantum Cryptography* (1999); Steven Levy, *Crypto: How the Code Rebels Beat the Government — Saving Privacy in the Digital Age* (2002); A. Michael Froomkin, *The Metaphor Is the Key: Cryptography, the Clipper Chip, and the Constitution*, 143 U. Pa. L. Rev. 709 (1995); Robert C. Post, *Encryption Source Code and the First Amendment*, 15 Berkeley Tech. L.J. 713 (2000); A. Michael Froomkin, *The Constitution and Encryption Regulation: Do We Need a "New Privacy"?,* 3 N.Y.U. J. Legis. & Pub. Pol'y 25 (1999).

> The explosion in cryptography and the US government's attempts to control it have given rise to a debate between those who hail the new technology's contribution to privacy, business, and security and those who fear both its interference with the work of police and its adverse effect on the collection of intelligence. Positions have often been extreme. The advocates for unfettered cryptography maintain that a free society depends on privacy to protect freedom of association, artistic creativity, and political discussion. The advocates of control hold that there will be no freedom at all unless we can protect ourselves from criminals, terrorists, and foreign threats. Many have tried to present themselves as seeking to maintain or restore the status quo. For the police, the status quo is the continued ability to wiretap. For civil libertarians, it is the ready availability of conversational privacy that prevailed at the time of the country's founding.[64]

The Clipper Chip. The U.S. government has become increasingly concerned that the growing sophistication of encryption would make it virtually impossible for the government to decrypt. In 1994, the government proposed implementing the "Clipper Chip," a federal encryption standard in which the government would retain a copy of the key in a system called "key escrow." By holding a "spare key," the government could readily decrypt encrypted communications if it desired. The Clipper Chip was strongly criticized, and the government's encryption standard has not been widely used.

Encryption and the First Amendment. In *Junger v. Daley*, 209 F.3d 481 (6th Cir. 2000), the Sixth Circuit concluded that encryption was protected speech under the First Amendment:

> Much like a mathematical or scientific formula, one can describe the function and design of encryption software by a prose explanation; however, for individuals fluent in a computer programming language, source code is the most efficient and precise means by which to communicate ideas about cryptography.

Junger relied on the reasoning of *Bernstein v. United States Dep't of Justice,* 176 F.3d 1132 (9th Cir. 1999) (opinion withdrawn), where the Ninth Circuit struck down a licensing scheme on encryption source code as a violation of the First Amendment:

> Bernstein has submitted numerous declarations from cryptographers and computer programmers explaining that cryptographic ideas and algorithms are conveniently expressed in source code. . . . [T]he chief task for cryptographers is the development of secure methods of encryption. While the articulation of such a system in layman's English or in general mathematical terms may be useful, the devil is, at least for cryptographers, often in the algorithmic details. By utilizing source code, a cryptographer can express algorithmic ideas with precision and methodological rigor that is otherwise difficult to achieve. . . .
>
> Thus, cryptographers use source code to express their scientific ideas in much the same way that mathematicians use equations or economists use graphs. . . .

---

[64] Whitfield Diffie & Susan Landau, *Privacy on the Line: The Politics of Wiretapping and Encryption* (1998).

> In light of these considerations, we conclude that encryption software, in its source code form and as employed by those in the field of cryptography, must be viewed as expressive for First Amendment purposes. . . .

Orin Kerr takes issue with *Junger*'s holding: "the court viewed source code using the close-up paradigm of what the code looked like, rather than the deeper functional perspective of what the code was actually supposed to do. . . . Just as viewing a Seurat painting from inches away reveals only dots, the *Junger* court's myopic view of source code revealed only communications that looked like speech in form, but lacked the deeper significance required to establish constitutional expression."[65]

Consider *Karn v. United States Dep't of State*, 925 F. Supp. 1 (D.D.C. 1996), where the court came to the contrary conclusion from *Junger*:

> . . . The government regulation at issue here is clearly content-neutral. . . . The defendants are not regulating the export of the diskette because of the expressive content of the comments and or source code, but instead are regulating because of the belief that the combination of encryption source code on machine readable media will make it easier for foreign intelligence sources to encode their communications. . . .
>
> . . . [A] content-neutral regulation is justified . . . if it is within the constitutional power of the government, it "furthers an important or substantial governmental interest," and "the incidental restriction on alleged First Amendment freedoms is no greater than is essential to the furtherance of that interest." . . .
>
> . . . By placing cryptographic products on the ITAR, the President has determined that the proliferation of cryptographic products will harm the United States. . . .
>
> . . . [T]he plaintiff has not advanced any argument that the regulation is "substantially broader than necessary" to prevent the proliferation of cryptographic products. Nor has the plaintiff articulated any present barrier to the spreading of information on cryptography "by any other means" other than those containing encryption source code on machine-readable media. Therefore, the Court holds that the regulation of the plaintiff's diskette is narrowly tailored to the goal of limiting the proliferation of cryptographic products and that the regulation is justified. . . .

Encryption and the Fourth Amendment. Suppose law enforcement officials legally obtain an encrypted communication. Does the Fourth Amendment require a warrant before the government can decrypt an encrypted communication? Consider the following argument by Orin Kerr:

> Encryption is often explained as a lock-and-key system, in which a "key" is used to "lock" plaintext by turning it into ciphertext, and then a "key" is used to "unlock" the ciphertext by turning it into plaintext. We know that locking a container is a common way to create a reasonable expectation of privacy in its contents: the government ordinarily cannot break the lock and search a closed container without a warrant. . . .

---

[65] Orin S. Kerr, *Are We Overprotecting Code? Thoughts on First-Generation Internet Law*, 57 Wash. & Lee L. Rev. 1287, 1292-93 (2000).

> When we use a "lock" and "unlock" in the metaphorical sense to denote understanding, however, a lock cannot trigger the rights-based Fourth Amendment. If I tell you a riddle, I do not have a right to stop you from figuring it out. Although figuring out the secret of an inscrutable communication may "unlock" its meaning, the Fourth Amendment cannot regulate such a cognitive discovery. . . .[66]

Encryption and the Fifth Amendment. Can the government compel the production of a private key if it is stored on a personal computer? What if the key is known only to the individual and not stored or recorded?

3. E-MAIL

STEVE JACKSON GAMES, INC. V. UNITED STATES SECRET SERVICE

36 F.3d 457 (5th Cir. 1994)

BARKSDALE, J. Appellant Steve Jackson Games, Incorporated (SJG), publishes books, magazines, role-playing games, and related products. Starting in the mid-1980s, SJG operated an electronic bulletin board system, called "Illuminati" (BBS), from one of its computers. SJG used the BBS to post public information about its business, games, publications, and the role-playing hobby; to facilitate play-testing of games being developed; and to communicate with its customers and free-lance writers by electronic mail (E-mail).

Central to the issue before us, the BBS also offered customers the ability to send and receive private E-mail. Private E-mail was stored on the BBS computer's hard disk drive temporarily, until the addressees "called" the BBS (using their computers and modems) and read their mail. After reading their E-mail, the recipients could choose to either store it on the BBS computer's hard drive or delete it. In February 1990, there were 365 BBS users. Among other uses, appellants Steve Jackson, Elizabeth McCoy, William Milliken, and Steffan O'Sullivan used the BBS for communication by private E-mail. . . . [In addition, Lloyd Blankenship, an employee of Steve Jackson Games, operated a computer bulletin bulletin board system (BBS).] Blankeship had the ability to review, and perhaps delete any data on the BBS.

On February 28, 1990, [Secret Service] Agent Foley applied for a warrant to search SJG's premises and Blankenship's residence for evidence of violations of 18 U.S.C. §§ 1030 (proscribes interstate transportation of computer access information) and 2314 (proscribes interstate transportation of stolen property). A search warrant for SJG was issued that same day, authorizing the seizure of [computer hardware, software, and computer data.]

The next day, March 1, the warrant was executed by the Secret Service, including Agents Foley and Golden. Among the items seized was the computer which operated the BBS. At the time of the seizure, 162 items of unread, private

---

[66] Orin S. Kerr, *The Fourth Amendment in Cyberspace: Can Encryption Create a "Reasonable Expectation of Privacy?,"* 33 Conn. L. Rev. 503, 520-21, 522 (2001).

E-mail were stored on the BBS, including items addressed to the individual appellants. . . .

Appellants filed suit in May 1991 against, among others, the Secret Service and the United States, claiming [among other things, a violation of] the Federal Wiretap Act, as amended by Title I of the Electronic Communications Privacy Act (ECPA), 18 U.S.C. §§ 2510-2521; and Title II of the ECPA, 18 U.S.C. §§ 2701-2711. . . .

As stated, the sole issue is a very narrow one: whether the seizure of a computer on which is stored private E-mail that has been sent to an electronic bulletin board, but not yet read (retrieved) by the recipients, constitutes an "intercept" proscribed by 18 U.S.C. § 2511(1)(a).

Section 2511 was enacted in 1968 as part of Title III of the Omnibus Crime Control and Safe Streets Act of 1968, often referred to as the Federal Wiretap Act. Prior to the 1986 amendment by Title I of the ECPA, it covered only wire and oral communications. Title I of the ECPA extended that coverage to electronic communications. In relevant part, § 2511(1)(a) proscribes "intentionally intercept[ing] . . . any wire, oral, or electronic communication," unless the intercept is authorized by court order or by other exceptions not relevant here. Section 2520 authorizes, *inter alia*, persons whose electronic communications are intercepted in violation of § 2511 to bring a civil action against the interceptor for actual damages, or for statutory damages of $10,000 per violation or $100 per day of the violation, whichever is greater. 18 U.S.C. § 2520.

The Act defines "intercept" as "the aural or other acquisition of the contents of any wire, electronic, or oral communication through the use of any electronic, mechanical, or other device." 18 U.S.C. § 2510(4). . . .

Webster's Third New International Dictionary (1986) defines "aural" as "of or relating to the ear" or "of or relating to the sense of hearing." And, the Act defines "aural transfer" as "a transfer containing the human voice at any point between and including the point of origin and the point of reception." 18 U.S.C. § 2510(18). This definition is extremely important for purposes of understanding the definition of a "wire communication," which is defined by the Act as

> any aural transfer made in whole or in part through the use of facilities for the transmission of communications by the aid of wire, cable, or other like connection between the point of origin and the point of reception (including the use of such connection in a switching station) . . . *and such term includes any electronic storage of such communication.*

18 U.S.C. § 2510(1) (emphasis added). In contrast, as noted, an "electronic communication" is defined as "any *transfer* of signs, signals, writing, images, sounds, data, or intelligence of any nature transmitted in whole or in part by a wire, radio, electromagnetic, photoelectronic or photooptical system . . . but does not include . . . any wire or oral communication. . . ." 18 U.S.C. § 2510(12) (emphasis added).

Critical to the issue before us is the fact that, unlike the definition of "wire communication," *the definition of "electronic communication" does not include electronic storage of such communications. See* 18 U.S.C. § 2510(12). "Electronic storage" is defined as

> (A) any *temporary*, intermediate *storage* of a wire or *electronic communication incidental to the electronic transmission thereof;* and
> (B) any storage of such communication by an electronic communication service for purposes of backup protection of such communication. . . .

18 U.S.C. § 2510(17) (emphasis added). The E-mail in issue was in "electronic storage." Congress' use of the word "transfer" in the definition of "electronic communication," and its omission in that definition of the phrase "any electronic storage of such communication" (part of the definition of "wire communication") reflects that Congress did not intend for "intercept" to apply to "electronic communications" when those communications are in "electronic storage." . . .

Title II generally proscribes unauthorized access to stored wire or electronic communications. Section 2701(a) provides:

> Except as provided in subsection (c) of this section whoever —
>
> (1) intentionally accesses without authorization a facility through which an electronic communication service is provided; or
> (2) intentionally exceeds an authorization to access that facility; and thereby obtains, alters, or prevents authorized access to a wire or electronic communication *while it is in electronic storage in such system* shall be punished. . . .

18 U.S.C. § 2701(a) (emphasis added).

As stated, the district court found that the Secret Service violated § 2701 when it

> intentionally accesse[d] without authorization a facility [the computer] through which an electronic communication service [the BBS] is provided . . . and thereby obtain[ed] [and] prevent[ed] authorized access [by appellants] to a[n] . . . electronic communication while it is in electronic storage in such system.

18 U.S.C. § 2701(a). The Secret Service does not challenge this ruling. We find no indication in either the Act or its legislative history that Congress intended for conduct that is clearly prohibited by Title II to furnish the basis for a civil remedy under Title I as well. . . .

NOTES & QUESTIONS

1. ***Interception vs. Electronic Storage.*** Is unread e-mail in storage because it is sitting on a hard drive at the ISP? Or is it in transmission because the recipient hasn't read it yet? Is the court applying an overly formalistic and strict reading of "interception"?
2. ***The Fourth Amendment and E-mail: A Question of Perspective?*** Suppose the police sought to obtain a person's unread e-mail messages that were stored with her ISP waiting to be downloaded. *Steve Jackson Games* demonstrates how ECPA would apply — the weaker provisions of the Stored Communications Act rather than the stronger protections of the Wiretap Act apply to e-mail temporarily stored with a person's ISP. *Steve Jackson Games* is a civil case. In the criminal law context, the Stored Communications Act requires a warrant to obtain e-mails stored at the ISP for 180 days or less. If the e-mails

have been stored over 180 days, then the government can obtain them with a mere subpoena.

Would the Fourth Amendment apply? Orin Kerr argues that the answer depends upon the perspective by which one views the Internet. In the "internal perspective," the Internet is viewed as a virtual world, analogous to real space. From the "external perspective," we view the Internet as a network and do not analogize to real space. Kerr provides the following example:

> Does the Fourth Amendment require [the police] to obtain a search warrant [to obtain an e-mail]? . . . The answer depends largely upon whether they apply an internal or external perspective of the Internet.
>
> Imagine that the first officer applies an internal perspective of the Internet. To him, e-mail is the cyberspace equivalent of old-fashioned postal mail. His computer announces, "You've got mail!" when an e-mail message arrives and shows him a closed envelope. When he clicks on the envelope, it opens, revealing the message. From his internal perspective, the officer is likely to conclude that the Fourth Amendment places the same restriction on government access to e-mail that it places on government access to ordinary postal mail. He will then look in a Fourth Amendment treatise for the black letter rule on accessing postal mail. That treatise will tell him that accessing a suspect's mail ordinarily violates the suspect's "reasonable expectation of privacy," and that therefore the officer must first obtain a warrant. Because e-mail is the equivalent of postal mail, the officer will conclude that the Fourth Amendment requires him to obtain a warrant before he can access the e-mail.
>
> Imagine that the second police office approaches the same problem from an external perspective. To him, the facts look quite different. Looking at how the Internet actually works, the second police officer sees that when A sent the e-mail to B, A was instructing his computer to send a message to his Internet Service Provider (ISP) directing the ISP to forward a text message to B's ISP. To simplify matters, let's say that A's ISP is EarthLink, and B's ISP is America Online (AOL). . . .
>
> What process does the Fourth Amendment require? The second officer will reason that A sent a copy of the e-mail communication to a third party (the EarthLink computer), disclosing the communication to the third party and instructing it to send the communication to yet another third party (AOL). The officer will ask, what process does the Fourth Amendment require to obtain information that has been disclosed to a third party and is in the third party's possession? The officer will look in a Fourth Amendment treatise and locate to the black letter rule that the Fourth Amendment permits the government to obtain information disclosed to a third party using a mere subpoena. The officer can simply subpoena the system administrator to compel him to produce the e-mails. No search warrant is required.
>
> Who is right? The first officer or the second? The answer depends on whether you approach the Internet from an internal or external perspective. From an internal perspective, the officers need a search warrant; from the external perspective, they do not.[67]

[67] Orin S. Kerr, *The Problem of Perspective in Internet Law,* 91 Geo. L.J. 357, 361-62, 365-67 (2003).

3. ***Previously Read E-mail Stored at an ISP.*** The e-mail stored on the ISP server in *Steve Jackson Games* had not yet been downloaded and read by the recipients. Many people continue to store their e-mail messages with their ISP even after having read them. Does the Stored Communications Act protect them in the same way? The answer to this question is currently in dispute. Daniel Solove observes:

> Because these messages are now stored indefinitely, according to the DOJ's interpretation . . . the e-mail is no longer in temporary storage and is "simply a remotely stored file." Therefore, under this view, it falls outside of much of the Act's protections. Since many people store their e-mail messages after reading them and the e-mail they send out, this enables the government to access their communications with very minimal limitations.[68]

In *Theofel v. Farey-Jones,* 359 F.3d 1066 (9th Cir. 2004), the court concluded that

> [t]he [Stored Communications] Act defines "electronic storage" as "(A) any temporary, intermediate storage of a wire or electronic communication incidental to the electronic transmission thereof; and (B) any storage of such communication by an electronic communication service for purposes of backup protection of such communication." Id. § 2510(17), incorporated by id. § 2711(1). Several courts have held that subsection (A) covers e-mail messages stored on an ISP's server pending delivery to the recipient. Because subsection (A) applies only to messages in "temporary, intermediate storage," however, these courts have limited that subsection's coverage to messages not yet delivered to their intended recipient.
>
> Defendants point to these cases and argue that messages remaining on an ISP's server after delivery no longer fall within the Act's coverage. But, even if such messages are not within the purview of subsection (A), they do fit comfortably within subsection (B). . . .
>
> An obvious purpose for storing a message on an ISP's server after delivery is to provide a second copy of the message in the event that the user needs to download it again — if, for example, the message is accidentally erased from the user's own computer. The ISP copy of the message functions as a "backup" for the user. Notably, nothing in the Act requires that the backup protection be for the benefit of the ISP rather than the user. Storage under these circumstances thus literally falls within the statutory definition.

See also Fraser v. Nationwide Mutual Insurance Co., 352 F.3d 108 (3d Cir. 2003) (suggesting that such e-mail messages were in backup storage under the definition of electronic storage).

4. ***What Constitutes an Interception?*** In *United States v. Councilman,* 373 F.3d 197 (1st Cir. 2004), an Internet bookseller, Interloc, Inc., provided e-mail service for its customers, who were book dealers. Councilman, the vice president of Interloc, directed Interloc employees to draft a computer program to intercept all incoming communications from Amazon.com to the book dealers and make copies of them. Councilman and other Interloc then read the

---

[68] Daniel J. Solove, *Reconstructing Electronic Surveillance Law,* 72 Geo. Wash. L. Rev. 1264 (2004).

e-mails in order to gain a commercial advantage. Councilman was charged with criminal violations of the Wiretap Act. Councilman argued that he did not violate the Wiretap Act because the e-mails were in electronic storage, albeit very briefly, when they were copied. The court followed *Steve Jackson Games* and concluded that the e-mail was in temporary storage and therefore subject to the Stored Communications Act, not the Wiretap Act. However, unlike *Steve Jackson Games,* Interloc accessed the e-mails "as they were being transmitted and in real time."

The *Councilman* case received significant criticism by academic commentators and experts in electronic surveillance law for misunderstanding the fundamental distinction between the interception of a communication and the accessing of a stored communication. An interception occurs contemporaneously — as the communication is being transmitted. Accessing a stored communication occurs later, as the communication sits on a computer. This distinction has practical consequences, since interceptions are protected by the much more protective Wiretap Act rather than the Stored Communications Act. Does such a distinction still make sense? Is the contemporaneous interception of communications more troublesome than the accessing of the communications in *Steve Jackson Games*?

The case was reheard en banc, and the en banc court reversed the panel. *See United States v. Councilman*, 418 F.3d 67 (1st Cir. 2005) (en banc). The court concluded that "the term 'electronic communication' includes transient electronic storage that is intrinsic to the communication process, and hence that interception of an e-mail message in such storage is an offense under the Wiretap Act." The court declined to further elaborate on what constitutes and "interception."

5. ***Carnivore.*** Beginning in 1998, the FBI began using a hardware and software mechanism called "Carnivore" to intercept people's e-mail and instant messaging information from their Internet Service Providers (ISPs). After obtaining judicial authorization, the FBI would install Carnivore by connecting a computer directly to the ISP's server and initiating the program. Carnivore was designed to locate the e-mails of a suspect at the ISP when the ISP did not have the capacity to do so.

Carnivore was capable of analyzing the entire e-mail traffic of an ISP, although the FBI maintained it was only used to search for the e-mails of a suspect. The program filtered out the e-mail messages of ISP subscribers who are not the subject of the investigation; but to do so, it had to scan the e-mail headers that identify the senders and recipients. The FBI likened e-mail headers to the information captured by a pen register, a device that registers the phone numbers a person dials.

However, Carnivore could be programmed to search through the entire text of all e-mails, to capture e-mails with certain key words. In this way, Carnivore resembles a wiretap. Recall that under federal wiretap law, judicial approval for obtaining pen register information only requires a certification that "the information likely to be obtained by such installation and use is relevant to an ongoing investigation." 18 U.S.C. § 3123. In contrast, judicial approval of a wiretap requires a full panoply of requirements under Title I, including a showing of probable cause.

To eliminate the negative associations with the term "Carnivore," the device was renamed "DCS1000." Many members of Congress viewed Carnivore with great suspicion. Congress held hearings over the summer of 2000 pertaining to Carnivore, and several bills were proposed to halt or limit the use of Carnivore.

The anti-Carnivore sentiment abruptly ended after the September 11, 2001, World Trade Center and Pentagon terrorist attacks. Section 216 of the USA PATRIOT Act of 2001, in anticipation of the use of Carnivore, required reports on the use of Carnivore to be filed with a court. These reports, filed under seal, require (1) the names of the officers using the device; (2) when the device was installed, used, and removed; (3) the configuration of the device; and (4) the information collected by the device. 18 U.S.C. § 3133(a)(3).

The FBI discontinued use of Carnivore because ISPs can readily produce the information the FBI desires without the assistance of the Carnivore device and because commercially available software has similar functionality.

4. ISP RECORDS

UNITED STATES V. HAMBRICK

55 F. Supp. 2d 504 (W.D. Va. 1999)

MICHAEL, J. Defendant Scott M. Hambrick seeks the suppression of all evidence obtained from his Internet Service Provider ("ISP"), MindSpring, and seeks the suppression of all evidence seized from his home pursuant to a warrant issued by this court. For the reasons discussed below, the court denies the defendant's motion.

On March 14, 1998, J. L. McLaughlin, a police officer with the Keene, New Hampshire Police Department, connected to the Internet and entered a chat room called "Gay dads 4 sex." McLaughlin's screen name was "Rory14." In this chat room, Detective McLaughlin encountered someone using the screen name "Blowuinva." Based on a series of online conversations between "Rory14" (Det. McLaughlin) and "Blowuinva," McLaughlin concluded that "Blowuinva" sought to entice a fourteen-year-old boy to leave New Hampshire and live with "Blowuinva." Because of the anonymity of the Internet, Detective McLaughlin did not know the true identity of the person with whom he was communicating nor did he know where "Blowuinva" lived. "Blowuinva" had only identified himself as "Brad."

To determine Blowuinva's identity and location, McLaughlin obtained a New Hampshire state subpoena that he served on Blowuinva's Internet Service Provider, MindSpring, located in Atlanta, Georgia. The New Hampshire state subpoena requested that MindSpring produce "any records pertaining to the billing and/or user records documenting the subject using your services on March 14th, 1998 at 1210HRS (EST) using Internet Protocol Number 207.69.169.92." MindSpring complied with the subpoena. On March 20, 1998, MindSpring supplied McLaughlin with defendant's name, address, credit card number, e-mail address, home and work telephone numbers, fax number, and the fact that the Defendant's account was connected to the Internet at the Internet Protocol (IP) address.

A justice of the peace, Richard R. Richards, signed the New Hampshire state subpoena. Mr. Richards is not only a New Hampshire justice of the peace, but he is also a detective in the Keene Police Department, Investigation Division. Mr. Richards did not issue the subpoena pursuant to a matter pending before himself, any other judicial officer, or a grand jury. At the hearing on the defendant's motion, the government conceded the invalidity of the warrant. The question before this court, therefore, is whether the court must suppress the information obtained from MindSpring, and all that flowed from it, because the government failed to obtain a proper subpoena. . . .

. . . [Under *Katz v. United States*,] the Fourth Amendment applies only where: (1) the citizen has manifested a subjective expectation of privacy, and (2) the expectation is one that society accepts as "objectively reasonable." . . . Applying the first part of the *Katz* analysis, Mr. Hambrick asserts that he had a subjective expectation of privacy in the information that MindSpring gave to the government. However, resolution of this matter hinges on whether Mr. Hambrick's expectation is one that society accepts as "objectively reasonable."

The objective reasonableness prong of the privacy test is ultimately a value judgment and a determination of how much privacy we should have as a society. In making this constitutional determination, this court must employ a sort of risk analysis, asking whether the individual affected should have expected the material at issue to remain private. The defendant asserts that the Electronic Communications Privacy Act ("ECPA") "legislatively resolves" this question. . .

The information obtained through the use of the government's invalid subpoena consisted of the defendant's name, address, social security number, credit card number, and certification that the defendant was connected to the Internet on March 14, 1998. Thus, this information falls within the provisions of Title II of the ECPA.

The government may require that an ISP provide stored communications and transactional records only if (1) it obtains a warrant issued under the Federal Rules of Criminal Procedure or state equivalent, or (2) it gives prior notice to the online subscriber and then issues a subpoena or receives a court order authorizing disclosure of the information in question. *See* 18 U.S.C. § 2703(a)-(c)(1)(B). When an ISP discloses stored communications or transactional records to a government entity without the requisite authority, the aggrieved customer's sole remedy is damages.

Although Congress is willing to recognize that individuals have some degree of privacy in the stored data and transactional records that their ISPs retain, the ECPA is hardly a legislative determination that this expectation of privacy is one that rises to the level of "reasonably objective" for Fourth Amendment purposes. Despite its concern for privacy, Congress did not provide for suppression where a party obtains stored data or transactional records in violation of the Act. Additionally, the ECPA's concern for privacy extends only to government invasions of privacy. ISPs are free to turn stored data and transactional records over to nongovernmental entities. *See* 18 U.S.C. § 2703(c)(1)(A) ("[A] provider of electronic communication service or remote computing service may disclose a record or other information pertaining to a subscriber to or customer of such service . . . to any person other than a governmental entity."). For Fourth Amendment purposes, this court does not find that the ECPA has legislatively determined that an individual has a reasonable expectation of privacy in his name, address, social security number, credit card number, and proof of Internet connection. The fact that the ECPA does not proscribe turning over such information to private entities buttresses the conclusion that the ECPA does not create a reasonable expectation of privacy in that information. This, however, does not end the court's inquiry. This court must determine, within the constitutional framework that the Supreme Court has established, whether Mr. Hambrick's subjective expectation of privacy is one that society is willing to recognize.

To have any interest in privacy, there must be some exclusion of others. To have a reasonable expectation of privacy under the Supreme Court's risk-analysis approach to the Fourth Amendment, two conditions must be met: (1) the data must not be knowingly exposed to others, and (2) the Internet service provider's ability to access the data must not constitute a disclosure. In *Katz*, the Supreme Court expressly held that "what a person knowingly exposes to the public, even in his home or office, is not a subject of Fourth Amendment protection." Further, the Court "consistently has held that a person has no legitimate expectation of privacy in information he voluntarily turns over to third parties." *Smith v. Maryland*, 442 U.S. 735, 743-44 (1979). . . .

When Scott Hambrick surfed the Internet using the screen name "Blowuinva," he was not a completely anonymous actor. It is true that an average member of the public could not easily determine the true identity of "Blowuinva." Nevertheless, when Mr. Hambrick entered into an agreement to obtain Internet access from MindSpring, he knowingly revealed his name, address, credit card number, and telephone number to MindSpring and its employees. Mr. Hambrick also selected the screen name "Blowuinva." When the defendant selected his screen name it became tied to his true identity in all MindSpring records. MindSpring employees had ready access to these records in the normal course of MindSpring's business, for example, in the keeping of its records for billing purposes, and nothing prevented MindSpring from revealing this information to nongovernmental actors.[69] Also, there is nothing in the record to suggest that there was a restrictive agreement between the defendant and MindSpring that would limit the right of MindSpring to reveal the defendant's personal information to nongovernmental entities. Where such dissemination of information to nongovernment entities is not prohibited, there can be no reasonable expectation of privacy in that information.

Although not dispositive to the outcome of this motion, it is important to note that the court's decision does not leave members of cybersociety without privacy protection. Under the ECPA, Internet Service Providers are civilly liable when they reveal subscriber information or the contents of stored communications to

---

[69] It is apparently common for ISPs to provide certain information that Mr. Hambrick alleges to be private to marketing firms and other organizations interested in soliciting business from Internet users.

the government without first requiring a warrant, court order, or subpoena. Here, nothing suggests that MindSpring had any knowledge that the facially valid subpoena submitted to it was in fact an invalid subpoena. Had MindSpring revealed the information at issue in this case to the government without first requiring a subpoena, apparently valid on its face, Mr. Hambrick could have sued MindSpring. This is a powerful deterrent protecting privacy in the online world and should not be taken lightly. . . .

NOTES & QUESTIONS

1. ***Is There a Reasonable Expectation of Privacy in ISP Records?*** The court in *Hambrick* concludes that there is no reasonable expectation of privacy in ISP records based on the third party doctrine in *Smith v. Maryland.* In *United States v. Kennedy,* 81 F. Supp. 2d 1103 (D. Kan. 2000), the court reached a similar conclusion:

   > Defendant has not demonstrated an objectively reasonable legitimate expectation of privacy in his subscriber information. . . . "[A] person has no legitimate expectation of privacy in information he voluntarily turns over to third parties." *Smith v. Maryland,* 442 U.S. 735 (1979). When defendant entered into an agreement with [his ISP], he knowingly revealed all information connected to [his IP address]. He cannot now claim to have a Fourth Amendment privacy interest in his subscriber information.

   Is *Smith v. Maryland* controlling on this issue? Is there a way to distinguish *Smith*?
2. ***Statutes as a Basis for a Reasonable Expectation of Privacy?*** Hambrick was not seeking relief directly under the Stored Communications Act of ECPA. Why not? Instead, Hambrick asserted he had Fourth Amendment protection in his subscriber records. He argued that under the *Katz* reasonable expectation of privacy test, the ECPA "legislatively resolves" that there is a reasonable expectation of privacy in information that Mindspring gave to the government. Should statutes that protect privacy serve as an indication of a societal recognition of a reasonable expectation of privacy? What are the consequences of using statutes such as ECPA to conclude that the Fourth Amendment applies?
3. ***Is There a Remedy?*** Mindspring couldn't release information to the government without a warrant or subpoena or else it would face civil liability. However, in this case, the government presented Mindspring with a subpoena that Mindspring had no knowledge was invalid. Therefore, it is unlikely that Mindspring would be liable. If the court is correct in its conclusion that 18 U.S.C. § 2703(a)–(c)(1)(B) of the ECPA only applies to the conduct of Internet Service Providers, then is there any remedy against Officer Richards's blatantly false subpoena? Could a police officer obtain a person's Internet subscriber information by falsifying a subpoena and escape without any civil liability or exclusionary rule?

McVeigh v. Cohen

983 F. Supp. 215 (D.D.C. 1998)

SPORKIN, J. . . . Plaintiff Timothy R. McVeigh, who bears no relation to the Oklahoma City bombing defendant, seeks to enjoin the United States Navy from discharging him under the statutory policy colloquially known as "Don't Ask, Don't Tell, Don't Pursue." See 10 U.S.C. § 654 ("new policy"). In the course of investigating his sexual orientation, the Plaintiff contends that the Defendants violated his rights under the Electronic Communications Privacy Act ("ECPA"), 18 U.S.C. § 2701 et seq., the Administrative Procedure Act ("APA") 5 U.S.C. § 706, the Department's own policy, and the Fourth and Fifth Amendments of the U.S. Constitution. Absent an injunction, the Plaintiff avers that he will suffer irreparable injury from the discharge, even if he were ultimately to prevail on the merits of his claims.

The Plaintiff, Senior Chief Timothy R. McVeigh, is a highly decorated seventeen-year veteran of the United States Navy who has served honorably and continuously since he was nineteen years old. At the time of the Navy's decision to discharge him, he was the senior-most enlisted man aboard the United States nuclear submarine U.S.S. Chicago.

On September 2, 1997, Ms. Helen Hajne, a civilian Navy volunteer, received an electronic mail ("email") message through the America Online Service ("AOL") regarding the toy-drive that she was coordinating for the Chicago crew members' children. The message box stated that it came from the alias "boysrch," but the text of the email was signed by a "Tim." Through an option available to AOL subscribers, the volunteer searched through the "member profile directory" to find the member profile for this sender. The directory specified that "boysrch" was an AOL subscriber named Tim who lived in Honolulu, Hawaii, worked in the military, and identified his marital status as "gay." Although the profile included some telling interests such as "collecting pics of other young studs" and "boy watching," it did not include any further identifying information such as full name, address, or phone number. . . .

Ms. Hajne proceeded to forward the email and directory profile to her husband, who, like Plaintiff, was also a noncommissioned officer aboard the U.S.S. Chicago. The material eventually found its way to Commander John Mickey, the captain of the ship and Plaintiff's commanding officer. In turn, Lieutenant Karin S. Morean, the ship's principal legal adviser and a member of the Judge Advocate General's ("JAG") Corps was called in to investigate the matter. By this point, the Navy suspected the "Tim" who authored the email might be Senior Chief Timothy McVeigh. Before she spoke to the Plaintiff and without a warrant or court order, Lieutenant Morean requested a Navy paralegal on her staff, Legalman First Class Joseph M. Kaiser, to contact AOL and obtain information from the service that could "connect" the screen name "boysrch" and accompanying user profile to McVeigh. Legalman Kaiser called AOL's toll-free customer service number and talked to a representative at technical services. Legalman Kaiser did not identify himself as a Naval serviceman. According to his testimony at the administrative hearing, he stated that he was "a third party in receipt of a fax sheet and wanted to confirm the profile sheet, [and] who it belonged to." The AOL representative affirmatively identified Timothy R. McVeigh as the customer in question.

Upon verification from AOL, Lieutenant Morean notified Senior Chief McVeigh that the Navy had obtained "some indication[] that he made a statement of homosexuality" in violation of § 654(b)(2) of "Don't Ask, Don't Tell." In light of the Uniform Code of Military Justice prohibition of sodomy and indecent acts, she then advised him of his right to remain silent. Shortly thereafter, in a memorandum dated September 22, 1997, the Navy advised Plaintiff that it was commencing an administrative discharge proceeding (termed by the Navy as an "administrative separation") against him. The reason stated was for "homosexual conduct, as evidenced by your statement that you are a homosexual."

On November 7, 1997, the Navy conducted an administrative discharge hearing before a three-member board. . . . At the conclusion of the administrative hearing, the board held that the government had sufficiently shown by a preponderance of the evidence that Senior Chief McVeigh had engaged in "homosexual conduct," a dischargeable offense. . . .

. . . Plaintiff is now scheduled to be discharged barring relief from this Court. . . .

. . . At its core, the Plaintiff's complaint is with the Navy's compliance, or lack thereof, with its new regulations under the "Don't Ask, Don't Tell, Don't Pursue" policy. Plaintiff contends that he did not "tell," as prescribed by the statute, but that nonetheless, the Navy impermissibly "asked" and zealously "pursued."

In short, this case raises the central issue of whether there is really a place for gay officers in the military under the new policy, "Don't Ask, Don't Tell, Don't Pursue." [This policy was adopted in 1993, and it prohibits the military from investigating sexual orientation unless there is "credible information" that a gay serviceman or servicewoman has the "propensity or intent to engage in homosexual acts."] . . .

The facts as stated above clearly demonstrate that the Plaintiff did not openly express his homosexuality in a way that compromised this "Don't Ask, Don't Tell" policy. Suggestions of sexual orientation in a private, anonymous email account did not give the Navy a sufficient reason to investigate to determine whether to commence discharge proceedings. In its actions, the Navy violated its own regulations. An investigation into sexual orientation may be initiated "only when [a commander] has received credible information that there is a basis for discharge," such as when an officer "has said that he or she is a homosexual or bisexual, or made some other statement that indicates a propensity or intent to engage in homosexual acts." Yet in this case, there was no such credible information that Senior Chief McVeigh had made such a statement. Under the Guidelines, "credible information" requires more than "just a belief or suspicion" that a Service member has engaged in homosexual conduct. In the examples provided, the Guidelines state that "credible information" would exist in this case only if "a reliable person" stated that he or she directly observed or heard a Service member make an oral or written statement that "a reasonable person would believe was intended to convey the fact that he or she engages in or has a propensity or intent to engage in homosexual acts."

Clearly, the facts as stated above in this case demonstrate that there was no such "credible information." All that the Navy had was an email message and user profile that it suspected was authored by Plaintiff. Under the military regulation, that information alone should not have triggered any sort of investigation. When the Navy affirmatively took steps to confirm the identity of the email respondent, it violated the very essence of "Don't Ask, Don't Pursue" by launching a search and destroy mission. Even if the Navy had a factual basis to believe that the email message and profile were written by Plaintiff, it was unreasonable to infer that they were necessarily intended to convey a propensity or intent to engage in homosexual conduct. Particularly in the context of cyberspace, a medium of "virtual reality" that invites fantasy and affords anonymity, the comments attributed to McVeigh do not by definition amount to a declaration of homosexuality. At most, they express "an abstract preference or desire to engage in homosexual acts." Yet the regulations specify that a statement professing homosexuality so as to warrant investigation must declare "more than an abstract preference or desire"; they must indicate a likelihood actually to carry out homosexual acts.

The subsequent steps taken by the Navy in its "pursuit" of the Plaintiff were not only unauthorized under its policy, but likely illegal under the Electronic Communications Privacy Act of 1986 ("ECPA"). The ECPA, enacted by Congress to address privacy concerns on the Internet, allows the government to obtain information from an online service provider — as the Navy did in this instance from AOL — but only if a) it obtains a warrant issued under the Federal Rules of Criminal Procedure or state equivalent; or b) it gives prior notice to the online subscriber and then issues a subpoena or receives a court order authorizing disclosure of the information in question. See 18 U.S.C. § 2703(b)(1)(A)-(B), (c)(1)(B).

In soliciting and obtaining over the phone personal information about the Plaintiff from AOL, his private on-line service provider, the government in this case invoked neither of these provisions and thus failed to comply with the ECPA. From the record, it is undisputed that the Navy directly solicited by phone information from AOL. Lieutenant Karin S. Morean, the ship's principal legal counsel and a member of the JAG corps, personally requested Legalman Kaiser to contact AOL and obtain the identity of the subscriber. Without this information, Plaintiff credibly contends that the Navy could not have made the necessary connection between him and the user profile which was the sole basis on which to commence discharge proceedings.

The government, in its defense, contends that the Plaintiff cannot succeed on his ECPA claim. It argues that the substantive provision of the statute that Plaintiff cites, 18 U.S.C. § 2703(c)(1)(B), puts the obligation on the online service provider to withhold information from the government, and not vice versa. In support of its position, Defendants cite to the Fourth Circuit opinion in *Tucker v. Waddell*, 83 F.3d 688 (4th Cir. 1996), which held that § 2703(c)(1)(B) only prohibits the actions of online providers, not the government. Accordingly, Defendants allege that Plaintiff has no cause of action against the government on the basis of the ECPA. . . .

. . . [However,] Section 2703(c)(1)(B) must be read in the context of the statute as a whole. In comparison, § 2703(a) and (b) imposes on the government a reciprocal obligation to obtain a warrant or the like before requiring disclosure. It appears from the face of the statute that all of the subsections of § 2703 were intended to work in tandem to protect consumer privacy. Even if, however, the government ultimately proves to be right in its assessment of § 2703(c)(1)(B), the Plaintiff has plead § 2703(a) and (b) as alternative grounds for relief. In his claim that the government, at the least, solicited a violation of the ECPA by AOL, the Court finds that there is likely success on the merits with regard to this issue. The government knew, or should have known, that by turning over the information without a warrant, AOL was breaking the law. Yet the Navy, in this case, directly solicited the information anyway. What is most telling is that the Naval investigator did not identify himself when he made his request. While the government makes much of the fact that § 2703(c)(1)(B) does not provide a cause of action against the government, it is elementary that information obtained improperly can be suppressed where an individual's rights have been violated. In these days of "big brother," where through technology and otherwise the privacy interests of individuals from all walks of life are being ignored or marginalized, it is imperative that statutes explicitly protecting these rights be strictly observed. . . .

. . . With literally the entire world on the world-wide web, enforcement of the ECPA is of great concern to those who bare the most personal information about their lives in private accounts through the Internet. . . .

. . . Although Officer McVeigh did not publicly announce his sexual orientation, the Navy nonetheless impermissibly embarked on a search and "outing" mission.

NOTES & QUESTIONS

1. ***A Suppression Remedy?*** Recall the following statement in *McVeigh*: "The government knew, or should have known, that by turning over the information without a warrant, AOL was breaking the law. . . . While the government makes much of the fact that § 2703(c)(1)(B) does not provide a cause of action against the government, it is elementary that information obtained improperly can be suppressed where an individual's rights have been violated." Is this last statement correct? The Stored Communications Act does not have a suppression remedy; the court is creating an exclusionary rule for the Stored Communications Act. Is this appropriate? Without a suppression remedy for the conduct of the government in this case, what would deter the government from violating the Stored Communications Act?
2. ***Postscript.*** Subsequent to *McVeigh v. Cohen,* Congress amended §§ 2703(a)-(c) to make it clear that these provisions applied not just to ISPs but also to government conduct. In *Freedman v. America Online, Inc.*, 303 F. Supp. 2d 121 (D. Conn. 2004), two police detectives signed a warrant themselves (rather than bring it before a judge) and served it to AOL. AOL responded by faxing plaintiff's name, address, phone numbers, account status, membership information, and his other AOL screen names. The district court concluded that the government had violated ECPA: "To conclude that the government may circumvent the legal processes set forth in the ECPA by merely

requesting subscriber information from an ISP contradicts Congress's intent to protect personal privacy."

5. IP ADDRESSES AND URLS

UNITED STATES V. FORRESTER

512 F.3d 500 (9th Cir. 2008)

FISHER, J. . . . Defendants-appellants Mark Stephen Forrester and Dennis Louis Alba were charged with various offenses relating to the operation of a large Ecstasy-manufacturing laboratory, and were convicted on all counts following a jury trial. They now appeal their convictions and sentences. . . .

During its investigation of Forrester and Alba's Ecstasy-manufacturing operation, the government employed various computer surveillance techniques to monitor Alba's e-mail and Internet activity. The surveillance began in May 2001 after the government applied for and received court permission to install a pen register analogue known as a "mirror port" on Alba's account with PacBell Internet. The mirror port was installed at PacBell's connection facility in San Diego, and enabled the government to learn the to/from addresses of Alba's e-mail messages, the IP addresses of the websites that Alba visited and the total volume of information sent to or from his account. Later, the government obtained a warrant authorizing it to employ imaging and keystroke monitoring techniques, but Alba does not challenge on appeal those techniques' legality or the government's application to use them.

Forrester and Alba were tried by jury. At trial, the government introduced extensive evidence showing that they and their associates built and operated a major Ecstasy laboratory. . . .

Alba contends that the government's surveillance of his e-mail and Internet activity violated the Fourth Amendment and fell outside the scope of the then-applicable federal pen register statute. We hold that the surveillance did not constitute a Fourth Amendment search and thus was not unconstitutional. We also hold that whether or not the computer surveillance was covered by the then-applicable pen register statute — an issue that we do not decide — Alba is not entitled to the suppression of any evidence (let alone the reversal of his convictions) as a consequence.

The Supreme Court held in *Smith v. Maryland* that the use of a pen register (a device that records numbers dialed from a phone line) does not constitute a search for Fourth Amendment purposes. According to the Court, people do not have a subjective expectation of privacy in numbers that they dial because they "realize that they must 'convey' phone numbers to the telephone company, since it is through telephone company switching equipment that their calls are completed." Even if there were such a subjective expectation, it would not be one that society is prepared to recognize as reasonable because "a person has no legitimate expectation of privacy in information he voluntarily turns over to third parties." Therefore the use of a pen register is not a Fourth Amendment search. Importantly, the Court distinguished pen registers from more intrusive surveillance techniques on the ground that "pen registers do not acquire the *contents* of communications" but rather obtain only the addressing information associated with phone calls.

Neither this nor any other circuit has spoken to the constitutionality of computer surveillance techniques that reveal the to/from addresses of e-mail messages, the IP addresses of websites visited and the total amount of data transmitted to or from an account. We conclude that the surveillance techniques the government employed here are constitutionally indistinguishable from the use of a pen register that the Court approved in *Smith.* First, e-mail and Internet users, like the telephone users in *Smith,* rely on third-party equipment in order to engage in communication. *Smith* based its holding that telephone users have no expectation of privacy in the numbers they dial on the users' imputed knowledge that their calls are completed through telephone company switching equipment. Analogously, e-mail and Internet users have no expectation of privacy in the to/from addresses of their messages or the IP addresses of the websites they visit because they should know that this information is provided to and used by Internet service providers for the specific purpose of directing the routing of information. Like telephone numbers, which provide instructions to the "switching equipment that processed those numbers," e-mail to/from addresses and IP addresses are not merely passively conveyed through third party equipment, but rather are voluntarily turned over in order to direct the third party's servers.

Second, e-mail to/from addresses and IP addresses constitute addressing information and do not necessarily reveal any more about the underlying contents of communication than do phone numbers. When the government obtains the to/from addresses of a person's e-mails or the IP addresses of websites visited, it does not find out the contents of the messages or know the particular pages on the websites the person viewed. At best, the government may make educated guesses about what was said in the messages or viewed on the websites based on its knowledge of the e-mail to/from addresses and IP addresses — but this is no different from speculation about the contents of a phone conversation on the basis of the identity of the person or entity that was dialed. Like IP addresses, certain phone numbers may strongly indicate the underlying contents of the communication; for example, the government would know that a person who dialed the phone number of a chemicals company or a gun shop was likely seeking information about chemicals or firearms. Further, when an individual dials a pre-recorded information or subject-specific line, such as sports scores, lottery results or phone sex lines, the phone number may even show that the caller had access to specific content information. Nonetheless, the Court in *Smith* and *Katz* drew a clear line between unprotected addressing information and protected content information that the government did not cross here.[70]

[70] Surveillance techniques that enable the government to determine not only the IP addresses that a person accesses but also the uniform resource locators ("URL") of the pages visited might be more constitutionally problematic. A URL, unlike an IP address, identifies the particular document within a website that a person views and thus reveals much more information about the person's Internet activity. For instance, a surveillance technique that captures IP addresses would show only that a person visited the New York Times' website at http://www.nytimes.com, whereas a technique that captures URLs would also divulge the particular articles the person viewed.

The government's surveillance of e-mail addresses also may be technologically sophisticated, but it is conceptually indistinguishable from government surveillance of physical mail. In a line of cases dating back to the nineteenth century, the Supreme Court has held that the government cannot engage in a warrantless search of the contents of sealed mail, but can observe whatever information people put on the outside of mail, because that information is voluntarily transmitted to third parties. E-mail, like physical mail, has an outside address "visible" to the third-party carriers that transmit it to its intended location, and also a package of content that the sender presumes will be read only by the intended recipient. The privacy interests in these two forms of communication are identical. The contents may deserve Fourth Amendment protection, but the address and size of the package do not. . . .

We therefore hold that the computer surveillance techniques that Alba challenges are not Fourth Amendment searches. However, our holding extends only to these particular techniques and does not imply that more intrusive techniques or techniques that reveal more content information are also constitutionally identical to the use of a pen register. . . .

Alba claims that the government's computer surveillance was not only unconstitutional but also beyond the scope of the then-applicable pen register statute, 18 U.S.C. § 3121-27 (amended October 2001). Under both the old and new versions of 18 U.S.C. § 3122, the government must apply for and obtain a court order before it can install and use a pen register. When the surveillance at issue here took place in May-July 2001, the applicable statute defined a pen register as a "device which records or decodes electronic or other impulses which identify the numbers dialed or otherwise transmitted on the telephone line to which such device is attached." 18 U.S.C. § 3127(3). Notwithstanding the government's invocation of this provision and application for and receipt of a court order, Alba maintains that the computer surveillance at issue here did not come within the statutory definition of a "pen register."

Even assuming that Alba is correct in this contention, he would not be entitled to the suppression of the evidence obtained through the computer surveillance. As both the Supreme Court and this court have emphasized, suppression is a disfavored remedy, imposed only where its deterrence benefits outweigh its substantial social costs or (outside the constitutional context) where it is clearly contemplated by the relevant statute. . . . Alba does not point to any statutory language requiring suppression when computer surveillance that is similar but not technically equivalent to a pen register is carried out. Indeed, he does not even identify what law or regulation the government may have violated if its surveillance did not come within the scope of the then-applicable pen register statute. The suppression of evidence under these circumstances is plainly inappropriate.

Our conclusion is bolstered by the fact that suppression still would not be appropriate even if the computer surveillance was covered by the pen register statute. Assuming the surveillance violated the statute, there is no mention of suppression of evidence in the statutory text. Instead, the only penalty specified is that "[w]hoever knowingly violates subsection (a)" by installing or using a pen register without first obtaining a court order "shall be fined under this title or imprisoned not more than one year, or both." 18 U.S.C. § 3121(d).

NOTES & QUESTIONS

1. ***IP Addresses vs. URLs.*** The *Forrester* court concludes that e-mail headers and IP addresses are akin to pen registers and that the controlling case is *Smith v. Maryland.* Does *Smith* control because IP address and e-mail header information are not revealing of the contents of the communications or because this information is conveyed to a third party? Recall that in a footnote, the court observes that URLs "might be more constitutionally problematic" because a "URL, unlike an IP address, identifies the particular document within a website that a person views and thus reveals much more information about the person's Internet activity." However, although IP addresses do not reveal specific parts of a websites that a person visits, they do reveal the various websites that a person visits. Why isn't this revealing enough to trigger constitutional protections?
2. ***Content vs. Envelope Information.*** A key distinction under ECPA, as well as Fourth Amendment law, is between "content" and "envelope" information. Orin Kerr explains the distinction:

> . . . [E]very communications network features two types of information: the contents of communications, and the addressing and routing information that the networks use to deliver the contents of communications. The former is "content information," and the latter is "envelope information."
>
> The essential distinction between content and envelope information remains constant across different technologies, from postal mail to email. With postal mail, the content information is the letter itself, stored safely inside its envelope. The envelope information is the information derived from the outside of the envelope, including the mailing and return addresses, the stamp and postmark, and the size and weight of the envelope when sealed.
>
> Similar distinctions exist for telephone conversations. The content information for a telephone call is the actual conversation between participants that can be captured by an audio recording of the call. The envelope information includes the number the caller dials, the number from which the caller dials, the time of the call, and its duration.[71]

Under ECPA, content information is generally given strong protection (e.g., the Wiretap Act), whereas envelope information is not (e.g., the Pen Register Act). But is such a distinction viable?

Daniel Solove contends that the distinction breaks down:

> When applied to IP addresses and URLs, the envelope/content distinction becomes even more fuzzy. An IP address is a unique number that is assigned to each computer connected to the Internet. Each website, therefore, has an IP address. On the surface, a list of IP addresses is simply a list of numbers; but it is actually much more. With a complete listing of IP addresses, the government can learn quite a lot about a person because it can trace how that person surfs the Internet. The government can learn the names of stores at which a person shops, the political organizations a person finds interesting, a person's sexual fetishes and fantasies, her health concerns, and so on.

---

[71] Orin S. Kerr, Internet *Surveillance Law After the USA PATRIOT Act: The Big Brother That Isn't,* 97 Nw. U. L. Rev. 607, 611 (2003).

> Perhaps even more revealing are URLs. A URL is a pointer — it points to the location of particular information on the Internet. In other words, it indicates where something is located. When we cite to something on the Web, we are citing to its URL. . . . URLs can reveal the specific information that people are viewing on the Web. URLs can also contain search terms. . . .
>
> [Therefore,] the content/envelope distinction is not always clear. In many circumstances, to adapt Marshall McLuhan, the "envelope" *is* the "content." Envelope information can reveal a lot about a person's private activities, sometimes as much (and even more) than can content information.[72]

Orin Kerr disagrees:

> Professor Solove appears to doubt the wisdom of offering lower privacy protection for non-content information. He suggests that the acquisition of non-content information should require a full search warrant based on probable cause. . . .
>
> Despite this, Solove's suggestion that the law should not offer lesser privacy protection for non-content information is unpersuasive. The main reason is that it is quite rare for non-content information to yield the equivalent of content information. It happens in very particular circumstances, but it remains quite rare, and usually in circumstances that are difficult to predict ex ante. In the Internet context, for example, non-content surveillance typically consists of collecting Internet packets; the packets disclose that a packet was sent from one IP address to another IP address at a particular time. This isn't very private information, at least in most cases. Indeed, it is usually impossible to know who asked for the packet, or what the packet was about, or what the person who asked for the packet wanted to do, or even if it was a person (as opposed to the computer) who sent for the packet in the first place. Solove focuses on the compelling example of Internet search terms as an example of non-content information that can be the privacy equivalent of content information. This is a misleading example, however, as Internet search terms very well may be contents. . . . Thus, despite the fact that non-content information can yield private information, in the great majority of cases contents of communications implicate privacy concerns on a higher order of magnitude than non-content information, and it makes sense to give greater privacy protections for the former and lesser to the latter.[73]

Solove replies:

> Kerr assumes that a compilation of envelope information is generally less revealing than content information. However, a person may care more about protecting the identities of people with whom she communicates than the content of those communications. Indeed, the identities of the people one communicates with implicates freedom of association under the First Amendment. The difficulty is that the distinction between content and envelope information does not correlate well to the distinction between sensitive and innocuous information. Envelope information can be quite sensitive; content information can be quite innocuous. Admittedly, in many cases, people do not care very much about maintaining privacy over the identities of their friends and

---

[72] Solove, *Surveillance Law, supra*, at 1287-88.

[73] Orin S. Kerr, *A User's Guide to the Stored Communications Act — and a Legislator's Guide to Amending It,* 72 Geo. Wash. L. Rev. 1208, 1229 n.142 (2004).

associates. But it is also true that in many cases, the contents of communications are not very revealing as well. Many e-mails are short messages which do not reveal any deep secrets, and even Kerr would agree that this should not lessen their protection under the law. This is because content information has the potential to be quite sensitive — but this is also the case with envelope information.[74]

3. ***The Scope of the Pen Register Act.*** The version of the Pen Register Act in effect when the search took place in *Forrester* was the pre-USA PATRIOT Act version, which defined pen registers more narrowly as "numbers dialed." The USA PATRIOT Act expanded the definition of pen register to include "dialing, routing, addressing, or signaling information . . . provided, however, that such information shall not include the contents of any communication." Prior to the USA PATRIOT Act changes, it was an open question as to whether the Pen Register Act applied to e-mail headers, IP addresses, and URLs. The USA PATRIOT Act changes aimed to clarify that the Pen Register Act did apply beyond telephone numbers. E-mail headers seem to fit readily into the new Pen Register Act definition. But what about IP addresses and URLs? They involve "routing" and "addressing" information, but they may also include "the contents" of communications. Do they involve "contents" or are they merely "envelope" information?
4. ***Text Messages.*** In *Quon v. Arch Wireless Operating Co., Ltd.,* 2008 WL 2440559 (9th Cir. 2008), the court held that accessing text messages can constitute a violation of the Stored Communications Act because the messages were stored by the communication service provider as "backup" protection for the user. The court also concluded that the Fourth Amendment protects text message communications because they are "content" information: "We see no meaningful difference between the e-mails at issue in *Forrester* and the text messages at issue here."
5. ***ECPA and the Exclusionary Rule.*** The *Forrester* court concludes that even if the acquisition of information violated the Pen Register Act, the exclusionary rule is not a remedy under the Act. As discussed earlier in this chapter, many provisions of electronic surveillance law lack an exclusionary rule. In the Wiretap Act, wire and oral communications are protected with an exclusionary rule, but electronic communications are not. Solove argues that "[s]ince e-mail has become a central mode of communication, this discrepancy is baseless."[75] Is it? Can you think of a reason why e-mail should receive lesser protection than a phone conversation, which would be protected by the exclusionary rule under the Wiretap Act? Additionally, the Stored Communications Act and Pen Register Act have no exclusionary remedies for any type of communication.

---

[74] Solove, *Surveillance Law, supra,* at 1288. Susan Freiwald contends that "the current categories of the ECPA do not cover web traffic data. At least one other category of protection is needed. Search terms entered, web-pages visited, and items viewed are neither message contents nor their to/from information." Freiwald, *Online Surveillance, supra,* at 71.

[75] Solove, *Surveillance Law, supra*, at 1282.

Orin Kerr argues the absence of an exclusionary rule in many of ECPA's provisions leads to inadequate judicial attention to ECPA. Without an exclusionary rule, Kerr contends, "criminal defendants have little incentive to raise challenges to the government's Internet surveillance practices." Therefore, many challenges to Internet surveillance practices "tend to be in civil cases between private parties that raise issues far removed from those that animated Congress to pass the statutes." Adding an exclusionary remedy, Kerr argues, would "benefit both civil libertarian and law enforcement interests alike." He writes:

> On the civil libertarian side, a suppression remedy would considerably increase judicial scrutiny of the government's Internet surveillance practices in criminal cases. The resulting judicial opinions would clarify the rules that the government must follow, serving the public interest of greater transparency. Less obviously, the change could also benefit law enforcement by altering the type and nature of the disputes over the Internet surveillance laws that courts encounter. Prosecutors would have greater control over the types of cases the courts decided, enjoy more sympathetic facts, and have a better opportunity to explain and defend law enforcement interests before the courts. The statutory law of Internet surveillance would become more like the Fourth Amendment law: a source of vital and enforceable rights that every criminal defendant can invoke, governed by relatively clear standards that by and large respect law enforcement needs and attempt to strike a balance between those needs and privacy interests.[76]

6. *The Internet vs. the Telephone.* Susan Freiwald contends that while the 1968 Wiretap Act (Title III) provided powerful and effective protection for telephone communications, ECPA in 1986 did not do the same for online communications:

> . . . [O]nline surveillance is even more susceptible to law enforcement abuse and even more threatening to privacy. Therefore, one might expect regulation of online surveillance to be more privacy-protective than traditional wiretapping law. That could not be further from the truth. The law provides dramatically less privacy protection for online activities than for traditional telephone calls and videotapings. Additionally, what makes the Wiretap Act complex makes online surveillance law chaotic. Almost all of the techniques designed to rein in law enforcement have been abandoned in the online context. And, while Congress resolved much of its ambivalence towards wiretapping in 1968, current law suggests the outright hostility of all branches of government to online privacy.[77]

In what ways does federal electronic surveillance law protect Internet communication differently from telephone communication? Should the privacy protections differ in these areas?

---

[76] Orin S. Kerr, *Lifting the "Fog" of Internet Surveillance: How a Suppression Remedy Would Change Computer Crime Law*, 54 Hastings L.J. 805, 824, 807-08 (2003).

[77] Susan Freiwald, *Online Surveillance: Remembering the Lessons of the Wiretap Act*, 56 Ala. L. Rev. 9, 14 (2004).

6. KEY LOGGING DEVICES

UNITED STATES V. SCARFO

180 F. Supp. 2d 572 (D.N.J. 2001)

POLITAN, J. . . . Acting pursuant to federal search warrants, the F.B.I. on January 15, 1999, entered Scarfo and Paolercio's business office, Merchant Services of Essex County, to search for evidence of an illegal gambling and loansharking operation. During their search of Merchant Services, the F.B.I. came across a personal computer and attempted to access its various files. They were unable to gain entry to an encrypted file named "Factors."

Suspecting the "Factors" file contained evidence of an illegal gambling and loansharking operation, the F.B.I. returned to the location and, pursuant to two search warrants, installed what is known as a "Key Logger System" ("KLS") on the computer and/or computer keyboard in order to decipher the passphrase to the encrypted file, thereby gaining entry to the file. The KLS records the keystrokes an individual enters on a personal computer's keyboard. The government utilized the KLS in order to "catch" Scarfo's passphrases to the encrypted file while he was entering them onto his keyboard. Scarfo's personal computer features a modem for communication over telephone lines and he possesses an America Online account. The F.B.I. obtained the passphrase to the "Factors" file and retrieved what is alleged to be incriminating evidence.

On June 21, 2000, a federal grand jury returned a three count indictment against the Defendants charging them with gambling and loansharking. The Defendant Scarfo then filed his motion for discovery and to suppress the evidence recovered from his computer. After oral argument was heard on July 30, 2001, the Court ordered additional briefing by the parties. In an August 7, 2001, Letter Opinion and Order, this Court expressed serious concerns over whether the government violated the wiretap statute in utilizing the KLS on Scarfo's computer. Specifically, the Court expressed concern over whether the KLS may have operated during periods when Scarfo (or any other user of his personal computer) was communicating via modem over telephone lines, thereby unlawfully intercepting wire communications without having applied for a wiretap pursuant to Title III, 18 U.S.C. § 2510.

As a result of these concerns, on August 7, 2001, this Court ordered the United States to file with the Court a report explaining fully how the KLS device functions and describing the KLS technology and how it works vis-à-vis the computer modem, Internet communications, e-mail and all other uses of a computer. In light of the government's grave concern over the national security implications such a revelation might raise, the Court permitted the United States to submit any additional evidence which would provide particular and specific reasons how and why disclosure of the KLS would jeopardize both ongoing and future domestic criminal investigations and national security interests.

The United States responded by filing a request for modification of this Court's August 7, 2001, Letter Opinion and Order so as to comply with the procedures set forth in the Classified Information Procedures Act, Title 18, United States Code, Appendix III, § 1 *et seq.* ("CIPA"). [The FBI contended that a detailed disclosure of how the KLS worked would negatively affect national security and that this information was classified. After an in camera, ex parte hearing with several officials from the Attorney General's office and the FBI, the court granted the government's request not to release the details of how KLS functioned. Instead, the government would provide Scarfo and his attorneys with an unclassified summary about how KLS worked. Based on that summary, Scarfo contended that the KLS violated the Fourth Amendment because the KLS had the capability of collecting data on all of his keystrokes, not merely those of his passphrase.]

Where a search warrant is obtained, the Fourth Amendment requires a certain modicum of particularity in the language of the warrant with respect to the area and items to be searched and/or seized. The particularity requirement exists so that law enforcement officers are constrained from undertaking a boundless and exploratory rummaging through one's personal property. . . . Because the encrypted file could not be accessed via traditional investigative means, Judge Haneke's Order permitted law enforcement officers to "install and leave behind software, firmware, and/or hardware equipment which will monitor the inputted data entered on Nicodemo S. Scarfo's computer in the TARGET LOCATION so that the F.B.I. can capture the password necessary to decrypt computer files by recording the key related information as they are entered." The Order also allowed the F.B.I. to

> search for and seize business records in whatever form they are kept (e.g., written, mechanically or computer maintained and any necessary computer hardware, including computers, computer hard drives, floppy disks or other storage disks or tapes as necessary to access such information, as well as, seizing the mirror hard drive to preserve configuration files, public keys, private keys, and other information that may be of assistance in interpreting the password) — including address and telephone books and electronic storage devices; ledgers and other accounting-type records; banking records and statements; travel records; correspondence; memoranda; notes; calendars; and diaries — that contain information about the identities and whereabouts of conspirators, betting customers and victim debtors, and/or that otherwise reveal the origin, receipt, concealment or distribution of criminal proceeds relating to illegal gambling, loansharking and other racketeering offenses.

On its face, the Order is very comprehensive and lists the items, including the evidence in the encrypted file, to be seized with more than sufficient specificity. *See Andresen v. Maryland,* 427 U.S. 463, 480-81 (1976) (defendant's general warrant claim rejected where search warrant contained, among other things, a lengthy list of specified and particular items to be seized). One would be hard pressed to draft a more specified or detailed search warrant than the May 8, 1999 Order. Indeed, it could not be written with more particularity. It specifically identifies each piece of evidence the F.B.I. sought which would be linked to the particular crimes the F.B.I. had probable cause to believe were committed. Most importantly, Judge Haneke's Order clearly specifies the key piece of the puzzle the F.B.I. sought — Scarfo's passphrase to the encrypted file.

That the KLS certainly recorded keystrokes typed into Scarfo's keyboard *other* than the searched-for passphrase is of no consequence. This does not, as Scarfo argues, convert the limited search for the passphrase into a general exploratory search. During many lawful searches, police officers may not know the exact nature of the incriminating evidence sought until they stumble upon it. Just like searches for incriminating documents in a closet or filing cabinet, it is true that during a search for a passphrase "some innocuous [items] will be at least cursorily perused in order to determine whether they are among those [items] to be seized."

Hence, "no tenet of the Fourth Amendment prohibits a search merely because it cannot be performed with surgical precision." Where proof of wrongdoing depends upon documents or computer passphrases whose precise nature cannot be known in advance, law enforcement officers must be afforded the leeway to wade through a potential morass of information in the target location to find the particular evidence which is properly specified in the warrant. . . . Accordingly, Scarfo's claim that the warrants were written and executed as general warrants is rejected. . . .

The principal mystery surrounding this case was whether the KLS intercepted a wire communication in violation of the wiretap statute by recording keystrokes of e-mail or other communications made over a telephone or cable line while the modem operated. These are the only conceivable wire communications which might emanate from Scarfo's computer and potentially fall under the wiretap statute. . . .

The KLS, which is the exclusive property of the F.B.I., was devised by F.B.I. engineers using previously developed techniques in order to obtain a target's key and key-related information. As part of the investigation into Scarfo's computer, the F.B.I. "did not install and operate any component which would search for and record data entering or exiting the computer from the transmission pathway through the modem attached to the computer." Neither did the F.B.I. "install or operate any KLS component which would search for or record any fixed data stored within the computer."

Recognizing that Scarfo's computer had a modem and thus was capable of transmitting electronic communications via the modem, the F.B.I. configured the KLS to avoid intercepting electronic communications typed on the keyboard and simultaneously transmitted in real time via the communication ports. . . . Hence, when the modem was operating, the KLS did not record keystrokes. It was designed to prohibit the capture of keyboard keystrokes whenever the modem operated. Since Scarfo's computer possessed no other means of communicating with another computer save for the modem, the KLS did not intercept any wire communications. Accordingly, the Defendants' motion to suppress evidence for violation of Title III is denied. . . .

NOTES & QUESTIONS

1. ***Did the Court Need to Reach the Main Issue?*** Judge Politan discusses the government's actions in *Scarfo* as if a suppression remedy were available for Scarfo. He finds that a search warrant was not required under the Wiretap Act because of the way in which the FBI's keylogging device worked; the KLS did not function when the modem was operating. But there was a simpler way to deny Scarfo's motion: the Wiretap Act does not provide a suppression

remedy for electronic communications. Did Judge Politan assume that a remedy existed according to some theory similar to the *McVeigh* case? Was he simply eager to rule on the KLS issue?

2. ***Recording Thoughts and Ideas.*** Consider the following argument by Raymond Ku:

> . . . By monitoring what an individual enters into her computer as she enters it, the government has the ability to monitor thought itself. Keystroke-recording devices allow the government to record formless thoughts and ideas an individual never intended to share with anyone, never intended to save on the hard drive and never intended to preserve for future reference in any form. The devices also allow the government to record thoughts and ideas the individual may have rejected the moment they were typed. . . .
>
> . . . [T]he techniques used in the Scarfo case bring us closer to a world in which the only privacy we are guaranteed is the privacy found in the confines of our own minds.[78]

3. ***Old Technologies in New Bottles?*** A common defense of new technological surveillance devices is that they are analogous to existing technologies. Carnivore can be likened to pen registers; the keystroke monitor in the Scarfo case can be analogized to a bug. To what extent are these analogies apt? Are new surveillance technologies, simply old forms of surveillance in new bottles? Or is there something different involved? If so, what is new with these technologies, and how ought they be regulated?

4. ***Magic Lantern.*** The FBI has developed technology through which a keystroke logging device can be installed into a person's computer through a computer virus that is e-mailed to the suspect's computer. The virus keeps track of keystrokes and secretly transmits the information to the government. Thus, the government can install a keystroke logging device without ever having to physically enter one's office or home. Recall your Fourth Amendment analysis of Carnivore. How does Magic Lantern differ with respect to its Fourth Amendment implications? How does your Fourth Amendment analysis of Magic Lantern differ from that of the keystroke logging device in *Scarfo*?

D. NATIONAL SECURITY AND FOREIGN INTELLIGENCE

1. IS NATIONAL SECURITY DIFFERENT?

Should the law treat investigations involving national security differently than other criminal investigations? In Fourth Amendment law, this question has long remained unresolved. In a footnote to *Katz v. United States,* 389 U.S. 347 (1967), the Court stated that perhaps a warrant might not be required in situations involving national security:

---

[78] Raymond Ku, *Think Twice Before You Type*, 163 N.J. L.J. 747 (Feb. 19, 2001).

> Whether safeguards other than prior authorization by a magistrate would satisfy the Fourth Amendment in a situation involving the national security is a question not presented by this case.

Justice White, in a concurring opinion, declared:

> In joining the Court's opinion, I note the Court's acknowledgment that there are circumstance in which it is reasonable to search without a warrant. In this connection . . . the Court points out that today's decision does not reach national security cases. Wiretapping to protect the security of the Nation has been authorized by successive Presidents. The present Administration would apparently save national security cases from restrictions against wiretapping. We should not require the warrant procedure and the magistrate's judgment if the President of the United States or his chief legal officer, the Attorney General, has considered the requirements of national security and authorized electronic surveillance as reasonable.

Justices Douglas and Brennan, in another concurring opinion, took issue with Justice White:

> . . . Neither the President nor the Attorney General is a magistrate. In matters where they believe national security may be involved they are not detached, disinterested, and neutral as a court or magistrate must be. . . .
>
> There is, so far as I understand constitutional history, no distinction under the Fourth Amendment between types of crimes. Article III, § 3, gives "treason" a very narrow definition and puts restrictions on its proof. But the Fourth Amendment draws no lines between various substantive offenses. The arrests on cases of "hot pursuit" and the arrests on visible or other evidence of probable cause cut across the board and are not peculiar to any kind of crime.
>
> I would respect the present lines of distinction and not improvise because a particular crime seems particularly heinous. When the Framers took that step, as they did with treason, the worst crime of all, they made their purpose manifest.

UNITED STATES V. UNITED STATES DISTRICT COURT (THE *KEITH* CASE)

407 U.S. 297 (1972)

POWELL, J. . . . The issue before us is an important one for the people of our country and their Government. It involves the delicate question of the President's power, acting through the Attorney General, to authorize electronic surveillance in internal security matters without prior judicial approval. Successive Presidents for more than one-quarter of a century have authorized such surveillance in varying degrees, without guidance from the Congress or a definitive decision of this Court. This case brings the issue here for the first time. Its resolution is a matter of national concern, requiring sensitivity both to the Government's right to protect itself from unlawful subversion and attack and to the citizen's right to be secure in his privacy against unreasonable Government intrusion.

This case arises from a criminal proceeding in the United States District Court for the Eastern District of Michigan, in which the United States charged three defendants with conspiracy to destroy Government property. . . . One of the defendants, Plamondon, was charged with the dynamite bombing of an office of the Central Intelligence Agency in Ann Arbor, Michigan.

Title III of the Omnibus Crime Control and Safe Streets Act, 18 U.S.C. §§ 2510-2520, authorizes the use of electronic surveillance for classes of crimes carefully specified in 18 U.S.C. § 2516. Such surveillance is subject to prior court order. Section 2518 sets forth the detailed and particularized application necessary to obtain such an order as well as carefully circumscribed conditions for its use. The Act represents a comprehensive attempt by Congress to promote more effective control of crime while protecting the privacy of individual thought and expression. Much of Title III was drawn to meet the constitutional requirements for electronic surveillance enunciated by this Court in *Berger v. New York,* and *Katz v. United States*.

The Government relies on § 2511(3). It argues that "in excepting national security surveillances from the Act's warrant requirement Congress recognized the President's authority to conduct such surveillances without prior judicial approval." The section thus is viewed as a recognition or affirmance of a constitutional authority in the President to conduct warrantless domestic security surveillance such as that involved in this case.

We think the language of § 2511(3), as well as the legislative history of the statute, refutes this interpretation. The relevant language is that: "Nothing contained in this chapter . . . shall limit the constitutional power of the President to take such measures as he deems necessary to protect . . ." against the dangers specified. At most, this is an implicit recognition that the President does have certain powers in the specified areas. Few would doubt this, as the section refers — among other things — to protection "against actual or potential attack or other hostile acts of a foreign power." But so far as the use of the President's electronic surveillance power is concerned, the language is essentially neutral.

Section 2511(3) certainly confers no power, as the language is wholly inappropriate for such a purpose. It merely provides that the Act shall not be interpreted to limit or disturb such power as the President may have under the Constitution. In short, Congress simply left presidential powers where it found them.

Our present inquiry, though important, is . . . a narrow one. It addresses a question left open by *Katz*:

> Whether safeguards other than prior authorization by a magistrate would satisfy the Fourth Amendment in a situation involving the national security. . . .

We begin the inquiry by noting that the President of the United States has the fundamental duty, under Art. II, § 1, of the Constitution, to "preserve, protect and defend the Constitution of the United States." Implicit in that duty is the power to protect our Government against those who would subvert or overthrow it by unlawful means. In the discharge of this duty, the President — through the Attorney General — may find it necessary to employ electronic surveillance to obtain intelligence information on the plans of those who plot unlawful acts against the Government. The use of such surveillance in internal security cases has been sanctioned more or less continuously by various Presidents and Attorneys General since July 1946.

Though the Government and respondents debate their seriousness and magnitude, threats and acts of sabotage against the Government exist in sufficient number to justify investigative powers with respect to them.[79] The covertness and complexity of potential unlawful conduct against the Government and the necessary dependency of many conspirators upon the telephone make electronic surveillance an effective investigatory instrument in certain circumstances. The marked acceleration in technological developments and sophistication in their use have resulted in new techniques for the planning, commission, and concealment of criminal activities. It would be contrary to the public interest for Government to deny to itself the prudent and lawful employment of those very techniques which are employed against the Government and its lawabiding citizens. . . .

But a recognition of these elementary truths does not make the employment by Government of electronic surveillance a welcome development — even when employed with restraint and under judicial supervision. There is, understandably, a deep-seated uneasiness and apprehension that this capability will be used to intrude upon cherished privacy of law-abiding citizens. We look to the Bill of Rights to safeguard this privacy. Though physical entry of the home is the chief evil against which the wording of the Fourth Amendment is directed, its broader spirit now shields private speech from unreasonable surveillance. Our decision in *Katz* refused to lock the Fourth Amendment into instances of actual physical trespass.

. . . [N]ational security cases, moreover, often reflect a convergence of First and Fourth Amendment values not present in cases of "ordinary" crime. Though the investigative duty of the executive may be stronger in such cases, so also is there greater jeopardy to constitutionally protected speech. . . . The danger to political dissent is acute where the Government attempts to act under so vague a concept as the power to protect "domestic security." Given the difficulty of defining the domestic security interest, the danger of abuse in acting to protect that interest becomes apparent.

The price of lawful public dissent must not be a dread of subjection to an unchecked surveillance power. Nor must the fear of unauthorized official eavesdropping deter vigorous citizen dissent and discussion of Government action in private conversation. For private dissent, no less than open public discourse, is essential to our free society.

As the Fourth Amendment is not absolute in its terms, our task is to examine and balance the basic values at stake in this case: the duty of Government to protect the domestic security, and the potential danger posed by unreasonable surveillance to individual privacy and free expression. If the legitimate need of Government to safeguard domestic security requires the use of electronic surveillance, the question is whether the needs of citizens for privacy and the free expression may not be better protected by requiring a warrant before such surveillance is undertaken. We must also ask whether a warrant requirement

[79] The Government asserts that there were 1,562 bombing incidents in the United States from January 1, 1971, to July 1, 1971, most of which involved Government related facilities. Respondents dispute these statistics as incorporating many frivolous incidents as well as bombings against nongovernmental facilities. The precise level of this activity, however, is not relevant to the disposition of this case.

would unduly frustrate the efforts of Government to protect itself from acts of subversion and overthrow directed against it. . . .

[C]ontentions in behalf of a complete exemption from the warrant requirement, when urged on behalf of the President and the national security in its domestic implications, merit the most careful consideration. We certainly do not reject them lightly, especially at a time of worldwide ferment and when civil disorders in this country are more prevalent than in the less turbulent periods of our history. There is, no doubt, pragmatic force to the Government's position.

[W]e do not think a case has been made for the requested departure from Fourth Amendment standards. The circumstances described do not justify complete exemption of domestic security surveillance from prior judicial scrutiny. Official surveillance, whether its purpose be criminal investigation or ongoing intelligence gathering, risks infringement of constitutionally protected privacy of speech. Security surveillances are especially sensitive because of the inherent vagueness of the domestic security concept, the necessarily broad and continuing nature of intelligence gathering, and the temptation to utilize such surveillances to oversee political dissent. We recognize, as we have before, the constitutional basis of the President's domestic security role, but we think it must be exercised in a manner compatible with the Fourth Amendment. In this case we hold that this requires an appropriate prior warrant procedure.

We cannot accept the Government's argument that internal security matters are too subtle and complex for judicial evaluation. Courts regularly deal with the most difficult issues of our society. There is no reason to believe that federal judges will be insensitive to or uncomprehending of the issues involved in domestic security cases. . . . If the threat is too subtle or complex for our senior law enforcement officers to convey its significance to a court, one may question whether there is probable cause for surveillance.

Nor do we believe prior judicial approval will fracture the secrecy essential to official intelligence gathering. The investigation of criminal activity has long involved imparting sensitive information to judicial officers who have respected the confidentialities involved. Judges may be counted upon to be especially conscious of security requirements in national security cases. Title III of the Omnibus Crime Control and Safe Streets Act already has imposed this responsibility on the judiciary in connection with such crimes as espionage, sabotage, and treason, §§ 2516(1)(a) and (c), each of which may involve domestic as well as foreign security threats. Moreover, a warrant application involves no public or adversary proceedings: it is an ex parte request before a magistrate or judge. Whatever security dangers clerical and secretarial personnel may pose can be minimized by proper administrative measures, possibly to the point of allowing the Government itself to provide the necessary clerical assistance. . . .

We emphasize, before concluding this opinion, the scope of our decision. As stated at the outset, this case involves only the domestic aspects of national security. We have not addressed and express no opinion as to, the issues which may be involved with respect to activities of foreign powers or their agents. . . .

Moreover, we do not hold that the same type of standards and procedures prescribed by Title III are necessarily applicable to this case. We recognize that domestic security surveillance may involve different policy and practical considerations from the surveillance of "ordinary crime." The gathering of security intelligence is often long range and involves the interrelation of various sources and types of information. The exact targets of such surveillance may be more difficult to identify than in surveillance operations against many types of crime specified in Title III. Often, too, the emphasis of domestic intelligence gathering is on the prevention of unlawful activity or the enhancement of the Government's preparedness for some possible future crisis or emergency. Thus, the focus of domestic surveillance may be less precise than that directed against more conventional types of crime.

Given those potential distinctions between Title III criminal surveillances and those involving the domestic security, Congress may wish to consider protective standards for the latter which differ from those already prescribed for specified crimes in Title III. Different standards may be compatible with the Fourth Amendment if they are reasonable both in relation to the legitimate need of Government for intelligence information and the protected rights of our citizens. For the warrant application may vary according to the governmental interest to be enforced and the nature of citizen rights deserving protection. . . .

DOUGLAS, J. concurring. While I join in the opinion of the Court, I add these words in support of it. . . .

If the Warrant Clause were held inapplicable here, then the federal intelligence machine would literally enjoy unchecked discretion. Here, federal agents wish to rummage for months on end through every conversation, no matter how intimate or personal, carried over selected telephone lines, simply to seize those few utterances which may add to their sense of the pulse of a domestic underground. . . .

That "domestic security" is said to be involved here does not draw this case outside the mainstream of Fourth Amendment law. Rather, the recurring desire of reigning officials to employ dragnet techniques to intimidate their critics lies at the core of that prohibition. For it was such excesses as the use of general warrants and the writs of assistance that led to the ratification of the Fourth Amendment. . . .

[W]e are currently in the throes of another national seizure of paranoia, resembling the hysteria which surrounded the Alien and Sedition Acts, the Palmer Raids, and the McCarthy era. Those who register dissent or who petition their governments for redress are subjected to scrutiny by grand juries, by the FBI, or even by the military. Their associates are interrogated. Their homes are bugged and their telephones are wiretapped. They are befriended by secret government informers. Their patriotism and loyalty are questioned. . . .

We have as much or more to fear from the erosion of our sense of privacy and independence by the omnipresent electronic ear of the Government as we do from the likelihood that fomenters of domestic upheaval will modify our form of governing.

NOTES & QUESTIONS

1. ***Domestic Security vs. Foreign Threats.*** The *Keith* Court draws a distinction between electronic surveillance in (1) criminal investigations, regulated under Title III (now ECPA); (2) domestic security investigations; and (3) investigations involving "activities of foreign powers and their agents."

   Regarding the first category, the *Keith* Court stated that there was no debate regarding "the necessity of obtaining a warrant in the surveillance of crimes unrelated to the national security interest." Regarding the second category, the focus of the *Keith* Court's opinion, its holding was that the Fourth Amendment required the issuing of a warrant in domestic security investigations. It also held that the precise requirements for issuing a requirement to investigate domestic security need not be the same as for Title III criminal surveillance. Finally, it stated that it did not address issues involving foreign powers and their agents. Does this tripartite distinction seem useful as a policy matter?

   How does one distinguish between security surveillance (category two) and surveillance for ordinary crime (category one)? Daniel Solove argues that such a distinction ought not to be made: "'National security' has often been abused as a justification not only for surveillance but also for maintaining the secrecy of government records as well as violating the civil liberties of citizens." He further contends that "the line between national security and regular criminal activities is very blurry, especially in an age of terrorism."[80] On the other hand, Richard Posner contends that the word "unreasonable" in the Fourth Amendment "invites a wide-ranging comparison between the benefits and costs of a search or seizure." He proposes a "sliding scale" standard where "the level of suspicion require to justify the search or seizure should fall . . . as the magnitude of the crime under investigation rises."[81] Paul Rosenzweig argues: "In this time of terror, some adjustment of the balance between liberty and security is both necessary and appropriate. . . . [T]he very text of the Fourth Amendment — with its prohibition only of 'unreasonable' searches and seizures — explicitly recognizes the need to balance the harm averted against the extent of governmental intrusion."[82]

2. ***The Church Committee Report.*** In 1976, a congressional committee led by Senator Frank Church (called the "Church Committee") engaged in an extensive investigation of government national security surveillance. It found extensive abuses, which it chronicled in its famous report known as the Church Committee Report:

   > Too many people have been spied upon by too many Government agencies and too much information has been collected. The Government has often undertaken the secret surveillance of citizens on the basis of their political beliefs, even when those beliefs posed no threat of violence or illegal acts on

---

[80] Solove, *Surveillance Law,* 72 Geo. Wash. L. Rev. 1264, 1301-02 (2004).

[81] Richard Posner, *Law, Pragmatism, and Democracy* 303 (2003); *see also* Akhil Reed Amar, *The Constitution and Criminal Procedure* 31 (1997) ("The core of the Fourth Amendment . . . is neither a warrant nor probable cause but reasonableness.").

[82] Paul Rosenzweig, *Civil Liberty and the Response to Terrorism,* 42 Duq. L. Rev. 663 (2004).

> behalf of a hostile foreign power. The Government, operating primarily through secret informants, but also using other intrusive techniques such as wiretaps, microphone "bugs," surreptitious mail opening, and break-ins, has swept in vast amounts of information about the personal lives, views, and associations of American citizens. . . . Groups and individuals have been harassed and disrupted because of their political views and their lifestyles. Investigations have been based upon vague standards whose breadth made excessive collection inevitable. . . .
>
> The FBI's COINTELPRO — counterintelligence program — was designed to "disrupt" groups and "neutralize" individuals deemed to be threats to domestic security. The FBI resorted to counterintelligence tactics in part because its chief officials believed that existing law could not control the activities of certain dissident groups, and that court decisions had tied the hands of the intelligence community. Whatever opinion one holds about the policies of the targeted groups, many of the tactics employed by the FBI were indisputably degrading to a free society. . . .
>
> Since the early 1930's, intelligence agencies have frequently wiretapped and bugged American citizens without the benefit of judicial warrant. . . .
>
> There has been, in short, a clear and sustained failure by those responsible to control the intelligence community and to ensure its accountability.[83]

The Church Committee Report was influential in the creation of FISA as well as the Attorney General Guidelines.

3. ***National Security vs. Civil Liberties.*** Eric Posner and Adrian Vermeule argue that the legislature and judiciary should defer to the executive in times of emergency and that it is justified to curtail civil liberties when national security is threatened:

> The essential feature of the emergency is that national security is threatened; because the executive is the only organ of government with the resources, power, and flexibility to respond to threats to national security, it is natural, inevitable, and desirable for power to flow to this branch of government. Congress rationally acquiesces; courts rationally defer. . . .
>
> During emergencies, when new threats appear, the balance shifts; government should and will reduce civil liberties in order to enhance security in those domains where the two must be traded off. . . .
>
> In emergencies . . . judges are at sea, even more so than are executive officials. The novelty of the threats and of the necessary responses makes judicial routines and evolved legal rules seem inapposite, even obstructive. There is a premium on the executive's capacities for swift, vigorous, and secretive action.[84]

4. ***The Fourth Amendment and Foreign Intelligence Surveillance.*** *Keith* did not address how the Fourth Amendment would govern foreign intelligence surveillance (category three). Circuit courts examining the issue have

---

[83] *Intelligence Activities and the Rights of Americans* (Vol. 2), Final Report of the Select Committee to Study Government Operations with Respect to Intelligence Activities 5, 10, 15 (Apr. 26, 1976).

[84] Eric A. Posner & Adrian Vermeule, *Terror in the Balance: Security, Liberty, and the Courts* 4, 5, 18 (2006). For another defense of the curtailment of civil liberties for national security, see Richard A. Posner, *Not a Suicide Pact: The Constitution in a Time of National Emergency* (2006).

concluded that at a minimum, no warrant is required by the Fourth Amendment for foreign intelligence surveillance. In *United States v. Butenko*, 494 F.2d 593 (3d Cir. 1974) (en banc), the court justified this conclusion by reasoning that "foreign intelligence gathering is a clandestine and highly unstructured activity, and the need for electronic surveillance often cannot be anticipated in advance." Reaching a similar conclusion in *United States v. Truong Dinh Hung*, 629 F.2d 908 (4th Cir. 1980), the court reasoned: "[T]he needs of the executive are so compelling in the area of foreign intelligence, unlike the area of domestic security, that a uniform warrant requirement would, following *Keith,* 'unduly frustrate' the President in carrying out his foreign affairs responsibilities."

2. THE FOREIGN INTELLIGENCE SURVEILLANCE ACT

In the *Keith* case, the Court explicitly refused to address whether the Fourth Amendment would require a warrant for surveillance of agents of foreign powers: "[T]his case involves only the domestic aspects of national security. We have not addressed and express no opinion as to, the issues which may be involved with respect to activities of foreign powers or their agents but that surveillance without a warrant might be constitutional in cases where the target was an agent of a foreign power."

The Foreign Intelligence Surveillance Act (FISA) of 1978, Pub. L. No. 95-511, codified at 50 U.S.C. §§ 1801–1811, establishes standards and procedures for use of electronic surveillance to collect "foreign intelligence" within the United States. § 1804(a)(7)(B). FISA creates a different regime than ECPA, the legal regime that governs electronic surveillance for law enforcement purposes. The regime created by FISA is designed primarily for intelligence gathering agencies to regulate how they gain general intelligence about foreign powers and agents of foreign powers within the borders of the United States. In contrast, the regime of ECPA is designed for domestic law enforcement to govern the gathering of information for criminal investigations involving people in United States.

Applicability of FISA. When does FISA govern rather than ECPA? FISA generally applies when foreign intelligence gathering is "a significant purpose" of the investigation. 50 U.S.C. § 1804(a)(7)(B) and §1823(a)(7)(B). The language of "a significant purpose" comes from the USA PATRIOT Act of 2001. Prior to the USA PATRIOT Act, FISA as interpreted by the courts required that the collection of foreign intelligence be the primary purpose for surveillance. After the USA PATRIOT Act, foreign intelligence gathering need no longer be the primary purpose. A further expansion of the FISA occurred in 2008 with amendments to that law, which we discuss below.

The Foreign Intelligence Surveillance Court (FISC). Requests for FISA orders are reviewed by a special court of federal district court judges. The USA PATRIOT Act increased the number of judges on the FISC from 7 to 11. 50 U.S.C. § 1803(a). The proceedings are ex parte, with the Department of Justice

(DOJ) making the applications to the court on behalf of the CIA and other agencies. The Court meets in secret, and its proceedings are generally not revealed to the public or to the targets of the surveillance.

Court Orders. The legal test for surveillance under FISA is not whether probable cause exists that the party to be monitored is involved in criminal activity. Rather, the court must find probable cause that the party to be monitored is a "foreign power" or "an agent of a foreign power." § 1801. Therefore, unlike ECPA or the Fourth Amendment, FISA surveillance is not tied to any required showing of a connection to criminal activity. However, if the monitored party is a "United States person" (a citizen or permanent resident alien), the government must establish probable cause that the party's activities "may" or "are about to" involve a criminal violation. § 1801(b)(2)(A).

The number of FISA electronic surveillance orders expanded from 199 orders (1979) to 886 (1999).[85] In 2001, the FISA court approved 934 applications for electronic surveillance orders. None were denied.[86] The USA PATRIOT Act of 2001 eased the standard for obtaining a FISA order. There were 1,228 orders in 2002, 1,727 orders in 2003 (4 were denied), and 1,758 applications in 2004. This represents an increase of 88 percent from 2001.

Surveillance Without Court Orders. In certain circumstances, FISA authorizes surveillance without having to first obtain a court order. § 1802. In particular, the surveillance must be "solely directed at" obtaining intelligence exclusively from "foreign powers." § 1802(a). There must be "no substantial likelihood that the surveillance will acquire the contents of any communications to which a United States person is a party." § 1802(a)(1)(B). Electronic surveillance without a court order requires the authorization of the President, through the Attorney General, in writing under oath. § 1802(a)(1).

Video Surveillance. Unlike ECPA, FISA explicitly regulates video surveillance. In order to have court approval for video surveillance, the FISA requires the government to submit, among other things, "a detailed description of the nature of the information sought and the type of communications or activities to be subjected to the surveillance," § 1804(a)(6); "a certification . . . that such information cannot reasonably be obtained by normal investigative techniques," § 1804(a)(7); and "a statement of the period of time for which the electronic surveillance is required to be maintained," § 1804(a)(10). Video surveillance orders can last for 90 days.

The FISA Amendments Act. In 2008, Congress enacted significant amendments to FISA. The FISA Amendments Act (FAA) was passed in response to the revelation in 2005 that since 9/11 the National Security Agency (NSA) was engaging in an extensive program of warrantless wiretapping of international phone

---

[85] Foreign Intelligence Surveillance Act Orders 1979-1999, http://www/epic.org/privacy/wiretap/stats/fisa_stats.html.

[86] Office of Attorney General, *2001 Annual FISA Report to Congress,* available at www.usdoj.gov/o4foia/readingrooms/2001annualfisareporttocongress.htm.

calls. Subsequently, several lawsuits were brought against the telecommunications companies that participated in the surveillance for violating FISA and ECPA. One of the most controversial aspects of the FAA was a grant of retroactive immunity to these companies. The NSA surveillance program and the ensuing litigation will be discussed later on in this chapter.

In its other aspects, the FAA both expanded the government's surveillance abilities and added new privacy protections. The FAA explicitly permits collection of information from U.S. telecommunications facilities where it is not possible in advance to know whether a communication is purely international (that is, all parties to it are located outside of the United States) or whether the communication involves a foreign power or its agents. David Kris explains, "With the advent of web-based communication and other developments, the government cannot always determine — consistently, reliably, and in real time — the location of parties to an e-mail message."[87] It is also possible to collect information and then examine it (through data mining) to look for links with a foreign power or its agents. The perceived need, Kris states, was for a kind of "vacuum-cleaner" capacity that would enable the government to sift through large amounts of information without meeting FISA's traditional warrant requirements.

FAA amends FISA to permit "targeting of persons reasonably believed to be located outside the United States to acquire foreign intelligence information." § 702(a). The person targeted must be a non-USA person, or certain more restrictive measures apply. §§ 703–04. The critical substantive requirements are that the "target" of the surveillance be someone overseas and that a "significant purpose" of the surveillance be to acquire "foreign intelligence information," which is broadly defined.

The collection of this information must be carried out in accordance with certain "targeting procedures" to ensure that the collection is directed at persons located outside the United States. § 702(c)(1)(A). The acquisition must also involve new minimization procedures, which the Attorney General is to adopt. § 702(e). The Justice Department and the Director of National Intelligence must certify in advance of the surveillance activity that targeting and minimization procedures meet the statutory standards and that "a significant purpose" of the surveillance is to acquire foreign intelligence information. § 702(g)(2). The FAA also states that the government may not engage in a kind of "reverse-targeting" — the government cannot target "a person reasonably believed to be outside the United States if the purpose of such acquisition is to target a particular, known person reasonably believed to be in the United States." § 702(b)(2).

The FISC is to review certifications and the targeting and minimization procedures adopted. If a certification does not "contain all the required elements" or the procedures "are not consistent with the requirements" of the FAA or the

---

[87] David Kris, *A Guide to the New FISA Bill, Part I*, Balkanization (June 21, 2008), at http://balkin.blogspot.com/2008/06/guide-to-new-fisa-bill-part-i.html. Kris is co-author of the leading treatise, J. Douglas Wilson & David Kris, *National Security Investigations and Prosecutions* (2007).

Fourth Amendment to the U.S. Constitution, the FISC is to issue an order directing the government to correct any deficiencies. § 702(i)(3).

As for its expansion of privacy protections, the FAA requires that the FISC approve surveillance of a U.S. citizen abroad based on a showing that includes a finding that the person is "an agent of a foreign power, or an officer or employee of a foreign power." Previously, FISA did not regulate surveillance of targets, whether U.S. citizens or not, when located outside the United States. The FAA also contains new mechanisms for congressional oversight and crafts new audit functions for the Inspector Generals of the Department Justice.

GLOBAL RELIEF FOUNDATION, INC. V. O'NEIL

207 F. Supp. 779 (N.D. Ill. 2002)

. . . [A]gents of the FBI arrived at the corporate headquarters of Global Relief [a U.S.-based Islamic humanitarian relief organization] and the home of its executive director on December 14, 2001 and seized a considerable amount of material they felt was relevant to their investigation of Global Relief's activities. As the defendants have conceded in their briefs, no warrant had been obtained before the FBI arrived either at Global Relief's headquarters or the executive director's residence. Nevertheless, FISA includes a provision which states that, when the Attorney General declares that "an emergency situation exists with respect to the execution of a search to obtain foreign intelligence information" prior to the Foreign Intelligence Surveillance Court acting on the application, a warrantless search is authorized. 50 U.S.C. § 1824(e)(1)(B)(i). When such an emergency situation arises, the government must submit a warrant application to the Foreign Intelligence Surveillance Court within 72 hours of the warrantless search for approval. *See* 50 U.S.C. § 1824(e). In this case, the failure of the FBI agents to present a FISA warrant on December 14 was caused by the Assistant Attorney General's declaration that an emergency situation existed with respect to the targeted documents and material. The defendants did submit a warrant application to the Foreign Intelligence Surveillance Court on December 15, as required by 50 U.S.C. § 1824(e). We have reviewed the warrant that issued and the submissions to the Foreign Intelligence Surveillance Court in support of that warrant.

We conclude that the FISA application established probable cause to believe that Global Relief and the executive director were agents of a foreign power, as that term is defined for FISA purposes, at the time the search was conducted and the application was granted. . . . Given the sensitive nature of the information upon which we have relied in making this determination and the Attorney General's sworn assertion that disclosure of the underlying information would harm national security, it would be improper for us to elaborate further on this subject.

This Court has concluded that disclosure of the information we have reviewed could substantially undermine ongoing investigations required to apprehend the conspirators behind the September 11 murders and undermine the ability of law enforcement agencies to reduce the possibility of terrorist crimes in the future. Furthermore, this Court is persuaded that the search and seizure made by the FBI on December 14 were authorized by FISA. Accordingly, we decline plaintiff's request that we declare the search invalid and order the immediate return of all items seized.

NOTES & QUESTIONS

1. ***Probable Cause.*** Searches under the Wiretap Act require a "super warrant," including a showing of probable cause that an individual has committed or is about to commit an enumerated offense. 18 U.S.C. § 2518(3). What is the required showing of probable cause for a FISA search? FISA requires a judicial finding, as the *O'Neill* case indicates, that probable cause exists to believe that the target is an agent of a foreign power. It also states that no U.S. person can be considered an agent of a foreign power based solely on First Amendment activities.
2. ***Defendants' Rights?*** In *Global Relief Foundation*, the court finds that disclosure of the information that it reviewed in deciding on the validity of the search was not to be revealed to the defendant because it "could substantially undermine ongoing investigations required to apprehend the conspirators behind the September 11 murders and undermine the ability of law enforcement agencies to reduce the possibility of terrorist crimes in the future." However, FISA requires that defendants receive notice about "any information obtained or derived from an electronic surveillance of that aggrieved person" pursuant to FISA when the government seeks to use information at trial or other official proceedings. 50 U.S.C. § 1806(c).
3. ***The Three* Keith *Categories.*** Recall the *Keith* Court's distinction between electronic surveillance in (1) criminal investigations; (2) domestic security investigations; and (3) investigations involving "activities of foreign powers and their agents." Today, ECPA regulates electronic surveillance in criminal investigations (category one above). The Foreign Intelligence Surveillance Act (FISA), as enacted in 1978, regulates electronic and other kinds of surveillance in cases involving foreign powers and their agents (category three).

   What then of the *Keith* category of "domestic security investigations" (category two)? Recall that the defendants in the underlying criminal proceeding were charged with a conspiracy to destroy government property. One of the defendants, for example, was charged with "the dynamite bombing" of a CIA office in Michigan. *Keith* makes it clear that it would be consistent with the Fourth Amendment for Congress to create different statutory requirements for issuing warrants for surveillance in cases involving domestic security. But Congress has not enacted such rules, and, as a consequence, law enforcement is required to carry out surveillance of criminal activities similar to those in *Keith* under the requirements of Title III and other parts of ECPA.

   This state of affairs remains unaltered by the "lone wolf" amendment to FISA in 2004. That year, Congress amended FISA to include any non-U.S. person who "engages in international terrorism or activities in preparation therefor" in the definition of "agent of a foreign power." This revised definition sunsets on December 31, 2009. The change means that the "lone wolf" terrorist need not be tied to a foreign power, but must be a non-U.S. person engaged in or plotting "international terrorism." FISA defines "international terrorism" as involving, among other things, activities that "[o]ccur totally outside the U.S., or transcend national boundaries in terms of the means by which they accomplished, the persons they appear intended to coerce or intimidate, or the locale in which their perpetrators operate or seek asylum." 50 U.S.C. § 1801(c). As an illustration of the coverage of the "Lone Wolf" amendment, it would not cover Timothy McVeigh, the Oklahoma City bomber.

4. ***A New Agency for Domestic Intelligence?*** Francesca Bignami notes that in Europe, one agency gathers intelligence on threats abroad posed by foreign governments, and one agency "is charged with gathering intelligence at home, on activities sponsored by foreign powers (counter-intelligence) as well as on home-grown security threats."[88] Both of these agencies are generally overseen not by judiciary, but by legislative and executive branches. Both intelligence agencies generally carry out surveillance under a more permissive set of legal rules than the domestic police. In contrast, in the United States, the FBI is charged with both domestic intelligence investigations and criminal investigations of violations of federal law.

   Judge Richard Posner has emerged as the leading critic of the assignment of this double function to the FBI. He contends that the combination of criminal investigation and domestic intelligence at the FBI has not been successful: "If the incompatibility between the law enforcement and intelligence cultures is conceded, then it follows that an agency 100 percent dedicated to domestic intelligence would be likely to do a better job than the FBI, which is at most 20 percent intelligence and thus at least 80 percent criminal investigation and in consequence dominated by the criminal investigations."[89] Posner calls for creation of a "pure" domestic intelligence agency, one without any law enforcement responsibilities and located outside of the FBI. For Posner, the new U.S. Security Intelligence Surveillance can be modeled on the United Kingdom's MI5 or the Canadian Security Intelligence Service. What should the rules be for such a domestic intelligence agency concerning telecommunications surveillance? Should the FISA rules be applied to it?

UNITED STATES V. ISA

923 F.2d 1300 (8th Cir. 1991)

[The FBI obtained an order pursuant to FISA to bug the home of Zein Hassan Isa and his wife, Maria Matias. The FBI suspected Isa, a naturalized U.S. citizen, of being an agent of the Palestine Liberation Organization (PLO). One evening, the

---

[88] Francesca Bignami, *European versus American Liberty*, 48 B.C. L. Rev. 609, 621 (2007).

[89] Richard A. Posner, *Uncertain Shield* 101-02 (2006).

FBI's recording tapes of the bugged home captured Zein and Maria's murder of their 16-year-old daughter, Tina. Zein and Maria became angry at Tina's general rebelliousness and her defiance of their order not to date a particular young man. On the tape, Zein said to Tina: "Here, listen, my dear daughter, do you know that this is the last day? Tonight, you're going to die!" Tina responded in disbelief: "Huh?" Maria held Tina down while Zein stabbed her six times in the chest. While Tina screamed, Zein said: "Quiet, little one! Die my daughter, die!" The FBI turned the tapes over to the State of Missouri, where the Isas resided, where they were used to convict the Isas of murder. The Isas were sentenced to death.[90] Zein Isa argued that the recording should be suppressed because it captured events that had no relevance to the FBI's foreign intelligence gathering.]

GIBSON, J. . . . [A]ppellant argues that his fourth amendment rights were violated because the government failed to comply with the minimization procedures defined in 50 U.S.C. § 1801(h). Specifically, he contends that the tapes turned over to the State of Missouri record a "private domestic matter," which is not relevant material under the Foreign Intelligence Surveillance Act and must therefore be destroyed. In support of this argument, he cites isolated sentences regarding required minimization procedures from the legislative history of the Foreign Intelligence Surveillance Act:

> Minimization procedures might also include restrictions on the use of surveillance to times when foreign intelligence information is likely to be obtained, . . . [Furthermore, a target's] communications which are clearly not relevant to his clandestine intelligence activities should be destroyed. S. Rep. No. 95-701, 95th Cong., 2d Sess. 4.

Notwithstanding the minimization procedures required by [FISA], the Act specifically authorizes the retention of information that is "evidence of a crime", 50 U.S.C. § 1801(h)(3), and provides procedures for the retention and dissemination of such information. 50 U.S.C. § 1806(b)-(f). There is no requirement that the "crime" be related to foreign intelligence. . .

Thus, we conclude that the tapes are "evidence of crime" and that the district court correctly denied appellant's motion to suppress. 50 U.S.C. § 1801(h)(3).

NOTES & QUESTIONS

1. ***Use of Information Obtained Through FISA Orders.*** As the *Isa* court notes, information obtained via FISA can be used in criminal trials. However, the standard to obtain a FISA order does not require probable cause. Is it appropriate to allow the use of evidence that would ordinarily required a warrant with probable cause to obtain? On the other hand, the FISA order in *Isa* was properly obtained, and the agents unexpectedly obtained evidence of a murder. If the order is obtained properly in good faith, and evidence of a

[90] The Eighth Circuit opinion contains a very meager account of the facts on this case. The facts contained in this book are taken from *Terror and Death at Home Are Caught in F.B.I. Tape,* N.Y. Times, Oct. 28, 1991, at A14.

crime is unexpectedly gathered, why should it be excluded from use in a criminal prosecution?

2. ***Minimization Procedures and Information Screening "Walls."*** As illustrated by *Isa,* FISA allows the use of information properly obtained under FISA to be used in a criminal prosecution. What prevents the government from using the often more lax standards of FISA to gather evidence in a criminal investigation? The standards of FISA are often much less stringent than those of ECPA. Government officials would merely need to say that they are conducting "intelligence gathering" and obtain a FISA order rather than an order under ECPA — and then, if they uncover evidence of a crime, they could use it to prosecute. FISA has some built-in protections against this. For example, it requires that "the purpose" of the surveillance be foreign intelligence gathering. This language was interpreted by courts as the "primary" purpose.

   FISA requires that procedures be implemented to minimize the collection, retention, and dissemination of information about United States persons. § 1801(h)(1). Minimization procedures are designed to prevent the broad power of "foreign intelligence gathering" from being used for routine criminal investigations. In a number of instances, however, there are overlaps between foreign intelligence gathering and criminal investigations.

   One common minimization procedure is what is known as an "information screening wall." With the "wall," an official not involved in the criminal investigation must review the raw materials gathered by FISA surveillance and only pass on information that might be relevant evidence. The wall is designed to prevent criminal justice personnel from initiating or directing the FISA surveillance. The wall does not prevent the sharing of information; rather, it prevents criminal prosecutors from becoming involved in the front end of the investigation rather than on the back end.

   How should terrorism investigations, which involve both intelligence gathering and the collection of evidence for criminal prosecution, fit into this scheme?

THE 9/11 COMMISSION REPORT

Excerpt from pp. 254-75 (2004)

"The System Was Blinking Red"

As 2001 began, counterterrorism officials were receiving frequent but fragmentary reports about threats. Indeed, there appeared to be possible threats almost everywhere the United States had interests — including at home. . . .

Threat reports surged in June and July, reaching an even higher peak of urgency. The summer threats seemed to be focused on Saudi Arabia, Israel, Bahrain, Kuwait, Yemen, and possibly Rome, but the danger could be anywhere — including a possible attack on the G-8 summit in Genoa. . . .

A terrorist threat advisory distributed in late June indicated a high probability of near-term "spectacular" terrorist attacks resulting in numerous casualties.

Other reports' titles warned, "Bin Ladin Attacks May Be Imminent" and "Bin Ladin and Associates Making Near-Term Threats." . . .

Most of the intelligence community recognized in the summer of 2001 that the number and severity of threat reports were unprecedented. Many officials told us that they knew something terrible was planned, and they were desperate to stop it. Despite their large number, the threats received contained few specifics regarding time, place, method, or target. . . .

["Jane," an FBI analyst assigned to the FBI's investigation of the terrorist attack on the USS *Cole*] began drafting what is known as a lead for the FBI's New York Field Office. A lead relays information from one part of the FBI to another and requests that a particular action be taken. . . . [H]er draft lead was not sent until August 28. Her email told the New York agent that she wanted him to get started as soon as possible, but she labeled the lead as "Routine" — a designation that informs the receiving office that it has 30 days to respond.

The agent who received the lead forwarded it to his squad supervisor. That same day, the supervisor forwarded the lead to an intelligence agent to open an intelligence case — an agent who thus was behind "the wall" keeping FBI intelligence information from being shared with criminal prosecutors. He also sent it to the *Cole* case agents and an agent who had spent significant time in Malaysia searching for another Khalid: Khalid Sheikh Mohammad.

The suggested goal of the investigation was to locate Mihdhar, [a member of al Qaeda and a 9/11 hijacker] determine his contacts and reasons for being in the United States, and possibly conduct an interview. Before sending the lead, "Jane" had discussed it with "John," the CIA official on detail to the FBI. . . . The discussion seems to have been limited to whether the search should be classified as an intelligence investigation or as a criminal one. It appears that no one informed higher levels of management in either the FBI or CIA about the case. . . .

One of the *Cole* case agents read the lead with interest, and contacted "Jane" to obtain more information. "Jane" argued, however, that because the agent was designated a "criminal" FBI agent, not an intelligence FBI agent, the wall kept him from participating in any search for Mihdhar. In fact, she felt he had to destroy his copy of the lead because it contained NSA information from reports that included caveats ordering that the information not be shared without OIPR's permission. The agent asked "Jane" to get an opinion from the FBI's National Security Law Unit (NSLU) on whether he could open a criminal case on Mihdhar.

"Jane" sent an email to the *Cole* case agent explaining that according to the NSLU, the case could be opened only as an intelligence matter, and that if Mihdhar was found, only designated intelligence agents could conduct or even be present at any interview. She appears to have misunderstood the complex rules that could apply to this situation.

The FBI agent angrily responded:

> Whatever has happened to this — someday someone will die — and the wall or not — the public will not understand why we were not more effective at throwing every resource we had at certain "problems." . . .

"Jane" replied that she was not making up the rules; she claimed that they were in the relevant manual and "ordered by the [FISA] Court and every office of the FBI is required to follow them including FBI NY."

It is now clear that everyone involved was confused about the rules governing the sharing and use of information gathered in intelligence channels. Because Mihdhar was being sought for his possible connection to or knowledge of the *Cole* bombing, he could be investigated or tracked under the existing *Cole* criminal case. No new criminal case was need for the criminal agent to begin searching for Mihdhar. And as NSA had approved the passage of its information to the criminal agent, he could have conducted a search using all available information. As a result of this confusion, the criminal agents who were knowledgeable about al Qaeda and experienced with criminal investigative techniques, including finding suspects and possible criminal charges, were thus excluded from the search. . . .

We believe that if more resources had been applied and a significantly different approach taken, Mihdhar and Hazmi might have been found. They had used their true names in the United States. Still, the investigators would have needed luck as well as skill to find them prior to September 11 even if such searches had begun as early as August 23, when the lead was first drafted.

Many FBI witnesses have suggested that even if Mihdhar had been found, there was nothing the agents could have done except follow him onto the planes. We believe this is incorrect. Both Hazmi and Mihdhar could have been held for immigration violations or as material witnesses in the *Cole* bombing case. Investigation or interrogation of them, and investigation of their travel and financial activities, could have yielded evidence of connections to other participants in the 9/11 plot. The simple fact of their detention could have derailed the plan. In any case, the opportunity did not arise. . . .

On August 15, 2001, the Minneapolis FBI Field Office initiated an intelligence investigation on Zacarias Moussaoui. . . . [H]e had entered the United States in February 2001, and had begun flight lessons at Airman Flight School in Norman, Oklahoma. He resumed his training at the Pan Am International Flight Academy in Eagan, Minnesota, starting on August 13. He had none of the usual qualifications for light training on Pan Am's Boeing 747 flight simulators. He said he did not intend to become a commercial pilot but wanted the training as an "ego boosting thing." Moussaoui stood out because with little knowledge of flying, he wanted to learn to "take off and land" a Boeing 747.

The agent in Minneapolis quickly learned that Moussaoui possessed jihadist beliefs. Moreover, Moussaoui had $32,000 in a bank account but did not provide a plausible explanation for this sum of money. He traveled to Pakistan but became agitated when asked if he had traveled to nearby countries while in Pakistan. He planned to receive martial arts training, and intended to purchase a global positioning receiver. The agent also noted that Moussaoui became extremely agitated whenever he was questioned regarding his religious beliefs. The agent concluded that Moussaoui was "an Islamic extremist preparing for some future act in furtherance of radical fundamentalist goals." He also believed Moussaoui's plan was related to his flight training.

Moussaoui can be seen as an al Qaeda mistake and a missed opportunity. An apparently unreliable operative, he had fallen into the hands of the FBI. . . . If Moussaoui had been connected to al Qaeda, questions should instantly have arisen about a possible al Qaeda plot that involved piloting airliners, a possibility that had never been seriously analyzed by the intelligence community. . . .

As a French national who had overstayed his visa, Moussaoui could be detained immediately. The INS arrested Moussaoui on the immigration violation. A deportation order was signed on August 17, 2001.

The agents in Minnesota were concerned that the U.S. Attorney's office in Minneapolis would find insufficient probable cause of a crime to obtain a criminal warrant to search Moussaoui's laptop computer. Agents at FBI headquarters believed there was insufficient probable cause. Minneapolis therefore sought a special warrant under the Foreign Intelligence Surveillance Act. . . .

To do so, however, the FBI needed to demonstrate probable cause that Moussaoui was an agent of a foreign power, a demonstration that was not required to obtain a criminal warrant but was a statutory requirement for a FISA warrant. The agent did not have sufficient information to connect Moussaoui to a "foreign power," so he reached out for help, in the United States and overseas. . .

[Based on information supplied by the French government, Moussaoui was linked to a rebel leader in Chechnya.] This set off a spirited debate between the Minneapolis Field Office, FBI headquarters, and the CIA as to whether Chechen rebels . . . were sufficiently associated with a terrorist organization to constitute a "foreign power" for purposes of the FISA statute. FBI headquarters did not believe this was good enough, and its National Security Law Unit declined to submit a FISA application. . . .

Although the Minneapolis agents wanted to tell the FAA from the beginning about Moussaoui, FBI headquarters instructed Minneapolis that it could not share the more complete report the case agent had prepared for the FAA. . . .

NOTES & QUESTIONS

1. ***Confusion About the Law Before 9/11.*** The 9/11 Commission Report excerpted above indicated that many law enforcement officials were confused about what FISA required and how information could be shared. The 9/11 Commission Report stated that the FBI headquarters concluded that Moussaoui's association with Chechen rebels was not adequate to justify a FISA order because Chechen rebels were not "sufficiently associated with a terrorist organization to constitute a 'foreign power' for purposes of the FISA statute." Does FISA require that a foreign power involve a terrorist organization? Consider the following excerpt from a Senate Report discussing the problems with the Moussaoui investigation:

> *First,* key FBI personnel responsible for protecting our country against terrorism did not understand the law. The SSA at FBI Headquarters responsible for assembling the facts in support of the Moussaoui FISA application testified before the Committee in a closed hearing that he did not know that "probable cause" was the applicable legal standard for obtaining a

> FISA warrant. In addition, he did not have a clear understanding of what the probable cause standard meant. . . . In addition to not understanding the probable cause standard, the SSA's supervisor (the Unit Chief) responsible for reviewing FISA applications did not have a proper understanding of the legal definition of the "agent of a foreign power" requirement.[91]

A footnote in the report explained that the FBI agent "was under the incorrect impression that the statute required a link to an already identified or 'recognized' terrorist organization, an interpretation that the FBI and the supervisor himself admitted was incorrect."

According to Senator Arlen Specter (R-PA), the consequences of this misunderstanding of law were grave:

> The failure to obtain a warrant under the Foreign Intelligence Surveillance Act for Zacarias Moussaoui was a matter of enormous importance, and it is my view that if we had gotten into Zacarias Moussaoui's computer, a treasure trove of connections to Al-Qeada, in combination with the FBI report from Phoenix where the young man with Osama bin Laden's picture seeking flight training, added to [the fact that] the CIA knew about two men who turned out to be terrorist pilots on 9/11 . . . there was a veritable blueprint and 9/11 might well have been prevented. . . .
>
> [I]n a way which was really incredulous, the FBI agents didn't know the standard. They didn't know it when they were dealing with the Moussaoui case, and they didn't know it almost a year later when we had the closed-door hearing.[92]

Does this indication regarding law enforcement confusion point to a need for changes in the law, changes in FBI training, or some other action?

2. ***What Did the FISA "Wall" Require?*** Since information validly obtained pursuant to a FISA court order can be used for criminal prosecution, the FISA "wall" prevented criminal enforcement officials from directing the implementation of FISA orders. Consider the following remarks by Jamie Gorelick, who was part of the 9/11 Commission:

> At last week's hearing, Attorney General John Ashcroft, facing criticism, asserted that "the single greatest structural cause for September 11 was the wall that segregated criminal investigations and intelligence agents" and that I built that wall through a March 1995 memo. This simply is not true.
>
> First, I did not invent the "wall," which is not a wall but a set of procedures implementing a 1978 statute (the Foreign Intelligence Surveillance Act, or FISA) and federal court decisions interpreting it. In a nutshell, that law, as the courts read it, said intelligence investigators could conduct electronic surveillance in the United States against foreign targets under a more lenient standard than is required in ordinary criminal cases, but only if the "primary purpose" of the surveillance were foreign intelligence rather than a criminal prosecution.
>
> Second, according to the FISA Court of Review, it was the justice departments under Presidents Ronald Reagan and George H.W. Bush in the

---

[91] Senate Report No. 108-040.

[92] *The USA Patriot Act in Practice: Shedding Light on the FISA Process,* S. Hearing 107-947 (Sept. 10, 2002).

> 1980s that began to read the statute as limiting the department's ability to obtain FISA orders if it intended to bring a criminal prosecution. . . .
>
> [N]othing in the 1995 guidelines prevented the sharing of information between criminal and intelligence investigators. Indeed, the guidelines require that FBI foreign intelligence agents share information with criminal investigators and prosecutors whenever they uncover facts suggesting that a crime has been or may be committed. . . .[93]

According to Gorelick, why was the "wall" in place? What function did it serve? What precisely did it require?

3. ***FISA and the USA PATRIOT Act.*** Prior to the USA PATRIOT Act, FISA applied when foreign intelligence gathering was "the purpose" of the investigation. Courts interpreted "the purpose" to mean that the primary purpose of the investigation had to be foreign intelligence gathering. Criminal enforcement could be a secondary purpose, but not the primary one. The USA PATRIOT Act, § 204, changed this language to make FISA applicable when foreign intelligence gathering is "a significant purpose" of the investigation. 50 U.S.C. §§ 1804(a)(7)(B) and 1823(a)(7)(B). Why do you think that this change was made in the USA PATRIOT Act?

IN RE SEALED CASE

310 F.3d 717 (FIS Ct. Rev. 2002)

[In 2002, Attorney General John Ashcroft submitted to the FISA court new procedures for minimization, which significantly curtailed the screening walls. The procedures were reviewed by the FISA court in *In re All Matters Submitted to the Foreign Intelligence Surveillance Court* (May 17, 2002). The court expressed concern over the new procedures in light of the fact that in September 2000, the government had confessed error in about 75 FISA applications, including false statements that the targets of FISA surveillance were not under criminal investigations, that intelligence and criminal investigations were separate, and that information was not shared with FBI criminal investigators and assistant U.S. attorneys. The FISA court rejected the proposed procedures because they would allow criminal prosecutors to advise on FISA information gathering activities. The government appealed to the Foreign Intelligence Surveillance (FIS) Court of Review, which is composed of three judges on the D.C. Circuit. In 2002, the FIS Court of Review published its first and, thus far, only opinion.]

PER CURIAM. This is the first appeal from the Foreign Intelligence Surveillance Court to the Court of Review since the passage of the Foreign Intelligence Surveillance Act (FISA) in 1978. The appeal is brought by the United States from a FISA court surveillance order which imposed certain restrictions on the government. . . .

---

[93] Jamie S. Gorelick, *The Truth About "the Wall,"* Wash. Post, Apr. 18, 2004, at B7.

The court's decision from which the government appeals imposed certain requirements and limitations accompanying an order authorizing electronic surveillance of an "agent of a foreign power" as defined in FISA. There is no disagreement between the government and the FISA court as to the propriety of the electronic surveillance; the court found that the government had shown probable cause to believe that the target is an agent of a foreign power and otherwise met the basic requirements of FISA. . . . The FISA court authorized the surveillance, but imposed certain restrictions, which the government contends are neither mandated nor authorized by FISA. Particularly, the court ordered that law enforcement officials shall not make recommendations to intelligence officials concerning the initiation, operation, continuation or expansion of FISA searches or surveillances. Additionally, the FBI and the Criminal Division [of the Department of Justice] shall ensure that law enforcement officials do not direct or control the use of the FISA procedures to enhance criminal prosecution, and that advice intended to preserve the option of a criminal prosecution does not inadvertently result in the Criminal Division's directing or controlling the investigation using FISA searches and surveillances toward law enforcement objectives.

To ensure the Justice Department followed these strictures the court also fashioned what the government refers to as a "chaperone requirement"; that a unit of the Justice Department, the Office of Intelligence Policy and Review (OIPR) (composed of 31 lawyers and 25 support staff), "be invited" to all meetings between the FBI and the Criminal Division involving consultations for the purpose of coordinating efforts "to investigate or protect against foreign attack or other grave hostile acts, sabotage, international terrorism, or clandestine intelligence activities by foreign powers or their agents." . . .

[The FISA court opinion below] appears to proceed from the assumption that FISA constructed a barrier between counterintelligence/intelligence officials and law enforcement officers in the Executive Branch — indeed, it uses the word "wall" popularized by certain commentators (and journalists) to describe that supposed barrier.

The "wall" emerges from the court's implicit interpretation of FISA. The court apparently believes it can approve applications for electronic surveillance only if the government's objective is *not* primarily directed toward criminal prosecution of the foreign agents for their foreign intelligence activity. But the court neither refers to any FISA language supporting that view, nor does it reference the Patriot Act amendments, which the government contends specifically altered FISA to make clear that an application could be obtained even if criminal prosecution is the primary counter mechanism.

Instead the court relied for its imposition of the disputed restrictions on its statutory authority to approve "minimization procedures" designed to prevent the acquisition, retention, and dissemination within the government of material gathered in an electronic surveillance that is unnecessary to the government's need for foreign intelligence information. 50 U.S.C. § 1801(h). . . .

. . . [I]t is quite puzzling that the Justice Department, at some point during the 1980s, began to read the statute as limiting the Department's ability to obtain FISA orders if it intended to prosecute the targeted agents — even for foreign intelligence crimes. To be sure, section 1804, which sets forth the elements of an application for an order, required a national security official in the Executive Branch — typically the Director of the FBI — to certify that "the purpose" of the surveillance is to obtain foreign intelligence information (amended by the Patriot Act to read "a significant purpose"). But as the government now argues, the definition of foreign intelligence information includes evidence of crimes such as espionage, sabotage or terrorism. Indeed, it is virtually impossible to read the 1978 FISA to exclude from its purpose the prosecution of foreign intelligence crimes, most importantly because, as we have noted, the definition of an agent of a foreign power — if he or she is a U.S. person — is grounded on criminal conduct. . . .

. . . In October 2001, Congress amended FISA to change "the purpose" language in § 1804(a)(7)(B) to "a significant purpose." It also added a provision allowing "Federal officers who conduct electronic surveillance to acquire foreign intelligence information" to "consult with Federal law enforcement officers to coordinate efforts to investigate or protect against" attack or other grave hostile acts, sabotage or international terrorism, or clandestine intelligence activities, by foreign powers or their agents. 50 U.S.C. § 1806(k)(1). . . . Although the Patriot Act amendments to FISA expressly sanctioned consultation and coordination between intelligence and law enforcement officials, in response to the first applications filed by OIPR under those amendments, in November 2001, the FISA court for the first time adopted the 1995 Procedures, as augmented by the January 2000 and August 2001 Procedures, as "minimization procedures" to apply in all cases before the court.

The Attorney General interpreted the Patriot Act quite differently. On March 6, 2002, the Attorney General approved new "Intelligence Sharing Procedures" to implement the Act's amendments to FISA. The 2002 Procedures supersede prior procedures and were designed to permit the complete exchange of information and advice between intelligence and law enforcement officials. They eliminated the "direction and control" test and allowed the exchange of advice between the FBI, OIPR, and the Criminal Division regarding "the initiation, operation, continuation, or expansion of FISA searches or surveillance." . . .

Unpersuaded by the Attorney General's interpretation of the Patriot Act, the court ordered that the 2002 Procedures be adopted, *with modifications,* as minimization procedures to apply in all cases. . . .

. . . [W]hen Congress explicitly authorizes consultation and coordination between different offices in the government, without even suggesting a limitation on who is to direct and control, it necessarily implies that either could be taking the lead. . . .

That leaves us with something of an analytic conundrum. On the one hand, Congress did not amend the definition of foreign intelligence information which, we have explained, includes evidence of foreign intelligence crimes. On the other hand, Congress accepted the dichotomy between foreign intelligence and law enforcement by adopting the significant purpose test. Nevertheless, it is our task to do our best to read the statute to honor congressional intent. The better reading, it seems to us, excludes from the purpose of gaining foreign intelligence information a sole objective of criminal prosecution. We therefore reject the government's argument to the contrary. Yet this may not make much practical difference. Because, as the government points out, when it commences an electronic surveillance of a foreign agent, typically it will not have decided whether to prosecute the agent (whatever may be the subjective intent of the investigators or lawyers who initiate an investigation). So long as the government entertains a realistic option of dealing with the agent other than through criminal prosecution, it satisfies the significant purpose test.

The important point is — and here we agree with the government — the Patriot Act amendment, by using the word "significant," eliminated any justification for the FISA court to balance the relative weight the government places on criminal prosecution as compared to other counterintelligence responses. If the certification of the application's purpose articulates a broader objective than criminal prosecution — such as stopping an ongoing conspiracy — and includes other potential non-prosecutorial responses, the government meets the statutory test. Of course, if the court concluded that the government's sole objective was merely to gain evidence of past criminal conduct — even foreign intelligence crimes — to punish the agent rather than halt ongoing espionage or terrorist activity, the application should be denied. . . .

It can be argued, however, that by providing that an application is to be granted if the government has only a "significant purpose" of gaining foreign intelligence information, the Patriot Act allows the government to have a primary objective of prosecuting an agent for a non-foreign intelligence crime. Yet we think that would be an anomalous reading of the amendment. . . . That is not to deny that ordinary crimes might be inextricably intertwined with foreign intelligence crimes. For example, if a group of international terrorists were to engage in bank robberies in order to finance the manufacture of a bomb, evidence of the bank robbery should be treated just as evidence of the terrorist act itself. But the FISA process cannot be used as a device to investigate wholly unrelated ordinary crimes.

Having determined that FISA, as amended, does not oblige the government to demonstrate to the FISA court that its primary purpose in conducting electronic surveillance is *not* criminal prosecution, we are obliged to consider whether the statute as amended is consistent with the Fourth Amendment. . . . [I]n asking whether FISA procedures can be regarded as reasonable under the Fourth Amendment, we think it is instructive to compare those procedures and requirements with their Title III counterparts. Obviously, the closer those FISA procedures are to Title III procedures, the lesser are our constitutional concerns. . . .

With limited exceptions not at issue here, both Title III and FISA require prior judicial scrutiny of an application for an order authorizing electronic surveillance. 50 U.S.C. § 1805; 18 U.S.C. § 2518. And there is no dispute that a FISA judge satisfies the Fourth Amendment's requirement of a "neutral and detached magistrate."

The statutes differ to some extent in their probable cause showings. Title III allows a court to enter an *ex parte* order authorizing electronic surveillance if it determines on the basis of the facts submitted in the government's application that "there is probable cause for belief that an individual is committing, has committed, or is about to commit" a specified predicate offense. 18 U.S.C. § 2518(3)(a). FISA by contrast requires a showing of probable cause that the target is a foreign power or an agent of a foreign power. 50 U.S.C. § 1805(a)(3).

We have noted, however, that where a U.S. person is involved, an "agent of a foreign power" is defined in terms of criminal activity. . . . FISA surveillance would not be authorized against a target engaged in purely domestic terrorism because the government would not be able to show that the target is acting for or on behalf of a foreign power. . . .

FISA's general programmatic purpose, to protect the nation against terrorists and espionage threats directed by foreign powers, has from its outset been distinguishable from "ordinary crime control." After the events of September 11, 2001, though, it is hard to imagine greater emergencies facing Americans than those experienced on that date.

We acknowledge, however, that the constitutional question presented by this case — whether Congress' disapproval of the primary purpose test is consistent with the Fourth Amendment — has no definitive jurisprudential answer.

. . . Our case may well involve the most serious threat our country faces. Even without taking into account the President's inherent constitutional authority to conduct warrantless foreign intelligence surveillance, we think the procedures and government showings required under FISA, if they do not meet the minimum Fourth Amendment warrant standards, certainly come close.

NOTES & QUESTIONS

1. ***Assessing the Benefits and Problems of the "Wall."*** Paul Rosenzweig argues: "Prior to the Patriot Act, a very real wall existed. . . . While information could be 'thrown over the wall' from intelligence officials to prosecutors, the decision to do so always rested with national security personnel — even though law-enforcement agents are in a better position to determine what evidence is pertinent to their case."[94]

Consider Peter Swire:

> The principal argument [in favor of the wall] is that criminal prosecutions should be based on the normal rules of criminal procedure, not on evidence gathered in a secret court system. The norm should be the usual constitutional protections rather than the exceptional circumstances that arise in foreign intelligence investigations. . . .
>
> "[T]he wall" serves essential purposes. . . . [R]emoval of "the wall" may violate the Constitution for investigations that are primarily not for foreign intelligence purposes. At some point an investigation is so thoroughly domestic and criminal that the usual Fourth Amendment and other protections apply. . . . Second, "the wall" may be important in preventing the spread of the secret FISA system over time. As of 2002, seventy-one percent of the federal electronic surveillance orders were FISA orders rather than Title III orders. The Patriot Act reduction of safeguards in the FISA system means that this figure may climb in the future. . . .
>
> . . . [E]arly in an investigation, it may be difficult or impossible for investigators to know whether the evidence will eventually be used for intelligence purposes or in an actual prosecution. For instance, imagine that a FISA wiretap is sought for a group of foreign agents who are planning a bomb

[94] Paul Rosenzweig, *Civil Liberty and the Response to Terrorism,* 42 Duq. L. Rev. 663 (2004).

> attack. On these facts, there would be a strong foreign intelligence purpose, to frustrate the foreign attack. In addition, there would be a strong law enforcement basis for surveillance, to create evidence that would prove conspiracy beyond a reasonable doubt. On these facts, it would be difficult for officials to certify honestly that "the primary purpose" of the surveillance was for foreign intelligence rather than law enforcement. The honest official might say that the surveillance has a dual use — both to create actionable foreign intelligence information and to create evidence for later prosecution.
>
> Faced with this possibility of dual use, the Patriot Act amendment was to require only that "a significant purpose" of the surveillance be for foreign intelligence. Under the new standard, an official could honestly affirm both a significant purpose for foreign intelligence and a likely use for law enforcement.

Swire is troubled by the USA PATRIOT Act's changing FISA's requirement that "the purpose" of the investigation be foreign intelligence gathering to a looser requirement that "a significant purpose" of the investigation constituting foreign intelligence gathering:

> The problem with the "significant purpose" standard, however, is that it allows too much use of secret FISA surveillance for ordinary crimes. The FISCR interpreted the new statute in a broad way: "So long as the government entertains a realistic option of dealing with the agent other than through criminal prosecution, it satisfies the significant purpose test." The range of "realistic options" would seem to be so broad, however, that FISA orders could issue for an enormous range of investigations that ordinarily would be handled in the criminal system. . . . The Patriot Act amendment, as interpreted by the FISCR, thus allows the slippery slope to occur. A potentially immense range of law enforcement surveillance could shift into the secret FISA system.[95]

In lieu of the standard that "a significant purpose" of the investigation consist of foreign intelligence gathering, Swire recommends that FISA orders should be granted only if the surveillance is "sufficiently important for foreign intelligence purposes." Will Swire's proposed standard ("sufficiently important for foreign intelligence purposes") make a material difference from that of "a significant purpose"?

2. ***The Constitutionality of FISA.*** At the end of *In re Sealed Case,* the court concludes: "[W]e think the procedures and government showings required under FISA, if they do not meet the minimum Fourth Amendment warrant standards, certainly come close." Is coming close to meeting minimum warrant standards adequate enough to be constitutional?

   Prior to the USA PATRIOT Act amendments, a few courts considered the constitutionality of FISA, with all concluding that the statute passed constitutional muster. For example, in *United States v. Duggan,* 743 F.2d 59 (2d Cir. 1984), the Second Circuit concluded that FISA did not violate the Fourth Amendment because

[95] Peter Swire, *The System of Foreign Intelligence Surveillance Law,* 72 Geo. Wash. L. Rev. 1306, 1342, 1360-65 (2004).

> [p]rior to the enactment of FISA, virtually every court that had addressed the issue had concluded that the President had the inherent power to conduct warrantless electronic surveillance to collect foreign intelligence information, and that such surveillances constituted an exception to the warrant requirement of the Fourth Amendment. The Supreme Court specifically declined to address this issue in *United States v. United States District Court*, but it had made clear that the requirements of the Fourth Amendment may change when differing governmental interests are at stake, and it observed . . . that the governmental interests presented in national security investigations differ substantially from those presented in traditional criminal investigations. . . .
>
> Against this background, Congress passed FISA to settle what it believed to be the unresolved question of the applicability of the Fourth Amendment warrant requirement to electronic surveillance for foreign intelligence purposes, and to "remove any doubt as to the lawfulness of such surveillance." . . .
>
> We regard the procedures fashioned in FISA as a constitutionally adequate balancing of the individual's Fourth Amendment rights against the nation's need to obtain foreign intelligence information. . . .

Why should different Fourth Amendment requirements exist for foreign intelligence purposes as opposed to regular domestic law enforcement? Is the distinction between foreign intelligence and domestic law enforcement tenable in light of international terrorism, where investigations often have both a foreign intelligence and domestic law enforcement purpose? Do the USA PATRIOT Act amendments affect FISA's constitutionality?

3. ***After-the-Fact Reasonableness Review?*** In a critique of the FISA warrant-procedure as amended by the PATRIOT Act, a Note in the *Yale Law Journal* proposes that FISA be repealed and that the United States return to use of warrantless foreign intelligence surveillance in which "targets could challenge the reasonableness of the surveillance in an adversary proceeding in an Article III court after the surveillance was complete."[96]

Do you think that the foreign intelligence context is well-suited to the proposed warrantless regime? For the Note, "the possibility after-the-fact reasonableness review of the merits of their decisions in Article III courts (in camera or note) would help guarantee careful and calm DOJ decisionmaking." Is reasonableness a sufficiently strict standard of review? Furthermore, one of the hallmarks of the Fourth Amendment's warrant procedure is before-the-fact review; law enforcement officials must seek judicial authorization *before* they conduct their search. Would after-the-fact review result in hindsight bias? Another consideration is the extent to which warrantless surveillance would allow the government to "bootstrap" an investigation — the government could undertake broad, unregulated surveillance knowing that it could lead to evidence that may be admissible in court.

[96] Nola K. Breglio, Note, *Leaving FISA Behind: The Need to Return to Warrantless Foreign Intelligence Surveillance*, 113 Yale L.J. 179, 203-04, 209, 212 (2003).

3. THE ATTORNEY GENERAL'S FBI GUIDELINES

Unlike many government agencies, the FBI was not created by Congress through a statute. In 1907, Attorney General Charles Bonaparte requested that Congress authorize him to create a national detective force in the Department of Justice (DOJ). The DOJ had been using investigators from the Secret Service, but Bonaparte wanted a permanent force. Congress rejected his request due to concerns over this small group developing into a secret police system. Nevertheless, Bonaparte went ahead with his plans and formed a new subdivision of the DOJ, called the "Bureau of Investigation." President Theodore Roosevelt later authorized the subdivision through an executive order in 1908. J. Edgar Hoover began running the Bureau, which was renamed the Federal Bureau of Investigation in 1935.[97]

The FBI grew at a great pace. In 1933, the FBI had 353 agents and 422 support staff; in 1945, it had 4,380 agents and 7,422 support staff.[98] Today, the FBI has 11,000 agents and 16,000 support staff, as well as 56 field offices, 400 satellite offices, and 40 foreign liaison posts.[99]

FBI surveillance activities are regulated through the U.S. Constitution and electronic surveillance laws, as well as by guidelines promulgated by the Attorney General. In 1976, responding to Hoover's abuses of power, Attorney General Edward Levi established guidelines to control FBI surveillance activities.[100] As William Banks and M.E. Bowman observe:

> The most pertinent Levi Guidelines focused on freedom of speech and freedom of the press. First, investigations based solely on unpopular speech, where there is no threat of violence, were prohibited. Second, techniques designed to disrupt organizations engaged in protected First Amendment activity, or to discredit individuals would not be used in any circumstance.
>
> At the same time, Attorney General Levi emphasized that the Guidelines were intended to permit domestic security investigations where the activities under investigation "involve or will involve the use of force or violence and the violation of criminal law." . . .
>
> On March 7, 1983, Attorney General William French Smith revised the Guidelines regarding domestic security investigations. . . .
>
> The Smith Guidelines were intended to increase the investigative avenues available to the FBI in domestic terrorism cases. Where the Levi/Civiletti Guidelines had established a predicate investigative standard of "specific and articulable facts," the Smith version lowered the threshold to require only a "reasonable indication" as the legal standard for opening a "full" investigation. . . . The "reasonable indication" standard is significantly lower than the Fourth Amendment standard of probable cause required in law enforcement. To balance the lowered threshold for opening an investigation, Attorney General Smith emphasized that investigations would be regulated and would "not be based solely on activities protected by the First Amendment or the lawful exercise of other rights secured by the Constitution."

---

[97] Curt Gentry, *J. Edgar Hoover: The Man and the* Secrets 111-13 (1991).

[98] Ronald Kessler, *The Bureau: The Secret History of the FBI* 57 (2002).

[99] Federal Bureau of Investigation, Frequently Asked Questions, http://www.fbi.gov/aboutus/faqs/faqsone.html (Dec. 4, 2003).

[100] *See* United States Attorney General Guidelines on Domestic Security Investigation (1976).

> Nonetheless, the Smith Guidelines authorized FBI Headquarters to approve the use of informants to infiltrate a group "in a manner that may influence the exercise of rights protected by the First Amendment." The Smith Guidelines also stated: "In the absence of any information indicating planned violence by a group or enterprise, mere speculation that force or violence might occur during the course of an otherwise peaceable demonstration is not sufficient grounds for initiation of an investigation." . . .
>
> According to the criminal guidelines, a full investigation may be opened where there is "reasonable indication" that two or more persons are engaged in an enterprise for the purpose of furthering political or social goals wholly or in part through activities that involve force or violence and are a violation of the criminal laws of the United States. . . .
>
> In order to determine whether an investigation should be opened, the FBI must also take into consideration the magnitude of the threat, the likelihood that the threat will come to fruition, and the immediacy of the jeopardy. In addition to physical danger, the FBI must consider the danger to privacy and free expression posed by an investigation. For example, unless there is a reasonable indication that force or violence might occur during the course of a demonstration, initiation of an investigation is not appropriate. . . .[101]

In 2002, Attorney General John Ashcroft issued revised FBI guidelines. Whereas under the preexisting guidelines, the FBI could engage in surveillance of public political activity and search the Internet when "facts or circumstances reasonably indicate that a federal crime has been, is being, or will be committed,"[102] Ashcroft's guidelines eliminate this requirement. The FBI is permitted to gather "publicly available information, whether obtained directly or through services or resources (whether nonprofit or commercial) that compile or analyze such information; and information voluntarily provided by private entities." The FBI can also "carry out general topical research, including conducting online searches and accessing online sites and forums."[103]

Daniel Solove argues that Congress should pass a legislative charter to regulate the FBI:

> . . . [E]xecutive orders and guidelines can all be changed by executive fiat, as demonstrated by Ashcroft's substantial revision to the guidelines in 2002. Moreover, the Attorney General Guidelines are not judicially enforceable. The problem with the current system is that it relies extensively on self-regulation by the executive branch. Much of this regulation has been effective, but it can too readily be changed in times of crisis without debate or discussion. Codifying the internal executive regulations of the FBI would also allow for public input into the process. The FBI is a very powerful arm of the executive branch, and if we believe in separation of powers, then it is imperative that the legislative branch, not the executive alone, become involved in the regulation of the FBI. The

---

[101] William C. Banks & M.E. Bowman, *Executive Authority for National Security Surveillance,* 50 Am. U. L. Rev. 1, 69-74 (2000).

[102] The Attorney General's Guidelines on General Crimes, Racketeering Enterprise and Domestic Security/Terrorism Investigations § II.C.1 (Mar. 21, 1989).

[103] The Attorney General's Guidelines on General Crimes, Racketeering Enterprise and Terrorism Enterprise Investigations § VI (May 30, 2002).

guidelines should be judicially enforceable to ensure that they are strictly followed.[104]

Should other government security agencies have more oversight? Does Solove overlook the FBI's internal administrative processes that serve to limit its power?

4. THE HOMELAND SECURITY ACT

In 2002, Congress passed the Homeland Security Act, 6 U.S.C. § 222, which consolidated 22 federal agencies into the Department of Homeland Security (DHS). Agencies and other major components at the DHS include the Transportation Security Administration, Customs and Border Protection, Federal Emergency Management Agency, U.S. Citizenship and Immigration Services, U.S. Coast Guard, and U.S. Secret Service. The Office of the Secretary of DHS includes the Office of the Chief Privacy Officer, the Office of Civil Rights and Civil Liberties, the Office of Counter Narcotics, and the Office of State and Local Government Coordination.

Among other things, the Act creates a Privacy Office. 6 U.S.C. § 222. The Secretary must "appoint a senior official to assume primary responsibility for privacy policy." The privacy official's responsibilities include ensuring compliance with the Privacy Act of 1974; evaluating "legislative and regulatory proposals involving the collection, use, and disclosure of personal information by the Federal Government"; and preparing an annual report to Congress.

5. THE INTELLIGENCE REFORM AND TERRORISM PREVENTION ACT

Information Sharing and Institutional Culture. The 9/11 Commission found that in addition to the legal restrictions on sharing of foreign intelligence information, limitations in the FBI's institutional culture as well as technology had also prevented the circulation of data. In its final report, the 9/11 Commission stated: "The importance of integrated, all-source analysis cannot be overstated. Without it, it is not possible to 'connect the dots.'"[105] The 9/11 Commission called for a restructuring of the United States Intelligence Community (USIC) through creation of a National Intelligence Director to oversee this process.

In an Executive Order of August 27, 2004, President Bush required executive branch agencies to establish an environment to facilitate sharing of terrorism information.[106] Responding to the 9/11 Commission Report, Congress passed the Intelligence Reform and Terrorism Prevention Act of 2004 (IRPTA), codifying the requirements in Bush's Executive Order. The Act mandates that intelligence be "provided in its most shareable form" that the heads of intelligence agencies and federal departments "promote a culture of information sharing."

---

[104] Daniel J. Solove, *Reconstructing Electronic Surveillance Law,* 72 Geo. Wash. L. Rev. 1264, 1304 (2004).

[105] The 9/11 Commission Report 408 (2004).

[106] Exec. Order No. 13356, 69 Fed. Reg. 53599, 53600-01 (Sept. 1, 2004).

The Privacy and Civil Liberties Oversight Board. The IRTPA seeks to establish protection of privacy and civil liberties by setting up a five-member Privacy and Civil Liberties Oversight Board. The Board gives advice to the President and agencies of the executive branch and provides an annual report of activities to Congress. Among its oversight activities, the Board is to review whether "the information sharing practices of the departments, agencies, and elements of the executive branch . . . appropriately protect privacy and civil liberties." The Board is also to "ensure that privacy and civil liberties are appropriately considered in the development and implementation of . . . regulations and executive branch policies." Regarding FISA surveillance, IRTPA mandates that the Attorney General provide more detailed reporting to Congress on governmental surveillance practices and the government's legal interpretations of FISA.

The Privacy and Civil Liberties Board has been the subject of controversy. A year after its creation, in February 2006, the Board still had not met a single time. When the Board issued its first annual report in May 2007, it led to the resignation of Lanny Davis, the Board's only Democratic member. The Bush Administration made more than 200 revisions to the report. The White House defending the actions as "standard operating procedure," and stated that it was appropriate because the board was legally under the President's supervision. In his resignation letter, Davis contested "the extensive redlining of the board's report to Congress by administration officials and the majority of the Board's willingness to accept most [of the edits.]"

Later that year, Congress enacted legislation to strengthen the independence and authority of the Board. It is now an "independent agency" located within the executive branch. No more than three members of the same political party can be appointed to the Board, and the Senate is to confirm all appointments to it. As before, however, the Board cannot issue subpoenas itself. Rather, a majority of Board members have the power to ask the Attorney General to issue a subpoena.[107]

6. THE NSA SURVEILLANCE PROGRAM

In December 2005, a front page article in the *New York Times* first revealed that the National Security Agency (NSA) was intercepting communications where one party was located outside the United States and another party inside the United States.[108] The Bush Administration named this surveillance program the "Terrorist Surveillance Program" (TSP).

Created in 1952, the NSA collects and analyzes foreign communications. As Frederick Schwarz and Aziz Huq explain, "The NSA collects signals intelligence from telegrams, telephones, faxes, e-mails, and other electronic communications, and then disseminates this information among other agencies of the executive branch."[109] Schwarz and Huq also point out that the Church Committee

---

[107] Ronald D. Lee & Paul M. Schwartz, *Beyond the "War on Terrorism": Towards the New Intelligence Network*, 103 Mich. L. Rev. 1446 (2005).

[108] James Risen & Eric Lichtblau, *Bush Lets U.S. Spy on Callers Without Courts*, N.Y. Times, Dec. 16. 2005, at A1.

[109] Frederick A.O. Schwarz Jr. & Aziz Z. Huq, *Unchecked and Unbalanced: Presidential Power in a Time of Terror* 127 (2007).

investigation in 1975-76 found that "the NSA had not exercised its vast power with restraint or due regard for the Constitution." In the past, the NSA had engaged in activities such as collecting every international telegram sent from the United States and maintaining watch lists of U.S. citizens involved in political protests.

After 9/11, the NSA again began secret surveillance activities within the United States. Although the Bush Administration has discussed aspects of the NSA surveillance of telecommunications, the complete dimensions of the NSA activities remain unknown. And while the Department of Justice has issued a white paper justifying these activities,[110] the legal opinions said to declare the program lawful are secret.

Several lawsuits ensued, challenging the legality of the NSA surveillance. Some of these cases were brought against telecommunications companies that cooperated with the NSA in conducting the surveillance. Plaintiffs alleged that these companies violated FISA and ECPA.

Early in 2007, a secret FISC decision denied permission for certain NSA surveillance activities. The FISC judgment was said to concern a NSA request for a so-called "basket warrant," under which warrants are issued not on a case-by-case basis for specific suspects, but more generally for surveillance activity involving multiple targets. One anonymous official was quoted as saying that the FISC ruling concerned cases "where one end is foreign and you don't know where the other is."[111] The Administration leaked information about this ruling and argued that it impeded the government's ability to investigate threats of imminent terrorist attacks.

In the summer of 2007, Congress enacted the Protect America Act to authorize the NSA surveillance program.[112] This statute was subject to sunset in 120 days, and it expired without Congress enacting a new law or renewing it. At that point, without the Protect America Act's amendments, the original FISA once again took effect, until Congress enacted FAA in July 2008.

A major roadblock to amending FISA had been the subject of immunity for the telecommunications companies that participated or participate in TSP or similar programs. President Bush stated that telecommunications immunity was needed to provide "meaningful liability protection to those who are alleged to have assisted our nation following the attacks of September 11, 2001." FISA already did contain immunity provisions, and this language was in effect at the time that the TSP began. *See* 18 U.S.C. § 2511(2)(a)(ii). The cooperation of the telecommunication companies with the NSA must have been outside the existing safe harbor language.

The FAA of 2008, discussed earlier in this chapter, establishes new rules for at least some of this NSA behavior. Title II of the FAA raises a new challenge to

---

[110] United States Department of Justice, *Legal Authorities Supporting the Activities of the National Security Agency Described by the President* (Jan. 19, 2006).

[111] Greg Miller, *Court Puts Limits on Surveillance Abroad*, L.A. Times, Aug. 2, 2007.

[112] The Protect America Act created an exception to FISA's requirements. The exception was found in the statute's § 105A. This part of the law exempted all communications "directed at" people outside of the United States from FISA's definition of "electronic surveillance." Once a communication fell within § 105A, the government could carry it out subject to § 105B and its requirements — rather than FISA and its obligation to seek a warrant from the FISC.

the litigation against the NSA behavior prior to its enactments — it provides statutory defenses for the telecommunications companies that assisted the NSA. Specifically, the FAA prohibits "a civil action" against anyone "for providing assistance to an element of the intelligence community" in connection "with an intelligence activity involving communications" following a specific kind of certification by the Attorney General. § 802. The certification in question requires a determination that the assistance was (1) authorized by the President during the period beginning on September 11, 2001 and ending on January 17, 2007; (2) designed to detect or prevent a terrorist attack; and (3) the subject of a written request from the Attorney General or the head of the intelligence community. A court presented with such a certificate is to review it for the support of "substantial evidence."

Before enactment of FAA, several courts heard challenges to the NSA warrantless wiretapping program. One of the most important issues in this litigation is the state secrets privilege, which is a common law evidentiary rule. The state secrets privilege protects information from discovery when disclosure of it would harm national security. As you read the following judicial decisions, consider the impact of the state secrets privilege as well as what effect the FAA will have on these cases.

AL-HARAMAIN ISLAMIC FOUNDATION V. BUSH

507 F.3d 1190 (9th Cir. 2007)

MCKEOWN, J. Following the terrorist attacks on September 11, 2001, President George W. Bush authorized the National Security Agency ("NSA") to conduct a warrantless communications surveillance program. The program intercepted international communications into and out of the United States of persons alleged to have ties to Al Qaeda and other terrorist networks. Though its operating parameters remain murky, and certain details may forever remain so, much of what is known about the Terrorist Surveillance Program ("TSP") was spoon-fed to the public by the President and his administration.

After *The New York Times* first revealed the program's existence in late 2005, government officials moved at lightning-speed to quell public concern and doled out a series of detailed disclosures about the program. Only one day after *The New York Times'* story broke, President Bush informed the country in a public radio address that he had authorized the interception of international communications of individuals with known links to Al Qaeda and related terrorist organizations. Two days after President Bush's announcement, then-Attorney General Alberto Gonzales disclosed that the program targeted communications where the government had concluded that one party to the communication was a member of, or affiliated with, Al Qaeda. The Department of Justice followed these and other official disclosures with a lengthy white paper in which it both confirmed the existence of the surveillance program and also offered legal justification of the intercepts.

The government's plethora of voluntary disclosures did not go unnoticed. Al-Haramain Islamic Foundation, a designated terrorist organization, and two of its attorneys (collectively, "Al-Haramain") brought suit against President Bush and other executive branch agencies and officials. They claimed that they were subject to warrantless electronic surveillance in 2004 in violation of the Foreign Intelligence Surveillance Act ("FISA"), various provisions of the United States Constitution, and international law. The government countered that the suit is foreclosed by the state secrets privilege, an evidentiary privilege that protects national security and military information in appropriate circumstances.

Essential to substantiating Al-Haramain's allegations against the government is a classified "Top Secret" document (the "Sealed Document") that the government inadvertently gave to Al-Haramain in 2004 during a proceeding to freeze the organization's assets. Faced with the government's motions to dismiss and to bar Al-Haramain from access to the Sealed Document, the district court concluded that the state secrets privilege did not bar the lawsuit altogether. The court held that the Sealed Document was protected by the state secrets privilege and that its inadvertent disclosure did not alter its privileged nature, but decided that Al-Haramain would be permitted to file *in camera* affidavits attesting to the contents of the document based on the memories of lawyers who had received copies. . . .

Al-Haramain is a Muslim charity which is active in more than 50 countries. Its activities include building mosques and maintaining various development and education programs. The United Nations Security Council has identified Al-Haramain as an entity belonging to or associated with Al Qaeda. In February 2004, the Office of Foreign Assets Control of the Department of Treasury temporarily froze Al-Haramain's assets pending a proceeding to determine whether to declare it a "Specially Designated Global Terrorist" due to the organization's alleged ties to Al Qaeda. Ultimately, Al-Haramain and one of its directors, Soliman Al-Buthi, were declared "Specially Designated Global Terrorists."

In August 2004, during Al-Haramain's civil designation proceeding, the Department of the Treasury produced a number of unclassified materials that were given to Al-Haramain's counsel and two of its directors. Inadvertently included in these materials was the Sealed Document, which was labeled "TOP SECRET." Al-Haramain's counsel copied and disseminated the materials, including the Sealed Document, to Al-Haramain's directors and co-counsel, including Wendell Belew and Asim Ghafoor. In August or September of 2004, a reporter from *The Washington Post* reviewed these documents while researching an article. In late August, the FBI was notified of the Sealed Document's inadvertent disclosure. In October of 2004, the FBI retrieved all copies of the Sealed Document from Al-Haramain's counsel, though it did not seek out Al-Haramain's directors to obtain their copies. The Sealed Document is located in a Department of Justice Sensitive Compartmented Information Facility.

Al-Haramain alleges that after *The New York Times* story broke in December 2005, it realized that the Sealed Document was proof that it had been subjected to warrantless surveillance in March and April of 2004. Though the government has acknowledged the existence of the TSP, it has not disclosed the identities of the specific persons or entities surveilled under the program, and disputes whether Al-Haramain's inferences are correct. . . .

Although we have not previously addressed directly the standard of review for a claim of the state secrets privilege, we have intimated that our review is de novo. De novo review as to the legal application of the privilege and clear error review as to factual findings make sense, as the determination of privilege is essentially a legal matter based on the underlying facts. . . .

The state secrets privilege is a common law evidentiary privilege that permits the government to bar the disclosure of information if "there is a reasonable danger" that disclosure will "expose military matters which, in the interest of national security, should not be divulged." *United States v. Reynolds,* 345 U.S. 1, 10 (1953). The privilege is not to be lightly invoked. . . .

We agree with the district court's conclusion that the very subject matter of the litigation — the government's alleged warrantless surveillance program under the TSP — is not protected by the state secrets privilege. Two discrete sets of unclassified facts support this determination. First, President Bush and others in the administration publicly acknowledged that in the months following the September 11, 2001, terrorist attacks, the President authorized a communications surveillance program that intercepted the communications of persons with suspected links to Al Qaeda and related terrorist organizations. Second, in 2004, Al-Haramain was officially declared by the government to be a "Specially Designated Global Terrorist" due to its purported ties to Al Qaeda. The subject matter of the litigation — the TSP and the government's warrantless surveillance of persons or entities who, like Al-Haramain, were suspected by the NSA to have connections to terrorists — is simply not a state secret. At this early stage in the litigation, enough is known about the TSP, and Al-Haramain's classification as a "Specially Designated Global Terrorist," that the subject matter of Al-Haramain's lawsuit can be discussed, as it has been extensively in publicly-filed pleadings, televised arguments in open court in this appeal,[113] and in the media and the blogosphere, without disturbing the dark waters of privileged information.

Because cases in this area are scarce, no court has put a fine point on how broadly or narrowly "subject matter" is defined in the context of state secrets. Application of this principle must be viewed in the face of the specific facts alleged and the scope of the lawsuit. In this case, the analysis is not difficult because Al-Haramain challenges warrantless surveillance authorized under the TSP. Significantly, until disclosure of the program in 2005, the program and its details were a highly prized government secret.

The first disclosure may have come from *The New York Times,* but President Bush quickly confirmed the existence of the TSP just one day later, on December 17, 2005, in a radio address to the nation. The President's announcement that he had authorized the NSA to intercept the international communications of individuals with known links to Al Qaeda cast the first official glimmer of light on the TSP. Since then, government officials have made voluntary disclosure after voluntary disclosure about the TSP, selectively coloring in the contours of the surveillance program and even hanging some of it in broad daylight.

Two days after President Bush's announcement, Attorney General Gonzales disclosed that the TSP intercepted communications where one party was outside the United States, and the government had "a reasonable basis to conclude that

---

[113] Pursuant to a camera request filed before argument, we permitted C-SPAN to record the proceeding for later broadcast.

one party to the communication is a member of al Qaeda, affiliated with al Qaeda, or a member of an organization affiliated with al Qaeda, or working in support of al Qaeda." Attorney General Gonzales confirmed that surveillance occurred without FISA warrants . . . and that American citizens could be surveilled only if they communicated with a suspected or known terrorist . . . .

In an address to the National Press Club on January 23, 2006, General Hayden volunteered further details about the TSP . . . General Hayden's statements provided to the American public a wealth of information about the TSP. The public now knows the following additional facts about the program, beyond the general contours outlined by other officials: (1) at least one participant for each surveilled call was located outside the United States; (2) the surveillance was conducted without FISA warrants; (3) inadvertent calls involving purely domestic callers were destroyed and not reported; (4) the inadvertent collection was recorded and reported; and (5) U.S. identities are expunged from NSA records of surveilled calls if deemed non-essential to an understanding of the intelligence value of a particular report. These facts alone, disclosed by General Hayden in a public address, provide a fairly complete picture of the scope of the TSP.

. . . [T]he government's many attempts to assuage citizens' fears that *they* have not been surveilled now doom the government's assertion that the very subject matter of this litigation, the existence of a warrantless surveillance program, is barred by the state secrets privilege. . . .

Al-Haramain's case does involve privileged information, but that fact alone does not render the very subject matter of the action a state secret. Accordingly, we affirm the district court's denial of dismissal on that basis.

Although the very subject matter of this lawsuit does not result in automatic dismissal, we must still address the government's invocation of the state secrets privilege as to the Sealed Document and its assertion that Al-Haramain cannot establish either standing or a prima facie case without the use of state secrets. . . .

Having reviewed it *in camera,* we conclude that the Sealed Document is protected by the state secrets privilege, along with the information as to whether the government surveilled Al-Haramain. We take very seriously our obligation to review the documents with a very careful, indeed a skeptical, eye, and not to accept at face value the government's claim or justification of privilege. Simply saying "military secret," "national security" or "terrorist threat" or invoking an ethereal fear that disclosure will threaten our nation is insufficient to support the privilege. Sufficient detail must be-and has been-provided for us to make a meaningful examination. . . . That said, we acknowledge the need to defer to the Executive on matters of foreign policy and national security and surely cannot legitimately find ourselves second guessing the Executive in this arena. . . . [O]ur judicial intuition about this proposition is no substitute for documented risks and threats posed by the potential disclosure of national security information. . . .

It is no secret that the Sealed Document has something to do with intelligence activities. Beyond that, we go no further in disclosure. The filings involving classified information, including the Sealed Document, declarations and portions of briefs, are referred to in the pleadings as *In Camera or Ex Parte* documents. Each member of the panel has had unlimited access to these documents.

We have spent considerable time examining the government's declarations (both publicly filed and those filed under seal). We are satisfied that the basis for the privilege is exceptionally well documented. Detailed statements underscore that disclosure of information concerning the Sealed Document and the means, sources and methods of intelligence gathering in the context of this case would undermine the government's intelligence capabilities and compromise national security. Thus, we reach the same conclusion as the district court: the government has sustained its burden as to the state secrets privilege.

We must next resolve how the litigation should proceed in light of the government's successful privilege claim. . . .

After correctly determining that the Sealed Document was protected by the state secrets privilege, the district court then erred in forging an unusual path forward in this litigation. Though it granted the government's motion to deny Al-Haramain access to the Sealed Document based on the state secrets privilege, the court permitted the Al-Haramain plaintiffs to file *in camera* affidavits attesting to the contents of the document from their memories.

The district court's approach—a commendable effort to thread the needle—is contrary to established Supreme Court precedent. If information is found to be a privileged state secret, there are only two ways that litigation can proceed: (1) if the plaintiffs can prove "the essential facts" of their claims "without resort to material touching upon military secrets," *Reynolds,* 345 U.S. at 11, or (2) in accord with the procedure outlined in FISA. By allowing *in camera* review of affidavits attesting to individuals' memories of the Sealed Document, the district court sanctioned "material touching" upon privileged information, contrary to *Reynolds.* Although FISA permits district court judges to conduct an *in camera* review of information relating to electronic surveillance, there are detailed procedural safeguards that must be satisfied before such review can be conducted. *See, e.g.,* 50 U.S.C. § 1806(f). The district court did not address this issue nor do we here.

Moreover, the district court's solution is flawed: if the Sealed Document is privileged because it contains very sensitive information regarding national security, permitting the same information to be revealed through reconstructed memories circumvents the document's absolute privilege. *See Reynolds,* 345 U.S. at 10 (A court "should not jeopardize the security which the privilege is meant to protect by insisting upon an examination of the evidence, even by the judge alone, in chambers."). That approach also suffers from a worst of both worlds deficiency: either the memory is wholly accurate, in which case the approach is tantamount to release of the document itself, or the memory is inaccurate, in which case the court is not well-served and the disclosure may be even more problematic from a security standpoint. The state secrets privilege, because of its unique national security considerations, does not lend itself to a compromise solution in this case. The Sealed Document, its contents, and any individuals' memories of its contents, even well-reasoned speculation as to its contents, are completely barred from further disclosure in this litigation by the common law state secrets privilege.

The requirements for standing are well known to us from the Supreme Court's decision in *Lujan v. Defenders of Wildlife,* 504 U.S. 555 (1992). Standing requires that (1) the plaintiff suffered an injury in fact, *i.e.,* one that is sufficiently "concrete and particularized" and "actual or imminent, not conjectural or hypothetical," (2) the injury is "fairly traceable" to the challenged conduct, and (3) the injury is "likely" to be "redressed by a favorable decision."

Al-Haramain cannot establish that it suffered injury in fact, a "concrete and particularized" injury, because the Sealed Document, which Al-Haramain alleges proves that its members were unlawfully surveilled, is protected by the state secrets privilege. At oral argument, counsel for Al-Haramain essentially conceded that Al-Haramain cannot establish standing without reference to the Sealed Document. . . . It is not sufficient for Al-Haramain to speculate that it might be subject to surveillance under the TSP simply because it has been designated a "Specially Designated Global Terrorist." . . .

Because we affirm the district court's conclusion that the Sealed Document, along with data concerning surveillance, are privileged, and conclude that no testimony attesting to individuals' memories of the document may be admitted to establish the contents of the document, Al-Haramain cannot establish that it has standing, and its claims must be dismissed, unless FISA preempts the state secrets privilege.

Under FISA, 50 U.S.C. §§ 1801 *et seq.,* if an "aggrieved person" requests discovery of materials relating to electronic surveillance, and the Attorney General files an affidavit stating that the disclosure of such information would harm the national security of the United States, a district court may review *in camera* and ex parte the materials "as may be necessary to determine whether the surveillance of the aggrieved person was lawfully authorized and conducted." 50 U.S.C. § 1806(f). The statute further provides that the court may disclose to the aggrieved person, using protective orders, portions of the materials "where such disclosure is necessary to make an accurate determination of the legality of the surveillance." *Id.* The statute, unlike the common law state secrets privilege, provides a detailed regime to determine whether surveillance "was lawfully authorized and conducted." *Id.*

As an alternative argument, Al-Haramain posits that FISA preempts the state secrets privilege. The district court chose not to rule on this issue. Now, however, the FISA issue remains central to Al-Haramain's ability to proceed with this lawsuit. Rather than consider the issue for the first time on appeal, we remand to the district court to consider whether FISA preempts the state secrets privilege and for any proceedings collateral to that determination.

HEPTING V. AT&T CORP.

439 F. Supp. 974 (N.D. Cal. 2006)

WALKER, J. Plaintiffs allege that AT&T Corporation (AT&T) and its holding company, AT&T Inc, are collaborating with the National Security Agency (NSA) in a massive warrantless surveillance program that illegally tracks the domestic and foreign communications and communication records of millions of Americans. . . .

In determining whether a factual statement is a secret for purposes of the state secrets privilege, the court should look only at publicly reported information that possesses substantial indicia of reliability and whose verification or substantiation possesses the potential to endanger national security. That entails assessing the value of the information to an individual or group bent on threatening the security of the country, as well as the secrecy of the information. . . .

Accordingly, in determining whether a factual statement is a secret, the court considers only public admissions or denials by the government, AT&T and other telecommunications companies, which are the parties indisputably situated to disclose whether and to what extent the alleged programs exist. In determining what is a secret, the court at present refrains from relying on the declaration of Mark Klein. Although AT&T does not dispute that Klein was a former AT&T technician and he has publicly declared under oath that he observed AT&T assisting the NSA in some capacity and his assertions would appear admissible in connection with the present motions, the inferences Klein draws have been disputed. To accept the Klein declaration at this juncture in connection with the state secrets issue would invite attempts to undermine the privilege by mere assertions of knowledge by an interested party. Needless to say, this does not reflect that the court discounts Klein's credibility, but simply that what is or is not secret depends on what the government and its alleged operative AT&T and other telecommunications providers have either admitted or denied or is beyond reasonable dispute.

Likewise, the court does not rely on media reports about the alleged NSA programs because their reliability is unclear. To illustrate, after Verizon and BellSouth denied involvement in the program described in *USA Today* in which communication records are monitored, *USA Today* published a subsequent story somewhat backing down from its earlier statements and at least in some measure substantiating these companies' denials.

Finally, the court notes in determining whether the privilege applies, the court is not limited to considering strictly admissible evidence. . . . [T]he court may rely upon reliable public evidence that might otherwise be inadmissible at trial because it does not comply with the technical requirements of the rules of evidence.

With these considerations in mind, the court at last determines whether the state secrets privilege applies here. . . .

In sum, the government has disclosed the general contours of the "terrorist surveillance program," which requires the assistance of a telecommunications provider, and AT&T claims that it lawfully and dutifully assists the government in classified matters when asked. . . .

[I]t is important to note that even the state secrets privilege has its limits. While the court recognizes and respects the executive's constitutional duty to protect the nation from threats, the court also takes seriously its constitutional duty to adjudicate the disputes that come before it. See *Hamdi v. Rumsfeld,* 542 U.S. 507, 536 (2004) (plurality opinion) ("Whatever power the United States Constitution envisions for the Executive in its exchanges with other nations or with enemy organizations in times of conflict, it most assuredly envisions a role for all three branches when individual liberties are at stake."). To defer to a blanket assertion of secrecy here would be to abdicate that duty, particularly because the very subject matter of this litigation has been so publicly aired. The compromise between liberty and security remains a difficult one. But dismissing this case at the outset would sacrifice liberty for no apparent enhancement of security. . . .

The government also contends the issue whether AT&T received a certification authorizing its assistance to the government is a state secret.

The procedural requirements and impact of a certification under Title III are addressed in 18 U.S.C. § 2511(2)(a)(ii):

> Notwithstanding any other law, providers of wire or electronic communication service, their officers, employees, and agents, . . . are authorized to provide information, facilities, or technical assistance to persons authorized by law to intercept wire, oral, or electronic communications or to conduct electronic surveillance, as defined in section 101 of [FISA] . . . . if such provider, its officers, employees, or agents, . . . has been provided with — . . .
>
> (B) a certification in writing by a person specified in section 2518(7) of this title [18 U.S.C.S. § 2518(7)] or the Attorney General of the United States that no warrant or court order is required by law, that all statutory requirements have been met, and that the specified assistance is required. . . .

Although it is doubtful whether plaintiffs' *constitutional* claim would be barred by a valid certification under section 2511(2)(a)(ii), this provision on its face makes clear that a valid certification would preclude the *statutory* claims asserted here. See 18 U.S.C. § 2511(2)(a)(ii) ("No cause of action shall lie in any court against any provider of wire or electronic communication service . . . . for providing information, facilities, or assistance in accordance with the terms of a . . . certification under this chapter.").

As noted above, it is not a secret for purposes of the state secrets privilege that AT&T and the government have some kind of intelligence relationship. Nonetheless, the court recognizes that uncovering whether and to what extent a certification exists might reveal information about AT&T's assistance to the government that has not been publicly disclosed. Accordingly, in applying the state secrets privilege to the certification question, the court must look deeper at what information has been publicly revealed about the alleged electronic surveillance programs. The following chart summarizes what the government has disclosed about the scope of these programs in terms of (1) the individuals whose communications are being monitored, (2) the locations of those individuals and (3) the types of information being monitored:

<table>
<tr><td></td><td>Purely Domestic</td><td colspan="2">Domestic-Foreign</td></tr>
<tr><td></td><td>Communication Content</td><td>Communication Content</td><td>Communication Records</td></tr>
<tr><td>General Public</td><td>Government DENIES</td><td>Government DENIES</td><td rowspan="2">Government NEITHER CONFIRMS NOR DENIES</td></tr>
<tr><td>Al Qaeda or affiliate member/agent</td><td>Government DENIES</td><td>Government CONFIRMS</td></tr>
</table>

As the chart relates, the government's public disclosures regarding monitoring of "communication content" (i.e., wiretapping or listening in on a communication) differ significantly from its disclosures regarding "communication records" (i.e., collecting ancillary data pertaining to a communication, such as the telephone numbers dialed by an individual). . . .

Beginning with the warrantless monitoring of "communication content," the government has confirmed that it monitors "contents of communications where . . . one party to the communication is outside the United States" and the government has "a reasonable basis to conclude that one party to the communication is a member of al Qaeda, affiliated with al Qaeda, or a member of an organization affiliated with al Qaeda, or working in support of al Qaeda." The government denies listening in without a warrant on any purely domestic communications or communications in which neither party has a connection to al Qaeda or a related terrorist organization. In sum, regarding the government's monitoring of "communication content," the government has disclosed the universe of possibilities in terms of *whose* communications it monitors and *where* those communicating parties are located.

Based on these public disclosures, the court cannot conclude that the existence of a certification regarding the "communication content" program is a state secret. If the government's public disclosures have been truthful, revealing whether AT&T has received a certification to assist in monitoring communication content should not reveal any new information that would assist a terrorist and adversely affect national security. And if the government has not been truthful, the state secrets privilege should not serve as a shield for its false public statements. In short, the government has opened the door for judicial inquiry by publicly confirming and denying material information about its monitoring of communication content.

Accordingly, the court concludes that the state secrets privilege will not prevent AT&T from asserting a certification-based defense, as appropriate, regarding allegations that it assisted the government in monitoring communication content. The court envisions that AT&T could confirm or deny the existence of a certification authorizing monitoring of communication content through a combination of responses to interrogatories and *in camera* review by the court. Under this approach, AT&T could reveal information at the level of generality at which the government has publicly confirmed or denied its monitoring of communication content. This approach would also enable AT&T to disclose the non-privileged information described here while withholding any incidental privileged information that a certification might contain.

Turning to the alleged monitoring of communication records, the court notes that despite many public reports on the matter, the government has neither confirmed nor denied whether it monitors communication records and has never publicly disclosed whether the NSA program reported by *USA Today* on May 11, 2006, actually exists. Although BellSouth, Verizon and Qwest have denied participating in this program, AT&T has neither confirmed nor denied its involvement. Hence, unlike the program monitoring communication content, the general contours and even the existence of the alleged communication records program remain unclear. . . .

[T]he court recognizes that it is not in a position to estimate a terrorist's risk preferences, which might depend on facts not before the court. For example, it may be that a terrorist is unable to avoid AT&T by choosing another provider or, for reasons outside his control, his communications might necessarily be routed through an AT&T facility. Revealing that a communication records program exists might encourage that terrorist to switch to less efficient but less detectable forms of communication. And revealing that such a program does not exist might encourage a terrorist to use AT&T services when he would not have done so otherwise. Accordingly, for present purposes, the court does not require AT&T to disclose what relationship, if any, it has with this alleged program.

The court stresses that it does not presently conclude that the state secrets privilege will necessarily preclude AT&T from revealing later in this litigation information about the alleged communication records program. While this case has been pending, the government and telecommunications companies have made substantial public disclosures on the alleged NSA programs. It is conceivable that these entities might disclose, either deliberately or accidentally, other pertinent information about the communication records program as this litigation proceeds. The court recognizes such disclosures might make this program's existence or non-existence no longer a secret. Accordingly, while the court presently declines to permit any discovery regarding the alleged communication records program, if appropriate, plaintiffs can request that the court revisit this issue in the future.

Finally, the court notes plaintiffs contend that Congress, through various statutes, has limited the state secrets privilege in the context of electronic surveillance and has abrogated the privilege regarding the existence of a government certification. Because these arguments potentially implicate highly complicated separation of powers issues regarding Congress' ability to abrogate what the government contends is a constitutionally protected privilege, the court declines to address these issues presently, particularly because the issues might very well be obviated by future public disclosures by the government and AT&T. If necessary, the court may revisit these arguments at a later stage of this litigation. . . .

[F]or purposes of the present motion to dismiss, plaintiffs have stated sufficient facts to allege injury-in-fact for all their claims. "At the pleading stage, general factual allegations of injury resulting from the defendant's conduct may suffice, for on a motion to dismiss we 'presume that general allegations embrace those specific facts that are necessary to support the claim.'" *Lujan,* 504 U.S. at 561 (quoting *Lujan v. National Wildlife Federation,* 497 U.S. 871 (1990)). Throughout the complaint, plaintiffs generally describe the injuries they have allegedly suffered because of AT&T's illegal conduct and its collaboration with the government. . . . Here, the alleged injury is concrete even though it is widely shared. Despite AT&T's alleged creation of a dragnet to intercept all or substantially all of its customers' communications, this dragnet necessarily inflicts a concrete injury that affects each customer in a distinct way, depending on the content of that customer's communications and the time that customer spends using AT&T services. Indeed, the present situation resembles a scenario in which "large numbers of individuals suffer the same common-law injury (say, a widespread mass tort)."

NOTES & QUESTIONS

1. ***Background on* Al-Haramain: *The Sealed Document.*** How did the Sealed Document in *Al-Haramain* wind up sealed? Where did it come from? Patrick Radden Keefe has interviewed Al-Haramain's attorneys, including Lynne Bernabei, to whom the Treasury Department had accidently sent the top secret material.[114] Based on these interviews, he explains:

> The document that the Treasury Department turned over to Bernabei appears to have been a summary of intercepted telephone conversations between two of Al Haramain's American lawyers, in Washington, and one of the charity's officers, in Saudia Arabia. The government had evidently passed along proof of surveillance to the targets of that surveillance, and supplied the Oregon branch of Al Haramian — a suspected terrorist organization — with ammunition to challenge the constitutionality of the warrantless-wiretapping program.

Keefe explains that the FBI itself retrieved almost all copies of this document from Bernabei, her fellow attorneys, and her clients. It did not, however, seek to retrieve the copies of these documents that went to two of her clients then living in the Middle East. At some point in the litigation, these copies were sent back to Al-Haramain's attorneys, who turned them over to the district court, which then segregated them from the other evidence.

2. ***State Secrets and Standing I:* Al-Haramain Islamic Foundation.** In *Al-Haramain Islamic Foundation*, the Ninth Circuit decided that the Bush administration had revealed too much about the TSP to claim that the very subject matter of the litigation was a state secret. Yet, it did agree that the Sealed Document, which the Treasury Department had inadvertently provided to the Al-Haramain Islamic Foundation, was protected by the state secret doctrine. The Ninth Circuit also found that the state secrets privilege prevented the plaintiffs, the Al-Haramain Foundation, from reconstructing "the essence of the document through memory." Without reference to the Sealed Document, Al-Haramain could not establish that it suffered injury-in-fact. Hence, it lacked standing.

   As a final matter, the Ninth Circuit remanded the case back to the lower court on the issue whether FISA preempts the state secrets privilege. If this statutory framework is found to displace the evidentiary privilege, its "detailed regime" would be used to determine the legality of the NSA surveillance.

3. ***State Secrets and Standing II:* Hepting.** In *Hepting*, the plaintiffs alleged that AT&T was collaborating with the NSA in a massive warrantless surveillance program, namely, the TSP. As customers of AT&T, the plaintiffs alleged that they suffered injury from this surveillance. But what about the state secrets privilege? Recall that in *Al-Haramain*, the plaintiffs' ability to demonstrate an injury turned on access to the Sealed Document or their memories of it. Without access to the documents, the Ninth Circuit found that the Al-

[114] Patrick Radden Keefe, *Annals of Surveillance: State Secrets*, New Yorker, Apr. 28, 2008.

Haramain Foundation and other plaintiffs could not show standing. In contrast, the *Hepting* plaintiffs alleged injury due to *non-targeted* surveillance under the TSP.

The *Hepting* court found that the existence of the TSP was itself not a state secret. It found that (1) the Bush administration had disclosed "the general contours" of the TSP, which (2) "requires the assistance of a telecommunications provider," and (3) AT&T helps the government in classified matters when asked. Do you agree that these allegations are sufficient to establish standing?

4. ***State Secrets and Standing III: Other Cases.*** Two federal courts have found plaintiffs lacking in standing in attempted litigation against the NSA surveillance. First, the Sixth Circuit in *ACLU v. NSA*, 493 F.3d 644 (6th Cir. 2007), ruled that the plaintiffs lacked standing under the (1) First Amendment, (2) Fourth Amendment, (3) separation of powers, (4) the Wiretap Act, and (5) FISA. As an illustration of its approach, it rejected the plaintiff's Fourth Amendment standing claim because there was no "evidence that the plaintiffs themselves have been subjected to an illegal search or seizure." As for FISA, the Sixth Circuit declared that the plaintiffs have not shown that they were subject to NSA surveillance; "[T]hus — for the same reason they could not maintain their Fourth Amendment claim — they cannot establish that they are 'aggrieved persons' under FISA's statutory scheme."

In dissent, Judge Ronald Gilman argued that plaintiffs had standing to challenge the program because of "specific present harms" that the attorney-plaintiffs faced due to conflicting duties to their clients in light of the real risk that their communications with them would be overhead. Gilman stated: "The TSP forces them to decide between breaching their duty of confidentiality to their clients and breaching their duty to provide zealous representation. Neither position is tenable." Gillman's dissent also argued that TSP violated FISA and the Wiretap Act

Like the Sixth Circuit in *ACLU v. NSA*, the district court in *Terkel v. AT&T*, 441 F. Supp. 2d 899 (N.D. Ill. 2006), found that the plaintiffs lacked standing. According to the *Terkel* court, the plaintiffs had no standing because of their inability to prove that AT&T had disclosed their records to the government. The *Terkel* court also observed that the case before it differed from *Hepting* in two significant ways. First, the *Terkel* plaintiffs challenged the alleged disclosure of *records* about customer communications and not *contents,* as was the case in *Hepting.* Second, the *Terkel* plaintiffs sought prospective relief only, while the *Hepting* plaintiffs also sought damages for past violations.

The *Terkel* court found that disclosures about past governmental activities were of limited value to the plaintiffs before it. Due to the lack of public disclosure of whether or not AT&T had surrendered records to the NSA, the plaintiffs were unable "to prove their standing to sue for prospective relief." The court declared that "based on the government's public submission," it was "persuaded that requiring AT&T to confirm or deny whether it has disclosed large quantities of telephone records to the federal government could give adversaries of this country valuable insight into the government's intelligence activities." It concluded: "Because requiring such disclosures would therefore adversely affect our national security, such disclosures are barred by the state secrets privilege."

5. ***The* Reynolds *Precedent.*** The birth of the modern states secret privilege is *Reynolds v. United States*, 345 U.S. 1 (1953). In this Cold War era case, the Supreme Court drew on English precedents regarding crown privilege. The *Reynolds* Court found that the "occasion for the privilege is appropriate when a court finds "from all the circumstances of the case, that there is a reasonable danger that compulsion of the evidence will expose military matters, which, in the interests of national security, should not be divulged."

   In *Reynolds*, a B-29 military aircraft had crashed and killed members of its crew as well as three civilian observers on board the flight. Their widows sued the government under the Federal Tort Claims Act and sought discovery of the official accident investigation of the Air Force. The Supreme Court found both a "reasonable danger that the accident investigation report would contain" state secrets and a "dubious showing of necessity" by the plaintiffs. It reversed the Third Circuit's decision and sustained the government's claim of privilege.

   In 2000, the Air Force declassified the accident report at stake in *Reynolds*. As William Weaver and Robert M. Pallitto summarize, "The material originally requested by the plaintiffs in *Reynolds* has recently been made public through Freedom of Information Act requests, and it contained no classified or national security information."[115] In 2005, the Third Circuit heard a claim from a surviving widow and five heirs of the other, now deceased widows, in the original action. In this case, *Herring v. United States*, 424 F.3d 383 (3d Cir. 2005), the plaintiff's claim was that the officials "fraudulently misrepresented the nature of the [accident] report in a way that caused the widows to settle their case for less than its full value."

   The Third Circuit rejected this claim. The plaintiffs failed to show a fraud upon the court related to the Air Force's assertions of military secrets privilege for the contested accident report in the *Reynolds*. It found that the statements of the government officials at the time of the *Reynolds* litigation were "susceptible of a truthful interpretation." For the *Herring* court, the question was not whether the accident report actually contained sensitive information about the mission and the electronic equipment involvement. Rather, it would be enough if these reports could reasonably be read "to assert privilege over technical information about the B-29." The statements could be read in that fashion; "the claim of privilege referred to the B-29 itself rather than solely the secret mission and equipment."

   Note as well that the *Reynolds* Court had not examined the documents itself, or sought to release the information to plaintiffs in redacted form. Courts continue to be reluctant to examine information about which the government has claimed the states secret privilege. As Weaver and Pallitto state, "In less than one-third of reported cases in which the privilege has been

---

[115] William G. Weaver & Robert M. Pallitto, *State Secrets and Executive Power*, 120 Pol. Sci. Q. 85, 99 (2005).

invoked have the courts required in camera inspection of documents, and they have only required such inspection five times out of the twenty-three reported cases since the presidency of George H.W. Bush."[116]

6. ***Statutory Reform?*** The state secrets privilege is a common law privilege; and it is one without a formal expression in any federal statute. Weaver and Pallitto observe:

> our own attempts to obtain policies governing assertion of the state secrets privilege met with failure, inasmuch as there appear to be no policy guidelines on the use of the privilege in any major department or agency of the executive branch. Freedom of Information Act requests to some three dozen agencies and their various subcomponents yielded nothing in the way of documentation of guidance for use of the privilege. Any limitations on assertion of the privilege appear to be self-imposed by the individual agencies, and use of the privilege seems to be carried out ad hoc at the discretion of the agency heads and their assistants.[117]

A bi-partisan bill, introduced by Senator Edward Kennedy and co-sponsored by Senator Arlen Specter, S. 2533, would limit the state secret doctrine. The bill would require the government to explain why it is invoking the privilege and to attempt to "craft a non-privileged substitute" for the privileged evidence. It also does much to strengthen the judiciary's power. For example, it instructs the court to review a specific item of evidence to determine whether the claim of the government is valid. Its rule for determining the applicability of the privilege is as follows: "Evidence is subject to the states secret privilege if it contains a state secret, or there is no possible means of effectively segregating it from other evidence that contains a state secret."

Is the state secrets doctrine in need of reform? If so, how ought it to be reshaped?

7. ***Checking the Executive.*** Neal Katyal and Richard Caplan have traced the history of "one of the most important periods of presidentially imposed surveillance in wartime" — President Franklin Delano Roosevelt's (FDR) wiretapping and his secret defiance of a congressional prohibition on wiretapping, enacted in § 605 of the 1934 Communications Act. FDR's secret wiretapping also defied the Supreme Court's decisions in two cases. Nonetheless, FDR in a secret memo authorized the Attorney General to wiretap in cases "involving the defense of the nation." Katyal and Caplan state, "[T]here is evidence suggesting that the wiretapping policy was extensively implemented. . . ."

Katyal and Caplan strongly reject the precedential value of FDR's action as a defense of the Bush Administration's program. They note that the FDR program's precedential value is limited because it was secret, and, moreover, that the fact "that a President — even a great one — acted in a certain way does not mean that future Presidents are justified in following his lead." And they also observe:

---

[116] *Id.* at 101.
[117] *Id.* at 111.

> . . . [A]s a matter of constitutional governance, it is exceptionally dangerous to vest a President with the power to break the laws, at least at a time when Congress can act. . . . If the President is unable to persuade Congress to authorize a measure he believes necessary to national security, there is likely to be good reason for that refusal. . . .
>
> [A]n obvious exception to the above analysis [is] for those short-term emergencies in which Congress is incapable of action. . . . But that emergency power must, in a constitutional democracy, be tightly circumscribed. . . . Emergency power would otherwise convert itself into a tool for lawbreaking in perpetuity. So the theory of emergency power might justify the first days of the Administration's NSA program, but certainly not one many months (or years) later. Indeed, Congress passed over a dozen pieces of post 9-11 legislation (including, most obviously, the Patriot Act), within three months of the attacks. The notion that an emergency precluded Congress from altering FISA to permit the NSA program is simply implausible. . . .

Katyal and Caplan go on to argue that Congress has proven ineffective to check the President during times of crisis:

> Congress's ineffectiveness stems partially from the fact that it is often dominated by security interests and unable to vote for "liberty" when such decisions will be portrayed as against "security." But it also stems from the reality that the President holds the veto pen. So Congress, even once apprised (and aghast) about a massive electronic surveillance program, cannot easily act. So long as the President claims to ground his surveillance program in some law, no matter how dubious, it will require Congress to pass a new law to trump that interpretation. And because Article I, section 7, requires a bicameral supermajority to override a veto, the only way such legislation can pass is with widespread support in both houses. Given the American political-party system, loyalty to the President alone will stymie such efforts. As a result of Congress's appreciation of this voting problem ex ante, it often does not even try to launch reforms.[118]

To effectively check the Executive Branch, Katyal and Caplan recommend creating "institutional friction" — that is, tensions and rivalries within government. But won't this approach just make the Executive Branch less effective — and in an area with important consequences for national security?

In its defense of the legality of the TSP, the Department of Justice points to "the President's well-recognized inherent constitutional authority as Commander in Chief and sole organ for the Nation in foreign affairs to conduct warrantless surveillance of enemy forces for intelligence purposes to detect and disrupt armed attacks on the United States."[119] Given "[t]he Government's overwhelming interest in detecting and thwarting further al Qaeda attacks," why should the Executive Branch be burdened with more "institutional friction"?

8. ***The End of FISA?*** William Banks argues: "At a minimum, the unraveling of FISA and emergence of the TSP call into question the virtual disappearance

[118] Neal Katyal & Richard Caplan, *The Surprisingly Strong Case for the Legality of the NSA Surveillance Program: The FDR Precedent*, 60 Stan. L. Rev. 1023 (2008).

[119] U.S. Department of Justice, *Legal Authorities Supporting the Activities of the National Security Agency Described by the President* 39-40 (Jan. 19, 2006).

of effective oversight of our national security surveillance. The Congress and federal courts have become observers of the system, not even participants, much less overseers."[120] He proposes: "If FISA is to have any meaningful role for the next thirty years, its central terms will have to be restored, one way or another."

In contrast, John Yoo argues that such surveillance should be permitted where there is a reasonable chance that terrorists will appear, or communicate, even if we do not know their specific identities. Yoo argues that in cases where there is a likelihood, perhaps "a 50 percent chance" that terrorists would use a certain kind of avenue for reaching each other, "[a] FISA-based approach would prevent computers from searching through that channel for keywords or names that might suggest terrorist communications."[121]

A third approach is proposed by Orin Kerr, who would update FISA beyond its current approach, which depends "on the identity and location of who is being monitored.[122] In contrast to this "person-focused" approach, Kerr would add "a complementary set of data-focused authorities" to the statute. Under this second approach, "Surveillance practices should be authorized when the government establishes a likelihood that surveillance would yield what I call 'terrorist intelligence information' — information relevant to terrorism investigations. . . ." Kerr is unwilling to state, however, whether the data-focused approach ("used when identities and/or location are unknown") should or should not require any kind of warrant.

9. ***The FISA Amendments Act.*** Considerable controversy accompanied the congressional enactment of the FAA. Senator Russ Feingold stated that the FAA was "not a compromise" but "a capitulation." Further, he declared:

> [T]he FISA Amendments Act, like the Protect America Act, would authorize the government to collect all communications between the U.S. and the rest of the world. That could mean millions upon millions of communications between innocent Americans and their friends, families, or business associates overseas could legally be collected. Parents calling their kids studying abroad, emails to friends serving in Iraq — all of these communications could be collected, with absolutely no suspicion of any wrongdoing, under this legislation. . . .
>
> The bill's supporters like to say that the government needs additional powers to target terrorists overseas. But under this bill, the government is not limited to targeting foreigners outside the U.S. who are terrorists, or who are suspected of some wrongdoing, or who are members or agents of some foreign government or organization. In fact, the government does not even need a specific purpose for wiretapping anyone overseas. All it needs to have is a general "foreign intelligence" purpose, which is a standard so broad that it covers all international communications.[123]

---

[120] William C. Banks, *The Death of FISA*, 91 Minn. L. Rev. 1209, 1297 (2007).

[121] John Yoo, *War By Other Means: An Insider's Accounts of the War on Terror* 112 (2006).

[122] Orin Kerr, *Updating the Foreign Intelligence Surveillance Act*, 75 U. Chi. L. Rev. 238 (2008).

[123] Russ Feingold, Remarks of U.S. Senator Russ Feingold, Opposing H.R. 6304, at http://feingold.senate.gov/~feingold/statements/08/06/20080625f.htm.

In contrast, President Bush, in signing the FAA, stated that it would "ensure that our intelligence community professionals have the tools they need to protect our country in the years to come. The Director of National Intelligence and the Attorney General both report that, once enacted, this law will provide vital assistance to our intelligence officials in their work to thwart terrorist plots."[124]

The FAA also provided retroactive immunity to cooperating telecommunications companies. What impact will the FAA have on *Al-Haramain*? On *Hepting*?

10. ***Inherent Executive Power.*** As noted above, the Department of Justice issued a white paper on January 19, 2006 in defense of the NSA warrantless wiretapping. A large part of its defense concerned the inherent authority of the Executive in this area. It states, "In exercising his constitutional powers, the President has wide discretion, consistent with the Constitution, over the methods of gathering intelligence about the Nation's enemies in a time of armed conflict." This power extends to the Executive's "inherent constitutional power to conduct warrantless searches and surveillance within the United States for foreign intelligence purposes."

Others have questioned the President's inherent power to engage in warrantless wiretapping in light of congressional legislation in this area through the Wiretap Act and FISA. The Congressional Research Service (CRS), a nonpartisan research branch of the Library of Congress, notes the importance in resolving this question of the enactment of the Wiretap Act, FISA, and the Wiretap Act's exclusivity language (the Wiretap Act states that FISA is to be "exclusive means" for carrying out the interception of foreign or international communications, 18 U.S.C. § 1511(2)(f)).[125] Thus, Congress did intend "to cabin the President's exercise of any inherent constitutional authority to engage in foreign intelligence electronic surveillance." Yet, the CRS also points to language in the Court of Review's decision in *In re Sealed Case*, which we excerpt above, that suggests that the President continues to have power to authorize electronic surveillance outside of FISA. It concludes, "Whether such authority may exist only to those areas which were not addressed by FISA in its definition of 'electronic surveillance' or is of broader sweep appears to be a matter with respect to which they are differing views."

In contrast, in a letter to Congress, 14 legal experts, including Curtis Bradley, David Cole, Walter Dellinger, Ronald Dworkin, Richard Epstein, William S. Sessions (former FBI director), Geoffrey Stone, Laurence Tribe, and Kathleen Sullivan found that the President did not have inherent power that would allow overriding FISA.[126] The experts find that Congress expressly prohibited the NSA domestic spying program by enactment of FISA, and that FISA's limitations are consistent with the President's role under Article II of

---

[124] The White House, *President Bush Signs H.R. 6304, FISA Amendments Act of 2008* (July 10, 2008), at http://www.whitehouse.gov/news/releases/2008/07/20080710-2.html.

[125] Congressional Research Service, *Presidential Authority to Conduct Warrantless Electronic Surveillance to Gather Foreign Intelligence Information* (Jan. 5, 2006).

[126] Curtis Bradley et al., *On NSA Spying: A Letter to Congress*, N.Y. Rev. Books (Feb. 9, 2006).

the Constitution. The letter observes, the DOJ "fails to offer a plausible legal defense of the NSA domestic spying program. If the administration felt that FISA was insufficient, the proper course was to seek legislative amendment, as it did with other aspects of FISA in the Patriot Act . . . [I]t is also beyond dispute that, . . . the President cannot simply violate criminal laws behind closed doors because he deems them obsolete or impracticable." To what extent, are these arguments against the President's inherent power to override FISA now moot with Congressional granting immunity to the tele-communication companies with FAA in 2008?

CHAPTER 4

HEALTH AND GENETIC PRIVACY

Health and genetic information is considered by many to be among the most private of information. People desire to keep matters about their health confidential because certain diseases have long been associated with great stigma (e.g., leprosy); other diseases are correlated in other people's minds with certain lifestyles and behaviors (e.g., sexually transmitted diseases), and certain debilitating or fatal illnesses might alter people's perception of the sufferer's capabilities and potentialities. Further, people want to keep illnesses private because they want to prevent others from viewing them differently. Knowledge of a person's health can result in being turned down for a job, being fired, being discriminated against, being rejected for a loan, and so on.

Today's health care system is vast and complex. Medical data is frequently disclosed to doctors and is widely circulated among hospitals, insurers, employers, and government agencies. At hospitals, dozens of nurses and staff have access to a patient's records. Currently, the United States is undergoing a transformation in medical recordkeeping, as more and more medical records are computerized. The increasing transformation of medical records into digital format will greatly facilitate the flow of health data. One health care provider has even announced plans to build the world's first all-digital hospital.[1] This hospital will have computerized medical records, patient beds equipped with computer screens and Internet access, and wireless communications for physicians and health care workers.

The move toward computerized medical records can bring great benefits, as it will enhance the accuracy of people's medical histories as well as the ease with which doctors can learn about important and relevant aspects of their patient's health. However, the increasing flow of health information raises substantial privacy concerns as well.

Health privacy in the United States is governed by a myriad of different laws and regulations. States have traditionally been the primary source for health privacy law. The privacy torts can provide remedies for intrusions into areas where one is receiving health care or public disclosures of private medical

[1] Michelle C. Pierre, Note, *New Technology, Old Issues: The All-Digital Hospital and Medical Information Privacy*, 56 Rutgers L. Rev. 541, 541-42 (2004).

information. Tort law also regulates the confidentiality of the relationship between patients and their physicians or other health caregivers. Additionally, many states have passed a variety of statutes to regulate health privacy. The level of protection, however, varies widely from state to state.

At the federal level, health privacy was unregulated until the last years of the twentieth century. Pursuant to its authority under the Health Insurance Portability and Accountability Act (HIPAA), enacted in 1996, the Department of Health and Human Services promulgated regulations under HIPAA. It issued its final HIPAA Rule in December 2000. The ensuing framework provides a minimum level of protection for all states. State regulations more protective of privacy still remain in effect. Health privacy is also protected by the constitutional right to privacy, but this protection applies only to data maintained by government officials and entities. This limitation flows from the requirement in the U.S. Constitution that there be "state action" before most constitutional rights apply.

By the end of the twentieth century, enormous changes began to take place in how medical professionals provided their services in the United States. A widening audience of outsiders now collects patient medical information in order to monitor and shape how health care is administered.[2]

In addition to allowing this external monitoring of physicians and patients, the sharing of personal medical data has played a central role in the shift to large, integrated systems for providing health care in the United States. Such integrated delivery systems coordinate the services of numerous health care professionals, whether located in hospitals, clinics, or outpatient facilities. The computer is essential to this transformation; it allows both the collection of extensive personal health data and the rapid sharing of such information throughout a corporate structure. The introduction of electronic health care records is playing an important role in this transformation of medical services.

A. CONFIDENTIALITY OF MEDICAL INFORMATION

1. PROFESSIONAL ETHICS AND EVIDENTIARY PRIVILEGES

(a) Ethical Rules

OATH AND LAW OF HIPPOCRATES

(circa 400 B.C.)

Whatever, in connection with my professional service, or not in connection with it, I see or hear, in the life of men, which ought not to be spoken of abroad, I will not divulge, as reckoning that all such should be kept secret.

---

[2] Paul M. Schwartz, *Privacy and the Economics of Health Care Information*, 76 Tex. L. Rev. 1 (1997).

CURRENT OPINIONS OF THE JUDICIAL COUNCIL OF THE AMERICAN MEDICAL ASSOCIATION CANON 5.05

. . . [T]he information disclosed to a physician during the course of the relationship between physician and patient is confidential to the greatest possible degree. . . . The physician should not reveal confidential communications or information without the express consent of the patient, unless required to do so by law.

(b) Evidentiary Privileges

An evidentiary privilege confers on an individual the right to refuse to testify or reveal facts about certain matters or the right to prevent another from doing so. Evidentiary privileges apply to almost all governmental proceedings, particularly judicial proceedings. Privileges permit the suppression of truthful and relevant evidence. For example, a client may tell her attorney certain confidential inculpatory information. The attorney-client privilege protects the confidentiality of that communication; generally, an attorney cannot be forced to testify as to that information.

There are a number of recognized privileges — and certain exceptions to them. The central privilege is the attorney-client privilege. In *Upjohn Co. v. United States*, 449 U.S. 383 (1981), the Supreme Court explained the rationale behind this privilege:

> The attorney-client privilege is the oldest of the privileges for confidential communications known to the common law. Its purpose is to encourage full and frank communication between attorneys and their clients and thereby promote broader public interests in the observance of law and administration of justice. The privilege recognizes that sound legal advice or advocacy serves public ends and that such advice or advocacy depends upon the lawyer's being fully informed by the client. As we stated last Term in *Trammel v. United States*, "The lawyer-client privilege rests on the need for the advocate and counselor to know all that relates to the client's reasons for seeking representation if the professional mission is to be carried out." And in *Fisher v. United States*, we recognized the purpose of the privilege to be "to encourage clients to make full disclosure to their attorneys."

In *Upjohn*, the Court found that the attorney-client privilege extended to in-house counsel at corporations. It also held communications between Upjohn's general counsel and lower level employees to be privileged. These communications were made "within the scope of the employees' corporate duties, and the employees themselves were sufficiently aware that they were being questioned in order that the corporation could obtain legal advice." The Court observed, "Consistent with the underlying purposes of the attorney-client privilege, these communications must be protected against compelled disclosure."

Evidentiary privileges protect only certain confidential relationships. Some recognized privileges include the (1) spousal privilege whereby a person can refuse to testify against his or her spouse in a criminal case; (2) spousal privilege in preventing one's spouse or former spouse from disclosing marital communications in criminal or civil cases; (3) accountant-client privilege; (4) priest-penitent privilege, whereby a person can prevent the disclosure of confidential communications made when seeking spiritual advice from his or her clergy member; (5) physician-patient privilege; (6) voter privilege, whereby a person can refuse to testify as to how he or she voted in any political election; (7) journalist privilege, where journalists can refuse to divulge information sources; and (8) executive privilege, permitting the President of the United States from divulging secrets necessary to the carrying out of his or her constitutional functions. Not all of these privileges are recognized in every state or in the federal courts. Further, the precise contours of each privilege sometimes vary from state to state.

Not all confidential relationships are protected by privileges. Although spousal privileges are widely recognized, the vast majority of jurisdictions do not recognize a parent-child privilege.

Privileges protect communications by both parties to a confidential relationship. Thus, with regard to the physician-patient privilege, statements made by the holder of the privilege (the patient) as well as by the physician to the patient are privileged.

The holder of the privilege may waive the privilege, but the professional remains bound by the privilege and is not permitted to waive it without the holder's consent. It is well settled that a voluntary knowing disclosure waives a privilege. *See Gray v. Bicknell,* 86 F.3d 1472 (8th Cir. 1996). However, courts are split as to whether inadvertent disclosures waive the privilege. *See, e.g., Georgetown Manor, Inc. v. Ethan Allen, Inc.*, 753 F. Supp. 936 (S.D. Fla. 1991) (inadvertent disclosure does not waive the privilege); *In re Sealed Case*, 877 F.2d 976 (D.C. Cir. 1989) (inadvertent disclosure waives the privilege); *Gray v. Bicknell*, 86 F.3d 1472 (8th Cir. 1996) (inadvertent disclosure sometimes waives the privilege based on application of a five-factor test).

In certain circumstances the privilege does not apply. For example, if a patient sues a physician or a client sues an attorney, the physician or attorney can testify as to confidential matters at issue in the lawsuit. Another limitation is the crime-fraud exception, which provides that if the communication is made in furtherance of a crime, fraud, or other misconduct, then it is not privileged. *See United States v. Zolin*, 491 U.S. 554 (1989).

Unlike certain other privileges, such as the attorney-client privilege and priest-penitent privilege, the common law did not recognize the physician-patient privilege. In contrast, a majority of states have established a physician-patient privilege.[3] States make exceptions in the physician-patient privilege for the reporting of certain diseases or injuries that implicate public health and safety.

JAFFEE V. REDMOND

518 U.S. 1 (1996)

STEVENS, J. . . . Petitioner is the administrator of the estate of Ricky Allen. Respondents are Mary Lu Redmond, a former police officer, and the Village of

---

[3] *See* Glen Weissenberger, *Federal Evidence* § 501.8 (1996).

Hoffman Estates, Illinois, her employer during the time that she served on the police force. Petitioner commenced this action against respondents after Redmond shot and killed Allen while on patrol duty.

On June 27, 1991, Redmond was the first officer to respond to a "fight in progress" call at an apartment complex. As she arrived at the scene, two of Allen's sisters ran toward her squad car, waving their arms and shouting that there had been a stabbing in one of the apartments. Redmond testified at trial that she relayed this information to her dispatcher and requested an ambulance. She then exited her car and walked toward the apartment building. Before Redmond reached the building, several men ran out, one waving a pipe. When the men ignored her order to get on the ground, Redmond drew her service revolver. Two other men then burst out of the building, one, Ricky Allen, chasing the other. According to Redmond, Allen was brandishing a butcher knife and disregarded her repeated commands to drop the weapon. Redmond shot Allen when she believed he was about to stab the man he was chasing. Allen died at the scene. Redmond testified that before other officers arrived to provide support, "people came pouring out of the buildings," and a threatening confrontation between her and the crowd ensued.

Petitioner filed suit in Federal District Court alleging that Redmond had violated Allen's constitutional rights by using excessive force during the encounter at the apartment complex. The complaint sought damages under Rev. Stat. § 1979, 42 U.S.C. § 1983, and the Illinois wrongful-death statute. At trial, petitioner presented testimony from members of Allen's family that conflicted with Redmond's version of the incident in several important respects. They testified, for example, that Redmond drew her gun before exiting her squad car and that Allen was unarmed when he emerged from the apartment building.

During pretrial discovery petitioner learned that after the shooting Redmond had participated in about 50 counseling sessions with Karen Beyer, a clinical social worker licensed by the State of Illinois and employed at that time by the Village of Hoffman Estates. Petitioner sought access to Beyer's notes concerning the sessions for use in cross-examining Redmond. Respondents vigorously resisted the discovery. They asserted that the contents of the conversations between Beyer and Redmond were protected against involuntary disclosure by a psychotherapist-patient privilege. The district judge rejected this argument. Neither Beyer nor Redmond, however, complied with his order to disclose the contents of Beyer's notes. At depositions and on the witness stand both either refused to answer certain questions or professed an inability to recall details of their conversations.

In his instructions at the end of the trial, the judge advised the jury that the refusal to turn over Beyer's notes had no "legal justification" and that the jury could therefore presume that the contents of the notes would have been unfavorable to respondents. The jury awarded petitioner $45,000 on the federal claim and $500,000 on her state-law claim. . . .

Rule 501 of the Federal Rules of Evidence authorizes federal courts to define new privileges by interpreting "common law principles . . . in the light of reason and experience." . . . The Senate Report accompanying the 1975 adoption of the Rules indicates that Rule 501 "should be understood as reflecting the view that the recognition of a privilege based on a confidential relationship . . . should be determined on a case-by-case basis." The Rule thus did not freeze the law governing the privileges of witnesses in federal trials at a particular point in our history, but rather directed federal courts to "continue the evolutionary development of testimonial privileges."

The common-law principles underlying the recognition of testimonial privileges can be stated simply. "For more than three centuries it has now been recognized as a fundamental maxim that the public . . . has a right to every man's evidence. When we come to examine the various claims of exemption, we start with the primary assumption that there is a general duty to give what testimony one is capable of giving, and that any exemptions which may exist are distinctly exceptional, being so many derogations from a positive general rule." Exceptions from the general rule disfavoring testimonial privileges may be justified, however, by a "public good transcending the normally predominant principle of utilizing all rational means for ascertaining truth."

Guided by these principles, the question we address today is whether a privilege protecting confidential communications between a psychotherapist and her patient "promotes sufficiently important interests to outweigh the need for probative evidence. . . ." Both "reason and experience" persuade us that it does. . . .

Like the spousal and attorney-client privileges, the psychotherapist-patient privilege is "rooted in the imperative need for confidence and trust." Treatment by a physician for physical ailments can often proceed successfully on the basis of a physical examination, objective information supplied by the patient, and the results of diagnostic tests. Effective psychotherapy, by contrast, depends upon an atmosphere of confidence and trust in which the patient is willing to make a frank and complete disclosure of facts, emotions, memories, and fears. Because of the sensitive nature of the problems for which individuals consult psychotherapists, disclosure of confidential communications made during counseling sessions may cause embarrassment or disgrace. For this reason, the mere possibility of disclosure may impede development of the confidential relationship necessary for successful treatment. . . .

The psychotherapist privilege serves the public interest by facilitating the provision of appropriate treatment for individuals suffering the effects of a mental or emotional problem. The mental health of our citizenry, no less than its physical health, is a public good of transcendent importance.

In contrast to the significant public and private interests supporting recognition of the privilege, the likely evidentiary benefit that would result from the denial of the privilege is modest. If the privilege were rejected, confidential conversations between psychotherapists and their patients would surely be chilled, particularly when it is obvious that the circumstances that give rise to the need for treatment will probably result in litigation. Without a privilege, much of the desirable evidence to which litigants such as petitioner seek access — for example, admissions against interest by a party — is unlikely to come into being. This unspoken "evidence" will therefore serve no greater truth-seeking function than if it had been spoken and privileged.

That it is appropriate for the federal courts to recognize a psychotherapist privilege under Rule 501 is confirmed by the fact that all 50 States and the District of Columbia have enacted into law some form of psychotherapist privilege. . . .

. . . [W]e hold that confidential communications between a licensed psychotherapist and her patients in the course of diagnosis or treatment are protected from compelled disclosure under Rule 501 of the Federal Rules of Evidence. . . .

. . . The reasons for recognizing a privilege for treatment by psychiatrists and psychologists apply with equal force to treatment by a clinical social worker such as Karen Beyer. Today, social workers provide a significant amount of mental health treatment. Their clients often include the poor and those of modest means who could not afford the assistance of a psychiatrist or psychologist, but whose counseling sessions serve the same public goals. . . .

SCALIA, J. joined by REHNQUIST, C. J. dissenting. . . . The Court has discussed at some length the benefit that will be purchased by creation of the evidentiary privilege in this case: the encouragement of psychoanalytic counseling. It has not mentioned the purchase price: occasional injustice. That is the cost of every rule which excludes reliable and probative evidence — or at least every one categorical enough to achieve its announced policy objective. . . . For the rule proposed here, the victim is more likely to be some individual who is prevented from proving a valid claim — or (worse still) prevented from establishing a valid defense. The latter is particularly unpalatable for those who love justice, because it causes the courts of law not merely to let stand a wrong, but to become themselves the instruments of wrong. . . .

When is it, one must wonder, that the psychotherapist came to play such an indispensable role in the maintenance of the citizenry's mental health? For most of history, men and women have worked out their difficulties by talking to, *inter alios*, parents, siblings, best friends, and bartenders — none of whom was awarded a privilege against testifying in court. Ask the average citizen: Would your mental health be more significantly impaired by preventing you from seeing a psychotherapist, or by preventing you from getting advice from your mom? I have little doubt what the answer would be. Yet there is no mother-child privilege. . . .

Even where it is certain that absence of the psychotherapist privilege will inhibit disclosure of the information, it is not clear to me that that is an unacceptable state of affairs. Let us assume the very worst in the circumstances of the present case: that to be truthful about what was troubling her, the police officer who sought counseling would have to confess that she shot without reason, and wounded an innocent man. . . . [There is no] reason why she should be enabled to deny her guilt in the criminal trial — or in a civil trial for negligence — while yet obtaining the benefits of psychotherapy by confessing guilt to a social worker who cannot testify. It seems to me entirely fair to say that if she wishes the benefits of telling the truth she must also accept the adverse consequences. . . .

NOTES & QUESTIONS

1. ***Mental Health as a Public Good? Privacy as a Public Good?*** Justice Stevens's opinion for the Court speaks of mental health for the citizenry as providing "a public good of transcendent importance." The protection of confidential communications between a psychotherapist and her patient from involuntary disclosure serves this important public interest. More generally, Paul Schwartz has argued that privacy is such a public good. He writes: "A public good benefits all of society and is generally viewed as something that cannot be created through an unregulated market."[4] Schwartz also proposes that "information privacy can be seen as a commons that requires some degree of social and legal control to construct and then maintain." Will people decline to engage in a given social interaction (e.g., seeking psychotherapy) without the evidentiary privilege that *Jaffee* recognizes? Most people are unaware of evidence law when speaking with their therapist or doctor. Are privileges necessary to encourage frank disclosures by patients to therapists?
2. ***Is There a Dangerous Patient Exception to the Privilege?*** Are there any limits to the privilege? In a footnote the Court indicated that there might be certain limits:

   > Although it would be premature to speculate about most future developments in the federal psychotherapist privilege, we do not doubt that there are situations in which the privilege must give way, for example, if a serious threat of harm to the patient or to others can be averted only by means of a disclosure by the therapist.

   Following *Jaffee*, three federal appellate courts considered whether there was in fact a "dangerous patient exception" to the privilege as suggested by the footnote above. In *United States v. Glass*, 113 F.3d 1356 (10th Cir. 1998), the court acknowledged that there may be "situations in which the privilege must give way." In contrast, the court in *United States v. Hayes*, 227 F.3d 578 (6th Cir. 2000), concluded that there is no "'dangerous patient' exception to the federal psychotherapist/patient testimonial privilege." In *United States v. Chase*, 340 F.3d. 978 (9th Cir. 2003) (en banc), the Ninth Circuit agreed with *Hayes*:

   > A dangerous-patient exception to the federal psychotherapist-patient testimonial privilege would significantly injure the interests justifying the existence of the privilege; would have little practical advantage; would encroach significantly on the policy prerogatives of the states; and would go against the experience of all but one of the states in our circuit, as well as the persuasive Proposed Rules. We therefore decline to recognize a dangerous-patient exception to the federal psychotherapist-patient privilege.

---

[4] Paul M. Schwartz, *Property, Privacy, and Personal Data*, 117 Harv. L. Rev. 2055, 2087-88 (2004).

2. TORT LIABILITY FOR DISCLOSURE OF PATIENT INFORMATION

MCCORMICK V. ENGLAND

494 S.E.2d 431 (S.C. Ct. App. 1997)

ANDERSON, J. . . . Dr. England was the family physician for McCormick, her former husband, and their children. McCormick and her husband became involved in a divorce action in which custody of the children was at issue. In support of his Motion for Emergency Relief and a Restraining Order, McCormick's husband submitted . . . letters to the family court regarding McCormick's emotional status. . . . [One] letter was prepared by Dr. England and was addressed "To Whom It May Concern." In his letter, Dr. England diagnosed McCormick as suffering from "major depression and alcoholism, acute and chronic." Further, Dr. England stated the children had experienced school difficulties due to the family discord caused by McCormick's drinking. He stated it was his medical opinion that McCormick was "a danger to herself and to her family with her substance abuse and major depressive symptoms," and concluded that she required hospitalization. There is no indication in the record that the letter was prepared under court order. [Among other things, McCormick sued for public disclosure of private facts and breach of confidentiality. The trial court dismissed her breach of confidentiality claim, stating that "It is well known that South Carolina does not recognize the physician-patient privilege at common law." McCormick appeals.] . . .

Whether a separate tort action for a physician's breach of a duty of confidentiality exists under the common law is a novel issue in this state. Dr. England contends South Carolina courts have previously ruled that no duty of confidentiality exists between a physician and patient; therefore, there can be no action for its breach. . . .

"At common law neither the patient nor the physician has the privilege to refuse to *disclose in court* a communication of one to the other, nor does either have a privilege that the communication not be disclosed to a third person." Although many states have statutorily created a "physician-patient testimonial privilege," South Carolina has not enacted a similar statute and does not recognize the physician-patient privilege. However, the absence of a testimonial privilege prohibiting certain in-court disclosures is not determinative of our issue because this evidentiary privilege is distinguishable from a duty of confidentiality. As our Supreme Court recently observed in *South Carolina State Board of Medical Examiners v. Hedgepath,* 480 S.E.2d 724 (S.C. 1997): "The terms 'privilege' and 'confidences' are not synonymous, and a professional's duty to maintain his client's confidences is independent of the issue whether he can be legally compelled to reveal some or all of those confidences, that is, whether those communications are privileged." . . .

A person who lacks medical training usually must disclose much information to his or her physician which may have a bearing upon diagnosis and treatment. Such disclosures are not totally voluntary; therefore, in order to obtain cooperation, it is expected that the physician will keep such information confidential. "Being a fiduciary relationship, mutual trust and confidence are essential."

The belief that physicians should respect the confidences revealed by their patients in the course of treatment is a concept that has its genesis in the Hippocratic Oath, which states in pertinent part: "Whatever, in connection with my professional practice, or not in connection with it, I see or hear, in the life of men, which ought not to be spoken of abroad, I will not divulge as reckoning that all such should be kept secret."

The modern trend recognizes that the confidentiality of the physician-patient relationship is an interest worth protecting. A majority of the jurisdictions faced with the issue have recognized a cause of action against a physician for the unauthorized disclosure of confidential information unless the disclosure is compelled by law or is in the patient's interest or the public interest.

In the absence of express legislation, courts have found the basis for a right of action for wrongful disclosure in four main sources: (1) state physician licensing statutes, (2) evidentiary rules and privileged communication statutes which prohibit a physician from testifying in judicial proceedings, (3) common law principles of trust, and (4) the Hippocratic Oath and principles of medical ethics which proscribe the revelation of patient confidences. The jurisdictions that recognize the duty of confidentiality have relied on various theories for the cause of action, including invasion of privacy, breach of implied contract, medical malpractice, and breach of a fiduciary duty or a duty of confidentiality. . . .

We find the reasoning of the cases from other jurisdictions persuasive on this issue and today we join the majority and hold that an actionable tort lies for a physician's breach of the duty to maintain the confidences of his or her patient in the absence of a compelling public interest or other justification for the disclosure. . . .

[Breach of confidentiality is a distinct tort from the tort of public disclosure of private facts.] Invasion of privacy consists of the public disclosure of private facts about the plaintiff, and the gravamen of the tort is publicity as opposed to mere publication. The defendant must intentionally reveal facts which are of no legitimate public interest, as there is no right of privacy in public matters. In addition, the disclosure must be such as would be highly offensive and likely to cause serious mental injury to a person of ordinary sensibilities.

Thus, an invasion of privacy claim narrowly proscribes the conduct to that which is "highly offensive" and "likely to cause serious mental injury." This standard is not consistent with the duty attaching to a confidential relationship because it focuses on the *content,* rather than the *source* of the information. The unauthorized revelation of confidential medical information should be protected without regard to the degree of its offensiveness. The privacy standard would not protect information that happens to be very distressing to a particular patient, even though the individual would likely not have revealed it without the expectation of confidentiality.

Further, the requirement of "publicity" is a limitation which would preclude many cases involving a breach of confidentiality. Publicity involves disclosure to the public, not just an individual or a small group. However, where the information disclosed is received in confidence, "one can imagine many cases where the greatest injury results from disclosure to a single person, such as a spouse, or to a small group, such as an insurance company resisting a claim. A confidential relationship is breached if unauthorized disclosure is made to only one person not a party to the confidence, but the right of privacy does not cover such a case." . . .

HAMMONDS V. AETNA CASUALTY & SURETY CO.

243 F. Supp. 793 (D. Ohio 1965)

CONNELL, C.J. Plaintiff has complained that the defendant insurance company, without just cause, had persuaded the plaintiff's treating physician to discontinue that relationship, and, further, that the defendant induced the doctor to divulge confidential information gained through the physician-patient relationship. In particular, it is alleged that the defendant, at the behest of a prominent defense attorney, persuaded Dr. Alexander Ling, the plaintiff's treating physician, to surrender certain undisclosed confidential information for use in pending litigation against the plaintiff on the false pretext that the plaintiff was contemplating a malpractice suit against Dr. Ling. . . .

In all medical jurisprudence there are few problems which have deserved and received more concentrated attention than the protection of the personal information which a patient remits to his physician. This relationship "is one of trust and confidence. It is submitted that the best interest of the patient is served in trusting his welfare to the skill and industry of his physician." To foster the best interest of the patient and to insure a climate most favorable to a complete recovery, men of medicine have urged that patients be totally frank in their discussions with their physicians. To encourage the desired candor, men of law have formulated a strong policy of confidentiality to assure patients that only they themselves may unlock the doctor's silence in regard to those private disclosures. . . .

. . . We conclude, therefore, that ordinarily a physician receives information relating to a patient's health in a confidential capacity and should not disclose such information without the patient's consent, except where the public interest or the private interest of the patient so demands. . . .

Any time a doctor undertakes the treatment of a patient, and the consensual relationship of physician and patient is established, two jural obligations (of significance here) are simultaneously assumed by the doctor. Doctor and patient enter into a simple contract, the patient hoping that he will be cured and the doctor optimistically assuming that he will be compensated. As an implied condition of that contract, this Court is of the opinion that the doctor warrants that any confidential information gained through the relationship will not be released without the patient's permission. Almost every member of the public is aware of the promise of discretion contained in the Hippocratic Oath, and every patient has a right to rely upon this warranty of silence. The promise of secrecy is as much an express warranty as the advertisement of a commercial entrepreneur. Consequently, when a doctor breaches his duty of secrecy, he is in violation of part of his obligations under the contract.

When a patient seeks out a doctor and retains him, he must admit him to the most private part of the material domain of man. Nothing material is more important or more intimate to man than the health of his mind and body. Since the layman is unfamiliar with the road to recovery, he cannot sift the circumstances of his life and habits to determine what is information pertinent to his health. As a consequence, he must disclose all information in his consultations with his doctor — even that which is embarrassing, disgraceful or incriminating. To promote full disclosure, the medical profession extends the promise of secrecy referred to above. The candor which this promise elicits is necessary to the effective pursuit of health; there can be no reticence, no reservation, no reluctance when patients discuss their problems with their doctors. But the disclosure is certainly intended to be private. If a doctor should reveal any of these confidences, he surely effects an invasion of the privacy of his patient. We are of the opinion that the preservation of the patient's privacy is no mere ethical duty upon the part of the doctor; there is a legal duty as well. The unauthorized revelation of medical secrets, or any confidential communication given in the course of treatment, is tortious conduct which may be the basis for an action in damages. . . .

However, we are not critically concerned here solely with an alleged disclosure by a doctor since the complaint accuses Dr. Ling only of a misfeasance predicated upon misinformation and directs its plea for redress not against the doctor but against the defendant insurance company which allegedly supplied this inaccurate information. . . . As we have noted above, the patient necessarily reposes a great deal of trust not only in the skill of the physician but in his discretion as well. The introduction into the relationship of this aura of trust, and the expectation of confidentiality which results therefrom, imposes the fiduciary obligations upon the doctor. As a consequence, all reported cases dealing with this point hold that the relationship of physician and patient is a fiduciary one. . . .

By its very definition, the term "fiduciary relationship" imports the notion that "if a wrong arises, the same remedy exists against the wrongdoer on behalf of the principal as would exist against a trustee on behalf of the cestui que trust." Therefore it is readily apparent that the legal obligations of a trustee are imposed upon any person operating in a fiduciary capacity and the same principles of law participation in breaches of trust must applicable to all fiduciaries.

It also follows that the same principles of law governing third party participation in breaches of trust must also apply to one who participates in or induces the breach of any fiduciary duty. The law is settled in Ohio and elsewhere participation in breaches of trust must also apply to one who participates in or induces the breach of any fiduciary duty. The law is settled in Ohio and elsewhere that a third party who induces a breach of a trustee's duty of loyalty, or participates in such a breach, or knowingly accepts any benefit from such a breach, becomes directly liable to the aggrieved party. . . . [W]hen one induces a doctor to divulge confidential information in violation of that doctor's legal responsibility to his patient, the third party may also be held liable in damages to the patient.

NOTES & QUESTIONS

1. ***The Breach of Confidentiality Tort.*** The "clear modern consensus of the case law" is to recognize the breach of confidentiality tort.[5] The tort creates liability when a duty of confidentiality exists and is breached. In *McCormick,* the court found the existence of a duty of confidentiality in various licensing statutes, evidentiary rules, ethical rules, and the common law principles of trust (fiduciary relationships). Courts have also found duties of confidentiality based on implied contracts of confidentiality.

   One of the sources of a duty of confidentiality is the existence of a fiduciary relationship. "A fiduciary relationship is one founded on trust or confidence reposed by one person in the integrity and fidelity of another. Out of such a relation, the laws raise the rule that neither party may exert influence or pressure upon the other, take selfish advantage of his trust[,] or deal with the subject matter of the trust in such a way as to benefit himself or prejudice the other except in the exercise of utmost good faith." *Mobile Oil Corp. v. Rubenfeld*, 339 N.Y.S.2d 623, 632 (1972). According to the Restatement: "[O]ne standing in a fiduciary relation with another is subject to liability to the other for harm resulting from a breach of duty imposed by the relation." Restatement (Second) of Torts § 874. There are no fixed sets of relationships that are fiduciary ones, and courts "have carefully refrained from defining instances of fiduciary relations in such a manner that other and perhaps new cases might be excluded." *Swerhun v. General Motors Corp.*, 812 F. Supp. 1218 (M.D. Fla. 1993). Courts look to the following factors in defining a fiduciary relationship: "[T]he degree of kinship of the parties; the disparity in age, health, and mental condition; education and business experience between the parties; and the extent to which the allegedly subservient party entrusted the handling of . . . business affairs to the other and reposed faith and confidence in [that person or entity]." *Pottinger v. Pottinger*, 605 N.E.2d 1130 (Ill. App. 1992).[6]

   The breach of confidentiality tort is not just limited to disclosures by physicians. For example, it has been applied to bankers and other professionals and entities. *See, e.g., Peterson v. Idaho First Nat'l Bank,* 367 P.2d 284 (Idaho 1961) (bankers); *Rich v. New York C. & H. R. R. Co.*, 87 N.Y. 382, 390 (N.Y. 1882) (attorneys); *Wagenheim v. Alexander Grant & Co.,* 482 N.E.2d 955, 961 (Ohio Ct. App. 1983) (accountants). The tort applies whenever a duty of confidentiality exists.

   As Neil Richards and Daniel Solove explain:

   > Slighted by Warren and Brandeis and virtually ignored by Prosser, confidentiality had a stunted development in the United States during the twentieth century, and it still has not fully penetrated into the culture of

---

[5] David A. Elder, *Privacy Torts* § 5:2 (2002).

[6] For more background about the breach of confidentiality tort, see Alan B. Vickery, Note, *Breach of Confidence: An Emerging Tort*, 82 Colum. L. Rev. 1426, 1426 (1982); G. Michael Harvey, Comment, *Confidentiality: A Measured Response to the Failure of Privacy*, 140 U. Pa. L. Rev. 2385, 2396 (1992); Susan M. Gilles, *Promises Betrayed: Breach of Confidence as a Remedy for Invasions of Privacy*, 43 Buff. L. Rev. 1, 20-25 (1995).

> American privacy law. In the United States, the breach of confidentiality tort has grown up in the shadow of the Warren and Brandeis torts. Not only did Prosser overlook breach of confidentiality, but also in many privacy cases, breach of confidentiality could have been an option but often was not explored. Breach of confidentiality remained ignored and underdeveloped while the Warren and Brandeis torts enjoyed the spotlight. Although the tort of breach of confidence has seen some development in recent decades, it remains in a relatively obscure and frequently overlooked corner of American tort law. . . .
>
> The American breach of confidentiality tort has yet to come close to reaching its fullest potential. The tort still applies only to a limited set of relationships, with most cases involving the patient-physician relationship. . . . Having only recently gained momentum, the breach of confidentiality tort often has not been raised in many cases where it might have relevance.

In England, the courts have rejected the Warren and Brandeis privacy torts, but have developed a robust tort of breach of confidence:

> The law of confidentiality in England also has attributes that the American privacy torts lack. In America, the prevailing belief is that people assume the risk of betrayal when they share secrets with each other. But in England, spouses, ex-spouses, friends, and nearly anyone else can be liable for divulging confidences. As one English court noted, "when people kiss and later one of them tells, that second person is almost certainly breaking a confidential arrangement." Confidentiality thus recognizes that nondisclosure expectations emerge not only from norms of individual dignity, but also from norms of relationships, trust, and reliance on promises. American privacy law has never fully embraced privacy within relationships; it typically views information exposed to others as no longer private. Although a tort remedying breach of confidence would emerge later on in American law, it developed slowly in comparison to the Warren and Brandeis privacy torts.[7]

One important exception to the tort is that physicians will not be liable for disclosing confidential medical information when it is necessary to protect others from danger or when it is required by law. For example, the court in *Simonsen v. Swenson,* 177 N.W. 831 (Neb. 1920), concluded that a doctor was not liable for disclosing the fact that a patient had syphilis, which at the time was believed to be highly contagious without sexual contact.[8]

2. ***Inducing Breaches of Confidentiality.*** Recall the following statement in the court's opinion: "The law is settled in Ohio and elsewhere that a third party who induces a breach of a trustee's duty of loyalty, or participates in such a breach, or knowingly accepts any benefit from such a breach, becomes directly liable to the aggrieved party." The Restatement provides: "A person who knowingly assists a fiduciary in committing a breach of trust is himself guilty of tortious conduct." Restatement (Second) of Torts § 874 comment (c).

---

[7] Neil M. Richards & Daniel J. Solove, *Privacy's Other Path: Recovering the Law of Confidentiality,* 96 Geo. L.J. 123, 156-58, 126 (2007).

[8] For more on this issue, see Lawrence O. Gostin & James G. Hodge, Jr., *Piercing the Veil of Secrecy in HIV/AIDS and Other Sexually Transmitted Diseases: Theories of Privacy and Disclosure in Partner Notification*, 5 Duke J. Gender L. & Pol'y 9, 16-23 (1998).

3. ***Holding a Hospital Liable for Breach of Confidentiality.*** In *Biddle v. Warren General Hospital,* 715 N.E.2d 518 (Ohio 1999), a law firm decided to earn extra money by making a deal to assist a hospital in determining whether unpaid patient bills could be submitted to the Social Security Administration (SSA) for payment. Under the plan, the hospital released its patient registration forms to the law firm, which would evaluate which patients could qualify for Social Security benefits and then contact those patients and urge them to apply for benefits. In this way, the hospital would be paid by the SSA for these patients. However, the hospital released the patient data to the firm without obtaining the consent of the patients. The patients brought a class action against the hospital and the firm. The court held that not only was there a viable breach of confidentiality claim against the hospital, but also the firm could be liable for inducing such a breach:

> We hold that a third party can be held liable for inducing the unauthorized, unprivileged disclosure of nonpublic medical information that a physician or hospital has learned within a physician-patient relationship. To establish liability the plaintiff must prove that: (1) the defendant knew or reasonably should have known of the existence of the physician-patient relationship; (2) the defendant intended to induce the physician to disclose information about the patient or the defendant reasonably should have anticipated that his actions would induce the physician to disclose such information; and (3) the defendant did not reasonably believe that the physician could disclose that information to the defendant without violating the duty of confidentiality that the physician owed the patient.

Suppose a person's physician were to disclose, without the patient's consent, the patient's medical file to a journalist. The journalist, knowing that the medical file was disclosed in breach of the doctor's fiduciary duty to the patient, accepted it anyway and published details about the patient's medical condition in the newspaper. Would the patient have a cause of action against the journalist in addition to the doctor? Would your conclusion be different in light of *Bartnicki v. Vopper* (Chapter 2)?

4. ***The Breach of Confidentiality Tort in the Modern Health Care System.*** Consider Lawrence Gostin:

> The rule of confidentiality is widely respected in law and medicine, and rightfully so. Indeed, in the past, confidentiality has worked reasonably well in safeguarding privacy. Much, if not all, of the intimate knowledge of the patient was generated within the physician-patient relationship, which was often meaningful and enduring. The patient's health record contained information primarily obtained during sessions between the physician and patient, so that the entire record was regarded as confidential. The record keepers, moreover, were the physicians themselves who took primary responsibility for the security of medical records.
>
> The rule of confidentiality does not work nearly as well in a modern information society. Health data today, in an era of electronic information gathering, is based only in small part on the physician-patient relationship. Many therapeutic encounters in a managed care context are not with a primary care physician. Patients may see many different physicians, nonphysician

specialists, nurse practitioners and other ancillary health care professionals within and outside of the health care plan. The information obtained in these encounters has uncertain protection under traditional rules of confidentiality. Focusing legal protection on a single therapeutic relationship within this information environment is an anachronistic vestige of an earlier and simpler time in medicine. The health record, moreover, contains a substantial amount of information gathered from numerous primary and secondary sources: laboratories, pharmacies, schools, public health officials, researchers, insurers, and other individuals and institutions. The health records of patients are kept not only in the office of a private physician or in a health plan, but also may be kept by government agencies, regional health database organizations, or information brokers. Databases maintained in each of these settings will be collected and transmitted electronically, reconfigured, and linked.

Rules enforcing informational privacy in health care place a duty on the entity that possesses the information. Thus, the keeper of the record — whether it is in a private physician's office, a hospital, or an HMO — holds the primary duty to maintain the confidentiality of the data. The development of electronic health care networks permitting standardized patient-based information to flow nationwide, and perhaps worldwide, means that the current privacy protection system, which focuses on requiring the institution to protect its records, needs to be reconsidered. Our past thinking assumed a paper or automated record created and protected by the provider. We must now envision a patient-based record that anyone in the system can call up on a screen. Because location has less meaning in an electronic world, protecting privacy requires attaching protection to the health record itself, rather than to the institution that generates it. . . .[9]

In contrast, Peter Winn argues that the breach of confidentiality tort might be strengthened with the new HIPAA regulations and may prove to be quite effective in providing a remedy against privacy invasions:

[A]lthough the HIPAA Privacy Rules create no federal cause of action, an analysis of the case law suggests that the Rules may well be adopted by common law courts to establish a national minimum standard for liability for breach of confidentiality under state law. . . .

With respect to the second perceived weakness of the Rules, because the breach of confidentiality tort traditionally requires that the patient be in a professional or contractual relationship with the person responsible for the wrongful disclosure, and because many harmful disclosures take place by entities such as Business Associates who are not in such a relationship, the breach of confidentiality tort has been viewed as unable to address the problems caused by the widespread dissemination of electronic health information among "downstream" users not in a relationship of confidentiality with the injured person. . . . [U]nder the developing case law, such federally required agreements with Business Associates, while ostensibly creating no liability other than between the contracting parties, are likely to facilitate the establishment of claims for breach of confidentiality against Business

[9] Lawrence O. Gostin, *Health Information Privacy*, 80 Cornell L. Rev. 451 (1995).

Associates by patients for misuse of their personal information in spite of the lack of a professional or contractual relationship.[10]

3. TORT LIABILITY FOR FAILURE TO DISCLOSE PATIENT INFORMATION

TARASOFF V. REGENTS OF UNIVERSITY OF CALIFORNIA

551 P.2d 334 (Cal. 1976)

TOBRINER, J. On October 27, 1969, Prosenjit Poddar killed Tatiana Tarasoff. Plaintiffs, Tatiana's parents, allege that two months earlier Poddar confided his intention to kill Tatiana to Dr. Lawrence Moore, a psychologist employed by the Cowell Memorial Hospital at the University of California at Berkeley. They allege that on Moore's request, the campus police briefly detained Poddar, but released him when he appeared rational. They further claim that Dr. Harvey Powelson, Moore's superior, then directed that no further action be taken to detain Poddar. No one warned plaintiffs of Tatiana's peril.

Plaintiffs' complaints predicate liability on . . . defendants' failure to warn plaintiffs of the impending danger. . . . Defendants, in turn, assert that they owed no duty of reasonable care to Tatiana. . . .

We shall explain that defendant therapists cannot escape liability merely because Tatiana herself was not their patient. When a therapist determines, or pursuant to the standards of his profession should determine, that his patient presents a serious danger of violence to another, he incurs an obligation to use reasonable care to protect the intended victim against such danger. The discharge of this duty may require the therapist to take one or more of various steps, depending upon the nature of the case. Thus it may call for him to warn the intended victim or others likely to apprise the victim of the danger, to notify the police, or to take whatever other steps are reasonably necessary under the circumstances. . . .

. . . [O]n August 20, 1969, Poddar was a voluntary outpatient receiving therapy at Cowell Memorial Hospital. Poddar informed Moore, his therapist, that he was going to kill an unnamed girl, readily identifiable as Tatiana, when she returned home from spending the summer in Brazil. Moore, with the concurrence of Dr. Gold, who had initially examined Poddar, and Dr. Yandell, Assistant to the director of the department of psychiatry, decided that Poddar should be committed for observation in a mental hospital. Moore orally notified Officers Atkinson and Teel of the campus police that he would request commitment. He then sent a letter to Police Chief William Beall requesting the assistance of the police department in securing Poddar's confinement.

Officers Atkinson, Brownrigg, and Halleran took Poddar into custody, but, satisfied that Poddar was rational, released him on his promise to stay away from Tatiana. Powelson, director of the department of psychiatry at Cowell Memorial Hospital, then asked the police to return Moore's letter, directed that all copies of the letter and notes that Moore had taken as therapist be destroyed, and "ordered

---

[10] Peter A. Winn, *Confidentiality in Cyberspace: The HIPAA Privacy Rules and the Common Law*, 33 Rutgers L.J. 617 (2002).

no action to place Prosenjit Poddar in 72-hour treatment and evaluation facility." . . .

. . . Poddar persuaded Tatiana's brother to share an apartment with him near Tatiana's residence; shortly after her return from Brazil, Poddar went to her residence and killed her.

Plaintiffs contend that [the defendants were negligent in not notifying them of Poddar's intent to kill Tatiana]. Defendants, however, contend that in the circumstances of the present case they owed no duty of care to Tatiana or her parents and that, in the absence of such duty, they were free to act in careless disregard of Tatiana's life and safety. . . .

. . . As a general principle, a "defendant owes a duty of care to all persons who are foreseeably endangered by his conduct, with respect to all risks which make the conduct unreasonably dangerous." As we shall explain, however, when the avoidance of foreseeable harm requires a defendant to control the conduct of another person, or to warn of such conduct, the common law has traditionally imposed liability only if the defendant bears some special relationship to the dangerous person or to the potential victim. Since the relationship between a therapist and his patient satisfies this requirement, we need not here decide whether foreseeability alone is sufficient to create a duty to exercise reasonable care to protect a potential victim of another's conduct.

Although, as we have stated above, under the common law, as a general rule, one person owed no duty to control the conduct of another, nor to warn those endangered by such conduct, the courts have carved out an exception to this rule in cases in which the defendant stands in some special relationship to either the person whose conduct needs to be controlled or in a relationship to the foreseeable victim of that conduct. Applying this exception to the present case, we note that a relationship of defendant therapists to either Tatiana or Poddar will suffice to establish a duty of care; as explained in section 315 of the Restatement Second of Torts, a duty of care may arise from either "(a) a special relation . . . between the actor and the third person which imposes a duty upon the actor to control the third person's conduct, or (b) a special relation . . . between the actor and the other which gives to the other a right of protection."

Although plaintiffs' pleadings assert no special relation between Tatiana and defendant therapists, they establish as between Poddar and defendant therapists the special relation that arises between a patient and his doctor or psychotherapist. Such a relationship may support affirmative duties for the benefit of third persons. Thus, for example, a hospital must exercise reasonable care to control the behavior of a patient which may endanger other persons. A doctor must also warn a patient if the patient's condition or medication renders certain conduct, such as driving a car, dangerous to others. . . .

. . . Decisions of other jurisdictions hold that the single relationship of a doctor to his patient is sufficient to support the duty to exercise reasonable care to protect others against dangers emanating from the patient's illness. The courts hold that a doctor is liable to persons infected by his patient if he negligently fails to diagnose a contagious disease or, having diagnosed the illness, fails to warn members of the patient's family. . . .

". . . [T]here now seems to be sufficient authority to support the conclusion that by entering into a doctor-patient relationship the therapist becomes sufficiently involved to assume some responsibility for the safety, not only of the patient himself, but also of any third person whom the doctor knows to be threatened by the patient." (Fleming & Maximov, The Patient or His Victim: The Therapist's Dilemma (1974) 62 Cal. L. Rev. 1025, 1030.)

Defendants contend, however, that imposition of a duty to exercise reasonable care to protect third persons is unworkable because therapists cannot accurately predict whether or not a patient will resort to violence. In support of this argument amicus representing the American Psychiatric Association and other professional societies cites numerous articles which indicate that therapists, in the present state of the art, are unable reliably to predict violent acts; their forecasts, amicus claims, tend consistently to overpredict violence, and indeed are more often wrong than right. Since predictions of violence are often erroneous, amicus concludes, the courts should not render rulings that predicate the liability of therapists upon the validity of such predictions.

The role of the psychiatrist, who is indeed a practitioner of medicine, and that of the psychologist who performs an allied function, are like that of the physician who must conform to the standards of the profession and who must often make diagnoses and predictions based upon such evaluations. Thus the judgment of the therapist in diagnosing emotional disorders and in predicting whether a patient presents a serious danger of violence is comparable to the judgment which doctors and professionals must regularly render under accepted rules of responsibility.

We recognize the difficulty that a therapist encounters in attempting to forecast whether a patient presents a serious danger of violence. Obviously we do not require that the therapist, in making that determination, render a perfect performance; the therapist need only exercise "that reasonable degree of skill, knowledge, and care ordinarily possessed and exercised by members of (that professional specialty) under similar circumstances." Within the broad range of reasonable practice and treatment in which professional opinion and judgment may differ, the therapist is free to exercise his or her own best judgment without liability; proof, aided by hindsight, that he or she judged wrongly is insufficient to establish negligence.

In the instant case, however, the pleadings do not raise any question as to failure of defendant therapists to predict that Poddar presented a serious danger of violence. On the contrary, the present complaints allege that defendant therapists did in fact predict that Poddar would kill, but were negligent in failing to warn. . . .

The risk that unnecessary warnings may be given is a reasonable price to pay for the lives of possible victims that may be saved. We would hesitate to hold that the therapist who is aware that his patient expects to attempt to assassinate the President of the United States would not be obligated to warn the authorities because the therapist cannot predict with accuracy that his patient will commit the crime. . . .

We realize that the open and confidential character of psychotherapeutic dialogue encourages patients to express threats of violence, few of which are ever executed. Certainly a therapist should not be encouraged routinely to reveal such threats; such disclosures could seriously disrupt the patient's relationship with his therapist and with the persons threatened. To the contrary, the therapist's obligations to his patient require that he not disclose a confidence unless such disclosure is necessary to avert danger to others, and even then that he do so discreetly, and in a fashion that would preserve the privacy of his patient to the fullest extent compatible with the prevention of the threatened danger.

The revelation of a communication under the above circumstances is not a breach of trust or a violation of professional ethics; as stated in the Principles of Medical Ethics of the American Medical Association (1957), section 9: "A physician may not reveal the confidence entrusted to him in the course of medical attendance . . . unless he is required to do so by law or unless it becomes necessary in order to protect the welfare of the individual or of the community." We conclude that the public policy favoring protection of the confidential character of patient-psychotherapist communications must yield to the extent to which disclosure is essential to avert danger to others. The protective privilege ends where the public peril begins. . . .

CLARK, J. dissenting. . . . Overwhelming policy considerations weigh against imposing a duty on psychotherapists to warn a potential victim against harm. While offering virtually no benefit to society, such a duty will frustrate psychiatric treatment, invade fundamental patient rights and increase violence.

The importance of psychiatric treatment and its need for confidentiality have been recognized by this court. "It is clearly recognized that the very practice of psychiatry vitally depends upon the reputation in the community that the psychiatrist will not tell."

Assurance of confidentiality is important for three reasons.

First, without substantial assurance of confidentiality, those requiring treatment will be deterred from seeking assistance. It remains an unfortunate fact in our society that people seeking psychiatric guidance tend to become stigmatized. Apprehension of such stigma — apparently increased by the propensity of people considering treatment to see themselves in the worst possible light — creates a well-recognized reluctance to seek aid. This reluctance is alleviated by the psychiatrist's assurance of confidentiality.

Second, the guarantee of confidentiality is essential in eliciting the full disclosure necessary for effective treatment. The psychiatric patient approaches treatment with conscious and unconscious inhibitions against revealing his innermost thoughts. "Every person, however well-motivated, has to overcome resistances to therapeutic exploration. These resistances seek support from every possible source and the possibility of disclosure would easily be employed in the service of resistance." Until a patient can trust his psychiatrist not to violate their confidential relationship, "the unconscious psychological control mechanism of repression will prevent the recall of past experiences."

Third, even if the patient fully discloses his thoughts, assurance that the confidential relationship will not be breached is necessary to maintain his trust in his psychiatrist — the very means by which treatment is effected. "(T)he essence of much psychotherapy is the contribution of trust in the external world and ultimately in the self, modeled upon the trusting relationship established during therapy." Patients will be helped only if they can form a trusting relationship with the psychiatrist. All authorities appear to agree that if the trust relationship cannot be developed because of collusive communication between the psychiatrist and others, treatment will be frustrated. . . .

Both the legal and psychiatric communities recognize that the process of determining potential violence in a patient is far from exact, being fraught with complexity and uncertainty. In fact precision has not even been attained in predicting who of those having already committed violent acts will again become violent, a task recognized to be of much simpler proportions.

This predictive uncertainty means that the number of disclosures will necessarily be large. As noted above, psychiatric patients are encouraged to discuss all thoughts of violence, and they often express such thoughts. However, unlike this court, the psychiatrist does not enjoy the benefit of overwhelming hindsight in seeing which few, if any, of his patients will ultimately become violent. Now, confronted by the majority's new duty, the psychiatrist must instantaneously calculate potential violence from each patient on each visit. The difficulties researchers have encountered in accurately predicting violence will be heightened for the practicing psychiatrist dealing for brief periods in his office with heretofore nonviolent patients. And, given the decision not to warn or commit must always be made at the psychiatrist's civil peril, one can expect most doubts will be resolved in favor of the psychiatrist protecting himself.

Neither alternative open to the psychiatrist seeking to protect himself is in the public interest. The warning itself is an impairment of the psychiatrist's ability to treat, depriving many patients of adequate treatment. It is to be expected that after disclosing their threats, a significant number of patients, who would not become violent if treated according to existing practices, will engage in violent conduct as a result of unsuccessful treatment. In short, the majority's duty to warn will not only impair treatment of many who would never become violent but worse, will result in a net increase in violence.

The second alternative open to the psychiatrist is to commit his patient rather than to warn. Even in the absence of threat of civil liability, the doubts of psychiatrists as to the seriousness of patient threats have led psychiatrists to overcommit to mental institutions. This overcommitment has been authoritatively documented in both legal and psychiatric studies. This practice is so prevalent that it has been estimated that "as many as twenty harmless persons are incarcerated for every one who will commit a violent act." . . .

NOTES & QUESTIONS

1. ***Background and Postscript.*** Peter Schuck and Daniel Givelber have discovered a strange background fact about the case: Alex Tarasoff, Tatiana's brother, shared an apartment with Poddar for about three months before the tragic killing:

> Alex had once answered the phone at the Tarasoff home when Poddar was calling for Tatiana; although Alex warned Poddar to "lay off," Poddar — undaunted — asked to meet him. Alex agreed and met Tanya and Poddar at the gas station where Alex worked. . . . The two men had some technical interests in common and became close friends and then roommates . . . Although Alex later testified that he did not believe that Poddar meant to kill

his sister, Poddar's friendship with Alex enabled Poddar to learn when he would find Tatiana alone at her family's home on October 27, 1969, the day of her death.

Schuck and Givelber also examined the intertwining of the California Supreme Court's decision in the criminal case, *People v. Poddar*, 518 P.2d 342 (Cal. 1974), with the tort case excerpted above. In the criminal case, the California Supreme Court had ordered a retrial because the trial court did not instruct the jury about how diminished capacity might affect the specific interest necessary for a verdict of second-degree murder. Poddar was not, however, subjected to another trial; the prosecutors allowed him to return to India. Schuck and Givelber propose that "the California Supreme Court, unable to condemn the therapists' passivity in the criminal case, did so indirectly in the tort case by creating the Tarasoff duty and allowing the jury to apply that duty to the university clinicians. The Court in effect lifted some of the burden of criminal responsibility from Poddar's shoulders while imposing a burden of civil responsibility on the clinicians."[11]

2. ***Warning Patients of a Duty to Disclose.*** Today, a majority of jurisdictions have adopted the *Tarasoff* rule. Given the *Tarasoff* rule, should psychotherapists have an ethical duty to warn patients that they may have to disclose to others when a patient makes a threat? In a study after *Tarasoff*, only 26 percent of psychotherapists informed patients of the possibility of disclosure at the outset of therapy; 51 percent informed patients when the patient threatened violence.[12]
3. ***Too Much Disclosure?*** In a footnote in his dissent, Justice Clark argues:

   > However compassionate, the psychiatrist hearing the threat remains faced with potential crushing civil liability for a mistaken evaluation of his patient and will be forced to resolve even the slightest doubt in favor of disclosure or commitment.

   Will the result in *Tarasoff* lead to too many disclosures by psychotherapists?
4. ***How Broadly Could the* Tarasoff *Rule Apply?*** *Tarasoff*, although it involved a psychotherapist, would seemingly apply to physicians, nurses, and social workers. Could it apply even more broadly — to marriage counselors or any professional having knowledge of a person's dangerous propensities?
5. ***Ethical vs. Legal Duties to Disclose.*** The psychiatric community was highly critical of *Tarasoff*. Ironically, however, even before *Tarasoff*, almost 80 percent of therapists believed they had an ethical duty to warn under circumstances akin to those in *Tarasoff*. In a 1987 study, almost all therapists had warned a potential victim, and most believed their duty to warn was based on an ethical obligation regardless of the law.[13] Does it matter whether this is a

[11] Peter H. Schuck & Daniel J. Givelber, Tarasoff v. Regents of the University of California, *in Torts Stories* 99 (Robert L. Rabin & Stephen D. Sugarman, 2003).

[12] *See* D.L. Rosenhan, Terri Wolff Teitelbaum, Kathi Weiss Teitelbaum, & Martin Davidson, *Warning Third Parties: The Ripple Effects of* Tarasoff, 24 Pac. L.J. 1165, 1208 (1993).

[13] *See* Fillmore Buckner & Marvin Firestone, *"Where the Public Peril Begins": 25 Years After* Tarasoff, 21 J. Legal Med. 187, 219 (2000).

legal duty or merely an ethical one? What if the option to disclose were simply left to the conscience of medical professionals?

6. **Tarasoff *and the Attorney-Client Privilege.*** Under the ABA Model Rule 1.6(b)(1), an attorney *may* reveal a client's intention to commit future crimes that are likely to cause imminent death or substantial bodily harm. This rule differs among the states, although the majority agrees with this rule. About one-fifth of the states provide that an attorney *must* disclose under such circumstances. Suppose an attorney were in a similar position to the therapist in *Tarasoff*. Although the ethical obligations of each state suggest that the attorney may disclose, the attorney does not. Would the attorney be liable under a *Tarasoff* theory?
7. **Tarasoff *and the Psychotherapist-Patient Privilege.*** In *Menendez v. Superior Court*, 834 P.2d 786 (Cal. 1992), law enforcement officials sought audiotape recordings and written notes of psychotherapy sessions of Erik and Lyle Menendez, two brothers who had murdered their parents. The case of the Menendezes garnered great publicity. Their psychotherapist was Dr. Leon Oziel, and the tapes contained information related to the killings. The tapes also involved threats made by Erik and Lyle to Dr. Oziel. The threats were aimed at him alone, but Dr. Oziel believed that his wife (Laurel Oziel) as well as his lover (Judalon Smyth) could also be endangered, so he warned them. Neither Lyle nor Erik attempted any harm to Dr. Oziel, Laurel, or Smyth. Both Laurel Oziel and Smyth were employed in Dr. Oziel's psychotherapy practice. The police served a search warrant on Dr. Oziel for the recordings and/or notes for three therapy sessions.

   The Menendezes claimed psychotherapist-patient privilege. The government argued that under Evidence Code § 1024 no privilege exists if "the psychotherapist has reasonable cause to believe that the patient is in such mental or emotional condition as to be dangerous to himself or to the person or property of another and that disclosure of the communication is necessary to prevent the threatened danger." The Supreme Court of California concluded that one of the sessions was not privileged, but that the other two were. First, the court held that even though the Menendezes' communications were publicly disclosed to Smyth, the Menendezes did not lose their privilege. "[T]he privilege can cover a communication that has lost its 'confidential' status." Second, the court held that all of the sessions should not be considered one communication; each therapy session should be treated separately. Third, the court concluded that if the conditions for a valid Tarasoff warning exist, a communication is not privileged, regardless of whether the therapist actually gave a Tarasoff warning or not. The exception to the privilege is "not keyed to . . . disclosure or warning, but to the existence of the specified factual predicate, viz., reasonable cause for belief in the dangerousness of the patient and the necessity of disclosure." Thus, the one session where the Menendezes made the threat to Dr. Oziel, which gave him reason to believe his wife and lover could be in danger, was not privileged.

McIntosh v. Milano

403 A.2d 500 (N.J. Super. 1979)

PETRELLA, J. Defendant [Michael Milano, M.D., a board-certified psychiatrist] first met Lee Morgenstein, then age 15, and began his treatment on May 5, 1973, after the latter's school psychologist had given Morgenstein's parents defendant's name and that of certain other therapists, partially because of Morgenstein's involvement with drugs. His treatment was on a weekly basis for what was initially diagnosed as "an adjustment reaction of adolescence." Initially it also included family therapy. During the course of therapy over the approximate two-year period, Morgenstein related many "fantasies" to defendant on various subjects, including fantasies of fear of other people, being a hero or an important villain, and using a knife to threaten people who might intimidate or frighten him.

Morgenstein also related certain alleged experiences and emotional involvements with decedent, who in 1973 was about 20 years old and at that time lived with her parents next door to the Morgensteins. Decedent's father was a doctor who from time to time had treated Lee Morgenstein for minor ailments. Defendant considered all such "fantasies" referred to above as just that, but he came to accept, after initial reservations, that the experiences related to him by Morgenstein as to his eventual victim represented truth and not fantasy. Dr. Milano stated he was somewhat "nonplussed" initially about the revelations of Morgenstein concerning Miss [Kimberly] McIntosh and alleged sexual experiences because of the five-year age difference. However, he said that he came to believe it because the way Morgenstein responded emotionally fit with what he told him, and Milano claimed he never had any reason to doubt Morgenstein. The doctor testified at Morgenstein's criminal trial that "(h)e (Morgenstein) didn't spend a lot of time describing in detail what he and Kim did, but that also sort of fit, if anything, his character in that he thought that nobody would believe him." Defendant did indicate in his deposition that he advised Morgenstein to break off the relationship.

Morgenstein had possessive feelings towards Kimberly, according to the doctor, and was "overwhelmed" by the relationship. Although Morgenstein is said to have repeatedly expressed anxiety to defendant over his relationship with Miss McIntosh, defendant asserts she was not the dominant theme of the therapy.

It is undisputed, and Dr. Milano admits, that Morgenstein had confided that he had fired a B.B. gun at what he recalled to be a car (Miss McIntosh's or her boyfriend's) on one occasion when he was upset because she was going on a date with her boyfriend. There is evidence proffered by plaintiff that other windows in the McIntosh house and another vehicle had been shot at and damaged by a B.B. or some other gun, and a factfinder might infer that these were actions of Morgenstein. It is also undisputed that Dr. Milano had been told by Morgenstein that he had purchased and carried a knife to show to people to scare them away if they should attempt to frighten or intimidate him, and brought it to a therapy session to show the doctor.

Although Dr. Milano said that Morgenstein wished Miss McIntosh would "suffer" as he did and had expressed jealousy and a very possessive attitude towards her, was jealous of other men and hateful towards her boyfriends, had difficulty convincing himself that fights or things were really over or finished, he denied that Morgenstein ever indicated or exhibited any feelings of violence toward decedent or said that he intended to kill her or inflict bodily harm. Morgenstein was also very angry that he had not been able to obtain Miss McIntosh's phone number when she moved from the family home. He may not even have known where she lived in 1975. Plaintiff proffered testimony that Miss McIntosh had told her family of Morgenstein's drug problems, felt sorry for him, and hoped he could get help.

Following an incident in which Morgenstein fell off a bicycle and injured his face the day before the July 8, 1975 therapy session, and after an incident during the course of that day's therapy (apparently when Dr. Milano briefly left the room), he stole a prescription form from the doctor's desk. Later that day he attempted to obtain 30 Seconal tablets from a pharmacist with the stolen form. The pharmacist apparently became suspicious and called Dr. Milano, who instructed him to retain the unauthorized prescription form, not to fill it, and to send Morgenstein home. He later tried to reach Morgenstein at home, but between then and the early evening hours Morgenstein was involved in the tragedy which took Miss McIntosh's life. Whatever exactly transpired thereafter, it would appear that Morgenstein left the pharmacy upset and at some point either late that afternoon or early evening obtained a pistol which he had kept hidden at his home, and knowing Miss McIntosh was expected to visit her parents, waited for her and either got her to go with him, wittingly or unwittingly, to a local park area where he fatally shot her in the back.

Dr. Milano had indicated in his testimony at the criminal trial that sometimes he inquired further when he felt that a patient was in some ways endangering himself or someone else, and in those instances he would contact his patient's parents, school, or people like that. In his deposition in this civil case Dr. Milano said he had spoken to Morgenstein's parents about a problem with a car accident and this resulted in their withholding certain privileges from their son. He also indicated he spoke to a school teacher about one of Morgenstein's problems. Apparently this was usually with Morgenstein's consent. Dr. Milano had said he would "look into it" if he felt the patient was endangering himself or someone else. He apparently talked to Morgenstein's parents in some fashion about the relationship between their son and Miss McIntosh a number of times in late 1974 and in 1975, but never attempted to contact decedent or her parents. Despite Morgenstein's fantasies and the incidents previously recited, and wishes for her suffering, he felt that Morgenstein had never expressed a desire for retaliation or "fantasies" of retaliation. Dr. Milano had said at the criminal trial that Morgenstein had fantasies of magical power and violence, which meant that if somebody said he was a scrawny little runt and wouldn't dare fight back, that he would be able to pull out a gun and shoot them. But he denied that Morgenstein ever had fantasies of pulling out a gun, and claimed that his fantasies apparently related to pulling out a knife and scaring people off. Morgenstein, nevertheless, was quoted as saying that if he had a gun, that would scare men and then nobody would dare threaten him. . . .

Plaintiff [McIntosh's mother] instituted this wrongful death action based in large part on the trial testimony of Dr. Milano. She relies also on a report of a psychiatrist retained as an expert witness expressing the opinion that defendant had a duty to warn Kimberly McIntosh, her parents or appropriate authorities that Morgenstein posed a physical threat or danger to decedent. Plaintiff asserts defendant breached that duty. . . .

The argument in this case is whether principles analogous to those expressed in *Tarasoff* apply or should be applied in New Jersey.

Plaintiff in the instant case asserts that a duty of a therapist towards third parties or potential victims is appropriate under the law of this State and forms a basis for a claim of actionable negligence analogous to that in *Tarasoff*. Defendant asserts such a duty is unworkable. . . .

It may be true that there cannot be 100% accurate prediction of dangerousness in all cases. However, a therapist does have a basis for giving an opinion and a prognosis based on the history of the patient and the course of treatment. Where reasonable men might differ and a fact issue exists, the therapist is only held to the standard for a therapist in the particular field in the particular community. Unless therapists clearly state when called upon to treat patients or to testify that they have no ability to predict or even determine whether their treatment will be efficacious or may even be necessary with any degree of certainty, there is no basis for a legal conclusion negating any and all duty with respect to a particular class of professionals. This is not to say that isolated or vague threats will of necessity give rise in all circumstances and cases to a duty. . . .

The *Tarasoff* duty has received criticism from some, but not all authors, mostly those in the medical professions. However, the concept of legal duties for the medical profession is not new. A doctor-patient relationship in some circumstances admittedly places a duty to warn others of contagious diseases. New Jersey recognizes the general rule that a person who negligently exposes another to a contagious disease, which the other contracts, is liable in damages. Specifically, a physician has the duty to warn third persons against possible exposure to contagious or infectious diseases, e.g., tuberculosis, venereal diseases, and so forth. That duty extends to instances where the physician should have known of the infectious disease.

Physicians also must report tuberculosis, venereal disease, and various other contagious diseases, see, e.g., N.J.S.A. 26:4-15, as well as certain other conditions. There is, to be sure, a relative certainty and uniformity present in a diagnosis of most physical illnesses, conditions and injuries as opposed to a psychiatric prediction of dangerousness based on symptoms and historical performance. Nevertheless, psychiatrists diagnose, treat and give opinions based on medical probabilities, particularly relying on a patient's history, without any clear indication of an inability to predict that is here asserted.

As a further illustration of types of duties imposed by statutes, N.J.S.A. 2A:97-2 provides that any person who has knowledge of actual commission of high misdemeanors and certain other crimes, but fails to report or disclose same, is himself guilty of a misdemeanor. No exception is set forth therein for a physician. To threaten to take the life of another person is also a crime. . . . Disclosure is, therefore, required in numerous situations. . . . [E]ven the Principles of Medical Ethics recognize that confidentiality gives way where "it becomes necessary in order to protect the welfare of the individual or of the community." . . .

. . . [T]his court holds that a psychiatrist or therapist may have a duty to take whatever steps are reasonably necessary to protect an intended or potential victim of his patient when he determines, or should determine, in the appropriate factual setting and in accordance with the standards of his profession established at trial, that the patient is or may present a probability of danger to that person. The relationship giving rise to that duty may be found either in that existing between the therapist and the patient, as was alluded to in *Tarasoff*, or in the more broadly based obligation a practitioner may have to protect the welfare of the community, which is analogous to the obligation a physician has to warn third persons of infectious or contagious disease. . . .

NOTES & QUESTIONS

1. ***Liability for Nondisclosure, Liability for Disclosure.*** Does it seem foreseeable for Dr. Milano to know that Morgenstein would harm McIntosh? Even if Dr. Milano prevails in court, there still is a strong incentive for him to disclose — to avoid a very costly litigation. Does the fear of a long court battle make therapists more likely to err on the side of disclosure? If Dr. Milano did disclose, would Morgenstein have a tort action for breach of confidentiality?
2. ***The Legal Duty: Sources and Scope.*** *McIntosh* recognizes a broader source for the legal duty to disclose than does *Tarasoff*. Consider the following passage at the conclusion of *McIntosh*:

   > The relationship giving rise to that duty may be found either in that existing between the therapist and the patient, as was alluded to in *Tarasoff*, or in the more broadly based obligation a practitioner may have to protect the welfare of the community, which is analogous to the obligation a physician has to warn third persons of infectious or contagious disease.

   If the duty arises in this "more broadly based obligation" to protect the public welfare, does this suggest that the duty itself may be broader than that in *Tarasoff*? Do therapists and medical personnel have a duty to warn the public at large if they believe a patient is generally dangerous and the patient has not made any threats to specific individuals?
3. ***The Duty to Warn About Relatives' Genetic Conditions.*** In *Pate v. Threlkel*, 661 So. 2d 278 (Fla. 1995), plaintiff Heidi Pate's mother received treatment for medullary thyroid carcinoma, a disorder believed to have a genetic component. When Pate learned that she also had the disease, she sued the doctors who treated her mother, alleging that the doctors were under a duty to warn Pate's mother that her children should be tested for the disease. Pate alleged that had she been tested, she would have taken preventative action that might have made her condition curable. The physicians argued that they lacked a duty of care to Pate. The court held that Pate had a valid claim:

   > . . . [T]o whom does the alleged duty to warn [the patient] of the nature of her disease run? The duty obviously runs to the patient who is in privity with the physician. In the past, courts have held that in order to maintain a cause of

action against a physician, privity must exist between the plaintiff and the physician. In other professional relationships, however, we have recognized the rights of identified third party beneficiaries to recover from a professional because that party was the intended beneficiary of the prevailing standard of care. . . .

Here, the alleged prevailing standard of care was obviously developed for the benefit of the patient's children as well as the patient. We conclude that when the prevailing standard of care creates a duty that is obviously for the benefit of certain identified third parties and the physician knows of the existence of those third parties, then the physician's duty runs to those third parties. . . .

. . . If there is a duty to warn, to whom must the physician convey the warning? Our holding should not be read to require the physician to warn the patient's children of the disease. In most instances the physician is prohibited from disclosing the patient's medical condition to others except with the patient's permission. Moreover, the patient ordinarily can be expected to pass on the warning. To require the physician to seek out and warn various members of the patient's family would often be difficult or impractical and would place too heavy a burden upon the physician. Thus, we emphasize that in any circumstances in which the physician has a duty to warn of a genetically transferable disease, that duty will be satisfied by warning the patient. . . .

Compare *Pate* to *Safer v. Estate of Pack*, 677 A.2d 1188 (N.J. Super. 1996). The plaintiff, Donna Safer, sued the estate of the deceased physician (Dr. Pack) who treated her father for colon cancer and multiple polyposis. After seven years of treatment, Safer's father died of cancer. Safer was ten years old at the time. About 25 years later, when Safer was 36 years old and newly married, she was diagnosed with colon cancer and multiple polyposis. She had a complete colectomy and one of her ovaries had to be removed. Safer contended that multiple polyposis is a hereditary condition that if untreated leads to colorectal cancer. Since the hereditary nature of the disease was known at the time Dr. Pack was treating Safer's father, Dr. Pack had a duty to warn Safer's father, and perhaps Safer herself. The court agreed with Safer:

. . . We see no impediment, legal or otherwise, to recognizing a physician's duty to warn those known to be at risk of avoidable harm from a genetically transmissible condition. In terms of foreseeability especially, there is no essential difference between the type of genetic threat at issue here and the menace of infection, contagion or a threat of physical harm. *See generally, e.g., McIntosh v. Milano*; *Tarasoff v. Regents of Univ. of Cal.* . . . The individual or group at risk is easily identified, and substantial future harm may be averted or minimized by a timely and effective warning. . . .

We need not decide, in the present posture of this case, how, precisely, that duty is to be discharged, especially with respect to young children who may be at risk, except to require that reasonable steps be taken to assure that the information reaches those likely to be affected or is made available for their benefit. . . .

We decline to hold as the Florida Supreme Court did in *Pate v. Threlkel,* that, in all circumstances, the duty to warn will be satisfied by informing the patient. It may be necessary, at some stage, to resolve a conflict between the physician's broader duty to warn and his fidelity to an expressed preference of the patient that nothing be said to family members about the details of the disease. . . .

How does the holding in *Pate* differ from that in *Safer*? Are these holdings a logical extension of *Tarasoff* and *McIntosh*? What are the potential privacy risks created by these holdings? Do the potential benefits of the rules established in *Pate* and *Safer* outweigh these privacy risks?

4. STATUTORY REPORTING REQUIREMENTS

HIV Notification Statutes. New York, along with many other states, has enacted a partner notification law when people are diagnosed with HIV. According to N.Y. Pub. Health L. § 2130, an HIV-positive diagnosis shall be reported to public health officials. The report "shall include information identifying the protected individual as well as the names, if available, of any contacts of the protected individual . . . known to the physician or provided to the physician by the infected person."

After the information is collected, any "contacts" of the individual may be notified by public health officials. *See* § 2133. A "contact" means "an identified spouse or sex partner of the protected individual, a person identified as having shared hypodermic needles or syringes with the protected individual or a person who the protected individual may have exposed to HIV under circumstances that present a risk of transmission of HIV, as determined by the commissioner." § 2180(10). The identity of the patient shall not be revealed to the contact. § 2133. "No criminal or civil liability shall arise against any protected individual solely due to his or her failure to cooperate in contact tracing conducted pursuant to section twenty-one hundred thirty-three of this title." § 2136(3).

Thirty-three states have partner notification laws. Thirty-one states collect HIV names. An argument in support of the laws is the difficulty many infected people have telling others of infection. In one study, 40 percent didn't disclose their HIV status to their partners. According to the Centers for Disease Control, 70 percent of partners are not informed. The argument against such disclosure laws is that they might deter people from getting tested. Further, HIV-positive women sometimes experience violence when their partners find out they have HIV. Almost half fear violence. Twenty-five percent were actually assaulted. Finally, it remains unclear whether such notification laws are effective.[14]

Consider Robert Gellman's conclusion about the preferability of legislation rather than existing case law and ethical principles to define the responsibilities of physicians with respect to patient privacy:

> Existing legal and ethical principles that guide physicians with respect to their obligations to protect the confidentiality of medical records are generally out of date and are not comprehensive. Physicians faced with requests or demands for patient information will find little in law or ethics to define their responsibilities with any precision. Yet the physician frequently is the only one who is in a

[14] *See* Sonia Bhatnager, Note, *HIV Name Reporting and Partner Notification in New York State*, 26 Fordham Urb. L.J. 1457, 1458 (1999).

> position to take action to protect the confidentiality of his records and the privacy of his patients. . . .
>
> . . . [A]s demand for medical records increases, the physician is being called upon to play a more central role in the protection of confidentiality. But the role that a physician should play is undefined because the physician's responsibilities are unclear. The result may be increased litigation over medical confidentiality issues and the obligations of physicians.
>
> . . . [B]ecause of the magnitude and complexity of privacy issues today, the courts cannot be expected to develop appropriate solutions in a timely fashion. . . .
>
> Therefore, the only practical way to develop suitable guidance defining the responsibilities of physicians, the right of patients, and the proper protection for medical information is through legislation.[15]

Consider the following argument by Richard Turkington about HIV notification:

> Are cases involving notification of HIV-related information sufficiently different from infectious disease notification cases and *Tarasoff* to consider adopting policies other than mandatory notification? There is a strong case for treating notification of HIV status differently. Disclosure without consent constitutes a serious invasion of privacy and involves risks of adverse consequences to the patient, such as discrimination or violence, through further publication by the sexual partner. Mandatory disclosure may also exacerbate psychiatric disorders caused by infection. Unless the patient is informed by the professional that HIV status would be disclosed to known current contacts at risk, disclosure threatens the trust necessary for free communication and the integrity of the professional-patient relationship. If the patient is informed of contact notification, he or she may be deterred from being tested. Third-party notification might save some lives in the short run but, in the long run, if it damages the trust between professional and client, and deters persons from voluntary testing, more transmission and deaths may result.
>
> Also, unlike the *Tarasoff* situation, the health professional is not the only potential source of notification to the third party. The infected person and the health department are both in the position to notify third parties, and the infected person is arguably in a better position to do so. Only the subject knows who is at risk. The physician may only know that a spouse is at risk. Imposing a duty upon the physician to discover those that may be sexually involved with the patient requires the physician to undertake a police-type activity that many are reluctant to perform and that ought not to be imposed. . . .
>
> The possibility of significant tort damage awards for disclosure under breach of confidentiality theories and the lack of clarity in the existing law on the duty to disclose to contacts leave the health care professional between a rock and a hard place. . . .[16]

---

[15] Robert M. Gellman, *Prescribing Privacy: The Uncertain Role of the Physician in the Protection of Patient Privacy*, 62 N.C. L. Rev. 255 (1984).

[16] Richard C. Turkington, *Confidentiality Policy for HIV-Related Information: An Analytical Framework for Sorting Out Hard and Easy Cases*, 34 Vill. L. Rev. 871 (1989); *see also* Lawrence O. Gostin & James G. Hodge, Jr., *Piercing the Veil of Secrecy in HIV/AIDS and Other Sexually Transmitted Diseases: Theories of Privacy and Disclosure in Partner Notification*, 5 Duke J. Gender & Pol'y 9 (1998).

Other Disclosure Requirements. Many states have statutory requirements for physicians to disclose health information for certain types of diseases or injuries. Recall from earlier in this chapter the New York statute upheld in *Whalen v. Roe,* which required the disclosure to the state of information about patients using certain prescription medications. Similar to the statute in *Whalen,* many state statutes require the collection of medical data for state registries. For example, New Jersey maintains a registry of birth defects, see N.J. Stat. 26:8-40.21; blindness, see N.J. Stat. 30:6-1.2; and cancer, see N.J. Stat. 26:2-106.

Other statutes require the reporting of certain conditions to various state agencies and officials. Ohio mandates the disclosure to appropriate government officials of occupational diseases (R.C. 3701.25 and 4123.71); diseases that are infectious, contagious, or dangerous to public health (R.C. 3701.24, 3701.52, 3707.06); health injuries indicative of child abuse or neglect (R.C. 2151.421); and injuries indicative of criminal conduct (R.C. 2921.22). Other states have similar reporting requirements. As discussed above, some states require, or provide for, disclosure of a person's medical condition to other individuals, such as partners and spouses.

A number of states place statutory bars on liability for the disclosure of certain conditions. For example, South Carolina has eliminated the "[t]he privileged quality of [patient-physician] communication" regarding the abuse or neglect of children. *See* S.C. Code Ann. § 20-7-550. Further, in South Carolina, "[a] physician or state agency identifying and notifying a spouse or known contact of a person having . . . (HIV) infection or . . . (AIDS) is not liable for damages resulting from the disclosure." S.C. Code Ann. § 44-29-146.

5. STATE LAW PRIVACY PROTECTIONS FOR MEDICAL INFORMATION

Until the Health Insurance Portability and Accountability Act (HIPAA) of 1996, which mandated federal privacy regulation for medical information, health privacy was a concern of the states. As we have seen, the constitutional right to information privacy and the Fourth Amendment provide some protection for personal health care information, but of a limited nature. While state regulation can be more extensive, it is also uneven in its protection. The Health Privacy Project at Georgetown University has prepared a comprehensive overview and analysis of every state's health privacy statutes and regulations.[17]

Privacy Torts. The Warren and Brandeis privacy torts protect medical information. Recall *Shulman v. Group W Productions, Inc.* from Chapter 2, where the court found that a TV show that taped the plaintiff as she was being rescued from a car accident and transported to the hospital via helicopter could give rise to a cause of action for intrusion upon seclusion (but not for public disclosure of private facts). In *Estate of Berthiaume v. Pratt,* 365 A.2d 792 (Me. 1976), a doctor attempted to take photographs of his patient, who was dying of

---

[17] *See* Joy Pritts, Janlori Goldman, Zoe Hudson, Aimee Berenson, & Elizabeth Hadley, *The State of Health Privacy: An Uneven Terrain (A Comprehensive Survey of State Health Privacy Statutes),* at http://www.healthprivacy.org.

cancer of the larynx. The patient raised a clenched fist and tried to remove his head from the camera's range. The patient died later that day. The court held that the patient had a claim for intrusion upon seclusion because the doctor did not have the right, against the patient's wishes, to complete his photographic record by taking pictures of the patient in his dying hours.

Many courts have found that the disclosure of medical information can give rise to a claim for public disclosure of private facts. In *Urbaniak v. Newton*, 277 Cal. Rptr. 354 (Cal. App. 1991), the court held that the disclosure of a patient's HIV status was "clearly a 'private fact' of which the disclosure may 'be offensive and objectionable to a reasonable [person] of ordinary sensibilities.'" *See also Susan S. v. Israels*, 67 Cal. Rptr. 2d 42 (Cal. App. 1997) (public disclosure action for disclosure of mental health records). In *Doe v. Mills*, 536 N.W.2d 824 (Mich. App. 1995), a group of abortion protestors held up large signs displaying the names of the plaintiffs outside the abortion clinic where they were getting abortions. The court held that the plaintiffs could bring a claim for public disclosure:

> . . . [A]bortion concerns matters of sexual relations and medical treatment, both of which are regarded as private matters. Furthermore, even though the abortion issue may be regarded as a matter of public interest, the plaintiffs' identities in this case were not matters of legitimate public concern, nor a matter of public record, but, instead, were purely private matters.

Likewise, in *Y.G. & L.G. v. Jewish Hospital of St. Louis,* 795 S.W.2d 488 (Mo. App. 1990), the court held that the plaintiffs had a viable public disclosure claim against a television station that broadcast the plaintiffs' involvement in a hospital's in vitro fertilization plan: "The in vitro program and its success may well have been matters of public interest, but the identity of the plaintiffs participating in the program was, we conclude, a private matter."

Tort Law Regulation of Patient-Physician Confidentiality. In addition to the privacy torts, a number of states recognize tort liability for instances where physicians disclose a patient's medical information. In certain circumstances, physicians can be liable for failing to disclose medical data about a patient.

Mandatory Reporting Laws. Many states require that medical personnel or institutions report certain health information to state agencies or to others. Depending on the state, the reporting requirements can extend to knife and gunshot wounds, sexually transmitted diseases, including HIV infection, and communicable diseases, such as tuberculosis. Reports are also required in many jurisdictions about injuries occurring to children and to elderly injuries, which are of the type that might indicate abuse.

Research Disclosure Laws. A number of states regulate the use of medical data for research purposes. For example, California generally prohibits nonconsensual disclosure of alcohol and drug abuse data, but permits such nonconsensual disclosure for the purpose of conducting research provided that the individual cannot be identified. *See* Cal. Health & Safety Code § 11977.

Medical Confidentiality Laws. Many states have specific statutes providing civil and criminal protection against the disclosure of medical information. Some laws restrict disclosure of medical data by particular entities: government agencies, HMOs, insurance companies, employers, pharmacists, and health data clearinghouses.

Other laws prohibit the disclosure by any entity of particular types of medical data, such as AIDS/HIV, alcohol or drug abuse, mental health, and genetic information. *See*, *e.g.*, Cal. Health & Safety Code § 199.21 (prohibiting disclosure of HIV test results); N.Y. Pub. Health L. § 17 (prohibiting the nonconsensual disclosure of medical records of minors relating to sexually transmitted diseases and abortion; even the disclosure to parents is prohibited without consent); Pa. Cons. Stat. § 1690.108 (prohibiting the disclosure of all records prepared during alcohol or drug abuse treatment).

Patient Access Laws. The vast majority of states (44) have statutes providing patients with a right to access certain medical records. A few states grant wide access to medical records held by all types of entities. On the other end of the spectrum, some states have no right of access, and others only have a limited right to access mental health records. The remaining states fall somewhere in between, permitting access to records from certain health care providers but not others (e.g., from some but not all of the following entities: hospitals, HMOs, insurers, and pharmacists).[18]

Comprehensive Health Privacy Laws. Most states do not have a comprehensive law governing medical privacy. According to the Health Privacy Project Report, only three states have a comprehensive law: Hawaii, Rhode Island, and Wisconsin. As the Report notes, most states regulate specific entities handling health data:

> The end result of this legislating by entity is that state laws — with a few notable exceptions — do not extend *comprehensive* protections to people's medical records. Thus, a state statute may impose privacy rules on hospitals but not dentists. The state may restrict the use and disclosure of information derived from a genetic test but not information obtained in a routine physical.[19]

6. HEALTH INSURANCE PORTABILITY AND ACCOUNTABILITY ACT

In 1996, Congress enacted the Health Insurance Portability and Accountability Act (HIPAA). The primary purpose of HIPAA was to permit employees to change jobs without having their new health plans exclude pre-existing conditions. Congress also mandated a uniform set of transaction codes to process insurance claims more easily. Given the greater ease of data sharing and transmission that uniform codes would enable, Congress was concerned about the privacy and security of medical data. However, Congress did not legislate privacy rules

---

[18] *See id.*

[19] *See id.*

within HIPAA itself. Rather, Congress established a deadline of August 21, 1999, for it to return to this topic and enact comprehensive legislation to provide for privacy of medical information. The Act also provided that if Congress failed to act by that date, then the Department of Health and Human Services (HHS) was to promulgate regulations with regard to health privacy.

No congressional majority could coalesce around a particular statutory solution, and the deadline passed without congressional action. Accordingly, HHS issued regulations, initially in the form of proposed regulations subject to revision. These were published at 64 Fed. Reg. 59,917 (Nov. 3, 1999). HHS received more than 50,000 comment letters on the proposed rule. *See HHS Rule Protecting Health Care Privacy Irks Some Employers, Likely to Affect Many*, 68 U.S.L.W. 2627, 2628 (Apr. 25, 2000).

The final version of the regulations was issued in December 2000 at the end of the Clinton Administration. Due to a procedural error, implementation of the regulations was delayed, and the Bush Administration initially criticized the regulations and vowed to delay and possibly to reconsider them. Later, the Administration changed course and announced that the regulations would go into effect. However, in 2002, the Bush Administration made significant changes in the regulations. *See* 67 Fed. Reg. 53,182 (Aug. 14, 2002).

The HIPAA regulations are the first comprehensive federal rules on health privacy; these rules are published at 45 C.F.R. parts 160 through 164.[20]

ENTITIES SUBJECT TO THE REGULATIONS

Covered Entities. The regulations do not apply to all people or entities that have access to an individual's health information. Rather, they apply "to health plans, health care clearinghouses, and health care providers." 45 C.F.R. § 160.102. Health care plans, clearinghouses, and providers that are covered by the regulation are called "covered entities."

A "health care provider" is a "provider of medical or health services . . . and any other person or organization who furnishes, bills, or is paid for health care in the normal course of business." § 160.103. Examples of health care providers are physicians, hospitals, and pharmacists.

A "health plan" is "an individual or group plan that provides, or pays the cost of, medical care." § 160.103. This definition encompasses health insurers and HMOs.

A "health care clearinghouse" is a public or private entity that processes health information into various formats — either into a standard format or into specialized formats for the needs of specific entities. § 160.103.

---

[20] For analysis of the HIPAA privacy rules, see Tamela J. White & Charlotte A. Hoffman, *The Privacy Standards Under the Health Insurance Portability and Accountability Act*, 106 W. Va. L. Rev. 709 (2004); Stacey A. Tovino, *The Use and Disclosure of Protected Health Information for Research Under the HIPAA Privacy Rule*, 49 S.D. L. Rev. 447 (2004); Lawrence O. Gostin & James G. Hodge, Jr., *Personal Privacy and Common Goods: A Framework for Balancing Under the National Health Information Privacy Rule*, 86 Minn. L. Rev. 1439 (2002); Peter D. Jacobson, *Medical Records and HIPAA: Is It Too Late to Protect Privacy?*, 86 Minn. L. Rev. 1497 (2002); Peter P. Swire & Lauren B. Steinfeld, *Security and Privacy After September 11: The Health Care Example*, 86 Minn. L. Rev. 1515 (2002); Mike Hatch, *HIPAA: Commercial Interests Win Round Two*, 86 Minn. L. Rev. 1481 (2002).

Electronic Processing. There is one other important consideration for determining the applicability of the HIPAA regulations — whether the person or entity processes and transmits health information electronically in a "standard" format as described in the HIPAA statute. The HIPAA statute was passed in order to standardize the format of the way health care information is transmitted, and only those entities using that format are covered under the regulations. A few critical definitions establish the jurisdictional scope of the regulations. The Pew Internet and American Life Project explains:

> If a person or an organization is a "health care provider" under the regulation, the next question to ask is whether it engages in the type of "standard transactions" that will bring it within the scope of the privacy rule. Since the intent of the administrative simplification provisions of HIPAA (including the privacy rule) is to simplify the processing of health insurance claims, the privacy rule applies only to providers who conduct insurance related transactions. Some of the electronic transaction that trigger application of HIPAA to a provider include: submitting health claims or equivalent information related to physician-patient interactions; determining eligibility for a health plan; receiving health care payment and remittance advice; and receiving referral certification and authorization. . . .
>
> In a very general sense, the question can be boiled down to: "Does the provider accept health insurance (including Medicaid) or participate in an HMO?"[21]

Hybrid Entities. Many entities provide a variety of products and services, only some of which pertain to health care. These entities are called "hybrid entities." § 164.504. An example of a hybrid entity is an employer that provides health care or a large company that has a division or subsidiary that provides health care or health insurance. Hybrid entities are less stringently regulated than covered entities. With a hybrid entity, the entity as a whole does not have to comply with the regulations — only the component that is actually performing the health care functions must comply. To address the danger that health information will spread beyond the health care component of a hybrid entity, the regulations require that firewalls be erected to protect against improper uses or disclosures within the entity. *See* § 164.504(c)(2).

Under the initial rule, only when the entity's primary mission was not health care related could it be deemed a hybrid rather than a covered entity. Under the revised rule proposed by the Bush Administration, any entity that provides a mixture of health care and other functions can elect to be a hybrid rather than a covered entity.

---

[21] Pew Internet & American Life Project, *Exposed Online: Why the New Federal Health Privacy Regulation Doesn't Offer Much Protection to Internet Users* 13 (Nov. 2001).

TYPE OF INFORMATION AND RECORDS COVERED

Individually Identifiable Health Information. The proposed regulations only applied to electronic records, not paper records. In the final rule, HHS extended the regulations to all individually identifiable health information in any form, electronic or nonelectronic. The information covered by the regulations is called "protected health information," and it generally consists of "individually identifiable health information." Under § 160.103, such information was defined as follows:

> *Individually identifiable health information* is information that is a subset of health information, including demographic information collected from an individual, and:
>
> (1) Is created or received by a health care provider, health plan, employer, or health care clearinghouse; and
>
> (2) Relates to the past, present, or future physical or mental health or condition of an individual; the provision of health care to an individual; or the past, present, or future payment for the provision of health care to an individual; and
>
> (i) That identifies the individual; or
>
> (ii) With respect to which there is a reasonable basis to believe the information can be used to identify the individual.

PRIVACY PROTECTIONS

Authorization. Covered health care providers do not need to obtain a person's authorization to use her protected health information for purposes of treatment, payment, and health care operations. § 164.502. For all uses and disclosures beyond those for treatment, payment, or health care operations, a patient's authorization is required. § 164.508(a).

A "covered entity may not condition the provision to an individual of treatment, payment, enrollment in the health plan, or eligibility for benefits on the provision of an authorization." § 164.508(b)(4). There are a number of exceptions to this rule. First, treatment can be conditioned on the provision of research-related disclosure. In other words, a physician or health care facility can make research-related disclosure a quid pro quo for treatment. Second, treatment can be conditioned if authorization is necessary to determine whether the individual is eligible for benefits or enrollment under a health plan, and for underwriting or risk rating determinations (this does not include psychotherapy notes). Third, payment of a claim or benefits can be conditioned upon authorization if the disclosure is necessary to determine a payment and is not for the use or disclosure of psychotherapy notes.

Marketing. Authorization is required for the use and disclosure of health data for the marketing of items and services. If a covered entity wants to provide a person's health data to a third party who wants to use it to peddle goods or services, it must first obtain that person's authorization. Authorization is required even if the marketing is done by the covered entity or one of its divisions.

In its revision of the regulations, the Bush Administration narrowed the definition of the activities that would constitute "marketing." In other words, it acted to permit broader use of health data. Excluded from the definition of "marketing" is the covered entity's own provision of health-related services and products. § 164.501. A covered entity can use an individual's health information without authorization to try to sell to her its own different products, treatments, and services — so long as they are health care related. Since these activities are not defined as "marketing," the individual cannot opt out or remove herself from the mailing list. In the conclusion of one observer, the HIPAA rules permit "marketing . . . to be disguised under operational activities."[22]

Psychotherapy Notes. Authorization is required "for any use or disclosure of psychotherapy notes" even if that use or disclosure is for treatment, payment, and health care operations. § 164.508. According to the regulation commentary, the reason why psychotherapy notes require authorization is because "psychotherapy notes do not include information that covered entities typically need for treatment, payment, or other types of health care operations."

The Right to Request Restrictions. An individual retains the right to request restrictions on the use or disclosure of health information by all covered entities. § 164.502(c). Covered entities must permit individuals to make such requests. § 164.522(a). If an entity agrees to an individual's request, it must adhere to its agreement. However, an entity is not required to agree to a restriction. § 164.522(a).

In emergency treatment situations, an entity can break this agreement, but if it discloses health information to other health care providers, it must request that the provider not further use or disclose the information. § 164.522(a).

Accommodation of Communication Preferences. Under § 164.502(h), individuals have the right to require covered providers to accommodate their requests about how providers communicate with the individual. According to the regulation's commentary,

> [A]n individual who does not want his or her family members to know about a certain treatment may request that the provider communicate with the individual at his or her place of employment, or to send communications to a designated address. Covered providers must accommodate the request unless it is unreasonable.

Minimum Necessary Uses and Disclosures. When using or disclosing protected health information, covered entities must "make reasonable efforts to limit protected health information to the minimum necessary" to accomplish their

---

[22] June Mary Zekan Makdisi, *Commercial Use of Protected Health Information Under HIPAA's Privacy Rule: Reasonable Disclosure or Disguised Marketing?*, 82 Neb. L. Rev. 741, 781 (2004).

goal. § 164.502(b)(1). This provision does not apply to disclosures to health care providers for treatment or to disclosures to the individual.

Under § 164.502(e)(1), a covered entity may disclose protected health information to a "business associate" so long as the "covered entity obtains satisfactory assurance that the business associate will appropriately safeguard the information."

Notice of Privacy Practices. Under § 164.520, covered entities must produce a notice of privacy practices.

Right of Access. Individuals have a right to access any protected health information that is used in whole or in part to make decisions about the individual.

EXCEPTIONS

Nonauthorized Uses and Disclosures. The regulation provides for a number of situations where health information can be used or disclosed without either authorization: (1) required by law; (2) for public health activities; (3) regarding victims of abuse, neglect, or domestic violence (under certain circumstances); (4) for health oversight activities; (5) for judicial and administrative proceedings; (6) for law enforcement purposes; (7) to avert a serious threat to health or safety; (8) for specialized government functions; and (9) for workers' compensation. § 164.512.

Disclosure to Law Enforcement Officials. Pursuant to § 164.512(f), health information may be disclosed to law enforcement officials without consent or authorization if required by a court order, warrant, or subpoena:

> (f) *Standard: disclosures for law enforcement purposes.* A covered entity may disclose protected health information for a law enforcement purpose to a law enforcement official . . .
>
> (ii) In compliance with and as limited by the relevant requirements of:
>
> (A) A court order or court-ordered warrant, or a subpoena or summons issued by a judicial officer;
>
> (B) A grand jury subpoena; or
>
> (C) An administrative request, including an administrative subpoena or summons, a civil or an authorized investigative demand, or similar process authorized under law, provided that:
>
> (1) The information sought is relevant and material to a legitimate law enforcement inquiry;
>
> (2) The request is specific and limited in scope to the extent reasonably practicable in light of the purpose for which the information is sought; and
>
> (3) De-identified information could not reasonably be used.

Moreover, certain health information may also be disclosed "in response to a law enforcement official's request for such information for the purpose of identifying or locating a suspect, fugitive, material witness, or missing person." *Id.*

COMPLIANCE AND ENFORCEMENT

Privacy Officials and Contact Persons. Covered entities must designate an individual as the covered entity's privacy official, responsible for the implementation and development of the entity's privacy policies and procedures. A person must be designated as a contact person to receive complaints about privacy and provide information about the matters covered by the entity's notice. The contact person can be the same person as the privacy official.

Enforcement. The regulations provide for criminal penalties for wrongful disclosures and civil damages of up to $25,000. Certain wrongful disclosures of medical data can also result in up to ten years' imprisonment and/or a $250,000 fine. The HIPAA regulations, however, do not grant a private cause of action. Enforcement of the statute is solely through the Secretary of Health and Human Services. *See Acara v. Banks*, 470 F.3d 569, 571-72 (5th Cir. 2006) ("[W]e are not alone in our conclusion that Congress did not intend for private enforcement of HIPAA. Every district court that has considered this issue is in agreement that the statute does not support a private right of action.").

EFFECT ON EXISTING LAW

State Law Preemption. HIPAA provides a baseline of protections but still allows states to pass more stringent requirements. § 160.203(b).

NOTES & QUESTIONS

1. ***Constitutionality of HIPAA.*** In *South Carolina Medical Ass'n v. Thompson,* 327 F.3d 346 (4th Cir. 2003), a group of doctors and doctors' associations challenged the constitutionality of HIPAA. They first argued that HIPAA is an improper delegation of congressional authority because Congress "relinquished its lawmaking function" by allowing an agency to establish privacy regulations rather than directly legislating to protect privacy. The court rejected this argument, contending that "Congress did not abdicate its legislative responsibilities in passing HIPAA, but outlined a broad set of principles to guide HHS action." The plaintiffs also argued that HHS improperly expanded HIPAA's scope beyond electronic health information to all health records maintained by covered entities. The court, however, concluded that "the plain language of HIPAA indicates that HHS could reasonably determine that the regulation of individually identifiable health information should include non-electronic forms of that information."
2. ***Compliance and Confusion.*** Consider the following from an article by Laura Parker in *USA Today*:

> In thousands of instances, [HIPAA] has been interpreted in extreme — and often incorrect — ways that critics say have been impractical at best and nonsensical at worst. . . .
>
> Thousands of doctors, for example, have stopped sending out appointment-reminder postcards, figuring the cards could be read by someone other than the patient. Some doctors have stopped leaving messages on patients' telephone answering machines, fearing that other family members might listen to them. Wives have been told they could no longer verify dental appointments for their husbands.[23]

Does HIPAA require these measures? HHS provides HIPAA questions and answers on its website:

> Question: *May health care providers use sign-in sheets or call out the names in waiting rooms?*
>
> Answer: Yes. Covered entities, such as physician's offices, may use patient sign-in sheets or call out patient names in waiting rooms, so long as the information disclosed is appropriately limited. . . . For example, the sign-in sheet may not display medical information that is not necessary for the purpose of signing in. . . .
>
> Question: *May health care providers leave messages at patients' homes or mail reminders to their homes?*
>
> Answer: Yes. . . . [T]he Rule does not prohibit covered entities from leaving messages for patients on their answering machines. However, to reasonably safeguard the individual's privacy, covered entities should take care to limit the amount of information disclosed on the answering machine. . . . The Privacy Rule permits covered entities to disclose limited information to family members, friends, or other persons regarding an individual's care. . . . However, covered entities should use professional judgment to assure that such disclosures are in the best interest of the individual and limit the information disclosed. . . .
>
> In situations where a patient has requested that the covered entity communicate with him in a confidential manner, such as by alternative means or at an alternative location, the covered entity must accommodate that request.
>
> Question: *Can a patient have a friend or family member pick up a prescription for her?*
>
> Answer: Yes. A pharmacist may use professional judgment and experience with common practice to make reasonable inferences of the patient's best interest in allowing a person other than the patient to pick up a prescription.
>
> Question: *May a doctor discuss a patient's health status, treatment, or payment with the patient's family and friends?*
>
> Answer: Yes. The HIPAA Privacy Rule at 45 CFR 164.510(b) specifically permits covered entities to share information that is directly relevant to the involvement of a spouse, family members, friends, or other persons identified by a patient.[24]

---

[23] Laura Parker, *Medical Privacy Law Creates Wide Confusion,* USA Today, Oct. 16, 2003.

[24] http://www.hhs.gov/ocr/hipaa/

3. ***Criminal Enforcement, the Richard Gibson Case, and the OLC Opinion.*** The HIPAA statute, 42 U.S.C. § 1320d-6(a), contains civil and criminal penalties for when:

> A person who knowingly and in violation of this part —
>
> (1) uses or causes to be used a unique health identifier;
>
> (2) obtains individually identifiable health information relating to an individual; or
>
> (3) discloses individually identifiable health information to another person.

The statute further provides: "A person described in subsection (a) shall . . . be fined not more than $50,000, imprisoned not more than 1 year, or both." According to Peter Swire, who worked on the HIPAA rule under the Clinton Administration, despite 13,000 HIPAA privacy complaints from 2003 to 2005, the federal government had brought no civil enforcement actions. During that time period, there was a single criminal action:

> In 2004 the U.S. attorney in Seattle announced that Richard Gibson was being indicted for violating the HIPAA privacy law. Gibson was a phlebotomist — a lab assistant — in a hospital. While at work he accessed the medical records of a person with a terminal cancer condition. Gibson then got credit cards in the patient's name and ran up over $9,000 in charges, notably for video game purchases. In a statement to the court, the patient said he "lost a year of life both mentally and physically dealing with the stress" of dealing with collection agencies and other results of Gibson's actions. Gibson signed a plea agreement and was sentenced to 16 months in jail.[25]

On June 1, 2005, the Office of Legal Counsel (OLC) issued a controversial opinion on the criminal enforcement of the HIPAA:

> We conclude that health plans, health care clearinghouses, those health care providers specified in the statute, and Medicare prescription drug card sponsors may be prosecuted for violations of section 1320d-6. In addition, depending on the facts of a given case, certain directors, officers, and employees of these entities may be liable directly under section 1320d-6, in accordance with general principles of corporate criminal liability, as these principles are developed in the course of particular prosecutions. Other persons may not be liable directly under this provision.[26]

According to Swire, based on this opinion, "Gibson could no longer be prosecuted under HIPAA." Swire criticized the OLC opinion:

> When Congress targeted these information crimes, and called for jail time, it created a criminal provision that is different from the civil provision. The OLC opinion essentially assumes that the scope of the civil and criminal provisions is the same. The OLC opinion tries to suppress the clear text of the

---

[25] Peter P. Swire, *Justice Department Opinion Undermines Protection of Medical Privacy* (Jun 7, 2005), at http://www.americanprogress.org/site/pp.asp?c 5 biJRJ8OVF&b 5 743281.

[26] *Scope of Criminal Enforcement Under 42 U.S.C. § 1320d-6*, Memorandum Opinion for the General Counsel Department of HHS and the Senior Counsel to the Deputy Attorney General, at http://www.usdoj.gov/olc/hipaa_final.htm.

criminal provision about "person," "false pretenses," "obtaining" and other terms. A fairer and more neutral reading of the statute would be to recognize the different scope that follows from the different language and different goals of the civil and criminal provisions.[27]

Since this controversy in 2005, however, three additional criminal prosecutions have occurred for HIPAA violations — in all of these cases, moreover, an employee, rather than a covered entity, was prosecuted. How was the prosecution possible in light of the OLC opinion?

As Assistant U.S. Attorney Peter Winn points out, 18 U.S.C. § 2(b) "provides a path for prosecutions of employees and business associates of HIPAA covered-entities."[28] This statute states: "Whoever wilfully causes an act to be done which if directly performed by him or another would be an offense against the United States, is punishable as a principal." Winn observes that U.S.C. § 2(b) codifies the common law maxim: "He who acts through another, acts himself." It permits an employee to be punished as a principal as if the covered entity, itself, had performed the act. In sum, the necessary connection is that the employee commit "an act that would be an offense *if committed directly by the covered entity.*"

The "Winn theory" has proved highly influential. As a 2007 article in the United States Attorneys' Bulletin by Ian DeWaal stated: "The bottom line is that [Assistant United States Attorneys] should be increasingly comfortable investigating and prosecuting HIPAA medical privacy criminal violations by individuals who do not fall within the enumerated classes of covered entities."[29] Thus, despite the OLC opinion, it is possible to hold an employee criminally liable in HIPAA enforcement cases — even when an employer is not prosecuted.[30]

To update the statistics cited by Swire above, through January 2008, the public filed 33,277 complaints with the Department of Health & Human Services' Office of Civil Rights (OCR), which is responsible for the civil enforcement of HIPAA.[31] In this time, there have been no fines levied on noncompliant organizations. The OCR investigated 8,405 of these complaints. Of those investigations, 5,653 led a regulated entity to change its privacy practices or to take some other corrective behavior. In the other cases, the investigators found no violation. In March 2008, Marilou King, senior advisor of HIPAA privacy enforcement at OCR, warned in a public presentation: "The pipeline is starting to fill up with cases that will be going to more formal forms of enforcement."

[27] Swire, Justice Department Opinion, supra.

[28] Peter A. Winn, *Criminal Prosecutions Under HIPAA*, 53 U.S. Att'ys Bull. 21 (Sept. 2005). *See* Peter A. Winn, *Who Is Subject to Criminal Prosecutions Under HIPAA?*, A.B.A. (Nov. 1, 2005), at http://www.abanet.org/health/01_interest_groups/01_media/WinnABA2005-11.pdf.

[29] Ian C. Smith DeWaal, *Successfully Prosecuting Health Insurance Portability and Accountability Act Medical Privacy Violations Against Noncovered Entities*, 55 U.S. Att'ys Bull., 10, 15, (July 2007).

[30] Cicely N. Tingle, *Developments in HIPAA and Health Information Technology*, 3 I/S 677, 686 (2008).

[31] *Enforcement of Privacy Rule Stresses Voluntary Compliance, HHS Official Says*, 7 Privacy & Sec. L. 479 (Mar. 31, 2008).

4. ***HIPAA and Health-Related Web Sites.*** A study by the Pew Internet and American Life Project in the year 2000 concluded that over 65 million Americans sought health information on the Internet.[32] A report by the same organization in November 2001 concluded that "a significant portion of activities at health-related web sites are not covered [by the HIPAA regulations] for several reasons. The major reason is that a great many web sites are run by organizations that are not 'covered entities.'" The report further stated:

> Most health-related Web sites engage in a number of different activities, from providing general educational health information to allowing patients to review test results online. Only some of these activities will be protected by the privacy regulations. For example, drugstore.com sells both drugs pursuant to a prescription and over-the-counter products. While information related to the prescription drug will be covered by the privacy regulation, information related to the over-the-counter product will not. The privacy rule covers only identifiable information related to "health care." This term does not include selling or distributing non-prescription health care items. . . .
>
> Many Web sites offer a "health assessment" feature where users may enter all sorts of information from height and weight to drug and alcohol use. . . . For example, HealthStatus.com offers free general health assessments as well as disease specific assessments to determine an individual's risk for some of the leading causes of death. . . . [B]ecause HealthStatus.com does not accept any insurance it will not be covered by the privacy rule.[33]

5. ***Law Enforcement Access.*** Section 164.512(f) has come under significant criticism by commentators who argue that it too broadly allows law enforcement officials to have access to health information.

   The Fourth Amendment generally requires a warrant supported by probable cause in order to search a person's documents. However, in what has become known as the "third party doctrine," the Court has held that there is no reasonable expectation of privacy (and hence, no Fourth Amendment protection) when a person's records are maintained by another party. For example, the Court has concluded that people lack a reasonable expectation of privacy in the records of the phone numbers they dial because these records are maintained by the phone company. *See Smith v. Maryland,* 442 U.S. 735 (1979) (Chapter 3). Likewise, bank records are not private because the bank, a third party, maintains control over them. *See United States v. Miller,* 425 U.S. 435 (1976) (Chapter 7).

   Suppose the government obtains a person's medical records under § 164.512(f). The person raises a Fourth Amendment challenge, contending that the government needed a search warrant to obtain the records. Would the person prevail? These records are maintained by third parties (doctors, hospitals, insurers). But these parties have statutory, common law, and ethical duties to maintain the confidentiality of health information. Does the third party doctrine extend to medical records?

---

[32] Pew Internet & American Life Project, *Exposed Online: Why the New Federal Health Privacy Regulation Doesn't Offer Much Protection to Internet Users* 7, 14, 17 (Nov. 2001).

[33] Pew Internet & American Life Project, *The Online Health Care Revolution: How the Web Helps Americans Take Better Care of Themselves* (Nov. 2000).

Other federal privacy statues generally provide stronger protection for third-party records than does the HIPAA rule. For example, the privacy subscriber provision in the Cable Communications Policy Act requires (1) "clear and convincing evidence that the subject of the information is reasonably suspected of engaging in criminal activity and that the information sought would be material evidence in the case"; and (2) "the subject of the information is afforded the opportunity to appear and contest such entity's claim." 47 U.S.C. § 551(h). Should cable subscriber records receive greater privacy protection than medical records? What factors might explain this outcome?

Consider *New York City Health & Hospitals Corp. v. Morgenthau*, 779 N.E.2d 773 (N.Y. Ct. App. 2002). A district attorney subpoenaed 23 hospitals to obtain emergency room data to investigate a homicide in which the suspect was thought to have been bleeding when he fled the crime scene. The subpoena sought records of those treated for stab wounds. A group of four hospitals refused to turn over the records, citing to Civil Practice Law and Rule § 4504(a), which provided:

> Unless the patient waives the privilege, a person authorized to practice medicine, registered professional nursing [or] licensed practical nursing . . . shall not be allowed to disclose any information which he acquired in attending a patient in a professional capacity, and which was necessary to enable him to act in that capacity. The relationship of a physician and patient shall exist between a medical corporation . . . and the patients to whom [it] . . . render[s] professional medical services.

The court quashed the subpoena:

> We conclude, however, that [*Matter of Grand Jury Investigation of Onondaga County,* 450 N.E.2d 678 (N.Y. 1983)] controls this appeal and directs that the challenged subpoenas be quashed. In *Onondaga County,* as in the instant case, the victim was stabbed to death under circumstances that led investigators to conclude that the assailant may have left the scene bleeding. Endeavoring to identify the assailant, the District Attorney of Onondaga County issued a grand jury subpoena on a hospital, seeking "all medical records pertaining to treatment of any person with stab wounds or other wounds caused by a knife." In quashing the subpoena, the Court held that compliance might have "require[d] the hospital to which it is addressed to divulge information protected by the physician-patient privilege." The Court concluded that under those circumstances, it was "not . . . possible to comply with a demand for names and addresses of all persons treated for a knife wound without disclosing privileged information concerning diagnosis and treatment."
>
> We perceive no difference of any actual substance between the subpoena quashed in *Onondaga County* and the ones challenged here. The records potentially responsive to the HHC subpoenas are precisely the same as those sought in *Onondaga County.* Though the District Attorney crafted the instant subpoenas with *Onondaga County* in mind by broadening their scope (to include most bleeding wounds rather than only knife wounds) and narrowing their reach (to include only wounds "plainly observable to a lay person"), the subpoenas still run afoul of *Onondaga County.* . . .

In light of this court's reasoning, consider HIPAA, § 164.512(f). Is there a conflict? If so, and if a subpoena pursuant to § 164.5129(f) were issued in that case, would HIPAA or the New York statute control?

NORTHWESTERN MEMORIAL HOSPITAL V. ASHCROFT

362 F.3d 923 (7th Cir. 2004)

POSNER, J. The government appeals from an order by the district court quashing a subpoena commanding Northwestern Memorial Hospital in Chicago to produce the medical records of certain patients on whom Dr. Cassing Hammond had performed late-term abortions at the hospital using the controversial method known [as partial birth abortion]. . . .

The subpoenaed records, apparently some 45 in number, are sought for use in the forthcoming trial in the Southern District of New York of a suit challenging the constitutionality of the Partial-Birth Abortion Ban Act of 2003, 18 U.S.C. § 1531. Dr. Hammond is one of the plaintiffs in that suit and will also be testifying as an expert witness. The district court held that the production of the records is barred by regulations issued under the Health Insurance Portability and Accountability Act of 1996 (HIPAA), Pub. L. 104-191, 110 Stat. 1936, and let us begin there.

[HIPAA provides that its regulations] "shall not supercede a contrary provision of State law, if the provision of State law imposes requirements, standards, or implementation specifications that are more stringent than the requirements, standards, or implementation specifications imposed under the regulation." See also 45 C.F.R. § 160.203(b). A standard is "more stringent" if it "provides greater privacy protection for the individual who is the subject of the individually identifiable health information" than the standard in the regulation.

The particular focus of the appeal is an HHS regulation . . . which authorizes a "covered entity" (such as Northwestern Memorial Hospital) to disclose private health information in judicial or administrative proceedings "in response to an order of a court." § 164.512(e)(1)(i). . . .

The district court in our case ruled that the Illinois law, because it sets a "more stringent" standard for disclosure than the HIPAA regulation, trumps that regulation by virtue of HIPAA's supersession provision. So he quashed the subpoena, precipitating this appeal.

Although the issue is not free from doubt, we agree with the government that the HIPAA regulations do not impose state evidentiary privileges on suits to enforce federal law. Illinois is free to enforce its more stringent medical records privilege (there is no comparable federal privilege) in suits in state court to enforce state law and, by virtue of an express provision in Fed. R. Evid. 501, in suits in federal court (mainly diversity suits) as well in which state law supplies the rule of decision. But the Illinois privilege does not govern in federal-question suits. . . .

All that 45 C.F.R. § 164.512(e) should be understood to do, therefore, is to create a procedure for obtaining authority to use medical records in litigation. Whether the records are actually admissible in evidence will depend among other things on whether they are privileged. And the evidentiary privileges that are applicable to federal-question suits are given not by state law but by federal law, Fed. R. Evid. 501, which does not recognize a physician-patient (or hospital-patient) privilege. . . .

The district court did not reach a further ground urged by Northwestern Memorial Hospital for quashing the government's subpoena, which is simply that the burden of compliance with it would exceed the benefit of production of the material sought by it. Fed. R. Civ. P. 45(c)(3)(A)(iv). . . .

The hospital had urged both the lack of probative value of the records and the loss of privacy by the patients. The government had responded in generalities, arguing that redaction would eliminate any privacy concern and that since Dr. Hammond had "made assertions of fact about his experience and his patients that plaintiffs are using to support their claim that, without a health exception, the Act is unconstitutional," the government should be permitted to test those assertions; but the government had not indicated what assertions these were or how the records might bear on them. Although on appeal the hospital repeated at length its reasons for believing that the records sought by the government would have little or no probative value, the government's response in both its opening brief and its reply brief remained vague to the point of being evasive.

At the oral argument we pressed the government's lawyer repeatedly and hard for indications of what he hoped to learn from the hospital records, and drew a blank. . . .

Like the district judge, we think the balance weighs in favor of quashing the subpoena. The government does not deny that the hospital is an appropriate representative of the privacy interests of its patients. But it argues that since it is seeking only a limited number of records and they would be produced to it minus the information that would enable the identity of the patient to be determined, there is no hardship to either the hospital or the patients of compliance. The argument is unrealistic and incomplete. What is true is that the *administrative* hardship of compliance would be modest. But it is not the only or the main hardship. The natural sensitivity that people feel about the disclosure of their medical records — the sensitivity that lies behind HIPAA — is amplified when the records are of a procedure that Congress has now declared to be a crime. Even if all the women whose records the government seeks know what "redacted" means, they are bound to be skeptical that redaction will conceal their identity from the world. This is hardly a typical case in which medical records get drawn into a lawsuit. Reflecting the fierce emotions that the long-running controversy over the morality and legality of abortion has made combustible, the Partial-Birth Abortion Ban Act and the litigation challenging its constitutionality — and even more so the rash of suits around the country in which the Department of Justice has been seeking the hospital records of abortion patients — have generated enormous publicity. These women must know that, and doubtless they are also aware that hostility to abortion has at times erupted into violence, including criminal obstruction of entry into abortion clinics, the firebombing of clinics, and the assassination of physicians who perform abortions.

Some of these women will be afraid that when their redacted records are made a part of the trial record in New York, persons of their acquaintance, or skillful "Googlers," sifting the information contained in the medical records concerning each patient's medical and sex history, will put two and two together, "out" the 45 women, and thereby expose them to threats, humiliation, and obloquy. As the court pointed out in *Parkson v. Central DuPage Hospital,* "whether the patients' identities would remain confidential by the exclusion of their names and identifying numbers is questionable at best. The patients' admit and discharge summaries arguably contain histories of the patients' prior and present medical conditions, information that in the cumulative can make the possibility of recognition very high." In its opening brief, as throughout the district court proceeding, the government expressly reserved the right, at a later date, to seek the identity of the patients whose records are produced. Pressed at argument, the government's lawyer abandoned the reservation; but we do not know what would prevent reconsideration should the government, the subpoena having been enforced, discover that particular medical records that it had obtained were incomplete, opaque, or ambiguous.

Even if there were no possibility that a patient's identity might be learned from a redacted medical record, there would be an invasion of privacy. Imagine if nude pictures of a woman, uploaded to the Internet without her consent though without identifying her by name, were downloaded in a foreign country by people who will never meet her. She would still feel that her privacy had been invaded. The revelation of the intimate details contained in the record of a late-term abortion may inflict a similar wound.

If Northwestern Memorial Hospital cannot shield its abortion patients' records from disclosure in judicial proceedings, moreover, the hospital will lose the confidence of its patients, and persons with sensitive medical conditions may be inclined to turn elsewhere for medical treatment. . . .

[Therefore, the subpoena is quashed] on the basis of relative hardship under Fed. R. Civ. P. 45(c).

MANION, J. concurring in part, dissenting in part. . . . This court should enforce the subpoena. I therefore concur in part and dissent in part. . . .

In this case, the government seeks only redacted medical records and agrees that all identifying information may be removed before Northwestern makes the records available for its review. Because the records will be redacted, they will not identify the individual. Nor is there a reasonable basis to believe that the information can be used to identify the individual. . . .

. . . [T]he relevance [of the subpoenaed records] cannot be overstated: Congress made explicit findings that a partial-birth abortion is never medically necessary to protect a women's health. Yet, Dr. Hammond claims Congress is wrong. . . . Dr. Hammond seeks to testify accordingly, and it is therefore imperative that the government be able to determine the veracity of his testimony. There is no better way than by determining if Dr. Hammond's actual practice supports his testimony. And this is not a question only of impeachment, but rather concerns the heart of this case. . . .

NOTES & QUESTIONS

1. ***Postscript.*** Not all courts facing the issue agreed with the Seventh Circuit. The judge in New York ordered that hospitals there turn over the records. *National Abortion Federation v. Ashcroft*, 2004 WL 555701 (S.D.N.Y. 2004) (not reported in F. Supp. 2d). Partially in response to considerable criticism, however, the DOJ abandoned its request for the records in that case.
2. ***De-Identified Records.*** The Seventh Circuit in *Northwestern Memorial Hospital* concluded that even though the patients' identities were not disclosed along with the records, the records should still be protected. Part of the court's holding appears to rest on the fact that the patients' identities could not be protected with the complete assurance that they would not be revealed down the road. However, another part of the court's holding suggests that even in a system where the patients' identities would be completely protected, the release of the records would still interfere with the patient-physician relationship. Is the court giving too much protection to the records here? Assuming that the records can be properly de-identified, is there any valid reason to withhold their disclosure in discovery if they bear some relevance to the case?
3. ***"More stringent state law."*** HIPAA and its regulations preempt state law unless that state law relates to the privacy of individually identifiable health information and is "more stringent" than HIPAA's requirements. In Law v. Zuckerman, 307 F. Supp. 2d 705 (D. Md. 2004), a plaintiff was suing her surgeon for malpractice. The surgeon's lawyers attempted to engage in ex parte communications with another physician of hers, who had carried out an elective procedure on her. The defendant in the malpractice lawsuit thought that the plaintiff's damages were caused by that other procedure, and not by his allegedly negligent care. The plaintiff was not notified that the defendant's attorneys would be communicating with her physician, and she contended that such communication is a violation of HIPAA. The court concluded that in a lawsuit based on diversity of citizenship in federal court, Maryland substantive law was to be applied where it did not conflict with controlling federal law. Whether or not this conflict existed turned on whether Maryland law was more stringent than HIPAA. According to the court:

> The key component in analyzing HIPAA's "more stringent" requirement is the ability of the patient to withhold permission and to effectively block disclosure. HIPAA's permissive disclosure requirements give each patient more control over the dissemination of their medical records than [the Maryland Confidentiality of Medical Records Act (MCMRA), which] sacrifices the patient's control of their private health information in order to expedite medical litigation. If state law can force disclosure without a court order, or the patient's consent, it is not "more stringent" than the HIPAA regulation. MCMRA is designed to give adverse counsel access to a patient's medical records without consent.

Under the circumstances of the case, therefore, ex parte communications were to be conducted in accordance with HIPAA procedures.

B. CONSTITUTIONAL PROTECTION OF MEDICAL INFORMATION

1. THE CONSTITUTIONAL RIGHT TO PRIVACY

Although the U.S. Constitution does not explicitly mention privacy, in a line of cases commonly referred to as "substantive due process," the Supreme Court has held that there exists a "right to privacy" in the U.S. Constitution.

As early as 1891, in *Union Pacific Railway v. Botsford*, 141 U.S. 250 (1891), the Court articulated some of the basic reasoning that would later develop into the "right to privacy" as it exists today. There, in holding that a court could not compel a plaintiff in a civil action to submit to a surgical examination, the Court declared:

> No right is held more sacred, or is more carefully guarded by the common law, than the right of every individual to the possession and control of his own person, free from all restraint or interference of others, unless by clear and unquestionable authority of law. As well said by Judge Cooley: "The right to one's person may be said to be a right of complete immunity; to be let alone." . . . The inviolability of the person is as much invaded by a compulsory stripping and exposure as by a blow. To compel any one, and especially a woman, to lay bare the body, or to submit it to the touch of a stranger, without lawful authority, is an indignity, an assault, and a trespass.

Later, in *Pierce v. Society of Sisters*, 268 U.S. 510 (1925), the Court held that parents cannot be compelled to have their children attend public schools because of the "liberty of parents and guardians to direct the upbringing and education of children under their control." In *Meyer v. Nebraska*, 262 U.S. 390 (1923) the Court declared:

> Fourteenth Amendment due process "denotes not merely freedom from bodily restraint but also the right of the individual to contract, to engage in any of the common occupations of life, to acquire useful knowledge, to marry, establish a home and bring up children, to worship God according to the dictates of his own conscience, and generally to enjoy those privileges long recognized at common law as essential to the orderly pursuit of happiness by free men."

The watershed case for substantive due process privacy was *Griswold v. Connecticut*, 381 U.S. 479 (1965).

GRISWOLD V. CONNECTICUT

381 U.S. 479 (1965)

DOUGLAS, J. [The directors of Planned Parenthood Association challenged a Connecticut law criminalizing contraceptives and counseling about contraceptives to married couples.]

Coming to the merits, we are met with a wide range of questions that implicate the Due Process Clause of the Fourteenth Amendment. Overtones of some arguments suggest that *Lochner v. State of New York*, 198 U.S. 45, should be our guide. But we decline that invitation. . . . We do not sit as a super-legislature to determine the wisdom, need, and propriety of laws that touch economic problems, business affairs, or social conditions. This law, however, operates directly on an intimate relation of husband and wife and their physician's role in one aspect of that relation.

The association of people is not mentioned in the Constitution nor in the Bill of Rights. The right to educate a child in a school of the parents' choice — whether public or private or parochial — is also not mentioned. Nor is the right to study any particular subject or any foreign language. Yet the First Amendment has been construed to include certain of those rights.

By *Pierce v. Society of Sisters*, the right to educate one's children as one chooses is made applicable to the States by the force of the First and Fourteenth Amendments. By *Meyer v. State of Nebraska*, the same dignity is given the right to study the German language in a private school. In other words, the State may not, consistently with the spirit of the First Amendment, contract the spectrum of available knowledge. The right of freedom of speech and press includes not only the right to utter or to print, but the right to distribute, the right to receive, the right to read and freedom of inquiry, freedom of thought, and freedom to teach — indeed the freedom of the entire university community. Without those peripheral rights the specific rights would be less secure. And so we reaffirm the principle of the *Pierce* and the *Meyer* cases.

In *NAACP v. State of Alabama*, 357 U.S. 449, we protected the "freedom to associate and privacy in one's associations," noting that freedom of association was a peripheral First Amendment right. Disclosure of membership lists of a constitutionally valid association, we held, was invalid "as entailing the likelihood of a substantial restraint upon the exercise by petitioner's members of their right to freedom of association." Ibid. In other words, the First Amendment has a penumbra where privacy is protected from governmental intrusion. In like context, we have protected forms of "association" that are not political in the customary sense but pertain to the social, legal, and economic benefit of the members. . . .

Those cases involved more than the "right of assembly" — a right that extends to all irrespective of their race or ideology. The right of "association," like the right of belief (*West Virginia State Board of Education v. Barnette*, 319 U.S. 624), is more than the right to attend a meeting; it includes the right to express one's attitudes or philosophies by membership in a group or by affiliation with it or by other lawful means. Association in that context is a form of expression of opinion; and while it is not expressly included in the First Amendment its existence is necessary in making the express guarantees fully meaningful.

The foregoing cases suggest that specific guarantees in the Bill of Rights have penumbras, formed by emanations from those guarantees that help give them life and substance. Various guarantees create zones of privacy. The right of association contained in the penumbra of the First Amendment is one, as we have seen. The Third Amendment in its prohibition against the quartering of soldiers "in any house" in time of peace without the consent of the owner is another facet of that privacy. The Fourth Amendment explicitly affirms the "right of the people to be secure in their persons, houses, papers, and effects, against unreasonable searches and seizures." The Fifth Amendment in its Self-Incrimination Clause enables the citizen to create a zone of privacy which government may not force him to surrender to his detriment. The Ninth Amendment provides: "The enumeration in the Constitution, of certain rights, shall not be construed to deny or disparage others retained by the people."

The Fourth and Fifth Amendments were described in *Boyd v. United States*, 116 U.S. 616, as protection against all governmental invasions "of the sanctity of a man's home and the privacies of life." We recently referred in *Mapp v. Ohio*, 367 U.S. 643, to the Fourth Amendment as creating a "right to privacy, no less important than any other right carefully and particularly reserved to the people."

We have had many controversies over these penumbral rights of "privacy and repose." These cases bear witness that the right of privacy which presses for recognition here is a legitimate one.

The present case, then, concerns a relationship lying within the zone of privacy created by several fundamental constitutional guarantees. And it concerns a law which, in forbidding the use of contraceptives rather than regulating their manufacture or sale, seeks to achieve its goals by means having a  maximum destructive impact upon that relationship. Such a law cannot stand in light of the familiar principle, so often applied by this Court, that a "governmental purpose to control or prevent activities constitutionally subject to state regulation may not be achieved by means which sweep unnecessarily broadly and thereby invade the area of protected freedoms." Would we allow the police to search the sacred precincts of marital bedrooms for telltale signs of the use of contraceptives? The very idea is repulsive to the notions of privacy surrounding the marriage relationship.

We deal with a right of privacy older than the Bill of Rights — older than our political parties, older than our school system. Marriage is a coming together for better or for worse, hopefully enduring, and intimate to the degree of being sacred. It is an association that promotes a way of life, not causes; a harmony in living, not political faiths; a bilateral loyalty, not commercial or social projects. Yet it is an association for as noble a purpose as any involved in our prior decisions.

BLACK & STEWART, J.J. dissenting. . . . I do not to any extent whatever base my view that this Connecticut law is constitutional on a belief that the law is wise or that its policy is a good one. In order that there may be no room at all to doubt why I vote as I do, I feel constrained to add that the law is every bit as offensive to me as it is my Brethren of the majority. . . .

Had the doctor defendant here, or even the nondoctor defendant, been convicted for doing nothing more than expressing opinions to persons coming to the clinic that certain contraceptive devices, medicines or practices would do them good and would be desirable, or for telling people how devices could be used, I can think of no reasons at this time why their expressions of views would not be protected by the First and Fourteenth Amendments, which guarantee freedom of speech. But speech is one thing; conduct and physical activities are quite another. The two defendants here were active participants in an organization which gave physical examinations to women, advised them what kind of contraceptive devices or medicines would most likely be satisfactory for them, and then supplied the devices themselves, all for a graduated scale of fees, based on the family income. Thus these defendants admittedly engaged with others in a planned course of conduct to help people violate the Connecticut law. Merely because some speech was used in carrying on the conduct — just as in ordinary life some speech accompanies most kinds of conduct — we are not in my view justified in holding that the First Amendment forbids the State to punish their conduct. Strongly as I desire to protect all First Amendment freedoms, I am unable to stretch the Amendment so as to afford protection to the conduct of these defendants in violating the Connecticut law. What would be the constitutional fate of the law if hereafter applied to punish nothing but speech is, as I have said, quite another matter.

The Court talks about a constitutional "right of privacy" as though there is some constitutional provision or provisions forbidding any law ever to be passed which might abridge the "privacy" of individuals. But there is not. There are, of course, guarantees in certain specific constitutional provisions which are designed in part to protect privacy at certain times and places with respect to certain activities. Such, for example, is the Fourth Amendment's guarantee against "unreasonable searches and seizures." But I think it belittles that Amendment to talk about it as though it protects nothing but "privacy." To treat it that way is to give it a niggardly interpretation, not the kind of liberal reading I think any Bill of Rights provision should be given. The average man would very likely not have his feelings soothed any more by having his property seized openly than by having it seized privately and by stealth. He simply wants his property left alone. And a person can be just as much, if not more, irritated, annoyed and injured by an unceremonious public arrest by a policeman as he is by a seizure in the privacy of his office or home.

One of the most effective ways of diluting or expanding a constitutionally guaranteed right is to substitute for the crucial word or words of a constitutional guarantee another word or words, more or less flexible and more or less restricted in meaning. This fact is well illustrated by the use of the term "right of privacy" as a comprehensive substitute for the Fourth Amendment's guarantee against "unreasonable searches and seizures." "Privacy" is a broad, abstract and ambiguous concept which can easily be shrunken in meaning but which can also, on the other hand, easily be interpreted as a constitutional ban against many things other than searches and seizures. I have expressed the view many times that First Amendment freedoms, for example, have suffered from a failure of the courts to stick to the simple language of the First Amendment in construing it, instead of invoking multitudes of words substituted for those the Framers used. For these reasons I get nowhere in this case by talk about a constitutional "right or privacy" as an emanation from one or more constitutional provisions. I like my privacy as well as the next one, but I am nevertheless compelled to admit that government has a right to invade it unless prohibited by some specific constitutional provision. For these reasons I cannot agree with the Court's judgment and the reasons it gives for holding this Connecticut law unconstitutional. . . .

NOTES & QUESTIONS

1. ***Finding "Privacy" in the Constitution.*** There is no explicit "right to privacy" mentioned in the Constitution. Does the Court make a persuasive case that (a) rights need not be explicitly mentioned to be constitutionally protected; and (b) that the right to privacy can be inferred from the penumbras of several other rights?

Recall Warren and Brandeis's article, *The Right to Privacy* (Chapter 1). They located the "right to be let alone" as an overarching principle in the common law based on examining specific common law rights. The *Griswold* Court applies a similar logic to its interpretation of the Constitution. Warren and Brandies claimed that they were not legislating; rather, they located the "right to be let alone" by interpreting the common law. Can the *Griswold* Court make the same claim?

Consider Robert Bork:

> Justice Douglas called the amendments and their penumbras "zones of privacy," though of course they are not that at all. They protect both private and public behavior and so would more properly be labeled "zones of freedom." If we follow Justice Douglas in his next step, these zones would then add up to an independent right of freedom, which is to say, a general constitutional right to be free of legal coercion, a manifest impossibility in any imaginable society. . . .
>
> *Griswold*, then, is an unprincipled decision, both in the way in which it derives a new constitutional right and in the way it defines that right, or rather fails to define it. We are left with no idea of the sweep of the right of privacy and hence no notion of the cases to which it may or may not be applied in the future.[34]

2. ***Is* Griswold *a Decisional or Informational Privacy Case?*** Consider Neil Richards:

> Many commentators see *Griswold* as the first of the line of constitutional cases culminating in *Roe v. Wade* and its progeny protecting the right to make intimate decisions including the right to abortion. Understandings of the privacy right recognized in *Griswold* as being related to informational meanings of the word are generally considered by scholars to be beside the point. . . . For example, although he notes the peculiarity of the label "privacy," Louis Henkin asserts that *Griswold* was about autonomy in marital relationships and not about information.
>
> Nevertheless, *Griswold* can, and perhaps should, be read as an information privacy case as well. . . . First, as Henkin himself notes, if *Griswold* were merely about reproductive autonomy, "privacy" is indeed a peculiar label to attach to the doctrine used to strike down the Connecticut law criminalizing the use of contraceptives. Second, the text of the opinion seems to be concerned with government access to information, albeit information about a specially protected relationship (marriage) in a specially protected place (the bedroom). . . .

---

[34] Robert H. Bork, *Neutral Principles and Some First Amendment Problems*, 47 Ind. L.J. 1, 8-9 (1971).

> . . . [A] fear of government intrusion into private zones (both physical and social) in pursuit of information was a large part of the rationale behind the conclusion that the Constitution protects a right of privacy. The Court was not recognizing a fundamental individual right to contraception, but rather invalidating the government's power to regulate commercial products where such regulation requires intrusion into private spaces and confidential relationships. . . .
>
> The third reason that *Griswold* can be read as an information privacy case is slightly more subtle than its rhetoric — but it perhaps is even more revealing. In marshalling precedent for his holding that the Constitution protected the right of marital privacy, Douglas relied extensively upon several lines of cases now commonly considered as falling on the information privacy side of the informational/decisional binary by information privacy scholars. Thus, he relied heavily upon the "associational privacy" cases of *NAACP v. Alabama* and *NAACP v. Button*; Fourth Amendment privacy cases such as *Boyd v. United States* and *Mapp v. Ohio*, and scholarship dealing with the privacy aspects of Fourth Amendment search and seizure; and Fifth Amendment self-incrimination law. . . .
>
> When viewed against this larger intellectual context, an information privacy reading of *Griswold* begins to take shape. According to Douglas, the First Amendment created a zone of privacy, not only in a person's home but also in the various intimate associations into which he might enter. The "free society" envisioned by the framers of the Constitution and embodied in the text of the First Amendment placed a substantive bar upon the state when it sought to probe or investigate those intimate associations. And when the state sought to investigate the most intimate association of all — that between a married man and woman — the prohibition on the state's power of scrutiny was just as complete. The hallmark of Douglas's analysis, however, was expressly informational. The focus of the analysis was on the state's ability to monitor, and the individual right was conceived not in terms of individual autonomy but in freedom from intrusion and scrutiny — the classic "right to be let alone" of Warren and Brandeis's article and Brandeis's *Olmstead* dissent. . . .[35]

The constitutional right to privacy cases are often referred to as "decisional privacy" because they involve certain decisions people make regarding their family life, health, body, reproduction, and child rearing. Is *Griswold* about decisional privacy? Information privacy? Or both?

3. ***The Privacy Rights of Non-Married Couples.*** Subsequent to *Griswold*, the Court elaborated upon the right to privacy in *Eisenstadt v. Baird*, 405 U.S. 438 (1972). *Eisenstadt* involved a statute that permitted the use of contraceptives only to married couples. Although *Griswold* rested upon the sanctity of the marital bedroom, the Court held that this law was also unconstitutional because right of privacy "is the right of the individual, married or single, to be free from unwarranted government intrusion into matters so fundamentally affecting a person as the decision whether to bear or beget a child."

---

[35] Neil M. Richards, *The Information Privacy Law Project*, 94 Geo. L.J. 1087, 1107-12 (2006); *see also* Daniel J. Solove, *A Taxonomy of Privacy*, 154 U. Pa. L. Rev. 477, 557-62 (2006).

4. ***The Right to Marry.*** In *Loving v. Virginia,* 388 U.S. 1 (1967), the Supreme Court struck down a statute that banned interracial marriage: "The freedom to marry has long been recognized as one of the vital personal rights essential to the orderly pursuit of happiness by free men." As the Court declared later in *Cleveland Board of Education v. LaFleur* 414 U.S. 642 (1974): "This Court has long recognized that freedom of personal choice in matters of marriage and family life is one of the liberties protected by the Due Process Clause of the Fourteenth Amendment."
5. **Roe v. Wade.** A year after *Eisenstadt,* the Court decided *Roe v. Wade*, 410 U.S. 113 (1973), one of the most controversial cases. There, the Court concluded that a Texas statute criminalizing abortion was unconstitutional as "violative of the Due Process Clause of the Fourteenth Amendment." As the Court explained:

> The Constitution does not explicitly mention any right of privacy. In a line of decisions, however, going back perhaps as far as *Union Pacific R.R. Co. v. Botsford*, the Court has recognized that a right of personal privacy, or a guarantee of certain areas or zones of privacy, does exist under the Constitution. In varying contexts, the Court or individual Justices have, indeed, found at least the roots of that right in the First Amendment; in the Fourth and Fifth Amendments; in the penumbras of the Bill of Rights; or in the concept of liberty guaranteed by the first section of the Fourteenth Amendment. These decisions make it clear that only personal rights that can be deemed "fundamental" or "implicit in the concept of ordered liberty" are included in this guarantee of personal privacy. They also make it clear that the right has some extension to activities relating to marriage; procreation; contraception; family relationships; and child rearing and education.
>
> This right of privacy, whether it be founded in the Fourteenth Amendment's concept of personal liberty and restrictions upon state action, as we feel it is, or, as the District Court determined, in the Ninth Amendment's reservation of rights to the people, is broad enough to encompass a woman's decision whether or not to terminate her pregnancy. The detriment that the State would impose upon the pregnant woman by denying this choice altogether is apparent. Specific and direct harm medically diagnosable even in early pregnancy may be involved. Maternity, or additional offspring, may force upon the woman a distressful life and future. Psychological harm may be imminent. Mental and physical health may be taxed by child care. There is also the distress, for all concerned, associated with the unwanted child, and there is the problem of bringing a child into a family already unable, psychologically and otherwise, to care for it. In other cases, as in this one, the additional difficulties and continuing stigma of unwed motherhood may be involved. All these are factors the woman and her responsible physician necessarily will consider in consultation.

John Ely contends that *Roe* does not follow logically from *Griswold*:

> [The regulation of contraceptives in *Griswold*] *would have been virtually impossible without* the most outrageous sort of governmental prying into the privacy of the home. [No] such rationalization is [possible in *Roe v. Wade*],

> for whatever else may be involved, it is not a case about governmental snooping.[36]

Is *Griswold* a "case about governmental snooping"? Should only laws where enforcement would require extensive governmental snooping be restricted under the constitutional right to privacy?

6. ***What Should the Constitutional Right to Privacy Protect?*** Consider Louis Henkin:

> [What] is it that makes my right to use contraceptives a right of Privacy, and fundamental, but my right to contract to work 16 hours a day or to pay more for milk than the law fixes, not a right of Privacy and not fundamental? Is it, as some suspect, that the game is being played backwards: that the private right which intuitively commends itself as valuable in our society in our time, or at least to a majority of our Justices at this time, is called fundamental, and if it cannot fit comfortably into specific constitutional provisions it is included in Privacy?[37]

What kinds of activities and decisions fall within the protection of the constitutional right to privacy? They generally involve matters of family, health, and body. Recall Robert Bork's criticism that *Griswold* provided "no idea of the sweep of the right of privacy." Is this correct?

David Meyer notes: "Current constitutional protection for family privacy is comprised of various distinct, though related, strands of rights against the state. It includes the right to marry, to procreate or to avoid procreation, to rear children, and to cohabit with family members. Although the Court occasionally groups these rights together in describing a more all-encompassing right of family privacy, it has never seriously attempted to offer a comprehensive theory which might explain why some intimate conduct or relationships, but not others, are entitled to special constitutional solicitude."[38]

Jed Rubenfeld argues that the laws that the right to privacy restricts are ones that go to the heart of one's existence: "These laws do not simply proscribe one act or remove one liberty; they inform the totality of a person's life. . . . It is the fundamental freedom not to have one's life too totally determined by a progressively more normalizing state."[39] In this way, laws that restrict contraception and abortion are different from laws that restrict contract or that regulate behavior.

One way of defining the scope of the right to privacy is to use John Stuart Mill's formulation in *On Liberty*:

> The only part of the conduct of anyone, for which he is amenable to society, is that which concerns others. In the part which merely concerns himself, his independence is, of right, absolute. Over himself, over his own body and mind, the individual is sovereign.[40]

---

[36] John H. Ely, *The Wages of Crying Wolf: A Comment on* Roe v. Wade, 82 Yale L.J. 920, 930 (1973).

[37] Louis Henkin, *Privacy and Autonomy*, 74 Colum. L. Rev. 1410, 1427 (1974).

[38] David D. Meyer, *The Paradox of Family Privacy*, 53 Vand. L .Rev. 527, 532 (2000).

[39] Jed Rubenfeld, *The Right to Privacy*, 102 Harv. L. Rev. 737, 784 (1989).

[40] John Stuart Mill, *On Liberty* (1859).

Is this a workable principle? Do marriage, contraception, and abortion merely concern the individuals involved, or do they concern others?

PLANNED PARENTHOOD OF SOUTHEASTERN PENNSYLVANIA V. CASEY

505 U.S. 833 (1992)

O'CONNOR, KENNEDY, AND SOUTER, J.J. . . . Liberty finds no refuge in a jurisprudence of doubt. Yet 19 years after our holding that the Constitution protects a woman's right to terminate her pregnancy in its early stages, *Roe v. Wade,* 410 U.S. 113 (1973), that definition of liberty is still questioned. . . .

At issue in these cases are five provisions of the Pennsylvania Abortion Control Act of 1982, as amended in 1988 and 1989. 18 Pa. Cons. Stat. §§ 3203-3220 (1990). The Act requires that a woman seeking an abortion give her informed consent prior to the abortion procedure, and specifies that she be provided with certain information at least 24 hours before the abortion is performed. For a minor to obtain an abortion, the Act requires the informed consent of one of her parents, but provides for a judicial bypass option if the minor does not wish to or cannot obtain a parent's consent. Another provision of the Act requires that, unless certain exceptions apply, a married woman seeking an abortion must sign a statement indicating that she has notified her husband of her intended abortion. The Act exempts compliance with these three requirements in the event of a "medical emergency." . . .

Before any of these provisions took effect, the petitioners, who are five abortion clinics and one physician representing himself as well as a class of physicians who provide abortion services, brought this suit seeking declaratory and injunctive relief. Each provision was challenged as unconstitutional on its face. . . .

Constitutional protection of the woman's decision to terminate her pregnancy derives from the Due Process Clause of the Fourteenth Amendment. It declares that no State shall "deprive any person of life, liberty, or property, without due process of law." The controlling word in the cases before us is "liberty." Although a literal reading of the Clause might suggest that it governs only the procedures by which a State may deprive persons of liberty, for at least 105 years, . . . the Clause has been understood to contain a substantive component as well, one "barring certain government actions regardless of the fairness of the procedures used to implement them." As Justice Brandeis (joined by Justice Holmes) observed, "[d]espite arguments to the contrary which had seemed to me persuasive, it is settled that the due process clause of the Fourteenth Amendment applies to matters of substantive law as well as to matters of procedure. Thus all fundamental rights comprised within the term liberty are protected by the Federal Constitution from invasion by the States." *Whitney v. California,* 274 U.S. 357 (1927) (concurring opinion). . . .

The most familiar of the substantive liberties protected by the Fourteenth Amendment are those recognized by the Bill of Rights. . . . It is tempting, as a means of curbing the discretion of federal judges, to suppose that liberty encompasses no more than those rights already guaranteed to the individual against federal interference by the express provisions of the first eight Amendments to the Constitution. But of course this Court has never accepted that view. . . .

Neither the Bill of Rights nor the specific practices of States at the time of the adoption of the Fourteenth Amendment marks the outer limits of the substantive sphere of liberty which the Fourteenth Amendment protects. See U.S. Const., Amdt. 9. As the second Justice Harlan recognized:

> [T]he full scope of the liberty guaranteed by the Due Process Clause cannot be found in or limited by the precise terms of the specific guarantees elsewhere provided in the Constitution. This "liberty" is not a series of isolated points pricked out in terms of the taking of property; the freedom of speech, press, and religion; the right to keep and bear arms; the freedom from unreasonable searches and seizures; and so on. It is a rational continuum which, broadly speaking, includes a freedom from all substantial arbitrary impositions and purposeless restraints, . . . and which also recognizes, what a reasonable and sensitive judgment must, that certain interests require particularly careful scrutiny of the state needs asserted to justify their abridgment. *Poe v. Ullman.*

Justice Harlan wrote these words in addressing an issue the full Court did not reach in *Poe v. Ullman,* but the Court adopted his position four Terms later in *Griswold v. Connecticut*. . . .

Our law affords constitutional protection to personal decisions relating to marriage, procreation, contraception, family relationships, child rearing, and education. Our cases recognize "the right of the *individual,* married or single, to be free from unwarranted governmental intrusion into matters so fundamentally affecting a person as the decision whether to bear or beget a child." *Eisenstadt v. Baird*. Our precedents "have respected the private realm of family life which the state cannot enter." *Prince v. Massachusetts,* 321 U.S. 158 (1944). These matters, involving the most intimate and personal choices a person may make in a lifetime, choices central to personal dignity and autonomy, are central to the liberty protected by the Fourteenth Amendment. At the heart of liberty is the right to define one's own concept of existence, of meaning, of the universe, and of the mystery of human life. Beliefs about these matters could not define the attributes of personhood were they formed under compulsion of the State.

These considerations begin our analysis of the woman's interest in terminating her pregnancy but cannot end it, for this reason: though the abortion decision may originate within the zone of conscience and belief, it is more than a philosophic exercise. Abortion is a unique act. It is an act fraught with consequences for others: for the woman who must live with the implications of her decision; for the persons who perform and assist in the procedure; for the spouse, family, and society which must confront the knowledge that these procedures exist, procedures some deem nothing short of an act of violence against innocent human life; and, depending on one's beliefs, for the life or potential life that is aborted. Though abortion is conduct, it does not follow that the State is entitled to proscribe it in all instances. That is because the liberty of the woman is at stake in a sense unique to the human condition and so unique to the law. The mother who carries a child to full term is subject to anxieties, to physical constraints, to pain that only she must bear. That these sacrifices have from the beginning of the human race been endured by woman with a pride that ennobles her in the eyes of others and gives to the infant a bond of love cannot alone be grounds for the State to insist she make the sacrifice. Her suffering is too intimate and personal for the State to insist, without more, upon its own vision of the woman's role, however dominant that vision has been in the course of our history and our culture. The destiny of the woman must be shaped to a large extent on her own conception of her spiritual imperatives and her place in society.

It should be recognized, moreover, that in some critical respects the abortion decision is of the same character as the decision to use contraception, to which *Griswold v. Connecticut, Eisenstadt v. Baird,* and *Carey v. Population Services International* afford constitutional protection. We have no doubt as to the correctness of those decisions. They support the reasoning in *Roe* relating to the woman's liberty because they involve personal decisions concerning not only the meaning of procreation but also human responsibility and respect for it. As with abortion, reasonable people will have differences of opinion about these matters. One view is based on such reverence for the wonder of creation that any pregnancy ought to be welcomed and carried to full term no matter how difficult it will be to provide for the child and ensure its well-being. Another is that the inability to provide for the nurture and care of the infant is a cruelty to the child and an anguish to the parent. These are intimate views with infinite variations, and their deep, personal character underlay our decisions in *Griswold, Eisenstadt,* and *Carey.* The same concerns are present when the woman confronts the reality that, perhaps despite her attempts to avoid it, she has become pregnant.

It was this dimension of personal liberty that *Roe* sought to protect, and its holding invoked the reasoning and the tradition of the precedents we have discussed, granting protection to substantive liberties of the person. . . .

Section 3209 of Pennsylvania's abortion law provides, except in cases of medical emergency, that no physician shall perform an abortion on a married woman without receiving a signed statement from the woman that she has notified her spouse that she is about to undergo an abortion. The woman has the option of providing an alternative signed statement certifying that her husband is not the man who impregnated her; that her husband could not be located; that the pregnancy is the result of spousal sexual assault which she has reported; or that the woman believes that notifying her husband will cause him or someone else to inflict bodily injury upon her. A physician who performs an abortion on a married woman without receiving the appropriate signed statement will have his or her license revoked, and is liable to the husband for damages. . . .

In well-functioning marriages, spouses discuss important intimate decisions such as whether to bear a child. But there are millions of women in this country who are the victims of regular physical and psychological abuse at the hands of their husbands. Should these women become pregnant, they may have very good reasons for not wishing to inform their husbands of their decision to obtain an abortion. Many may have justifiable fears of physical abuse, but may be no less fearful of the consequences of reporting prior abuse to the Commonwealth of Pennsylvania. Many may have a reasonable fear that notifying their husbands will provoke further instances of child abuse; these women are not exempt from § 3209's notification requirement. Many may fear devastating forms of psychological abuse from their husbands, including verbal harassment, threats of future violence, the destruction of possessions, physical confinement to the home, the withdrawal of financial support, or the disclosure of the abortion to family and friends. These methods of psychological abuse may act as even more of a deterrent to notification than the possibility of physical violence, but women who are the victims of the abuse are not exempt from § 3209's notification requirement. And many women who are pregnant as a result of sexual assaults by their husbands will be unable to avail themselves of the exception for spousal sexual assault, § 3209(b)(3), because the exception requires that the woman have notified law enforcement authorities within 90 days of the assault, and her husband will be notified of her report once an investigation begins, § 3128(c). If anything in this field is certain, it is that victims of spousal sexual assault are extremely reluctant to report the abuse to the government; hence, a great many spousal rape victims will not be exempt from the notification requirement imposed by § 3209.

The spousal notification requirement is thus likely to prevent a significant number of women from obtaining an abortion. It does not merely make abortions a little more difficult or expensive to obtain; for many women, it will impose a substantial obstacle. We must not blind ourselves to the fact that the significant number of women who fear for their safety and the safety of their children are likely to be deterred from procuring an abortion as surely as if the Commonwealth had outlawed abortion in all cases. . . .

This conclusion is in no way inconsistent with our decisions upholding parental notification or consent requirements. Those enactments, and our judgment that they are constitutional, are based on the quite reasonable assumption that minors will benefit from consultation with their parents and that children will often not realize that their parents have their best interests at heart. We cannot adopt a parallel assumption about adult women.

We recognize that a husband has a "deep and proper concern and interest . . . in his wife's pregnancy and in the growth and development of the fetus she is carrying." With regard to the children he has fathered and raised, the Court has recognized his "cognizable and substantial" interest in their custody. . . .

Before birth, however, the issue takes on a very different cast. It is an inescapable biological fact that state regulation with respect to the child a woman is carrying will have a far greater impact on the mother's liberty than on the father's. The effect of state regulation on a woman's protected liberty is doubly deserving of scrutiny in such a case, as the State has touched not only upon the private sphere of the family but upon the very bodily integrity of the pregnant woman. . . . The Constitution protects individuals, men and women alike, from unjustified state interference, even when that interference is enacted into law for the benefit of their spouses.

There was a time, not so long ago, when a different understanding of the family and of the Constitution prevailed. In *Bradwell v. State,* 16 Wall. 130 (1873), three Members of this Court reaffirmed the common-law principle that "a woman had no legal existence separate from her husband, who was regarded as her head and representative in the social state; and, notwithstanding some recent modifications of this civil status, many of the special rules of law flowing from and dependent upon this cardinal principle still exist in full force in most States."

Only one generation has passed since this Court observed that "woman is still regarded as the center of home and family life," with attendant "special responsibilities" that precluded full and independent legal status under the Constitution. *Hoyt v. Florida,* 368 U.S. 57 (1961). These views, of course, are no longer consistent with our understanding of the family, the individual, or the Constitution. . . .

The husband's interest in the life of the child his wife is carrying does not permit the State to empower him with this troubling degree of authority over his wife. The contrary view leads to consequences reminiscent of the common law. A husband has no enforceable right to require a wife to advise him before she exercises her personal choices. If a husband's interest in the potential life of the child outweighs a wife's liberty, the State could require a married woman to notify her husband before she uses a postfertilization contraceptive. Perhaps next in line would be a statute requiring pregnant married women to notify their husbands before engaging in conduct causing risks to the fetus. After all, if the husband's interest in the fetus' safety is a sufficient predicate for state regulation, the State could reasonably conclude that pregnant wives should notify their husbands before drinking alcohol or smoking. Perhaps married women should notify their husbands before using contraceptives or before undergoing any type of surgery that may have complications affecting the husband's interest in his wife's reproductive organs. And if a husband's interest justifies notice in any of these cases, one might reasonably argue that it justifies exactly what the *Danforth* Court held it did not justify a requirement of the husband's consent as well. A State may not give to a man the kind of dominion over his wife that parents exercise over their children.

Section 3209 embodies a view of marriage consonant with the common-law status of married women but repugnant to our present understanding of marriage and of the nature of the rights secured by the Constitution. Women do not lose their constitutionally protected liberty when they marry. The Constitution protects all individuals, male or female, married or unmarried, from the abuse of governmental power, even where that power is employed for the supposed benefit of a member of the individual's family. These considerations confirm our conclusion that § 3209 is invalid. . . .

SCALIA, REHNQUIST, WHITE, AND THOMAS, J.J. concurring in part and dissenting in part. . . . The States may, if they wish, permit abortion on demand, but the Constitution does not require them to do so. The permissibility of abortion, and the limitations upon it, are to be resolved like most important questions in our democracy: by citizens trying to persuade one another and then voting. . . . A State's choice between two positions on which reasonable people can disagree is constitutional even when (as is often the case) it intrudes upon a "liberty" in the absolute sense. Laws against bigamy, for example — with which entire societies of reasonable people disagree — intrude upon men and women's liberty to marry and live with one another. But bigamy happens not to be a liberty specially "protected" by the Constitution.

That is, quite simply, the issue in these cases: not whether the power of a woman to abort her unborn child is a "liberty" in the absolute sense; or even whether it is a liberty of great importance to many women. Of course it is both.

The issue is whether it is a liberty protected by the Constitution of the United States. I am sure it is not. I reach that conclusion not because of anything so exalted as my views concerning the "concept of existence, of meaning, of the universe, and of the mystery of human life." *Ibid*. Rather, I reach it for the same reason I reach the conclusion that bigamy is not constitutionally protected — because of two simple facts: (1) the Constitution says absolutely nothing about it, and (2) the longstanding traditions of American society have permitted it to be legally proscribed. . . .

Roe's mandate for abortion on demand destroyed the compromises of the past, rendered compromise impossible for the future, and required the entire issue to be resolved uniformly, at the national level. At the same time, *Roe* created a vast new class of abortion consumers and abortion proponents by eliminating the moral opprobrium that had attached to the act. ("If the Constitution guarantees abortion, how can it be bad?" — not an accurate line of thought, but a natural one.) Many favor all of those developments, and it is not for me to say that they are wrong. . . .

The Imperial Judiciary lives. It is instructive to compare this Nietzschean vision of us unelected, life-tenured judges — leading a Volk who will be "tested by following," and whose very "belief in themselves" is mystically bound up in their "understanding" of a Court that "speak[s] before all others for their constitutional ideals" — with the somewhat more modest role envisioned for these lawyers by the Founders. . . .

We should get out of this area, where we have no right to be, and where we do neither ourselves nor the country any good by remaining.

NOTES & QUESTIONS

1. ***The Most Intimate and Personal Choices.*** Recall the following passage in *Casey*:

> These matters, involving the most intimate and personal choices a person may make in a lifetime, choices central to personal dignity and autonomy, are central to the liberty protected by the Fourteenth Amendment. At the heart of liberty is the right to define one's own concept of existence, of meaning, of the universe, and of the mystery of human life. Beliefs about these matters could not define the attributes of personhood were they formed under compulsion of the State.

In what ways does the rationale for protecting substantive due process differ in *Griswold* and *Casey*? What choices are "central to personal dignity and autonomy"?

2. ***The "Undue Burden" Standard.*** Although affirming *Roe,* the plurality opinion sets forth a new standard to evaluate whether regulations on abortion pass constitutional muster:

> *Roe v. Wade* was express in its recognition of the State's "important and legitimate interest[s] in preserving and protecting the health of the pregnant woman [and] in protecting the potentiality of human life." The trimester framework, however, does not fulfill *Roe*'s own promise that the State has an interest in protecting fetal life or potential life. *Roe* began the contradiction by

> using the trimester framework to forbid any regulation of abortion designed to advance that interest before viability. Before viability, *Roe* and subsequent cases treat all governmental attempts to influence a woman's decision on behalf of the potential life within her as unwarranted. This treatment is, in our judgment, incompatible with the recognition that there is a substantial state interest in potential life throughout pregnancy.
>
> The very notion that the State has a substantial interest in potential life leads to the conclusion that not all regulations must be deemed unwarranted. Not all burdens on the right to decide whether to terminate a pregnancy will be undue. In our view, the undue burden standard is the appropriate means of reconciling the State's interest with the woman's constitutionally protected liberty. . . .
>
> A finding of an undue burden is a shorthand for the conclusion that a state regulation has the purpose or effect of placing a substantial obstacle in the path of a woman seeking an abortion of a nonviable fetus. . . .

Justice Scalia criticizes the "undue burden" standard, contending that it was "inherently manipulable and will prove hopelessly unworkable in practice." He elaborates:

> The joint opinion explains that a state regulation imposes an "undue burden" if it "has the purpose or effect of placing a substantial obstacle in the path of a woman seeking an abortion of a nonviable fetus." An obstacle is "substantial," we are told, if it is "calculated[,] [not] to inform the woman's free choice, [but to] hinder it." This latter statement cannot possibly mean what it says. *Any* regulation of abortion that is intended to advance what the joint opinion concedes is the State's "substantial" interest in protecting unborn life will be "calculated [to] hinder" a decision to have an abortion. It thus seems more accurate to say that the joint opinion would uphold abortion regulations only if they do not *unduly* hinder the woman's decision. That, of course, brings us right back to square one: Defining an "undue burden" as an "undue hindrance" (or a "substantial obstacle") hardly "clarifies" the test. Consciously or not, the joint opinion's verbal shell game will conceal raw judicial policy choices concerning what is "appropriate" abortion legislation. . . .

The "undue burden" test, endorsed only by a plurality in *Casey,* became the standard of the Court in *Stenberg v. Carhart,* 530 U.S. 914 (2000), when the Court struck down a statute restricting partial-birth abortions.

3. ***Spousal Notification.*** The spousal notification provision the Court struck down in *Casey* only required that the woman notify her husband if she was going to have an abortion. Should this be something a husband is entitled to know? Note that the notification provision is not directed toward the biological father — it is the husband who must be notified. Does this notification, as the Court notes, give the husband a "troubling degree of authority over his wife"? Suppose a statute required that the biological father be notified. Does he have a right to learn that the fetus is being aborted?
4. ***Partial Birth Abortion.*** In *Gonzales v. Carhart*, 127 S. Ct. 1610 (2007), the Supreme Court upheld the Partial-Birth Abortion Act, which prohibited abortions in which a living fetus is partially delivered through the vagina and is killed. The Act makes an exception to save the mother's life but does not make an exception to protect the woman's health.

5. ***The Right to Refuse Medical Treatment.*** In *Cruzan v. Director, Missouri Dep't of Health,* 497 U.S. 261 (1990), the Court held that a competent person has a liberty interest in refusing unwanted medical treatment, but that the state could require proof of "clear and convincing" evidence that an incompetent person would have wanted to discontinue medical treatment.
6. ***The Right to Die.*** The Court refused to extend the right to privacy to the so-called right to die. *Washington v. Glucksberg*, 521 U.S. 702 (1997). The plaintiffs challenged a state's ban on assisted suicide. The Court reasoned:

> First, Washington has an "unqualified interest in the preservation of human life." The State's prohibition on assisted suicide, like all homicide laws, both reflects and advances its commitment to this interest. . . . This interest is symbolic and aspirational as well as practical. . . .
>
> Those who attempt suicide — terminally ill or not — often suffer from depression or other medical disorders. . . . Research indicates, however, that many people who request physician-assisted suicide withdraw that request if their depression and pain are treated.
>
> The State also has an interest in protecting the integrity and ethics of the medical profession. . . . And physician-assisted suicide could, it is argued, undermine the trust that is essential to the doctor-patient relationship by blurring the time-honored line between healing and harming.

7. ***Homosexual Sodomy.*** In *Bowers v. Hardwick*, 478 U.S. 186 (1986), the Court upheld a Georgia statute criminalizing sodomy because the Constitution does not confer "a fundamental right upon homosexuals to engage in sodomy." The Court rejected a reading of *Pierce, Meyer, Griswold, Roe,* and *Eisenstadt* as protecting acts homosexual sodomy in the home:

> [W]e think it evident that none of the rights announced in those cases bears any resemblance to the claimed constitutional right of homosexuals to engage in acts of sodomy that is asserted in this case. No connection between family, marriage, or procreation on the one hand and homosexual activity on the other has been demonstrated, either by the Court of Appeals or by respondent. Moreover, any claim that these cases nevertheless stand for the proposition that any kind of private sexual conduct between consenting adults is constitutionally insulated from state proscription is unsupportable. . . .
>
> Precedent aside, however, respondent would have us announce, as the Court of Appeals did, a fundamental right to engage in homosexual sodomy. This we are quite unwilling to do.

Frank Easterbrook considers *Roe* and *Bowers* to be "irreconcilable."[41] Do you agree?

LAWRENCE V. TEXAS
539 U.S. 558 (2003)

KENNEDY, J. Liberty protects the person from unwarranted government intrusions into a dwelling or other private places. In our tradition the State is not

[41] Frank Easterbrook, *Abstraction and Authority*, 59 U. Chi. L. Rev. 349 (1992).

omnipresent in the home. And there are other spheres of our lives and existence, outside the home, where the State should not be a dominant presence. Freedom extends beyond spatial bounds. Liberty presumes an autonomy of self that includes freedom of thought, belief, expression, and certain intimate conduct. The instant case involves liberty of the person both in its spatial and more transcendent dimensions.

The question before the Court is the validity of a Texas statute making it a crime for two persons of the same sex to engage in certain intimate sexual conduct.

In Houston, Texas, officers of the Harris County Police Department were dispatched to a private residence in response to a reported weapons disturbance. They entered an apartment where one of the petitioners, John Geddes Lawrence, resided. The right of the police to enter does not seem to have been questioned. The officers observed Lawrence and another man, Tyron Garner, engaging in a sexual act. The two petitioners were arrested, held in custody over night, and charged and convicted before a Justice of the Peace.

The complaints described their crime as "deviate sexual intercourse, namely anal sex, with a member of the same sex (man)." The applicable state law is Tex. Penal Code Ann. § 21.06(a) (2003). It provides: "A person commits an offense if he engages in deviate sexual intercourse with another individual of the same sex." The statute defines "[d]eviate sexual intercourse" as follows:

> (A) any contact between any part of the genitals of one person and the mouth or anus of another person; or
>
> (B) the penetration of the genitals or the anus of another person with an object. § 21.01(1). . . .

[The men were convicted, and they challenged their conviction as violative of substantive due process. Their challenge was rejected by Texas courts based on *Bowers v. Hardwick,* 478 U.S. 186 (1986).]

We conclude the case should be resolved by determining whether the petitioners were free as adults to engage in the private conduct in the exercise of their liberty under the Due Process Clause of the Fourteenth Amendment to the Constitution. For this inquiry we deem it necessary to reconsider the Court's holding in *Bowers*. . . .

The Court began its substantive discussion in *Bowers* as follows: "The issue presented is whether the Federal Constitution confers a fundamental right upon homosexuals to engage in sodomy and hence invalidates the laws of the many States that still make such conduct illegal and have done so for a very long time." That statement, we now conclude, discloses the Court's own failure to appreciate the extent of the liberty at stake. To say that the issue in *Bowers* was simply the right to engage in certain sexual conduct demeans the claim the individual put forward, just as it would demean a married couple were it to be said marriage is simply about the right to have sexual intercourse. The laws involved in *Bowers* and here are, to be sure, statutes that purport to do no more than prohibit a particular sexual act. Their penalties and purposes, though, have more far-reaching consequences, touching upon the most private human conduct, sexual behavior, and in the most private of places, the home. The statutes do seek to control a personal relationship that, whether or not entitled to formal recognition in the law, is within the liberty of persons to choose without being punished as criminals.

This, as a general rule, should counsel against attempts by the State, or a court, to define the meaning of the relationship or to set its boundaries absent injury to a person or abuse of an institution the law protects. It suffices for us to acknowledge that adults may choose to enter upon this relationship in the confines of their homes and their own private lives and still retain their dignity as free persons. When sexuality finds overt expression in intimate conduct with another person, the conduct can be but one element in a personal bond that is more enduring. The liberty protected by the Constitution allows homosexual persons the right to make this choice. . . .

At the outset it should be noted that there is no longstanding history in this country of laws directed at homosexual conduct as a distinct matter. . . . Nineteenth-century commentators similarly read American sodomy, buggery, and crime-against-nature statutes as criminalizing certain relations between men and women and between men and men. . . .

Laws prohibiting sodomy do not seem to have been enforced against consenting adults acting in private. A substantial number of sodomy prosecutions and convictions for which there are surviving records were for predatory acts against those who could not or did not consent, as in the case of a minor or the victim of an assault. As to these, one purpose for the prohibitions was to ensure there would be no lack of coverage if a predator committed a sexual assault that did not constitute rape as defined by the criminal law. . . . Instead of targeting relations between consenting adults in private, 19th-century sodomy prosecutions typically involved relations between men and minor girls or minor boys, relations between adults involving force, relations between adults implicating disparity in status, or relations between men and animals. . . .

It was not until the 1970's that any State singled out same-sex relations for criminal prosecution, and only nine States have done so. . . . Over the course of the last decades, States with same-sex prohibitions have moved toward abolishing them.

In summary, the historical grounds relied upon in *Bowers* are more complex than the majority opinion and the concurring opinion by Chief Justice Burger indicate. Their historical premises are not without doubt and, at the very least, are overstated. . . .

In 1955 the American Law Institute promulgated the Model Penal Code and made clear that it did not recommend or provide for "criminal penalties for consensual sexual relations conducted in private." ALI, Model Penal Code § 213.2, Comment 2, p. 372 (1980). It justified its decision on three grounds: (1) The prohibitions undermined respect for the law by penalizing conduct many people engaged in; (2) the statutes regulated private conduct not harmful to others; and (3) the laws were arbitrarily enforced and thus invited the danger of blackmail. ALI, Model Penal Code, Commentary 277-280 (Tent. Draft No. 4, 1955). . . .

Of even more importance, almost five years before *Bowers* was decided the European Court of Human Rights considered a case with parallels to *Bowers* and to today's case. An adult male resident in Northern Ireland alleged he was a practicing homosexual who desired to engage in consensual homosexual conduct. The laws of Northern Ireland forbade him that right. He alleged that he had been questioned, his home had been searched, and he feared criminal prosecution. The court held that the laws proscribing the conduct were invalid under the European Convention on Human Rights. *Dudgeon v. United Kingdom,* 45 Eur. Ct. H.R. (1981) & ¶ 52. Authoritative in all countries that are members of the Council of Europe (21 nations then, 45 nations now), the decision is at odds with the premise in *Bowers* that the claim put forward was insubstantial in our Western civilization.

In our own constitutional system the deficiencies in *Bowers* became even more apparent in the years following its announcement. The 25 States with laws prohibiting the relevant conduct referenced in the *Bowers* decision are reduced now to 13, of which 4 enforce their laws only against homosexual conduct. In those States where sodomy is still proscribed, whether for same-sex or heterosexual conduct, there is a pattern of nonenforcement with respect to consenting adults acting in private. . . .

Two principal cases decided after *Bowers* cast its holding into even more doubt. In *Planned Parenthood of Southeastern Pa. v. Casey,* 505 U.S. 833 (1992), the Court reaffirmed the substantive force of the liberty protected by the Due Process Clause. The *Casey* decision again confirmed that our laws and tradition afford constitutional protection to personal decisions relating to marriage, procreation, contraception, family relationships, child rearing, and education. In explaining the respect the Constitution demands for the autonomy of the person in making these choices, we stated as follows:

> These matters, involving the most intimate and personal choices a person may make in a lifetime, choices central to personal dignity and autonomy, are central to the liberty protected by the Fourteenth Amendment. At the heart of liberty is the right to define one's own concept of existence, of meaning, of the universe, and of the mystery of human life. Beliefs about these matters could not define the attributes of personhood were they formed under compulsion of the State.

Persons in a homosexual relationship may seek autonomy for these purposes, just as heterosexual persons do. The decision in *Bowers* would deny them this right.

The second post-*Bowers* case of principal relevance is *Romer v. Evans,* 517 U.S. 620 (1996). There the Court struck down class-based legislation directed at homosexuals as a violation of the Equal Protection Clause. *Romer* invalidated an amendment to Colorado's constitution which named as a solitary class persons who were homosexuals, lesbians, or bisexual either by "orientation, conduct, practices or relationships," and deprived them of protection under state antidiscrimination laws. We concluded that the provision was "born of animosity toward the class of persons affected" and further that it had no rational relation to a legitimate governmental purpose. . . .

Equality of treatment and the due process right to demand respect for conduct protected by the substantive guarantee of liberty are linked in important respects, and a decision on the latter point advances both interests. If protected conduct is made criminal and the law which does so remains unexamined for its substantive validity, its stigma might remain even if it were not enforceable as drawn for equal protection reasons. When homosexual conduct is made criminal by the law of the State, that declaration in and of itself is an invitation to subject homosexual persons to discrimination both in the public and in the private spheres. The central holding of *Bowers* has been brought in question by this case, and it should be addressed. Its continuance as precedent demeans the lives of homosexual persons. . . .

Bowers was not correct when it was decided, and it is not correct today. It ought not to remain binding precedent. *Bowers v. Hardwick* should be and now is overruled. . . .

The present case does not involve minors. It does not involve persons who might be injured or coerced or who are situated in relationships where consent might not easily be refused. It does not involve public conduct or prostitution. It does not involve whether the government must give formal recognition to any relationship that homosexual persons seek to enter. The case does involve two adults who, with full and mutual consent from each other, engaged in sexual practices common to a homosexual lifestyle. The petitioners are entitled to respect for their private lives. The State cannot demean their existence or control their destiny by making their private sexual conduct a crime. Their right to liberty under the Due Process Clause gives them the full right to engage in their conduct without intervention of the government. "It is a promise of the Constitution that there is a realm of personal liberty which the government may not enter." The Texas statute furthers no legitimate state interest which can justify its intrusion into the personal and private life of the individual. . . .

SCALIA, REHNQUIST, & THOMAS, J.J. DISSENTING. . . . [W]hile overruling the *outcome* of *Bowers,* the Court leaves strangely untouched its central legal conclusion: "[R]espondent would have us announce . . . a fundamental right to engage in homosexual sodomy. This we are quite unwilling to do." Instead the Court simply describes petitioners' conduct as "an exercise of their liberty" — which it undoubtedly is — and proceeds to apply an unheard-of form of rational-basis review that will have far-reaching implications beyond this case. . . .

State laws against bigamy, same-sex marriage, adult incest, prostitution, masturbation, adultery, fornication, bestiality, and obscenity are likewise sustainable only in light of *Bowers'* validation of laws based on moral choices. Every single one of these laws is called into question by today's decision; the Court makes no effort to cabin the scope of its decision to exclude them from its holding. The impossibility of distinguishing homosexuality from other traditional "morals" offenses is precisely why *Bowers* rejected the rational-basis challenge. . . .

Texas Penal Code Ann. § 21.06(a) (2003) undoubtedly imposes constraints on liberty. So do laws prohibiting prostitution, recreational use of heroin, and, for that matter, working more than 60 hours per week in a bakery. But there is no right to "liberty" under the Due Process Clause, though today's opinion repeatedly makes that claim. The Fourteenth Amendment *expressly allows* States to deprive their citizens of "liberty," *so long as "due process of law" is provided:*

> No state shall . . . deprive any person of life, liberty, or property, *without due process of law.* Amdt. 14 (emphasis added).

Our opinions applying the doctrine known as "substantive due process" hold that the Due Process Clause prohibits States from infringing *fundamental* liberty interests, unless the infringement is narrowly tailored to serve a compelling state interest. We have held repeatedly, in cases the Court today does not overrule, that *only* fundamental rights qualify for this so-called "heightened scrutiny" protection — that is, rights which are "deeply rooted in this Nation's history and tradition." All other liberty interests may be abridged or abrogated pursuant to a validly enacted state law if that law is rationally related to a legitimate state interest. . . .

Whether homosexual sodomy was prohibited by a law targeted at same-sex sexual relations or by a more general law prohibiting both homosexual and heterosexual sodomy, the only relevant point is that it *was* criminalized — which suffices to establish that homosexual sodomy is not a right "deeply rooted in our Nation's history and tradition." The Court today agrees that homosexual sodomy was criminalized and thus does not dispute the facts on which *Bowers actually* relied.

Next the Court makes the claim, again unsupported by any citations, that "[l]aws prohibiting sodomy do not seem to have been enforced against consenting adults acting in private." The key qualifier here is "acting in private" — since the Court admits that sodomy laws *were* enforced against consenting adults (although the Court contends that prosecutions were "infrequent"). I do not know what "acting in private" means; surely consensual sodomy, like heterosexual intercourse, is rarely performed on stage. If all the Court means by "acting in private" is "on private premises, with the doors closed and windows covered," it is entirely unsurprising that evidence of enforcement would be hard to come by. (Imagine the circumstances that would enable a search warrant to be obtained for a residence on the ground that there was probable cause to believe that consensual sodomy was then and there occurring.) Surely that lack of evidence would not sustain the proposition that consensual sodomy on private premises with the doors closed and windows covered was regarded as a "fundamental right," even though all other consensual sodomy was criminalized. . . . *Bowers*' conclusion that homosexual sodomy is not a fundamental right "deeply rooted in this Nation's history and tradition" is utterly unassailable. . . .

Today's opinion is the product of a Court, which is the product of a law-profession culture, that has largely signed on to the so-called homosexual agenda, by which I mean the agenda promoted by some homosexual activists directed at eliminating the moral opprobrium that has traditionally attached to homosexual conduct. I noted in an earlier opinion the fact that the American Association of Law Schools (to which any reputable law school *must* seek to belong) excludes from membership any school that refuses to ban from its job-interview facilities a law firm (no matter how small) that does not wish to hire as a prospective partner a person who openly engages in homosexual conduct.

One of the most revealing statements in today's opinion is the Court's grim warning that the criminalization of homosexual conduct is "an invitation to subject homosexual persons to discrimination both in the public and in the private spheres." It is clear from this that the Court has taken sides in the culture war, departing from its role of assuring, as neutral observer, that the democratic rules of engagement are observed. Many Americans do not want persons who openly engage in homosexual conduct as partners in their business, as scoutmasters for their children, as teachers in their children's schools, or as boarders in their home. They view this as protecting themselves and their families from a lifestyle that they believe to be immoral and destructive. The Court views it as "discrimination" which it is the function of our judgments to deter. . . .

Let me be clear that I have nothing against homosexuals, or any other group, promoting their agenda through normal democratic means. Social perceptions of sexual and other morality change over time, and every group has the right to persuade its fellow citizens that its view of such matters is the best. That homosexuals have achieved some success in that enterprise is attested to by the fact that Texas is one of the few remaining States that criminalize private, consensual homosexual acts. But persuading one's fellow citizens is one thing, and imposing one's views in absence of democratic majority will is something else. I would no more *require* a State to criminalize homosexual acts — or, for that matter, display *any* moral disapprobation of them — than I would *forbid* it to do so. What Texas has chosen to do is well within the range of traditional democratic action, and its hand should not be stayed through the invention of a brand-new "constitutional right" by a Court that is impatient of democratic change. It is indeed true that "later generations can see that laws once thought necessary and proper in fact serve only to oppress"; and when that happens, later generations can repeal those laws. But it is the premise of our system that those judgments are to be made by the people, and not imposed by a governing caste that knows best. . . .

NOTES & QUESTIONS

1. ***Decisional vs. Informational Privacy.*** Recall Neil Richards's argument that *Griswold* can be read as an informational privacy case. Can *Lawrence*?

   Lior Strahilevitz notes four possible interpretations of the primary rationale of *Lawrence*:

   > Perhaps *Lawrence* is about keeping Texas police officers from coming into a bedroom and arresting him on the basis of what they see. Perhaps *Lawrence* is about permitting gay couples to make decisions about how to live their lives without the state's interference. Perhaps *Lawrence* is about respecting intimacy established within homosexual relationships. Or perhaps *Lawrence* is about protecting the dignity of homosexuals and rejecting Texas's efforts to make second-class citizens out of them because anti-sodomy laws stigmatized and triggered further discrimination against gays and lesbians.[42]

2. ***The Victorian Compromise.*** The Court notes that "[l]aws prohibiting sodomy do not seem to have been enforced against consenting adults acting in private." This conclusion is an example of what Lawrence Friedman calls the "Victorian compromise":

[42] Lior Jacob Strahilevitz, *Consent, Aesthetics, and the Boundaries of Sexual Privacy after* Lawrence v. Texas, 54 DePaul L. Rev. 671, 678 n.35 (2005).

> The first two-thirds or so of the nineteenth century is the heyday of what I have called the Victorian compromise. This compromise comes out most clearly in laws about sex and morality. These laws lost some of their absolute all-or-nothing quality. It is as if society — or most of society, at any rate — was aware that vice, crime, and sexual misconduct were never going to go away. Vice at least was tolerable, although only in small amounts and only if discreet and under a good deal of control. . . .
>
> Law and norms performed this function by making a sharp distinction between the surface of the law and its dark underbelly. It was important to maintain purity and high ideals in the external, visible sphere, the *public* and official sphere. What went on underneath was another story. The dark underbelly was meant to be kept invisible. Its secrets should never be leached out into daylight — and should never be granted legitimacy. . . .
>
> Sex was strictly a private affair. Decent people never talked about it. Sex was meant for the privacy of the home.[43]

Friedman notes that the laws and norms regulating sex (sodomy, prostitution, adultery, etc.) were selectively enforced and focused primarily on keeping deviant sex in the shadows.

3. ***Blackmail.*** The Court notes that the Model Penal Code recommended against criminalizing sodomy to prevent the crime of blackmail. Blackmail involves threatening to disclose a secret in return for "hush money." Consider Angus McLaren:

> Modern blackmail first emerged when criminals in the eighteenth century recognized that the laws against sodomy provided them with the means by which they could extort money from those whom they could entrap. . . .
>
> In the eighteenth century English men were so alarmed by the thought of criminals extorting money by threatening to accuse innocent victims of sodomy — which at the time was a capital offense — that the government made the leveling of such charges a felony. In the nineteenth century men began to fear that even their heterosexual peccadilloes could put them at the mercy of a blackmailer. With the increasing centrality of family life, an unsullied sexual reputation increased in importance. . . .
>
> The courts for the most part did not want to know if the blackmailers made up their stories or if the victims actually had engaged in homosexual practices. . . . Victims who appeared to have engaged in same-sex activities put the courts in a potentially awkward position. On the one hand the law stated that the truth of the blackmailer's accusation in no way mitigated the offence. On the other hand the courts did not want to be seen as defending immoralists. The way out for the prosecution and judge was to assert that there was no truth to the charge.[44]

Why is blackmail a crime? Why should courts prohibit contracts to keep secrets? Consider James Lindgren:

> In blackmail, the heart of the problem is that two separate acts, each of which is a moral and legal right, can combine to make a moral and legal wrong. For example, if I threaten to expose a criminal act unless I am paid money, I have

---

[43] Lawrence M. Friedman, *Guarding Life's Dark Dark Secrets: Legal and Social Controls over Reputation, Propriety, and Privacy* 66-68 (2007).

[44] Angus McLaren, *Sexual Blackmail: A Modern History* 3, 6, 21 (2002).

> committed blackmail. Or if I threaten to expose a sexual affair unless I am given a job, once again I have committed blackmail. I have a legal right to expose or threaten to expose the crime or affair, and I have a legal right to seek a job or money, but if I combine these rights it is blackmail. If both a person's ends — seeking a job or money — and his means — threatening to expose — are otherwise legal, why is it illegal to combine them? Therein lies what has been called the "paradox of blackmail."[45]

4. ***The "Culture War."*** In his dissent, Justice Scalia declares that "the Court has taken sides in the culture war, departing from its role of . . . [serving as a] neutral observer." Robert Post contends that the Supreme Court must "take sides" in a "culture war" and cannot remain neutral: "Instead of pursuing the chimerical objective of neutrality, the Court would do better to analyze the conditions under which courts should properly make cultural judgments."[46] Can the Court be neutral? Should it be?

   The Court discusses and cites foreign authorities in its decision. Some have criticized the Court for doing so. Is the Court's use of foreign authorities appropriate?[47]

2. THE CONSTITUTIONAL RIGHT TO INFORMATION PRIVACY

WHALEN V. ROE

429 U.S. 589 (1977)

STEVENS, J. . . . Many drugs have both legitimate and illegitimate uses. In response to a concern that such drugs were being diverted into unlawful channels, in 1970 the New York Legislature created a special commission to evaluate the State's drug-control laws. The commission found the existing laws deficient in several respects. There was no effective way to prevent the use of stolen or revised prescriptions, to prevent unscrupulous pharmacists from repeatedly refilling prescriptions, to prevent users from obtaining prescriptions from more than one doctor, or to prevent doctors from over-prescribing, either by authorizing an excessive amount in one prescription or by giving one patient multiple prescriptions. . . .

The new New York statute classified potentially harmful drugs in five schedules. Drugs, such as heroin, which are highly abused and have no recognized medical use, are in Schedule I; they cannot be prescribed. Schedules II through V include drugs which have a progressively lower potential for abuse

---

[45] James Lindgren, *Unravelling the Paradox of Blackmail*, 84 Colum. L. Rev. 670, 670-71 (1984).

[46] Robert C. Post, *Foreword: Fashioning the Legal Constitution: Culture, Courts and Law*, 117 Harv. L. Rev. 4 (2003).

[47] For an excellent discussion of the issue, see Rex D. Glensy. *Which Countries Count?: Lawrence v. Texas and the Selection of Foreign Persuasive Authority*, 45 Va. J. Int'l L. 347 (2005).

but also have a recognized medical use. Our concern is limited to Schedule II which includes the most dangerous of the legitimate drugs.[48]

With an exception for emergencies, the Act requires that all prescriptions for Schedule II drugs be prepared by the physician in triplicate on an official form. The completed form identifies the prescribing physician; the dispensing pharmacy; the drug and dosage; and the name, address, and age of the patient. One copy of the form is retained by the physician, the second by the pharmacist, and the third is forwarded to the New York State Department of Health in Albany. A prescription made on an official form may not exceed a 30-day supply, and may not be refilled.

The District Court found that about 100,000 Schedule II prescription forms are delivered to a receiving room at the Department of Health in Albany each month. They are sorted, coded, and logged and then taken to another room where the data on the forms is recorded on magnetic tapes for processing by a computer. Thereafter, the forms are returned to the receiving room to be retained in a vault for a five-year period and then destroyed as required by the statute.[49] The receiving room is surrounded by a locked wire fence and protected by an alarm system. The computer tapes containing the prescription data are kept in a locked cabinet. When the tapes are used, the computer is run "off-line," which means that no terminal outside of the computer room can read or record any information. Public disclosure of the identity of patients is expressly prohibited by the statute and by a Department of Health regulation. Willful violation of these prohibitions is a crime punishable by up to one year in prison and a $2,000 fine. At the time of trial there were 17 Department of Health employees with access to the files; in addition, there were 24 investigators with authority to investigate cases of overdispensing which might be identified by the computer. Twenty months after the effective date of the Act, the computerized data had only been used in two investigations involving alleged overuse by specific patients.

A few days before the Act became effective, this litigation was commenced by a group of patients regularly receiving prescriptions for Schedule II drugs, by doctors who prescribe such drugs, and by two associations of physicians. After various preliminary proceedings, a three-judge District Court conducted a one-day trial. Appellees offered evidence tending to prove that persons in need of treatment with Schedule II drugs will from time to time decline such treatment because of their fear that the misuse of the computerized data will cause them to be stigmatized as "drug addicts."[50]

---

[48] These include opium and opium derivatives, cocaine, methadone, amphetamines, and methaqualone. Pub. Health Law § 3306. These drugs have accepted uses in the amelioration of pain and in the treatment of epilepsy, narcolepsy, hyperkinesia, schizo-affective disorders, and migraine headaches.

[49] Pub. Health Law § 3370(3), 1974 N.Y.Laws, c. 965, § 16. The physician and the pharmacist are required to retain their copies for five years also, but they are not required to destroy them.

[50] Two parents testified that they were concerned that their children would be stigmatized by the State's central filing system. One child had been taken off his Schedule II medication because of this concern. Three adult patients testified that they feared disclosure of their names would result from central filing of patient identifications. One of them now obtains his drugs in another State. The other two continue to receive Schedule II prescriptions in New York, but continue to fear disclosure and stigmatization. Four physicians testified that the prescription system entrenches on

Appellees contend that the statute invades a constitutionally protected "zone of privacy." The cases sometimes characterized as protecting "privacy" have in fact involved at least two different kinds of interests. One is the individual interest in avoiding disclosure of personal matters, and another is the interest in independence in making certain kinds of important decisions. Appellees argue that both of these interests are impaired by this statute. The mere existence in readily available form of the information about patients' use of Schedule II drugs creates a genuine concern that the information will become publicly known and that it will adversely affect their reputations. This concern makes some patients reluctant to use, and some doctors reluctant to prescribe, such drugs even when their use is medically indicated. It follows, they argue, that the making of decisions about matters vital to the care of their health is inevitably affected by the statute. Thus, the statute threatens to impair both their interest in the nondisclosure of private information and also their interest in making important decisions independently.

We are persuaded, however, that the New York program does not, on its face, pose a sufficiently grievous threat to either interest to establish a constitutional violation.

Public disclosure of patient information can come about in three ways. Health Department employees may violate the statute by failing, either deliberately or negligently, to maintain proper security. A patient or a doctor may be accused of a violation and the stored data may be offered in evidence in a judicial proceeding. Or, thirdly, a doctor, a pharmacist, or the patient may voluntarily reveal information on a prescription form.

The third possibility existed under the prior law and is entirely unrelated to the existence of the computerized data bank. Neither of the other two possibilities provides a proper ground for attacking the statute as invalid on its face. There is no support in the record, or in the experience of the two States that New York has emulated, for an assumption that the security provisions of the statute will be administered improperly. And the remote possibility that judicial supervision of the evidentiary use of particular items of stored information will provide inadequate protection against unwarranted disclosures is surely not a sufficient reason for invalidating the entire patient-identification program.

Even without public disclosure, it is, of course, true that private information must be disclosed to the authorized employees of the New York Department of Health. Such disclosures, however, are not significantly different from those that were required under the prior law. Nor are they meaningfully distinguishable from a host of other unpleasant invasions of privacy that are associated with many facets of health care. Unquestionably, some individuals' concern for their own privacy may lead them to avoid or to postpone needed medical attention. Nevertheless, disclosures of private medical information to doctors, to hospital

---

patients' privacy, and that each had observed a reaction of shock, fear, and concern on the part of their patients whom they had informed of the plan. One doctor refuses to prescribe Schedule II drugs for his patients. On the other hand, over 100,000 patients per month have been receiving Schedule II drug prescriptions without their objections, if any, to central filing having come to the attention of the District Court. The record shows that the provisions of the Act were brought to the attention of the section on psychiatry of the New York State Medical Society, but that body apparently declined to support this suit.

personnel, to insurance companies, and to public health agencies are often an essential part of modern medical practice even when the disclosure may reflect unfavorably on the character of the patient. Requiring such disclosures to representatives of the State having responsibility for the health of the community, does not automatically amount to an impermissible invasion of privacy.

Appellees also argue, however, that even if unwarranted disclosures do not actually occur, the knowledge that the information is readily available in a computerized file creates a genuine concern that causes some persons to decline needed medication. The record supports the conclusion that some use of Schedule II drugs has been discouraged by that concern; it also is clear, however, that about 100,000 prescriptions for such drugs were being filled each month prior to the entry of the District Court's injunction. Clearly, therefore, the statute did not deprive the public of access to the drugs. . . .

We hold that neither the immediate nor the threatened impact of the patient-identification requirements in the New York State Controlled Substances Act of 1972 on either the reputation or the independence of patients for whom Schedule II drugs are medically indicated is sufficient to constitute an invasion of any right or liberty protected by the Fourteenth Amendment. . . .

A final word about issues we have not decided. We are not unaware of the threat to privacy implicit in the accumulation of vast amounts of personal information in computerized data banks or other massive government files. The collection of taxes, the distribution of welfare and social security benefits, the supervision of public health, the direction of our Armed Forces, and the enforcement of the criminal laws all require the orderly preservation of great quantities of information, much of which is personal in character and potentially embarrassing or harmful if disclosed. The right to collect and use such data for public purposes is typically accompanied by a concomitant statutory or regulatory duty to avoid unwarranted disclosures. Recognizing that in some circumstances that duty arguably has its roots in the Constitution, nevertheless New York's statutory scheme, and its implementing administrative procedures, evidence a proper concern with, and protection of, the individual's interest in privacy. We therefore need not, and do not, decide any question which might be presented by the unwarranted disclosure of accumulated private data whether intentional or unintentional or by a system that did not contain comparable security provisions. We simply hold that this record does not establish an invasion of any right or liberty protected by the Fourteenth Amendment. . . .

BRENNAN, J. concurring. . . . The information disclosed by the physician under this program is made available only to a small number of public health officials with a legitimate interest in the information. As the record makes clear, New York has long required doctors to make this information available to its officials on request, and that practice is not challenged here. Such limited reporting requirements in the medical field are familiar and are not generally regarded as an invasion of privacy. Broad dissemination by state officials of such information, however, would clearly implicate constitutionally protected privacy rights, and would presumably be justified only by compelling state interests.

What is more troubling about this scheme, however, is the central computer storage of the data thus collected. Obviously, as the State argues, collection and storage of data by the State that is in itself legitimate is not rendered unconstitutional simply because new technology makes the State's operations more efficient. However, as the example of the Fourth Amendment shows the Constitution puts limits not only on the type of information the State may gather, but also on the means it may use to gather it. The central storage and easy accessibility of computerized data vastly increase the potential for abuse of that information, and I am not prepared to say that future developments will not demonstrate the necessity of some curb on such technology. . . .

NOTES & QUESTIONS

1. ***The Constitutional Right to Information Privacy.*** The *Whalen* Court characterizes the line of substantive due process cases protecting the right to privacy as involving two "different kinds of interests" — (1) "the individual interest in avoiding disclosure of personal matters" and (2) "the interest in independence in making certain kinds of important decisions." In one reading, the latter interest can be referred to as decisional privacy because it involves the extent to which the state can become involved with the decisions an individual makes with regard to her body and family. The former interest involves the privacy implications of the collection, use, and disclosure of personal information. This former interest is often referred to as the "constitutional right to information privacy." What is the Court's implicit conception of privacy as manifested by this interest?

   In a different reading of *Whalen*, the Court identified a bifurcated information privacy interest. In other words, both *Whalen* interests serve to protect informational privacy. Regarding the second *Whalen* interest, for example, Paul Schwartz argues that the Court "extends the constitutional protection offered important activities or decisions to *information* that reports activities or decisions."[51] Schwartz notes, however, that lower courts "have been reluctant to use the second *Whalen* interest as a bar to the state's information gathering practices." In this reading of the case, one open question is whether the second *Whalen* interest should be restricted only to information about fundamental interests, such as those typically protected by substantive due process cases, or extended more generally to situations in which the government's collection and processing of information will chill decision making. Moreover, Schwartz calls for use of this second interest in judicial exploration of "the means of processing, the types of data bases to be linked, and the purposes for which the processing information will be utilized." How practical is this constitutional standard?
2. **Nixon v. Administrator of General Services.** After *Whalen*, the Court affirmed this notion of constitutional protection for information privacy in *Nixon v. Administrator of General Services*, 433 U.S. 425 (1977), concluding that President Nixon had a constitutional privacy interest in records of his private communications with his family but not in records involving his

---

[51] Paul M. Schwartz, *Privacy and Participation: Personal Information and Public Sector Regulation in the United States*, 80 Iowa L. Rev. 553, 581-82 (1995).

official duties. Although ex-president Nixon had a legitimate expectation of privacy in private communications with his family, doctor, and minister, it was outweighed by the public interest in Nixon's papers.

3. ***The Constitutional Right to Information Privacy After* Whalen *and* Nixon.** Subsequent to *Whalen* and *Nixon*, the Court did little to develop the right of information privacy. As one court observed, the right "has been infrequently examined; as a result, its contours remain less than clear." *Davis v. Bucher*, 853 F.2d 718, 720 (9th Cir. 1988). Most federal circuit courts have recognized the right. *See, e.g., Barry v. City of New York*, 712 F.2d 1554, 1559 (2d Cir. 1983); *United States v. Westinghouse Electric Corp.*, 638 F.2d 570, 577-80 (3d Cir. 1980); *Walls v. City of Petersburg*, 895 F.2d 188, 192 (4th Cir. 1990); *Plante v. Gonzalez*, 575 F.2d 1119, 1132, 1134 (5th Cir.1978); *Kimberlin v. United States Dep't of Justice*, 788 F.2d 434 (7th Cir. 1986); *In re Crawford*, 194 F.3d 954, 959 (9th Cir. 1999).

In contrast to other circuits, the Sixth Circuit has adopted the constitutional right to information privacy in a very narrow manner. In *J.P. v. DeSanti*, 653 F.2d 1080, 1090 (6th Cir. 1981), the Sixth Circuit concluded that "[a]bsent a clear indication from the Supreme Court we will not construe isolated statements in *Whalen* and *Nixon* more broadly than their context allows to recognize a general constitutional right to have disclosure of private information measured against the need for disclosure." *Id.* at 1089; *see also Bloch v. Ribar*, 156 F.3d 673, 684 (6th Cir. 1998) ("[T]he right to informational privacy will be triggered only when the interest at stake relates to those personal rights that can be deemed 'fundamental' or 'implicit in the concept of ordered liberty.'") (quoting *J.P. v. DeSanti*, 653 F.2d 1080, 1090 (6th Cir. 1981)).

At least one other Circuit court has expressed doubts as to whether the constitutional right to information privacy exists at all. In *American Federation of Government Employees, AFL-CIO v. Department of Housing & Urban Development*, 118 F.3d 786 (D.C. Cir. 1997), the court observed:

> We begin our analysis by expressing our grave doubts as to the existence of a constitutional right of privacy in the nondisclosure of personal information. Were we the first to confront the issue we would conclude with little difficulty that such a right does not exist, but we do not, of course, write on a blank slate. The Supreme Court [in *Whalen v. Roe*] has addressed the issue in recurring dicta without, we believe, resolving it. . . .
>
> The Court was equally Delphic in *Nixon v. Administrator of General Services*. . . .

Based upon your reading of *Whalen*, do you conclude (1) there is a broad constitutional right to information privacy that pertains to a variety of kinds of personal information; (2) there is a narrow constitutional right to information privacy that only pertains to personal information relating to one's health, family, children, and other interests protected by the Court's substantive due process right to privacy decisions; or (3) there is no constitutional right to information privacy, and the passage in *Whalen* was mere dicta?

4. ***The* Westinghouse *Test.*** Since the constitutional right to information privacy has yet to develop a distinctive identity, courts applying the right often draw from other types of privacy law. At least one court has observed that the constitutional right to information privacy "closely resembles — and may be identical to — the interest protected by the common law prohibition against unreasonable publicity given to one's private life." *Smith v. City of Artesia*, 772 P.2d 373, 376 (N.M. App. 1989). One court has looked to the "reasonable expectations of privacy" test to determine whether information is entitled to protection under the constitutional right to information privacy. *See Fraternal Order of Police, Lodge No. 5, Philadelphia* 812 F.2d 105, 112 (3d Cir. 1987).

The Third Circuit has developed the most well-known test for deciding constitutional right to information privacy cases. In *United States v. Westinghouse Electric Corp*., 638 F.2d 570, 578 (3d Cir. 1980), the court articulated seven factors that "should be considered in deciding whether an intrusion into an individual's privacy is justified": (1) "the type of record requested"; (2) "the information it does or might contain"; (3) "the potential for harm in any subsequent nonconsensual disclosure"; (4) "the injury from disclosure to the relationship in which the record was generated"; (5) "the adequacy of safeguards to prevent unauthorized disclosure"; (6) "the degree of need for access"; and (7) "whether there is an express statutory mandate, articulated public policy, or other recognizable public interest militating toward access." In addition to the Third Circuit, the *Westinghouse* test is used by some other circuit courts.

5. ***The Constitutionality of Disclosure and Reporting Requirements.*** Consider *Greenville Women's Clinic v. Commissioner*, 317 F.3d 357 (4th Cir. 2002). A state regulation required that abortion clinics disclose to state officials patients' names and records. The abortion clinics argued that this regulation ran afoul of *Whalen v. Roe.* The state argued that it needed "the information to monitor abortions and to assure complaints with the health-care standards . . . aimed at preserving maternal health." The court concluded that the regulation did not violate the constitutional right to information privacy because the regulation "explicitly requires [that the state maintain the] confidentiality of patients' records." Judge King dissented, arguing that the state does not adequately safeguard patient confidentiality because the state statutes mandating confidentiality "contain gaping holes in the protections they afford against public disclosures" and because "despite the State's assurances of confidentiality, private medical information has been leaked to the public." This case, argued King, presents more severe privacy threats than in *Whalen* because the plaintiffs in *Whalen* feared the stigma of disclosure, whereas "women seeking abortions in South Carolina have a great deal more to fear than stigma. The protests designed to harass and intimidate women entering abortion clinics, and the violence inflicted on abortion providers, provide women with ample reason to fear for their physical safety."

In *Planned Parenthood of Central Missouri v. Danforth*, 428 U.S. 52 (1976), Missouri required that physicians report abortions to the state, which would keep the data confidential, except that the data can "be inspected and health data acquired by local, state, or national public health officers." The records must also be retained for seven years in the permanent files of the health facility where the abortion was performed. The reporting requirements were challenged "on the ground that they . . . impose an extra layer and burden of regulation" on a woman's right to seek an abortion. The Court held that the regulations were constitutional: "Recordkeeping and reporting requirements that are reasonably directed to the preservation of maternal health and that properly respect a patient's confidentiality and privacy are permissible."

42 U.S.C. § 1983 AND "CONSTITUTIONAL TORTS"

Most cases involving the constitutional right to information privacy are litigated by way of 42 U.S.C. § 1983. This statute was part of the Civil Rights Act of 1871 and was designed to facilitate the enforcement of civil rights protected by the Constitution and federal law. This famous civil rights statute provides:

> Every person who, under color of any statute, ordinance, regulation, custom, or usage, of any state or territory, subjects, or causes to be subjected, any citizen of the United States or other person within the jurisdiction thereof to the deprivation of any rights, privileges, or immunities secured by the Constitution and laws, shall be liable to the party injured in an action at law, suit at equity, or other proper proceeding for redress.

Section 1983 provides a way to remedy constitutional violations in the civil law (as opposed to criminal) context. Section 1983 creates a cause of action against those who, acting under state governmental authority, violate federal law and the federal Constitution. Section 1983 transforms constitutional violations into tort actions and enables plaintiffs to collect damages and obtain injunctive relief.

Section 1983 requires that the wrongful conduct be "under color of state law, custom, or usage." This is often referred to as the "state action" requirement.

The word "person" in § 1983 includes government entities and officials. However, state governments are not "persons," and the Eleventh Amendment immunizes states against suits by private citizens. The Eleventh Amendment provides:

> The Judicial power of the United States shall not be construed to extend to any suit in law or equity, commenced or prosecuted against one of the United States by Citizens of another State, or by Citizens or Subjects of any Foreign State.

The Supreme Court has interpreted the Eleventh Amendment not just to bar a citizen of one state from suing another state, but also to bar a citizen from suing his or her own state. *See Hans v. Louisiana*, 134 U.S. 1 (1890). Therefore, instead of suing states directly, plaintiffs sue state officials.

Although states cannot be sued directly, municipalities and local governments can. In *Monell v. New York City Dep't of Social Services*, 436 U.S. 658 (1978), the Court held that municipalities can be sued as "persons" under § 1983. However, municipalities cannot be sued for the acts of their employees. In other words, municipalities are not liable under § 1983 on the basis of the *respondeat superior* doctrine. Municipalities are liable "when execution of a government's policy or custom, whether made by its lawmakers or by those whose edicts or acts may fairly represent official policy, inflicts the injury." Of course, *Monell* does not bar a suit against a local official directly.

In short, any state or local official can be sued directly under § 1983. State governments cannot be sued. Local governments can be sued, but only when their policy or custom inflicts the injury, not merely because they employ the officials who caused the injury.

What about federal officials? Section 1983 does not authorize suits against federal officials. However, the Supreme Court held that federal officials can be sued for violating constitutional rights. *See Bivens v. Six Unknown Named Agents of Federal Bureau of Narcotics*, 403 U.S. 388 (1971). *Bivens* claims are addressed in a similar way as § 1983 claims.

When sued, government officials (both state and local) can raise certain defenses known as "immunities." Certain officials are absolutely immune from liability under § 1983 — they cannot be liable at all if they are acting in their capacities as officials. Such officials include legislators and judges. Executive officials such as police officers only receive a limited immunity defense known as "qualified immunity." They are immune if "their conduct does not violate *clearly established* statutory or constitutional rights of which a reasonable person would have known." *Harlow v. Fitzgerald*, 457 U.S. 800 (1982). Immunities are generally the same for federal officials, with at least one notable exception. Although state governors only receive qualified immunity, see *Scheuer v. Rhodes*, 416 U.S. 232 (1974), the President of the United States receives absolute immunity, see *Nixon v. Fitzgerald*, 457 U.S. 731 (1982).

This introduction is by no means a comprehensive background into § 1983. It is important, however, to understand the basic structure of § 1983 because constitutional right to information privacy cases are often litigated by way of § 1983.

CARTER V. BROADLAWNS MEDICAL CENTER

667 F. Supp. 1269 (S.D. Iowa 1987)

[The Broadlawns Medical Center (BMC), a public county hospital located in Des Moines, Iowa, decided to employ a full-time chaplain. Its previous reliance on volunteer chaplains proved to be inadequate because it was difficult for volunteer chaplains to visit patients regularly. The Board of Trustees for BMC hired Maggie Alenzo Rogers, a female who was not an ordained minister. Rogers graduated from the University of Dubuque Theological Seminary in 1984 and was "endorsed" by the United Church of Christ. Her job description stated that she would "provide consistent pastoral care throughout the Medical Center, adding spiritual support and counseling to the ongoing healing effort." BMC had a policy of allowing Rogers to have open access to patient medical records. A group of plaintiffs challenged this policy as a violation of the constitutional right to information privacy.]

O'BRIEN, C. J. . . . The Court also concludes that the policy of chaplains having open access to patient medical records is constitutionally infirm under the Fourteenth Amendment. Patients at BMC have a right of privacy founded on the Fourteenth Amendment's concept of personal liberty. *Whalen v. Roe*, 429 U.S. 589 (1977). One facet of the right of privacy "is the right of an individual not to have his private affairs made public by the government." In *Planned Parenthood v. Danforth*, 428 U.S. 52 (1976), the Supreme Court refused to strike down record-keeping and reporting requirements regarding abortions that were (1) reasonably directed to the preservation of maternal health and which (2) properly respect a patient's confidentiality and privacy. In allowing chaplains free access to medical records, BMC is not properly respecting a patient's confidentiality and privacy. The Court concludes that patient medical records can only be accessed by a chaplain upon prior express approval of the individual patient or his guardian. This will not be so broad as to bar doctors, medical and psychiatric professionals and nurses to provide to the chaplain basic information, not privileged, which would enable the chaplain to understand what the patient's basic problem was, e.g., a suicide attempt. The Court shall enter injunctive relief regarding this violation. . . .

DOE V. BOROUGH OF BARRINGTON

729 F. Supp. 376 (D.N.J. 1990)

BROTMAN, J. . . . On March 25, 1987, Jane Doe, her husband, and their friend James Tarvis were traveling in the Doe's pickup truck through the Borough of Barrington ("Barrington"). At approximately 9:00 A.M., a Barrington police officer stopped the truck and questioned the occupants. As a result of the vehicle stop, Barrington officers arrested Jane Doe's husband and impounded the pickup truck. Barrington officers escorted Jane Doe, her husband, and James Tarvis to the Barrington Police Station.

When he was initially arrested, Jane Doe's husband told the police officers that he had tested HIV positive and that the officers should be careful in searching him because he had "weeping lesions." . . Barrington police released Jane Doe and James Tarvis from custody, but detained Jane Doe's husband on charges of unlawful possession of a hypodermic needle and a burglary detainer entered by Essex County.

Sometime in the late afternoon of the same day, Jane Doe and James Tarvis drove Tarvis's car to the Doe residence in the Borough of Runnemede ("Runnemede"). The car engine was left running, and the car apparently slipped into gear, rolling down the driveway into a neighbor's fence. The neighbors owning the fence are Michael DiAngelo and defendant Rita DiAngelo. Rita DiAngelo is an employee in the school district in Runnemede.

Two Runnemede police officers, Steven Van Camp and defendant Russell Smith, responded to the radio call about the incident. While they were at the scene, Detective Preen of the Barrington police arrived and, in a private conversation with Van Camp, revealed that Jane Doe's husband had been arrested earlier in the day and had told Barrington police officers that he had AIDS. Van Camp then told defendant Smith.

After Jane Doe and Tarvis left the immediate vicinity, defendant Smith told the DiAngelos that Jane Doe's husband had AIDS and that, to protect herself, Rita DiAngelo should wash with disinfectant. . . . Defendant Rita DiAngelo became upset upon hearing this information. Knowing that the four Doe children attended the Downing School in Runnemede, the school that her own daughter attended, DiAngelo contacted other parents with children in the school. She also contacted the media. The next day, eleven parents removed nineteen children from the Downing School due to a panic over the Doe children's attending the school. The media was present, and the story was covered in the local newspapers and on television. At least one of the reports mentioned the name of the Doe family. Plaintiffs allege that as a result of the disclosure, they have suffered harassment, discrimination, and humiliation. They allege they have been shunned by the community.

Plaintiffs brought this civil rights action against the police officer Smith and the municipalities of Barrington and Runnemede for violations of their federal constitutional rights pursuant to 42 U.S.C. § 1983. The federal constitutional right is their right to privacy under the fourteenth amendment. . . .

AIDS is a viral disease that weakens or destroys the body's immune system. The disease is caused by the presence of the Human Immunodeficiency Virus ("HIV"), which attacks the body's T-lymphocyte cells that are a critical part of the body's immune system. As a result, the body is unable to withstand infections it would normally suppress. These resulting infections, known as "opportunistic diseases," eventually cause permanent disability and death. . . .

HIV is transmitted through contact with contaminated blood, semen, or vaginal fluids. The virus is transmitted through activities such as sexual intercourse, anal sex, use of nonsterile hypodermic needles, and transfusions of contaminated blood or blood products. Additionally, women infected with HIV can transmit the virus to their children before or during birth. Although HIV has been detected in other bodily fluids such as saliva and urine, the virus is much less concentrated, and there are no known cases of transmission of the virus by such means. The Centers for Disease Control ("CDC") terms the risk of infection from such fluids as "extremely low or nonexistent."

In 1986, the Surgeon General announced that HIV is not transmitted through casual contact with an infected person, such as shaking hands, kissing, or contacting an object used by an infected person. . . .

This court finds that the Constitution protects plaintiffs from governmental disclosure of their husband's and father's infection with the AIDS virus. The United States Supreme Court has recognized that the fourteenth amendment protects two types of privacy interests. "One is the individual interest in avoiding disclosure of personal matters, and another is the interest in independence in making certain kinds of important decisions." *Whalen v. Roe*, 429 U.S. 589, 599-600 (1977). Disclosure of a family member's medical condition, especially exposure to or infection with the AIDS virus, is a disclosure of a "personal matter."

The Third Circuit recognizes a privacy right in medical records and medical information. *United States v. Westinghouse*, 638 F.2d 570 (3d Cir. 1980). . . .

Lower courts have held that, once the government has confidential information, it has the obligation to avoid disclosure of the information. In *Carter v. Broadlawns Medical Center*, the court held that a public hospital had violated plaintiffs' constitutional rights by giving chaplains open access to patient medical records without patient authorization. The court noted that, in permitting free access to medical records, the hospital did not properly respect a patient's confidentiality and privacy as recognized in *Whalen v. Roe*. . . . The case demonstrates that, not only is the government restricted from collecting personal medical information, it may be restricted from disclosing such private information it lawfully receives. . . .

The sensitive nature of medical information about AIDS makes a compelling argument for keeping this information confidential. Society's moral judgments about the high-risk activities associated with the disease, including sexual relations and drug use, make the information of the most personal kind. Also, the privacy interest in one's exposure to the AIDS virus is even greater than one's privacy interest in ordinary medical records because of the stigma that attaches with the disease.

The hysteria surrounding AIDS extends beyond those who have the disease. The stigma attaches not only to the AIDS victim, but to those in contact with AIDS patients. Revealing that one's family or household member has AIDS causes the entire family to be ostracized. The right to privacy in this information extends to members of the AIDS patient's immediate family. Those sharing a household with an infected person suffer from disclosure just as the victim does. Family members, therefore, have a substantial interest in keeping this information confidential. Disclosures about AIDS cause a violation of the family's privacy much greater than simply revealing any other aspect of their family medical history.

An individual's privacy interest in medical information and records is not absolute. The court must determine whether the societal interest in disclosure outweighs the privacy interest involved. To avoid a constitutional violation, the government must show a compelling state interest in breaching that privacy.

The government's interest in disclosure here does not outweigh the substantial privacy interest involved. The government has not shown a compelling state interest in breaching the Does' privacy. The government contends that Officer Smith advised the DiAngelos to wash with disinfectant because of his concern for the prevention and avoidance of AIDS, an incurable and contagious disease. While prevention of this deadly disease is clearly an appropriate state objective, this objective was not served by Smith's statement that the DiAngelos should wash with disinfectant. Disclosure of the Does' confidential information did not advance a compelling governmental interest in preventing the spread of the disease because there was no risk that Mr. or Mrs. DiAngelo might be exposed to the HIV virus through casual contact with Jane Doe. The state of medical knowledge at the time of this incident established that AIDS is not transmitted by casual contact. Smith's statement could not prevent the transmission of AIDS because there was no threat of transmission present.

This court concludes that the Does have a constitutional right of privacy in the information disclosed by Smith and the state had no compelling interest in revealing that information. As such, the disclosure violated the Does' constitutional rights. . . .

. . . [Defendant Smith] argues that plaintiffs have no standing to bring this action because Smith's statement violated only the privacy rights of Jane Doe's husband. . . .

Plaintiffs here do not assert the constitutional rights of Jane Doe's husband. Jane Doe sues as guardian for her minor children for the violation of their own rights to privacy. The children have standing to sue for the violation of their right to privacy from governmental disclosure of their father's infection with AIDS. Likewise, Jane Doe individually asserts a violation of her constitutional right to privacy. That the officer did not reveal information about the children's own medical condition is immaterial. A family member's diagnosis with AIDS is a personal matter, as defined in *Whalen v. Roe*, that falls within the protection of the Constitution.

This court rejects the standing argument because Smith's statement communicated private, confidential information about Jane Doe and her children. The stigma of AIDS extends to all family members, whether or not they actually have the disease. Smith's statement also implicitly suggested that Jane Doe herself might somehow transmit the disease to the DiAngelos. Jane Doe clearly has standing to assert a violation of her right to privacy. . . .

. . . [Next, the Defendant] asserts that, because Jane Doe's husband told police that he had AIDS, the husband "published" the information, giving up any right to privacy in the information. . . .

Clearly, an arrestee's disclosure to police that he or she has AIDS is preferable to nondisclosure. Police can take whatever precautions are necessary to prevent transmission of the disease. Police have more than "casual contact" with arrestee, increasing the likelihood that the disease can be transmitted. For example, by frisking an arrested person, police may come into contact with hypodermic needles. Thus, disclosure should be encouraged to protect police officers. Common sense demands that persons with AIDS be able to make such disclosures without fear that police will inform neighbors, employers, or the media. Smith's publication argument, therefore, is rejected as contrary to public policy. . . .

NOTES & QUESTIONS

1. ***Private Parties.*** Suppose only private parties had disclosed that Mr. Doe had AIDS. Would there be a cause of action?
2. ***Does It Matter Who Is Being Informed?*** Suppose Mrs. Doe didn't know that her husband had HIV. Would the police violate Mr. Doe's constitutional right to information privacy by telling her?
3. ***Public Health Concerns.*** What if the disease were highly contagious with casual contact? Does that matter for the application of the constitutional right to information privacy? The facts of this case occurred early on in the AIDS epidemic, when information about AIDS was just beginning to dispel some of the myths and hysteria surrounding AIDS. What effect should this have on the liability of the police?

DOE V. SOUTHEASTERN PENNSYLVANIA TRANSPORTATION AUTHORITY

72 F.3d 1133 (3d Cir. 1995)

ROSENN, J. This appeal requires that we probe the depth and breadth of an employee's conditional right to privacy in his prescription drug records. John Doe, an employee of the Southeastern Pennsylvania Transportation Authority (SEPTA), initiated this action under 42 U.S.C. § 1983 against his self-insured employer, alleging that the defendants violated his right to privacy. Plaintiff claims that, in monitoring the prescription drug program put in place by SEPTA for fraud, drug abuse and excessive costs, the Chief Administrative Officer, Judith Pierce, and the Director of Benefits, Jacob Aufschauer, learned that John Doe had contracted Acquired Immunodeficiency Syndrome (AIDS). This, he alleges, invaded his right to privacy.

A jury found for the plaintiff and awarded him $125,000 in compensatory damages for his emotional distress. . . .

We set forth the facts as the jury could have found them in support of its verdict. Accordingly, all evidence and inferences therefrom must be taken in the light most favorable to the verdict winner. In 1990, Judith Pierce became the Chief Administrative Officer for SEPTA. Her responsibilities included containing the costs of SEPTA's self-insured health program. In 1992, a bargaining agreement with Local Union 234 required SEPTA to provide, inter alia, prescription drugs for the employees. SEPTA entered into a contract with Rite-Aid Drug Store to be the sole provider for all of SEPTA's prescription drug programs. As part of this contract, Rite-Aid provided SEPTA with an estimate of the yearly costs of this program. If, at the end of the year, the actual cost to Rite-Aid amounted to over 115% of that estimate, SEPTA would have to pay substantial penalties; however, if the actual cost was 90% or less of that estimate, SEPTA would be entitled to rebates. Pierce was responsible for monitoring those costs.

John Doe is a SEPTA employee. At all times relevant to this appeal, Doe was HIV-positive, and had contracted AIDS by the time of trial. In 1991, Doe began to take Retrovir for his condition. Retrovir is a prescription drug used solely to treat HIV. Before filling his prescription, Doe asked Dr. Richard Press, the head of SEPTA's Medical Department and Doe's direct supervisor, if he or anyone else reviewed employee names in association with the drugs the employees were taking. Doe wished to keep his condition a secret from his co-workers. Dr. Press assured Doe that he had only been asked to review names on prescriptions in cases of suspected narcotics abuse and knew of no other review that included names. After receiving this information, Doe filled his prescription through the employer's health insurance. He continued to do so after SEPTA switched to Rite-Aid; he was never informed that this change might alter his confidentiality status.

In November of 1992, Pierce requested and received utilization reports from Rite-Aid. These reports were part of the contract between Rite-Aid and SEPTA. Pierce did not request the names of SEPTA employees in the reports, and Rite-Aid sent the reports in their standard format. . . . [One report] listed employees who were filling prescriptions at a cost of $100 or more per employee in the past month. Each line of the report included the name of an employee or dependent, a code to identify the prescribing doctor, the dispense date of the prescription, the name of the drug, the number of days supplied, and the total cost. Pierce called Aufschauer into her office, and the two of them reviewed the report. It was immediately apparent to Pierce that the reports would reveal employees' medications; however, she reviewed them in the format as submitted. . . .

Pierce stated that her purpose in reviewing the reports with Aufschauer was several-fold. First, she wanted to look for signs of fraud and drug abuse. . . . Second, Pierce wanted to determine if Rite-Aid was fulfilling its promise to use generic rather than brand name drugs whenever possible. Third, although they were both covered in the Rite-Aid contract, Pierce wanted to determine the cost to SEPTA of fertility drugs and medications to help employees stop smoking, such as nicotine patches. Finally, Pierce wanted to determine whether the reports were in a summary form and whether they would permit an audit. Her review, however, focused almost entirely on the current report, which included employees' names. . . .

Pierce and Aufschauer scanned the reports. When they came across a drug name neither one recognized, they would look it up in a Physician's Desk Reference (PDR) that Pierce had. Pierce then called Dr. Louis Van de Beek, a SEPTA staff physician, and inquired about the drugs not listed in the PDR. She asked the doctor for what Retrovir was used. When Dr. Van de Beek told her it was used in the treatment of AIDS, she inquired whether there was any other use for it. He told her no. She then asked about the three other medications that Doe was taking, and was informed that they were all AIDS medications as well. Pierce discreetly never mentioned Doe by name; however, Dr. Van de Beek was aware of Doe's condition and Doe's medications because Doe himself had disclosed this information to him. Therefore, Dr. Van de Beek deduced that Pierce was asking about Doe. He told her that if she were trying to diagnose employees' conditions through prescriptions, he felt this was improper and possibly illegal. Pierce immediately ended the conversation and told him not to speak of the conversation to anyone.

Pierce then took the report to Dr. Press. She asked him if he would be able to perform an audit using the information in the report. Press noted that Pierce had highlighted certain lines on the report, including employees' names and the drugs that each of those highlighted employees were taking. Press testified that the drugs highlighted were all HIV or AIDS-related. Pierce asked Press if he knew whether any of the people whose names were highlighted were HIV-positive. Press said that he was aware of Doe's condition. He then told Pierce that he was uncomfortable with the presence of the names on the report. . . .

Dr. Van de Beek informed Doe of Pierce's questions. He told Doe that Pierce had likely found out that Doe was HIV-positive. Doe claims he became upset at this news. He avers that he became more upset upon discovering from Dr. Press that Pierce had his name highlighted on a list because he didn't know who had access to or had seen this "AIDS list" and only a few SEPTA employees knew of his HIV-status. He had told Press and Van de Beek, as well as his acting supervisor and the administrative assistant of his department that he had AIDS. . . .

After these incidents, Doe remained at SEPTA in his current position. He makes no claim of personal discrimination or of any economic deprivation. He later received a salary upgrade and promotion. However, he testified that he felt as though he were being treated differently. A proposal he had made for an in house employee assistance program met with scant interest; he felt that this was because of his HIV condition. In addition, an administrator who reported to Pierce did not call on Doe to assist in the same way that he had called on Doe earlier. Doe testified that he felt as though there was less social chitchat, co-workers ate less of the baked goods he brought to the office to share, and that his work space seemed more lonely than before. He also became fearful of Pierce, who never told Doe that she knew of his illness. Doe alleges that he became depressed and requested a prescription for Zoloft, an antidepressant, from his physician. Later, another antidepressant called Elavil was added to the medications Doe was taking. . . .

As a preliminary matter, this court must decide if a person's medical prescription record is within the ambit of information protected by the Constitution. If there is no right to privacy, our inquiry stops. A § 1983 action cannot be maintained unless the underlying act violates a plaintiff's Constitutional rights. . . .

. . . The Supreme Court, in *Whalen v. Roe*, noted that the right to privacy encompasses two separate spheres. One of these is an individual's interest in independence in making certain decisions. The other is an interest in avoiding disclosure of personal information. Medical records fall within the second category. Therefore, the Court held that individuals do have a limited right to privacy in their medical records. . . .

An individual using prescription drugs has a right to expect that such information will customarily remain private. The district court, therefore, committed no error in its holding that there is a constitutional right to privacy in one's prescription records. . . .

As with many individual rights, the right of privacy in one's prescription drug records must be balanced against important competing interests.

Before we can perform this balancing test, we must first assess whether, and to what extent, Pierce disclosed Doe's prescription drug information. . . .

Both Pierce and Aufschauer learned of Doe's illness through the Rite-Aid report. Pierce's initial discovery of the names on the report was inadvertent. . . . However, Pierce then spent some time and effort researching the report with the names on it. She highlighted, for her research purposes, those names on the report whose medications she was unfamiliar with and which were expensive, including Doe's, and called two SEPTA staff physicians to ask about medications she did not recognize. It was through this inquiry that Pierce learned about Doe's condition. She did not know the uses of Retrovir before she did this research.

Aufschauer learned of Doe's condition through his work as Director of Benefits and Pierce's subordinate. Pierce disclosed the information to him in the course of their work. SEPTA argues that this disclosure was necessary, as Aufschauer also had reasons for needing this information. Aufschauer's legitimate need for this information may affect whether the disclosure is an actionable one. It does not alter the existence of disclosure.

Nor can Pierce and Aufschauer be considered as a single unit for the purpose of determining disclosure. A disclosure occurs in the workplace each time private information is communicated to a new person, regardless of the relationship between the co-workers sharing that information. . . . Therefore, we hold that each person who learned of Doe's condition constitutes a separate disclosure for the purposes of Doe's invasion of privacy action.

To hold differently would lead us to a decision that Doe had waived his right to privacy by voluntarily disclosing his medical condition to co-workers at SEPTA. We are not faced with a situation where persons to whom Doe disclosed this information told others. Rather, Pierce and Aufschauer learned his condition completely independently of Doe's disclosures. His decision to give private information to some co-workers does not give carte blanche to other co-workers to invade his privacy.

However, we are not persuaded that the impingement on Doe's privacy by the disclosure to SEPTA's Chief Medical Officer, Dr. Press, amounts to a constitutional violation. Doe himself had already voluntarily informed Dr. Press of his condition. Dr. Press did not learn any new information from Pierce's actions. . . . Van de Beek, like Dr. Press, had already heard of Doe's condition from Doe himself. . . . [These disclosures] did not "amount to an impermissible invasion of privacy," because John Doe had already provided [the doctors] with this information. . . .

As we noted earlier, an individual's privacy interest in his or her prescription records is not an absolute right against disclosure. This interest must be weighed against the interests of the employer in obtaining the information. We apply an intermediate standard of review in making this determination. . . . The intrusion upon Doe's privacy was minimal at worst.

This court has previously enumerated the factors to be weighed in determining whether a given disclosure constitutes an actionable invasion of privacy in *United States v. Westinghouse Electric Corp.*, 638 F.2d 570 (3d Cir. 1980). . . . *Westinghouse* mandates a consideration of seven different factors. They are: (1) the type of record requested; (2) the information it does or might contain; (3) the potential for harm in any subsequent nonconsensual disclosure; (4) the injury from disclosure to the relationship in which the record was generated; (5) the adequacy of safeguards to prevent unauthorized disclosure; (6) the degree of need for access; and (7) whether there is an express statutory mandate, articulated public policy, or other recognizable public interest favoring access. Although some of these factors may be in Doe's favor, overall, we believe the balance weighs on the side of permitting the disclosures present here. There is a strong public interest of the Transportation Authority, and the many thousands of people it serves, in containing its costs and expenses by permitting this sort of research by authorized personnel. This interest outweighs the minimal intrusion, particularly given the lack of any economic loss, discrimination, or harassment actually suffered by plaintiff. . . .

. . . In *Doe v. Borough of Barrington*, a borough police officer, without justification, told the neighbors of a man suffering from AIDS that the entire family had AIDS. The neighbors reacted by organizing a protest, and trying to prevent the man's children from attending public school. In that case, the court quite rightly held such conduct violated the plaintiffs' privacy rights, and there was no competing interest to justify the disclosure.

By contrast, SEPTA had legitimate reasons for obtaining the prescription information from Rite-Aid. Pierce had requested the information in Rite-Aid's standard format; she did not request the names of any employees. She did not disclose the information relating to Doe except to Aufschauer, in connection with their review, and to Dr. Press, for purposes of an audit. Dr. Press, the Chief Medical Officer, already knew of Doe's condition through Doe's voluntary disclosure. Moreover, Pierce destroyed the first report. Under these circumstances, we cannot conclude that Westinghouse factor (3) would impose liability on SEPTA. . . .

Factors six and seven strongly favor the defendants. Pierce had a genuine, legitimate and compelling need for the document she requested. Aufschauer, as Director of Benefits, also had a need for the document. Each had a responsibility and obligation to keep insurance costs down and to detect fraudulent and abusive behavior. The report was intended for that purpose. Employers have a legitimate need for monitoring the costs and uses of their employee benefit programs, especially employers who have fiscal responsibilities, as does SEPTA, to the public. . . .

Employers also have a right to ensure that their health plan is only being used by those who are authorized to be covered. Finally, the employers have a right to contain costs by requiring that employees use generic drugs rather than brand name when an adequate substitute exists. To accomplish these goals, employers must have access to reports from their prescription suppliers, and they must inspect and audit those reports. That is precisely what Pierce and Aufschauer were engaged in, and this was a legitimate function of their positions. They had a legitimate need for access to information from the drug supplier, and they carefully controlled its use. . . .

We hold that a self-insured employer's need for access to employee prescription records under its health insurance plan, when the information disclosed is only for the purpose of monitoring the plans by those with a need to know, outweighs an employee's interest in keeping his prescription drug purchases confidential. Such minimal intrusion, although an impingement on privacy, is insufficient to constitute a constitutional violation. . . .

NOTES & QUESTIONS

1. ***Private vs. Public Sector Employers.*** What if SEPTA were a private sector employer. Would Doe have a good case under the public disclosure of private facts tort?
2. ***Medical Privacy in the Workplace.*** Should employers be permitted to ask for or receive health information from their employees? Does it matter whether the employer is providing health insurance? Should parents be permitted to ask their babysitter for health information (such as mental health, HIV, and other diseases) as part of the hiring decision?
3. ***Conceptualizing Doe's Privacy Harm.*** Daniel Solove argues that the court in *Doe v. SEPTA* misconceptualized Doe's claim that his privacy was invaded:

> [The court] missed the nature of Doe's complaint. Regardless of whether he was imagining how his co-workers were treating him, he was indeed suffering a real palpable fear. His real injury was the powerlessness of having no idea who else knew he had HIV, what his employer thought of him, or how the

> information could be used against him. This feeling of unease changed the way he perceived everything at his place of employment. The privacy problem was not merely the fact that Pierce divulged his secret or that Doe himself had lost control over his information, but rather that the information appeared to be entirely out of anyone's control.[52]

Is this a type of injury that the law should recognize? Had the court recognized the injury in this way, how would its analysis have been different?

4. ***The Storm Lake Case.*** In 2002, in Storm Lake, Iowa, a baby's mangled body was found in a trash bin. Law enforcement officials sought and obtained a court order to obtain all of the pregnancy records at medical facilities in the area. In particular, the officials were seeking the names and addresses of women who had positive pregnancy tests. Planned Parenthood of Greater Iowa challenged the order. When the case made it up to the Iowa Supreme Court, the law enforcement officials stated that they would no longer seek the records, and the case was dismissed. Suppose, however, that the officials did not drop their request. Based on the privacy laws you learned thus far, how would you resolve this case?[53]
5. ***Subpoenas for Abortion Records.*** In *Alpha Medical Clinic v. Anderson,* 128 P.3d 364 (Kan. 2006), Kansas Attorney General Phill Kline subpoenaed the records of 90 females who received abortions at two clinics. Kline sought the subpoenas to investigate whether there were violations of Kansas law. In particular, he sought information about whether abortions were being performed after 22 weeks' gestational age, which K.S.A. § 65-6703 prohibits except to protect the physical health of the woman. Kline also sought information about whether Kansas child abuse statutes were violated. The trial court, Judge Anderson, ordered that the records be produced to the court for an *in camera* review. The clinics brought an action for mandamus. The Supreme Court of Kansas concluded that the clinics had "third-party standing to assert their patients' information privacy rights." The court analyzed whether Kline's subpoenas infringed upon the patients' constitutional right to information privacy. The court concluded:

> The type of information sought by the State here could hardly be more sensitive, or the potential harm to patient privacy posed by disclosure more substantial. Judge Anderson's order does not do all it can to narrow the information gathered or to safeguard that information from unauthorized disclosure once it is in the district court's hands. Although the criminal inquisition statutes do not speak to the need for such narrowing and safeguards, the constitutional dimensions of this case compel them. . . .
>
> Only if Judge Anderson is satisfied that the attorney general is on firm legal ground should he permit the inquisition to continue and some version of the subpoenas to remain in effect. Then he also must enter a protective order

[52] Daniel J. Solove, *Privacy and Power: Computer Databases and Metaphors for Information Privacy*, 53 Stan. L. Rev. 1393, 1438-39 (2001).

[53] For more information about the case, see Poornima L. Ravishankar, Comment, *Planned Parenthood Is Not a Bank: Closing the Clinic Doors to the Fourth Amendment Third Party Doctrine,* 34 Seton Hall L. Rev. 1093 (2004).

that sets forth at least the following safeguards: (1) Petitioners' counsel must redact patient-identifying information from the files before they are delivered to the judge under seal; (2) the documents should be reviewed initially in camera by a lawyer and a physician or physicians appointed by the court, who can then advise the court if further redactions should be made to eliminate information unrelated to the legitimate purposes of the inquisition.

3. THE FOURTH AMENDMENT

FERGUSON V. CITY OF CHARLESTON

532 U.S. 67 (2001)

[A Charleston public hospital operated by the Medical University of South Carolina (MUSC) developed a policy of testing pregnant patients suspected of drug use. The drug testing was done by examining urine samples. Patients with positive results were provided with referrals for education and treatment and were sometimes arrested and prosecuted for drug offenses or child neglect. In rejecting a Fourth Amendment challenge to the testing, the Fourth Circuit concluded that the testing was reasonable under the "special needs" doctrine. Under this doctrine, a search without a warrant or probable cause can be reasonable under the Fourth Amendment if special needs make the warrant or probable cause requirements impractical.]

STEVENS, J. . . . Because MUSC is a state hospital, the members of its staff are government actors, subject to the strictures of the Fourth Amendment. Moreover, the urine tests conducted by those staff members were indisputably searches within the meaning of the Fourth Amendment. Neither the District Court nor the Court of Appeals concluded that any of the nine criteria used to identify the women to be searched provided either probable cause to believe that they were using cocaine, or even the basis for a reasonable suspicion of such use. Rather, the District Court and the Court of Appeals viewed the case as one involving MUSC's right to conduct searches without warrants or probable cause. Furthermore, given the posture in which the case comes to us, we must assume for purposes of our decision that the tests were performed without the informed consent of the patients.

Because the hospital seeks to justify its authority to conduct drug tests and to turn the results over to law enforcement agents without the knowledge or consent of the patients, this case differs from the four previous cases in which we have considered whether comparable drug tests "fit within the closely guarded category of constitutionally permissible suspicionless searches." In three of those cases, we sustained drug tests for railway employees involved in train accidents, *Skinner v. Railway Labor Executives' Assn.*, 489 U.S. 602 (1989), for United States Customs Service employees seeking promotion to certain sensitive positions, *Treasury Employees v. Von Raab*, 489 U.S. 656 (1989), and for high school students participating in interscholastic sports, *Vernonia School Dist. v. Acton*, 515 U.S. 646 (1995). In the fourth case, we struck down such testing for candidates for designated state offices as unreasonable. *Chandler v. Miller*, 520 U.S. 305, 513 (1997).

In each of those cases, we employed a balancing test that weighed the intrusion on the individual's interest in privacy against the "special needs" that supported the program. As an initial matter, we note that the invasion of privacy in this case is far more substantial than in those cases. In the previous four cases, there was no misunderstanding about the purpose of the test or the potential use of the test results, and there were protections against the dissemination of the results to third parties. The use of an adverse test result to disqualify one from eligibility for a particular benefit, such as a promotion or an opportunity to participate in an extracurricular activity, involves a less serious intrusion on privacy than the unauthorized dissemination of such results to third parties. The reasonable expectation of privacy enjoyed by the typical patient undergoing diagnostic tests in a hospital is that the results of those tests will not be shared with nonmedical personnel without her consent. . . .

The critical difference between those four drug-testing cases and this one, however, lies in the nature of the "special need" asserted as justification for the warrantless searches. In each of those earlier cases, the "special need" that was advanced as a justification for the absence of a warrant or individualized suspicion was one divorced from the State's general interest in law enforcement. . . . In this case, however, the central and indispensable feature of the policy from its inception was the use of law enforcement to coerce the patients into substance abuse treatment. This fact distinguishes this case from circumstances in which physicians or psychologists, in the course of ordinary medical procedures aimed at helping the patient herself, come across information that under rules of law or ethics is subject to reporting requirements, which no one has challenged here.

Respondents argue in essence that their ultimate purpose — namely, protecting the health of both mother and child — is a beneficent one. . . . In this case, a review of the M-7 policy plainly reveals that the purpose actually served by the MUSC searches "is ultimately indistinguishable from the general interest in crime control." . . .

. . . [T]hroughout the development and application of the policy, the Charleston prosecutors and police were extensively involved in the day-to-day administration of the policy. . . .

While the ultimate goal of the program may well have been to get the women in question into substance abuse treatment and off of drugs, the immediate objective of the searches was to generate evidence *for law enforcement purposes* in order to reach that goal. . . . Given the primary purpose of the Charleston program, which was to use the threat of arrest and prosecution in order to force women into treatment, and given the extensive involvement of law enforcement officials at every stage of the policy, this case simply does not fit within the closely guarded category of "special needs." . . .

As respondents have repeatedly insisted, their motive was benign rather than punitive. Such a motive, however, cannot justify a departure from Fourth Amendment protections, given the pervasive involvement of law enforcement with the development and application of the MUSC policy. . . . The Fourth Amendment's general prohibition against nonconsensual, warrantless, and suspicionless searches necessarily applies to such a policy. . . .

NOTES & QUESTIONS

1. ***Mandatory AIDS Testing of Firefighters and Paramedics.*** In contrast to *Ferguson*, consider *Anonymous Fireman v. City of Willoughby,* 779 F. Supp. 402 (N.D. Ohio 1991). In *Anonymous Fireman*, firefighters and paramedics challenged a city's mandatory annual testing for the AIDS virus as part of their annual physical examination. They claimed that the testing violated their Fourth Amendment rights. The court found that the "protection of the public from the contraction and transmission of AIDS by firefighters and paramedics is a compelling governmental interest." It also declared:

> The medical evidence demonstrates that the risk of HIV transmission in the performance of the duties of firefighter paramedic is high. . . .
>
> State and local authorities have compelling interests in ensuring that its firefighters and paramedics are performing their duties free of having AIDS. Reasonable and particularized suspicion is not necessary as a precondition to mandatory AIDS testing of firefighters and paramedics.

Does *Ferguson* affect the reasoning of this case?

2. ***Medical Testing of Accused Sex Offenders.*** In *In re J.G.,* 701 A.2d 1260 (N.J. 1997), New Jersey enacted statutes providing for AIDS testing at the request of the victim of assailants who were charged with sexual assault. Three juveniles charged with sexual assault violations and required to submit to AIDS testing challenged the statutes on Fourth Amendment grounds. Experts testifying on behalf of the juveniles stated that the harms of testing would be outweighed by the benefits:

> In the opinion of Dr. James Oleske, testing sexual assailants for HIV would provide no medical benefit in the diagnosis or treatment of victims because the test would not reveal whether transmission, which does not occur in all cases, had in fact occurred, and because testing the assailant might produce a false-negative result due to the three- to six-month latency period. . . .
>
> The experts offered their opinions about whether there was any "psycho-social benefit" to the victim in knowing the HIV status of the assailant. In Dr. Oleske's view, victims may suffer actual harm from knowing their assailants' status. They may wrongly rely on a false-negative result and discontinue medical care and testing, or they may react to a positive result without considering their actual risk of infection or their own status. He acknowledged, however, that for the victim and the victim's family "[t]he question of peace of mind, . . . in lay terms, may be real." . . .

The court, however, concluded that on balance, the alleged offenders' Fourth Amendment rights were outweighed by the benefits of the testing:

> . . . A court must balance the encroachment on an individual's Fourth Amendment interests against the advancement of legitimate state goals. When a search is conducted in furtherance of a criminal investigation, the balance is most often tipped "in favor of the procedures described by the Warrant Clause of the Fourth Amendment," that is, toward a finding that the search "is not reasonable unless it is accomplished pursuant to a judicial warrant issued upon probable cause."

An exception to the Warrant Clause may apply "when 'special needs, beyond the normal need for law enforcement, make the warrant and probable-cause requirement impracticable.'" . . .

Serological testing of sex offenders . . . is not intended to facilitate the criminal prosecution of those offenders. HIV test results are required to be kept confidential (with certain limited exceptions). Notably, the statute does not authorize disclosure to the prosecutor's office. The State has said that the tests are not intended to be used to gain evidence for criminal prosecutions and do not place offenders at risk of a new conviction or longer sentence. We agree, and hold that the results of HIV tests . . . may not be used against an accused sex offender in a criminal prosecution.

Moreover, both the warrant and individualized suspicion requirements are impractical in this context. . . . "HIV infected sexual offenders often have no outward manifestations of infection," which means that probable cause or individualized suspicion that an assailant is infected with the AIDS virus could not be found without testing. Requiring probable cause or individualized suspicion before testing could be conducted would create the proverbial Catch-22 and would "frustrate the governmental purpose behind the search." . . .

Unquestionably, the state has a compelling interest in making information available when it directly affects the physical and mental well-being of survivors of sexual assault. . . .

. . . Survivors of sexual assault, and those close to them, face significant psychological as well as physical trauma. [The statutes] respond to these significant concerns by requiring the testing of offenders at the victim's request, and by establishing counseling, testing, and other support services for victims. . . .

The dissemination of test results . . . is carefully restricted. It is, therefore, reasonable to require assailants to submit to this intrusion upon their privacy. . . .

. . . [However, only if] . . . a demonstration of a risk that the AIDS virus may have been transmitted from the offender to the victim . . . is made will the interests of the state in enacting the testing statutes outweigh the privacy interests of the offender. . . .

C. GENETIC INFORMATION

1. BACKGROUND: GENETIC PRIVACY

Deoxyribonucleic acid, otherwise known as DNA, is present in all cellular organisms and contains the information an organism needs to live and to transfer genetic material. The DNA molecule's structure consists of two strands coiled around one another forming a double helix. Each strand of DNA is comprised of different sequences of four chemical compounds. The chemical compounds are adenine, guanine, thymine, and cytosine, denoted with A, G, T, and C, respectively. A "nucleotide" is a subunit of a DNA strand that contains one of these four chemical compounds. Nucleotides, each containing A, G, T, or C, are arranged in sequences along each strand of DNA. The nucleotides in one strand of DNA are paired with the nucleotides in the other DNA strand. Each pair of nucleotides is known as a base pair. The base pairs are joined to each other by chemical bonds called "hydrogen bonds." There are about 3 billion base pairs in the human genome.

DNA contains the recipe for the creation of proteins. A protein consists of smaller molecules known as amino acids. The structure of each protein is determined by the sequence of its amino acids. The sequence of base pairs of nucleotides in DNA determines the sequence of amino acids.

A "gene" is a sequence of nucleotides that codes for the production of a particular protein. Genes are responsible for transmitting inherited traits. Genes are located inside chromosomes, which are contained in the nucleus of each cell.[54] Humans have 23 pairs of chromosomes. It had been previously estimated that there are about 100,000 genes in the 23 chromosomes, but recent research suggests that the number is between 20,000 and 25,000.

Every cell in the human body, which is comprised of about 100 trillion cells, contains DNA (except red blood cells). DNA can be isolated from white blood cells, sperm cells, cells in saliva, nasal secretions, sweat, and the cells surrounding the roots of hair.

An individual's complete genetic makeup is known as a "genome." With the exception of identical twins, no two humans have an identical genome. However, only a small portion of DNA differs among individuals. About 99 percent of the 3 billion base pairs of nucleotides are the same in all humans. The 1 percent that is different enables DNA forensic analysis.

The Human Genome Project, the first draft of which was completed in 2000, has mapped out all of the genes in the human chromosomes. With further study, the Human Genome Project will enable the identification of the particular genes that cause certain diseases.

Along with these developments comes a new threat to privacy. Once genes and gene mutations are better understood, and are linked to particular diseases and traits, one's genetic information can reveal one's medical history and even the future of one's health. Further, one's genetic information can reveal information about one's family members. As Anita Allen explains:

> According to legal doctrine, to appropriate a person's name or likeness is a way of invading his or her privacy. Privacy, it appears, has something to do with controlling one's identity. . . .
>
> The question whether our genes comprise our identities is a difficult one. Proprietary genetic privacy is suggested by the idea that the human DNA is a repository of valuable human personality. Proprietary genetic privacy is further suggested by the related notion that human DNA is owned by the persons from whom it is taken, as a species of private property.
>
> If DNA is the human essence — that is, the thing that makes individuals special and perhaps unique — it arguably ought to belong to the individual from whom it was ultimately derived. If DNA "belongs" to individual sources, it might belong to them exclusively and inalienably. Or DNA could qualify as

[54] Some cells, such as red blood cells, do not contain a nucleus and do not have nuclear DNA (but they may have mitochondrial DNA).

alienable property that others can acquire both lawfully through voluntary private transactions and wrongfully through nonconsensual appropriation. . . .[55]

2. PROPERTY RIGHTS IN BODY PARTS AND DNA

MOORE V. REGENTS OF THE UNIVERSITY OF CALIFORNIA

793 P.2d 479 (Cal. 1990)

PANELLI, J. . . . The plaintiff is John Moore (Moore), who underwent treatment for hairy-cell leukemia at the Medical Center of the University of California at Los Angeles (UCLA Medical Center). The five defendants are: (1) Dr. David W. Golde (Golde), a physician who attended Moore at UCLA Medical Center; (2) the Regents of the University of California (Regents), who own and operate the university; (3) Shirley G. Quan, a researcher employed by the Regents; (4) Genetics Institute, Inc. (Genetics Institute); and (5) Sandoz Pharmaceuticals Corporation and related entities (collectively Sandoz).

Moore first visited UCLA Medical Center on October 5, 1976, shortly after he learned that he had hairy-cell leukemia. After hospitalizing Moore and "withdr[awing] extensive amounts of blood, bone marrow aspirate, and other bodily substances," Golde confirmed that diagnosis. At this time all defendants, including Golde, were aware that "certain blood products and blood components were of great value in a number of commercial and scientific efforts" and that access to a patient whose blood contained these substances would provide "competitive, commercial, and scientific advantages."

On October 8, 1976, Golde recommended that Moore's spleen be removed. Golde informed Moore "that he had reason to fear for his life, and that the proposed splenectomy operation . . . was necessary to slow down the progress of his disease." Based upon Golde's representations, Moore signed a written consent form authorizing the splenectomy.

Before the operation, Golde and Quan "formed the intent and made arrangements to obtain portions of [Moore's] spleen following its removal" and to take them to a separate research unit. Golde gave written instructions to this effect on October 18 and 19, 1976. These research activities "were not intended to have . . . any relation to [Moore's] medical . . . care." However, neither Golde nor Quan informed Moore of their plans to conduct this research or requested his permission. Surgeons at UCLA Medical Center, whom the complaint does not name as defendants, removed Moore's spleen on October 20, 1976.

Moore returned to the UCLA Medical Center several times between November 1976 and September 1983. He did so at Golde's direction and based upon representations "that such visits were necessary and required for his health and well-being, and based upon the trust inherent in and by virtue of the physician-patient relationship. . . ." On each of these visits Golde withdrew additional samples of "blood, blood serum, skin, bone marrow aspirate, and sperm." On each occasion Moore traveled to the UCLA Medical Center from his

---

[55] Anita L. Allen, Genetic *Privacy: Emerging Concepts and Values, in Genetic Secrets: Protecting Privacy and Confidentiality in the Genetic Era* (Mark A. Rothstein, ed. 1997).

home in Seattle because he had been told that the procedures were to be performed only there and only under Golde's direction.

"In fact, [however,] throughout the period of time that [Moore] was under [Golde's] care and treatment, . . . the defendants were actively involved in a number of activities which they concealed from [Moore]. . . ." Specifically, defendants were conducting research on Moore's cells and planned to "benefit financially and competitively . . . [by exploiting the cells] and [their] exclusive access to [the cells] by virtue of [Golde's] on-going physician-patient relationship. . . ."

Sometime before August 1979, Golde established a cell line from Moore's T-lymphocytes.[56] [In 1984, the Regents had the cell line patented. The potential market value for products derived from the cell line was estimated to be in the billions of dollars.] . . .

Moore attempted to state 13 causes of action, [which included among them a cause of action for conversion, for breach of fiduciary duty, and for lack of informed consent]. . . .

A. *Breach of Fiduciary Duty and Lack of Informed Consent.* Moore repeatedly alleges that Golde failed to disclose the extent of his research and economic interests in Moore's cells before obtaining consent to the medical procedures by which the cells were extracted. These allegations, in our view, state a cause of action against Golde for invading a legally protected interest of his patient. This cause of action can properly be characterized either as the breach of a fiduciary duty to disclose facts material to the patient's consent or, alternatively, as the performance of medical procedures without first having obtained the patient's informed consent.

Our analysis begins with three well-established principles. First, "a person of adult years and in sound mind has the right, in the exercise of control over his own body, to determine whether or not to submit to lawful medical treatment." Second, "the patient's consent to treatment, to be effective, must be an informed consent." Third, in soliciting the patient's consent, a physician has a fiduciary duty to disclose all information material to the patient's decision.

These principles lead to the following conclusions: (1) a physician must disclose personal interests unrelated to the patient's health, whether research or economic, that may affect the physician's professional judgment; and (2) a physician's failure to disclose such interests may give rise to a cause of action for performing medical procedures without informed consent or breach of fiduciary duty.

To be sure, questions about the validity of a patient's consent to a procedure typically arise when the patient alleges that the physician failed to disclose

---

[56] A T-lymphocyte is a type of white blood cell. T-lymphocytes produce lymphokines, or proteins that regulate the immune system. Some lymphokines have potential therapeutic value. If the genetic material responsible for producing a particular lymphokine can be identified, it can sometimes be used to manufacture large quantities of the lymphokine through the techniques of recombinant DNA. . . . While the genetic code for lymphokines does not vary from individual to individual, it can nevertheless be quite difficult to locate the gene responsible for a particular lymphokine. Because T-lymphocytes produce many different lymphokines, the relevant gene is often like a needle in a haystack. Moore's T-lymphocytes were interesting to the defendants because they overproduced certain lymphokines, thus making the corresponding genetic material easier to identify.

medical risks, as in malpractice cases, and not when the patient alleges that the physician had a personal interest, as in this case. The concept of informed consent, however, is broad enough to encompass the latter. "The scope of the physician's communication to the patient . . . must be measured by the patient's need, and that need is whatever information is material to the decision."

Indeed, the law already recognizes that a reasonable patient would want to know whether a physician has an economic interest that might affect the physician's professional judgment. As the Court of Appeal has said, "[c]ertainly a sick patient deserves to be free of any reasonable suspicion that his doctor's judgment is influenced by a profit motive." . . .

A physician who adds his own research interests to this balance may be tempted to order a scientifically useful procedure or test that offers marginal, or no, benefits to the patient. The possibility that an interest extraneous to the patient's health has affected the physician's judgment is something that a reasonable patient would want to know in deciding whether to consent to a proposed course of treatment. It is material to the patient's decision and, thus, a prerequisite to informed consent. . . .

B. *Conversion.* Moore also attempts to characterize the invasion of his rights as a conversion — a tort that protects against interference with possessory and ownership interests in personal property. He theorizes that he continued to own his cells following their removal from his body, at least for the purpose of directing their use, and that he never consented to their use in potentially lucrative medical research. Thus, to complete Moore's argument, defendants' unauthorized use of his cells constitutes a conversion. As a result of the alleged conversion, Moore claims a proprietary interest in each of the products that any of the defendants might ever create from his cells or the patented cell line. . . .

1. *Moore's Claim Under Existing Law.* "To establish a conversion, plaintiff must establish an actual interference with his ownership or right of possession. . . Where plaintiff neither has title to the property alleged to have been converted, nor possession thereof, he cannot maintain an action for conversion."

Since Moore clearly did not expect to retain possession of his cells following their removal, to sue for their conversion he must have retained an ownership interest in them. But there are several reasons to doubt that he did retain any such interest. First, no reported judicial decision supports Moore's claim, either directly or by close analogy. Second, California statutory law drastically limits any continuing interest of a patient in excised cells. Third, the subject matters of the Regents' patent — the patented cell line and the products derived from it — cannot be Moore's property. . . .

Lacking direct authority for importing the law of conversion into this context, Moore relies, as did the Court of Appeal, primarily on decisions addressing privacy rights. One line of cases involves unwanted publicity. These opinions hold that every person has a proprietary interest in his own likeness and that unauthorized, business use of a likeness is redressible as a tort. But in neither opinion did the authoring court expressly base its holding on property law. Each court stated, following Prosser, that it was "pointless" to debate the proper characterization of the proprietary interest in a likeness. For purposes of determining whether the tort of conversion lies, however, the characterization of the right in question is far from pointless. Only property can be converted.

Not only are the wrongful-publicity cases irrelevant to the issue of conversion, but the analogy to them seriously misconceives the nature of the genetic materials and research involved in this case. Moore, adopting the analogy originally advanced by the Court of Appeal, argues that "[i]f the courts have found a sufficient proprietary interest in one's persona, how could one not have a right in one's own genetic material, something far more profoundly the essence of one's human uniqueness than a name or a face?" However, as the defendants' patent makes clear — and the complaint, too, if read with an understanding of the scientific terms which it has borrowed from the patent — the goal and result of defendants' efforts has been to manufacture lymphokines. Lymphokines, unlike a name or a face, have the same molecular structure in every human being and the same, important functions in every human being's immune system. Moreover, the particular genetic material which is responsible for the natural production of lymphokines, and which defendants use to manufacture lymphokines in the laboratory, is also the same in every person; it is no more unique to Moore than the number of vertebrae in the spine or the chemical formula of hemoglobin.[57]

Another privacy case offered by analogy to support Moore's claim establishes only that patients have a right to refuse medical treatment. In this context the court in *Bouvia* wrote that "'[e]very human being of adult years and sound mind has a right to determine what shall be done with his own body. . . .'" Relying on this language to support the proposition that a patient has a continuing right to control the use of excised cells, the Court of Appeal in this case concluded that "[a] patient must have the ultimate power to control what becomes of his or her tissues. To hold otherwise would open the door to a massive invasion of human privacy and dignity in the name of medical progress." Yet one may earnestly wish to protect privacy and dignity without accepting the extremely problematic conclusion that interference with those interests amounts to a conversion of personal property. Nor is it necessary to force the round pegs of "privacy" and "dignity" into the square hole of "property" in order to protect the patient, since the fiduciary-duty and informed-consent theories protect these interests directly by requiring full disclosure.

The next consideration that makes Moore's claim of ownership problematic is California statutory law, which drastically limits a patient's control over excised cells. Pursuant to Health and Safety Code section 7054.4, "[n]otwithstanding any other provision of law, recognizable anatomical parts, human tissues, anatomical human remains, or infectious waste following conclusion of scientific use shall be disposed of by interment, incineration, or any other method determined by the state department [of health services] to protect the public health and safety." Clearly the Legislature did not specifically intend

---

[57] By definition, a gene responsible for producing a protein found in more than one individual will be the same in each. It is precisely because everyone needs the same basic proteins that proteins produced by one person's cells may have therapeutic value for another person. (See generally OTA Rep., supra, at pp. 38-40.) Thus, the proteins that defendants hope to manufacture — lymphokines such as interferon — are in no way a "likeness" of Moore. Because all normal persons possess the genes responsible for production of lymphokines, it is sometimes possible to make normal cells into overproducers. According to a research paper to which defendants contributed, Moore's cells overproduced lymphokines because they were infected by a virus, HTLV-II (human T-cell leukemia virus type II). The same virus has been shown to transform normal T-lymphocytes into overproducers like Moore's.

this statute to resolve the question of whether a patient is entitled to compensation for the nonconsensual use of excised cells. A primary object of the statute is to ensure the safe handling of potentially hazardous biological waste materials. Yet one cannot escape the conclusion that the statute's practical effect is to limit, drastically, a patient's control over excised cells. By restricting how excised cells may be used and requiring their eventual destruction, the statute eliminates so many of the rights ordinarily attached to property that one cannot simply assume that what is left amounts to "property" or "ownership" for purposes of conversion law. . . .

Finally, the subject matter of the Regents' patent—the patented cell line and the products derived from it—cannot be Moore's property. This is because the patented cell line is both factually and legally distinct from the cells taken from Moore's body. Federal law permits the patenting of organisms that represent the product of "human ingenuity," but not naturally occurring organisms. Human cell lines are patentable because "[l]ong-term adaptation and growth of human tissues and cells in culture is difficult — often considered an art . . . ," and the probability of success is low. It is this inventive effort that patent law rewards, not the discovery of naturally occurring raw materials. . . .

2. *Should Conversion Liability Be Extended?* As we have discussed, Moore's novel claim to own the biological materials at issue in this case is problematic, at best. Accordingly, his attempt to apply the theory of conversion within this context must frankly be recognized as a request to extend that theory. . . .

There are three reasons why it is inappropriate to impose liability for conversion based upon the allegations of Moore's complaint. First, a fair balancing of the relevant policy considerations counsels against extending the tort. Second, problems in this area are better suited to legislative resolution. Third, the tort of conversion is not necessary to protect patients' rights. For these reasons, we conclude that the use of excised human cells in medical research does not amount to a conversion.

Of the relevant policy considerations, two are of overriding importance. The first is protection of a competent patient's right to make autonomous medical decisions. That right, as already discussed, is grounded in well-recognized and long-standing principles of fiduciary duty and informed consent. This policy weighs in favor of providing a remedy to patients when physicians act with undisclosed motives that may affect their professional judgment. The second important policy consideration is that we not threaten with disabling civil liability innocent parties who are engaged in socially useful activities, such as researchers who have no reason to believe that their use of a particular cell sample is, or may be, against a donor's wishes. . . .

Liability based upon existing disclosure obligations, rather than an unprecedented extension of the conversion theory, protects patients' rights of privacy and autonomy without unnecessarily hindering research. . . .

Research on human cells plays a critical role in medical research. This is so because researchers are increasingly able to isolate naturally occurring, medically useful biological substances and to produce useful quantities of such substances through genetic engineering. . . .

The extension of conversion law into this area will hinder research by restricting access to the necessary raw materials. . . . At present, human cell lines are routinely copied and distributed to other researchers for experimental purposes, usually free of charge. This exchange of scientific materials, which still is relatively free and efficient, will surely be compromised if each cell sample becomes the potential subject matter of a lawsuit. . . .

. . . [T]he theory of liability that Moore urges us to endorse threatens to destroy the economic incentive to conduct important medical research. If the use of cells in research is a conversion, then with every cell sample a researcher purchases a ticket in a litigation lottery. Because liability for conversion is predicated on a continuing ownership interest, "companies are unlikely to invest heavily in developing, manufacturing, or marketing a product when uncertainty about clear title exists." . . .

BROUSSARD, J. concurring and dissenting. [Justice Broussard concurred in the majority's holding that the complaint states a cause of action for breach of fiduciary duty.]

With respect to the conversion cause of action, I dissent from the majority's conclusion that the facts alleged in this case do not state a cause of action for conversion. . . .

Because plaintiff alleges that defendants wrongfully interfered with his right to determine, prior to the removal of his body parts, how those parts would be used after removal, I conclude that the complaint states a cause of action under traditional, common law conversion principles. . . .

Although the majority opinion, at several points, appears to suggest that a removed body part, by its nature, may never constitute "property" for purposes of a conversion action, there is no reason to think that the majority opinion actually intends to embrace such a broad or dubious proposition. If, for example, another medical center or drug company had stolen all of the cells in question from the UCLA Medical Center laboratory and had used them for its own benefit, there would be no question but that a cause of action for conversion would properly lie against the thief, and the majority opinion does not suggest otherwise. Thus, the majority's analysis cannot rest on the broad proposition that a removed body part is not property, but rather rests on the proposition that a patient retains no ownership interest in a body part once the body part has been removed from his or her body.

The majority opinion fails to recognize, however, that, in light of the allegations of the present complaint, the pertinent inquiry is not whether a patient generally retains an ownership interest in a body part after its removal from his body, but rather whether a patient has a right to determine, before a body part is removed, the use to which the part will be put after removal. Although the majority opinion suggests that there are "reasons to doubt" that a patient retains "any" ownership interest in his organs or cells after removal, the opinion fails to identify any statutory provision or common law authority that indicates that a patient does not generally have the right, before a body part is removed, to choose among the permissible uses to which the part may be put after removal. On the contrary, the most closely related statutory scheme — the Uniform Anatomical Gift Act (Health & Saf. Code, § 7150 et seq.) — makes it quite clear that a patient does have this right.

The Uniform Anatomical Gift Act is a comprehensive statutory scheme that was initially adopted in California in 1970 and most recently revised in 1988. . . . [T]he act clearly recognizes that it is the donor of the body part, rather than the hospital or physician who receives the part, who has the authority to designate, within the parameters of the statutorily authorized uses, the particular use to which the part may be put.

Although, as noted, the Uniform Anatomical Gift Act applies only to anatomical gifts that take effect on or after the death of the donor, the general principle of "donor control" which the act embodies is clearly not limited to that setting. In the transplantation context, for example, it is common for a living donor to designate the specific donee — often a relative — who is to receive a donated organ. If a hospital, after removing an organ from such a donor, decided on its own to give the organ to a different donee, no one would deny that the hospital had violated the legal right of the donor by its unauthorized use of the donated organ. Accordingly, it is clear under California law that a patient has the right, prior to the removal of an organ, to control the use to which the organ will be put after removal.

It is also clear, under traditional common law principles, that this right of a patient to control the future use of his organ is protected by the law of conversion. As a general matter, the tort of conversion protects an individual not only against improper interference with the right of possession of his property but also against unauthorized use of his property or improper interference with his right to control the use of his property. . . . California cases have also long recognized that "unauthorized use" of property can give rise to a conversion action.

The application of these principles to the present case is evident. If defendants had informed plaintiff, prior to removal, of the possible uses to which his body part could be put and plaintiff had authorized one particular use, it is clear under the foregoing authorities that defendants would be liable for conversion if they disregarded plaintiff's decision and used the body part in an unauthorized manner for their own economic benefit. Although in this case defendants did not disregard a specific directive from plaintiff with regard to the future use of his body part, the complaint alleges that, before the body part was removed, defendants intentionally withheld material information that they were under an obligation to disclose to plaintiff and that was necessary for his exercise of control over the body part; the complaint also alleges that defendants withheld such information in order to appropriate the control over the future use of such body part for their own economic benefit. If these allegations are true, defendants clearly improperly interfered with plaintiff's right in his body part at a time when he had the authority to determine the future use of such part, thereby misappropriating plaintiff's right of control for their own advantage. Under these circumstances, the complaint fully satisfies the established requirements of a conversion cause of action. . . .

Finally, the majority maintains that plaintiff's conversion action is not viable because "the subject matter of the Regents' patent — the patented cell line and the products derived from it — cannot be Moore's property." Even if this is an accurate statement of federal patent law, it does not explain why plaintiff may not maintain a conversion action for defendants' unauthorized use of his own body parts, blood, blood serum, bone marrow, and sperm. Although the damages which plaintiff may recover in a conversion action may not include the value of the patent and the derivative products, the fact that plaintiff may not be entitled to all of the damages which his complaint seeks does not justify denying his right to maintain any conversion action at all. . . .

MOSK, J. dissenting. . . . The majority claim that a conversion cause of action threatens to "destroy the economic incentive" to conduct the type of research here in issue. . . .

In any event, in my view whatever merit the majority's single policy consideration may have is outweighed by two contrary considerations, i.e., policies that are promoted by recognizing that every individual has a legally protectible property interest in his own body and its products. First, our society acknowledges a profound ethical imperative to respect the human body as the physical and temporal expression of the unique human persona. One manifestation of that respect is our prohibition against direct abuse of the body by torture or other forms of cruel or unusual punishment. Another is our prohibition against indirect abuse of the body by its economic exploitation for the sole benefit of another person. The most abhorrent form of such exploitation, of course, was the institution of slavery. Lesser forms, such as indentured servitude or even debtor's prison, have also disappeared. Yet their specter haunts the laboratories and boardrooms of today's biotechnological research-industrial complex. It arises wherever scientists or industrialists claim, as defendants claim here, the right to appropriate and exploit a patient's tissue for their sole economic benefit — the right, in other words, to freely mine or harvest valuable physical properties of the patient's body: "Research with human cells that results in significant economic gain for the researcher and no gain for the patient offends the traditional mores of our society in a manner impossible to quantify. Such research tends to treat the human body as a commodity — a means to a profitable end. The dignity and sanctity with which we regard the human whole, body as well as mind and soul, are absent when we allow researchers to further their own interests without the patient's participation by using a patient's cells as the basis for a marketable product." (Danforth, *supra.*) . . .

The majority's final reason for refusing to recognize a conversion cause of action on these facts is that "there is no pressing need" to do so because the complaint also states another cause of action that is assuredly adequate to the task; that cause of action is "the breach of a fiduciary duty to disclose facts material to the patient's consent or, alternatively, . . . the performance of medical procedures without first having obtained the patient's informed consent" . . . I disagree . . . with the majority's further conclusion that in the present context a nondisclosure cause of action is an adequate — in fact, a superior — substitute for a conversion cause of action. . . .

The remedy is largely illusory. . . . There are two barriers to recovery. First, "the patient must show that if he or she had been informed of all pertinent information, he or she would have declined to consent to the procedure in question." . . .

The second barrier to recovery is still higher, and is erected on the first: it is not even enough for the plaintiff to prove that he personally would have refused consent to the proposed treatment if he had been fully informed; he must also prove that in the same circumstances no reasonably prudent person would have given such consent. . . .

. . . [I]t may be difficult for a plaintiff to prove that no reasonably prudent person would have consented to the proposed treatment if the doctor had disclosed the particular risk of physical harm that ultimately caused the injury. This is because in many cases the potential benefits of the treatment to the plaintiff clearly outweigh the undisclosed risk of harm. . . . Few if any judges or juries are likely to believe that disclosure of such a possibility of research or development would dissuade a reasonably prudent person from consenting to the treatment. For example, in the case at bar no trier of fact is likely to believe that if defendants had disclosed their plans for using Moore's cells, no reasonably prudent person in Moore's position — i.e., a leukemia patient suffering from a grossly enlarged spleen — would have consented to the routine operation that saved or at least prolonged his life. . . .

The second reason why the nondisclosure cause of action is inadequate for the task that the majority assign to it is that it fails to solve half the problem before us: it gives the patient only the right to refuse consent, i.e., the right to prohibit the commercialization of his tissue; it does not give him the right to grant consent to that commercialization on the condition that he share in its proceeds. "Even though good reasons exist to support informed consent with tissue commercialization, a disclosure requirement is only the first step toward full recognition of a patient's right to participate fully. Informed consent to commercialization, absent a right to share in the profits from such commercial development, would only give patients a veto over their own exploitation. But recognition that the patient[s] [have] an ownership interest in their own tissues would give patients an affirmative right of participation. Then patients would be able to assume the role of equal partners with their physicians in commercial biotechnology research." . . .

Third, the nondisclosure cause of action fails to reach a major class of potential defendants: all those who are outside the strict physician-patient relationship with the plaintiff. . . . [T]he nondisclosure cause of action will thus be inadequate to reach a number of parties to the commercial exploitation of his tissue. Such parties include, for example, any physician-researcher who is not personally treating the patient, any other researcher who is not a physician, any employer of the foregoing (or even of the treating physician), and any person or corporation thereafter participating in the commercial exploitation of the tissue. Yet some or all of those parties may well have participated more in, and profited more from, such exploitation than the particular physician with whom the plaintiff happened to have a formal doctor-patient relationship at the time. . . .

NOTES & QUESTIONS

1. ***A Right to Own or Control Genetic Information?*** The *Moore* case asks us to examine whether we can own our body parts (specifically, a spleen) once they are removed from our bodies. This suggests a broader question: Do we own our genetic information? To what extent can we control this information?

Moore certainly had a property right in his spleen when it was in his body. Why does he lose that right when the spleen is removed?

2. ***Fiduciary Duties.*** The majority concludes that the interests of privacy and dignity can adequately be protected with a fiduciary duty; therefore, it is unnecessary to resort to property rights. Is a fiduciary duty sufficient to protect Moore's privacy interest?

3. ***Property or Privacy?*** Compare Broussard's view of Moore's claim of harm to that of the majority. Is the real harm to Moore, as Broussard argues, that he lost control over his body parts rather than, as the majority characterizes Moore's claim, that his property was taken? Is Broussard's view not one of property but of privacy? Is ownership of the spleen the same as control over it?

   Suppose Moore had a privacy interest in his cells—a right to control future use. Moore would be entitled to damages for his loss of privacy (i.e., for the emotional harm of knowing his cells were used without his consent). Are these damages likely to deter the doctors considering the billions of dollars that the cell line was worth?

4. ***What Is the Privacy Interest in Genetic Information?*** If Moore has a privacy interest in his genetic information, how would you characterize it? According to James Boyle, it is difficult to view genetic information alone as implicating privacy. Only when genetic information is deciphered (to reveal certain traits or diseases) will it yield the type of information we consider to be private:

   > [O]ur intuitive notions of privacy are constructed around the notion of preventing disclosure of intimate, embarrassing, or simply "personal" *socially constructed facts* about ourselves to others like ourselves. I could stare at my genetic code all day and not even know it was mine. . . .
   >
   > The difficulty with Moore's case is, first, that no one would think worse of him for having a genetic make-up that could be mined for a socially valuable drug and, second, that specialized knowledge would be necessary to make the connection between the "facts revealed" and the "inner life." . . .
   >
   > If Moore's claim is not to the protection of his "privacy" . . . but rather to the protection of his ability to commodify the genetic information derived from his cells, then the inquiry shifts from privacy to [property], from the home and the secret to the market and the commodity. . . .[58]

5. ***Methods of Protecting Genetic Privacy.*** How should genetic privacy be protected? With a property right that gives people complete ownership of their genetic information? With a fiduciary duty that remedies duplicitous actions to take one's genetic information or the unlawful disclosure of one's genetic information? With tort damages for the loss of a privacy right in one's genetic information (i.e., for the loss of control over one's genetic information)? With a limited right to control one's genetic information short of complete ownership? Or with a rule that genetic information is in the public domain and belongs to society as a whole?

---

[58] James Boyle, *Shamans, Software, and Spleens: Law and the Construction of the Information Society* 105-106 (1996).

6. ***Is Genetic Information Property?*** Consider Radhika Rao:

> [P]roperty traditionally implies alienability — the power to transfer rights to others. Although many categories of inalienable property exist, alienability is the norm for property. The law views limits upon alienability as exceptions, justifiable only in response to market failure or other externalities. Consequently, inalienable property is an inherently unstable and precarious category, destined to be the target of sustained assault.
>
> Privacy, on the other hand, does not carry the same connotations. Personal privacy encompasses the right to possess one's own body and the right to exclude others, but does not embrace the power to give, sell, or otherwise transfer body rights to other individuals. And relational privacy safeguards intimate and consensual relationships, but affords little shelter to commercial transactions. Accordingly, we should adopt the language of privacy rather than that of property when we seek to protect self-ownership without suggesting that rights in the human body can be conveyed to others and when we wish to distinguish gifts of the body to family members from sales to strangers.
>
> The principal feature of bodily property may be this power to transfer rights to others, whether by sale, gift, or disposition after death. By contrast, the right of personal privacy can be curtailed or relinquished altogether, but it cannot be conveyed to another. . . .
>
> As a result, the lines that courts draw in many of these decisions precisely track the parameters of privacy jurisprudence. Common law cadaver cases, for example, grant the right to control disposition of a dead body to decedents and their close relatives, but repeatedly deny the right to treat the corpse as an article of commerce. Similarly, *Moore v. Regents of the University of California* affirms the patient's autonomy over his own body but rejects his claim to receive a share of the profits reaped from the valuable cell line derived from his spleen cells. In addition, *Hecht v. Superior Court* ultimately held that a man may bestow his sperm upon a lover, but the recipient may not trade the sperm to others. These decisions differentiate between self-ownership and sale of the body to others, while separating the rights of intimate relatives from the interests of strangers. Although such subtle distinctions are alien to property law, they are entirely consistent with the right of privacy.[59]

Also consider the following argument by Sonia Suter:

> As property rights increasingly dominate the world of genetics, it seems only natural to use property rights to protect an individual's interest in his or her own genetic information. . . [However,] the property model is deeply problematic as a tool to protect our interests in genetic information. . . . At heart, the term "property" connotes control within the marketplace and therefore protects economic interests in genetic information. "Privacy," in contrast, connotes a different kind of control — control over access to the self as well as things close to, intimately connected to, and about the self. It therefore has the potential to protect us against the many ways in which we and our relationships are made vulnerable by improper uses of genetic information. . . .

---

[59] Radhika Rao, *Property, Privacy, and the Human Body*, 80 B.U. L. Rev. 359 (2000).

> [When viewed as property,] [g]enetic information is seen as a commodity, disaggregated from the self, rather than something in which we have a dignitary and personhood interest. In addition, even when the property model successfully protects some of the interests we have in our genetic information, the property model undermines the relationships in which we share this information, pushing them toward arms-length transactions as opposed to relationships of trust. Using property rights in this context, in other words, harms the individual and the relationships around which genetic information is disclosed in a way that privacy does not.[60]

7. ***State Genetic Privacy Statutes.*** At least 18 states have passed statutes protecting the privacy of genetic information.[61] In 1996, New Jersey passed the Genetic Privacy Act, N.J.S.A. §§ 10:5-43 *et seq.,* one of the broadest state protections of genetic privacy. The Act prohibits discrimination based on genetic information. The Act further limits the collection, retention, or disclosure of genetic information about an individual without first obtaining the individual's informed consent. Exceptions include the use of genetic information by law enforcement for the purposes of establishing the identity of a person in the course of a criminal investigation, to determine paternity, to determine the identity of deceased individuals, and a number of other exceptions. Section 7 declares: "An individual's genetic information is the property of the individual." Among exceptions to the retention restriction, Section 7 provides for retention if it "is for anonymous research where the identity of the subject will not be released." Section 8 provides, subject to certain exceptions, that "[r]egardless of the manner of receipt or the source of genetic information, including information received from an individual, a person may not disclose or be compelled, by subpoena or other means, to disclose the identity of an individual upon whom a genetic test has been performed or to disclose genetic information about the individual in a manner that permits identification of the individual."

   How does the Act deal with the trade-off in *Moore* between property rights and research? How does the Act affect the case of *Safer v. Estate of Pack,* where the court held that a duty of care may require a doctor to disclose genetic information about a parent to a child?

8. ***The "Future Diary" Metaphor.*** Consider George Annas, who contends that genetic information constitutes a "future diary" about individuals:

   > First, let us examine the nature of privacy and why genetic information is private. The first thing that must be understood is that all your genetic information is contained in the nucleus of each of your cells. All that a geneticist needs is one cell from you to read your genetic code. It could be a blood cell — most genetic testing is done with blood cells. It could also be hair cells or even saliva. Once someone has a drop of your blood, or, perhaps,

---

[60] Sonia M. Suter, *Disentangling Privacy from Property: Toward a Deeper Understanding of Genetic Privacy,* 72 Geo. Wash. L. Rev. 737, 739-40, 746-47 (2004).

[61] *See* Joy Pritts, Janlori Goldman, Zoe Hudson, Aimee Berenson & Elizabeth Hadley, *The State of Health Privacy: An Uneven Terrain (A Comprehensive Survey of State Health Privacy Statutes)* (1999), available at http://www.georgetown.edu/research/ihcrp/privacy/statereport.pdf.

> hair or saliva, they have your DNA from which your genetic code can be extracted.
>
> Therefore, we have to think of one drop of blood as a medical record. It is in code, it is a code that has not been broken yet, and it will require sophisticated codebreakers to break it. But the fact remains that it is a complete record of your DNA. You do not have to agree with many boosters of the Genome Project who think it is the Book of Life, that your DNA is going to tell the story of your life. I would not get that carried away, but it does contain an enormous amount of information about you and your probable medical future.[62]

Pauline Kim argues that "[t]he metaphor of genes as a 'blueprint' or 'future diary' is misleading. It suggests that our genetic material determines our future in some fixed, unalterable way."[63] Consider Judge Douglas Ginsburg's critique of the "future diary" metaphor:

> I believe it was Dr. Annas who coined the term "future diary" to describe the information in our genes. The metaphor derives its power from the jealousy with which people guard the secrets in their written diaries and therefore implicitly supports genetic exceptionalism. Upon analysis, however, the metaphor breaks down. First, our future diaries are much less diverse than our written ones: "while a child is 99.95 percent the same as its genetic mother at the level of the DNA molecule, it is also 99.90 percent the same as any randomly chosen person on the planet earth." Second, unlike the past thoughts and actions contained in our written diaries, the secrets that our future diaries are supposed to hold, like our family histories, speak only to probabilities. . . .
>
> The sober, unexciting realization that genetic information is but the latest iteration of our evolving medical knowledge yields one final suggestion: areas in which changes in degree are endemic are not well suited to statutory solutions. Courts, following in the common law tradition, can address the issues that genetic information raises as the extension of an existing phenomenon. Recognizing that genetic information is not qualitatively different from other types of medical information allows courts to draw upon past experience and to adapt that experience to meet new challenges. Engrafting a unique statutory solution for genetic information onto this common law landscape will simply create two divergent legal regimes for what is essentially a single problem.[64]

Which of these views of genetic information do you find most convincing? Which metaphor is likely to help shape the best legal approach?

3. GENETIC TESTING AND DISCRIMINATION

Information About Genetic Disorders. A genetic disorder occurs as a result of a particular genetic mutation. Sometimes, a mutation of a single gene alone can cause the disorder. Sometimes, disorders are caused by many mutated genes

---

[62] George J. Annas, *Genetic Privacy: There Ought to Be a Law,* 4 Tex. Rev. L. & Pol. 9 (1999).

[63] Pauline T. Kim, *Genetic Discrimination, Genetic Privacy: Rethinking Employee Protections for a Brave New Workplace*, 96 Nw. U. L. Rev. 1497, 1536-37 (2002).

[64] Douglas H. Ginsburg, *Genetics and Privacy,* 4 Tex. Rev. L. & Pol. 17 (1999).

and environmental factors. Genetic testing can give people the opportunity to find out if they have a high risk of contracting certain genetic disorders — such as cystic fibrosis, muscular dystrophy, Huntington's disease, and some rare forms of breast and colon cancer. Often, genetic testing does not predict with 100 percent accuracy whether a person will come down with a particular disorder. But it can predict that the risks will be very high for contracting certain disorders.

The information that a person has a high risk to contract a disorder that is disabling or fatal is not merely of use to that person, but also is of great interest to one's spouse, fiancée, or partner. Additionally, such information is useful to one's health or life insurer, since having the disorder dramatically affects the potential risk the insurer expects as well as the level of insurance payments it demands. It may be of interest to one's creditors, who might not want to risk lending money to a borrower who is at high risk of contracting a fatal disorder. Further, it may be of interest to one's employer, who may not want to spend the time, resources, and money training a worker who may have to retire earlier than expected. Employers that self-insure may also be interested in the information, as the potential employee will affect the employer's financial condition.

Genetic Testing by Employers. Currently, most companies do not require genetic testing, but 20 percent require data about the medical history of employees' families, which can serve as a source for genetic information.[65] In 2001, Burlington Northern Santa Fe Railroad secretly tested employees suffering from carpal tunnel syndrome to see if they were genetically predisposed to coming down with the condition. When the testing came to light, and the company was sued by the EEOC and a workers' union, the company settled, agreeing to halt the testing. Thirty states have statutes restricting employers from gathering, using, and/or disclosing employee genetic data.[66]

The Genetic Information Nondiscrimination Act. In 2008, Congress enacted the Genetic Information Nondiscrimination Act (GINA). This statute prevents insurance companies and employers from using genetic tests to deny individuals health coverage or employment. In enacting the statute, Congress found, "Federal law addressing genetic discrimination in health insurance and employment is incomplete in both the scope and depth and its protections." The findings to the statute also noted that state laws "vary widely with respect to their approach, application, and level of protection."

In its Title I, GINA prohibits genetic discrimination in health insurance. It does so by forbidding insurers, whether in the group or individual market, from adjusting "premium or contribution amounts" on the basis of genetic information. In its Title II, it prohibits employment discrimination on the basis of genetic information. It is an unfair employment practice for an employer "to fail, or refuse to hire, or to discharge, any employee, or otherwise to discriminate against any employee" because of genetic information. GINA also prohibits an employee

---

[65] *See* Health Privacy Project, *Report: Genetics and Privacy: A Patchwork of Protections* 19 (2002).

[66] National Conference of State Legislatures, http://www.ncsl.org/programs/health/genetics/ndiscrim.htm.

from requesting, requiring, or purchasing genetic information about any employee, subject, however, to some exception.

The Equal Employment Opportunity Commission is to enforce the statute. GINA does not, however, cover the use of genetic testing results in life insurance, or long term care and disability insurance. Before enactment of this statute, Richard Epstein and Paul Schwartz considered the merits of such legislation. Epstein was against such a law; Schwartz was in favor.

RICHARD A. EPSTEIN, *THE LEGAL REGULATION OF GENETIC DISCRIMINATION: OLD RESPONSES TO NEW TECHNOLOGY*

74 B.U. L. Rev. 1 (1994)

. . . Must the person disclose the information [learned from a genetic test] to other parties? I think that in the case of Huntington's disease it is immoral for a person to marry (or even take a job) and conceal the condition from the potential spouse or employer. This conclusion is valid in commercial settings as well as in marital ones so long as the concealment results in selective knowledge to one side that is denied to the other. When an individual has knowledge that he is at risk of incapacitation, perhaps from family history, then full disclosure should be the norm. When the individual knows to a certainty that he is a carrier of the trait, from a reliable genetic test, the same is true. The principle does not change; all that changes is the information that must be disclosed. . . .

At this point it is critical to note that the plea for privacy is often a plea for the right to misrepresent one's self to the rest of the world. In and of itself that may not be a bad thing. We are certainly not obligated to disclose all of our embarrassing past to persons in ordinary social conversations; and it is certainly acceptable to use long sleeves to cover an ugly scar. White lies are part of the glue that makes human interaction possible without shame and loss of face. Strictly speaking, people may be deceived, but they are rarely hurt, and they may even be relieved to be spared an awkward encounter. However, when a major change in personal or financial status is contemplated by another party, the white lies that make human interaction possible turn into frauds of a somewhat deeper dye. In order to see why this is the case, recall that the traditional tort of misrepresentation stressed the usual five fingers: a false statement, known to be false, material to the listener, and relied on, to the listener's detriment. There is little question, whether we deal with marriage or with business, that concealment of relevant genetic information satisfies each element. The only question, therefore, is whether one can justify what is a prima facie wrong.

I am hard pressed to see what that justification might be. No doubt the individual who engages in this type of deception has much to gain. But equally there can be no doubt that this gain exists in all garden variety cases of fraud as well. To show the advantage of the fraud to the party who commits it is hardly to excuse or to justify it, for the same can be said of all cases of successful wrongs. On the other side of the transaction, there is a pronounced loss from not knowing the information when key decisions have to be made. . . .

False statements about or deliberate concealment of genetic information is as much a fraud as false statements about or concealment of any other issue. The only possible justification for concealment, therefore, would be that it is unfair for the person with the pending disorder to deal alone with the suffering and financial loss. Yet, that loss is not sustained because of the wrong of another. Could the victim of a natural catastrophe keep it secret, and single out one other person to bear some substantial fraction of the loss? If not, then why give that same privilege to the victim of a genetic defect? Today, it is easy to find strong support for socializing losses. But why should a person laboring under a genetic defect be entitled to pick the person or group that has to pay the subsidy? . . .

PAUL M. SCHWARTZ, *PRIVACY AND THE ECONOMICS OF HEALTH CARE INFORMATION*

76 Tex. L. Rev. 1 (1997)

. . . Most people who receive health benefits in this country obtain it at their place of employment. In the United States approximately 140 million people, or nearly two-thirds of the population under sixty-five, receive medical benefits through their job. Because these benefits are an increasingly costly part of the overall package of compensation, employers have a great incentive to weed out workers with expensive health care needs. Despite any amount of soothing statements about the rationality of employers, the actual use of genetic information and health records in employment decisions is far from efficient. . . .

The argument against [Richard Epstein's] position is greatly strengthened by the generally poor societal record in this area; a considerable historical pattern exists of misapplication of [genetic] information. This story begins with the eugenics movement, whose misunderstanding and deformation of genetic science encouraged public policies that included the sterilization of "inferior" members of society. As for the recent era of modern genetics, the United States has far from a perfect record. Genetic discrimination already takes place in the United States. Studies by scientists at Stanford and Harvard have documented numerous instances of genetic discrimination in the public and private sectors. Another study found a high rate of discrimination in obtaining insurance and employment for people who have a genetic condition or for their family members. Many of these individuals will never suffer from any genetic illness; yet, the testing process itself creates a category of individuals now deemed to be genetically unfit. . . .

Like genetic information, health care data are also being used to make employment decisions. According to one empirical study of privacy in the workplace, over one-third of Fortune 500 companies surveyed in 1995 admitted to using the medical records of their personnel in employment-related decisions. In previous years, this survey found that as many as one-half of these companies admitted to engaging in such behavior. Evidence also indicates that some of this reliance on employees' health data is leading to economically inefficient employment decisions. According to a recent nationwide survey, for example, cancer patients currently lose their jobs at over five times the rate of those who do not have the disease. Considerable ignorance has also been found regarding the workplace implications of this disease; another survey found common overestimation by supervisors of the actual experience of cancer patients regarding fatigue, infections, and nausea during treatment. To consider another socially charged illness, one can point to evidence that greater insurance discrimination is faced by those who are HIV-positive than individuals who suffer from equally serious illnesses with similar costs. Discrimination between employees with different health conditions can be based on social stigma and misunderstandings rather than the relative costs of different workers' medical conditions. . . .

. . . The individual to whom these data refer faces a high price when attempting to explain the significance or insignificance of the information, and these explanatory costs can exceed the value of unrestricted disclosure to society. Indeed, many parties, including employers, believe that they are not ignorant about the full dimensions or implications of certain personal data, and will continue to (mis)apply genetic personal information based simply on their popular beliefs. Thus, achieving economic efficiency necessitates placing certain kinds of limits on access to personal information because of the excessive social costs of placing such data in the proper context under a policy of unrestricted access. . .

An excessive disclosure norm for certain kinds of information will distort or eliminate the kinds of personal information that health care consumers share in future transactions with physicians. . . . Inadequate safeguards for protecting medical data will make the encounters that take place between physicians and patients less effective because of the likelihood that patients will withhold important information. . .

Open access to health care or genetic information has a final negative effect on individual behavior. It ties individuals to current jobs out of the fear that they will be denied new employment or health insurance. . . . These workers were afraid that their health history or that of family members would lead a new insurer to reject or limit their coverage. As this Article has indicated, such fears are far from baseless. The resulting phenomenon, which has been termed "job lock," introduces significant distortions in the labor market. As health care economist Victor Fuchs notes, "[L]abor market efficiency suffers" when health insurance considerations affect workers' choices of jobs and decisions about job change. . .

To summarize our argument thus far, employers are not making purely rational use of medical and genetic data. Rather, this information provides an excuse for the exercise of social stigma and misunderstandings of science. Open access to these data also distorts individual behavior by encouraging patients to share incomplete data with physicians and by causing employees to be locked in jobs that they would otherwise leave. Moreover, open disclosure permits certain workers to be cast off into an increasingly strained public insurance market. This process has contributed to an increase in aggregate health care costs. . .

NOTES & QUESTIONS

1. ***Executive Order 13145.*** On February 8, 2000, President Clinton issued Executive Order 13145: To Prohibit Discrimination in Federal Employment Based on Genetic Information. It applies to all Executive departments and agencies with regard to all employees covered by § 717 of Title VII of the Civil Rights Act of 1964. The Order protects "protected genetic information," which is defined as "information about an individual's genetic tests," "information about the genetic tests of an individual's family members," or "information about the occurrence of a disease, or medical condition or disorder in family members of the individual." Pursuant to the Order:

> (a) The employing department or agency shall not discharge, fail or refuse to hire, or otherwise discriminate against any employee with respect to the compensation, terms, conditions, or privileges of employment of that employee, because of protected genetic information with respect to the employee, or because of information about a request for or the receipt of genetic services by such employee.
>
> (b) The employing department or agency shall not limit, segregate, or classify employees in any way that would deprive or tend to deprive any employee of employment opportunities or otherwise adversely affect that employee's status, because of protected genetic information with respect to the employee or because of information about a request for or the receipt of genetic services by such employee.
>
> (c) The employing department or agency shall not request, require, collect, or purchase protected genetic information with respect to an employee, or information about a request for or the receipt of genetic services by such employee.

2. ***State Law, Genetic Discrimination, and Preemption Under GINA.*** As of 2002, 30 states have laws prohibiting employment discrimination based on genetic information.[67] Thirty-four states have statutes barring the use of genetic data by insurers for risk classification.[68] GINA states that it does not "limit the rights or protections of an individual under any other Federal or State statute that provides equal or greater protection to an individual than the rights or protections provided for under this title." § 209(a). GINA therefore sets a federal preemptive "floor" and not a "ceiling." State laws may exceed its protection, but GINA supplants weaker state laws, or adds protections for those states that lack a law prohibiting employment discrimination based on genetic data.
3. ***Is Genetic Information Different?*** Recall from Chapter 1 Judge Posner's view that privacy is a desire to misrepresent oneself, a type of fraud. How does this compare to Epstein's view of privacy? Suppose a person has diabetes, heart disease, or cancer. In an application for health or life insurance, that person would have to disclose all preexisting conditions. Otherwise, the individual would be committing a fraud if she deliberately left out health conditions that she was aware of. Why not view the knowledge of genetic predisposition the same way? What is the difference between the nondisclosure of regular medical information versus genetic information?

[67] National Conference of State Legislatures, http://www.ncsl.org/programs/health/genetics/ndiscrim.htm.

[68] National Conference of State Legislatures, http://www.ncsl.org/programs/health/genetics/ndishlth.htm.

4. ***Combating Genetic Discrimination: Discrimination Law vs. Privacy Law.*** What is the best way to combat genetic discrimination? Consider the following argument by Pauline Kim:

> [T]he analogy between genetic discrimination, and race and sex discrimination, is fundamentally flawed. . . . For example, the societal consensus condemning race discrimination emerged in reaction to a history of systematic social disadvantage imposed on identifiable groups of people because of their race. By contrast, the threat of genetic discrimination is entirely prospective; advocates fear new technologies will be misused to reveal hidden information that will disadvantage certain individuals. In the employment context, race and sex discrimination are believed to be wrong because those characteristics are irrelevant to a worker's ability to perform the job. However, genetic technologies offer the potential to provide information that is arguably relevant to an employee's future job performance.

Kim suggests that the law of privacy is more suited to redressing the harms of genetic discrimination than discrimination law:

> As a practical matter, then, prohibiting employer reliance on genetic traits presents a different challenge than prohibiting discrimination based on an easily observed characteristic such as race or sex. Because employer knowledge of an employee's race or sex is nearly always unavoidable, preventing race discrimination requires direct prohibition of a discriminatory motive. By contrast, employers cannot detect genetic anomalies by casual observation. The issue of genetic privacy, then, is prior to that of discrimination. If employers have access to workers' genetic information, divining when they have used that information improperly will be extremely difficult. If, however, that information is unavailable, discrimination on the basis of genetic traits becomes impossible. Those concerned about preventing genetic discrimination, then, ought to be concerned first and foremost with protecting the privacy of workers' genetic information.[69]

4. DNA DATABASES AND IDENTIFICATION

One current use of DNA is known as "DNA fingerprinting" or "DNA typing."[70] This involves the comparison of DNA from two samples. At a crime scene, most often with violent crimes, the criminal might have unwittingly deposited genetic material. A pulled-out hair, a drop of blood, a scratched-off skin cell, semen, and so on can enable forensic scientists to extract DNA. The entire genome is not used, only particular portions or fragments of DNA that are known to contain differences among individuals. An early method of analyzing DNA was restriction fragment length polymorphism (RFLP). DNA was extracted from samples using special enzymes and cut into fragments and organized by size. These fragments were then exposed on X-ray film, where they formed a pattern of dark bands, which are unique to each type of DNA. Today, a newer

---

[69] Pauline T. Kim, *Genetic Discrimination, Genetic Privacy: Rethinking Employee Protections for a Brave New Workplace*, 96 Nw. U. L. Rev. 1497, 1500, 1537 (2002).

[70] For a legal discussion of DNA fingerprinting, see Dan L. Burk & Jennifer A. Hess, *Genetic Privacy: Constitutional Considerations in Forensic DNA Testing*, 5 Geo. Mason U. Civ. Rts. L.J. 1 (1994).

technology called "short tandem repeat" (STR) analysis is the most common method of DNA typing. STR analysis examines length polymorphisms known as "short tandem repeats."[71]

The fact that a suspect's DNA matches the DNA found at a crime scene does not indicate with certainty that the suspect is likely to be the culprit or even is likely to have been at the crime scene. Statistically, a portion of the population will match the DNA found at a crime scene. What DNA evidence can determine with near certainty is that certain individuals do not match the DNA at the scene. In other words, DNA evidence can more accurately exclude individuals as suspects than include them.

Since DNA has proven to be a very useful tool for forensic scientists in solving crimes, the states and the FBI are assembling DNA databases of felons. All states permit DNA to be taken from sex offenders and other violent criminals. There is currently a push to expand DNA collection to all arrestees. The FBI maintains a national DNA database known as the "Combined DNA Indexing System" (CODIS).[72] These DNA databases do not contain a person's entire genetic code, just fragments useful for identification. Currently, in the United States, the collection of DNA is limited to those convicted or accused of a crime. There are some notable exceptions, one of which is the U.S. military, which maintains a DNA database for identification of the remains of soldiers in combat. For the most part, however, the government does not collect DNA from ordinary citizens to help solve crimes.

In contrast, Britain more widely collects DNA from its citizens. In 1987, British authorities collected DNA samples from every male citizen in Leicestershire after two young women were raped. This technique has been dubbed a "DNA dragnet," and this case was explored in depth in Joseph Wambaugh's *The Blooding* (1989). Since 1995, British authorities have been collecting DNA from everybody taken into police custody. The British government has plans to expand its DNA database to allow the retention of the DNA of individuals later found to be innocent. In many other countries, such DNA profiles are destroyed.

DNA databases can be used for purposes other than solving crimes. As scientists better understand the human genome, additional uses for genetic information will arise.

The following case involves a Fourth Amendment challenge to the creation of a DNA database. For the purposes of understanding this case, the Fourth Amendment requires that searches (looking around for evidence) and seizures (taking of items and evidence) be "reasonable" and generally be authorized by a warrant supported by probable cause. The warrant requirement ensures that a neutral judge or magistrate approves of the search and that the police have a good justification for a search. This typically means "individualized suspicion" — that there is a good reason to suspect that a particular individual has engaged in a crime. This requirement prevents searches that are "fishing expeditions."

---

[71] *See* William C. Thompson, *DNA Testing*, in 2 *Encyclopedia of Crime and Punishment* 537 (David Levinson, ed. 2002).

[72] *See id.*

However, there are exceptions to the warrant requirement, as indicated by the case below.

UNITED STATES V. KINCADE

379 F.3d 813 (9th Cir. 2004) (en banc)

O'SCANNLAIN, J. (for the plurality). . . . Pursuant to the DNA Analysis Backlog Elimination Act of 2000 ("DNA Act"), individuals who have been convicted of certain federal crimes[73] and who are incarcerated, or on parole, probation, or supervised release must provide federal authorities with "a tissue, fluid, or other bodily sample . . . on which a[n] . . . analysis of the [sample's] deoxyribonucleic acid (DNA) identification information" can be performed. . . .

Once collected by a phlebotomist, qualified federal offenders' blood samples are turned over to the [FBI] for DNA analysis — the identification and recording of an individual's "genetic fingerprint." Through the use of short tandem repeat technology ("STR"), the Bureau analyzes the presence of various alleles located at 13 markers (or loci) on DNA present in the specimen. These STR loci are each found on so-called "junk DNA" — that is, non-genic stretches of DNA not presently recognized as being responsible for trait coding — and "were purposely selected because they are not associated with any known physical or medical characteristics." Because there are observed group variances in the representation of various alleles at the STR loci, however, DNA profiles derived by STR may yield probabilistic evidence of the contributor's race or sex. . . .

Once STR has been used to produce an individual's DNA profile, the resulting record is loaded into the Bureau's Combined DNA Index System ("CODIS") — a massive centrally-managed database linking DNA profiles culled from federal, state, and territorial DNA collection programs, as well as profiles drawn from crime-scene evidence, unidentified remains, and genetic samples voluntarily provided by relatives of missing persons. 42 U.S.C. §§ 14132(a)-(b) As of March 2004, CODIS contained DNA profiles drawn from 1,641,076 offenders and 78,475 crime scenes. . . .

CODIS can be used in two different ways. First, law enforcement can match one forensic crime scene sample to another forensic crime scene sample, thereby allowing officers to connect unsolved crimes through a common perpetrator.

---

[73] As enumerated by the initial terms of the DNA Act, these "qualifying federal offenses" included murder, voluntary manslaughter, aggravated assault, sexual abuse, child abuse, kidnapping, robbery, burglary, arson, and any attempt or conspiracy to commit such crimes. *See* 42 U.S.C. § 14135a(d)(1). With passage of the PATRIOT Act, Pub. L. No. 107-56, § 503, 115 Stat. 272, 364 (2001), acts of terrorism (as defined in 18 U.S.C. 2332b(g)(5)(B)) and additional crimes of violence (as defined in 18 U.S.C. § 16) have been added to the ranks of qualifying federal offenses. *See* 42 U.S.C. § 14135a(d)(2). A complete list of qualifying federal offenses can be found at 28 C.F.R. § 28.2. Although the federal offender provisions of the DNA Act are most relevant here, we note that the Act reaches beyond the federal arena. Subsidiary provisions provide for collection and storage of DNA information from offenders subject to the jurisdiction of the District of Columbia, 42 U.S.C. § 14135b, and the Armed Forces, 10 U .S.C. § 1565. The Act also appropriates $170 million to support state efforts to collect and to store DNA profiles from state offenders and crime scene evidence. 42 U.S.C. §§ 14135(a) & (j). Partially as a result, every state in the Union now operates a DNA collection program. A regularly updated summary of state DNA legislation can be found at http://www.dnaresource.com.

Second, and of perhaps greater significance, CODIS enables officials to match evidence obtained at the scene of a crime to a particular offender's profile. In this latter capacity, CODIS serves as a potent tool for monitoring the criminal activity of known offenders. Through March 2004, Bureau data indicated that CODIS has aided some 16,160 investigations nationwide. . . .

On July 20, 1993, driven by escalating personal and financial troubles, decorated Navy seaman Thomas Cameron Kincade robbed a bank using a firearm. . . . He pleaded guilty . . . and was sentenced to 97 months imprisonment, followed by three years' supervised release. . . .

On March 25, 2002, Kincade's probation officer asked him to submit a blood sample pursuant to the DNA Act. He refused, eventually explaining that his objections were purely a matter of personal preference — in his words, "not a religious conviction." . . . [The court concluded that Kincade's refusal to follow his probation officer's order was a violation of his supervised release. Kincade was sentenced to four months' imprisonment. Kincade challenges the DNA Act under the Fourth Amendment.]

"The touchstone of our analysis under the Fourth Amendment is always 'the reasonableness in all the circumstances of the particular governmental invasion of a citizen's personal security.'" *Pennsylvania v. Mimms,* 434 U.S. 106 (1977) (quoting *Terry v. Ohio,* 392 U.S. 1 (1968)).

Ordinarily, the reasonableness of a search depends on governmental compliance with the Warrant Clause, which requires authorities to demonstrate probable cause to a neutral magistrate and thereby convince him to provide formal authorization to proceed with a search by issuance of a particularized warrant. However, the general rule of the Warrant Clause is not unyielding. . . .

[T]he Court's more recent "special needs" cases have emphasized the absence of any law enforcement motive underlying the challenged search and seizure. . . .

In [*Indianapolis v. Edmond,* 531 U.S. 32 (2000)], the Court addressed whether the . . . police department lawfully could operate a program of random vehicle checkpoints in an effort to interdict illegal drugs. . . . Two of the detained motorists eventually sued, alleging that such suspicionless law enforcement detentions violated the Fourth Amendment. Siding with the motorists, the Court explained that it had never approved a checkpoint program "whose primary purpose was to detect evidence of ordinary criminal wrongdoing." . . .

In [*Ferguson v. City of Charleston,* 532 U.S. 67 (2001)], the Court addressed whether a public hospital lawfully could share pregnant women's positive drug tests with law enforcement in an effort to help solve the epidemic of "crack babies." . . . [B]ecause "the immediate objective of the searches was to generate evidence *for law enforcement purposes,*" and in light of "the extensive involvement of law enforcement officials at every stage of the policy," the Court concluded that "this case simply does not fit within the closely guarded category of 'special needs.'" . . .

While these recent cases may seem to be moving toward requiring that *any* search conducted primarily for law enforcement purposes must be accompanied by at least some quantum of individualized suspicion, the Court signaled the existence of possible limitations in *United States v. Knights,* 534 U.S. 112 (2001). At issue there was a warrantless search of a probationer long suspected of having committed crimes targeting Pacific Gas & Electric ("PG & E") facilities. [The police engaged in a warrantless search of the probationer's (Knights) home.] . . .

. . . [The Court balanced] the invasion of Knights's interest in privacy against the State's interest in searching his home without a warrant supported by probable cause. . . . With regard to Knights's interest in privacy, the Court observed:

> Inherent in the very nature of probation is that probationers do not enjoy the absolute liberty to which every citizen is entitled. . . . The judge who sentenced Knights to probation determined that it was necessary to condition the probation on Knights's acceptance of the search provision. . . . The probation condition thus significantly diminished Knights's reasonable expectation of privacy. . . .

Having thus upheld a warrantless probation search designed purely to further law enforcement purposes, and having done so wholly outside the confines of special needs analysis, *Knights* suggests something of a departure from *Edmond* and *Ferguson*. . . .

One possible distinction between *Knights,* on one hand, and *Edmond* and *Ferguson,* on the other, suggests a possible reconciliation: The search conducted in *Knights* was supported by reasonable suspicion, while the Court's most recent special needs cases have focused on suspicionless searches and seizures, such as the DNA profiling at issue here. *See, e.g., Lidster,* 124 S. Ct. at 889; *Ferguson,* 532 U.S. at 76-77; *Edmond,* 531 U.S. at 37-38. One might therefore be tempted to conclude that the quantum of suspicion supporting the search of Knights's apartment was what pushed the Court beyond special needs analysis.

We do not think so. . . .

. . . [I]t remains *entirely* an open question whether suspicionless searches of conditional releasees pass constitutional muster when such searches are conducted for law enforcement purposes. . . .

[The court concluded that the totality of the circumstances test, rather than the special needs approach, should govern in this case because "conditional releasees enjoy severely constricted expectations of privacy relative to the general citizenry — and that the government has a far more substantial interest in invading their privacy than it does in interfering with the liberty of law-abiding citizens."]

We also wish to emphasize the limited nature of our holding. With its alarmist tone and obligatory reference to George Orwell's *1984,* Judge Reinhardt's dissent repeatedly asserts that our decision renders every person in America subject to DNA sampling for CODIS purposes, including "attendees of public high schools or universities, persons seeking to obtain drivers' licenses, applicants for federal employment, or persons requiring any form of federal identification, and those who desire to travel by airplane," "political opponents," "disfavored minorities," "all newborns," "passengers of vehicles," "arrestees," — no, really, "the entire population." Nothing could be further from the truth — and we respectfully suggest that our dissenting colleague ought to recognize the obvious and significant distinction between the DNA profiling of law-abiding citizens who are passing through some transient status (*e.g.,* newborns, students, passengers in a car or on a plane) and lawfully adjudicated criminals whose proven conduct substantially heightens the government's interest in monitoring them and quite properly carries lasting consequences that simply do not attach from the simple fact of having been born, or going to public school, or riding in a car.

With this framework in mind, we can now appraise the reasonableness of the federal DNA Act's compulsory DNA profiling of qualified federal offenders. In evaluating the totality of the circumstances, we must balance the degree to which DNA profiling interferes with the privacy interests of qualified federal offenders against the significance of the public interests served by such profiling.

As we have recognized, compulsory blood tests implicate the individual's interest in bodily integrity — "a cherished value of our society." *Schmerber v. California,* 384 U.S. 757 (1966). Nonetheless, it is firmly established that "the intrusion occasioned by a blood test is not significant, since such 'tests are a commonplace in these days of periodic physical examinations.'" . . .

At the same time, the DNA profile derived from the defendant's blood sample establishes only a record of the defendant's identity — otherwise personal information in which the qualified offender can claim no right of privacy once lawfully convicted of a qualifying offense (indeed, once lawfully arrested and booked into state custody). . . .

The concerns raised by amici and by Judge Reinhardt in his dissent are indeed weighty ones, and we do not dismiss them lightly. . . . In our system of government, courts base decisions not on dramatic Hollywood fantasies. . . . If, as Kincade's aligned amici and Judge Reinhardt's dissent insist, and when, some future program permits the parade of horribles the DNA Act's opponents fear . . . we have every confidence that courts will respond appropriately. As currently structured and implemented, however, the DNA Act's compulsory profiling of qualified federal offenders can only be described as minimally invasive — both in terms of the bodily intrusion it occasions, and the information it lawfully produces.

In contrast, the interests furthered by the federal DNA Act are undeniably compelling. By establishing a means of identification that can be used to link conditional releasees to crimes committed while they are at large, compulsory DNA profiling serves society's "'overwhelming interest' in ensuring that a parolee complies with the requirements [of his release] and is returned to prison if he fails to do so." The deterrent effect of such profiling similarly fosters society's enormous interest in reducing recidivism. . . . Finally, by contributing to the solution of past crimes, DNA profiling of qualified federal offenders helps bring closure to countless victims of crime who long have languished in the knowledge that perpetrators remain at large. Together, the weight of these interests is monumental. . . .

. . . [We] conclude that compulsory DNA profiling of qualified federal offenders is reasonable under the totality of the circumstances. . . . [T]he DNA Act satisfies the requirements of the Fourth Amendment. . . .

REINHARDT, PREGERSON, KOZINSKI, AND WARDLAW, J.J. dissenting. Today this court approves the latest installment in the federal government's effort to construct a comprehensive national database into which basic information concerning American citizens will be entered and stored for the rest of their lives

— although no majority exists with respect to the legal justification for this conclusion. . . . We would be lucky indeed if it were possible to so limit the effect of their opinions. For, under the rationales they espouse, . . . all Americans will be at risk, sooner rather than later, of having our DNA samples permanently placed on file in federal cyberspace, and perhaps even worse, of being subjected to various other governmental programs providing for suspicionless searches conducted for law enforcement purposes.

Neither Supreme Court precedent nor any established rule of Fourth Amendment law supports today's plurality or concurring opinion. Never has the Court approved of a search like the one we confront today: a programmatic search designed to produce and maintain evidence relating to ordinary criminal wrongdoing, yet conducted without any level of individualized suspicion. . . .

The approval of such a program carries with it all of the dangers inherent in allowing the government to collect and store information about its citizens in a centralized place. J. Edgar Hoover terrorized leaders of the civil rights movement by exploiting the information he collected in his files. Our government's surveillance and shameful harassment of suspected communists and alleged communist-sympathizers in the middle of the twentieth century depended largely on the centralization of information collected about countless numbers of non-communist members of our citizenry — often by means that violated the Fourth Amendment. The same was true of the Palmer Raids a few decades earlier and of our roundup of Japanese Americans and their placement in internment camps during World War Two. *See generally* Daniel J. Solove, *Digital Dossiers and the Dissipation of Fourth Amendment Privacy,* 75 S. Cal. L. Rev. 1083 (2002).

Even governments with benign intentions have proven unable to regulate or use wisely vast stores of information they collect regarding their citizens. The problem with allowing the government to collect and maintain private information about the intimate details of our lives is that the bureaucracy most often in charge of the information "is poorly regulated and susceptible to abuse. This [ ] has profound social effects because it alters the balance of power between the government and the people, exposing individuals to a series of harms, increasing their vulnerability and decreasing the degree of power that they exercise over their lives." *Id.* at 1105. To allow such information to be collected through the compulsory extraction of blood from the bodies of non-consenting Americans runs contrary to the values on which this country was founded. . . .

The unequivocal purpose of the searches performed pursuant to the DNA Act is to generate the sort of ordinary investigatory evidence used by law enforcement officials for everyday law enforcement purposes. The government maintained from the outset of this litigation that the purpose of the searches authorized by the DNA Act is to "help law enforcement solve unresolved and future cases." Moreover, it is plain that in passing the DNA Act, Congress's primary concern was the swift and accurate solution and prosecution of crimes as a general matter. . . .

The searches are designed to reveal at some point in time whether the individuals whose blood samples are involuntarily extracted have "committed some crime." This is the paradigmatic search condemned by the special needs doctrine. . . .

[The totality of the circumstances approach does not apply in this context.]

Indeed, the "totality of the circumstances" test was designed to guide the Court in its probable cause and reasonable suspicion determinations. The test has never been used, however, to justify suspicionless law enforcement searches. To the contrary, in "totality of the circumstances" cases, the presence of *some level* of suspicion has always been a given and a *sine qua non.* Cases involving suspicionless programmatic search regimes are not "general" Fourth Amendment cases. That is why the plurality cannot cite a single case that has applied the totality of the circumstances test to a regime of suspicionless searches. . . .

KOZINSKI, J. dissenting: . . . Once Kincade completes his period of supervised release, he becomes an ordinary citizen just like everyone else. Having paid his debt to society, he recovers his full Fourth Amendment rights, and police have no greater authority to invade his private sphere than anyone else's. The difficult question is whether the government may exploit Kincade's diminished Fourth Amendment rights while he is still a probationer to obtain his DNA signature, so it can use it in investigating thousands of crimes nationwide, past and future, for the rest of Kincade's life. . . . Stripped of its bells and whistles, the plurality's theory seems to be this: We have a pretty good idea that people who have committed crimes in the past are more likely than others to commit crimes in the future. It is thus very, very, very useful for us to get their DNA fingerprints now so we can use them later to investigate crimes. . . .

If collecting DNA fingerprints can be justified on the basis of the plurality's multi-factor, gestalt high-wire act, then it's hard to see how we can keep the database from expanding to include everybody. Of course, anyone who already has to give up bodily fluids for alcohol or drug testing — airline pilots, high school athletes, customs inspectors and people suspected of driving while intoxicated — would be easy prey under the mushy multi-factor test. But, with only a little waggling, we can shoehorn the rest of us in. As the plurality notes, blood is taken from us from the day we are born pretty much till the day we die, and on many days in between. What exactly happens to that blood after it leaves our veins? Most of us don't know or care, presuming (if we consider it at all) that whatever isn't used for testing is discarded. But what if Congress were to require medical labs to submit the excess blood for DNA fingerprinting so it can be included in CODIS? . . .

This isn't an issue we can leave for another day. Later, when further expansions of CODIS are proposed, information from the database will have been credited with solving hundreds or thousands of crimes, and we will have become inured to the idea that the government is entitled to hold large databases of DNA fingerprints. This highlights an important aspect of Fourth Amendment opinions: Not only do they reflect today's values by giving effect to people's reasonable expectations of privacy, they also shape future values by changing our experience and altering what we come to expect from our government. A highly expansive opinion like the plurality's, one that draws no hard lines and revels in the boon that new technology will provide to law enforcement, is an engraved invitation to future expansion. And when that inevitable expansion comes, we will look to the regime we approved today as the new baseline and say, this too must be OK because it's just one small step beyond the last thing we approved. My colleagues in the plurality assure us that, when that day comes, they will stand vigilant and guard the line, but by then the line — never very clear to begin with — will have shifted. The fishbowl will look like home. . . .

For the reasons eloquently expressed by Judge Reinhardt in his dissent, and those stated above, I cannot agree that the suspicionless extraction of blood to include Kincade's DNA in the CODIS database can be upheld under the Fourth Amendment. The time to put the cork back in the brass bottle is now — before the genie escapes.

NOTES & QUESTIONS

1. ***DNA Databases: Defining the Privacy Injury.*** What is the privacy injury with regard to the use of DNA databases? Is it the physical invasion of the body to remove the blood? Or is it the fact that DNA can include significant information about a person? Currently, DNA identification only involves a small portion of one's DNA. The entire genome is not mapped out. Sequencing is done for certain known sites where particular genes show a significant variability, as much of our DNA is identical. DNA databases do not contain the entire DNA of an individual but only samples of certain genes. Should this fact alleviate any concern over DNA databases? What if one's entire genome were included in the database?

   According to Gaia Bernstein, DNA samples used in government databases threaten part of a "liberal meta-narrative," one that "posits [the] individual as separate from others." In her view: "What [individuals] hold dearly as signifying their soul is collected together with other samples and at best considered as just another statistic." She concludes: "The knowledge that this 'copy' of the self is out there, merged in insignificantly with those of others and utilized to serve communal goals, is a great source of unease for individuals whose life-narrative is governed by the liberal postulates."[74]

2. ***The Law of DNA Databases.*** Thus far, every other circuit to examine whether DNA databases violate the Fourth Amendment has upheld them. *See, e.g., Jones v. Murray*, 962 F.2d 302 (4th Cir. 1992); *Boling v. Romer,* 101 F.3d 1336 (10th Cir. 1996); *Shaffer v. Saffle*, 148 F.3d 1180 (10th Cir. 1998); *Roe v. Marcotte*, 193 F.3d 72 (2d Cir. 1999).

   However, in *Maryland v. Raines*, 383 Md. 1 (Md. 2003), the appellee contended that the Fourth Amendment proscribes searches similar to the one eventually upheld in *Kincade*. Relying on *Indianapolis v. Edmond*, 531 U.S. 32 (2000), and *Ferguson v. City of Charleston*, 532 U.S. 67 (2001), Raines argued that a search cannot satisfy the reasonableness requirement of the Fourth Amendment where the DNA was seized without any individualized suspicion of criminal conduct. The appellee also argued that the search allowed under the Act cannot fall into the special needs doctrine because the primary purpose of the Act is to assist in the prosecution of crimes. The Maryland court rejected both claims. The court concluded:

---

[74] Gaia Bernstein, *Accommodating Technological Innovation: Identity, Genetic Testing and the Internet,* 57 Vand. L. Rev. 965, 1009-12 (2004).

> [A]ppellee and other incarcerated individuals have little, if any, expectation of privacy in their identity. Therefore, a search like the one authorized by the Act in this case, whose primary purpose is to identify individuals with lessened expectations of privacy, is totally distinguishable from search of ordinary individuals for the purpose of gathering evidence against them in order to prosecute them for the very crimes that the search reveals.

3. ***A National DNA Database?*** What is wrong with the government having a DNA database of convicts and doing searches to identify the perpetrators of crimes? Would your opinion change if the database contained the DNA of everybody, not just those who were convicted of a crime? Would a national DNA database consisting of DNA for every citizen collected through a mandatory collection program be constitutional? Suppose that the DNA were obtained without requiring a physical intrusion into the body. Would this affect your view of the constitutionality of the national DNA database?
4. ***Are DNA Databases Different?*** Does the existence of the DNA databases mean that for offenders in the database, they will always be investigated (by a search in the database) every time there is a sexual or violent crime? Is this any different from what is already done through the use of fingerprints and mug shots?
5. ***DNA Dragnets.*** As Erin Murphy explains, a DNA dragnet involves law enforcement officials investigating an offense by descending on a community and requesting "voluntary submission of DNA samples from the entire eligible population."[75] In 2000, in a small rural Australian village, police used a mass DNA screening investigation technique to identify the man who raped a 91-year-old woman. Villagers were free to refuse the DNA test, but critics said that the DNA testing was not really voluntary because a person who refused would appear guilty in the eyes of the rest of the village. As of 2004, DNA dragnets occurred in the United States in at least 18 instances.[76] They have occurred in Los Angeles, Wichita, San Diego, Ann Arbor, Miami, Oklahoma City, Baton Rouge, Omaha, and other locations. In February 2008, the Daytona Beach Police responded to a serial killer targeting prostitutes by taking DNA samples from "persons of interest" during traffic stops and announcing plans to take DNA samples from anyone arrested in that locality beginning in the near future. Will the scope of DNA "dragnets" spread to involve more and more people? Consider the collection of DNA samples in Daytona Beach during traffic stops. What legal challenges can be raised to DNA dragnets?[77]
6. ***The New Forensics.*** Erin Murphy proposes that a group of modern forensic sciences, which she terms "second-generation sciences," offers both a new degree of certainty as well as a new potential for misuse:

---

[75] Erin Murphy, *The New Forensics,* 95 Cal. L. Rev. 721 (2007).

[76] Police Professionalism Initiative, *Police DNA "Sweeps" Extremely Unproductive*, Dep't of Criminal Justice, University of Nebraska-Omaha (Samuel Walker, Coordinator) (Sept. 2004), at http://www.unomaha.edu/criminaljustice/PDF/dnareport.pdf.

[77] For more information about DNA dragnet searches, see Jeffrey S. Grand, Note, *The Blooding of America: Privacy and the DNA Dragnet,* 23 Cardozo L. Rev. 2277 (2002).

> [E]ven within the short lifetime of the most advanced second-generation science, DNA typing, examples of both questionable methodological assertions and erroneous technical application abound. . . . Both Virginia and Texas wrongly jailed individuals for years on the basis of falsely inculpating DNA evidence. . . .
>
> As is already apparent from the short history of DNA typing, many of the characteristics that make second-generation sciences so appealing in fact places them at equal, if not greater, risk for error in the current regime.
>
> First, with regard to admissibility determinations, the technical complexity of second-generation techniques make close and continuous judicial scrutiny of their methodological soundness less likely. . . . Even well-meaning judges may struggle to comprehend complicated scientific or mathematical principles, and the heightened likelihood of error may discourage a court from delving too deeply into such complicated scientific knowledge. . . .
>
> Given the rigor of second-generation techniques, defense attorneys, like judges, may find themselves susceptible to the temptation simply to trust the integrity of the evidence, thus making the case seem insurmountable or "open-and-shut." Many lawyers will reasonably conclude that it requires too great an effort, and reaps too little a reward, to study such evidence in the hopes of uncovering a flawed methodological approach. . . .
>
> [T]he database-dependency of second-generation sciences, and the privacy and proprietary secrets concerns they raise, effectively prohibit access to the material necessary for independent research. Manufacturers of DNA typing kits, cell phone or search engine technologies, or biometric scanning software may bristle at disclosing broadly the technology underlying their particular techniques, even under a court "gag" order. Similarly, the relinquishment of data stored indiscriminately in databanks for exploratory purposes — whether iris patterns, DNA profiles, or cell records — understandably raises legitimate concerns about personal privacy.[78]

Murphy proposes to loosen "the government's grip" on the technology. Independent forensic laboratories should be created. Moreover, a centralized oversight group should carry out research and audit functions—and encourage others to pursue these activities as well. Murphy also contends that "the courtroom's grip on the law" should be loosened. She proposes greater centralization of the defense function to allow pooling of resources. She also advocates defense entitlements to DNA evidence and greater governmental duties, including the burden to place before a trial court continued evidence of a technique's legitimacy. Do you think these remedies will cure the ills that Murphy has diagnosed in her article?

7. ***"Abandoned" DNA?*** Frequently, the law views the police's collection of discarded DNA as similar to its examination of trash. In *California v. Greenwood,* 486 U.S. 35 (1988), the Supreme Court held that there was no reasonable expectation of privacy in trash set out at the curb for collection. Law enforcement officials have collected discarded DNA from a smoked cigarette, a recently used coffee cup, and a licked envelope sent through the mail. In a *New York Times* article, Amy Harmon warns: "The police could collect DNA deemed 'abandoned' from targeted individuals and monitor their

[78] Erin Murphy, *The New Forensics*, 95 Cal. L. Rev. 721 (2007).

movements even if they are not suspected of committing a serious crime. Innocent people whose DNA turns up unexpectedly may find themselves identified by a database." Several hundred suspects over the last few years have been implicated by traces of DNA collected from them secretly. In addition, "[m]any more were eliminated from suspicion without ever knowing that their coffee cups, tissue, straws, utensils and cigarette butts were subject to DNA analysis by the police." Harmon also notes that most people fail to realize that there may be no way to avoid shedding DNA in public "short of living in a bubble."[79] Does *Greenwood* foreclose finding a reasonable expectation of privacy in DNA from discarded items? Should DNA in discarded items be treated differently from regular trash?

For Elizabeth Joh, however, instead of thinking of the collection and analysis of such samples as involving "abandoned" DNA, we should view it as "covert involuntary DNA sampling." Joh argues that the law should end its grant of virtually limitless discretion to the police in collecting such DNA. More limits on police procedures are needed in this context because of the vast potential uses of this information, and the rapidity of scientific research in genetics, which makes it difficult to predict the amount of information about an individual that a single genetic sample might reveal. In Joh's view, the police should be required to obtain a warrant whenever they seek covert, involuntary DNA from a target. She also calls for the more modest step of having legislatures clarify "the applicability of DNA database laws, both federal and state, to the collection of abandoned DNA."[80] What standard, if any, should be required in order for law enforcement officials to collect "abandoned" DNA?

---

[79] Amy Harmon, *Lawyers Fight Gene Material Gained on Sly*, N.Y. Times, Apr. 3, 2008, at A1.

[80] Elizabeth E. Joh, *Reclaiming "Abandoned" DNA*, 100 Nw. U. L. Rev. 857, 860, 881 (2006).

CHAPTER 5

PRIVACY OF ASSOCIATION AND IDENTITY

This chapter focuses on the privacy of association and identity. It begins with group association. The groups to which we belong form an important component of our personal identity. As Oscar Gandy observes:

> [I]ndividual identities are formed in interaction with others. The characteristics of those interactions help to determine the salience, as well as the level of comfort with which different aspects of one's identity co-exist. Self-esteem, or how an individual feels about herself is determined, in part, by the ways in which her relevant reference groups are evaluated by others.[1]

Consider as well the following argument of Edward Bloustein:

> Group privacy is an extension of individual privacy. The interest protected by group privacy is the desire and need of people to come together, to exchange information, share feelings, make plans and act in concert to attain their objectives. This requires that people reveal themselves to one another — breach their individual privacy — and rely on those with whom they associate to keep within the group what was revealed.[2]

Identification as a member of an unpopular group may result in severe social and financial repercussions. For example, people who were identified as members of the Communist Party often lost their jobs and were blacklisted from future employment during the McCarthy era in the 1950s. People may also belong to groups that they want to conceal from their parents, siblings, or certain friends. Privacy is essential to preserving one's ability to form bonds and associate with others having similar beliefs and views. The First Amendment recognizes the importance of preserving the freedom to associate: "Congress shall make no law . . . abridging . . . the right of the people peacefully to assemble." Additionally, group association is often central to political expression, implicating the First Amendment's protection of speech. Without privacy, people

---

[1] Oscar H. Gandy, Jr., *Exploring Identity and Identification in Cyberspace*, 14 Notre Dame J.L. Ethics & Pub. Pol'y 1085 (2000).

[2] Edward J. Bloustein, *Individual and Group Privacy* 125 (1978).

will be deterred from engaging in these important identity forming and expressive activities.

In a similar way, the ability to communicate anonymously helps to promote freedom of expression. People often express, listen to, and read unpopular ideas. The identification of a speaker or reader can severely chill these activities. As Gary Marx notes, anonymity can "facilitate the flow of information and communication on public issues" and "encourage experimentation and risk taking without facing large consequences, risk of failure or embarrassment since one's identity is protected."[3] Consider the following argument by A. Michael Froomkin:

> . . . Not everyone is so courageous as to wish to be known for everything they say, and some timorous speech deserves encouragement. Corporate whistle-blowers, even junior professors, may fear losing their jobs. People criticizing a religious cult or other movement from which they might fear retaliation may fear losing their lives. In some countries, even this one in some times and places, it is unsafe to be heard to criticize the government. Persons who wish to criticize a repressive government or foment a revolution against it may find anonymity invaluable. Indeed, given the ability to broadcast messages widely using the Internet, anonymous e-mail may become the modern replacement of the anonymous handbill.
>
> Communicative anonymity encourages people to post requests for information to public bulletin boards about matters they may find too personal to discuss if there were any chance that the message might be traced back to its origin. In addition to the obvious psychological benefits to people who thus find themselves enabled to communicate, there may be external benefits to the entire community. . . .[4]

This chapter also explores identification by way of various identification systems (such as numbers assigned to individuals, identification cards, biometric identifiers, and so on). This form of systematic social identification has profound implications for the type of society we wish to create. Identity systems have both social benefits and costs. Identification is increasingly important for a society as large and sophisticated as ours, where many transactions occur impersonally among strangers. It is, for example, possible with the right identity documents and credit cards to buy an automobile on the spot at a car dealership. These identification systems also allow the easy linking of different databases, and the tying together of scattered data crumbs and the tracking of this information back to a single person.

Further, proponents of identification systems have contended that they will promote security. However, such systems have been criticized because they can impede one's ability to travel freely in society. Such systems can also threaten the individual's freedom to define her own identity by imposing on her a government-mandated identity that reduces her to a mere number and associated

---

[3] Gary T. Marx, *Identity and Anonymity: Some Conceptual Distinctions and Issues for Research*, in Jane Caplan & John Torpey, *Documenting Individual Identity* 311, 316, 318 (2001).

[4] A. Michael Froomkin, *Flood Control on the Information Ocean: Living with Anonymity, Digital Cash, and Distributed Databases*, 15 J.L. & Comm. 395, 408 (1996).

data in a database. Further, such systems may facilitate dangerous forms of social control and subject individuals to a variety of bureaucratic abuses.

A. PRIVACY OF GROUP ASSOCIATIONS

1. COMPELLED DISCLOSURE OF GROUP MEMBERSHIP LISTS

NATIONAL ASSOCIATION FOR THE ADVANCEMENT OF COLORED PEOPLE V. STATE OF ALABAMA

357 U.S. 449 (1958)

HARLAN, J. . . . Alabama has a statute similar to those of many other States which requires a foreign corporation, except as exempted, to qualify before doing business by filing its corporate charter with the Secretary of State and designating a place of business and an agent to receive service of process. The statute imposes a fine on a corporation transacting intrastate business before qualifying and provides for criminal prosecution of officers of such a corporation. The National Association for the Advancement of Colored People is a nonprofit membership corporation organized under the laws of New York. . . . [Although operating an office in Alabama, the] Association has never complied with the qualification statute, from which it considered itself exempt.

In 1956 the Attorney General of Alabama brought an equity suit in the State Circuit Court, Montgomery County, to enjoin the Association from conducting further activities within, and to oust it from, the State. . . . The bill [in equity] recited that the Association, by continuing to do business in Alabama without complying with the qualification statute, was ". . . causing irreparable injury to the property and civil rights of the residents and citizens of the State of Alabama. . . ." On the day the complaint was filed, the Circuit Court issued ex parte an order restraining the Association, pendente lite, from engaging in further activities within the State and forbidding it to take any steps to qualify itself to do business therein.

Petitioner demurred to the allegations of the bill and moved to dissolve the restraining order. . . . Before the date set for a hearing on this motion, the State moved for the production of a large number of the Association's records and papers, including bank statements, leases, deeds, and records containing the names and addresses of all Alabama "members" and "agents" of the Association. It alleged that all such documents were necessary for adequate preparation for the hearing, in view of petitioner's denial of the conduct of intrastate business within the meaning of the qualification statute. Over petitioner's objections, the court ordered the production of a substantial part of the requested records, including the membership lists, and postponed the hearing on the restraining order to a date later than the time ordered for production. . . .

Petitioner argues that in view of the facts and circumstances shown in the record, the effect of compelled disclosure of the membership lists will be to abridge the rights of its rank-and-file members to engage in lawful association in support of their common beliefs. It contends that governmental action which, although not directly suppressing association, nevertheless carries this consequence, can be justified only upon some overriding valid interest of the State.

Effective advocacy of both public and private points of view, particularly controversial ones, is undeniably enhanced by group association, as this Court has more than once recognized by remarking upon the close nexus between the freedoms of speech and assembly. It is beyond debate that freedom to engage in association for the advancement of beliefs and ideas is an inseparable aspect of the "liberty" assured by the Due Process Clause of the Fourteenth Amendment, which embraces freedom of speech. Of course, it is immaterial whether the beliefs sought to be advanced by association pertain to political, economic, religious or cultural matters, and state action which may have the effect of curtailing the freedom to associate is subject to the closest scrutiny.

The fact that Alabama, so far as is relevant to the validity of the contempt judgment presently under review, has taken no direct action to restrict the right of petitioner's members to associate freely, does not end inquiry into the effect of the production order. In the domain of these indispensable liberties, whether of speech, press, or association, the decisions of this Court recognize that abridgement of such rights, even though unintended, may inevitably follow from varied forms of governmental action. . . .

It is hardly a novel perception that compelled disclosure of affiliation with groups engaged in advocacy may constitute as effective a restraint on freedom of association as the forms of governmental action in the cases above were thought likely to produce upon the particular constitutional rights there involved. This Court has recognized the vital relationship between freedom to associate and privacy in one's associations. When referring to the varied forms of governmental action which might interfere with freedom of assembly, it said in *American Communications Ass'n v. Douds*: "A requirement that adherents of particular religious faiths or political parties wear identifying arm-bands, for example, is obviously of this nature." Compelled disclosure of membership in an organization engaged in advocacy of particular beliefs is of the same order. Inviolability of privacy in group association may in many circumstances be indispensable to preservation of freedom of association, particularly where a group espouses dissident beliefs.

We think that the production order, in the respects here drawn in question, must be regarded as entailing the likelihood of a substantial restraint upon the exercise by petitioner's members of their right to freedom of association. Petitioner has made an uncontroverted showing that on past occasions revelation of the identity of its rank-and-file members has exposed these members to economic reprisal, loss of employment, threat of physical coercion, and other manifestations of public hostility. Under these circumstances, we think it apparent that compelled disclosure of petitioner's Alabama membership is likely to affect adversely the ability of petitioner and its members to pursue their collective effort to foster beliefs which they admittedly have the right to advocate, in that it may induce members to withdraw from the Association and dissuade others from joining it because of fear of exposure of their beliefs shown through their associations and of the consequences of this exposure.

It is not sufficient to answer, as the State does here, that whatever repressive effect compulsory disclosure of names of petitioner's members may have upon participation by Alabama citizens in petitioner's activities follows not from state action but from private community pressures. The crucial factor is the interplay of governmental and private action, for it is only after the initial exertion of state power represented by the production order that private action takes hold.

We turn to the final question whether Alabama has demonstrated an interest in obtaining the disclosures it seeks from petitioner which is sufficient to justify the deterrent effect which we have concluded these disclosures may well have on the free exercise by petitioner's members of their constitutionally protected right of association. Such a ". . . subordinating interest of the State must be compelling." . . .

Whether there was "justification" in this instance turns solely on the substantiality of Alabama's interest in obtaining the membership lists. . . . The issues in the litigation commenced by Alabama by its bill in equity were whether the character of petitioner and its activities in Alabama had been such as to make petitioner subject to the registration statute, and whether the extent of petitioner's activities without qualifying suggested its permanent ouster from the State. Without intimating the slightest view upon the merits of these issues, we are unable to perceive that the disclosure of the names of petitioner's rank-and-file members has a substantial bearing on either of them. . . .

NOTES & QUESTIONS

1. ***Bates v. City of Little Rock.*** In *Bates v. City of Little Rock*, 361 U.S. 516 (1960), the Court struck down a Little Rock, Arkansas, ordinance requiring the disclosure of the NAACP's members and contributors:

> On this record it sufficiently appears that compulsory disclosure of the membership lists of the local branches of the National Association for the Advancement of Colored People would work a significant interference with the freedom of association of their members. There was substantial uncontroverted evidence that public identification of persons in the community as members of the organizations had been followed by harassment and threats of bodily harm. There was also evidence that fear of community hostility and economic reprisals that would follow public disclosure of the membership lists had discouraged new members from joining the organizations and induced former members to withdraw. This repressive effect, while in part the result of private attitudes and pressures, was brought to bear only after the exercise of governmental power had threatened to force disclosure of the members' names.

2. ***Political Campaign Contributions.*** Pursuant to the Federal Election Campaign Act (FECA), the personal information of people making contributions to candidates over a certain amount ($100 at the time *Buckley* was decided, and $200 today) are disclosed publicly. The revealed information includes one's name, employer, and occupation. In *Buckley v. Valeo,* 424 U.S. 1

(1976), one of the issues the Court considered was whether mandatory political campaign disclosures pursuant to the FECA violated the First Amendment. The Court recognized that such disclosures implicate First Amendment rights:

> We long have recognized that significant encroachments on First Amendment rights of the sort that compelled disclosure imposes cannot be justified by a mere showing of some legitimate governmental interest. Since *NAACP v. Alabama* we have required that the subordinating interests of the State must survive exacting scrutiny. . . .
>
> The strict test established by *NAACP v. Alabama* is necessary because compelled disclosure has the potential for substantially infringing the exercise of First Amendment rights.

The Court concluded, however, that the disclosure requirements were the least restrictive means for achieving compelling government interests:

> First, disclosure provides the electorate with information "as to where political campaign money comes from and how it is spent by the candidate" in order to aid the voters in evaluating those who seek federal office. . . . The sources of a candidate's financial support also alert the voter to the interests to which a candidate is most likely to be responsive and thus facilitate predictions of future performance in office.
>
> Second, disclosure requirements deter actual corruption and avoid the appearance of corruption by exposing large contributions and expenditures to the light of publicity. . . .
>
> Third, and not least significant, recordkeeping, reporting, and disclosure requirements are an essential means of gathering the data necessary to detect violations of the contribution limitations described above.

The challengers of the law argued that the disclosure rules should not apply to minor parties and independent candidates because their views are less likely to be mainstream, heightening the potential chilling effects of disclosure. Despite this claim, the Court concluded:

> We are not unmindful that the damage done by disclosure to the associational interests of the minor parties and their members and to supporters of independents could be significant. These movements are less likely to have a sound financial base and thus are more vulnerable to falloffs in contributions. In some instances fears of reprisal may deter contributions to the point where the movement cannot survive. The public interest also suffers if that result comes to pass, for there is a consequent reduction in the free circulation of ideas both within and without the political arena.

William McGeveran contends that *Buckley*'s holding on disclosure requirements should be revisited. He notes that modern technology has made political contribution records significantly more accessible, as organizations are now creating searchable online databases of such records. McGeveran argues that people might be chilled from making political contributions because of negative professional consequences or the stigma of being associated with unpopular non-mainstream candidates: "Political contributions label us, and disclosure displays that label to others without our consent. Forced revelations are intrusions into a sphere of personal liberty." He contends:

> [D]isclosure is more likely to deter contributions aligned with certain ideological positions — more controversial ones — a correlation that threatens both the First Amendment protection of contributions and the open debate we strive for in elections. Those with mainstream views who choose to sacrifice privacy may contribute an amount above the threshold while others, whose views are more likely to be unorthodox, are chilled from doing so.

Regarding *Buckley*'s stated compelling government interests, they often fail "to justify disclosure of modest-sized contributions." Most small contributions are too insignificant to have a corrupting influence. Moreover, "very few voters actually give much consideration to the nature of candidates' donors when choosing whether to support them."[5]

2. INTERROGATION ABOUT GROUP ASSOCIATIONS

BARENBLATT V. UNITED STATES

360 U.S. 109 (1959)

[In 1954, a Subcommittee of the House Un-American Activities Committee summoned Lloyd Barenblatt, a 31-year-old teacher of psychology at Vassar College, to testify. The House Un-American Activities Committee was a long-standing Committee that investigated Communist activities by forcing suspected Communist Party members to disclose that they were Party members and reveal the names of other members. Before Barenblatt appeared, his contract with Vassar expired and was not renewed. The Committee wanted to question Barenblatt because another witness had stated that when Barenblatt was a graduate student, he had been associated with a small group of Communists. When called before the Committee, Barenblatt refused to answer questions pertaining to his current and past membership in the Communist Party. He was found in contempt, tried in federal district court, and sentenced to six months in prison.]

HARLAN, J. . . . The precise constitutional issue confronting us is whether the Subcommittee's inquiry into petitioner's past or present membership in the Communist Party transgressed the provisions of the First Amendment, which of course reach and limit congressional investigations.

. . . Undeniably, the First Amendment in some circumstances protects an individual from being compelled to disclose his associational relationships. However, the protections of the First Amendment, unlike a proper claim of the privilege against self-incrimination under the Fifth Amendment, do not afford a witness the right to resist inquiry in all circumstances. Where First Amendment rights are asserted to bar governmental interrogation resolution of the issue

---

[5] William McGeveran, *McIntyre's Checkbook: Privacy Costs of Political Contribution Disclosure*, 6 U. Pa. J. Const. L. 1, 19, 30, 38 (2003).

always involves a balancing by the courts of the competing private and public interests at stake in the particular circumstances shown. These principles were recognized in *Watkins* [*v. United States*, 354 U.S. 178], where, in speaking of the First Amendment in relation to congressional inquiries, we said: "It is manifest that despite the adverse effects which follow upon compelled disclosure of private matters, not all such inquiries are barred. . . . The critical element is the existence of, and the weight to be ascribed to, the interest of the Congress in demanding disclosures from an unwilling witness." . .

The first question is whether this investigation was related to a valid legislative purpose, for Congress may not constitutionally require an individual to disclose his political relationships or other private affairs except in relation to such a purpose.

That Congress has wide power to legislate in the field of Communist activity in this Country, and to conduct appropriate investigations in aid thereof, is hardly debatable. . . . Justification for its exercise in turn rests on the long and widely accepted view that the tenets of the Communist Party include the ultimate overthrow of the Government of the United States by force and violence, a view which has been given formal expression by the Congress. . . .

. . . [T]he record is barren of other factors which in themselves might sometimes lead to the conclusion that the individual interests at stake were not subordinate to those of the state. There is no indication in this record that the Subcommittee was attempting to pillory witnesses. Nor did petitioner's appearance as a witness follow from indiscriminate dragnet procedures, lacking in probable cause for belief that he possessed information which might be helpful to the Subcommittee. And the relevancy of the questions put to him by the Subcommittee is not open to doubt.

We conclude that the balance between the individual and the governmental interests here at stake must be struck in favor of the latter, and that therefore the provisions of the First Amendment have not been offended. . .

BLACK, J. joined by WARREN, C.J. and DOUGLAS, J. dissenting. . . . The First Amendment says in no equivocal language that Congress shall pass no law abridging freedom of speech, press, assembly or petition. The activities of this Committee, authorized by Congress, do precisely that, through exposure, obloquy and public scorn. . . .

I do not agree that laws directly abridging First Amendment freedoms can be justified by a congressional or judicial balancing process. . . .

But even assuming what I cannot assume, that some balancing is proper in this case, I feel that the Court after stating the test ignores it completely. At most it balances the right of the Government to preserve itself, against Barenblatt's right to refrain from revealing Communist affiliations. Such a balance, however, mistakes the factors to be weighed. In the first place, it completely leaves out the real interest in Barenblatt's silence, the interest of the people as a whole in being able to join organizations, advocate causes and make political "mistakes" without later being subjected to governmental penalties for having dared to think for themselves. . . .

The fact is that once we allow any group which has some political aims or ideas to be driven from the ballot and from the battle for men's minds because some of its members are bad and some of its tenets are illegal, no group is safe. Today we deal with Communists or suspected Communists. In 1920, instead, the New York Assembly suspended duly elected legislators on the ground that, being Socialists, they were disloyal to the country's principles. In the 1830's the Masons were hunted as outlaws and subversives, and abolitionists were considered revolutionaries of the most dangerous kind in both North and South. Earlier still, at the time of the universally unlamented alien and sedition laws, Thomas Jefferson's party was attacked and its members were derisively called "Jacobins." Fisher Ames described the party as a "French faction" guilty of "subversion" and "officered, regimented and formed to subordination." Its members, he claimed, intended to "take arms against the laws as soon as they dare." History should teach us then, that in times of high emotional excitement minority parties and groups which advocate extremely unpopular social or governmental innovations will always be typed as criminal gangs and attempts will always be made to drive them out. It was knowledge of this fact, and of its great dangers, that caused the Founders of our land to enact the First Amendment as a guarantee that neither Congress nor the people would do anything to hinder or destroy the capacity of individuals and groups to seek converts and votes for any cause, however radical or unpalatable their principles might seem under the accepted notions of the time. . . .

Finally, I think Barenblatt's conviction violates the Constitution because the chief aim, purpose and practice of the House Un-American Activities Committee, as disclosed by its many reports, is to try witnesses and punish them because they are or have been Communists or because they refuse to admit or deny Communist affiliations. The punishment imposed is generally punishment by humiliation and public shame. There is nothing strange or novel about this kind of punishment. It is in fact one of the oldest forms of governmental punishment known to mankind; branding, the pillory, ostracism and subjection to public hatred being but a few examples of it. . . .

. . . [T]he Committee has called witnesses who are suspected of Communist affiliation, has subjected them to severe questioning and has insisted that each tell the name of every person he has ever known at any time to have been a Communist, and, if possible, to give the addresses and occupations of the people named. These names are then indexed, published, and reported to Congress, and often to the press. The same technique is employed to cripple the job opportunities of those who strongly criticize the Committee or take other actions it deems undesirable. . . .

NOTES & QUESTIONS

1. ***Shelton v. Tucker.*** In *Shelton v. Tucker*, 364 U.S. 479 (1960), the Court struck down a law requiring teachers to list the organizations they belonged or contributed to within the past five years. The Court held that "the statute's comprehensive interference with associational freedom goes far beyond what might be justified in the exercise of the State's legitimate inquiry into the fitness and competency of its teachers":

> The scope of the inquiry required by [the statute] is completely unlimited. The statute requires a teacher to reveal the church to which he belongs, or to which he has given financial support. It requires him to disclose his political party, and every political organization to which he may have contributed over a five-year period. It requires him to list, without number, every conceivable kind of associational tie — social, professional, political, vocational, or religious. Many such relationships could have no possible bearing upon the teacher's occupational competence or fitness.

Can you reconcile the Court's decision in *Barenblatt* with *Shelton v. Tucker* and *NAACP v. Alabama*?

2. ***Communist Party Membership.*** Cases involving privacy of group associations have frequently arisen when various legislative committees or licensing boards questioned individuals about their membership in Communist organizations. Many cases, like *Barenblatt*, involved questioning before the House Un-American Activities Committee (HUAC). In *Wilkinson v. United States*, 365 U.S. 399 (1961), an individual refused to answer a question by the Committee about membership in the Communist Party. The individual contended that the reason he was being questioned was because he had voiced public criticism of the Committee. The Court, however, concluded that *Barenblatt* still controlled, and that the Committee had "reasonable ground to suppose that the petitioner was an active Communist Party member." Dissenting, Justices Black and Douglas and Chief Justice Warren argued that "this case involves nothing more nor less than an attempt by the Un-American Activities Committee to use the contempt power of the House of Representatives as a weapon against those who dare to criticize it." *See also Braden v. United States*, 365 U.S. 431 (1961).

   A number of cases involved challenges to questions asked by state bar committees. In *Konigsberg v. State Bar of California*, 366 U.S. 36 (1961), an applicant for membership in the California Bar refused to answer questions about his membership in the Communist Party. The committee refused to certify him. The Court held that the applicant's First Amendment rights were not violated because "[t]here is here no likelihood that deterrence of association may result from foreseeable private action, for bar committee interrogations such as this are conducted in private." *See also In re Anastalpo*, 366 U.S. 82 (1961) (questioning of applicant by Illinois Bar about his Communist Party membership was proper under the First Amendment). Can these cases be reconciled with *NAACP v. Alabama*? If so, how?

3. ***Prior vs. Current Communist Party Membership.*** In *DeGregory v. Attorney General*, 383 U.S. 825 (1966), an individual was jailed for contempt for refusing to answer questions by the New Hampshire Attorney General about his past (rather than current) membership in the Communist Party. The individual feared that "the details of his political associations to which he might testify would be reported in a pamphlet purporting to describe the nature of subversion in New Hampshire." The court held that the First Amendment prohibited the inquiry into the individual's prior group activities:

> There is no showing of "overriding and compelling state interest" that would warrant intrusion into the realm of political and associational privacy protected by the First Amendment. The information being sought was historical, not current. Lawmaking at the investigatory stage may properly probe historic events for any light that may be thrown on present conditions and problems. But the First Amendment prevents use of the power to investigate enforced by the contempt power to probe at will and without relation to existing need. The present record is devoid of any evidence that there is any Communist movement in New Hampshire.

4. ***The Scope of the Inquiry.*** In *Baird v. State Bar*, 401 U.S. 1 (1971), an applicant before the Arizona Bar Committee refused to answer whether she was a member of the Communist Party or any organization "that advocates overthrow of the United States Government by force or violence." As a result, the applicant was denied admission to the bar. The Court held that the questioning was improper because the government cannot attempt to conduct "[b]road and sweeping state inquiries" into people's political views or group associations. "In effect this young lady was asked by the State to make a guess as to whether any organization to which she ever belonged 'advocates overthrow of the United States Government by force or violence.'" The Court reasoned:

> The First Amendment's protection of association prohibits a State from excluding a person from a profession or punishing him solely because he is a member of a particular political organization or because he holds certain beliefs. Similarly, when a State attempts to make inquiries about a person's beliefs or associations, its power is limited by the First Amendment. Broad and sweeping state inquiries into these protected areas, as Arizona has engaged in here, discourage citizens from exercising rights protected by the Constitution.
>
> When a State seeks to inquire about an individual's beliefs and associations a heavy burden lies upon it to show that the inquiry is necessary to protect a legitimate state interest. Of course Arizona has a legitimate interest in determining whether petitioner has the qualities of character and the professional competence requisite to the practice of law. But here petitioner has already supplied the Committee with extensive personal and professional information to assist its determination. By her answers to questions other than No. 25, and her listing of former employers, law school professors, and other references, she has made available to the Committee the information relevant to her fitness to practice law. And whatever justification may be offered, a State may not inquire about a man's views or associations solely for the purpose of withholding a right or benefit because of what he believes.

Can you distinguish *Baird* from *Barenblatt*, *Konigsberg*, and the other Communist Party membership cases?

3. SURVEILLANCE OF GROUP ACTIVITIES

LAIRD V. TATUM

408 U.S. 1 (1972)

BURGER, C.J. . . . The President is authorized by 10 U.S.C. § 331 to make use of the armed forces to quell insurrection and other domestic violence if and when the conditions described in that section obtain within one of the States. Pursuant to those provisions, President Johnson ordered federal troops to assist local authorities at the time of the civil disorders in Detroit, Michigan, in the summer of 1967 and during the disturbances that followed the assassination of Dr. Martin Luther King. Prior to the Detroit disorders, the Army had a general contingency plan for providing such assistance to local authorities, but the 1967 experience led Army authorities to believe that more attention should be given to such preparatory planning. The data-gathering system here involved is said to have been established in connection with the development of more detailed and specific contingency planning designed to permit the Army, when called upon to assist local authorities, to be able to respond effectively with a minimum of force. . . .

The system put into operation as a result of the Army's 1967 experience consisted essentially of the collection of information about public activities that were thought to have at least some potential for civil disorder, the reporting of that information to Army Intelligence headquarters at Fort Holabird, Maryland, the dissemination of these reports from headquarters to major Army posts around the country, and the storage of the reported information in a computer data bank located at Fort Holabird. The information itself was collected by a variety of means, but it is significant that the principal sources of information were the news media and publications in general circulation. Some of the information came from Army Intelligence agents who attended meetings that were open to the public and who wrote field reports describing the meetings, giving such data as the name of the sponsoring organization, the identity of speakers, the approximate number of persons in attendance, and an indication of whether any disorder occurred. And still other information was provided to the Army by civilian law enforcement agencies. . . .

By early 1970 Congress became concerned with the scope of the Army's domestic surveillance system; hearings on the matter were held before the Subcommittee on Constitutional Rights of the Senate Committee on the Judiciary. Meanwhile, the Army, in the course of a review of the system, ordered a significant reduction in its scope. For example, information referred to in the complaint as the "blacklist" and the records in the computer data bank at Fort Holabird were found unnecessary and were destroyed, along with other related records. One copy of all the material relevant to the instant suit was retained, however, because of the pendency of this litigation. The review leading to the destruction of these records was said at the time the District Court ruled on petitioners' motion to dismiss to be a "continuing" one, and the Army's policies at that time were represented as follows in a letter from the Under Secretary of the Army to Senator Sam J. Ervin, Chairman of the Senate Subcommittee on Constitutional Rights:

> [R]eports concerning civil disturbances will be limited to matters of immediate concern to the Army — that is, reports concerning outbreaks of violence or incidents with a high potential for violence beyond the capability of state and local police and the National Guard to control. These reports will be collected by liaison with other Government agencies and reported by teletype to the Intelligence Command. They will not be placed in a computer. . . . These reports are destroyed 60 days after publication or 60 days after the end of the disturbance. This limited reporting system will ensure that the Army is prepared to respond to whatever directions the President may issue in civil disturbance situations and without "watching" the lawful activities of civilians. . . .

In recent years this Court has found in a number of cases that constitutional violations may arise from the deterrent, or "chilling," effect of governmental regulations that fall short of a direct prohibition against the exercise of First Amendment rights. In none of these cases, however, did the chilling effect arise merely from the individual's knowledge that a governmental agency was engaged in certain activities or from the individual's concomitant fear that, armed with the fruits of those activities, the agency might in the future take some other and additional action detrimental to that individual. Rather, in each of these cases, the challenged exercise of governmental power was regulatory, proscriptive, or compulsory in nature, and the complainant was either presently or prospectively subject to the regulations, proscriptions, or compulsions that he was challenging.

For example, the petitioner in *Baird v. State Bar of Arizona* had been denied admission to the bar solely because of her refusal to answer a question regarding the organizations with which she had been associated in the past. In announcing the judgment of the Court, Mr. Justice Black said that "a State may not inquire about a man's views or associations solely for the purpose of withholding a right or benefit because of what he believes." Some of the teachers who were the complainants in *Keyishian v. Board of Regents* had been discharged from employment by the State, and the others were threatened with such discharge, because of their political acts or associations. The Court concluded that the State's "complicated and intricate scheme" of laws and regulations relating to teacher loyalty could not withstand constitutional scrutiny. . . .

The decisions in these cases fully recognize that governmental action may be subject to constitutional challenge even though it has only an indirect effect on the exercise of First Amendment rights. At the same time, however, these decisions have in no way eroded the

> established principle that to entitle a private individual to invoke the judicial power to determine the validity of executive or legislative action he must show that he has sustained, or is immediately in danger of sustaining, a direct injury as the result of that action. . . . *Ex parte Levitt*, 302 U.S. 633 (1937).

The respondents do not meet this test; their claim, simply stated, is that they disagree with the judgments made by the Executive Branch with respect to the type and amount of information the Army needs and that the very existence of the Army's data-gathering system produces a constitutionally impermissible chilling effect upon the exercise of their First Amendment rights. That alleged "chilling" effect may perhaps be seen as arising from respondents' very perception of the system as inappropriate to the Army's role under our form of government, or as arising from respondents' beliefs that it is inherently dangerous for the military to be concerned with activities in the civilian sector, or as arising from respondents' less generalized yet speculative apprehensiveness that the Army may at some future date misuse the information in some way that would cause direct harm to respondents. Allegations of a subjective "chill" are not an adequate substitute for a claim of specific present objective harm or a threat of specific future harm; "the federal courts established pursuant to Article III of the Constitution do not render advisory opinions." . . .

DOUGLAS, J. joined by MARSHALL, J. dissenting. . . . If Congress had passed a law authorizing the armed services to establish surveillance over the civilian population, a most serious constitutional problem would be presented. There is, however, no law authorizing surveillance over civilians, which in this case the Pentagon concededly had undertaken. The question is whether such authority may be implied. One can search the Constitution in vain for any such authority. . . .

. . . [T]he Armed Services — as distinguished from the "militia" — are not regulatory agencies or bureaus that may be created as Congress desires and granted such powers as seem necessary and proper. The authority to provide rules "governing" the Armed Services means the grant of authority to the Armed Services to govern themselves, not the authority to govern civilians. Even when "martial law" is declared, as it often has been, its appropriateness is subject to judicial review. . . .

Our tradition reflects a desire for civilian supremacy and subordination of military power. The tradition goes back to the Declaration of Independence, in which it was recited that the King "has affected to render the Military independent of and superior to the Civil power." . . .

The action in turning the "armies" loose on surveillance of civilians was a gross repudiation of our traditions. The military, though important to us, is subservient and restricted purely to military missions. . . .

The claim that respondents have no standing to challenge the Army's surveillance of them and the other members of the class they seek to represent is too transparent for serious argument. The surveillance of the Army over the civilian sector — a part of society hitherto immune from its control — is a serious charge. It is alleged that the Army maintains files on the membership, ideology, programs, and practices of virtually every activist political group in the country, including groups such as the Southern Christian Leadership Conference, Clergy and Laymen United Against the War in Vietnam, the American Civil Liberties Union, Women's Strike for Peace, and the National Association for the Advancement of Colored People. The Army uses undercover agents to infiltrate these civilian groups and to reach into confidential files of students and other groups. The Army moves as a secret group among civilian audiences, using cameras and electronic ears for surveillance. The data it collects are distributed to civilian officials in state, federal, and local governments and to each military intelligence unit and troop command under the Army's jurisdiction (both here and abroad); and these data are stored in one or more data banks.

Those are the allegations; and the charge is that the purpose and effect of the system of surveillance is to harass and intimidate the respondents and to deter them from exercising their rights of political expression, protest, and dissent "by invading their privacy, damaging their reputations, adversely affecting their employment and their opportunities for employment, and in other ways." Their fear is that "permanent reports of their activities will be maintained in the Army's data bank, and their 'profiles' will appear in the so-called 'Blacklist' and that all of this information will be released to numerous federal and state agencies upon request." . . .

One need not wait to sue until he loses his job or until his reputation is defamed. To withhold standing to sue until that time arrives would in practical effect immunize from judicial scrutiny all surveillance activities, regardless of their misuse and their deterrent effect. . . .

This case involves a cancer in our body politic. It is a measure of the disease which afflicts us. Army surveillance, like Army regimentation, is at war with the principles of the First Amendment. Those who already walk submissively will say there is no cause for alarm. But submissiveness is not our heritage. The First Amendment was designed to allow rebellion to remain as our heritage. The Constitution was designed to keep government off the backs of the people. The Bill of Rights was added to keep the precincts of belief and expression, of the press, of political and social activities free from surveillance. The Bill of Rights was designed to keep agents of government and official eavesdroppers away from assemblies of people. The aim was to allow men to be free and independent and to assert their rights against government. There can be no influence more paralyzing of that objective than Army surveillance. When an intelligence officer looks over every nonconformist's shoulder in the library, or walks invisibly by his side in a picket line, or infiltrates his club, the America once extolled as the voice of liberty heard around the world no longer is cast in the image which Jefferson and Madison designed, but more in the Russian image. . . .

NOTES & QUESTIONS

1. ***First Amendment Injuries.*** Why doesn't surveillance create a cognizable injury under the First Amendment? Being watched inhibits one's ability to be free and candid in one's expression. How broad is the Supreme Court's holding? Would the plaintiffs have established standing if they produced evidence that the surveillance was deterring their First Amendment activities? Would the case have come out differently had the surveillance involved gatherings in private as opposed to in public?

   If *Laird* had been decided in the plaintiffs' favor, could individuals challenge wiretapping and other forms of police surveillance as a violation of the First Amendment? Such a holding could have far-reaching implications because many forms of police monitoring and investigation would be subject not only to Fourth Amendment limitations but to First Amendment ones as well. Where should the line be drawn?
2. ***Military vs. FBI Surveillance.*** Justice Douglas's dissent expresses great alarm that the Army is engaging in surveillance. Does the fact that the Army

is doing the surveillance make it more problematic than if the FBI were engaging in the same activity?

3. ***Army Surveillance in America: An Historian's Take.*** Joan Jensen observes that throughout American history the executive branch frequently "used the army to maintain internal security." She notes that "[t]he use of the army in civil disturbances provoked emotionally charged debates over civil liberties and the limits of governmental power." Jensen also examines the involvement in the *Laird* case of Senator Sam Ervin, Jr., a conservative Democratic senator from North Carolina, who led a campaign against army surveillance. Through a hearing in the Senate and litigation that led to *Laird v. Tatum*, Ervin sought to challenge the army's practices. Although Ervin lost the case before the Court, Jensen finds that the litigation had a positive effect:

> Public discussion of *Laird v. Tatum* probably hurried the curtailment of army surveillance that was already under way in the Department of Defense. Negative public criticism also acted as a restraint upon President Nixon's use of army agents when he expanded domestic surveillance shortly after. The case served a practical purpose; it fostered greater control by the army of its own structure and gave additional public support for congressional action.[6]

4. ***The Pentagon's Directive.*** In 1980, the Department of Defense (DoD) issued a directive regulating collection of information regarding persons and organizations that were unaffiliated with the DoD. Directive Number 5200.27 was not applicable to "DoD intelligence components." It expressed a DoD policy that "prohibits collecting, reporting, processing or storing information on individuals or organizations not affiliated with the [DoD], except in those limited circumstances where such information is essential to the accomplishment of the DoD missions outlined below." The authorized missions were: (1) protection of DoD functions and property; (2) personnel security; and (3) operations related to civil disturbances.

   Directive 5200.27 also spelled out a list of prohibited activities. These include:

> 5.1. The acquisition of information on individuals or organizations not affiliated with the DoD will be restricted to that which is essential to the accomplishment of assigned DoD missions under this Directive.
>
> 5.2. No information shall be acquired about a person or organization solely because of lawful advocacy of measures in opposition to Government policy.
>
> 5.3. There shall be no physical or electronic surveillance of Federal, State, or local officials or of candidates for such offices.
>
> 5.4. There shall be no electronic surveillance of any individual or organization, except as authorized by law.
>
> 5.5. There shall be no covert or otherwise deceptive surveillance or penetration of civilian organizations unless specifically authorized by the Secretary of Defense, or his designee.

---

[6] Joan M. Jensen, *Army Surveillance in America 1775-1980*, at 255 (1991).

> 5.6. No DoD personnel will be assigned to attend public or private meetings, demonstrations, or other similar activities for the purpose of acquiring information, the collection of which is authorized by this Directive without specific prior approval by the Secretary of Defense, or his designee. An exception to this policy may be made by the local commander concerned, or higher authority, when, in his judgment, the threat is direct and immediate and time precludes obtaining prior approval. In each such case a report will be made immediately to the Secretary of Defense, or his designee.
>
> 5.7. No computerized data banks shall be maintained relating to individuals or organizations not affiliated with the Department of Defense, unless authorized by the Secretary of Defense, or his designee.

The Directive also requires that "[i]nformation within the purview of this Directive" to "be destroyed within 90 days unless its retention is required by law or unless its retention is specifically authorized under criteria established by the Secretary of Defense, or his designee."

Are these provisions adequate to regulate DoD information collection? Or are they excessive in binding the DoD's ability to act?

5. ***Operation TALON.*** In late 2005, journalists revealed that information about political gatherings, mostly aimed at protesting the Iraq war or military recruitment, were being kept in a Pentagon database. Part of the DoD, the Counterintelligence Field Agency (CIFA), had collected information about domestic political organizations and their activities. The Pentagon called the data collection system in question "TALON," which stood for "Threats and Local Observation Notices." It was a data collection system of potential threats against U.S. military bases, both at home and overseas, that civilians and service members reported to military intelligence.

   The ACLU filed a FOIA request seeking information about the reports in TALON; in its view, "the inclusion within the Pentagon's TALON database of traditional and constitutionally protected activities was more widespread than previously known." It noted that even threat reports deemed "not credible" remained in the database. Finally, the ACLU found numerous unanswered questions about the DoD's collection and maintenance of information about the lawful protest activities of U.S. citizens: "We do not know whether the Department of Defense maintains other threat databases that include similar information, or whether Department of Defense personnel are engaged in other information-gathering about United States citizens."[7]

   In April 2007, the Pentagon announced that it was closing down TALON. The Pentagon also announced that it would task its homeland defense office with creating a system for collecting and assessing information about domestic threats to military bases and assets.

6. ***Surveillance Cameras in Public Places.*** Do surveillance cameras in public places implicate the right to free association and anonymity? Consider Christopher Slobogin:

---

[7] American Civil Liberties Union, *No Real Threat: the Pentagon's Secret Database on Peaceful Protest* 6 (Jan. 2007).

> [I]f public conduct is expressive — for instance, a speech at a park rally — and public associations are speech-related — such as joining the rally — then the First Amendment should be implicated by camera surveillance. That is because . . . such surveillance can chill conduct, even though it takes place in public and is meant to be seen by others.
>
> Admittedly, the Supreme Court rejected a similar claim in *Laird v. Tatum*. . . . The Court has since indicated, however, that a government action the sole effect of which is to chill speech is justifiable under some circumstances. *Tatum* thus does not necessarily foreclose a First Amendment argument against camera surveillance. The latter method of data collection is quite different from the government's efforts in *Tatum*. Most of the "surveillance" in *Tatum* consisted of perusing published material and public records, and the rest involved undercover agents who attended meetings; furthermore, the plaintiffs in *Tatum* alleged no specific acts by the Army against them, and may not have been "chilled" in any event. In short, *Tatum* did not involve overt surveillance. The conspicuous presence of cameras aimed at participants engaging in First Amendment activity, in contrast, is closer to the type of "present . . . compulsion" directed at speech that has concerned the Court in cases where it has found violations of the First Amendment. . . .
>
> The chilling phenomenon has also long been recognized in other settings, particularly in labor cases involving suits under the National Labor Relations Act (NLRA) against employers who have photographed or videotaped employees engaging in authorized strikes and demonstrations. . . .[8]

7. *Census Disclosures.* Following 9/11, the Department of Homeland Security obtained from the Census Bureau specially tabulated statistics on Arab-Americans living in the United States. The tabulations were produced in August 2002 and December 2003 in response to requests from what is now the Customs and Border Protection division of the Department of Homeland Security. One set listed cities with more than 1,000 Arab-Americans. The second, far more detailed, provided ZIP-code-level breakdowns of Arab-American populations, sorted by country of origin. The categories provided were Egyptian, Iraqi, Jordanian, Lebanese, Moroccan, Palestinian, Syrian, and two general categories, "Arab/Arabic" and "Other Arab." Because the disclosure did not reveal the names of individuals, proponents of the disclosure argued that it did not violate any laws. Moreover, Census officials contended that the information was already publicly available; they merely had provided it in a specially tabulated form. But civil liberties groups said that the release was a dangerous breach of public trust and likened it to the Census Bureau's compilation of similar information about Japanese-Americans during World War II. An official with the Census Bureau also expressed concern about the disclosure since it was not clear how the information would be used. Later in 2004, the Census Bureau announced that it would no longer assist law enforcement or intelligence agencies with

---

[8] Christopher Slobogin, *Public Privacy: Camera Surveillance of Public Places and the Right to Anonymity*, 72 Miss. L.J. 213, 253-55 (2002).

special tabulations on ethnic groups and other "sensitive populations" without the approval of senior bureau officials.

8. ***Surveillance of Public Political Activity.*** After 9/11, the government has indicated a heightened interest in surveillance of political events. Linda Fisher suggests that law enforcement officials must have some suspicion of wrongdoing to justify the surveillance:

> [T]he Constitution should prohibit domestic surveillance of U.S. persons' First Amendment activity in the absence of a reasonable suspicion of criminal activity. Politically motivated investigations are not permissible, since the mission of law enforcement is to enforce the criminal laws, not to monitor political or religious expression. The history and purposes of the constitutional right of association corroborate this conclusion.[9]

However, one argument in favor of surveillance is that monitoring volatile political activity might provide insight on potential terrorist plots or activities. Terrorism often involves group activities and associational networks. Should the government be restricted in monitoring those expressing strong political views in favor of causes championed by terrorist organizations — such as the plight of the Palestinians and the curtailment of U.S. involvement in the Middle East?

PHILADELPHIA YEARLY MEETING OF THE RELIGIOUS SOCIETY OF FRIENDS V. TATE

519 F.2d 1335 (3d Cir. 1975)

SEITZ, C.J. Plaintiffs, two organizations and six individuals, appeal an order of the district court dismissing their complaint for failure to state a claim. Defendants are the former Mayor of Philadelphia, the Managing Director and certain police officers of the City of Philadelphia. . . .

Plaintiffs allege that at many public assemblies or demonstrations attended by citizen groups whose general political or social views conflict with those of government officials and/or the Philadelphia Police Department, members of the Philadelphia Police Department, under the command of some of the defendants, are present, photograph many of those in attendance, and make a record of the event, regardless of whether or not such demonstrations are peaceful or lawful.

Plaintiffs further allege that the Philadelphia Police Department, through its Political Disobedience Unit, has compiled intelligence files on numerous individuals and groups. These files, about 18,000 in number, are separate from police interrogation and investigation records. They contain basic information plus information concerning the individual subject's political views, associations and personal life and habits. The files are allegedly kept indefinitely and sometimes without the knowledge of the subjects of the files.

Plaintiffs allege, on information and belief, that no safeguards exist as to the disposition of or access to the political and personal information contained in the

---

[9] Linda E. Fisher, *Guilt by Expressive Association: Political Profiling, Surveillance and the Privacy of Groups*, 46 Ariz. L. Rev. 621, 627 (2004).

files; that such information is available to other law enforcement agencies and, on information and belief, to private employers, to governmental agencies for purposes of considering employment, promotion, granting of licenses, passports, etc., to private political organizations which seek to suppress "subversive" or dissident political activity or views, and to the press.

It is also charged that Philadelphia Police Department has improperly and unlawfully publicized its political intelligence gathering system by the unauthorized public disclosure of information concerning certain named individuals and groups who are the subject of police intelligence files. On June 2, 1970, in a network television broadcast the above named defendants and their agents publicly discussed their system and disclosed the names of certain groups and individuals on whom such files were kept, without the approval of such groups and individuals, including plaintiff organizations and four individual plaintiffs.

After the foregoing factual allegations the plaintiffs allege that such facts resulted in violations of their rights under the First and Fourteenth Amendments. . . .

Plaintiffs sought declaratory, injunctive and other relief under 42 U.S.C. §§ 1983 and 1985 and 28 U.S.C. § 2201. This appeal followed the dismissal of the complaint for failure to state a claim upon which relief could be granted. . . .

In [*Laird v.*] *Tatum*, the Supreme Court was confronted by the claims of a plaintiff who alleged "that the exercise of his First Amendment rights is being chilled by the mere existence, without more, of a governmental investigative and data-gathering activity that is alleged to be broader in scope than is reasonably necessary for the accomplishment of a valid government purpose." The Court held that the jurisdiction of a federal court could not be invoked in such circumstances, where there was no immediate threat to the individual's constitutional rights and any chilling effect was subjective. . . .

We think it is clear that *Tatum* supports the action of the district court here to the extent the complaint alleges a constitutional violation on the basis of mere police photographing and data gathering at public meetings. We say this because such activity by law enforcement authorities, without more, is legally unobjectionable and creates at best a so-called subjective chill which the Supreme Court has said is not a substitute for a claim of specific present harm or a threat of specific future harm.

Nor does the sharing of this information with other agencies of government having a legitimate law enforcement function give rise to a constitutional violation. We cannot see where the traditional exchange of information with other law enforcement agencies results in any more objective harm than the original collation of such information. Although plaintiffs would distinguish their case from *Tatum* on the ground that they are direct targets of the intelligence system and their dossiers contain information about their individual political views, etc., we think that this is not sufficient to distinguish *Tatum* insofar as plaintiffs rely on the mere existence of police intelligence gathering and the sharing of information with other enforcement agencies. . . .

. . . [Next, we consider] plaintiffs' allegation that no safeguards exist on the disposition of or access to the political and personal information and conclusions contained in the dossiers and lists which defendants maintain and that such information is actually or potentially available, *inter alia*, to a wide spectrum of individuals, governmental agencies, private political organizations and the press.

It is not apparent how making information concerning the lawful activities of plaintiffs available to non-police groups or individuals could be considered within the proper ambit of law enforcement activity, particularly since it is alleged that plaintiffs are subject to surveillance only because their political views deviate from those of the "establishment." We think these allegations, at a minimum, show immediately threatened injury to plaintiffs by way of a chilling of their rights of freedom of speech and associational privacy. Some examples of immediately threatened harm come readily to mind. The general availability of such materials and lists could interfere with the job opportunities, careers or travel rights of the individual plaintiffs and such practical consequences may ensue without any specific awareness on plaintiffs' part. The mere anticipation of the practical consequences of joining or remaining with plaintiff organizations may well dissuade some individuals from becoming members, or may persuade others to resign their membership. We therefore conclude that, except for the allegation concerning the availability of the material to other law enforcement agencies, the allegations of paragraph 3 above state a claim sufficient to withstand a motion to dismiss. . . .

In paragraph 4 above, it is alleged that the Philadelphia Police Department described their political intelligence gathering system in a nationwide television show and specifically identified the plaintiff organizations and four of the individual plaintiffs as being the subjects of police dossiers.

The district court held that the allegations summarized in paragraph 4 amounted to no more than a subjective complaint of a chilling effect based on the "mere existence" of governmental information gathering activities. The court indicated that in order to create a justiciable controversy, plaintiffs were required to allege tangible consequences, such as a contempt citation, a criminal prosecution, exclusion from a profession, a threat of conscription and the like. However, we cannot believe that the *Tatum* opinion was meant to find non-justiciable a case such as the one before us where the alleged threatened injury, although not concrete, is nonetheless strikingly apparent. It cannot be doubted that disclosure on nationwide television that certain named persons or organizations are subjects of police intelligence files has a potential for a substantial adverse impact on such persons and organizations even though tangible evidence of the impact may be difficult, if not impossible, to obtain. . . .

. . . If plaintiffs' allegations are true, this type of activity strikes at the heart of a free society. We therefore conclude that the allegations of paragraph 4 as well as the improper dispersal claims of paragraph 3 set forth justiciable claims.

NOTES & QUESTIONS

1. **Tate *vs.* Laird.** Does *Tate* adequately distinguish *Laird* ? Is public disclosure always a more injurious privacy violation than government surveillance and information collection?
2. ***The Constitutional Right to Information Privacy.*** Is the result of *Tate* also supported by the constitutional right to information privacy in *Whalen*? Under

several cases involving this right, courts viewed information in public records as not private. As a consequence, these courts found that use of such information cannot give rise to a claim for a violation of the constitutional right to information privacy. *See, e.g., Cline v. Rogers,* 87 F.3d 176 (6th Cir. 1996). Suppose that in *Tate*, the police made their dossiers available as public records. Would the plaintiffs still have a viable claim under the constitutional right to information privacy? Would the plaintiffs have any other constitutional claims?

B. ANONYMITY

1. ANONYMOUS SPEECH

TALLEY V. STATE OF CALIFORNIA
362 U.S. 60 (1960)

BLACK, J. The question presented here is whether the provisions of a Los Angeles City ordinance restricting the distribution of handbills "abridge the freedom of speech and of the press secured against state invasion by the Fourteenth Amendment of the Constitution." The ordinance, § 28.06 of the Municipal Code of the City of Los Angeles, provides:

> No person shall distribute any hand-bill in any place under any circumstances, which does not have printed on the cover, or the face thereof, the name and address of the following:
>
> (a) The person who printed, wrote, compiled or manufactured the same.
>
> (b) The person who caused the same to be distributed; provided, however, that in the case of a fictitious person or club, in addition to such fictitious name, the true names and addresses of the owners, managers or agents of the person sponsoring said hand-bill shall also appear thereon.

The petitioner was arrested and tried in a Los Angeles Municipal Court for violating this ordinance. . . .

Anonymous pamphlets, leaflets, brochures and even books have played an important role in the progress of mankind. Persecuted groups and sects from time to time throughout history have been able to criticize oppressive practices and laws either anonymously or not at all. The obnoxious press licensing law of England, which was also enforced on the Colonies was due in part to the knowledge that exposure of the names of printers, writers and distributors would lessen the circulation of literature critical of the government. The old seditious libel cases in England show the lengths to which government had to go to find out who was responsible for books that were obnoxious to the rulers. John Lilburne was whipped, pilloried and fined for refusing to answer questions designed to get evidence to convict him or someone else for the secret distribution of books in England. Two Puritan Ministers, John Penry and John Udal, were sentenced to death on charges that they were responsible for writing, printing or publishing books. Before the Revolutionary War colonial patriots frequently had to conceal their authorship or distribution of literature that easily could have brought down on them prosecutions by English-controlled courts. Along about that time the Letters of Junius were written and the identity of their author is unknown to this day. Even the Federalist Papers, written in favor of the adoption of our Constitution, were published under fictitious names. It is plain that anonymity has sometimes been assumed for the most constructive purposes.

We have recently had occasion to hold in two cases that there are times and circumstances when States may not compel members of groups engaged in the dissemination of ideas to be publicly identified. *Bates v. City of Little Rock*, 361 U.S. 516; *N.A.A.C.P. v. State of Alabama*, 357 U.S. 449. The reason for those holdings was that identification and fear of reprisal might deter perfectly peaceful discussions of public matters of importance. This broad Los Angeles ordinance is subject to the same infirmity. We hold that it, like the Griffin, Georgia, ordinance, is void on its face. . . .

CLARK, J., joined by FRANKFURTER, J. and WHITTAKER, J., dissenting. . . . The record is barren of any claim, much less proof, that [Talley] will suffer any injury whatever by identifying the handbill with his name. Unlike *NAACP v. Alabama*, 357 U.S. 449 (1958), which is relied upon, there is neither allegation nor proof that Talley or any group sponsoring him would suffer "economic reprisal, loss of employment, threat of physical coercion [or] other manifestations of public hostility." Talley makes no showing whatever to support his contention that a restraint upon his freedom of speech will result from the enforcement of the ordinance. The existence of such a restraint is necessary before we can strike the ordinance down.

But even if the State had this burden, which it does not, the substantiality of Los Angeles' interest in the enforcement of the ordinance sustains its validity. Its chief law enforcement officer says that the enforcement of the ordinance prevents "fraud, deceit, false advertising, negligent use of words, obscenity, and libel," and, as we have said, that such was its purpose. In the absence of any showing to the contrary by Talley, this appears to me entirely sufficient.

I stand second to none in supporting Talley's right of free speech — but not his freedom of anonymity. The Constitution says nothing about freedom of anonymous speech. . . .

MCINTYRE V. OHIO ELECTIONS COMMISSION

514 U.S. 334 (1995)

STEVENS, J. . . . On April 27, 1988, Margaret McIntyre distributed leaflets to persons attending a public meeting at the Blendon Middle School in Westerville, Ohio. At this meeting, the superintendent of schools planned to discuss an imminent referendum on a proposed school tax levy. The leaflets expressed Mrs. McIntyre's opposition to the levy. There is no suggestion that the text of her message was false, misleading, or libelous. She had composed and printed it on her home computer and had paid a professional printer to make additional copies. Some of the handbills identified her as the author; others merely purported to express the views of "CONCERNED PARENTS AND TAX PAYERS." Except for the help provided by her son and a friend, who placed some of the leaflets on car windshields in the school parking lot, Mrs. McIntyre acted independently.

While Mrs. McIntyre distributed her handbills, an official of the school district, who supported the tax proposal, advised her that the unsigned leaflets did not conform to the Ohio election laws. Undeterred, Mrs. McIntyre appeared at another meeting on the next evening and handed out more of the handbills.

The proposed school levy was defeated at the next two elections, but it finally passed on its third try in November 1988. Five months later, the same school official filed a complaint with the Ohio Elections Commission charging that Mrs. McIntyre's distribution of unsigned leaflets violated § 3599.09(A) of the Ohio Code [which prohibited the distribution of political literature without the name and address of the person or organization responsible for the distribution]. The commission agreed and imposed a fine of $100. . . .

Mrs. McIntyre passed away during the pendency of this litigation. Even though the amount in controversy is only $100, petitioner, as the executor of her estate, has pursued her claim in this Court. Our grant of certiorari reflects our agreement with his appraisal of the importance of the question presented. . . .

Ohio maintains that the statute under review is a reasonable regulation of the electoral process. . . .

"Anonymous pamphlets, leaflets, brochures and even books have played an important role in the progress of mankind." *Talley v. California*. Great works of literature have frequently been produced by authors writing under assumed names.[10] Despite readers' curiosity and the public's interest in identifying the creator of a work of art, an author generally is free to decide whether or not to disclose his or her true identity. The decision in favor of anonymity may be motivated by fear of economic or official retaliation, by concern about social ostracism, or merely by a desire to preserve as much of one's privacy as possible. Whatever the motivation may be, at least in the field of literary endeavor, the interest in having anonymous works enter the marketplace of ideas unquestionably outweighs any public interest in requiring disclosure as a condition of entry. Accordingly, an author's decision to remain anonymous, like other decisions concerning omissions or additions to the content of a publication, is an aspect of the freedom of speech protected by the First Amendment.

. . . On occasion, quite apart from any threat of persecution, an advocate may believe her ideas will be more persuasive if her readers are unaware of her identity. Anonymity thereby provides a way for a writer who may be personally unpopular to ensure that readers will not prejudge her message simply because they do not like its proponent. Thus, even in the field of political rhetoric, where "the identity of the speaker is an important component of many attempts to

[10] American names such as Mark Twain (Samuel Langhorne Clemens) and O. Henry (William Sydney Porter) come readily to mind. Benjamin Franklin employed numerous different pseudonyms. Distinguished French authors such as Voltaire (François Marie Arouet) and George Sand (Amandine Aurore Lucie Dupin), and British authors such as George Eliot (Mary Ann Evans), Charles Lamb (sometimes wrote as "Elia"), and Charles Dickens (sometimes wrote as "Boz"), also published under assumed names. . . .

persuade," the most effective advocates have sometimes opted for anonymity. The specific holding in *Talley* related to advocacy of an economic boycott, but the Court's reasoning embraced a respected tradition of anonymity in the advocacy of political causes.[11] This tradition is perhaps best exemplified by the secret ballot, the hard-won right to vote one's conscience without fear of retaliation. . . .

California had defended the Los Angeles ordinance at issue in *Talley* as a law "aimed at providing a way to identify those responsible for fraud, false advertising and libel." We rejected that argument because nothing in the text or legislative history of the ordinance limited its application to those evils. We then made clear that we did "not pass on the validity of an ordinance limited to prevent these or any other supposed evils." The Ohio statute likewise contains no language limiting its application to fraudulent, false, or libelous statements; to the extent, therefore, that Ohio seeks to justify § 3599.09(A) as a means to prevent the dissemination of untruths, its defense must fail for the same reason given in *Talley*. As the facts of this case demonstrate, the ordinance plainly applies even when there is no hint of falsity or libel. . . .

. . . [Section] 3599.09(A) of the Ohio Code does not control the mechanics of the electoral process. It is a regulation of pure speech. Moreover, even though this provision applies evenhandedly to advocates of differing viewpoints, it is a direct regulation of the content of speech. Every written document covered by the statute must contain "the name and residence or business address of the chairman, treasurer, or secretary of the organization issuing the same, or the person who issues, makes, or is responsible therefor." Furthermore, the category of covered documents is defined by their content — only those publications containing speech designed to influence the voters in an election need bear the required markings. Consequently, we are not faced with an ordinary election restriction; this case "involves a limitation on political expression subject to exacting scrutiny." . . .

When a law burdens core political speech, we apply "exacting scrutiny," and we uphold the restriction only if it is narrowly tailored to serve an overriding state interest. . . .

Nevertheless, the State argues that, even under the strictest standard of review, the disclosure requirement in § 3599.09(A) is justified by two important and legitimate state interests. Ohio judges its interest in preventing fraudulent and libelous statements and its interest in providing the electorate with relevant information to be sufficiently compelling to justify the anonymous speech ban. These two interests necessarily overlap to some extent, but it is useful to discuss them separately.

Insofar as the interest in informing the electorate means nothing more than the provision of additional information that may either buttress or undermine the argument in a document, we think the identity of the speaker is no different from other components of the document's content that the author is free to include or exclude. . . . The simple interest in providing voters with additional relevant

[11] That tradition is most famously embodied in the Federalist Papers, authored by James Madison, Alexander Hamilton, and John Jay, but signed "Publius." Publius' opponents, the Anti-Federalists, also tended to publish under pseudonyms. . . .

information does not justify a state requirement that a writer make statements or disclosures she would otherwise omit. Moreover, in the case of a handbill written by a private citizen who is not known to the recipient, the name and address of the author add little, if anything, to the reader's ability to evaluate the document's message. . . .

The state interest in preventing fraud and libel stands on a different footing. We agree with Ohio's submission that this interest carries special weight during election campaigns when false statements, if credited, may have serious adverse consequences for the public at large. Ohio does not, however, rely solely on § 3599.09(A) to protect that interest. Its Election Code includes detailed and specific prohibitions against making or disseminating false statements during political campaigns. These regulations apply both to candidate elections and to issue-driven ballot measures. Thus, Ohio's prohibition of anonymous leaflets plainly is not its principal weapon against fraud. Rather, it serves as an aid to enforcement of the specific prohibitions and as a deterrent to the making of false statements by unscrupulous prevaricators. Although these ancillary benefits are assuredly legitimate, we are not persuaded that they justify § 3599.09(A)'s extremely broad prohibition. . . .

Under our Constitution, anonymous pamphleteering is not a pernicious, fraudulent practice, but an honorable tradition of advocacy and of dissent. Anonymity is a shield from the tyranny of the majority. It thus exemplifies the purpose behind the Bill of Rights, and of the First Amendment in particular: to protect unpopular individuals from retaliation — and their ideas from suppression — at the hand of an intolerant society. . . .

THOMAS, J. concurring. . . . I agree with the majority's conclusion that Ohio's election law . . . is inconsistent with the First Amendment. I would apply, however, a different methodology to this case. Instead of asking whether "an honorable tradition" of anonymous speech has existed throughout American history, or what the "value" of anonymous speech might be, we should determine whether the phrase "freedom of speech, or of the press," as originally understood, protected anonymous political leafleting. I believe that it did. . . .

Unfortunately, we have no record of discussions of anonymous political expression either in the First Congress, which drafted the Bill of Rights, or in the state ratifying conventions. Thus, our analysis must focus on the practices and beliefs held by the Founders concerning anonymous political articles and pamphlets. . . .

There is little doubt that the Framers engaged in anonymous political writing. The essays in the *Federalist Papers*, published under the pseudonym of "Publius," are only the most famous example of the outpouring of anonymous political writing that occurred during the ratification of the Constitution. . . .

The large quantity of newspapers and pamphlets the Framers produced during the various crises of their generation show the remarkable extent to which the Framers relied upon anonymity. During the break with Great Britain, the revolutionaries employed pseudonyms both to conceal their identity from Crown authorities and to impart a message. Often, writers would choose names to signal their point of view or to invoke specific classical and modern "crusaders in an agelong struggle against tyranny." Thus, leaders of the struggle for independence would adopt descriptive names such as "Common Sense," a "Farmer," or "A True Patriot," or historical ones such as "Cato" (a name used by many to refer to the Roman Cato and to Cato's letters), or "Mucius Scaevola." The practice was even more prevalent during the great outpouring of political argument and commentary that accompanied the ratification of the Constitution. Besides "Publius," prominent Federalists signed their articles and pamphlets with names such as "An American Citizen," "Marcus," "A Landholder," "Americanus"; Anti-Federalists replied with the pseudonyms "Cato," "Centinel," "Brutus," the "Federal Farmer," and "The Impartial Examiner." The practice of publishing one's thoughts anonymously or under pseudonym was so widespread that only two major Federalist or Anti-Federalist pieces appear to have been signed by their true authors, and they may have had special reasons to do so. . . .

Because the majority has adopted an analysis that is largely unconnected to the Constitution's text and history, I concur only in the judgment.

SCALIA, J. joined by REHNQUIST, C.J. dissenting. . . . The Court's unprecedented protection for anonymous speech does not even have the virtue of establishing a clear (albeit erroneous) rule of law. . . . It may take decades to work out the shape of this newly expanded right-to-speak-incognito, even in the elections field. And in other areas, of course, a whole new boutique of wonderful First Amendment litigation opens its doors. Must a parade permit, for example, be issued to a group that refuses to provide its identity, or that agrees to do so only under assurance that the identity will not be made public? Must a municipally owned theater that is leased for private productions book anonymously sponsored presentations? Must a government periodical that has a "letters to the editor" column disavow the policy that most newspapers have against the publication of anonymous letters? Must a public university that makes its facilities available for a speech by Louis Farrakhan or David Duke refuse to disclose the on-campus or off-campus group that has sponsored or paid for the speech? Must a municipal "public-access" cable channel permit anonymous (and masked) performers? The silliness that follows upon a generalized right to anonymous speech has no end. . . .

The Court says that the State has not explained "why it can more easily enforce the direct bans on disseminating false documents against anonymous authors and distributors than against wrongdoers who might use false names and addresses in an attempt to avoid detection." I am not sure what this complicated comparison means. I am sure, however, that (1) a person who is required to put his name to a document is much less likely to lie than one who can lie anonymously, and (2) the distributor of a leaflet which is unlawful because it is anonymous runs much more risk of immediate detection and punishment than the distributor of a leaflet which is unlawful because it is false. Thus, people will be more likely to observe a signing requirement than a naked "no falsity" requirement; and, having observed that requirement, will then be significantly less likely to lie in what they have signed.

But the usefulness of a signing requirement lies not only in promoting observance of the law against campaign falsehoods (though that alone is enough to sustain it). It lies also in promoting a civil and dignified level of campaign debate — which the State has no power to command, but ample power to encourage by such undemanding measures as a signature requirement. Observers of the past few national elections have expressed concern about the increase of character assassination — "mudslinging" is the colloquial term — engaged in by political candidates and their supporters to the detriment of the democratic process. Not all of this, in fact not much of it, consists of actionable untruth; most is innuendo, or demeaning characterization, or mere disclosure of items of personal life that have no bearing upon suitability for office. Imagine how much all of this would increase if it could be done anonymously. The principal impediment against it is the reluctance of most individuals and organizations to be publicly associated with uncharitable and uncivil expression. Consider, moreover, the increased potential for "dirty tricks." It is not unheard-of for campaign operatives to circulate material over the name of their opponents or their opponents' supporters (a violation of election laws) in order to attract or alienate certain interest groups. How much easier — and sanction free! — it would be to circulate anonymous material (for example, a really tasteless, though not actionably false, attack upon one's own candidate) with the hope and expectation that it will be attributed to, and held against, the other side. . . .

I do not know where the Court derives its perception that "anonymous pamphleteering is not a pernicious, fraudulent practice, but an honorable tradition of advocacy and of dissent." I can imagine no reason why an anonymous leaflet is any more honorable, as a general matter, than an anonymous phone call or an anonymous letter. It facilitates wrong by eliminating accountability, which is ordinarily the very purpose of the anonymity. . . .

NOTES & QUESTIONS

1. ***Why Is Anonymity in Speaking Protected by the First Amendment?*** *Talley* and *McIntyre* conclude that anonymous speech is protected under the First Amendment but do so based on different rationales. What are those rationales? Which rationale seems most persuasive to you?
2. ***Identification Requirements.*** In *Buckley v. ACLF*, 525 U.S. 182 (1999), the Court struck down part of a Colorado statute requiring individuals handing out petitions to wear name tags. The Court reasoned:

   > [T]he name badge requirement forces circulators to reveal their identities at the same time they deliver their political message, it operates when reaction to the circulator's message is immediate and may be the most intense, emotional, and unreasoned. . . . The injury to speech is heightened for the petition circulator because the badge requirement compels personal name identification at the precise moment when the circulator's interest in anonymity is the greatest.

   In *Watchtower Bible & Tract Society v. Village of Stratton,* 536 U.S. 150 (2002), a local ordinance required all solicitors of private residences to obtain a permit, which required that the individuals supply data about their cause as well as their name, home addresses, and employers or affiliated organizations. In upholding the ordinance, the Sixth Circuit distinguished *McIntyre* because "individuals going door-to-door to engage in political speech are not anonymous by virtue of the fact that they reveal a portion of their identities — their physical identities — to the residents they canvass." Therefore, the appellate court reasoned, the right to speak anonymously did not apply. *See* 240 F.3d 553 (6th Cir. 2001). The Supreme Court reversed:

> It is offensive — not only to the values protected by the First Amendment, but to the very notion of a free society — that in the context of everyday public discourse a citizen must first inform the government of her desire to speak to her neighbors and then obtain a permit to do so. Even if the issuance of permits by the mayor's office is a ministerial task that is performed promptly and at no cost to the applicant, a law requiring a permit to engage in such speech constitutes a dramatic departure from our national heritage and constitutional tradition. . . .

The Supreme Court concluded that the ordinance was invalid under the First Amendment because it was not narrowly tailored to the Village's interest in preventing fraud, since much canvassing involves finding support for political campaigns or unpopular causes. As to an interest in crime prevention, "there is an absence of any evidence of a special crime problem related to door-to-door solicitation in the record before us."

In dissent, Chief Justice Rehnquist argued that the "ordinance is content neutral" and "merely regulates the manner in which one must canvass." The ordinance survives intermediate scrutiny because it produces "[s]ome deterrence of serious criminal activity."

2. ANONYMITY IN CYBERSPACE

E-mail and the Internet enable people to communicate anonymously with ease. People can send e-mail or post messages to electronic bulletin boards under pseudonyms. However, this anonymity is quite fragile, and in some cases illusory.

First, many people believe that their web surfing is anonymous — in other words, that when they visit various websites, their identities are not known to the operators of those sites unless they choose to disclose who they are. However, the use of "cookies" — small text files that are downloaded into the user's computer when a user visits a website — means that web surfing is far from an anonymous activity. With cookies, users are tagged with an identification number, which can in some circumstances be used to look up a variety of information collected about them, often including their identity. Beyond cookies, there are also other ways that websites track and identify their visitors. These include website log files, which contain a user's Internet protocol (IP) address, time online, any information that the user entered into a webpage, pages downloaded, the last page where the user clinked a link which led to the present page (also known as the "Referrer"), and Internet cookies. Information can also be collected through "web bugs," also known as "clear GIF," which is a graphic on a web page created for the purpose of online tracking. Web bugs are typically only 1 x 1 pixel in size, and hence invisible to the viewer.

Second, an individual's Internet Service Provider (ISP) has information linking one's screen name (the pseudonym one writes under) to one's actual identity. The security of this information depends upon the policies and carefulness of one's ISP. Under federal wiretap law, an ISP must disclose information identifying a particular user to the government pursuant to a subpoena. However, no subpoena is required for private parties. An ISP "may disclose a record or other information pertaining to a subscriber . . . to any person other than a governmental entity." 18 U.S.C. § 2703(c)(1)(A).

As David Sobel observes:

> Since 1998, scores of civil lawsuits have been filed against "John Doe" defendants by plaintiffs allegedly harmed by anonymous Internet postings. The underlying causes of action vary, ranging from defamation to unauthorized disclosure of proprietary information.
>
> The common denominator in these suits is that they all raise novel yet fundamental questions of fairness and due process. Upon the filing of civil complaints, plaintiffs' counsel serve subpoenas on message board operators and Internet service providers seeking the identities of anonymous posters. Some service providers, including America Online, notify subscribers when civil subpoenas are received and allow them a period of time to challenge the process. But many online services — most notably Yahoo! — comply with such subpoenas as a matter of course, without notice to their users. As a result, "John Doe" defendants frequently have no opportunity to quash subpoenas and the courts have no role in evaluating the propriety of requests for identifying information.[12]

Anonymity creates dangers of potential fraud and abuse. For example, "cybersmearers" anonymously post false information about a company to manipulate stock prices. How should one's interest in anonymity be reconciled with the interests of preventing fraud and permitting people to sue for defamatory statements?

ACLU v. Miller

977 F. Supp. 1228 (N.D. Ga. 1997)

SHOOB, J. This action is before the Court on plaintiffs' motion for preliminary injunction and defendants' motion to dismiss. . . .

Plaintiffs bring this action for declaratory and injunctive relief challenging the constitutionality of Act No. 1029, Ga. Laws 1996, p. 1505, codified at O.C.G.A. § 16-9-93.1 ("act" or "statute"). The act makes it a crime for

> any person . . . knowingly to transmit any data through a computer network . . . for the purpose of setting up, maintaining, operating, or exchanging data with an electronic mailbox, home page, or any other electronic information storage bank or point of access to electronic information if such data uses any individual name . . . to falsely identify the person . . .

and for

---

[12] David L. Sobel, *The Process That "John Doe" Is Due: Addressing the Legal Challenge to Internet Anonymity*, 5 Va. J.L. & Tech. 3 (2000). For more background, see generally Lyrissa Barnett Lidsky, *Silencing John Doe: Defamation and Discourse in Cyberspace*, 49 Duke L.J. 855 (2000); Philip Giordano, *Invoking Law as a Basis for Identity in Cyberspace*, 1998 Stan. Tech. L. Rev. 1.

> any person . . . knowingly to transmit any data through a computer network . . . if such data uses any . . . trade name, registered trademark, logo, legal or official seal, or copyrighted symbol . . . which would falsely state or imply that such person . . . has permission or is legally authorized to use [it] for such purpose when such permission or authorization has not been obtained.

. . . Plaintiffs, a group of individuals and organization members who communicate over the internet, interpret it as imposing unconstitutional content-based restrictions on their right to communicate anonymously and pseudonymously over the internet, as well as on their right to use trade names, logos, and other graphics in a manner held to be constitutional in other contexts.

Plaintiffs argue that the act has tremendous implications for internet users, many of whom "falsely identify" themselves on a regular basis for the purpose of communicating about sensitive topics without subjecting themselves to ostracism or embarrassment. Plaintiffs further contend that the trade name and logo restriction frustrates one of the internet's unique features — the "links" that connect web pages on the World Wide Web and enable users to browse easily from topic to topic through the computer network system. Plaintiffs claim that the act's broad language is further damaging in that it allows for selective prosecution of persons communicating about controversial topics.

Defendants contend that the act prohibits a much narrower class of communications. They interpret it as forbidding only fraudulent transmissions or the appropriation of the identity of another person or entity for some improper purpose. . . .

. . . It appears from the record that plaintiffs are likely to prove that the statute imposes content-based restrictions which are not narrowly tailored to achieve the state's purported compelling interest. Furthermore, plaintiffs are likely to show that the statute is overbroad and void for vagueness.

First, because "the identity of the speaker is no different from other components of [a] document's contents that the author is free to include or exclude," *McIntyre v. Ohio Elections Comm'n*, 514 U.S. 334 (1995), the statute's prohibition of internet transmissions which "falsely identify" the sender constitutes a presumptively invalid content-based restriction. The state may impose content-based restrictions only to promote a "compelling state interest" and only through use of "the least restrictive means to further the articulated interest." Thus, in order to overcome the presumption of invalidity, defendants must demonstrate that the statute furthers a compelling state interest and is narrowly tailored to achieve it.

Defendants allege that the statute's purpose is fraud prevention, which the Court agrees is a compelling state interest. However, the statute is not narrowly tailored to achieve that end and instead sweeps innocent, protected speech within its scope. Specifically, by its plain language the criminal prohibition applies regardless of whether a speaker has any intent to deceive or whether deception actually occurs. Therefore, it could apply to a wide range of transmissions which "falsely identify" the sender, but are not "fraudulent" within the specific meaning of the criminal code. . . .

For similar reasons, plaintiffs are likely to succeed on their overbreadth claim because the statute "sweeps protected activity within its proscription." In the first amendment context, the overbreadth doctrine, which invalidates overbroad statutes even when some of their applications are valid, is based on the recognition that "the very existence of some broadly written laws has the potential to chill the expressive activity of others not before the Court."

The Court concludes that the statute was not drafted with the precision necessary for laws regulating speech. On its face, the act prohibits such protected speech as the use of false identification to avoid social ostracism, to prevent discrimination and harassment, and to protect privacy, as well as the use of trade names or logos in non-commercial educational speech, news, and commentary — a prohibition with well-recognized first amendment problems. Therefore, even if the statute could constitutionally be used to prosecute persons who intentionally "falsely identify" themselves in order to deceive or defraud the public, or to persons whose commercial use of trade names and logos creates a substantial likelihood of confusion or the dilution of a famous mark, the statute is nevertheless overbroad because it operates unconstitutionally for a substantial category of the speakers it covers. . . .

NOTES & QUESTIONS

1. ***Retaining Identifying Information.*** In *ACLU v. Miller*, suppose that instead of passing the law that it did, Georgia passed a narrower law that provided:

   > Any anonymous remailer service or Internet Service Provider must retain identifying information for all communications it transmits or helps to transmit. This identifying information must be provided pursuant to a search warrant, court order, or subpoena.

   Would such a law be constitutional?

2. ***Privacy Enhancing Technologies.*** Given the fragile state of privacy on the Internet, individuals can resort to certain technological devices to help preserve their anonymity. Technologies that enhance privacy are referred to as "Privacy Enhancing Technologies" or PETs. According to Marc Rotenberg: "The concept of PETs has resonated in the privacy world. Governments have undertaken studies to explore how PETs, oftentimes based on pseudonyms, could be implemented in the world of the Internet and e-commerce. PETs typically seek to implement Fair Information Practices and where possible to minimize or eliminate the collection of personally identifiable information."[13]

   One example of a PET that protects anonymity is an "anonymous remailer" — a computer service that enables people to send e-mail anonymously. A person sends a message through a remailer, which removes a person's actual name and e-mail address, substitutes it with a pseudonym, and sends it on its way. Certain remailers maintain accounts with individuals, and as a result, the individual's identifying information is known to the remailer and can be obtained by getting a court order to force the remailer to divulge the identity. Other remailers operate in such a way that even the remailer does not know the identities of its clients. There are a number of remailer services on the

---

[13] Marc Rotenberg, *Fair Information Practices and the Architecture of Privacy (What Larry Doesn't Get)*, 2001 Stan. Tech. L. Rev. 1.

Internet. However, remailers do not offer foolproof anonymity. One's e-mail messages to a remailer can be intercepted by the government, by one's employer, by one's ISP, or by others.

Consider A. Michael Froomkin:

> Remailer operators already have come under various forms of attack, most recently lawsuits or subpoenas instigated by officials of the Church of Scientology who sought to identify the person they allege used remailers to disseminate copyrighted and secret Church teachings. As a result, operating a remailer is not a risk-free activity today. Indeed, one can imagine a number of creative lawsuits that might reasonably be launched at the operator of a remailer. Examples include a new tort of concealment of identity, a claim of conspiracy with the wrong-doer, and a RICO claim. A remailer operator whose remailer was used to harass someone might face a common law tort claim of harassment. . . . Although it is far from obvious that any of these legal theories would or should succeed, some raise non-frivolous issues and thus would be expensive to defend.[14]

3. ***The WHOIS Database.*** Currently, the Internet Corporation for Assigned Names and Numbers (ICANN) Registrar Accreditation Agreement (RAA) requires that the identity and addresses of domain name holders be publicly disclosed, as well as the identities, addresses, e-mail addresses, and telephone numbers for technical and administrative contacts. Domain names are the names assigned to particular websites (e.g., cnn.com). In other words, an individual who wants to create her own website must publicly disclose personal information and cannot remain anonymous. The registration scheme extends to anyone who owns a domain name, including commercial services and publishers of political newsletters.

Dawn Nunziato observes that the ICANN identification policy was enacted "[a]t the behest of interested intellectual property owners, who were concerned about their ability to police infringing content on the Internet." She argues:

> Because of the important role anonymous speech serves within expressive forums — which in turn are integral to democratic governments — ICANN should, in reevaluating its policies to accord meaningful protection for freedom of expression, revise its policy requiring domain name holders publicly to disclose their names and addresses. While protecting anonymous Internet speech is clearly an important component of free speech within the United States, it is even more important for ICANN to protect the identity of speakers from countries that are more inclined to retaliate against speakers based on the ideas they express.

Nunziato suggests that ICANN should still collect registrants' names and addresses, but only make public their e-mail addresses. Only upon a

---

[14] A. Michael Froomkin, *Flood Control on the Information Ocean: Living with Anonymity, Digital Cash, and Distributed Databases*, 15 J.L. & Comm. 395, 425-26 (1996).

"heightened showing by a rights holder" should ICANN release a registrant's name and address.[15]

Should registrants of Internet domain names be able to obtain "proxy registrations" that hide their information from the general public? In February 2005, the National Telecommunication and Information Administration of the Department of Commerce decided that registrars, such as Go Daddy, could not offer proxy registrations for the U.S. domain. Does this decision implicate First Amendment interests?

DOE V. CAHILL

884 A.2d 451 (Del. 2005)

STEELE, C.J. . . . On November 2, 2004, the plaintiffs below, Patrick and Julia Cahill, both residents of Smyrna, Delaware, filed suit against four John Doe defendants asserting defamation and invasion of privacy claims. This appeal involves only one of the John Doe defendants, John Doe No. 1 below and "Doe" in this opinion. Using the alias "Proud Citizen," Doe posted two statements on an internet website sponsored by the Delaware State News called the "Smyrna/Clayton Issues Blog" concerning Cahill's performance as a City Councilman of Smyrna. The "Guidelines" at the top of the blog stated "[t]his is your hometown forum for opinions about public issues." The first of Doe's statements, posted on September 18, 2004, said:

> If only Councilman Cahill was able to display the same leadership skills, energy and enthusiasm toward the revitalization and growth of the fine town of Smyrna as Mayor Schaeffer has demonstrated! While Mayor Schaeffer has made great strides toward improving the livelihood of Smyrna's citizens, Cahill has devoted all of his energy to being a divisive impediment to any kind of cooperative movement. *Anyone who has spent any amount of time with Cahill would be keenly aware of such character flaws, not to mention an obvious mental deterioration.* Cahill is a prime example of failed leadership — his eventual ousting is exactly what Smyrna needs in order to move forward and establish a community that is able to thrive on its own economic stability and common pride in its town.

The next day, Doe posted another statement:

> *Gahill* [sic] *is as paranoid* as everyone in the town thinks he is. The mayor needs support from his citizens and protections from unfounded attacks. . . .

Pursuant to Superior Court Rule 30, the Cahills sought and obtained leave of the Superior Court to conduct a pre-service deposition of the owner of the internet blog, Independent Newspapers. After obtaining the IP addresses associated with the blog postings from the blog's owner, the Cahills learned that Comcast Corporation owned Doe's IP address. An IP address is an electronic number that specifically identifies a particular computer using the internet. IP addresses are often owned by internet service providers who then assign them to

---

[15] Dawn C. Nunziato, *Freedom of Expression, Democratic Norms, and Internet Governance*, 52 Emory L.J. 187, 202, 257, 259 (2003).

subscribers when they use the internet. These addresses are unique and assigned to only one ISP subscriber at a time. Thus, if the ISP knows the time and the date that postings were made from a specific IP address, it can determine the identity of its subscriber.

Armed with Doe's IP address, the Cahills obtained a court order requiring Comcast to disclose Doe's identity. As required by Federal Statute,[16] when Comcast received the discovery request, it notified Doe. On January 4, 2005, Doe filed an "Emergency Motion for a Protective Order" seeking to prevent the Cahills from obtaining his identity from Comcast. . . .

On June 14, 2005, the trial judge issued a memorandum opinion denying Doe's motion for a protective order. The Superior Court judge adopted a "good faith" standard for determining when a defamation plaintiff could compel the disclosure of the identity of an anonymous plaintiff. Under the good faith standard, the Superior Court required the Cahills to establish: (1) that they had a legitimate, good faith basis upon which to bring the underlying claim; (2) that the identifying information sought was directly and materially related to their claim; and (3) that the information could not be obtained from any other source. Applying this standard, the Superior Court held that the Cahills could obtain Doe's identity from Comcast. Doe filed an interlocutory appeal, which we accepted on June 28, 2005. . . .

The internet is a unique democratizing medium unlike anything that has come before. The advent of the internet dramatically changed the nature of public discourse by allowing more and diverse people to engage in public debate. . . .

Internet speech is often anonymous. "Many participants in cyberspace discussions employ pseudonymous identities, and, even when a speaker chooses to reveal her real name, she may still be anonymous for all practical purposes." . . .

It is clear that speech over the internet is entitled to First Amendment protection. This protection extends to anonymous internet speech. Anonymous internet speech in blogs or chat rooms in some instances can become the modern equivalent of political pamphleteering. As the United States Supreme Court recently noted, "anonymous pamphleteering is not a pernicious, fraudulent practice, but an honorable tradition of advocacy and dissent." The United States Supreme Court continued, "[t]he right to remain anonymous may be abused when it shields fraudulent conduct. But political speech by its nature will sometimes have unpalatable consequences, and, in general, our society accords greater weight to the value of free speech than to the dangers of its misuse."

It also is clear that the First Amendment does not protect defamatory speech. "[I]t is well understood that the right of free speech is not absolute at all times and under all circumstances." Certain classes of speech, including defamatory and libelous speech, are entitled to no Constitutional protection. . . . Accordingly, we must adopt a standard that appropriately balances one person's right to speak anonymously against another person's right to protect his reputation. . . .

In this case, this Court is called upon to adopt a standard for trial courts to apply when faced with a public figure plaintiff's discovery request that seeks to unmask the identity of an anonymous defendant who has posted allegedly

[16] 47 U.S.C. 551(c)(2) requires a court order to a cable ISP and notice to the ISP subscriber before an ISP can disclose the identity of its subscriber to a third party.

defamatory material on the internet. Before this Court is an entire spectrum of "standards" that could be required, ranging (in ascending order) from a good faith basis to assert a claim, to pleading sufficient facts to survive a motion to dismiss, to a showing of *prima facie* evidence sufficient to withstand a motion for summary judgment, and beyond that, hurdles even more stringent. The Cahills urge this Court to adopt the good faith standard applied by the Superior Court. We decline to do so. Instead we hold that a defamation plaintiff must satisfy a "summary judgment" standard before obtaining the identity of an anonymous defendant.

We are concerned that setting the standard too low will chill potential posters from exercising their First Amendment right to speak anonymously. The possibility of losing anonymity in a future lawsuit could intimidate anonymous posters into self-censoring their comments or simply not commenting at all. A defamation plaintiff, particularly a public figure, obtains a very important form of relief by unmasking the identity of his anonymous critics. The revelation of identity of an anonymous speaker "may subject [that speaker] to ostracism for expressing unpopular ideas, invite retaliation from those who oppose her ideas or from those whom she criticizes, or simply give unwanted exposure to her mental processes." Plaintiffs can often initially plead sufficient facts to meet the good faith test applied by the Superior Court, even if the defamation claim is not very strong, or worse, if they do not intend to pursue the defamation action to a final decision. After obtaining the identity of an anonymous critic through the compulsory discovery process, a defamation plaintiff who either loses on the merits or fails to pursue a lawsuit is still free to engage in extra-judicial self-help remedies; more bluntly, the plaintiff can simply seek revenge or retribution.

Indeed, there is reason to believe that many defamation plaintiffs bring suit merely to unmask the identities of anonymous critics. As one commentator has noted, "[t]he sudden surge in John Doe suits stems from the fact that many defamation actions are not really about money." "The goals of this new breed of libel action are largely symbolic, the primary goal being to silence John Doe and others like him." This "sue first, ask questions later" approach, coupled with a standard only minimally protective of the anonymity of defendants, will discourage debate on important issues of public concern as more and more anonymous posters censor their online statements in response to the likelihood of being unmasked. . . .

Long-settled doctrine governs this Court's review of dismissals under Rule 12(b)(6). Under that doctrine, the threshold for the showing a plaintiff must make to survive a motion to dismiss is low. Delaware is a notice pleading jurisdiction. Thus, for a complaint to survive a motion to dismiss, it need only give "general notice of the claim asserted." A court can dismiss for failure to state a claim on which relief can be granted only if "it appears with reasonable certainty that the plaintiff could not prove any set of facts that would entitle him to relief." On a motion to dismiss, a court's review is limited to the well-pleaded allegations in the complaint. An allegation, "though vague or lacking in detail" can still be well-pleaded so long as it puts the opposing party on notice of the claim brought against it. Finally, in ruling on a motion to dismiss under Rule 12(b)(6), a trial court must draw all reasonable factual inferences in favor of the party opposing the motion. . . .

[E]ven silly or trivial libel claims can easily survive a motion to dismiss where the plaintiff pleads facts that put the defendant on notice of his claim, however vague or lacking in detail these allegations may be. Clearly then, if the stricter motion to dismiss standard is incapable of screening silly or trivial defamation suits, then the even less stringent good faith standard is less capable of doing so. . . .

[A] summary judgment proceeding can dispense with weak or even "silly" libel cases before trial (but even then only after significant expense and anxiety to the parties). Applying a summary judgment standard to a public figure defamation plaintiff's discovery request to obtain an anonymous defendant's identity will more appropriately protect against the chilling effect on anonymous First Amendment internet speech that can arise when plaintiffs bring trivial defamation lawsuits primarily to harass or to unmask their critics. . . .

We conclude that the summary judgment standard is the appropriate test by which to strike the balance between a defamation plaintiff's right to protect his reputation and a defendant's right to exercise free speech anonymously. We accordingly hold that before a defamation plaintiff can obtain the identity of an anonymous defendant through the compulsory discovery process he must support his defamation claim with facts sufficient to defeat a summary judgment motion.

. . . . [T]o the extent reasonably practicable under the circumstances, the plaintiff must undertake efforts to notify the anonymous poster that he is the subject of a subpoena or application for order of disclosure. The plaintiff must also withhold action to afford the anonymous defendant a reasonable opportunity to file and serve opposition to the discovery request. Moreover, when a case arises in the internet context, the plaintiff must post a message notifying the anonymous defendant of the plaintiff's discovery request on the same message board where the allegedly defamatory statement was originally posted. . . .

Although a good faith or motion to dismiss standard sets the bar too low to protect a defendant's First Amendment right to speak anonymously on the internet, a summary judgment standard does not correspondingly set the bar too high for a defamation plaintiff seeking redress for reputational harm to obtain relief. . . .

[T]o obtain discovery of an anonymous defendant's identity under the summary judgment standard, a defamation plaintiff "must submit sufficient evidence to establish a *prima facie* case for each essential element of the claim in question." In other words, the defamation plaintiff, as the party bearing the burden of proof at trial, must introduce evidence creating a genuine issue of material fact for all elements of a defamation claim *within the plaintiff's control.*

Under Delaware law, a public figure defamation plaintiff in a libel case must plead and ultimately prove that: 1) the defendant made a defamatory statement; 2) concerning the plaintiff; 3) the statement was published; and 4) a third party would understand the character of the communication as defamatory. In addition, the public figure defamation plaintiff must plead and prove that 5) the statement is false and 6) that the defendant made the statement with actual malice. Finally, "[p]roof of damages proximately caused by a publication deemed libelous need not be shown in order for a defamed plaintiff to recover nominal or compensatory damages." . . .

[W]e are mindful that public figures in a defamation case must prove that the defendant made the statements with actual malice. Without discovery of the defendant's identity, satisfying this element may be difficult, if not impossible. Consequently, we do NOT hold that the public figure defamation plaintiff is required to produce evidence on this element of the claim. We hold only that a public figure plaintiff must plead the first five elements and offer *prima facie* proof on each of the five elements to create a genuine issue of material fact requiring trial. In other words, a public figure defamation plaintiff must only plead and prove facts with regard to elements of the claim that are within his control. . . .

Having adopted a summary judgment standard, we now apply it to the facts of this case. . . .

In deciding whether or not a statement is defamatory we determine, "*first,* whether alleged defamatory statements are expressions of fact or protected expressions of opinion; and [*second*], whether the challenged statements are capable of a defamatory meaning." . . .

Applying a good faith standard, the trial judge concluded, "it is enough to meet the 'good faith' standard that the Cahills articulate a legitimate basis for claiming defamation in the context of their particular circumstances." He continued "[g]iven that Mr. Cahill is a married man, [Doe's] statement referring to him as "Gahill" might reasonably be interpreted as indicating that Mr. Cahill has engaged in an extra-marital same-sex affair. Such a statement may form the basis of an actionable defamation claim." We disagree. Using a "G" instead of a "C" as the first letter of Cahill's name is just as likely to be a typographical error as an intended misguided insult. Under the summary judgment standard, no reasonable person would interpret this statement to indicate that Cahill had an extra-marital same-sex affair. With respect to Doe's other statements, the trial judge noted:

> Again, the context in which the statements were made is probative. [Doe's] statements might give the reader the impression that [Doe] has personal knowledge that Mr. Cahill's mental condition is deteriorating and that he is becoming "paranoid." Given that Mr. Cahill is a member of the Smyrna Town Council, an elected position of public trust, the impression that he is suffering from diminished mental capacity might be deemed capable of causing harm to his reputation, particularly when disseminated over the internet for all of his constituents to read.

We agree that the context in which the statements were made is probative, but reach the opposite conclusion. Given the context, no reasonable person could have interpreted these statements as being anything other than opinion. The guidelines at the top of the blog specifically state that the forum is dedicated to *opinions* about issues in Smyrna. . . .

At least one reader of the blog quickly reached the conclusion that Doe's comments were no more than unfounded and unconvincing opinion. Given the context of the statement and the normally (and inherently) unreliable nature of assertions posted in chat rooms and on blogs, this is the only supportable conclusion. Read in the context of an internet blog, these statements did not imply any assertions of underlying objective facts. Accordingly, we hold that as a matter of law a reasonable person would not interpret Doe's statements as stating facts about Cahill. The statements are, therefore, incapable of a defamatory meaning. Because Cahill has failed to plead an essential element of his claim, he *ipso facto* cannot produce *prima facie* proof of that first element of a libel claim, and thus, cannot satisfy the summary judgment standard we announce today. Doe's statements simply are not sufficient to give rise to a *prima facie* case for defamation liability. . . .

NOTES & QUESTIONS

1. ***Postscript.*** The anonymous speaker in *Doe v. Cahill* turned out to be Mayor Schaeffer's 25-year-old stepdaughter. Her identity was revealed inadvertently in discovery. The Schaeffers and Cahills were next door neighbors, and they had feuded since 2003. Until the mayor's stepdaughter was unmasked, he had denied that anybody in his household made the statements against Cahill. Subsequently, Cahill settled his defamation lawsuit against Schaeffer's stepdaughter.

   After the Delaware Supreme Court decision was issued, Patrick and Julia Cahill were arrested following a shouting match with the Schaeffers. The Cahills were charged with terroristic threatening, harassment, and disorderly conduct. They were subsequently acquitted of these charges, but Patrick Cahill was convicted of violating a police order to avoid contacting the Schaeffers. He was fined $100 and sentenced to a year of probation.
2. ***The Standard for Unmasking an Anonymous Speaker.*** Do you agree with the court in *Doe v. Cahill* that the summary judgment standard as opposed to the good faith standard is the appropriate one for unmasking an anonymous speaker? Not all courts have adopted the summary judgment standard. Several courts use the standard in *Columbia Insurance Co. v. Seescandy.com,* 185 F.R.D. 573 (N.D. Cal. 1999):

   > First, the plaintiff should identify the missing party with sufficient specificity such that the Court can determine that defendant is a real person or entity who could be sued in federal court. . . .
   >
   > Second, the party should identify all previous steps taken to locate the elusive defendant. . . .
   >
   > Third, plaintiff should establish to the Court's satisfaction that plaintiff's suit against defendant could withstand a motion to dismiss. . . .
   >
   > Lastly, the plaintiff should file a request for discovery with the Court, along with a statement of reasons justifying the specific discovery requested as well as identification of a limited number of persons or entities on whom discovery process might be served and for which there is a reasonable likelihood that the discovery process will lead to identifying information about defendant that would make service of process possible.

   Compare the *Cahill* standard with the *Seescandy* standard. What the pros and cons of each approach?
3. ***The Identities of Third Parties to the Litigation.*** In *Doe v. 2TheMart.com, Inc.* 140 F. Supp.2d 1088 (W.D. Wash. 2001), shareholders of 2TheMart.com,

Inc. brought a derivative class action against the corporation. The company, in preparing its defense, subpoenaed the identity of 23 anonymous speakers who posted messages on an online message board. These postings were very critical of 2TheMart. One of the anonymous speakers challenged the subpoena. The court concluded:

> The standard for disclosing the identity of a non-party *witness* must be higher than that [required for a party to the litigation]. . . . When the anonymous Internet user is not a party to the case, the litigation can go forward without the disclosure of their identity. Therefore, non-party disclosure is only appropriate in the exceptional case where the compelling need for the discovery sought outweighs the First Amendment rights of the anonymous speaker.
>
> Accordingly, this Court adopts the following standard for evaluating a civil subpoena that seeks the identity of an anonymous Internet user who is not a party to the underlying litigation. The Court will consider four factors in determining whether the subpoena should issue. These are whether: (1) the subpoena seeking the information was issued in good faith and not for any improper purpose, (2) the information sought relates to a core claim or defense, (3) the identifying information is directly and materially relevant to that claim or defense, and (4) information sufficient to establish or to disprove that claim or defense is unavailable from any other source. . . .
>
> Only when the identifying information is needed to advance core claims or defenses can it be sufficiently material to compromise First Amendment rights. If the information relates only to a secondary claim or to one of numerous affirmative defenses, then the primary substance of the case can go forward without disturbing the First Amendment rights of the anonymous Internet users.
>
> The information sought by TMRT does not relate to a core defense. Here, the information relates to only one of twenty-seven affirmative defenses raised by the defendant, the defense that "no act or omission of any of the Defendants was the cause in fact or the proximate cause of any injury or damage to the plaintiffs." . . .
>
> [Moreover,] TMRT has failed to demonstrate that the identity of the Internet users is directly and materially relevant to a core defense. These Internet users are not parties to the case and have not been named as defendants as to any claim, cross-claim or third-party claim. . . .

Doe v. 2TheMart.com based its heightened standard on *Seescandy.* What should a standard for third parties be if based on the *Cahill* standard?

4. ***The Costs of Anonymity.*** Although anonymity has benefits such as enabling people to engage in expression, to consume ideas, and to surf the Internet without fear of reprisal or social opprobrium, anonymity can also facilitate undesirable activity, such as crime and spam. As Dennis Bailey argues:

> Empowered with anonymity, Internet users can engage in any number of malicious activities with a reduced chance of getting caught. They can spread hate or libel without fear of reprisal. They can break copyright infringement laws through free P2P software networks like Kazaa. Or far worse, they can

engage in detestable actions like trafficking in child pornography or electronic stalking.[17]

In cases involving libel over the Internet, a person cannot successfully recover damages from the poster of defamatory comments without first knowing who to sue. We see in libel lawsuits subpoenas served on ISPs to reveal the identity of the poster of a message. Should ISPs be required to (1) keep records of people's identities so that such information can be recovered and (2) disclose such information if there is a libel suit?

5. ***Anonymity vs. Privacy?*** Anonymity can also pose a threat to privacy. Anonymity permits people to get away with defamation, public disclosure of private facts, intrusion, and other privacy torts. For example, a person can anonymously post gossip about a person or post a candid photograph of a person in the nude. Without being able to discover the identity of the poster, the victim has little legal recourse against the poster. Should a victim be able to obtain the name of an anonymous poster from an ISP? How could this authority be misused?

6. ***Anonymity vs. Pseudonymity.*** Tal Zarsky argues that anonymity "come[s] at a high price to society" because "[i]n an anonymous society where locations, interactions, and transactions are hidden behind a veil of anonymity, the lack of accountability will spread to all areas of conduct, interfering with the formation of business and other relationships and allowing individuals to act without inhibitions." Zarsky contends that "traceable pseudonymity" is preferable because it "allows us to interact with consistent personalities" yet protects our "physical identity" and because it provides "accountability with partial anonymity."[18] What are the relative benefits and costs of traceable pseudonymity versus anonymity?

3. ANONYMOUS READING AND RECEIVING OF IDEAS

TATTERED COVER, INC. V. CITY OF THORNTON

44 P.3d 1044 (Colo. 2002)

[Law enforcement officials (local City of Thornton police and a federal DEA agent) suspected that a methamphetamine lab was being operated out of a trailer home. On searching through some garbage from the trailer, an officer discovered evidence of drug operations and a mailing envelope from the Tattered Cover bookstore addressed to one of the suspects (Suspect A). There was an invoice and order number corresponding to the books shipped in the envelope, but no evidence about what those books were. Subsequently, a search warrant was obtained for the trailer home. In the bedroom, the police discovered a methamphetamine laboratory and drugs. Although there were a number of

[17] Dennis Bailey, *The Open Society Paradox* 31 (2004).

[18] Tal Z. Zarsky, *Thinking Outside the Box: Considering Transparency, Anonymity, and Pseudonymity as Overall Solutions to the Problems of Information Privacy in the Internet Society*, 58 U. Miami L. Rev. 991, 1028, 1032, 1044 (2004).

suspects, the police believed that Suspect A occupied the bedroom. Among the items seized from the bedroom were two books: *Advanced Techniques of Clandestine Psychedelic and Amphetamine Manufacture*, by Uncle Fester, and *The Construction and Operation of Clandestine Drug Laboratories*, by Jack B. Nimble. The officers believed that these books were the ones mailed to Suspect A in the mailing envelope from the Tattered Cover found in the trash. The officers served the Tattered Cover with a DEA administrative subpoena. The subpoena requested the title of the books corresponding to the order and invoice numbers of the mailer, as well as information about all other book orders Suspect A had made. Joyce Meskis, the owner of the Tattered Cover, refused to comply with the subpoena, citing concern for its customers' privacy and First Amendment rights. The officers then approached prosecutors from the Adams County District Attorney's office to obtain a search warrant for the Tattered Cover. The prosecutors believed that the warrant sought was too broad and refused to sign off on it. The officers then went to the Denver DA's office, which approved the warrant. A Denver county court judge authorized the warrant. The Tattered Cover sued to enjoin the officers from executing the warrant.]

BENDER, J. . . . The First Amendment to the United States Constitution protects more than simply the right to speak freely. It is well established that it safeguards a wide spectrum of activities, including the right to distribute and sell expressive materials, the right to associate with others, and, most importantly to this case, the right to receive information and ideas. . . .

Without the right to receive information and ideas, the protection of speech under the United States and Colorado Constitutions would be meaningless. It makes no difference that one can voice whatever view one wishes to express if others are not free to listen to these thoughts. The converse also holds true. Everyone must be permitted to discover and consider the full range of expression and ideas available in our "marketplace of ideas." As Justice Brandeis so eloquently stated, "[Our founders] believed that freedom to think as you will and to speak as you think are means indispensable to the discovery and spread of political truth.". . .

Bookstores are places where a citizen can explore ideas, receive information, and discover myriad perspectives on every topic imaginable. When a person buys a book at a bookstore, he engages in activity protected by the First Amendment because he is exercising his right to read and receive ideas and information. Any governmental action that interferes with the willingness of customers to purchase books, or booksellers to sell books, thus implicates First Amendment concerns. . .

The need to protect anonymity in the context of the First Amendment has particular applicability to book-buying activity. . . . The right to engage in expressive activities anonymously, without government intrusion or observation, is critical to the protection of the First Amendment rights of book buyers and sellers, precisely because of the chilling effects of such disclosures. Search warrants directed to bookstores, demanding information about the reading history of customers, intrude upon the First Amendment rights of customers and bookstores because compelled disclosure of book-buying records threatens to destroy the anonymity upon which many customers depend. . . .

Like the Federal Constitution, our Colorado Constitution protects speech rights. Specifically, Article II, Section 10, entitled "Freedom of speech and press," provides that:

> No law shall be passed impairing the freedom of speech; every person shall be free to speak, write or publish whatever he will on any subject, being responsible for all abuse of that liberty. . . .

The United States Supreme Court has repeatedly acknowledged that its interpretation of the Federal Constitution defines the minimum level of protections that must be afforded, through the Fourteenth Amendment, by the states. However, the Supreme Court has also recognized that a state may, if it so chooses, afford its residents a greater level of protection under its state constitution than that bestowed by the Federal Constitution.

With respect to expressive freedoms, this court has recognized that the Colorado Constitution provides broader free speech protections than the Federal Constitution. . . .

Having defined the right at issue in this case, we next address the collision between the exercise of this right and the investigative efforts of law enforcement officials. We consider the legal test that applies to determine when law enforcement officials may use a search warrant to obtain customer book purchase records from an innocent, third-party bookstore, and the circumstances that trigger application of that test. . . .

Search warrants are the mechanism used to protect against unjustified police intrusions that would otherwise violate the dictates of the Fourth Amendment and Article II, Section 7. In order to obtain a search warrant, law enforcement officials must demonstrate, prior to any search, that probable cause exists to believe that the legitimate object of such a search is located in a specific place. The warrant itself must describe with particularity the place to be searched and the objects that may be seized. . . .

Conflicts between First Amendment and Fourth Amendment rights are inevitable when law enforcement officials attempt to use search warrants to obtain expressive materials. . . .

. . . [T]he Supreme Court has made clear that, when expressive rights are implicated, a search warrant must comply with the particularity requirements of the Fourth Amendment with "scrupulous exactitude." *Zurcher v. Stanford Daily*, 436 U.S. 547, 564 (1978); *Stanford v. Texas*, 379 U.S. 476, 485 (1965). . . .

. . . [In *Zurcher*, the Court held] that First Amendment concerns can never entirely preclude the execution of a search warrant that complies with the Fourth Amendment: "Properly administered, the preconditions for a warrant — probable cause, specificity with respect to the place to be searched and the things to be seized, and overall reasonableness — should afford sufficient protection against the harms that are assertedly threatened by warrants for searching newspaper offices."

The Supreme Court's pronouncements in *Zurcher* can be read to mean that, beyond the "scrupulous exactitude" requirement, the First Amendment places no special limitation on the ability of the government to seize expressive materials under the Fourth Amendment. We acknowledge that this is arguably the import of *Zurcher*. Thus, we ground the holding in this case in our Colorado Constitution. . . .

. . . [W]e find the protections afforded to fundamental expressive rights by federal law, under the above interpretation of *Zurcher*, to be inadequate. We turn to our Colorado Constitution, which we now hold requires a more substantial justification from the government than is required by the Fourth Amendment of the United States Constitution when law enforcement officials attempt to use a search warrant to obtain an innocent, third-party bookstore's customer purchase records. . . .

. . . [C]ourts have recognized that a very high level of review, referred to as "strict scrutiny" or "exacting scrutiny" is to be undertaken when government action collides with First Amendment rights. This heightened standard is necessary because governmental action that burdens the exercise of First Amendment rights compromises the core principles of an open, democratic society. . . .

We hold that law enforcement officials must demonstrate a sufficiently compelling need for the specific customer purchase record sought from the innocent, third-party bookstore. . . .

. . . [T]he court must engage in a more specific inquiry as to whether law enforcement officials have a compelling need *for the precise and specific information sought*. . . .

. . . [W]e [also] hold that an innocent, third-party bookstore must be afforded an opportunity for a hearing prior to the execution of any search warrant that seeks to obtain its customers' book-purchasing records. At the hearing, the court will apply the balancing test described above to determine whether law enforcement officials have a sufficiently compelling need for the book purchase record that outweighs the harms associated with enforcement of the search warrant. . . .

. . . [Turning to the case at bar,] the City describes three reasons that it is important for it to know whether Suspect A purchased the two "how to" books found at the scene of the crime. First, the City states that this will help them to prove the mens rea of the crime, that Suspect A "intentionally or knowingly" operated the methamphetamine lab. Second, the City contends that proof that Suspect A purchased the "how to" books will help them to prove that Suspect A occupied the master bedroom, the place where the books and methamphetamine lab were found. Finally, the City asserts that the Tattered Cover invoice "connects" Suspect A to the crime. . . .

With respect to the argument that evidence that Suspect A purchased the books will help prove that he knowingly or intentionally operated a methamphetamine lab, we note that the City's search of the bedroom revealed a fully operational and functional methamphetamine lab as well as a small quantity of the manufactured drug. The two "how to" books were found in the immediate vicinity of the lab. The physical presence of the lab itself, and of these books, goes a long way towards proving that the operator of the lab did not accidentally manufacture methamphetamines. These facts leave no doubt that the person or persons who operated this lab did so intentionally. . . .

Thus, we turn to the City's second justification, that the invoice will help them to demonstrate that Suspect A occupied the master bedroom and, hence, must have operated the methamphetamine lab. In essence, the City wishes to use the purchasing record to place Suspect A at the scene of the crime. . . .

If the City needs evidence of who occupied the master bedroom, as indirect evidence of who must have operated the lab, the record reveals a number of alternative ways in which this information could have been ascertained. . . . Clothes and shoes could have been examined to see if the sizes matched Suspect A. Objects could have been fingerprinted. The bed and flooring could have been examined for hair or other DNA samples. Beyond this physical evidence, there are numerous witnesses that the City likely could have interviewed without compromising the integrity of their criminal investigation. . . .

The City's final justification is that proof that Suspect A bought the two books will "connect" him to the crime. The City's argument is somewhat amorphous because it never elaborates on the specific reason as to why the connection exists. At its core, however, the argument rests on the premise that if Suspect A bought the "how to" books, he must have operated the lab. The rationale for this argument is thus directly tied to the contents of the books Suspect A may have purchased. This is precisely the reason that this search warrant is likely to have chilling effects on the willingness of the general public to purchase books about controversial topics.

The dangers, both to Suspect A and to the book-buying public, of permitting the government to access the information it seeks, and to use this proof of purchase as evidence of Suspect A's guilt, are grave. Assuming that Suspect A purchased the books in question, he may have done so for any of a number of reasons, many of which are in no way linked to his commission of any crime. He might have bought them for a friend or roommate, unaware that they would subsequently be placed in the vicinity of an illegal drug lab. He might have been curious about the process of making drugs, without having any intention to act on what he read. It may be that none of these scenarios is as likely as that suggested by the City, that Suspect A bought the books intending to use them to help him make an illegal drug. Nonetheless, Colorado's long tradition of protecting expressive freedoms cautions against permitting the City to seize the Tattered Cover's book purchase record. . . .

NOTES & QUESTIONS

1. ***The Right to Read Anonymously.*** Do you agree with the decision in *Tattered Cover* that, in addition to the right to speak anonymously, there is also a right to read anonymously? Does such a right follow logically from the Supreme Court's freedom of association and anonymity cases?

   Consider the following argument by Julie Cohen:

   > For the most part, First Amendment jurisprudence has defined readers' rights only incidentally. Historically, both courts and commentators have been more concerned with protecting speakers than with protecting readers. . . .
   >
   > . . . All speech responds to prior speech of some sort. The person who expresses vigorous disapproval of Hillary Clinton after months of reading electronic bulletins on "femi-nazis" from Rush Limbaugh and subscribing to anti-feminist Usenet newsgroups is no different in this regard than the person

> who reads a judicious mixture of New York Times op-ed pieces and scholarly literature on feminism before venturing to express an opinion regarding Mrs. Clinton's conduct. When the two readers choose to express their own views, the First Amendment protects both speakers equally. Logically, that zone of protection should encompass the entire series of intellectual transactions through which they formed the opinions they ultimately chose to express. Any less protection would chill inquiry, and as a result, public discourse, concerning politically and socially controversial issues — precisely those areas where vigorous public debate is most needed, and most sacrosanct. . . .
>
> The freedom to read anonymously is just as much a part of our tradition, and the choice of reading materials just as expressive of identity, as the decision to use or withhold one's name. Indeed, based purely on tradition, the freedom to read anonymously may be even more fundamental than the freedom to engage in anonymous political speech. Anonymous advocacy has always been controversial. Anonymous reading, in contrast, is something that is taken for granted. The material conditions for non-anonymous reading — the technologies that enable content providers to monitor readers' activities and choices — have only recently come to exist. With them has come the realization that the act of reading communicates, and that our tradition of anonymous exploration and inquiry is threatened. Reader profiles are valuable to marketers precisely because they disclose information about the reader's tastes, preferences, interests, and beliefs. That information is content that the reader should have a constitutionally protected interest in refusing to share.[19]

Cohen argues that the government should recognize and pass legislation to protect one's right to read anonymously. If there were such a right to read anonymously, then under Cohen's reasoning, should the government necessarily enact a law to restrict the use of cookies on public websites?

Marc Blitz contends that the First Amendment also protects seeking information in libraries:

> [T]he First Amendment right to receive information . . . not only protects paths for citizens' communication of ideas, but also the somewhat different paths that information-seekers use to track down ideas that are lying dormant. Crucial to this second activity is the protection of public libraries. As the British liberal statesman, Herbert Samuel, once said: "A library is thought in cold storage." It is a place where ideas are frozen and preserved for information-seekers — put in the form of what George Simmel called "objectified knowledge" — so that they remain available during the many years it might take an individual find them (along with thousands or millions of other cultural and intellectual sources).[20]

Consider the Supreme Court's view of asking a librarian to unblock access to a website so that adult material may be viewed. In *United States v. American Library Ass'n*, 539 U.S. 194 (2003), a plurality of the Court upheld the Children's Internet Protection Act (CIPA), which required libraries to have filters to block pornography on Internet terminals. The plurality noted

---

[19] Julie E. Cohen, *A Right to Read Anonymously: A Closer Look at "Copyright Management" in Cyberspace*, 28 Conn. L. Rev. 981 (1996).

[20] Marc Jonathan Blitz, *Constitutional Safeguards For Silent Experiments in Living Libraries, the Right to Read, and a First Amendment Theory for an Unaccompanied Right to Receive Information*, 74 U. Mo. Kan. City L. Rev. 799, 881-82 (2006).

that those who wished to have material unblocked could easily ask the librarians to do so, and it concluded that "the Constitution does not guarantee the right to acquire information at a public library without any risk of embarrassment." Writing in dissent, Justice Stevens suggested that

> because the procedures that different libraries are likely to adopt to respond to unblocking requests will no doubt vary, it is impossible to measure the aggregate effect of the statute on patrons' access to blocked sites. Unless we assume that the statute is a mere symbolic gesture, we must conclude that it will create a significant prior restraint on adult access to protected speech. A law that prohibits reading without official consent, like a law that prohibits speaking without consent, "constitutes a dramatic departure from our national heritage and constitutional tradition." *Watchtower Bible & Tract Soc. of N.Y., Inc. v. Village of Stratton*, 536 U.S. 150 (2002).

2. ***A Slippery Slope?*** How far can the rationale of *Tattered Cover* be extended? Suppose the police obtained a search warrant for one's home and sought to seize a person's diary? Would such a seizure be subject to strict scrutiny? What about the search of one's computer, which can reveal anonymous speech as well as one's online reading activities? Isn't the government's questioning of various witnesses to whom a person spoke also likely to interfere with that person's expressive activities? Why are books different (or are they)?
3. ***The First Amendment and Postal Mail.*** In *Lamont v. Postmaster General of the United States*, 381 U.S. 301 (1965), a 1962 federal statute required that all mail (except sealed letters) that originates or is prepared in a foreign country and is determined by the Secretary of the Treasury to be "communist political propaganda" be detained at the post office. The addressee would be notified of the matter, and the mail would be delivered to the addressee only upon her request. The Court struck down the statute on First Amendment grounds:

> We rest on the narrow ground that the addressee in order to receive his mail must request in writing that it be delivered. This amounts in our judgment to an unconstitutional abridgment of the addressee's First Amendment rights. The addressee carries an affirmative obligation which we do not think the Government may impose on him. This requirement is almost certain to have a deterrent effect, especially as respects those who have sensitive positions. Their livelihood may be dependent on a security clearance. Public officials like schoolteachers who have no tenure, might think they would invite disaster if they read what the Federal Government says contains the seeds of treason. Apart from them, any addressee is likely to feel some inhibition in sending for literature which federal officials have condemned as "communist political propaganda." The regime of this Act is at war with the "uninhibited, robust, and wide-open debate and discussion" that are contemplated by the First Amendment.

4. ***The First Amendment and Government Searches.*** In *Smith v. Maryland*, 442 U.S. 735 (1979) and *United States v. Miller,* 425 U.S. 435 (1976), the U.S. Supreme Court held that a person does not have a reasonable expectation of privacy in records held by third parties. Recall that under the Stored Commu-

nications Act, the government can obtain identifying information (as well as other personal information) from one's ISP with a court order. 18 U.S.C. § 2703(c)(1)(B). This is how the government obtains the identities of people engaging in illegal activity who use screen names. However, based on the cases you have read in this chapter about the right to anonymity, does the First Amendment have a role to play in these situations? Consider the following argument by Daniel Solove:

> Extensive government information gathering from third party records also implicates the right to speak anonymously. . . . With government information gathering from third parties, namely ISPs, the government can readily obtain an anonymous or pseudonymous speaker's identity. Only computer-savvy users can speak with more secure anonymity. When private parties attempt to obtain the identifying information, courts have held that subpoenas for this information must contain heightened standards. However, no such heightened standards apply when the *government* seeks to obtain the information.[21]

Recall *Doe v. Cahill* from the previous section. If private parties must satisfy heightened scrutiny under the First Amendment to obtain information relating to an anonymous speaker on the Internet, shouldn't the government also have to satisfy such scrutiny? What kind of standard should the government have to satisfy under the First Amendment?

5. ***The First Amendment as Criminal Procedure.*** Daniel Solove contends that the First Amendment should be employed to protect against many forms of government searches and surveillance:

> The First Amendment is usually taught separately from the Fourth and Fifth Amendments, and judicial decisions on criminal procedure only occasionally mention the First Amendment. I contend in this Article, however, that the First Amendment must be considered alongside the Fourth and Fifth Amendments as a source of criminal procedure.
>
> First Amendment activities are implicated by a wide array of law enforcement data-gathering activities. Government information gathering about computer and Internet use, for example, can intrude on a significant amount of First Amendment activity. Searching or seizing a computer can reveal personal and political writings. Obtaining e-mail can provide extensive information about correspondence and associations. Similarly, ISP records often contain information about speech, as they can link people to their anonymous communications. AOL, for example, receives about a thousand requests per month for use of its customer records in criminal cases.

Solove contends that there is a doctrinal foundation for First Amendment protection against government information gathering. If the First Amendment were to apply to certain government law enforcement activities, what level of protections would it provide? Solove argues:

> Even if an instance of government information gathering triggers First Amendment protection, collection of the data will not necessarily be prohibited. Rather, the First Amendment will require the government to

[21] Daniel J. Solove, *Digital Dossiers and the Dissipation of Fourth Amendment Privacy*, 75 S. Cal. L. Rev. 1083 (2002).

> demonstrate (1) a significant interest in gathering the information and (2) that the manner of collection is narrowly tailored to achieving that interest. . . . [T]he use of a warrant supported by probable cause will, in most cases, suffice to satisfy the narrow tailoring requirement. In other words, in cases where the First Amendment applies, it often will require procedures similar to those required by the Fourth Amendment.[22]

Solove also posits that the First Amendment would be enforced by way of an exclusionary rule. To what extent does the First Amendment apply to government law enforcement activities? Should the First Amendment require similar protections to those of the Fourth Amendment or greater protections as in *Tattered Cover*?

6. ***Library Records.*** Forty-eight states have laws protecting the privacy of library records. New York's statute, for example, provides:

> Library records, which contain names or other personally identifying details regarding the users of public, free association, school, college and university libraries and library systems of this state . . . shall be confidential and shall not be disclosed except that such records may be disclosed to the extent necessary for the proper operation of such library and shall be disclosed upon request or consent of the user or pursuant to subpoena, court order or where otherwise required by statute. N.Y. CPLR § 4509.

Like New York's statute, most library records statutes allow for the disclosure of records pursuant to a court order or subpoena. *See, e.g.,* Fla. Stat. § 257.261; Cal. Gov't Code § 6267. Would the reasoning of *Doe v. Cahill* or *Doe v. 2TheMart.com* apply to such a court order or subpoena to require heightened requirements? Pennsylvania's law has a narrower court order and subpoena provision:

> Records related to the circulation of library materials which contain the names or other personally identifying details regarding the users of the State Library or any local library . . . shall be confidential and shall not be made available to anyone except by a court order in a criminal proceeding. 24 P.S. § 4428.

More generally, the FBI may gain access to "tangible things" such as "books, records, papers, documents and other items" if it receives authorization from the FISA court. It must certify to the court that the records are sought "for an investigation to obtain foreign intelligence information not concerning a U.S. person or to protect against international terrorism or clandestine intelligence activities, provided that such investigation of a U.S. person is not conducted solely upon the basis of activities protected by the First Amendment to the Constitution." 50 U.S.C. § 1861.

4. ANONYMITY AND COPYRIGHT

The DMCA and Privacy. Congress enacted the Digital Millennium Copyright Act (DMCA) of 1998, 17 U.S.C. § 512, to strengthen the rights of

---

[22] Daniel J. Solove, *The First Amendment as Criminal Procedure*, 82 N.Y.U. L. Rev. 112, 114-15, 159 (2007).

copyright holders. It mandates civil and criminal penalties for those who create or distribute devices to circumvent copyright protection. Critics of the Act argue that many anti-circumvention tools can be used not only to defeat antipiracy protections but also to engage in legitimate activities, such as scientific research and free speech. The DMCA contains a provision that states: "Nothing in this chapter abrogates, diminishes, or weakens the provisions of, nor provides any defense or element of mitigation in a criminal prosecution or civil action under, any Federal or State law that prevents the violation of the privacy of an individual in connection with the individual's use of the Internet." 17 U.S.C. § 1205. As Julie Cohen observes: "This provision is probably best interpreted as preserving information providers' obligations under the federal Electronic Communications Privacy Act and analogous state laws; thus, for example, a software company caught monitoring customers' use of its e-mail program could not claim that the DMCA allows it to do so."[23]

The DMCA and Anonymous Speech. The Recording Industry Association of America (RIAA) began using the subpoena provisions of the DMCA, 17 U.S.C. § 512(h) to force ISPs to reveal the identities of subscribers that the RIAA thought were engaging in music piracy. Verizon Internet Services refused to comply with the RIAA subpoenas and litigation ensued. In *In Re Verizon Internet Services, Inc*., 240 F. Supp.2d 24 (D.D.C. 2003), a federal district court concluded that the DMCA authorized copyright holders to subpoena identifying information about people who traded music and that the RIAA could obtain the information it wanted from Verizon. In part of its decision, the district court raised the issue of whether such subpoenas would be valid under the First Amendment. The court concluded:

> It is . . . clear that the First Amendment does not protect copyright infringement. *See Harper & Row, Publs., Inc. v. Nation Enters.,* 471 U.S. 539 (1985); *Zacchini v. Scripps-Howard,* 433 U.S. 562 (1977). Moreover, the Supreme Court recently confirmed in *Eldred v. Ashcroft,* 123 S. Ct. 769 (2003), that the proximity of the Copyright Clause and the First Amendment demonstrates "the Framers' view [that] copyright's limited monopolies are compatible with free speech principles," and that copyright serves to promote First Amendment ideals as "the engine of free expression."). The Court noted "built-in First Amendment accommodations" in copyright law, including the distinction between ideas and expression and the "fair use" doctrine, which it found "are generally adequate to address" First Amendment concerns relating to asserted rights to use the speech of others. Here, of course, the various protections incorporated into subsection (h), and discussed *supra,* further guard against First Amendment concerns.
>
> Nor is this an instance where the anonymity of an Internet user merits free speech and privacy protections. Certainly, the Supreme Court has recognized that, in some situations, the First Amendment protects a speaker's anonymity. *See, e.g., Watchtower Bible & Tract Society v. Village of Stratton; Buckley v. Am. Constitutional Law Found., Inc.*; *McIntyre v. Ohio Elections Comm.* Lower federal courts have specifically recognized that the First Amendment may protect an individual's anonymity on the Internet. *See, e.g., Doe v. 2TheMart.com, Inc.; ACLU of Georgia v. Miller.* . . .

---

[23] Julie E. Cohen, *DRM and Privacy,* 18 Berkeley Tech. L.J. 575, 594 n.54 (2003).

> But neither Verizon nor any *amici* has suggested that anonymously downloading more than 600 songs from the Internet without authorization is protected expression under the First Amendment. To be sure, this is not a case where Verizon's customer is anonymously using the Internet to distribute speeches of Lenin, Biblical passages, educational materials, or criticisms of the government — situations in which assertions of First Amendment rights more plausibly could be made. As the Supreme Court explained in *Watchtower Bible & Tract Society,* the purpose of protecting anonymous expression is to safeguard those "who support causes anonymously" and those who "fear economic or official retaliation," "social ostracism," or an unwanted intrusion into "privacy." The materials RIAA alleges are being infringed include more than 600 copyrighted recordings by well-known artists. RIAA has shown that the copyright owners have not authorized such use; moreover, the fact that these copyrighted materials were shared over the peer-to-peer software of KaZaA only reinforces the belief that copyrights are being infringed. There is no evidence, or even suggestion, in the record to indicate that downloading or transmitting these recordings is somehow protected expression. . . .

In *Recording Industry Ass'n of America v. Verizon Internet Services, Inc.,* 351 F.3d 1229 (3d Cir. 2003), the Third Circuit reversed the district court. It concluded that the DMCA did not authorize such subpoenas because "a subpoena may be issued only to an ISP engaged in storing on its servers material that is infringing or the subject of infringing activity" and the users who were sharing music files were storing them on their own personal computers, not on the ISP's servers. As the court noted, "Verizon cannot remove or disable one user's access to infringing material resident on another user's computer because Verizon does not control the content on its subscribers' computers."

The court did not reach the First Amendment issue. Would such a provision in the DMCA — one that allowed copyright holders to obtain the identities of those they suspect of copyright infringement from ISPs — run afoul of the First Amendment? Why would the RIAA or other copyright holder want to obtain the identities of anonymous Internet users prior to filing a lawsuit? What are the privacy implications of permitting the RIAA to assemble a list of people that it believes have infringed upon their copyrights? Do the benefits of this procedure under the DMCA outweigh the costs to privacy? What procedures could be established to permit the enforcement of copyright interests and to protect the privacy rights of Internet users?

Anonymous Expression and Consumption. In the context of copyright and privacy, the anonymity of both speakers and listeners is implicated. *In re Verizon Internet Services, Inc.* implicates the anonymity of speakers (those who distribute copyrighted works) as well as of listeners or readers (those who download and receive the works distributed by others). Do speakers and listeners have equal rights to anonymity?

Digital Rights Management (DRM) Technologies. In several articles, Julie Cohen has pointed out the danger of copyright holders taking steps to erode the privacy of individuals. In particular, Cohen focuses on digital rights management (DRM) technologies, which aim to prevent copying of copyrighted works. Some

DRM technologies constrain individual freedom by restricting people's ability to copy for "space-shifting purposes" or limit the geographic region or type of equipment in which people can use a copyrighted work. Cohen observes, "Technologies of direct constraint shape individual practices of intellectual consumption in ways that shift the locus of choice about those practices away from the individual." Other DRM technologies engage in surveillance of the individual user:

> DRM technologies that monitor user behavior create records of intellectual consumption. Indirectly, then, they create records of intellectual exploration, one of the most personal and private of activities. They also create records of behavior within private spaces, spaces within which one might reasonably expect that one's behavior is not subject to observation.[24]

What limits, if any, should the law place on the use of DRM technologies? Currently, the DMCA might prevent the users of copyrighted materials from tampering with DRM in order to preserve their anonymity. Could the First Amendment apply in these instances? Note that there must be state action for the First Amendment to apply. Cohen argues that that there may be state action:

> On their face, these provisions would reach both the conduct of the willful infringer and that of the concerned libertarian who tampers with copyright management soft-ware only, and only to the extent necessary, to preserve his or her anonymity. Arguably, enforcement of these provisions supplies the requisite government action.[25]

Beyond the First Amendment, Cohen contends that common law privacy protections are not well-suited to regulate DRM technologies because they may be waived by consent: "Because the privacy invasions effected by DRM technologies occur in the context of consensual commercial transactions, the mechanisms for establishing effective consent can easily be put in place."[26]

Privacy and Copyright Enforcement. In testimony on the Digital Millennium Copyright Act, Marc Rotenberg observed:

> It should be clear that copyright holders have no special claim on what you or I wish to read, watch, or hear. Copyright law has never established a right to know the identity of a user of a copyrighted work. Where identity has been disclosed, it is generally pursuant to a licensing scheme (ASCAP) or some secondary purpose (shipping a product) and not federal legislation. It may also be necessary to determine the identity of a user of a work to establish infringement. But there is no general right of a copyright owner to know the identity of the user. . . .
>
> It is not enough to note the special circumstances when users may be required to defeat copyright management schemes to further important ends, it is necessary to ask whether it is appropriate and fair for copyright holders to

---

[24] Cohen, *DRM and Privacy*, *supra*, at 585.

[25] Julie E. Cohen, *The Right to Read Anonymously: A Closer Look at "Copyright Management" in Cyberspace,* 28 Conn. L. Rev. 981, 1020 (1996).

[26] Cohen, *DRM and Privacy, supra*, at 608.

demand disclosure of one's identity as an additional cost of gaining access to a copyrighted work.[27]

For Sonia Katyal, like Marc Rotenberg, intellectual property and privacy are at an impasse in cyberspace. She finds that the two areas face inherent conflicts: "[T]he law has displayed a persistent failure to recognize that expansions of control of intellectual property cause tradeoffs in other areas of consumer protection — particularly where privacy is concerned."[28] Katyal proposes amending the Digital Millennium Copyright Act (DMCA) to track the federal Privacy Protection Act (PPA) (Chapter 7).

Katyal argues that "the DMCA could establish that it is illegal for private piracy surveillance measures to force an ISP to seize or silence expression that falls under fair use or First Amendment protection without first requesting a court order." Such a court order would be for a special subpoena modeled on the PPA; it would exempt from disclosure any "work product materials, intended for publication." Second, "the DMCA, following its own notice-and-takedown provision, could provide for a requirement of notice to be given to the end user prior to disclosure of identity, and could provide for specific procedures to challenge the disclosure of one's identity in the event of an asserted defense of fair use." Finally, Katyal makes clear that the amended DMCA should go beyond the outcome of *Verizon*; in contexts where the First Amendment is implicated, the amended DMCA should "require the immediate appealability of any proposed termination of access, the use of specially trained magistrates or marshals to carry out Internet searches, and other procedures that reflect a concern for individual civil liberties and expression." In contrast, what are the requirements of the *Verizon* court to safeguard end user identity? Which safeguards establish the best balance between privacy copyright?

C. IDENTIFICATION

1. IDENTIFICATION DEVICES AND TECHNIQUES

Many transactions occur without the need for identification. A person selects a magazine at a bookstore and pays with cash. She buys a metro card and takes a train across a city without revealing her identity. She walks into a public museum or enters a coffee shop to visit a friend. Most activities in our daily lives take place without any need for identification. In other circumstances, it may be possible to provide a credential that enables a transaction without disclosing one's actual identity.

But in certain circumstances, actual identification may be required. This raises a critical question: How do we know whether a person is who she says she is? For many economic transactions, this question is a fundamental one. A person

[27] Marc Rotenberg, Testimony and Statement for the Record on The WIPO Copyright Treaties Implementation Act and Privacy Issues Before the Subcommittee on Telecommunications, Trade, and Consumer Protection, Committee on Commerce, U.S. House of Representatives (June 5, 1998).

[28] Sonia K. Katyal, *The New Surveillance*, 54 Case W. Res. L. Rev. 297, 375, 378-79 (2003).

visits her bank to make a withdrawal. A teller who has never seen or met that person must find some way to verify that she is the true owner of the bank account. A person calls her school to obtain a copy of her transcript. The registrar needs to be able to verify that the caller is who she claims to be. Roger Clarke defines identification as "the association of data with a particular human being."[29] What system should we adopt to identify people? Different devices to authenticate identity differ in effectiveness, potential for error and abuse, and social benefits and costs.

Identification Cards. One type of identification system is for people to carry cards. Cards can contain a variety of information — typically, one's photograph, name, date of birth, address, and physical characteristics. Modern identification cards often not only have information printed on the card, but have data encoded in a magnetic strip on the card. Data can either be stored on the card or consist of a number that corresponds to a record of information in a database. In the United States, drivers' licenses are often used as identification cards.

Passwords and Secret Codes. Another way to verify identity is through the use of passwords and secret codes. These devices require the person to memorize a password or code. Examples include a combination to open a lock, a personal identification number (PIN) to use with a bank card, and a password to log onto a computer network or e-mail server.

Biometric Identification. Biometric identification and authentication use unique and time-invariant biological or behavioral characteristics. Fingerprints are a long-standing form of biometric identification. Modern technology has enabled sophisticated devices to detect hand prints, voice patterns, iris and retina patterns, facial appearance, and gait.

Computer Chip Implants. A new form of identification under development is a computer chip implanted beneath one's skin. This chip is generally called a Radio Frequency Identification Device (RFID). In the past, chips have been implanted into animals to track them. In December 2001, a Florida company announced that it had developed a small chip (about the size of a grain of rice) that could be surgically implanted in humans. The chip, called VeriChip, can transmit a signal that can be detected several feet away by a scanner. The chip can either directly contain personal data or transmit a number that corresponds to personal data in a database.

What then of the costs and benefits of identification? The ability to authenticate identity has important social benefits. It enables greater accountability and efficiency in economic transactions. Quickly and accurately linking people to data can also be useful when others need to learn information about them (e.g., when doctors need to obtain a person's medical history). According to Lynn LoPucki, difficulties in identification make possible the crime of identity theft. This crime occurs where the thief impersonates the victim and

---

[29] Roger Clarke, *Human Identification and Identity Authentication* (1998), available at http://www.anu.edu.au/people/Roger.Clarke/DV/SCTISK3.html.

gains access to the victim's records and accounts as well as opens up new accounts and conducts business by pretending to be the victim. LoPucki contends: "The problem is not that thieves have access to personal information, but that creditors and credit-reporting agencies often lack both the means and the incentives to correctly identify the persons who seek credit from them or on whom they report."[30] Further, identification systems can promote security by enabling the better screening and detection of criminals and terrorists.

However, greater identification makes anonymity more difficult, and in many instances, impossible. Further, identification can alter the type of society we are building, curtailing freedom and subjecting people to the ills of bureaucracy. As Roger Clarke observes:

> The need to identify oneself may be intrinsically distasteful to some people. For example, they may regard it as demeaning, or implicit recognition that the organisation with whom they are dealing exercises power over them. Many people accept that, at least in particular contexts, an organisation with which they are dealing needs to have their name. Some, however, feel it is an insult to human dignity to require them to use a number or code instead of a name. Some feel demeaned by demands, as part of the identification process, that they reveal information about themselves or their family, or embarrassed at having to memorize a password or PIN.
>
> Some people are unwilling to submit to the regimen of carrying tokens, or unprepared to produce them, on the grounds that this reeks of a totalitarian regime, reflects and perpetuates a power relationship that they despise (such as the South African pass laws during the period of apartheid), or carries with it the seeds of discrimination (as reflected by the content of the token).
>
> Another factor which forces compromise between the interests of accountability and law and order on the one hand, and civil liberties on the other, is the importance of multiple identities as a means of avoiding physical harm and death at the hands of violent opponents.[31]

For what purposes should we require identification? Identification may be necessary for certain purposes but not others. The remainder of this chapter explores identification in the United States.

2. IDENTIFICATION AND THE CONSTITUTION

In *Kolender v. Lawson*, 461 U.S. 352 (1983), the Court considered a facial challenge to a law that required any person who "loiters or wanders . . . without apparent reason or business" to "identify himself and to account for his presence when requested by any peace officer to do so." The Court struck down the statute as unconstitutionally vague:

> . . . [The statute] as presently drafted and construed by the state courts, contains no standard for determining what a suspect has to do in order to satisfy the

[30] Lynn M. LoPucki, *Human Identification Theory and the Identity Theft Problem*, 80 Tex. L. Rev. 89 (2001).

[31] Roger Clarke, *Human Identification in Information Systems: Management Challenges and Public Policy Issues*, 7 Information Tech. & People 6 (1994), available at http://www.anu.edu.au/people/Roger.Clarke/DV/HumanID.html.

> requirement to provide a "credible and reliable" identification. As such, the statute vests virtually complete discretion in the hands of the police to determine whether the suspect has satisfied the statute and must be permitted to go on his way in the absence of probable cause to arrest. An individual, whom police may think is suspicious but do not have probable cause to believe has committed a crime, is entitled to continue to walk the public streets "only at the whim of any police officer" who happens to stop that individual under § 647(e). Our concern here is based upon the potential for arbitrarily suppressing First Amendment liberties. In addition, [the statute] implicates consideration of the constitutional right to freedom of movement.

Justice Brennan concurred, arguing that the statute also violated the Fourth Amendment:

> . . . [U]nder the Fourth Amendment, police officers with reasonable suspicion that an individual has committed or is about to commit a crime may detain that individual, using some force if necessary, for the purpose of asking investigative questions. They may ask their questions in a way calculated to obtain an answer. But they may not compel an answer, and they must allow the person to leave after a reasonably brief period of time unless the information they have acquired during the encounter has given them probable cause sufficient to justify an arrest.

In *Carey v. Nevada Gaming Control Board*, 279 F.3d 873 (9th Cir. 2002), James Carey was detained by an official of the Nevada Gaming Control Board on suspicion of cheating while gambling. When asked to identify himself verbally or through identification documents, Carey refused. Although the official determined that there was no probable cause that Carey violated gaming laws, the official arrested Carey for refusing to identify himself. The official cited two statutes that required individuals detained by officials to identify themselves or else face criminal sanctions. Carey spent the evening in prison. No charges were brought against him. Carey sued under § 1983 alleging a violation of, among other things, his Fourth Amendment rights. The court agreed with Carey:

> [S]uch [identification] statutes violate the Fourth Amendment because as a result of the demand for identification, the statutes bootstrap the authority to arrest on less than probable cause and because the serious intrusion on personal security outweighs the mere possibility that identification might provide a link leading to arrest. . . . [The official] was able to arrest Carey even though there was no probable cause to believe that Carey had violated the gaming laws, and even though Carey's name was not relevant to determining whether Carey had cheated. An arrest under such circumstances is unreasonable. We therefore hold that Carey's arrest violated the Fourth Amendment.

HIIBEL V. SIXTH JUDICIAL DISTRICT COURT

542 U.S. 177 (2004)

KENNEDY, J. The petitioner was arrested and convicted for refusing to identify himself during a stop allowed by *Terry v. Ohio,* 392 U.S. 1 (1968). [Hiibel] challenges his conviction under the Fourth and Fifth Amendments to the United States Constitution. . . .

The sheriff's department in Humboldt County, Nevada, received an afternoon telephone call reporting an assault. The caller reported seeing a man assault a woman in a red and silver GMC truck on Grass Valley Road. Deputy Sheriff Lee Dove was dispatched to investigate. When the officer arrived at the scene, he found the truck parked on the side of the road. A man was standing by the truck, and a young woman was sitting inside it. The officer observed skid marks in the gravel behind the vehicle, leading him to believe it had come to a sudden stop.

The officer approached the man and explained that he was investigating a report of a fight. The man appeared to be intoxicated. The officer asked him if he had "any identification on [him]," which we understand as a request to produce a driver's license or some other form of written identification. The man refused and asked why the officer wanted to see identification. The officer responded that he was conducting an investigation and needed to see some identification. The unidentified man became agitated and insisted he had done nothing wrong. The officer explained that he wanted to find out who the man was and what he was doing there. After continued refusals to comply with the officer's request for identification, the man began to taunt the officer by placing his hands behind his back and telling the officer to arrest him and take him to jail. This routine kept up for several minutes: the officer asked for identification 11 times and was refused each time. After warning the man that he would be arrested if he continued to refuse to comply, the officer placed him under arrest.

We now know that the man arrested on Grass Valley Road is Larry Dudley Hiibel. Hiibel was charged with "willfully resist[ing], delay[ing], or obstruct[ing] a public officer in discharging or attempting to discharge any legal duty of his office". . . . The government reasoned that Hiibel had obstructed the officer in carrying out his duties under § 171.123, a Nevada statute that defines the legal rights and duties of a police officer in the context of an investigative stop. Section 171.123 provides in relevant part:

> 1. Any peace officer may detain any person whom the officer encounters under circumstances which reasonably indicate that the person has committed, is committing or is about to commit a crime. . . .
>
> 3. The officer may detain the person pursuant to this section only to ascertain his identity and the suspicious circumstances surrounding his presence abroad. Any person so detained shall identify himself, but may not be compelled to answer any other inquiry of any peace officer.

. . . Hiibel was convicted and fined $250. . . .

NRS § 171.123(3) is an enactment sometimes referred to as a "stop and identify" statute. . . .

Stop and identify statutes often combine elements of traditional vagrancy laws with provisions intended to regulate police behavior in the course of investigatory stops. The statutes vary from State to State, but all permit an officer to ask or require a suspect to disclose his identity. . . . In some States, a suspect's refusal to identify himself is a misdemeanor offense or civil violation; in others, it is a factor to be considered in whether the suspect has violated loitering laws. In other States, a suspect may decline to identify himself without penalty.

. . . In *Brown v. Texas,* 443 U.S. 47 (1979), the Court invalidated a conviction for violating a Texas stop and identify statute on Fourth Amendment grounds. The Court ruled that the initial stop was not based on specific, objective facts establishing reasonable suspicion to believe the suspect was involved in criminal activity. Absent that factual basis for detaining the defendant, the Court held, the risk of "arbitrary and abusive police practices" was too great and the stop was impermissible. Four Terms later, the Court invalidated a modified stop and identify statute on vagueness grounds. *See Kolender v. Lawson,* 461 U.S. 352 (1983). The California law in *Kolender* required a suspect to give an officer "'credible and reliable'" identification when asked to identify himself. The Court held that the statute was void because it provided no standard for determining what a suspect must do to comply with it, resulting in "'virtually unrestrained power to arrest and charge persons with a violation.'"

The present case begins where our prior cases left off. Here there is no question that the initial stop was based on reasonable suspicion, satisfying the Fourth Amendment requirements noted in *Brown.* Further, the petitioner has not alleged that the statute is unconstitutionally vague, as in *Kolender.* Here the Nevada statute is narrower and more precise. The statute in *Kolender* had been interpreted to require a suspect to give the officer "credible and reliable" identification. In contrast, the Nevada Supreme Court has interpreted NRS § 171.123(3) to require only that a suspect disclose his name. As we understand it, the statute does not require a suspect to give the officer a driver's license or any other document. Provided that the suspect either states his name or communicates it to the officer by other means — a choice, we assume, that the suspect may make — the statute is satisfied and no violation occurs. . . .

Hiibel argues that his conviction cannot stand because the officer's conduct violated his Fourth Amendment rights. We disagree.

Asking questions is an essential part of police investigations. In the ordinary course a police officer is free to ask a person for identification without implicating the Fourth Amendment. Beginning with *Terry v. Ohio,* 392 U.S. 1 (1968), the Court has recognized that a law enforcement officer's reasonable suspicion that a person may be involved in criminal activity permits the officer to stop the person for a brief time and take additional steps to investigate further. . . .

Obtaining a suspect's name in the course of a *Terry* stop serves important government interests. Knowledge of identity may inform an officer that a suspect is wanted for another offense, or has a record of violence or mental disorder. On the other hand, knowing identity may help clear a suspect and allow the police to concentrate their efforts elsewhere. Identity may prove particularly important in cases such as this, where the police are investigating what appears to be a domestic assault. Officers called to investigate domestic disputes need to know whom they are dealing with in order to assess the situation, the threat to their own safety, and possible danger to the potential victim. . . .

The threat of criminal sanction helps ensure that the request for identity does not become a legal nullity. On the other hand, the Nevada statute does not alter the nature of the stop itself: it does not change its duration or its location. A state law requiring a suspect to disclose his name in the course of a valid *Terry* stop is consistent with Fourth Amendment prohibitions against unreasonable searches and seizures.

Petitioner argues that the Nevada statute circumvents the probable cause requirement, in effect allowing an officer to arrest a person for being suspicious. According to petitioner, this creates a risk of arbitrary police conduct that the Fourth Amendment does not permit. These are familiar concerns; they were central to the opinion in *Papachristou,* and also to the decisions limiting the operation of stop and identify statutes in *Kolender* and *Brown.* Petitioner's concerns are met by the requirement that a *Terry* stop must be justified at its inception and "reasonably related in scope to the circumstances which justified" the initial stop. Under these principles, an officer may not arrest a suspect for failure to identify himself if the request for identification is not reasonably related to the circumstances justifying the stop. . . . It is clear in this case that the request for identification was "reasonably related in scope to the circumstances which justified" the stop. The officer's request was a commonsense inquiry, not an effort to obtain an arrest for failure to identify after a *Terry* stop yielded insufficient evidence. The stop, the request, and the State's requirement of a response did not contravene the guarantees of the Fourth Amendment. . . .

Petitioner further contends that his conviction violates the Fifth Amendment's prohibition on compelled self-incrimination. The Fifth Amendment states that "[n]o person . . . shall be compelled in any criminal case to be a witness against himself." To qualify for the Fifth Amendment privilege, a communication must be testimonial, incriminating, and compelled.

Respondents urge us to hold that the statements NRS § 171.123(3) requires are nontestimonial, and so outside the Clause's scope. We decline to resolve the case on that basis. Even if these required actions are testimonial, . . . petitioner's challenge must fail because in this case disclosure of his name presented no reasonable danger of incrimination. . . .

In this case petitioner's refusal to disclose his name was not based on any articulated real and appreciable fear that his name would be used to incriminate him, or that it "would furnish a link in the chain of evidence needed to prosecute" him. As best we can tell, petitioner refused to identify himself only because he thought his name was none of the officer's business. Even today, petitioner does not explain how the disclosure of his name could have been used against him in a criminal case. While we recognize petitioner's strong belief that he should not have to disclose his identity, the Fifth Amendment does not override the Nevada Legislature's judgment to the contrary absent a reasonable belief that the disclosure would tend to incriminate him.

The narrow scope of the disclosure requirement is also important. One's identity is, by definition, unique; yet it is, in another sense, a universal characteristic. Answering a request to disclose a name is likely to be so insignificant in the scheme of things as to be incriminating only in unusual circumstances. Even witnesses who plan to invoke the Fifth Amendment privilege answer when their names are called to take the stand. Still, a case may arise where there is a substantial allegation that furnishing identity at the time of a stop would have given the police a link in the chain of evidence needed to convict the individual of a separate offense. In that case, the court can then consider whether the privilege applies, and, if the Fifth Amendment has been violated, what remedy must follow. We need not resolve those questions here.

STEVENS, J. dissenting. . . . [O]ur cases have afforded Fifth Amendment protection to statements that are "incriminating" in a much broader sense than the Court suggests. It has "long been settled that [the Fifth Amendment's] protection encompasses compelled statements that lead to the discovery of incriminating evidence even though the statements themselves are not incriminating and are not introduced into evidence." By "incriminating" we have meant disclosures that "could be used in a criminal prosecution or could lead to other evidence that might be so used,"— communications, in other words, that "would furnish a link in the chain of evidence needed to prosecute the claimant for a federal crime." . .

Given a proper understanding of the category of "incriminating" communications that fall within the Fifth Amendment privilege, it is clear that the disclosure of petitioner's identity is protected. The Court reasons that we should not assume that the disclosure of petitioner's name would be used to incriminate him or that it would furnish a link in a chain of evidence needed to prosecute him. But why else would an officer ask for it? And why else would the Nevada Legislature require its disclosure only when circumstances "reasonably indicate that the person has committed, is committing or is about to commit a crime"? If the Court is correct, then petitioner's refusal to cooperate did not impede the police investigation. Indeed, if we accept the predicate for the Court's holding, the statute requires nothing more than a useless invasion of privacy. I think that, on the contrary, the Nevada Legislature intended to provide its police officers with a useful law enforcement tool, and that the very existence of the statute demonstrates the value of the information it demands.

A person's identity obviously bears informational and incriminating worth, "even if the [name] itself is not inculpatory." A name can provide the key to a broad array of information about the person, particularly in the hands of a police officer with access to a range of law enforcement databases. And that information, in turn, can be tremendously useful in a criminal prosecution. It is therefore quite wrong to suggest that a person's identity provides a link in the chain to incriminating evidence "only in unusual circumstances." . .

BREYER, SOUTER, & GINSBURG, J.J. dissenting. . . . [T]his Court's Fourth Amendment precedents make clear that police may conduct a *Terry* stop only within circumscribed limits. And one of those limits invalidates laws that compel responses to police questioning.

In *Terry v. Ohio*, the Court considered whether police, in the absence of probable cause, can stop, question, or frisk an individual at all. . . Justice White, in a separate concurring opinion, set forth further conditions. Justice White wrote: "Of course, the person stopped is not obliged to answer, answers may not be compelled, and refusal to answer furnishes no basis for an arrest, although it may alert the officer to the need for continued observation." . . .

The majority presents no evidence that the rule enunciated by Justice White and then by the *Berkemer* Court, which for nearly a generation has set forth a settled *Terry* stop condition, has significantly interfered with law enforcement. Nor has the majority presented any other convincing justification for change. I would not begin to erode a clear rule with special exceptions. I consequently dissent.

NOTES & QUESTIONS

1. **Hiibel *and* Terry *Stops.*** A *Terry* stop is a special exception to ordinary Fourth Amendment procedures. Ordinarily, if a police officer wants to search a person, she needs a warrant supported by probable cause. If she wants to seize a person (i.e., detain or arrest a person), then she needs probable cause. *Terry* permits limited searches and seizures based on less than probable cause — reasonable suspicion that criminal activity is afoot. Prior to *Hiibel*, the only search permitted under *Terry* was a "frisk" for weapons. *Hiibel* suggests that the state can allow an officer to search in a different way — to compel a person to identify herself under penalty of law. To what extent can such an expansion be justified under *Terry*?
2. ***The Fifth Amendment and Identification.*** The majority states: "Still, a case may arise where there is a substantial allegation that furnishing identity at the time of a stop would have given the police a link in the chain of evidence needed to convict the individual of a separate offense. In that case, the court can then consider whether the privilege applies, and, if the Fifth Amendment has been violated, what remedy must follow." Is the majority admitting that under certain circumstances, the application of the Nevada statute will violate the Fifth Amendment? How are such violations to be prevented? The opinion suggests that the privilege can be enforced after the fact, in court. Is this post-hoc remedy sufficient to protect people's Fifth Amendment rights?
3. ***The Breadth of* Hiibel.** How broad or narrow is *Hiibel*? Does the opinion imply that the police can request of every citizen an identity document? Several aspects of the opinion suggest it is quite narrow. First, the majority notes that "the statute does not require a suspect to give the officer a driver's license or any other document." The suspect is merely required to state his name. Second, the request for identification must be "reasonably related" to the purpose of a *Terry* stop, which itself requires reasonable suspicion that criminal activity is afoot. The majority states that "an officer may not arrest a suspect for failure to identify himself if the request for identification is not reasonably related to the circumstances justifying the stop." Under what circumstances may a person who is stopped by the police lawfully withhold their name? For example, could a person with an outstanding warrant invoke a Fifth Amendment right not to reveal her name? How might the police respond in such a situation? Based on *Hiibel,* what other questions can a state demand a person answer?
4. ***Identification at the Airport.*** In *Gilmore v. Gonzales*, 435 F.3d 1125 (9th Cir. 2006), the court considered whether the requirement to show identification before boarding an airplane constituted a violation of the right to travel and the Fourth Amendment. On July 4, 2002, John Gilmore, a California resident and U.S. citizen, attempted to fly from Oakland International Airport to

Baltimore-Washington International Airport. He later attempted to fly to Washington, D.C., from San Francisco International Airport. There, a United Airlines agent explained that a traveler without identification was subject to secondary screening, which involved a more intensive search than that to which most air travelers were subject.

Regarding the right to travel, the Ninth Circuit concluded that a person "does not possess a fundamental right to travel by airplane even though it is the most convenient mode of travel for him." The court stated that "the Constitution does not guarantee the right to travel by any particular form of transportation." Additionally, the court held that "the identification policy's 'burden' is not unreasonable. The identification policy requires that airline passengers either present identification or be subjected to a more extensive search. The more extensive search is similar to searches that we have determined were reasonable."

As for the Fourth Amendment, the Ninth Circuit concluded that the request for identification was not a seizure. An individual is seized within the meaning of the Fourth Amendment when, in light of all the circumstances, a reasonable person would have believed that she was not free to leave. Since people who fail to present identification are not arrested or otherwise detained, no seizure is involved. As the court noted, "Gilmore twice tried to board a plane without presenting identification and twice left the airport when he was unsuccessful." There was no threatened punishment for his noncompliance with the identification requirement; he was simply not permitted to board the plane.

Finally, the court held that if a passenger were to choose the search option, this would not be an unreasonable search under the Fourth Amendment because the passenger had consented to the search and the search is reasonable in light of its purpose and scope. Moreover, Gilmore has a meaningful choice. As the Ninth Circuit summarized: "He could have presented identification, submitted to a search, or left the airport."

3. SOCIAL SECURITY NUMBERS

The closest thing that the United States has to a national identifier is the Social Security number (SSN). A nine-digit identifier, the SSN was created in 1936 as part of the Social Security System. Because Social Security benefits would not be paid until a worker's retirement or death, a unique number was necessary to identify his or her account. At the time of its introduction, some observers worried that the new system would depersonalize individuals "by treating them as numbers."[32]

Over time, various federal agencies began to use the SSN for other purposes. In 1961, for example, the IRS was authorized by Congress to use SSNs as taxpayer identification numbers. Subsequently, throughout the 1960s and 1970s, the SSN began to be used for military personnel, legally admitted aliens, anyone receiving or applying for federal benefits, food stamps, school lunch program

[32] James R. Beniger, *The Control Revolution* 409 (1986).

eligibility, draft registration, and federal loans. State and local governments, as well as private sector entities such as schools and banks, began to use SSNs as well — for driver's licenses, birth certificates, blood donation, jury selection, workers' compensation, occupational licenses, and marriage licenses.[33]

In the early 1970s, the early spurt in the growing uses of the SSN raised serious concerns that the SSN would become a de facto universal identifier. In 1973, the Department of Health, Education, and Welfare issued a major report on privacy, criticizing the use of the SSN for identification purposes.[34]

In the Privacy Act of 1974, Congress partially responded to these concerns by prohibiting any governmental agency from denying any right, benefit, or privilege merely because an individual refused to disclose his or her SSN. Pursuant to § 7 of the Privacy Act:

> (a)(1) It shall be unlawful for any federal, state or local government agency to deny to any individual any right, benefit, or privilege provided by law because of such individual's refusal to disclose his Social Security account number.
>
> (2) The provisions of paragraph (1) of this subsection shall not apply with respect to —
>
> (A) Any disclosure which is required by federal statute, or
>
> (B) The disclosure of a social security number to any federal, state, or local agency maintaining a system of records in existence and operating before January 1, 1975, if such disclosure was required under statute or regulation adopted prior to such date to verify the identity of an individual.
>
> (b) Any federal, state, or local government agency which requests an individual to disclose his social security account number shall inform that individual whether that disclosure is mandatory or voluntary, by what statutory or other authority such number is solicited, and what uses will be made of it. 5 U.S.C. § 552a note.

The Privacy Act was passed to "curtail the expanding use of social security numbers by federal and local agencies and, by so doing, to eliminate the threat to individual privacy and confidentiality of information posed by common numerical identifiers." *Doyle v. Wilson*, 529 F. Supp. 1343, 1348 (D. Del. 1982).

Nevertheless, the use of SSNs continued to escalate after the Privacy Act. In 1977, a Privacy Protection Study Commission acknowledged a belief of some individuals "that being labeled with the SSN is dehumanizing." At the same time, it argued against further restrictions on the collection and use of the SSN; in its view, such measures "would be costly and cumbersome in the short run, ineffectual in the long run, and would also distract public attention from the need to formulate general policies on record exchanges."

Today, SSNs continue to be widely used. SSNs are collected by private-sector database firms from a number of public and nonpublic sources, such as

---

[33] For a chart of the increasing uses of the SSN, see Simson Garfinkel, *Database Nation: The Death of Privacy in the 21st Century* 33-34 (2000). *See also* Social Security Administration, *Social Security: Your Number* (1998), available at http://www.ssa.gov/pubs/10002.html.

[34] U.S. Department of Health, Education, and Welfare, *Report of the Secretary's Advisory Committee on Automated Personal Data Systems: Records, Computers, and the Rights of Citizens* xxxii (1973).

court records and credit reports. It is currently legal for private firms to sell or disclose SSNs. As one commentator has observed:

> . . . [W]ith respect to collecting SSNs from individuals (1) federal law does not bar private actors from requesting SSNs or refusing to do business with someone if they refuse; and (2) state laws, although reaching a few private actors, contain no general prohibitions against SSN use or collection. . . . [G]overnmental use of SSNs is forbidden by Section 7 of the Privacy Act unless an exception applies, but . . . over the years Congress has made so many exceptions, that the collection of SSNs in government is quite widespread. This is the case for two reasons: Congress has passed many mandates of SSN use, and where states or private actors are left to decide whether or not to require the SSN, these entities generally choose to use it. . . .
>
> . . . [T]he fact remains that governmental dissemination of personal identifying numbers is still widespread, and limits on private actors are also virtually nonexistent.[35]

GREIDINGER V. DAVIS

988 F.2d 1344 (4th Cir. 1993)

HAMILTON, J. The Constitution of Virginia requires all citizens otherwise qualified to vote and possessing a [Social Security number (SSN)] (registering after July 1, 1971) to provide their SSN on their Virginia Voter Registration Application (Application) in order to become registered to vote. Va. Const. art. II, § 2. If an individual otherwise qualified to vote does not possess a SSN, a "dummy" number will be provided. The scheme also provides that any registered voter may inspect the voter registration books in the Office of the General Registrar. In practice, these books contain the registration application of a registered voter.

The scheme further provides that Statewide Voter Registration lists containing the SSNs of voters can be obtained by: (a) candidates for election to further their candidacy, (b) political party committees for political purposes only, (c) incumbent office holders to report to their constituents, and (d) nonprofit organizations which promote voter participation and registration for that purpose only.

On July 24, 1991, appellant, Marc Alan Greidinger, filled out an Application, but refused to disclose his SSN. Because of this omission, Greidinger received a Denial of Application for Virginia Voter Registration from the General Registrar of Stafford County. Consequently, the Virginia State Board of Elections (the Board) prevented Greidinger from voting in the November 5, 1991, general election. . . .

Greidinger argues that the "public disclosure" accompanying Virginia's requirement that he provide his SSN on his voter registration application unconstitutionally burdens his right to vote as protected by the First and Fourteenth Amendments. In making this argument, Greidinger attacks two components of

---

[35] Flavio L. Komuves, *We've Got Your Number: An Overview of Legislation and Decisions to Control the Use of Social Security Numbers as Personal Identifiers*, 16 J. Marshall J. Computer & Info. L. 529, 569 (1998).

Virginia's voter registration scheme. He objects to Virginia's permitting registered voters to obtain another registered voter's SSN via § 24.1-56, which provides that all registration books, containing all of the registration forms, "shall be opened to the inspection of any qualified voter." He also objects to § 24.1-23(8) which allows dissemination of a registered voter's SSN to a candidate for election or political party nomination, political party committee or official, incumbent office holder, and nonprofit organization which promotes voter participation and registration.

Notably, Greidinger does not challenge Virginia's receipt and internal use of his SSN. He challenges only the dissemination of the SSN to the public pursuant to § 24.1-23(8) (candidates, political parties and officials, incumbents, and nonprofit organizations which promote voter participation and voter registration) and § 24.1-56 (general public). In addition, Greidinger does not assert any constitutional right to privacy in his SSN. Rather, he argues that the privacy interest in his SSN is sufficiently strong that his right to vote cannot be predicated on the disclosure of his SSN to the public or political entities.

It is axiomatic that "[n]o right is more precious in a free country than that of having a voice in the election of those who make the laws under which, as good citizens, we must live. Other rights, even the most basic, are illusory if the right to vote is undermined." Despite the fundamental nature of the right to vote, states may nevertheless impose certain qualifications on and regulate access to the franchise. . . .

. . . If a substantial burden exists [on the right to vote, the restriction] on the right to vote must serve a compelling state interest and be narrowly tailored to serve that state interest. . . .

Before we begin examining the burden on Greidinger's right to vote, we note that the Virginia statutes at issue, for all practical purposes, condition Greidinger's right to vote on the public disclosure of his SSN. . . .

Because Virginia's voter registration scheme conditions Greidinger's right to vote on the public disclosure of his SSN, we must examine whether this condition imposes a substantial burden. . . .

Since the passage of the Privacy Act, an individual's concern over his SSN's confidentiality and misuse has become significantly more compelling. For example, armed with one's SSN, an unscrupulous individual could obtain a person's welfare benefits or Social Security benefits, order new checks at a new address on that person's checking account, obtain credit cards, or even obtain the person's paycheck. Succinctly stated, the harm that can be inflicted from the disclosure of a SSN to an unscrupulous individual is alarming and potentially financially ruinous. These are just examples, and our review is by no means exhaustive; we highlight a few to elucidate the egregiousness of the harm. . . .

The statutes at issue compel a would-be voter in Virginia to consent to the possibility of a profound invasion of privacy when exercising the fundamental right to vote. As illustrated by the examples of the potential harm that the dissemination of an individual's SSN can inflict, Greidinger's decision not to provide his SSN is eminently reasonable. In other words, Greidinger's fundamental right to vote is substantially burdened to the extent the statutes at issue permit the public disclosure of his SSN.

Having identified that Greidinger's right to vote is substantially burdened by the public disclosure of his SSN, we must next determine whether Virginia has advanced a compelling state interest that justifies the disclosure and dissemination of his SSN. If Virginia advances a compelling state interest, we must determine whether disclosure of the SSN is narrowly tailored to fulfill that state interest.

. . . Unquestionably, Virginia has a compelling state interest in preventing voter fraud and promoting voter participation. However, the inquiry does not end here. We must determine whether the disclosure of the SSN under § 24.1-23(8) and/or § 24.1-56 is narrowly tailored to fulfill that state interest. We conclude that it is not.

Virginia's voter registration form requires a registrant to supply, among other things, his name, address, SSN, age, place of birth, and county of previous registration. Virginia's interest in preventing voter fraud and voter participation could easily be met without the disclosure of the SSN and the attendant possibility of a serious invasion of privacy that would result from that disclosure. . . . Most assuredly, an address or date of birth would sufficiently distinguish among voters that shared a common name. Moreover, the same state interest could be achieved through the use of a voter registration number as opposed to a SSN. . . . Thus, to the extent § 24.1-23(8) and § 24.1-56 allow Virginia's voter registration scheme to "sweep [ ] broader than necessary to advance electoral order," it creates an intolerable burden on Greidinger's fundamental right to vote.

NOTES & QUESTIONS

1. ***Is There a Reasonable Expectation of Privacy in SSNs?*** Consider *Beacon Journal v. City of Akron*, 70 Ohio St. 3d 605 (Ohio 1994). There, private parties requested that a city provide them with public employees' personnel records containing employees' names, addresses, telephone numbers, birth dates, education, employment status, and SSNs. The city provided the records with the SSNs deleted. The private parties sued to obtain the SSNs. The court concluded that the SSNs were not "public records" for the purposes of Ohio's Public Records Act:

> . . . R.C. 149.43(A) expressly excludes the release of records which would violate state or federal law. Because we find that the disclosure of the SSNs would violate the federal constitutional right to privacy, we find them to be excluded from mandatory disclosure. . . .
>
> We must determine whether the city employees have a legitimate expectation of privacy in their SSNs and then whether their privacy interests outweigh those interests benefited by disclosure of the numbers. . . .
>
> Due to the federal legislative scheme involving the use of SSNs, city employees have a legitimate expectation of privacy in their SSNs. [The court quoted § 7 of the Privacy Act of 1974.] . . .
>
> Congress when enacting the Privacy Act of 1974 was codifying the societal perception that SSNs should not to be available to all. This legislative scheme is sufficient to create an expectation of privacy in the minds of city employees concerning the use and disclosure of their SSNs. . . .

> The city's refusal to release its employees' SSNs does not significantly interfere with the public's right to monitor governmental conduct. The numbers by themselves reveal little information about the city's employees. The city provided appellees with enormous amounts of other information about each city employee; only the SSNs numbers were deleted. . . .
>
> While the release of all city employees' SSNs would provide inquirers with little useful information about the organization of their government, the release of the numbers could allow an inquirer to discover the intimate, personal details of each city employee's life, which are completely irrelevant to the operations of government. As the *Greidinger* court warned, a person's SSN is a device which can quickly be used by the unscrupulous to acquire a tremendous amount of information about a person. . . .
>
> Thanks to the abundance of data bases in the private sector that include the SSNs of persons listed in their files, an intruder using an SSN can quietly discover the intimate details of a victim's personal life without the victim ever knowing of the intrusion.
>
> We find today that the high potential for fraud and victimization caused by the unchecked release of city employee SSNs outweighs the minimal information about governmental processes gained through the release of the SSNs. . . .

How does the legal theory in *Beacon* differ from that in *Greidinger*?

2. ***Disclosure of Social Security Numbers and the First Amendment.*** In *City of Kirkland v. Sheehan*, 29 Media L. Rep. 2367 (Wash. Sup. Ct. 2001), a group of law enforcement personnel sued the operators of a website critical of the police that listed the names, addresses, dates of birth, phone numbers, Social Security numbers, and other personal data. Although the court held that the disclosure of most of the personal data was protected under the First Amendment, the disclosure of Social Security numbers was different:

> In this case, as in numerous others, in the absence of a credible specific threat of harm, the publication of lawfully obtained addresses and telephone numbers, while certainly unwelcome to those who had desired a greater degree of anonymity, is traditionally viewed as having the ability to promote political speech. Publication may arguably expose wrongdoers and/or facilitate peaceful picketing of homes or worksites and render other communication possible.
>
> However, Social Security numbers are different from addresses and telephone numbers. The blanket identification of the Social Security numbers of a group of people, without more, does not provide a similar opportunity for or otherwise facilitate or promote substantive communication. It cannot reasonably be disputed that at its core the SSN is simply a government-originated identifying number. It is a key or a tool, created by the government and unique for each individual. Access to an individual's SSN enables a new holder to obtain access to and to control, manipulate or alter other personal information. In effect, access to an SSN allows a person, agency or company to more efficiently and effectively search for and seize information and assets of another, a power originally available only to the government and one which was subject to direct Constitutional restraint.
>
> On its face, the SSN is a tag or an identifier which at best has only a distant possibility of a substantive communicative purpose. Keeping Social

Security numbers private is a compelling interest for the government and citizens alike. . . .

4. NATIONAL IDENTIFICATION SYSTEMS

A national identification system is a nationwide system for identifying individuals. It consists of linking a database of information about individuals to an identifier, so that individuals can be readily connected to a stream of data about them.

More than 100 countries have some form of national identification card. These countries include most nations in Europe (including Germany, France, Spain, Greece, Finland, and others), Malaysia, Singapore, Thailand, and many others. However, Americans have repeatedly eschewed such systems. Throughout the latter half of the twentieth century, government officials entertained the idea of creating a national identification system on a number of occasions, but each time, the idea was rejected.

Proponents of national identification systems point to greater efficiencies, ease of use, prevention of fraud, and greater capacity to screen for terrorists and criminals. Critics contend that having one single identification card can vastly increase the dangers if the card is lost or stolen. Such a system of national identification could magnify the effects of fraud. To the extent that the card would bring added efficiency in terms of cardholders having to undergo less stringent security checks, the possessors of forged or stolen cards could better avoid such screenings. Cards could impede free movement throughout the country. Errors in the bureaucratic system administering the cards and linking the cardholders to information in a database could have a severe impact on people's lives. Further, national identifiers would be used by the private sector to link together data about individuals.

RICHARD SOBEL, *THE DEGRADATION OF POLITICAL IDENTITY UNDER A NATIONAL IDENTIFICATION SYSTEM*

8 B.U. J. Sci. & Tech. L. 37 (2002)

America is moving toward a system of national identification numbers, databanks, and identity cards that contradicts the constitutional and philosophical bases of democratic government and undermines the moral economy of political and personal identity. Because the kinds of problems that a national identification system ("NIDS") is supposed to solve tend to occur in relatively closed societies, the troubles a NIDS creates as a bureaucratic scheme may soon foreclose options and opportunities central to a free society. . . . The growing impact of NIDS on due process, burden of proof, freedom from search, free expression, freedom of travel, the right to employment, and federalism makes this issue particularly appropriate for contemporary ethical and policy analysis. . . .

The ongoing developments toward a NIDS, as privacy advocate Robert Ellis Smith notes, fundamentally contradict what it means to be an American. In an open democratic society, the government derives its powers from the consent of the governed, constitutions are developed to circumscribe state power, and activities such as work, travel, and medical care are readily available and treated in ways respectful of privacy. In contrast, the government in authoritarian societies bestows, or denies, identities and opportunities through identification numbers or documents, intruding into individuals' lives. In addition, especially because the government has the power to coerce individuals and to control their lives, people confront force when they must follow, or if they disobey, the government's directions. . . .

A formal NIDS would require an identity number, databank, and ID card. The system would begin by assigning each American resident a unique national identity number. Each citizen and identifiable immigrant would be uniquely identified by a numeral. Resident enumeration and data collection would begin at birth, defining each newborn as a data point to be tracked from cradle to grave through a government-issued number. Such a process has already begun with the relatively recent practice of issuing Social Security numbers at birth and requiring them to obtain marriage licenses and tax deductions for one's children of any age. . . .

For the existence and implementation of a NIDS, particularly a national identity card, there must also be a national computer databank organized by ID numbers. An individual would have to be entered into the databank to exist in a legal sense or to have a bureaucratic existence. Receiving an ID card would require meeting the criteria for being registered in the databank. ID numbers would be used for multiple purposes, and computer databanks would collect disparate pieces of information. For reasons of proposed efficiency, such a computer system would centralize and interconnect with educational, employment, social security, tax, and medical information. These data would paint a detailed portrait of each individual's habits and preference even though such collections would not be fully accurate or secure. One would not, moreover, have a political identity or be able to exercise political rights without proper ID. Inclusion in the databank would create a paper, plastic, or electronic person. . . .

Citizens or residents might be required to carry their national ID at all times or produce it when entering school, applying for a job or government benefits, and traveling away from home. . . .

Identity systems and documents have a long history of uses and abuses for social control and discrimination. Through the Civil War, slaves were required to carry passes in order to travel outside of plantations. . . .

A system of identification cards was used to isolate and round up Jews in Germany and other Nazi-occupied territories prior to World War II and in the occupied countries once the war began. All German Jews were required to apply for such cards by December 31, 1938. . . .

Even before the Japanese attack on Pearl Harbor, however, President Franklin Delano Roosevelt . . . ordered the Census Bureau to collect all information on "foreign-born and American-born Japanese" from the Census data lists. Within days, information from the 1930 and 1940 censuses on all Japanese Americans was gathered and distributed to the Federal Bureau of Investigation, the governors, and the top military officials in western states. Its use facilitated the internment of Japanese Americans on the West Coast.

NOTES & QUESTIONS

1. ***National Identification Systems: Pro and Con.*** As a policy matter, do you agree with Richard Sobel that efforts to collect and combine information should be blocked or perhaps undone? Consider the contrary view of Amitai Etzioni:

   > American society incurs high costs — social, economic, and other kinds — because of its inability to identify many hundreds of thousands of violent criminals, white-collar criminals, welfare and credit card cheats, parents who do not pay child support, and illegal immigrants. If individuals could be properly identified, public safety would be significantly enhanced and social and economic costs would be reduced significantly. . . .
   >
   > In response to the claim that universal identifiers will cause a police state or totalitarian regime to arise, it should be noted that ID cards are quite common in European democracies and have been in place for quite some time without undermining these democracies. . . .
   >
   > If a totalitarian regime were to arise, and no universal identification system was in place, the new secret police would have only to consolidate existing private databases and add existing public ones (those maintained by the IRS, INS, FBI, and SSA, among others) to have a very elaborate description of most Americans. . . .[36]

   What are the benefits of a national identification system? What are the costs? What privacy interests could a national identification card in the United States implicate?

2. ***Anonymity.*** Consider the cases on anonymity. What would be the impact of a national identification system on First Amendment values?

3. ***The Intelligence Reform and Terrorism Prevention Act of 2004.*** The Intelligence Reform and Terrorism Prevention Act of 2004 requires standardization of birth certificates and driver's licenses for acceptance by federal agencies. § 7212. The law also establishes standards for common machine-readable identity information to be included on each driver's license or personal identification card, including minimum data elements. Identification security standards are required to ensure that driver's licenses and personal identification cards are resistant to tampering, alteration, or counterfeiting. The cards must be capable of accommodating and ensuring the security of a digital photograph or other unique identifier. A state may confiscate a driver's license or personal identification card if any component or security feature of the document is compromised.

4. ***The REAL ID Act.*** In May 2005, the Senate unanimously approved legislation, already passed by the House, creating standardization requirements for state driver's licenses. The REAL ID Act, sponsored by Representative James Sensenbrenner, was enacted as part of spending legislation (Pub. L. No. 109-13) rather than as a stand-alone bill, which effectively limited debate on it. This law sets minimum document requirements for state driver's licenses or

---

[36] Amitai Etzioni, *The Limits of Privacy* 103-104, 126, 130 (1999).

identification cards; unless these standards are met, a federal agency is not to accept the state document in question for any official purposes.

The REAL ID Act establishes the kinds of multiple documents that must be shown to verify identity before a license can be issued or renewed. Moreover, it requires states to produce standardized, tamper-resistant licenses that include machine-readable data. It also mandates states to store digital images of "identity source documents" (such as birth certificates) as well as the photographs on driver's licenses. It requires driver license data to be kept in linked databases available to all states. Finally, undocumented immigrants will not be able to obtain a driver's license as the REAL ID Act requires evidence of lawful status in the United States to obtain a driver's license or ID card.

The REAL ID Act proved controversial from its time of enactment. Proponents of the law say it will help prevent terrorists and illegal immigrants from obtaining ID documents. Opponents of the law argue that it creates a national ID card and a de facto national ID database, and that it will not improve security. As security expert Bruce Schneier contends: "It's a bad idea, and is going to make us all less safe. It's also very expensive." He further argues:

> [T]he main problem with any strong identification system is that it requires the existence of a database. In this case, it would have to be 50 linked databases of private and sensitive information on every American — one widely and instantaneously accessible from airline check-in stations, police cars, schools, and so on.
>
> The security risks of this database are enormous. It would be a kludge of existing databases that are incompatible, full of erroneous data, and unreliable. Computer scientists don't know how to keep a database of this magnitude secure, whether from outside hackers or the thousands of insiders authorized to access it.
>
> But even if we could solve all these problems, and within the putative $11 billion budget, we still wouldn't be getting very much security. A reliance on ID cards is based on a dangerous security myth, that if only we knew who everyone was, we could pick the bad guys out of the crowd.[37]

In contrast, Michael Chertoff, Secretary of the Department of Homeland Security (DHS), declared: "Do you think your privacy is better protected if someone can walk around with phony docs with your name and your social security number, or is your privacy better protected if you have the confidence that the identification relied upon is in fact reliable and uniquely tied to a single individual?"

In February 2007, the DHS issued new guidelines for the program and agreed to extend the deadline for implementation beyond May 2008, the original deadline. The guidelines set a long phase-in period for the program with full compliance for all driver's licenses and identification cards set for December 2017. Licenses for those under 50 years old are to be compliant by May 11, 2014, and for those 50 and over, by December 1, 2017. According to

---

[37] Bruce Schneier, *REAL ID: Costs and Benefits*, Schneier on Security (Jan. 30, 2007), http://www.schneier.com/blog/archives/2007/01/realid_costs_an.html.

Chertoff, the phase-in represented “risk management” because older people were less likely to be terrorists than younger people.

At least 21 states have passed resolutions of some kind that oppose REAL ID. In seven of these states, legislatures enacted laws that ban state implementation of the REAL ID Act. In response, the DHS has said that if states fail to comply, driver’s licenses from these states will no longer be considered valid ID documents for many purposes, such as getting on an airplane or obtaining a passport.

CHAPTER 6

PRIVACY AND GOVERNMENT RECORDS AND DATABASES

In the United States, government began to use records widely about citizens after the rise of the administrative state in the early part of the twentieth century. The administrative state's extensive and complex systems of regulation, licensing, and entitlements demanded the collection of a significant amount of personal information. For example, the Social Security system, created in 1935, required that records be kept about every employed individual's earnings. To ensure that each record was correctly identified, the Social Security Administration assigned each individual a unique nine-digit number known as a Social Security number (SSN).

Technology has also been developed that helps government create detailed databases of personal information. Indeed, one of the greatest catalysts for the creation of government records has been technology — namely, the computer. The invention of the mainframe computer in 1946 sparked a revolution in recordkeeping. By the 1960s, computers provided a fast, efficient, and inexpensive way to store, analyze, and transfer information. Federal and state agencies began to computerize their records, often using SSNs as identifiers for these records.[1]

Today, federal agencies maintain thousands of databases. States also keep a panoply of public records, pertaining to births, marriages, divorces, property ownership, licensing, voter registration, and the identity and location of sex offenders. State public records will be covered later in this chapter.

The vast stores of personal information spread throughout government databases have given rise to significant fears that one day this information might be combined to create a file on each citizen. In his influential book on privacy from 1971, Arthur Miller warned of the "possibility of constructing a

[1] *See* Alan F. Westin & Michael A. Baker, *Databanks in a Free Society: Computers, Record-Keeping and Privacy* 229 (1972); Priscilla Regan, *Legislating Privacy* 69 (1995); Daniel J. Solove, *Privacy and Power: Computer Databases and Metaphors for Information Privacy*, 53 Stan. L. Rev. 1393, 1400-03 (2001).

sophisticated data center capable of generating a comprehensive womb-to-tomb dossier on every individual and transmitting it to a wide range of data users over a national network."[2] Several times, the federal government has seriously considered the idea of creating a national database of personal information. In the 1960s, for example, the Johnson Administration proposed a National Data Center that would combine data held by various federal agencies into one large computer database. However, the plan was abandoned after a public outcry. Following the terrorist attacks on September 11, 2001, there was a new effort to build a national database based on records contained in state motor vehicle agencies. Unlike the earlier proposal that envisioned a centralized system of records management, the new system would be based on standardized record formats and data linkages to enable information sharing among federal and state agencies.

A. PUBLIC ACCESS TO GOVERNMENT RECORDS

1. PUBLIC RECORDS AND COURT RECORDS

As noted above, states maintain a panoply of records about individuals, many available to the public. These records contain varying kinds of information. Birth records often disclose one's name, date of birth, place of birth, the names and ages of one's parents, and one's mother's maiden name. States also maintain driver's license records, as well as accident reports. Voting records, which can disclose one's political party affiliation, date of birth, e-mail address, home address, and telephone number, are publicly available in many states. Several types of professions require state licensing, such as doctors, attorneys, engineers, nurses, police, and teachers. Property ownership records contain a physical description of one's property, including the number and size of rooms as well as the value of the property. Police records, such as records of arrests, are also frequently made publicly available.

Court records are public in all states, though settlements in civil actions are sometimes sealed. A significant amount of personal data can find its way into court records. In a civil case, for example, medical and financial information often is entered into evidence. The names, addresses, and occupations of jurors become part of the court record, as well as the jurors' answers to voir dire questions. In some states, family court proceedings are public.

For information in court records, privacy is protected by way of protective orders, which are issued at the discretion of trial court judges. Courts also have the discretion to seal certain court proceedings or portions of court proceedings from the public, as well as to permit parties to proceed anonymously under special circumstances.

Privacy in records maintained by state agencies is protected under each state's freedom of information law. Most states have some form of exemption for privacy, often patterned after the federal Freedom of Information Act's (FOIA)

---

[2] Arthur Miller, *Assault on Privacy* 39 (1971).

privacy exemptions. Not all states interpret their privacy exemptions as broadly as the Supreme Court has interpreted FOIA's. Further, certain state FOIAs do not have privacy exemptions.

Until recently, public and court records were difficult to access. These documents were only available in local offices. The Internet revolution has now made it possible to access records from anywhere. Furthermore, private sector entities have consolidated these records into gigantic new databases.

DOE V. SHAKUR

164 F.R.D. 359 (S.D.N.Y. 1996)

CHIN, J. This diversity action raises the difficult question of whether the victim of a sexual assault may prosecute a civil suit for damages under a pseudonym. Plaintiff has brought this action charging that defendants Tupac A. Shakur and Charles L. Fuller sexually assaulted her on November 18, 1993. On December 1, 1994, a jury trial in Supreme Court, New York County, found Shakur and Fuller guilty of sexual abuse and not guilty of sodomy, attempted sodomy and weapons violations. They were sentenced on February 7, 1995 and an appeal is pending.

This civil suit was filed approximately two weeks after Shakur and Fuller were sentenced. The complaint seeks $10 million in compensatory damages and $50 million in punitive damages. Before filing her complaint, plaintiff obtained an order *ex parte* from Judge Sprizzo, sitting as Part I judge, sealing the complaint and permitting plaintiff to file a substitute complaint using a pseudonym in place of her real name. Neither defendant filed a timely answer and thus the Clerk of the Court entered a default.

Shakur has moved to vacate the entry of default. In his motion papers, which have not yet been filed with the Clerk of the Court but which have been served on plaintiff, Shakur identifies plaintiff by her real name. Shakur justifies his use of plaintiff's name by noting that Judge Sprizzo's order allowing plaintiff to file her complaint using a pseudonym was signed after an *ex parte* appearance and merely sealed the complaint. That order did not provide that this entire proceeding was to be conducted under seal. In response, plaintiff claims that Judge Sprizzo's order requires all papers filed with the Court to use plaintiff's pseudonym. In the alternative, plaintiff requests that I issue such an order now.

As a threshold matter, it is plain from the face of Judge Sprizzo's order that he did not decide the issue now before me. Judge Sprizzo's order merely allowed plaintiff to file the *complaint* under seal. Judge Sprizzo did not order that all documents filed in this case be sealed. Nor did Judge Sprizzo hold that plaintiff could prosecute the entire lawsuit under a pseudonym. Nor do I believe that Judge Sprizzo, sitting as Part I judge on the basis of an *ex parte* application, intended to foreclose defendants from being heard on the issue.

Rule 10(a) of the Federal Rules of Civil Procedure provides that a complaint shall state the names of all the parties. The intention of this rule is to apprise parties of who their opponents are and to protect the public's legitimate interest in knowing the facts at issue in court proceedings. Nevertheless, in some circumstances a party may commence a suit using a fictitious name.

It is within a court's discretion to allow a plaintiff to proceed anonymously. *Doe v. Bell Atlantic Business Sys. Servs., Inc.,* 162 F.R.D. 418, 420 (D. Mass. 1995). In exercising its discretion, a court should consider certain factors in determining whether plaintiffs may proceed anonymously. These factors include (1) whether the plaintiff is challenging governmental activity; (2) whether the plaintiff would be required to disclose information of the utmost intimacy; (3) whether the plaintiff would be compelled to admit his or her intention to engage in illegal conduct, thereby risking criminal prosecution; (4) whether the plaintiff would risk suffering injury if identified; and (5) whether the party defending against a suit brought under a pseudonym would be prejudiced.

In considering these and other factors, a court must engage in a balancing process. As the Eleventh Circuit has held,

> The ultimate test for permitting a plaintiff to proceed anonymously is whether the plaintiff has a substantial privacy right which outweighs the "customary and constitutionally-embedded presumption of openness in judicial proceedings." It is the exceptional case in which a plaintiff may proceed under a fictitious name.

Frank, 951 F.2d at 323 (*citing Doe v. Stegall,* 653 F.2d 180, 186 (5th Cir. 1981)).

The present case is a difficult one. If the allegations of the complaint are true, plaintiff was the victim of a brutal sexual assault. Quite understandably, she does not want to be publicly identified and she has very legitimate privacy concerns. On balance, however, these concerns are outweighed by the following considerations.

First, plaintiff has chosen to bring this lawsuit. She has made serious charges and has put her credibility in issue. Fairness requires that she be prepared to stand behind her charges publicly.

Second, this is a civil suit for damages, where plaintiff is seeking to vindicate primarily her own interests. This is not a criminal case where rape shield laws might provide some anonymity to encourage victims to testify to vindicate the public's interest in enforcement of our laws. *See id.* (rape shield laws "apply to situations where the government chooses to prosecute a case, and offer[ ] anonymity to a victim who does not have a choice in or control over the prosecution"). Indeed, the public's interest in bringing defendants to justice for breaking the law — assuming that they did — is being vindicated in the criminal proceedings.

Third, Shakur has been publicly accused. If plaintiff were permitted to prosecute this case anonymously, Shakur would be placed at a serious disadvantage, for he would be required to defend himself publicly while plaintiff could make her accusations from behind a cloak of anonymity.

Finally, the public has a right of access to the courts. Indeed, "lawsuits are public events and the public has a legitimate interest in knowing the facts involved in them. Among those facts is the identity of the parties." . . .

Plaintiff argues that Shakur's notoriety will likely cause this case to attract significant media attention, and she contends that disclosure of her name will cause her to be "publicly humiliated and embarrassed." Such claims of public humiliation and embarrassment, however, are not sufficient grounds for allowing a plaintiff in a civil suit to proceed anonymously, as the cases cited above demonstrate. Moreover, plaintiff has conceded that the press has known her name for some time. Indeed, plaintiff makes it clear that the press has been aware of both her residence and her place of employment. Hence, her identity is not unknown.

Plaintiff's allegation that she has been subjected to death threats would provide a legitimate basis for allowing her to proceed anonymously. Plaintiff has not, however, provided any details, nor has she explained how or why the use of her real name in court papers would lead to harm, since those who presumably would have any animosity toward her already know her true identity. Thus, plaintiff simply has not shown that she is entitled to proceed under a pseudonym in this action.

It may be, as plaintiff suggests, that victims of sexual assault will be deterred from seeking relief through civil suits if they are not permitted to proceed under a pseudonym. That would be an unfortunate result. For the reasons discussed above, however, plaintiff and others like her must seek vindication of their rights publicly.

NOTES & QUESTIONS

1. ***Pseudonymous Litigation.*** *Doe v. Shakur* involved a party's request to proceed under a pseudonym. The court refused this request. The standard for allowing a party to proceed with a fictitious name gives significant room for judicial discretion. Consider *Doe v. Blue Cross & Blue Shield United of Wisconsin*, 112 F.3d 869 (7th Cir. 1997):

> The plaintiff is proceeding under a fictitious name because of fear that the litigation might result in the disclosure of his psychiatric records. The motion to proceed in this way was not opposed, and the district judge granted it without comment. The judge's action was entirely understandable given the absence of objection and the sensitivity of psychiatric records, but we would be remiss if we failed to point out that the privilege of suing or defending under a fictitious name should not be granted automatically even if the opposing party does not object. The use of fictitious names is disfavored, and the judge has an independent duty to determine whether exceptional circumstances justify such a departure from the normal method of proceeding in federal courts. *See United States v. Microsoft Corp.,* 56 F.3d 1448, 1463-64 (D.C. Cir. 1995) (per curiam), and cases cited there, and our recent dictum in *K.F.P. v. Dane County,* 110 F.3d 516, 518-19 (7th Cir. 1997). Rule 10(a) of the Federal Rules of Civil Procedure, in providing that the complaint shall give the names of all the parties to the suit (and our plaintiff's name is *not* "John Doe"), instantiates the principle that judicial proceedings, civil as well as criminal, are to be conducted in public. Identifying the parties to the proceeding is an important dimension of publicness. The people have a right to know who is using their courts.
>
> There are exceptions. Records or parts of records are sometimes sealed for good reasons, including the protection of state secrets, trade secrets, and informers; and fictitious names are allowed when necessary to protect the privacy of children, rape victims, and other particularly vulnerable parties or witnesses. But the fact that a case involves a medical issue is not a sufficient reason for allowing the use of a fictitious name, even though many people are

> understandably secretive about their medical problems. "John Doe" suffers, or at least from 1989 to 1991 suffered, from a psychiatric disorder — obsessive-compulsive syndrome. This is a common enough disorder — some would say that most lawyers and judges suffer from it to a degree — and not such a badge of infamy or humiliation in the modern world that its presence should be an automatic ground for concealing the identity of a party to a federal suit. To make it such would be to propagate the view that mental illness is shameful. Should "John Doe"'s psychiatric records contain material that would be highly embarrassing to the average person yet somehow pertinent to this suit and so an appropriate part of the judicial record, the judge could require that this material be placed under seal.

Also consider *Doe No. 2 v. Kolko*, 242 F.R.D. 193 (2006). An adult plaintiff alleged that he was sexually abused as a child by a rabbi at a private Jewish school. The court allowed the plaintiff to proceed anonymously by looking to several factors, including: the public's strong interest in protecting sexual abuse victims; the opinion of the plaintiff's psychologist that the alleged abuse had caused the plaintiff severe psychological and emotional injuries; plaintiff's assertion that he feared retaliation and ostracism if his name was disclosed; a lack of showing that knowledge of plaintiff's identity was widespread; any additional prejudice to defendant's reputation due to pursuit of legal action under pseudonym was minimal due to two similar lawsuits against the rabbi by named plaintiffs; and, finally, a lack of showing that defendants' ability to conduct discovery or impeach plaintiff's credibility would be impaired by allowing plaintiff to proceed anonymously. On the final point, the court noted that defendants would need to make redactions and take measures not to disclose plaintiff's identity, but would otherwise not be hampered by plaintiff's mere anonymity in court papers. These restrictions could also be reconsidered before the case went to trial.

When is it appropriate for a judge to allow a party to proceed under a pseudonym? Does the test give too much discretion to judges to make this determination? If so, how would you draft a rule that limits judicial discretion in approaching this issue?

2. ***Protective Orders.*** Federal Rule of Civil Procedure 26(c) provides that judges may, "for good cause shown," issue protective orders where disclosure of information gleaned in discovery might cause a party "annoyance, embarrassment, oppression, or undue burden or expense." In other words, a protective order serves to place limits on the process of discovery. Most states have protective order provisions similar to the federal one. There is a presumption in favor of access to information through discovery, and the party seeking the protective order must overcome this presumption. Courts will issue a protective order when a party's interest in privacy outweighs the public interest in disclosure.[3] Although the standard for obtaining a protective order is easier to satisfy than the standard for proceeding under a pseudonym,

---

[3] For more information about court records, see Gregory M. Silverman, *Rise of the Machines: Justice Information Systems and the Question of Public Access to Court Records Over the Internet*, 79 Wash. L. Rev. 175 (2004).

the thumb on the scale is on the side of public access. Consider the "good cause shown" standard of Federal Rule of Civil Procedure 26(c). Does it grant too much discretion to a court in granting protective orders?

3. ***Personal Information in Court Records.*** Under some court practices, certain information is categorically excluded from court records. As Natalie Gomez-Velez notes:

> The list of data elements categorically excluded from case records varies from state to state, depending to some extent on the degree to which case records are being made available and the extent to which a particular state precludes public access to certain categories of cases and information. . . .
>
> To a great extent, the federal courts, New York, Indiana, and courts in other states that exclude whole classes of sensitive cases like matrimonial, adoption, juvenile, and family law cases from public access, have fewer problems to solve than courts that permit public access to these kinds of cases.[4]

2. THE FREEDOM OF INFORMATION ACT

Until the second half of the twentieth century, only a few states had created a statutory right of public access to government records. The federal government had no such statute until the passage in 1966 of the Freedom of Information Act (FOIA). President Lyndon Johnson, in signing FOIA into law, stated:

> This legislation springs from one of our most essential principles: A democracy works best when the people have all the information that the security of the Nation permits. No one should be able to pull curtains of secrecy around decisions which can be revealed without injury to the public interest.[5]

Significant amendments to FOIA in 1974 strengthened the Act. *See* Pub. L. No. 93-502. Key provisions established administrative deadlines, reduced fees, imposed sanctions for arbitrary and capricious withholding of agency records, and provided for attorneys' fees and costs.

Right to Access. FOIA grants all persons the right to inspect and copy records and documents maintained by any federal agency, federal corporation, or federal department. Certain documents must be disclosed automatically — without anybody explicitly requesting them. FOIA requires disclosure in the Federal Register of descriptions of agency functions, procedures, rules, and policies. 5 U.S.C. § 552(a)(1). FOIA also requires that opinions, orders, administrative staff manuals, and other materials be automatically released into the public domain. § 552(a)(2).

To obtain a document under FOIA, a requester must invoke FOIA in the request and follow the "published rules stating the time, place, fees (if any), and procedures to be followed." § 552(a)(3)(A). The agency must make a "reasonable

---

[4] Natalie Gomez-Velez, *Internet Access to Court Records — Balancing Public Access and Privacy*, 51 Loy. L. Rev. 365, 434-35 (2005).

[5] 2 *Public Papers of the Presidents of the United States: Lyndon B. Johnson* 699 (1967), quoted in H.R. Rep. 104-795 (104th Cong. 2d Sess.), at 8 (1996).

effort[]" to answer any request that "reasonably describe[s]" the information sought. §§ 552(a)(3)(A)-(C). A requester can submit a request by mail or through an online form. The agency receiving the request is required to respond to the request within 20 business days unless the agency requests extra time based on "unusual circumstances." § 552(a)(6)(A). A requester may ask for expedited processing upon a showing of "compelling need." § 552(a)(6)(E)(i)(I).

There is an administrative appeals process to challenge any agency denial of a request that an agency must detail in its denial letter. § 552(a)(6)(A). The requester has 20 business days to invoke the process. After exhausting any administrative appeals or if any agency fails to adhere to statutory time limits, a requester may also file a complaint against the agency in federal court. § 552(a)(4)(B).

Exemptions. FOIA contains nine enumerated exemptions to disclosure. Pursuant to § 552(b):

> (b) This section does not apply to matters that are —
>
> (1)(A) specifically authorized under criteria established by an Executive order to be kept secret in the interest of national defense or foreign policy and (B) are in fact properly classified pursuant to such Executive order;
>
> (2) related solely to the internal personnel rules and practices of an agency;
>
> (3) specifically exempted from disclosure by statute (other than section 552b of this title), provided that such statute (A) requires that the matters be withheld from the public in such a manner as to leave no discretion on the issue, or (B) establishes particular criteria for withholding or refers to particular types of matters to be withheld;
>
> (4) trade secrets and commercial or financial information obtained from a person and privileged or confidential;
>
> (5) inter-agency or intra-agency memorandums or letters which would not be available by law to a party other than an agency in litigation with the agency;
>
> (6) personnel and medical files and similar files the disclosure of which would constitute a clearly unwarranted invasion of personal privacy;
>
> (7) records or information compiled for law enforcement purposes, but only to the extent that the production of such law enforcement records or information (A) could reasonably be expected to interfere with enforcement proceedings, (B) would deprive a person of a right to a fair trial or an impartial adjudication, (C) could reasonably be expected to constitute an unwarranted invasion of personal privacy, (D) could reasonably be expected to disclose the identity of a confidential source, including a State, local, or foreign agency or authority or any private institution which furnished information on a confidential basis, and, in the case of a record or information compiled by a criminal law enforcement authority in the course of a criminal investigation or by an agency conducting a lawful national security intelligence investigation, information furnished by a confidential source, (E) would disclose techniques and procedures for law enforcement investigations or prosecutions, or would disclose guidelines for law enforcement investigations or prosecutions if

such disclosure could reasonably be expected to risk circumvention of the law, or (F) could reasonably be expected to endanger the life or physical safety of any individual;

(8) contained in or related to examination, operating, or condition reports prepared by, on behalf of, or for the use of an agency responsible for the regulation or supervision of financial institutions; or

(9) geological and geophysical information and data, including maps, concerning wells.

Redaction. If a portion of a document that falls under an exemption can be redacted (blacked out), then the remainder of the document must be provided to the requester:

> Any reasonably segregable portion of a record shall be provided to any person requesting such record after deletion of the portions which are exempt under this subsection. § 552(b).

The Privacy Exemptions. Two of the exemptions involve privacy concerns. Exemption (6) exempts from disclosure "personnel and medical files and similar files the disclosure of which would constitute a clearly unwarranted invasion of personal privacy." § 552(b)(6). Exemption (7)(C) exempts from disclosure "records or information compiled for law enforcement purposes . . . which could reasonably be expected to constitute an unwarranted invasion of personal privacy." § 552(b)(7)(C). Further, FOIA provides that "[t]o the extent required to prevent a clearly unwarranted invasion of personal privacy, an agency may delete identifying details when it makes available or publishes an opinion, statement of policy, interpretation, or staff manual or instruction." § 552(a)(2). Consider the textual differences between Exemptions (6) and 7(c). Which exemption is more protective of privacy interests?

The exemptions are permissive; that is, agencies are not required to apply the exemptions. Only the government agency can raise Exemptions 6 and 7(C). The individual to whom the information pertains has no right to litigate the issue if the agency does not choose to; nor does the individual have a right to be given notice that her personal information falls within a FOIA request.[6]

The Law Enforcement Exemption. Exemption § 552(b)(7) depends upon the agency demonstrating "that the files were generated during legitimate law enforcement activity." *Freeman v. United States Dep't of Justice,* 723 F. Supp. 1115 (D. Md. 1988). "Exemption 7(E) may not be used to withhold information regarding investigative techniques that are illegal or of questionable legality." *Wilkinson v. FBI,* 633 F. Supp. 336, 349-50 (C.D. Cal. 1986). However, even if people become "an object of investigation because their names were obtained from an unlawful search," FOIA does not "require that documents generated in

[6] For more background about FOIA's privacy exemptions, see James T. O'Reilly, *Expanding the Purpose of Federal Records Access: New Private Entitlement or New Threat to Privacy?*, 50 Admin. L. Rev. 371 (1998); Patricia M. Wald, *The Freedom of Information Act: A Short Case Study in the Perils and Paybacks of Legislating Democratic Values*, 33 Emory L.J. 649 (1984); Anthony T. Kronman, *The Privacy Exemption to the Freedom of Information Act*, 9 J. Legal Stud. 727 (1980).

the investigation . . . be turned over." *Becker v. Internal Revenue Service,* 34 F.2d 398 (7th Cir. 1994).

State FOIAs. Since the passage of FOIA in 1966, a number of states have enacted their own open records statutes. Today, every state has an open records law, most of which are patterned after the federal FOIA. These statutes are often referred to as "freedom of information," "open access," "right to know," or "sunshine" laws.

UNITED STATES DEPARTMENT OF JUSTICE V. REPORTERS COMMITTEE FOR FREEDOM OF THE PRESS

489 U.S. 749 (1989)

STEVENS, J. The Federal Bureau of Investigation (FBI) has accumulated and maintains criminal identification records, sometimes referred to as "rap sheets," on over 24 million persons. The question presented by this case is whether the disclosure of the contents of such a file to a third party "could reasonably be expected to constitute an unwarranted invasion of personal privacy" within the meaning of the Freedom of Information Act (FOIA), 5 U.S.C. § 552(b)(7)(C). . . .

In 1924 Congress appropriated funds to enable the Department of Justice (Department) to establish a program to collect and preserve fingerprints and other criminal identification records. That statute authorized the Department to exchange such information with "officials of States, cities and other institutions." Six years later Congress created the FBI's identification division, and gave it responsibility for "acquiring, collecting, classifying, and preserving criminal identification and other crime records and the exchanging of said criminal identification records with the duly authorized officials of governmental agencies, of States, cities, and penal institutions." Rap sheets compiled pursuant to such authority contain certain descriptive information, such as date of birth and physical characteristics, as well as a history of arrests, charges, convictions, and incarcerations of the subject. Normally a rap sheet is preserved until its subject attains age 80. . . .

. . . As a matter of executive policy, the Department has generally treated rap sheets as confidential and, with certain exceptions, has restricted their use to governmental purposes. . . .

Although much rapsheet information is a matter of public record, the availability and dissemination of the actual rap sheet to the public is limited. Arrests, indictments, convictions, and sentences are public events that are usually documented in court records. In addition, if a person's entire criminal history transpired in a single jurisdiction, all of the contents of his or her rap sheet may be available upon request in that jurisdiction. That possibility, however, is present in only three States. All of the other 47 States place substantial restrictions on the availability of criminal-history summaries even though individual events in those summaries are matters of public record. Moreover, even in Florida, Wisconsin, and Oklahoma, the publicly available summaries may not include information about out-of-state arrests or convictions. . . .

The statute known as FOIA is actually a part of the Administrative Procedure Act (APA). Section 3 of the APA as enacted in 1946 gave agencies broad discretion concerning the publication of governmental records. In 1966 Congress amended that section to implement "'a general philosophy of full agency disclosure.'" . . . The amendment . . . requires every agency "upon any request for records which . . . reasonably describes such records" to make such records "promptly available to any person." If an agency improperly withholds any documents, the district court has jurisdiction to order their production. Unlike the review of other agency action that must be upheld if supported by substantial evidence and not arbitrary or capricious, FOIA expressly places the burden "on the agency to sustain its action" and directs the district courts to "determine the matter de novo."

Congress exempted nine categories of documents from FOIA's broad disclosure requirements. Three of those exemptions are arguably relevant to this case. Exemption 3 applies to documents that are specifically exempted from disclosure by another statute. § 552(b)(3). Exemption 6 protects "personnel and medical files and similar files the disclosure of which would constitute a clearly unwarranted invasion of personal privacy." § 552(b)(6). Exemption 7(C) excludes records or information compiled for law enforcement purposes, "but only to the extent that the production of such [materials] . . . could reasonably be expected to constitute an unwarranted invasion of personal privacy." § 552(b)(7)(C). . . .

This case arises out of requests made by a CBS news correspondent and the Reporters Committee for Freedom of the Press (respondents) for information concerning the criminal records of four members of the Medico family. The Pennsylvania Crime Commission had identified the family's company, Medico Industries, as a legitimate business dominated by organized crime figures. Moreover, the company allegedly had obtained a number of defense contracts as a result of an improper arrangement with a corrupt Congressman.

FOIA requests sought disclosure of any arrests, indictments, acquittals, convictions, and sentences of any of the four Medicos. Although the FBI originally denied the requests, it provided the requested data concerning three of the Medicos after their deaths. In their complaint in the District Court, respondents sought the rap sheet for the fourth, Charles Medico (Medico), insofar as it contained "matters of public record." . . .

Exemption 7(C) requires us to balance the privacy interest in maintaining, as the Government puts it, the "practical obscurity" of the rap sheets against the public interest in their release.

The preliminary question is whether Medico's interest in the nondisclosure of any rap sheet the FBI might have on him is the sort of "personal privacy" interest that Congress intended Exemption 7(C) to protect.[7] . . . Because events summarized in a rap sheet have been previously disclosed to the public, respondents contend that Medico's privacy interest in avoiding disclosure of a

[7] The question of the statutory meaning of privacy under the FOIA is, of course, not the same as the question whether a tort action might lie for invasion of privacy or the question whether an individual's interest in privacy is protected by the Constitution. *See, e.g., Cox Broadcasting Corp. v. Cohn*, 420 U.S. 469 (1975) (Constitution prohibits State from penalizing publication of name of deceased rape victim obtained from public records). . . .

federal compilation of these events approaches zero. We reject respondents' cramped notion of personal privacy.

To begin with, both the common law and the literal understandings of privacy encompass the individual's control of information concerning his or her person. In an organized society, there are few facts that are not at one time or another divulged to another. Thus the extent of the protection accorded a privacy right at common law rested in part on the degree of dissemination of the allegedly private fact and the extent to which the passage of time rendered it private. According to Webster's initial definition, information may be classified as "private" if it is "intended for or restricted to the use of a particular person or group or class of persons: not freely available to the public." Recognition of this attribute of a privacy interest supports the distinction, in terms of personal privacy, between scattered disclosure of the bits of information contained in a rap sheet and revelation of the rap sheet as a whole. The very fact that federal funds have been spent to prepare, index, and maintain these criminal-history files demonstrates that the individual items of information in the summaries would not otherwise be "freely available" either to the officials who have access to the underlying files or to the general public. Indeed, if the summaries were "freely available," there would be no reason to invoke the FOIA to obtain access to the information they contain. Granted, in many contexts the fact that information is not freely available is no reason to exempt that information from a statute generally requiring its dissemination. But the issue here is whether the compilation of otherwise hard-to-obtain information alters the privacy interest implicated by disclosure of that information. Plainly there is a vast difference between the public records that might be found after a diligent search of courthouse files, county archives, and local police stations throughout the country and a computerized summary located in a single clearinghouse of information. . . .

We have also recognized the privacy interest in keeping personal facts away from the public eye. In *Whalen v. Roe*, 429 U.S. 589 (1977), we held that "the State of New York may record, in a centralized computer file, the names and addresses of all persons who have obtained, pursuant to a doctor's prescription, certain drugs for which there is both a lawful and an unlawful market." In holding only that the Federal Constitution does not prohibit such a compilation, we recognized that such a centralized computer file posed a "threat to privacy":

> We are not unaware of the threat to privacy implicit in the accumulation of vast amounts of personal information in computerized data banks or other massive government files. The collection of taxes, the distribution of welfare and social security benefits, the supervision of public health, the direction of our Armed Forces, and the enforcement of the criminal laws all require the orderly preservation of great quantities of information, much of which is personal in character and potentially embarrassing or harmful if disclosed. The right to collect and use such data for public purposes is typically accompanied by a concomitant statutory or regulatory duty to avoid unwarranted disclosures. Recognizing that in some circumstances that duty arguably has its roots in the Constitution, nevertheless New York's statutory scheme, and its implementing administrative procedures, evidence a proper concern with, and protection of, the individual's interest in privacy.

In sum, the fact that "an event is not wholly 'private' does not mean that an individual has no interest in limiting disclosure or dissemination of the information." The privacy interest in a rap sheet is substantial. The substantial character of that interest is affected by the fact that in today's society the computer can accumulate and store information that would otherwise have surely been forgotten long before a person attains age 80, when the FBI's rap sheets are discarded. . . .

Exemption 7(C), by its terms, permits an agency to withhold a document only when revelation "could reasonably be expected to constitute an unwarranted invasion of personal privacy." We must next address what factors might warrant an invasion of the interest described [above].

Our previous decisions establish that whether an invasion of privacy is warranted cannot turn on the purposes for which the request for information is made. Except for cases in which the objection to disclosure is based on a claim of privilege and the person requesting disclosure is the party protected by the privilege, the identity of the requesting party has no bearing on the merits of his or her FOIA request. . . . As we have repeatedly stated, Congress "clearly intended" the FOIA "to give any member of the public as much right to disclosure as one with a special interest [in a particular document]."

Thus whether disclosure of a private document under Exemption 7(C) is warranted must turn on the nature of the requested document and its relationship to "the basic purpose of the Freedom of Information Act 'to open agency action to the light of public scrutiny,'" rather than on the particular purpose for which the document is being requested. In our leading case on FOIA, we declared that the Act was designed to create a broad right of access to "official information." *EPA v. Mink,* 410 U.S. 73, 80, (1973). In his dissent in that case, Justice Douglas characterized the philosophy of the statute by quoting this comment by Henry Steele Commager:

> "'The generation that made the nation thought secrecy in government one of the instruments of Old World tyranny and committed itself to the principle that a democracy cannot function unless the people are permitted to know *what their government is up to.*'" (quoting from *The New York Review of Books*, Oct. 5, 1972, p. 7) (emphasis added).

. . . This basic policy of "'full agency disclosure unless information is exempted under clearly delineated statutory language,'" indeed focuses on the citizens' right to be informed about "what their government is up to." Official information that sheds light on an agency's performance of its statutory duties falls squarely within that statutory purpose. That purpose, however, is not fostered by disclosure of information about private citizens that is accumulated in various governmental files but that reveals little or nothing about an agency's own conduct. In this case — and presumably in the typical case in which one private citizen is seeking information about another — the requester does not intend to discover anything about the conduct of the agency that has possession of the requested records. Indeed, response to this request would not shed any light on the conduct of any Government agency or official. . . .

Respondents argue that there is a two-fold public interest in learning about Medico's past arrests or convictions: He allegedly had improper dealings with a corrupt Congressman, and he is an officer of a corporation with defense contracts. But if Medico has, in fact, been arrested or convicted of certain crimes, that information would neither aggravate nor mitigate his allegedly improper relationship with the Congressman; more specifically, it would tell us nothing directly about the character of the Congressman's behavior. Nor would it tell us anything about the conduct of the Department of Defense (DOD) in awarding one or more contracts to the Medico Company. . . . Conceivably Medico's rap sheet would provide details to include in a news story, but, in itself, this is not the kind of public interest for which Congress enacted the FOIA. In other words, although there is undoubtedly some public interest in anyone's criminal history, especially if the history is in some way related to the subject's dealing with a public official or agency, the FOIA's central purpose is to ensure that the Government's activities be opened to the sharp eye of public scrutiny, not that information about private citizens that happens to be in the warehouse of the Government be so disclosed. . . .

. . . The privacy interest in maintaining the practical obscurity of rap-sheet information will always be high. When the subject of such a rap sheet is a private citizen and when the information is in the Government's control as a compilation, rather than as a record of "what the Government is up to," the privacy interest protected by Exemption 7(C) is in fact at its apex while the FOIA-based public interest in disclosure is at its nadir. Such a disparity on the scales of justice holds for a class of cases without regard to individual circumstances; the standard virtues of bright-line rules are thus present, and the difficulties attendant to ad hoc adjudication may be avoided. Accordingly, we hold as a categorical matter that a third party's request for law enforcement records or information about a private citizen can reasonably be expected to invade that citizen's privacy, and that when the request seeks no "official information" about a Government agency, but merely records that the Government happens to be storing, the invasion of privacy is "unwarranted." . . .

BLACKMUN J., joined by BRENNAN, J. concurring in the judgment: I concur in the result the Court reaches in this case, but I cannot follow the route the Court takes to reach that result. In other words, the Court's use of "categorical balancing" under Exemption 7(C), I think, is not basically sound. Such a bright-line rule obviously has its appeal, but I wonder whether it would not run aground on occasion, such as in a situation where a rap sheet discloses a congressional candidate's conviction of tax fraud five years before. Surely, the FBI's disclosure of that information could not "reasonably be expected" to constitute an invasion of personal privacy, much less an unwarranted invasion, inasmuch as the candidate relinquished any interest in preventing the dissemination of this information when he chose to run for Congress. In short, I do not believe that Exemption 7(C)'s language and its legislative history, or the case law, support interpreting that provision as exempting all rap-sheet information from the FOIA's disclosure requirements.

NOTES & QUESTIONS

1. ***The Privacy Interest and "Practical Obscurity."*** Many courts, including the Supreme Court in other contexts, have held that once information is exposed to the public, it can no longer be considered private. In *Reporters Committee,* however, the Court recognizes a privacy interest in the rap sheets despite the fact that they are compiled from information in public records. The Court concludes that "there is a vast difference between the public records that might be found after a diligent search of courthouse files, county archives, and local police stations throughout the country and a computerized summary located in a single clearinghouse of information." Is the Court stretching privacy too far by claiming it can be violated by altering "practical obscurity"?

   Daniel Solove argues in support of the Court's conception of privacy: "Privacy involves an expectation of a certain degree of accessibility of information. . . . Privacy can be violated by altering levels of accessibility, by taking obscure facts and making them widely accessible."[8] Is such a conception of privacy feasible?
2. ***The Interest in Public Access.*** The Court also denies access to the rap sheets because "this [FOIA] request would not shed any light on the conduct of any Government agency or official." What kind of use of government records is being sought in *Reporters Committee*? Does this use contribute to the public interest? Does the use comport with the purpose of FOIA?
3. ***The Court's Rationale Beyond the FOIA Context.*** In a footnote, the Court stated that the reasoning of this case is confined to the FOIA context. As a hypothetical case, imagine that there were no privacy exemptions to FOIA, and the FBI disclosed the rap sheets. The Medicos sue, claiming a violation of their constitutional right to information privacy. What would the result likely be? Can the Court coherently claim that people have a privacy interest in their rap sheet information under FOIA but not in the context of the constitutional right to information privacy?
4. ***Exemption 6.*** The *Reporters Committee* case concerned Exemption 7(C). Exemption 6 provides that FOIA's disclosure provisions do not apply to "*personnel and medical files and similar files* the disclosure of which would constitute a clearly unwarranted invasion of personal privacy." § 552(b)(6) (emphasis added). Does Exemption 6 only apply to "personnel and medical files"? What does "similar files" mean?

   The Supreme Court answered these questions in *United States Dep't of State v. Washington Post Co.*, 456 U.S. 595 (1982). There, the *Washington Post* requested documents indicating whether two Iranian nationals were holding valid United States passports. According to the Department of State, the two individuals were prominent figures in Iran's Revolutionary Government; several Iranian revolutionary leaders had been strongly criticized in Iran for ties to the United States; and the two could be subject to

---

[8] Daniel J. Solove, *Access and Aggregation: Public Records, Privacy, and the Constitution*, 86 Minn. L. Rev. 1137, 1176-78 (2002).

violence if United States ties, such as passports, were disclosed. The *Washington Post* contended that the language of Exemption 6 simply did not cover these types of documents. The Court disagreed:

> The language of Exemption 6 sheds little light on what Congress meant by "similar files." Fortunately, the legislative history is somewhat more illuminating. The House and Senate Reports, although not defining the phrase "similar files," suggest that Congress' primary purpose in enacting Exemption 6 was to protect individuals from the injury and embarrassment that can result from the unnecessary disclosure of personal information. . . .
>
> . . . Congress' statements that it was creating a "general exemption" for information contained in "great quantities of files," suggest that the phrase "similar files" was to have a broad, rather than a narrow, meaning. This impression is confirmed by the frequent characterization of the "clearly unwarranted invasion of personal privacy" language as a "limitation" which holds Exemption 6 "within bounds." Had the words "similar files" been intended to be only a narrow addition to "personnel and medical files," there would seem to be no reason for concern about the exemption's being "held within bounds," and there surely would be clear suggestions in the legislative history that such a narrow meaning was intended. We have found none.
>
> A proper analysis of the exemption must also take into account the fact that "personnel and medical files," the two benchmarks for measuring the term "similar files," are likely to contain much information about a particular individual that is not intimate. Information such as place of birth, date of birth, date of marriage, employment history, and comparable data is not normally regarded as highly personal, and yet respondent does not disagree that such information, if contained in a "personnel" or "medical" file, would be exempt from any disclosure that would constitute a clearly unwarranted invasion of personal privacy. . . .
>
> . . . "[T]he protection of an individual's right of privacy" which Congress sought to achieve by preventing "the disclosure of [information] which might harm the individual," surely was not intended to turn upon the label of the file which contains the damaging information. . . .
>
> In sum, we do not think that Congress meant to limit Exemption 6 to a narrow class of files containing only a discrete kind of personal information. Rather, "[t]he exemption [was] intended to cover detailed Government records on an individual which can be identified as applying to that individual." When disclosure of information which applies to a particular individual is sought from Government records, courts must determine whether release of the information would constitute a clearly unwarranted invasion of that person's privacy. . . .

5. ***Definition of Agency.*** FOIA requires only that "agencies" respond to requesters. Congress is not a federal agency and is therefore not subject to the Act. Nor is the President or his advisors, whose "sole function" is to "advise and assist" the President. For similar reasons, the National Security Council is not an agency. *Armstrong v. Executive Office of the President*, 90 F.3d 556 (D.C. Cir. 1996).

NATIONAL ARCHIVES AND RECORDS ADMINISTRATION V. FAVISH

541 U.S. 157 (2004)

KENNEDY, J. This is case requires us to interpret the Freedom of Information Act (FOIA), 5 U.S.C. § 552. FOIA does not apply if the requested data fall within one or more exemptions. Exemption 7(C) excuses from disclosure "records or information compiled for law enforcement purposes" if their production "could reasonably be expected to constitute an unwarranted invasion of personal privacy." § 552(b)(7)(C).

In *Department of Justice v. Reporters Comm. for Freedom of Press,* 489 U.S. 749 (1989), we considered the scope of Exemption 7(C) and held that release of the document at issue would be a prohibited invasion of the personal privacy of the person to whom the document referred. The principal document involved was the criminal record, or rap sheet, of the person who himself objected to the disclosure. Here, the information pertains to an official investigation into the circumstances surrounding an apparent suicide. The initial question is whether the exemption extends to the decedent's family when the family objects to the release of photographs showing the condition of the body at the scene of death. If we find the decedent's family does have a personal privacy interest recognized by the statute, we must then consider whether that privacy claim is outweighed by the public interest in disclosure.

Vincent Foster, Jr., deputy counsel to President Clinton, was found dead in Fort Marcy Park, located just outside Washington, D.C. The United States Park Police conducted the initial investigation and took color photographs of the death scene, including 10 pictures of Foster's body. The investigation concluded that Foster committed suicide by shooting himself with a revolver. Subsequent investigations by the Federal Bureau of Investigation, committees of the Senate and the House of Representatives, and independent counsels Robert Fiske and Kenneth Starr reached the same conclusion. Despite the unanimous finding of these five investigations, a citizen interested in the matter, Allan Favish, remained skeptical. Favish is now a respondent in this proceeding. . . .

It is common ground among the parties that the death-scene photographs in [the Office of Independent Counsel's, or] OIC's possession are "records or information compiled for law enforcement purposes" as that phrase is used in Exemption 7(C). This leads to the question whether disclosure of the four photographs "could reasonably be expected to constitute an unwarranted invasion of personal privacy." Favish contends the family has no personal privacy interest covered by Exemption 7(C). . . .

We disagree. The right to personal privacy is not confined, as Favish argues, to the "right to control information about oneself." . . To say that the concept of personal privacy must "encompass" the individual's control of information about himself does not mean it cannot encompass other personal privacy interests as well. *Reporters Committee* had no occasion to consider whether individuals whose personal data are not contained in the requested materials also have a recognized privacy interest under Exemption 7(C). *Reporters Committee* explained, however, that the concept of personal privacy under Exemption 7(C) is not some limited or "cramped notion" of that idea. 489 U.S. at 763. Records or information are not to be released under the Act if disclosure "could reasonably be expected to constitute an unwarranted invasion of personal privacy." 5 U.S.C. § 552(b)(7). This provision is in marked contrast to the language in Exemption 6, pertaining to "personnel and medical files," where withholding is required only if disclosure "would constitute a clearly unwarranted invasion of personal privacy." § 552(b)(6). The adverb "clearly," found in Exemption 6, is not used in Exemption 7(C). In addition, "whereas Exemption 6 refers to disclosures that 'would constitute' an invasion of privacy, Exemption 7(C) encompasses any disclosure that 'could reasonably be expected to constitute' such an invasion." *Reporters Committee,* 489 U.S., at 756. . . .

Law enforcement documents obtained by Government investigators often contain information about persons interviewed as witnesses or initial suspects but whose link to the official inquiry may be the result of mere happenstance. There is special reason, therefore, to give protection to this intimate personal data, to which the public does not have a general right of access in the ordinary course. In this class of cases where the subject of the documents "is a private citizen," "the privacy interest . . . is at its apex."

. . . Foster's relatives . . . invoke their own right and interest to personal privacy. They seek to be shielded by the exemption to secure their own refuge from a sensation-seeking culture for their own peace of mind and tranquility, not for the sake of the deceased. . . .

. . . We have little difficulty . . . in finding in our case law and traditions the right of family members to direct and control disposition of the body of the deceased and to limit attempts to exploit pictures of the deceased family member's remains for public purposes.

Burial rites or their counterparts have been respected in almost all civilizations from time immemorial. See generally 26 *Encyclopaedia Britannica* 851 (15th ed. 1985) (noting that "[t]he ritual burial of the dead" has been practiced "from the very dawn of human culture and . . . in most parts of the world"); 5 *Encyclopedia of Religion* 450 (1987) ("[F]uneral rites . . . are the conscious cultural forms of one of our most ancient, universal, and unconscious impulses"). They are a sign of the respect a society shows for the deceased and for the surviving family members. The power of Sophocles' story in Antigone maintains its hold to this day because of the universal acceptance of the heroine's right to insist on respect for the body of her brother. *See* Antigone of Sophocles, 8 *Harvard Classics: Nine Greek Dramas* 255 (C. Eliot ed. 1909). The outrage at seeing the bodies of American soldiers mutilated and dragged through the streets is but a modern instance of the same understanding of the interests decent people have for those whom they have lost. Family members have a personal stake in honoring and mourning their dead and objecting to unwarranted public exploitation that, by intruding upon their own grief, tends to degrade the rites and respect they seek to accord to the deceased person who was once their own.

In addition this well-established cultural tradition acknowledging a family's control over the body and death images of the deceased has long been recognized at common law. Indeed, this right to privacy has much deeper roots in the common law than the rap sheets held to be protected from disclosure in *Reporters Committee.* An early decision by the New York Court of Appeals is typical:

> It is the right of privacy of the living which it is sought to enforce here. That right may in some cases be itself violated by improperly interfering with the character or memory of a deceased relative, but it is the right of the living, and not that of the dead, which is recognized. A privilege may be given the surviving relatives of a deceased person to protect his memory, but the privilege exists for the benefit of the living, to protect their feelings, and to prevent a violation of their own rights in the character and memory of the deceased. *Schuyler v. Curtis,* 147 N.Y. 434 (1895). . . .

We can assume Congress legislated against this background of law, scholarship, and history when it enacted FOIA and when it amended Exemption 7(C) to extend its terms. . . .

We have observed that the statutory privacy right protected by Exemption 7(C) goes beyond the common law and the Constitution. See *Reporters Committee,* 489 U.S., at 762, n.13 (contrasting the scope of the privacy protection under FOIA with the analogous protection under the common law and the Constitution). . . . It would be anomalous to hold in the instant case that the statute provides even less protection than does the common law.

The statutory scheme must be understood, moreover, in light of the consequences that would follow were we to adopt Favish's position. As a general rule, withholding information under FOIA cannot be predicated on the identity of the requester. See *Reporters Committee, supra,* at 771. We are advised by the Government that child molesters, rapists, murderers, and other violent criminals often make FOIA requests for autopsies, photographs, and records of their deceased victims. Our holding ensures that the privacy interests of surviving family members would allow the Government to deny these gruesome requests in appropriate cases. We find it inconceivable that Congress could have intended a definition of "personal privacy" so narrow that it would allow convicted felons to obtain these materials without limitations at the expense of surviving family members' personal privacy.

. . . [W]e hold that FOIA recognizes surviving family members' right to personal privacy with respect to their close relative's death-scene images. Our holding is consistent with the unanimous view of the Courts of Appeals and other lower courts that have addressed the question. . . .

Our ruling that the personal privacy protected by Exemption 7(C) extends to family members who object to the disclosure of graphic details surrounding their relative's death does not end the case. Although this privacy interest is within the terms of the exemption, the statute directs nondisclosure only where the information "could reasonably be expected to constitute an unwarranted invasion" of the family's personal privacy. The term "unwarranted" requires us to balance the family's privacy interest against the public interest in disclosure. . . .

FOIA is often explained as a means for citizens to know "what the Government is up to." This phrase should not be dismissed as a convenient formalism. It defines a structural necessity in a real democracy. The statement confirms that, as a general rule, when documents are within FOIA's disclosure provisions, citizens should not be required to explain why they seek the information. A person requesting the information needs no preconceived idea of the uses the data might serve. The information belongs to citizens to do with as they choose. Furthermore, as we have noted, the disclosure does not depend on the identity of the requester. As a general rule, if the information is subject to disclosure, it belongs to all.

When disclosure touches upon certain areas defined in the exemptions, however, the statute recognizes limitations that compete with the general interest in disclosure, and that, in appropriate cases, can overcome it. In the case of Exemption 7(C), the statute requires us to protect, in the proper degree, the personal privacy of citizens against the uncontrolled release of information compiled through the power of the state. The statutory direction that the information not be released if the invasion of personal privacy could reasonably be expected to be unwarranted requires the courts to balance the competing interests in privacy and disclosure. To effect this balance and to give practical meaning to the exemption, the usual rule that the citizen need not offer a reason for requesting the information must be inapplicable.

Where the privacy concerns addressed by Exemption 7(C) are present, the exemption requires the person requesting the information to establish a sufficient reason for the disclosure. First, the citizen must show that the public interest sought to be advanced is a significant one, an interest more specific than having the information for its own sake. Second, the citizen must show the information is likely to advance that interest. Otherwise, the invasion of privacy is unwarranted.

. . . In the case of photographic images and other data pertaining to an individual who died under mysterious circumstances, the justification most likely to satisfy Exemption 7(C)'s public interest requirement is that the information is necessary to show the investigative agency or other responsible officials acted negligently or otherwise improperly in the performance of their duties. . . .

We hold that, where there is a privacy interest protected by Exemption 7(C) and the public interest being asserted is to show that responsible officials acted negligently or otherwise improperly in the performance of their duties, the requester must establish more than a bare suspicion in order to obtain disclosure. Rather, the requester must produce evidence that would warrant a belief by a reasonable person that the alleged Government impropriety might have occurred. In *Department of State v. Ray,* 502 U.S. 164 (1991), we held there is a presumption of legitimacy accorded to the Government's official conduct. The presumption perhaps is less a rule of evidence than a general working principle. However the rule is characterized, where the presumption is applicable, clear evidence is usually required to displace it. . . . Given FOIA's prodisclosure purpose, however, the less stringent standard we adopt today is more faithful to the statutory scheme. Only when the FOIA requester has produced evidence sufficient to satisfy this standard will there exist a counterweight on the FOIA scale for the court to balance against the cognizable privacy interests in the requested records. . . . It would be quite extraordinary to say we must ignore the fact that five different inquiries into the Foster matter reached the same conclusion. . . . Favish has not produced any evidence that would warrant a belief by a reasonable person that the alleged Government impropriety might have occurred to put the balance into play. . . .

NOTES & QUESTIONS

1. ***Coffins of U.S. Soldiers.*** In 2004, Russ Kick obtained 361 photos on a CD-ROM of the coffins of U.S. soldiers who had been killed in combat in Iraq. The photos depicted coffins that were closed and draped with U.S. flags. The Air Force released the photos pursuant to a FOIA-request by Kick for "photographs showing caskets (or other devices) containing the remains of US military personnel at Dover [Air Force Base]."[9] Kick had selected Dover Air Force Base because "they process the remains of most, if not all, US military personnel killed overseas." The Air Force initially denied Kick's request; when he appealed the decision, it reversed and released the photos. The photos of the coffins contain no name tags or any other information that might identify the deceased soldier.

   The Bush Administration criticized the release of the photos. According to a Bush spokesperson: "[T]he sensitivity and privacy of families of the fallen must be the first priority."[10] Is there a privacy interest in the photos? Some are skeptical of efforts to keep the photos secret because of privacy concerns; they contend that the real reason is to deprive the public of images that vividly depict the number of fallen soldiers. Based on FOIA, would the photos be exempt under one of the privacy exemptions?
2. ***The Implications of Post-Mortem Privacy.*** Apart from the narrow context of FOIA, how will post-mortem privacy interests function in other areas of law? Are there other privacy interests that should or should not exist after one's death?
3. ***National Security and Critical Infrastructure Information.*** Post 9/11, the federal government has taken a new restrictive approach to FOIA. First, as part of the Homeland Security Act, the Bush Administration oversaw enactment of a new exemption to FOIA in the Critical Infrastructure Information Act of 2002 (CIIA). The CIIA exempts from FOIA disclosure any information that a private party voluntarily provides to the Department of Homeland Security (DHS) if the information relates to the security of vital infrastructure.

   "Critical infrastructure information" is "information not customarily in the public domain and related to the security of critical infrastructure or protected [computer] systems." 6 U.S.C. § 131. In a report prepared for Rep. Henry A. Waxman (Waxman Report), the Minority Staff, Special Investigation Division, Committee on Government Reform, stated:

   > Communications from the private sector to government agencies are routinely released under FOIA (apart from confidential business information). This is an important check against capture of governmental agencies by special interests.

---

[9] The Memory Hole, *Photos of Military Coffins*, at http://www.thememoryhole.com/war/coffin_photos/dover/.

[10] Associated Press, *White House: Military Should Respect Family Privacy on Photos of Coffins*, USA Today, Apr. 23, 2004.

> But under the critical infrastructure information exemption even routine communications can be withheld from disclosure.[11]

In an op-ed in the *Washington Post*, Mark Tapscott of the Heritage Foundation asked for clarification of "what constitutes vulnerabilities" of infrastructure in order to prevent the CIIA from being "manipulated by clever corporate and government operators to hide endless varieties of potentially embarrassing and/or criminal information from public view."

The Waxman Report also noted that CIIA exempts from FOIA all information that is marked critical infrastructure information. As a consequence, the CIIA may not permit the redaction that is otherwise normally carried out under FOIA. As the Report states, "None of the information in a submission marked as critical infrastructure information is likely to be disclosed, even when portions of the information do not themselves constitute critical infrastructure information."[12]

Second, beyond the enactment of CIIA, a further move toward a restrictive approach to FOIA was made through the Executive Branch's introduction of the concept of "sensitive but unclassified information." On March 19, 2002, Andrew Card, White House Chief of Staff, issued an important memorandum that instructs federal agencies to deny disclosure of "sensitive but unclassified information."[13] The Card Memorandum urged agencies to safeguard records regarding weapons of mass destruction and "other information that could be misused to harm the security of our Nation and the safety of our people." The Card Memorandum urged agencies to apply FOIA's Exemption 2 or Exemption 4 in withholding such records. Please reread these exemptions reprinted earlier in this section. How do you think they are being extended to apply to "sensitive but unclassified information"?

Consider the following argument by Mary-Rose Papandrea:

> FOIA is riddled with large, undefined exceptions. When information arguably involves national security, courts are too timid to force the executive branch to provide a thorough explanation for continued secrecy. . . .
>
> The "right to know" has encountered additional and more disturbing problems since the terrorist attacks of September 11. Not only has the courts' tendency to defer to the Executive's national security risk assessment become exaggerated, but courts now appear overtly hostile to the very existence of a right of access during a time of crisis. Instead, they suggest that an enforceable right to know is unnecessary because the political process is adequate to force government disclosure.[14]

How should open government be reconciled with national security concerns?

---

[11] U.S. House of Representatives, *Committee on Government Reform, Minority Staff, Special Investigations Division, Secrecy in the Bush Administration* 9 (Sept. 14, 2004).

[12] *Id.* at 10.

[13] Andrew H. Card, Jr., Assistant to the President and Chief of Staff, *Memorandum for the Heads of Executive Departments and Agencies; Subject: Action to Safeguard Information Regarding Weapons of Mass Destruction and Other Sensitive Documents Relating to Homeland Security* (Mar. 19, 2002), at http://www.usdoj.gov/oip/foiapost/2002foiapost10.htm.

[14] Mary-Rose Papandrea, *Under Attack: The Public's Right to Know and the War on Terror*, 25 B.C. Third World L.J. 35, 79-80 (2005).

3. CONSTITUTIONAL REQUIREMENTS OF PUBLIC ACCESS

The Common Law Right to Access Public Records. As the Supreme Court held in *Nixon v. Warner Communications, Inc.,* 435 U.S. 589 (1978): "It is clear that the courts of this country recognize a general right to inspect and copy public records and documents, including judicial records and documents." The right to access public records is justified by "the citizen's desire to keep a watchful eye on the workings of public agencies, and in a newspaper publisher's intention to publish information concerning the operation of government." Thus, under the common law, the Court concluded, there is a general right to access public records and court records. The Court noted that the right to access is not absolute.

Court Records. Courts have a long tradition of allowing open access to court records. In *Nixon v. Warner Communications, Inc.,* 435 U.S. 589 (1978), the Supreme Court stated: "Every court has supervisory power over its own records and files, and access has been denied where court files might have become a vehicle for improper purposes." Access to court records is "best left to the sound discretion of the trial court, a discretion to be exercised in light of the relevant facts and circumstances of the particular case." In *Seattle Times Co. v. Rhinehart*, 467 U.S. 20, 33 (1984), the Court held that "pretrial depositions and interrogatories are not public components of a civil trial. Such proceedings were not open to the public at common law, and, in general, they are conducted in private as a matter of modern practice."

The First Amendment Right to Access. The First Amendment requires that certain judicial proceedings be open to the public. In *Globe Newspaper v. Superior Court*, 457 U.S. 596 (1982), the Supreme Court articulated a test to determine whether the First Amendment requires public access to a proceeding: (1) whether the proceeding "historically has been open to the press and general public" and (2) whether access "plays a particularly significant role in the functioning of the judicial process and the government as a whole." The court in *Globe* concluded that the First Amendment requires public access to criminal trials, and the government can deny access only if "the denial is necessitated by a compelling governmental interest and is narrowly tailored to serve that interest." According to the Court, the First Amendment right to access extends to voir dire in a capital murder trial. *Press-Enterprise Co. v. Superior Court* ("*Press-Enterprise I*"), 464 U.S. 501 (1984). It also extends to pre-trial proceedings. *Press-Enterprise Co. v. Superior Court* ("*Press-Enterprise II*"), 478 U.S. 1 (1986).

Privacy of Litigants and Jurors. A court can permit plaintiffs to proceed under a pseudonym, although "it is the exceptional case in which a plaintiff may proceed under a fictitious name." *Doe v. Frank*, 951 F.2d 320, 323 (11th Cir. 1992). Courts can also provide for jurors to remain anonymous. Is such anonymity appropriate?

Consider the case of Juror Number Four. In a well-publicized criminal trial against Tyco International executive L. Dennis Kozlowski, during the jury's 12 days of deliberating, newspapers identified Juror Number Four by name because she appeared to gesture an "O.K." sign to the defense table. The articles stated that she lived on the Upper East Side of Manhattan and that the apartment building staff found her to be cold and stingy. The newspapers reported that friends described her as opinionated and stubborn. Extensive coverage of the juror continued. As a result of the coverage, the juror received a threatening note, and the judge declared a mistrial. On the one hand, the media was reporting on possible juror misconduct. On the other hand, the media coverage interfered with the trial. Suppose on retrial, the judge were to order that the identities of all the jurors shall not be disclosed. Would such an order be constitutional?

In some jurisdictions, the court records of divorce cases are made public. Is such a policy advisable? This issue is best illustrated by what happened in June 2004, when at the request of the *Chicago Tribune* and a TV station, a judge ordered the unsealing of the divorce records of Illinois Republican Senate candidate Jack Ryan and his wife, actress Jeri Ryan. Both Jack and Jeri had vigorously objected to the unsealing of the records, which they contended would cause harm to them as well as their nine-year-old child. The records revealed Jeri's accusations that Jack had taken her to sex clubs and asked her to perform sex acts that made her uncomfortable. A few days after the release of the records, Jack abandoned his quest for the Senate. Was the release of the records appropriate in this case? Jack was a political candidate, and Jeri was a well-known actress. Does their public figure status affect the analysis? Should it? To what extent should the effect of the release of the information on a couple's children be a factor in the analysis?

LOS ANGELES POLICE DEPARTMENT V. UNITED REPORTING PUBLISHING CORP.

528 U.S. 32 (1999)

REHNQUIST, C.J. California Government Code § 6254(f)(3) places two conditions on public access to arrestees' addresses — that the person requesting an address declare that the request is being made for one of five prescribed purposes, and that the requestor also declare that the address will not be used directly or indirectly to sell a product or service.

The District Court permanently enjoined enforcement of the statute, and the Court of Appeals affirmed, holding that the statute was facially invalid because it unduly burdens commercial speech. We hold that the statutory section in question was not subject to a "facial" challenge.

Petitioner, the Los Angeles Police Department, maintains records relating to arrestees. Respondent, United Reporting Publishing Corporation, is a private publishing service that provides the names and addresses of recently arrested individuals to its customers, who include attorneys, insurance companies, drug and alcohol counselors, and driving schools.

Before July 1, 1996, respondent received arrestees' names and addresses under the old version of § 6254, which generally required state and local law enforcement agencies to make public the name, address, and occupation of every individual arrested by the agency. Cal. Govt. Code § 6254(f). Effective July 1, 1996, the state legislature amended § 6254(f) to limit the public's access to arrestees' and victims' current addresses. The amended statute provides that state and local law enforcement agencies shall make public:

> [T]he current address of every individual arrested by the agency and the current address of the victim of a crime, where the requester declares under penalty of perjury that the request is made for a scholarly, journalistic, political, or governmental purpose, or that the request is made for investigation purposes by a licensed private investigator . . . except that the address of the victim of [certain crimes] shall remain confidential. Address information obtained pursuant to this paragraph shall not be used directly or indirectly to sell a product or service to any individual or group of individuals, and the requester shall execute a declaration to that effect under penalty of perjury. Cal. Govt. Code § 6254(f)(3).

Sections 6254(f)(1) and (2) require that state and local law enforcement agencies make public, inter alia, the name, occupation, and physical description, including date of birth, of every individual arrested by the agency, as well as the circumstances of the arrest. Thus, amended § 6254(f) limits access only to the arrestees' addresses.

Before the effective date of the amendment, respondent sought declaratory and injunctive relief pursuant to 42 U.S.C. § 1983 to hold the amendment unconstitutional under the First and Fourteenth Amendments to the United States Constitution. On the effective date of the statute, petitioner and other law enforcement agencies denied respondent access to the address information because, according to respondent, "[respondent's] employees could not sign section 6254(f)(3) declarations." Respondent did not allege, and nothing in the record before this Court indicates, that it ever "declar[ed] under penalty of perjury" that it was requesting information for one of the prescribed purposes and that it would not use the address information to "directly or indirectly . . . sell a product or service," as would have been required by the statute. *See* § 6254(f)(3).

Respondent then amended its complaint and sought a temporary restraining order. The District Court issued a temporary restraining order, and, a few days later, issued a preliminary injunction. Respondent then filed a motion for summary judgment, which was granted. In granting the motion, the District Court construed respondent's claim as presenting a facial challenge to amended § 6254(f). The court held that the statute was facially invalid under the First Amendment.

The Court of Appeals affirmed the District Court's facial invalidation. The court concluded that the statute restricted commercial speech, and, as such, was entitled to "'a limited measure of protection, commensurate with its subordinate position in the scale of First Amendment values.'" The court applied the test set out in *Central Hudson Gas & Elec. Corp. v. Public Serv. Comm'n of N.Y.*, 447 U.S. 557 (1980), and found that the asserted governmental interest in protecting arrestees' privacy was substantial. But, the court held that "the numerous exceptions to § 6254(f)(3) for journalistic, scholarly, political, governmental, and investigative purposes render the statute unconstitutional under the First Amendment." The court noted that "[h]aving one's name, crime, and address printed in the local paper is a far greater affront to privacy than receiving a letter from an attorney, substance abuse counselor, or driving school eager to help one overcome his present difficulties (for a fee, naturally)," and thus that the exceptions "undermine and counteract" the asserted governmental interest in preserving arrestees' privacy. Thus, the Court of Appeals affirmed the District Court's grant of summary judgment in favor of respondent and upheld the injunction against enforcement of § 6254(f)(3). We granted certiorari.

We hold that respondent was not, under our cases, entitled to prevail on a "facial attack" on § 6254(f)(3).

Respondent's primary argument in the District Court and the Court of Appeals was that § 6254(f)(3) was invalid on its face, and respondent maintains that position here. But we believe that our cases hold otherwise.

The traditional rule is that "a person to whom a statute may constitutionally be applied may not challenge that statute on the ground that it may conceivably be applied unconstitutionally to others in situations not before the Court."

Prototypical exceptions to this traditional rule are First Amendment challenges to statutes based on First Amendment overbreadth. "At least when statutes regulate or proscribe speech . . . the transcendent value to all society of constitutionally protected expression is deemed to justify allowing 'attacks on overly broad statutes with no requirement that the person making the attack demonstrate that his own conduct could not be regulated by a statute drawn with the requisite narrow specificity.'" "This is deemed necessary because persons whose expression is constitutionally protected may well refrain from exercising their right for fear of criminal sanctions provided by a statute susceptible of application to protected expression." . . .

Even though the challenge be based on the First Amendment, the overbreadth doctrine is not casually employed. "Because of the wide-reaching effects of striking down a statute on its face at the request of one whose own conduct may be punished despite the First Amendment, we have recognized that the overbreadth doctrine is 'strong medicine' and have employed it with hesitation, and then 'only as a last resort.'" . . .

The Court of Appeals held that § 6254(f)(3) was facially invalid under the First Amendment. Petitioner contends that the section in question is not an abridgment of anyone's right to engage in speech, be it commercial or otherwise, but simply a law regulating access to information in the hands of the police department.

We believe that, at least for purposes of facial invalidation, petitioner's view is correct. This is not a case in which the government is prohibiting a speaker from conveying information that the speaker already possesses. The California statute in question merely requires that if respondent wishes to obtain the addresses of arrestees it must qualify under the statute to do so. Respondent did not attempt to qualify and was therefore denied access to the addresses. For purposes of assessing the propriety of a facial invalidation, what we have before us is nothing more than a governmental denial of access to information in its possession. California could decide not to give out arrestee information at all without violating the First Amendment.

To the extent that respondent's "facial challenge" seeks to rely on the effect of the statute on parties not before the Court — its potential customers, for example — its claim does not fit within the case law allowing courts to entertain facial challenges. No threat of prosecution, for example, or cutoff of funds hangs over their heads. They may seek access under the statute on their own just as respondent did, without incurring any burden other than the prospect that their request will be denied. Resort to a facial challenge here is not warranted because there is "no possibility that protected speech will be muted." . . .

GINSBURG, J. joined by O'CONNOR, SOUTER, and BREYER, J.J. concurring. I join the Court's opinion, which recognizes that California Government Code § 6254(f)(3) is properly analyzed as a restriction on access to government information, not as a restriction on protected speech. That is sufficient reason to reverse the Ninth Circuit's judgment.

As the Court observes, the statute at issue does not restrict speakers from conveying information they already possess. Anyone who comes upon arrestee address information in the public domain is free to use that information as she sees fit. It is true, as Justice Scalia suggests, that the information could be provided to and published by journalists, and § 6254(f)(3) would indeed be a speech restriction if it then prohibited people from using that published information to speak to or about arrestees. But the statute contains no such prohibition. Once address information is in the public domain, the statute does not restrict its use in any way.

California could, as the Court notes, constitutionally decide not to give out arrestee address information at all. It does not appear that the selective disclosure of address information that California has chosen instead impermissibly burdens speech. To be sure, the provision of address information is a kind of subsidy to people who wish to speak to or about arrestees, and once a State decides to make such a benefit available to the public, there are no doubt limits to its freedom to decide how that benefit will be distributed. California could not, for example, release address information only to those whose political views were in line with the party in power. But if the award of the subsidy is not based on an illegitimate criterion such as viewpoint, California is free to support some speech without supporting other speech.

Throughout its argument, respondent assumes that § 6254(f)(3)'s regime of selective disclosure burdens speech in the sense of reducing the total flow of information. Whether that is correct is far from clear and depends on the point of comparison. If California were to publish the names and addresses of arrestees for everyone to use freely, it would indeed be easier to speak to and about arrestees than it is under the present system. But if States were required to choose between keeping proprietary information to themselves and making it available without limits, States might well choose the former option. In that event, disallowing selective disclosure would lead not to more speech overall but to more secrecy and less speech. As noted above, this consideration could not justify limited disclosures that discriminated on the basis of viewpoint or some other proscribed criterion. But it does suggest that society's interest in the free flow of information might argue for upholding laws like the one at issue in this case rather than imposing an all-or-nothing regime under which "nothing" could be a State's easiest response.

STEVENS, J. joined by KENNEDY, J. dissenting. . . . To determine whether the Amendment is valid as applied to respondent, it is similarly not necessary to invoke the overbreadth doctrine. That doctrine is only relevant if the challenger needs to rely on the possibility of invalid applications to third parties. In this case, it is the application of the Amendment to respondent itself that is at issue. Nor, in my opinion, is it necessary to do the four-step *Central Hudson* dance, because I agree with the majority that the Amendment is really a restriction on access to government information rather than a direct restriction on protected speech. For this reason, the majority is surely correct in observing that "California could decide not to give out arrestee information at all without violating the First Amendment." Moreover, I think it equally clear that California could release the information on a selective basis to a limited group of users who have a special, and legitimate, need for the information.

A different, and more difficult, question is presented when the State makes information generally available, but denies access to a small disfavored class. In this case, the State is making the information available to scholars, news media, politicians, and others, while denying access to a narrow category of persons solely because they intend to use the information for a constitutionally protected purpose. As Justice Ginsburg points out, if the State identified the disfavored persons based on their viewpoint, or political affiliation, for example, the discrimination would clearly be invalid.

What the State did here, in my opinion, is comparable to that obviously unconstitutional discrimination. In this case, the denial of access is based on the fact that respondent plans to publish the information to others who, in turn, intend to use it for a commercial speech purpose that the State finds objectionable. Respondent's proposed publication of the information is indisputably lawful — petitioner concedes that if respondent independently acquires the data, the First Amendment protects its right to communicate it to others. Similarly, the First Amendment supports the third parties' use of it for commercial speech purposes. Thus, because the State's discrimination is based on its desire to prevent the information from being used for constitutionally protected purposes, I think it must assume the burden of justifying its conduct.

The only justification advanced by the State is an asserted interest in protecting the privacy of victims and arrestees. Although that interest would explain a total ban on access, or a statute narrowly limiting access, it is insufficient when the data can be published in the news media and obtained by private investigators or others who meet the Amendment's vague criteria. . . . By allowing such widespread access to the information, the State has eviscerated any rational basis for believing that the Amendment will truly protect the privacy of these persons.

That the State might simply withhold the information from all persons does not insulate its actions from constitutional scrutiny. For even though government may withhold a particular benefit entirely, it "may not deny a benefit to a person on a basis that infringes his constitutionally protected interests — especially his interest in freedom of speech." A contrary view would impermissibly allow the government to "'produce a result which [it] could not command directly.'" It is perfectly clear that California could not directly censor the use of this information or the resulting speech. It follows, I believe, that the State's discriminatory ban on access to information — in an attempt to prohibit persons from exercising their constitutional rights to publish it in a truthful and accurate manner — is equally invalid.

Accordingly, I respectfully dissent.

NOTES & QUESTIONS

1. ***Reconciling Privacy and Transparency.*** Consider the following argument by Daniel Solove:

> How can the tension between transparency and privacy be reconciled? Must access to public records be sacrificed at the altar of privacy? Or must privacy be compromised as the price for a government disinfected by sunlight?
>
> It is my thesis that both transparency and privacy can be balanced through limitations on the access and use of personal information in public records. . . . We can make information accessible for certain purposes only. When government discloses information, it can limit how it discloses that information by preventing it from being amassed by companies for commercial purposes, to be sold to others, or to be combined with other information and sold back to the government. . . .
>
> . . . [B]y making access conditional on accepting certain responsibilities when using data — such as using it for specific purposes, not disclosing it to others, and so on, certain functions of transparency can be preserved at the same time privacy is protected.[15]

However, does this approach, as Justice Stevens contends in his dissent, impermissibly single out certain types of speakers? What if the California statute limited disclosure of the information to anybody who would use a form of mass communication or widespread publicity to disclose that information? In other words, what if it excluded journalists and the media from access?

2. **Florida Star v. B.J.F.** In *Florida Star v. B.J.F.*, 491 U.S. 524 (1989), the Supreme Court struck down a Florida law that prohibited the press from publishing a rape victim's name that inadvertently appeared in a public record. The Court held: "[W]here a newspaper publishes truthful information which it has lawfully obtained, punishment may lawfully be imposed, if at all, only when narrowly tailored to a state interest of the highest order." Daniel Solove notes:

> Governments can make a public record available *on the condition that* certain information is not disclosed or used in a certain manner. However, governments cannot establish post-access restrictions on the disclosure or use of information that is publicly available. Once the information is made available to the public, the *Florida Star* cases prohibit a state from restricting use.[16]

Is *United Reporting* consistent with *Florida Star*? Suppose Florida passed a law that in order for the press to access its police reports about sexual assaults,

---

[15] Daniel J. Solove, *Access and Aggregation: Public Records, Privacy, and the Constitution*, 86 Minn. L. Rev. 1137 (2002).

[16] *Id.*

journalists would have to agree to not disclose rape victims' names from the reports. Would this law be constitutional?

4. CONSTITUTIONAL LIMITATIONS ON PUBLIC ACCESS

(a) Public Records

Like the federal FOIA, many states have privacy exemptions in their freedom of information laws. But not all states balance privacy and transparency equally. Are there limitations on what information governments can release to the public? Consider the cases below:

KALLSTROM V. CITY OF COLUMBUS [*KALLSTROM I*]

136 F.3d 1055 (6th Cir. 1998)

MOORE, J. . . . The three plaintiffs, Melissa Kallstrom, Thomas Coelho, and Gary Householder, are undercover officers employed by the Columbus Police Department. All three were actively involved in the drug conspiracy investigation of the Short North Posse, a violent gang in the Short North area of Columbus, Ohio. In *United States v. Derrick Russell, et al.*, No. CR-2 95-044, (S.D. Ohio), forty-one members of the Short North Posse were prosecuted on drug conspiracy charges. Plaintiffs testified at the trial of eight of the *Russell* defendants.

During the *Russell* criminal trial, defense counsel requested and obtained from the City Kallstrom's personnel and pre-employment file, which defense counsel appears to have passed on to several of the *Russell* defendants. Officers Coelho and Householder also suspect that copies of their personnel and pre-employment files were obtained by the same defense attorney. The City additionally released Officer Coelho's file to the Police Officers for Equal Rights organization following its request for the file in the fall of 1995 in order to investigate possible discriminatory hiring and promotion practices by the City. The officers' personnel files include the officers' addresses and phone numbers; the names, addresses, and phone numbers of immediate family members; the names and addresses of personal references; the officers' banking institutions and corresponding account information, including account balances; their social security numbers; responses to questions regarding their personal life asked during the course of polygraph examinations; and copies of their drivers' licenses, including pictures and home addresses. The district court found that in light of the Short North Posse's propensity for violence and intimidation, the release of these personnel files created a serious risk to the personal safety of the plaintiffs and those relatives named in the files.

Prior to accepting employment with the City, the plaintiffs were assured by the City that personal information contained in their files would be held in strict confidence. Despite its earlier promise of confidentiality, however, the City believed Ohio's Public Records Act, Ohio Rev. Code Ann. § 149.43, required it to release the officers' files upon request from any member of the public.

The officers brought suit under 42 U.S.C. §§ 1983 and 1988 against the City, claiming that the dissemination of personal information contained in their personnel files violates their right to privacy as guaranteed by the Due Process Clause of the Fourteenth Amendment. . . . In addition to seeking compensatory damages, the officers request an injunction restraining the City from releasing personal information regarding them. . . .

Section 1983 imposes civil liability on a person acting under color of state law who deprives another of the "rights, privileges, or immunities secured by the Constitution and laws." 42 U.S.C. § 1983. The threshold question, therefore, is whether the City deprived the officers of a right "secured by the Constitution and laws." . . .

In *Whalen v. Roe,* the Supreme Court declared that the constitutional right to privacy grounded in the Fourteenth Amendment respects not only individual autonomy in intimate matters, but also the individual's interest in avoiding divulgence of highly personal information. The court echoed these sentiments in *Nixon v. Administrator of Gen. Servs.,* 433 U.S. 425 (1977), acknowledging that "[o]ne element of privacy has been characterized as 'the individual interest in avoiding disclosure of personal matters.'" Although *Whalen* and *Nixon* appear to recognize constitutional protection for an individual's interest in safeguarding personal matters from public view, in both cases the Court found that public interests outweighed the individuals' privacy interests.

This circuit has read *Whalen* and *Nixon* narrowly, and will only balance an individual's interest in nondisclosure of informational privacy against the public's interest in and need for the invasion of privacy where the individual privacy interest is of constitutional dimension. . . . We hold that the officers' privacy interests do indeed implicate a fundamental liberty interest, specifically their interest in preserving their lives and the lives of their family members, as well as preserving their personal security and bodily integrity. . . .

In light of the Short North Posse's propensity for violence and intimidation, the district court found that the City's release of the plaintiffs-appellants' addresses, phone numbers, and driver's licenses to defense counsel in the *Russell* case, as well as their family members' names, addresses, and phone numbers, created a serious risk to the personal safety of the plaintiffs and those relatives named in the files. We see no reason to doubt that where disclosure of this personal information may fall into the hands of persons likely to seek revenge upon the officers for their involvement in the *Russell* case, the City created a very real threat to the officers' and their family members' personal security and bodily integrity, and possibly their lives. Accordingly, we hold that the City's disclosure of this private information about the officers to defense counsel in the *Russell* case rises to constitutional dimensions, thereby requiring us . . . to balance the officers' interests against those of the City.

The district court found that although there was no indication that the Police Officers for Equal Rights organization posed any threat to the officers and their family members, disclosure even to that group of the officers' phone numbers, addresses, and driver's licenses, and their family members' names, addresses and phone numbers "increases the risk that the information will fall into the wrong hands." . . . Since the district court did not indicate its view of the severity of risks inherent in disclosure of information to the Police Officers for Equal Rights organization, we remand to the district court for reconsideration in light of this opinion of issues regarding disclosure of personal information to that organization.

In finding that the City's release of private information concerning the officers to defense counsel in the *Russell* case rises to constitutional dimensions by threatening the personal security and bodily integrity of the officers and their family members, we do not mean to imply that every governmental act which intrudes upon or threatens to intrude upon an individual's body invokes the Fourteenth Amendment. But where the release of private information places an individual at substantial risk of serious bodily harm, possibly even death, from a perceived likely threat, the "magnitude of the liberty deprivation . . . strips the very essence of personhood." . . .

Where state action infringes upon a fundamental right, such action will be upheld under the substantive due process component of the Fourteenth Amendment only where the governmental action furthers a compelling state interest, and is narrowly drawn to further that state interest. Having found that the officers have a fundamental constitutional interest in preventing the release of personal information contained in their personnel files where such disclosure creates a substantial risk of serious bodily harm, we must now turn to whether the City's actions narrowly serve a compelling public purpose.

The City believed Ohio's Public Records Act, Ohio Rev. Code Ann. § 149.43, required it to disclose the personal information contained in the officers' records. Ohio's Public Records Act requires the state to make available all public records to any person, unless the record falls within one of the statute's enumerated exceptions. The State mandates release of state agency records in order to shed light on the state government's performance, thereby enabling Ohio citizens to understand better the operations of their government. In the judicial setting, courts have long recognized the importance of permitting public access to judicial records so that citizens may understand and exercise oversight over the judicial system. We see no reason why public access to government agency records should be considered any less important. For purposes of this case, we assume that the interests served by allowing public access to agency records rises to the level of a compelling state interest. Nevertheless, the City's release to the criminal defense counsel of the officers' and their family members' home addresses and phone numbers, as well as the family members' names and the officers' driver's licenses, does not narrowly serve these interests.

While there may be situations in which the release of the this type of personal information might further the public's understanding of the workings of its law enforcement agencies, the facts as presented here do not support such a conclusion. The City released the information at issue to defense counsel in a large drug conspiracy case, who is asserted to have passed the information onto his clients. We simply fail to see how placing this personal information into the hands of the *Russell* defendants in any way increases public understanding of the City's law enforcement agency where the *Russell* defendants and their attorney make no claim that they sought this personal information about the officers in order to shed light on the internal workings of the Columbus Police Department. We therefore cannot conclude that the disclosure narrowly serves the state's interest in ensuring accountable governance. Accordingly, we hold that the City's actions in automatically disclosing this information to any member of the public requesting it are not narrowly tailored to serve this important public interest. . . .

Injunctive relief involving matters subject to state regulation may be no broader than necessary to remedy the constitutional violation. . . . [T]he constitutional violation arises when the release of private information about the officers places their personal security, and that of their families, at substantial risk without narrowly serving a compelling state interest. Thus, the officers are entitled to notice and an opportunity to be heard prior to the release of private information contained in their personnel files only where the disclosure of the requested information could potentially threaten the officers' and their families' personal security. As discussed above, release of the officers' addresses, phone numbers, and driver's licenses, as well as their family members' names, addresses, and phone numbers, is likely to result in a substantial risk to their personal security. On remand, the district court should consider whether release of other private information contained in the officers' personnel files also poses the same risk. . . . [B]ecause the City's decision to continue releasing this information potentially places the officers and their families at risk of irreparable harm that cannot be adequately remedied at law, the officers are entitled to injunctive relief prohibiting the City from again disclosing this information without first providing the officers meaningful notice.

KALLSTROM V. CITY OF COLUMBUS [*KALLSTROM II*]

165 F. Supp. 2d 686 (S.D. Ohio 2001)

SMITH, J. In this case, the Court is being asked to limit the freedom of the press by preventing the news media from obtaining public information contained in the city's personnel files. City police officers fear its publication may endanger themselves and their families.

To deny members of the press access to public information solely because they have the ability to disseminate it would silence the most important critics of governmental activity. This not only violates the Constitution, but eliminates the very protections the Founders envisioned a free press would provide.

Plaintiffs, who are three Columbus police officers ("Officers"), filed suit against defendant City of Columbus ("City") seeking compensatory damages under 42 U.S.C. §§ 1983 and 1988 and an injunction to prevent further dissemination of their personal information. Specifically, plaintiffs claim defendant violated their rights to privacy as guaranteed by the Due Process Clause of the Fourteenth Amendment by making their personnel records available to a criminal defense attorney pursuant to the Ohio Public Records Act, Ohio Rev. Code § 149.43. In October 1998, intervenors, a group of ten Ohio news organizations, joined the lawsuit without opposition after the City, citing the Sixth Circuit decision in this case, denied their request to see plaintiffs' personnel files. . . .

Using the Sixth Circuit's framework, the Court finds the Fourteenth Amendment does not prevent the City from allowing intervenors to inspect or copy the requested information from plaintiffs' personnel files. . . .

Intervenors have requested the home addresses of each plaintiff; summaries of investigations of plaintiffs' backgrounds; memos and reports of any assaults in which the plaintiffs were either perpetrators or victims; memos and reports related to any motor vehicle accidents in which City vehicles operated by plaintiffs were damaged or caused property damage or personal injury to others; memos and notices related to any disciplinary charges; and, answers to personal history questions. The request specifically excludes information identifying the Officers' banking institutions and financial account numbers; personal credit card numbers; social security numbers; information about any psychological conditions the Officers may have; responses to polygraph examinations; and, "medical records" or any other recorded information exempt from mandatory disclosure under Ohio Revised Code § 149.43. Further, intervenors do not object to the City redacting the names of any minor dependents of plaintiffs unless the dependent is employed by the City, any information made confidential by the Americans with Disabilities Act, 42 U.S.C. § 12101 et seq., or records which the Ohio Public Records Act would not require the City to disclose.

The Court finds plaintiffs do not have a constitutional privacy interest in the information requested by intervenors. Under the Sixth Circuit standard, plaintiffs must show that the release of information they wish to keep private would place them "at substantial risk of serious bodily harm, possibly even death, from a perceived likely threat." *Kallstrom,* 136 F.3d at 1064. The Court could fathom information contained in plaintiffs' personnel files that satisfies this stringent constitutional standard. Yet, that is not the Court's responsibility. The Sixth Circuit requires this Court to look at a "clear development of the factual circumstances" surrounding any future release of personal information from the Officers' personnel files. Plaintiffs have failed to provide any potentially admissible evidence to suggest that the release of any information contained in the three personnel files may place any of the plaintiffs at any risk of serious bodily harm. Nor have they identified a current "perceived likely threat."[17] This is fatal to their claims. By not identifying any real potential danger that could arise from the release of information in their personnel files, plaintiffs have failed to make a showing sufficient to establish the existence of an element essential to their case for which they carry the burden.

Further, the majority of intervenors' request focuses on each plaintiff's disciplinary records, incident complaints from citizens, and other documents detailing how each officer is performing his or her job. Although plaintiffs may wish maintain the confidentiality of their employment histories, the Constitution does not provide a shield against disclosure of potentially embarrassing or even improper activities by public servants.

Finally, plaintiffs' interests in their home addresses also fail to meet the stringent constitutional standard set by the Sixth Circuit. Addresses are part of the public domain. Anyone with an individual's name and either Internet access or the initiative to visit a local government office can scan county property

---

[17] The Court sympathizes with plaintiffs' initial fears of retaliation from the Short North Posse. . . . [H]owever, plaintiffs have not developed clear and factual circumstances, outside of mere speculation, that this threat still exists. The only evidence in the record suggests, fortunately, the threat never developed.

records, court records, or voter registration records for such information as an individual's address, the exact location of his or her residence, and even a floor plan of the home. The Supreme Court has found that "[t]he interests in privacy fade when the information involved already appears on the public record." *Cox Broad. Corp. v. Cohn,* 420 U.S. 469 (1975). In this case, plaintiffs have voluntarily revealed their own identities. For instance, plaintiffs initiated this lawsuit in their own names and describe their profession in the pleadings as "undercover narcotics officers." Plaintiffs also chose to testify without a pseudonym in the Posse trial. As plaintiffs have revealed their identities, their addresses are easily accessible in the public domain.

Even assuming plaintiffs have a constitutional interest in the information contained in their personnel files, the balancing test described by the Sixth Circuit still weighs in favor of disclosure. Where a state action infringes upon a fundamental right, the action will be upheld only where it furthers a compelling state interest and is narrowly drawn to further that state interest. In *Kallstrom,* the Sixth Circuit assumed that the state interests served by allowing public access to agency records were compelling, but held that the City's release of plaintiffs' personnel files to counsel for a criminal defendant did not narrowly achieve these interests.

Ohio's Public Records Act requires the state to make available all public records to any person unless the record falls within one of the statute's exceptions. Ohio Rev. Code § 149.43(B). The state has an interest in releasing its governmental agency records to "ensure accountability of government to those being governed." *See State ex rel. Strothers v. Wertheim,* 80 Ohio St.3d 155 (1997). In *Kallstrom,* the Sixth Circuit acknowledged "there may be situations in which the release of this type of personal information might further the public's understanding of the workings of its law enforcement agencies." *Kallstrom,* 136 F.3d at 1065. This is one of those situations. The information intervenors request details the functioning of the City's police force. The personnel files reveal, among other things, the character and background of the City's police officers, whether the officers are using City property responsibly, and whether the City is enforcing the residency requirement for City employees as required by the City's charter. The state has a compelling interest in releasing this type of information to enlighten the public about the performance of its law enforcement agencies and ensure government accountability. The importance of public access to these files as a restraint on government activity is evident from cases such as the U.S. Justice Department's civil rights action against the City concerning police practices, which is currently pending in this courthouse.

Further, the City's disclosure of public records, including police officer personnel files, is narrowly tailored to achieve this compelling state interest. In *Kallstrom,* the Sixth Circuit failed "to see how placing [the Officers'] personal information into the hands of the *Russell* defendants in any way increases public understanding of the City's law enforcement agency." The press, however, is a different entity. . . .

The full disclosure of these personnel files is necessary to enable the press to do its job. As nothing less than full disclosure will ensure transparency in government, the Court finds full disclosure is narrowly tailored to meet the state's compelling interest. . . .

The intervenors seek a second declaration that the City is violating the First Amendment by denying the news organizations a state law right because they might publish accurate reports of the contents of public records. The Court agrees and grants summary judgment for intervenors on their second ground for declaratory judgment. . . .

Neither the First Amendment nor the Fourteenth Amendment mandates a right of access to government information or sources of information within the government's control. . . . In this case, the doors have been opened by the Ohio Public Records Act. Thus, the issue becomes whether the City can deny intervenors their state law right to these public records because, as members of the news media, they have the ability to disseminate the information contained in plaintiffs' personnel files.

The Supreme Court has held that the government may not single out the press to bear special burdens without violating the First Amendment. *Minneapolis Star & Tribune Co. v. Minnesota Comm'r of Revenue,* 460 U.S. 575 (1983). In *Minneapolis Star,* the Supreme Court found that Minnesota's use tax on paper and ink violated the First Amendment for "singling out the press for taxation" that did not apply to other enterprises. Courts, however, have not been hesitant to extend this rationale beyond taxation. *See, e.g., Legi-Tech, Inc. v. Keiper,* 766 F.2d 728 (2d Cir. 1985) (suggesting denial of press access to a public legislative database would face "hostile scrutiny" as singling out the press for a special burden). . . .

Due to these important considerations, a state-imposed burden on the press is always "subject to at least some degree of heightened First Amendment scrutiny." When the government specially burdens the press, "the appropriate method of analysis thus is to balance the burden implicit in singling out the press against the interest asserted by the State." The burden "can survive only if the governmental interest outweighs the burden and cannot be achieved by means that do not infringe First Amendment rights as significantly."

In its pleadings, the City states its interest as preventing members of the press from accessing plaintiffs' personnel records because news organizations have the ability to disseminate the information to "wide and diverse audiences, including the Short North Posse." Since the second part of the *Minneapolis Star* test is dispositive, the Court finds it unnecessary to balance the City's interest with the burden implicit in singling out the press. The Court concludes the City's decision to single out the press for disparate treatment does not satisfactorily accomplish its stated purpose.

Treating the press differently will not prevent the harm the City is seeking to avoid. The City's denial of the intervenors' public records request because of their ability to disseminate information suggests that the same records would have been provided to anyone who did not have this capability. Any member of the public would have access to these records — including Short North Posse members, their friends, and their families. Silencing the press makes no difference as to whether these people have access to plaintiffs' personal information.

Further, this distinction does not prevent the press from gaining access to the materials. The news organizations could have a surrogate request the records and provide copies to the press. Even a reporter for one of the intervenors could request the records as a citizen, without revealing his or her professional affiliation, and use plaintiffs' personal information in the same manner as if the news organization had requested the records as an entity. Allowing the City to impose these arbitrary burdens threatens to eviscerate the ability of the press to serve as a restraint on government activity, poses inherent dangers to free expression, and presents great potential for censorship or manipulation. . . .

In choosing to deny intervenors' request based on their ability to disseminate the information, however, the City placed a burden on the press that would not have attached to any other request for those public records. The City's arbitrary treatment of the press is not only thoroughly ineffective at achieving its objective, but also highly offensive to the First Amendment. . . .

NOTES & QUESTIONS

1. ***How Broad Is the* Kallstrom II *Decision?*** In his reading of *Kallstrom I*, Paul Schwartz argues that the case showed that "[o]nly the threat of life-threatening harm to officers and their families and the City of Columbus' plan for automatic disclosure of this information" allowed an interest in nondisclosure to triumph.[18] Schwartz also notes that the Sixth Circuit granted merely a limited injunction to the undercover officers that allowed them a chance to object when someone requested their personal data. In this fashion, the *Kallstrom II* court left the door open for release of this information under other circumstances. What is left of the Sixth Circuit's opinion after *Kallstrom II*? Under what basis did the district court in *Kallstrom II* decide that the information should be released to the press?

   In *Barber v. Overton*, 496 F.3d 449 (6th Cir. 2007), the Sixth Circuit revisited the *Kallstrom I* and found that this decision was not implicated by a (mistaken) release of Social Security numbers and birth dates of prison officers to prisoners: "*Kallstrom* created a narrowly tailored right, limited to circumstances where the information was particularly sensitive and the persons to whom it was disclosed were particularly dangerous *vis-à-vis the plaintiffs*" (emphasis in original). In sum, the *Barber* court stated that the release of the information "was not sensitive enough nor the threat of retaliation apparent enough to warrant constitution protection here."
2. ***Statutory vs. Constitutional Privacy Exemptions.*** Contrast the operation of statutory privacy exemptions to FOIA and exceptions based on the constitutional right to information privacy, as in *Kallstrom I*. How does the presence of the Ohio Public Records Act affect the analysis in *Kallstrom II*?
3. ***The Scope of Privacy Exemptions.*** In *Moak v. Philadelphia Newspapers, Inc.*, 336 A.2d 920 (Pa. 1975), the court held that the employee records of a police department, which contained the name, gender, date of birth, salary, and other personal information about the employees, did not fall within the privacy exemption to Pennsylvania's Right to Know Law because the records would not "operate to the prejudice or impairment of a person's reputation or

---

[18] Paul M. Schwartz, *Internet Privacy and the State*, 32 Conn. L. Rev. 815, 828-29 (2000).

personal security." Should the privacy of personal information turn on whether it will harm a person's reputation or security?

4. ***Public Records in a Digital World.*** Public records are increasingly being stored in electronic format. The paper records of the past were difficult to access. Now, they can be collected in databases and searched en masse. To what extent should the increased accessibility of records created by the digital age affect open record laws?

In 2001, the Judicial Conference Committee on Court Administration and Case Management issued a report with policies regarding public access to electronic case files. As Peter Winn describes it:

> Before the Judicial Conference Committee on Court Administration and Case Management (Committee) issued the Report, a study of the problem was prepared by the staff of the Administrative Office of the United States Courts. The staff white paper described two general approaches to the problem. One approach was to treat electronic judicial records as governed by exactly the same rules as paper records — what the white paper calls the "public is public" approach. The second approach advocated treating electronic and paper files differently in order to respect the practical obscurity of paper case files, urging that the rules regulating electronic court records reflect the fact that unrestricted online access to court records would undoubtedly, as a practical matter, compromise privacy, as well as increase the risk of personal harm to litigants and third parties whose private information appeared in case files. The white paper suggested that different levels of privileges could be created to govern electronic access to court records. Under this approach, judges and court staff would generally have broad, although not unlimited, remote access to all electronic case files, as would other key participants in the judicial process, such as the U.S. Attorney, the U.S. Trustee, and bankruptcy case trustees. Litigants and their attorneys would have unrestricted access to the files relevant to their own cases. The general public would have remote access to a subset of the full case file, including, in most cases, pleadings, briefs, orders, and opinions. Under this approach, the entire electronic case file could still be viewed at the clerk's office, just as the paper file is available now for inspection, but would not generally be made available on the Internet.
>
> Unfortunately, at least with respect to civil cases and bankruptcy cases, few, if any, of the suggestions contained in the staff white paper were ultimately adopted in the Report. Instead, the Committee adopted the "public is public" approach to the problem, rejecting the view that courts have a responsibility to adopt rules governing the use of their computer systems to try to recreate in cyberspace the practical balance that existed in the world of paper judicial records. In supporting this decision, the Committee took the position that attempting to recreate the "practical obscurity" of the brick and mortar world was simply too complicated an exercise for the courts to undertake. The Report does appear to recognize a limited responsibility on the part of the courts to adopt rules in order to limit the foreseeable harms of identity theft and online stalking. The Report recommends that certain "personal data identifiers," such as Social Security numbers, dates of birth, financial account numbers, and names of minor children, be partially redacted by the litigants. . . .
>
> The Report recommends that criminal court records not be placed online, for the present, finding that any benefits of remote electronic access to

> criminal files would be outweighed by the safety and law enforcement risks such access would create. The Report expressed the concern that allowing defendants and others easy access to information regarding the cooperation and other activities of co-defendants would increase the risk that the information would be used to intimidate, harass, and possibly harm victims, defendants, and their families. In addition, the Report noted that merely sealing such documents would not adequately address the problems of online access, since the fact that a document is sealed signals probable defendant cooperation and covert law enforcement initiatives.[19]

In March 2004, the Judicial Conference issued a report recommending that, with certain exceptions, all criminal records be placed online accessible to the public.[20]

(b) Police Records

PAUL V. DAVIS

424 U.S. 693 (1976)

REHNQUIST, J. . . . Petitioner Paul is the Chief of Police of the Louisville, Ky., Division of Police, while petitioner McDaniel occupies the same position in the Jefferson County, Ky., Division of Police. In late 1972 they agreed to combine their efforts for the purpose of alerting local area merchants to possible shoplifters who might be operating during the Christmas season. In early December petitioners distributed to approximately 800 merchants in the Louisville metropolitan area a "flyer," which began as follows:

> TO: BUSINESS MEN IN THE METROPOLITAN AREA
>
> The Chiefs of The Jefferson County and City of Louisville Police Departments, in an effort to keep their officers advised on shoplifting activity, have approved the attached alphabetically arranged flyer of subjects known to be active in this criminal field.
>
> This flyer is being distributed to you, the business man, so that you may inform your security personnel to watch for these subjects. These persons have been arrested during 1971 and 1972 or have been active in various criminal fields in high density shopping areas.
>
> Only the photograph and name of the subject is shown on this flyer, if additional information is desired, please forward a request in writing. . . .

The flyer consisted of five pages of "mug shot" photos, arranged alphabetically. [Each page had the heading: "ACTIVE SHOPLIFTERS."]

In approximately the center of page 2 there appeared photos and the name of the respondent, Edward Charles Davis III.

Respondent appeared on the flyer because on June 14, 1971, he had been arrested in Louisville on a charge of shoplifting. He had been arraigned on this charge in September 1971, and, upon his plea of not guilty, the charge had been

---

[19] Peter A. Winn, *Online Court Records: Balancing Judicial Accountability and Privacy in an Age of Electronic Information*, 79 Wash. L. Rev. 307, 322-25 (2004).

[20] http://www.privacy.uscourts.gov/crimimpl.htm

"filed away with leave (to reinstate)," a disposition which left the charge outstanding. Thus, at the time petitioners caused the flyer to be prepared and circulated respondent had been charged with shoplifting but his guilt or innocence of that offense had never been resolved. Shortly after circulation of the flyer the charge against respondent was finally dismissed by a judge of the Louisville Police Court.

At the time the flyer was circulated respondent was employed as a photographer by the Louisville Courier-Journal and Times. The flyer, and respondent's inclusion therein, soon came to the attention of respondent's supervisor, the executive director of photography for the two newspapers. This individual called respondent in to hear his version of the events leading to his appearing in the flyer. Following this discussion, the supervisor informed respondent that although he would not be fired, he "had best not find himself in a similar situation" in the future.

Respondent thereupon brought this § 1983 action in the District Court for the Western District of Kentucky, seeking redress for the alleged violation of rights guaranteed to him by the Constitution of the United States. . . .

Respondent's due process claim is grounded upon his assertion that the flyer, and in particular the phrase "Active Shoplifters" appearing at the head of the page upon which his name and photograph appear, impermissibly deprived him of some "liberty" protected by the Fourteenth Amendment. His complaint asserted that the "active shoplifter" designation would inhibit him from entering business establishments for fear of being suspected of shoplifting and possibly apprehended, and would seriously impair his future employment opportunities. Accepting that such consequences may flow from the flyer in question, respondent's complaint would appear to state a classical claim for defamation actionable in the courts of virtually every State. Imputing criminal behavior to an individual is generally considered defamatory per se, and actionable without proof of special damages.

Respondent brought his action, however, not in the state courts of Kentucky, but in a United States District Court for that State. He asserted not a claim for defamation under the laws of Kentucky, but a claim that he had been deprived of rights secured to him by the Fourteenth Amendment of the United States Constitution. Concededly if the same allegations had been made about respondent by a private individual, he would have nothing more than a claim for defamation under state law. But, he contends, since petitioners are respectively an official of city and of county government, his action is thereby transmuted into one for deprivation by the State of rights secured under the Fourteenth Amendment. . . .

If respondent's view is to prevail, a person arrested by law enforcement officers who announce that they believe such person to be responsible for a particular crime in order to calm the fears of an aroused populace, presumably obtains a claim against such officers under § 1983. And since it is surely far more clear from the language of the Fourteenth Amendment that "life" is protected against state deprivation than it is that reputation is protected against state injury, it would be difficult to see why the survivors of an innocent bystander mistakenly shot by a policeman or negligently killed by a sheriff driving a government vehicle, would not have claims equally cognizable under § 1983.

It is hard to perceive any logical stopping place to such a line of reasoning. Respondent's construction would seem almost necessarily to result in every legally cognizable injury which may have been inflicted by a state official acting under "color of law" establishing a violation of the Fourteenth Amendment. We think it would come as a great surprise to those who drafted and shepherded the adoption of that Amendment to learn that it worked such a result, and a study of our decisions convinces us they do not support the construction urged by respondent. . . .

The second premise upon which the result reached by the Court of Appeals could be rested that the infliction by state officials of a "stigma" to one's reputation is somehow different in kind from infliction by a state official of harm to other interests protected by state law is equally untenable. The words "liberty" and "property" as used in the Fourteenth Amendment do not in terms single out reputation as a candidate for special protection over and above other interests that may be protected by state law. While we have in a number of our prior cases pointed out the frequently drastic effect of the "stigma" which may result from defamation by the government in a variety of contexts, this line of cases does not establish the proposition that reputation alone, apart from some more tangible interests such as employment, is either "liberty" or "property" by itself sufficient to invoke the procedural protection of the Due Process Clause. . . .

Respondent's complaint also alleged a violation of a "right to privacy guaranteed by the First, Fourth, Fifth, Ninth, and Fourteenth Amendments." . . .

While there is no "right of privacy" found in any specific guarantee of the Constitution, the Court has recognized that "zones of privacy" may be created by more specific constitutional guarantees and thereby impose limits upon government power. *See Roe v. Wade*, 410 U.S. 113 (1973). Respondent's case, however, comes within none of these areas. He does not seek to suppress evidence seized in the course of an unreasonable search. *See Katz v. United States*, 389 U.S. 347 (1967). And our other "right of privacy" cases, while defying categorical description, deal generally with substantive aspects of the Fourteenth Amendment. In *Roe* the Court pointed out that the personal rights found in this guarantee of personal privacy must be limited to those which are "fundamental" or "implicit in the concept of ordered liberty" as described in *Palko v. Connecticut*, 302 U.S. 319 (1937). The activities detailed as being within this definition were ones very different from that for which respondent claims constitutional protection matters relating to marriage, procreation, contraception, family relationships, and child rearing and education. In these areas it has been held that there are limitations on the States' power to substantively regulate conduct.

Respondent's claim is far afield from this line of decisions. He claims constitutional protection against the disclosure of the fact of his arrest on a shoplifting charge. His claim is based, not upon any challenge to the State's ability to restrict his freedom of action in a sphere contended to be "private," but instead on a claim that the State may not publicize a record of an official act such as an arrest. None of our substantive privacy decisions hold this or anything like this, and we decline to enlarge them in this manner. . . .

NOTES & QUESTIONS

1. **Wisconsin v. Constantineau.** Five years prior to *Paul*, the Court was more receptive to constitutional protection for reputational harms in *Wisconsin v. Constantineau*, 400 U.S. 433 (1971). There, the Court struck down a law authorizing the posting of names of people who had been designated excessive drinkers in retail liquor outlets. Alcohol was not to be sold to these individuals. The Court reasoned:

   > Where a person's good name, reputation, honor, or integrity is at stake because of what the government is doing to him, notice and an opportunity to be heard are essential. "Posting" under the Wisconsin Act may to some be merely the mark of illness, to others it is a stigma, an official branding of a person. The label is a degrading one. Under the Wisconsin Act, a resident of Hartford is given no process at all. This appellee was not afforded a chance to defend herself. She may have been the victim of an official's caprice. Only when the whole proceedings leading to the pinning of an unsavory label on a person are aired can oppressive results be prevented.

   Is *Paul* consistent with this case?

2. **Paul v. Davis *vs.* Whalen v. Roe.** *Paul v. Davis* was decided one year prior to *Whalen v. Roe,* 429 U.S. 589 (1977), where the Supreme Court recognized that the constitutional right to privacy involves "the individual interest in avoiding disclosure of personal matters." How does *Paul* square with *Whalen*? Does *Whalen* implicitly overrule *Paul* by recognizing a constitutional right to avoid disclosure of certain information? How can these cases be reconciled?

CLINE V. ROGERS

87 F.3d 176 (6th Cir. 1996)

BATCHELDER, J. . . . The plaintiff-appellant, Jackie Ray Cline ("Cline"), alleges that in 1992, a private citizen contacted the Sheriff's Department of McMinn County, Tennessee ("the County"), and asked Sheriff George Rogers to check Cline's arrest record. According to Cline, Rogers searched state and local records and requested a computer search of National Crime Information Center ("NCIC") records of the Federal Bureau of Investigation ("FBI"). Cline alleges that Rogers disclosed to the private citizen the information Rogers obtained regarding Cline's criminal history, in violation of both Tennessee and federal law.

Cline filed this lawsuit against Rogers, individually and in his official capacity as sheriff. Cline also named the County as a defendant, alleging that improper searches of criminal records is "a routine and customary practice in McMinn County," that the County "lacks adequate controls to ensure that access to criminal records is for authorized purposes only," that the County did not have in place an adequate system to detect misuse of criminal records, that the County had provided inadequate training to prevent such abuse, and that the County had "been indifferent to the civil rights of private citizens by allowing such abuses to continue."

Cline's complaint sought damages under 42 U.S.C. § 1983 for violation of his federal civil rights. . . . [The district court dismissed Cline's complaint, and Cline appealed.]

There is no violation of the United States Constitution in this case because there is no constitutional right to privacy in one's criminal record. Nondisclosure of one's criminal record is not one of those personal rights that is "fundamental" or "implicit in the concept of ordered liberty." *See Whalen v. Roe*. In *Whalen*, the Supreme Court distinguished fundamental privacy interests in "matters relating to marriage, procreation, contraception, family relationships, and child rearing and education" and "individual interest in avoiding disclosure of personal matters."

Moreover, one's criminal history is arguably not a private "personal matter" at all, since arrest and conviction information are matters of public record. *See Paul v. Davis* (rejecting a similar claim based on facts more egregious than those alleged here). Although there may be a dispute among the circuit courts regarding the existence and extent of an individual privacy right to nondisclosure of "personal matters," see *Slayton v. Willingham*, 726 F.2d 631 (10th Cir. 1984); *Fadjo v. Coon*, 633 F.2d 1172, 1176 (5th Cir. Unit B 1981) (both opining that *Paul* has been at least partially overruled by the Supreme Court's decisions in *Whalen* and *Nixon*), this circuit does not recognize a constitutional privacy interest in avoiding disclosure of, e.g., one's criminal record. See *DeSanti*, 653 F.2d at 1090 (regarding disclosure of juvenile delinquents' "social histories"); see also *Doe v. Wigginton*, 21 F.3d 733 (6th Cir. 1994) (disclosure of inmate's HIV infection did not violate constitutional right of privacy).

Because there is no privacy interest in one's criminal record that is protected by the United States Constitution, Cline could prove no set of facts that would entitle him to relief; therefore, the district court correctly dismissed this claim. . .

SCHEETZ V. THE MORNING CALL, INC.

946 F.2d 202 (3d Cir. 1991)

NYGAARD, J. . . . Kenneth Scheetz is a police officer in the City of Allentown. Rosann Scheetz is his wife. In the course of an argument between them in their home in January of 1988, Kenneth struck Rosann. Rosann left the house, but returned approximately a half an hour later. The argument resumed, and Kenneth again struck Rosann.

Rosann called the Allentown police. Two officers responded and prepared a standard "offense/incident" report, consisting of a face sheet and supplemental reports. The "face sheet" of this report[21] stated that Rosann Scheetz had reported a domestic disturbance, that two police cars had responded, and that Rosann had left the home.

In the meantime, Rosann had driven to the Allentown police station, apparently with the intention of filing a Pennsylvania Protection From Abuse

---

[21] The "face sheet" is a public document similar to a police blotter. The parties agree that this document is a public record. The parties dispute whether the "supplemental reports" are public records available under Pennsylvania's Right to Know Law. There is some evidence that these reports were generally available, subject to the approval of a police supervisor.

Petition. The officers who interviewed Rosann prepared two "supplemental reports" and made them part of the file. They reveal that Rosann stated that her husband had beaten her before and had refused counseling. The police gave Rosann three options: file criminal charges, request a protection from abuse order, or initiate department disciplinary action against Kenneth. These supplements also note that Rosann had visible physical injuries, that Rosann did not want to return home and that she was permitted to spend the night in the shift commander's office.

Chief Wayne Stephens filed a third supplement to the report. He had spoken to Kenneth about the incident, and the third supplement memorialized this fact, as well as Kenneth's statement to the Chief that he and his wife were scheduled to speak with a marriage counselor. None of the supplements indicated that the Chief took any disciplinary action against Kenneth.

Shortly after the incident, Kenneth Scheetz was named "Officer of the Year" by Chief Stephens. Several months later, as part of "Respect for Law Week," press releases and photos of Kenneth were released. A dinner and official ceremony were held in Kenneth's honor. The Morning Call ("The Call"), a local newspaper, published a story and photo on this honor.

Terry Mutchler, a reporter for The Call, became interested in investigating the prior incident involving Kenneth and Rosann. Another reporter from the paper had tried to get the police report from the police, who refused to release it. Mutchler's request for a copy of the report from the department was also formally refused. Mutchler nonetheless managed to get a copy of the report.

Mutchler then interviewed Chief Stephens about the incident. Chief Stephens initially denied the incident, but when confronted with Mutchler's information, he claimed that the report was stolen and refused further comment. Chief Stephens did, however, offer his insights into the subject of spousal abuse, stating "people fake it" and "women . . . tear their dresses and rip up their bras and say they were raped." Mutchler also interviewed Deputy Chief Monaghan, who offered assorted rationalizations for why no follow-up had been done on the Scheetz incident. The Scheetzes refused comment on the incident.

The Call published an article by Mutchler titled "Police didn't investigate assault complaint against officer." Eight paragraphs of the article were comprised of quotes from the police report of the beating incident which detailed the injuries Rosann received. The bulk of the article, however, focused on the lack of investigation and follow-up by the police department. Chief Stephens was quoted as saying that the incident had not been investigated. The article also quoted the comments Chief Stephens had made to Mutchler about domestic abuse, as well as Deputy Chief Monaghan's explanations for why no charges were pressed. The last two columns of the article consisted of quotes from Kenneth's superiors praising his work. . . .

. . . Kenneth and Rosann then sued Mutchler, The Call, and "John or Jane Doe." The complaint alleged that Mutchler and The Call had conspired with an unknown state actor (the Doe defendant) to deprive the Scheetzes of their constitutional right to privacy in violation of 42 U.S.C. § 1983. The complaint also raised several pendent state law claims. . . .

The district court granted the defendants' motion for summary judgment in part, denied it in part, granted judgment to the defendants on the § 1983 claim, dismissed the pendent state claims, dismissed the Doe defendant and dismissed all remaining motions as moot. The Scheetzes appeal. . . .

. . . Because we conclude that the Scheetzes have not alleged a violation of a constitutionally protected privacy interest, we will affirm.

The defendants rely on dicta in *Paul v. Davis* to support their argument that "garden variety" invasion of privacy claims are not actionable under section 1983. . . . The Supreme Court rejected the proposition that reputation alone was a liberty or property interest within the meaning of the due process clause. In dicta, the Court went on to consider the alternative argument that the police chiefs' action constituted a violation of the plaintiff's right to privacy. After first noting that privacy decisions had been limited in the past to family and procreative matters, the Court concluded that publication by the state of an official act such as an arrest could not constitute invasion of the constitutional right to privacy.

The very next year, however, the Court held in *Whalen v. Roe*, that the right to privacy extends to both "the individual interest in avoiding disclosure of personal matters, and . . . the interest in independence in making certain kinds of important decisions." *Whalen* recognized that the information contained in medical records is constitutionally protected under the confidentiality branch of the privacy right.

Thus, some confidential information is protected under the confidentiality branch of the right to privacy, the dicta in *Paul* notwithstanding.[22] Accordingly, the Scheetzes in this case contend that the information contained in the police incident report is similarly protected by the federal right.

Although cases exploring the autonomy branch of the right of privacy are legion, the contours of the confidentiality branch are murky. We have recognized that some confidential information, such as medical records, is constitutionally protected under the confidentiality branch of the federal privacy right. Other courts have similarly recognized that § 1983 may be used to redress violations of a constitutional confidentiality right.

Concluding that violations of the confidentiality right of privacy may be actionable under § 1983 does not, however, end our inquiry. Although defendants are wrong in arguing that *Paul* prohibits any privacy § 1983 action, we conclude that they correctly argue that the Scheetzes did not have a constitutionally protected privacy interest in the information they divulged in a police report. . . .

Although the outlines of the confidentiality right are not definite, the information that has been protected in other cases was information that the disclosing person reasonably expected to remain private. In reporting this potential crime to the police, Rosann Scheetz could not reasonably expect the information to remain secret. The police could have brought charges without her concurrence, at which point all the information would have wound up on the public record, where it would have been non-confidential. *See Cox Broadcasting Corp. v. Cohn*, 420 U.S. 469 (1975) (privacy interest fades when information is in the public record). This information is not like medical or financial records (which have been accorded some constitutional protection by this court) where there is a reasonable expectation that privacy will be preserved. When police are

[22] *Paul* can be reconciled with *Whalen* since the information at issue in *Paul* (the fact of plaintiff's arrest for shoplifting) is not the kind of information entitled to constitutional protection.

called, a private disturbance loses much of its private character. We conclude that the information Rosann Scheetz disclosed in the police reports is not constitutionally protected. . . .

MANSMANN, J. dissenting. . . . I agree that some of the information contained in the police report, specifically that information contained in the "Offense/Incident Report," is not protected under a constitutional privacy interest. Because the "Offense/Incident Report" is classified as a public document under the police department's policy, that information was not treated as confidential. . . .

Some of the information reported by The Call, however, was contained only in confidential portions of the police report entitled "Investigative Supplements" and was not discernable from the public portion of the report. That information detailed the private facts of the Scheetzes' marital counseling and precise details of their marital disturbance, including a description of Rosann's injuries and her statements. Since this information is clearly confidential, I would then examine the nature of the Scheetzes' privacy interest in keeping it confidential. . . .

. . . The majority suggests that because the information could have been publicly disclosed, the Scheetzes had no privacy interest. While it is true that criminal charges could have been brought without Rosann's concurrence, it does not necessarily follow that in spite of the fact that she declined to press charges or take alternative legal action, and no legal action ensued, Rosann Scheetz could have reasonably expected public disclosure of the confidential information that had remained quietly dormant in confidential police department reports.

This is especially true where the public disclosure occurred 16 months after the incident. *See, e.g.*, *Briscoe v. Reader's Digest Ass'n*, 483 P.2d 34 (Cal. 1971) (common law right to privacy infringed by publication of truck hijacking conviction of 11 years ago); *Melvin v. Reid*, 297 P. 91 (Cal. 1931) (liability for common law invasion of privacy imposed upon producers of movie that revealed prior life of prostitution and crime of woman who had long since taken a new name and established a respectable life). . . .

. . . Because this confidential information had lain undisclosed in the confidential police department files for over a year and Rosann Scheetz had not pursued any legal action, the Scheetzes could reasonably have expected that the confidential information would never be publicly disclosed. In light of this delay, I cannot agree with the majority's otherwise appropriate assertion that "[w]hen police are called, a private disturbance loses much of its private character." Information that has remained confidential over a period of time, absent any legal action, can reasonably be expected to recede from public notice. . . .

NOTES & QUESTIONS

1. ***Privacy as a Way to Conceal a Scandal.*** The information about the police department's treatment of Ken Scheetz's abuse of his wife is highly newsworthy. The information reveals a police department that praised rather than disciplined Ken Scheetz and virtually ignored his wife's complaints of

abuse. Is privacy being used to cover up the scandalous way the police department reacted to Rosann Scheetz's complaint?

2. ***Deterring Reporting of Spousal Abuse.*** Would routine disclosure of complaints of spousal abuse inhibit victims such as Rosann Scheetz from coming forward? Keep in mind that it is Rosann Scheetz, in addition to her husband, who is suing for a violation of her privacy.
3. ***Limits on Police Reports.*** The court concluded that Rosann Scheetz lacked an expectation of privacy in the information because it was included in a police report: "In reporting this potential crime to the police, Rosann Scheetz could not reasonably expect the information to remain secret. The police could have brought charges without her concurrence, at which point all the information would have wound up on the public record, where it would have been non-confidential." Are there limits to what information the police should include in a police report?
4. ***Police Threats to Disclose.*** Consider *Sterling v. Borough of Minersville*, 232 F.3d. 190 (3d Cir. 2000). Marcus Wayman, 18 years old, was in a parked car along with a 17-year-old male friend. The car was parked in a lot adjacent to a beer distributor. F. Scott Wilinsky, a police officer, observed the vehicle and became suspicious that the youths might be attempting to burglarize the beer distributor. Wilinsky called for backup. After investigating, the officers determined that a break-in had not occurred at the beer distributor, but that the youths had been drinking. Wilinsky searched the vehicle and discovered two condoms and asked about the boys' sexual orientation. The boys said that they were gay, and that they were in the lot to engage in consensual sex. The boys were arrested for underage drinking and taken to the police station, where Wilinsky lectured them that homosexual activity was contrary to the dictates of the Bible. Wilinsky then told Wayman that he must inform his grandfather about his homosexuality or else Wilinsky himself would inform Wayman's grandfather. When he was released from custody, Wayman committed suicide. Wayman's mother filed a § 1983 suit against the Borough of Minersville, Wilinksy, and other officers and officials alleging, among other things, a violation of the constitutional right to information privacy. The court reasoned:

> We first ask whether Wayman had a protected privacy right concerning Wilinsky's threat to disclose his suspected sexual orientation. . . .
>
> It is difficult to imagine a more private matter than one's sexuality and a less likely probability that the government would have a legitimate interest in disclosure of sexual identity.
>
> We can, therefore, readily conclude that Wayman's sexual orientation was an intimate aspect of his personality entitled to privacy protection under *Whalen*. . . .
>
> Before we can definitely conclude that a constitutional tort has occurred, however, we must further ask whether Wilinsky's threat of disclosure, rather than actual disclosure, constituted a violation of Wayman's right to privacy. . .
>
> The threat to breach some confidential aspect of one's life . . . is tantamount to a violation of the privacy right because the security of one's

> privacy has been compromised by the threat of disclosure. Thus, Wilinsky's threat to disclose Wayman's suspected homosexuality suffices as a violation of Wayman's constitutionally protected privacy interest. . . .

(c) Megan's Laws

In 1994, in New Jersey, a seven-year-old girl, Megan Kanka, was brutally raped and murdered by her neighbor, Jesse Timmendequas, who had two earlier sexual assault convictions. Nobody in Megan's family knew about Timmendequas's prior criminal record. Seventeen days after Megan's death, New Jersey Assembly Speaker Chuck Haytaian declared a legislative emergency. A law was proposed, called "Megan's Law," to establish a system for people to learn of the whereabouts of sexual offenders who were released from prison. The statute passed without committee hearings and without supportive research. Within three months of Megan's death, the law was signed by Governor Christie Whitman and became law. Similar laws appeared in other states. These laws, commonly called "Megan's Laws," set up databases of personal information about sexual offenders so that people can learn their identities and where they live.

In 1996, Congress passed a federal Megan's Law restricting states from receiving federal anti-crime funds unless they agreed to "release relevant information that is necessary to protect the public" from released sex offenders. *See* Pub. L. No. 104-145, codified at 42 U.S.C. § 14071(d)(2). Today, all 50 states have passed a version of Megan's Law. Sex offender registries under Megan's Law often contain information such as the sex offender's Social Security number, photograph, address, prior convictions, and places of employment.

States differ in how they disseminate sexual offender information. In California, booths are set up at county fairs so that individuals can browse through the registry. Some states have 1-800 or 1-900 numbers where people can call in and ask if particular people are sex offenders. At least 16 states have made their registries available on the Internet.

PAUL P. V. VERNIERO

170 F.3d 396 (3d Cir. 1999)

SLOVITER, J. Plaintiff Paul P. sues on his behalf and on behalf of a class of persons who, having been convicted of specified sex crimes, are required to comply with N.J. Stat. Ann. § 2c:7-1 et seq., known as "Megan's Law," which provides for a system of registration and community notification. . . .

In a related action, *E.B. v. Verniero*, 119 F.3d 1077 (3d Cir. 1997), this court rejected the claims of comparably situated persons that the community notification requirements violate the Double Jeopardy Clause or the Ex Post Facto Clause of the United States Constitution. That holding of *E.B.* was predicated on the conclusion that the notification required by Megan's Law does not constitute punishment. . . .

In this case, plaintiffs raise a challenge to Megan's Law that they claim is different from that considered in *E.B.* They argue that the statutory requirement that the class members provide extensive information to local law enforcement personnel, including each registrant's current biographical data, physical description, home address, place of employment, schooling, and a description and license plate number of the registrant's vehicle, and the subsequent community notification is a violation of their constitutionally protected right to privacy.

The statutory scheme is described in detail in *E.B.*, and we refer only briefly to the salient details. We explained the registration requirements as follows:

The registrant must provide the following information to the chief law enforcement officer of the municipality in which he resides: name, social security number, age, race, sex, date of birth, height, weight, hair and eye color, address of legal residence, address of any current temporary legal residence, and date and place of employment. N.J.S.A. 2C:7-4b(1). He must confirm his address every ninety days, notify the municipal law enforcement agency if he moves, and re-register with the law enforcement agency of any new municipality. N.J.S.A. 2C:7-2d to e.

The information provided by the registrant is put into a central registry, open to other law enforcement personnel but not to public inspection. Law enforcement officials then use the data provided to apply a "Risk Assessment Scale," a numerical scoring system, to determine the registrant's "risk of offense" and the tier in which the registrant should be classified. In the case of Tier 1 registrants, notification is given only to law enforcement agents "likely to encounter" the registrant. Tier 2, or "moderate risk," notification is given to law enforcement agents, schools, and community organizations "likely to encounter" the registrant. Tier 3, or "high risk," notification goes to all members of the public "likely to encounter" the registrant. Notifications generally contain a warning that the information is confidential and should not be disseminated to others, as well as an admonition that actions taken against the registrant, such as assaults, are illegal.

The prosecutor must provide the registrant with notice of the proposed notification. A pre-notification judicial review process is available for any registrant who wishes to challenge his or her classification.

The plaintiffs are Tier 2 and Tier 3 registrants who have been certified as a class and whose offenses were committed after the enactment of Megan's Law. . . .

The legal foundation for plaintiffs' claim is the Supreme Court's recognition that there is "a right of personal privacy, or a guarantee of certain areas or zones of privacy," protected by the United States Constitution. *Roe v. Wade*, 410 U.S. 113, 152 (1973). This "guarantee of personal privacy" covers "only personal rights that can be deemed 'fundamental' or 'implicit in the concept of ordered liberty.'" This privacy right "has some extension to activities relating to marriage, procreation, contraception, family relationships, and child rearing and education."

Plaintiffs argue that Megan's Law infringes upon their constitutionally protected privacy interests in two ways. One is by the dissemination of information about them, most particularly by disseminating both their home addresses and a "compilation of information which would otherwise remain 'scattered' or 'wholly forgotten.'" Their other claim is that the community notification infringes upon their "privacy interests in their most intimate relationships — those with their spouses, children, parents, and other family members."

Plaintiffs thus seek to invoke the two categories of privacy interests identified by the Supreme Court in *Whalen v. Roe*. . . .

The parties dispute the extent to which our decision in *E.B.* is dispositive of the privacy issue before us in this case. Plaintiffs contend that no privacy issue was raised, briefed, or argued in *E.B.* and that the discussion in *E.B.* relating to cases on which they rely is dictum. The State defendants, on the other hand, regard "[t]he portions of the *E.B.* decision holding that community notification does not implicate a fundamental privacy interest and the finding of a compelling state interest in protecting the public from recidivist sex offenders," as "control[ling] the decision in this case." We thus turn to examine the *E.B.* decision.

The privacy issue arose in *E.B.* during our analysis of whether community notification mandated by Megan's Law constitutes punishment for purposes of the Ex Post Facto and Double Jeopardy Clauses. In that context, we stated that the "primary sting from Megan's law notification comes by way of injury to what is denoted . . . as reputational interests. This includes . . . the myriad of . . . ways in which one is treated differently by virtue of being known as a potentially dangerous sex offender." *E.B.*, 119 F.3d at 1102. We then referred to the Supreme Court's holding in *Paul v. Davis*, stating:

> Just as Davis sought constitutional protection from the consequences of state disclosure of the fact of his shoplifting arrest and law enforcement's assessment that he was a continuing risk, so registrants seek protection from what may follow disclosure of facts related to their sex offense convictions and the resulting judgment of the state that they are a continuing risk. It follows that, just as the officers' publication of the official act of Davis' arrest did not violate any fundamental privacy right of Davis', neither does New Jersey's publication (through notification) of registrants' convictions and findings of dangerousness implicate any interest of fundamental constitutional magnitude.

We rejected the contention that dissemination of information about criminal activity beyond law enforcement personnel is analogous to historical punishments, such as the stocks, cages, and scarlet letters. We found instead that the dissemination is more like the dissemination of "rap sheet" information to regulatory agencies, bar associations, prospective employers, and interested members of the public that public indictment, public trial, and public imposition of sentence necessarily entail. We noted that although the Supreme Court later recognized in *United States Department of Justice v. Reporters Committee for Freedom of the Press*, 489 U.S. 749 (1989), that the dissemination of "rap sheets" implicates a privacy interest, the Court there was determining whether a "rap sheet" fell under the "privacy interest" protected by an exemption to the Freedom of Information Act ("FOIA"), not that protected by the Constitution. We pointed out that the Supreme Court itself made the distinction between the two types of privacy interest, and we quoted its statement in *Reporters*

Committee, that "[t]he question of the statutory meaning of privacy under the FOIA is, of course, not the same as the question . . . whether an individual's interest in privacy is protected by the Constitution." . . .

. . . Finally, we concluded in *E.B.* that even if a "fundamental right" were implicated, "the state's interest here would suffice to justify the deprivation." . . .

The District Court here concluded that there was no privacy interest in the plaintiffs' home addresses, stating that "[b]ecause such information is public, plaintiffs' privacy interests are not implicated." As to the argument based on the "compilation" of various information, the court held that "[i]t is of little consequence whether this public information is disclosed piecemeal or whether it is disclosed in compilation."

To the extent that plaintiffs' alleged injury stems from the disclosure of their sex offender status, alone or in conjunction with other information, the District Court's opinion is in line with other cases in this court and elsewhere holding specifically that arrest records and related information are not protected by a right to privacy. See *Fraternal Order of Police*, 812 F.2d at 117 (holding that "arrest records are not entitled to privacy protection" because they are public); *Cline v. Rogers*, 87 F.3d 176, 179 (6th Cir.) (holding that "there is no constitutional right to privacy in one's criminal record" because "arrest and conviction information are matters of public record"). . . .

We are not insensitive to the argument that notification implicates plaintiffs' privacy interest by disclosing their home addresses. The compilation of home addresses in widely available telephone directories might suggest a consensus that these addresses are not considered private were it not for the fact that a significant number of persons, ranging from public officials and performers to just ordinary folk, choose to list their telephones privately, because they regard their home addresses to be private information. Indeed, their view is supported by decisions holding that home addresses are entitled to privacy under FOIA, which exempts from disclosure personal files "the disclosure of which would constitute a clearly unwarranted invasion of personal privacy." 5 U.S.C. § 552(b)(6). . . .

Although these cases are not dispositive, they reflect the general understanding that home addresses are entitled to some privacy protection, whether or not so required by a statute. We are therefore unwilling to hold that absent a statute, a person's home address is never entitled to privacy protection. . . .

Accepting therefore the claim by the plaintiffs that there is some nontrivial interest in one's home address by persons who do not wish it disclosed, we must engage in the balancing inquiry repeatedly held appropriate in privacy cases. . . .

The nature and significance of the state interest served by Megan's Law was considered in *E.B.* There, we stated that the state interest, which we characterized as compelling, "would suffice to justify the deprivation even if a fundamental right of the registrant's were implicated." We find no reason to disagree. The public interest in knowing where prior sex offenders live so that susceptible individuals can be appropriately cautioned does not differ whether the issue is the registrant's claim under the Double Jeopardy or Ex Post Facto Clauses, or is the registrant's claim to privacy. . . .

The other argument raised by plaintiffs as part of their privacy claim is that community notification infringes upon their fundamental interest in family relationships. . . . In *E.B.*, we recognized that Megan's Law "impose[s] no restrictions on a registrant's ability to live and work in a community," but that plaintiffs complain of the law's "indirect effects: Actions that members of the community may take as a result of learning of the registrant's past, his potential danger, and his presence in the community." Even if we concede, as the District Court did, that "being subject to Megan's Law community notification places a constitutionally cognizable strain upon familial relationships," these indirect effects which follow from plaintiffs' commission of a crime are too substantially different from the government actions at issue in the prior cases to fall within the penumbra of constitutional privacy protection. Megan's Law does not restrict plaintiffs' freedom of action with respect to their families and therefore does not intrude upon the aspect of the right to privacy that protects an individual's independence in making certain types of important decisions. . . .

During the pendency of this appeal, appellants filed a series of motions under seal, six in all, seeking to supplement the record with evidence of recent incidents which have caused serious adverse consequences to them and their families. . . .

. . . [T]his court has previously held that "[t]he fact that protected information must be disclosed to a party who has a particular need for it . . . does not strip the information of its protection against disclosure to those who have no similar need," and we have required the government to implement adequate safeguards against unnecessary disclosure. Because these motions were filed in this court in the first instance, the District Court has not had the opportunity to consider the information contained therein and to determine whether any action is appropriate in light of our precedent.

[We] will remand this matter so that the District Court can consider whether plaintiffs' interest in assuring that information is disclosed only to those who have a particular need for it has been accorded adequate protection in light of the information set forth in the motions. . . .

NOTES & QUESTIONS

1. ***The Privacy Interest.*** In *Russell v. Gregoire*, 124 F.3d 1079 (9th Cir. 1997), the court considered a similar challenge under the constitutional right to information privacy to Washington's version of Megan's Law, which involved public dissemination of the offender's photo, name, age, birth date, other identifying information, and a summary of his or her crime. It includes the general vicinity of his or her residence, but not the exact address. Wash. Rev. Code § 9A.44.130(1). The court held that the statute did not run afoul of the constitutional right to information privacy:

> In this case, the collection and dissemination of information is carefully designed and narrowly limited. Even if *Whalen* and *Nixon* had established a broad right to privacy in data compilations, the Act does not unduly disseminate private information about Russell and Stearns.
>
> Moreover, any such right to privacy, to the extent it exists at all, would protect only personal information. The information collected and disseminated by the Washington statute is already fully available to the public and is not constitutionally protected, with the exception of the general vicinity of the offender's residence (which is published) and the offender's employer (which

is collected but not released to the public). Neither of these two items are generally considered "private."

Recall that in *Paul P. v. Verniero,* the court held that the reasoning of *United States Department of Justice v. Reporters Committee for Freedom of the Press*, 489 U.S. 749 (1989), was inapplicable to the constitutional right to information privacy. In *Reporters Committee*, the Court concluded that the disclosure of FBI "rap sheets" (compilations of a person's arrests, charges, and convictions) under the Freedom of Information Act (FOIA) implicated a privacy interest:

> In an organized society, there are few facts that are not at one time or another divulged to another. Thus, the extent of the protection accorded a privacy right at common law rested in part on the degree of dissemination of the allegedly private fact and the extent to which the passage of time rendered it private. . . . Recognition of this attribute of a privacy interest supports the distinction, in terms of personal privacy, between scattered disclosure of the bits of information contained in a rap sheet and revelation of the rap sheet as a whole.

The reasoning of this case suggests that sexual offenders have a privacy interest in their prior convictions. Should the reasoning of *Reporters Committee* apply to the constitutional right to information privacy?

Prior to *Paul P.*, the New Jersey Supreme Court had upheld New Jersey's Megan's Law in *Doe v. Poritz*, 662 A.2d 367 (N.J. 1995). There, the court, relying on *Reporters Committee*, recognized a privacy interest in some of the information divulged by New Jersey's Megan's Law:

> . . . We find . . . that considering the totality of the information disclosed to the public, the Notification Law implicates a privacy interest. That the information disseminated under the Notification Law may be available to the public, in some form or other, does not mean that plaintiff has no interest in limiting its dissemination. As the Court recognized in *United States Department of Justice v. Reporters Committee for Freedom of the Press*, 489 U.S. 749 (1989), privacy "encompass[es] the individual's control of information concerning his or her person." . . .
>
> . . . [T]he Court recognized a "distinction . . . between scattered disclosure of the bits of information contained in a rap sheet and revelation of the rap sheet as a whole." . . . The Court noted, furthermore, that there was a "privacy interest inherent in the nondisclosure of certain information even when the information may have been at one time public." . . .
>
> In exposing those various bits of information to the public, the Notification Law links various bits of information — name, appearance, address, and crime — that otherwise might remain unconnected. However public any of those individual pieces of information may be, were it not for the Notification Law, those connections might never be made. We believe a privacy interest is implicated when the government assembles those diverse pieces of information into a single package and disseminates that package to the public, thereby ensuring that a person cannot assume anonymity — in this case, preventing a person's criminal history from fading into obscurity and being wholly forgotten. Those convicted of crime may have no cognizable privacy interest in the fact of their conviction, but the Notification Law, given the compilation and dissemination of information, nonetheless implicates a

> privacy interest. The interests in privacy may fade when the information is a matter of public record, but they are not non-existent. . . .

The court, however, concluded that the state interest outweighed the sexual offender's privacy interest:

> There is an express public policy militating toward disclosure: the danger of recidivism posed by sex offenders. The state interest in protecting the safety of members of the public from sex offenders is clear and compelling. The Legislature has determined that there is a substantial danger of recidivism by sex offenders, and public notification clearly advances the purpose of protecting the public from that danger. . . .

Compare the treatment of *Reporters Committee* in *Paul P.* and *Poritz*. How do the cases differ in the way they deal with the import of *Reporters Committee*?[23]

2. ***Postscript to* Paul P.** Following the Third Circuit's decision in *Paul P.*, the district court on remand held that the Megan's Law regulations in New Jersey did not sufficiently protect against unauthorized disclosures. The plaintiffs had cited to 45 instances where information had been released to unauthorized persons, with one disclosure resulting in the offender's name and address being printed in an article on the front page of a newspaper. Although noting that zero leakage is unattainable, the court stated that the government must avoid "unreasonably impinging on the 'nontrivial' privacy interests" of the plaintiffs and that the current Megan's Law regulations failed to meet this standard. *Paul P. v. Farmer*, 80 F. Supp. 2d 320 (D.N.J. 2000). The state attorney general promulgated new guidelines that were approved by the district court and affirmed on appeal. *See Paul P. v. Farmer*, 227 F.3d 98 (3d Cir. 2000). The new guidelines permit two forms of notice. An "unredacted notice" contains all information. A "redacted notice" omits the specific home address of the offender as well as the name and address of the employer. To receive an unredacted notice, the recipient must sign a form agreeing to be bound by court order and submitting to the jurisdiction of the court. The recipient must agree to share information only with her household and those caring for her children. If the person refuses to sign the receipt, then she can only receive the redacted notice.

    In 2000, New Jersey amended its constitution by a referendum that provided that nothing in the New Jersey Constitution shall prohibit the disclosure of Megan's Law information over the Internet. New Jersey subsequently posted its sexual offender data on a website, excluding the offenders' current home addresses.

    In *A.A. v. New Jersey,* 341 F.3d 206 (3d Cir. 2003), the Third Circuit upheld New Jersey's Megan's Law against a privacy claim against a public Internet registry posting personal information against convicted sex offenders. The court found that the Internet registry, which contains information about

---

[23] *See also Cutshall v. Sundquist*, 193 F.3d 466 (6th Cir. 1999) (rejecting reliance on *Reporters Committee* and concluding that constitutional right to information privacy is not implicated by Megan's Law).

certain high-risk and moderate-risk sex offenders, was permissible due to the state's compelling interest to prevent sex offenses. Although the convicted sex offenders have a "nontrivial" privacy interest in their home addresses, the court concluded that a need exists to access information in a mobile society. The court stated: "Consider parents with young children who want to purchase a new home in New Jersey. Without the Registry, they would not be notified of the presence of convicted sex offenders, even those with a high risk of re-offense, until they had already purchased their new home which may be in the proximity of a Registrant's home. . . . So too a family planning a vacation at the New Jersey shore."

Like New Jersey, many states are placing their Megan's Law information on the Internet. Is such a practice going too far? Or is it necessary to make accessing the information more convenient? Consider Daniel Solove's critique of posting Megan's Law disclosures on the Internet:

> Megan's Law disclosures may be relevant for certain types of relationships, such as child care. Still, what most Megan's Laws lose sight of the use of the information in question. Megan's Law data is beneficial when disclosed for certain purposes, but not necessarily for all purposes. When placed on the Internet for any curious individual around the world to see, Megan's Law information becomes disconnected from its goals.[24]

3. ***The Breadth of Megan's Laws.*** Megan's Law does not merely involve offenses against children. It encompasses a wide range of sex offenses, which can range from sodomy, prostitution, consensual homosexual acts, masturbation in public places, flashing, and statutory rape. In some states, the disclosure does not indicate what particular sexual offense the offender committed. Is such a general listing appropriate? Is Megan's Law justified under the constitutional right to information privacy for every offense that a state classifies as a sexual offense? Or does the balance weigh in favor of Megan's Law only for specific offenses? If so, how should such offenses be distinguished from ones in which the balance does not weigh in favor of Megan's Law?[25]
4. ***Recidivism Rates.*** One of the justifications for Megan's Law is that sexual offenders have a high recidivism rate and, hence, pose a threat to the community. But sexual offenders have a lower recidivism rate than those who commit other forms of violent crime, such as robbers. In one study of offenders re-arrested within three years for any crime, previously convicted murderers had approximately a 42 percent re-arrest rate; rapists had a 51.5 percent re-arrest rate; other sexual offenders had a 48 percent re-arrest rate; and robbers had a 66 percent re-arrest rate. However, re-arrest rates, without more information, are misleading. Of the 51.5 percent of rapists who were re-

[24] Daniel J. Solove, *The Virtues of Knowing Less: Justifying Privacy Protections Against Disclosure*, 53 Duke L.J. 967, 1061 (2003).

[25] For more on the privacy implications of Megan's Laws, see Caroline Louise Lewis, *The Jacob Wetterling Crimes Against Children and Sexually Violent Offender Registration Act: An Unconstitutional Deprivation of the Right to Privacy and Substantive Due Process*, 31 Harv. C.R.-C.L. L. Rev. 89 (1996); Symposium, *Critical Perspectives on Megan's Law: Protection vs. Privacy*, 13 N.Y.L. Sch. J. Hum. Rts. 1 (1996).

arrested within three years after being released, only 7.7 percent were re-arrested for a sex crime. Further, different types of sexual offenders have different recidivism rates.[26]

5. ***Family Stigma.*** The majority of sexual offenses against children are committed by family members or close friends of the family (estimated at about 92 percent).[27] When a child's parent is released and is listed in the sex offender registry, the child's privacy can also be compromised because the entire family is under the stigma of harboring a sexual offender.

   In *Doe v. Quiring,* 686 N.W.2d 918 (S.D. 2004), a young woman, who was the victim of incest by her father, brought suit to have her father's name removed from the sex offender public registry. Among the information that the registry contains is the type of crime that the offender committed. The victim argued that "public access to incest offenders and their crimes through the Registry 'necessarily' involves the 'release of . . . identifying information regarding the victim of the crime.'" Pursuant to South Dakota's Megan's Law: "Nothing in this section allows the release of the name or any identifying information regarding the victim of the crime to any person other than law enforcement agencies, and such victim identifying information is confidential." SDCL 22-22-40. The victim contended that "because the crime of incest involves familial relationships, the very definition of the crime of incest 'so narrows the group of possible victims that identification of the victim is necessarily implicated by the name of the offense.'" The court, however, disagreed:

   > [B]ecause the Registry does not reveal the victim's familial relationship, age, physical description, address, or gender, a victim could be any one of a number of less than 21-year-old relatives of the offender. Under these circumstances, we believe that the mere listing of the offender and type of offense is not the disclosure of the "identifying information" that the Legislature intended to prohibit. . . .

   In dissent, Justices Meierhenry and Sabers argued:

   > Initially, the legislative purpose "of alerting the public in the interest of community safety" is satisfied by identifying the crime as "rape" or "sexual contact." To note the crime specifically as incest only serves to narrow the class of victims to a small number capable of being identified. The size of the class of incest victims is limited to family members. The number of family members under the age of twenty-one is even smaller and, in some cases, may include only a couple of children. Publicly identifying the crime as "incest" significantly increases the risk of providing "identifying information of the victim" and may bring opprobrium on family members who were not victims. It may also have the effect of making victims or family members reluctant to

---

[26] *See* Jane A. Small, *Who Are the People in Your Neighborhood? Due Process, Public Protection, and Sex Offender Notification Laws*, 74 N.Y.U. L. Rev. 1451 (1999). For a contrary view regarding recidivism rates for sex offenders, see Daniel L. Feldman, *The "Scarlet Letter Laws" of the 1990s: A Response to Critics*, 60 Alb. L. Rev. 1081 (1997).

[27] Michele L. Earl-Hubbard, Comment, *The Child Sex Offender Registration Laws: The Punishment, Liberty Deprivation, and Unintended Results Associated with the Scarlet Letter Laws of the 1990s*, 90 Nw. U. L. Rev. 788, 851-52 (1996).

report the crimes knowing the registry will list the crime as incest. Often incest crimes go unreported because of the fear of public exposure and embarrassment created for the family, victim, and perpetrator. Michele L. Earl-Hubbard, *The Child Sex Offender Registration Laws: The Punishment, Liberty Deprivation, and Unintended Results Associated with the Scarlet Letter Laws of the 1990s,* 90 N.W. U. L. Rev. 788, 856 (1996). As one author noted, "Ironically, Megan's Laws may stigmatize the very victims of sex offenses whom they are designed to protect, many of whom are children living in the same house as the sex offender." Daniel J. Solove, *The Virtues of Knowing Less: Justifying Privacy Protections Against Disclosure,* 53 Duke L.J. 967, 1060 (2003).

6. ***Shaming Punishments.*** In colonial America, marking criminals with branding, mutilation, or letter-wearing (such as the scarlet letter) was common. Marks would be burned into the convict's hand or forehead. This was often done because there was no way of imprisoning people. Nathaniel Hawthorne's *The Scarlet Letter* involves a famous example of a shaming punishment where Hester Prynne was made to stitch a red letter "A" to her clothing to punish her for adultery. Does Megan's Law amount to a shaming punishment? Is this form of punishment appropriate?

   Amitai Etzioni has praised shaming in the context of Megan's Law. He argues: "[S]haming is particularly communitarian in that it does not occur unless the community approves of the values at stake."[28] In his view, moreover, due to recidivism among sex offenders, a likely alternative to publicizing the presence of the sex offender in the community plus shaming will be "to keep the offender longer in jail" to protect the community. Will antisocial behavior expand in the absence of shaming?

7. ***Shaming in Other Contexts.*** Today, shaming punishments are making a comeback. In a move broader than Megan's Law, some localities are publicizing the names of certain arrestees. For example, in 1997, Kansas City created "John TV," broadcasting on television the names, photographs, addresses, and ages of people who had been arrested for soliciting prostitutes. Similar programs have been started in other cities. Is this activity more or less problematic to you than Megan's Law?

8. ***Is Megan's Law a Punishment?*** In *Smith v. Doe,* 538 U.S. 84 (2003), the Supreme Court examined whether Alaska's Megan's Law violated the constitutional prohibitions on ex post facto laws. An ex post facto law is a law that applies after the fact. In other words, the federal government and the states cannot pass a law that criminalizes past actions. Pursuant to U.S. Constitution art. I, § 9, "No . . . ex post facto Law shall be passed" by the federal government. U.S. Constitution art. I, § 10 provides that "No state shall . . . pass any . . . ex post facto Law."

   Alaska's Megan's Law makes public the following information: "name, aliases, address, photograph, physical description, description [,] license [and] identification numbers of motor vehicles, place of employment, date of birth, crime for which convicted, date of conviction, place and court of conviction,

[28] Amitai Etzioni, The *Limits of Privacy* 60-61 (1999).

length and conditions of sentence, and a statement as to whether the offender or kidnapper is in compliance with [the update] requirements . . . or cannot be located." Alaska Stat. § 18.65.087(b). The Supreme Court noted that if the sex offender registration and notification law is designed to "impose punishment," then it "constitutes retroactive punishment" and is an impermissible ex post facto law. The Court concluded that "the intent of the Alaska Legislature was to create a civil, nonpunitive regime." Further, the Court concluded that the effect of the law did not "negate Alaska's intention to establish a civil regulatory scheme." In reaching this latter conclusion, the Court dismissed an argument that Megan's Law resembles the "shaming punishments of the colonial period."

> Any initial resemblance to early punishments is, however, misleading. Punishments such as whipping, pillory, and branding inflicted physical pain and staged a direct confrontation between the offender and the public. Even punishments that lacked the corporal component, such as public shaming, humiliation, and banishment, involved more than the dissemination of information. They either held the person up before his fellow citizens for face-to-face shaming or expelled him from the community. By contrast, the stigma of Alaska's Megan's Law results not from public display for ridicule and shaming but from the dissemination of accurate information about a criminal record, most of which is already public. Our system does not treat dissemination of truthful information in furtherance of a legitimate governmental objective as punishment. On the contrary, our criminal law tradition insists on public indictment, public trial, and public imposition of sentence. Transparency is essential to maintaining public respect for the criminal justice system, ensuring its integrity, and protecting the rights of the accused. The publicity may cause adverse consequences for the convicted defendant, running from mild personal embarrassment to social ostracism. In contrast to the colonial shaming punishments, however, the State does not make the publicity and the resulting stigma an integral part of the objective of the regulatory scheme.

The Court reasoned that although the "reach of the Internet is greater than anything which could have been designed in colonial times," the goal of the notification is "to inform the public for its own safety, not to humiliate the offender. . . . The Internet makes the document search more efficient, cost effective, and convenient for Alaska's citizenry."

Justices Stevens, Ginsburg, and Breyer dissented. In Justices Ginsburg and Breyer's dissent, they observed:

> And meriting heaviest weight in my judgment, the Act makes no provision whatever for the possibility of rehabilitation: Offenders cannot shorten their registration or notification period, even on the clearest demonstration of rehabilitation or conclusive proof of physical incapacitation. However plain it may be that a former sex offender currently poses no threat of recidivism, he will remain subject to long-term monitoring and inescapable humiliation.
>
> John Doe I, for example, pleaded *nolo contendere* to a charge of sexual abuse of a minor nine years before the Alaska Act was enacted. He successfully completed a treatment program, and gained early release on supervised probation in part because of his compliance with the program's

requirements and his apparent low risk of re-offense. He subsequently remarried, established a business, and was reunited with his family. He was also granted custody of a minor daughter, based on a court's determination that he had been successfully rehabilitated. The court's determination rested in part on psychiatric evaluations concluding that Doe had "a very low risk of re-offending" and is "not a pedophile." Notwithstanding this strong evidence of rehabilitation, the Alaska Act requires Doe to report personal information to the State four times per year, and permits the State publicly to label him a "Registered Sex Offender" for the rest of his life.

9. ***Megan's Law Disclosures for All Crimes?*** A growing number of states are furnishing online databases of all of their current inmates and parolees. Do these databases serve the statutory purpose of protecting the community? Should registries of felons stop at sexual offenders? Why not all people convicted of a crime?
10. ***How Far Can Disclosure Go?*** In May 2001, Judge J. Manuel Banales of Texas ordered 21 convicted sex offenders to post signs in their front yards stating: "Danger! Registered Sex Offender Lives Here." Additionally, the offenders must place bumper stickers on their cars stating: "Danger! Registered Sex Offender in Vehicle." Other offenders were ordered to send letters to all the people who lived within three blocks of their homes. Compliance is monitored by the probation department. "The whole idea is that everybody is looking at you," Judge Banales said to the offenders. "You have no one else to blame but yourself." Under the reasoning of either *Russell* or *Paul P.*, is this court order a violation of the constitutional right to information privacy?
11. ***A Prison-Privacy Trade-off?*** Suppose that instead of enacting Megan's Laws, society just decided to extend the sentences for sexual offenses and lock up sexual offenders for life. Perhaps if states could not enact a Megan's Law, they would resort to more life sentences for sexual offenders. Most likely, many offenders would choose a regime where they would be released from prison and subject to Megan's Law to a regime where they would spend the rest of their lives in prison. What do you think about this potential trade-off?

B. GOVERNMENT RECORDS OF PERSONAL INFORMATION

1. FAIR INFORMATION PRACTICES

In the 1960s, the increasing use of computers gave rise to a significant public debate about privacy. In particular, commentators expressed opposition to the increasing amount of personal information collected by government agencies and stored in computer databases.

In 1973, the Department of Housing, Education, and Welfare (HEW) issued a highly influential report about government records maintained in computer databases. The HEW Report characterized the growing concern over privacy:

> It is no wonder that people have come to distrust computer-based record-keeping operations. Even in non-governmental settings, an individual's control over the personal information that he gives to an organization or that an organization obtains about him, is lessening as the relationship between the giver and receiver of personal data grows more attenuated, impersonal, and diffused. There was a time when information about an individual tended to be elicited in face-to-face contacts involving personal trust and a certain symmetry, or balance, between giver and receiver. Nowadays, an individual must increasingly give information about himself to large and relatively faceless institutions, for handling and use by strangers — unknown, unseen, and, all too frequently, unresponsive. Sometimes the individual does not even know that an organization maintains a record about him. Often he may not see it, much less contest its accuracy, control its dissemination, or challenge its use by others. . . .
>
> The poet, the novelist, and the social scientist tell us, each in his own way, that the life of a small-town man, woman, or family is an open book compared to the more anonymous existence of urban dwellers. Yet the individual in a small town can retain his confidence because he can be more sure of retaining control. He lives in a face-to-face world, in a social system where irresponsible behavior can be identified and called to account. By contrast, the impersonal data system, and faceless users of the information it contains, tend to be accountable only in the formal sense of the word. In practice they are for the most part immune to whatever sanctions the individual can invoke.

To remedy these growing concerns over the accumulation and use of personal information by the government, the HEW Report recommended that a Code of Fair Information Practices be established:

- There must be no personal-data record-keeping systems whose very existence is secret.
- There must be a way for an individual to find out what information about him is in a record and how it is used.
- There must be a way for an individual to prevent information about him obtained for one purpose from being used or made available for other purposes without his consent.
- There must be a way for an individual to correct or amend a record of identifiable information about him.
- Any organization creating, maintaining, using, or disseminating records of identifiable personal data must assure the reliability of the data for their intended use and must take reasonable precautions to prevent misuse of the data.[29]

---

[29] U.S. Dep't of Health, Educ. & Welfare, Records, *Computers, and the Rights of Citizens: Report of the Secretary's Advisory Comm. on Automated Personal Data Systems* 29-30, 41-42 (1973) ("HEW Report").

Fair Information Practices can be understood most simply as the rights and responsibilities that are associated with the transfer and use of personal information. Since the intent is to correct information asymmetries that result from the transfer of personal data from an individual to an organization, Fair Information Practices typically assign rights to individuals and responsibilities to organizations.

MARC ROTENBERG, *FAIR INFORMATION PRACTICES AND THE ARCHITECTURE OF PRIVACY (WHAT LARRY DOESN'T GET)*

2001 Stan. Tech. L. Rev. 1

. . . Not only have Fair Information Practices played a significant role in framing privacy laws in the United States, these basic principles have also contributed to the development of privacy laws around the world and even to the development of important international guidelines for privacy protection. The most well known of these international guidelines are the Organization for Economic Cooperation and Development's Recommendations Concerning and Guidelines Governing the Protection of Privacy and Transborder Flows of Personal Data ("OECD Guidelines"). The OECD Guidelines set out eight principles for data protection that are still the benchmark for assessing privacy policy and legislation: Collection Limitation; Data Quality; Purpose Specification; Use Limitation; Security Safeguards; Openness; Individual Participation; and Accountability. The principles articulate in only a couple of pages a set of rules that have guided the development of national law and increasingly the design of information systems.

It is generally understood that the challenge of privacy protection in the information age is the application and enforcement of Fair Information Practices and the OECD Guidelines. While some recommendations for improvement have been made, the level of consensus, at least outside of the United States, about the viability of Fair Information Practices as a general solution to the problem of privacy protection is remarkable. As recently as 1998 the OECD reaffirmed support for the 1980 guidelines, and countries that are adopting privacy legislation have generally done so in the tradition of Fair Information Practices.

While some commentators have made recommendations for updating or expanding the principles, there is general agreement that the concept of Fair Information Practices and the specific standards set out in the OECD Guidelines continue to provide a useful and effective framework for privacy protection in information systems.

Commentators have also noted a remarkable convergence of privacy policies. Countries around the world, with very distinct cultural backgrounds and systems of governance, nonetheless have adopted roughly similar approaches to privacy protection. Perhaps this is not so surprising. The original OECD Guidelines were drafted by representatives from North America, Europe, and Asia. The OECD Guidelines reflect a broad consensus about how to safeguard the control and use of personal information in a world where data can flow freely across national borders. Just as it does today on the Internet. . . .

Viewed against this background, the problem of privacy protection in the United States in the early 1990s was fairly well understood. The coverage of U.S. law was uneven: Fair Information Practices were in force in some sectors and not others. There was inadequate enforcement and oversight. Technology continued to outpace the law. And the failure to adopt a comprehensive legal framework to safeguard privacy rights could jeopardize transborder data flows with Europe and other regions. These factors should all have played a significant role in coding a solution to the privacy problem. . . .

2. THE PRIVACY ACT

Influenced by the HEW Report's Fair Information Practices and inspired by the Watergate scandal, Congress enacted the Privacy Act of 1974 four months after President Nixon resigned from office. In passing the Privacy Act, Congress found that "the privacy of an individual is directly affected by the collection, maintenance, use, and dissemination of personal information by Federal agencies" and that "the increasing use of computers and sophisticated information technology, while essential to the efficient operations of the Government, has greatly magnified the harm to individual privacy that can occur from any collection, maintenance, use, or dissemination of personal information."

Purposes of the Privacy Act. The Privacy Act's stated purposes are, among other things, to: (1) "permit an individual to determine what records pertaining to him are collected, maintained, used, or disseminated by [federal] agencies"; (2) "permit an individual to prevent records pertaining to him obtained by such agencies for a particular purpose from being used or made available for another purpose without his consent"; (3) allow an individual to access and correct his personal data maintained by federal agencies; and (4) ensure that information is "current and accurate for its intended use, and that adequate safeguards are provided to prevent misuse of such information."

Applicability and Scope. The Privacy Act applies to federal agencies. It does not apply to businesses or private sector organizations. Moreover, it does not apply to state and local agencies—only federal ones.

In order to establish a violation of the Privacy Act, a plaintiff must prove several things:

First, the plaintiff must prove that the agency violated its obligations under the Act (most often, that the agency improperly disclosed information).

Second, the information disclosed must be a "record" contained within a "system of records." A "record" must be identifiable to an individual (contain her name or other identifying information) and must contain information about the individual. § 552a(a)(4). The record must be kept as part of a "system of records," which is "a group of any records under the control of any agency from which information is retrieved by the name of the individual or by some identifying number, symbol, or other identifying particular assigned to the individual." § 552a(a)(5).

Third, to collect damages, the plaintiff must show that an adverse impact resulted from the Privacy Act violation and that the violation was "willful or intentional."

Limits on Disclosure. Pursuant to the Privacy Act:

> No agency shall disclose any record which is contained in a system of records by any means of communication to any person, or to another agency, except pursuant to a written request by, or with prior written consent of, the individual to whom the record pertains. 5 U.S.C. § 552a(b).

Responsibilities for Recordkeeping. The Privacy Act establishes restrictions and responsibilities for agencies maintaining records about individuals. Agencies shall maintain "only such information about an individual as is relevant and necessary to accomplish a purpose of the agency required to be accomplished by statute or by executive order of the President." § 552a(e)(1). Additionally, agencies shall "collect information to the greatest extent practicable directly from the subject individual when the information may result in adverse determinations about an individual's rights, benefits, and privileges under Federal programs." § 552a(e)(2). Agencies shall inform individuals who make a request about how their personal information will be used. § 552a(e)(3). Agencies must publish in the Federal Register notices about the systems of records they maintain. § 552a(e)(4). Agencies must also "establish appropriate administrative, technical, and physical safeguards to insure the security and confidentiality of records." § 552a(e)(10).

Right to Access and Correct Records. Pursuant to the federal Privacy Act, upon request, individuals can review their records and can ask that the agency correct any inaccuracies in their records. § 552a(d).

Enforcement. If an agency fails to comply with any provision of the Privacy Act, or refuses to comply with an individual's request to obtain access to her records or correct her records, individuals can bring a civil action in federal court. § 552a(g)(1). The court can enjoin the agency from withholding access of records. § 552a(g)(3). In limited circumstances, monetary damages may be awarded:

> (4) In any suit brought under the provisions of subsection (g)(1)(C) or (D) of this section in which the court determines that the agency acted in a manner which was intentional or willful, the United States shall be liable to the individual in an amount equal to the sum of—
>
> (A) actual damages sustained by the individual as a result of the refusal or failure, but in no case shall a person entitled to recovery receive less than the sum of $1,000; and
>
> (B) the costs of the action together with reasonable attorney fees as determined by the court. § 552a(g)(4).

Law Enforcement Exceptions. Pursuant to § 552a(j), the "head of any agency may promulgate rules . . . to exempt any system of records within the agency from any part of [the Privacy Act] if the system of records" is (1) maintained by the CIA or (2) maintained by a law enforcement agency and consists of (A) identifying and criminal history information compiled to identify criminal offenders or (B) "information compiled for the purpose of criminal investigation, including reports of informants and investigators, and associated with an identifiable individual"; or (C) "reports identifiable to an individual compiled at any stage of the process of enforcement of the criminal laws from arrest or indictment through release from supervision." This exception does not apply to § 552a(b), §§ 552a(c)(1) and (2), and certain portions of § 552(e).

Additionally, § 552(k)(2) allows the head of any agency to promulgate rules to exempt "investigatory material compiled for law enforcement purposes" from the Act's accounting and access provisions. However, "if any individual is denied any right, privilege, or benefit that we would otherwise be entitled by Federal law . . . as a result of the maintenance of such material, such material shall be provided to the individual, except to the extent that the disclosure of such material would reveal the identity of a [government informant]."

FOIA Exception. When FOIA requires that information be released, the Privacy Act does not apply. § 552a(b)(3).

Routine Use Exception. The broadest exception under the Privacy Act is that information may be disclosed for any "routine use" if disclosure is "compatible" with the purpose for which the agency collected the information. § 552a(b)(3).

Information Sharing Among Agencies. The Privacy Act permits one agency to disclose information "to another agency or to an instrumentality of any governmental jurisdiction within or under the control of the United States for a civil or criminal law enforcement activity" if the agency or instrumentality's head makes "a written request to the agency which maintains the record." § 552a(b)(7).

Other Exceptions. In all, there are about a dozen exceptions to the Privacy Act. Other exceptions allow disclosure to the Census Bureau, "to a person pursuant to a showing of compelling circumstances affecting the health or safety of an individual"; to Congress; to the Comptroller General, pursuant to a court order, or to a credit reporting agency. § 552a(b).

State Privacy Acts. Although every state has a statute comparable to the federal FOIA, requiring public access to government records, most states do not have a statute comparable to the federal Privacy Act. Only about a third of states have adopted such a statute.

QUINN V. STONE

978 F.2d 126 (3d Cir. 1992)

HIGGINBOTHAM, J. Appellants Randall Quinn (Quinn) and Marianne Merritt (Merritt) are married to each other and work at the Letterkenny Army Depot (LEAD) in Chambersburg, Pennsylvania as civilian employees. Appellee Michael P.W. Stone is the Secretary of the Army and the second appellee is the Department of the Army. At LEAD, Quinn is a natural resource manager and Merritt is an environmentalist. Quinn is responsible for controlling the deer population on LEAD property by setting the length of the hunting season and determining the types of deer to be killed. . . .

In addition to their professional interest in LEAD's wildlife, Quinn and Merritt are both deer hunters and hunt deer on LEAD property with other hunters. Quinn and Merritt are registered with the Pennsylvania Game Commission and possess valid Pennsylvania hunting licenses. Quinn and Merritt also have "bonus tags" which allow the holder to kill one additional deer during the hunting season. Both also possess valid LEAD hunting permits.

On January 6, 1990, Quinn and Merritt went hunting on LEAD property. At check-in Post 2, both Quinn and Merritt complied with the LEAD procedures whereby all hunters are required to produce their Pennsylvania hunting licenses and LEAD hunting permits. As part of this check-in procedure, the LEAD Security employees annotate a computer-generated hunting roster, which lists all hunters with LEAD hunting permits. Each entry on this roster corresponds to a single hunter and consists of:

a. the LEAD permit number
b. the Pennsylvania hunting license number
c. the name of the hunter
d. the address of the hunter
e. the phone number of the hunter.

The hunting roster is computer-generated at the beginning of the hunting day, with the check-in time, check-out time, and kill information added by hand as the day progresses.

The computer-generated LEAD hunting roster for January 6, 1990 incorrectly gave separate addresses and phone numbers for Quinn and Merritt. The roster indicated that Quinn lived at an address in St. Thomas, Pennsylvania and Merritt in Chambersburg, Pennsylvania. Both parties agree that Merritt's listed address was incorrect and out-of-date. Apparently, her prior address was never changed in the LEAD files, even though Merritt had written her new address on her LEAD hunting permit application, her LEAD hunting license, her application for a Pennsylvania hunting license, and her Pennsylvania hunting license for the 1988-89 and 1989-90 hunting seasons.

Two of Security personnel conducting the check-in at Post 2 during the day were Lark Myers (Myers) and Statler. Statler personally observed Quinn and Merritt checking in to hunt. Shortly after Quinn and Merritt checked in, Myers mentioned to Statler that Quinn had previously brought a deer to Myers' fiance's butcher shop to be butchered. Statler questioned how Quinn could still be hunting this season if he had already killed one deer. Statler reviewed the roster and found Quinn's name. Statler then looked for Quinn's wife's name but did not recognize Merritt's name. He then asked Myers what Quinn's wife's name was and Myers told him that she thought Merritt continued to go by the name of Merritt after her marriage to Quinn. Statler again reviewed the hunting roster and found Merritt's entry. Statler noted that the home address listed for Merritt was different from that listed for Quinn and remarked on this to Myers.

Later that morning, Statler reported to David Miller (Miller), an investigator in LEAD Security, the information that Quinn and Merritt were hunting and that they had taken a deer to be butchered earlier during the hunting season. Miller then informed Jody Eyer (Eyer), a part-time Deputy Wildlife Conservation Officer with the Pennsylvania Game Commission, of Quinn's and Merritt's hunting even though Quinn had previously killed a deer that season. Eyer believed that there were grounds to suspect that a hunting violation had occurred since a hunter is generally allowed to kill only one deer a season. Eyer contacted Statler and spoke with him directly. He also reviewed the hunting roster. Eyer turned the case over to Frank Clark (Clark), a full-time PGC Wildlife Conservation Officer, for investigation, although Eyer continued to aid in the investigation.

On January 9, 1990, LEAD's Miller met with PGC's Clark. In this meeting, Clark reviewed the hunting roster generated at Post 2 and noted the discrepancies between Quinn's and Merritt's listed addresses. To Clark, the two addresses raised the possibility that Quinn and Merritt "had used two addresses to illegally obtain two sets of hunting licenses." At this meeting, Clark requested that LEAD review available files to determine the correct addresses. LEAD investigator Fox (Fox) did so but was unable to determine the correct addresses. . . .

[After an extensive investigation, Clark concluded that there "was no evidence to charge Quinn and Merritt with hunting violations."]

The appellants allege that both suffered occupational and health damage as a result of the disclosures. Quinn alleges that he suffered damage to his professional image, reputation, integrity and working relationship with LEAD and PGC personnel. Merritt alleges that her reputation for "law-abidingness and integrity" was damaged. Quinn also alleges suffering from stress, headaches, hypertension, chest pains, sinusitis, nervousness, and inability to sleep. Merritt alleges she suffered stress, nervousness, and inability to sleep. Both allege they suffered emotional anguish.

Quinn and Merritt filed separate actions alleging violations of the Privacy Act, 5 U.S.C. § 552a, and seeking an order directing the Army to purge its files of records relating to the plaintiffs and damages for violations of the Act. The district court granted the defendants' motion to consolidate the actions and on September 18, 1991 granted the defendants' motion for summary judgment. Plaintiffs filed a timely appeal. . . .

This appeal presents several different issues relating to three of the four necessary elements for a damages suit under the Privacy Act. As we explain in this opinion, in order to maintain a suit for damages under the catch-all provision of 5 U.S.C. § 552a(g)(1)(D) for a violation of the Act's central prohibition against disclosure, § 552a(b), a plaintiff must advance evidence to support a jury's finding of four necessary elements: (1) the information is covered by the Act as a "record" contained in a "system of records"; (2) the agency "disclose[d]" the information; (3) the disclosure had an "adverse effect" on the plaintiff (an element which separates itself into two components: (a) an adverse effect standing requirement and (b) a causal nexus between the disclosure and the adverse effect); and (4) the disclosure was "willful or intentional."

The appellees first argue that the district court properly granted summary judgment because the information relating to Merritt on the LEAD hunting roster and on her time card is not information covered by the Act. We disagree.

The Act defines a "record" to mean:

> any item, collection, or grouping of information about an individual that is maintained by an agency, including, but not limited to, his education, financial transactions, medical history, and criminal or employment history and that contains his name, or the identifying particular assigned to the individual, such as a finger or voice print or a photograph.

5 U.S.C. § 552a(a)(4). Further, the Act's prohibition on disclosure relates to "any record which is contained in a system of records." § 552a(b). Fitting the statutory definitions of a protected record, the information allegedly disclosed from both the hunting roster and the time card contained an identifying particular (the plaintiff's name) and was maintained within a system of records.

Appellees propose two separate arguments that the information contained in the hunting roster is not a "record" within the meaning of the Act. First, they argue that stale or incorrect information, such as Merritt's out-of-date address and telephone number, is not covered by the Act because this information is not meaningful. We cannot accept this argument in this case. The Third Circuit has recently re-affirmed that, at the very least, there is a "meaningful" privacy interest in home addresses. *Federal Labor Relations Authority v. U.S. Department of the Navy,* 966 F.2d 747 (3d Cir. 1992) (en banc). As we noted there, the disclosure of home addresses "can identify specific and sometimes personal characteristics about residents." In the light of the other information disclosed in this case, the disclosure of the existence of an out-of-date address, different from the one at which Merritt was currently living, revealed the meaningful information that Merritt had maintained an address apart from Quinn's, an address that might be used to manipulate Pennsylvania's hunting laws. As this case demonstrates, the meaningful privacy interest in a particular piece of information may be lessened by the passage of time, but such an interest is unlikely to be extinguished. We conclude that this out-of-date home address was meaningful information and was protected by the Privacy Act.

Second, the appellees argue that the Act protects only information which discloses a characteristic or quality of an individual. The appellees contend that Merritt's information on the hunting roster did not constitute a "record" because "none of the information disclosed a characteristic or quality about her." Applying this argument also to the time card, appellees argue that "[t]he fact that an individual was working or not on a weekday is not information which discloses a characteristic [or] quality about the person."

At first blush, this argument seems close to the requirement that the information must be meaningful, but appellees here propose a different gloss on the statute than that of meaningfulness. They would read the Act to protect only that category of information which is intimate or personal, information which directly reflects a specific or personal characteristic about a person (as opposed to information which might reveal such specific and personal characteristics but only in conjunction with other pieces of information). . . .

[W]e think that such information does reveal a "quality or characteristic" about that person. Time card information regarding taking time off from work as compensation for overtime, as sick leave, or for vacation can easily be considered descriptive of an individual.

More significantly, we reject appellees' underlying argument that the information covered by the Act as a "record" is limited to the information that directly reflects a characteristic or quality of the individual. . . . [W]e find such an interpretation contrary to the language of the statute. On its face, § 552a(a)(4)'s statutory definition of a record as "any item, collection, or grouping of information about an individual" appears to us to have a broad meaning encompassing *any* information about an individual that is linked to that individual through an identifying particular and is not to be restricted to information that reflects a characteristic or quality of an individual. Moreover, our interpretation is consistent with the thrust of the statutory definition. A "record" may be "any item, collection, or grouping of information about an individual." 5 U.S.C. § 552a(a)(4). While a record can therefore consist of a single piece of information, it may also be a collection or grouping of pieces of information. Thus, even if a piece of information could not meet a "characteristic or quality" test standing alone, it could still be included within a "record" as statutorily defined and protected by the Act if that piece of information were linked with an identifying particular (or was itself an identifying particular) and maintained within a system of records.

We thus . . . conclude in this case that both the information on the hunting roster and time card was information that was covered by the Act.

Even if the information on the hunting roster and on the time card were covered by the Act, appellees make two arguments that this information was not "disclosed" within the meaning of 552a(b). The appellees contend that, while Quinn's home address and telephone number were records, they were not disclosed within the meaning of 5 U.S.C. § 552a(b) because the information had been previously disclosed by Quinn to the Pennsylvania Game Commission. Appellees argue that disclosure contemplates release of information not otherwise known to the recipient.

We agree the Act is not violated where the agency makes available information which is already known by the recipient.

There is no basis, however, in this record to make such an argument. Clearly, there was no prior knowledge of the information on the time card. Likewise, there is no evidence on this record that Eyer and Clark, the investigators in the field, already had any actual knowledge of the home address information. There is, by contrast, evidence that Eyer and Clark received the partially out-of-date information about Quinn's and Merritt's addresses by means of a disclosure of the hunting roster. Without evidence that Eyer and Clark otherwise knew the information disclosed, the appellees' argument fails.

The appellees next contend that no disclosure of information occurs when the information, even if not actually known by the recipient, is otherwise public. Appellees may be making either of two arguments here. To say that information is public can mean either that such information is readily accessible to the members of the public or that each individual member of the public should be presumed to know this information. We reject both arguments.

Appellees have cited to this court no case that stands for the proposition that there is no violation of the Act if the information is merely readily accessible to the members of the public (such as in the local telephone book) and our research has discovered none. We doubt if any court would so hold. To do so would eviscerate the Act's central prohibition, the prohibition against disclosure. For instance, such an argument would short-circuit the delicate balancing courts now engage in between the FOIA and the Privacy Act under 5 U.S.C. § 552a(b)(2). See *FLRA v. U.S. Department of the Navy,* 966 F.2d 747 (3d Cir. 1992) (en banc). To define disclosure so narrowly as to exclude information that is readily accessible to the public would render superfluous the detailed statutory scheme of twelve exceptions to the prohibition on disclosure. We conclude that making available information which is readily accessible to the members of the public is a disclosure under 552a(b), subject, of course, to the Act's exceptions. . . .

We thus conclude that not only was the information contained in the hunting roster and the time card covered by the Act, but it was also disclosed within the Act's terms.

What remains is to examine the Act's "adverse effect" requirement. The Privacy Act's civil remedies section, in relevant part, provides as follows:

> (g)(1) Civil remedies. — Whenever any agency . . .
>
> (D) fails to comply with any other provision of this section, or any rule promulgated thereunder, in such a way as to have an adverse effect on an individual,
>
> the individual may bring a civil action against the agency, and the district courts of the United States shall have jurisdiction in the matters under the provisions of this subsection.

This section thus gives an individual adversely affected by any agency violation of the Act a judicial remedy whereby the individual may seek damages. Thus, there are two limitations placed on the right to sue. First, the adverse effect requirement of (g)(1)(D) is, in effect, a standing requirement. Allegations of mental distress, emotional trauma, or embarrassment have been held sufficient to confer standing. *Albright v. United States,* 732 F.2d 181 (D.C. Cir. 1984). Second, to state a claim under the Act, the plaintiff must also allege a causal connection between the agency violation and the adverse effect. . . .

Appellees argue that neither of these two requirements were met in this case. First, they argue that Merritt makes no assertion that the release of time card information had an adverse effect on her sufficient to confer standing. Upon any fair reading of the record, however, appellees' argument cannot be sustained. As we have recounted above, both appellants allege that they have undergone stress and emotional anguish. Both also allege that they have suffered occupational losses due to the PGC investigation allegedly caused by the disclosures. We think these allegations sufficient to satisfy the Act's adverse effect standing requirement.

With greater vigor, appellees argue there is no causal connection between the disclosures and the adverse effects. They assert that the PGC's investigation was begun prior to and independent of the disclosure of the hunting roster. Appellees claim that the only information passed along to the PGC was Statler's personal observation that plaintiffs were hunting on Jan. 6, 1990 and Myers' observation that they had previously taken a deer to the butcher's. Defendants also claim that the time card disclosure had no causal connection to the adverse effects suffered by the plaintiffs.

We believe, however, that the record amply shows a causal connection between the disclosures and the alleged adverse effects on Quinn and Merritt by means of the PGC investigation. First, there is sufficient evidence for a jury to find that the PGC investigation was initially caused in significant part by the disclosure of the discrepant addresses. There is evidence that the varying addresses were passed along by LEAD Security employee Statler to Eyer of the PGC from the beginning of the investigation. . . .

A trier of fact could infer that the address discrepancy was part of the impetus for Eyer to turn the investigation over to Clark, the full-time investigator.

We thus cannot agree with the district court that the difference in addresses which initially raised the suspicion of the PGC investigator was "only a small part of his investigation." This piece of information was present from the very beginning of the investigation and may have played a significant role in the crucial decisions to initiate and pursue the investigation.

Second, there is sufficient evidence for a jury to conclude that the disclosure of Merritt's time card information served to fuel and to keep the investigation going even after the discrepancy in the addresses had been resolved. . . .

The issue of the "routine use" exception to the Act's prohibition on disclosure has been argued before this court by both parties. However, the issue was not argued before the district court in support of the defendants' motion for summary judgment and the district court did not consider the issue. We thus consider this issue waived for purposes of this appeal. . . .

We recognize that some persons might feel that a lengthy opinion such as this that explores whether or not it was permissible to reveal matters so mundane as information on a hunting record and a time card is a trivialization of the federal litigation process. However, Congress has made the choice that there are some areas of privacy which must be recognized by the federal government in its management of information and, as we read the present record, the appellants should not be precluded from proving their allegations. The district court's grant of summary judgment in favor of the appellees will be reversed in part and affirmed in part and the case remanded for further proceedings consistent with this opinion.

NYGAARD, J. dissenting. While I agree with most of the conclusions reached by the majority, because I believe that the disclosure of the contents of these records was pursuant to a "routine use," I respectfully dissent.

The Privacy Act states that records are not protected from disclosure if the disclosure is pursuant to a "routine use." 5 U.S.C. § 552a(b)(3). A routine use is defined as "the use of such record for a purpose which is compatible with the purpose for which it was collected." 5 U.S.C. § 552a(a)(7). In addition, the Privacy Act states that the agencies must publish a notice each year in the Federal Register indicating the routine uses for which protected records may be used. 5 U.S.C. § 552a(e)(4). This information must include "the categories of users and the purpose of such use." 5 U.S.C. § 552a(e)(4)(D).

In compliance with the Privacy Act, the DOD published in the Federal Register, "blanket routine uses" which are applicable to every record system maintained by its various branches, including the army.

One of these provisions entitled "Routine Use-Law Enforcement," states:

> In the event that a system of records maintained by this component to carry out its functions indicates a violation or potential violation of law . . . the relevant records in the system of records may be referred, as a routine use, to the appropriate agency, whether federal, state, local, or foreign, charged with the responsibility of *investigating or prosecuting such violation* [.] Fed. Reg., May 29, 1985. (emphasis added.) . . . .

These routine uses fairly cover the facts of this case. The disclosure of the hunting roster information was for use by the Pennsylvania Game Commission's wildlife conservation officers to investigate possible violations of state hunting laws. This was precisely the type of "state law enforcement" the regulations covered.

Here, one of the main purposes for the collection of the information on the hunting roster was to monitor hunting in order to prevent unlawful overkilling of deer. The disclosure was made to help PGC find out if appellants were trying to hunt deer lawfully. . . .

The disclosure of Merritt's time card information to PGC investigator Clark creates a tougher question. . . .

In general, the main reason time cards are collected is to determine employees' work hours in order to compute payroll. It is not to collect information about an employee which can be used against him in a criminal investigation.

Nonetheless, the *main* purpose for which time cards are collected certainly is not the *only* purpose. One of the reasons time card information is collected is to find out if an employee was at work on a given day-the precise reason for which it was used in this case. LEAD disclosed information on Merritt's time card precisely for this purpose. . . .

For this reason, I would affirm the district court's grant of summary judgment as to both Merritt's time card and the hunting roster.

NOTES & QUESTIONS

1. ***Information in the Public Domain.*** The court in *Quinn* holds that even publicly accessible information is protected against disclosure by the Privacy Act because holding otherwise "would eviscerate the Act's central prohibition, the prohibition against disclosure." The court noted that it could find no court to conclude that information already in the public domain would not be protected. Subsequently, some courts have so concluded. For example,

in *Barry v. U.S. Department of Justice*, 63 F. Supp. 2d 25 (D.D.C. 1999), the court concluded that a record widely accessible to the public was not protected by the Privacy Act. It distinguished *Quinn* along with other "decisions involving information that may have been 'public,' but that could be found only in isolated public records." The court concluded that because the record in question was publicly available in a way not "isolated or obscure," it was not protected by the Privacy Act. Did *Quinn* turn on the fact that the addresses were "obscure or isolated"? Should information already available to the public be protected against disclosure by the Privacy Act?

2. ***The "Routine Use" Exemption: "The Biggest Loophole."*** Consider Robert Gellman:

> The act limits use of personal data to those officers and employees of the agency maintaining the data who have a need for the data in the performance their duties. This vague standard is not a significant barrier to the sharing of personal information within agencies. . . . No administrative process exists to control or limit internal agency uses. Suits have been brought by individuals who objected to specific uses, but most uses have been upheld. . . .
>
> The legislation left most decisions about external uses to the agencies, and this created the biggest loophole in the law.
>
> An agency can establish a "routine use" if it determines that a disclosure is compatible with the purpose for which the record was collected. This vague formula has not created much of a substantive barrier to external disclosure of personal information. . . Later legislation, political pressures, and bureaucratic convenience tended to overwhelm the law's weak limitations. Without any effective restriction on disclosure, the Privacy Act lost much of its vitality and became more procedural and more symbolic.[30]

Other observers have noted the problematic nature of the Privacy Act's "routine use" exemption. According to the Privacy Act's language, a routine use must be "a purpose which is compatible with the purpose for which it was collected." 5 U.S.C. § 552a(7). Paul Schwartz observes:

> Not only is the "routine use" exemption applied in a fashion that ignores relevant statutory language, such agency practice continues despite prolonged and well-placed criticism of it. As early as 1977, the Privacy Protection Study Commission, a blue-ribbon commission created by Congress at the time of the Privacy Act's enactment, noted its disapproval of overbroad applications of the routine use exemption. In 1983, the House Committee on Government Operations issued a condemnation of such agency practice. Three years later, the Congressional Office of Technology Assessment complained that the routine use exemption had become "a catchall exemption." . . . David Flaherty, in a pathbreaking comparative study of data protection law, *Protecting Privacy in Surveillance Societies*, called the American routine use exemption "a huge loophole." Despite these comments, agencies continue to justify almost any use of information as a "routine use" of the data.[31]

---

[30] Robert Gellman, *Does Privacy Law Work? in Technology and Privacy: The New Landscape* (Philip E. Agre & Marc Rotenberg eds. 1997).

[31] Paul M. Schwartz, *Privacy and Participation*, 80 Iowa L. Rev. 553, 586 (1995).

Only a few courts have placed substantive limits on an agency's proposed "routine use" of personal information. Justin Franklin and Robert Bouchard conclude: "In practice, many of the cases where a 'routine use' defense is raised are resolved in favor of the government."[32]

3. ***What Is an "Agency"?*** The Privacy Act only applies to federal agencies. In *Tripp v. Executive Office of the President,* 200 F.R.D. 140 (D.D.C. 2001), Linda Tripp sued the Executive Office of the President (EOP), the Department of Defense (DOD), and the FBI. Tripp, the friend of Monica Lewinsky who secretly recorded their conversations to assist Kenneth Starr in his investigation of President Clinton, contended that the EOP, DOD, and FBI leaked confidential information about her to the media in retaliation for her role in the Clinton investigation. The EOP moved to dismiss claiming that it was not an "agency" within the meaning of the Privacy Act. The Privacy Act adopts FOIA's definition of "agency," which "includes any executive department . . . . or other establishment in the executive branch of the Government (including the Executive Office of the President), or any independent regulatory agency." 5 U.S.C. § 552(f). However, the court concluded:

   > The plain language of the Privacy Act directs one to look to the FOIA for the definition of "agency." 5 U.S.C. § 552a(1). While on its face, the FOIA states that the definition of "agency" includes the Executive Office of the President, the U.S. Supreme Court, the D.C. Circuit, and Congress, through the FOIA's legislative history, have all made it abundantly clear this does not include the Office of the President.

   Unlike the EOP, the FBI and DOD are agencies under the Privacy Act. In 2003, Tripp settled her Privacy Act suit against the Defense Department for $590,000.

4. ***What Constitutes a "Record" in a "System of Records"?*** The Privacy Act does not apply to all information or records that an agency maintains. Rather, it applies to records contained in a "system of records." A "system of records" is a group of records where data is retrieved by an individual's name or other identifying information. 5 U.S.C. § 552a(a)(4). A "record" is "any item, collection, or grouping of information about an individual . . . that contains his name [or other identifying information]." In *Albright v. United States,* 631 F.2d 915 (D.C. Cir. 1980), the court analyzed whether a videotape of a meeting constituted a "record" under the Privacy Act. The court concluded that it was: "As long as the tape contains a means of identifying an individual by picture or voice, it falls within the definition of 'record' under the Privacy Act."

---

[32] Justin D. Franklin & Robert E. Bouchard, *Guidebook to the Freedom of Information and Privacy Acts* §2:18 (2007).

DOE V. CHAO

540 U.S. 614 (2004)

SOUTER, J. The United States is subject to a cause of action for the benefit of at least some individuals adversely affected by a federal agency's violation of the Privacy Act of 1974. The question before us is whether plaintiffs must prove some actual damages to qualify for a minimum statutory award of $1,000. We hold that they must.

Petitioner Buck Doe filed for benefits under the Black Lung Benefits Act, 83 Stat. 792, 30 U.S.C. § 901 *et seq.,* with the Office of Workers' Compensation Programs, the division of the Department of Labor responsible for adjudicating it. The application form called for a Social Security number, which the agency then used to identify the applicant's claim, as on documents like "multicaptioned" notices of hearing dates, sent to groups of claimants, their employers, and the lawyers involved in their cases. The Government concedes that following this practice led to disclosing Doe's Social Security number beyond the limits set by the Privacy Act. See 5 U.S.C. § 552a(b).

Doe joined with six other black lung claimants to sue the Department of Labor, alleging repeated violations of the Act and seeking certification of a class of "'all claimants for Black Lung Benefits since the passage of the Privacy Act.'" Pet. for Cert. 6a. Early on, the United States stipulated to an order prohibiting future publication of applicants' Social Security numbers on multicaptioned hearing notices, and the parties then filed cross-motions for summary judgment. The District Court denied class certification and entered judgment against all individual plaintiffs except Doe, finding that their submissions had raised no issues of cognizable harm. As to Doe, the court accepted his uncontroverted evidence of distress on learning of the improper disclosure, granted summary judgment, and awarded $1,000 in statutory damages under 5 U.S.C. § 552a(g)(4).

A divided panel of the Fourth Circuit affirmed in part but reversed on Doe's claim, holding the United States entitled to summary judgment across the board. 306 F.3d 170 (2002). The Circuit treated the $1,000 statutory minimum as available only to plaintiffs who suffered actual damages because of the agency's violation, and then found that Doe had not raised a triable issue of fact about actual damages, having submitted no corroboration for his claim of emotional distress, such as evidence of physical symptoms, medical treatment, loss of income, or impact on his behavior. In fact, the only indication of emotional affliction was Doe's conclusory allegations that he was " 'torn . . . all to pieces' " and " 'greatly concerned and worried' " because of the disclosure of his Social Security number and its potentially " 'devastating' " consequences.

Doe petitioned for review of the holding that some actual damages must be proven before a plaintiff may receive the minimum statutory award. . . .

"[I]n order to protect the privacy of individuals identified in information systems maintained by Federal agencies, it is necessary . . . to regulate the collection, maintenance, use, and dissemination of information by such agencies." Privacy Act of 1974. The Act gives agencies detailed instructions for managing their records and provides for various sorts of civil relief to individuals aggrieved by failures on the Government's part to comply with the requirements.

Subsection (g)(1) recognizes a civil action for agency misconduct fitting within any of four categories (the fourth, in issue here, being a catchall), 5 U.S.C. §§ 552a(g)(1)(A)–(D), and then makes separate provision for the redress of each. The first two categories cover deficient management of records: subsection (g)(1)(A) provides for the correction of any inaccurate or otherwise improper material in a record, and subsection (g)(1)(B) provides a right of access against any agency refusing to allow an individual to inspect a record kept on him. . . .

Like the inspection and correction infractions, breaches of the statute with adverse consequences are addressed by specific terms governing relief:

> In any suit brought under the provisions of subsection (g)(1)(C) or (D) of this section in which the court determines that the agency acted in a manner which was intentional or willful, the United States shall be liable to the individual in an amount equal to the sum of —
>
> (A) actual damages sustained by the individual as a result of the refusal or failure, but in no case shall a person entitled to recovery receive less than the sum of $1,000; and
>
> (B) the costs of the action together with reasonable attorney fees as determined by the court. § 552a(g)(4).

Doe argues that subsection (g)(4)(A) entitles any plaintiff adversely affected by an intentional or willful violation to the $1,000 minimum on proof of nothing more than a statutory violation: anyone suffering an adverse consequence of intentional or willful disclosure is entitled to recovery. The Government claims the minimum guarantee goes only to victims who prove some actual damages. We think the Government has the better side of the argument.

To begin with, the Government's position is supported by a straightforward textual analysis. When the statute gets to the point of guaranteeing the $1,000 minimum, it not only has confined any eligibility to victims of adverse effects caused by intentional or willful actions, but has provided expressly for liability to such victims for "actual damages sustained." It has made specific provision, in other words, for what a victim within the limited class may recover. When the very next clause of the sentence containing the explicit provision guarantees $1,000 to a "person entitled to recovery," the simplest reading of that phrase looks back to the immediately preceding provision for recovering actual damages, which is also the Act's sole provision for recovering anything (as distinct from equitable relief). With such an obvious referent for "person entitled to recovery" in the plaintiff who sustains "actual damages," Doe's theory is immediately questionable in ignoring the "actual damages" language so directly at hand and instead looking for "a person entitled to recovery" in a separate part of the statute devoid of any mention either of recovery or of what might be recovered.

Nor is it too strong to say that Doe does ignore statutory language. When Doe reads the statute to mean that the United States shall be liable to any adversely affected subject of an intentional or willful violation, without more, he treats willful action as the last fact necessary to make the Government "liable," and he is thus able to describe anyone to whom it is liable as entitled to the $1,000 guarantee. But this way of reading the statute simply pays no attention to the fact that the statute does not speak of liability (and consequent entitlement to recovery) in a freestanding, unqualified way, but in a limited way, by reference to enumerated damages.

Doe's manner of reading "entitle[ment] to recovery" as satisfied by adverse effect caused by intentional or willful violation is in tension with more than the text, however. It is at odds with the traditional understanding that tort recovery requires not only wrongful act plus causation reaching to the plaintiff, but proof of some harm for which damages can reasonably be assessed. Doe, instead, identifies a person as entitled to recover without any reference to proof of damages, actual or otherwise. Doe might respond that it makes sense to speak of a privacy tort victim as entitled to recover without reference to damages because analogous common law would not require him to show particular items of injury in order to receive a dollar recovery. Traditionally, the common law has provided such victims with a claim for "general" damages, which for privacy and defamation torts are presumed damages: a monetary award calculated without reference to specific harm. . . .

This [conclusion] . . . is underscored by drafting history showing that Congress cut out the very language in the bill that would have authorized any presumed damages. The Senate bill would have authorized an award of "actual and general damages sustained by any person," with that language followed by the guarantee that "in no case shall a person entitled to recovery receive less than the sum of $1,000." S. 3418, 93d Cong., 2d Sess., § 303(c)(1) (1974). Although the provision for general damages would have covered presumed damages, this language was trimmed from the final statute, subject to any later revision that might be recommended by the Commission. The deletion of "general damages" from the bill is fairly seen, then, as a deliberate elimination of any possibility of imputing harm and awarding presumed damages. The deletion thus precludes any hope of a sound interpretation of entitlement to recovery without reference to actual damages.

Finally, Doe's reading is open to the objection that no purpose is served by conditioning the guarantee on a person's being entitled to recovery. As Doe treats the text, Congress could have accomplished its object simply by providing that the Government would be liable to the individual for actual damages "but in no case . . . less than the sum of $1,000" plus fees and costs. Doe's reading leaves the reference to entitlement to recovery with no job to do, and it accordingly accomplishes nothing. . . .

Next, Doe also suggests there is something peculiar in offering some guaranteed damages, as a form of presumed damages not requiring proof of amount, only to those plaintiffs who can demonstrate actual damages. But this approach parallels another remedial scheme that the drafters of the Privacy Act would probably have known about. At common law, certain defamation torts were redressed by general damages but only when a plaintiff first proved some "special harm," *i.e.,* "harm of a material and generally of a pecuniary nature." 3 Restatement of Torts § 575, Comments *a* and *b* (1938) (discussing defamation torts that are "not actionable per se"). Plaintiffs claiming such torts could recover presumed damages only if they could demonstrate some actual, quantifiable pecuniary loss. Because the recovery of presumed damages in these cases was supplemental to compensation for specific harm, it was hardly unprecedented for

Congress to make a guaranteed minimum contingent upon some showing of actual damages, thereby avoiding giveaways to plaintiffs with nothing more than "abstract injuries." . . .

The "entitle[ment] to recovery" necessary to qualify for the $1,000 minimum is not shown merely by an intentional or willful violation of the Act producing some adverse effect. The statute guarantees $1,000 only to plaintiffs who have suffered some actual damages.

GINSBURG, STEVENS, & BREYER, J.J. dissenting. "It is 'a cardinal principle of statutory construction' that 'a statute ought, upon the whole, to be so construed that, if it can be prevented, no clause, sentence, or word shall be superfluous, void, or insignificant.'" The Court's reading of § 552a(g)(4) is hardly in full harmony with that principle. Under the Court's construction, the words "a person entitled to recovery" have no office, and the liability-determining element "adverse effect" becomes superfluous, swallowed up by the "actual damages" requirement. Further, the Court's interpretation renders the word "recovery" nothing more than a synonym for "actual damages," and it turns the phrase "shall be liable" into "may be liable." . . .

The purpose and legislative history of the Privacy Act, as well as similarly designed statutes, are in harmony with the reading of § 552a(g)(4) most federal judges have found sound. Congress sought to afford recovery for "*any* damages" resulting from the "willful or intentional" violation of "any individual's rights under th[e] Act." § 2(b)(6), 88 Stat. 1896 (emphasis added). Privacy Act violations commonly cause fear, anxiety, or other emotional distress — in the Act's parlance, "adverse effects." Harm of this character must, of course, be proved genuine. In cases like Doe's, emotional distress is generally the only harm the claimant suffers, *e.g.,* the identity theft apprehended never materializes. . . .

The Government, although recognizing that "actual damages" may be slender and easy to generate, fears depletion of the federal fisc were the Court to adopt Doe's reading of § 552a(g)(4). Experience does not support those fears. As the Government candidly acknowledged at oral argument: "[W]e have not had a problem with enormous recoveries against the Government up to this point." No doubt mindful that Congress did not endorse massive recoveries, the District Court in this very case denied class-action certification, and other courts have similarly refused to certify suits seeking damages under § 552a(g)(4) as class actions. Furthermore, courts have disallowed the runaway liability that might ensue were they to count every single wrongful disclosure as a discrete basis for a $1,000 award.

The text of § 552a(g)(4), it is undisputed, accommodates two concerns. Congress sought to give the Privacy Act teeth by deterring violations and providing remedies when violations occur. At the same time, Congress did not want to saddle the Government with disproportionate liability. . . .

Congress has used language similar to § 552a(g)(4) in other privacy statutes. See 18 U.S.C. § 2707(c); 26 U.S.C. § 6110(j)(2); 26 U.S.C. § 7217(c) (1976 ed., Supp. V). These other statutes have been understood to permit recovery of the $1,000 statutory minimum despite the absence of proven actual damages. . . .

Doe has standing to sue, the Court agrees, based on "allegations that he was 'torn . . . all to pieces' and 'greatly concerned and worried' because of the disclosure of his Social Security number and its potentially 'devastating' consequences." Standing to sue, but not to succeed, the Court holds, unless Doe also incurred an easily arranged out-of-pocket expense. In my view, Congress gave Privacy Act suitors like Doe not only standing to sue, but the right to a recovery if the fact trier credits their claims of emotional distress brought on by an agency's intentional or willful violation of the Act. For the reasons stated in this dissenting opinion, which track the reasons expressed by Circuit Judge Michael dissenting in part in the Fourth Circuit, I would reverse the judgment of the Court of Appeals.

NOTES & QUESTIONS

1. ***Postscript.*** In subsequent litigation, the district court concluded that Buck Doe was still entitled to attorneys' fees and costs under the Privacy Act because he established that the government had willfully violated the Act. The court awarded $57,520.97 for attorneys' fees and costs. On appeal, in *Doe v. Chao*, 435 F.3d 492 (4th Cir. 2006), the Fourth Circuit held that attorneys' fees and costs could still be recovered despite failing to show actual damages. However, the court concluded that the district court erred in assessing the amount of the award because it failed to "give primary consideration to the amount of damages awarded as compared to the amount sought." On remand, the district court awarded $15,887.50 in attorneys' fees and costs to Doe's counsel.
2. ***Damages Under the Privacy Act.*** One of the difficulties in privacy cases that involve the leakage of personal information is establishing damages. In most cases, people might be made more vulnerable to harms like identity theft, but they might not yet be victimized. Damages for the violation of many Privacy Act violations will involve emotional distress rather than overt physical or psychological harm. By requiring "actual damages" in order to receive statutory damages, does the Court's holding in *Doe v. Chao* make it nearly impossible to recover for a Privacy Act violation? On the other hand, should any violation of the Privacy Act result in automatic damages for thousands of dollars?

   What constitutes "actual damages" under the Privacy Act? The *Chao* Court did not reach an opinion on the issue, noting in a footnote:

   > The Courts of Appeals are divided on the precise definition of actual damages. Compare *Fitzpatrick v. IRS,* 665 F.2d 327, 331 (11th Cir. 1982) (actual damages are restricted to pecuniary loss), with *Johnson v. Department of Treasury, IRS,* 700 F.2d 971, 972-974 (5th Cir. 1983) (actual damages can cover adequately demonstrated mental anxiety even without any out-of-pocket loss). That issue is not before us. . . . We assume without deciding that the Fourth Circuit was correct to hold that Doe's complaints in this case did not rise to the level of alleging actual damages. We do not suggest that out-of-pocket expenses are necessary for recovery of the $1,000 minimum; only that they suffice to qualify under any view of actual damages.

3. ***The Linda Tripp Case.*** Recall the Linda Tripp case above in the notes to *Quinn v. Stone.* The Department of Defense (DOD) settled the case for $590,000. In light of *Doe v. Chao,* should the DOD have settled?
4. ***Willful vs. Negligent Violations of the Privacy Act.*** In *Andrews v. Veterans Administration*, 838 F.2d 418 (10th Cir. 1988), an employee of the Veterans Administration (VA) was responding to a FOIA request for proficiency reports of various nurses. The VA employee attempted to redact the identities of nurses from the reports, but failed to do so properly. As a result, several nurses could be identified on their reports. At trial, the district court concluded that the nurses "suffered some degree of anguish, embarrassment, or other mental trauma" from the disclosure and that the VA employee "acted conscientiously, in good faith, though inadvertently negligently, in releasing the proficiency reports in an inadequately sanitized condition." Furthermore, the district court concluded that the VA was grossly negligent in failing to adequately train the employee about the release of personal information. On appeal, the Tenth Circuit concluded that the disclosure of the information was improper. The identities of the nurses were protected under Exemption 6 of FOIA. However, the VA, despite acting with gross negligence, could not be held liable to the nurses:

> . . . [E]ven if the Privacy Act is violated, no punishment may be imposed unless the agency acted in a manner which was intentional or willful. In this case the district court equated "intentional or willful" with gross negligence. . . .
>
> . . . [T]he term "willful or intentional" clearly requires conduct amounting to more than gross negligence. We are persuaded by the District of Columbia Circuit's definitions of willful or intentional that contemplate action "so 'patently egregious and unlawful' that anyone undertaking the conduct should have known it 'unlawful,'" or conduct committed "without grounds for believing it to be lawful" or action "flagrantly disregarding others' rights under the Act," and we adopt those definitions, and add the view . . . that the conduct must amount to, at the very least, reckless behavior. Those, and similar definitions, describe conduct more extreme than gross negligence.
>
> Applying that standard to this case, our review of the record convinces us that the VA's conduct falls far short of a "willful or intentional" violation of the Privacy Act. Indeed, we find that it falls short of even the gross negligence standard applied by the district court to that conduct. . . .

According to Paul Schwartz, "individuals who seek to enforce their rights under the Privacy Act face numerous statutory hurdles, limited damages, and scant chance to affect an agency's overall behavior."[33] The most common form of improper disclosure of records is due to carelessness rather than willful behavior. Does the requirement that disclosure be done "willfully and intentionally" make damages under the Privacy Act virtually impossible to collect? What if the standard for collecting damages were negligence? Would agencies that must handle millions of records and respond to thousands of FOIA requests be exposed to too great a risk of liability?

Consider Robert Gellman:

---

[33] Paul M. Schwartz, *Privacy and Participation*, 80 Iowa L. Rev. 553, 596 (1995).

> The Privacy Act contains civil and criminal penalties for violations, but it is far from clear that the enforcement methods are useful. . . . In more than 20 years, federal prosecutors have brought no more than a handful of criminal cases, and perhaps only one, under the Privacy Act.
>
> The basic method for enforcing the Privacy Act is the individual lawsuit. Aggrieved individuals can sue the government for violations. . . . The former General Counsel to the Privacy Protection Study Commission testified that the act was "to a large extent, unenforceable by individuals." The main reasons are that it is difficult to recover damages and that limited injunctive relief is available under the law. Individual enforcement does not offer any significant incentive for agencies to comply more carefully with the Privacy Act's provisions.[34]

5. ***The Interaction Between the Privacy Act and FOIA.*** The Privacy Act does not apply to information that must be disclosed pursuant to FOIA. § 552a(k)(1). However, if one of FOIA's privacy exceptions applies, then the Privacy Act would require that the government refrain from disclosing certain information.

United States Dep't of Defense v. Federal Labor Relations Authority, 510 U.S. 487 (1994), clearly illustrates the interaction between these two statutes. There, two local unions requested the names and home addresses of employees in federal agencies. The agencies disclosed the employees' names and work stations to the unions but refused to release their home addresses. The unions filed unfair labor practice charges with the Federal Labor Relations Authority (FLRA), arguing that federal labor law required the agencies to disclose the addresses. Pursuant to the Federal Service Labor-Management Relations Statute, 5 U.S.C. §§ 7101–7135, agencies must, "to the extent not prohibited by law," furnish unions with data necessary for collective-bargaining purposes. § 7114(b)(4). The agencies argued that disclosure of the home addresses was prohibited by the Privacy Act. The Court agreed with the agencies:

> The employee addresses sought by the unions are "records" covered by the broad terms of the Privacy Act. Therefore, unless FOIA would require release of the addresses, their disclosure is "prohibited by law," and the agencies may not reveal them to the unions.
>
> We turn, then, to FOIA. . . . The exemption potentially applicable to employee addresses is Exemption 6, which provides that FOIA's disclosure requirements do not apply to "personnel and medical files and similar files the disclosure of which would constitute a clearly unwarranted invasion of personal privacy." 5 U.S.C. § 552(b)(6).
>
> Thus, although this case requires us to follow a somewhat convoluted path of statutory cross-references, its proper resolution depends upon a discrete inquiry: whether disclosure of the home addresses "would constitute a clearly unwarranted invasion of [the] personal privacy" of bargaining unit employees within the meaning of FOIA. . . .

---

[34] Robert Gellman, *Does Privacy Law Work?* in *Technology and Privacy: The New Landscape* (Philip E. Agre & Marc Rotenberg eds. 1997).

We must weigh the privacy interest of bargaining unit employees in nondisclosure of their addresses against the only relevant public interest in the FOIA balancing analysis — the extent to which disclosure of the information sought would "she[d] light on an agency's performance of its statutory duties" or otherwise let citizens know "what their government is up to."

The relevant public interest supporting disclosure in this case is negligible, at best. Disclosure of the addresses might allow the unions to communicate more effectively with employees, but it would not appreciably further "the citizens' right to be informed about what their government is up to." Indeed, such disclosure would reveal little or nothing about the employing agencies or their activities. . . .

Against the virtually nonexistent FOIA-related public interest in disclosure, we weigh the interest of bargaining unit employees in nondisclosure of their home addresses. . . .

It is true that home addresses often are publicly available through sources such as telephone directories and voter registration lists, but "[i]n an organized society, there are few facts that are not at one time or another divulged to another." *Reporters Comm.* The privacy interest protected by Exemption 6 "encompass[es] the individual's control of information concerning his or her person." An individual's interest in controlling the dissemination of information regarding personal matters does not dissolve simply because that information may be available to the public in some form. Here, for the most part, the unions seek to obtain the addresses of nonunion employees who have decided not to reveal their addresses to their exclusive representative. . . . Whatever the reason that these employees have chosen not to become members of the union or to provide the union with their addresses, however, it is clear that they have *some* nontrivial privacy interest in nondisclosure, and in avoiding the influx of union-related mail, and, perhaps, union-related telephone calls or visits, that would follow disclosure.

Many people simply do not want to be disturbed at home by work-related matters. . . . Moreover, when we consider that other parties, such as commercial advertisers and solicitors, must have the same access under FOIA as the unions to the employee address lists sought in this case, it is clear that the individual privacy interest that would be protected by nondisclosure is far from insignificant.

Because the privacy interest of bargaining unit employees in nondisclosure of their home addresses substantially outweighs the negligible FOIA-related public interest in disclosure, we conclude that disclosure would constitute a "clearly unwarranted invasion of personal privacy." 5 U.S.C. § 552(b)(6). FOIA, thus, does not require the agencies to divulge the addresses, and the Privacy Act, therefore, prohibits their release to the unions. . . .

Suppose the agencies opted not to litigate and disclosed the addresses of their employees. Would an employee have a cause of action under the Privacy Act for the disclosure of her address? Would that employee likely prevail in such an action? What type of remedy could the employee obtain?

6. ***The Complementary Values of the Privacy Act and FOIA.*** Although the Privacy Act restricts disclosures and the FOIA promotes disclosures, Marc Rotenberg contends that these statutes promote "complementary values." He observes:

> In enacting both the Privacy Act of 1974 and adopting the amendments that same year which significantly strengthened the Freedom of Information Act, Congress sought to ensure that personal information collected and maintained by federal agencies would be properly protected while also seeking to ensure that public information in the possession of federal agencies would be widely available to the public. The complementary goals of safeguarding individual liberty and ensuring government accountability were enabled by legislation that protected privacy on the one hand and promoted government oversight on the other.[35]

7. ***The Accuracy of the National Crime Information Center Database.*** In 2003, the Justice Department stated that the FBI would no longer be required to ensure the accuracy of its National Crime Information Center (NCIC) database, which consists of nearly 40 million criminal records. The NCIC provides access to fingerprints, mug shots, people with outstanding arrest warrants, missing persons, suspected terrorists, and gang members. The NCIC database is used by law enforcement officials around the country. Under the Privacy Act, can the FBI be exempted from maintaining the accuracy of NCIC?

8. ***Government Access to Private Sector Databases.*** The Privacy Act also applies to private companies that contract with the government to administer systems of records. 5 U.S.C. § 552a(m). However, as Christopher Hoofnagle observes, "a database of information that originates at a [commercial data broker] would not trigger the requirements of the Privacy Act." Hoofnagle goes on to observe:

> This limitation to the Privacy Act is critical — it allows [commercial data brokers] to amass huge databases that the government is legally prohibited from creating. Then, when the government needs the information, it can request it from the [commercial data broker].[36]

9. ***Law Enforcement Access to Privacy Act Records.*** After 9/11, there were extensive complaints about restrictions on the ability of agencies to share personal information. To what extent does the Privacy Act permit such information sharing? Examine § 552a(b)(7).

10. ***The First Amendment Restriction.*** Pursuant to the Privacy Act, 5 U.S.C. § 552a(e)(7), agencies shall

> maintain no record describing how any individual exercises rights guaranteed by the First Amendment unless expressly authorized by statute or by the individual about whom the record is maintained or unless pertinent to and within the scope of an authorized law enforcement activity.

In *Becker v. Internal Revenue Service,* 34 F.2d 398 (7th Cir. 1994), three brothers, Thomas, Jeffrey, and Steven Becker, sought to have IRS records

---

[35] Marc Rotenberg, *Privacy and Secrecy After September 11*, 86 Minn. L. Rev. 1115, 1129 (2002).

[36] Christopher Jay Hoofnagle, *Big Brother's Little Helpers: How ChoicePoint and Other Commercial Data Brokers Collect and Package Your Data for Law Enforcement*, 29 N.C. J. Int'l L. & Com. Reg. 595, 623 (2004).

about them expunged pursuant to the Privacy Act. The files pertained to a criminal investigation of their failure to pay taxes and their activities as "tax protestors." Some of the records in the IRS's files pertained to the brothers' First Amendment rights, such as "a flyer advertising a book and a collection of newspaper articles regarding various IRS actions against certain individuals and groups who are alleged tax protesters or cheats."

The district court concluded that maintaining these materials in the Beckers' records "unquestionably implies that they are associated with the tax protesters and cheats described in the newspaper articles" and thus describes "how the plaintiffs exercise their First Amendment rights of speech and association." However, the district court concluded that the documents are "pertinent to and within the scope of an authorized law enforcement activity." Accordingly, the district court concluded, "the IRS may lawfully maintain these records and may withhold this information from plaintiffs under the Privacy Act pursuant to 5 U.S.C. § 552a(k)(2)." Section 552a(k)(2) allows agencies to exempt certain systems of records from individual access. The IRS claimed that it exempted the records because "to grant access to an investigative file could interfere with investigative and enforcement proceedings . . . and disclose investigative techniques and procedures."

The Seventh Circuit, however, concluded that § 551a(k)(2) does not allow agencies to be exempt from the First Amendment activities exclusion. The court noted that these documents were contained in files closed several years ago, and that the Beckers' ultimate objective was to have the records removed from their files, not just to gain access. The court reasoned:

> We conclude that the IRS has not sufficiently justified the maintenance of the documents in the Beckers' files. The IRS asserts that it may maintain these articles for possible future uses. Under some circumstances, this may be a legitimate justification for maintaining documents in a file for an extended period of time. We have examined the material, and any thought that it could be helpful in future enforcement activity concerning the Beckers is untenable. The material consists of newspaper articles dating from the middle to late 1980s, with no reference to the Beckers; any potential advantage to having these documents in the Beckers' files, at some uncertain date, is minuscule (and the IRS does not elaborate on how this material would be helpful). This indefinite use must be viewed in light of the fact that Judge Alesia found the Beckers' First Amendment rights are implicated. As the Senate Report on the Privacy Act pointed out,
>
> > This section's [5 U.S.C. § 552a(e)(7)] restraint is aimed particularly at preventing collection of protected information not immediately needed, about law-abiding Americans, on the off-chance that Government or the particular agency might possibly have to deal with them in the future. S. Rep. No. 1183, 93d Cong., 2d Sess., *reprinted in* 1974 U.S.C.C.A.N. 6916, 6971.
>
> There is a remote possibility that a part of the newspaper articles (describing practices of tax protesters) would be helpful in investigation of persons in general. We are not, however, presented with a situation where documents are maintained in a general file rather than in a specific individual's file.

> Because we conclude that the IRS has not carried its burden in establishing that the materials are exempt from Privacy Act requirements, the documents should be expunged. . . .

Consider the following case, which came to a different conclusion regarding the First Amendment restriction:

J. RODERICK MACARTHUR FOUNDATION V. FEDERAL BUREAU OF INVESTIGATION

102 F.3d 600 (D.C. Cir. 1996)

GINSBURG, J. . . . The J. Roderick MacArthur Foundation and its former president Lance E. Lindblom seek to compel the Federal Bureau of Investigation to expunge its records relating to their associational activities and to refrain from maintaining such records in the future. Lindblom invokes both the Privacy Act, 5 U.S.C. § 552a, and the First Amendment to the Constitution of the United States; the Foundation relies solely upon the first amendment. . . .

As president of the Foundation, which provides grants to organizations involved with various political, social, and economic issues, Lindblom occasionally met with foreign leaders and political dissidents. At some point Lindblom's associations caught the attention of the FBI. When Lindblom and the Foundation later got wind of the FBI's interest they asked the Bureau, pursuant to the Freedom of Information Act, 5 U.S.C. § 552(a), for copies of all documents it had relating to them. The FBI informed them that it had a file on Lindblom consisting of 23 pages of materials and that, although the FBI did not have a file on the Foundation, it had located in other files five pages on which the Foundation's name appears. . . . The FBI released redacted copies of several of the documents relating to Lindblom and the Foundation but refused to release others. . . . At least some of the documents that the FBI released from the Lindblom file refer to Lindblom's associational activities. . . .

Section (e)(7) of the [Privacy] Act provides in relevant part that a government agency "shall . . . maintain no record describing how any individual exercises rights guaranteed by the First Amendment unless . . . pertinent to and within the scope of an authorized law enforcement activity." 5 U.S.C. § 552a(e)(7). . . .

Lindblom does not challenge the FBI's having collected information about him, and we assume that the information was pertinent to an authorized law enforcement activity when it was collected. Lindblom's claim is that an agency may not maintain (that is, retain) such lawfully collected information unless there is a current law enforcement necessity to do so. More specifically, he claims that "information which may have been properly collected as part of a legitimate law enforcement investigation may not be permanently kept under the name of the individual, especially when that individual is not the target of the investigation." . . .

Lindblom's primary assertion, that the Act forbids maintenance of information about first amendment activities unless that information serves a "current law enforcement necessity," requires more extended analysis. . . .

Looking at the terms of § (e)(7), we find no support for Lindblom's argument that the Act authorizes an agency to maintain a record describing first amendment activities only if and so long as there is a "current law enforcement necessity" to do so. The noun "record" in § (e)(7) is modified in only two ways: the record must be "[1] pertinent to and [2] within the scope of an authorized law enforcement activity." We do not understand this to mean, as Lindblom would in essence require, that the record must be pertinent to an active investigation; "an authorized law enforcement activity" such as foreign counter-intelligence, is a concept far broader than either an active investigation or a "current law enforcement necessity." . . .

Information that was pertinent to an authorized law enforcement activity when collected does not later lose its pertinence to that activity simply because the information is not of current interest (let alone "necessity") to the agency — a point seemingly lost upon our dissenting colleague. . . .

. . . Lindblom's interpretation of the Act would place new and daunting burdens, both substantive and administrative, upon the FBI and other government agencies, with little or no gain to individual privacy. If a law enforcement agency were required to purge its files of information regarding an individual so requesting whenever it had closed a particular investigation, then its ability to accomplish its mission would inevitably suffer. As we have said before, intelligence gathering is "akin to the construction of a mosaic"; to appreciate the full import of a single piece may require the agency to take a broad view of the whole work. Suppose, for example, that a citizen is contacted by a foreign agent but the FBI, after investigation, determines that the contact is innocent. If the same individual is later contacted by another foreign agent and perhaps thereafter by a third, then what had earlier appeared to be innocent when viewed in isolation may, when later viewed as part of a larger whole, acquire a more sinister air. Simply put, information that was once collected as part of a now-closed investigation may yet play a role in a new or reopened investigation. If the earlier record had been purged, however, then the agency's later investigation could not be informed by the earlier event(s).

Furthermore, if federal law enforcement agencies were required upon request to purge all such records, then they would surely be inundated with requests to do so. Responding to each such request could be difficult and time-consuming. . . . [W]e are reluctant to think that the Congress required so formidable an undertaking, with so little potential benefit, absent a clear statement to that effect. . . .

Accordingly, we hold that the Privacy Act does not prohibit an agency from maintaining records about an individual's first amendment activities if the information was pertinent to an authorized law enforcement activity when the agency collected the information. The Act does not require an agency to expunge records when they are no longer pertinent to a current law enforcement activity. . . .

The Foundation and Lindblom both claim that the FBI violated the first amendment by creating files on them based upon their associational activity. The FBI responds that it has no file on the Foundation and that its maintenance of lawfully gathered information about Lindblom does not violate his rights under the first amendment. We need not, however, decide whether the FBI violated the Constitution because the appellants lack standing so to claim.

"In order to establish standing under Article III, a complainant must allege (1) a personal injury-in-fact that is (2) 'fairly traceable' to the defendant's conduct and (3) redressable by the relief requested." *Branton v. FCC,* 993 F.2d 906 (D.C. Cir. 1992). The injury-in-fact requirement has two elements: The plaintiff must show that it has suffered "an invasion of a legally protected interest which is (a) concrete and particularized and (b) actual or imminent, not conjectural or hypothetical." *Lujan v. Defenders of Wildlife,* 504 U.S. 555, 560 (1992).

Consider first the case of the Foundation. It claims to have been injured because the FBI's maintenance of records on the Foundation inhibited its pursuit of activities protected by the first amendment. More specifically, the Foundation claims that the FBI's maintenance of records regarding the Foundation (1) may deter potential grantees from seeking money from the Foundation and (2) may make it more difficult for current Foundation employees to find jobs elsewhere in the future. . . .

The affiants declare, among other things, that "in the close-knit philanthropic community, an FBI file potentially limits the future employability of foundation personnel" and that "it is likely that some grantees' behavior will be affected by the maintenance of FBI files on foundations."

These affidavits speak broadly of stigma and harm to the Foundation's reputation. A "potential" limitation upon employees' future "employability" lacks concreteness. The Foundation points to not a single Foundation employee whose job prospects have been dimmed because of the FBI records. Nor does either affidavit indicate even generally how "some grantees' behavior will be affected" by the FBI records on the Foundation. The Foundation does not point to a single grantee or even type of grantee that would be any less likely to seek money from the Foundation because the FBI maintains records on it. This is not enough to establish an injury to the Foundation.

The Foundation's claim of injury also lacks immediacy. Because the Foundation does not allege that it has yet suffered any injury in the form of diminished job prospects for its employees or decreased interest from potential grantees, its only hope for standing rests upon showing that a threatened harm is "*certainly* impending." It is not enough for the Foundation to assert that it might suffer an injury in the future, or even that it is likely to suffer an injury at some unknown future time. Such "someday" injuries are insufficient. . . .

Lindblom also raises a first amendment claim, but he offers no separate arguments or affidavits in support of his standing. . . . Lindblom does not claim that the FBI's interest in him has limited or may limit his prospects for employment. . . . Lindblom has failed to show that he has suffered any injury in his individual capacity, we hold that Lindblom lacks standing to press a constitutional claim against the FBI. . . .

TATEL, J. concurring in part and dissenting in part. . . . The statute defines "maintain" as including both "maintain" and "collect." 5 U.S.C. § 552a(a)(3) (1994). To collect means "to gather together." To maintain means "to keep in existence or continuance; preserve." *Random House Unabridged Dictionary* 403, 1160 (2d ed.1993).In order to give each of these verbs its meaning, I would interpret section (e)(7), as a whole, to require that records be pertinent to "an authorized law enforcement activity" — words undefined in the statute — not only at the time of gathering, i.e., collecting, but also at the time of keeping, i.e., maintaining. In other words, if there is no *current* law enforcement activity to which a record has pertinence, the agency may not maintain it. Not only does this approach avoid effectively reading the word "maintain" out of that term's statutory definition, but it furthers the Act's purpose to protect citizens from the unnecessary collection *and* retention of personal information by the government. . . .

Because Congress chose to use the word "maintain" in section (e)(7), and to define that term as both "maintain" and "collect," we know that Congress must have meant something more than just "collect." . . .

Congress passed the Privacy Act to give individuals some defenses against governmental tendencies towards secrecy and "Big Brother" surveillance. *See* S. Rep. No. 93-1183, at 1 (Privacy Act "is designed to prevent the kind of illegal, unwise, overbroad, investigation and record surveillance of law-abiding citizens produced in recent years from actions of some over-zealous investigators, and the curiosity of some government administrators, or the wrongful disclosure and use, in some cases, of personal files held by Federal agencies."). The fewer unnecessary files describing First Amendment activities the government keeps on law-abiding citizens, the lesser the chance of any future abuse of those files.

NOTES & QUESTIONS

1. ***The Scope of the First Amendment Restriction.*** Which court, *Becker* or *MacArthur Foundation,* comes to a more convincing interpretation of the First Amendment restriction? Based on the *MacArthur Foundation* court's interpretation, to what would the First Amendment restriction apply?
2. ***The Fourth Amendment and Information Collection and Recordkeeping.*** Does the Fourth Amendment have any applicability in this context? Or does the Fourth Amendment only focus on information gathering activities?
3. ***What Constitutes "Law Enforcement Activity" Under § 552a(e)(7)?*** In *Bassiouni v. FBI,* 436 F.3d 712 (7th Cir. 2006), a law professor sought to have his records amended or expunged pursuant to the Privacy Act. Mahmoud Cherif Bassiouni, a DePaul University law professor, obtained access to FBI records about himself. The records listed groups labeled as "terrorist" groups, including the Popular Front for the Liberation of Palestine, a group currently designated by the Department of State as a terrorist group. The records did not conclude that Bassiouni was a member of any of these groups. The FBI stated "that it does not suspect him of ties to terrorist groups." Contending that he was not a member of these groups, Bassiouni demanded that the FBI amend or expunge his records because they were outdated and inaccurate. Among other things, Bassiouni contended that the maintenance of the records was a violation of § 552a(e)(7). The court, however, disagreed because § 552a(e)(7) does not apply to information "pertinent to and within the scope of an authorized law enforcement activity." According to the court:

In this case, the Bureau, through Special Agent Krupkowski's declaration, identifies the ways in which Mr. Bassiouni's file is related to its law enforcement activities. First, the FBI notes its ongoing investigations into the threats posed by terrorist groups, specifically those originating in the Middle East. According to the declaration, "the FBI has amended its investigative priorities, naming as its number one priority to 'protect the United States from terrorist attack.'" Because of the nature of these investigative activities, and because of the breadth of Mr. Bassiouni's contacts with the Middle East, the FBI anticipates that it will continue to receive information about Mr. Bassiouni. The Bureau's file on Mr. Bassiouni will provide context for evaluating that new information.

Perhaps more importantly, the public Krupkowski Declaration states that the records are important for evaluating the continued reliability of its intelligence sources. The Declaration explains that the process of verifying source information, and therefore determining whether a source is reliable, takes place over "years, even decades." . . .

We believe that the purposes identified by the Bureau fall within "authorized law enforcement activity" conducted by the FBI. We note at the outset that the realm of national security belongs to the executive branch, and we owe considerable deference to that branch's assessment in matters of national security. Furthermore, although the Privacy Act certainly does not authorize collection and maintenance of information of private citizens on the "off-hand" chance that such information may someday be useful, it does not require law enforcement agencies to purge, on a continuous basis, properly collected information with respect to individuals that the agency has good reason to believe may be relevant on a continuing basis in the fulfillment of the agency's statutory responsibilities. The Privacy Act does not give any indication that Congress intended law enforcement agencies to begin from scratch with every investigation. Nor do we believe that Congress meant to deprive such agencies of the benefit of historical analysis.

Mr. Bassiouni, however, urges us to reject the proffered law enforcement justifications as inadequate. He maintains, first, that, in order to fall within the law enforcement exception of (e)(7) the FBI must be "*currently* involved in a law enforcement investigation of Plaintiff." However, as we have noted already, no court that has considered the meaning of law enforcement activity in (e)(7) has interpreted the term so narrowly.

3. THE USE OF GOVERNMENT DATABASES

(a) The Computer Matching and Privacy Protection Act

In 1977 the federal government initiated Project Match, a program where it compared computer employee records to records of people receiving benefits through Aid to Families with Dependent Children to detect fraud. This was considered by the government to be exempted from the Privacy Act under the "routine use" exception. According to Priscilla Regan:

> . . . The scope of computer matches . . . raises Fourth Amendment questions. Computer matches are generalized electronic searches of millions of records. Under the Fourth Amendment, the Supreme Court has determined that searches must not be overly inclusive; no "fishing expeditions" or "dragnet investigations" are allowed. Yet in computer matches, many people who have

> not engaged in fraud or are not actually suspected of criminal activity are subject to the computer search. This raises questions about the presumption of innocence, as reflected in Fourth and Fifth Amendment case law. If matches are considered a Fourth Amendment search, then some limitations on the breadth of the match and/or justifications for a match are necessary. For example, a government agency could be required to show that a less intrusive means of carrying out the search was not available and that procedural safeguards limiting the dangers of abuse and agency discretion were applied. Additionally, procedural safeguards are required under due process protections. A final constitutional issue is whether matching conflicts with the equal protection clause because categories of people, not individual suspects, are subject to computer matches. Two groups — federal employees and welfare recipients — are most often the subjects of computer matching.
>
> Despite these arguments about the constitutionality of computer matches, the courts have generally not upheld individual privacy claims in cases challenging computer-matching programs. Moreover, there has been little litigation in this area for two reasons. First, the damage requirements of the Privacy Act are so difficult to prove that they serve as a deterrent to its use. . . . Secondly, in large-scale computer matching, single individuals are rarely sufficiently harmed to litigate claims and most individuals are not even aware of the match. . . .[37]

In 1988, Congress passed the Computer Matching and Privacy Protection Act (CMPPA), Pub. L. No. 100-503, to regulate the practice of computer matching. The CMPPA amends the Privacy Act and provides that in order for agencies to disclose records to engage in computer matching programs, they must establish "a written agreement between the source agency and the recipient agency or non-Federal agency stating" the purpose and legal authority for the program, a justification for the program, a description of the records to be matched, procedures for the accuracy of the information, and prohibitions on redisclosure of the records. § 552a(o)(1). These agreements must be available upon request to the public.

The CMPPA establishes Data Integrity Boards within each agency to oversee matching, requires agencies to perform a cost-benefit analysis of proposed matching endeavors, and requires agencies to notify individuals of the termination of benefits due to computer matching and permit them an opportunity to refute the termination. § 552a(p).

Is computer matching a violation of the Fourth Amendment? If you believe that matching contravenes the Fourth Amendment, are the due process rights provided by the CMPPA sufficient to cure the constitutional deficiencies?[38]

[37] Priscilla Regan, *Legislating Privacy* 89-90 (1995).

[38] For an interesting account of the psychological effects and other harms caused by endeavors such as computer matching on welfare recipients, see John Gilliom, *Overseers of the Poor: Surveillance, Resistance, and the Limits of Privacy* (2001).

(b) Airline Passenger Screening

THE 9/11 COMMISSION REPORT

Excerpts from pp. 1-4, 392-95 (2004)

Boston: American 11 and United 175. [Mohamed] Atta and [Abdul Aziz al] Omari boarded a 6:00 A.M. flight from Portland [Maine] to Boston's Logan International Airport.

When he checked in for his flight to Boston, Atta was selected by a computerized prescreening system known as CAPPS (Computer Assisted Passenger Prescreening System), created to identify passengers who should be subject to special security measures. Under the security rules in place at the time, the only consequence of Atta's selection by CAPPS was that his checked bags were held off the plane until it was confirmed that he boarded the aircraft. This did not hinder Atta's plans. . . .

While Atta had been selected by CAPPS in Portland, three members of his hijacking team — Suqami, Wail al Shehri, and Waleed al Shehri — were selected in Boston. Their selection affected only the handling of their checked bags, not their screening at the checkpoint.

Washington Dulles: American 77. Hundreds of miles southwest of Boston, at Dulles International Airport . . . five more men were preparing to take their early morning flight. At 7:15, a pair of them, Khalid al Mihdhar and Majed Moqed, checked in at the American Airlines ticket counter for Flight 77, bound for Los Angeles. Within the next 20 minutes, they would be followed by Nani Hanjour and two brothers, Nawaf al Hazmi and Salem al Hazmi.

Hani Hanjour, Khalid al Mihdhar, and Majed Moqed were flagged by CAPPS. The Hazmi brothers were also selected for extra scrutiny by the airline's customer service representative at the check-in counter. He did so because one of the brothers did not have photo identification nor could he understand English, and because the agent found both of the passengers to be suspicious. The only consequence of their selection was that their checked bags were held off the plane until it was confirmed that they had boarded the aircraft. . . .

[Overall, on] 9/11, the 19 hijackers were screened by a computer-assisted screening system called CAPPS. More than half were identified for further inspection, which applied only to their checked luggage.

Under current practices, air carriers enforce government orders to stop certain known and suspected terrorists from boarding commercial flights and to apply secondary screening procedures to others. The "no-fly" and "automatic selectee" lists include only those individuals who the U.S. government believes pose a direct threat of attacking aviation.

Because air carriers implement the program, concerns about sharing intelligence information with private firms and foreign countries keep the U.S. government from listing all terrorist and terrorist suspects who should be included. The TSA has planned to take over this function when it deploys a new screening system to take the place of CAPPS. The deployment of this system has been delayed because of claims it may violate civil liberties.

Recommendation: Improved use of "no-fly" and "automatic selectee" lists should not be delayed while the argument about a successor to CAPPS continues. This screening function should be performed by the TSA, and it should utilize the larger set of watchlists maintained by the federal government. Air carriers should be required to supply the information needed to test and implement this new system. . . .

NOTES & QUESTIONS

1. ***False Positives.*** The 9/11 Report mentioned the number of "hits" that the CAPPS system made, flagging more than half of the 19 terrorists. Each day, there are approximately 1.9 million airline passengers. Imagine a false positive rate of just 1 percent, which by current estimates of such rates would be quite a good rate. At a 1 percent error rate, 19,000 people would be flagged as false positives. Merely talking about the "hits" rather than the "misses" paints only a partial picture of the effectiveness of the system.

   After 9/11, the airline screening system incorrectly singled out a number of high-profile individuals. For example, Senator Edward Kennedy (D-Mass.) and Rep. Donald E. Young (R-Alaska) were tapped for secondary screening. Cat Stevens, a singer who now goes by the name Yusuf Islam, was placed on the no-fly list. According to *Time* magazine, this incident rested in a spelling mistake: "According to aviation sources with access to the list, there is no Yusuf Islam on the no-fly registry, though there is a 'Youssouf Islam.'" The article goes on, however, to state that the U.S. Transportation Safety Administration "alleges that Islam has links to terrorist groups, which he has denied; British foreign minister Jack Straw said the TSA action 'should never have been taken.'"[39]

   Supporters of computerized airline screening argue that even with a significant number of false positives, CAPPS is useful in singling out passengers for extra scrutiny, since the most extensive screening cannot be done on 1.9 million passengers each day.

   Some argue that if the government were able to collect more data, the false positives would drop. Is the answer obtaining more data? Are screening systems like CAPPS effective security measures? Bruce Schneier, a noted security expert, discusses whether a system like CAPPS might in the end be worth the trade-offs:

   > System like CAPPS will be likely to single out lone terrorists who meet the profile, or a terrorist group whose entire membership fits the profile, or copycat terrorist groups without the wisdom, time, and resources to probe [the system]. But terrorists are a surprisingly diverse group . . . CAPPS works best combined with random screening.

   Schneier also notes two basic problems with CAPPS. First, it can be probed. In other words, "a terrorist organization can probe the system repeatedly and identify which of its people, or which ticket characteristics, are

[39] Sally B. Donnelly, *You Say Yusuf, I Say Youssouf* . . . , Time.com, Sept. 25, 2004, www.time.com/time/nation/article/0,8599,702062,00.html.

less likely to be searched." Second, a system "that is more likely to select a certain class of passenger is also less likely to select other classes of passengers."[40] As a consequence, terrorists who do not fit a profile may slip by unnoticed.

2. ***The Evolution of Airline Passenger Screening.*** Since September 11th, the government has been attempting to design an airline passenger screening program. In 2001, the FAA created two lists — a list of people who were barred from flying and a list of people selected for secondary screening. In 2002, the Transportation Security Administration (TSA) was created, and it took over the security functions from the FAA. The Terrorist Screening Center in the FBI maintains the no-fly list as well as the selectee list. The no-fly list, which had only 16 names on it in 2001, now has over 20,000 names. The precise number remains unknown. The names on these lists are kept secret.

In 2003, the federal government announced the creation of CAPPS II, which was to be the successor to CAPPS. CAPPS II would have classified people according to their "threat level" when flying. Passengers would be classified as green, yellow, or red. Green passengers would be screened normally; yellow ones would be given extra scrutiny; and red passengers would not be allowed to fly.

Critics of CAPPS II criticized the lack of transparency in the system. They objected that the data used in the profiling along with the factors that go into the profiles would not be publicly disclosed. What are the costs and benefits of requiring public disclosure of the types of information and the logic used in the profiling?

In July 2004, the government announced that it was abandoning CAPPS II. Shortly thereafter, the Transportation Security Agency proposed a new screening system called "Secure Flight." This system has also been troubled. It was suspended in 2006, revised, and is not yet operational. One official estimate predicts it will not yet start until 2010. On February 28, 2008, the General Accountability Office reported to Congress on Secure Flight: "While TSA has made considerable progress in the development and implementation of Secure Flight, it has not fully addressed program management issues including (1) developing cost and schedule estimates consistent with best practices, (2) fully implementing its risk management plan, (3) developing a comprehensive testing strategy, and (4) ensuring that information security requirements are fully implemented."[41]

Some argue that the benefit of a computerized airline passenger screening system is that without such a system, more individuals must be subjected to extensive searching. With the system, only those individuals profiled as a risk will be subject to extra scrutiny. Therefore, airline screening systems such as Secure Flight protect privacy by narrowing the number of people who must be intrusively searched. On the other hand, the system has costs in terms of both

---

[40] Bruce Schneier, *Beyond Fear* 164-65 (2003).

[41] GAO, *Aviation Security: Transportation Security Administration Has Strengthened Planning to Guide Investments in Key Aviation Security Programs, but More Work Remains*, GAO-08-456T (Feb. 28, 2008).

privacy and equality. Privacy is affected not just in a search, but in the gathering of data for profiling. Equality is implicated because some passengers, very possibly based on race and nationality, will be treated differently than other passengers. How do you weigh the costs and benefits? What about the people who are banned from flying? What kind of legal challenge would they have?

3. ***PNR Data.*** Airline passenger screening systems rely on passenger name record (PNR) data, which commercial airlines maintain for each passenger. This record includes financial information, such as credit card numbers, as well as itineraries for travel, phone numbers, and any special meal requests. After 9/11, the government requested that airlines turn over their PNR data. Although sharing the information with the government was not authorized in their privacy policies, many airlines willingly complied. Is it problematic for the government to have PNR data? What can be learned about an individual through PNR data?

   In 2005, it was revealed that the FBI was keeping 257.5 million PNR records on people who flew between June and September 2001.[42] To what extent does the Privacy Act restrict the FBI from retaining this information?

(c) Government Data Mining

Data mining involves examining personal information in databases to look for patterns or unusual activity, or to identify links between a suspect and other individuals. Computer matching programs are an example of data mining — they seek to detect fraud by making comparisons in personal information residing in different databases.

Total Information Awareness. In 2002, the press reported that the Department of Defense was developing a project called "Total Information Awareness" (TIA), headed by Admiral John Poindexter. TIA would consist of a database of dossiers of people constructed with information about their finances, education, travel, health, and more. The information would be obtained from various private sector companies. The information would then be used to profile people to single out those engaged in terrorist activities. TIA generated a significant public outcry, and the Senate amended its spending bill early in 2003 to bar funding for TIA until the details of the program were explained to Congress.

In its report to Congress on May 20, 2003, the Department of Defense renamed the program "Terrorism Information Awareness" and stated that the program would be protective of privacy. Later in 2003, the Senate voted to deny funding for TIA. According to some media reports, however, classified part of the federal budget still contain funding for certain aspects of TIA.[43] What laws or constitutional rights would be implicated by TIA or a similar program?

Consider K.A. Taipale:

---

[42] Leslie Miller, *FBI Keeping Records on Pre-9/11 Travelers*, Associated Press, Jan. 14, 2005.

[43] Ira S. Rubinstein, Ronald D. Lee & Paul M. Schwartz, *Data Mining and Internet Profiling*, 75 U. Chi. L. Rev. 261, 265 (2008).

> [I]t is my view that the recent defunding of DARPA's Information Awareness Office ("IAO") and its Terrorism Information Awareness program and related projects will turn out to be a pyrrhic "victory" for civil liberties as the program provided a focused opportunity around which to publicly debate the rules and procedures for the future use of these technologies and, importantly, to oversee the development of the appropriate technical features required to support any concurred upon implementation or oversight policies to protect privacy.[44]

Daniel Solove predicted in 2004 that TIA was far from dead:

> . . . TIA is only one part of the story of government access to personal information and its creation of dossiers on American citizens. In fact, for quite some time, the government has been increasingly contracting with businesses to acquire databases of personal information. Database firms are willing to supply the information and the government is willing to pay for it. Currently, government agencies such as the FBI and IRS are purchasing databases of personal information from private-sector companies. A private company called ChoicePoint, Inc. has amassed a database of 10 billion records and has contracts with at least 35 federal agencies to share the data with them. . . .
>
> Thus, we are increasingly seeing collusion, partly voluntary, partly coerced, between the private sector and the government. While public attention has focused on the Total Information Awareness project, the very same goals and techniques of the program continue to be carried out less systematically by various government agencies and law enforcement officials. We are already closer to Total Information Awareness than we might think.[45]

Pattern-Based vs. Subject-Based Data Mining. There are at least two general types of data mining. "Subject-based" data mining involves searching the data of a specific identified person. It might involve examining whom that person associates and does business with. "Pattern-based" data mining involves starting with a particular profile for terrorist activity and then analyzing databases to see which individuals' patterns of activity match that profile. Do these forms of data mining present different privacy concerns? If so, what are they? How should each type of data mining be regulated?

DATA MINING: FEDERAL EFFORTS COVER A WIDE RANGE OF USES

U.S. General Accountability Office, excerpt from pp. 2-3 (May 2004)

Federal agencies are using data mining for a variety of purposes, ranging from improving service or performance to analyzing and detecting terrorist patterns and activities. Our survey of 128 federal departments and agencies on their use of data mining shows that 52 agencies are using or are planning to use data mining. These departments and agencies reported 199 data mining efforts, of which 68 were planned and 131 were operational. . . .

The Department of Defense reported having the largest number of data mining efforts aimed at improving service or performance and at managing

[44] K.A. Taipale, *Data Mining and Domestic Security: Connecting the Dots to Make Sense of Data*, 5 Colum. Sci. & Tech. L. Rev. 9-12 (2003).

[45] Daniel J. Solove, *The Digital Person: Technology and Privacy in the Information Age* 169, 175 (2004).

human resources. Defense was also the most frequent user of efforts aimed at analyzing intelligence and detecting terrorist activities, followed by the Departments of Homeland Security, Justice, and Education. . . .

Data mining efforts for detecting criminal activities or patterns, however, were spread relatively evenly among the reporting agencies.

In addition, out of all 199 data mining efforts identified, 122 used personal information. For these efforts, the primary purposes were detecting fraud, waste, and abuse; detecting criminal activities or patterns; analyzing intelligence and detecting terrorist activities; and increasing tax compliance.

Agencies also identified efforts to mine data from the private sector and data from other federal agencies, both of which could include personal information. Of 54 efforts to mine data from the private sector (such as credit reports or credit card transactions), 36 involve personal information. Of 77 efforts to mine data from other federal agencies, 46 involve personal information (including student loan application data, bank account numbers, credit card information, and taxpayer identification numbers).

Data mining enables corporations and government agencies to analyze massive volumes of data quickly and relatively inexpensively. The use of this type of information retrieval has been driven by the exponential growth in the volumes and availability of information collected by the public and private sectors, as well as by advances in computing and data storage capabilities. In response to these trends, generic data mining tools are increasingly available for — or built into — major commercial database applications. Today, mining can be performed on many types of data. . . .

MARY DEROSA, DATA MINING AND DATA ANALYSIS FOR COUNTERTERRORISM

Center for Strategic and International Studies (CSIS) 6-8 (2004)

A relatively simple and useful data-analysis tool for counterterrorism is subject-based "link analysis." This technique uses aggregated public records or other large collections of data to find links between a subject — a suspect, an address, or other piece of relevant information — and other people, places, or things. This can provide additional clues for analysts and investigators to follow. Link analysis is a tool that is available now and is used for, among other things, background checks of applicants for sensitive jobs and as an investigatory tool in national security and law enforcement investigations.

A hindsight analysis of the September 11 attacks provides an example of how simple, subject-based link analysis could be used effectively to assist investigations or analysis of terrorist plans. By using government watch list information, airline reservation records, and aggregated public record data, link analysis could have identified all 19 September 11 terrorists — for follow-up investigation — before September 11. The links can be summarized as follows:

Direct Links — Watch List Information

- Khalid Almihdhar and Nawaf Alhazmi, both hijackers of American Airlines (AA) Flight 77, which crashed into the Pentagon, appeared on a U.S.

government terrorist watch list. Both used their real names to reserve their flights. . . .

Link Analysis — One Degree of Separation

- Two other hijackers used the same contact address for their flight reservations that Khalid Almihdhar listed on his reservation. These were Mohamed Atta, who hijacked AA Flight 11, which crashed into the World Trade Center North Tower, and Marwan Al Shehhi, who hijacked UA Flight 175.
- Salem Alhazmi, who hijacked AA Flight 77, used the same contact address on his reservation as Nawaf Alhazmi.
- The frequent flyer number that Khalid Almihdhar used to make his reservation was also used by hijacker Majed Moqed to make his reservation on AA Flight 77.
- Hamza Alghamdi, who hijacked UA Flight 175, used the same contact address on his reservation as Ahmed Alghamdi used on his.
- Hani Hanjour, who hijacked AA Flight 77, lived with both Nawaf Alhazmi and Khalid Almihdhar, a fact that searches of public records could have revealed. . .

Thus, if the government had started with watch list data and pursued links, it is at least possible that all of the hijackers would have been identified as subjects for further investigation. Of course, this example does not show the false positives — names of people with no connection to the terror attacks that might also have been linked to the watch list subjects.

Pattern-based data analysis also has potential for counterterrorism in the longer term, if research on uses of those techniques continues. . . . [D]ata-mining research must find ways to identify useful patterns that can predict an extremely rare activity — terrorist planning and attacks. It must also identify how to separate the "signal" of pattern from the "noise" of innocent activity in the data. One possible advantage of pattern-based searches — if they can be perfected — would be that they could provide clues to "sleeper" activity by unknown terrorists who have never engaged in activity that would link them to known terrorists. Unlike subject-based queries, pattern-based searches do not require a link to a known suspicious subject.

Types of pattern-based searches that could prove useful include searches for particular combinations of lower-level activity that together are predictive of terrorist activity. For example, a pattern of a "sleeper" terrorist might be a person in the country on a student visa who purchases a bomb-making book and 50 medium-sized loads of fertilizer. Or, if the concern is that terrorists will use large trucks for attacks, automated data analysis might be conducted regularly to identify people who have rented large trucks, used hotels or drop boxes as addresses, and fall within certain age ranges or have other qualities that are part of a known terrorist pattern. Significant patterns in e-mail traffic might be discovered that could reveal terrorist activity and terrorist "ringleaders." Pattern-based searches might also be very useful in response and consequence management. For example, searches of hospital data for reports of certain combinations of symptoms, or of other databases for patterns of behavior, such as pharmaceutical purchases or work absenteeism might provide an early signal of a terrorist attack using a biological weapon. . . .

NOTES & QUESTIONS

1. ***The TAPAC Committee Report.*** The Technology and Privacy Advisory Committee (TAPAC) was appointed by Secretary of Defense Donald Rumsfeld to examine the privacy implications of data mining. In its report, it noted that TIA was "a flawed effort to achieve worthwhile ends. It was flawed by its perceived insensitivity to critical privacy issues, the manner in which it was presented to the public, and the lack of clarity and consistency with which it was described." The report recommended:

   > If the data mining is limited to searches based on particularized suspicion about a specific individual, we believe existing law should govern. Because, by definition, there is enough evidence about such a person to warrant further investigation, and that investigation is clearly subject to the protections of the Fourth Amendment, supplemented by federal statutes, we rely on existing law. We understand this category of data mining to include searches seeking to identify or locate a specific individual (e.g., a suspected terrorist) from airline or cruise ship passenger manifests or other lists of names or other non-sensitive information about U.S. persons. . . .
   >
   > For all other government data mining that involves personally identifiable information about U.S. persons, we recommend below that the government be required to first establish a predicate demonstrating the need for the data mining to prevent or respond to terrorism, and second, unless exigent circumstances are present, obtain authorization from the Foreign Intelligence Surveillance Court for its data mining activities. As we stress, that authorization may be sought either for programs that include data mining known or likely to include information on U.S. persons, or for specific applications of data mining where the use of personally identifiable information concerning U.S. persons is clearly anticipated. Legislation will be required for the Foreign Intelligence Surveillance Court to fulfill the role we recommend.[46]

   The TAPAC Report's central recommendation is for a secret Foreign Intelligence Surveillance Act (FISA) court to approve various data mining projects. Is this a viable way to regulate data mining?

2. ***The Markle Foundation Reports.*** The Markle Foundation, a private sector philanthropic organization, established a Task Force on National Security in the Information Age that has issued two reports about government data mining. In these reports, the Markle Task Force is enthusiastic about the potential benefits of government data mining and recommends moving ahead with projects that will draw on this technique. The Markle Task Force recommends that government have ready access to private sector databases,

---

[46] Technology and Privacy Advisory Committee (TAPAC), *Safeguarding Privacy in the Fight Against Terrorism*, vii-x, 45-49 (2004).

but that the databases not be combined into a centralized database like the one envisioned for TIA:

> Attempting to centralize [databases of personal] information is not the answer because it would not link the information to the dispersed analytical capabilities of the network. Centralization could also lead to information becoming obsolete, since a centralized analytical entity would not have the ability to keep up-to-date much of the information collected from dispersed sources. . . .
>
> Our Task Force's fundamental objective, then, is to identify the technological tools and infrastructure, the policies, and the processes necessary to link these different communities so that important information can be shared among the people who need it, and as rapidly as possible. . . .
>
> Today, the private sector is on the frontline of the homeland security effort. Its members are holders of the data that may prove crucial to identifying and locating terrorists or thwarting terrorist attacks. . . . We therefore start from the premise that the government must have access to that information, which is needed to protect our country, and that through a combination of well-crafted guidelines, careful articulation of the types of information needed for identified purposes, and effective oversight using modern information technology, it will be possible to assure that government gets that information in a way that protects our essential liberties.[47]

Is decentralization sufficient to safeguard privacy? While mentioning privacy and civil liberty concerns, the Markle Foundation Task Force does not suggest much in the way of legal controls, but it mentions the possibility of technology to help protect privacy. The report does not, however, explain what concrete limitations should be established to protect privacy.

3. ***The CMPPA and Government Data Mining.*** To what extent does the Computer Matching and Privacy Protection Act (CMPPA) regulate government data mining? Consider the view of the Markle Foundation:

> Based upon past applications of the routine use exception [to the Privacy Act], it seems likely that future government initiatives promoting increased interagency information sharing to protect national security will meet with little resistance. A routine use need only meet [two requirements] to be valid: (1) compatible with the purpose of the information collection and (2) published in the Federal Register. . . .
>
> In today's age of information, data mining has the potential to become one of the government's most powerful tools for analyzing information on terrorism. Congress, however, has restricted the kinds of data mining federal agencies can do. In 1977, the Department of Health, Education, and Welfare initiated Project Match to identify federal employees fraudulently receiving welfare payments. . . . Over the next decade, such computer matching became pervasive. In a 1986 study, the Office of Technology Assessment reported that in 1984, eleven cabinet level departments and four independent agencies conducted 110 separate computer matching programs, consisting of 700 total matches and involving seven billion records. . . .

---

[47] Markle Foundation Task Force, *Creating a Trusted Information Network for Homeland Security* 14-15 (2003).

> The widespread disclosure of information across agencies promoted Congress to act in 1988. To address these problems, Congress amended the Privacy Act by passing the Computer Matching Act, which precluded government agencies from treating computer matching as a routine use in most cases. Congress, however, explicitly excluded "matches performed for foreign counterintelligence purposes or to produce background checks for security clearances of Federal personnel." . . . Thus, so long as an agency lists something like "analyzing information to improve national security or prevent terrorism" as a routine use for the agency's information, a counterterrorism intelligence agency should be able to data mine the agency's records.[48]

4. ***The Privacy Act and Government Data Mining.*** What, if any, limits would the Privacy Act place on the kinds of government data mining discussed earlier in this section? Do any other laws discussed thus far regulate the practice?

Consider the following observation by Stewart Baker in the Markle Foundation Report regarding the limitations of the Privacy Act:

> [The Privacy Act] requirements are just restrictive enough to make it awkward for the government to take direct access of private databases for data-mining analysis. As a result, one of the emerging solutions being adopted by the government is to encourage or even require industry to keep the databases in private hands, run pattern recognition themselves, and report suspicious results to the government. . . . [T]his approach has been used in the anti-money-laundering context. The Administration has discussed adopting similar approaches with respect to other records that might be of interest in counter-terrorism investigations.[49]

UNITED STATES V. SOKOLOW

490 U.S. 1 (1989)

Respondent Andrew Sokolow was stopped by Drug Enforcement Administration (DEA) agents upon his arrival at Honolulu International Airport. The agents found 1,063 grams of cocaine in his carry-on luggage. When respondent was stopped, the agents knew, *inter alia,* that (1) he paid $2,100 for two airplane tickets from a roll of $20 bills; (2) he traveled under a name that did not match the name under which his telephone number was listed; (3) his original destination was Miami, a source city for illicit drugs; (4) he stayed in Miami for only 48 hours, even though a round-trip flight from Honolulu to Miami takes 20 hours; (5) he appeared nervous during his trip; and (6) he checked none of his luggage. A divided panel of the United States Court of Appeals for the Ninth Circuit held that the DEA agents did not have a reasonable suspicion to stop respondent, as required by the Fourth Amendment. 831 F.2d 1413 (CA9 1987). We take the contrary view.

---

[48] Markle Foundation Task Force, *Protecting America's Freedom in the Information Age* 131 (2002).

[49] Markle Foundation Task Force, *Protecting America's Freedom in the Information Age* 169 (2002).

This case involves a typical attempt to smuggle drugs through one of the Nation's airports. On a Sunday in July 1984, respondent went to the United Airlines ticket counter at Honolulu Airport, where he purchased two round-trip tickets for a flight to Miami leaving later that day. The tickets were purchased in the names of "Andrew Kray" and "Janet Norian" and had open return dates. Respondent paid $2,100 for the tickets from a large roll of $20 bills, which appeared to contain a total of $4,000. He also gave the ticket agent his home telephone number. The ticket agent noticed that respondent seemed nervous; he was about 25 years old; he was dressed in a black jumpsuit and wore gold jewelry; and he was accompanied by a woman, who turned out to be Janet Norian. Neither respondent nor his companion checked any of their four pieces of luggage.

After the couple left for their flight, the ticket agent informed Officer John McCarthy of the Honolulu Police Department of respondent's cash purchase of tickets to Miami. Officer McCarthy determined that the telephone number respondent gave to the ticket agent was subscribed to a "Karl Herman," who resided at 348-A Royal Hawaiian Avenue in Honolulu. Unbeknownst to McCarthy (and later to the DEA agents), respondent was Herman's roommate. The ticket agent identified respondent's voice on the answering machine at Herman's number. Officer McCarthy was unable to find any listing under the name "Andrew Kray" in Hawaii. McCarthy subsequently learned that return reservations from Miami to Honolulu had been made in the names of Kray and Norian, with their arrival scheduled for July 25, three days after respondent and his companion had left. He also learned that Kray and Norian were scheduled to make stopovers in Denver and Los Angeles.

On July 25, during the stopover in Los Angeles, DEA agents identified respondent. He "appeared to be very nervous and was looking all around the waiting area." Later that day, at 6:30 p.m., respondent and Norian arrived in Honolulu. As before, they had not checked their luggage. Respondent was still wearing a black jumpsuit and gold jewelry. The couple proceeded directly to the street and tried to hail a cab, where Agent Richard Kempshall and three other DEA agents approached them. Kempshall displayed his credentials, grabbed respondent by the arm, and moved him back onto the sidewalk. Kempshall asked respondent for his airline ticket and identification; respondent said that he had neither. He told the agents that his name was "Sokolow," but that he was traveling under his mother's maiden name, "Kray."

Respondent and Norian were escorted to the DEA office at the airport. There, the couple's luggage was examined by "Donker," a narcotics detector dog, which alerted on respondent's brown shoulder bag. The agents arrested respondent. He was advised of his constitutional rights and declined to make any statements. The agents obtained a warrant to search the shoulder bag. They found no illicit drugs, but the bag did contain several suspicious documents indicating respondent's involvement in drug trafficking. The agents had Donker reexamine the remaining luggage, and this time the dog alerted on a medium-sized Louis Vuitton bag. By now, it was 9:30 p.m., too late for the agents to obtain a second warrant. They allowed respondent to leave for the night, but kept his luggage. The next morning, after a second dog confirmed Donker's alert, the agents obtained a warrant and found 1,063 grams of cocaine inside the bag.

Respondent was indicted for possession with the intent to distribute cocaine in violation of 21 U.S.C. § 841(a)(1). The United States District Court for Hawaii denied his motion to suppress the cocaine and other evidence seized from his luggage, finding that the DEA agents had a reasonable suspicion that he was involved in drug trafficking when they stopped him at the airport. . . .

The United States Court of Appeals for the Ninth Circuit reversed respondent's conviction by a divided vote, holding that the DEA agents did not have a reasonable suspicion to justify the stop. The majority divided the facts bearing on reasonable suspicion into two categories. In the first category, the majority placed facts describing "ongoing criminal activity," such as the use of an alias or evasive movement through an airport; the majority believed that at least one such factor was always needed to support a finding of reasonable suspicion. In the second category, it placed facts describing "personal characteristics" of drug couriers, such as the cash payment for tickets, a short trip to a major source city for drugs, nervousness, type of attire, and unchecked luggage. The majority believed that such characteristics, "shared by drug couriers and the public at large," were only relevant if there was evidence of ongoing criminal behavior and the Government offered "[e]mpirical documentation" that the combination of facts at issue did not describe the behavior of "significant numbers of innocent persons." Applying this two-part test to the facts of this case, the majority found that there was no evidence of ongoing criminal behavior, and thus that the agents' stop was impermissible. . . .

Our decision . . . turns on whether the agents had a reasonable suspicion that respondent was engaged in wrongdoing when they encountered him on the sidewalk. In *Terry v. Ohio,* 392 U.S. 1 (1968), we held that the police can stop and briefly detain a person for investigative purposes if the officer has a reasonable suspicion supported by articulable facts that criminal activity "may be afoot," even if the officer lacks probable cause.

The officer, of course, must be able to articulate something more than an "inchoate and unparticularized suspicion or 'hunch.'" The Fourth Amendment requires "some minimal level of objective justification" for making the stop. That level of suspicion is considerably less than proof of wrongdoing by a preponderance of the evidence. We have held that probable cause means "a fair probability that contraband or evidence of a crime will be found," *Illinois v. Gates,* 462 U.S. 213 (1983), and the level of suspicion required for a *Terry* stop is obviously less demanding than that for probable cause. . . .

In evaluating the validity of a stop such as this, we must consider "the totality of the circumstances — the whole picture." . . .

The rule enunciated by the Court of Appeals, in which evidence available to an officer is divided into evidence of "ongoing criminal behavior," on the one hand, and "probabilistic" evidence, on the other, is not in keeping with the quoted statements from our decisions. It also seems to us to draw a sharp line between types of evidence, the probative value of which varies only in degree. The Court of Appeals classified evidence of traveling under an alias, or evidence that the suspect took an evasive or erratic path through an airport, as meeting the test for showing "ongoing criminal activity." But certainly instances are conceivable in which traveling under an alias would not reflect ongoing criminal activity: for example, a person who wished to travel to a hospital or clinic for an operation and wished to concealed that fact. One taking an evasive path through an airport might be seeking to avoid a confrontation with an angry acquaintance or with a creditor. This is not to say that each of these types of evidence is not highly probative, but they do not have the sort of ironclad significance attributed to them by the Court of Appeals.

On the other hand, the factors in this case that the Court of Appeals treated as merely "probabilistic" also have probative significance. Paying $2,100 in cash for two airplane tickets is out of the ordinary, and it is even more out of the ordinary to pay that sum from a roll of $20 bills containing nearly twice that amount of cash. Most business travelers, we feel confident, purchase airline tickets by credit card or check so as to have a record for tax or business purposes, and few vacationers carry with them thousands of dollars in $20 bills. We also think the agents had a reasonable ground to believe that respondent was traveling under an alias; the evidence was by no means conclusive, but it was sufficient to warrant consideration. While a trip from Honolulu to Miami, standing alone, is not a cause for any sort of suspicion, here there was more: surely few residents of Honolulu travel from that city for 20 hours to spend 48 hours in Miami during the month of July.

Any one of these factors is not by itself proof of any illegal conduct and is quite consistent with innocent travel. But we think taken together they amount to reasonable suspicion. Indeed, *Terry* itself involved "a series of acts, each of them perhaps innocent" if viewed separately, "but which taken together warranted further investigation." . . .

We do not agree with respondent that our analysis is somehow changed by the agents' belief that his behavior was consistent with one of the DEA's "drug courier profiles." A court sitting to determine the existence of reasonable suspicion must require the agent to articulate the factors leading to that conclusion, but the fact that these factors may be set forth in a "profile" does not somehow detract from their evidentiary significance as seen by a trained agent. . . .

We hold that the agents had a reasonable basis to suspect that respondent was transporting illegal drugs on these facts. . . .

MARSHALL & BRENNAN, J.J. dissenting. Because the strongest advocates of Fourth Amendment rights are frequently criminals, it is easy to forget that our interpretations of such rights apply to the innocent and the guilty alike. In the present case, the chain of events set in motion when respondent Andrew Sokolow was stopped by Drug Enforcement Administration (DEA) agents at Honolulu International Airport led to the discovery of cocaine and, ultimately, to Sokolow's conviction for drug trafficking. But in sustaining this conviction on the ground that the agents reasonably suspected Sokolow of ongoing criminal activity, the Court diminishes the rights of *all* citizens "to be secure in their persons," U.S. Const., Amdt. 4, as they traverse the Nation's airports. Finding this result constitutionally impermissible, I dissent.

The Fourth Amendment cabins government's authority to intrude on personal privacy and security by requiring that searches and seizures usually be supported by a showing of probable cause. The reasonable-suspicion standard is a derivation of the probable-cause command, applicable only to those brief detentions which fall short of being full-scale searches and seizures and which are necessitated by law enforcement exigencies such as the need to stop ongoing crimes, to prevent imminent crimes, and to protect law enforcement officers in highly charged situations. By requiring reasonable suspicion as a prerequisite to such seizures, the Fourth Amendment protects innocent persons from being subjected to "overbearing or harassing" police conduct carried out solely on the basis of imprecise stereotypes of what criminals look like, or on the basis of irrelevant personal characteristics such as race.

To deter such egregious police behavior, we have held that a suspicion is not reasonable unless officers have based it on "specific and articulable facts." It is not enough to suspect that an individual has committed crimes in the past, harbors unconsummated criminal designs, or has the propensity to commit crimes. On the contrary, before detaining an individual, law enforcement officers must reasonably suspect that he is engaged in, or poised to commit, a criminal act *at that moment*. . . .

Evaluated against this standard, the facts about Andrew Sokolow known to the DEA agents at the time they stopped him fall short of reasonably indicating that he was engaged at the time in criminal activity. It is highly significant that the DEA agents stopped Sokolow because he matched one of the DEA's "profiles" of a paradigmatic drug courier. In my view, a law enforcement officer's mechanistic application of a formula of personal and behavioral traits in deciding whom to detain can only dull the officer's ability and determination to make sensitive and fact-specific inferences "in light of his experience," *Terry, supra*, particularly in ambiguous or borderline cases. Reflexive reliance on a profile of drug courier characteristics runs a far greater risk than does ordinary, case-by-case police work of subjecting innocent individuals to unwarranted police harassment and detention. This risk is enhanced by the profile's "chameleon-like way of adapting to any particular set of observations." *Compare, e.g., United States v. Moore,* 675 F.2d 802 (CA6 1982) (suspect was first to deplane), cert. denied, 460 U.S. 1068 (1983), *with United States v. Mendenhall,* 446 U.S. 544 (1980) (last to deplane), *with United States v. Buenaventura-Ariza,* 615 F.2d 29 (CA2 1980) (deplaned from middle); *United States v. Sullivan,* 625 F.2d 9 (CA4 1980) (one-way tickets), *with United States v. Craemer,* 555 F.2d 594 (CA6 1977) (round-trip tickets), with *United States v. McCaleb,* 552 F.2d 717 (CA6 1977) (nonstop flight), with *United States v. Sokolow,* 808 F.2d 1366, (CA9) (changed planes); *Craemer, supra* (no luggage), *with United States v. Sanford,* 658 F.2d 342 (CA5 1981) (gym bag), with *Sullivan, supra,* at 12 (new suitcases); *United States v. Smith,* 574 F.2d 882 (CA6 1978) (traveling alone), *with United States v. Fry,* 622 F.2d 1218 (CA5 1980) (travelling with companion); *United States v. Andrews,* 600 F.2d 563 (CA6 1979) (acted nervously), *with United States v. Himmelwright*, 551 F.2d 991 (CA5) (acted too calmly). . . . In asserting that it is not "somehow" relevant that the agents who stopped Sokolow did so in reliance on a prefabricated profile of criminal characteristics, the majority thus ducks serious issues relating to a questionable law enforcement practice, to address the validity of which we granted certiorari in this case. . . .

[T]raveler Sokolow gave no indications of evasive activity. On the contrary, the sole behavioral detail about Sokolow noted by the DEA agents was that he was nervous. With news accounts proliferating of plane crashes, near collisions, and air terrorism, there are manifold and good reasons for being agitated while awaiting a flight, reasons that have nothing to do with one's involvement in a criminal endeavor.

The remaining circumstantial facts known about Sokolow, considered either singly or together, are scarcely indicative of criminal activity. . . . [T]he fact that Sokolow took a brief trip to a resort city for which he brought only carry-on luggage also "describe[s] a very large category of presumably innocent travelers." That Sokolow embarked from Miami, "a source city for illicit drugs," is no more suggestive of illegality; thousands of innocent persons travel from "source cities" every day and, judging from the DEA's testimony in past cases, nearly every major city in the country may be characterized as a source or distribution city. That Sokolow had his phone listed in another person's name also does not support the majority's assertion that the DEA agents reasonably believed Sokolow was using an alias; it is commonplace to have one's phone registered in the name of a roommate, which, it later turned out, was precisely what Sokolow had done. That Sokolow was dressed in a black jumpsuit and wore gold jewelry also provides no grounds for suspecting wrongdoing, the majority's repeated and unexplained allusions to Sokolow's style of dress notwithstanding. For law enforcement officers to base a search, even in part, on a "pop" guess that persons dressed in a particular fashion are likely to commit crimes not only stretches the concept of reasonable suspicion beyond recognition, but also is inimical to the self-expression which the choice of wardrobe may provide.

Finally, that Sokolow paid for his tickets in cash indicates no imminent or ongoing criminal activity. The majority "feel[s] confident" that "[m]ost business travelers . . . purchase airline tickets by credit card or check." Why the majority confines its focus only to "business travelers" I do not know, but I would not so lightly infer ongoing crime from the use of legal tender. Making major cash purchases, while surely less common today, may simply reflect the traveler's aversion to, or inability to obtain, plastic money. . . .

NOTES & QUESTIONS

1. ***Profiling.*** What sorts of criteria would be sufficient to find reasonable suspicion for a *Terry* stop for potential terrorist activity at an airport? Having a one-way ticket? Having only carry-on luggage? One of the difficulties in creating a profile of a terrorist, Anita Ramasastry notes, is that "[t]here is no well-defined and reinforced profile for terrorists. Further, attacks are relatively infrequent, making it harder to reinforce any profiles that do exist."[50]

   Is the use of profiles to detain or search people problematic? Fred Schauer contends that making generalizations is not necessarily problematic, even when doing so leads to some mistakes:

   > Here Justice Marshall [dissenting in *Sokolow*] went right to the heart of the matter. He recognized that the question of the profile is not about profiles as

[50] Anita Ramasastry, *Lost in Translation? Data Mining, National Security, and the "Adverse Inference" Problem*, 22 Santa Clara Computer & High Tech. L.J. 757, 773 (2006).

> such, but is about *rules*. The issue is whether preexisting and general rules should be employed to determine which people to stop, as the majority was willing to permit, or whether that determination must, as Justice Marshall insisted, be made on a particularistic basis by individual officers using their own best judgment in each case, even if that best judgment can itself be seen as just another version of profiling. Once we understand that the issue is not about whether to use profiles or not but instead about whether to use (or to prefer) formal written profiles or informal unwritten ones, it becomes clear that this is not a question of profiles or not, but a question about discretion. Should individual customs officers have the discretion to create their own profiles, as Justice Marshall preferred, or is it at least permissible, even if not constitutionally mandatory, for formal written profiles to be used as a way of regularizing the process and limiting the discretion of individual officers?
>
> Once we understand the choice as being one between profiles that are constructed in advance and have the potential to be both under- and overinclusive, on the one hand, and profiles that are constructed on a case-by-case basis by law-enforcement officials making, in Justice Marshall's words, "sensitive and fact-specific inferences in light of [their] experience," on the other, we can see that the issue is not about profiling at all, for profiling is inevitable.[51]

Is the use of data mining laudable because it involves a computer searching for written pre-established patterns rather than the ad hoc discretion of airline screening officials at the security checkpoints? Pre-established profiles can eliminate the use of race or other problematic factors that might be used in an official's ad hoc discretion. Then again, even pre-established profiles can employ improper factors.

What factors should be considered to be improper? Should information about a person's associations and group memberships be included? Information about a person's political and expressive activity? Information about a person's religion or race?

Fred Schauer examines the issue of whether race should be a factor in the profile:

> Those who commit acts of airplane terrorism, both before and after September 11, 2001, are disproportionately younger Muslim men of Middle Eastern background. . . .
>
> On the evidence we now have, it is more than plausible to suppose that Middle Eastern ethnicity is a significant contributory factor, such that including it in the algorithm will make the algorithm substantially more effective than excluding it.
>
> Because allowing the use of race and ethnicity imposes a cost on those members of the targeted groups who are in the area of overinclusion — Middle Easterners who have done nothing wrong — it might be preferable to distribute the cost more broadly, and in doing so raise the cost without lowering the degree of security. If excluding the relevant factor of Middle Eastern appearance from the algorithm made it necessary to increase the scrutiny of everyone — if excluding ethnicity while still including everything else increased waiting time at airports an average of thirty minutes per passenger — this might still be a price worth paying. . . . Put starkly, the

[51] Frederick Schauer, *Profiles, Probabilities, and Stereotypes* 173-74 (2003).

> question of racial or ethnic profiling in air travel is not the question of whether racial and ethnic sensitivity must be bought at the price of thousands of lives. Rather, it is most often the question of whether racial and ethnic sensitivity should be bought at the price of arriving thirty minutes earlier at the airport.[52]

Consider the following document obtained by the Electronic Privacy Information Center from NASA regarding airline passenger data:

> ISLE ran a simple anomaly detection algorithm that it developed as part of this project on a subset of the census database, and it found some interesting anomalies. Many of the anomalies were people from unusual countries. One anomaly was a 22-year-old African American man who was not a college graduate but had over $100,000 in capital gains.
>
> We ran Gritbot on a subset of the census database. It discovered many interesting anomalies, including a woman whose ancestry is Mexican but who speaks Chinese at home, a 16-year-old veteran, and some people who reported their race to be white and their ancestry to be African-American. . . .[53]

Profiles ultimately involve human judgment about what patterns should be singled out as suspicious. One difficulty with data mining is that if the profiles remain secret, how can there be oversight to prevent improper factors from being used? Who decides what factors are appropriate?

2. *An Assessment of Government Data Mining.* Consider the following account of the problems of government data mining by Daniel Solove:

> Usually, the government has some form of particularized suspicion, a factual basis to believe that a particular person may be engaged in illegal conduct. Particularized suspicion keeps the government's profound investigative powers in check, preventing widespread surveillance and snooping into the lives and affairs of all citizens. Computer matches . . . investigate everyone, and most people who are investigated are innocent.
>
> With the new information supplied by the private sector, there is an increased potential for more automated investigations, such as searches for all people who purchase books about particular topics or those who visit certain websites, or perhaps even people whose personal interests fit a profile for those likely to engage in certain forms of criminal activity. Profiles work similarly to the way that Amazon.com predicts which products customers will want to buy. They use particular characteristics and patterns of activity to predict how people will behave in the future. Of course, profiles can be mistaken, but they are often accurate enough to tempt people to rely on them. But there are even deeper problems with profiles beyond inaccuracies. Profiles can be based on stereotypes, race, or religion. A profile is only as good as its designer. Profiles are often kept secret, enabling prejudices and faulty assumptions to exist unchecked by the public.[54]

3. *A Hypothetical Data Mining Problem.* Suppose the FBI receives a tip from a credible source that two young males, both naturalized U.S. citizens, who are Muslim and who were originally born in Saudi Arabia, have rented a U-Haul

---

[52] *Id.* at 181-90.

[53] NASA Documents, available at http://www.epic.org/privacy/airtravel/nasa/

[54] Daniel J. Solove, *The Digital Person: Technology and Privacy in the Information Age* 179-85 (2004).

truck and are planning to use it to detonate a bomb at a crowded building or place in Los Angeles, CA within the next week. The source says he met the two males at his mosque, which has over 1,000 worshippers. This is all the information the FBI agents have. The FBI would like to: (1) obtain the records of the people who attend the mosque; (2) obtain the records of U-Haul. The FBI would like to engage in data mining on the records to narrow their search for the two males. Notwithstanding existing law, should the FBI agents be permitted to obtain the records? If so, what privacy protections should be established?

ARIZONA V. EVANS

514 U.S. 1 (1995)

REHNQUIST, J. This case presents the question whether evidence seized in violation of the Fourth Amendment by an officer who acted in reliance on a police record indicating the existence of an outstanding arrest warrant — a record that is later determined to be erroneous — must be suppressed by virtue of the exclusionary rule regardless of the source of the error. . . .

In January 1991, Phoenix police officer Bryan Sargent observed respondent Isaac Evans driving the wrong way on a one-way street in front of the police station. The officer stopped respondent and asked to see his driver's license. After respondent told him that his license had been suspended, the officer entered respondent's name into a computer data terminal located in his patrol car. The computer inquiry confirmed that respondent's license had been suspended and also indicated that there was an outstanding misdemeanor warrant for his arrest. Based upon the outstanding warrant, Officer Sargent placed respondent under arrest. While being handcuffed, respondent dropped a hand-rolled cigarette that the officers determined smelled of marijuana. Officers proceeded to search his car and discovered a bag of marijuana under the passenger's seat.

The State charged respondent with possession of marijuana. When the police notified the Justice Court that they had arrested him, the Justice Court discovered that the arrest warrant previously had been quashed and so advised the police. Respondent argued that because his arrest was based on a warrant that had been quashed 17 days prior to his arrest, the marijuana seized incident to the arrest should be suppressed as the fruit of an unlawful arrest. Respondent also argued that "[t]he 'good faith' exception to the exclusionary rule [was] inapplicable . . . because it was police error, not judicial error, which caused the invalid arrest." . . .

"The question whether the exclusionary rule's remedy is appropriate in a particular context has long been regarded as an issue separate from the question whether the Fourth Amendment rights of the party seeking to invoke the rule were violated by police conduct." The exclusionary rule operates as a judicially created remedy designed to safeguard against future violations of Fourth Amendment rights through the rule's general deterrent effect. As with any remedial device, the rule's application has been restricted to those instances where its remedial objectives are thought most efficaciously served. Where the exclusionary rule does not result in appreciable deterrence, then, clearly, its use . . . is unwarranted. . . .

If court employees were responsible for the erroneous computer record, the exclusion of evidence at trial would not sufficiently deter future errors so as to warrant such a severe sanction. First, as we noted in [*United States v. Leon,* 468 U.S. 897 (1984)], the exclusionary rule was historically designed as a means of deterring police misconduct, not mistakes by court employees. Second, respondent offers no evidence that court employees are inclined to ignore or subvert the Fourth Amendment or that lawlessness among these actors requires application of the extreme sanction of exclusion. To the contrary, the Chief Clerk of the Justice Court testified at the suppression hearing that this type of error occurred once every three or four years.

Finally, and most important, there is no basis for believing that application of the exclusionary rule in these circumstances will have a significant effect on court employees responsible for informing the police that a warrant has been quashed. Because court clerks are not adjuncts to the law enforcement team engaged in the often competitive enterprise of ferreting out crime, they have no stake in the outcome of particular criminal prosecutions. The threat of exclusion of evidence could not be expected to deter such individuals from failing to inform police officials that a warrant had been quashed. . . .

In fact, once the court clerks discovered the error, they immediately corrected it, and then proceeded to search their files to make sure that no similar mistakes had occurred. There is no indication that the arresting officer was not acting objectively reasonably when he relied upon the police computer record. Application of the *Leon* framework supports a categorical exception to the exclusionary rule for clerical errors of court employees. . . .

O'CONNOR, SOUTER, AND BREYER, J.J. concurring. The evidence in this case strongly suggests that it was a court employee's departure from established recordkeeping procedures that caused the record of respondent's arrest warrant to remain in the computer system after the warrant had been quashed. Prudently, then, the Court limits itself to the question whether a court employee's departure from such established procedures is the kind of error to which the exclusionary rule should apply. . . .

In limiting itself to that single question, however, the Court does not hold that the court employee's mistake in this case was necessarily the *only* error that may have occurred and to which the exclusionary rule might apply. While the police were innocent of the court employee's mistake, they may or may not have acted reasonably in their reliance *on the recordkeeping system itself.* Surely it would *not* be reasonable for the police to rely, say, on a recordkeeping system, their own or some other agency's, that has no mechanism to ensure its accuracy over time and that routinely leads to false arrests, even years after the probable cause for any such arrest has ceased to exist (if it ever existed). . . .

In recent years, we have witnessed the advent of powerful, computer-based recordkeeping systems that facilitate arrests in ways that have never before been possible. The police, of course, are entitled to enjoy the substantial advantages this technology confers. They may not, however, rely on it blindly. With the benefits of more efficient law enforcement mechanisms comes the burden of corresponding constitutional responsibilities.

GINSBURG & STEVENS, J.J. dissenting. This case portrays the increasing use of computer technology in law enforcement; it illustrates an evolving problem this Court need not, and in my judgment should not, resolve too hastily. . . .

Widespread reliance on computers to store and convey information generates, along with manifold benefits, new possibilities of error, due to both computer malfunctions and operator mistakes. Most germane to this case, computerization greatly amplifies an error's effect, and correspondingly intensifies the need for prompt correction; for inaccurate data can infect not only one agency, but the many agencies that share access to the database. The computerized data bases of the Federal Bureau of Investigation's National Crime Information Center (NCIC), to take a conspicuous example, contain over 23 million records, identifying, among other things, persons and vehicles sought by law enforcement agencies nationwide. NCIC information is available to approximately 71,000 federal, state, and local agencies. Thus, any mistake entered into the NCIC spreads nationwide in an instant.

Isaac Evans' arrest exemplifies the risks associated with computerization of arrest warrants. Though his arrest was in fact warrantless — the warrant once issued having been quashed over two weeks before the episode in suit — the computer reported otherwise. Evans' case is not idiosyncratic. . .

In the instant case, the Court features testimony of the Chief Clerk of the Justice Court in East Phoenix to the effect that errors of the kind Evans encountered are reported only "on[c]e every three or four years." But the same witness also recounted that, when the error concerning Evans came to light, an immediate check revealed that three other errors of the very same kind had occurred on "that same day.". . .

In the Court's view, exclusion of evidence, even if capable of deterring police officer errors, cannot deter the carelessness of other governmental actors. Whatever federal precedents may indicate — an issue on which I voice no opinion — the Court's conclusion is not the lesson inevitably to be drawn from logic or experience.

In this electronic age, particularly with respect to recordkeeping, court personnel and police officers are not neatly compartmentalized actors. Instead, they serve together to carry out the State's information-gathering objectives. Whether particular records are maintained by the police or the courts should not be dispositive where a single computer data base can answer all calls. Not only is it artificial to distinguish between court clerk and police clerk slips; in practice, it may be difficult to pinpoint whether one official, *e.g.,* a court employee, or another, *e.g.,* a police officer, caused the error to exist or to persist. Applying an exclusionary rule as the Arizona court did may well supply a powerful incentive to the State to promote the prompt updating of computer records. . . .

NOTES & QUESTIONS

1. ***Accuracy.*** Pattern-based data mining is often not a highly accurate way of identifying suspects. Daniel Steinbock explores the arguments relating to data mining's accuracy:

> It must be noted at the outset that, in one sense, accuracy is not a particularly high priority in data matching and data mining. To the extent that their results are used for heightened scrutiny or for terrorist profiling, even the staunchest advocates would not pretend that these indicators are foolproof, but would simply respond that they do not need to be. This is especially true for predictive uses; the goal is simply to sort the higher from the lower risks and, perhaps, to see if a certain threshold of risk has been reached. On the other hand, even with predictive uses, errors in the data will produce a larger number of falsely positive results, thereby imposing unnecessary harms. This effectively externalizes the error costs of the computer-generated decision onto its subjects.[55]

Anita Ramasastry notes that data can often be "lost in translation" when it is taken from other contexts and used for government data mining purposes:

> First, data may not be accurate when provided initially by a consumer or may only reflect a partial truth. Second, data may get mistranslated due to human error (e.g. typing in a birth date incorrectly) when placed into a database. Third, when data is used in a new context, it may not be interpreted in the same way as previously used, because the new party using the data may not understand how the data was originally classified. For example, racial or ethnic classifications in one database may be different than in a new database. Fourth, when data from different sources is combined into a larger database, it may be incorrectly integrated. In other words, data from different people who share the same surname might be incorrectly merged, creating a new profile that is incorrect. Thus, there are multiple ways in which data may be erroneous. Where human agents are involved in compiling or aggregating different data, data sources can be mistranslated.[56]

2. ***Due Process.*** Consider Daniel Steinbock:

> The most striking aspect of virtually all antiterrorist and data mining decisions is the total absence of even the most rudimentary procedures for notice, hearing, or other opportunities for meaningful participation before, or even after, the deprivation is imposed.

Steinbock examines four ways to bring due process to data mining programs:

> One is summary hearings, along the lines of those required in brief school suspensions, prior to denial of access to flights or infringements of other liberty or property rights. A second involves correction opportunities after the initial data matching or data mining consequence, in a fuller process with

---

[55] Daniel J. Steinbock, *Data Matching, Data Mining, and Due Process*, 40 Ga. L. Rev. 1, 82-83 (2005).

[56] Anita Ramasastry, *Lost in Translation? Data Mining, National Security, and the "Adverse Inference" Problem*, 22 Santa Clara Computer & High Tech. L.J. 757, 778 (2006).

disclosure and a right to respond. A third means of redress is after-the-fact compensatory damages for false positives in outcome. This solution allows for less process but makes wrongly identified persons whole, at least monetarily. Finally, given the frequent need for secrecy in data matching and data mining decision algorithms and the difficulty of addressing challenges to them in individual hearings, this Article proposes examination of their validity by independent oversight bodies. Evaluating whether a decisional system meets constitutional demands of due process requires attention to all stages of the process.[57]

3. *Transparency.* Consider Daniel Solove:

> The problem with many data mining programs is that they lack adequate transparency. The reason for the secrecy of the programs is that exposing the algorithms and patterns that trigger identification as a possible future terrorist will tip off terrorists about what behaviors to avoid. This is indeed a legitimate concern. Our society, however, is one of open government, public accountability, and oversight of government officials — not one of secret blacklists maintained in clandestine bureaucracies. Without public accountability, unelected bureaucrats can administer data mining programs in ways often insulated from any scrutiny at all. For example, the information gathered about people for use in data mining might be collected from sources that do not take sufficient steps to maintain its accuracy. Without oversight, it is unclear what level of accuracy the government requires for the information it gathers and uses. If profiles are based on race, speech, or other factors that society might not find desirable to include, how is this to be aired and discussed? If a person is routinely singled out based on a profile and wants to challenge the profile, there appears no way to do so unless the profile is revealed.
>
> The lack of transparency in data mining programs makes it nearly impossible to balance the liberty and security interests. Given the significant potential privacy issues and other constitutional concerns, combined with speculative and unproven security benefits as well as many other alternative means of promoting security, should data mining still be on the table as a viable policy option?[58]

UNITED STATES V. ELLISON

462 F.3d 557 (6th Cir. 2006)

GIBBONS, J. . . . The central issue in this case is whether the Fourth Amendment is implicated when a police officer investigates an automobile license plate number using a law enforcement computer database. While on routine patrol, Officer Mark Keeley of the Farmington Hills (Michigan) Police Department pulled into a two-lane service drive adjacent to a shopping center. Keeley testified that a white van, with a male driver inside, was idling in the lane closest to the stores, in an area marked with "Fire Lane" and "No Parking" signs. Keeley did not issue the van a citation for being illegally parked, nor did he request that

---

[57] Steinbock, Data Mining, supra, at 57.

[58] Daniel J. Solove, *Data Mining and the Security-Liberty Debate*, 74 U. Chi. L. Rev. 343 (2008).

the driver move the van. Rather, he moved into a parking spot to observe the van and entered the vehicle's license plate number into his patrol car's Law Enforcement Information Network ("LEIN") computer. The LEIN search revealed that the vehicle was registered to Curtis Ellison, who had an outstanding felony warrant. Following standard procedure, Keeley radioed for back-up and continued observing the van. After two minutes, another male got into the van, and it drove away. Officer Keeley followed the van until his back-up was nearby, and then activated his lights and stopped the van.

Officer Keeley approached the driver's-side window as his back-up arrived. He advised the driver that he was being stopped for parking in a fire lane and asked for license, registration and proof of insurance. The driver, identified as Edward Coleman, stated that he had only stopped in front of the store to wait for the passenger. At this time the passenger stated that he was the registered owner of the vehicle. Keeley verified the passenger's identity as Curtis Ellison and moved to the passenger side of the van. Keeley notified Ellison that he was being arrested on the outstanding warrant. Ellison stepped out of the van, and during the routine safety pat-down, two firearms were found. Coleman was released with a warning about parking in a fire lane.

Ellison was indicted for being a felon in possession of a firearm in violation of 18 U.S.C. § 922(g). Prior to trial, he made a timely motion to suppress the firearm as the fruit of an illegal search. After holding a hearing, the district court made a factual finding that the van was not parked illegally, and thus, the officer did not have probable cause to run the LEIN check of Ellison's license plate. The court issued a Memorandum Opinion and Order granting the motion to suppress under the "fruit of the poisonous tree" doctrine. . . .

The government argues on appeal that Ellison had no reasonable expectation of privacy in the information contained on his license plate, and thus, no probable cause was required for Officer Keeley to run the LEIN check. . . .

Although the district court did not expressly state that Ellison had a reasonable expectation of privacy in the information contained on his license plate, such a conclusion was necessarily implied by the court's ruling that a Fourth Amendment violation occurred. Thus, the district court could only find that the LEIN search violated the Fourth Amendment if it first concluded that Ellison had a "constitutionally protected reasonable expectation of privacy" in his license plate number. . . .

A tenet of constitutional jurisprudence is that the Fourth Amendment protects only what an individual seeks to keep private. *Katz,* 389 U.S. at 351-52. "What a person knowingly exposes to the public . . . is not a subject of Fourth Amendment protection." It is also settled that "objects falling in the plain view of an officer who has a right to be in the position to have that view are subject to seizure." . . .

No argument can be made that a motorist seeks to keep the information on his license plate private. The very purpose of a license plate number, like that of a Vehicle Identification Number, is to provide identifying information to law enforcement officials and others. . . .

The dissent implies that even if an individual has no expectation of privacy in a license plate number, a privacy interest is somehow created by the entry of this information into a law-enforcement computer database. This argument flies in the face of established Fourth Amendment doctrine. First, despite the dissent's concerns over the information available in a LEIN search, Ellison had no privacy interest in the information retrieved by Officer Keely. The obvious purpose of maintaining law enforcement databases is to make information, such as the existence of outstanding warrants, readily available to officers carrying out legitimate law enforcement duties. The dissent fails to state how using a license plate number-in which there is no expectation of privacy-to retrieve other non-private information somehow creates a "search" for the purposes of the Fourth Amendment. . . . This is not a case where the police used a technology not available to the public to discover evidence that could not otherwise be obtained without "intrusion into a constitutionally-protected area." *Kyllo v. United States,* 533 U.S. 27, 34-35 (2001) (holding that the use of thermal-imaging technology to detect heat inside a private home violates the Fourth Amendment). The technology used in this case does not allow officers to access any previously-unobtainable information; it simply allows them to access information more quickly. As the information was obtained without intruding upon a constitutionally-protected area, there was no "search" for Fourth Amendment purposes. . . .

MOORE, J. dissenting. . . . The majority rests its conclusion that the Fourth Amendment was not implicated by the LEIN search on the relatively uncontroversial fact that the operator of a vehicle has no privacy interest in the particular combination of letters and numerals that make up his license-plate number, but pays short shrift to the crucial issue of how the license-plate information is used. . . . This approach misses the crux of the issue before the court: even if there is no privacy interest in the license-plate number per se, can the police, without any measure of heightened suspicion or other constraint on their discretion, conduct a search using the license-plate number to access information about the vehicle and its operator that may not otherwise be public or accessible by the police without heightened suspicion? . . . .

The use of a computer database to acquire information about drivers through their license-plate numbers without any heightened suspicion is in tension with many of the Fourth Amendment concerns expressed in *Delaware v. Prouse,* 440 U.S. 648, 655-63 (1979). In *Prouse,* the Supreme Court held that an officer may not stop a vehicle to check the operator's license and registration without "at least articulable and reasonable suspicion that a motorist is unlicensed or that an automobile is not registered, or that either the vehicle or an occupant is otherwise subject to seizure for violation of law," despite the fact that the state requires drivers to be licensed and vehicles to be registered. The Court stated that the Fourth Amendment aims "to safeguard the privacy and security of individuals against arbitrary invasions. . . . Thus, the permissibility of a particular law enforcement practice is judged by balancing its intrusion on the individual's Fourth Amendment interests against its promotion of legitimate governmental interests." The Court then explained the constitutional concerns that flow from the unbridled discretion associated with permitting random searches of drivers' information:

> To insist neither upon an appropriate factual basis for suspicion directed at a particular automobile nor upon some other substantial and objective standard or rule to govern the exercise of discretion "would invite intrusions upon constitutionally guaranteed rights based on nothing more substantial than inarticulate hunches. . . ." *Terry v. Ohio,* 392 U.S. [1], at 22 [1968]. . . . When there is not probable cause to believe that a driver is violating any one of the multitude of applicable traffic and equipment regulations — or other articulable basis amounting to reasonable suspicion that the driver is unlicensed or his vehicle unregistered — we cannot conceive of any legitimate basis upon which a patrolman could decide that stopping a particular driver for a spot check would be more productive than stopping any other driver. This kind of standardless and unconstrained discretion is the evil the Court has discerned when in previous cases it has insisted that the discretion of the official in the field be circumscribed, at least to some extent. . . .

Although the license-plate search at issue here is arguably less invasive than a license-and-registration check, the constitutional concerns regarding abuse of discretion do not disappear simply because drivers are not stopped to conduct the license-plate search. First, a search can implicate the Fourth Amendment even when the individual does not know that she is being searched. Second, the balancing of Fourth Amendment interests also requires consideration of "psychological intrusion[s] visited upon" the individuals searched in assessing the extent of intrusion that a particular police practice imposes. *See Prouse,* 440 U.S. at 657. The psychological invasion that results from knowing that one's personal information is subject to search by the police, for no reason, at any time one is driving a car is undoubtedly grave.

Because the government incorrectly limits its Fourth Amendment analysis to the plain view of the license plate without exploring the constitutional implications of the subsequent LEIN search, it does not provide any explanation as to the governmental interests promoted by license-plate searches. . . .

In addition, the possibility and the reality of errors in the computer databases accessed by MDT systems lead to great concern regarding the potential for license-plate searches to result in unwarranted intrusions into privacy in the form of stops made purely on the basis of incorrect information. . . .

NOTES & QUESTIONS

1. ***The Fourth Amendment and Government Data Mining.*** Does the Fourth Amendment provide any limits on government data mining? Lee Tein argues that it does:

> The use of patterns discovered through data mining raises . . . particularity issues. Imagine a database of a million people and a hypothesis that those who meet certain criteria are highly likely to be terrorists. But you don't know whether any of these million people actually do meet these criteria; if you did, you wouldn't need to run the search. The basic problem is lack of particularized suspicion; data about these persons would be "searched"

> without any reason to believe either that the database contains evidence of terrorist activity or that any person "in" the database is a terrorist. . . .[59]

When the government engages in data mining, it often analyzes information that it already possesses. Is this a search? If the government has information about a person in its records and analyzes it, does this trigger the Fourth Amendment?

In contrast, Richard Posner argues in favor of data mining: "Computer searches do not invade privacy because search programs are not sentient beings. Only the human search should raise constitutional or other legal issues."[60] Consider the following argument in response to Posner: "[T]here is human intervention in data mining even before the first automated search is run; humans will write the software, shape the database parameters, and decide on the kinds of matches that count. And the task of data mining itself is guided by some degree of human interaction."[61] To the extent there is a human element in data mining, how ought it to be regulated? Do the problems of data mining stem solely from the human element?

4. THE DRIVER'S PRIVACY PROTECTION ACT

For decades, many states had been selling to private sector companies their motor vehicle records. Motor vehicle records contain information such as one's name, address, phone number, Social Security number, medical information, height, weight, gender, eye color, photograph, and date of birth. This information was highly desired by marketers, who paid states millions of dollars to obtain these records. In 1994, Congress passed the Driver's Privacy Protection Act (DPPA), 18 U.S.C. §§ 2721–2725, to halt this practice.

Restriction on Disclosure. Pursuant to DPPA:

> [A] State department of motor vehicles . . . shall not knowingly disclose or otherwise make available to any person or entity personal information about any individual obtained by the department in connection with a motor vehicle record. 18 U.S.C. § 2721(a).

"Personal information" is defined as data "that identifies an individual, including an individual's photograph, social security number, driver identification number, name, address (but not the 5-digit zip code), telephone number, and medical or disability information." § 2725(3). The definition of "personal information" specifically excludes "information on vehicular accidents, driving violations, and driver's status." § 2725(3).

DPPA applies to state DMVs and their officials and employees. Further, DPPA only applies to motor vehicle records.

---

[59] Lee Tien, Privacy, *Technology and Data Mining*, 30 Ohio N.U. L. Rev. 389, 405 (2004).

[60] Richard Posner, *Privacy, Surveillance, and Law*, 75 U. Chi. L. Rev. 245 (2008).

[61] Ira Rubinstein, Ronald D. Lee & Paul M. Schwartz, *Data Mining and Internet Profiling*, 75 U. Chi. L. Rev. 261 (2008).

Consent. State DMVs can disclose personal information in motor vehicle records if the individual consents. In order to disclose a driver's personal information for marketing or other restricted uses, the driver must affirmatively indicate her consent (opt in). § 2721(b) and (d).

Exceptions. The DPPA contains a number of exceptions. Personal information can be disclosed for purposes of law enforcement, recalls, legal proceedings, and insurance claims investigations. § 2721(b). Additionally, DPPA permits disclosure to licensed private investigative agencies. § 2721(b). Ironically, the event that motivated Congress to pass the DPPA was the murder of actress Rebecca Shaeffer. Her murderer ascertained her address from a private detective, who had received it from the DMV.[62]

Restrictions on Further Dissemination. If private entities obtain motor vehicle record information, they cannot resell or further disseminate that information. 18 U.S.C. § 2721(c). However, if the driver consents to the disclosure of her data, then information may be disseminated for any purpose.

Enforcement. The DPPA establishes criminal fines for any "person" who knowingly obtains or discloses motor vehicle record data in ways prohibited by the DPPA. §§ 2722, 2723(a), 2725(2).

The DPPA, § 2724, provides for a private right to action for violations:

> A person who knowingly obtains, discloses or uses personal information, from a motor vehicle record, for a purpose not permitted under this chapter shall be liable to the individual to whom the information pertains, who may bring a civil action in a United States district court.

Note that this section purportedly applies to any "person who knowingly obtains, discloses or uses personal information, from a motor vehicle record." In other words, it does not just apply to state DMVs but to anybody who uses data from a motor vehicle record. States and state agencies are generally excluded from the DPPA, but the U.S. Attorney General may impose a civil penalty of up to $5,000 per day for state agencies that maintain a "policy or practice of substantial noncompliance" with the DPPA. § 2723(b).

In *Margan v. Niles*, 250 F. Supp. 2d 63 (N.D.N.Y. 2003), the court found that the DPPA provided a cause of action beyond the motor operator whose motor vehicle record was disclosed. The court found that "any individual whose address was obtained from a motor vehicle record is a proper plaintiff." Hence, in *Niles*, the spouse and children of an individual whose address was obtained from a motor vehicle record could "maintain an action under the DPPA where the spouse and children share the same address as that individual." The court also found that a municipality whose agent violated the DPPA could be held vicariously liable under this statute. *See also Luparello v. The Incorporated Village of Garden City,* 290 F. Supp. 2d 341 (E.D.N.Y. 2003).

---

62 *See* Charles J. Sykes, *The End of Privacy: Personal Rights in the Surveillance Society* 30-31 (1999).

The Scope of Congressional Power. In *Reno v. Condon*, 528 U.S. 141 (2000), the Supreme Court upheld the DPPA against a constitutional challenge that DPPA violated the Tenth and Eleventh Amendments:

> The United States asserts that the DPPA is a proper exercise of Congress' authority to regulate interstate commerce under the Commerce Clause, U.S. Const., Art. I, § 8, cl. 3. The United States bases its Commerce Clause argument on the fact that the personal, identifying information that the DPPA regulates is a "thin[g] in interstate commerce," and that the sale or release of that information in interstate commerce is therefore a proper subject of congressional regulation. We agree with the United States' contention. The motor vehicle information which the States have historically sold is used by insurers, manufacturers, direct marketers, and others engaged in interstate commerce to contact drivers with customized solicitations. The information is also used in the stream of interstate commerce by various public and private entities for matters related to interstate motoring. Because drivers' information is, in this context, an article of commerce, its sale or release into the interstate stream of business is sufficient to support congressional regulation.

Based on *Reno v. Condon*, what is the extent of Congress's power to regulate information maintained by the states? Suppose Congress amended the Privacy Act to apply not just to federal agencies but to all state and local governments as well. Would such an extension of the Privacy Act be constitutional?

CHAPTER 7

PRIVACY OF FINANCIAL AND COMMERCIAL DATA

A. THE FINANCIAL SERVICES INDUSTRY AND PERSONAL DATA

1. THE FAIR CREDIT REPORTING ACT

Increasingly, companies in the United States make sales based on credit. Since 1980, almost all homes and most new cars are purchased on credit. Well over half of retail items are purchased on credit as well.[1]

As a result of the centrality of different forms of consumer borrowing, credit reporting agencies play an ever-greater role in economic transactions. Credit reporting agencies prepare credit reports about people's credit history for use by creditors seeking to loan people money. Credit reports contain financial information such as bankruptcy filings, judgments and liens, mortgage foreclosures, and checking account data. Some companies also prepare investigative consumer reports, which supplement the credit report with information about an individual's character and lifestyle. Creditors depend upon credit reports to determine whether or not to offer a person a loan as well as what interest rate to charge that person. Credit reports are also reviewed by some landlords before renting out an apartment.

Credit reports contain a "credit score" that is used to assess a person's credit risk. In many cases, a low score will not necessarily mean the denial of a loan, mortgage, or credit card; rather, it means that a higher rate of interest will be charged. As Evan Hendricks notes:

> According to the Fair Isaac Corporation, a leading developer of credit scoring models, one delinquent account can lower a credit score from 70 to 120 points. A consumer with excellent credit (credit score of 720-850) would pay about 7.85% interest rate for a home equity loan, while a consumer with marginal

---

[1] *See generally* Robert Ellis Smith, *Ben Franklin's Web Site: Privacy and Curiosity from Plymouth Rock to the Internet* 313-25 (2000); Steven L. Nock, *The Costs of Privacy: Surveillance and Reputation in America* (1993).

> credit (640-659) would pay 9.2% and one with poor credit (500-559) would pay a 12.1% rate. The rate swings for a new car loan are even greater, with good credit risks paying a 5.2% rate, moderate risks paying 11.4% and poor risks paying 17.2%.[2]

Credit reports are not only used in connection with granting credit. Employers use credit reports to make hiring and promotion decisions. The issuance of professional licenses, such as admittance to the bar, also can require the examination of one's credit report.

There are three major national credit reporting agencies: Experian, Equifax, and Trans Union. Each of these three companies has information on virtually every adult American citizen, and they routinely prepare credit reports about individuals.

According to Peter Swire, our financial system has been shifting toward more traceable payment transactions: "The shift from cash to checks to credit and debit cards shows an evolution toward creating records, placing the records automatically in databases, and potentially linking the databases to reveal extremely detailed information about an individual's purchasing history."[3] This evolution is generating new problems for the protection of privacy.

In 1970, Congress passed the Fair Credit Reporting Act (FCRA), Pub. L. No. 90-321, to regulate credit reporting agencies. The Act was inspired by allegations of abuse and lack of responsiveness of credit agencies to consumer complaints. In its statement of purpose, the FCRA states: "There is a need to insure that consumer reporting agencies exercise their grave responsibilities with fairness, impartiality, and a respect for the consumer's right to privacy." 15 U.S.C. § 1681. The FCRA requires credit reporting companies to provide an individual access to her records, establishes procedures for correcting information, and sets limitations on disclosure.

Scope. FCRA applies to "any consumer reporting agency" that furnishes a "consumer report." 15 U.S.C. § 1681b. As a consequence, the scope of the FCRA turns on the definitions of "consumer report" and "consumer reporting agencies." Pursuant to § 1681b(d):

> The term "consumer report" means any written, oral, or other communication of any information by a consumer reporting agency bearing on a consumer's credit worthiness, credit standing, credit capacity, character, general reputation, personal characteristics, or mode of living which is used or expected to be used or collected in whole or in part for the purpose of serving as a factor in establishing the consumer's eligibility for
>
> (A) credit or insurance to be used primarily for personal, family, or household purposes;
>
> (B) employment purposes; or
>
> (C) any other purpose authorized under [§ 1681b].

---

[2] Evan Hendricks, *Credit Scores and Credit Reports: How the System Really Works, What You Can Do* 3-4 (2004).

[3] Peter P. Swire, *Financial Privacy and the Theory of High-Tech Government Surveillance*, 77 Wash. U. L.Q. 461 (1999).

A "consumer reporting agency" is defined as

> [a]ny person which, for monetary fees, dues, or on a cooperative nonprofit basis, regularly engages in whole or in part in the practice of assembling or evaluating consumer credit information or other information on consumers for the purpose of furnishing consumer reports to third parties, and which uses means or facility of interstate commerce for the purpose of preparing or furnishing consumer reports. § 1681b(f).

Courts have held that "even if a report is used or expected to be used for a non-consumer purpose, it may still fall within the definition of a consumer report if it contains information that was originally collected by a consumer reporting agency with the expectation that it would be used for a consumer purpose." *Ippolito v. WNS, Inc.*, 864 F.2d 440 (7th Cir. 1988); *Bakker v. McKinnon*, 152 F.3d 1007 (8th Cir. 1998).

Permissible Uses of Credit Reports. Pursuant to 15 U.S.C. § 1681(b)(a), a consumer reporting agency can furnish a consumer report only under certain circumstances or for certain uses: (1) in response to a court order or grand jury subpoena; (2) to the person to whom the report pertains; (3) to a "person which [the agency] has reason to believe" intends to use the information in connection with (a) the extension of credit to a consumer; (b) employment purposes; (c) insurance underwriting; (d) licensing or the conferral of government benefits; (e) assessment of credit risks associated with an existing credit obligation; (f) "legitimate business need" when engaging in "a business transaction involving the consumer"; (4) to establish a person's capacity to pay child support.

Credit Reports for Employment Purposes. When an employer or potential employer seeks a credit report for employment purposes, she must first disclose in writing to the consumer that a credit report may be obtained, and the consumer must authorize in writing that the report can be obtained. The person seeking the report from a credit reporting agency must certify that she obtained the consent of the individual and that she will not use the information in violation of any equal employment opportunity law or regulation. § 1681b(b). If the person who obtained the report takes adverse action based in any way on the report, she must provide the consumer a copy of the report and a description of the consumer's rights under the FCRA. § 1681b(b).

Pursuant to § 1681b(g):

> A consumer reporting agency shall not furnish for employment purposes, or in connection with a credit or insurance transaction or a direct marketing transaction, a consumer report that contains medical information about a consumer, unless the consumer consents to the furnishing of the report.

Law Enforcement Access. Pursuant to FCRA, "a consumer reporting agency may furnish identifying information respecting any customer, limited to his name, address, former addresses, places of employment, or former places of employment, to a governmental agency." § 1681f. The FBI can obtain "the names and addresses of all financial institutions . . . at which a consumer maintains or has maintained an account" by presenting a written request to a consumer reporting agency. § 1681u(a). Additionally, pursuant to a written request by the FBI, a consumer reporting agency must disclose "identifying information respecting a consumer, limited to name, address, former addresses, places of employment, or former places of employment." The FBI, however, must certify that the information is sought in an investigation to protect against "international terrorism or clandestine intelligence activities" and that the investigation "is not conducted solely upon the basis of activities protected by the first amendment to the Constitution of the United States." § 1681u(b). To obtain additional information from a credit report, the FBI must obtain a court order and meet the same standard as above. § 1681u(c).

Moreover, § 1681v provides a broad release exemption "to a government agency authorized to conduct investigations of, or intelligence or counterintelligence activities or analysis related to, international terrorism." These entities can obtain a consumer report on an individual when the government agency provides "a written certification" to a consumer reporting agency that the information is "necessary" for an agency investigation or other agency activity.

Unauthorized Disclosures of Credit Reports: Prescreening. A typical American receives a flood of credit cards offers each year. These offers follow due to the practice of "prescreening" consumers for such offers, which FCRA permits. A credit reporting agency can furnish a credit report, without the consumer's authorization, if

> (i) the transaction consists of a firm offer of credit or insurance;
>
> (ii) the consumer reporting agency has complied with subsection (e); and
>
> (iii) there is not in effect the election by the consumer, made in accordance with subsection (e), to have the consumer's name and address excluded from lists of names provided by the agency pursuant to this paragraph. § 1681b(c).

Subsection (e) of § 1681b provides the consumer with a right to opt out of such unauthorized disclosures. If the consumer notifies the credit reporting agency by phone, the opt out shall last for two years and then expire. If the consumer notifies the credit reporting agency by submitting a signed opt-out form, then the opt out remains effective until the consumer notifies the agency otherwise. § 1681b(e).

Limitations on Information Contained in Credit Reports. Credit reporting agencies are excluded from providing certain information in credit reports, such as bankruptcy proceedings more than ten years old; suits and judgments more than seven years old; paid tax liens more than seven years old; and records of arrest, indictment, or conviction of a crime more than seven years old. § 1681c(a). These limitations do not apply, however, when a company is preparing a credit report used in connection with a credit transaction more than $150,000; underwriting a life insurance policy more than $150,000; or employing an individual with an annual salary more than $75,000. § 1681c(b).

Investigative Consumer Reports. An "investigative consumer report" is "a consumer report or portion thereof in which information on a consumer's character, general reputation, personal characteristics, or mode of living is obtained through personal interviews, with neighbors, friends, or associates." § 1681a(f). The FCRA provides limitations on investigative consumer reports. These reports cannot be prepared unless "it is clearly and accurately disclosed to the consumer that an investigative consumer report including information as to his character, general reputation, personal characteristics and mode of living, whichever are applicable, may be made." § 1681d(a)(1). The consumer, if she requests, can require disclosure "of the nature and scope of the investigation requested." § 1681d(b). Further, if the report contains any adverse information about a person gleaned from interviews with neighbors, friends, or associates, the agency must take reasonable steps to corroborate that information "from an additional source that has independent and direct knowledge of the information" or ensure that "the person interviewed is the best possible source of the information." § 1681d(d).

Accuracy. "Whenever a consumer reporting agency prepares a consumer report it shall follow reasonable procedures to assure maximum possible accuracy of the information concerning the individual about whom the report relates." § 1681e(b).

Disclosures to the Consumer. The FCRA requires that credit reporting agencies, upon request of the consumer, disclose, among other things:

> (1) All information in the consumer's file at the time of the request, except . . . any information concerning credit scores or any other risk scores or predictors relating to the consumer.
> (2) The sources of the information. . .
> (3) Identification of each person . . . that procured a consumer report [within two years for employment purposes; within one year for all other purposes] . . . .
> (4) The dates, original payees, and amounts of any checks upon which is based any adverse characterization of the consumer, included in the file at the time of disclosure. . . . § 1681g.

Responsiveness to Consumer Complaints. National credit reporting agencies must provide consumers who request disclosures under the FCRA with a toll-free telephone number at which personnel are accessible to respond to consumer inquiries during normal business hours. § 1681g(c).

Procedures in Case of Disputed Accuracy. Pursuant to § 1681i(a)(1):

> If the completeness or accuracy of any item of information contained in a consumer's file at a consumer reporting agency is disputed by the consumer and the consumer notifies the agency directly of such dispute, the agency shall reinvestigate free of charge and record the current status of the disputed information or delete the item from the file. . . .

The consumer reporting agency must provide written notice to a consumer of the results of a reinvestigation within five business days after completing the investigation. § 1681i.

If the information is found to be inaccurate or incomplete or cannot be verified, the consumer reporting agency must promptly delete it from the file. § 1681i. At the request of the consumer, the credit reporting agency must furnish notification that the item has been deleted to "any person specifically designated by the consumer who has within two years prior thereto received a consumer report for employment purposes, or within six months prior thereto received a consumer report for any other purpose." § 1681i(d).

"If the reinvestigation does not resolve the dispute, the consumer may file a brief statement setting forth the nature of the dispute." § 1681i(b).

In any subsequent credit report, the agency must clearly note that the information in question is disputed by the consumer and provide the consumer's statement. § 1681i(c).

Public Record Information for Employment Purposes. If a credit reporting agency furnishes a credit report for employment purposes containing information obtained in public records that is likely to have an adverse effect on the consumer, it must either notify the consumer of the fact that public record information is being reported along with the name and address of the person to whom the information is being reported or "maintain strict procedures designed to insure that whenever public record information which is likely to have an adverse effect on a consumer's ability to obtain employment is reported it is complete and up to date." § 1681k.

Requirements on Users of Consumer Reports. If a user of a credit report takes any adverse action on a consumer based in any way on the report, the user shall provide notice of the adverse action to the consumer, information for the consumer to contact the credit reporting agency that prepared the report, and notice of the consumer's right to obtain a free copy of the report and to dispute the accuracy of the report. § 1681m(a). Whenever credit is denied based on information obtained through sources other than a credit report, upon the consumer's written request, the person or entity denying credit shall disclose the nature of that information. § 1681m(b).

Civil Liability. A person who "willfully fails to comply with any requirement" of the FCRA is liable to the consumer for actual damages or damages between $100 and $1,000, as well as punitive damages and attorneys' fees and costs. § 1681n. Negligent failure to comply with any requirement of the FCRA results in liability to the consumer for actual damages as well as attorneys' fees and costs. § 1681n. The FTC also has the power to enforce the FCRA.

The FCRA states that an action to enforce liability under the Act must be brought within two years "from the date on which the liability arises." § 1681p. However, when the defendant has "willfully misrepresented any information required under [the FCRA] to be disclosed and the information . . . is material to [a claim under the FCRA], the actions may be brought at a time within two years after [the plaintiff's] discovery of the misrepresentation." § 1681p.

The Fair and Accurate Credit Transactions Act. In 2003, Congress passed the Fair and Accurate Credit Transactions Act (FACTA), which amended FCRA. Evan Hendricks explains the impetus for passing the FACTA:

> [K]ey provisions of the FCRA that preempted State law were set to expire on December 31, 2003. These provisions dealt with issues affecting billions of dollars in commerce: pre-approved credit card offers, duties on creditors (furnishers) to report accurately and to reinvestigate, and the sharing of personal data among corporate affiliates. Industry expressed fears that if legislation was not passed and the preemption expired, state legislatures would begin passing conflicting laws that would raise compliance costs, and worse, interfere with profits.
>
> To consumer and privacy groups, legislation was long overdue because the 1996 FCRA Amendments were not getting the job done. All of the long-standing problems related to privacy and fair information practices persisted: inaccuracy, faulty reinvestigations, reinsertion, non-responsiveness, and lax security. More dramatically, identity theft had been crowned the nation's "fastest growing crime," and the biggest harm from identity theft, everyone knew, was to the privacy of credit reports. . . .
>
> Both sides wanted legislation, but not the same legislation. Industry wanted a simple, straightforward bill that would do nothing more than make FCRA preemption permanent.
>
> Consumer privacy groups called for a detailed reform bill that would set a "floor" of new protections, but which would leave the states free to go further.[4]

One-Call Fraud Alerts. The FACTA amends FCRA to enable consumers to alert only one credit reporting agency of potential fraud rather than all of them. That agency must notify the other credit reporting agencies. 15 U.S.C. § 1681c-1.

Business Transaction Data. The FACTA gives victims of identity theft the right to require certain disclosures from the creditors used by the identity thief; these disclosures concern information about the fraudulent transactions carried out in the victim's name. 15 U.S.C. § 1681g(e)(1). To obtain this information from the creditors, however, the victim must provide one form of identification from a list (that the business gets to pick) as well as proof of the claim of identity theft (police report, affidavit). The victim's request must be in writing and must specify the date of the transaction and other transaction data. Business entities can decline this request if they believe in good faith that there is not "a high degree of confidence in knowing the true identity of the individual requesting the information." § 1681g(e)(2). Further, business entities cannot be sued if they make a disclosure in good faith under these provisions. § 1681g(e)(7). Business entities are not required to alter their record-keeping practices to provide the information required by these provisions. § 1681g(e)(8).

Block of Identity Theft Information. The FACTA amends the FCRA to provide:

[4] Hendricks, *Credit Scores, supra*, at 307-08.

> (a) *Block.* Except as otherwise provided in this section, a consumer reporting agency shall block the reporting of any information in the file of a consumer that the consumer identifies as information that resulted from an alleged identity theft, not later than 4 business days after the date of receipt by such agency of —
>
> (1) appropriate proof of the identity of the consumer;
> (2) a copy of an identity theft report;
> (3) the identification of such information by the consumer; and
> (4) a statement by the consumer that the information is not information relating to any transaction by the consumer.
>
> (b) *Notification.* A consumer reporting agency shall promptly notify the furnisher of information identified by the consumer under subsection (a) —
>
> (1) that the information may be a result of identity theft;
> (2) that an identity theft report has been filed;
> (3) that a block has been requested under this section; and
> (4) of the effective dates of the block. § 1681c-2.

SSN Truncation. If a consumer requests it, credit reporting agencies must not disclose the first five digits of the consumer's SSN. § 1681g(a)(1)(A).

Free Credit Reports. The FACTA requires credit reporting agencies to provide a free credit report once a year at the request of a consumer. § 1681j.

Disclosure of Credit Scores. The FACTA requires credit reporting agencies to disclose to a consumer her credit score. Many credit reporting agencies previously would not divulge a person's credit score. § 1681g.

Statute of Limitations. FCRA's statute of limitation extends to two years after the date when the plaintiff discovers the violation or five years after the date of the violation, whichever occurs earlier.

Preemption. The FACTA preempts state laws that address many business practices. State laws that deal with these topics — even if they provide more protection to consumers — are preempted. However, the FACTA does provide that it does not "annul, affect, or exempt any person subject to the provisions of this title from complying with the laws of any State with respect to the collection, distribution, or use of any information on consumers or for the prevention or mitigation of identity theft, except to the extent that those laws are inconsistent with any provision of this title, and then only to the extent of the inconsistency." 15 U.S.C. § 1681t. Nevertheless, the FACTA has numerous exceptions to this provision. *See* Pub. L. No. 108-159 (2003), §§ 605, 615.

SMITH V. BOB SMITH CHEVROLET, INC.

275 F. Supp. 2d 808 (W.D. Ky. 2003)

HEYBURN, J. Christopher Smith ("Plaintiff") alleges that Defendant Bob Smith Chevrolet, Inc. violated the Fair Credit Reporting Act, 15 U.S.C. § 1681 *et seq.*, and invaded his privacy in violation of Kentucky common law. . . . [B]oth parties have moved for summary judgment on the issue of whether Smith Chevrolet lacked a permissible purpose when it accessed Plaintiff's credit report; Smith Chevrolet moved to dismiss the Kentucky invasion of privacy claim. . . .

The underlying facts concern the disputed sale of a 2001 GMC Suburban. Having decided that he wanted to purchase a car, on December 13, 2000, Plaintiff completed a GMAC credit application to determine his eligibility for financing. On December 23, 2000, Plaintiff went to Smith Chevrolet with the intention of purchasing the Suburban to use on a family Christmas vacation.

After arriving at the dealership, Plaintiff met with a company employee to discuss the terms of the sale. Two factors complicated the sale. First, Plaintiff wanted to trade in his 1997 Mercury Villager. Second, as an employee of General Electric — a General Motors ("GM") supplier — he was entitled to a standard discount upon proof of employment. Although Plaintiff did have the 1997 Mercury Villager to trade-in on December 23, 2000, he did not have the proper documentation needed to secure the discount. Notwithstanding this fact, a Smith Chevrolet representative agreed to sell Plaintiff the Suburban at the GM discounted price provided he proved his entitlement to the full discount at a later date. After calculating the Villager's trade-in value and the GM discount, the two sides agreed on a price and set forth the terms of the sale in a handwritten purchase order. . . .

On January 10, 2001, Plaintiff faxed and mailed proof of his eligibility for the GM discount. Shortly thereafter, Plaintiff's bank issued Smith Chevrolet a check in the amount of the balance due.

About a week or ten days later, another dispute arose which gives rise to the current litigation. At that point Smith Chevrolet claims it realized the employee who generated the typewritten Purchase Agreement inadvertently doubled the amount of Plaintiff's discount. Smith Chevrolet contacted Plaintiff, explained the calculation error and told Plaintiff that he owed the dealership more money. Furthermore, Smith Chevrolet told Plaintiff that, until he paid the difference, it refused to transfer the Suburban's title and pay off the outstanding loan attached on the Villager trade-in. These were both actions Smith Chevrolet had promised Plaintiff it would take when Plaintiff left the lot on December 23, 2000.

Following from this dispute, on February 21, 2000, Smith Chevrolet accessed Plaintiff's consumer report. The decision to access Plaintiff's report was made by Drew Smith, Smith Chevrolet's chief executive officer and part-owner. Smith Chevrolet says it accessed Plaintiff's report to determine whether Plaintiff was (1) continuing to make payments on the Villager's loan and (2) maintaining insurance on the Villager. Plaintiff disputes Smith Chevrolet's motivations in this regard and claims that it simply wanted to invade Plaintiff's privacy.

When the parties could not agree on the amount due, Plaintiff sued Smith Chevrolet in Jefferson Circuit Court for breach of the sale contract. He demanded specific performance so that he could receive the Suburban's title and transfer the Villager loan obligations to Smith Chevrolet. About a year later, a state court jury found in Plaintiff's favor. One day earlier, on May 13, 2002, Plaintiff filed this suit in federal court. . . .

The heart of [Plaintiff's] case is the contention that Smith Chevrolet violated the FCRA when it accessed Plaintiff's credit report on February 21, 2001. Specifically, Plaintiff contends Smith Chevrolet is liable for negligently and willfully violating the responsibilities imposed by the FCRA. *See* 15 U.S.C. § 1681o (creating a private cause of action for negligent violations of the FCRA); 15 U.S.C. § 1681n (creating a private cause of action for willful violations). Both sides have filed motions for summary judgment addressing whether Smith Chevrolet had a "permissible purpose" for accessing Plaintiff's credit report. The facts central to this claim are not in dispute. Smith Chevrolet may access Plaintiff's credit report only if, as a matter of law, its actions are consistent with one of the permissible purposes set forth in 15 U.S.C. § 1681b(a)(3).

The FCRA identifies a limited set of "permissible purposes" for obtaining and using a consumer report. *See* 15 U.S.C. § 1681b(a)(3); *see also* 15 U.S.C. § 1681b(f). Those permissible purposes provide that a person may only access a consumer report if he:

> (A) intends to use the information in connection with a credit transaction involving the consumer on whom the information is to be furnished and involving the extension of credit to, or review or collection of an account of, the consumer; or
>
> (B) intends to use the information for employment purposes; or
>
> (C) intends to use the information in connection with the underwriting of insurance involving the consumer; or
>
> (D) intends to use the information in connection with a determination of the consumer's eligibility for a license or other benefit granted by a governmental instrumentality required by law to consider an applicant's financial responsibility or status; or
>
> (E) intends to use the information, as a potential investor or servicer, or current insurer, in connection with a valuation of, or an assessment of the credit or prepayment risks associated with, an existing credit obligation; or
>
> (F) otherwise has a legitimate business need for the information—
>
> (i) in connection with a business transaction that is initiated by the consumer; or
>
> (ii) to review an account to determine whether the consumer continues to meet the terms of the account.

15 U.S.C. § 1681b(a)(3).

In its summary judgment motion, Smith Chevrolet contends it had three bases for accessing Plaintiff's credit report. The Court now addresses each of these arguments.

First and most persuasively, Smith Chevrolet contends its actions complied with § 1681b(a)(3)(f)(i). That section provides that one may obtain a consumer report if it "has a legitimate business need for the information . . . in connection with a business transaction that is initiated by the consumer. . ." Smith Chevrolet argues that because the transaction was in dispute, it needed to ascertain the value of its collateral. If it appeared that Plaintiff was not current on his payments for the Mercury Villager, then his indebtedness would have increased over and above the amount owed Smith Chevrolet.

As a starting point, the Court begins with the FCRA's text. The applicability of this permissible purpose boils down to whether Smith Chevrolet's use of the credit report was "in connection with a transaction initiated by the consumer," as the statute uses those terms. That restriction to the actual statutory usage is important here because, in the abstract, it is true Smith Chevrolet accessed Plaintiff's credit report in connection with a transaction Plaintiff at one point initiated. The Court concludes, however, that the statute uses the terms "in connection with a transaction initiated by the consumer" more restrictively.

Turning to the text at issue, when Congress defined the term "consumer report," it stated:

> The term "consumer report" means any written, oral, or other communication of any information by a consumer reporting agency bearing on a consumer's credit worthiness, credit standing, credit capacity, character, general reputation, personal characteristics, or mode of living which is used or expected to be used or collected in whole or in part for the purpose of serving as a factor in establishing the consumer's eligibility for—
>
> (A) credit or insurance to be used primarily for personal, family, or household purposes;
>
> (B) employment purposes; or
>
> (C) any other purpose authorized under section 604 [15 U.S.C. § 1681b].

15 U.S.C. § 1681a(d).

This definition suggests that Congress primarily envisioned consumer reports being disseminated for the purposes of assessing "eligibility." Then, in § 1681b(a)(3), Congress listed additional specific permissible purposes pertaining to the extension of credit, collection of an account, employment purposes, the underwriting of insurance for a consumer, determining a consumer's eligibility for a governmental benefit, and the valuation of a consumer's credit risk. The rule of *ejusdem generis* provides that when general words follow an enumeration of specific terms, the general words are construed to embrace only objects similar in nature to those objects enumerated by the preceding specific words. The definition of "consumer report" therefore includes those reports needed to assess a consumer's eligibility for a benefit, as well as other predictable needs — such as collecting money owed under an agreement and assessing a particular consumer's credit or insurance risk — that arise in the midst of a typical business transaction. In fact, in every one of these situations, the consumer report is obtained either to provide a benefit to a consumer or to collect a pre-existing debt.

Tellingly, the two permissible purposes stated in § 1681b(a)(3)(F) can also be read to effectuate these same ends. That is, § 1681b(a)(3)(F)(i) suggests the retention of a credit report for the purpose of furthering a business transaction initiated by a consumer and § 1681b(a)(3)(F)(ii) permits the use of a credit report to determine whether a consumer continues to be eligible for a benefit. It is a basic principle of statutory construction that a statute should be read and construed as a whole. Like the definition of "consumer report" and consistent with the other five specific permissible purposes, these two permissible purposes also suggest that Congress intended to allow access to a consumer report either when that access would benefit a consumer or would facilitate the collection of pre-existing debt.

To be precise, Smith Chevrolet's stated reason for accessing the credit report was not in connection with a standard business transaction that Plaintiff initiated. Instead, and quite significantly in this Court's view, Smith Chevrolet accessed the credit report to determine how much additional money it could collect, apart from what the two parties agreed upon in a standard business transaction. Almost certainly, it did not access Plaintiff's credit report for a reason beneficial to the consumer. Nor did it access the credit report to collect on a pre-existing debt. Rather, it accessed the report for its own business purposes and as part of a new event: the recovery of the duplicative discount. Although this is a fine distinction, it may be an important one. Smith Chevrolet's interpretation of the phrase "in connection with" is limitless. Under its reading, so long as any company had a reason to question any part of a transaction, it could access a consumer's credit report "in connection with a business transaction" that at some point was "initiated by the consumer." That is, five weeks, five months, or five years down the line, Smith Chevrolet could access Plaintiff's credit report if some dispute ever arose about the contracted price. In the Court's view, such an interpretation would give commercial entities an unlimited blank check to access and *reaccess* a consumer credit report long after the typical issues of eligibility, price, and financing were determined. Neither the specific language nor the overall scope of the FCRA can be said to support such an interpretation. . . .

Moreover, nearly every federal court addressing this issue has similarly held that the "legitimate business need" permissible purpose should be narrowly construed in the context of the other five enumerated purposes. . . .

The Court concludes, therefore, that when Smith Chevrolet accessed Plaintiff's credit report it was not, as a practical matter, part of the transaction which Plaintiff initiated. That transaction, in so far as Plaintiff's eligibility and debt was concerned, ended when the parties created a contract for the car's price and Plaintiff paid that price in full. Under any conceivable interpretation of the facts in this case, Smith Chevrolet cannot be said to have a "legitimate business need" for Plaintiff's credit report "in connection with a transaction initiated by the consumer." § 604(a)(3)(F)(i).

Smith Chevrolet also argues that its actions were protected both by §§ 1681b(3)(A) and 1681b(a)(1)(F)(ii) which provide that:

> Any consumer reporting agency may furnish a consumer report under the following circumstances and no other: . . .
>
> (A) to a person which it has reason to believe intends to use the information in connection with a credit transaction involving the consumer on whom the information is to be furnished and involving the extension of credit to, or review or collection of an account of the consumer; or . . .
>
> (F) otherwise has a legitimate business need for the information . . . (ii) to review an account to determine whether the consumer continues to meet the terms of the account.

Smith Chevrolet claims that it had a permissible purpose under both of these provisions because, due to its own error, Plaintiff received twice the discount he was entitled to and so a debt remained. Therefore, Smith Chevrolet says that it was reviewing whether Plaintiff owed any additional debt. And, because reviewing the size of the debt Plaintiff owed is synonymous with "collection of an account" and with determining "whether [Chris Smith] continue[d] to meet the terms of the account," Smith Chevrolet contends it therefore clearly had a permissible purpose.

The problem with this argument is that there was no outstanding debt and, consequently, there was no "account" to collect on. To be sure, Smith Chevrolet thought there *should be* an outstanding debt. Thinking there *should be* a debt, Smith Chevrolet contacted Plaintiff and ordered him to pay. At that point, Plaintiff refused to pay. Only then did Smith Chevrolet access Plaintiff's credit report.

Whether a debt or existing account exists simply cannot be a function of whether Smith Chevrolet alleges the existence of a debt. To do so would allow Smith Chevrolet infinite opportunities to access Plaintiff's credit report, so long as he could come up with a reason for thinking the account should continue in existence. As this Court has explained elsewhere, the FCRA intended to strike a balance between protecting the needs of commerce and the consumer's privacy interest. The Court finds that Smith Chevrolet must have a reasonable belief that the debt existed. Here, Smith Chevrolet's decision to investigate Plaintiff's credit report was not based on a reasonable belief that debt was owed; it was based on a belief that the original transaction was mistaken. Plaintiff had no reason to suspect that any new debt would arise after the initial transaction was completed. For all practical purposes that transaction was closed when the vehicle was delivered and Plaintiff made his payment. To find these permissible purposes applicable in this instance would extend the FCRA's language well beyond its intended purpose. . . .

Both sides have also moved for summary judgment on Plaintiff's claim of willful non-compliance. Section 1681n provides for civil liability in cases where the defendant willfully fails to comply with FCRA. In such a case, punitive damages may be awarded. 15 U.S.C. § 1681n(a)(2). This Court has recently explained the standard for liability under § 1681n, stating that, "[t]o show willful noncompliance with the FCRA, [the Plaintiff] must show that [defendant] knowingly and intentionally committed an act in conscious disregard for the rights of others, but need not show malice or evil motive."

Questions involving a party's state of mind are generally appropriately resolved by a jury rather than on summary judgment. From what the Court can ascertain at this point, the following facts are undisputed. Carol Hodges, a former Finance and Insurance Manager for Smith Chevrolet, has testified that the company did not have "written polices" regarding the acquisition of credit reports. She said that salespeople could freely access consumer credit reports. Hodges also said that the company had some unwritten rules for accessing customer credit reports, but these rules were not strictly followed. In fact, Smith Chevrolet's practices were "haphazard" and "very sloppy." Hodges had no part in the February 21, 2001, events and has no idea if Smith Chevrolet acted responsibly the day it accessed Plaintiff's credit report.

Based on these disputed facts, the Court cannot enter summary judgment on the issue of Smith Chevrolet's state of mind and will therefore deny the parties cross motions for summary judgment as they pertain to § 1681n.

Last, Smith Chevrolet has moved for summary judgment on Plaintiff's invasion of privacy claim. The Supreme Court of Kentucky adopted the principles for invasion of privacy as enunciated in the Restatement (Second) of Torts (1976) in *McCall v. Courier-Journal and Louisville Times Co.,* 623 S.W.2d 882, 887 (Ky. 1981). . . .

NOTES & QUESTIONS

1. ***Legitimate Business Need.*** In *Smith Chevrolet*, a critical element in the court's decision is its finding that the auto dealership must have a "reasonable belief" that the debt existed to access the credit report. But the decision to investigate the credit report was based, in fact, on a belief that the Plaintiff should owe the car dealer more than he did (due to the mistaken double discount). How does the court interpret the FCRA's statutory provision that allows businesses access to consumer credit reports when there is "a legitimate business need for the information"?
2. ***Permissible Uses of Consumer Reports.*** The FCRA contains a provision for civil liability for "obtaining a consumer report under false pretenses or knowingly without a permissible purpose." 15 U.S.C. § 1681n(a)(1)(B). But what, exactly, is a "consumer report"? A consumer report is defined based on the purposes for which it is used. These purposes include credit, insurance, and employment background checks, among others. 15 U.S.C. § 1681b.

   In *Phillips v. Grendahl,* 312 F.3d 357 (8th Cir. 2002), Mary Grendahl became suspicious of her daughter Sarah's fiancée, Lavon Phillips. She believed he was lying about being an attorney as well as his ex-wives and girlfriends. Grendahl contacted Kevin Fitzgerald, a friend who worked for a detective agency. By searching computer databases, Fitzgerald obtained Phillips's Social Security number and previous addresses. He then submitted the data to Econ Control to obtain a report called a "Finder's Report." A Finder's Report includes a person's "address, aliases, birthdate, employer addresses, and the identity of firms with which the consumer had credit accounts and firms that had made inquiries about the consumer."

   When Phillips discovered the investigation, he sued Grendahl, the detective agency Fitzgerald worked for, and Econ Control. The court concluded that the Finder's Report was a "consumer report" under FCRA. It also concluded that the defendants did not have a valid purpose under FCRA for obtaining the report:

   > The only purpose for obtaining the report was to obtain information on Mary Grendahl's prospective son-in-law. Investigating a person because he wants to marry one's daughter is not a statutory consumer purpose under section 1681b(a). Even if getting married can be characterized as a consumer transaction under section 1681b(a)(3), it was not Mary Grendahl, but her

> daughter, whom Phillips was engaged to marry. He had no business transaction pending with Mary Grendahl. There was no permissible purpose for obtaining or using a consumer report.

3. ***Liability Under FCRA.*** FCRA creates liability for willfully or negligently failing to comply with its requirements. People can recover actual damages or statutory damages between $100 and $1,000 for willful violations, plus punitive damages and attorneys' fees and costs. § 1681n. People can recover actual damages and attorneys' fees and costs for negligent violations. § 1681n. Willful means that one intentionally commits an act "in conscious disregard for the rights of others." In *Safeco Insurance Co. v. Burr,* 127 S. Ct. 2201 (2007), the Supreme Court held that acting in "reckless disregard" of a consumer's rights under FCRA was sufficient to establish willfulness.

   Jeff Sovern notes that the FCRA's fault standard for liability — negligence — is inadequate to allow many victims to pursue relief because victims "are not normally aware of the procedures a credit bureau uses when issuing an erroneous credit report or what constitutes reasonable procedures." Because each individual consumer's losses will not be very high, consumers may not bring valid cases because of high litigation costs. Therefore, Sovern argues, credit reports should "be made strictly liable for attributing the transactions of identity thieves to innocent customers." Sovern also recommends liquidated damages for identity theft cases in order to reduce litigation costs.[5]

4. ***Furnishing Information to a Consumer Reporting Agency.*** In *Lema v. Citibank,* 935 F. Supp. 695 (D. Md. 1996), Citibank issued the plaintiff a credit card. When the plaintiff's account became delinquent, Citibank reported the information to consumer reporting agencies. The plaintiff sued Citibank under FCRA, claiming that the information it supplied to the consumer reporting agencies was inaccurate. The court dismissed the claim:

   > The FCRA imposes civil liability only on consumer reporting agencies and users of consumer information. Thus, plaintiff must show that defendants are either of those entities in order to withstand defendants' summary judgment motion. . . .
   >
   > Plaintiff alleges only that defendants reported to third parties information regarding transactions between defendants and plaintiff. Defendants did not therefore furnish a consumer report regarding plaintiff, nor did they act as a consumer reporting agency with respect to him.

   The court noted that the FCRA, § 1681h, provides qualified immunity for those that furnish allegedly false information to consumer reporting agencies. Plaintiffs can "bring a state law claim of defamation, invasion of privacy or negligence, provided such plaintiff alleges that defendants acted with malice or wilful intent to injure plaintiff."

---

[5] Jeff Sovern, *The Jewel of Their Souls: Preventing Identity Theft Through Loss Allocation Rules,* 64 U. Pitt. L. Rev. 343, 393, 406-07 (2003).

SARVER V. EXPERIAN INFORMATION SOLUTIONS

390 F.3d 969 (7th Cir. 2004)

EVANS, J. Lloyd Sarver appeals from an order granting summary judgment to Experian Information Solutions, Inc., a credit reporting company, on his claim under the Fair Credit Reporting Act (FCRA), 15 U.S.C. §§ 1681 *et seq.*

Experian reported inaccurate information on Sarver's credit report, which on August 2, 2002, caused the Monogram Bank of Georgia to deny him credit. Monogram cited the Experian credit report and particularly a reference to a bankruptcy which appeared on the report. Both before and after Monogram denied him credit, Sarver asked for a copy of his credit report. He received copies both times and both reports showed that accounts with Cross Country Bank were listed as having been "involved in bankruptcy." No other accounts had that notation, although other accounts had significant problems. A Bank One installment account had a balance past due 180 days, and another company, Providian, had written off $3,099 on a revolving account.

On August 29, 2002, Sarver wrote Experian informing it that the bankruptcy notation was inaccurate and asking that it be removed from his report. Sarver provided his full name and address but no other identifying information. On September 11, Experian sent Sarver a letter requesting further information, including his Social Security number, before it could begin an investigation. Sarver did not provide the information, but instead filed the present lawsuit, which resulted in summary judgment for Experian. It was later confirmed that the notation on the Cross Country Bank account was inaccurate and, as it turned out, another Lloyd Sarver was the culprit on that account.

In this appeal from the judgment dismissing his case, Sarver claims summary judgment was improper because issues of fact exist as to whether Experian violated FCRA, §§ 1681i and 1681e(b). . . .

Section 1681i requires a credit reporting agency to reinvestigate items on a credit report when a consumer disputes the validity of those items. An agency can terminate a reinvestigation if it determines the complaint is frivolous, "including by reason of a failure by a consumer to provide sufficient information to investigate the disputed information." § 1681i(a)(3). We do not need to decide whether Sarver's failure to provide the information Experian requested rendered his complaint frivolous; his claim under § 1681i(a) fails for another reason, a lack of evidence of damages. In order to prevail on his claims, Sarver must show that he suffered damages as a result of the inaccurate information. As we have said in *Crabill v. Trans Union, L.L.C.,* 259 F.3d 662, 664 (7th Cir. 2001):

> Without a causal relation between the violation of the statute and the loss of credit, or some other harm, a plaintiff cannot obtain an award of "actual damages."

On this point, the district court concluded that there were no damages. Our review of the record leads us to agree.

Sarver, however, disagrees and claims that he suffered damages when he was denied credit from Monogram Bank of Georgia on August 2, 2002. This letter cannot be a basis for his damage claim, however, because as of August 2,

Experian had no notice of any inaccuracies in the report. Even though Sarver asked for a copy of his report on July 18, he did not notify Experian of a problem until a month and a half later. Experian must be notified of an error before it is required to reinvestigate. As we have made clear, the FCRA is not a strict liability statute. *Henson v. CSC Credit Servs.,* 29 F.3d 280 (7th Cir. 1994).

Sarver also does not show that he suffered pecuniary damages between August 29 (when he notified Experian of the error) and February 20, 2003 (when the Cross Country account was removed from his file). He does not claim that he applied for credit during that time period or that a third party looked at his report. In addition, his claim for emotional distress fails. We have maintained a strict standard for a finding of emotional damage "because they are so easy to manufacture." *Aiello v. Providian Fin. Corp.,* 239 F.3d 876, 880 (7th Cir. 2001). We have required that when "the injured party's own testimony is the only proof of emotional damages, he must explain the circumstances of his injury in reasonable detail; he cannot rely on mere conclusory statements." *Denius v. Dunlap,* 330 F.3d 919, 929 (7th Cir. 2003). Finally, to obtain statutory damages under FCRA § 1681n(a), Sarver must show that Experian willfully violated the Act. There is similarly no evidence of willfulness. Summary judgment was properly granted on this claim.

We turn to Sarver's claim under § 1681e(b), which requires that a credit reporting agency follow "reasonable procedures to assure maximum possible accuracy" when it prepares a credit report. The reasonableness of a reporting agency's procedures is normally a question for trial unless the reasonableness or unreasonableness of the procedures is beyond question. *Crabill,* 259 F.3d at 663. However, to state a claim under the statute,

> a consumer must sufficiently allege "that a credit reporting agency prepared a report containing 'inaccurate' information." However, the credit reporting agency is not automatically liable even if the consumer proves that it prepared an inaccurate credit report because the FCRA "does not make reporting agencies strictly liable for all inaccuracies." A credit reporting agency is not liable under the FCRA if it followed "reasonable procedures to assure maximum possible accuracy," but nonetheless reported inaccurate information in the consumer's credit report.

Henson, 29 F.3d at 284. The Commentary of the Federal Trade Commission to the FCRA, 16 C.F.R. pt. 600, app., section 607 at 3.A, states that the section does not hold a reporting agency responsible where an item of information, received from a source that it reasonably believes is reputable, turns out to be inaccurate unless the agency receives notice of systemic problems with its procedures.

Experian has provided an account of its procedures. The affidavit of David Browne, Experian's compliance manager, explains that the company gathers credit information originated by approximately 40,000 sources. The information is stored in a complex system of national databases, containing approximately 200 million names and addresses and some 2.6 billion trade lines, which include information about consumer accounts, judgments, etc. The company processes over 50 million updates to trade information each day. Lenders report millions of accounts to Experian daily; they provide identifying information, including address, social security number, and date of birth. The identifying information is used to link the credit items to the appropriate consumer. Mr. Browne also notes that Experian's computer system does not store complete credit reports, but rather stores the individual items of credit information linked to identifying information. The credit report is generated at the time an inquiry for it is received.

One can easily see how, even with safeguards in place, mistakes can happen. But given the complexity of the system and the volume of information involved, a mistake does not render the procedures unreasonable. In his attempt to show that Experian's procedures are unreasonable, Sarver argues that someone should have noticed that only the Cross Country accounts were shown to have been involved in bankruptcy. That anomaly should have alerted Experian, Sarver says, to the fact that the report was inaccurate. What Sarver is asking, then, is that each computer-generated report be examined for anomalous information and, if it is found, an investigation be launched. In the absence of notice of prevalent unreliable information from a reporting lender, which would put Experian on notice that problems exist, we cannot find that such a requirement to investigate would be reasonable given the enormous volume of information Experian processes daily.

We found in *Henson* that a consumer reporting agency was not liable, as a matter of law, for reporting information from a judgment docket unless there was prior notice from the consumer that the information might be inaccurate. We said that a

> contrary rule of law would require credit reporting agencies to go beyond the face of numerous court records to determine whether they correctly report the outcome of the underlying action. Such a rule would also require credit reporting agencies to engage in background research which would substantially increase the cost of their services. In turn, they would be forced to pass on the increased costs to their customers and ultimately to the individual consumer.

Henson, 29 F.3d at 285. The same could be said for records from financial institutions. As we said, in his affidavit Mr. Browne proclaims, and there is nothing in the record to make us doubt his statement, that lenders report many millions of accounts to Experian daily. Sarver's report, dated August 26, 2002, contains entries from six different lenders. The increased cost to Experian to examine each of these entries individually would be enormous. We find that as a matter of law there is nothing in this record to show that Experian's procedures are unreasonable.

NOTES & QUESTIONS

1. *A Critical Perspective on* Sarver. Consider Elizabeth De Armond:

> In justifying the agency's failure to resolve the anomalies within the records attributed to the plaintiff, the court emphasized the 200 million names and addresses, the 2.6 billion trade lines, and the complexity of the system. This reasoning overlooks that the very complexity of the system reveals the ability of the agency to control the high volume of individuals and records, and that ability should alert the agency to the high risk of misattributing information.

The court ruled that the agency's failure to investigate the inconsistency was not unreasonable because the agency had no notice that the specific lender who had provided information about the impaired accounts was unreliable. However, the question, in order to protect individuals from reckless attribution, should not be whether any single provider is unreliable. The question should have been whether reporting it as the plaintiff's without checking it, given the obvious inconsistency, was reckless. Where the agency was aware of the risk of misattribution from fuzzy matching, and that matching produced a record that was unlike the others, a jury should decide whether the failure to take any steps to verify the anomalous data breached the FCRA's accuracy standard.

The *Sarver* court also reasoned that to require an agency to further investigate the accuracy of a consumer's records when an anomaly appeared would impose "enormous" increased costs. However, the court did not refer to any estimate of the costs or explain why an already complex system capable of making many comparisons among different records could not inexpensively adjust to cross-checking data when reliability was at issue. Furthermore, when an anomaly appears that would work to the consumer's detriment, an agency could simply decline to attribute the negative data should it not want to take the extra effort of verifying it. The decision allows the agency all of the benefits of its database technology with none of the responsibilities.[6]

This criticism raises a baseline issue: who should bear the costs of relative degrees of inaccuracy and accuracy in the credit system? If credit agency's need investigate more kinds of inconsistencies in credit reports, will consumers as a group bear the additional costs?

2. ***Is FCRA too Deferential to Industry Interests?*** Consider De Armond on the flaws of FCRA:

> [FCRA] inadequately protects individuals from the consequential and emotional damages caused by misattributed acts for several reasons. . . .
>
> The Act's most significant flaw is that it imposes meaningful accuracy requirements only after a false and negative item has been reported, has already been put into the data sea. However, given that digitized data is far more available, accessible, duplicable, and transmittable than old paper records, once a false record has been put into the data sea, it is very hard to ever completely cull it out. . . .
>
> The Act is designed to impose meaningful accuracy standards only after inaccurate information has already been provided by a data provider and reported by a data aggregator. The Act permits the original data provider, called a furnisher under the Act, to furnish nearly any item in a consumer's name without first verifying that it belongs to that consumer. But the Act only prohibits the furnisher from furnishing information that the furnisher either "knows or has reasonable cause to believe" to be inaccurate. A furnisher only has "'reasonable cause to believe that an item of information is inaccurate'" if the furnisher has "specific knowledge, other than solely allegations by the consumer, that would cause a reasonable person to have substantial doubts about the accuracy of the information." . . .

[6] Elizabeth D. De Armond, *Frothy Chaos: Modern Data Warehousing and Old-Fashioned Defamation*, 41 Val. U. L. Rev. 1061, 1099-1102, 1108 (2007).

> Thus, the agency acquires information that likely has not been subjected to any scrutiny, let alone verified. The agency acquires the information, either electronically or via magnetic tape from the provider, and stores it electronically, where it sits until needed for a report. Just as the Act imposes a relatively weak accuracy requirement on data providers at the point of initial provision, the Act places only loose limits on aggregators that then report the information. When a subscriber requests a report on a particular consumer, the aggregator, the consumer reporting agency, must only follow "reasonable procedures to assure maximum possible accuracy" of the information that it returns to the subscriber. The provision does not in fact require agencies to ensure the maximum possible accuracy of every item of information, or to do much if anything to match, verify, or cross-check the information. . . .
>
> It is only after an individual has learned that an agency has falsely charged him or her with negative data that the individual can require an aggregator to examine the data. . . .

As *Sarver* also points out, the Experian computer system does not store computer credit reports, but only generates them when an inquiry is received. Individual items of credit information are stored linked to identifying information, which allows their retrieval and compilation into a credit report. Should individual items of information be reviewed for accuracy at the initial time that the credit agency collects them?

3. ***What Constitutes Negligence in Investigating Errors in Consumer Reports?*** In *Dennis v. BEH-1, LLC*, 504 F.3d 892 (9th Cir. 2007), Jason Dennis was sued by his landlord, but the parties agreed to drop the lawsuit after reaching a settlement. The parties filed a "Request for Dismissal" with the court clerk, and the court register properly registered the dismissal. Later on, Experian Information Solutions, Inc. stated on Dennis's credit report that a civil claim judgment had been entered against him for $1,959. Dennis contacted Experian to complain about the error. Experian had Hogan Information Services, a third party contractor, verify Dennis's claims. Hogan replied that Experian's information was correct and sent along a copy of the stipulation of settlement between Dennis and his landlord. Experian told Dennis that it would not correct his report. Dennis sued under FCRA, contending that Experian failed to maintain "reasonable procedures" under § 1681e(b) to ensure the accuracy of credit reports and that it failed to adequately reinvestigate the disputed information under § 1681i. The district court dismissed Dennis's case on summary judgment. The court of appeals, however, concluded:

> The district court erred insofar as it held that Dennis couldn't make the prima facie showing of inaccurate reporting required by sections 1681e and 1681i. Experian's credit report on Dennis *is* inaccurate. Because the case against Dennis was dismissed, there could have been no "Civil claim judgment" against him: "A dismissal without prejudice . . . has the effect of a final judgment *in favor* of the defendant." Dennis has made the prima facie showing of inaccuracy required by sections 1681e and 1681i.
>
> The district court also seems to have awarded summary judgment to Experian because Dennis didn't offer evidence of "actual damages" as required by section 1681*o*(a)(1). Here, too, the district court erred. Dennis testified that he hoped to start a business and that he diligently paid his bills on

> time for years so that he would have a clean credit history when he sought financing for the venture. The only blemish on his credit report in April 2003 was the erroneously reported judgment. According to Dennis, that was enough to cause several lenders to decline his applications for credit, dashing his hopes of starting a new business. Dennis also claims that Experian's error caused his next landlord to demand that Dennis pay a greater security deposit. In addition to those tangible harms, Dennis claims that Experian's inaccurate report caused him emotional distress, which we've held to be "actual damages."

The court of appeals reasoned that Hogan failed to understand the meaning of the Request for Dismissal document and that Experian could readily have detected this mistake:

> Experian could have caught Hogan's error if it had consulted the Civil Register in Dennis's case, which can be viewed free of charge on the Los Angeles Superior Court's excellent website. As described above, the Register clearly indicates that the case against Dennis was dismissed. Experian apparently never looked at the Register.
>
> Experian also could have detected Hogan's mistake by examining the document Hogan retrieved from Dennis's court file. Hogan mistakenly believed that this document proved that judgment had been entered against Dennis; in fact, the document confirms Dennis's account of what happened. The document is a written stipulation between Dennis and his landlord that no judgment would be entered against Dennis so long as Dennis complied with the payment schedule. The parties couldn't have been clearer on this point: "If paid, case dismissed. If not paid, judgment to enter upon [landlord's] declaration of non-payment. . . ."

The court of appeals further concluded that it had no need to remand the case for a jury trial regarding Experian's negligence:

> Even accepting as true everything Experian has claimed, no rational jury could find that the company wasn't negligent. The stipulation Hogan retrieved from Dennis's court file may be unusual, but it's also unambiguous, and Experian was negligent in mis-interpreting it as an entry of judgment. Experian is also responsible for the negligence of Hogan, the investigation service it hired to review Dennis's court file. . . .
>
> When conducting a reinvestigation pursuant to 15 U.S.C. § 1681i, a credit reporting agency must exercise reasonable diligence in examining the court file to determine whether an adverse judgment has, in fact, been entered against the consumer. A reinvestigation that overlooks documents in the court file expressly stating that *no* adverse judgment was entered falls far short of this standard. On our own motion, therefore, we grant summary judgment to Dennis on his claim that Experian negligently failed to conduct a reasonable reinvestigation in violation of section 1681i. Whether Experian's failure was also willful, in violation of section 1681n, is a question for the jury on remand.
>
> This case illustrates how important it is for Experian, a company that traffics in the reputations of ordinary people, to train its employees to understand the legal significance of the documents they rely on. Because Experian negligently failed to conduct a reasonable reinvestigation, we grant summary judgment to Dennis on this claim. We remand only so that the district court may calculate damages and award attorney's fees. As to all other

> claims under the Fair Credit Reporting Act, we reverse summary judgment for Experian and remand for trial. Dennis is also entitled to attorney's fees for an entirely successful appeal. 15 U.S.C. § 1681*o*(a)(2). . . .

4. ***Defamation, Privacy, and FCRA's Qualified Immunity.*** Can the credit reporting agencies be sued under state tort law for defamation or for invasion of privacy? Regarding defamation, recall that the Supreme Court held in *Dun & Bradstreet, Inc. v. Greenmoss Builders, Inc.,* 472 U.S. 749 (1985), that a credit reporting agency reporting on an individual is engaging in "speech on matters of purely private concern" and, consequently, receives less First Amendment protection than other forms of speech. Therefore, for such cases of defamation, the First Amendment limits established by *New York Times v. Sullivan,* 376 U.S. 254 (1964), and *Gertz v. Robert Welch, Inc.,* 418 U.S. 323 (1974), do not apply. All forms of damages (compensatory, presumed, and punitive) are available without showing "actual malice."

   However, FCRA provides qualified immunity to credit reporting agencies and to the furnishers of information to credit reporting agencies:

   > Except as provided in sections 1681n and 1681o of this title, no consumer may bring any action or proceeding in the nature of defamation, invasion of privacy, or negligence with respect to the reporting of information against any consumer reporting agency, or any user of information, or any person who furnishes information to a consumer reporting agency, based on information disclosed pursuant to section 1681g, 1681h, or 1681m of this title, or based on information disclosed by a user of a consumer report to or for a consumer against whom the user has taken adverse action, based in whole or in part on the report except as to false information furnished with malice or wilful intent to injure such consumer. § 1681h(e).

   Therefore, although the Constitution doesn't require actual malice to establish defamation for the false reporting of credit information, the FCRA does. Actual malice exists if one states false information with knowledge of its falsity or in reckless disregard for the truth.

   Establishing malice can be difficult. Consider *Morris v. Equifax Information Services, L.L.C.*, 457 F.3d 460 (5th Cir. 2006):

   > While Morris has presented evidence that Equifax knew that Morris claimed that there were false statements in the information that Equifax was publishing about Morris, this evidence does not show that Equifax knew these statements were false. Morris also argues that Equifax had a reckless disregard for whether the statements were false because "Equifax continued to publish the same false information about Morris without lifting a finger to determine whether the information was false or not." To show "reckless disregard," however, Morris must present "sufficient evidence to permit the conclusion that the defendant *in fact entertained serious doubts* as to the truth of his publication." *St. Amant v. Thompson*, 390 U.S. 727 (1968) (emphasis added). In this case, there is no such evidence.

   How does a person establish that a credit reporting agency "entertained serious doubts" about the truth of its report? The difficulty is that the reporting is an automated process involving hundreds of millions of people. If a person calls to point out an error, should that be sufficient to show that the credit reporting agency had knowledge? Or does it make it too easy for any person to establish reckless disregard, as it would be established anytime a person merely made an allegation of falsity?

Elizabeth De Armond recommends that notwithstanding the requirement of proving actual malice, defamation and false light can serve as a good way to protect victims of credit reporting mistakes. She argues that credit reporting agencies offer special services to protect people from identity theft if people pay for it, but the existence of these services demonstrates that credit reporting agencies "have the analytical capacity to discern unusual activity in a particular consumer's name, at least if the consumer is willing to pay for it." De Armond contends that "data providers and data aggregators should be well aware that data may not belong to whom it appears. Failing to acknowledge that risk, by verifying identities of doers of the deeds they report, surpasses the standard of recklessness." Specifically, with regard to the *Sarver* case, she argues: "In *Sarver,* where the aggregator, a consumer reporting agency, attributed accounts that indicated the borrower's bankruptcy to the wrong individual, the agency acted recklessly . . . when it repeated the misattribution, even after the plaintiff had notified the agency of its error."[7]

2. THE USE AND DISCLOSURE OF FINANCIAL INFORMATION

(a) The Breach of Confidentiality Tort and Financial Institutions

Recall the breach of confidentiality tort from Chapter 4. Under the common law, a doctor can be liable to a patient if she discloses the patient's personal information. A number of jurisdictions extend the tort of breach of confidentiality to disclosures by banks and financial institutions of their customers' financial information. In *Peterson v. Idaho First Nat'l Bank*, 367 P.2d 284 (Idaho 1961), the court held that a bank could be sued for breach of confidentiality for disclosing customer information:

> It is generally stated that the relation between a bank and its general depositor is that of debtor and creditor. . . . But it is also said that in discharging its obligation to a depositor a bank must do so subject to the rules of agency. . . .
>
> All agree that a bank should protect its business records from the prying eyes of the public, moved by curiosity or malice. No one questions its right to protect its fiduciary relationship with its customers, which, in sound banking practice, as a matter of common knowledge, is done everywhere. . . .
>
> To give such information to third persons or to the public at the instance of the customer or depositor is certainly not beyond the scope of banking powers. It is a different matter, however, when such information is sought from the bank without the consent of the depositor or customer of the bank. Indeed, it is an implied term of the contract between the banker and his customer that the banker will not divulge to third persons, without the consent of the customer, express or implied, either the state of the customer's account or any of his

[7] De Armond, *supra,* at 1139, 1132, 1130.

> transactions with the bank, or any information relating to the customer acquired through the keeping of his account. . . .
>
> It is inconceivable that a bank would at any time consider itself at liberty to disclose the intimate details of its depositors' accounts. Inviolate secrecy is one of the inherent and fundamental precepts of the relationship of the bank and its customers or depositors.

Several other jurisdictions have held likewise. *See, e.g., Barnett Bank of West Florida v. Hooper*, 498 So. 2d 923 (Fla. 1986); *Indiana Nat'l Bank v. Chapman*, 482 N.E.2d 474 (Ind. App. 1985); *Suburban Trust Co. v. Waller*, 408 A.2d 758 (Md. App. 1979); *Richfield Bank & Trust Co. v. Sjogren*, 244 N.W.2d 648 (Minn. 1976); *McGuire v. Shubert,* 722 A.2d 1087 (Pa. Super. 1998).

(b) The Gramm-Leach-Bliley Act

In 1999, Congress passed the Financial Services Modernization Act, more commonly known as the Gramm-Leach-Bliley (GLB) Act, Pub. L. No. 106-102, codified at 15 U.S.C. §§ 6801–6809. The GLB Act was designed to restructure financial services industries, which had long been regulated under the Glass-Steagall Act of 1933. The Glass-Steagall Act, passed in response to the Great Depression, prevented different types of financial institutions (e.g., banks, brokerage houses, insurers) from affiliating with each other. The GLB Act enables the creation of financial conglomerates that provide a host of different forms of financial services.

The law authorizes widespread sharing of personal information by financial institutions such as banks, insurers, and investment companies. The law permits sharing of personal information between companies that are joined together or affiliated with each other as well as sharing of information between unaffiliated companies. To protect privacy, the Act requires a variety of agencies (FTC, Comptroller of Currency, SEC, and a number of others) to establish "appropriate standards for the financial institutions subject to their jurisdiction" to "insure security and confidentiality of customer records and information" and "protect against unauthorized access" to the records. 15 U.S.C. § 6801.

Nonpublic Personal Information. The privacy provisions of the GLB Act only apply to "nonpublic personal information" that consists of "personally identifiable financial information." § 6809(4). Thus, the law only protects *financial* information that is *not public*.

Sharing of Information with Affiliated Companies. The GLB Act permits financial institutions that are joined together to share the "nonpublic personal information" that each affiliate possesses. For example, suppose an affiliate has access to a person's medical information. This information could be shared with an affiliate bank that could then turn down a person for a loan. Affiliates must tell customers that they are sharing such information. § 6802(a). The disclosure can be in the form of a general disclosure in a privacy policy. § 6803(a). There is no way for individuals to block this sharing of information.

Sharing of Information with Nonaffiliated Companies. Financial institutions can share personal information with nonaffiliated companies only if they first provide individuals with the ability to opt out of the disclosure. § 6802(b). However, people cannot opt out if the financial institution provides personal data to nonaffiliated third parties "to perform services for or functions on behalf of the financial institution, including marketing of the financial institution's own products and services, or financial products or services offered pursuant to joint agreements between two or more financial institutions." § 6802(b)(2). The financial institution must disclose the information sharing and must have a contract with the third party requiring the third party to maintain the confidentiality of the information. § 6802(b)(2). Third parties receiving personal data from a financial institution cannot reuse that information. § 6802(c). These provisions do not apply to disclosures to credit reporting agencies.

Limits on Disclosure. Financial institutions cannot disclose (other than to credit reporting agencies) account numbers or credit card numbers for use in direct marketing (telemarketing, e-mail, or mail). § 6802(d).

Privacy Notices. The GLB Act requires that financial institutions inform customers of their privacy policies. In particular, customers must be informed about policies concerning the disclosure of personal information to affiliates and other companies and categories of information that are disclosed and the security of personal data. § 6803(a).

Security. The GLB Act requires the FTC and other agencies to establish security standards for nonpublic personal information. *See* 15 U.S.C. §§ 6801(b), 6805(b)(2). The FTC issued its final regulations on May 23, 2002. According to the regulations, financial institutions "shall develop, implement, and maintain a comprehensive information security program" that is appropriate to the "size and complexity" of the institution, the "nature and scope" of the institution's activities, and the "sensitivity of any customer information at issue." 16 C.F.R. § 314.3(a). An "information security program" is defined as "the administrative, technical, or physical safeguards [an institution uses] to access, collect, distribute, process, store, use, transmit, dispose of, or otherwise handle customer information." § 314.2(b).

Preemption. The GLB Act does not preempt state laws that provide greater protection to privacy. § 6807(b). As will be discussed below, Vermont has made use of this provision and requires opt in, or affirmative consumer consent, before a financial institution can share nonpublic personal financial information pertaining to a consumer to a nonaffiliated third party.

Critics and Supporters. Consider the following critique by Ted Janger and Paul Schwartz:

> The GLB Act has managed to disappoint both industry leaders and privacy advocates alike. Why are so many observers frustrated with the GLB Act? We have already noted the complaint of financial services companies regarding the

> expense of privacy notices. These organizations also argue that there have been scant pay-off from the costly mailings — and strong evidence backs up this claim. For example, a survey from the American Banker's Association found that 22% of banking customers said that they received a privacy notice but did not read it, and 41% could not even recall receiving a notice. The survey also found only 0.5% of banking customers had exercised their opt-out rights. . . .
>
> Not only are privacy notices difficult to understand, but they are written in a fashion that makes it hard to exercise the opt-out rights that GLB Act mandates. For example, opt-out provisions are sometimes buried in privacy notices. As the Public Citizen Litigation Group has found, "Explanations of how to opt-out invariably appear at the end of the notices. Thus, before they learn how to opt-out, consumers must trudge through up to ten pages of fine print. . . ." Public Citizen also identified many passages regarding opt-out that "are obviously designed to discourage consumers from exercising their rights under the statute." For example, some financial institutions include an opt-out box only "in a thicket of misleading statements.". . . A final tactic of GLB Act privacy notices is to state that consumers who opt-out may fail to receive "valuable offers." . . .
>
> The GLB Act merely contains an opt-out requirement; as a result, information can be disclosed to non-affiliated entities unless individuals take affirmative action, namely, informing the financial entity that they refuse this sharing of their personal data. By setting its default as an opt-out, the GLB Act fails to create any penalty on the party with superior knowledge, the financial entity, should negotiations fail to occur. In other words, the GLB leaves the burden of bargaining on the less informed party, the individual consumer. These doubts about the efficacy of opt-out are supported, at least indirectly, by the evidence concerning sometimes confusing, sometimes misleading privacy notices. . . . An opt-out default creates incentives for privacy notices that lead to *inaction* by the consumer.[8]

Marcy Peek argues that the GLB Act has actually done more to facilitate information sharing than to protect privacy. Enabling greater information uses so long as customers have a right to opt out has resulted in much more information sharing since "the opt-out right is meaningless in practice; the right to opt out of the trafficking of one's personal information is explained in lengthy, legalistic privacy policies that most people throw away as just more junk mail." More broadly, Peek argues, several laws purporting to protect privacy often "represent a façade of protection for consumers, keeping them complacent in the purported knowledge that someone is protecting their privacy interests." In the end, Peek argues, "corporate power drives information privacy law."[9]

In contrast, Peter Swire argues that the GLB Act "works surprisingly well as privacy legislation":

> Recognizing the criticisms to date, and the limits of the available evidence, I would like to make the case for a decidedly more optimistic view of the effect of the GLB notices. Even in their current flawed form and even if not a single consumer exercised the opt-out right, I contend that a principal effect of the

---

[8] Ted Janger & Paul M. Schwartz, *The Gramm-Leach-Bliley Act, Information Privacy, and the Limits of Default Rules*, 86 Minn. L. Rev. 1219, 1230-32, 1241 (2002).

[9] Marcy E. Peek, Information *Privacy and Corporate Power: Towards a Re-Imagination of Information Privacy Law*, 37 Seton Hall L. Rev. 127, 147-49, 137 (2006).

> notices has been to require financial institutions to inspect their own practices. In this respect, the detail and complexity of the GLB notices is actually a virtue. In order to draft the notice, many financial institutions undertook an extensive process, often for the first time, to learn just how data is and is not shared between different parts of the organization and with third parties. Based on my extensive discussions with people in the industry, I believe that many institutions discovered practices that they decided, upon deliberation, to change. One public example of this was the decision of Bank of America no longer to share its customers' data with third parties, even subject to opt-out. The detailed and complex notice, in short, created a more detailed roadmap for privacy compliance.[10]

The critics of the GLB Act and Swire appear to be looking at the statute from two different perspectives. The critics are looking at it from a consumer-centric view; Swire sees the positive effect that the statute has on practices within institutions. Is there a way for a statute to have a positive impact in both areas?

(c) State Financial Regulation

The Vermont Opt-in Approach. In contrast to the GLB approach, Vermont permits sharing of personal data by financial institutions with nonaffiliated companies only if companies obtain an individual's consent. This requirement of a positive response before information can be shared is termed an "opt in." State of Vermont, Department, Insurance, Securities & Health Care Administration, Banking Division, Regulation B-2001-01, Privacy of Consumer Financial and Health Information Regulation. This regulation also carefully defines the acceptable form of and process for opt-in notice. For example, when consumers want to revoke their opting in to information sharing, financial institutions cannot force "the consumer to write his or her own letter." Financial institutions also cannot make consumers "use a check-off box that was provided with the initial notice but [that] is not included with subsequent notices."

California's SB1. California's Financial Information Privacy Act, known as "SB1," Cal. Fin. Code §§ 4050–4060, was enacted "to afford persons greater privacy protections that those provided in . . . the federal Gramm-Leach-Bliley Act." § 4051. Specifically, the California legislature found that the Gramm-Leach-Bliley Act "increases the likelihood that the personal financial information of California residents will be widely shared among, between, and within companies" and that "the policies intended to protect financial privacy imposed by the Gramm-Leach-Bliley Act are inadequate to meet the privacy concerns of California residents." § 4051.5.

In contrast to the Gramm-Leach-Bliley Act, which provides people with an opt-out right, SB1, like the Vermont regulation, requires opt in:

> [A] financial institution shall not sell, share, transfer, or otherwise disclose nonpublic personal information to or with any nonaffiliated third parties without

---

[10] Peter P. Swire, *The Surprising Virtues of the New Financial Privacy Law*, 86 Minn. L. Rev. 1263, 1315-16 (2002).

> the explicit prior consent of the consumer to whom the nonpublic personal information relates. § 4052.5.

SB1 permits financial institutions to offer incentives or discounts for people to opt in. § 4053.

Financial institutions challenged SB1, arguing that it was preempted by the FCRA. In *American Bankers Association v. Gould*, 412 F.3d 1081 (9th Cir. 2005), the court concluded that "SB1 is preempted [by FCRA] to the extent that it applies to information shared between affiliates concerning consumers' 'credit worthiness, credit standing, credit capacity, character, general reputation, personal characteristics, or mode of living' that is used, expected to be used, or collected for the purpose of establishing eligibility for 'credit or insurance,' employment, or other authorized purpose." The court remanded for the district court to determine which portions of SB1 survived preemption.

On remand, *American Bankers Association v. Lockyer*, 2005 WL 2452798 (E.D. Cal. 2005) (not reported in F. Supp. 2d), the court held that "no portion of SB1's affiliate sharing provision survives" preemption. Among the difficulties for the court was that, as plaintiffs argued before it, "it would be virtually impossible to ascertain in advance whether or not information collected and shared by a financial institution would satisfy a FCRA authorized purpose." The district court explained:

> A financial institution may gather and share information with its affiliates believing in good faith that it is not required to comply with SB1 because the information will be used for an FCRA authorized purpose. If, in fact, the information is not so used, the financial institution would have acted in violation of SB1 exposing it to the penalties thereunder. This creates the untenable situation of forcing California financial institutions to either risk violation of SB1 or comply therewith whether or not the information is for an FCRA authorized purpose.

The North Dakota Opt-in Referendum and Other States. In June 2002, North Dakotans overwhelmingly rejected, by a 73 percent vote, a 2001 state law that had established an opt-out rather than opt-in standard for financial institutions in North Dakota. The Privacy Rights Clearinghouse noted: "The referendum in North Dakota was the first time this issue has been taken directly to voters."[11] New Mexico has also provided an opt-in requirement for financial institutions before sharing of personal consumer data is permitted with nonaffiliated companies.

3. IDENTITY THEFT

Identity theft is one of the most rapidly growing forms of crime. Identity theft occurs when a criminal obtains an individual's personal information and uses it to open new bank accounts, acquire credit cards, and obtain loans in that individual's name. Consider the following example from journalist Bob Sullivan:

---

[11] Privacy Rights Clearinghouse, *North Dakota Votes for "Opt-In" Financial Privacy*, June 21, 2002, at www.privacyrights.org/ar/nd_optin.htm.

> Starting in August 1998, Anthony Lemar Taylor spent a year successfully pretending to be the golf superstar [Tiger Woods]. Taylor's $50,000 spending spree included a big-screen television, stereo speakers, a living room set, even a U-Haul to move all the stolen goods. Taylor, who looks nothing like the golf legend, simply obtained a driver's license using Tiger's real name, Eldrick Woods; then, he used Wood's Social Security number to get credit in his name. . . .
>
> When Tiger himself testified during the case in 2001, Taylor, a 30-year-old career criminal, didn't stand a chance. Wood's star power helped the state throw the book at Taylor. . . . The firm, swift justice might have made other potential identity thieves think twice, but for this: Precious few identity thefts are even investigated, let alone prosecuted to the full extent of the law. The average victim has enough trouble getting the police to bother filling out an incident report. . . .
>
> The real world of identity theft . . . is . . . a haunting, paperwork nightmare, one often compared to financial rape, littered with small and large tragedies. . . . Couples can't buy homes because their credit is damaged. Identity theft victims are often denied access to the lowest interest rates and can pay as much as 50 percent more to borrow money. . . . And thousands of people face hundreds of hours of electronic trials against their erroneous credit reports and eventually end with fraudulent debts and endless nightly threatening calls from collection agencies.[12]

According to a 2007 report to the FTC, "approximately 8.3 million U.S. adults discovered that they were victims of some form of ID theft in 2005."[13] According to this report's estimates, the total losses from ID theft in that year were $15.6 billion. Moreover, "victims of all types of ID theft spent hours of their time resolving the various problems that result from ID theft. The median value for the number of hours spent resolving problems by all victims was four. However, 10 percent of all victims spent at least 55 hours resolving their problems."

In an important caveat, however, this report also notes that it may not capture all types of identity theft. In particular, it does not measure "synthetic ID theft." This activity involves a criminal creating a fictitious identity by combining information from one or more consumers. Affected consumers face considerable obstacles in detecting synthetic ID theft; therefore, any survey of identity theft, which depends on consumer self-reporting, is likely to underreport it.

Chris Hoofnagle proposes that policy responses to identity theft are hobbled by a lack of information about the dimensions of the problem.[14] He argues: "We are asking the wrong people about the crime. . . . Victims often do not know how their personal data were stolen or who stole the information." Hoofnagle's solution is to create a reporting requirement on financial institutions, including all lenders and organizations that control access to accounts (such as PayPal and Western Union). There would be three disclosure requirements for these entities: "(1) the number of identity theft incidents suffered or avoided; (2) the forms of

---

[12] Bob Sullivan, *Your Evil Twin: Behind the Identity Theft Epidemic* 35-36 (2004).

[13] Synovate, Federal Trade Commission — 2006 Identity Theft Survey Report (Nov. 2007).

[14] Chris Jay Hoofnagle, *Identity Theft: Making the Known Unknowns Known*, 21 Harv. J. L. & Tech. 97 (2007).

identity theft attempted and the financial products targeted (e.g., mortgage loan or credit card); and (3) the amount of loss suffered or avoided."

Hoofnagle's larger hope is that if statistics were available by individual institution on identity theft, financial institutions would have a "new product differentiator, similar to low interest rates and fee-free access accounts." In other words, consumers would be able to choose to have a financial relationship with one organization rather than another based on its track record in providing safe financial products. Do you think that consumers would respond to such market information and actually switch accounts from one organization to another? Personal information might be stolen from nonfinancial institutions, such as a college, and then used by a criminal for fraud at a bank. How can incentives be provided for nonfinancial institutions to have adequate security?

(a) Identity Theft Statutes

The Identity Theft Assumption and Deterrence Act. Congress responded to the growth of identity theft by passing the Identity Theft and Assumption Deterrence Act in 1998. The Act makes it a federal crime to "knowingly transfer or use, without lawful authority, a means of identification of another person with the intent to commit, or to aid or abet, any unlawful activity that constitutes a violation of Federal law, or that constitutes a felony under any applicable State or local law." 18 U.S.C. § 1028.

The Fair Credit Reporting Act. The Fair Credit Reporting Act (FCRA), as amended by the Fair and Accurate Credit Transactions Act (FACTA), has provisions that address identity theft. We discuss these provisions below.

State Legislative Responses. The vast majority of states now have statutes concerning identity theft. Before 1998, only three states had enacted statutes dealing explicitly with identity theft.[15] Arizona was one of these states; it punishes identity thefts as low-grade felony, but its statute does not address victims' rights and remedies. Ariz. Rev. Stat. Ann. § 13-2008(D). The passage of the federal Identity Theft Assumption and Deterrence Act in 1998 sparked most states to pass their own identity theft legislation — more than 40 states now have identity theft statutes on the books.[16]

Many identity theft statutes focus on defining criminal penalties for the crime. Penalties are tied to the amount of money the thief steals. For example, in Florida, identity theft is a second-degree felony if it results in an injury of $75,000 or more, Fla. Stat. Ann. § 817.568(2)(b), but is only a first-degree misdemeanor if the individual is harassed without having reached the $75,000 threshold. Fla. Stat. Ann. § 817.568(3). New Jersey likewise penalizes identity thefts resulting in injury over $75,000 as a second-degree crime; injuries between $500 and $75,000 constitute a third-degree crime; injuries between $200 and

---

[15] U.S. General Accountability Office, *Report to the Honorable Sam Johnson House of Representatives, Identity Theft: Greater Awareness and Use of Existing Data Are Needed* 7 (June 2002).

[16] *Id.* at 6.

$500 constitute a fourth-degree crime; and injuries less than $200 constitute a disorderly persons offense. N.J.S.A. §§ 2C:21-17(c)(1)–(2). Pennsylvania punishes identity thefts in a similar manner. *See* Pa. Stat. Ann. tit. 18, § 4120(c)(1).

Should penalties be tied to the dollar value of the things the thief wrongfully took or to the mental distress and harm caused to the victims, which might not be correlated to such a dollar value?

California, in contrast to most other states, has some of the most comprehensive and powerful identity theft laws. For example, California permits victims to obtain the fraudulent applications that the identity thief made as well as a record of the thief's transactions in the victim's name. Cal. Penal Code § 530.8; Cal. Civil Code § 1748.95. California also assists victims in stopping debt collectors from continuing to try to collect debts that the thief created. Cal. Civ. Code § 1788.18. The central difference between California's approach and that of other states is that California grants powerful rights to victims to assist them in fixing the damage of an identity theft. California also requires companies to notify consumers of data security breaches where personal information about consumers is compromised. Cal. Civ. Code § 1798.82(a).

Assessing Identity Theft Statutes. Daniel Solove contends that many statutes addressing identity theft focus mainly on enhancing criminal penalties and ignore the real roots of the problem:

> [T]he prevailing approach toward dealing with identity theft — by relying on increasing criminal penalties and by depending upon individuals to take great lengths to try to protect themselves against their vulnerabilities to identity theft — has the wrong focus. . . . The underlying cause of identity theft is an architecture that makes us vulnerable to such crimes and unable to adequately repair the damage. . . .
>
> This architecture is not created by identity thieves; rather, it is exploited by them. It is an architecture of vulnerability, one where personal information is not protected with adequate security, where identity thieves have easy access to data and the ability to use it in detrimental ways. We are increasingly living with what I call "digital dossiers" about our lives, and these dossiers are not controlled by us but by various entities, such as private-sector companies and the government. These dossiers play a profound role in our lives in modern society. The identity thief taps into these dossiers and uses them, manipulates them, and pollutes them. The identity thief's ability to so easily access and use our personal data stems from an architecture that does not provide adequate security to our personal information and that does not afford us with a sufficient degree of participation in the collection, dissemination, and use of that information. Consequently, it is difficult for the victim to figure out what is going on and how she can remedy the situation. . . .
>
> Private sector entities lack adequate ways of controlling access to records and accounts in a person's name, and numerous companies engage in the common practice of using SSNs, mother's maiden names, and addresses for access to

account information. Additionally, creditors give out credit and establish new accounts if the applicant supplies a name, SSN, and address.[17]

Lynn LoPucki and Solove agree that the problem of identity theft is caused by the frequent use of SSNs as identifiers. According to LoPucki:

> The problem is not that thieves have access to personal information, but that creditors and credit-reporting agencies often lack both the means and the incentives to correctly identify the persons who seek credit from them or on whom they report.[18]

LoPucki suggests that the problem is caused by the lack of a reliable means for identification. He proposes a system where the government maintains a database of identification information that people submit, such as biometric data, photographs, and other personal information. Solove argues that more sophisticated identification systems come with other problems, such as an increase in data gathering about people and an inability of people who are the victims of abusive spouses or stalkers to hide. However, both Solove and LoPucki agree that identity theft is, in large part, a problem caused by the system in which credit is granted in the United States.

(b) Tort Law

WOLFE v. MBNA AMERICA BANK

485 F. Supp. 2d 874 (W.D. Tenn. 2007)

DONALD, J. Before the Court is Defendant MBNA America Bank's ("Defendant") Motion to Dismiss Plaintiff's Fourth Amended Complaint made pursuant to Rule 12(b)(6) of the Federal Rules of Civil Procedure. Plaintiff Mark Wolfe ("Plaintiff") filed his Fourth Amended Complaint on September 15, 2006, alleging a claim under the Tennessee Consumer Protection Act of 1977 ("TCPA"), Tenn. Code Ann. § 47-18-104(a)-(b), as well as claims for negligence, gross negligence, and defamation.

Plaintiff, now a twenty-seven year old male, is a resident of the State of Tennessee. In or about April 2000, Defendant received a credit account application in Plaintiff's name from a telemarketing company. The application listed Plaintiff's address as 3557 Frankie Carolyn Drive, Apartment 4, Memphis, Tennessee 38118. Plaintiff did not reside and had never resided at this address.

Upon receipt of the application, Defendant issued a credit card bearing Plaintiff's name to an unknown and unauthorized individual residing at the address listed on the application. Plaintiff alleges that Defendant, prior to issuing the card, did not attempt to verify whether the information contained in the credit account application was authentic and accurate. After receiving the card, the

---

[17] Daniel J. Solove, *Identity Theft, Privacy, and the Architecture of Vulnerability,* 54 Hastings L.J. 1227 (2003). For a response to Solove's proposals for solutions and a defense of his own proposed solution, see Lynn M. LoPucki, *Did Privacy Cause Identity Theft?*, 54 Hastings L.J. 1277 (2003).

[18] Lynn M. LoPucki, *Human Identification Theory and the Identity Theft Problem,* 80 Tex. L. Rev. 89, 94 (2001).

unknown and unauthorized individual charged $864.00 to the credit account, exceeding the account's $500.00 credit limit. When no payments were made on the account, Defendant, without investigating whether the account was obtained using a stolen identity, declared the account delinquent and transferred the account to NCO Financial Systems, Inc. ("NCO"), a debt collection agency. Defendant also notified various credit reporting agencies that the account was delinquent.

In order to collect the debt on the delinquent account, NCO hired an attorney, who discovered Plaintiff's actual address. The attorney, in a letter dated November 29, 2004, notified Plaintiff of the delinquent account and requested payment. Upon receipt of this letter, Plaintiff contacted the attorney to inquire about the account, but was told that he would receive information about the account in thirty (30) days. Plaintiff never received any further information.

In January 2005, Plaintiff applied for a job with a bank, but Plaintiff was not hired due to his poor credit score. Following this denial, Plaintiff contacted Defendant numerous times to dispute the delinquent account but was unable to obtain any "adequate or real explanation" from Defendant. At some point in time, Defendant mailed a notice of arbitration proceedings to the address listed on the credit account application, which subsequently resulted in an arbitration award against Plaintiff. Despite Plaintiff notifying Defendant that his identity was stolen, Defendant continues to list the credit account bearing Plaintiff's name as delinquent and has not corrected the information provided to credit reporting agencies regarding the account. . . .

A motion to dismiss for failure to state a claim only tests whether the plaintiff has pleaded a cognizable claim. . . .

Plaintiff alleges that Defendant had a *duty to verify* "the accuracy and authenticity of a credit application completed in Plaintiff's name before issuing a credit card." . . . Plaintiff alleges that Defendant failed to comply with [its duty to verify], and thus, is negligent and/or grossly negligent.

In Tennessee, negligence is established if a plaintiff demonstrates: "(1) a duty of care owed by the defendant to the plaintiff; (2) conduct falling below the applicable standard of care amounts to a breach of that duty; (3) an injury or loss; (4) causation in fact; and (5) proximate, or legal cause." To establish gross negligence, a plaintiff "must demonstrate ordinary negligence and must then prove that the defendant acted 'with utter unconcern for the safety of others, or . . . with such reckless disregard for the rights of others that a conscious indifference to consequences is implied in law'". . . .

Addressing the first context or duty, Defendant asserts that Plaintiff's negligence and gross negligence claims should be dismissed because Tennessee negligence law does not impose a duty on Defendant to verify the authenticity and accuracy of a credit account application prior to issuing a credit card. Defendant, characterizing Plaintiff's claim as one for the "negligent enablement of identity theft," argues that a duty to verify essentially constitutes a duty to prevent third-party criminal activity. Defendant argues that Tennessee courts have never held that commercial banks have a common law duty to prevent the theft of a non-customer's identity. Defendant further argues that it, like Plaintiff, is a victim of identity theft.

Under Tennessee negligence law, a duty is defined as "the legal obligation a defendant owes to a plaintiff to conform to the reasonable person standard of care in order to protect against unreasonable risks of harm." "Whether a defendant owes a duty to a plaintiff in any given situation is a question of law for the court." The "existence and scope of the duty of the defendant in a particular case rests on all the relevant circumstances, including the foreseeability of harm to the plaintiff and other similarly situated persons." A harm is foreseeable "if a reasonable person could foresee the probability of its occurrence or if the person was on notice that the likelihood of danger to the party to whom is owed a duty is probable."

Because Tennessee courts have not specifically addressed whether Tennessee negligence law imposes a duty to verify on commercial banks, Defendant cites in support of its argument the Supreme Court of South Carolina's decision in *Huggins v. Citibank, N.A.,* 585 S.E.2d 275 (S.C. 2003). In *Huggins,* the plaintiff alleged, among other things, that the defendant bank was negligent for issuing a credit card in the plaintiff's name to an unknown and unauthorized person "without any investigation, verification, or corroboration" of the authenticity and accuracy of the credit account application. The defendant argued that under South Carolina negligence law, it had no duty to verify the accuracy and authenticity of the credit account application because plaintiff was technically a non-customer. The South Carolina Supreme Court, despite finding that "it is foreseeable that injury may arise by the negligent issuance of a credit card," ultimately found that no duty to verify existed because "[t]he relationship, if any, between credit card issuers and potential victims of identity theft is far too attenuated to rise to the level of a duty between them." Noting the similarity between negligence law in Tennessee and South Carolina, Defendant argues that its relationship with Plaintiff, like the parties in *Huggins,* was and is too attenuated to warrant the imposition of a duty to verify.

Upon review, the Court finds the South Carolina Supreme Court's conclusion in *Huggins* to be flawed. In reaching its conclusion, the *Huggins* court relied heavily on the fact that there was no prior business relationship between the parties, that is, the plaintiff was not a customer of the defendant bank. The Court believes that the court's reliance on this fact is misplaced. While the existence of a prior business relationship might have some meaning in the context of a contractual dispute, a prior business relationship has little meaning in the context of negligence law. Instead, to determine whether a duty exists between parties, the Court must examine all relevant circumstances, with emphasis on the foreseeability of the alleged harm. As to the issue of foreseeability, the South Carolina Supreme Court found that "it is foreseeable that injury may arise by the negligent issuance of a credit card" and that such injury "could be prevented if credit card issuers carefully scrutinized credit card applications." The Court agrees with and adopts these findings.

With the alarming increase in identity theft in recent years, commercial banks and credit card issuers have become the first, and often last, line of defense in preventing the devastating damage that identity theft inflicts. Because the injury resulting from the negligent issuance of a credit card is foreseeable and preventable, the Court finds that under Tennessee negligence law, Defendant has a duty to verify the authenticity and accuracy of a credit account application before issuing a credit card. The Court, however, emphasizes that this duty to verify does not impose upon Defendant a duty to prevent all identity theft. The Court recognizes that despite banks utilizing the most reasonable and vigilant verification methods, some criminals will still be able to obtain enough personal information to secure a credit card with a stolen identity. Rather, this duty to verify merely requires Defendant to implement reasonable and cost-effective verification methods that can prevent criminals, in some instances, from obtaining a credit card with a stolen identity. Whether Defendant complied with this duty before issuing a credit card in Plaintiff's name is an issue for the trier of fact. Accordingly, Defendant's motion to dismiss Plaintiff's negligence and gross negligence claims in the first factual context is DENIED.

NOTES & QUESTIONS

1. ***Tort Law to the Rescue?*** In *Wolfe*, the district court located a duty in tort law that required a bank to take steps to verify identity before issuing a credit card in the plaintiff's name to a person. The court operated under a negligence theory: the bank need not prevent all identity theft (strict liability), but merely to use reasonable verification methods. What kind of practical steps might a bank take to make sure that the person to whom it issues a credit card is, in fact, the intended person? In light of the Lo Pucki-Solove debate (excerpted above) about the flawed system for checking and otherwise verifying identity, how successful are any "reasonable" means likely to be?

(c) The Fair Credit Reporting Act

A significant amount of identity theft involves the credit reporting system. When an identity thief starts creating delinquent debts in a person's name, creditors report the delinquencies to the credit reporting agencies, and the delinquencies begin to appear on the person's credit report. This can severely affect the person's credit score and make it impossible for the person to secure credit. What are the responsibilities of credit reporting agencies in ensuring that the data it reports about individuals really pertains to them rather than to the identity thief who impersonated them?

SLOANE V. EQUIFAX INFORMATION SERVICES, LLC

510 F.3d 495 (4th Cir. 2007)

DIANA GRIBBON MOTZ, J. After Suzanne Sloane discovered that a thief had stolen her identity and ruined her credit, she notified the police and sought to have Equifax Information Services, LLC, a credit reporting service, correct the resulting errors in her credit report. The police promptly arrested and jailed the thief. But twenty-one months later, Equifax still had not corrected the errors in Suzanne's credit report. Accordingly, Suzanne brought this action against Equifax for violations of the Fair Credit Reporting Act (FCRA), 15 U.S.C.A. §§ 1681 *et seq.* A jury found that Equifax had violated the Act in numerous respects and awarded Suzanne $351,000 in actual damages ($106,000 for economic losses and $245,000 for mental anguish, humiliation, and emotional distress). The district court entered judgment in the amount of $351,000. In addition, without permitting Equifax to file a written opposition, the court also awarded Suzanne attorney's fees in the amount of $181,083. On appeal, Equifax challenges the award of damages and attorney's fees. We affirm in part and reverse and remand in part.

On June 25, 2003, Suzanne Sloane entered Prince William Hospital to deliver a baby. She left the hospital not only a new mother, but also the victim of identity theft. A recently hired hospital employee named Shovana Sloan noticed similarity in the women's names and birth dates and, in November and December 2003, began using Suzanne's social security number to obtain credit cards, loans, cash advances, and other goods and services totaling more than $30,000. At the end of January 2004, Suzanne discovered these fraudulent transactions when Citibank notified her that it had cancelled her credit card and told her to contact Equifax if she had any concerns.

Unable to reach Equifax by telephone on a Friday evening, Suzanne went instead to the Equifax website, where she was able to access her credit report and discovered Shovana Sloan's name and evidence of the financial crimes Shovana had committed. Suzanne promptly notified the police, and contacted Equifax, which assertedly placed a fraud alert on her credit file. Equifax told Suzanne to "roll up her sleeves" and start calling all of her "20-some" creditors to notify them of the identity theft. Suzanne took the next two days off from work to contact each of her creditors, and, at their direction, she submitted numerous notarized forms to correct her credit history.

Suzanne, however, continued to experience problems with Equifax. On March 31, 2004, almost two months after reporting the identity theft to Equifax and despite her efforts to work with individual creditors as Equifax had advised, Suzanne and her husband, Tracey, tried to secure a pre-qualification letter to buy a vacation home, but were turned down. The loan officer told them that Suzanne's credit score was "terrible" — in fact, the "worst" the loan officer had ever seen — and that no loan would be possible until the numerous problems in Suzanne's Equifax credit report had been corrected. The loan officer also told Suzanne not to apply for additional credit in the meantime, because each credit inquiry would appear on her credit report and further lower her score.

Chagrined that Equifax had not yet corrected these errors in her credit report, Suzanne refrained from applying for any type of consumer credit for seven months. But, in October 2004, after the repeated breakdown of their family car, Suzanne and Tracey attempted to rely on Suzanne's credit to purchase a used car at a local dealership. Following a credit check, the car salesman pulled Tracey aside and informed him that it would be impossible to approve the financing so long as Suzanne's name appeared on the loan. Similarly, when the Sloanes returned to the mortgage company to obtain a home loan in January 2005, eight months after their initial visit, they were offered only an adjustable rate loan instead of a less expensive 30-year fixed rate loan in part because of Equifax's still inaccurate credit report.

In frustration, on March 9, 2005, more than thirteen months after first reporting the identity theft to Equifax, Suzanne sent a formal letter to the credit reporting agency, disputing twenty-four specific items in her credit report and requesting their deletion. Equifax agreed to delete the majority of these items, but after assertedly verifying two accounts with Citifinancial, Inc., Equifax notified Suzanne that it would not remove these two items. At trial, Equifax admitted that under its "verified victim policy," it should have automatically removed these Citifinancial items at Suzanne's request, but it failed to do so in violation of its own written procedures.

Two months later, on May 9, 2005, Suzanne again wrote to Equifax, still disputing the two Citifinancial accounts, and now also contesting two Washington Mutual accounts that Equifax had previously deleted but had mistakenly restored to Suzanne's report. When Equifax attempted to correct these mistakes, it exacerbated matters further by generating a second credit file bearing Shovana Sloan's name but containing Suzanne's social security number. Compounding this mistake, on May 23, 2005, Equifax sent a letter to Suzanne's house addressed to Shovana Sloan, warning Shovana that *she* was possibly the victim of identity theft and offering to sell her a service to monitor her credit file. Then, on June 7, 2005, Equifax sent copies of *both* credit reports to Suzanne; notably, both credit reports still contained the disputed Citifinancial accounts.

The stress of these problems weighed on Suzanne and significantly contributed to the deterioration of her marriage to Tracey. . . . In May 2005, the credit situation forced Tracey, a high school teacher, to abandon his plans to take a sabbatical during which he had hoped to develop land for modular homes with his father. The Sloanes frequently fought during the day and slept in separate rooms at night. . . . Also, during this period, Suzanne was frequently unable to sleep at night, and as her insomnia worsened, she found herself nodding off while driving home from work in the evening. Even after the couple took a vacation to reconcile in August 2005, when they returned home, they were greeted with the denial of a line of credit from Wachovia Bank. . . .

On November 4, 2005 — following twenty-one months of struggle to correct her credit report — Suzanne filed this action against Equifax, Trans Union, LLC, Experian Information Solutions, Inc., and Citifinancial, alleging violations of the FCRA. After settling a separate suit against Prince William Hospital and the personnel company that placed Shovana Sloan in the hospital's accounting department, Suzanne settled her claims in this action against Experian, Trans Union, and Citifinancial. Equifax, however, refused to settle. Thus, the case proceeded to trial with Equifax the sole remaining defendant. The jury returned a verdict against Equifax, awarding Suzanne $106,000 for economic loss and $245,000 for mental anguish, humiliation, and emotional distress.

Equifax moved for judgment as a matter of law and for a new trial or remittitur on the jury's award of damages for emotional distress. The district court denied Equifax's post-trial motions and then, without permitting Equifax to submit an opposition to Suzanne's request for attorney's fees, ordered Equifax to pay $181,083 in attorney's fees. This appeal followed. . . .

In this case, the jury specifically found, via a special verdict, that Suzanne proved by a preponderance of the evidence that Equifax violated the FCRA by negligently: (1) failing to follow reasonable procedures designed to assure maximum accuracy on her consumer credit report; (2) failing to conduct a reasonable investigation to determine whether disputed information in her credit report was inaccurate; (3) failing to delete information from the report that it found after reinvestigation to be inaccurate, incomplete, or unverified; and (4) reinserting information into her credit file that it had previously deleted. On appeal, Equifax does not challenge the jury's findings that Suzanne proved that it violated the FCRA in all of these respects.

The FCRA provides a private cause of action for those damaged by violations of the statute. *See* 15 U.S.C.A. §§ 1681n, 1681o. A successful plaintiff can recover both actual and punitive damages for willful violations of the FCRA, *id.* § 1681n(a), and actual damages for negligent violations, *id.* § 1681o(a). Actual damages may include not only economic damages, but also damages for humiliation and mental distress. The statute also provides that a successful plaintiff suing under the FCRA may recover reasonable attorney's fees. 15 U.S.C.A. §§ 1681n(a)(3), 1681o(a)(2). . . .

Equifax first argues that because Suzanne assertedly suffered a single, indivisible injury, she should not recover any damages from Equifax or, alternatively, her recovery should be reduced to take account of her prior settlements with other defendants. According to Equifax, the prior settlements have fully, or almost fully, compensated Suzanne for all of her injuries.

Equifax relies on the "one satisfaction rule" to support its argument. *See Chisholm v. UHP Projects, Inc.,* 205 F.3d 731, 737 (4th Cir. 2000) ("[T]his equitable doctrine operates to reduce a plaintiff's recovery from the nonsettling defendant to prevent the plaintiff from recovering twice from the same assessment of liability."). But, in the case at hand, we cannot find, as a matter of law, that Suzanne has suffered from a "single, indivisible harm" that has already been redressed by other parties. . . .

To the contrary, Suzanne provided credible evidence that her emotional and economic damages resulted from separate acts by separate parties. She did not attempt to hold any of the credit reporting agencies responsible for damages arising from either the identity theft itself or the initial inaccuracies that the theft generated in her credit reports. Moreover, although some of Suzanne's interactions with Equifax overlapped with exchanges with other credit reporting agencies, her encounters with Equifax both predate and postdate these other exchanges. . . .

Further, during the period when Suzanne attempted to correct the mistakes made by all three agencies, each agency produced reports with different inaccuracies, and each agency either corrected or exacerbated these mistakes independently of the others. Thus, even during this period, the inaccuracies in Equifax's credit reports caused Suzanne discrete injuries independent of those caused by the other credit reporting agencies.

For all of these reasons, we reject Equifax's argument that Suzanne has suffered from a single, indivisible injury or has been doubly compensated as a consequence of her prior settlements.

Equifax next argues that the evidence does not support any award for economic losses. Equifax claims that only speculation and conjecture support such an award, and so the district court erred in denying Equifax's motion for judgment as to this award.

We disagree. The evidence at trial in this case clearly demonstrates that on numerous occasions Suzanne attempted to secure lines of credit from a variety of financial institutions, only to be either denied outright or offered credit on less advantageous terms that she might have received absent Equifax's improper conduct. At times, these financial institutions consulted credit reports from other agencies, but at other times these institutions relied exclusively on the erroneous credit information provided by Equifax. Based on these incidents, we find that there is a legally sufficient evidentiary basis for a reasonable jury to have found that Equifax's conduct resulted in economic losses for Suzanne. Therefore, the district court did not err in denying Equifax's motion regarding this award.

Additionally, Equifax asserts that the district court erred in refusing to order remittitur of the mental anguish, humiliation, and emotional distress damages award to no more than $25,000. Equifax contends that the jury's award of $245,000 is inconsistent with awards in similar cases and is disproportionate to any actual injury proved at trial. Suzanne, by contrast, contends that the evidence provides more than adequate support for the jury's award. To resolve this question, we set forth the relevant governing principles, apply these principles to the evidence before the jury, and compare the evidence and emotional distress award in Suzanne's case with the evidence and award in all assertedly relevant cases. . . .

We begin with Federal Rule of Civil Procedure 59(a), which provides that if a court concludes that a jury award of compensatory damages is excessive, it may order a new trial nisi remittitur. . . . A district court abuses its discretion only by upholding an award of damages when "the jury's verdict is against the weight of the evidence or based on evidence which is false."

In this case, the district court found that the jury's emotional distress award was "not an unreasonable conclusion from this evidence." The court noted that the jury could base its award on Equifax's specific actions, as distinct from those of the other credit reporting agencies, and that Equifax's actions directly led to the mounting frustration and distress that Suzanne felt for almost two years. As one example of Equifax's specific actions, the court recalled the letter that Equifax sent to Suzanne, many months after she had notified Equifax of the identity theft, bearing the name of the identity thief and warning the thief, not Suzanne, that the thief's personal information was in peril. . . .

Moreover, Equifax does not deny that Suzanne suffered emotional distress. Nor does Equifax contend that Suzanne failed to produce sufficient evidence to sustain some award for this injury. Rather, Equifax simply proposes replacing the jury's number with one of its own invention — offering $25,000 in place of $245,000. Yet when asked at oral argument to explain the basis for the proposed remittitur, Equifax's counsel could offer no legal or factual basis for this amount, conceding that the number had been taken "out of the air." Not only is such an unprincipled approach intrinsically unsound, but it also directly contravenes the Seventh Amendment, which precludes an appellate court from replacing an award of compensatory damages with one of the court's own choosing. In short, the issue before us is neither whether Suzanne offered sufficient evidence at trial to sustain an award for emotional distress nor whether we believe that Equifax's "out of the air" $25,000 represents a fair estimate of those damages, but whether the jury's award is *excessive* in light of evidence presented at trial.

Our previous cases establish the type of evidence required to support an award for emotional damages. We have warned that "[n]ot only is emotional distress fraught with vagueness and speculation, it is easily susceptible to fictitious and trivial claims." *Price v. City of Charlotte,* 93 F.3d 1241, 1250 (4th Cir. 1996). For this reason, although specifically recognizing that a plaintiff's testimony can provide sufficient evidence to support an emotional distress award, we have required a plaintiff to "reasonably and sufficiently explain the circumstances of [the] injury and not resort to mere conclusory statements." Thus, we have distinguished between plaintiff testimony that amounts only to "conclusory statements" and plaintiff testimony that "sufficiently articulate[s]" true "demonstrable emotional distress."

In *Knussman v. Maryland,* 272 F.3d 625 (4th Cir. 2001), we summarized the factors properly considered in determinating the potential excessiveness of an award for emotional distress. They include the factual context in which the emotional distress arose; evidence corroborating the testimony of the plaintiff; the nexus between the conduct of the defendant and the emotional distress; the degree of such mental distress; mitigating circumstances, if any; physical injuries suffered due to the emotional distress; medical attention resulting from the emotional duress; psychiatric or psychological treatment; and the loss of income, if any.

In the present case, Suzanne offered considerable objective verification of her emotional distress, chronic anxiety, and frustration during the twenty-one months that she attempted to correct Equifax's errors. First, her repeated denials of credit and continuous problems with Equifax furnish an objective and inherently reasonable "factual context" for her resulting claims of emotional distress. Suzanne also corroborated her account in two ways. She offered "sufficiently articulated" descriptions of her protracted anxiety through detailed testimony of specific events and the humiliation and anger she experienced as a result of each occurrence. She also provided evidence that the distress was apparent to others, particularly her family; Tracey, for instance, described in detail his wife's ongoing struggles with Equifax and the emotional toll these events took upon her. In addition, substantial trial evidence attested to the direct "nexus" between Equifax's violations of the FCRA and Suzanne's emotional distress. Furthermore, Suzanne's emotional distress manifested itself in terms of physical symptoms, particularly insomnia. . . .

Reviewing this evidence in light of the appropriate factors already set forth, we conclude that substantial, if not overwhelming, objective evidence supports an emotional distress award. Equifax ignores much of this evidence, however, and insists that an award of $245,000 is "inconsistent with awards in other similar cases." But Equifax relies on cases which are in fact not very "similar" to the case at hand and so provide little assistance in assessing the amount of the emotional distress award here. . . .

As Equifax's authorities indicate, finding helpful precedent for comparison here is not a simple task. The recent emergence of identity theft and the rapid growth of the credit-reporting industry present a unique dilemma without clear precedent. When Congress enacted the FCRA in 1970, it recognized the vital role that credit-reporting agencies had assumed within the burgeoning culture of American consumerism. Since the mid-1980s, the introduction of computerized information technology and data-warehousing has led to the national consolidation of the credit-reporting industry into the "Big Three" — Equifax, Experian, and Trans Union — and rendered credit reporting an integral part of our most ordinary consumer transactions. According to recent data, each of these national credit-reporting agencies has perhaps 1.5 billion credit accounts held by approximately 190 million individuals. Each receives more than two billion items of information every month, and together these three agencies issue approximately two million consumer credit reports each day.

Against this backdrop, identity theft has emerged over the last decade as one of the fastest growing white-collar crimes in the United States. . . . Given the rapid emergence of identity theft in the last decade, it comes as no surprise that past precedent fails to fully reflect the unfortunate current reality. . . .

A survey of the other, more recent FCRA cases that involve requests for remittitur of emotional distress awards suggests that approved awards more typically range between $20,000 and $75,000.

This handful of cases, while helpful, differs from the case at hand. For, unlike the plaintiffs in those cases, Suzanne did not suffer from isolated or accidental reporting errors. Rather, as a victim of identity theft, she suffered the systematic manipulation of her personal information, which, despite her best efforts, Equifax failed to correct over a protracted period of time. Of course, Equifax bore no responsibility for the initial theft, but the FCRA makes the company responsible for taking reasonable steps to correct Suzanne's credit report once she brought the theft to the company's attention; this Equifax utterly failed to do. A reasonable jury could conclude that Equifax's repeated errors engendered more emotional distress than that found in these other FCRA cases.

We also believe that some guidance can be gained from case law concerning defamation. Prior to the enactment of the FCRA, defamation was one of several common-law actions used by plaintiffs in response to the dissemination of inaccurate credit information.[19] These common-law causes of action parallel those offered under the FCRA in that they typically involve a defendant found liable for propagating inaccurate information about the plaintiff, and the effects, while unquestionably harmful, are difficult to translate into monetary terms. . . . [C]ourts frequently sustain emotional distress awards in the range of $250,000 in defamation cases.

We do not believe the evidence presented here permits an award of this magnitude because, after all, this case does not involve actual defamation. Moreover, Suzanne presented almost no evidence at trial to suggest that Equifax's violations of the FCRA resulted in harm to her reputation, and it appears that few people beyond Suzanne's family and potential creditors knew of her disastrous credit file. We therefore believe that the maximum award supported by the evidence here must be significantly less than these defamation awards. But, considering the extensive corroboration offered at trial concerning the many months of emotional distress, mental anguish, and humiliation suffered by Suzanne, we believe that the evidence does support an award in the maximum amount of $150,000. We recognize that even this amount is appreciably more than that awarded for emotional distress in most other FCRA cases. But, as explained earlier, the case at hand differs significantly from those cases. A

[19] A provision of the FCRA bars consumers from bringing actions "in the nature of defamation, invasion of privacy, or negligence" in certain specified contexts, except as those causes of action arise under sections 1681n and 1681o of the FCRA. 15 U.S.C.A. § 1681h(e).

$150,000 award reflects those differences—the repeated violations of the FCRA found by the jury in its special verdict, the number of errors contained in Equifax's credit reports, and the protracted length of time during which Equifax failed to correct Suzanne's credit file. Accordingly, we reduce the emotional distress award to $150,000 and grant a new trial nisi remittitur at Suzanne's option. . . .

[The court vacated the district court's grant of attorney's fees in the amount of $181,083 because the district court failed to allow Equifax to submit a written opposition to Sloane's motion for attorney's fees. The case was remanded to allow Equifax to file its opposition.]

NOTES & QUESTIONS

1. ***Damages.*** Was the remittitur to $150,000 appropriate? Why should damage awards be limited based on the damage awards in other cases? As the court noted, they involve very different facts than the case at bar.

   Also recall the court's statement that "this case does not involve actual defamation. . . . Suzanne presented almost no evidence at trial to suggest that Equifax's violations of the FCRA resulted in harm to her reputation, and it appears that few people beyond Suzanne's family and potential creditors knew of her disastrous credit file." Why doesn't this case involve "harm to her reputation"? Don't reports on people's creditworthiness affect their financial reputations, that is, their ability to pay back their debts, their trustworthiness and dependability?
2. ***The Harm of Identity Theft.*** When assessing the damages Sloane suffered from her identity theft ordeal, how much of the harm was caused by Equifax's actions? Purportedly, the entire incident of identity theft caused her marital discord, insomnia, and emotional distress. Yet, the identity theft did involve, after all, not only Equifax, but the identity thief, creditors, and other credit reporting agencies. Are the damages assessed to Equifax proportionate to Equifax's contribution to Sloane's ordeal? Or should Equifax be viewed as the "least cost avoider," the party who can internalize the costs of preventing this harm at the least overall cost?

B. COMMERCIAL ENTITIES AND PERSONAL DATA

Thus far, this chapter has examined the use of personal information within the financial sector. This part examines the use of personal information by commercial entities and how the law has attempted different ways to regulate in this area.

1. GOVERNANCE BY TORT

DWYER V. AMERICAN EXPRESS CO.

652 N.E.2d 1351 (Ill. App. 1995)

BUCKLEY, J. Plaintiffs, American Express cardholders, appeal the circuit court's dismissal of their claims for invasion of privacy and consumer fraud against defendants, American Express Company, American Express Credit Corporation, and American Express Travel Related Services Company, for their practice of renting information regarding cardholder spending habits.

On May 13, 1992, the New York Attorney General released a press statement describing an agreement it had entered into with defendants. The following day, newspapers reported defendants' actions which gave rise to this agreement. According to the news articles, defendants categorize and rank their cardholders into six tiers based on spending habits and then rent this information to participating merchants as part of a targeted joint-marketing and sales program. For example, a cardholder may be characterized as "Rodeo Drive Chic" or "Value Oriented." In order to characterize its cardholders, defendants analyze where they shop and how much they spend, and also consider behavioral characteristics and spending histories. Defendants then offer to create a list of cardholders who would most likely shop in a particular store and rent that list to the merchant.

Defendants also offer to create lists which target cardholders who purchase specific types of items, such as fine jewelry. The merchants using the defendants' service can also target shoppers in categories such as mail-order apparel buyers, home-improvement shoppers, electronics shoppers, luxury lodgers, card members with children, skiers, frequent business travelers, resort users, Asian/European travelers, luxury European car owners, or recent movers. Finally, defendants offer joint-marketing ventures to merchants who generate substantial sales through the American Express card. Defendants mail special promotions devised by the merchants to its cardholders and share the profits generated by these advertisements. . . .

Plaintiffs have alleged that defendants' practices constitute an invasion of their privacy [in particular, a violation of the intrusion upon seclusion tort]. . .

. . . [There are] four elements [to intrusion upon seclusion] which must be alleged in order to state a cause of action: (1) an unauthorized intrusion or prying into the plaintiff's seclusion; (2) an intrusion which is offensive or objectionable to a reasonable man; (3) the matter upon which the intrusion occurs is private; and (4) the intrusion causes anguish and suffering. . . .

Plaintiffs' allegations fail to satisfy the first element, an unauthorized intrusion or prying into the plaintiffs' seclusion. The alleged wrongful actions involve the defendants' practice of renting lists that they have compiled from information contained in their own records. By using the American Express card, a cardholder is voluntarily, and necessarily, giving information to defendants that, if analyzed, will reveal a cardholder's spending habits and shopping preferences. . . .

Plaintiffs claim that because defendants rented lists based on this compiled information, this case involves the disclosure of private financial information and most closely resembles cases involving intrusion into private financial dealings, such as bank account transactions. Plaintiffs cite several cases in which courts have recognized the right to privacy surrounding financial transactions.

However, we find that this case more closely resembles the sale of magazine subscription lists, which was at issue in *Shibley v. Time, Inc.* In *Shibley*, the plaintiffs claimed that the defendant's practice of selling and renting magazine subscription lists without the subscribers' prior consent "constitut[ed] an invasion of privacy because it amount[ed] to a sale of individual 'personality profiles,' which subjects the subscribers to solicitations from direct mail advertisers." The plaintiffs also claimed that the lists amounted to a tortious appropriation of their names and "personality profiles." . . .

The *Shibley* court found that an Ohio statute, which permitted the sale of names and addresses of registrants of motor vehicles, indicated that the defendant's activity was not an invasion of privacy. . . .

Defendants rent names and addresses after they create a list of cardholders who have certain shopping tendencies; they are not disclosing financial information about particular cardholders. These lists are being used solely for the purpose of determining what type of advertising should be sent to whom. We also note that the Illinois Vehicle Code authorizes the Secretary of State to sell lists of names and addresses of licensed drivers and registered motor-vehicle owners. Thus, we hold that the alleged actions here do not constitute an unreasonable intrusion into the seclusion of another. We so hold without expressing a view as to the appellate court conflict regarding the recognition of this cause of action.

Considering plaintiffs' appropriation claim, the elements of the tort are: an appropriation, without consent, of one's name or likeness for another's use or benefit. This branch of the privacy doctrine is designed to protect a person from having his name or image used for commercial purposes without consent. According to the Restatement, the purpose of this tort is to protect the "interest of the individual in the exclusive use of his own identity, in so far as it is represented by his name or likeness." Illustrations of this tort provided by the Restatement include the publication of a person's photograph without consent in an advertisement; operating a corporation named after a prominent public figure without the person's consent; impersonating a man to obtain information regarding the affairs of the man's wife; and filing a lawsuit in the name of another without the other's consent.

Plaintiffs claim that defendants appropriate information about cardholders' personalities, including their names and perceived lifestyles, without their consent. Defendants argue that their practice does not adversely affect the interest of a cardholder in the "exclusive use of his own identity," using the language of the Restatement. Defendants also argue that the cardholders' names lack value and that the lists that defendants create are valuable because "they identify a useful aggregate of potential customers to whom offers may be sent.". . .

To counter defendants' argument, plaintiffs point out that the tort of appropriation is not limited to strictly commercial situations.

Nonetheless, we again follow the reasoning in *Shibley* and find that plaintiffs have not stated a claim for tortious appropriation because they have failed to allege the first element. Undeniably, each cardholder's name is valuable to defendants. The more names included on a list, the more that list will be worth. However, a single, random cardholder's name has little or no intrinsic value to defendants (or a merchant). Rather, an individual name has value only when it is associated with one of defendants' lists. Defendants create value by categorizing and aggregating these names. Furthermore, defendants' practices do not deprive any of the cardholders of any value their individual names may possess. . . .

NOTES & QUESTIONS

1. **Shibley v. Time.** In *Shibley v. Time, Inc.* 341 N.E.2d 337 (Ohio Ct. App. 1975), the plaintiff sued the publishers of a number of magazines for selling subscription lists to direct mail advertising businesses. The plaintiff sued under the public disclosure tort and the appropriation tort. Despite the fact that the purchasers of the lists can learn about the plaintiff's lifestyle from the data, the court dismissed the plaintiff's public disclosure action. The court found that the sale of the lists did not "cause mental suffering, shame or humiliation to a person of ordinary sensibilities." The court also rejected the plaintiff's argument that by selling the lists, the defendants were appropriating his name and likeness because the tort of appropriation is available only in those "situations where the plaintiff's name or likeness is displayed to the public to indicate that the plaintiff indorses the defendant's product or business."

   According to *Shibley* and *Dwyer*, why does the public disclosure tort fail to provide a remedy for the disclosure of personal information to other companies? Why does the tort of intrusion upon seclusion fail? Why does the tort of appropriation fail? More generally, can tort law adequately remedy the privacy problems created by profiling and databases?[20]
2. ***A Fair Information Practices Tort?*** Sarah Ludington recommends that a new tort should be developed in the common law, one that "would impose on data traders a duty to use Fair Information Practices (based on the principles of notice, choice, access, and security)." Why the common law rather than legislation? Ludington argues:

   > [B]ecause it is now clear that industry lobbying has succeeded while self-regulation has failed, and that legislatures have either failed to act or provided solutions that inadequately address the injuries, individuals must — indeed, should — look to the judiciary to help resolve the misuse of personal information.[21]

---

[20] For an interesting argument about how the tort of breach of confidentiality might provide a weak but potential solution to the problem, see Jessica Litman, *Information Privacy/Information Property*, 52 Stan. L. Rev. 1283 (2000). For a discussion of the use of the tort of appropriation, see Andrew J. McClurg, *A Thousand Words Are Worth a Picture: A Privacy Tort Response to Consumer Data Profiling,* 98 Nw. U. L. Rev. 63 (2003).

[21] Sarah Ludington, *Reining in the Data Traders: A Tort for the Misuse of Personal Information*, 66 Md. L. Rev. 140, 172-73 (2007).

Would the use of the common law to regulate the collection and use of personal data be effective or appropriate? What would be the strengths and weaknesses of such a regulatory approach?

3. ***Defining the Harm.*** What is the harm of commercial entities collecting and using personal information? One might contend that the kind of information that companies collect about individuals is not very sensitive or intimate. How much is a person harmed by sharing data that she prefers Coke to Pepsi or Puffs to Kleenex? Is there a significant privacy problem in revealing that a person has purchased tennis products, designer sunglasses, orange juice, or other things? One might view the harm as so minimal as to be trivial.

   Does information about a person's consumption patterns reveal something about that person's identity? Stan Karas argues that "consumption patterns may identify one as a liberal, moderate Republican, radical feminist or born-again Christian. . . . For some individuals, consumption is no longer a way of expressing identity but is synonymous with identity. . . . [T]he identity of many subcultures is directly related to distinctive patterns of consumption. One need only think of the personal styles of punk rockers, hip-hoppers, or Harley-fetishizing bikers."[22]

   According to Jerry Kang, data collection and compiling is a form of surveillance that inhibits individual freedom and choice: "[I]information collection in cyberspace is more like surveillance than like casual observation." He notes that "surveillance leads to self-censorship. This is true even when the observable information would not be otherwise misused or disclosed."[23]

   Daniel Solove contends that the problem of computer databases does not stem from surveillance. He argues that numerous theorists describe the problem in terms of the metaphor of Big Brother, the ruthless totalitarian government in George Orwell's *1984*, which constantly monitors its citizens. Solove contends that the Big Brother metaphor fails to adequately conceptualize the problem:

   > A large portion of our personal information involves facts that we are not embarrassed about: our financial information, race, marital status, hobbies, occupation, and the like. Most people surf the web without wandering into its dark corners. The vast majority of the information collected about us concerns relatively innocuous details. The surveillance model does not explain why the recording of this non-taboo information poses a problem.[24]

   In contrast, Solove proposes that data collection and processing is most aptly captured by Franz Kafka's *The Trial*, where the protagonist (Joseph K.) is arrested by officials from a clandestine court system but is not informed of the reason for his arrest. From what little he manages to learn about the court system, which operates largely in secret, Joseph K. discovers that a vast bureaucratic court has examined his life and assembled a dossier on him. His

---

[22] Stan Karas, *Privacy, Identity, Databases,* 52 Am. U. L. Rev. 393, 438-39 (2002).

[23] Jerry Kang, *Information Privacy in Cyberspace Transactions*, 50 Stan. L. Rev. 1193 (1998).

[24] Daniel J. Solove, *Privacy and Power: Computer Databases and Metaphors for Information Privacy*, 53 Stan. L. Rev. 1393 (2001).

records, however, are "inaccessible," and K.'s life gradually becomes taken over by his frustrating quest for answers:

> *The Trial* captures the sense of helplessness, frustration, and vulnerability one experiences when a large bureaucratic organization has control over a vast dossier of details about one's life. At any time, something could happen to Joseph K.; decisions are made based on his data, and Joseph K. has no say, no knowledge, and no ability to fight back. He is completely at the mercy of the bureaucratic process. . . .
>
> The problem with databases emerges from subjecting personal information to the bureaucratic process with little intelligent control or limitation, resulting in a lack of meaningful participation in decisions about our information. . . .
>
> Under this view, the problem with databases and the practices currently associated with them is that they disempower people. They make people vulnerable by stripping them of control over their personal information. There is no diabolical motive or secret plan for domination; rather, there is a web of thoughtless decisions made by low-level bureaucrats, standardized policies, rigid routines, and a way of relating to individuals and their information that often becomes indifferent to their welfare.[25]

Joel Reidenberg points out that the lack of protection of information privacy will "destroy anonymity" and take away people's "freedom to choose the terms of personal information disclosure."[26] According to Paul Schwartz, the lack of privacy protection can threaten to expose not just information about what people purchase, but also information about their communication and consumption of ideas:

> In the absence of strong rules for information privacy, Americans will hesitate to engage in cyberspace activities—including those that are most likely to promote democratic self-rule. . . Current polls already indicate an aversion on the part of some people to engage even in basic commercial activities on the Internet. Yet, deliberative democracy requires more than shoppers; it demands speakers and listeners. But who will speak or listen when this behavior leaves finely-grained data trails in a fashion that is difficult to understand or anticipate?[27]

4. *Is Privacy Still Possible?* Is privacy still possible in an Information Age? Scott McNealy, CEO of Sun Microsystems, Inc., once remarked: "You already have zero privacy. Get over it." Should we eulogize the death of privacy and move on? Or is it possible to protect privacy in modern times? Consider David Brin:

> . . . [I]t is already far too late to prevent the invasion of cameras and databases. The *djinn* cannot be crammed back into its bottle. No matter how many laws are passed, it will prove quite impossible to legislate away the new surveillance tools and databases. They are here to stay.
>
> Light *is* going to shine into nearly every corner of our lives. . . .

---

[25] *Id.*

[26] Joel R. Reidenberg, *Setting Standards for Fair Information Practice in the U.S. Private Sector*, 80 Iowa L. Rev. 497 (1995).

[27] Paul M. Schwartz, *Privacy and Democracy in Cyberspace,* 52 Vand. L. Rev. 1609, 1651 (1999).

> If neo-Western civilization has one great trick in its repertoire, a technique more responsible than any other for its success, that trick is *accountability*. Especially the knack — which no other culture ever mastered — of making accountability apply to the mighty. . . .
>
> Kevin Kelly, executive editor of *Wired* magazine, expressed the same idea with the gritty clarity of information-age journalism: "The answer to the whole privacy question is more knowledge. More knowledge about who's watching you. More knowledge about the information that flows between us — particularly the meta-information about who knows what and where it's going."
>
> In other words, we may not be able to eliminate the intrusive glare shining on citizens of the next century, but the glare just might be rendered harmless through the application of more light aimed in the other direction.[28]

Is greater transparency the solution to the increasing threats to privacy?

REMSBURG V. DOCUSEARCH, INC.

816 A.2d 1001 (N.H. 2003)

DALIANIS, J. . . . [Liam Youens contacted Docusearch and purchased the birth date of Amy Lynn Boyer for a fee. He again contacted Docusearch and placed an order for Boyer's SSN. Docusearch obtained Boyer's SSN from a credit reporting agency and provided it to Youens. Youens then asked for Boyer's employment address. Docusearch hired a subcontractor, Michele Gambino, who obtained it by making a "pretext" phone call to Boyer. Gambino lied about her identity and the purpose of the call, and she obtained the address from Boyer. The address was then given to Youens. Shortly thereafter, Youens went to Boyer's workplace and shot and killed her and then killed himself.]

All persons have a duty to exercise reasonable care not to subject others to an unreasonable risk of harm. Whether a defendant's conduct creates a risk of harm to others sufficiently foreseeable to charge the defendant with a duty to avoid such conduct is a question of law, because "the existence of a duty does not arise solely from the relationship between the parties, but also from the need for protection against reasonably foreseeable harm." Thus, in some cases, a party's actions give rise to a duty. Parties owe a duty to those third parties foreseeably endangered by their conduct with respect to those risks whose likelihood and magnitude make the conduct unreasonably dangerous.

In situations in which the harm is caused by criminal misconduct, however, determining whether a duty exists is complicated by the competing rule "that a private citizen has no general duty to protect others from the criminal attacks of third parties." This rule is grounded in the fundamental unfairness of holding private citizens responsible for the unanticipated criminal acts of third parties, because "[u]nder all ordinary and normal circumstances, in the absence of any reason to expect the contrary, the actor may reasonably proceed upon the assumption that others will obey the law."

---

[28] David Brin, *The Transparent Society* 8-23 (1998).

In certain limited circumstances, however, we have recognized that there are exceptions to the general rule where a duty to exercise reasonable care will arise. We have held that such a duty may arise because: (1) a special relationship exists; (2) special circumstances exist; or (3) the duty has been voluntarily assumed. The special circumstances exception includes situations where there is "an especial temptation and opportunity for criminal misconduct brought about by the defendant." This exception follows from the rule that a party who realizes or should realize that his conduct has created a condition which involves an unreasonable risk of harm to another has a duty to exercise reasonable care to prevent the risk from occurring. The exact occurrence or precise injuries need not have been foreseeable. Rather, where the defendant's conduct has created an unreasonable risk of criminal misconduct, a duty is owed to those foreseeably endangered.

Thus, if a private investigator or information broker's (hereinafter "investigator" collectively) disclosure of information to a client creates a foreseeable risk of criminal misconduct against the third person whose information was disclosed, the investigator owes a duty to exercise reasonable care not to subject the third person to an unreasonable risk of harm. In determining whether the risk of criminal misconduct is foreseeable to an investigator, we examine two risks of information disclosure implicated by this case: stalking and identity theft.

It is undisputed that stalkers, in seeking to locate and track a victim, sometimes use an investigator to obtain personal information about the victims.

Public concern about stalking has compelled all fifty States to pass some form of legislation criminalizing stalking. Approximately one million women and 371,000 men are stalked annually in the United States. Stalking is a crime that causes serious psychological harm to the victims, and often results in the victim experiencing post-traumatic stress disorder, anxiety, sleeplessness, and sometimes, suicidal ideations.

Identity theft, *i.e.*, the use of one person's identity by another, is an increasingly common risk associated with the disclosure of personal information, such as a SSN. A person's SSN has attained the status of a quasi-universal personal identification number. At the same time, however, a person's privacy interest in his or her SSN is recognized by state and federal statutes. . . .

Like the consequences of stalking, the consequences of identity theft can be severe. . . . Victims of identity theft risk the destruction of their good credit histories. This often destroys a victim's ability to obtain credit from any source and may, in some cases, render the victim unemployable or even cause the victim to be incarcerated.

The threats posed by stalking and identity theft lead us to conclude that the risk of criminal misconduct is sufficiently foreseeable so that an investigator has a duty to exercise reasonable care in disclosing a third person's personal information to a client. And we so hold. This is especially true when, as in this case, the investigator does not know the client or the client's purpose in seeking the information. . . .

[The plaintiff also brought an action for intrusion upon seclusion.] A tort action based upon an intrusion upon seclusion must relate to something secret, secluded or private pertaining to the plaintiff. Moreover, liability exists only if the defendant's conduct was such that the defendant should have realized that it would be offensive to persons of ordinary sensibilities.

In addressing whether a person's SSN is something secret, secluded or private, we must determine whether a person has a reasonable expectation of privacy in the number. . . . As noted above, a person's interest in maintaining the privacy of his or her SSN has been recognized by numerous federal and state statutes. As a result, the entities to which this information is disclosed and their employees are bound by legal, and, perhaps, contractual constraints to hold SSNs in confidence to ensure that they remain private. Thus, while a SSN must be disclosed in certain circumstances, a person may reasonably expect that the number will remain private.

Whether the intrusion would be offensive to persons of ordinary sensibilities is ordinarily a question for the fact-finder and only becomes a question of law if reasonable persons can draw only one conclusion from the evidence. The evidence underlying the certified question is insufficient to draw any such conclusion here, and we therefore must leave this question to the fact-finder. In making this determination, the fact-finder should consider "the degree of intrusion, the context, conduct and circumstances surrounding the intrusion as well as the intruder's motives and objectives, the setting into which he intrudes, and the expectations of those whose privacy is invaded." Accordingly, a person whose SSN is obtained by an investigator from a credit reporting agency without the person's knowledge or permission may have a cause of action for intrusion upon seclusion for damages caused by the sale of the SSN, but must prove that the intrusion was such that it would have been offensive to a person of ordinary sensibilities.

We next address whether a person has a cause of action for intrusion upon seclusion where an investigator obtains the person's work address by using a pretextual phone call. We must first establish whether a work address is something secret, secluded or private about the plaintiff.

In most cases, a person works in a public place. "On the public street, or in any other public place, [a person] has no legal right to be alone." . . . Thus, where a person's work address is readily observable by members of the public, the address cannot be private and no intrusion upon seclusion action can be maintained.

[Additionally, the plaintiff brought a cause of action for appropriation.] "One who appropriates to his own use or benefit the name or likeness of another is subject to liability to the other for invasion of his privacy." *Restatement (Second) of Torts* § 652E.

. . . Appropriation is not actionable if the person's name or likeness is published for "purposes other than taking advantage of [the person's] reputation, prestige or other value" associated with the person. Thus, appropriation occurs most often when the person's name or likeness is used to advertise the defendant's product or when the defendant impersonates the person for gain.

An investigator who sells personal information sells the information for the value of the information itself, not to take advantage of the person's reputation or prestige. The investigator does not capitalize upon the goodwill value associated with the information but rather upon the client's willingness to pay for the information. In other words, the benefit derived from the sale in no way relates to the social or commercial standing of the person whose information is sold. Thus, a person whose personal information is sold does not have a cause of action for appropriation against the investigator who sold the information. . . .

NOTES & QUESTIONS

1. ***The Scope of the Duty.*** The court concludes that Docusearch has a duty to people "foreseeably endangered" by its disclosure of personal information. Is this too broad a duty to impose on those who collect and disseminate personal data? What could Docusearch have done to avoid being negligent in this case? Suppose Jill tells Jack the address of Roe. Jack goes to Roe's house and kills her. Based on *Remsburg*, can Jill be liable?
2. ***Tort Liability and the First Amendment.*** Does liability for Docusearch implicate the First Amendment?

2. GOVERNANCE BY CONTRACT AND PROMISES

(a) Privacy Policies

Privacy policies are statements made by companies about their practices regarding personal information. Increasingly, companies on the Internet are posting privacy policies, and statutes such as the Gramm-Leach-Bliley Act require certain types of companies (financial institutions, insurance companies, and brokerage companies) to maintain privacy policies.

One of the common provisions of many privacy policies is an "opt-out" provision. An opt-out provision establishes a default rule that the company can use or disclose personal information in the ways it desires so long as the consumer does not indicate otherwise. The consumer must take affirmative steps, such as checking a box, calling the company, or writing a letter, to express her desire to opt out of a particular information use or disclosure. In contrast, an "opt-in" provision establishes a default rule that the company cannot use or disclose personal information without first obtaining the express consent of the individual.

JEFF SOVERN, *OPTING IN, OPTING OUT, OR NO OPTIONS AT ALL: THE FIGHT FOR CONTROL OF PERSONAL INFORMATION*

74 Wash. L. Rev. 1033 (1999)

. . . [F]ew consumers understand how much of their personal information is for sale, although they may have a general idea that there is a trade in personal data and that the specifics about that trade are kept from them. . . .

. . . [C]onsumers cannot protect their personal information when they are unaware of how it is being used by others. . . .

The second reason consumers have not acted to protect their privacy, notwithstanding surveys that suggest considerable consumer concern with confidentiality, has to do with how difficult it is to opt out. . . .

. . . Even if consumers can obtain the information needed to opt out, the cost in time and money of communicating and negotiating with all the relevant information gatherers may be substantial. . . .

Companies may not be eager to offer opt-outs because they may rationally conclude that they will incur costs when consumers opt out, while receiving few offsetting benefits. When consumers exercise the option of having their names deleted, mailing lists shrink and presumably become less valuable. . . .

Because of these added costs, companies might decide that while they must offer an opt-out plan, they do not want consumers to take advantage of it. . . . [C]ompanies that offer opt-outs have an incentive to increase the transaction costs incurred by consumers who opt out. . . .

Companies can increase consumers' transaction costs in opting out in a number of ways. A brochure titled "Privacy Notice," which my local cable company included with its bill, provides an example. This Privacy Notice discussed, among other things, how cable subscribers could write to the company to ask that the company not sell their names and other information to third parties. There are at least four reasons why this particular notice may not be effective in eliciting a response from consumers troubled by the sale of their names to others.

First, the Privacy Notice may be obscured by other information included in the mailing. . . .

The second reason why consumers may not respond to the Privacy Notice is its length. The brochure is four pages long and contains 17 paragraphs, 36 sentences, and 1062 words. . . .

Some companies have gone in the other direction, providing so little information in such vague terms that consumers are unable to discern what they are being told. . . .

A third reason why the Privacy Notice may not be effective stems from its prose. Notwithstanding the Plain Language Law in my home state, computer analysis of the text found it extremely difficult, requiring more than a college education for comprehension. By comparison, a similar analysis of this Article found that it required a lower reading level than that of the Privacy Notice.

Fourth, the Privacy Notice may be ineffective because it does not provide an easy or convenient mechanism for opting out. For example, the Privacy Notice invites consumers who object to the sale of their personal information to write to the cable company in a separate letter. By contrast, cable subscribers desiring to add a new premium channel can do so over the telephone, speaking either to a person or tapping buttons on their telephone, depending on their preference. The more difficult the opt-out process, the less likely consumers are to avail themselves of it. . . .

A third explanation for the failure of consumers to opt out as often as their survey answers might suggest is the consumers themselves. Extensive literature on consumer complaint behavior makes clear that many consumers who are distressed by merchant conduct cannot bring themselves to tell the merchant about it. This inability to communicate might translate into failure by consumers to add their names to opt-out lists. . . .

[Sovern suggests that an opt-in system would be more preferable than an opt-out system.]

One benefit of an opt-in system is that it minimizes transaction costs. While some transaction costs are inevitable in any system in which consumers can opt out or opt in, strategic-behavior transaction costs, at least, can be avoided by using a system which discourages parties from generating such costs. The current system encourages businesses to inflate strategic-behavior costs to increase their own gains, albeit at the expense of consumers and the total surplus from exchange. An opt-in system would encourage businesses to reduce strategic-behavior costs without giving consumers an incentive to increase these costs. Instead of an opt-out situation in which merchants are obligated to provide a message they do not wish consumers to receive, an opt-in regime would harness merchants' efforts in providing a message they want the consumer to receive. . . .

An opt-in system thus increases the likelihood that consumers will choose according to their preferences rather than choosing according to the default. . . .

An opt-in system also increases the prospect that direct mailing would be tailored to what consumers wish to receive, thus benefiting consumers who want to receive some, but not all, solicitations. . . .

The sale of information is troublesome in part because it creates externalities, or costs borne by others. Externalities are created when a person engages in an activity that imposes costs on others but is not required to take those costs into account when deciding whether to pursue the activity. The feelings experienced by consumers whose information is sold and used against their wishes constitute just such externalities. An opt-in system — or an opt-out system in which consumers who object to the trade in their personal information have a genuine opportunity to opt out — can shift costs and thereby "internalize" this externality. To put it another way, consumers could bar the sale of their information unless businesses paid them an amount they deemed adequate, thereby requiring businesses selling personal information to incur a cost otherwise borne by consumers. . . .

A regulated opt-out system is less likely than an opt-in system to solve the problem. Opt-out systems do not give businesses the incentive to minimize consumer transaction costs. Consequently, firms might respond to such regulation by generating formal, legalistic notices that consumers would likely ignore. An opt-out system might thus create only the illusion of a cure.

Accordingly, an opt-in system is preferable, chiefly because it eliminates the incentive firms have to engage in strategic behavior and thus inflate consumer transaction costs. An opt-in system would permit consumers who wish to protect their privacy to do so without incurring transaction costs. Consumers who permit the use of their personal information should also be able to realize their wish easily. Indeed, because firms profit from the use of consumer information, firms would have an incentive to make it as easy as possible for consumers to consent to the use of their personal information. . . . An opt-in system, therefore, seems to offer the best hope of accommodating consumer preferences while minimizing transaction costs. . . .

MICHAEL E. STATEN & FRED H. CATE, *THE IMPACT OF OPT-IN PRIVACY RULES ON RETAIL MARKETS: A CASE STUDY OF MBNA*

52 Duke L.J. 745, 750-51, 766, 770-74, 776 (2003)

To illustrate the costs of moving to an opt-in system, we examine MBNA Corporation, a financial institution that offers consumers a variety of loan and insurance products (primarily credit cards), takes deposits, but operates entirely without a branch network. Incorporated in 1981 and publicly traded since 1991, the company has compiled a stunning growth record in just two decades. As of the end of 2000, the company provided credit cards and other loan products to 51 million consumers, had $89 billion of loans outstanding, and serviced 15 percent of all Visa/MasterCard credit card balances outstanding in the United States.

MBNA's ability to access and use information about potential and existing customers is largely responsible for it becoming the second largest credit card issuer in the United States in less than twenty years. To appreciate the critical role that the sharing of information has played in MBNA's remarkable history, one need only reflect on the challenge of acquiring 51 million customers with no brick-and-mortar stores or branches. Like firms in a variety of businesses, but especially financial services, MBNA harnessed information technology as the engine for establishing and building customer relationships without ever physically meeting its customers. By using direct mail, telephone and, most recently, Internet contacts, the company has reached out to new prospects throughout the population, regardless of where they live, with offers tailored to their individual interests. . . .

At the core of its marketing and targeting strategies is the proposition that consumers who share a common institutional bond or experience will have an affinity for using a card that lets them demonstrate their affiliation each time they use it to pay for a purchase. The affinity for the institution raises the probability that a prospect will be converted to a customer. Equally important, the institution or organization usually maintains a list of members on which MBNA can focus its marketing efforts. Following this "affinity group" marketing strategy, MBNA designs a card product tailored to members of a particular group, negotiates a financial arrangement with the organization for the exclusive rights to market an affinity card to its members, and uses the member list as a source of potential names to contact via direct mail or telemarketing. . . .

Design of new affinity cards is an ongoing process. In 2000 alone, MBNA acquired the endorsements of 459 new groups, including the United States Tennis Association, the Atlanta Braves, National Audubon Society, barnesand-noble.com, and the Thurgood Marshall Scholarship Fund.

Although targeting prospects through affinity groups has proven to be a clever strategy, not every group member is offered a card product. The key to the company's profitability and earnings growth, especially given the rapid growth in the size of the customer base, has been in screening the prospects from each affinity group to identify those likely to be quality customers. Given that MBNA's fundamental business is lending money via an unsecured credit card with a revolving line of credit attached, the company wants to put the card in the hands of customers who will use it, but who will not default on their balances.

Consequently, MBNA uses information to screen prospects both before it makes card offers (the targeting process) and after it receives applications (the underwriting process). . . .

How large a drag does an "explicit-consent" system impose on economic efficiency? According to the U.S. Postal Service, 52 percent of unsolicited mail in this country is never read. If that figure translates to opt-in requests, then more than half of all consumers in an opt-in system would lose the benefits or services that could result from the use of personal information because the mandatory request for consent would never receive their attention. Moreover, even if an unsolicited offer is read, experience with company-specific and industry-wide opt-out lists demonstrates that less than 10 percent of the U.S. population ever opts out of a mailing list — often the figure is less than 3 percent. Indeed, the difficulty (and cost) of obtaining a response of any sort from consumers is the primary drawback of an opt-in approach. . . .

MBNA's core product is the affinity card tailored for and marketed to each of more than 4,700 affinity groups. . . . [T]he foundation of MBNA's affinity strategy is access to the member lists of each of its affinity organizations. This marketing partnership with thousands of member organizations nationwide makes MBNA unique among major credit card issuers and accounts for much of the company's superior financial performance and reputation for outstanding customer service. However, in the absence of an explicit joint-marketing exception in an opt-in law, a third-party opt-in regime could effectively end MBNA's unique direct marketing approach by sharply limiting an organization's ability to share its member list. . . .

Like all major credit card issuers, MBNA uses personal information to increase the chance that its credit card offer will reach an interested and qualified customer. This process greatly reduces the number of solicitations that must be sent to achieve a given target volume of new accounts, thereby reducing the cost of account acquisition. It also reduces the volume of junk mail in the form of card offers sent to consumers who are not qualified. Third-party or affiliate opt-in systems would eliminate MBNA's access to a significant portion of the information that it currently uses to identify which individuals on the member lists it receives would be good prospects for a given credit card or other product. A blanket opt-in system applicable to marketing activities would impose similar limits.

The MBNA direct mail marketing operations obtain and consider about 800 million consumer "leads" during the course of a year. The vast majority of these leads are names that appear on affinity group member lists (e.g., university alumni groups and professional associations), or names of consumers who are customers of institutions that have endorsed MBNA's credit card product. Because this is an annual figure, many names appear more than once because the individuals are on more than one list acquired during the course of a year, or may be considered in conjunction with a specific group's marketing campaign several times during the year. The most creditworthy names among them may receive multiple solicitations during the year.

MBNA does not wish to mail to all names on the list. Not all are equally likely to respond to a solicitation, nor will all meet the credit underwriting standards for a particular card product. In 2000, the MBNA direct marketing budget supported approximately 400 million mailings of card offers. The challenge to the company in managing the acquisition of new accounts is to cull the "lead list" of 800 million prospect names to identify and target the 400 million direct mail solicitations to consumers who are most likely to become new cardholders. Generally speaking, MBNA has developed a set of targeting criteria such that names reaching the final mailing list of 400 million: (1) are most likely to respond to the offer and the use of the credit card, and (2) are most likely to meet MBNA's creditworthiness standards for the card.

MBNA prepares hundreds of distinct solicitations throughout the year for its various affinity groups. As part of the targeting process for each new solicitation, the prospect list is scrubbed via comparison to a series of "suppression files" that the company maintains and routinely updates. These files pull information about either individuals or addresses from a variety of internal and external data sources. A few examples of the specific criteria illustrate the process.

[The authors describe how MBNA has proprietary response models to help it determine which customers are most likely to respond to its offer. It uses credit history information to find individuals who are likely to repay, but, at the same time, do not have "extraordinary creditworthiness" and are, hence, likely to be frequently solicited by card issuers and unlikely to respond to an MBNA offer.]

The bottom line from the culling process is that approximately 40 percent of the eight hundred million names are suppressed. The initial lead list is typically reduced by an additional 10 percent through a combination of eliminating duplicate records, suppressing undeliverable addresses, and dropping customer names that appear on various "do not mail" lists that record customer preferences not to be solicited. . . . The approximately four hundred million names remaining on the lead list receive targeted direct mail offers with the endorsement of the affinity group to which they belong. . . .

MBNA's proprietary response models indicate that its use of information in these three categories to cull likely prospects accounts for approximately a 19 percent reduction in names from the annual prospect list. In other words, by targeting offers under current rules, about 150 million names on the prospect list during the course of a typical annual solicitation cycle do not receive solicitations, because the direct mail piece would otherwise reach a consumer who was either not interested or not qualified for the card product. . . .

[Under an opt-in approach,] approximately 550 million names would remain, instead of 400 million under the current rules. Lacking the information necessary to further distinguish good prospects from poor prospects, the company's targeting efficiency would be impaired.

MBNA would have two choices. It could increase its direct mail volume to send solicitations to all 550 million names remaining on the prospect list after the culling process, or it could arbitrarily remove 150 million names from the list after the culling process so that its direct mail volume remained unchanged at 400 million. Under either scenario, approximately 27 percent of the solicitations (150 million of 550 million) would go to consumers who were less interested in, and/or less qualified for, the offer, and who would have been dropped from the target list had MBNA been allowed to access and use the information on which its presently relies under current privacy rules. . . .

Although MBNA's actual response rate and cost per account booked is proprietary, we can illustrate the impact of the decline by utilizing the credit card industry average response rate to direct mail solicitations for 2000, which was 0.6 percent. For every 100 million solicitations mailed to individuals under the opt-in scenario, only 492 thousand new accounts would be booked, as compared to 600 thousand if the offers were targeted under existing rules, an 18 percent reduction in new accounts for the same expenditure on direct mail solicitations. Of course, the higher cost per account booked is borne not only by MBNA, but by MBNA's customers as well, in the form of higher prices, reduced benefits, diminished service, and higher acceptance standards for new credit products.

But, the negative impact does not stop there. Regardless of whether MBNA's response to opt-in is to mail more solicitations or mail the same number to a less-targeted prospect list, under either scenario, the recipient group of four hundred million individuals will — on average — be more risky and less profitable than MBNA's target group reached under the current rules. As a result, MBNA's delinquency and charge-off rates will rise, relative to its current experience, thereby imposing additional costs that will be passed along to all of MBNA's customers. Card usage will also be affected by booking cardholders who are less likely to use the card.

NOTES & QUESTIONS

1. ***Opt out vs. Opt in.*** Do you agree with Sovern that an opt-in policy is more efficient than an opt-out policy? Do you think that an opt-in policy is feasible? Are the views of Staten and Cate convincing on this score? Do you think opt out or opt in should be required by law?
2. ***Internalizing Costs.*** Staten and Cate claim that MBNA's business model will be threatened by opt in. This business model relies in part, however, on sending out 400 million of mostly unwanted solicitations for credit in order to receive a 0.6 percent response rate. In other words, this model views as an externality the added cost of sorting through mail for 99.4 percent of those individuals solicited. Should MBNA be obliged to internalize these costs?

(b) Contract Law

A privacy policy can be thought of as a type of contract, though the terms are typically dictated by the company and are non-negotiable. Consider the following advice of Scott Killingsworth to the drafters of website privacy policies:

> Considering enforcement leads to the question: what is the legal effect of a privacy policy? As between the website and the user, a privacy policy bears all of the earmarks of a contract, but perhaps one enforceable only at the option of the user. It is no stretch to regard the policy as an offer to treat information in specified ways, inviting the user's acceptance, evidenced by using the site or submitting the information. The website's promise and the user's use of the site and submission of personal data are each sufficient consideration to support a contractual obligation. Under this analysis, users would have the right to sue and

seek all available remedies for breach of the privacy policy, without the need for private rights of action under such regulatory statutes as the FTC Act.[29]

Privacy policies can also be viewed simply as notices that warn consumers about the use of their personal information. Assuming that these notices are subject to change as business practices evolve, how effective are privacy policies as a means to protect privacy?

IN RE NORTHWEST AIRLINES PRIVACY LITIGATION

2004 WL 1278459 (D. Minn. 2004) (not reported in F. Supp. 2d)

MAGNUSON, J. . . . Plaintiffs are customers of Defendant Northwest Airlines, Inc. ("Northwest"). After September 11, 2001, the National Aeronautical and Space Administration ("NASA") requested that Northwest provide NASA with certain passenger information in order to assist NASA in studying ways to increase airline security. Northwest supplied NASA with passenger name records ("PNRs"), which are electronic records of passenger information. PNRs contain information such as a passenger's name, flight number, credit card data, hotel reservation, car rental, and any traveling companions.

Plaintiffs contend that Northwest's actions constitute violations of the Electronic Communications Privacy Act ("ECPA"), 18 U.S.C. § 2701 *et seq.,* the Fair Credit Reporting Act ("FCRA"), 15 U.S.C. § 1681, and Minnesota's Deceptive Trade Practices Act ("DTPA"), Minn. Stat. § 325D.44, and also constitute invasion of privacy, trespass to property, negligent misrepresentation, breach of contract, and breach of express warranties. The basis for most of Plaintiffs' claims is that Northwest's website contained a privacy policy that stated that Northwest would not share customers' information except as necessary to make customers' travel arrangements. Plaintiffs contend that Northwest's provision of PNRs to NASA violated Northwest's privacy policy, giving rise to the legal claims noted above.

Northwest has now moved to dismiss the Amended Consolidated Class Action Complaint (hereinafter "Amended Complaint"). . . .

The ECPA prohibits a person or entity from

> (1) intentionally access[ing] without authorization a facility through which an electronic communication service is provided; or
> (2) intentionally exceeds an authorization to access that facility; and thereby obtains, alters, or prevents authorized access to a wire or electronic communication while it is in electronic storage in such system shall be punished. 18 U.S.C. § 2701(a).

Plaintiffs argue that Northwest's access to its own electronic communications service is limited by its privacy policy, and that Northwest's provision of PNRs to NASA violated that policy and thus constituted unauthorized access to the "facility through which an electronic communication service is provided" within the meaning of this section. Plaintiffs also allege that Northwest violated § 2702

---

[29] Scott Killingsworth, *Minding Your Own Business: Privacy Policies in Principle and in Practice*, 7 J. Intell. Prop. L. 57, 91-92 (1999).

of the ECPA, which states that "a person or entity providing an electronic communications service to the public shall not knowingly divulge to any person or entity the contents of a communication while in electronic storage by that service." 18 U.S.C. § 2702(a)(1). Northwest argues first that it cannot violate § 2702 because it is not a "person or entity providing an electronic communications service to the public." . . .

Defining electronic communications service to include online merchants or service providers like Northwest stretches the ECPA too far. Northwest is not an internet service provider. . . .

Similarly, Northwest's conduct as outlined in the Amended Complaint does not constitute a violation of § 2701. Plaintiffs' claim is that Northwest improperly disclosed the information in PNRs to NASA. Section 2701 does not prohibit improper disclosure of information. Rather, this section prohibits improper access to an electronic communications service provider or the information contained on that service provider. . . .

Finally, Northwest argues that Plaintiffs' remaining claims fail to state a claim on which relief can be granted. These claims are: trespass to property, intrusion upon seclusion, breach of contract, and breach of express warranties.

To state a claim for trespass to property, Plaintiffs must demonstrate that they owned or possessed property, that Northwest wrongfully took that property, and that Plaintiffs were damaged by the wrongful taking. Plaintiffs contend that the information contained in the PNRs was Plaintiffs' property and that, by providing that information to NASA, Northwest wrongfully took that property.

As a matter of law, the PNRs were not Plaintiffs' property. Plaintiffs voluntarily provided some information that was included in the PNRs. It may be that the information Plaintiffs provided to Northwest was Plaintiffs' property. However, when that information was compiled and combined with other information to form a PNR, the PNR itself became Northwest's property. Northwest cannot wrongfully take its own property. Thus, Plaintiffs' claim for trespass fails. . . .

Intrusion upon seclusion exists when someone "intentionally intrudes, physically or otherwise, upon the solitude or seclusion of another or his private affairs or concerns . . . if the intrusion would be highly offensive to a reasonable person." . . . In this instance, Plaintiffs voluntarily provided their personal information to Northwest. Moreover, although Northwest had a privacy policy for information included on the website, Plaintiffs do not contend that they actually read the privacy policy prior to providing Northwest with their personal information. Thus, Plaintiffs' expectation of privacy was low. Further, the disclosure here was not to the public at large, but rather was to a government agency in the wake of a terrorist attack that called into question the security of the nation's transportation system. Northwest's motives in disclosing the information cannot be questioned. Taking into account all of the factors listed above, the Court finds as a matter of law that the disclosure of Plaintiffs' personal information would not be highly offensive to a reasonable person and that Plaintiffs have failed to state a claim for intrusion upon seclusion. . . .

Northwest contends that the privacy policy on Northwest's website does not, as a matter of law, constitute a unilateral contract, the breach of which entitles Plaintiffs to damages. Northwest also argues that, even if the privacy policy constituted a contract or express warranty, Plaintiffs' contract and warranty claims fail because Plaintiffs have failed to plead any contract damages. . . .

Plaintiffs' rely on the following statement from Northwest's website as the basis for their contract and warranty claims:

> When you reserve or purchase travel services through Northwest Airlines nwa.com Reservations, we provide only the relevant information required by the car rental agency, hotel, or other involved third party to ensure the successful fulfillment of your travel arrangements. . . .

The usual rule in contract cases is that "general statements of policy are not contractual." . . .

The privacy statement on Northwest's website did not constitute a unilateral contract. The language used vests discretion in Northwest to determine when the information is "relevant" and which "third parties" might need that information. Moreover, absent an allegation that Plaintiffs actually read the privacy policy, not merely the general allegation that Plaintiffs "relied on" the policy, Plaintiffs have failed to allege an essential element of a contract claim: that the alleged "offer" was accepted by Plaintiffs. Plaintiffs' contract and warranty claims fail as a matter of law.

Even if the privacy policy was sufficiently definite and Plaintiffs had alleged that they read the policy before giving their information to Northwest, it is likely that Plaintiffs' contract and warranty claims would fail as a matter of law. Defendants point out that Plaintiffs have failed to allege any contractual damages arising out of the alleged breach. . . .

[The case is dismissed.]

NOTES & QUESTIONS

1. ***Breach of Contract.*** In *Dyer v. Northwest Airlines Corp.*, 334 F. Supp. 2d 1196 (D.N.D. 2004), another action involving Northwest Airlines' disclosure of passenger records to the government, the court reached a similar conclusion on the plaintiffs' breach of contract claim:

> To sustain a breach of contract claim, the Plaintiffs must demonstrate (1) the existence of a contract; (2) breach of the contract; and (3) damages which flow from the breach. . . .
>
> . . . [T]he Court finds the Plaintiffs' breach of contract claim fails as a matter of law. First, broad statements of company policy do not generally give rise to contract claims. . . . Second, nowhere in the complaint are the Plaintiffs alleged to have ever logged onto Northwest Airlines' website and accessed, read, understood, actually relied upon, or otherwise considered Northwest Airlines' privacy policy. Finally, even if the privacy policy was sufficiently definite and the Plaintiffs had alleged they did read the policy prior to providing personal information to Northwest Airlines, the Plaintiffs have failed to allege any contractual damages arising out of the alleged breach.

2. ***Damages.*** In *In re Jet Blue Airways Corp. Privacy Litigation*, 379 F. Supp. 2d 299 (E.D.N.Y. 2005), a group of plaintiffs sued Jet Blue Airlines for breach of

contract for sharing passenger records with the government. The court granted Jet Blue's motion to dismiss:

> An action for breach of contract under New York law requires proof of four elements: (1) the existence of a contract, (2) performance of the contract by one party, (3) breach by the other party, and (4) damages. . . .
>
> JetBlue . . . argues that plaintiffs have failed to meet their pleading requirement with respect to damages, citing an absence of any facts in the Amended Complaint to support this element of the claim. Plaintiffs' sole allegation on the element of contract damages consists of the statement that JetBlue's breach of the company privacy policy injured plaintiffs and members of the class and that JetBlue is therefore liable for "actual damages in an amount to be determined at trial." . . . At oral argument, when pressed to identify the "injuries" or damages referred to in the Amended Complaint, counsel for plaintiffs stated that the "contract damage could be the loss of privacy," acknowledging that loss of privacy "may" be a contract damage. It is apparent based on the briefing and oral argument held in this case that the sparseness of the damages allegations is a direct result of plaintiffs' inability to plead or prove any actual contract damages. As plaintiffs' counsel concedes, the only damage that can be read into the present complaint is a loss of privacy. At least one recent case has specifically held that this is not a damage available in a breach of contract action. *See Trikas v. Universal Card Services Corp.,* 351 F. Supp. 2d 37 (E.D.N.Y. 2005). This holding naturally follows from the well-settled principle that "recovery in contract, unlike recovery in tort, allows only for economic losses flowing directly from the breach."
>
> Plaintiffs allege that in a second amended complaint, they could assert as a contract damage the loss of the economic value of their information, but while that claim sounds in economic loss, the argument ignores the nature of the contract asserted. . . . [T]he "purpose of contract damages is to put a plaintiff in the same economic position he or she would have occupied had the contract been fully performed." Plaintiffs may well have expected that in return for providing their personal information to JetBlue and paying the purchase price, they would obtain a ticket for air travel and the promise that their personal information would be safeguarded consistent with the terms of the privacy policy. They had no reason to expect that they would be compensated for the "value" of their personal information. In addition, there is absolutely no support for the proposition that the personal information of an individual JetBlue passenger had any value for which that passenger could have expected to be compensated. . . . . There is likewise no support for the proposition that an individual passenger's personal information has or had any compensable value in the economy at large.

If you were the plaintiffs' attorney, how would you go about establishing the plaintiffs' injury? Is there any cognizable harm when an airline violates its privacy policy by providing passenger information to the government?

3. ***Breach of Confidentiality Tort.*** Would the plaintiffs have a cause of action based on the breach of confidentiality tort?

4. ***Enforcing Privacy Policies as Contracts Against Consumers.*** Suppose privacy policies were enforceable as contracts. Would this be beneficial to consumers? It might not be, Allyson Haynes argues:

> [T]here is a distinct possibility that as website operators grow savvier with respect to the law, they will respond to the lack of substantive privacy protection (and lack of consumer awareness) by including in privacy policies terms that are not favorable to consumers.

On the flip side of consumers seeking to enforce privacy policies as contracts, companies might also desire to hold customers to be contractually bound to the companies' privacy policies. Would a privacy policy be enforceable as a contract against the customer? Haynes contends:

> [P]articularly in cases where consumers are deemed to have assented to privacy policies by virtue of their presence on the site or by giving information without affirmatively clicking acceptance, the consumer has a good argument that he or she did not assent to the privacy policy, preventing the formation of a binding contract, and preventing the website from enforcing any of its terms against the consumer.[30]

(c) FTC Enforcement

Beyond private law actions such as contract and promissory estoppel, the promises that companies make regarding their privacy practices can be enforced by the government through public law. Private law actions are initiated on behalf of harmed individuals, who can obtain monetary or other redress for their injuries. In contrast, public law actions are initiated by government agencies or officials, and they typically involve fines and penalties.

In 1995, Congress and privacy experts first asked the Federal Trade Commission (FTC) to become involved with consumer privacy issues.[31] Since 1998, the FTC has maintained the position that the use or dissemination of personal information in a manner contrary to a posted privacy policy is a deceptive practice under the FTC Act, 15 U.S.C. § 45. The Act prohibits "unfair or deceptive acts or practices in or affecting commerce." An "unfair or deceptive" act or practice is one that "causes or is likely to cause substantial injury to consumers which is not reasonably avoidable by consumers themselves and not outweighed by countervailing benefits to consumers or to competition." § 45(n).

The FTC does not have jurisdiction over all companies. Exempt from the FTC's jurisdiction are many types of financial institutions, airlines, telecommunications carriers, and other types of entities. § 45(a)(2). The Act authorizes the FTC to bring civil actions for penalties up to $10,000 for a knowing violation of the Act. § 45(m)(1)(A). Further, the FTC can obtain injunctive remedies. § 53. The Act does not provide for private causes of action; only the FTC can enforce the Act. Since it began enforcing the Act for breaches of privacy policies in 1998, the FTC has brought a number of actions, most of which have settled. Some of these enforcement cases concern companies not

---

[30] Allyson W. Haynes, *Online Privacy Policies: Contracting Away Control Over Personal Information?*, 111 Penn. St. L. Rev. 587, 612, 618 (2007).

[31] Letter from EPIC Director Marc Rotenberg to FTC Commissioner Christine Varney, Dec. 14, 1995.

keeping their privacy promises. As a more complicated example of a violation of the FTC Act, consider *In the Matter of Vision I Properties*.

IN THE MATTER OF VISION I PROPERTIES

2005 WL 1274741 (F.T.C. 2005)

[Vision I Properties licensed shopping cart software and provided related services to small online retail merchants through a website, www.cartmanager.com. The company's software created customizable shopping cart pages for client merchants' websites. The resulting pages resided on websites managed by Vision I Properties, but resembled the other pages on merchants' websites.

Some of the client merchants using this company's shopping cart software and services published various privacy policies on their websites. In its complaint, the FTC excerpted some of these privacy policies, including one that stated: "PRIVACY POLICY: It's simple. We don't sell, trade, or lend any information on our customers or visitors to anyone."

In fact, however, Vision I Properties in January 2003 rented consumers' personal information collected through its shopping cart and check out pages at client merchant sites. The FTC complaint noted: "Such personal information includes the name, address, phone number, and purchase history of nearly one million consumers. This personal information was used by third parties to send direct mail and make telemarketing calls to consumers who shopped at merchant sites using the software."

For the FTC, it was reasonable for consumers to rely on merchants' privacy policies. Moreover, Vision I Properties did not adequately inform merchants of its information sharing. It did assert, however, in its online license agreement that it would retain "full ownership of all data submitted by either Merchant or Purchaser." The FTC dismissed this statement, however, as (1) "buried in the middle of the online agreement" and also as (2) lacking an explanation of how Vision I Properties intended "to use the information or that such use may conflict with the merchants' privacy policies."

On April 19, 2005, the FTC and Vision I properties settled the case and the FTC issued a Decision and Order.]

DECISION AND ORDER

The Federal Trade Commission having initiated an investigation of certain acts and practices of the Respondent named in the caption hereof, and the Respondent having been furnished thereafter with a copy of a draft Complaint that the Bureau of Consumer Protection proposed to present to the Commission for its consideration and which, if issued by the Commission, would charge the Respondent with violation of the Federal Trade Commission Act. . . .

I.

IT IS ORDERED that Respondent, directly or through any corporation, subsidiary, division, or other device, in connection with the collection of personally identifiable information from or about consumers, shall not make, expressly or by implication, any false or misleading representation regarding the collection, use, or disclosure of personally identifiable information.

II.

IT IS FURTHER ORDERED that Respondent, directly or through any corporation, subsidiary, division, or other device, shall not sell, rent, or disclose to any third party for marketing purposes any personally identifiable information that was collected from consumers through shopping cart software used at a merchant customer's Web site prior to the date of service of this Order.

III.

IT IS FURTHER ORDERED that Respondent, directly or through any corporation, subsidiary, division, or other device, shall not sell, rent, or disclose to any third party for marketing purposes any personally identifiable information collected from consumers through shopping cart or other software used at a merchant customer's Web site after the date of service of this Order unless, prior to the date such information was collected, Respondent took one of the following two actions:

A. Provided to the merchant customer a clear and conspicuous written notice of its information practices and obtained from the merchant customer a written certification stating: (1) that the merchant customer received such notice; and (2) either (a) that its posted privacy policy states that consumers' information may be sold, rented, or disclosed to third parties, or (b) that it provides a clear and conspicuous disclosure, before any personally identifiable information is collected from consumers through Respondent's shopping cart or other software, stating that the consumer is leaving the merchant customer's Web site and entering Respondent's Web site, and that Respondent's site is governed by Respondent's own privacy policy.

The written notice to merchants required by this Paragraph shall be labeled "Important Notice to Merchants from CartManager" and must: (1) state that Respondent intends to sell, rent, or disclose such information; (2) identify the types or categories of any entities to which such information will be disclosed; (3) advise the merchant customer that it may be liable for any misrepresentations it makes about the use or disclosure of information collected from consumers at its Web site, including through software used at the site; and (4) contain no other information; OR

B. Provided a clear and conspicuous disclosure on the page(s) through which it collected such information stating: (1) that the consumer is on Respondent's Web site, and (2) that information provided by the consumer to Respondent will be used, sold, rented, or disclosed to third parties for marketing purposes.

IV.

IT IS FURTHER ORDERED that within five (5) days of the date of service of this Order, Respondent shall pay $9,101.63 to the United States Treasury as disgorgement. Such payment shall be by cashier's check or certified check made payable to the Treasurer of the United States. In the event of any default in payment, which default continues for more than ten (10) days beyond the due date of payment, Respondent shall also pay interest as computed under 28 U.S.C. § 1961, which shall accrue on the unpaid balance from the date of default until the date the balance is fully paid.

V.

IT IS FURTHER ORDERED that Respondent Vision One and its successors and assigns shall, for a period of five (5) years after the last date of dissemination of any representation covered by this Order, maintain and upon request make available to the Federal Trade Commission for inspection and copying a print or electronic copy of all documents demonstrating their compliance with the terms and provisions of this Order, including, but not limited to:

A. A sample copy of each different privacy statement or communication relating to the collection of personally identifiable information containing representations about how personally identifiable information will be used and/or disclosed. Each Web page copy shall be dated and contain the full URL of the Web page where the material was posted online. Electronic copies shall include all text and graphics files, audio scripts, and other computer files used in presenting the information on the Web; *provided, however*, that after creation of any Web page or screen in compliance with this Order, Respondent shall not be required to retain a print or electronic copy of any amended Web page or screen to the extent that the amendment does not affect Respondent's compliance obligations under this Order;

B. A sample copy of each different document containing the disclosures required by Part III.A. of this Order; a list of all merchant customers who received each different document containing such disclosures; all communications by merchant customers in response to such disclosures, including all written certifications received pursuant to Part III.A. and any complaints received from merchant customers; and a sample copy of each different document containing the disclosures required by Part III.B.; and

C. All invoices, communications, and records relating to the disclosure to third parties of personally identifiable information collected through merchant customer Web sites. . . .

VII.

IT IS FURTHER ORDERED that Respondent Vision One and its successors and assigns shall notify the Commission at least thirty (30) days prior to any change in the corporation(s) that may affect compliance obligations arising under this Order, including, but not limited to, a dissolution, assignment, sale, merger, or other action that would result in the emergence of a successor corporation; the creation or dissolution of a subsidiary, parent, or affiliate that engages in any acts or practices subject to this Order; the proposed filing of a bankruptcy petition; or a change in the corporate name or address. . . .

IX.

This Order will terminate on April 19, 2025, or twenty (20) years from the most recent date that the United States or the Federal Trade Commission files a complaint (with or without an accompanying consent decree) in federal court alleging any violation of the Order, whichever comes later. . . .

NOTES & QUESTIONS

1. ***Responsibility for Violating Another Company's Privacy Policy?*** In a typical "broken promise" privacy case, the FTC charges a company with breaking its own promise to provide certain kinds of privacy practices or protections. In contrast, the FTC in *Vision I Properties* was faced with a situation in which the behavior of Vision I broke the privacy promises of other parties (the merchants). Vision I Properties does not seem to be in privity with the end customers; it is a B2B (business-to-business) company rather than a B2C (business-to-consumer) company.

   To be sure, Vision I Properties prevented its merchant customers from delivering on their privacy policies. Yet, Vision I Properties had a provision in its contracts with the merchants explicitly claiming ownership of all information collected with use of its software. By pursuing an action against Vision I Properties, the FTC was claiming that its behavior was an unfair or deceptive trade practice. But if a merchant has a privacy policy, why isn't the burden on the merchant to police the behavior of the B2B entities with whom it contracts? Shouldn't the merchants be liable for lack of care in reading their contracts?
2. ***Damages.*** *In the Matter of Vision I Properties,* the FTC assesses damages of $9,101.63 "as disgorgement." A disgorgement measure of damages looks to the unjust enrichment of a defendant and requires her to surrender a profit improperly or illegally obtained. Is the proper measure of damages in this case the disgorgement of profits that Vision I Properties obtained through its practices in renting the information it collected through its shopping cart software?
3. ***Broken Promises:* Liberty Financial.** In *In re Liberty Financial Cos.,* No. 9823522, 1999 FTC LEXIS 99 (May 6, 1999), the FTC charged the operator of a website for child and teen investors with falsely promising that the personal information it collected in a survey would be kept anonymous. The website gathered data about the child and family's finances, but instead of being anonymously maintained, it was kept in an identifiable form. Liberty Financial settled with the FTC, agreeing to refrain from making future misrepresentations, to post a privacy notice on its website, and to obtain

parental consent prior to gathering personal data from children. FTC commissioners approved the settlement 4–0.

4. ***Deceptive Data Collection:* ReverseAuction.** In *FTC v. ReverseAuction.com, Inc.*, No. 00-CV-32 (D.D.C. Jan. 6, 2000), the FTC charged ReverseAuction.com with improperly obtaining personal information from eBay customers. ReverseAuction then used the information to spam eBay customers promoting its own auction website. The message falsely stated to the recipients that their eBay user IDs would expire soon. The FTC charged that ReverseAuction's practice was both unfair and deceptive.

   ReverseAuction settled, agreeing to be barred from making future misrepresentations. Further, ReverseAuction had to notify the consumers who received its spam and inform them that its eBay user IDs will not expire and that eBay did not authorize ReverseAuction's spam. Consumers also can delete their personal information from ReverseAuction's database. ReverseAuction must also display its own privacy policy on its website. FTC commissioners voted 5–0 to approve the settlement. However, two commissioners, Orson Swindle and Thomas B. Leary, agreeing that ReverseAuction acted deceptively, disagreed that ReverseAuction acted unfairly:

   > We do not, however, support the unfairness theory in Count One. The Commission has no authority to declare an act or practice unfair unless it "causes or is likely to cause *substantial injury* to consumers which is not reasonably avoidable by consumers themselves and not outweighed by countervailing benefits to consumers or to competition." 15 U.S.C. § 45(n) (emphasis added). . . .
   >
   > We do not say that privacy concerns can never support an unfairness claim. In this case, however, ReverseAuction's use of eBay members' information to send them e-mail did not cause substantial enough injury to meet the statutory standard. . . .
   >
   > The injury in this case was caused by deception: that is, by ReverseAuction's failure to honor its express commitments. It is not necessary or appropriate to plead a less precise theory.
   >
   > . . . The unfairness theory . . . posits substantial injury stemming from ReverseAuction's use of information readily available to millions of eBay members to send commercial e-mail. This standard for substantial injury overstates the appropriate level of government-enforced privacy protection on the Internet, and provides no rationale for when unsolicited commercial e-mail is unfair and when it is not.

   One commissioner, Mozelle W. Thompson, issued a separate statement to justify the unfairness theory:

   > I believe that ReverseAuction's behavior caused substantial injury to members of the eBay community, that the injury could not have been avoided by those members, and it was not outweighed by countervailing benefits. I believe the harm caused in this case is especially significant because it not only breached the privacy expectation of each and every eBay member, it also undermined consumer confidence in eBay and diminishes the electronic marketplace for all its participants. This injury is exacerbated because consumer concern about

privacy and confidence in the electronic marketplace are such critical issues at this time.

5. ***Retroactive Privacy Policy Changes:*** **Gateway Learning Corp.** When Gateway Learning Corp. collected personal information from its consumers, its privacy policy stated that it would not sell, rent, or loan personal information to third parties unless people consented. Subsequently, Gateway altered its privacy policy to allow the renting of personal information to third parties without informing customers or obtaining their consent. The FTC filed a complaint alleging that this practice was an "unfair" act. *See In re Gateway Learning Corp.,* No. C-4120 (Sept. 10, 2004). Gateway settled with the FTC, agreeing to avoid making deceptive claims or retroactively change its privacy policy without consumer consent. Gateway agreed to pay $4,608, the amount it earned from renting the information.

   Suppose a company puts the following line in its privacy policy: "Please be aware that we may change this policy at any time." Would this allow for the retroactive application of a revised policy? Or is there an argument that even with a statement such as this one, the revised policy could not be applied retroactively?

6. ***Privacy Promises and Bankruptcy:*** **Toysmart** ***and Amazon.com.*** In *FTC v. Toysmart.com, LLC,* Civ. Action No. 00-11341-RGS (July 21, 2000), an Internet toy retailer, Toysmart.com, went bankrupt in 2000. One of the company's most important assets was its database of personal information — it had a customer list with over 200,000 individual names. This list included addresses, names and ages of children, purchasing information, and a toy wish list. Toysmart was a member of TRUSTe, an e-commerce industry privacy protection organization that establishes rules for privacy policies and permits companies that follow them to display TRUSTe's privacy seal. Toysmart had agreed to follow TRUSTe's guidelines and had displayed the TRUSTe seal on its website.

   In its privacy policy, Toysmart promised: "Personal information voluntarily submitted by visitors to our site, such as name, address, billing information and shopping preferences, is never shared with a third party. All information obtained by toysmart.com is used only to personalize your experience online." To pay back creditors, Toysmart attempted to sell its database of personal information.

   The FTC filed a complaint objecting to this practice and argued that such a sale, in light of Toysmart's promises never to sell its customer's personal information, would be a deceptive practice. The FTC approved a settlement by a 3–2 vote restricting how Toysmart could sell its database. The settlement states that:

   > The Debtor shall only assign or sell its Customer Information as part of the sale of its Goodwill and only to a Qualified Buyer approved by the Bankruptcy Court. In the process of approving any sale of the Customer Information, the Bankruptcy Court shall require that the Qualified Buyer agree to and comply with the terms of this Stipulation.

> The Qualified Buyer shall treat Customer Information in accordance with the terms of the Privacy Statement and shall be responsible for any violation by it following the date of purchase. Among other things, the Qualified Buyer shall use Customer Information only to fulfill customer orders and to personalize customers' experience on the Web site, and shall not disclose, sell or transfer Customer Information to any Third Party.
>
> If the Qualified Buyer materially changes the Privacy Statement, prior notice will be posted on the Web site. Any such material change in policy shall apply only to information collected following the change in policy. The Customer Information shall be governed by the Privacy Statement, unless the consumer provides affirmative consent ("opt-in") to the previously collected information being governed by the new policy. . . .

Is this settlement adequate to resolve the problems raised by the FTC in its complaint? As a postscript, one should note that the settlement attracted the support of Toysmart's creditors, since it would allow the sale of the database to certain purchasers, and hence could be used to pay back the creditors. However, in August 2000, Judge Carol Kenner of the U.S. Bankruptcy Court rejected the settlement because there were currently no offers on the table to buy the database, and it would hurt the creditors to restrict the sale to certain types of purchasers without first having a potential buyer. In February 2001, Judge Kenner agreed to let Toysmart sell its customer database to Disney, the primary shareholder, for $50,000. Disney agreed, as part of the deal, to destroy the list.

The Toysmart bankruptcy also led Amazon.com, the Internet's largest retailer, to change its privacy policy. Prior to the Toysmart case, Amazon's privacy policy provided:

> Amazon.com does not sell, trade, or rent your personal information to others. We may choose to do so in the future with trustworthy third parties, but you can tell us not to by sending a blank e-mail message to never@amazon.com.

In its new policy, Amazon.com stated:

> Information about our customers is an important part of our business, and we are not in the business of selling it to others. We share customer information only with the subsidiaries Amazon.com, Inc., controls and as described below. . . .
>
> As we continue to develop our business, we might sell or buy stores or assets. In such transactions, customer information generally is one of the transferred business assets. Also, in the unlikely event that Amazon.com, Inc., or substantially all of its assets are acquired, customer information will of course be one of the transferred assets. . . .

Amazon.com's new policy was criticized by some privacy organizations. One of the criticisms was that the policy did not provide an opt-out right. Suppose Amazon.com went bankrupt and decided to sell all of its customer data. Can it sell data supplied by consumers under the old policy? Can the new policy apply retroactively?

7. ***Bankruptcy: Property Rights vs. Contract Rights.*** Edward Janger proposes that a property rights regime (as opposed to the contractual rights of a privacy

policy) will best protect the privacy of personal data when companies possessing such data go bankrupt:

> Property rules are viewed as reflecting undivided entitlements. They allocate, as Carol Rose puts it, the "whole meatball" to the "owner." Liability rules, by contrast are viewed as dividing an entitlement between two parties. One party holds the right, but the other party is given the option to take the right and compensate the right holder for the deprivation (to breach and pay damages). . . .
>
> Propertization has some crucial benefits, but it also has some serious costs. Both the bankruptcy and non-bankruptcy treatment of privacy policies turn on whether a privacy policy creates a right enforceable only through civil damages, or a right with the status of property. If bankruptcy courts treat privacy policies solely as contract obligations [liability rule], the debtor will be free to breach (or reject) the contract in bankruptcy. Any damage claim will be treated as a prepetition claim, paid, if at all, at a significant discount. Consumer expectations (contractual or otherwise) of privacy are likely to be defeated. By contrast, if personal information is deemed property subject to an encumbrance, then the property interest must be respected, or to use the bankruptcy term, "adequately protected."

In other words, Janger contends that giving individuals property rights in their personal data will provide more protection than giving individuals contract rights in the event a company goes bankrupt. Janger further argues that property rights alone will not be sufficient. Property rights must be "muddy" rather than "crystalline":

> . . . A crystalline rule places all of the relevant rights firmly in the hand of the entitlement holder or "owner." A muddier standard leaves the right subject to challenge by a competing claimant. Crystalline rules situate decisionmaking and norm-generating authority in either the legislature or the market. Muddy rules lead to decisions made and legal norms articulated by judges. . . .
>
> . . . [M]uddy standards force parties ex ante to recognize that they might have to justify their contractual terms and negotiating behavior ex post. This attribute of muddy rules operates to enforce behavioral norms in ways that crystalline rules do not. Efforts to resolve norm-based disputes force disclosure of information related to the norm. This norm-based information forcing effect has both public and private implications. Muddy rules may improve the contracting behavior of parties, but muddy rules also serve a more public purpose. Muddy rules force information into the legal system about transactions. They allow judges, and the judiciary, to develop rules incrementally, through common law reasoning, and inform legislative decisionmaking by placing disputes on the record. But muddiness alone is not enough. The benefits of the muddy liability rule may evaporate entirely when a debtor goes bankrupt. These behavior regulating and information forcing effects of muddy rules are maximized only when the muddy rule is given the status of property.[32]

---

[32] Edward J. Janger, *Muddy Property: Generating and Protecting Information Privacy Norms in Bankruptcy*, 44 Wm. & Mary L. Rev. 1801 (2002).

8. ***Customer Databases as Collateral.*** Xuan-Thao Nguyen points out that companies are using their customer databases as collateral for loans, since these databases are one of their most significant assets:

> Whether intentional or unintentional, many Internet companies ignore their own privacy policy statements when the companies pledge their customer database as collateral in secured financing schemes. This practice renders online privacy statements misleading because the statements are silent on collateralization of the company's assets. . . .
>
> The secured party can use the consumer database in its business or sell the consumer database to others. The collateralization of the consumer database and its end result may contradict the debtor's consumer privacy statement declaring that the debtor does not sell or lease the consumer information to others. Though there is no direct sale of the consumer database to the secured party, the effect of the collateralization of the consumer database is the same: the consumer database is in the hands of third parties with unfettered control and rights. Essentially, the collateralization of consumer databases violates the privacy policies publicized on debtors' Web sites.[33]

9. ***The FTC as an Enforcer of Privacy: An Assessment.*** In 2000, Steven Hetcher assessed the FTC's behavior in enforcing privacy in these terms:

> By the Agency's lights, its promotion of the fair practice principles should satisfy privacy advocates, as the fair information practice principles are derived from pre-existing norms of the advocacy community. Public interest advocates contend to the contrary, however, that privacy policies ill serve their aspirational privacy norms. They argue that privacy policies are typically not read by website users. They are written in legalese such that even if people read them, they will not understand them. Hence, they do not provide notice and thus cannot lead to consent. In addition, there is evidence that many sites do not adhere to their own policies. The policies are subject to change when companies merge, such that one company's policy is likely to go unheeded. Finally, very few privacy policies guarantee security or enforcement. Thus, the provision of a privacy policy by a website does not automatically promote the fair practice principles.
>
> Despite these problems, the FTC has strongly endorsed privacy policies. This raises a puzzle as to why the Agency should do so, given the severe criticism privacy policies have received. Why, for instance, is the FTC not coming out in support of the creation of a new agency to oversee privacy protection? . . .
>
> There is a public choice answer as to why the Agency has promoted privacy policies, despite their problems (and despite the fact that they do not appear to promote the interests of any industry groups whose favor the FTC might be seeking). It is through privacy policies that the FTC is gaining jurisdiction over the commercial Internet. Jurisdiction is power. In other words, the FTC acts as if it has a plan to migrate its activities to the Internet, and privacy policies have been at the core of this plan. . . .[34]

---

[33] Xuan-Thao N. Nguyen, *Collateralizing Privacy,* 78 Tul. L. Rev. 553, 571, 590 (2004).

[34] Steven Hetcher, *The FTC as Internet Privacy Norm Entrepreneur*, 53 Vand. L. Rev. 2041 (2000). *See also* Steven Hetcher, *Norms in a Wired World* (2004); Steven Hetcher, *Changing the Social Meaning of Privacy in Cyberspace*, 15 Harv. J. L. & Tech. 149 (2001); Steven A. Hetcher,

Joel Reidenberg argues that the FTC is the wrong choice to regulate privacy in the United States:

> Public enforcement of data privacy relies on an expedient set of actors who are generally mismatched to remedy public wrongs. The public actors do not have specific statutory privacy rights authority. Instead, they exploit derivative powers to play a role in privacy claims. At the federal level, the current enforcement agency is the Federal Trade Commission. In many ways, this agency is an illogical choice for the protection of citizens' privacy. The FTC's mission is to enforce antitrust and certain consumer protection laws:
>
> > The Commission seeks to ensure that the nation's markets function competitively, and are vigorous, efficient, and free of undue restrictions. The Commission also works to enhance the smooth operation of the marketplace by eliminating acts or practices that are unfair or deceptive.
>
> Reliance on the FTC as a primary enforcer of citizen privacy is misplaced. The prevention of privacy wrongs, and particularly the public wrongs, as such, is simply not part of the core mission of the FTC. The FTC is not charged with the enforcement of civil rights, nor is the agency equipped or permitted to handle employment or telecommunications privacy matters. In fact, the FTC only grudgingly accepted involvement with privacy issues. During the mid-1990s, Commissioner Christine Varney persistently raised privacy as an important issue. For many years, the FTC hoped that the market would self-regulate and did not want to intervene aggressively. The FTC even opposed new federal legislation to protect information privacy. . . .
>
> While the FTC seems to be the federal regulator of choice for a light touch in enforcement against privacy wrongs, the states' Attorneys General have taken a more aggressive stance. The National Association of Attorneys General has an Internet Law task force that studies and coordinates the enforcement of privacy. In effect, the states are unwilling to wait for federal results. This more aggressive stance of public enforcement at the state level is illustrated well by an enforcement action brought against DoubleClick. In February 2000, the Electronic Privacy Information Center ("EPIC"), a prominent privacy advocacy group, filed a complaint against DoubleClick with the Federal Trade Commission based on the company's practice of profiling web users without adequate disclosure. EPIC's complaint focused on the lack of disclosure and on profiling as an "unfair and deceptive practice." The FTC eventually closed its investigation with no action. However, a coalition of ten states pursued DoubleClick's practices and compelled DoubleClick to accept a binding agreement regarding privacy policies and disclosure; DoubleClick also accepted a fine of $450,000 to reimburse the states' investigative costs.
>
> Like the federal actions, the state cases that rely on "unfair and deceptive practices" statutory authority do not address the public wrongs directly. When states pursue claims, the results are only able to achieve company specific cessations of particular data processing practices. These remedies address specific harms to individuals rather than the broader harms caused by wide-spread practices.[35]

Norm Proselytizers Create a Privacy Entitlement in Cyberspace, 16 Berkeley Tech. L.J. 877 (2001).

[35] Joel R. Reidenberg, *Privacy Wrongs in Search of Remedies*, 54 Hastings L.J. 877 (2003).

After these writings by Hetcher and Reidenberg, however, the FTC developed an additional role — the agency began to enforce standards of data security. Does this role fit in with Hetcher's analysis ("through privacy policies . . . the FTC is gaining jurisdiction over the commercial Internet") or Reidenberg's ("the FTC seems to be the federal regulator of choice for a light touch in enforcement")?

10. ***State Deceptive Trade Practices Acts.*** In addition to the FTC Act, which is enforced exclusively by the FTC, every state has some form of deceptive trade practices act of its own. Many of these statutes not only enable a state attorney general to bring actions but also provide a private cause of action to consumers. Several of these laws have provisions for statutory minimum damages, punitive damages, and attorneys' fees. *See, e.g.,* Cal. Civ. Code § 1780(a)(4) (punitive damages); Conn. Gen. Stat. § 42-110g(a) (punitive damages); Mich. Comp. Laws § 445.911(2) (minimum damages); N.Y. Gen. Bus. Law § 349(h) (minimum damages). In interpreting these state laws, many state courts have been heavily influenced by FTC Act jurisprudence. However, as Jeff Sovern notes, many states "have been more generous to consumers than has the FTC," and "even if the FTC concludes that practices pass muster under the FTC Act, it is still at least theoretically possible for a state to find the practices deceptive under their own legislation." Thus, Sovern concludes, "information practices that are currently in widespread use may indeed violate state little FTC Acts. Marketers should think carefully about whether they wish to alter their practices."[36]

3. GOVERNANCE BY SELF-REGULATION

Pure Self-Regulation. Some commentators contend that the best solution to data collection and use is to allow companies to regulate themselves. Fred Cate points out that self-regulation is "more flexible and more sensitive to specific contexts and therefore allow[s] individuals to determine a more tailored balance between information uses and privacy than privacy laws do."[37]

Eric Goldman argues:

> Relatively few consumers have bought privacy management tools, such as software to browse anonymously and manage Internet cookies and e-mail. Many vendors are now migrating away from consumer-centric business models. So, although consumers can take technological control over their own situation, few consumers do.
>
> Plus, as most online marketers know, people will "sell" their personal data incredibly cheaply. As Internet pundit Esther Dyson has said: "You do a survey, and consumers say they are very concerned about their privacy. Then you offer them a discount on a book, and they'll tell you everything." Indeed, a recent Jupiter report said that 82% of respondents would give personal information to new shopping sites to enter a $100 sweepstakes.

[36] Jeff Sovern, *Protecting Privacy with Deceptive Trade Practices Legislation*, 69 Fordham L. Rev. 1305, 1352-53, 1357 (2001).

[37] Fred H. Cate, *Privacy in Perspective* 26 (2001); *see also* Fred H. Cate, *Privacy in the Information Age* (1997).

> Clearly consumers' stated privacy concerns diverge from what consumers do. Two theories might explain the divergence.
>
> First, asking consumers what they care about reveals only whether they value privacy. That's half the equation. Of more interest is how much consumers will pay — in time or money — for the corresponding benefits. For now the cost-benefit ratio is tilted too high for consumers to spend much time or money on privacy.
>
> Second, consumers don't have uniform interests. Regarding online privacy, consumers can be segmented into two groups: activists, who actively protect their online privacy, and apathetics, who do little or nothing to protect themselves. The activists are very vocal but appear to be a tiny market segment.
>
> Using consumer segmentation, the analytical defect of broad-based online privacy regulations becomes apparent. The activists, by definition, take care of themselves. They demand privacy protections from businesses and, if they don't get it, use technology to protect themselves or take their business elsewhere.
>
> In contrast, mainstream consumers don't change their behavior based on online privacy concerns. If these people won't take even minimal steps to protect themselves, why should government regulation do it for them?
>
> Further, online businesses will invest in privacy when it's profitable. . . . When companies believed that few consumers would change their behavior if they were offered greater privacy, those companies did nothing or put into place privacy policies that disabused consumers of privacy expectations. Of course, if companies later discovered that they were losing business because customers wanted more privacy, they would increase their privacy initiatives.
>
> Consumer behavior will tell companies what level of privacy to provide. Let the market continue unimpeded rather than chase phantom consumer fears through unnecessary regulation.[38]

In contrast, Peter Swire contends that privacy legislation need not be antithetical to business interests. According to Swire, privacy legislation should be viewed as similar to the "trustwrap" that Johnson & Johnson placed around bottles of Tylenol after a scare involving cyanide poisoning of the pain reliever.[39] Swire believes that "privacy legislation targeted at online practices" would provide the kind of safety to allow consumers to engage in cyberspace activities with confidence.

Default Rules. In contrast to a pure self-regulatory approach, in which personal information belongs to whatever entity happens to obtain it, Jerry Kang argues that a default rule that individuals retain control over information they surrender during Internet transactions is more efficient than a default rule where companies can use the data as they see fit. According to Kang, the latter default rule would create two inefficiencies for individuals in attempting to bargain around the rule:

> . . . First, [the individual] would face substantial research costs to determine what information is being collected and how it is being used. That is because individuals today are largely clueless about how personal information is

[38] Eric Goldman, *The Privacy Hoax,* Forbes (Oct. 14, 2002), available at http://www.ericgoldman.org/Articles/privacyhoax.htm.

[39] Peter P. Swire, *Trustwrap: the Importance of Legal Rules to Electronic Commerce and Internet Privacy*, 54 Hastings L.J. 847 (2003).

> processed through cyberspace. Transacting parties and transaction facilitators do not generally provide adequate, relevant notice about what information will be collected and how it will be used. What is worse, consumer ignorance is sometimes fostered by deceptive practices.
>
> Second, the individual would run into a collective action problem. Realistically, the information collector — the "firm" — would not entertain one person's idiosyncratic request to purchase back personal information because the costs of administering such an individually tailored program would be prohibitive. This explains the popular use of form contracts, even in cyberspace, that cannot be varied much, if at all. Therefore, to make it worth the firm's while, the individual would have to band together with like-minded individuals to renegotiate the privacy terms of the underlying transaction. These individuals would suffer the collective action costs of locating each other, coming to some mutual agreement and strategy, proposing an offer to the information collector and negotiating with it — all the while discouraging free riders. . . .

Therefore, Kang argues, the appropriate default is to give control of information to the individual:

> With this default, if the firm valued personal data more than the individual, then the firm would have to buy permission to process the data in functionally unnecessary ways. Note, however, two critical differences in contracting around this default. First, unlike the individual who had to find out what information is being collected and how it is being used, the collector need not bear such research costs since it already knows what its information practices are. Second, the collector does not confront collective action problems. It need not seek out other like-minded firms and reach consensus before coming to the individual with a request. This is because an individual would gladly entertain an individualized, even idiosyncratic, offer to purchase personal information. In addition, there will be no general "holdout" problem because one individual's refusal to sell personal information to the collector will not generally destroy the value of personal information purchased from others.[40]

Would Kang's approach serve as a dramatic change for the self-regulatory approach? Couldn't companies regularly bargain around Kang's default rule in order to obtain control of the data from individuals? Does assigning the initial entitlement make a practical difference?

Flexible Regulation. Some commentators contend that a middle ground can be found between traditional legal regulation and self-regulation. Dennis Hirsch argues that environmental law suggests ways to regulate privacy that are flexible and that mix legal regulation with self-regulation:

> Over the past forty years, environmental law has been at the epicenter of an intense and productive debate about the most effective way to regulate. Initial environmental laws took the form of prescriptive, uniform standards that have come to be known as "command-and-control" regulation. These methods, while effective in some settings, proved costly and controversial. In the decades that followed, governments, academics, environmental and business groups, and others poured tremendous resources into figuring out how to improve upon these

---

[40] Jerry Kang, *Information Privacy in Cyberspace Transactions*, 50 Stan. L. Rev. 1193, 1253-54, 1257 (1998).

> methods. This work has produced a "second generation" of environmental regulation. . . .
>
> Second generation initiatives encourage the regulated parties themselves to choose the means by which they will achieve environmental performance goals. That is what defines them and distinguishes them from first generation regulations under which the agency has the primary decisionmaking power over pollution control methods. This difference tends to make second generation strategies more cost-effective and adaptable than command-and-control rules. The proliferation of second generation strategies has led some to identify the environmental field as having "some of the most innovative regulatory instruments in all of American law."
>
> Privacy regulation today finds itself in a debate similar to the one that the environmental field has been engaged in for years. On the one hand, there is a growing sense that the digital age is causing unprecedented damage to privacy and that action must be taken immediately to mitigate these injuries. On the other, a chorus of voices warns against the dangers of imposing intrusive and costly regulation on the emerging business sectors of the information economy. Missing thus far from the dialogue is any significant discussion of the more flexible "second generation" regulatory strategies that might be able to bridge this gap. It took environmental law decades to arrive at these alternatives. The privacy field could capitalize on this experience by looking to these environmental policies as models for privacy regulation.[41]

Is the analogy of privacy law to environmental law an apt one? To what extent are the privacy statutes discussed in this book thus far command-and-control rules versus flexible rules? Is Hirsch calling less for self-regulation than for industry input into the form and content of rules?

Regulation by Technology. As part of the self-governance, technology can assist companies as well as consumers in making privacy choices. Privacy on the Internet can be protected by another form of regulatory mechanism — technology. According to Joel Reidenberg, "law and government regulation are not the only source of rule-making. Technological capabilities and system design choices impose rules on participants."[42] Reidenberg calls such forms of technological governance "Lex Informatica."

In the privacy context, Privacy Enhancing Technologies (PETs) have received much attention from scholars and the privacy policy community. Herbert Burkert describes PETs as "technical and organizational concepts that aim at protecting personal identity. These concepts usually involve encryption in the form digital signatures, blind signature or digital pseudonyms."[43]

---

[41] Dennis D. Hirsch, *Protecting the Inner Environment: What Privacy Regulation Can Learn from Environmental Law*, 41 Ga. L. Rev. 1, 8-10 (2006).

[42] Joel Reidenberg, *Lex Informatica: The Formulation of Information Policy Rules Through Technology*, 76 Tex. L. Rev. 553 (1998).

[43] Herbert Burkert, *Privacy-Enhancing Technologies: Typology, Critique, Vision*, in *Technology and Privacy: The New Landscape* 123, 125, 128 (Philip E. Agre & Marc Rotenberg, eds., 1997).

4. GOVERNANCE BY PROPERTY

A number of commentators propose that privacy can be protected by restructuring the property rights that people have in personal information. For example, according to Richard Murphy, personal information "like all information, is property." He goes on to conclude:

> . . . [I]n many instances, privacy rules are in fact implied contractual terms. To the extent that information is generated through a voluntary transaction, imposing nondisclosure obligations on the recipient of the information may be the best approach for certain categories of information. The value that information has ex post is of secondary importance; the primary question is what is the efficient contractual rule. Common-law courts are increasingly willing to impose an implied contractual rule of nondisclosure for many categories of transactions, including those with attorneys, medical providers, bankers, and accountants. Many statutes can also be seen in this light — that is, as default rules of privacy. And an argument can be made for the efficiency of a privacy default rule in the generic transaction between a merchant and a consumer.[44]

Lawrence Lessig also contends that privacy should be protected with property rights. He notes that "[p]rivacy now is protected through liability rules — if you invade someone's privacy, they can sue you and you must then pay." A "liability regime allows a taking, and payment later." In contrast, a property regime gives "control, and power, to the person holding the property right." Lessig argues: "When you have a property right, before someone takes your property they must negotiate with you about how much it is worth."[45]

Other commentators critique the translation of privacy into a form of property right that can be bartered and sold. For example, Katrin Schatz Byford argues that viewing "privacy as an item of trade . . . values privacy only to the extent it is considered to be of personal worth by the individual who claims it." She further contends: "Such a perspective plainly conflicts with the notion that privacy is a collective value and that privacy intrusions at the individual level necessarily have broader social implications because they affect access to social power and stifle public participation."[46]

Consider Pamela Samuelson's argument as to why property rights are inadequate to protect privacy:

> . . . Achieving information privacy goals through a property rights system may be difficult for reasons other than market complexities. Chief among them is the difficulty with alienability of personal information. It is a common, if not ubiquitous, characteristic of property rights systems that when the owner of a property right sells her interest to another person, that buyer can freely transfer to third parties whatever interest the buyer acquired from her initial seller. Free alienability works very well in the market for automobiles and land, but it is far

---

[44] Richard S. Murphy, *Property Rights in Personal Information: An Economic Defense of Privacy*, 84 Geo. L.J. 2381, 2416-17 (1996).

[45] Lawrence Lessig, *Code and Other Laws of Cyberspace* (1999).

[46] Katrin Schatz Byford, *Privacy in Cyberspace: Constructing a Model of Privacy for the Electronic Communications Environment*, 24 Rutgers Computer & Tech. L.J. 1 (1998). For an argument about the problems of commodifying certain goods and of viewing all human conduct in light of the market metaphor, see Margaret Jane Radin, *Contested Commodities* (1996).

> from clear that it will work well for information privacy. . . . Collectors of data may prefer a default rule allowing them to freely transfer personal data to whomever they wish on whatever terms they can negotiate with their future buyers. However, individuals concerned with information privacy will generally want a default rule prohibiting retransfer of the data unless separate permission is negotiated. They will also want any future recipient to bind itself to the same constraints that the initial purchaser of the data may have agreed to as a condition of sale. Information privacy goals may not be achievable unless the default rule of the new property rights regime limits transferability. . . .
>
> . . . From a civil liberties perspective, propertizing personal information as a way of achieving information privacy goals may seem an anathema. Not only might it be viewed as an unnecessary and possibly dangerous way to achieve information privacy goals, it might be considered morally obnoxious. If information privacy is a civil liberty, it may make no more sense to propertize personal data than to commodify voting rights. . . .[47]

Daniel Solove also counsels against protecting privacy as a form of property right because the "market approach has difficulty assigning the proper value to personal information":

> . . . [T]he aggregation problem severely complicates the valuation process. An individual may give out bits of information in different contexts, each transfer appearing innocuous. However, the information can be aggregated and could prove to be invasive of the private life when combined with other information. It is the totality of information about a person and how it is used that poses the greatest threat to privacy. As Julie Cohen notes, "[a] comprehensive collection of data about an individual is vastly more than the sum of its parts." From the standpoint of each particular information transaction, individuals will not have enough facts to make a truly informed decision. The potential future uses of that information are too vast and unknown to enable individuals to make the appropriate valuation. . . .
>
> [Property rights] cannot work effectively in a situation where the power relationship and information distribution between individuals and public and private bureaucracies is so greatly unbalanced. In other words, the problem with market solutions is not merely that it is difficult to commodify information (which it is), but also that a regime of default rules alone (consisting of property rights in information and contractual defaults) will not enable fair and equitable market transactions in personal information. . . .[48]

In contrast to these skeptics, Paul Schwartz develops a model of propertized personal data that would help fashion a market for data trade that would respect individual privacy and help maintain a democratic order. Schwartz calls for "limitations on an individual's right to alienate personal information; default rules that force disclosure of the terms of trade; a right of exit for participants in the market; the establishment of damages to deter market abuses; and institutions to police the personal information market and punish privacy violations." In his judgment, a key element of this model is its approach of "hybrid inalienability"

[47] Pamela Samuelson, *Privacy as Intellectual Property?*, 52 Stan. L. Rev. 1125, 1137-47 (2000).

[48] Daniel J. Solove, *Privacy and Power: Computer Databases and Metaphors for Information Privacy*, 53 Stan. L. Rev. 1393 (2001).

in which a law allows individuals to share their personal information, but also places limitations on future use of the information. Schwartz explains:

> This hybrid consists of a use-transferability restriction plus an opt-in default. In practice, it would permit the transfer for an initial category of use of personal data, but only if the customer is granted an opportunity to block further transfer or use by unaffiliated entities. Any further use or transfer would require the customer to opt in — that is, it would be prohibited unless the customer affirmatively agrees to it.
>
> As an initial example concerning compensated telemarketing, a successful pitch for Star Trek memorabilia would justify the use of personal data by the telemarketing company and the transfer of it both to process the order and for other related purposes. Any outside use or unrelated transfers of this information would, however, require obtaining further permission from the individual. Note that this restriction limits the alienability of individuals' personal information by preventing them from granting one-stop permission for all use or transfer of their information. A data processor's desire to carry out further transfers thus obligates the processor to supply additional information and provides another chance for the individual to bargain with the data collector. . . .
>
> To ensure that the opt-in default leads to meaningful disclosure of additional information, however, two additional elements are needed. First, the government must have a significant role in regulating the way that notice of privacy practices is provided. As noted above, a critical issue will be the "frame" in which information about data processing is presented.
>
> Second, meaningful disclosure requires addressing what Henry Hansmann and Reinier Kraakman term "verification problems." Their scholarship points to the critical condition that third parties must be able to verify that a given piece of personal information has in fact been propertized and then identify the specific rules that apply to it. As they explain, "[a] verification rule sets out the conditions under which a given right in a given asset will run with the asset." In the context of propertized personal information, the requirement for verification creates a role for nonpersonal metadata, a tag or kind of barcode, to provide necessary background information and notice.[49]

Finally, consider what Warren and Brandeis said about privacy as a property claim:

> The aim of [copyright] statutes is to secure to the author, composer, or artist the entire profits arising from publication. . . .
>
> But where the value of the production is found not in the right to take the profits arising from publication, but in the peace of mind or the relief afforded by the ability to prevent any publication at all, it is difficult to regard the right as one of property, in the common acceptation of that term.[50]

[49] Paul M. Schwartz, *Property, Privacy and Personal Data*, 117 Harv. L. Rev. 2055, 2056, 2098-99 (2004). *See also* Vera Bergelson, *It's Personal But Is It Mine? Toward Property Rights in Personal Information*, 37 U.C. Davis L. Rev. 379 (2003) (although a collector may have rights in individuals' personal information, a property approach would correctly subordinate these rights to the rights of the individuals).

[50] Samuel Warren & Louis Brandeis, *The Right to Privacy*, 4 Harv. L. Rev. 193 (1890).

5. GOVERNANCE BY STATUTORY REGULATION

Numerous statutes are directly and potentially applicable to the collection, use, and transfer of personal information by commercial entities. Congress's approach is best described as "sectoral," as each statute is narrowly tailored to particular types of businesses and services. The opposite of sectoral in this context is omnibus, and the United States lacks such a comprehensive statute regulating the private sector's collection and use of personal information. Such omnibus statutes are standard in much of the rest of the world. All member nations of the European Union have enacted omnibus information privacy laws.

In the United States, sectoral laws also do not regulate all commercial entities in their collection and use of personal information. Thus far, federal statutes regulate three basic areas: (a) entertainment records (video and cable television); (b) Internet use and electronic communications; and (c) marketing (telemarketing and spam). As you examine the existing statutes, think about the kinds of commercial entities that the law does not currently regulate. Consider whether these entities should be regulated. Also consider whether one omnibus privacy law can adequately apply to all commercial entities. Would the differences between types of commercial entities make a one-size-fits-all privacy law impractical?

The sectoral statutes embody the Fair Information Practices originally developed by HEW and incorporated into the Privacy Act. However, not all statutes embody all of the Fair Information Practices. As you study each statute, examine which of the Fair Information Practices are required by each statute and which are not.

(a) Entertainment Records

THE VIDEO PRIVACY PROTECTION ACT

Incensed when a reporter obtained a list of videos that Supreme Court Justice Nominee Robert Bork and his family had rented from a video store, Congress passed the Video Privacy Protection Act (VPPA) of 1988, Pub. L. No. 100-618. The VPPA is also known as the "Bork Bill."

What Is a Video Tape? Who Is a Video Tape Service Provider? The VPPA is written in technology-neutral terms. It defines a "video tape service provider" as "any person engaged in the business, in or affecting interstate or foreign commerce, of rental, sale, or delivery of prerecorded video cassette tapes or similar audio visual materials. . . ." § 2710(a)(4). This statutory language allows the VPPA to extend to DVDs (as opposed to video cassette tapes) and should also cover online delivery of movies and other content.

Restrictions on Disclosure. The VPPA prohibits videotape service providers from knowingly disclosing personal information, such as titles of videocassettes rented or purchased, without the individual's written consent. The VPPA creates a private cause of action when a videotape service provider "knowingly discloses

. . . personally identifiable information concerning any consumer of such provider." 18 U.S.C § 2710(b)(1).

Destruction of Records. The VPPA requires that records of personal information be destroyed as soon as practicable. § 2710(e).

Exceptions. The VPPA contains several exceptions, permitting videotape providers to disclose "to any person if the disclosure is incident to the ordinary course of business of the video tape service provider." § 2710(b)(2)(E).

The statute provides that "the subject matter of such materials may be disclosed if the disclosure is for the exclusive use of marketing goods and services directly to the consumer." § 2710(b)(2)(D)(ii). Videotape service providers can disclose the names and addresses of consumers if the consumer has been given the right to opt out, and the disclosure does not identify information about the videos the consumer rents. § 2710(b)(2)(D).

The statute also permits disclosure to the consumer, § 2710(b)(2)(A); disclosure with the informed written consent of the consumer, § 2710(b)(2)(B); disclosure to a law enforcement agency pursuant to a warrant or subpoena, § 2710(b)(2)(C); and disclosure for civil discovery if there is notice and an opportunity to object, § 2710(b)(2).

Preemption. VPPA does not block states from enacting statutes that are more protective of privacy. § 2710(f).

Enforcement. The VPPA's private right of action permits recovery of actual damages and provides for liquidated damages in the amount of $2,500. The Act also authorizes recovery for punitive damages, attorneys' fees, and enables equitable and injunctive relief. § 2710(c). The VPPA also includes a statutory exclusionary rule that prevents the admission into evidence of any information obtained in violation of the statute. § 2710(d).

DIRKES V. BOROUGH OF RUNNEMEDE

936 F. Supp. 235 (D.N.J. 1996)

BROTMAN, J. Presently before this Court is a motion for summary judgment brought by the Borough of Runnemede, the Borough of Runnemede Police Department, and Lieutenant Emil Busko. . . .

The present action arises from the investigation of and disciplinary action taken against Plaintiff Chester Dirkes, formerly an officer with the Department. On May 24, 1990, in the course of an investigation into a citizen's death, Plaintiff Dirkes allegedly removed pornographic magazines and videotapes from the decedent's apartment. Based on this allegation, the Camden County Grand Jury returned a one count indictment for misconduct in office against him on May 29, 1991. As a result of the indictment, on May 30, 1991, the Department issued a disciplinary notice to Plaintiff Dirkes and suspended him without pay and benefits. Plaintiff Dirkes' trial commenced on April 20, 1992 and on May 5, 1992, he was acquitted of the sole charge against him.

Following the acquittal, the Borough retained special counsel and resumed its internal affairs investigation against Plaintiff Dirkes. The Department assigned Lt. Busko to investigate the matter. On or about May 7, 1992, Lt. Busko obtained the names and rental dates of certain pornographic videotapes previously rented by Plaintiff Dirkes and his wife, co-plaintiff Marie Dirkes. Lt. Busko received this information from an employee of Videos To Go, the store from which Plaintiffs apparently regularly rent or buy video tapes for their private use. In seeking to obtain this information, Lt. Busko failed to secure a warrant, a subpoena or a court order. He simply requested and received the information from an employee of Videos to Go without question.

The internal affairs memorandum listing the video tape rental information was distributed to the Borough's special counsel, who in turn distributed it in connection with Plaintiff Dirkes' disciplinary hearing and in a proceeding before the Superior Court of New Jersey, Camden County.

On or about March 19, 1993, Plaintiffs filed their complaint with this Court alleging that Defendants violated the provisions of the Videotape Privacy Protection Act of 1988, as codified at 18 U.S.C. § 2710 (the "Act"), as well as Plaintiffs' common law privacy rights. . . . Subsequently, the video information was received into evidence at Plaintiff Dirkes' disciplinary hearing. As a result of that hearing, the Department terminated Plaintiff Dirkes from his employment. . . .

Defendants have moved for summary judgment on Count I of Plaintiffs' complaint, which asserts a violation of the Videotape Privacy Protection Act. . . .

Section 2710(c) of the Act provides broadly that "[a]ny person aggrieved by any act of a person in violation of [§ 2710] may bring a civil action" in an appropriate U.S. District Court. The Act can be violated in one or all of three ways. First, a "video tape service provider" violates § 2710(b) of the Act by disclosing "personally identifiable information" regarding a customer unless the person to whom the disclosure is made or the disclosure itself falls into one of six categories. 18 U.S.C. § 2710(b). Second, § 2710(d) of the Act is violated when personally identifiable information obtained in any manner other than as narrowly provided by the Act is "received in evidence" in almost any adversarial proceeding. 18 U.S.C. § 2710(d). Third, a person subject to the Act violates § 2710(e) by failing to timely destroy a customer's personally identifiable information. 18 U.S.C. § 2710(e). Upon finding any of these violations, a court may, but need not, award a range of relief including actual damages, punitive damages, attorneys' fees, or "such other . . . equitable relief as the Court may determine to be appropriate." 18 U.S.C. § 2710(c).

Because it is undisputed that subsections (b) and (d) have been violated in the instant matter, § 2710(c) authorizes the Plaintiffs to bring a suit. Videos to Go, the video tape service provider in this matter, violated subsection (b) of the Act by disclosing Plaintiffs' video rental information to Lt. Busko. It is undisputed that this disclosure does not fall into one of the six permissible disclosure exceptions delineated in subsection (b)(2) of the Act. A second violation of the Act occurred when Plaintiffs' personally identifiable information was received into evidence at Plaintiff Dirkes' disciplinary hearing. 18 U.S.C. § 2710(d).

Having found that there have been two violations of the Act, the Court must now determine whether Lt. Busko, the Department, or the Borough are proper defendants. As noted earlier, subsection (c) provides that "[a]ny person aggrieved by any act of a person in violation of [§ 2710] may bring a civil action." 18 U.S.C. § 2710(c). While it broadly provides relief for violations of § 2710, this subsection does not delineate those parties against whom an action may be instituted. 18 U.S.C. § 2710(c). In support of its current summary judgment motion, the Defendants argue collectively that they cannot be held liable under the Act because their actions did not violate the Act. For example, only the actions of a video tape service provider can cause a violation of § 2710(b). Because the Defendants are not video tape service providers as that term is defined under the Act, they argue that they cannot be held responsible under the Act.

This Court must reject the Defendants' narrow reading of the statute. Again, the plain language of the Act does not delineate those parties against whom an action under this Act may be maintained. Taking the Defendants' argument to its logical extension, this omission would prevent plaintiffs from bringing a cause of action against anyone. Such an absurd result must be rejected. The clear intent of the Act is to prevent the disclosure of private information. As established by its legislative history, the Act enables consumers "to maintain control over personal information divulged and generated in exchange for receiving services from video tape service providers." S. Rep. No. 100-599, at 8 (1988). This purpose is furthered by allowing parties, like these Plaintiffs, to bring suit against those individuals who have come to possess (and who could disseminate) the private information in flagrant violation of the purposes of the Act. While it need not identify all potential categories of defendants in this opinion, the Court finds that those parties who are in possession of personally identifiable information as a direct result of an improper release of such information are subject to suit under the Act. Because it is undisputed that Lt. Busko, the Department, and the Borough all possess the information as a direct result of a violation of the Act, each is a proper defendant.

Furthermore, the Supreme Court in *Local 28 of Sheet Metal Workers v. E.E.O.C.,* 478 U.S. 421 (1986), reinforced the principle that remedial statutes should be construed broadly. *Local 28* involved a violation of Title VII, a statute designed to address employment discrimination. Upon examining the legislative history of Title VII, the Court determined that "Congress reaffirmed the breadth of the [district] court's remedial powers under § 706(g) by adding language authorizing courts to order 'any other equitable relief as the court deems appropriate.'" This added language is identical to that used in subsection (c)(2)(D) of the Videotape Privacy Protection Act. 18 U.S.C. § 2710(c). It is evident throughout the *Local 28* opinion that the Supreme Court intended to give effect to the legislators' intent to provide as broad remedial powers as possible to the district courts to eliminate the effects of illegal discrimination. This Court will exercise the same broad powers to give effect to the intent of Videotape Privacy Protection Act's U.S. Senate sponsors. The importance of maintaining the privacy of an individual's personally identifiable information mandates that people who obtain such information from a violation of the Act be held as proper defendants to prevent the further disclosure of the information. . . .

For the reasons set forth above, the Court will deny Defendants' motion for summary judgment. . . .

DANIEL V. CANTELL

375 F.3d 377 (6th Cir. 2004)

CUDAHY, J. The plaintiff, Alden Joe Daniel, Jr. (Daniel) was charged with and eventually pleaded guilty to the sexual molestation of three underage girls. Allegedly, part of his *modus operandi* was showing pornographic movies to the underage girls. . . . Therefore, as part of the criminal investigation into his conduct, law enforcement officials sought and were able to obtain his video rental records. . . .

Daniel brings this suit against (1) various police officers, attorneys, and the parents of one of Daniel's victims, as well as (2) the employees and owners of two video stores where Daniel rented pornographic videos. There is no dispute that the defendants making up this second category are proper parties under the Act. The only question which we must answer is whether the defendants not associated with the video stores are proper parties under the Act. We believe that based on the plain language of the Act, this first group of defendants are *not* proper parties. . . .

Section (b) provides that "[a] *video tape service provider* who knowingly discloses, to any person, personally identifiable information concerning any consumer of such provider shall be liable to the aggrieved person for the relief provided in subsection (d)." 18 U.S.C. § 2710(b)(1) (emphasis added). Therefore, under the plain language of the statute, only a "video tape service provider" (VTSP) can be liable. The term VTSP is defined by the statute to mean "any person, engaged in the business, in or affecting interstate or foreign commerce, of rental, sale, or delivery of prerecorded video cassette tapes or similar audio video materials, or any person or other entity to whom a disclosure is made under subparagraph (D) or (E) of subsection (b)(2), but only with respect to the information contained in the disclosure." *Id.* at § 2710(a)(4). Daniel does not allege that the defendants in question are engaged in the business of rental, sale or delivery of prerecorded video cassette tapes. Therefore, the defendants may only be VTSPs if personal information was disclosed to them under subparagraph (D) or (E) of subsection (b)(2).

Subparagraph (D) applies "if the disclosure is solely the names and addresses of consumers." *Id.* at § 2710(b)(2)(D). Moreover, disclosure under subparagraph (D) must be "for the exclusive use of marketing goods and services directly to the consumer." *Id.* at § 2710(b)(2)(D)(ii). For instance, if a video store provided the names and addresses of its patrons to a movie magazine publisher, the publisher would be considered a VTSP, but only with respect to the information contained in the disclosure. No disclosure in this case was made under subparagraph (D). The information provided was not limited to Daniel's name and address. Instead, the disclosure was of Daniel's history of renting pornographic videotapes and included the specific titles of those videos. Additionally, the disclosure was not for marketing purposes but for purposes of a criminal investigation. Therefore, subparagraph (D) is inapplicable in this case.

Daniel properly does not argue that the disclosure falls within subparagraph (E). . . . Subparagraph (E) applies only to disclosures made "incident to the ordinary course of business" of the VTSP. *Id.* at § 2710(b)(2)(E). The term "ordinary course of business" is "narrowly defined" in the statute to mean "only debt collection activities, order fulfillment, request processing, and the transfer of ownership." *Id.* at § 2710(a)(2) . . . In sum, because Daniel has presented no evidence suggesting that a disclosure was made under subparagraph (D) or (E) in this case, the non-video store defendants are not VTSPs under the Act and therefore, are not proper parties to this litigation.

Daniel argues, however, that any person, not just a VTSP, can be liable under the Act based on *Dirkes v. Borough of Runnemede,* 936 F. Supp. 235 (D.N.J. 1996). *Dirkes* did reach this conclusion but only by misreading the Act. The court in *Dirkes* was focused on language in the Act stating that "[a]ny person aggrieved by any act of *a person* in violation of this section may bring a civil action in the United States district court." 18 U.S.C. § 2710(c)(1) (emphasis added). Because the statute states that a suit can be based upon an act of "a person" rather than an act of "a VTSP," *Dirkes* found that any person can be liable under the Act. *Dirkes*, however, ignored the rest of the sentence. A lawsuit under the Act must be based on an "act of a person *in violation of this section*. . . ." 18 U.S.C. § 2710(c)(1) (emphasis added). The statute makes it clear that only a VTSP can be in violation of section 2710(b). *See* § 2710(b)(1) ("A video tape service provider who knowingly discloses . . . personally identifiable information . . . shall be liable. . . ."). Moreover, if any person could be liable under the Act, there would be no need for the Act to define a VTSP in the first place. More tellingly, if any person could be liable under the Act, there is no reason that the definition of a VTSP would be limited to "any person . . . to whom a disclosure is made under subparagraph (D) or (E) of subsection (b)(2)." *Dirkes* would have us ignore this limitation and find that any person can be liable under the Act whether or not a disclosure was made to him under subparagraph (D) or (E). We avoid interpretations of a statute which would render portions of it superfluous.

The court in *Dirkes* found otherwise because the "clear intent of the Act," as demonstrated by its legislative history, "is to prevent the disclosure of private information." Where the plain language of a statute is clear, however, we do not consult the legislative history. . . . In any case, our interpretation of the statute — that only a VTSP can be liable under § 2710(b) — does not conflict with Congress' purpose in adopting the Act. One can "prevent the disclosure of private information" simply by cutting off disclosure at its source, i.e., the VTSP. Just because Congress' goal was to prevent the disclosure of private information, does not mean that Congress intended the implementation of every conceivable method of preventing disclosures. Printing all personal information in hieroglyphics instead of English would also help prevent the disclosure of such information. However, nothing in the legislative history suggests that Congress was encouraging hieroglyphics and, similarly, nothing suggests that Congress intended that anyone other than VTSPs would be liable under the Act. In sum, the Act is clear that only a VTSP can be liable under § 2710(b). Because the non-video store defendants do not fit within the definition of a VTSP, they are not proper parties.

NOTES & QUESTIONS

1. ***To Whom Does VPPA Apply?*** The key question in *Dirkes* and *Daniel* is whether the VPPA *only* regulates videotape service providers. The *Daniel* court answered this question affirmatively; the *Dirkes* court would apply the VPPA to additional parties, including law enforcement officers. Which interpretation of the statutory language do you find most convincing? Would policy reasons support a broader or narrower application of the statute?
2. ***Facebook, Beacon, Blockbuster, and a VPPA Violation*?** In April 2008, Cathryn Elain Harris filed a lawsuit against Blockbuster Video (a video tape service provider) and Facebook claiming violations of the VPPA. The complaint objected to Blockbuster reporting its customers' activities to Facebook through the Beacon program.

   Facebook introduced Beacon in November 2007; under it, partner companies shared information with Facebook about Facebook user activity that took place on their websites. Initially, this information became part of one's Facebook profile unless the user opted out. After consumer protest, Facebook changed its policy to require that a Facebook user would have to opt in to Beacon before information was disclosed on her Facebook page. It is not clear, however, whether opting out of Beacon stops partner companies from sharing information with Facebook.

   The Harris complaint alleges that Blockbuster's website is still reporting a user's activities back to Facebook, whether or not the consumer opts out of having the information associated with her Facebook profile. Does the Blockbuster-Beacon-Facebook behavior, if as alleged, violate the VPPA? If so, what measure of damages should be used?

THE CABLE COMMUNICATIONS POLICY ACT

In 1984, Congress passed the Cable Communications Policy Act (CCPA or "Cable Act"), Pub. L. No. 98-549. The Act applies to cable operators and service providers. 47 U.S.C. § 551(a)(1).

Notice and Access. The Cable Act requires cable service providers to notify subscribers (in a written privacy policy) of the nature and uses of personal information collected. § 551(a)(1). Subscribers must have access to their personal data held by cable operators. § 551(d).

Limitations on Data Collection. Cable operators "shall not use the cable system to collect personally identifiable information concerning any subscriber without the prior written or electronic consent of the subscriber concerned." § 551(b)(1).

Limitations on Data Disclosure. Cable operators cannot disclose personally identifiable information about any subscriber without the subscriber's consent:

> [A] cable operator shall not disclose personally identifiable information concerning any subscriber without the prior written or electronic consent of the

subscriber concerned and shall take such actions as are necessary to prevent unauthorized access to such information by a person other than the subscriber or cable operator. § 551(c)(1).

However, cable operators can disclose personal data under certain circumstances, such as when necessary for a "legitimate business activity" or pursuant to a court order if the subscriber is notified. Cable operators may disclose subscriber names and addresses if "the cable operator has provided the subscriber the opportunity to prohibit or limit such disclosure." § 551(c)(2).

Data Destruction. Cable operators must destroy personal data if the information is no longer necessary for the purpose for which it was collected. § 551(e).

Government Access to Cable Information. Pursuant to § 551(h):

> A governmental entity may obtain personally identifiable information concerning a cable subscriber pursuant to a court order only if, in the court proceeding relevant to such court order —
>
> (1) such entity offers clear and convincing evidence that the subject of the information is reasonably suspected of engaging in criminal activity and that the information sought would be material evidence in the case; and
>
> (2) the subject of the information is afforded the opportunity to appear and contest such entity's claim.

Note that a court order to obtain cable records requires "clear and convincing evidence," a standard higher than probable cause. There is no exclusionary rule for information obtained in violation of the Cable Act.

Enforcement. The Cable Act provides for a private cause of action and actual damages, with a minimum of $1,000 or $100 for each day of the violation, whichever is higher. The plaintiff can collect any actual damages that are more than the statutory minimum. Further, the Cable Act provides for punitive damages and attorneys' fees. § 551(f).

Cable Internet Service. Section 211 of the USA PATRIOT Act amended the Cable Act, 47 U.S.C. § 551(c)(2)(D), to provide disclosure to a government entity under federal wiretap law when the government seeks information from cable companies except that "such disclosure shall not include records revealing cable subscriber selection of video programming from a cable operator." This provision of the PATRIOT Act will not sunset.

New Cable Services and Products? In March 2008, the *New York Times* reported on a plan by the nation's six largest cable companies to create a joint venture to allow national advertisers to purchase custom as well as interactive ads.[51] The initiative is called Project Canoe. According to the report: "Cable companies have the ability to compile better data on users than Internet companies can gleam, which could make focused ads on television more effective." The kind of marketing planned will direct different targeted ads to the bachelor living in a Manhattan skyscraper and a retiree settled in Florida. In addition, interactive advertising allows TV viewers to use their remote control to "request a brochure or call up more information about a product." The key to Project Canoe is the cable set-top box, which collects "vast amounts of data." In light of the Cable Act, how would you advise executives at Project Canoe regarding their plans?

(b) Internet Use and Electronic Communications

CHILDREN'S ONLINE PRIVACY PROTECTION ACT

Passed in 1998, the Children's Online Privacy Protection Act (COPPA), Pub. L. No. 106-170, 15 U.S.C. §§ 6501–6506, regulates the collection and use of children's information by Internet websites. The COPPA applies to "an operator of a website or online service directed to children, or any operator that has actual knowledge that it is collecting personal information from a child." 15 U.S.C. § 6502(a)(1). COPPA only applies to websites that collect personal information from children under age 13. § 6502(1).

Notice. Children's websites must post privacy policies, describing "what information is collected from children by the operator, how the operator uses such information, and the operator's disclosure practices for such information." § 6502(b)(1)(A)(i).

Consent. Children's websites must "obtain verifiable parental consent for the collection, use or disclosure of personal information from children." § 6502(b)(1)(A)(ii). Websites cannot condition child's participation in a game or receipt of a prize on the disclosure of more personal information than is necessary to participate in that activity. § 6502(b)(1)(C). When information is not maintained in retrievable form, then consent is not required. § 6502(b)(2).

Right to Restrict Uses of Information. If parent requests it, the operator must provide to the parent a description of the "specific types of personal information collected," the right to "refuse to permit the operator's further use or maintenance in retrievable form, or future online collection, of personal information from that child," and the right to "obtain any personal information collected from the child." § 6502(b)(1)(B).

---

[51] Tim Arango, *Cable Firms Join Forces to Attract Focused Ads*, N.Y. Times, C1, Mar. 10, 2008.

Enforcement. Violations of the COPPA are "treated as a violation of a rule defining an unfair or deceptive act or practice" under 15 U.S.C. § 57a(a)(1)(B). Thus, the FTC enforces the law and can impose fines. There is no private cause of action for violations of the COPPA.

States can bring civil actions for violations of the COPPA in the interests of its citizens to obtain injunctions and damages. § 6504.

Preemption. The COPPA preempts state law. § 6502(d).

Safe Harbor. If an operator follows self-regulatory guidelines issued by marketing or online industry groups that are approved by the FTC, then the COPPA requirements will be deemed satisfied. § 6503.

Should the COPPA be extended to apply to everyone, not just children? Should there be a private cause of action under the COPPA? Note that the COPPA only applies when a website has "actual knowledge" that a user is under 13 or operates a website specifically targeted to children. Is this too limiting? Would a rule dispensing with the "actual knowledge" requirement be feasible?[52]

FTC Enforcement Actions. The FTC has engaged in several enforcement actions pursuant to COPPA. These cases have resulted in settlements simultaneously with the filing of complaints. Heavy penalties have been assessed as part of some of the settlements. For example, in September 2006, the FTC announced a settlement with Xanga.com, which included a $1 million civil penalty. The complaint charges that Xanga.com, a social networking website, had actual knowledge of its collection of disclosure of children's personal information. The Xanga website stated that children under 13 could not join its social network, but it allowed visitors to create Xanga accounts even if they provided a birth date indicating that they were younger than that age. Moreover, Xanga did not provide parents with access to and control over their children's information, and did not notify the parents of children who joined the site of its information practices. Finally, the FTC found that Xanga had created 1.7 million accounts for users who submitted age information that indicated they were younger than 13 years old.

In addition, the FTC has fined operators of websites in situations where they lacked actual knowledge that they were collecting information of someone who was under 13. Thus, the FTC found a violation of COPPA when a website was directed to children and provided a pull-down menu for the year of birth that did not include any of the last 12 years.[53]

Assessing the COPPA. Consider the following critique of the COPPA by Anita Allen:

---

[52] For more information about COPPA, see Dorothy A. Hertzel, Note, *Don't Talk to Strangers: An Analysis of Government and Industry Efforts to Protect Child's Privacy Online*, 52 Fed. Comm. L.J. 429 (2000).

[53] U.S. v. Lisa Frank, No. 01-CV-1516 (E.D. Va. 2001), Complaint at ¶ 15, at http://www.ftc.gov/os/2001/10/lfcmp.pdf.

> Not all parents welcome the veto power COPPA confers. New power has meant new responsibility. The statute forces parents who would otherwise be content to give their children free rein over their computers to get involved in children's use of Internet sites that are geared toward children and collect personal information. . . .
>
> Prohibiting voluntary disclosures by children lacking parental consent in situations in which they and their parents may be indifferent to privacy losses and resentful of government intervention, COPPA is among the most paternalistic and authoritarian of the federal privacy statutes thus far.[54]

ELECTRONIC COMMUNICATIONS PRIVACY ACT

In several cases, plaintiffs have attempted to use the Electronic Communications Privacy Act (ECPA) to prevent certain kinds of information collection, use, and disclosure by commercial entities. Recall from Chapter 3 that EPCA consists of three acts: (1) the Wiretap Act, 18 U.S.C. §§ 2510–2522, which regulates the interception of communications; (2) the Stored Communications Act (SCA), 18 U.S.C. §§ 2701–2711, which regulates communications in storage and ISP subscriber records; and (3) the Pen Register Act, 18 U.S.C. §§ 3121–3127, which regulates the use of pen register and trap and trace devices. The attempts to use ECPA to regulate commercial entities using personal information primarily seek to use the Wiretap Act or the SCA.

IN RE PHARMATRAK, INC. PRIVACY LITIGATION

220 F. Supp. 2d 4 (D. Mass. 2002)

TAURO, J. Plaintiffs . . . bring this consolidated action against Pharmatrak, Inc. and several pharmaceutical companies. . . .

Plaintiffs allege that Defendants "secretly intercepted and accessed Internet users' electronic communications with various health-related and medical-related Internet Web sites and secretly accessed their computer hard drives in order to collect private information about their Web browsing habits [and] confidential health information without their knowledge, authorization, or consent." Plaintiffs contend that the Pharmaceutical Defendants conspired with Plaintiff Pharmatrak to "collect and share this wrongfully obtained personal and sensitive information." This activity was allegedly accomplished through the use of "web bugs," "persistent cookies," and other devices.

The Pharmaceutical Defendants hired Defendant Pharmatrak to monitor their corporate web sites and provide monthly analysis of web site traffic. . . . Pharmatrak specifically represented to the Pharmaceutical Defendants that these products did not collect "personally identifiable information." Even though the Pharmaceutical Defendants may not have known precisely how Pharmatrak's software worked, Plaintiffs readily admit that "the Pharmaceutical Defendants did authorize Pharmatrak's presence upon their Web sites."

---

[54] Anita L. Allen, *Minor Distractions: Children, Privacy and E-Commerce*, 38 Houston L. Rev. 751, 752-53, 768-69, 775-76 (2001).

Pharmatrak's system operated through the use of HTML programming, JavaScript programming, cookies, and "web bugs." Each of the Pharmaceutical Defendants' web pages were programmed with Pharmatrak code, which allowed Pharmatrak to monitor web site activity. When a computer browser requested information from a Pharmaceutical Defendant's web page, the web page would send the requested information to the user, and the site's programming code would instruct the user's browser to contact Pharmatrak's web server and retrieve a "clear GIF" from it. A clear GIF is a one pixel-by-one pixel or two pixels-by-two pixels graphic image, and is sometimes called a web bug or a "pixel tag." The purpose of a clear GIF was to cause the user's computer browser to communicate directly with Pharmatrak's web server. . . .

Having caused the user's Internet browser to contact Pharmatrak, Pharmatrak then sent a cookie back to the browser. A cookie is an electronic file "attached" to a user's computer by a computer server. Plaintiffs concede that "[c]ookies generally perform many convenient and innocuous functions." Commonly, cookies are used to store users' preferences and other information, which allows users to easily access and utilize personalized services on the web or to maintain an online "shopping cart." Cookies also allow web sites to differentiate between users as they visit by assigning each individual browser a unique, randomly generated numeric or alphanumeric identifier. If an individual browser had already visited the "Pharmatrak-enabled" website, Pharmatrak would recognize the previously placed cookie and could therefore differentiate between a repeat visit and an initial visit. . . .

Plaintiffs allege that the JavaApplet used by Pharmatrak allowed Pharmatrak to monitor the length of time that a particular user viewed one of the Pharmaceutical Defendants' web pages. Plaintiffs also allege that the JavaScript programming allowed Pharmatrak to "intercept the full URL of the tracked Web page visited by the user," as well as "the full URL of the Web page visited by the Internet user *immediately prior* to the user's visit to the Pharmatrak-coded Web page. This prior Web page address is known as a 'referrer URL.'" According to Plaintiffs, Pharmatrak used JavaScript "to extract referring URLs from the client's history, thereby bypassing any security or privacy mechanisms put in place to control the flow of potentially sensitive data." The JavaScript and JavaApplet, therefore, also caused users' computer browsers to communicate with Pharmatrak's server while they intentionally communicated with the Pharmaceutical Defendants' servers.

The examination of Pharmatrak's logs "identified hundreds of people by name." . . . Plaintiffs claim that Pharmatrak collected information which included: names, addresses, telephone numbers, dates of birth, sex, insurance status, medical conditions, education levels, and occupations. Pharmatrak also collected data about email communications, including user names, email addresses, and subject lines from emails. . . .

In sum, Plaintiffs argue that "Pharmatrak's technology permits defendants to collect extensive, detailed information about plaintiffs and Class members." In addition to the personal information discussed above, the information collected allegedly included "Web sites the Internet users were at prior to the time they went to the Pharmaceutical Defendants' Web sites, questions they asked and typed in at those prior sites, information they entered while at the Pharmaceutical Defendants' web sites, and the types of computers they were using."

Title I of the Electronic Communication Privacy Act of 1986 ("ECPA"), Interception of Electronic Communications ("The Wiretap Act"), provides that:

> Except as otherwise specifically provided in this chapter[,] any person who — (a) intentionally intercepts, endeavors to intercept, or procures any other person to intercept, any wire, oral, or electronic communication . . . shall be punished as provided in subsection (4) or shall be subject to suit as provided in subsection (5). 18 U.S.C. § 2511(1)(a).

This criminal statute provides for a private right of action, and is subject the following statutory exception:

> (d) It shall not be unlawful under this chapter for a person not acting under color of law to intercept a wire, oral, or electronic communication where such person is a party to the communication or where one of the parties to the communication has given prior consent to such interception unless such communication is intercepted for the purpose of committing any criminal or tortious act. 18 U.S.C. § 2511(2)(d).

Plaintiffs argue that Defendants intentionally "intercepted plaintiffs' or Class members' electronic communications with the Web sites they visited without plaintiffs' or the Class' [sic] knowledge, authorization, or consent. . . ."

Plaintiffs claim that "Pharmatrak intercepted plaintiffs' transmission of their personal information to the Pharmaceutical Defendants' Web sites without the express or implied consent of either plaintiffs or the Pharmaceutical Defendants." Despite the fact that the Pharmaceutical Defendants may have consented to Pharmatrak's assembly of anonymous, aggregate information, Plaintiffs insist that the web sites never consented to Pharmatrak's collection of personally identifiable information. Absent this specific consent, Plaintiffs argue, the Wiretap Act's statutory exception simply does not apply. . . .

In the present case, Plaintiffs concede that the Pharmaceutical Defendants consented to the placement of code for Pharmatrak's . . . service on their web sites. . . . [C]onsent precludes a claim under the Wiretap Act. The Pharmaceutical companies contracted with Pharmatrak, and authorized Pharmatrak to communicate with any users who contacted the Pharmaceutical Web sites. . . . It is sufficient that the Pharmaceutical Defendants were parties to communications with Plaintiffs and consented to the monitoring service provided by Defendant Pharmatrak.

Plaintiffs are also unable to demonstrate that Defendants acted with a tortious purpose. Plaintiffs have produced no evidence "either (1) that the primary motivation, or (2) that a determinative factor in the actor [Pharmatrak's] motivation for intercepting the conversation was to commit a criminal [or] tortious . . . act." Without a showing of the requisite *mens rea,* Plaintiffs cannot succeed on their claim under the Wiretap Act. . . .

Title II of the ECPA, also known as the "Stored Wire and Electronic Communications and Transactional Records Act," "aims to prevent hackers from obtaining, altering, or destroying certain stored electronic communications." The statute provides:

> [W]hoever — (1) intentionally accesses without authorization a facility through which an electronic communication service is provided; or (2) intentionally exceeds an authorization to access that facility; and thereby obtains, alters, or prevents authorized access to a wire or electronic communication while it is in electronic storage in such system shall be punished as provided by subsection (b) of this section. 18 U.S.C. § 2701(a).

Plaintiffs acknowledge that § 2701 was primarily designed to provide a cause of action against computer hackers, and argue that "Defendants' conduct of accessing data in plaintiffs' computers, including the content of plaintiffs' e-mails, constitutes electronic trespassing and falls squarely within the ambit of Section 2701."

Defendants disagree, and claim that they are entitled to summary judgment on at least two separate grounds: (1) Plaintiffs' computers are not facilities which provide electronic communications services, an essential element of § 2701; and (2) any alleged access to "communications" was authorized.

Defendants are correct that an individual Plaintiff's personal computer is not a "facility through which an electronic communication service is provided" for the purposes of § 2701. Plaintiffs find it noteworthy that "[p]ersonal computers provide consumers with the opportunity to access the Internet and send or receive electronic communications," and that "[w]ithout personal computers, most consumers would not be able to access the Internet or electronic communications." Fair enough, but without a telephone, most consumers would not be able to access telephone lines, and without televisions, most consumers would not be able to access cable television. Just as telephones and televisions are necessary devices by which consumers access particular services, personal computers are necessary devices by which consumers connect to the Internet. While it is possible for modern computers to perform server-like functions, there is no evidence that any of the Plaintiffs used their computers in this way. While computers and telephones certainly provide services in the general sense of the word, that is not enough for the purposes of the ECPA. The relevant *service* is Internet access, and the service is provided through ISPs or other servers, not though Plaintiffs' PCs.

Even if the court were to assume that Plaintiffs' computers are "facilities" under § 2701, any access to stored communications was authorized and, thus, Defendants' conduct falls under the exception from liability created by § 2701(c)(2). . . . [T]he Pharmaceutical Defendants are "users" under the ECPA. . . . As users, the Pharmaceutical Defendants could consent to Pharmatrak's interception of Plaintiffs' communications. . . .

In addition, the ECPA does not prohibit Pharmatrak's actions with regard to the placing of cookies on Plaintiffs' computers. Section § 2701 seeks to target communications which are in "electronic storage" incident to their transmission. . . . "Title II only protects electronic communications stored 'for a limited time' in the 'middle' of a transmission, i.e. when an electronic communication service temporarily stores a communication while waiting to store it." Even if such cookies were covered by the ECPA, Pharmatrak created and sent the cookies, and thus any accessing of the cookies by Pharmatrak at a later date would certainly be "authorized." Because Pharmatrak's cookies fall outside the scope of § 2701, Plaintiffs' claim under that section must fail. . . .

NOTES & QUESTIONS

1. ***Postscript.*** On appeal, the First Circuit let stand the district court's holding dismissing the plaintiff's Stored Communications Act claim. *In re Pharmatrak, Inc. Privacy Litigation,* 392 F.3d 9 (1st Cir. 2003). As for the Wiretap Act claim, the court reversed. To prove a violation of the Wiretap Act, the court stated, the plaintiff must prove that "a defendant (1) intentionally (2) intercepted, endeavored to intercept or procured another person to intercept or endeavor to intercept (3) the contents of (4) an electronic communication (5) using a device." The court concluded that the "district court made an error of law . . . as to what constitutes consent." The court reasoned that the "client pharmaceutical companies did not give the requisite consent. The pharmaceutical clients sought and received assurances from Pharmatrak that its . . . service did not and could not collect personally identifiable information. . . . Nor did the users consent." The court remanded as to whether the interception had been intentional.

   Note that there was no consent here because Pharmatrak didn't adequately inform its pharmaceutical clients. Suppose that Pharmatrak told its pharmaceutical clients that it was gathering personal information, but that Pharmatrak did not inform the individual users of the pharmaceutical websites. Would the consent exception apply under these circumstances?

   On remand, the district court concluded that the interception was not intentional, and that at most, Pharmatrak had negligently gathered the personal data. Accordingly, the Wiretap Act claim was again dismissed. *In re Pharmatrak, Inc. Privacy Litigation,* 292 F. Supp. 2d 263 (D. Mass. 2003).

2. ***Does ECPA Prohibit Cookies?*** When a person interacts with a website, the site can record certain information about the person, such as what parts of the website the user visited, what the user clicked on, and how long the user spent reading different parts of the website. This information is called "clickstream data."

   Websites use "cookies" to identify particular users.[55] A cookie is a small text file that is downloaded into the user's computer when a user accesses a web page. The text in a cookie, which is often encoded, usually includes an identification number and several other data elements, such as the website and the expiration date. The cookie lets a website know that a particular user has returned. The website can then access any information it collected about that individual on her previous visits to the website. Cookies can also be used to track users as they visit multiple websites.

   In *In re Doubleclick Inc. Privacy Litigation*, 154 F. Supp. 2d 497 (S.D.N.Y. 2001), a group of plaintiffs challenged DoubleClick's use of cookies under the Stored Communications Act (SCA) and Wiretap Act. In 2001, DoubleClick was the leading company providing online advertising. DoubleClick helps advertisers distribute advertisements to websites based on

---

[55] For a discussion of the *DoubleClick* case, see Tal Zarsky, *Cookie Viewers and the Undermining of Data-Mining: A Critical Review of the DoubleClick Settlement*, 2002 Stan. Tech. L. Rev. 1.

information about specific web surfers. When a person visits a DoubleClick-affiliated website, DoubleClick places a cookie on that person's computer. As the person visits other sites that use DoubleClick, it builds a profile of that person's web surfing activity. DoubleClick then can target ads to specific people based on their profile. For example, suppose a news website uses DoubleClick. A person visits the news website. The website checks with DoubleClick to see if DoubleClick recognizes the person. If the person's computer has a DoubleClick cookie, DoubleClick then looks up the profile associated with the cookie and sends the website advertisements tailored to that person's interests. Suppose Person A likes tennis and Person B likes golf. When Person A goes to the news website, a banner ad for tennis might appear. When Person B visits the same site, a banner ad for golf might appear.

The plaintiffs in the *DoubleClick* case raised an SCA claim and a Wiretap Act claim. Regarding the SCA claim, the Act provides:

> [W]hoever (1) intentionally accesses without authorization a facility through which an electronic information service is provided; or (2) intentionally exceeds an authorization to access that facility; and thereby obtains . . . access to a wire or electronic communication while it is in electronic storage in such system shall be punished. . . . 18 U.S.C. § 2701(a).

Although the court ultimately concluded that the SCA did not apply, its reasoning was very controversial. The court first held that an individual's computer, when connected to the Internet, was a "facility through which an electronic information service is provided." This means that when DoubleClick accessed cookies on people's computers, it was "intentionally access[ing] without authorization a facility through which an electronic information service is provided." However, the consent exception to this provision of the SCA is that "users" may authorize access "with respect to a communication of or intended for that user." § 2701(c). The individuals whose computers were accessed were obviously users, and they did not consent. But the websites that the users visited that used DoubleClick cookies were also "users" in the court's interpretation, and they consented. Only one party needs to consent for the SCA consent exception to apply.

Moreover, the court noted that the SCA only applies to "temporary, intermediate storage of a wire or electronic communication," § 2510(17), and that DoubleClick's cookies were not "temporary" because they exist on people's hard drives for a virtually infinite time period.

Commentators argue that the court's application of the SCA is wrong because a "facility" refers to an Internet Service Provider, not an individual computer. Indeed, this was the conclusion of *In re Pharmatrak.* Consider Orin Kerr:

> [T]he Stored Communications Act regulates the privacy of Internet account holders at ISPs and other servers; the law was enacted to create by statute a set of Fourth Amendment-like set of rights in stored records held by ISPs. The theory of the *Doubleclick* plaintiffs turned this framework on its head, as it

> attempted to apply a law designed to give account holders privacy rights in information held at third-party ISPs to home PCs interacting with websites.[56]

Regarding the Wiretap Act claim, DoubleClick conceded, for the purposes of summary judgment, that it had "intercepted" electronic communications. Orin Kerr also takes issue with this concession:

> [T]he Wiretap Act prohibits a third-party from intercepting in real-time the contents of communications between two parties unless one of the two parties consents. This law had no applicability to Doubleclick's cookies, as the cookies did not intercept any contents and did not intercept anything in real-time. The cookies merely registered data sent to it from Doubleclick's servers.[57]

DoubleClick argued that even if it intercepted electronic communications, the consent exception applied, since one party (the websites using DoubleClick) consented. The court agreed. The consent exception, however, does not apply if even with consent the "communication is intercepted for the purpose of committing any criminal or tortious act." 18 U.S.C. § 2511(2)(d). The court concluded: "DoubleClick's purpose has plainly not been to perpetuate torts on millions of Internet users, but to make money by providing a valued service to commercial Web sites."

3. ***Web Bugs.*** Beyond cookies, another device for collecting people's data is called a "web bug." As one court describes it, web bugs (or "action tags") are very tiny pixels on a website that can record how a person navigates around the Internet. Unlike a cookie, which can be accepted or declined by a user, a web bug is a very small graphic file that is secretly downloaded to the user's computer. Web bugs enable the website to monitor a person's keystrokes and cursor movement. Web bugs can also be placed in e-mail messages that use HTML, or HyperText Markup Language. E-mail using HTML enables users to see graphics in an e-mail. A web bug in an e-mail message can detect whether the e-mail was read and to whom it was forwarded. According to computer security expert Richard M. Smith, a web bug can gather the IP address of the computer that fetched the web bug; the URL of the page that the web bug is located on; the URL of the web bug image; the time the web bug was viewed; the type of browser that fetched the web bug image; and a previously set cookie value. Is the use of a web bug a violation of federal electronic surveillance law?

DYER V. NORTHWEST AIRLINES CORP.

334 F. Supp. 2d 1196 (D.N.D. 2004)

HOVLAND, C.J. . . . Following September 11, 2001, the National Aeronautical and Space Administration ("NASA") requested system-wide passenger data from

[56] Orin S. Kerr, *Lifting the "Fog" of Internet Surveillance: How a Suppression Remedy Would Change Computer Crime Law*, 54 Hastings L.J. 805, 831 (2003).

[57] *Id.* at 831.

Northwest Airlines for a three-month period in order to conduct research for use in airline security studies. Northwest Airlines complied and, unbeknownst to its customers, provided NASA with the names, addresses, credit card numbers, and travel itineraries of persons who had flown on Northwest Airlines between July and December 2001.

The discovery of Northwest Airlines' disclosure of its customers' personal information triggered a wave of litigation. Eight class actions — seven in Minnesota and one in Tennessee — were filed in federal court prior to March 19, 2004. The seven Minnesota actions were later consolidated into a master file.

[In this case, t]he complaint alleges that Northwest Airlines' unauthorized disclosure of customers' personal information constituted a violation of the Electronic Communications Privacy Act ("ECPA"), 18 U.S.C. §§ 2702(a)(1) and (a)(3). . . .

The Electronic Communications Privacy Act (ECPA) provides in relevant part that, with certain exceptions, a person or entity providing either an electronic communication service or remote computing service to the public shall not:

- knowingly divulge to any person or entity the contents of a communication while in electronic storage by that service (18 U.S.C. § 2702(a)(1)); and
- knowingly divulge a record or other information pertaining to a subscriber to or customer of such service . . . to any governmental entity (18 U.S.C. § 2702(a)(3)).

In its complaint, the Plaintiffs asserted claims under both 18 U.S.C. §§ 2702(a)(1) and (a)(3) of the ECPA. The plaintiffs have conceded no claim exists under 18 U.S.C. § 2702(a)(1). Consequently, the Court's focus will be directed at the Plaintiffs' ability to sustain a claim against Northwest Airlines under 18 U.S.C. § 2702(a)(3). To sustain a claim under 18 U.S.C. § 2702(a)(3), the Plaintiffs must establish that Northwest Airlines provides either electronic communication services or remote computing services. It is clear that Northwest Airlines provides neither.

The ECPA defines "electronic communication service" as "any service which provides the users thereof the ability to send or receive wire or electronic communications." 18 U.S.C. § 2510(15). In construing this definition, courts have distinguished those entities that sell access to the internet from those that sell goods or services on the internet. 18 U.S.C. § 2702(a)(3) prescribes the conduct only of a "provider of a remote computing service or electronic communication service to the public." A provider under the ECPA is commonly referred to as an internet service provider or ISP. There is no factual allegation that Northwest Airlines, an airline that sells airline tickets on its website, provides internet services.

Courts have concluded that "electronic communication service" encompasses internet service providers as well as telecommunications companies whose lines carry internet traffic, but does not encompass businesses selling traditional products or services online. See *In re DoubleClick Inc. Privacy Litig.,* 154 F. Supp. 2d 497 (S.D.N.Y. 2001). . . .

The distinction is critical in this case. Northwest Airlines is not an electronic communications service provider as contemplated by the ECPA. Instead,

Northwest Airlines sells its products and services over the internet as opposed to access to the internet itself. The ECPA definition of "electronic communications service" clearly includes internet service providers such as America Online, as well as telecommunications companies whose cables and phone lines carry internet traffic. However, businesses offering their traditional products and services online through a website are not providing an "electronic communication service." As a result, Northwest Airlines falls outside the scope of 18 U.S.C. § 2702 and the ECPA claim fails as a matter of law. The facts as pled to not give rise to liability under the ECPA. 18 U.S.C. § 2702(a) does not prohibit or even address the dissemination of business records of passenger flights and information as described in the complaint. Instead, the focus of 18 U.S.C. § 2702(a) is on "communications" being stored by the communications service provider for the purpose of subsequent transmission or for backup purposes.

[The plaintiffs also raised a claim under the Minnesota Deceptive Trade Practices Act. The court held that the claim was barred by the federal Airline Deregulation Act, which preempts state regulation of "a price, route, or service of an airline carrier." 49 U.S.C. § 4173(b)(1).]

NOTES & QUESTIONS

1. ***ISPs vs. Non-ISPs.*** In this case, Northwest Airlines violated its privacy policy by disclosing its customer records to the government. Suppose Northwest Airlines had been an ISP like AOL or Earthlink. Would it have been liable under the Stored Communications Act?
2. ***Other Remedies.*** What other potential remedies might the plaintiffs have in this case? The plaintiffs brought an action for breach of contract, which was discussed earlier in this chapter in the section on privacy policies. Besides breach of contract, can you think of any other causes of action that might be brought?

COMPUTER FRAUD AND ABUSE ACT

The Computer Fraud and Abuse Act (CFAA) of 1984, 18 U.S.C. § 1030, provides criminal and civil penalties for unauthorized access to computers. Originally passed in 1984, the statue was amended updated throughout the 1990s. Several states have similar statutes regarding the misuse of computers. As Orin Kerr notes:

> While no two statutes are identical, all share the common trigger of "access without authorization" or "unauthorized access" to computers, sometimes in tandem with its close cousin, "exceeding authorized access" to computers.[58]

[58] Orin S. Kerr, *Cybercrime's Scope: Interpreting "Access" and "Authorization" in Computer Misuse Statutes*, 78 N.Y.U. L. Rev. 1596, 1615 (2003).

Scope. The CFAA applies to all "protected computer[s]." A "protected computer" is any computer used in interstate commerce or communication. Whereas the Stored Communications Act of ECPA appears to apply only to ISPs, the CFAA applies to both ISPs and individual computers.

Criminal Penalties. The CFAA creates seven crimes. Among these, it imposes criminal penalties when a person or entity "intentionally accesses a computer without authorization or exceeds authorized access, and thereby obtains . . . information from any protected computer." § 1030(a)(2)(c). It criminalizes unauthorized access to "any nonpublic computer of a department or agency of the United States." § 1030(a)(3). The CFAA also criminalizes unauthorized access to computers "knowingly with intent to defraud" and the obtaining of "anything of value, unless the object of the fraud and the thing obtained consists only of the use of the computer and the value of such use is not more than $5,000 in any 1-year period." § 1030(a)(4). Yet another crime created by the CFAA prohibits knowingly transmitting "a program, information, code, or command" or "intentionally access[ing] a protected computer without authorization" that causes damage to a protected computer. § 1030(5)(A)(i). Punishments range from fines to imprisonment for up to 20 years depending upon the provision violated.

Damage. The term "damage" means "any impairment to the integrity or availability of data, a program, a system, or information." § 1030(e). In many provisions in the CFAA, the damage must exceed $5,000 in a one-year period.

Civil Remedies. "Any person who suffers damage or loss by reason of a violation of this section may maintain a civil action against the violator to obtain compensatory damages or injunctive relief or other equitable relief." § 1030(g). "Damage" must cause a "loss aggregating at least $5,000 in value during any 1-year period to one or more individuals." § 1030(e).

Exceeding Authorized Access. Many provisions in the CFAA can be violated not just by unauthorized access, but also when one "exceeds authorized access." To exceed authorized access means "to access a computer with authorization and to use such access to obtain or alter information in the computer that the accesser is not entitled so to obtain and alter." § 1030(e)(6).

CREATIVE COMPUTING V. GETLOADED.COM LLC

386 F.3d 930 (9th Cir. 2004)

KLEINFELD, J. Truck drivers and trucking companies try to avoid dead heading. "Deadheading" means having to drive a truck, ordinarily on a return trip, without a revenue-producing load. If the truck is moving, truck drivers and their companies want it to be carrying revenue-producing freight. In the past, truckers and shippers used blackboards to match up trips and loads. Eventually television screens were used instead of blackboards, but the matching was still inefficient. Better information on where the trucks and the loads are — and quick, easy access to that information — benefits shippers, carriers, and consumers.

Creative Computing developed a successful Internet site, truckstop.com, which it calls "The Internet Truckstop," to match loads with trucks. The site is very easy to use. It has a feature called "radius search" that lets a truck driver in, say, Middletown, Connecticut, with some space in his truck, find within seconds all available loads in whatever mileage radius he likes (and of course lets a shipper post a load so that a trucker with space can find it). The site was created so early in Internet history and worked so well that it came to dominate the load-board industry.

Getloaded decided to compete, but not honestly. After Getloaded set up a load-matching site, it wanted to get a bigger piece of Creative's market. Creative wanted to prevent that, so it prohibited access to its site by competing loadmatching services. The Getloaded officers thought trucking companies would probably use the same login names and passwords on truckstop.com as they did on getloaded.com. Getloaded's president, Patrick Hull, used the login name and password of a Getloaded subscriber, in effect impersonating the trucking company, to sneak into truckstop.com. Getloaded's vice-president, Ken Hammond, accomplished the same thing by registering a defunct company, RFT Trucking, as a truckstop.com subscriber. These tricks enabled them to see all of the information available to Creative's bona fide customers.

Getloaded's officers also hacked into the code Creative used to operate its website. Microsoft had distributed a patch to prevent a hack it had discovered, but Creative Computing had not yet installed the patch on truckstop.com. Getloaded's president and vice-president hacked into Creative Computing's website through the back door that this patch would have locked. Once in, they examined the source code for the tremendously valuable radius-search feature. . . .

Getloaded argues that no action could lie under the Computer Fraud and Abuse Act because it requires a $5,000 floor for damages from each unauthorized access, and that Creative Computing submitted no evidence that would enable a jury to find that the floor was reached on any single unauthorized access. . . .

The briefs dispute which version of the statute we should apply — the one in effect when Getloaded committed the wrongs, or the one in effect when the case went to trial (which is still in effect). The old version of the statute made an exception to the fraudulent access provision if "the value of such use [unauthorized access to a protected computer] is not more than $5,000 in any 1-year period."[59] The new version, in effect now and during trial, says "loss . . . during any 1-year period . . . aggregating at least $5,000 in value."[60] These provisions are materially identical.

---

[59] 18 U.S.C. § 1030(a)(4) (2001) ("[Whoever] knowingly and with intent to defraud, accesses a protected computer without authorization, or exceeds authorized access, and by means of such conduct furthers the intended fraud and obtains anything of value, unless the object of the fraud and the thing obtained consists only of the use of the computer and the value of such use is not more than $5,000 in any 1-year period.").

[60] 18 U.S.C. § 1030(a)(5)(B)(i) ("[Whoever caused] loss to 1 or more persons during any 1-year period (and, for purposes of an investigation, prosecution, or other proceeding brought by the United States only, loss resulting from a related course of conduct affecting 1 or more other protected computers) aggregating at least $5,000 in value.").

The old version of the statute defined "damage" as "any impairment to the integrity or availability of data, a program, a system, or information" that caused the loss of at least $5,000. It had no separate definition of "loss." The new version defines "damage" the same way, but adds a definition of loss. "Loss" is defined in the new version as "any reasonable cost to any victim, including the cost of responding to an offense, conducting a damage assessment, and restoring the data . . . and any revenue lost, cost incurred, or other consequential damages incurred because of interruption of service."

For purposes of this case, we need not decide which version of the Act applies, because Getloaded loses either way. Neither version of the statute supports a construction that would require proof of $5,000 of damage or loss from a single unauthorized access. The syntax makes it clear that in both versions, the $5,000 floor applies to how much damage or loss there is to the victim over a one-year period, not from a particular intrusion. Getloaded argues that "impairment" is singular, so the floor has to be met by a single intrusion. The premise does not lead to the conclusion. The statute (both the earlier and the current versions) says "damage" means "any impairment to the integrity or availability of data[etc.] . . . that causes loss aggregating at least $5,000." Multiple intrusions can cause a single impairment, and multiple corruptions of data can be described as a single "impairment" to the data. The statute does not say that an "impairment" has to result from a single intrusion, or has to be a single corrupted byte. A court construing a statute attributes a rational purpose to Congress. Getloaded's construction would attribute obvious futility to Congress rather than rationality, because a hacker could evade the statute by setting up thousands of $4,999 (or millions of $4.99) intrusions. As the First Circuit pointed out in the analogous circumstance of physical impairment, so narrow a construction of the $5,000 impairment requirement would merely "reward sophisticated intruders." The damage floor in the Computer Fraud and Abuse Act contains no "single act" requirement.

NOTES & QUESTIONS

1. **DoubleClick, Pharmatrak, *and the CFAA*.** In both the *DoubleClick* and *Pharmatrak* cases, the plaintiffs brought CFAA claims. In both cases, the plaintiffs lost. In *In re Doubleclick Inc. Privacy Litigation*, 154 F. Supp. 2d 497 (S.D.N.Y. 2001), the plaintiffs contended that collectively they suffered more than $5,000 in damages, but the court held that the plaintiffs could not add up their damages. Damages could only be combined "for a single act" against "a particular computer." Since the plaintiffs' CFAA claims concerned multiple acts against many different computers, they could not be aggregated to reach the $5,000 threshold. In *In re Pharmatrak, Inc. Privacy Litigation*, 220 F. Supp. 2d 4 (D. Mass. 2002), the court concluded:

   > Plaintiffs do not allege that their computers were physically damaged in any way, or that they suffered any damage resulting from the repair or replacement of their computer systems. . . .
   >
   > Plaintiffs have not shown any evidence whatsoever that Defendants have caused them at least $5,000 of damage or loss. . . . Any damage or loss under

> the CFAA may be aggregated across victims and across time, but only for a single act. Because Plaintiffs have not shown any facts that demonstrate damage or loss of over $5,000 for any single act of the Defendants, [the CFAA claim is dismissed].

2. ***The Megan Meier Case and Lori Drew Indictment.*** Megan Meier was a 13-year old girl who became friends with a boy named "Josh Evans" on the social network website MySpace. After a while, Josh started sending Megan mean and nasty comments over the Internet. Tragically, Megan committed suicide. Josh was actually a fake MySpace profile created by Lori Drew, the mother of one of Megan's classmates. Drew created the profile in an apparent attempt to learn information about her daughter from Megan. The case generated significant media attention, as well as public outrage over Drew's actions.

   In 2008, Drew was indicted with violating the CFAA. The indictment charged four counts, including the one below:

   > On or about the following dates, defendant Drew, using a computer in O'Fallon, Missouri, intentionally accessed and caused to be accessed a computer used in interstate commerce, namely, the MySpace servers located in Los Angeles County, California, within the Central District of California, without authorization and in excess of authorized access, and, by means of interstate commerce obtained and caused to be obtained information from that computer to further tortious acts, namely intentional infliction of emotional distress on [Megan Meier].

   The prosecution's theory was that Drew exceeded authorized access to MySpace by violating its terms of service, which mandated that Drew provide "truthful and accurate information" when registering and to "refrain from using any information obtained from MySpace services to harass, abuse, or harm other people." The CFAA § 1020(a)(2)(C) makes it a criminal misdemeanor when one "intentionally accesses a computer without authorization or exceeds authorized access, and thereby obtains . . . information from any protected computer." The CFAA § 1030(c)(2)(B)(2) makes it a felony to exceed authorized access if the offense was committed in furtherance of any tortious act.

   Is the prosecutor's theory consistent with the CFAA's language and purpose? What are the implications of prosecutions under the CFAA for violating a website's terms of service? Is the CFAA unconstitutionally vague? A constitutionally vague law is one that either fails to provide the kind of notice that will enable ordinary people to understand what conduct it prohibits; or authorizes or encourages arbitrary and discriminatory enforcement.

3. ***Spyware.*** Spyware is a new kind of computer program that raises significant threats to privacy. Paul Schwartz distinguishes "spyware" from "adware" in terms of the notice provided to the user. He also explains how these programs come about through the linking of personal computers via the Internet: "Spyware draws on computer resources to create a network that can be used for numerous purposes, including collecting personal and nonpersonal information from computers and delivering adware or targeted advertisements

to individuals surfing the Web. Adware is sometimes, but not always, delivered as part of spyware; the definitional line between the two depends on whether the computer user receives adequate notice of the program's installation."[61] Would the CFAA apply to a company that secretly installs spyware in a person's computer that transmits her personal data back to the company without her awareness? Would the Wiretap Act apply?

4. ***State Spyware Statutes.*** The state of Utah became the first state to pass legislation to regulate spyware. The original Spyware Control Act, Utah Code Ann. §§ 13-40-101 *et seq.*, prohibited the installation of spyware on another person's computer, limited the display of certain types of advertising, created a private right of action, and empowered the Utah Division of Consumer Protection to collect complaints. WhenU, an advertising network, challenged the Act in 2004, arguing that it violated the Commerce Clause of the U.S. Constitution, and it obtained a preliminary injunction against the statute. A revised bill was signed by the Utah governor on March 17, 2005. The revised Act defines "spyware" as "software on a computer of a user who resides in this state that . . . collects information about an Internet website at the time the Internet website is being viewed in this state, unless the Internet website is the Internet website of the person who provides the software; and . . . uses the information . . . contemporaneously to display pop-up advertising on the computer."

   Following Utah's lead, California enacted a spyware bill, which was signed by Governor Arnold Schwarzenegger on September 28, 2004. The Consumer Protection Against Computer Spyware Act, SB 1426, prohibits a person from causing computer software to be installed on a computer and using the software to (1) take control of the computer; (2) modify certain settings relating to the computer's access to the Internet; (3) collect, through intentionally deceptive means, personally identifiable information; (4) prevent, without authorization, the authorized user's reasonable efforts to block the installation of or disable software; (5) intentionally misrepresent that the software will be uninstalled or disabled by the authorized user's action; or (6) through intentionally deceptive means, remove, disable, or render, inoperative security, anti-spyware, or antivirus software installed on the computer.

(c) Marketing

TELEPHONE CONSUMER PROTECTIONS ACT

The Telephone Consumer Protections Act (TCPA) of 1991, Pub. L. No. 102-243, 47 U.S.C. § 227, permits individuals to sue a telemarketer in small claims court for an actual loss or up to $500 (whichever is greater), for each call received after requesting to be placed on its "Do Not Call" list:

---

[61] Paul M. Schwartz, *Property, Privacy, and Personal Data*, 117 Harv. L. Rev. 2055 (2004).

> A person who has received more than one telephone call within any 12-month period by or on behalf of the same entity in violation of the regulations prescribed under this subsection may, if otherwise permitted by the laws or rules of a court of a State bring in an appropriate court of that State [an action for an injunction and to recover actual damages or $500 for each violation]. § 227(c)(5).

Telemarketers can offer as an affirmative defense that they established "reasonable practices and procedures to effectively prevent telephone solicitations in violation of the regulations prescribed under this subsection." § 227(c)(5). If telemarketer has acted "willfully or knowingly," then damages are trebled. § 227(c)(5).

The TCPA prohibits telemarketers from calling residences and using prerecorded messages without the consent of the called party. 47 U.S.C. § 227(b)(1)(B). The TCPA prohibits the use of a fax, computer, or other device to send an unsolicited advertisement to a fax machine. § 227(b)(1)(C). The Act also requires the FCC to promulgate rules to "protect residential telephone subscribers' privacy rights and to avoid receiving telephone solicitations to which they object." § 227(c)(1). In addition, the FCC is authorized to require that a "single national database" be established of a "list of telephone numbers of residential subscribers who object to receiving telephone solicitations." § 227(c)(3). It is within the discretion of the FCC to determine whether such a database is necessary or feasible.

States may initiate actions against telemarketers "engaging in a pattern or practice of telephone calls or other transmissions to residents of that State" in violation of the TCPA. § 227(f)(1).

In *Destination Ventures, Ltd. v. FCC,* 46 F.3d 54 (9th Cir. 1995), Destination Ventures challenged a provision of the TCPA banning unsolicited faxes that contained advertisements on First Amendment grounds. The court upheld the ban because it was designed to prevent shifting advertising costs to consumers, who would be forced to pay for the toner and paper to receive the ads.

CAN-SPAM ACT

In 2003, Congress enacted the Controlling the Assault of Non-Solicited Pornography and Marketing (CAN-SPAM) Act, Pub. L. No. 108-187, 15 U.S.C. §§ 7701 *et seq.*, to address the problem of spam. Spam is a term to describe unsolicited commercial e-mail sent to individuals to advertise products and services.[62] Companies that send unsolicited e-mail are referred to as spammers. Spam is often mailed out in bulk to large lists of e-mail addresses. A recent practice has been to insert hidden HTML tags (also known as "pixel tags") into spam. This enables the sender of the e-mail to detect whether the e-mail was opened. It can also inform the sender about whether the e-mail message was forwarded, to what e-mail address it was forwarded, and sometimes, even comments added by a user when forwarding the e-mail. This only works if the recipient has an HTML-enabled e-mail reader rather than a text-only reader.

---

[62] For more information on spam, see David E. Sorkin, *Technical and Legal Approaches to Unsolicited Electronic Mail*, 35 U.S.F. L. Rev. 325, 336 (2001).

HTML e-mail is e-mail that contains pictures and images rather than simply plain text. The practice has become known as a "web bug."

Applicability. The CAN-SPAM Act applies to commercial e-mail, which it defines as a "message with the primary purpose of which is the commercial advertisement or promotion of a commercial product or service."

Prohibitions. The Act prohibits the knowing sending of commercial messages with the intent to deceive or mislead recipients.

Opt Out. The CAN-SPAM Act also requires that a valid opt-out option be made available to e-mail recipients. To make opt out possible, the Act requires senders of commercial e-mail to contain a return address "clearly and conspicuously displayed." Finally, it creates civil and criminal penalties for violations of its provisions. For example, the law allows the DOJ to seek criminal penalties, including imprisonment, for commercial e-mailers who engage in activities such as using a computer to relay or retransmit multiple commercial e-mail messages to receive or mislead recipients or an Internet access service about the message's origin and falsifying header information in multiple e-mail messages and initiate the transmission of these messages.

Assessing the Act. A year after enactment of CAN-SPAM, media accounts faulted the law as ineffective. Indeed, reports stressed the increase in spam during this time. According to one anti-spam vendor, 67 percent of all e-mail was spam in February 2004, and 75 percent in November 2004. Some spammers employed new tactics after the passage of the Act, such as using "zombie networks," which involve hijacking computers with Trojan horse programs. Anti-spam activists faulted CAN-SPAM for preempting tougher state laws, failing to provide a private right of action, and providing an opt-out option instead of an opt in.

Consider Paul Schwartz's critique of the CAN-SPAM Act:

> The CAN-SPAM Act of 2003 fails to provide for an individual right of action. It does provide, however, for the FTC's study of "a system for rewarding those who supply information about violations of the Act." This proposed bounty system for those who assist the FTC follows a recommendation by Lawrence Lessig, a leading cyberlaw professor. As the CAN-SPAM Act states, the FTC is to develop "procedures . . . to grant a reward of not less than 20 percent of the total civil penalty collected for a violation of [the] Act to the first person" who both "identifies the person in violation of [the] Act" and "supplies information that leads to the successful collection of a civil penalty."
>
> The bounty system calls for a mix of public and private action to increase enforcement of legal norms. It assumes, however, that the FTC's central weakness in enforcement is either informational or technical. That is, the FTC may lack adequate evidence regarding spam or the technical skills to unmask those who send unsolicited commercial e-mails. Yet the FTC already has a procedure for collecting spam, and by 2003 it was already receiving as many as 130,000 forwarded e-mails a day as a result. Moreover, if the FTC lacks the technical skills to unmask spammers, it might simply hire additional computer scientists. The enforcement of laws against spam, junk faxes, and unauthorized use of personal data is frequently a drawn-out, resource-intensive process, and

> the bounty-hunter approach still leaves the central burden on the FTC or other governmental agencies. A final problem with the bounty approach, as presented by Lessig and the CAN-SPAM Act, is that it rewards only a single person per spamming case. A stronger mix of public and private action would encourage broader involvement by private individuals. As Diane Mey, the "Erin Brockovich of the anti-telemarketing movement," notes of the benefit of private rights of action: "[I]f enough people sting them a bunch of little stings, maybe they'll get the message and change their ways."[63]

State Anti-Spam Laws. At least 20 states have anti-spam statutes. For example, Cal. Bus. & Professions Code § 17538.4 mandates that senders of spam include in the text of their e-mails a way through which recipients can request to receive no further e-mails. The sender must remove the person from its list. A provider of an e-mail service located within the state of California can request that spammers stop sending spam through its equipment. If the spammer continues to send e-mail, it can be liable for $50 per message up to a maximum of $25,000 per day. *See* § 17538.45.

A Critique of Anti-Spam Legislation. Consumers don't always dislike marketing messages. As Eric Goldman reminds us, "consumers want marketing when it creates personal benefits for them, and marketing also can have spillover benefits that improve social welfare." Goldman is worried that current legal regulation will block the kinds of filters that will improve the ability of consumers to manage information and receive information that will advance their interests. He points to anti-adware laws in Utah and Alaska as especially problematic; these statutes "prohibit client-side software from displaying pop-up ads triggered by the consumer's use of a third party trademark or domain name — even if the consumer has fully consented to the software." For Goldman, these statutes are flawed because they try to "ban or restrict matchmaking technologies." The ideal filter would be a "mind-reading wonder" that "could costlessly — but accurately — read consumers' minds, infer their expressed and latent preferences without the consumer bearing any disclosure costs, and act on the inferred preferences to screen out unwanted content and proactively seek out wanted content." Goldman is confident that such filtering technology is not only possible, but "inevitable — perhaps imminently."[64] What kind of regulatory approach would encourage development and adoption of Goldman's favored filters while also blocking existing SPAM technology? Will surrendering more privacy help better target marketing and thus clear out our inboxes of unwanted spam?

Spam and Speech. Is spam a form of speech, protected by the First Amendment? In *Cyber Promotions, Inc. v. America Online, Inc.*, 948 F. Supp. 436 (E.D. Pa. 1996), Cyber Promotions, Inc. sought a declaratory judgment that America Online (AOL) was prohibited under the First Amendment from denying

---

[63] Paul M. Schwartz, *Property, Privacy and Personal Data*, 117 Harv. L. Rev. 2055, 2112-13 (2004).

[64] Eric Goldman, *A Cosean Analysis of Marketing*, 2006 Wisc. L. Rev. 1151, 1154-55, 1202, 1211-12.

it the ability to send AOL customers unsolicited e-mail. The court rejected Cyber Promotion's argument because of a lack of state action: "AOL is a private online company that is not owned in whole or part by the government." Today, the Internet is increasingly becoming a major medium of communication. Prior to modern communications media, individuals could express their views in traditional "public fora" — parks and street corners. These public fora are no longer the central place for public discourse. Perhaps the Internet is the modern public forum, the place where individuals come to speak and express their views. If this is the case, is it preferable for access to the Internet to be controlled by private entities?

(d) Federal Privacy Legislation: An Assessment

Consider the privacy statutes you have studied so far. Notice the sectoral approach — each statute addresses a particular industry or type of record or problem. Think about these laws together as a system of regulation for privacy. Do these laws adequately carry out the vision of the HEW Report's Code of Fair Information Practices? What, if anything, is missing from this system of regulation? What areas are not covered and should be?

Priscilla Regan contends that Congress has been slow to respond to privacy issues. According to Regan, those interests opposed to privacy protections (law enforcement entities, private industry, employers) were able to delay, block, and weaken Congress' statutory responses to privacy problems. Regan offers an explanation for this phenomenon:

> . . . Generally, the importance of privacy is rooted in traditional liberal thinking — privacy inheres in the individual as an individual and is important to the individual for self-development or for the establishment of intimate or human relationships. Given that the philosophical justification for privacy rests largely on its importance to the individual as an individual, policy discussions about protecting privacy focus on the goal of protecting an individual value or interest. The result has been an emphasis on an atomistic individual and the legal protection of his or her rights.
>
> But as illustrated in congressional attempts to protect privacy, defining privacy primarily in terms of its importance to the individual and in terms of an individual right has served as a weak basis for public policy. . . .
>
> [P]rivacy's importance does not stop with the individual and . . . a recognition of the social importance of privacy will clear a path for more serious policy discourse about privacy and for the formulation of more effective public policy to protect privacy.[65]

Also consider Paul Schwartz's assessment of privacy law:

> . . . At present, however, no successful standards, legal or otherwise, exist for limiting the collection and utilization of personal data in cyberspace. The lack of appropriate and enforceable privacy norms poses a significant threat to democracy in the emerging Information Age. Indeed, information privacy

---

[65] Priscilla M. Regan, *Legislating Privacy: Technology, Social Values, and Public Policy* (1995).

> concerns are the leading reason why individuals not on the Internet are choosing to stay off.
>
> The stakes are enormous; the norms that we develop for personal data use on the Internet will play an essential role in shaping democracy in the Information Age. . . .
>
> . . . [T]he traditional American legal approach to information privacy law emphasizes regulation of government use of personal data rather than private sector activities. From the earliest days of the Republic, American law has viewed the government as the entity whose data use raises the greatest threat to individual liberty. For example, federal and state constitutional protections seek to assure freedom from governmental interference for communications and for the press. This approach means that treatment of personal information in the private sector is often unaccompanied by the presence of basic legal protections. Yet, private enterprises now control more powerful resources of information technology than ever before. These organizations' information processing contributes to their power over our lives. As the Internet becomes more central to life in the United States, the weaknesses and illogic of this existing legal model for information privacy are heightened.[66]

Joel Reidenberg critiques the ad hoc approach the United States has taken toward the protection of privacy:

> The American legal system does not contain a comprehensive set of privacy rights or principles that collectively address the acquisition, storage, transmission, use and disclosure of personal information within the business community. The federal Constitution does not address privacy for information transactions wholly within the private sector and state constitutional provisions similarly do not afford rights for private transactions. Instead, legal protection is accorded exclusively through privacy rights created on an ad hoc basis by federal or state legislation or state common law rules. In addition, self-regulatory schemes have been adopted by some industries and by various companies. Although these schemes may offer privacy protection, they do not provide enforceable legal rights and do not seem to have permeated the vast majority of information processing entities.
>
> In general, the aggregation of the federal and state rights provides targeted protection for individuals in answer to defined problems. This mosaic approach derives from the traditional American fear of government intervention in private activities and the reluctance to broadly regulate industry. The result of the mosaic is a rather haphazard and unsatisfactory response to each of the privacy concerns.[67]

Reidenberg asserts that other countries, especially those in the European Union, have taken a more comprehensive approach toward protecting privacy.

In contrast, Marc Rotenberg has a mixed verdict on the development of United States privacy law. Rotenberg contends that Congress has been responsive to emerging privacy concerns by passing privacy laws in response to new challenges. He asserts that the privacy statutes have incorporated many of the Fair Information Practices, which continue to guide and shape privacy law in

---

[66] Paul M. Schwartz, *Privacy and Democracy in Cyberspace*, 52 Vand. L. Rev. 1609, 1611, 1633-34 (1999).

[67] Joel R. Reidenberg, *Privacy in the Information Economy: A Fortress or Frontier for Individual Rights?*, 44 Fed. Comm. L.J. 195 (1992).

the United States. However, Rotenberg also argues that recent efforts to promote self-regulation have slowed the adoption of necessary privacy statutes: "One cannot escape the conclusion that privacy policy in the United States today reflects what industry is prepared to do rather than what the public wants done."[68]

(e) State Statutory Regulation

Many states have passed legislation regulating business records and databases. Many state statutes have stronger protections of privacy than federal statutes. In particular, California has passed a series of strong privacy protections, and it is probably safe to generalize that California has the strongest privacy law in the United States.[69]

Office of Privacy Protection. In 2000, California created an Office of Privacy Protection. "The office's purpose shall be protecting the privacy of individuals' personal information in a manner consistent with the California Constitution by identifying consumer problems in the privacy area and facilitating development of fair information practices." Cal. Bus. & Prof. Code §§ 350–352. The office also is authorized to make recommendations to organizations about privacy policies and practices.

In its report of activity highlights for the fiscal year July 2006–June 2007, the Office of Privacy Protection noted that it responded to 4,777 calls and e-mails. The largest amount of contacts concerned identity theft (53 percent), with the next categories being business practices and privacy laws (14 percent) and online databases (8 percent).[70] The office also noted its implementation of "a train-the-trainers strategy." It provided training in assisting victims of identity theft to community organizations, and in basic privacy awareness to state information security officers. It also developed a law enforcement manual on investigation and prosecution of identity theft for use in law enforcement classes.

Destruction of Consumer Records. Pursuant to Cal. Civ. Code § 1798.81:

> A business shall take all reasonable steps to destroy, or arrange for the destruction of a customer's records within its custody or control containing personal information which is no longer to be retained by the business by (1) shredding, (2) erasing, or (3) otherwise modifying the personal information in those records to make it unreadable or undecipherable through any means.

"Shine the Light" Law. In 2003, California passed SB27, codified at Cal. Civ. Code § 1798.83. This statute allows consumers to obtain from businesses information about the personal data that the businesses disclosed to third parties for direct marketing purposes. People can find out what kinds of personal information were provided to third parties for their direct marketing purposes as

---

[68] Marc Rotenberg, *Fair Information Practices and the Architecture of Privacy (What Larry Doesn't Get)*, 2001 Stan. Tech. L. Rev. 1, 117-19.

[69] The California Office of Privacy Protection maintains a comprehensive summary of California's privacy statutes: http://www.privacy.ca.gov/lawenforcement/laws.htm.

[70] See Office of Privacy Protection, at http://www.privacy.ca.gov/.

well as the "names and addresses of all of the third parties that received personal information from the business." § 1798.83(1). The law applies to businesses with 20 or more employees. § 1798(c)(1). It does not apply to financial institutions. Companies with privacy policies that allow people to opt out of the sharing of their data with third parties are exempt. § 1798(c)(2).

C. DATA SECURITY

1. INTRODUCTION

The Database Industry. The database industry consists of companies that compile, analyze, and trade personal data. These companies are known as data brokers. Journalist Robert O'Harrow, Jr., describes several of the large database companies in detail. For example, Acxiom is "a billion-dollar player in the data industry, with details about nearly every adult in the United States." Acxiom provides information to marketers for profiling consumers, manages credit records, sells data for background checks, and provides data to government agencies. According to O'Harrow:

> It's not just names, ages, addresses, and telephone numbers. The computers in [Acxiom's] rooms also hold billions of records about marital status and families and ages of children. They track individuals' estimated incomes, the value of their homes, the make and price of their cars. They maintain unlisted phone numbers and details about people's occupations, religions, and ethnicities. They sometimes know what some people read, what they order over the phone and online, and where they go on vacation. . . .
>
> When someone makes a toll-free call to a client of Acxiom to inquire about clothing or to buy some shoes, information about who the caller is and where he or she lives pops up on a screen. . . . Using TeleSource, the agent can often find out the kind of home the caller lives in, the type of cars the people in the household drive, whether they exercise.

Another major database company is ChoicePoint, which was formed in 1997 as a spin-off from the credit reporting agency Equifax. O'Harrow observes: "ChoicePoint has a total of about 17 billion online public records, a figure that grows by more than 40,000 every day. . . . All told, the company has more than 250 terabytes of data regarding the lives of about 220 million adults."[71]

LexisNexis is another of the large data broker companies. It is commonly known for its legal research services, but it also processes personal information.

In addition to these large data brokers are numerous companies that compile, analyze, and sell data for marketing purposes. Daniel Solove describes some of these companies:

---

[71] Robert O'Harrow, Jr., *No Place to Hide* 34, 37-50, 145 (2005). For more background, see Chris Jay Hoofnagle, *Big Brother's Little Helpers: How ChoicePoint and Other Commercial Data Brokers Collect and Package Your Data for Law Enforcement,* 29 N.C. J Int'l L. & Commercial Reg. 595, 602-03 (2004).

> The most powerful database builders construct information empires, sometimes with information on more than half of the American population. For example, Donnelly Marketing Information Services of New Jersey keeps track of 125 million people. Wiland Services has constructed a database containing over 1,000 elements, from demographic information to behavioral data, on over 215 million people.[72]

Data Security Breaches. Several of the largest database companies have had significant security breaches. In 2003, Acxiom had two security breaches. In the first, a person "took the names, credit card numbers, Social Security numbers, addresses, and other details about an estimated 20 million people." In the second, hackers from Florida improperly gained access to Acxiom's records over a period of a few months.[73] In 2005, LexisNexis announced that unauthorized individuals had improperly accessed personal information on about 32,000 people from its Accurint database, which is part of Seisint that LexisNexis acquired in 2004.

The security breach that garnered the most attention, however, involved ChoicePoint. In 2005, ChoicePoint sent over 30,000 letters to California residents announcing that it had suffered a major security breach. It did so because of California's data security notification law, S.B. 1386, codified at Cal. Civ. Code § 1798.82(a), which required individual notification when a security breach involved people's data. At the time, California was the only state with such a law.

The security breach occurred because an identity theft crime ring set up fake businesses and then signed up to receive ChoicePoint's data. As a result, personal information, including names, addresses, and SSNs of over 145,000 people, were improperly accessed. Over 700 of these individuals were victimized by some form of identity theft.

The fraud was discovered in October 2004 by ChoicePoint, but victims were not notified until February 2005 to avoid impeding the law enforcement investigation. When news of the breach was announced, it sparked considerable public attention. After angry statements by many state attorneys general and a public outcry, ChoicePoint decided to voluntarily notify all individuals affected by the breach, not just Californians.

Beyond the ChoicePoint incident, there has been no shortage of other security breaches. LexisNexis announced that the personal information of about 310,000 people was improperly accessed. Beyond the database industry, several universities disclosed that personal information had been leaked or hacked. Bank of America announced that it lost computer data tapes containing data on about 1.2 million government employees. All told thus far, in 2005, at least 50 different announcements were made regarding data security breaches, implicating the personal data of over 50 million people. Today, data security breaches continue to be announced on a frequent basis.

In response, Congress initiated several hearings and bills to examine the database industry and address information privacy and identity theft issues. Bills

---

[72] Daniel J. Solove, *The Digital Person: Technology and Privacy in the Information Age* 20 (2004).

[73] O'Harrow, *supra,* at 71-72.

with various information privacy protections were proposed and passed in many states. For example, very shortly after the ChoicePoint security breach, numerous states enacted data security breach notification laws.

2. DATA SECURITY BREACH NOTIFICATION STATUTES

California was the first state to require companies that maintain personal information to notify individuals in the event of a security breach where personal information is leaked or improperly accessed. Pursuant to SB 1386, codified at Cal. Civ. Code § 1798.82(a):

> Any person or business that conducts business in California, and that owns or licenses computerized data that includes personal information, shall disclose any breach of the security of the system following discovery or notification of the breach in the security of the data to any resident of California whose unencrypted personal information was, or is reasonably believed to have been, acquired by an unauthorized person. The disclosure shall be made in the most expedient time possible and without unreasonable delay, consistent with the legitimate needs of law enforcement. . . .

The California security breach notice provision received national attention after the ChoicePoint data security breach in 2005. Afterwards, almost all states enacted data breach notification laws. At least 44 other states, the District of Columbia and Puerto Rico have enacted statutes that required governmental agencies and/or private companies to disclose security breaches involving personal information.[74] These laws vary according to the following criteria: (1) the entities that the law covers; (2) the law's trigger for notification; (3) any exceptions to the law's notification requirement; (4) the party to whom disclosure is required under the law; (5) whether there is a substantive requirement for data security; and (6) the presence or absence of a private right of action.[75]

Thirty states follow the California approach and rely on the "acquisition" standard for breach notification. These states generally require notification whenever there is a reasonable likelihood that an unauthorized party has "acquired" person information. Only eight states have adopted a higher standard. These states consider whether there is a reasonable likelihood of "misuse" of the information, or "material risk" of harm to the person. The idea is that a breach letter should not be sent to the affected public unless there is a more significant likelihood of harm.

A mere five states provide a private right of action for individuals whose information has been breached. Finally, only twelve of the state statutes create a substantive duty to take reasonable steps to safeguard data. Typically, these statutes provide open-ended, general standards, such as a requirement to provide "reasonable security procedures and practices appropriate to the nature of the

---

[74] National Conference of State Legislatures, State Security Breach Notifications Laws, http://www.ncsl.org/programs/lis/cip/priv/breachlaws.htm (last visited July 16, 2008. For an analysis of data security breach laws, see Paul Schwartz & Edward Janger, *Notification of Data Security Breaches*, 105 Mich. L. Rev. 913, 924-25 (2007).

[75] For a detailed chart examining these laws, state by state (as of 2007), see Schwartz & Janger, *Data Security, supra,* at 972-84.

information." In California, such standards are supplemented by nonbinding, albeit more specific, recommendations from the Office of Privacy Protection.

As noted, most states rely on the same basic trigger for notification: a reasonable belief of "acquisition" of the leaked data. A minority of states require the likelihood of outside "misuse" of the information. More generally, breach notification letters may lose their effectiveness if consumers become dulled by frequent cautions about harms that never materialize. In this sense, Fred Cate writes "if the California law were adopted nationally, like the boy who cried wolf, the flood of notices would soon teach consumers to ignore them. When real danger threatened, who would listen?"[76]

What kind of breach notification statute would be optimal? Schwartz and Janger contend that notification letters to people whose data was leaked play an important role. Within organizations, notification letters have the potential to (1) create a credible threat of negative costs or other punishments for the firm, (2) improve information flows within the firm, and (3) strengthen the position of the data security and privacy officers at the company. Moreover, breach notification letters can play an important role outside the breached organization. Mandated breach disclosure can trigger legislative and other regulatory activity. Schwartz and Janger argue:

> As information about data security breaches and industry practices becomes public, the public, media, and legislators learn about the kinds of errors that lead to data breaches and the types of mistakes that companies make. This situation creates an opportunity for legislators to suggest new regulations and for governmental agencies to provide pressure as to the appropriate content of existing legal standards.[77]

Schwartz and Janger propose that the critical need is for a "coordinated response architecture," which would include a "coordinated response agent" (CRA) to help tailor notice content and supervise the decision whether to give notice. Notification to the consumer would follow upon a reasonable likelihood of "misuse" of notification-triggering information, and notification to the CRA would require the lower standard of a reasonable likelihood of "unauthorized access." The CRA will help coordinate actions that companies take after a breach, tailor the content of the notification in light of the nature of the data breach, and help prepare comparative statistical information regarding data security events.

3. CIVIL LIABILITY

PISCIOTTA V. OLD NATIONAL BANCORP

499 F.3d 629 (7th Cir. 2007)

RIPPLE, J. Plaintiffs Luciano Pisciotta and Daniel Mills brought this action on behalf of a putative class of customers and potential customers of Old National

[76] *See, e.g.,* Fred H. Cate, *Another Notice Isn't an Answer*, USA Today, Feb. 27, 2005, at 14A.
[77] Schwartz & Janger, *Data Security, supra,* at 956.

Bancorp ("ONB"). They alleged that, through its website, ONB had solicited personal information from applicants for banking services, but had failed to secure it adequately. As a result, a third-party computer "hacker" was able to obtain access to the confidential information of tens of thousands of ONB site users. The plaintiffs sought damages for the harm that they claim to have suffered because of the security breach; specifically, they requested compensation for past and future credit monitoring services that they have obtained in response to the compromise of their personal data through ONB's website. ONB answered the allegations and then moved for judgment on the pleadings under Rule 12(c). The district court granted ONB's motion and dismissed the case. The plaintiffs timely appeal. For the reasons set forth in this opinion, we affirm the judgment of the district court. . . .

ONB operates a marketing website on which individuals seeking banking services can complete online applications for accounts, loans and other ONB banking services. The applications differ depending on the service requested, but some forms require the customer or potential customer's name, address, social security number, driver's license number, date of birth, mother's maiden name and credit card or other financial account numbers. In 2002 and 2004, respectively, Mr. Pisciotta and Mr. Mills accessed this website and entered personal information in connection with their applications for ONB banking services.

In 2005, NCR, a hosting facility that maintains ONB's website, notified ONB of a security breach. ONB then sent written notice to its customers. The results of the investigation that followed have been filed under seal in this court; for present purposes, it will suffice to note that the scope and manner of access suggests that the intrusion was sophisticated, intentional and malicious.

Mr. Pisciotta and Mr. Mills, on behalf of a putative class of other ONB website users, brought this action in the United States District Court for the Southern District of Indiana. They named ONB and NCR as defendants and asserted negligence claims against both defendants as well as breach of implied contract claims by ONB and breach of contract by NCR. The plaintiffs alleged that:

> [b]y failing to adequately protect [their] personal confidential information, [ONB and NCR] caused Plaintiffs and other similarly situated past and present customers to suffer substantial potential economic damages and emotional distress and worry that third parties will use [the plaintiffs'] confidential personal information to cause them economic harm, or sell their confidential information to others who will in turn cause them economic harm.

In pleading their damages, the plaintiffs stated that they and others in the putative class "have incurred expenses in order to prevent their confidential personal information from being used and will continue to incur expenses in the future." Significantly, the plaintiffs did not allege any *completed direct* financial loss to their accounts as a result of the breach. Nor did they claim that they or any other member of the putative class *already had been* the victim of identity theft as a result of the breach. The plaintiffs requested "[c]ompensation for all economic and emotional damages suffered as a result of the Defendants' acts which were negligent, in breach of implied contract or in breach of contract," and "[a]ny and all other legal and/or equitable relief to which Plaintiffs . . . are entitled, including establishing an economic monitoring procedure to insure [sic] prompt notice to Plaintiffs . . . of any attempt to use their confidential personal information stolen from the Defendants." . . .

The principal claims in this case are based on a negligence theory. The elements of a negligence claim under Indiana law are: "(1) a duty owed to plaintiff by defendant, (2) breach of duty by allowing conduct to fall below the applicable standard of care, and (3) a *compensable injury* proximately caused by defendant's breach of duty." The plaintiffs' complaint also alleges that ONB has breached an implied contract. Compensable damages are an element of a breach of contract cause of action as well.

As this case comes to us, both the negligence and the contractual issues can be resolved, and the judgment of the district court affirmed, *if* the district court was correct in its determination that Indiana law would not permit recovery for credit monitoring costs incurred by the plaintiffs. . . . We must determine whether Indiana would consider that the harm caused by identity information exposure, coupled with the attendant costs to guard against identity theft, constitutes an existing *compensable injury and consequent damages* required to state a claim for negligence or for breach of contract. Neither the parties' efforts nor our own have identified any Indiana precedent addressing this issue. Nor have we located the decision of any court (other than the district court in this case) that examines Indiana law in this context. We are charged with predicting, nevertheless, how we think the Supreme Court of Indiana would decide this issue. . . .

We begin our inquiry with the Indiana authority most closely addressed to the issue before us. On March 21, 2006, the Indiana legislature enacted a statute that applies to certain database security breaches. Specifically, the statute creates certain duties when a database in which personal data, electronically stored by private entities or state agencies, potentially has been accessed by unauthorized third parties. I.C. § 24-4.9 *et seq.* The statute took effect on July 1, 2006, after the particular incident involved in this case; neither party contends that the statute is directly applicable to the present dispute. We nevertheless find this enactment by the Indiana legislature instructive in our evaluation of the probable approach of the Supreme Court of Indiana to the allegations in the present case.

The provisions of the statute applicable to private entities storing personal information require only that a database owner *disclose* a security breach to potentially affected consumers; they do not require the database owner to take any other affirmative act in the wake of a breach. If the database owner fails to comply with the only affirmative duty imposed by the statute — the duty to disclose — the statute provides for enforcement *only* by the Attorney General of Indiana. It creates no private right of action against the database owner by an affected customer. It imposes no duty to compensate affected individuals for inconvenience or potential harm to credit that may follow. . . .

The plaintiffs maintain that the statute is evidence that the Indiana legislature believes that an individual has suffered a compensable injury at the moment his personal information is exposed because of a security breach. We cannot accept this view. Had the Indiana legislature intended that a cause of action should be available against a database owner for failing to protect adequately personal information, we believe that it would have made some more definite statement of that intent. Moreover, given the novelty of the legal questions posed by information exposure and theft, it is unlikely that the legislature intended to sanction the development of common law tort remedies that would apply to the same factual circumstances addressed by the statute. The narrowness of the defined duties imposed, combined with state-enforced penalties as the exclusive remedy, strongly suggest that Indiana law would not recognize the costs of credit monitoring that the plaintiffs seek to recover in this case as compensable damages.

The plaintiffs further submit that cases decided by the Indiana courts in analogous areas of the law instruct that they suffered an immediate injury when their information was accessed by unauthorized third parties. Specifically, the plaintiffs claim that Indiana law acknowledges special duties on the part of banks to prevent the disclosure of the personal information of their customers; they further claim that Indiana courts have recognized explicitly the significant harm that may result from a failure to prevent such a loss. . . . [One of these cases concerned disclosure to law enforcement that a bank account had been "marked for repossession"; the other, a creditor who was told that the plaintiff's bank account had insufficient funds to cover checks written.]

Whatever these cases say about the relationship of banks and customers in Indiana, they are of marginal assistance to us in determining whether the present plaintiffs are entitled to the remedy they seek as a matter of Indiana law. The reputational injuries suffered by the plaintiffs in [the previous Indiana cases] were direct and immediate; the plaintiffs sought to be compensated for that harm, rather than to be reimbursed for their efforts to guard against some future, anticipated harm. We therefore do not believe that the factual circumstances of the cases relied on by the plaintiffs are sufficiently analogous to the circumstances that we confront in the present case to instruct us on the probable course that the Supreme Court of Indiana would take if faced with the present question.

Although not raised by the parties, we separately note that in the somewhat analogous context of toxic tort liability, the Supreme Court of Indiana has suggested that compensable damage requires more than an exposure to a future potential harm. Specifically, in *AlliedSignal, Inc. v. Ott,* 785 N.E.2d 1068 (Ind. 2003), the Supreme Court of Indiana held that no cause of action accrues, despite incremental physical changes following asbestos exposure, until a plaintiff reasonably could have been diagnosed with an actual exposure-related illness or disease. . . . [E]xposure alone does not give rise to a legally cognizable injury.

Although some courts have allowed medical monitoring damages to be recovered or have created a special cause of action for medical monitoring under similar circumstances, *see Badillo v. American Brands, Inc.,* 16 P.3d 435 (Nev. 2001) (citing cases interpreting the law of seventeen states to allow medical monitoring in some form), no authority from Indiana is among them. Indeed, its recent holding in *AlliedSignal* indicates a contrary approach. To the extent the decision of the Supreme Court of Indiana in that matter provides us with guidance on the likely approach that court would adopt with respect to the information exposure injury in this case, we think it supports the view that no cause of action for credit monitoring is available.

Finally, without Indiana guidance directly on point, we next examine the reasoning of other courts applying the law of other jurisdictions to the question posed by this case. *Allstate Ins. Co.,* 392 F.3d at 952. In this respect, several district courts, applying the laws of other jurisdictions, have rejected similar claims on their merits. In addition to those cases in which the district court held that the plaintiff lacked standing, a series of cases has rejected information security claims on their merits. Most have concluded that the plaintiffs have not been injured in a manner the governing substantive law will recognize.

Although some of these cases involve different types of information losses, all of the cases rely on the same basic premise: Without more than allegations of increased risk of future identity theft, the plaintiffs have not suffered a harm that the law is prepared to remedy. Plaintiffs have not come forward with a single case or statute, from any jurisdiction, authorizing the kind of action they now ask this federal court, sitting in diversity, to recognize as a valid theory of recovery under Indiana law. We decline to adopt a "substantive innovation" in state law, or "to invent what would be a truly novel tort claim" on behalf of the state, absent some authority to suggest that the approval of the Supreme Court of Indiana is forthcoming.

In sum, all of the interpretive tools of which we routinely make use in our attempt to determine the content of state law point us to the conclusion that the Supreme Court of Indiana would not allow the plaintiffs' claim to proceed.

NOTES & QUESTIONS

1. ***Private Rights of Action?*** In *Pisciotta*, the court decides that the Indiana legislature did not create "a cause of action against the database owner for failing to protect adequately personal information." As an example of a statute with such a private right of action, California enacted AB 1950 in 2004, a year after passing SB 1386, its data breach notification law. AB 1950 provides: "A business that owns or licenses personal information about a California resident . . . [to] implement and maintain reasonable security procedures and practices appropriate to the nature of the information, to protect the personal information from unauthorized access, destruction, use, modification, or disclosure." Cal. Civ. Code § 1798.81(b). California law also provides a private right of action in its unfair competition law (which generally permits a private party to bring a lawsuit against any business practice otherwise forbidden by law) and in its breach notification law, § 1798.84 (which provides for a right of action for any "customer injured by a violation of this title"). What is the promise and peril of a private right of action for an organization's failure to maintain reasonable data security?
2. ***Tort Negligence for Data Security Breaches.*** In tort law, under a general negligence theory, litigants might sue a company after a data security incident and seek to collect damages. Thus far, however, class action lawsuits following data breaches have been notably unsuccessful. Among other problems, claimants are facing trouble convincing courts that the data processing entities owe a duty to the individuals whose data are leaked, or that

damages can be inferred from the simple fact of a data breach. For example, a South Carolina court declared in 2003 that "[t]he relationship, if any, between credit card issuers and potential victims of identity theft is far too attenuated to rise to the level of a duty between them." *Huggins v. Citibank*, 585 S.E.2d 275 (S.C. 2003).

3. ***Proving Harm from Data Security Breaches.*** Suppose a person has been notified that her personal information has been improperly accessed, but she has not yet suffered from identity theft. Should she be entitled to any form of compensation? Has she suffered an injury? One might argue that being made more vulnerable to future harm has made her worse off than before. The individual might live with greater unease knowing that she is less secure. On the other hand, no identity theft has occurred, and it may never occur. How should the law address this situation? Recognize a harm? If so, how should damages be assessed?

In *Forbes v. Wells Fargo Bank, N.A.*, 420 F. Supp. 2d 1018 (D. Minn. 2006), a contractor for Wells Fargo Bank had computers stolen containing unencrypted data about customers, such as names, addresses, Social Security numbers, and account numbers. A group of customers sued for breach of contract, breach of fiduciary duty, and negligence. The court, however, dismissed the case:

> Plaintiffs allege that Wells Fargo negligently allowed Regulus to keep customers' private information without adequate security. To establish a negligence claim, a plaintiff must prove that (1) the defendant owed plaintiff a duty of care, (2) the defendant breached that duty, (3) the plaintiff sustained damage and (4) the breach of the duty proximately caused the damage. A plaintiff may recover damages for an increased risk of harm in the future if such risk results from a present injury and indicates a reasonably certain future harm. Alone, however, "the threat of future harm, not yet realized, will not satisfy the damage requirement."
>
> Plaintiffs contend that the time and money they have spent monitoring their credit suffices to establish damages. However, a plaintiff can only recover for loss of time in terms of earning capacity or wages. Plaintiffs have failed to cite any Minnesota authority to the contrary. Moreover, they overlook the fact that their expenditure of time and money was not the result of any present injury, but rather the anticipation of future injury that has not materialized. In other words, the plaintiffs' injuries are solely the result of a perceived risk of future harm. Plaintiffs have shown no present injury or reasonably certain future injury to support damages for any alleged increased risk of harm. For these reasons, plaintiffs have failed to establish the essential element of damages. Therefore, summary judgment in favor of defendant on plaintiffs' negligence claim is warranted.
>
> Plaintiffs also bring a claim for breach of contract against Wells Fargo. To establish their claim, plaintiffs must show that they were damaged by the alleged breach. *See Jensen v. Duluth Area YMCA,* 688 N.W.2d 574, 578-79 (Minn. App. 2004). For all of the reasons discussed above, plaintiffs have failed to establish damages. Therefore, summary judgment in favor of defendant on plaintiffs' breach of contract claim is warranted.

Why aren't expenditures to reduce risks of future harm created by another recoverable? Suppose a company leaks a toxic chemical, causing a person to have an increased risk of cancer. The person sees a doctor and gets a prescription for a drug that will reduce the likelihood that the chemical will cause cancer. Would the expenses of seeing the doctor and purchasing the drug be recoverable? Is this hypothetical analogous to a data security breach?

4. ***Strict Liability for Data Security Breaches?*** Danielle Citron argues for strict liability for harms caused by data breaches. Computer databases of personal information, Citron contends, are akin to the water reservoirs of the early Industrial Age:

> The dynamics of the early Industrial Age, a time of great potential and peril, parallel those at the advent of the Information Age. Then, as now, technological change brought enormous wealth and comfort to society. Industry thrived as a result of machines powered by water reservoirs. But when the dams holding those reservoirs failed, the escaping water caused massive property and personal damage different from the interpersonal harms of the previous century. *Rylands v. Fletcher* provided the Industrial Age's strict-liability response to the accidents caused by the valuable reservoirs' escaping water. The history of *Rylands'*s reception in Britain and the United States reflects the tension between that era's desire for economic growth and its concern for security from industrial hazards.
>
> Computer databases are this century's reservoirs. . . . Much as water reservoirs drove the Industrial Age, computer databases fuel the Internet economy of our Information Age.

Citron argues that a strict liability regime is preferable to negligence tort liability:

> The rapidly changing nature of information technologies may create uncertainty as to what a negligence regime entails. . . .
>
> Due to the rapidly changing threats to information security, database operators will likely be uncertain as to what constitutes optimal care. Cyber-intruders employ increasingly innovative techniques to bypass security measures and steal personal data, thereby requiring an ever-changing information-security response to new threats, vulnerabilities, and technologies. . . .
>
> A negligence regime will fail to address the significant leaks that will occur despite database operators' exercise of due care over personal data. Security breaches are an inevitable byproduct of collecting sensitive personal information in computer databases. No amount of due care will prevent significant amounts of sensitive data from escaping into the hands of cyber-criminals. Such data leaks constitute the predictable residual risks of information reservoirs.
>
> Consequently, negligence will not efficiently manage the residual risks of hazardous databases. Negligence would neither induce database operators to change their activity level nor discourage marginal actors from collecting sensitive information because such operators need not pay for the accident costs of their residual risk.
>
> The high levels of residual risk suggest treating cyber-reservoirs as ultrahazardous activities — those with significant social utility and significant risk — that warrant strict liability. As Judge Richard Posner has explained,

> ultrahazardous activities often involve something "new" that society has "little experience" securing, where neither the injurer nor victim can prevent the accident by taking greater care. This characterized water reservoirs in nineteenth-century England. Strict liability creates an incentive for actors engaging in ultrahazardous activities to "cut back on the scale of the activity . . . to slow its spread while more is learned about conducting it safely."
>
> Classifying database collection as an ultrahazardous activity is a logical extension of Posner's analysis. Just as no clear safety standard governing the building and maintenance of water reservoirs had emerged in the 1850s, a stable set of information-security practices has not yet materialized today. . . .
>
> In this analysis, strict liability has the potential to encourage a change in activity level respecting the storage of sensitive personal information, unless and until more information allows operators to better assess optimal precaution levels and to respond to the persistent problem of residual risk. Because strict liability would force database operators to internalize the full costs of their activities, marginally productive database operators might refrain from maintaining cyber-reservoirs of personal data. Strict liability also may decrease the collection of ultrasensitive data among those who are at greatest risk of security breaches. Moreover, as insurance markets develop in this emerging area, database operators that continue collecting sensitive information will be better positioned to assess the cost of residual risk and the extent to which they can spread the cost of such risk onto consumers.[78]

Are you convinced by the analogy between the database industry and reservoirs? Will strict liability lead to the correct level of investment in security by companies? Could it lead to over-investment in data security?

5. ***Assessing the Federal Approach to Data Security.*** As discussed above, after the ChoicePoint data security breach in 2005 — along with the numerous other breaches that followed — a majority of states have now passed data security breach legislation. Despite several proposed bills, the federal government has yet to pass a comprehensive data security law. However, some existing federal privacy laws protect data security in the context of particular industries. Consider Andrea Matwyshyn:

> The current approach to information security, exemplified by statutes such as COPPA, HIPAA, and GLBA, attempts to regulate information security by creating legal "clusters" of entities based on the type of business they transact, the types of data they control, and that data's permitted and nonpermitted uses. In other words, the current regulatory approach has singled out a few points in the system for the creation of information security enclaves. . . .
>
> The current approach ignores the fundamental tenet of security that a system is only as strong as its weakest links, not its strongest points. . . . It will not prove adequate to only ensure that a few points or clusters in the system are particularly well-secured. . . .
>
> The biggest economic losses arise not out of illegal leveraging of these protected categories of data; rather, losses arise out of stolen personally identifiable information, such as credit card data and social security numbers,

[78] Danielle Keats Citron, *Reservoirs of Danger: The Evolution of Public and Private Law at the Dawn of the Information Age,* 80 S. Cal. L. Rev. 241, 243-44, 263-67 (2007).

which are warehoused frequently by entities that are not regulated by COPPA, HIPAA or GLBA. Therefore, creating enclaves of superior data security for data related to children online, some financial information, and some health data will not alleviate the weak information security in other parts of the system and will not substantially diminish information crime. . . .[79]

4. FTC REGULATION

The FTC has acted on numerous occasions to penalize merchants that fail to take reasonable measures to protect customer data. In a typical data security complaint, the FTC argues that the firm's data-handling practices constituted unfair acts or practices in violation of Section 5 of the Federal Trade Commission Act. In settling its enforcement actions, the FTC has required both general and specific pledges of reasonable data security.

The most dramatic of these FTC enforcement actions involved ChoicePoint. In settling the FTC charges, ChoicePoint agreed in January 2006 to pay $10 million in civil penalties and $5 million into a consumer redress fund.[80] The $10 million fine is the largest civil penalty in the FTC's history. ChoicePoint also promised changes to its business and improvements to its security practices.

The stipulated final judgment bars the company from furnishing consumer reports to customers without a permissible purpose and requires it to establish reasonable procedures to ensure that it will provide consumer reports only to those with a permissible purpose. One requirement placed on ChoicePoint is to verify the identity of businesses that apply to receive consumer reports by auditing subscribers' use of consumer reports and by making site visits to certain of its customers.

Finally, the settlement obligated ChoicePoint to establish and maintain a comprehensive information security program and to submit this program for two decades to outside independent audits. It agreed to "establish and implement, and thereafter maintain, a comprehensive information security program that is reasonably designed to protect the security, confidentiality, and integrity of personal information collected from or about consumers." In maintaining this "comprehensive information security program," ChoicePoint promised to engage in risk assessments and to design and implement regular testing of the effectiveness of its security program's key controls, systems, and procedures. It also agreed to obtain an initial and then biennial outside assessment of its data security safeguards from an independent third-party professional. The FTC has reached significant settlements in other data security cases as well. Consider the FTC's settlement in *In the Matter of Reed Elsevier, Inc. and Seisint* below.

---

[79] Andrea M. Matwyshyn, *Material Vulnerabilities: Data Privacy, Corporate Information Security, and Securities Regulation*, 3 Berkeley Bus. L.J. 129, 169-70 (2005).

[80] News Release, FTC, ChoicePoint *Settles Data Security Breach Charges* (Jan. 26, 2006), at http://www.ftc.gov/opa/2006/01/choicepoint.htm.

IN THE MATTER OF REED ELSEVIER, INC. AND SEISINT

2008 WL 903806 (F.T.C. 2008)

[Reed Elsevier acquired Seisint in September 2004 and operated it as a wholly owned subsidiary within LexisNexis, more widely known for providing legal information. Seisint collected and sold information about consumers, and did so under the trade name of "Accurint." According to the FTC's complaint, Seisint used its information "to locate assets and people, authenticate identities, and verify credentials." It also sold products about consumers to "insurance companies, debt collectors, employers, landlords, law firms, and law enforcement and other government agencies." In order to sell these products, Reed Elsevier and Seisint collected and aggregated information about millions of consumers from public and nonpublic sources.

The FTC alleged that in its security practices, Reed Elsevier and Seisint failed to provide "reasonable and appropriate security to prevent authorized access" to sensitive consumer information. It argued, "In particular, respondents failed to establish or implement reasonable policies and procedures governing the creation and authentication of user credentials for authorized customers. . . ." Among other flawed practices, the FTC pointed to the companies' failure to establish or enforce rules that would make it difficult to guess user credentials. It permitted their customers to use the same word as both password and user ID. In addition, it allowed the sharing of user credentials among multiple users at a single customer firm, which lowered the likely detection of unauthorized services. It also failed to mandate periodic changes of user credentials and did not implement simple, readily available defenses against common network attacks.

The consequences of the shortcomings in security practices at Reed Elsevier and Seisint were dramatic. In its complaint, the FTC stated:

> On multiple occasions since January 2003, attackers exploited respondent Seisint's user ID and password structures to obtain without authorization the user credentials of legitimate Accurint customers. The attackers then used these credentials to make thousands of unauthorized searches for consumer information in Accurint databases. These attacks disclosed sensitive information about several hundred thousand consumers, including, in many instances, names, current and prior addresses, dates of birth, and Social Security numbers. Although some of these attacks occurred before respondent REI acquired respondent Seisint, they continued for at least 9 months after the acquisition, during which time respondent Seisint was operating under the control of respondent REI. Since March 2005, respondent REI through LexisNexis has notified over 316,000 consumers that the attacks disclosed sensitive information about them that could be used to conduct identity theft.

These incidents also led to new credit accounts being opened in the name of customers.

On March 27, 2008, the FTC announced a settlement with Reed Elsevier and its Seisint subsidiary.]

AGREEMENT CONTAINING CONSENT ORDER

The Federal Trade Commission has conducted an investigation of certain acts and practices of Reed Elsevier Inc. and Seisint, Inc. ("proposed respondents"). Proposed respondents, having been represented by counsel, are willing to enter into an agreement containing a consent order resolving the allegations contained in the attached draft complaint. . . .

ORDER

For purposes of this order, the following definitions shall apply:

1. Unless otherwise specified, "respondents" shall mean Reed Elsevier Inc., its successors and assigns, officers, agents, representatives, and employees, and Seisint, Inc., and its successors and assigns, officers, agents, representatives, and employees.

2. "Personal information" shall mean individually identifiable information from or about a consumer including, but not limited to: (a) a first and last name; (b) a home or other physical address, including street name and name of city or town; (c) an email address or other online contact information, such as an instant messaging user identifier or a screen name that reveals a consumer's email address; (d) a telephone number; (e) a Social Security number; (f) a date of birth; (g) a driver's license number; (h) credit and/or debit card information, including but not limited to card number and expiration date and transaction detail data; (i) a persistent identifier, such as a customer number held in a "cookie" or processor serial number, that is combined with other available data that identifies a consumer; or (j) any other information from or about a consumer that is combined with (a) through (i) above.

3. "Information product or service" shall mean each product, service, or other means by which respondents individually or collectively provide direct or indirect access to personal information from or about consumers that is comprised in whole or part of nonpublic information; *provided, however*, that this term shall not include information products or services that: (a) provide access solely to personal information that is publicly available information, or (b) permit customers to upload or otherwise supply, organize, manage, or retrieve information that is under the customer's control.

4. "Publicly available information" shall mean information that respondents have a reasonable basis to believe is lawfully made available to the general public from: (a) Federal, State, or local government records, (b) widely distributed media, or (c) disclosures to the general public that are required to be made by Federal, State, or local law. Respondents shall have a reasonable basis to believe information is lawfully made available to the general public if respondents have taken reasonable steps to determine: (a) that the information is of the type that is available to the general public, and (b) whether an individual can direct that the information not be made available to the general public and, if so, that the individual has not done so.

I.

IT IS ORDERED that each respondent, directly or through any corporation, subsidiary, division, or other device, in connection with the advertising, marketing, promotion, offering for sale, or sale of personal information collected from or about consumers made available through any information product or service of LexisNexis ("the information"), in or affecting commerce, shall, no later than the date of service of this order, establish and implement, and thereafter maintain, a comprehensive information security program that is reasonably designed to protect the security, confidentiality, and integrity of the information. Such program, the content and implementation of which must be fully documented in writing, shall contain administrative, technical, and physical safeguards appropriate to each respondent's size and complexity, the nature and scope of each respondent's activities, and the sensitivity of the information, including:

A. the designation of an employee or employees to coordinate and be accountable for the information security program.

B. the identification of material internal and external risks to the security, confidentiality, and integrity of the information that could result in the unauthorized disclosure, misuse, loss, alteration, destruction, or other compromise of the information, and assessment of the sufficiency of any safeguards in place to control these risks. At a minimum, this risk assessment should include consideration of risks in each area of relevant operation, including, but not limited to: (1) employee training and management; (2) information systems, including network and software design, information processing, storage, transmission, and disposal; and (3) prevention, detection, and response to attacks, intrusions, or other systems failures.

C. the design and implementation of reasonable safeguards to control the risks identified through risk assessment, and regular testing or monitoring of the effectiveness of the safeguards' key controls, systems, and procedures.

D. the development and use of reasonable steps to select and retain service providers capable of appropriately safeguarding personal information they receive from respondent, and requiring service providers by contract to implement and maintain appropriate safeguards; *provided, however*, that this subparagraph shall not apply to personal information about a consumer that respondent provides to a government agency or lawful information supplier when the agency or supplier already possesses the information and uses it only to retrieve, and supply to respondent, additional personal information about the consumer.

E. the evaluation and adjustment of respondent's information security program in light of the results of the testing and monitoring required by subparagraph C, any material changes to respondent's operations or business arrangements, or any other circumstances that respondent knows or has reason to know may have a material impact on the effectiveness of its information security program.

II.

IT IS FURTHER ORDERED that, in connection with its compliance with Paragraph I of this order, each respondent shall obtain initial and biennial assessments and reports ("Assessments") from a qualified, objective, independent third-party professional, who uses procedures and standards generally accepted in the profession. The reporting period for the Assessments shall cover: (1) the first one hundred and eighty (180) days after service of the order for the initial Assessment, and (2) each two (2) year period thereafter for twenty (20) years after service of the order for the biennial Assessments. Each Assessment shall:

A. set forth the specific administrative, technical, and physical safeguards that respondent has implemented and maintained during the reporting period;

B. explain how such safeguards are appropriate to respondent's size and complexity, the nature and scope of respondent's activities, and the sensitivity of the personal information collected from or about consumers;

C. explain how the safeguards that have been implemented meet or exceed the protections required by Paragraph I of this order; and

D. certify that respondent's security program is operating with sufficient effectiveness to provide reasonable assurance that the security, confidentiality, and integrity of personal information is protected and has so operated throughout the reporting period.

Each Assessment shall be prepared and completed within sixty (60) days after the end of the reporting period to which the Assessment applies by a person qualified as a Certified Information System Security Professional (CISSP) or as a Certified Information Systems Auditor (CISA); a person holding Global Information Assurance Certification (GIAC) from the SysAdmin, Audit, Network, Security (SANS) Institute; or a similarly qualified person or organization. . . .

VII.

This order will terminate twenty (20) years from the date of its issuance, or twenty (20) years from the most recent date that the United States or the Federal Trade Commission files a complaint (with or without an accompanying consent decree) in federal court alleging any violation of the order, whichever comes later. . . .

NOTES & QUESTIONS

1. ***The Terms of Settlement.*** This settlement illustrates the FTC's classic approach in its data security settlements of imposing long-term requirements for an information security program. Do you think that the settlement terms in *Reed Elsevier* are appropriate? Does the FTC strike the correct balance in providing some flexibility to the companies in deciding the content of a reasonable security program?
2. ***Damages:* Reed Elsevier *vs.* ChoicePoint.** Unlike other companies with whom the FTC has settled claims, Reed Elsevier and Seisint avoided paying

fines. Should the FTC have sought to negotiate the payment of damages in *Reed Elsevier*? In its *ChoicePoint* settlement, discussed above, the FTC negotiated a payment of $10 million in civil penalties and $5 million for civil redress. It found that ChoicePoint violated the FCRA by furnishing credit histories to subscribers without a permissible purpose and violated the FTC Act by making false and misleading statements about its privacy practices. One possible difference in the FTC's ability to obtain damages in *ChoicePoint* concerned the company's FCRA violations. The FTC in its *ChoicePoint* complaint sought monetary civil penalties for each separate violation of the FCRA. A violation of FCRA, according to the FTC, occurred each time ChoicePoint (1) furnished a consumer report to a person without a permissible purpose for it, (2) failed to make a reasonable effort to verify the identity of the prospective user, or (3) furnished a consumer report to any person when it had reasonable grounds for believing the report would not be used for a FCRA permissible purpose. Is there a similar way to create a framework for assessing damages in *Reed Elsevier*?

3. ***Data Leaks:* Eli Lilly.** In *FTC v. Eli Lilly*, No. 012-3214, the FTC charged Eli Lilly, a pharmaceutical company, with disclosing people's health data that it collected through its Prozac.com website. Prozac is a drug used for treating depression. Lilly offered customers an e-mail service that would send them e-mail messages to remind them to take or refill their medication. In June 2001, the company sent e-mail messages to all 669 users of the reminder service announcing that the service was terminated. However, this message contained the e-mail addresses of all subscribers in the "To" line of the message. The FTC alleged that the company's privacy policy promising confidentiality was deceptive because the company failed to establish adequate security protections for its consumers' data. Specifically, the FTC complaint alleged that Eli Lilly failed to

   > provide appropriate training for its employees regarding consumer privacy and information security; provide appropriate oversight and assistance for the employee who sent out the e-mail, who had no prior experience in creating, testing, or implementing the computer program used; and implement appropriate checks and controls on the process, such as reviewing the computer program with experienced personnel and pretesting the program internally before sending out the e-mail.

   In January 2002, Eli Lilly settled. The settlement requires Eli Lilly to establish a new security program. It must designate personnel to oversee the program, identify and address various security risks, and conduct an annual review of the security program. FTC Commissioners voted 5–0 to approve the settlement.

   Consider the settlements in the cases described above. Do you think that these settlements are adequate to redress the rights of the individuals affected?

4. **Microsoft Passport *and* Guess*: Proactive FTC Enforcement?*** Microsoft launched Microsoft.NET Passport, an online authentication service. Passport allowed consumers to use a single username and password to access multiple

websites. The goal of Passport was to serve as a universal sign-on service, eliminating the need to sign on to each website separately. A related service, Wallet, permitted users to submit credit card and billing information in order to make purchases at multiple websites without having to reenter the information on each site.

The FTC initiated an investigation of the Passport services following a July 2001 complaint from a coalition of consumer groups. In the petition to the FTC, the privacy groups raised questions about the collection, use, and disclosure of personal information that Passport would make possible, and asserted that Microsoft's representations about the security of the system were both unfair and deceptive. In its privacy policy, Microsoft promised that ".NET Passport is protected by powerful online security technology and a strict privacy policy." Further, Microsoft stated: "Your .NET Passport information is stored on secure .NET Passport servers that are protected in controlled facilities."

On August 8, 2002, the FTC found that Microsoft had violated § 5 of the FTC Act and announced a proposed settlement with the company. *See In the Matter of Microsoft Corp.,* No. 012-3240. The Commission found that Microsoft falsely represented that (1) it employs reasonable and appropriate measures under the circumstances to maintain and protect the privacy and confidentiality of consumers' personal information collected through its Passport and Wallet services; (2) purchases made with Passport Wallet are generally safer or more secure than purchases made at the same site without Passport Wallet when, in fact, most consumers received identical security at those sites regardless of whether they used Passport Wallet to complete their transactions; (3) Passport did not collect any personally identifiable information other than that described in its privacy policy when, in fact, Passport collected and held, for a limited time, a personally identifiable sign-in history for each user; and (4) the Kids Passport program provided parents control over what information participating websites could collect from their children.

Under the terms of the proposed consent order, Microsoft may not make any misrepresentations, expressly or by implication, of any of its information practices. Microsoft is further obligated to establish a "comprehensive information security program," and conduct an annual audit to assess the security practices. Microsoft is also required to make available to the FTC for a period of five years all documents relating to security practices as well as compliance with the orders. The order remains in place for 20 years.

The FTC took a similar approach in *In re Guess.com, Inc.,* No. 022-3260 (July 30, 2003). Guess, a clothing company, had promised that all personal information "including . . . credit card information and sign-in password, are stored in an unreadable, encrypted format at all times." This assertion of company policy was false, and the FTC initiated an action even before data was leaked or improperly accessed. The case was eventually settled.

In both *Microsoft* and *Guess*, the FTC brought an action before any data security breach had occurred. Is this a form of proactive enforcement? Suppose a company merely makes a general promise to "keep customer data secure." The FTC believes that the company is not providing adequate security and brings an action. How should the adequacy of a company's security practices be evaluated, especially in cases in which privacy policies are vague about the precise security measures taken?

5. ***The Gramm-Leach-Bliley Act and the FTC.*** Consider the following observation by Daniel Solove:

> [O]ne problem with the FTC's jurisdiction is that it is triggered when a company breaches its own privacy policy. But what if a company doesn't make explicit promises about security? One hopeful development is the Gramm-Leach-Bliley (GLB) Act. The GLB Act requires a number of agencies that regulate financial institutions to promulgate "administrative, technical, and physical safeguards for personal information." In other words, financial institutions must adopt a security system for their data, and the minimum specifications of this system are to be defined by government agencies. . . .[81]

Solove argues that the security practices of many financial institutions are quite lax, as such institutions often provide access to accounts if a person merely supplies her Social Security number. Based on the GLB Act, could the FTC use its enforcement powers to curtail such practices?

D. FIRST AMENDMENT LIMITATIONS ON PRIVACY REGULATION

Although the First Amendment protects privacy, privacy restrictions can come into conflict with the First Amendment. In particular, many privacy statutes regulate the disclosure of true information. The cases in this section explore the extent to which the First Amendment limits the privacy statutes. Before turning to the cases, some background about basic First Amendment jurisprudence is necessary. The cases in this section often focus on commercial speech, and the Court analyzes commercial speech differently than other forms of expression.

First Amendment Protection of Commercial Speech. For a while, the Court considered commercial speech as a category of expression that is not accorded First Amendment protection. However, in *Virginia State Board of Pharmacy v. Virginia Citizens Consumer Council, Inc.,* 425 U.S. 748 (1976), the Court held that commercial speech deserves constitutional protection. However, the Court held that commercial speech has a lower value than regular categories of speech and therefore is entitled to a lesser protection. *Ohralik v. Ohio State Bar Ass'n,* 436 U.S. 447 (1978).

Defining Commercial Speech. What is "commercial speech"? The Court has defined it as speech that "proposes a commercial transaction," *Virginia State Board,* 425 U.S. 748 (1976), and as "expression related solely to the economic interests of the speaker and its audience." *Central Hudson Gas & Electric Corp.*

---

[81] Daniel J. Solove, *The Digital Person: Technology and Privacy in the Information Age* 107-08 (2004).

v. Public Service Comm'n of New York, 447 U.S. 557 (1980). The Court later held that neither of these are necessary requirements to define commercial speech; both are factors to be considered in determining whether speech is commercial. *See Bolger v. Youngs Drug Products Corp.,* 463 U.S. 60 (1983).

The* Central Hudson *Test. In *Central Hudson,* 447 U.S. 557 (1980), the Court established a four-part test for analyzing the constitutionality of restrictions on commercial speech:

> At the outset, we must determine whether the expression is protected by the First Amendment. For commercial speech to come within that provision, it at least must concern lawful activity and not be misleading. Next, we ask whether the asserted governmental interest is substantial. If both inquiries yield positive answers, we must determine whether the regulation directly advances the governmental interest asserted, and whether it is not more extensive than is necessary to serve that interest.

In *Board of Trustees of State University of New York v. Fox,* 492 U.S. 469 (1989), the Court revised the last part of the *Central Hudson* test — that speech "not [be] more extensive than is necessary to serve [the governmental] interest" — to a requirement that there be a "fit between the legislature's ends and the means chosen to accomplish the ends, . . . a fit that is not necessarily perfect, but reasonable."

In *Cincinnati v. Discovery Network, Inc.,* 507 U.S. 410 (1993), the Court, applying the commercial speech test in *Central Hudson* and *Fox*, struck down an ordinance that banned news racks with "commercial handbills." The ordinance did not apply to news racks for newspapers. The Court concluded that the ban was not a "reasonable fit" with the city's interest in aesthetics. Moreover, the Court concluded that the ordinance was not content-neutral. The Court held that Cincinnati "has enacted a sweeping ban on the use of newsracks that distribute 'commercial handbills,' but not 'newspapers.' Under the city's newsrack policy, whether any particular newsrack falls within the ban is determined by the content of the publication resting inside that newsrack. Thus, by any commonsense understanding of the term, the ban in this case is 'content based.' . . . [B]ecause the ban is predicated on the content of the publications distributed by the subject newsracks, it is not a valid time, place, or manner restriction on protected speech."

ROWAN V. UNITED STATES POST OFFICE DEPARTMENT

397 U.S. 728 (1970)

[A federal statute permitted individuals to require that entities sending unwanted mailings remove the individuals' names from their mailing lists and cease to send future mailings. A group of organizations challenged the statute on First Amendment grounds.]

BURGER, C.J. . . . The essence of appellants' argument is that the statute violates their constitutional right to communicate. . . . Without doubt the public postal system is an indispensable adjunct of every civilized society and communication is imperative to a healthy social order. But the right of every person "to be let alone" must be placed in the scales with the right of others to communicate.

In today's complex society we are inescapably captive audiences for many purposes, but a sufficient measure of individual autonomy must survive to permit every householder to exercise control over unwanted mail. To make the householder the exclusive and final judge of what will cross his threshold undoubtedly has the effect of impeding the flow of ideas, information, and arguments that, ideally, he should receive and consider. Today's merchandising methods, the plethora of mass mailings subsidized by low postal rates, and the growth of the sale of large mailing lists as an industry in itself have changed the mailman from a carrier of primarily private communications, as he was in a more leisurely day, and have made him an adjunct of the mass mailer who sends unsolicited and often unwanted mail into every home. It places no strain on the doctrine of judicial notice to observe that whether measured by pieces or pounds, Everyman's mail today is made up overwhelmingly of material he did not seek from persons he does not know. And all too often it is matter he finds offensive. . . .

The Court has traditionally respected the right of a householder to bar, by order or notice, solicitors, hawkers, and peddlers from his property. In this case the mailer's right to communicate is circumscribed only by an affirmative act of the addressee giving notice that he wishes no further mailings from that mailer.

To hold less would tend to license a form of trespass and would make hardly more sense than to say that a radio or television viewer may not twist the dial to cut off an offensive or boring communication and thus bar its entering his home. Nothing in the Constitution compels us to listen to or view any unwanted communication, whatever its merit; we see no basis for according the printed word or pictures a different or more preferred status because they are sent by mail. The ancient concept that "a man's home is his castle" into which "not even the king may enter" has lost none of its vitality, and none of the recognized exceptions includes any right to communicate offensively with another. . . .

If this prohibition operates to impede the flow of even valid ideas, the answer is that no one has a right to press even "good" ideas on an unwilling recipient. That we are often "captives" outside the sanctuary of the home and subject to objectionable speech and other sound does not mean we must be captives everywhere. The asserted right of a mailer, we repeat, stops at the outer boundary of every person's domain. . . .

MAINSTREAM MARKETING SERVICES, INC. V. FEDERAL TRADE COMMISSION

358 F.3d 1228 (10th Cir. 2004)

EBEL, J. . . . In 2003, two federal agencies—the Federal Trade Commission (FTC) and the Federal Communications Commission (FCC) — promulgated rules that together created the national do-not-call registry *See* 16 C.F.R. § 310.4(b)(1)(iii)(B) (FTC rule); 47 C.F.R. § 64.1200(c)(2) (FCC rule). The national do-not-call registry is a list containing the personal telephone numbers of telephone subscribers who have voluntarily indicated that they do not wish to receive unsolicited calls from commercial telemarketers. Commercial telemarketers are generally prohibited from calling phone numbers that have been placed on the do-not-call registry, and they must pay an annual fee to access the numbers on the registry so that they can delete those numbers from their telephone solicitation lists. So far, consumers have registered more than 50 million phone numbers on the national do-not-call registry.

The national do-not-call registry's restrictions apply only to telemarketing calls made by or on behalf of sellers of goods or services, and not to charitable or political fundraising calls. Additionally, a seller may call consumers who have signed up for the national registry if it has an established business relationship with the consumer or if the consumer has given that seller express written permission to call. Telemarketers generally have three months from the date on which a consumer signs up for the registry to remove the consumer's phone number from their call lists. Consumer registrations remain valid for five years, and phone numbers that are disconnected or reassigned will be periodically removed from the registry.

The national do-not-call registry is the product of a regulatory effort dating back to 1991 aimed at protecting the privacy rights of consumers and curbing the risk of telemarketing abuse. In the Telephone Consumer Protection Act of 1991 ("TCPA") — under which the FCC enacted its do-not-call rules — Congress found that for many consumers telemarketing sales calls constitute an intrusive invasion of privacy. . . . The TCPA therefore authorized the FCC to establish a national database of consumers who object to receiving "telephone solicitations," which the act defined as commercial sales calls. . . .

The national do-not-call registry's telemarketing restrictions apply only to commercial speech. Like most commercial speech regulations, the do-not-call rules draw a line between commercial and non-commercial speech on the basis of content. In reviewing commercial speech regulations, we apply the *Central Hudson* test. *Central Hudson Gas & Elec. Corp. v. Pub. Serv. Comm'n of N.Y.*, 447 U.S. 557 (1980).

Central Hudson established a three-part test governing First Amendment challenges to regulations restricting non-misleading commercial speech that relates to lawful activity. First, the government must assert a substantial interest to be achieved by the regulation. Second, the regulation must directly advance that governmental interest, meaning that it must do more than provide "only ineffective or remote support for the government's purpose." Third, although the regulation need not be the least restrictive measure available, it must be narrowly tailored not to restrict more speech than necessary. Together, these final two factors require that there be a reasonable fit between the government's objectives and the means it chooses to accomplish those ends. . . .

The government asserts that the do-not-call regulations are justified by its interests in 1) protecting the privacy of individuals in their homes, and 2) protecting consumers against the risk of fraudulent and abusive solicitation. Both of these justifications are undisputedly substantial governmental interests.

In *Rowan v. United States Post Office Dep't,* the Supreme Court upheld the right of a homeowner to restrict material that could be mailed to his or her house.

The Court emphasized the importance of individual privacy, particularly in the context of the home, stating that "the ancient concept that 'a man's home is his castle' into which 'not even the king may enter' has lost none of its vitality." In *Frisby v. Schultz,* the Court [held] . . .

> One important aspect of residential privacy is protection of the unwilling listener. . . . [A] special benefit of the privacy all citizens enjoy within their own walls, which the State may legislate to protect, is an ability to avoid intrusions. Thus, we have repeatedly held that individuals are not required to welcome unwanted speech into their own homes and that the government may protect this freedom.

A reasonable fit exists between the do-not-call rules and the government's privacy and consumer protection interests if the regulation directly advances those interests and is narrowly tailored. . . .

These criteria are plainly established in this case. The do-not-call registry directly advances the government's interests by effectively blocking a significant number of the calls that cause the problems the government sought to redress. It is narrowly tailored because its opt-in character ensures that it does not inhibit any speech directed at the home of a willing listener.

The telemarketers assert that the do-not-call registry is unconstitutionally underinclusive because it does not apply to charitable and political callers. First Amendment challenges based on underinclusiveness face an uphill battle in the commercial speech context. As a general rule, the First Amendment does not require that the government regulate all aspects of a problem before it can make progress on any front. . . . The underinclusiveness of a commercial speech regulation is relevant only if it renders the regulatory framework so irrational that it fails materially to advance the aims that it was purportedly designed to further. . .

As discussed above, the national do-not-call registry is designed to reduce intrusions into personal privacy and the risk of telemarketing fraud and abuse that accompany unwanted telephone solicitation. The registry directly advances those goals. So far, more than 50 million telephone numbers have been registered on the do-not-call list, and the do-not-call regulations protect these households from receiving most unwanted telemarketing calls. According to the telemarketers' own estimate, 2.64 telemarketing calls per week — or more than 137 calls annually — were directed at an average consumer before the do-not-call list came into effect. *Cf.* 68 Fed. Reg. at 44152 (discussing the five-fold increase in the total number of telemarketing calls between 1991 and 2003). Accordingly, absent the do-not-call registry, telemarketers would call those consumers who have already signed up for the registry an estimated total of 6.85 *billion* times each year.

To be sure, the do-not-call list will not block all of these calls. Nevertheless, it will prohibit a substantial number of them, making it difficult to fathom how the registry could be called an "ineffective" means of stopping invasive or abusive calls, or a regulation that "furnish[es] only speculative or marginal support" for the government's interests. . . .

Finally, the type of unsolicited calls that the do-not-call list does prohibit— commercial sales calls — is the type that Congress, the FTC and the FCC have all determined to be most to blame for the problems the government is seeking to redress. According to the legislative history accompanying the TCPA, "[c]omplaint statistics show that unwanted commercial calls are a far bigger problem than unsolicited calls from political or charitable organizations." H.R. Rep. No. 102-317, at 16 (1991). Additionally, the FTC has found that commercial callers are more likely than non-commercial callers to engage in deceptive and abusive practices. . . . The speech regulated by the do-not-call list is therefore the speech most likely to cause the problems the government sought to alleviate in enacting that list, further demonstrating that the regulation directly advances the government's interests. . . .

Although the least restrictive means test is not the test to be used in the commercial speech context, commercial speech regulations do at least have to be "narrowly tailored" and provide a "reasonable fit" between the problem and the solution. Whether or not there are "numerous and obvious less-burdensome alternatives" is a relevant consideration in our narrow tailoring analysis. . . . We hold that the national do-not-call registry is narrowly tailored because it does not over-regulate protected speech; rather, it restricts only calls that are targeted at unwilling recipients. . . .

The Supreme Court has repeatedly held that speech restrictions based on private choice (i.e., an opt-in feature) are less restrictive than laws that prohibit speech directly. In *Rowan,* for example, the Court approved a law under which an individual could require a mailer to stop all future mailings if he or she received advertisements that he or she believed to be erotically arousing or sexually provocative. Although it was the government that empowered individuals to avoid materials they considered provocative, the Court emphasized that the mailer's right to communicate was circumscribed only by an affirmative act of a householder. . . .

Like the do-not-mail regulation approved in *Rowan,* the national do-not-call registry does not itself prohibit any speech. Instead, it merely "permits a citizen to erect a wall . . . that no advertiser may penetrate without his acquiescence." *See Rowan,* 397 U.S. at 738. Almost by definition, the do-not-call regulations only block calls that would constitute unwanted intrusions into the privacy of consumers who have signed up for the list. . . .

NOTES & QUESTIONS

1. ***The Do Not Call List and* Rowan.** To what extent is this case controlled by *Rowan*? Does the Do Not Call (DNC) list go beyond the statute in *Rowan*?
2. ***Charitable and Political Calls.*** The DNC list permits calls based on charitable or political purposes. There is no way to block such calls. Suppose that Congress decided that all calls could be included. Would a charity or political group have a First Amendment ground to overturn the DNC list?

U.S. WEST, INC. V. FEDERAL COMMUNICATIONS COMMISSION

182 F.3d 1224 (10th Cir. 1999)

TACHA, J. . . . U.S. West, Inc. petitions for review of a Federal Communication Commission ("FCC") order restricting the use and disclosure of and access to customer proprietary network information ("CPNI"). *See* 63 Fed. Reg. 20,326 (1998) ("CPNI Order"). [U.S. West argues that FCC regulations, implementing 47 U.S.C. § 222, among other things, violate the First Amendment. These regulations require telecommunications companies to ask consumers for approval (to "opt-in") before they can use a customer's personal information for marketing purposes.] . . .

The dispute in this case involves regulations the FCC promulgated to implement provisions of 47 U.S.C. § 222, which was enacted as part of the Telecommunications Act of 1996. Section 222, entitled "Privacy of customer information," states generally that "[e]very telecommunications carrier has a duty to protect the confidentiality of proprietary information of, and relating to . . . customers." To effectuate that duty, § 222 places restrictions on the use, disclosure of, and access to certain customer information. At issue here are the FCC's regulations clarifying the privacy requirements for CPNI. The central provision of § 222 dealing with CPNI is § 222(c)(1), which states:

> Except as required by law or with the approval of the customer, a telecommunications carrier that receives or obtains customer proprietary network information by virtue of its provision of a telecommunications service shall only use, disclose, or permit access to individually identifiable customer proprietary network information in its provision of (A) the telecommunication service from which such information is derived, or (B) services necessary to, or used in, the provision of such telecommunications service, including the publishing of directories.

Section 222(d) provides three additional exceptions to the CPNI privacy requirements. [These exceptions permit the companies to use and disclose CPNI for billing purposes, to prevent fraud, and to provide services to the consumer if the consumer approves of the use of such information to provide the service. Any other uses or disclosures of CPNI not specifically permitted by § 222 require the consumer's consent. The regulations adopted by the CPNI Order implementing § 222 divides telecommunications services into three categories: (1) local, (2) long-distance, and (3) mobile or cellular. A telecommunications carrier can use or disclose CPNI to market products within one of these service categories if the customer already subscribes to that category of service. Carriers can't use or disclose CPNI to market categories of service to which the customer does not subscribe unless first obtaining the customer's consent. The regulations also prohibit using CPNI without consent to market other services such as voice mail or Internet access, to track customers that call competitors, or to try to regain the business of customers that switch carriers.] . . .

The regulations also describe the means by which a carrier must obtain customer approval. Section 222(c)(1) did not elaborate as to what form that approval should take. The FCC decided to require an "opt-in" approach, in which a carrier must obtain prior express approval from a customer through written, oral, or electronic means before using the customer's CPNI. The government acknowledged that the means of approval could have taken numerous other forms, including an "opt-out" approach, in which approval would be inferred from the customer-carrier relationship unless the customer specifically requested that his or her CPNI be restricted. . . .

Petitioner argues that the CPNI regulations interpreting 47 U.S.C. § 222 violate the First Amendment. . . .

Because petitioner's targeted speech to its customers is for the purpose of soliciting those customers to purchase more or different telecommunications services, it "does no more than propose a commercial transaction." Consequently, the targeted speech in this case fits soundly within the definition of commercial speech. It is well established that nonmisleading commercial speech regarding a lawful activity is a form of protected speech under the First Amendment, although it is generally afforded less protection than noncommercial speech. The parties do not dispute that the commercial speech based on CPNI is truthful and nonmisleading. Therefore, the CPNI regulations implicate the First Amendment by restricting protected commercial speech. . . .

We analyze whether a government restriction on commercial speech violates the First Amendment under the four-part framework set forth in *Central Hudson* [*Gas & Elec. Corp. v. Public Serv. Comm'n of N.Y.,* 477 U.S. 557 (1980)]. First, we must conduct a threshold inquiry regarding whether the commercial speech concerns lawful activity and is not misleading. If these requirements are not met, the government may freely regulate the speech. If this threshold requirement is met, the government may restrict the speech only if it proves: "(1) it has a substantial state interest in regulating the speech, (2) the regulation directly and materially advances that interest, and (3) the regulation is no more extensive than necessary to serve the interest." As noted above, no one disputes that the commercial speech based on CPNI is truthful and nonmisleading. We therefore proceed directly to whether the government has satisfied its burden under the remaining three prongs of the *Central Hudson* test. . . .

The respondents argue that the FCC's CPNI regulations advance two substantial state interests: protecting customer privacy and promoting competition. While, in the abstract, these may constitute legitimate and substantial interests, we have concerns about the proffered justifications in the context of this case. . . .

. . . Although we agree that privacy may rise to the level of a substantial state interest, the government cannot satisfy the second prong of the *Central Hudson* test by merely asserting a broad interest in privacy. It must specify the particular notion of privacy and interest served. Moreover, privacy is not an absolute good because it imposes real costs on society. Therefore, the specific privacy interest must be substantial, demonstrating that the state has considered the proper balancing of the benefits and harms of privacy. In sum, privacy may only constitute a substantial state interest if the government specifically articulates and properly justifies it.

In the context of a speech restriction imposed to protect privacy by keeping certain information confidential, the government must show that the dissemination of the information desired to be kept private would inflict specific and significant harm on individuals, such as undue embarrassment or ridicule, intimidation or harassment, or misappropriation of sensitive personal information for the purposes of assuming another's identity. Although we may feel uncomfortable knowing that our personal information is circulating in the world, we live in an open society where information may usually pass freely. A general level of discomfort from knowing that people can readily access information about us does not necessarily rise to the level of a substantial state interest under *Central Hudson* for it is not based on an identified harm.

Neither Congress nor the FCC explicitly stated what "privacy" harm § 222 seeks to protect against. The CPNI Order notes that "CPNI includes information that is extremely personal to customers . . . such as to whom, where, and when a customer places a call, as well as the types of service offerings to which the customer subscribes," and it summarily finds "call destinations and other details about a call . . . may be equally or more sensitive [than the content of the calls]." The government never states it directly, but we infer from this thin justification that disclosure of CPNI information could prove embarrassing to some and that the government seeks to combat this potential harm. . . .

Under the next prong of *Central Hudson,* the government must "demonstrate that the harms it recites are real and that its restriction will in fact alleviate them to a material degree.". . . On the record before us, the government fails to meet its burden.

The government presents no evidence showing the harm to either privacy or competition is real. Instead, the government relies on speculation that harm to privacy and competition for new services will result if carriers use CPNI. . . . While protecting against disclosure of sensitive and potentially embarrassing personal information may be important in the abstract, we have no indication of how it may occur in reality with respect to CPNI. Indeed, we do not even have indication that the disclosure might actually occur. The government presents no evidence regarding how and to whom carriers would disclose CPNI. . . . [T]he government has not explained how or why a carrier would disclose CPNI to outside parties, especially when the government claims CPNI is information that would give one firm a competitive advantage over another. This leaves us unsure exactly who would potentially receive the sensitive information. . . .

In order for a regulation to satisfy this final *Central Hudson* prong, there must be a fit between the legislature's means and its desired objective. . . .

. . . [O]n this record, the FCC's failure to adequately consider an obvious and substantially less restrictive alternative, an opt-out strategy, indicates that it did not narrowly tailor the CPNI regulations regarding customer approval. . . .

The respondents merely speculate that there are a substantial number of individuals who feel strongly about their privacy, yet would not bother to opt-out if given notice and the opportunity to do so. Such speculation hardly reflects the careful calculation of costs and benefits that our commercial speech jurisprudence requires. . . .

In sum, even assuming that respondents met the prior two prongs of *Central Hudson,* we conclude that based on the record before us, the agency has failed to satisfy its burden of showing that the customer approval regulations restrict no more speech than necessary to serve the asserted state interests. Consequently, we find that the CPNI regulations interpreting the customer approval requirement of 47 U.S.C. § 222(c) violate the First Amendment.

BRISCOE, J. dissenting. . . . After reviewing the CPNI Order and the administrative record, I am convinced the FCC's interpretation of § 222, more specifically its selection of the opt-in method for obtaining customer approval, is entirely reasonable. Indeed, the CPNI Order makes a strong case that, of the two options seriously considered by the FCC, the opt-in method is the only one that legitimately forwards Congress' goal of ensuring that customers give informed consent for use of their individually identifiable CPNI. . . .

. . . U.S. West suggests the CPNI Order unduly limits its ability to engage in commercial speech with its existing customers regarding new products and services it may offer. . . .

The problem with U.S. West's arguments is they are more appropriately aimed at the restrictions and requirements outlined in § 222 rather than the approval method adopted in the CPNI Order. As outlined above, it is the statute, not the CPNI Order, that prohibits a carrier from using, disclosing, or permitting access to individually identifiable CPNI without first obtaining informed consent from its customers. Yet U.S. West has not challenged the constitutionality of § 222, and this is not the proper forum for addressing such a challenge even if it was raised. . . .

The majority, focusing at this point on the CPNI Order rather than the statute, concludes the FCC failed to adequately consider the opt-out method, which the majority characterizes as "an obvious and substantially less restrictive alternative" than the opt-in method. Notably, however, the majority fails to explain why, in its view, the opt-out method is substantially less restrictive. Presumably, the majority is relying on the fact that the opt-out method typically results in a higher "approval" rate than the opt-in method. Were mere "approval" percentages the only factor relevant to our discussion, the majority would perhaps be correct. As the FCC persuasively concluded in the CPNI Order, however, the opt-out method simply does not comply with § 222's requirement of informed consent. In particular, the opt-out method, unlike the opt-in method, does not guarantee that a customer will make an informed decision about usage of his or her individually identifiable CPNI. To the contrary, the opt-out method creates the very real possibility of "uninformed" customer approval. In the end, I reiterate my point that the opt-in method selected by the FCC is the only method of obtaining approval that serves the governmental interests at issue while simultaneously complying with the express requirement of the statute (i.e., obtaining informed customer consent). . . .

In conclusion, I view U.S. West's petition for review as little more than a run-of-the-mill attack on an agency order "clothed by ingenious argument in the garb" of First Amendment issues. . . .

NOTES & QUESTIONS

1. ***Is Opt in Narrowly Tailored?*** Is the opt-in system involved in *U.S. West* more restrictive than the do-not-mail list in *Rowan* or the DNC list in *Mainstream*

Marketing? Is the privacy interest in *U.S. West* different than in *Rowan* and *Mainstream Marketing*?

2. ***Personal Information: Property, Contract, and Speech.*** Consider the following critique of *U.S. West* by Julie Cohen:

> The law affords numerous instances of regulation of the exchange of information as property or product. Securities markets, which operate entirely by means of information exchange, are subject to extensive regulation, and hardly anybody thinks that securities laws and regulations should be subjected to heightened or strict First Amendment scrutiny. Laws prohibiting patent, copyright, and trademark infringement, and forbidding the misappropriation of trade secrets, have as their fundamental purpose (and their undisputed effect) the restriction of information flows. The securities and intellectual property laws, moreover, are expressly content-based, and thus illustrate that (as several leading First Amendment scholars acknowledge) this characterization doesn't always matter. Finally, federal computer crime laws punish certain uses of information for reasons entirely unrelated to their communicative aspects. . . .
>
> The accumulation, use, and market exchange of personally-identified data don't fit neatly into any recognized category of "commercial speech" . . . because in the ways that matter, these activities aren't really "speech" at all. Although regulation directed at these acts may impose some indirect burden on direct-to-consumer communication, that isn't the primary objective of data privacy regulation. This suggests that, at most, data privacy regulation should be subject to the intermediate scrutiny applied to indirect speech regulation.[82]

3. ***Is Opt In Too Expensive?*** Michael Staten and Fred Cate have defended the *U.S. West* decision by noting the results of the testing of an opt-in system by U.S. West:

> In 1997, U.S. West (now Qwest Communications), one of the largest telecommunications companies in the United States, conducted one of the few affirmative consent trials for which results are publicly available. In that trial, the company sought permission from its customers to utilize information about their calling patterns (e.g., volume of calls, time and duration of calls, etc.) to market new services to them. The direct mail appeal for permission received a positive response rate between 5 and 11 percent for residential customers (depending upon the size of a companion incentive offered by the company). Residential customers opted in at a rate of 28 percent when called about the service.
>
> When U.S. West was actually communicating in person with the consumers, the positive response rate was three to six times higher than when it relied on consumers reading and responding to mail. But even with telemarketing, the task of reaching a customer is daunting. U.S. West determined that it required an average of 4.8 calls to each consumer household before they reached an adult who could grant consent. In one-third of households called, U.S. West never reached the customer, despite repeated attempts. In any case, many U.S. West customers received more calls than would have been the case in an opt-out system, and despite repeated contact

---

[82] Julie E. Cohen, *Examined Lives: Informational Privacy and the Subject as Object*, 52 Stan. L. Rev. 1373, 1416-18, 1421 (2000).

> attempts, one-third of their customers missed opportunities to receive new products and services. The approximately $20 cost per positive response in the telemarketing test and $29 to $34 cost per positive response in the direct mail test led the company to conclude that opt-in was not a viable business model because it was too costly, too difficult, and too time intensive.[83]

Robert Gellman, however, generally disputes the findings of industry studies about the costs of privacy protective measures. With regard to opt-in cost assessments, Gellman argues that industry studies often fail "to consider other ways [beyond direct mail and telemarketing] that business and charities can solicit individuals to replace any losses from opt-in requirements. Newspaper, Internet, radio, and television advertising may be effective substitutes for direct mail. There are other ways to approach individuals without the compilation of detailed personal dossiers. None of the alternatives is adequately considered."[84]

4. *Is Commercial Transaction Information Different from Other Speech?* Courts analyzing First Amendment challenges to regulation of data about commercial transactions have typically viewed the dissemination and use of such data as commercial speech, and they have applied the *Central Hudson* test. This test is less protective than regular First Amendment protection. Solveig Singleton contends that data about commercial transactions should be considered regular speech, not commercial speech:

> Is commercial tracking essentially different from gossip? . . .
>
> Gossip and other informal personal contacts serve an important function in advanced economies. In Nineteenth Century America, entrepreneurs would increase their sales by acquiring information about their customers. Customers relied on their neighborhood banker, whom they knew since childhood, to grant them credit. They would return again and again to the same stores for personalized service. . . .
>
> [E]conomic actors must develop new mechanisms of relaying information to each other about fraud, trust, and behavior of potential customers. Towards the end of the Nineteenth Century and throughout the Twentieth Century, formal credit reporting began to evolve out of gossip networks. . . .
>
> The equivalence of gossip and consumer databases suggests that there is no need to treat the evolution of databases as a crisis. Those who argue for a new legal regime for privacy, however, view new uses of information as having crossed an "invisible line" between permissible gossip and violative information collection. While the use of new technology to collect information may make people uneasy, is there any reason to suppose that any harm that might result will amount to greater harm than the harm that could come from being a victim of vicious gossip?[85]

---

[83] Michael E. Staten & Fred H. Cate, *The Impact of Opt-In Privacy Rules on Retail Credit Markets: A Case Study of MBNA*, 52 Duke L.J. 745, 767-68 (2003).

[84] Robert Gellman, *Privacy, Consumers, and Costs: How the Lack of Privacy Costs Consumers and Why Business Studies of Privacy Costs Are Biased and Incomplete* (March 2002), at http://www.epic.org/reports/dmfprivacy.html.

[85] Solveig Singleton, *Privacy Versus the First Amendment: A Skeptical Approach*, 11 Fordham Intell. Prop. Media & Ent. L.J. 97, 126-32 (2000).

Singleton goes on to contend that information collected by businesses in databases is less pernicious than gossip because few people have access to it and it is "likely to be much more accurate than gossip." Is the information in computer databases merely gossip on a more systemic scale? Compare how the First Amendment regulates gossip with how it regulates commercial speech.

5. ***The Value of Privacy.*** What is the value of protecting the privacy of consumer information maintained by telecommunications companies? Is it more important than the economic benefits that the telecommunications companies gain by using that information for marketing? How should policymakers go about answering such questions? Consider James Nehf:

> The choice of utilitarian reasoning — often reduced to cost-benefit analysis ("CBA") in policy debates — fixes the outcome in favor of the side that can more easily quantify results. In privacy debates, this generally favors the side arguing for more data collection and sharing. Although CBA can mean different things in various contexts, the term here means a strategy for making choices in which quantifiable weights are given to competing alternatives. . . .
>
> We should openly acknowledge that non-economic values are legitimate in privacy debates, just as they have been recognized in other areas of fundamental importance. Decisions about the societal acceptance of disabled citizens, the codification of collective bargaining rights for workers, and the adoption of fair trial procedures for the accused did not depend entirely, or even primarily, on CBA outcomes. Difficulties in quantifying costs and benefits do not present insurmountable obstacles when policymakers address matters of basic human dignity. The protection of personal data should be viewed in a similar way, and CBA should play a smaller role in privacy debates. . . .
>
> A similar phenomenon is at work in the formulation of public policy. Policymakers are often asked to compare incomparable alternatives. . . .
>
> By converting all values to money, the incomparability problem is lessened, but only if we accept the legitimacy of money as the covering value. In the privacy debate, the legitimacy of monetizing individual privacy preferences is highly suspect. Benefits are often personal, emotional, intangible, and not readily quantifiable. Preferences on privacy matters are generally muddled, incoherent, and ill-informed. If privacy preferences are real but not sufficiently coherent to form a sound basis for valuation, any attempt to place a monetary value on them loses meaning. The choice of CBA as the model for justifying decisions fixes the end, because the chosen covering value will usually result in a decision favoring data proliferation over data protection. . . .
>
> People make choices between seemingly incomparable things all the time, and they can do so rationally. A person is not acting irrationally by preferring a perceived notable value over an incomparable nominal value, even if she cannot state a normative theory to explain why the decision is right. A similar phenomenon may be seen in the formulation of public policy. Notable values may be preferred over nominal ones in the enactment of laws and the implementation of policies even if policymakers cannot explain why one alternative is better than the other. Moreover, by observing a number of such decisions over time, we may begin to see a pattern develop and covering

values emerge that can serve as guides to later decisions that are closer to the margin.[86]

TRANS UNION CORP. V. FEDERAL TRADE COMMISSION

245 F.3d 809 (D.C. Cir. 2001)

TATEL, J. . . . Petitioner Trans Union sells two types of products. First, as a credit reporting agency, it compiles credit reports about individual consumers from credit information it collects from banks, credit card companies, and other lenders. It then sells these credit reports to lenders, employers, and insurance companies. Trans Union receives credit information from lenders in the form of "tradelines." A tradeline typically includes a customer's name, address, date of birth, telephone number, Social Security number, account type, opening date of account, credit limit, account status, and payment history. Trans Union receives 1.4 to 1.6 billion records per month. The company's credit database contains information on 190 million adults.

Trans Union's second set of products — those at issue in this case — are known as target marketing products. These consist of lists of names and addresses of individuals who meet specific criteria such as possession of an auto loan, a department store credit card, or two or more mortgages. Marketers purchase these lists, then contact the individuals by mail or telephone to offer them goods and services. To create its target marketing lists, Trans Union maintains a database known as MasterFile, a subset of its consumer credit database. MasterFile consists of information about every consumer in the company's credit database who has (A) at least two tradelines with activity during the previous six months, or (B) one tradeline with activity during the previous six months plus an address confirmed by an outside source. The company compiles target marketing lists by extracting from MasterFile the names and addresses of individuals with characteristics chosen by list purchasers. For example, a department store might buy a list of all individuals in a particular area code who have both a mortgage and a credit card with a $10,000 limit. Although target marketing lists contain only names and addresses, purchasers know that every person on a list has the characteristics they requested because Trans Union uses those characteristics as criteria for culling individual files from its database. Purchasers also know that every individual on a target marketing list satisfies the criteria for inclusion in MasterFile.

The Fair Credit Reporting Act of 1970 ("FCRA"), 15 U.S.C. §§ 1681, 1681a-1681u, regulates consumer reporting agencies like Trans Union, imposing various obligations to protect the privacy and accuracy of credit information. The Federal Trade Commission, acting pursuant to its authority to enforce the FCRA, *see* 15 U.S.C. § 1681s(a), determined that Trans Union's target marketing lists were "consumer reports" subject to the Act's limitations. [The FTC concluded that targeted marketing was not an authorized use of consumer reports under the FCRA and ordered Trans Union to halt its sale of the lists.] . . . .

---

[86] James P. Nehf, *Incomparability and the Passive Virtues of Ad Hoc Privacy Policy*, 76 U. Colo. L. Rev. 1, 29-36, 42 (2005).

. . . [Trans Union challenges the FTC's application of the FCRA as violative of the First Amendment.] Banning the sale of target marketing lists, the company says, amounts to a restriction on its speech subject to strict scrutiny. Again, Trans Union misunderstands our standard of review. In *Dun & Bradstreet, Inc. v. Greenmoss Builders, Inc.,* 472 U.S. 749 (1985), the Supreme Court held that a consumer reporting agency's credit report warranted reduced constitutional protection because it concerned "no public issue." "The protection to be accorded a particular credit report," the Court explained, "depends on whether the report's 'content, form, and context' indicate that it concerns a public matter." Like the credit report in *Dun & Bradstreet,* which the Supreme Court found "was speech solely in the interest of the speaker and its specific business audience," the information about individual consumers and their credit performance communicated by Trans Union target marketing lists is solely of interest to the company and its business customers and relates to no matter of public concern. Trans Union target marketing lists thus warrant "reduced constitutional protection."

We turn then to the specifics of Trans Union's First Amendment argument. The company first claims that neither the FCRA nor the Commission's Order advances a substantial government interest. The "Congressional findings and statement of purpose" at the beginning of the FCRA state: "There is a need to insure that consumer reporting agencies exercise their grave responsibilities with . . . respect for the consumer's right to privacy." 15 U.S.C. § 1681 (a)(4). Contrary to the company's assertions, we have no doubt that this interest — protecting the privacy of consumer credit information — is substantial.

Trans Union next argues that Congress should have chosen a "less burdensome alternative," i.e., allowing consumer reporting agencies to sell credit information as long as they notify consumers and give them the ability to "opt out." Because the FCRA is not subject to strict First Amendment scrutiny, however, Congress had no obligation to choose the least restrictive means of accomplishing its goal.

Finally, Trans Union argues that the FCRA is underinclusive because it applies only to consumer reporting agencies and not to other companies that sell consumer information. But given consumer reporting agencies' unique "access to a broad range of continually-updated, detailed information about millions of consumers' personal credit histories," we think it not at all inappropriate for Congress to have singled out consumer reporting agencies for regulation. . . .

NOTES & QUESTIONS

1. **U.S. West *vs.* Trans Union.** Compare *U.S. West* with *Trans Union*. Are these cases consistent with each other? Which case's reasoning strikes you as more persuasive?
2. **Trans Union II.** In *Trans Union v. FTC*, 295 F.3d 42 (D.C. Cir. 2002) (*Trans Union II*), Trans Union sued to enjoin regulations promulgated pursuant to the Gramm-Leach-Bliley (GLB) Act, alleging, among other things, that they violated the First Amendment. Trans Union argued that these regulations would prevent it from selling credit headers, which consist of a consumer's

name, address, Social Security number, and phone number. Trans Union contended that the sale of credit headers is commercial speech. The court concluded that Trans Union's First Amendment arguments were "foreclosed" by its earlier opinion in *Trans Union v. FTC,* which resolved that "the government interest in 'protecting the privacy of consumer credit information' 'is substantial.'"

3. ***Free Speech and the Fair Information Practices.*** Recall the discussion of the Fair Information Practices from Chapter 6. The Fair Information Practices provide certain limitations on the uses and disclosure of personal information. Eugene Volokh contends:

> I am especially worried about the normative power of the notion that the government has a compelling interest in creating "codes of fair information practices" restricting true statements made by nongovernmental speakers. The protection of free speech generally rests on an assumption that it's not for the government to decide which speech is "fair" and which isn't; the unfairnesses, excesses, and bad taste of speakers are something that current First Amendment principles generally require us to tolerate. Once people grow to accept and even like government restrictions on one kind of supposedly "unfair" communication of facts, it may become much easier for people to accept "codes of fair reporting," "codes of fair debate," "codes of fair filmmaking," "codes of fair political criticism," and the like. . . .[87]

Consider Paul Schwartz, who contends that free discourse is promoted by the protection of privacy:

> When the government requires fair information practices for the private sector, has it created a right to stop people from speaking about you? As an initial point, I emphasize that the majority of the core fair information practices do not involve the government preventing disclosure of personal information. [The fair information practices generally require: (1) the creation of a statutory fabric that defines obligations with respect to the use of personal information; (2) the maintenance of processing systems that are understandable to the concerned individual (transparency); (3) the assignment of limited procedural and substantive rights to the individual; and (4) the establishment of effective oversight of data use, whether through individual litigation (self-help), a government role (external oversight), or some combination of these approaches.] . . . [F]air information practices one, two, and four regulate the business practices of private entities without silencing their speech. No prevention of speech about anyone takes place, for example, when the Fair Credit Reporting Act of 1970 requires that certain information be given to a consumer when an "investigative consumer report" is prepared about her.
>
> These nonsilencing fair information practices are akin to a broad range of other measures that regulate information use in the private sector and do not abridge the freedom of speech under any interpretation of the First Amendment. The First Amendment does not prevent the government from requiring product labels on food products or the use of "plain English" by

---

[87] Eugene Volokh, *Freedom of Speech and Information Privacy: The Troubling Implications of a Right to Stop People from Speaking About You*, 52 Stan. L. Rev. 1049, 1090 (2000).

> publicly traded companies in reports sent to their investors or Form 10-Ks filed with the Securities and Exchange Commission. Nor does the First Amendment forbid privacy laws such as the Children's Online Privacy Protection Act, which assigns parents a right of access to their children's online data profiles. The ultimate merit of these laws depends on their specific context and precise details, but such experimentation by the State should be viewed as noncontroversial on free speech grounds.
>
> Nevertheless, one subset of fair information practices does correspond to Volokh's idea of information privacy as the right to stop people from speaking about you. . . . [S]o long as [laws protecting personal information disclosure] are viewpoint neutral, these laws are a necessary element of safeguarding free communication in our democratic society. . . .
>
> . . . [A] democratic order depends on both an underlying personal capacity for self-governance and the participation of individuals in community and democratic self-rule. Privacy law thus has an important role in protecting individual self-determination and democratic deliberation. By providing access to one's personal data, information about how it will be processed, and other fair information practices, the law seeks to structure the terms on which individuals confront the information demands of the community, private bureaucratic entities, and the State. Attention to these issues by the legal order is essential to the health of a democracy, which ultimately depends on individual communicative competence.[88]

4. ***Is Information Speech?*** Is the collection, use, and/or transfer of personal information a form of speech? Or is it merely trade in property?

Eugene Volokh contends that such information processing constitutes speech:

> Many . . . databases — for instance, credit history databases or criminal record databases — are used by people to help them decide whom it is safe to deal with and who is likely to cheat them. Other databases, which contain less incriminating information, such as a person's shopping patterns . . . [contain] data [that] is of direct daily life interest to its recipients, since it helps them find out with whom they should do business.[89]

Further, Volokh contends: "[I]t is no less speech when a credit bureau sends credit information to a business. The owners and managers of a credit bureau are communicating information to decisionmakers, such as loan officers, at the recipient business."[90]

Daniel Solove recognizes that some forms of database information transfer and use can constitute speech:

> There are no easy analytic distinctions as to what is or is not "speech." The "essence" of information is neither a good, nor is it speech, for information can be used in ways that make it akin to either one. It is the *use* of the information that determines what information is, not anything inherent in the information itself. If I sell you a book, I have engaged in a commercial transaction. I sold the book as a good. However, the book is also expressing

---

[88] Paul M. Schwartz, *Free Speech vs. Information Privacy: Eugene Volokh's First Amendment Jurisprudence,* 52 Stan. L. Rev. 1559 (2000).

[89] Volokh, *Freedom of Speech, supra,* at 1093-94.

[90] *Id.* at 1083-84.

> something. Even though books are sold as goods, the government cannot pass a law restricting the topics of what books can be sold. . . .
>
> Volokh appears to view all information dissemination that is communicative as speech. Under Volokh's view, therefore, most forms of information dissemination would be entitled to equal First Amendment protection. . . .
>
> However, Volokh's view would lead to severe conflicts with much modern regulation. Full First Amendment protection would apply to statements about a company's earnings and other information regulated by the SEC, insider trading, quid pro quo sexual harassment, fraudulent statements, perjury, bribery, blackmail, extortion, conspiracy, and so on. One could neatly exclude these examples from the category of speech, eliminating the necessity for First Amendment analysis. Although this seems the easiest approach, it is conceptually sloppy or even dishonest absent a meaningful way to argue that these examples do not involve communication. I contend that these examples of highly regulated forms of communication have not received the full rigor of standard First Amendment analysis because of policy considerations. Categorizing them as nonspeech conceals these policy considerations under the façade of an analytical distinction that thus far has not been persuasively articulated.
>
> I am not eschewing all attempts at categorization between speech and nonspeech. To do so would make the First Amendment applicable to virtually anything that is expressive or communicative. Still, the distinction as currently constituted hides its ideological character. . . .
>
> Dealing with privacy issues by categorizing personal information as nonspeech is undesirable because it cloaks the real normative reasons for why society wants to permit greater regulation of certain communicative activity. Rather than focusing on distinguishing between speech and nonspeech, the determination about what forms of information to regulate should center on policy considerations. These policy considerations should turn on the uses of the information rather than on notions about the inherent nature of the information.[91]

Solove goes on to argue that although transfers of personal information may be speech, they are of lower value than other forms of free speech, such as political speech. He contends that whereas speech of public concern is of high value, speech of private concern is given a lower constitutional value, and hence less stringent scrutiny, as is commercial speech and other lower-value categories of speech.

Neil Richards, however, contends that "most privacy regulation that interrupts information flows in the context of an express or implied commercial relationship is neither 'speech' within the current meaning of the First Amendment, nor should it be viewed as such." He criticizes Schwartz and Solove because "they grant too much ground to the First Amendment critique, and may ultimately prove to be underprotective of privacy interests, particularly in the database context." Richards finds Solove's contextual balancing approach too messy to "provide meaningfully increased protection for privacy in the courts." Richards argues instead for a categorical solution

---

[91] Daniel J. Solove, *The Virtues of Knowing Less: Justifying Privacy Protections Against Disclosure,* 53 Duke L.J. 967, 979-80 (2003).

and contends that much regulation of speech in the commercial context should be seen as falling entirely outside the scope of the heightened First Amendment scrutiny:

> This might be the case because the speech is threatening, obscene, or libelous, and thus part of the "established" categories of "unprotected speech." But it might also be the case because the speech is an insider trading tip, . . . an offer to create a monopoly in restraint of trade, or a breach of the attorney-client privilege. In either case, the speech would be outside the scope of the First Amendment and could be regulated as long as a rational basis existed for so doing. . . .
>
> [I]nformation disclosure rules that are the product of generally applicable laws fall outside the scope of the First Amendment. Where information is received by an entity in violation of some other legal rule — whether breach of contract, trespass, theft, or fraud — the First Amendment creates no barrier to the government's ability to prevent and punish disclosure. This is the case even if the information is newsworthy or otherwise of public concern. . . .
>
> From a First Amendment perspective, no such equivalently important social function [as dissemination of information by the press] . . . is played by database companies engaged in the trade of personal data. Indeed, a general law regulating the commercial trade in personal data by database, profiling, and marketing companies is far removed from the core speech protected by the First Amendment, and is much more like the "speech" outside the boundaries of heightened review.

Richards goes on to equate the First Amendment critique of privacy regulation to *Lochnerism,* where the Supreme Court in *Lochner v. New York,* 198 U.S. 45 (1905), struck down a statute regulating the hours bakers could work per week based on "freedom of contract." *Lochner* was, and remains, highly criticized for being an impediment to New Deal legislation by an activist ideological Court. Richards notes:

> [T]here are some fairly strong parallels between the traditional conception of *Lochner* and the First Amendment critique of data privacy legislation. Both theories are judicial responses to calls for legal regulation of the economic and social dislocations caused by rapid technological change. *Lochnerism* addressed a major socio-technological problem of the industrial age — the power differential between individuals and businesses in industrial working conditions, while the First Amendment critique is addressed to a major socio-technological problem of our information age — the power differential between individuals and businesses over information in the electronic environment. Both theories place a libertarian gloss upon the Constitution, interpreting it to mandate either "freedom of contract" or "freedom of information." Both theories seek to place certain forms of economic regulation beyond the power of legislatures to enact. And both theories are eagerly supported by business interests keen to immunize themselves from regulation under the aegis of Constitutional doctrine. To the extent that the First Amendment critique is similar to the traditional view of *Lochner,* then, its elevation of an economic right to first-order constitutional magnitude seems similarly dubious.[92]

---

[92] Neil Richards, *Reconciling Data Privacy and the First Amendment,* 52 UCLA L. Rev. 1149, 1169, 1180, 1172-73, 1206, 1212-13 (2005).

E. GOVERNMENT ACCESS TO PRIVATE SECTOR RECORDS

1. INFORMATION GATHERING WITHOUT SEARCH WARRANTS

(a) Subpoenas

A subpoena is an order to obtain testimony or documents. Numerous statutes authorize federal agencies to issue subpoenas. In *Doe v. Ashcroft,* 334 F. Supp. 2d 471 (S.D.N.Y. 2004), the court explained:

> For example, the Internal Revenue Service (IRS) may issue subpoenas to investigate possible violations of the tax code, and the Securities Exchange Commission (SEC) may issue subpoenas to investigate possible violations of the securities laws. More obscure examples include the Secretary of Agriculture's power to issue subpoenas in investigating and enforcing laws related to honey research, and the Secretary of Commerce's power to issue subpoenas in investigating and enforcing halibut fishing laws. . . .
>
> Where an agency seeks a court order to enforce a subpoena against a resisting subpoena recipient, courts will enforce the subpoena as long as: (1) the agency's investigation is being conducted pursuant to a legitimate purpose, (2) the inquiry is relevant to that purpose, (3) the information is not already within the agency's possession, and (4) the proper procedures have been followed. The Second Circuit has described these standards as "minimal." Even if an administrative subpoena meets these initial criteria to be enforceable, its recipient may nevertheless affirmatively challenge the subpoena on other grounds, such as an allegation that it was issued with an improper purpose or that the information sought is privileged.

In contrast to an administrative subpoena, an ordinary subpoena may be issued in civil or criminal cases. For criminal cases, the government may obtain a subpoena from the clerk of court. Subpoenas are not issued directly by judges. Instead, "[t]he clerk must issue a blank subpoena — signed and sealed — to the party requesting it, and that party must fill in the blanks before the subpoena is served." Fed. R. Crim. P. 17(a). Failure to comply with a subpoena can lead to contempt of court sanctions. A subpoena can broadly compel the production of various documents and items:

> A subpoena may order the witness to produce any books, papers, documents, data, or other objects the subpoena designates. The court may direct the witness to produce the designated items in court before trial or before they are to be offered in evidence. When the items arrive, the court may permit the parties and their attorneys to inspect all or part of them. Fed. R. Crim. P. 17(c)(1).

If the party served with the subpoena has an objection, she may bring a motion to quash or modify the subpoena. "[T]he court may quash or modify the subpoena if compliance would be unreasonable or oppressive." Fed. R. Crim. P. 17(c)(2). As *Doe v. Ashcroft,* 334 F. Supp. 2d 471 (S.D.N.Y. 2004) explains:

> The reasonableness of a subpoena depends on the context. For example, to survive a motion to quash, a subpoena issued in connection with a criminal trial

> "must make a reasonably specific request for information that would be both relevant and admissible at trial." By contrast, a grand jury subpoena is generally enforced as long as there is a "reasonable possibility that the category of materials the Government seeks will produce information relevant to the general subject of the grand jury's investigation." Considering the grand jury's broad investigatory power and minimal court supervision, it is accurate to observe, as the Second Circuit did long ago, that "[b]asically the grand jury is a law enforcement agency."

When do subpoenas violate the Fourth or Fifth Amendments? Subpoenas can compel the production of documents with incriminating information. Recall that in *Boyd v. United States,* 116 U.S. 616 (1886), the Supreme Court concluded that the government was barred from obtaining a person's papers or documents via a subpoena. However, the Court reversed course in *Hale v. Henkel,* 201 U.S. 43 (1906), when it concluded that the administrative state depended upon the government's ability to subpoena business documents. The Court made a "clear distinction . . . between an individual and a corporation."

Later on, in *Couch v. United States,* 409 U.S. 322 (1973), the Court held that tax records could be subpoenaed without violating the Fourth or Fifth Amendments: "[In a] situation where obligations of disclosure exist and under a system largely dependent upon honest self-reporting even to survive . . . [people] cannot reasonably claim, either for Fourth or Fifth Amendment purposes, an expectation of protected privacy or confidentiality." Then, in *Fisher v. United States,* 425 U.S. 391 (1976), the Court expanded its holding in *Couch* to encompass the disclosure not just of corporate documents or tax records but of nearly all private papers. Christopher Slobogin notes that this was an alteration in the Court's jurisprudence because the Court had long maintained a distinction between corporate records and personal papers. Later cases cut back on the breadth of *Fisher,* holding that the act of a party producing a document can constitute a Fifth Amendment violation. *See, e.g., United States v. Hubbell,* 530 U.S. 27 (2000).[93] However, as Christopher Slobogin notes, the "lion's share of subpoenas that seek personal papers . . . are directed at third parties." In the next section, consider the Court's approach to the applicability of the Fourth Amendment to information held by third parties.

GONZALES V. GOOGLE

234 F.R.D. 674 (N.D. Cal. 2006)

[The government sought information for its use in *ACLU v. Gonzales*, No. 98-CV-5591, pending in the Eastern District of Pennsylvania. That case involved a challenge by the ACLU to the Children's Online Protection Act (COPA). Google was not a party to that case, but the government subpoenaed from Google: (1) URL samples: "[a]ll URL's that are available to be located to a query on your company's search engine as of July 31, 2005" and (2) search queries: "[a]ll queries that have been entered on your company's search engine between June 1,

---

[93] For an excellent history of the Supreme Court's jurisprudence regarding subpoenas, see Christopher Slobogin, *Subpoenas and Privacy,* 53 DePaul L. Rev. 805 (2005).

2005 and July 31, 2005 inclusive." Subsequently, the government narrowed its URL sample demand to 50,000 URLs and it narrowed its search query demand to all queries during a one-week period rather than the two-month period mentioned above. Google still raised a challenge, and the government again narrowed its search query request for only 5,000 entries from Google's query log. It continued to seek a sample of 50,000 URLs from Google's search index. Under Federal Rule of Civil Procedure 26, a subpoena sought must be "reasonably calculated to lead to admissible evidence." It may be quashed if the "burden or expense of the proposed discovery outweighs its likely benefit."]

WARE, J. . . . As narrowed by negotiations with Google and through the course of this Miscellaneous Action, the Government now seeks a sample of 50,000 URLs from Google's search index. In determining whether the information sought is reasonably calculated to lead to admissible evidence, the party seeking the information must first provide the Court with its plans for the requested information. The Government's disclosure of its plans for the sample of URLs is incomplete. The actual methodology disclosed in the Government's papers as to the search index sample is, in its entirety, as follows: "A human being will browse a random sample of 5,000-10,000 URLs from Google's index and categorize those sites by content" and from this information, the Government intends to "estimate . . . the aggregate properties of the websites that search engines have indexed." The Government's disclosure only describes its methodology for a study to categorize the URLs in Google's search index, and does not disclose a study regarding the effectiveness of filtering software. Absent any explanation of how the "aggregate properties" of material on the Internet is germane to the underlying litigation, the Government's disclosure as to its planned categorization study is not particularly helpful in determining whether the sample of Google's search index sought is reasonably calculated to lead to admissible evidence in the underlying litigation.

Based on the Government's statement that this information is to act as a "test set for the study" and a general statement that the purpose of the study is to "evaluate the effectiveness of content filtering software," the Court is able to envision a study whereby a sample of 50,000 URLs from the Google search index may be reasonably calculated to lead to admissible evidence on measuring the effectiveness of filtering software. In such a study, the Court imagines, the URLs would be categorized, run through the filtering software, and the effectiveness of the filtering software ascertained as to the various categories of URLs. The Government does not even provide this rudimentary level of general detail as to what it intends to do with the sample of URLs to evaluate the effectiveness of filtering software, and at the hearing neither confirmed nor denied the Court's speculations about the study. In fact, the Government seems to indicate that such a study is not what it has in mind: "[t]he government seeks this information *only* to perform a study, in the aggregate, of trends on the Internet" (emphasis added), with no explanation of how an aggregate study of Internet trends would be reasonably calculated to lead to admissible evidence in the underlying suit where the efficacy of filtering software is at issue. . . .

Given the broad definition of relevance in Rule 26, and the current narrow scope of the subpoena, despite the vagueness with which the Government has disclosed its study, the Court gives the Government the benefit of the doubt. The Court finds that 50,000 URLs randomly selected from Google's data base for use in a scientific study of the effectiveness of filters is relevant to the issues in the case of *ACLU v. Gonzales.*[94]

In its original subpoena the Government sought a listing of the text of all search queries entered by Google users over a two month period. As defined in the Government's subpoena, "queries" include only the text of the search string entered by a user, and not "any additional information that may be associated with such a text string that would identify the person who entered the text string into the search engine, or the computer from which the text string was entered." The Government has narrowed its request so that it now seeks only a sample of 5,000 such queries from Google's query log. The Government discloses its plans for the query log information as follows: "A random sample of approximately 1,000 Google queries from a one-week period will be run through the Google search engine. A human being will browse the top URLs returned by each search and categorize the sites by content." . . .

Google also argues that it will be unduly burdened by loss of user trust if forced to produce its users' queries to the Government. Google claims that its success is attributed in large part to the volume of its users and these users may be attracted to its search engine because of the privacy and anonymity of the service. According to Google, even a perception that Google is acquiescing to the Government's demands to release its query log would harm Google's business by deterring some searches by some users.

Google's own privacy statement indicates that Google users could not reasonably expect Google to guard the query log from disclosure to the Government. . . . Google's privacy policy does not represent to users that it keeps confidential any information other than "personal information." Neither Google's URLs nor the text of search strings with "personal information" redacted, are reasonably "personal information" under Google's stated privacy policy. Google's privacy policy indicates that it has not suggested to its users that non-"personal information" such as that sought by the Government is kept confidential.

However, even if an expectation by Google users that Google would prevent disclosure to the Government of its users' search queries is not entirely reasonable, the statistic cited by Dr. Stark that over a quarter of all Internet searches are for pornography indicates that at least some of Google's users expect some sort of privacy in their searches. The expectation of privacy by some Google users may not be reasonable, but may nonetheless have an appreciable impact on the way in which Google is perceived, and consequently the frequency with which users use Google. Such an expectation does not rise to the level of an absolute privilege, but does indicate that there is a potential burden as to Google's loss of goodwill if Google is forced to disclose search queries to the Government.

---

[94] To the extent that the Government is gathering this information for some other purpose than to run the sample of Google's search index through various filters to determine the efficacy of those filters, the Court would take a different view of the relevance of the information. For example, the Court would not find the information relevant if it is being sought just to characterize the nature of the URL's in Google's database.

Rule 45(c)(3)(B) provides additional protections where a subpoena seeks trade secret or confidential commercial information from a nonparty. . . . Because Google still continues to claim information about its entire search index and entire query log as confidential, the Court will presume that the requested information, as a small sample of proprietary information, may be somewhat commercially sensitive, albeit not independently commercially sensitive. Successive disclosures, whether in this lawsuit or pursuant to subsequent civil subpoenas, in the aggregate could yield confidential commercial information about Google's search index or query log. . . .

What the Government has not demonstrated, however, is a substantial need for *both* the information contained in the sample of URLs and sample of search query text. Furthermore, even if the information requested is not a trade secret, a district court may in its discretion limit discovery on a finding that "the discovery sought is unreasonably cumulative or duplicative, or is obtainable from some other source that is more convenient, less burdensome, or less expensive." Rule 26(b)(2)(i).

Faced with duplicative discovery, and with the Government not expressing a preference as to which source of the test set of URLs it prefers, this Court exercises its discretion pursuant to Rule 26(b)(2) and determines that the marginal burden of loss of trust by Google's users based on Google's disclosure of its users' search queries to the Government outweighs the duplicative disclosure's likely benefit to the Government's study. Accordingly, the Court grants the Government's motion to compel only as to the sample of 50,000 URLs from Google's search index.

The Court raises, sua sponte, its concerns about the privacy of Google's users apart from Google's business goodwill argument. . . .

Although the Government has only requested the text strings entered, basic identifiable information may be found in the text strings when users search for personal information such as their social security numbers or credit card numbers through Google in order to determine whether such information is available on the Internet. The Court is also aware of so-called "vanity searches," where a user queries his or her own name perhaps with other information. . . . This concern, combined with the prevalence of Internet searches for sexually explicit material — generally not information that anyone wishes to reveal publicly — gives this Court pause as to whether the search queries themselves may constitute potentially sensitive information.

The Court also recognizes that there may a difference between a private litigant receiving potentially sensitive information and having this information be produced to the Government pursuant to civil subpoena. . . . Even though counsel for the Government assured the Court that the information received will only be used for the present litigation, it is conceivable that the Government may have an obligation to pursue information received for unrelated litigation purposes under certain circumstances regardless of the restrictiveness of a protective order. The Court expressed this concern at oral argument as to queries such as "bomb placement white house," but queries such as "communist berkeley parade route protest war" may also raise similar concerns. In the end, the Court need not express an opinion on this issue because the Government's motion is granted only as to the sample of URLs and not as to the log of search queries.

The Court also refrains from expressing an opinion on the applicability of the Electronic Communications Privacy Act. . . . The Court only notes that the ECPA does not bar the Government's request for sample of 50,000 URLs from Google's index though civil subpoena.

NOTES & QUESTIONS

1. ***URL Samples vs. Search Queries.*** The sought-after subpoena in *Gonzales v. Google* concerned information about both URL samples and search queries. What decision did the district court reach for each type of data? Are there different privacy implications for governmental access to the two kinds of information?
2. ***Can People Be Identified from Anonymous Search Data?*** An incident involving AOL proved that individuals can be identified based on their search queries. In August 2006, AOL revealed that it had released to researchers about 20 million search queries made by over 650,000 users of its search engine. Although AOL had substituted numerical IDs for the subscribers' actual user names, the personal identity of the user could be found based on the search queries. The *New York Times* demonstrated as much by tracking down AOL user No. 4417749; it linked this person's data trail to a 62-year old widow who lived in Lilburn, Georgia, and admitted to the reporter, "Those are my searches."[95]

(b) Financial Information and the Third Party Doctrine

THE BANK SECRECY ACT

The Bank Secrecy Act, Pub. L. No. 91-508, was enacted by Congress in 1970. The Act requires the retention of bank records and creation of reports that would be useful in criminal, tax, or regulatory investigations or proceedings. The Bank Secrecy Act was passed because of worry that shifting from paper to computer records would make white collar law enforcement more complicated.[96] The Act requires that federally insured banks record the identities of account holders as well as copies of each check, draft, or other financial instrument. Not all records and financial instruments must be maintained; only those that the Secretary of the Treasury designates as having a "high degree of usefulness." 12 U.S.C. § 1829b. Further, the Act authorizes the Secretary of the Treasury to promulgate regulations for the reporting of domestic financial transactions. 31 U.S.C. § 1081. The regulations require that a report be made for every deposit, withdrawal, or other transfer of currency exceeding $10,000. *See* 31 C.F.R. § 103.22. For transactions exceeding $5,000 into or out of the United States, the amount, the date of receipt, the form of financial instrument, and the person who received it must be reported. *See* 31 C.F.R. §§ 103.23, 103.25.

---

[95] Michael Barbaro & Tom Zeller, Jr., A Face is Exposed for AOL Searcher No. 4417749, N.Y. Times, Aug. 9, 2006.

[96] H. Jeff Smith, *Managing Privacy* 24 (1994).

CALIFORNIA BANKERS ASSOCIATION V. SHULTZ

416 U.S. 21 (1974)

[A group of bankers as well as depositors challenged the Bank Secrecy Act as a violation of the First, Fourth, and Fifth Amendments. The Court held that the Act did not violate the Fourth Amendment. First, the Court held that the bankers did not possess Fourth Amendment rights in the information because "corporations can claim no equality with individuals in the enjoyment of a right to privacy." Second, as to the Fourth Amendment rights of the individual depositors, the Court concluded that they lacked standing to pursue their claims.]

REHNQUIST, J. . . . The complaint filed in the District Court by the ACLU and the depositors contains no allegation by any of the individual depositors that they were engaged in the type of $10,000 domestic currency transaction which would necessitate that their bank report it to the Government. . . . [W]e simply cannot assume that the mere fact that one is a depositor in a bank means that he has engaged or will engage in a transaction involving more than $10,000 in currency, which is the only type of domestic transaction which the Secretary's regulations require that the banks report. That being so, the depositor plaintiffs lack standing to challenge the domestic reporting regulations, since they do not show that their transactions are required to be reported. . . .

We therefore hold that the Fourth Amendment claims of the depositor plaintiffs may not be considered on the record before us. Nor do we think that the California Bankers Association or the Security National Bank can vicariously assert such Fourth Amendment claims on behalf of bank customers in general. . .

[The Court also rejected a Fifth Amendment challenge to the Act as well as a First Amendment challenge. With regard to the First Amendment challenge, the Court concluded that the "threat to any First Amendment rights of the ACLU or its members from the mere existence of the records in the hands of the bank is a good deal more remote than the threat assertedly posed by the Army's system of compilation and distribution of information which we declined to adjudicate in *Laird v. Tatum*, 408 U.S. 1 (1972)."]

DOUGLAS, J. dissenting. . . . One's reading habits furnish telltale clues to those who are bent on bending us to one point of view. What one buys at the hardware and retail stores may furnish clues to potential uses of wires, soap powders, and the like used by criminals. A mandatory recording of all telephone conversations would be better than the recording of checks under the Bank Secrecy Act, if Big Brother is to have his way. The records of checks — now available to the investigators — are highly useful. In a sense a person is defined by the checks he writes. By examining them the agents get to know his doctors, lawyers, creditors, political allies, social connections, religious affiliation, educational interests, the papers and magazines he reads, and so on ad infinitum. These are all tied to one's social security number; and now that we have the data banks, these other items will enrich that storehouse and make it possible for a bureaucrat — by pushing one button — to get in an instant the names of the 190 million Americans who are subversives or potential and likely candidates.

It is, I submit, sheer nonsense to agree with the Secretary that all bank records of every citizen "have a high degree of usefulness in criminal, tax, or regulatory investigations or proceedings." That is unadulterated nonsense unless we are to assume that every citizen is a crook, an assumption I cannot make.

Since the banking transactions of an individual give a fairly accurate account of his religion, ideology, opinions, and interests, a regulation impounding them and making them automatically available to all federal investigative agencies is a sledge-hammer approach to a problem that only a delicate scalpel can manage. Where fundamental personal rights are involved — as is true when as here the Government gets large access to one's beliefs, ideas, politics, religion, cultural concerns, and the like — the Act should be "narrowly drawn" to meet the precise evil. Bank accounts at times harbor criminal plans. But we only rush with the crowd when we vent on our banks and their customers the devastating and leveling requirements of the present Act. I am not yet ready to agree that America is so possessed with evil that we must level all constitutional barriers to give our civil authorities the tools to catch criminals. . . .

UNITED STATES V. MILLER

425 U.S. 435 (1976)

POWELL, J. . . . [A]gents from the Treasury Department's Alcohol, Tobacco and Firearms Bureau presented grand jury subpoenas issued in blank by the clerk of the District Court, and completed by the United States Attorney's office, to the presidents of the Citizens & Southern National Bank of Warner Robins and the Bank of Byron, where respondent maintained accounts. The subpoenas required the two presidents to appear on January 24, 1973, and to produce [all records of loans as well as savings and checking accounts in the name of Mitch Miller]. . . .

The banks did not advise respondent that the subpoenas had been served but ordered their employees to make the records available and to provide copies of any documents the agents desired. . . .

The grand jury met on February 12, 1973, 19 days after the return date on the subpoenas. Respondent and four others were indicted. . . . The record does not indicate whether any of the bank records were in fact presented to the grand jury. They were used in the investigation and provided "one or two" investigatory leads. Copies of the checks also were introduced at trial to establish the overt acts [in a conspiracy in which the defendants were charged].

In his motion to suppress, denied by the District Court, respondent contended that the bank documents were illegally seized. It was urged that the subpoenas were defective because they were issued by the United States Attorney rather than a court, no return was made to a court, and the subpoenas were returnable on a date when the grand jury was not in session. The Court of Appeals reversed. Citing the prohibition in *Boyd v. United States*, 116 U.S. 616, 622 (1886), against "compulsory production of a man's private papers to establish a criminal charge against him," the court held that the Government had improperly circumvented *Boyd*'s protections of respondent's Fourth Amendment right against "unreasonable searches and seizures" by "first requiring a third party bank to copy all of its depositors' personal checks and then, with an improper invocation of legal process, calling upon the bank to allow inspection and reproduction of those copies." . . . The subpoenas issued here were found not to constitute adequate "legal process." The fact that the bank officers cooperated voluntarily was found to be irrelevant, for "he whose rights are threatened by the improper disclosure here was a bank depositor, not a bank official." . . .

We find that there was no intrusion into any area in which respondent had a protected Fourth Amendment interest and that the District Court therefore correctly denied respondent's motion to suppress. . . .

On their face, the documents subpoenaed here are not respondent's "private papers." Unlike the claimant in *Boyd* [*v. United States*], respondent can assert neither ownership nor possession. Instead, these are the business records of the banks. Respondent argues, however, that the Bank Secrecy Act introduces a factor that makes the subpoena in this case the functional equivalent of a search and seizure of the depositor's "private papers." We have held, in *California Bankers Ass'n v. Shultz*, that the mere maintenance of records pursuant to the requirements of the Act "invade(s) no Fourth Amendment right of any depositor." But respondent contends that the combination of the recordkeeping requirements of the Act and the issuance of a subpoena to obtain those records permits the Government to circumvent the requirements of the Fourth Amendment by allowing it to obtain a depositor's private records without complying with the legal requirements that would be applicable had it proceeded against him directly. Therefore, we must address the question whether the compulsion embodied in the Bank Secrecy Act as exercised in this case creates a Fourth Amendment interest in the depositor where none existed before. This question was expressly reserved in *California Bankers Ass'n.*

Respondent urges that he has a Fourth Amendment interest in the records kept by the banks because they are merely copies of personal records that were made available to the banks for a limited purpose and in which he has a reasonable expectation of privacy. He relies on this Court's statement in *Katz v. United States*, 389 U.S. 347, 353 (1967), that "we have . . . departed from the narrow view" that "'property interests control the right of the Government to search and seize,'" and that a "search and seizure" become unreasonable when the Government's activities violate "the privacy upon which (a person) justifiably relie[s]." But in *Katz* the Court also stressed that "[w]hat a person knowingly exposes to the public . . . is not a subject of Fourth Amendment protection." We must examine the nature of the particular documents sought to be protected in order to determine whether there is a legitimate "expectation of privacy" concerning their contents.

Even if we direct our attention to the original checks and deposit slips, rather than to the microfilm copies actually viewed and obtained by means of the subpoena, we perceive no legitimate "expectation of privacy" in their contents. The checks are not confidential communications but negotiable instruments to be used in commercial transactions. All of the documents obtained, including financial statements and deposit slips, contain only information voluntarily conveyed to the banks and exposed to their employees in the ordinary course of business. The lack of any legitimate expectation of privacy concerning the information kept in bank records was assumed by Congress in enacting the Bank Secrecy Act, the expressed purpose of which is to require records to be maintained because they "have a high degree of usefulness in criminal tax, and regulatory investigations and proceedings." 12 U.S.C. § 1829b(a)(1).

The depositor takes the risk, in revealing his affairs to another, that the information will be conveyed by that person to the Government. This Court has held repeatedly that the Fourth Amendment does not prohibit the obtaining of information revealed to a third party and conveyed by him to Government authorities, even if the information is revealed on the assumption that it will be used only for a limited purpose and the confidence placed in the third party will not be betrayed.

This analysis is not changed by the mandate of the Bank Secrecy Act that records of depositors' transactions be maintained by banks. In *California Bankers Ass'n v. Shultz,* we rejected the contention that banks, when keeping records of their depositors' transactions pursuant to the Act, are acting solely as agents of the Government. But, even if the banks could be said to have been acting solely as Government agents in transcribing the necessary information and complying without protest with the requirements of the subpoenas, there would be no intrusion upon the depositors' Fourth Amendment rights. . . .

Since no Fourth Amendment interests of the depositor are implicated here, this case is governed by the general rule that the issuance of a subpoena to a third party to obtain the records of that party does not violate the rights of a defendant, even if a criminal prosecution is contemplated at the time of the subpoena is issued. Under these principles, it was firmly settled, before the passage of the Bank Secrecy Act, that an Internal Revenue Service summons directed to a third-party bank does not violate the Fourth Amendment rights of a depositor under investigation.

Many banks traditionally kept permanent records of their depositors' accounts, although not all banks did so and the practice was declining in recent years. By requiring that such records be kept by all banks, the Bank Secrecy Act is not a novel means designed to circumvent established Fourth Amendment rights. It is merely an attempt to facilitate the use of a proper and long-standing law enforcement technique by insuring that records are available when they are needed.

We hold that the District Court correctly denied respondent's motion to suppress, since he possessed no Fourth Amendment interest that could be vindicated by a challenge to the subpoenas. . . .

BRENNAN, J. dissenting. . . . The pertinent phrasing of the Fourth Amendment "The right of the people to be secure in their persons, houses, papers, and effects, against unreasonable searches and seizures, shall not be violated" is virtually in haec verba as Art. I, § 19, of the California Constitution "The right of the people to be secure in their persons, houses, papers, and effects, against unreasonable seizures and searches, shall not be violated." The California Supreme Court has reached a conclusion under Art. I, § 13, in the same factual situation, contrary to that reached by the Court today under the Fourth Amendment. I dissent because in my view the California Supreme Court correctly interpreted the relevant constitutional language. . . .

Addressing the threshold question whether the accused's right of privacy was invaded, and relying on part on the decision of the Court of Appeals in this case, Mr. Justice Mosk stated in his excellent opinion for a unanimous court:

> It cannot be gainsaid that the customer of a bank expects that the documents, such as checks, which he transmits to the bank in the course of his business operations, will remain private, and that such an expectation is reasonable. The prosecution concedes as much, although it asserts that this expectation is not constitutionally cognizable. Representatives of several banks testified at the suppression hearing that information in their possession regarding a customer's account is deemed by them to be confidential.
>
> In the present case, although the record establishes that copies of petitioner's bank statements rather than of his checks were provided to the officer, the distinction is not significant with relation to petitioner's expectation of privacy. That the bank alters the form in which it records the information transmitted to it by the depositor to show the receipt and disbursement of money on a bank statement does not diminish the depositor's anticipation of privacy in the matters which he confides to the bank. A bank customer's reasonable expectation is that, absent compulsion by legal process, the matters he reveals to the bank will be utilized by the bank only for internal banking purposes. Thus, we hold petitioner had a reasonable expectation that the bank would maintain the confidentiality of those papers which originated with him in check form and of the bank statements into which a record of those same checks had been transformed pursuant to internal bank practice. . . .
>
> The underlying dilemma in this and related cases is that the bank, a detached and disinterested entity, relinquished the records voluntarily. But that circumstance should not be crucial. For all practical purposes, the disclosure by individuals or business firms of their financial affairs to a bank is not entirely volitional, since it is impossible to participate in the economic life of contemporary society without maintaining a bank account. In the course of such dealings, a depositor reveals many aspects of his personal affairs, opinions, habits and associations. Indeed, the totality of bank records provides a virtual current biography. While we are concerned in the present case only with bank statements, the logical extension of the contention that the bank's ownership of records permits free access to them by any police officer extends far beyond such statements to checks, savings, bonds, loan applications, loan guarantees, and all papers which the customer has supplied to the bank to facilitate the conduct of his financial affairs upon the reasonable assumption that the information would remain confidential. To permit a police officer access to these records merely upon his request, without any judicial control as to relevancy or other traditional requirements of legal process, and to allow the evidence to be used in any subsequent criminal prosecution against a defendant, opens the door to a vast and unlimited range of very real abuses of police power.
>
> Cases are legion that condemn violent searches and invasions of an individual's right to the privacy of his dwelling. The imposition upon privacy, although perhaps not so dramatic, may be equally devastating when other methods are employed. Development of photocopying machines, electronic computers and other sophisticated instruments have accelerated the ability of government to intrude into areas which a person normally chooses to exclude from prying eyes and inquisitive minds. Consequently judicial interpretations of the reach of the constitutional protection of individual privacy must keep pace with the perils created by these new devices. . . .

NOTES & QUESTIONS

1. ***The Right to Financial Privacy Act.*** Two years after *Miller*, in 1978, Congress passed the Right to Financial Privacy Act (RFPA), Pub. L. No. 95-630, which partially filled the void left by *Miller*. The RFPA prevents banks and other financial institutions from disclosing a person's financial information to the government unless the records are disclosed pursuant to subpoena or search warrant. *See* 29 U.S.C. §§ 3401–3422.
2. ***State Law.*** As discussed throughout this book, many states have rejected the Supreme Court's interpretations of the Fourth Amendment, opting to provide additional protections. In 2004, a New Jersey court rejected the reasoning of *Miller*:

> The discomfort in finding a stranger pouring over one's checkbook, deposit slips and cancelled checks is equal to seeing someone sifting through his or her garbage, or reviewing a list of dialed telephone numbers called from home, like telephones, are an extension of one's desk or home office. Indeed, as in the case of the telephone, technological advances in the form of personal computers with access to the internet and electronic banking services have made those services available to the homes of its depositors. Bank records kept at home could not be seized in the absence of a duly issued search warrant based upon probable cause and they should not be vulnerable to viewing, copying, seizure or retrieval simply because they are readily available at a bank.
>
> Finally, the fact that financial affairs are memorialized in written records of banks or maintained in their electronic data systems to which, as part of its legitimate business, a bank's employees have access, does not suggest that persons have any sense that their private and personal traits and affairs are less confidential when they deal with their bank than when they make telephone calls or put out their garbage. The repose of confidence in a bank goes beyond entrustment of money, but extends to the expectation that financial affairs are confidential except as may be reasonable and necessary to conduct customary bank business. *State v. McAllister*, 840 A.2d 967 (2004).

3. ***Pen Registers and* Smith v. Maryland.** Recall the Court's reasoning in *Smith v. Maryland* (Chapter 3), where the Court held that the Fourth Amendment was inapplicable to pen registers of phone numbers. How does the Court's rationale in *Smith* compare to that in *Miller*?
4. ***The Implications of the Third Party Doctrine.*** Daniel Solove contends that *Miller* and *Smith* pose a substantial threat to privacy in the modern world given the dramatic extent to which third parties hold personal information:

> In the Information Age, an increasing amount of personal information is contained in records maintained by private sector entities, Internet Service Providers, phone companies, cable companies, merchants, bookstores, websites, hotels, landlords and employers. Many private sector entities are beginning to aggregate the information in these records to create extensive digital dossiers.
>
> The data in these digital dossiers increasingly flows from the private sector to the government, particularly for law enforcement use. . . . Detailed records of an individual's reading materials, purchases, magazines, diseases and

> ailments, and website activity, enable the government to assemble a profile of an individual's finances, health, psychology, beliefs, politics, interests, and lifestyle. This data can unveil a person's anonymous speech, groups and personal associations.
>
> The increasing amount of personal information flowing to the government poses significant problems with far-reaching social effects. Inadequately constrained government information gathering can lead to at least three types of harms. First, it can result in the slow creep toward a totalitarian state. Second, it can chill democratic activities and interfere with individual self-determination. Third, it can lead to the danger of harms arising in bureaucratic settings. Individuals, especially in times of crisis, are vulnerable to abuse from government misuse of personal information. Once government entities have collected personal information, there are few regulations in how it can be used and how long it can be kept. The bureaucratic nature of modern law enforcement institutions can enable sweeping searches, the misuse of personal data, improper exercises of discretion, unjustified interrogation, arrests, roundups of disfavored individuals, and discriminatory profiling.[97]

Because of the third party doctrine in *Miller* and *Smith*, the Fourth Amendment fails to limit the government from gathering personal information maintained by businesses. *Miller* and *Smith* were decided in the 1970s. Should they be reconsidered in light of the extensive computerized records maintained today? What would be the consequences of overruling *Miller* and *Smith*?

(c) The USA PATRIOT Act § 215

Section 215 of the USA PATRIOT Act adds a new § 501 to the Foreign Intelligence Surveillance Act (FISA):

> (a)(1) The Director of the Federal Bureau of Investigation or a designee of the Director (whose rank shall be no lower than Assistant Special Agent in Charge) may make an application for an order requiring the production of any tangible things (including books, records, papers, documents, and other items) for an investigation to protect against international terrorism or clandestine intelligence activities, provided that such investigation of a United States person is not conducted solely upon the basis of activities protected by the first amendment to the Constitution.
>
> (2) An investigation conducted under this section shall —
>
> (A) be conducted under guidelines approved by the Attorney General under Executive Order 12333 (or a successor order); and
>
> (B) not be conducted of a United States person solely upon the basis of activities protected by the first amendment to the Constitution of the United States.

Applications for court orders shall be made to a judge and "shall specify that the records are sought for an authorized investigation" and "to protect against

[97] Daniel J. Solove, *Digital Dossiers and the Dissipation of Fourth Amendment Privacy*, 75 S. Cal. L. Rev. 1083, 1084-86 (2002).

international terrorism or clandestine intelligence activities." § 501(b). This section also has a gag order:

> (d) No person shall disclose to any other person (other than those persons necessary to produce the tangible things under this section) that the Federal Bureau of Investigation has sought or obtained tangible things under this section. § 501(d).

The American Library Association (ALA) led a spirited campaign against § 215. It issued a resolution stating, in part, that

> the American Library Association encourages all librarians, library administrators, library governing bodies, and library advocates to educate their users, staff, and communities about the process for compliance with the USA PATRIOT Act and other related measures and about the dangers to individual privacy and the confidentiality of library records resulting from those measures.

In 2003, Attorney General John Ashcroft stated that § 215 had never been used to access library records. He further stated: "The fact is, with just 11,000 FBI agents and over a billion visitors to America's libraries each year, the Department of Justice has neither the staffing, the time nor the inclination to monitor the reading habits of Americans. . . . No offense to the American Library Association, but we just don't care." In 2005, the ALA revealed the results of a survey of librarians indicating a minimum of 137 formal law enforcement inquiries to library officials since 9/11, 49 of which were by federal officials and the remainder by state and local officials. The study did not indicate whether any of these were pursuant to § 215.

(d) National Security Letters

Provisions in several laws permit the FBI to obtain personal information from third parties merely by making a written request in cases involving national security. No court order is required. These requests are called "National Security Letters" (NSLs).

The Stored Communications Act. ECPA's Stored Communications Act contains an NSL provision, 18 U.S.C. § 2709. This provision allows the FBI to compel communications companies (ISPs, telephone companies) to release customer records when the FBI makes a particular certification. Before the USA PATRIOT Act, the FBI had to certify that the records were "relevant to an authorized foreign counterintelligence investigation" and that "there are specific and articulable facts giving reason to believe that the person or entity to whom the information sought pertains is a foreign power or an agent of a foreign power as defined in section 101 of the Foreign Intelligence Surveillance Act of 1978 (50 U.S.C. 1801)."

Section 505 of the USA PATRIOT Act amended the National Security Letters provision of ECPA by altering what must be certified. The existing requirements regarding counterintelligence and specific and articulable facts that the target was an agent of a foreign power were deleted. The FBI now needs to certify that the records are "relevant to an authorized investigation to protect against terrorism or clandestine intelligence activities, provided that such an investigation of a United States person is not conducted solely on the basis of activities protected by the first amendment of the Constitution to the United States." 18 U.S.C. § 2709.

This provision also has a gag order:

> No wire or electronic communication service provider, or officer, employee, or agent thereof, shall disclose to any person that the Federal Bureau of Investigation has sought or obtained access to information or records under this section. § 2709(c).

Unlike § 215, Ashcroft made no statement about § 505.[98]

The Right to Financial Privacy Act. The Right to Financial Privacy Act (RFPA) also contains an NSL provision. As amended by the Patriot Act, this provision states that the FBI can obtain an individual's financial records if it "certifies in writing to the financial institution that such records are sought for foreign counter intelligence purposes to protect against international terrorism or clandestine intelligence activities, provided that such an investigation of a United States person is not conducted solely upon the basis of activities protected by the first amendment to the Constitution of the United States." 12 U.S.C. § 3414(a)(5)(A). As with the Stored Communications Act NSL provision, the RFPA NSL provision contains a "gag" rule prohibiting the financial institution from disclosing the fact it received the NSL. § 3414(a)(5)(D).

The Fair Credit Reporting Act. Likewise, the Fair Credit Reporting Act provides for NSLs. Pursuant to a written FBI request, consumer reporting agencies "shall furnish to the Federal Bureau of Investigation the names and addresses of all financial institutions . . . at which a customer maintains or has maintained an account." 15 U.S.C. § 1681u(a). Consumer reporting agencies must also furnish "identifying information respecting a consumer, limited to name, address, former addresses, places of employment, or former places of employment." 15 U.S.C. § 1681u(b). To obtain a full consumer report, however, the FBI must obtain a court order ex parte. 15 U.S.C. § 1681u(c). Like the other NSL provisions, the FCRA NSL provisions restrict NSLs for investigations based "solely" upon First Amendment activities. The FCRA NSL also has a "gag" rule. 15 U.S.C. § 1681u(d).

The USA PATRIOT Reauthorization Act. In the USA PATRIOT Reauthorization Act of 2005, Congress made several amendments that affected NSLs. It explicitly provided for judicial review of NSLs. It also required a detailed examination by the DOJ's Inspector General "of the effectiveness and use, including any improper or illegal use" of NSLs. This kind of audit proved its value in March 2006 when the Inspector General issued its review of the FBI's use of NSLs. First, the Inspector General found a dramatic underreporting of NSLs. Indeed, the total number of NSL requests between 2003 and 2005 totaled

[98] Mark Sidel, *More Secure, Less Free?: Antiterrorism Policy and Civil Liberties After September 11*, at 14 (2004).

at least 143,074. Of these NSLs requests, as the Inspector General found, "[t]he overwhelming majority . . . sought telephone toll billing records information, subscriber information (telephone or e-mail) or electronic communication transaction records under the ECPA NSL statute." [99]

The Inspector General also carried out a limited audit of investigative case files, and found that 22 percent of them contained at least one violation of investigative guidelines or procedures that was not reported to any of the relevant internal authorities at the FBI. Finally, the Inspector General also found over 700 instances in which the FBI obtained telephone records and subscriber information from telephone companies based on the use of a so-called "exigent letter" authority. This authority, absent from the statute, was invented by the FBI's Counterterrorism Division. Having devised this new power, the FBI did not set limits on its use, or track how it was employed. Witnesses told the Inspector General that many of these letters "were not issued in exigent circumstances, and the FBI was unable to determine which letters were sent in emergency circumstances due to inadequate recordkeeping." Indeed, "in most instances, there was no documentation associating the requests with pending national security investigations."[100]

NSL Litigation. In *Doe v. Ashcroft*, 334 F. Supp. 2d 471 (S.D.N.Y. 2004), a federal district court invalidated 18 U.S.C. § 2709 (*Doe I*). It found that § 2709 violated the Fourth Amendment because, at least as applied, it barred or at least substantially deterred a judicial challenge to an NSL request. It did so by prohibiting an NSL recipient from revealing the existence of an NSL inquiry. The court also found that the "all inclusive sweep" of § 2709 violated the First Amendment as a prior-restraint and content-based restriction on sweep that was subject to strict scrutiny review. Additionally, the court found that in some instances the use of an NSL might infringe upon people's First Amendment rights. For example, suppose that the FBI uses an NSL to find out the identity of an anonymous speaker on the Internet. Does the First Amendment limit using an NSL in this manner? Does the First Amendment restriction on the NSL provisions, which prohibits NSLs for investigations based "solely" upon First Amendment activities, adequately address these potential First Amendment problems?

Shortly after *Doe I,* another district court invalidated 18 U.S.C. § 2709(c), which prevented a recipient of an NSL to disclose information about the government's action. *Doe v. Gonzales*, 386 F. Supp. 2d 66, 82 (D. Conn. 2005) (*Doe II*).

While appeals in *Doe I* and *Doe II* were pending, Congress enacted the USA PATRIOT Reauthorization Act of 2005, which made several changes to § 2709 and added several provisions concerning judicial review of NSLs, which were codified at 18 U.S.C. § 3511. Following enactment of these provisions, plaintiffs challenged the amended nondisclosure provisions of §§ 2709(c) and 3511. The same district court that issued the *Doe I* opinion then found §§ 2709(c) and

---

[99] Office of the Inspector General, *A Review of the Federal Bureau of Investigations Use of National Security Letters* x-xiv (Mar. 2007).

[100] *Id.* at xxxviii, xxxiv.

3511(b) to be facially unconstitutional. *Doe v. Gonzales*, 500 F. Supp. 2d 379 (S.D.N.Y. 2007) (*Doe III*).

The newly enacted § 3511 provided for judicial review of NSLs. As a result, the *Doe III* plaintiffs did not challenge it on Fourth Amendment grounds as in *Doe I*. Instead, they argued, and the court agreed, that the nondisclosure provisions of § 2709(c) remained an unconstitutional prior restraint and content-based restriction on speech. The court also concluded that § 3511(b) was unconstitutional under the First Amendment and the doctrine of separation of powers. Among its conclusions, the court noted that Congress in amending § 2709(c) allowed the FBI to certify on a case-by-case basis whether nondisclosure was necessary. Yet, this narrowing of the statute to reduce the possibility of unnecessary limitation of speech also means that the FBI could conceivably engage in viewpoint discrimination. As a consequence, the amended statute was a content-based restriction as well as a prior restraint on speech and, therefore, subject to strict scrutiny.

2. INFORMATION GATHERING WITH SEARCH WARRANTS

Under the Fourth Amendment, a search warrant may be issued if there is probable cause to believe that there is incriminating evidence in the place to be searched. This is not limited to places owned or occupied by the criminal suspect. In certain instances, incriminating documents or things may be possessed by an innocent party. What if that innocent party is a journalist or news entity, and the search implicates First Amendment rights? Consider the following case:

ZURCHER V. THE STANFORD DAILY

436 U.S. 547 (1978)

[A demonstration at the Stanford University Hospital turned violent when police tried to force demonstrators to leave. A group of demonstrators attacked and injured nine police officers. The officers were able to identify only two of the assailants. The *Stanford Daily*, a student newspaper, published articles and photographs about the incident. The District Attorney obtained a search warrant to search the *Daily*'s offices for negatives, film, and pictures about the incident. After the search, the *Daily* brought suit under 42 U.S.C. § 1983, alleging that the search was unconstitutional.]

WHITE, J. . . . The issue here is how the Fourth Amendment is to be construed and applied to the "third party" search, the recurring situation where state authorities have probable cause to believe that fruits, instrumentalities, or other evidence of crime is located on identified property but do not then have probable cause to believe that the owner or possessor of the property is himself implicated in the crime that has occurred or is occurring. . . .

Under existing law, valid warrants may be issued to search *any* property, whether or not occupied by a third party, at which there is probable cause to believe that fruits, instrumentalities, or evidence of a crime will be found.

Nothing on the face of the Amendment suggests that a third-party search warrant should not normally issue. . . .

As the Fourth Amendment has been construed and applied by this Court, "when the State's reason to believe incriminating evidence will be found becomes sufficiently great, the invasion of privacy becomes justified and a warrant to search and seize will issue." . . .

As we understand the structure and language of the Fourth Amendment and our cases expounding it, valid warrants to search property may be issued when it is satisfactorily demonstrated to the magistrate that fruits, instrumentalities, or evidence of crime is located on the premises. The Fourth Amendment has itself struck the balance between privacy and public need, and there is no occasion or justification for a court to revise the Amendment and strike a new balance by denying the search warrant in the circumstances present here and by insisting that the investigation proceed by subpoena *duces tecum*, whether on the theory that the latter is a less intrusive alternative or otherwise. . . .

[The *Daily* argues] that searches of newspaper offices for evidence of crime reasonably believed to be on the premises will seriously threaten the ability of the press to gather, analyze, and disseminate news. This is said to be true for several reasons: First, searches will be physically disruptive to such an extent that timely publication will be impeded. Second, confidential sources of information will dry up, and the press will also lose opportunities to cover various events because of fears of the participants that press files will be readily available to the authorities. Third, reporters will be deterred from recording and preserving their recollections for future use if such information is subject to seizure. Fourth, the processing of news and its dissemination will be chilled by the prospects that searches will disclose internal editorial deliberations. Fifth, the press will resort to self-censorship to conceal its possession of information of potential interest to the police.

It is true that the struggle from which the Fourth Amendment emerged "is largely a history of conflict between the Crown and the press," and that in issuing warrants and determining the reasonableness of a search, state and federal magistrates should be aware that "unrestricted power of search and seizure could also be an instrument for stifling liberty of expression." Where the materials sought to be seized may be protected by the First Amendment, the requirements of the Fourth Amendment must be applied with "scrupulous exactitude." . . . Where presumptively protected materials are sought to be seized, the warrant requirement should be administered to leave as little as possible to the discretion or whim of the officer in the field. . . .

Aware of the long struggle between Crown and press and desiring to curb unjustified official intrusions, the Framers took the enormously important step of subjecting searches to the test of reasonableness and to the general rule requiring search warrants issued by neutral magistrates. They nevertheless did not forbid warrants where the press was involved, did not require special showings that subpoenas would be impractical, and did not insist that the owner of the place to be searched, if connected with the press, must be shown to be implicated in the offense being investigated. Further, the prior cases do no more than insist that the courts apply the warrant requirements with particular exactitude when First Amendment interests would be endangered by the search. As we see it, no more than this is required where the warrant requested is for the seizure of criminal evidence reasonably believed to be on the premises occupied by a newspaper. Properly administered, the preconditions for a warrant — probable cause, specificity with respect to the place to be searched and the things to be seized, and overall reasonableness — should afford sufficient protection against the harms that are assertedly threatened by warrants for searching newspaper offices. . . .

STEWART, J. joined by MARSHALL, J. dissenting. It seems to me self-evident that police searches of newspaper offices burden the freedom of the press. The most immediate and obvious First Amendment injury caused by such a visitation by the police is physical disruption of the operation of the newspaper. Policemen occupying a newsroom and searching it thoroughly for what may be an extended period of time will inevitably interrupt its normal operations, and thus impair or even temporarily prevent the processes of newsgathering, writing, editing, and publishing. By contrast, a subpoena would afford the newspaper itself an opportunity to locate whatever material might be requested and produce it.

But there is another and more serious burden on a free press imposed by an unannounced police search of a newspaper office: the possibility of disclosure of information received from confidential sources, or of the identity of the sources themselves. . . .

It requires no blind leap of faith to understand that a person who gives information to a journalist only on condition that his identity will not be revealed will be less likely to give that information if he knows that, despite the journalist's assurance his identity may in fact be disclosed. And it cannot be denied that confidential information may be exposed to the eyes of police officers who execute a search warrant by rummaging through the files, cabinets, desks, and wastebaskets of a newsroom. Since the indisputable effect of such searches will thus be to prevent a newsman from being able to promise confidentiality to his potential sources, it seems obvious to me that a journalist's access to information, and thus the public's will thereby be impaired.

NOTES & QUESTIONS

1. ***Searches Implicating the First Amendment.*** In certain circumstances, a search may implicate the First Amendment, as it did in *Zurcher*. Suppose the police desire to search a bookstore's records to determine who purchased a particular book. The police obtain a valid warrant. However, First Amendment rights may be implicated, as such searches might chill people's ability to read. Would the government have to, in addition to securing a warrant, satisfy First Amendment scrutiny? For one court's answer, see *Tattered Cover v. City of Thornton* in Chapter 5.
2. ***Subpoenas vs. Warrants.*** In certain ways, subpoenas can be more protective of privacy than warrants. The person served with the subpoena can produce the requested documents herself rather than having government officials physically enter the person's office or dwelling to conduct the search. Further, the person can challenge the subpoena in court prior to complying; with a search warrant, judicial authorization is granted ex parte, and the warrant is

most often challenged only after it is executed. On the other hand, subpoenas can be obtained without any requirement of particularized suspicion or probable cause. The role for judicial oversight is rather minimal.

PRIVACY PROTECTION ACT

In 1980, Congress responded to *Zurcher* by passing the Privacy Protection Act (PPA), Pub. L. No. 96-440, 94 Stat. 1879, codified at 42 U.S.C. § 2000aa.

Work Product. Pursuant to the PPA:

> Notwithstanding any other law, it shall be unlawful for a government officer or employee, in connection with the investigation or prosecution of a criminal offense, to search for or seize any work product materials possessed by a person reasonably believed to have a purpose to disseminate to the public a newspaper, book, broadcast, or other similar form of public communication, in or affecting interstate or foreign commerce. . . . § 2000aa(a).

However, if "there is probable cause to believe that the person possessing such materials has committed or is committing the criminal offense to which the materials relate," then such materials may be searched or seized. The "criminal offense" cannot consist of the mere receipt, possession, or communication of the materials (except if it involves national defense data, classified information, or child pornography). § 2000aa(a)(1). The materials may be searched or seized if "there is reason to believe that the immediate seizure of such materials is necessary to prevent the death of, or serious bodily injury to, a human being." § 2000aa(a)(2).

Other Documents. The PPA also restricts the search or seizure of "documentary materials, other than work product materials, possessed by a person in connection with a purpose to disseminate to the public a newspaper, book, broadcast, or other similar form of public communication." § 2000aa(b). This provision has the same exceptions as the work product provision, with additional exceptions permitting search or seizure when there is reason to believe that the documents will be destroyed or concealed.

Subpoenas. The effect of the PPA is to require law enforcement officials to obtain a subpoena in order to obtain such information. Unlike search warrants, subpoenas permit the party subject to them to challenge them in court before having to comply. Further, instead of law enforcement officials searching through offices or records, the persons served with the subpoena must produce the documents themselves.

CHAPTER 8

PRIVACY AND PLACE

In *Katz v. United States*, 389 U.S. 347 (1967), the Court declared that the Fourth Amendment "protects people, not places." Nevertheless, in Fourth Amendment jurisprudence — as well as other forms of privacy law — different places receive vastly different privacy protection. This chapter explores privacy in three of the most central places of our lives: home, school, and work.

A. PRIVACY AT HOME

The home has long enjoyed significant protection as a private place. The maxim that the home is one's "castle" appeared as early as 1499.[1] *Semayne's Case,* 77 Eng. Rep. 194, 195 (K.B. 1604), was the first recorded case in which the sanctity of the home was mentioned: "[T]he house of every one is to him as his castle and fortress." According to William Blackstone, the law has "so particular and tender a regard to the immunity of a man's house that it stiles it his castle, and will never suffer it to be violated with impunity."[2] William Pitt once remarked: "The poorest man may in his cottage bid defiance to the Crown. It may be frail — its roof may shake — the wind may enter — the rain may enter — but the King of England cannot enter — all his force dares not cross the threshold of the ruined tenement!"[3]

In the United States, the importance of privacy in the home has long been recognized. The Supreme Court recognized in 1886 the importance of protecting "the sanctity of a man's home" in *Boyd v. United States,* 116 U.S. 616 (1886). As the Court later observed in *Payton v. New York,* 445 U.S. 573 (1980): "In none is the zone of privacy more clearly defined when bounded by the unambiguous physical dimensions of an individual's home." In a different case, it stated, "At the very core [of the Fourth Amendment] stands the right of a man to retreat into his own home and there be free from unreasonable governmental intrusion." *Silverman v. United States,* 365 U.S. 505 (1961).

---

[1] See Note, *The Right to Privacy in Nineteenth Century America*, 94 Harv. L. Rev. 1892, 1894 (1981).

[2] 4 William Blackstone, *Commentaries on the Laws of England* 223 (1769).

[3] Charles J. Sykes, *The End of Privacy* 83 (1999).

STANLEY V. GEORGIA

394 U.S. 557 (1969)

MARSHALL, J. . . . An investigation of appellant's alleged bookmaking activities led to the issuance of a search warrant for appellant's home. Under authority of this warrant, federal and state agents secured entrance. They found very little evidence of bookmaking activity, but while looking through a desk drawer in an upstairs bedroom, one of the federal agents, accompanied by a state officer, found three reels of eight-millimeter film. Using a projector and screen found in an upstairs living room, they viewed the films. The state officer concluded that they were obscene and seized them. Since a further examination of the bedroom indicated that appellant occupied it, he was charged with possession of obscene matter and placed under arrest. He was later indicted for "knowingly hav(ing) possession of . . . obscene matter" in violation of Georgia law. Appellant was tried before a jury and convicted. . . .

Appellant raises several challenges to the validity of his conviction. We find it necessary to consider only one. Appellant argues here, and argued below, that the Georgia obscenity statute, insofar as it punishes mere private possession of obscene matter, violates the First Amendment, as made applicable to the States by the Fourteenth Amendment. For reasons set forth below, we agree that the mere private possession of obscene matter cannot constitutionally be made a crime. . . .

It is true that *Roth* does declare, seemingly without qualification, that obscenity is not protected by the First Amendment. That statement has been repeated in various forms in subsequent cases. However, neither *Roth* nor any subsequent decision of this Court dealt with the precise problem involved in the present case. Roth was convicted of mailing obscene circulars and advertising, and an obscene book, in violation of a federal obscenity statute. . . . None of the statements cited by the Court in *Roth* for the proposition that "this Court has always assumed that obscenity is not protected by the freedoms of speech and press" were made in the context of a statute punishing mere private possession of obscene material; the cases cited deal for the most part with use of the mails to distribute objectionable material or with some form of public distribution or dissemination. Moreover, none of this Court's decisions subsequent to *Roth* involved prosecution for private possession of obscene materials. Those cases dealt with the power of the State and Federal Governments to prohibit or regulate certain public actions taken or intended to be taken with respect to obscene matter. . . .

In this context, we do not believe that this case can be decided simply by citing *Roth*. *Roth* and its progeny certainly do mean that the First and Fourteenth Amendments recognize a valid governmental interest in dealing with the problem of obscenity. But the assertion of that interest cannot, in every context, be insulated from all constitutional protections. Neither *Roth* nor any other decision of this Court reaches that far. . . . *Roth* and the cases following it discerned such an "important interest" in the regulation of commercial distribution of obscene material. That holding cannot foreclose an examination of the constitutional implications of a statute forbidding mere private possession of such material.

It is now well established that the Constitution protects the right to receive information and ideas. "This freedom (of speech and press) . . . necessarily protects the right to receive. . . ." This right to receive information and ideas, regardless of their social worth, is fundamental to our free society. Moreover, in the context of this case — a prosecution for mere possession of printed or filmed matter in the privacy of a person's own home — that right takes on an added dimension. For also fundamental is the right to be free, except in very limited circumstances, from unwanted governmental intrusions into one's privacy.

> The makers of our Constitution undertook to secure conditions favorable to the pursuit of happiness. They recognized the significance of man's spiritual nature, of his feelings and of his intellect. They knew that only a part of the pain, pleasure and satisfactions of life are to be found in material things. They sought to protect Americans in their beliefs, their thoughts, their emotions and their sensations. They conferred, as against the government, the right to be let alone — the most comprehensive of rights and the right most valued by civilized man. *Olmstead v. United States,* 277 U.S. 438, 478 (1928) (Brandeis, J., dissenting).

These are the rights that appellant is asserting in the case before us. He is asserting the right to read or observe what he pleases — the right to satisfy his intellectual and emotional needs in the privacy of his own home. He is asserting the right to be free from state inquiry into the contents of his library. Georgia contends that appellant does not have these rights, that there are certain types of materials that the individual may not read or even possess. Georgia justifies this assertion by arguing that the films in the present case are obscene. But we think that mere categorization of these films as "obscene" is insufficient justification for such a drastic invasion of personal liberties guaranteed by the First and Fourteenth Amendments. Whatever may be the justifications for other statutes regulating obscenity, we do not think they reach into the privacy of one's own home. If the First Amendment means anything, it means that a State has no business telling a man, sitting alone in his own house, what books he may read or what films he may watch. Our whole constitutional heritage rebels at the thought of giving government the power to control men's minds. . . .

Georgia asserts that exposure to obscene materials may lead to deviant sexual behavior or crimes of sexual violence. There appears to be little empirical basis for that assertion. But more important, if the State is only concerned about printed or filmed materials inducing antisocial conduct, we believe that in the context of private consumption of ideas and information we should adhere to the view that "(a)mong free men, the deterrents ordinarily to be applied to prevent crime are education and punishment for violations of the law. . . ." Given the present state of knowledge, the State may no more prohibit mere possession of obscene matter on the ground that it may lead to antisocial conduct than it may prohibit possession of chemistry books on the ground that they may lead to the manufacture of homemade spirits.

It is true that in *Roth* this Court rejected the necessity of proving that exposure to obscene material would create a clear and present danger of antisocial conduct or would probably induce its recipients to such conduct. But that case dealt with public distribution of obscene materials and such distribution is subject to different objections. For example, there is always the danger that obscene material might fall into the hands of children, or that it might intrude upon the sensibilities or privacy of the general public. No such dangers are present in this case. . . .

We hold that the First and Fourteenth Amendments prohibit making mere private possession of obscene material a crime. *Roth* and the cases following that decision are not impaired by today's holding. As we have said, the States retain broad power to regulate obscenity; that power simply does not extend to mere possession by the individual in the privacy of his own home. Accordingly, the judgment of the court below is reversed and the case is remanded for proceedings not inconsistent with this opinion.

NOTES & QUESTIONS

1. ***Possession of Obscenity Outside the Home.*** Stanley possessed obscene material that Georgia could constitutionally outlaw because the First Amendment does not protect obscenity. According to the Court, states can ban obscene films outside the home. Thus, were Stanley to step outside the door with his films, a police officer could arrest him. Should Stanley's location inside his home make any difference? Suppose Stanley possessed and used illegal narcotics in his home. Does the state have any business telling a person, sitting alone in her home, what substances she may or may not ingest?
2. ***The Limits of* Stanley.** In *Osborne v. Ohio,* 495 U.S. 103 (1990), the Court held that the rule in *Stanley* does not apply to the possession of child pornography in the home:

   > In *Stanley,* Georgia primarily sought to proscribe the private possession of obscenity because it was concerned that obscenity would poison the minds of its viewers. We responded that "[w]hatever the power of the state to control public dissemination of ideas inimical to the public morality, it cannot constitutionally premise legislation on the desirability of controlling a person's private thoughts." The difference here is obvious: The State does not rely on a paternalistic interest in regulating Osborne's mind. Rather, Ohio has enacted §2907.323(A)(3) in order to protect the victims of child pornography; it hopes to destroy a market for the exploitative use of children.

3. ***The Fourth Amendment and the Home.*** Although *Katz* declared that "the Fourth Amendment protects people, not places," *Katz v. United States,* 389 U.S. 347, 351 (1967), the Court has afforded the home the strongest protection under the Fourth Amendment. For example, automobiles can generally be searched without warrants, while homes rarely can be searched without warrants (except under exigent circumstances). Compare *Chambers v. Maroney,* 399 U.S. 42 (1970), with *Mincey v. Arizona,* 437 U.S. 385 (1978). The Court has even permitted "informational checkpoints" that allow the police to briefly stop a car and ask the occupants of the car whether they have any information about a recent crime that occurred in the area. *Illinois v. Lidster*, 540 U.S. 419 (2004). Arrests can be made without warrants outside the home; but within the home, warrantless arrests are generally not permissible. Compare *United States v. Watson,* 423 U.S. 411 (1976), with

Payton v. New York, 445 U.S. 573 (1980). In *Payton v. New York,* the Court struck down New York statutes that permitted the police to enter a home without a warrant in order to make a routine felony arrest:

> The Fourth Amendment protects the individual's privacy in a variety of settings. In none is the zone of privacy more clearly defined than when bounded by the unambiguous physical dimensions of an individual's home — a zone that finds its roots in clear and specific constitutional terms: "The right of the people to be secure in their . . . houses . . . shall not be violated." That language unequivocally establishes the proposition that "[a]t the very core [of the Fourth Amendment] stands the right of a man to retreat into his own home and there be free from unreasonable governmental intrusion." *Silverman v. United States,* 365 U.S. 505, 511. In terms that apply equally to seizures of property and to seizures of persons, the Fourth Amendment has drawn a firm line at the entrance to the house. Absent exigent circumstances, that threshold may not reasonably be crossed without a warrant.

4. ***The Scope of the Fourth Amendment Protection of the Home.*** In *Chapman v. United States,* 365 U.S. 610 (1961), the Court held that the Fourth Amendment protection of the home extends to apartment tenants, even though they do not own the apartment. Further, in *Bumper v. North Carolina,* 391 U.S. 543 (1968), the Court held that a person living in the home of another was entitled to the same Fourth Amendment protection as if it were her own home. Later, in *Minnesota v. Olson,* 495 U.S. 91 (1990), the Court extended the Fourth Amendment protection of the home to overnight guests in another's home or apartment:

> To hold that an overnight guest has a legitimate expectation of privacy in his host's home merely recognizes the every day expectations of privacy that we all share. Staying overnight in another's home is a long-standing social custom that serves functions recognized as valuable by society. We stay in others' homes when we travel to a strange city for business or pleasure, we visit our parents, children, or more distant relatives out of town, when we are in between jobs, or homes, or when we house-sit for a friend. . . .
>
> From the overnight guest's perspective, he seeks shelter in another's home precisely because it provides him with privacy, a place where he and his possessions will not be disturbed by anyone but his host and those his host allows inside. We are at our most vulnerable when we are asleep because we cannot monitor our own safety or the security of our belongings. It is for this reason that, although we may spend all day in public places, when we cannot sleep in our own home we seek out another private place to sleep, whether it be a hotel room, or the home of a friend.

However, in *Minnesota v. Carter,* 525 U.S. 83 (1998), the Court held that a visitor who was in a friend's apartment for a short duration (not overnight) had no reasonable expectation of privacy in that apartment:

> The text of the [Fourth] Amendment suggests that its protections extend only to people in "their" houses. But we have held that in some circumstances a person may have a legitimate expectation of privacy in the house of someone else. . . .

But whereas it is plausible to regard a person's overnight lodging as at least his "temporary" residence, it is entirely impossible to give that characterization to an apartment that he uses to package cocaine. Respondents here were not searched in "their . . . hous[e]" under any interpretation of the phrase that bears the remotest relationship to the well understood meaning of the Fourth Amendment.

Justices Ginsburg, Souter, and Stevens dissented:

A home dweller places her own privacy at risk, the Court's approach indicates, when she opens her home to others. . . . Human frailty suggests that today's decision will tempt police to pry into private dwellings without warrant, to find evidence incriminating guests who do not rest there through the night. As I see it, people are not genuinely "secure in their . . . houses . . . against unreasonable searches and seizures," U.S. Const., Amdt. 4, if their invitations to others increase the risk of unwarranted governmental peering and prying into their dwelling places.

Through the host's invitation, the guest gains a reasonable expectation of privacy in the home. *Minnesota v. Olson* so held with respect to an overnight guest. The logic of that decision extends to shorter term guests as well. One need not remain overnight to anticipate privacy in another's home. . . .

WILSON V. LAYNE

526 U.S. 603 (1999)

REHNQUIST, J. One of the dangerous fugitives identified as a target of "Operation Gunsmoke" [a national program where U.S. Marshals worked with state and local police to apprehend dangerous fugitives] was Dominic Wilson, the son of petitioners Charles and Geraldine Wilson. Dominic Wilson had violated his probation on previous felony charges of robbery, theft, and assault with intent to rob, and the police computer listed "caution indicators" that he was likely to be armed, to resist arrest, and to "assaul[t] police." The computer also listed his address as 909 North Stone Street Avenue in Rockville, Maryland. Unknown to the police, this was actually the home of petitioners, Dominic Wilson's parents. Thus, in April 1992, the Circuit Court for Montgomery County issued three arrest warrants for Dominic Wilson, one for each of his probation violations. The warrants were each addressed to "any duly authorized peace officer," and commanded such officers to arrest him and bring him "immediately" before the Circuit Court to answer an indictment as to his probation violation. The warrants made no mention of media presence or assistance.

In the early morning hours of April 16, 1992, a Gunsmoke team of Deputy United States Marshals and Montgomery County Police officers assembled to execute the Dominic Wilson warrants. The team was accompanied by a reporter and a photographer from the Washington Post, who had been invited by the Marshals to accompany them on their mission as part of a Marshal's Service ride-along policy.

At around 6:45 a.m., the officers, with media representatives in tow, entered the dwelling at 909 North Stone Street Avenue in the Lincoln Park neighborhood of Rockville. Petitioners Charles and Geraldine Wilson were still in bed when they heard the officers enter the home. Petitioner Charles Wilson, dressed only in a pair of briefs, ran into the living room to investigate. Discovering at least five men in street clothes with guns in his living room, he angrily demanded that they state their business, and repeatedly cursed the officers. Believing him to be an angry Dominic Wilson, the officers quickly subdued him on the floor. Geraldine Wilson next entered the living room to investigate, wearing only a nightgown. She observed her husband being restrained by the armed officers.

When their protective sweep was completed, the officers learned that Dominic Wilson was not in the house, and they departed. During the time that the officers were in the home, the Washington Post photographer took numerous pictures. The print reporter was also apparently in the living room observing the confrontation between the police and Charles Wilson. At no time, however, were the reporters involved in the execution of the arrest warrant. The Washington Post never published its photographs of the incident.

Petitioners sued the law enforcement officials in their personal capacities for money damages under *Bivens v. Six Unknown Fed. Narcotics Agents,* 403 U.S. 388 (1971) (the U.S. Marshals Service respondents) and 42 U.S.C. §1983 (the Montgomery County Sheriff's Department respondents). They contended that the officers' actions in bringing members of the media to observe and record the attempted execution of the arrest warrant violated their Fourth Amendment rights. The District Court denied respondents' motion for summary judgment on the basis of qualified immunity. . . .

In *Payton v. New York,* 445 U.S. 573 (1980), we noted that although clear in its protection of the home, the common law tradition at the time of the drafting of the Fourth Amendment was ambivalent on the question of whether police could enter a home without a warrant. We were ultimately persuaded that the "overriding respect for the sanctity of the home that has been embedded in our traditions since the origins of the Republic" meant that absent a warrant or exigent circumstances, police could not enter a home to make an arrest. . . .

Here, of course, the officers had such a warrant, and they were undoubtedly entitled to enter the Wilson home in order to execute the arrest warrant for Dominic Wilson. But it does not necessarily follow that they were entitled to bring a newspaper reporter and a photographer with them. In *Horton v. California,* 496 U.S. 128 (1990), we held "[i]f the scope of the search exceeds that permitted by the terms of a validly issued warrant or the character of the relevant exception from the warrant requirement, the subsequent seizure is unconstitutional without more." While this does not mean that every police action while inside a home must be explicitly authorized by the text of the warrant, the Fourth Amendment does require that police actions in execution of a warrant be related to the objectives of the authorized intrusion.

Certainly the presence of reporters inside the home was not related to the objectives of the authorized intrusion. Respondents concede that the reporters did not engage in the execution of the warrant, and did not assist the police in their task. The reporters therefore were not present for any reason related to the justification for police entry into the home — the apprehension of Dominic Wilson.

This is not a case in which the presence of the third parties directly aided in the execution of the warrant. Where the police enter a home under the authority of a warrant to search for stolen property, the presence of third parties for the purpose of identifying the stolen property has long been approved by this Court and our common law tradition.

Respondents argue that the presence of the Washington Post reporters in the Wilsons' home nonetheless served a number of legitimate law enforcement purposes. They first assert that officers should be able to exercise reasonable discretion about when it would "further their law enforcement mission to permit members of the news media to accompany them in executing a warrant." But this claim ignores the importance of the right of residential privacy at the core of the Fourth Amendment. It may well be that media ride-alongs further the law enforcement objectives of the police in a general sense, but that is not the same as furthering the purposes of the search. Were such generalized "law enforcement objectives" themselves sufficient to trump the Fourth Amendment, the protections guaranteed by that Amendment's text would be significantly watered down.

Respondents next argue that the presence of third parties could serve the law enforcement purpose of publicizing the government's efforts to combat crime, and facilitate accurate reporting on law enforcement activities. There is certainly language in our opinions interpreting the First Amendment which points to the importance of "the press" in informing the general public about the administration of criminal justice. . . . But the Fourth Amendment also protects a very important right, and in the present case it is in terms of that right that the media ride-alongs must be judged. . . .

Finally, respondents argue that the presence of third parties could serve in some situations to minimize police abuses and protect suspects, and also to protect the safety of the officers. While it might be reasonable for police officers to themselves videotape home entries as part of a "quality control" effort to ensure that the rights of homeowners are being respected, or even to preserve evidence, such a situation is significantly different from the media presence in this case. The Washington Post reporters in the Wilsons' home were working on a story for their own purposes. They were not present for the purpose of protecting the officers, much less the Wilsons. A private photographer was acting for private purposes, as evidenced in part by the fact that the newspaper and not the police retained the photographs. Thus, although the presence of third parties during the execution of a warrant may in some circumstances be constitutionally permissible, the presence of *these* third parties was not.

The reasons advanced by respondents, taken in their entirety, fall short of justifying the presence of media inside a home. We hold that it is a violation of the Fourth Amendment for police to bring members of the media or other third parties into a home during the execution of a warrant when the presence of the third parties in the home was not in aid of the execution of the warrant. . . .

NOTES & QUESTIONS

1. ***Liability for the Reporters?*** What causes of action would the Wilsons have against the news reporters? Are they likely to be successful in these causes of action?

2. ***Variations on the Facts.*** Suppose the police brought in their own video camera, and one of the officers filmed the arrest. The police then gave the videotape to the press. Would they violate the Fourth Amendment under *Wilson*? Suppose the police left open the door to the Wilsons' house, and a press camera person filmed the arrest through the open door without entering into the Wilson abode. Would this be unconstitutional under *Wilson*?
3. ***Filming as a Check on Police?*** One could argue that one of the central purposes of the Fourth Amendment is to keep police power in check. Furthermore, one could argue that the practice of filming the police during arrests serves the purposes of the Fourth Amendment by providing a significant check on police abuses. How does the *Wilson* Court respond to these arguments? Do you agree?
4. ***The Application of* Wilson *Outside the Home: "Perp Walks."*** In *Lauro v. Charles,* 219 F.3d 202 (2d Cir. 2000), the court applied *Wilson* to a widespread police practice in New York City known as a "perp walk," in which an arrestee (often in handcuffs and guided by police officers) is walked in front of the press to be photographed or filmed. Although sometimes the arrestee is filmed during the regular course of being transferred from one location to another, the police and the press often cooperate in staging the perp walk. In a perp walk, the police bring the arrestee outside the police station and lead her back inside for no other purpose than to allow the press to photograph her. In *Lauro,* the court held, relying on *Wilson,* that the staged perp walk violated an arrestee's Fourth Amendment rights:

> . . . In the instant case, Lauro was physically restrained, by handcuffs and by the grip of Detective Charles on his arm. In that humiliating position, he was made to walk outside the precinct house, was driven around the block, and was then forced to walk back into the precinct house, in front of television cameras. The fact that Lauro was lawfully under arrest when these events occurred does not mean that no Fourth Amendment interest of Lauro's was implicated. . . .
>
> Despite its adverse effects on Lauro's dignity and privacy, the perp walk might nevertheless have been reasonable under the Fourth Amendment, had it been sufficiently closely related to a legitimate governmental objective. In this respect, Charles argues that "the importance of the press in informing the general public about the administration of criminal justice has long been recognized by the Supreme Court," and that this interest suffices to justify the perp walk before us.
>
> The Supreme Court, however, in *Wilson* explicitly rejected an identical argument when it was proffered in support of the media ride-along in that case. . . .
>
> . . . The interests of the press, and of the public who might want to view perp walks, are far from negligible. In this case, however, the press and the public were not viewing the actual event of Lauro being brought to the police station, but rather, were offered a staged recreation of that event. Even assuming that there is a legitimate state interest in accurate reporting of police activity, that interest is not well served by an inherently fictional dramatization of an event that transpired hours earlier. . .

If the Fourth Amendment does not generally recognize a reasonable expectation of privacy when one is in public spaces, why does the staged perp walk in *Lauro* violate the arrestee's constitutional interest?

5. ***Tranquility of the Home.*** In addition to the Court affording the home greater protection under the Fourth Amendment than other places, the Court has sustained state regulation protecting the tranquility of the home from First Amendment challenges. In *Kovacs v. Cooper,* 336 U.S. 77 (1949), the Court upheld an ordinance prohibiting the use of sound trucks or other devices to amplify sound used in public streets:

> The right of free speech is guaranteed every citizen that he may reach the minds of willing listeners and to do so there must be opportunity to win their attention. This is the phase of freedom of speech that is involved here. We do not think the Trenton ordinance abridges that freedom. It is an extravagant extension of due process to say that because of it a city cannot forbid talking on the streets through a loud speaker in a loud and raucous tone. . . . The preferred position of freedom of speech in a society that cherishes liberty for all does not require legislators to be insensible to claims by citizens to comfort and convenience. To enforce freedom of speech in disregard of the rights of others would be harsh and arbitrary in itself. That more people may be more easily and cheaply reached by sound trucks, perhaps borrowed without cost from some zealous supporter, is not enough to call forth constitutional protection for what those charged with public welfare reasonably think is a nuisance when easy means of publicity are open. . . . We think that the need for reasonable protection in the homes or business houses from the distracting noises of vehicles equipped with such sound amplifying devices justifies the ordinance.

In *Kovacs,* the Court distinguished an earlier case, *Martin v. City of Struthers,* 319 U.S. 141 (1943), where it struck down an ordinance prohibiting people from going door to door to distribute pamphlets:

> We do not think that the *Struthers* case requires us to expand this interdiction of legislation to include ordinance against obtaining an audience for the broadcaster's ideas by way of sound trucks with loud and raucous noises on city streets. The unwilling listener is not like the passer-by who may be offered a pamphlet in the street but cannot be made to take it. In his home or on the street he is practically helpless to escape this interference with his privacy by loud speakers except through the protection of the municipality.

In *Frisby v. Schultz,* 487 U.S. 474 (1988), the Court upheld an ordinance completely banning picketing near any residence. The plaintiffs were a group of pro-life advocates who desired to picket an abortion doctor's residence. The Court concluded that the ordinance was a content neutral restriction on speech because it applied to all residential picketing regardless of the content of the expression. The Court also ruled that the ordinance satisfied the test accorded content neutral restrictions because it was narrowly tailored to serve a significant governmental interest (protecting privacy of the home) and it left open alternative channels for communications. As the Court reasoned:

> "The State's interest in protecting the well-being, tranquility, and privacy of the home is certainly of the highest order in a free and civilized society." Our

prior decisions have often remarked on the unique nature of the home, "the last citadel of the tired, the weary, and the sick," and have recognized that "[p]reserving the sanctity of the home, the one retreat to which men and women can repair to escape from the tribulations of their daily pursuits, is surely an important value."

One important aspect of residential privacy is protection of the unwilling listener. Although in many locations, we expect individuals simply to avoid speech they do not want to hear, the home is different. "That we are often 'captives' outside the sanctuary of the home and subject to objectionable speech . . . does not mean we must be captives everywhere." *Rowan v. Post Office Dept.,* 397 U.S. 728, 738 (1970). Instead, a special benefit of the privacy all citizens enjoy within their own walls, which the State may legislate to protect, is an ability to avoid intrusions. . . .

There simply is no right to force speech into the home of an unwilling listener.

It remains to be considered, however, whether the Brookfield ordinance is narrowly tailored to protect only unwilling recipients of the communications. A statute is narrowly tailored if it targets and eliminates no more than the exact source of the "evil" it seeks to remedy. A complete ban can be narrowly tailored, but only if each activity within the proscription's scope is an appropriately targeted evil. . . .

. . . The type of focused picketing prohibited by the Brookfield ordinance is fundamentally different from more generally directed means of communication that may not be completely banned in residential areas. Here, in contrast, the picketing is narrowly directed at the household, not the public. The type of picketers banned by the Brookfield ordinance generally do not seek to disseminate a message to the general public, but to intrude upon the targeted resident, and to do so in an especially offensive way. Moreover, even if some such picketers have a broader communicative purpose, their activity nonetheless inherently and offensively intrudes on residential privacy. The devastating effect of targeted picketing on the quiet enjoyment of the home is beyond doubt. . . .

GEORGIA V. RANDOLPH

547 U.S. 103 (2006)

SOUTER, J. . . . The Fourth Amendment recognizes a valid warrantless entry and search of premises when police obtain the voluntary consent of an occupant who shares, or is reasonably believed to share, authority over the area in common with a co-occupant who later objects to the use of evidence so obtained. *Illinois v. Rodriguez,* 497 U.S. 177 (1990); *United States v. Matlock,* 415 U.S. 164 (1974). The question here is whether such an evidentiary seizure is likewise lawful with the permission of one occupant when the other, who later seeks to suppress the evidence, is present at the scene and expressly refuses to consent. We hold that, in the circumstances here at issue, a physically present co-occupant's stated refusal to permit entry prevails, rendering the warrantless search unreasonable and invalid as to him.

Respondent Scott Randolph and his wife, Janet, separated in late May 2001, when she left the marital residence in Americus, Georgia, and went to stay with her parents in Canada, taking their son and some belongings. In July, she returned to the Americus house with the child, though the record does not reveal whether her object was reconciliation or retrieval of remaining possessions.

On the morning of July 6, she complained to the police that after a domestic dispute her husband took their son away, and when officers reached the house she told them that her husband was a cocaine user whose habit had caused financial troubles. She mentioned the marital problems and said that she and their son had only recently returned after a stay of several weeks with her parents. Shortly after the police arrived, Scott Randolph returned and explained that he had removed the child to a neighbor's house out of concern that his wife might take the boy out of the country again; he denied cocaine use, and countered that it was in fact his wife who abused drugs and alcohol.

One of the officers, Sergeant Murray, went with Janet Randolph to reclaim the child, and when they returned she not only renewed her complaints about her husband's drug use, but also volunteered that there were "items of drug evidence" in the house. Brief for Petitioner 3. Sergeant Murray asked Scott Randolph for permission to search the house, which he unequivocally refused.

The sergeant turned to Janet Randolph for consent to search, which she readily gave. She led the officer upstairs to a bedroom that she identified as Scott's, where the sergeant noticed a section of a drinking straw with a powdery residue he suspected was cocaine. He then left the house to get an evidence bag from his car and to call the district attorney's office, which instructed him to stop the search and apply for a warrant. When Sergeant Murray returned to the house, Janet Randolph withdrew her consent. The police took the straw to the police station, along with the Randolphs. After getting a search warrant, they returned to the house and seized further evidence of drug use, on the basis of which Scott Randolph was indicted for possession of cocaine.

He moved to suppress the evidence, as products of a warrantless search of his house unauthorized by his wife's consent over his express refusal. . . .

To the Fourth Amendment rule ordinarily prohibiting the warrantless entry of a person's house as unreasonable *per se,* one "jealously and carefully drawn" exception recognizes the validity of searches with the voluntary consent of an individual possessing authority. That person might be the householder against whom evidence is sought or a fellow occupant who shares common authority over property, when the suspect is absent, and the exception for consent extends even to entries and searches with the permission of a co-occupant whom the police reasonably, but erroneously, believe to possess shared authority as an occupant. None of our co-occupant consent-to-search cases, however, has presented the further fact of a second occupant physically present and refusing permission to search, and later moving to suppress evidence so obtained. The significance of such a refusal turns on the underpinnings of the co-occupant consent rule, as recognized since *Matlock.*

The defendant in that case was arrested in the yard of a house where he lived with a Mrs. Graff and several of her relatives, and was detained in a squad car parked nearby. When the police went to the door, Mrs. Graff admitted them and consented to a search of the house. . . .

The constant element in assessing Fourth Amendment reasonableness in the consent cases, then, is the great significance given to widely shared social expectations, which are naturally enough influenced by the law of property, but not controlled by its rules. *Matlock* accordingly not only holds that a solitary co-inhabitant may sometimes consent to a search of shared premises, but stands for the proposition that the reasonableness of such a search is in significant part a function of commonly held understanding about the authority that co-inhabitants may exercise in ways that affect each other's interests.

Matlock's example of common understanding is readily apparent. When someone comes to the door of a domestic dwelling with a baby at her hip, as Mrs. Graff did, she shows that she belongs there, and that fact standing alone is enough to tell a law enforcement officer or any other visitor that if she occupies the place along with others, she probably lives there subject to the assumption tenants usually make about their common authority when they share quarters. They understand that any one of them may admit visitors, with the consequence that a guest obnoxious to one may nevertheless be admitted in his absence by another. As *Matlock* put it, shared tenancy is understood to include an "assumption of risk," on which police officers are entitled to rely, and although some group living together might make an exceptional arrangement that no one could admit a guest without the agreement of all, the chance of such an eccentric scheme is too remote to expect visitors to investigate a particular household's rules before accepting an invitation to come in. So, *Matlock* relied on what was usual and placed no burden on the police to eliminate the possibility of atypical arrangements, in the absence of reason to doubt that the regular scheme was in place. . . .

Although we have not dealt directly with the reasonableness of police entry in reliance on consent by one occupant subject to immediate challenge by another, we took a step toward the issue in an earlier case dealing with the Fourth Amendment rights of a social guest arrested at premises the police entered without a warrant or the benefit of any exception to the warrant requirement. *Minnesota v. Olson,* 495 U.S. 91 (1990), held that overnight houseguests have a legitimate expectation of privacy in their temporary quarters because "it is unlikely that [the host] will admit someone who wants to see or meet with the guest over the objection of the guest." If that customary expectation of courtesy or deference is a foundation of Fourth Amendment rights of a houseguest, it presumably should follow that an inhabitant of shared premises may claim at least as much, and it turns out that the co-inhabitant naturally has an even stronger claim.

To begin with, it is fair to say that a caller standing at the door of shared premises would have no confidence that one occupant's invitation was a sufficiently good reason to enter when a fellow tenant stood there saying, "stay out." Without some very good reason, no sensible person would go inside under those conditions. Fear for the safety of the occupant issuing the invitation, or of someone else inside, would be thought to justify entry, but the justification then would be the personal risk, the threats to life or limb, not the disputed invitation.

The visitor's reticence without some such good reason would show not timidity but a realization that when people living together disagree over the use of their common quarters, a resolution must come through voluntary accommodation, not by appeals to authority. Unless the people living together fall within some recognized hierarchy, like a household of parent and child or barracks housing military personnel of different grades, there is no societal understanding of superior and inferior, a fact reflected in a standard formulation of domestic property law, that "[e]ach cotenant . . . has the right to use and enjoy the entire property as if he or she were the sole owner, limited only by the same right in the other cotenants." . . . In sum, there is no common understanding that one co-tenant generally has a right or authority to prevail over the express wishes of another, whether the issue is the color of the curtains or invitations to outsiders.

Since the co-tenant wishing to open the door to a third party has no recognized authority in law or social practice to prevail over a present and objecting co-tenant, his disputed invitation, without more, gives a police officer no better claim to reasonableness in entering than the officer would have in the absence of any consent at all. Accordingly, in the balancing of competing individual and governmental interests entailed by the bar to unreasonable searches, the cooperative occupant's invitation adds nothing to the government's side to counter the force of an objecting individual's claim to security against the government's intrusion into his dwelling place. Since we hold to the "centuries-old principle of respect for the privacy of the home," *Wilson v. Layne,* 526 U.S. 603 (1999), "it is beyond dispute that the home is entitled to special protection as the center of the private lives of our people," *Minnesota v. Carter,* 525 U.S. 83 (1998) (Kennedy, J., concurring). . . .

Disputed permission is thus no match for this central value of the Fourth Amendment, and the State's other countervailing claims do not add up to outweigh it. . . .

ROBERTS & SCALIA, J.J. dissenting. . . . The Fourth Amendment protects privacy. If an individual shares information, papers, *or places* with another, he assumes the risk that the other person will in turn share access to that information or those papers *or places* with the government. And just as an individual who has shared illegal plans or incriminating documents with another cannot interpose an objection when that other person turns the information over to the government, just because the individual happens to be present at the time, so too someone who shares a place with another cannot interpose an objection when that person decides to grant access to the police, simply because the objecting individual happens to be present.

A warrantless search is reasonable if police obtain the voluntary consent of a person authorized to give it. Co-occupants have "assumed the risk that one of their number might permit [a] common area to be searched." *United States v. Matlock,* 415 U.S. 164 (1974). Just as Mrs. Randolph could walk upstairs, come down, and turn her husband's cocaine straw over to the police, she can consent to police entry and search of what is, after all, her home, too. . . .

[T]he majority is confident in assuming — confident enough to incorporate its assumption into the Constitution — that an invited social guest who arrives at the door of a shared residence, and is greeted by a disagreeable co-occupant shouting "stay out," would simply go away. The Court observes that "no sensible person would go inside under those conditions," and concludes from this that the inviting co-occupant has no "authority" to insist on getting her way over the wishes of her co-occupant, But it seems equally accurate to say — based on the majority's conclusion that one does not have a right to prevail over the express wishes of his co-occupant — that the objector has no "authority" to insist on getting *his* way over his co-occupant's wish that her guest be admitted.

The fact is that a wide variety of differing social situations can readily be imagined, giving rise to quite different social expectations. A relative or good friend of one of two feuding roommates might well enter the apartment over the objection of the other roommate. The reason the invitee appeared at the door also affects expectations: A guest who came to celebrate an occupant's birthday, or one who had traveled some distance for a particular reason, might not readily turn away simply because of a roommate's objection. The nature of the place itself is also pertinent: Invitees may react one way if the feuding roommates share one room, differently if there are common areas from which the objecting roommate could readily be expected to absent himself. Altering the numbers might well change the social expectations: Invitees might enter if two of three co-occupants encourage them to do so, over one dissenter. . . .

In *United States v. White,* we held that one party to a conversation can consent to government eavesdropping, and statements made by the other party will be admissible at trial. This rule is based on privacy: "Inescapably, one contemplating illegal activities must realize and risk that his companions may be reporting to the police. . . . [I]f he has no doubts, or allays them, or risks what doubt he has, the risk is his." . . .

As the Court explained in *United States v. Jacobsen*:

> It is well settled that when an individual reveals private information to another, he assumes the risk that his confidant will reveal that information to the authorities, and if that occurs the Fourth Amendment does not prohibit governmental use of that information. Once frustration of the original expectation of privacy occurs, the Fourth Amendment does not prohibit governmental use of the now nonprivate information: "This Court has held repeatedly that the Fourth Amendment does not prohibit the obtaining of information revealed to a third party and conveyed by him to Government authorities, even if the information is revealed on the assumption that it will be used only for a limited purpose and the confidence placed in a third party will not be betrayed."

The same analysis applies to the question whether our privacy can be compromised by those with whom we share common living space. If a person keeps contraband in common areas of his home, he runs the risk that his co-occupants will deliver the contraband to the police. . . .

Even in our most private relationships, our observable actions and possessions are private at the discretion of those around us. A husband can request that his wife not tell a jury about contraband that she observed in their home or illegal activity to which she bore witness, but it is she who decides whether to invoke the testimonial marital privilege. . . .

There is no basis for evaluating physical searches of shared space in a manner different from how we evaluated the privacy interests in the foregoing cases. . . .

The common thread in our decisions upholding searches conducted pursuant to third-party consent is an understanding that a person "assume[s] the risk" that those who have access to and control over his shared property might consent to a search. *Matlock,* 415 U.S., at 171. In *Matlock,* we explained that this assumption of risk is derived from a third party's "joint access or control for most purposes" of shared property. And we concluded that shared use of property makes it "reasonable to recognize that any of the co-inhabitants has the right to permit the inspection in his own right."

In this sense, the risk assumed by a joint occupant is comparable to the risk assumed by one who reveals private information to another. If a person has incriminating information, he can keep it private in the face of a request from police to share it, because he has that right under the Fifth Amendment. If a person occupies a house with incriminating information in it, he can keep that information private in the face of a request from police to search the house, because he has that right under the Fourth Amendment. But if he shares the information — or the house — with another, that other can grant access to the police in each instance. . . .

Just as the source of the majority's rule is not privacy, so too the interest it protects cannot reasonably be described as such. That interest is not protected if a co-owner happens to be absent when the police arrive, in the backyard gardening, asleep in the next room, or listening to music through earphones so that only his co-occupant hears the knock on the door. That the rule is so random in its application confirms that it bears no real relation to the privacy protected by the Fourth Amendment. What the majority's rule protects is not so much privacy as the good luck of a co-owner who just happens to be present at the door when the police arrive. . . .

Rather than draw such random and happenstance lines — and pretend that the Constitution decreed them — the more reasonable approach is to adopt a rule acknowledging that shared living space entails a limited yielding of privacy to others, and that the law historically permits those to whom we have yielded our privacy to in turn cooperate with the government. Such a rule flows more naturally from our cases concerning Fourth Amendment reasonableness and is logically grounded in the concept of privacy underlying that Amendment. . . .

NOTES & QUESTIONS

1. ***Presence vs. Absence.*** In *United States v. Matlock,* 415 U.S. 164 (1974), the Supreme Court held that the "consent of one who possesses common authority over premises or effects is valid as against the absent, nonconsenting person with whom that authority is shared." In *Illinois v. Rodriguez,* 497 U.S. 177 (1990), the Court held that even if the police wrongly believe that the person consenting to the search has authority over the property, the search is valid so long as the police error was reasonable and in good faith. The difference in *Randolph* is that the defendant was home at the time and did not consent. Had he been absent, the police would have been able to search under the Fourth Amendment. Does this distinction make sense?
2. ***Assumption of Risk.*** Is Chief Justice Roberts correct that the assumption of risk doctrine should govern this case? Suppose Scott Randolph's wife went to the police and gave information about Scott's criminal activity. There would

be no Fourth Amendment problem here. So why can't she let the police into her house to show the police the same information?

B. PRIVACY AT SCHOOL

1. SCHOOL SEARCHES AND SURVEILLANCE

NEW JERSEY V. T.L.O.

469 U.S. 325 (1984)

WHITE, J. . . . On March 7, 1980, a teacher at Piscataway High School in Middlesex County, N.J., discovered two girls smoking in a lavatory. One of the two girls was the respondent T.L.O., who at that time was a 14-year-old high school freshman. Because smoking in the lavatory was a violation of a school rule, the teacher took the two girls to the Principal's office, where they met with Assistant Vice Principal Theodore Choplick. In response to questioning by Mr. Choplick, T.L.O.'s companion admitted that she had violated the rule. T.L.O., however, denied that she had been smoking in the lavatory and claimed that she did not smoke at all.

Mr. Choplick asked T.L.O. to come into his private office and demanded to see her purse. Opening the purse, he found a pack of cigarettes, which he removed from the purse and held before T.L.O. as he accused her of having lied to him. As he reached into the purse for the cigarettes, Mr. Choplick also noticed a package of cigarette rolling papers. In his experience, possession of rolling papers by high school students was closely associated with the use of marihuana. Suspecting that a closer examination of the purse might yield further evidence of drug use, Mr. Choplick proceeded to search the purse thoroughly. The search revealed a small amount of marihuana, a pipe, a number of empty plastic bags, a substantial quantity of money in one-dollar bills, an index card that appeared to be a list of students who owed T.L.O. money, and two letters that implicated T.L.O. in marihuana dealing.

Mr. Choplick notified T.L.O.'s mother and the police, and turned the evidence of drug dealing over to the police. At the request of the police, T.L.O.'s mother took her daughter to police headquarters, where T.L.O. confessed that she had been selling marihuana at the high school. On the basis of the confession and the evidence seized by Mr. Choplick, the State brought delinquency charges against T.L.O. in the Juvenile and Domestic Relations Court of Middlesex County. Contending that Mr. Choplick's search of her purse violated the Fourth Amendment, T.L.O. moved to suppress the evidence found in her purse as well as her confession, which, she argued, was tainted by the allegedly unlawful search. . . .

In determining whether the search at issue in this case violated the Fourth Amendment, we are faced initially with the question whether that Amendment's prohibition on unreasonable searches and seizures applies to searches conducted by public school officials. We hold that it does. . . .

. . . [T]he State of New Jersey has argued that the history of the Fourth Amendment indicates that the Amendment was intended to regulate only searches and seizures carried out by law enforcement officers; accordingly, although public school officials are concededly state agents for purposes of the Fourteenth Amendment, the Fourth Amendment creates no rights enforceable against them.

It may well be true that the evil toward which the Fourth Amendment was primarily directed was the resurrection of the pre-Revolutionary practice of using general warrants or "writs of assistance" to authorize searches for contraband by officers of the Crown. But this Court has never limited the Amendment's prohibition on unreasonable searches and seizures to operations conducted by the police. Rather, the Court has long spoken of the Fourth Amendment's strictures as restraints imposed upon "governmental action" — that is, "upon the activities of sovereign authority." Accordingly, we have held the Fourth Amendment applicable to the activities of civil as well as criminal authorities: building inspectors, Occupational Safety and Health Act inspectors, and even firemen entering privately owned premises to battle a fire, are all subject to the restraints imposed by the Fourth Amendment. As we observed in *Camara v. Municipal Court,* "[t]he basic purpose of this Amendment, as recognized in countless decisions of this Court, is to safeguard the privacy and security of individuals against arbitrary invasions by governmental officials." . . .

To hold that the Fourth Amendment applies to searches conducted by school authorities is only to begin the inquiry into the standards governing such searches. Although the underlying command of the Fourth Amendment is always that searches and seizures be reasonable, what is reasonable depends on the context within which a search takes place. The determination of the standard of reasonableness governing any specific class of searches requires "balancing the need to search against the invasion which the search entails." On one side of the balance are arrayed the individual's legitimate expectations of privacy and personal security; on the other, the government's need for effective methods to deal with breaches of public order.

We have recognized that even a limited search of the person is a substantial invasion of privacy. We have also recognized that searches of closed items of personal luggage are intrusions on protected privacy interests, for "the Fourth Amendment provides protection to the owner of every container that conceals its contents from plain view." A search of a child's person or of a closed purse or other bag carried on her person, no less than a similar search carried out on an adult, is undoubtedly a severe violation of subjective expectations of privacy.

. . . To receive the protection of the Fourth Amendment, an expectation of privacy must be one that society is "prepared to recognize as legitimate." The State of New Jersey has argued that because of the pervasive supervision to which children in the schools are necessarily subject, a child has virtually no legitimate expectation of privacy in articles of personal property "unnecessarily" carried into a school. This argument has two factual premises: (1) the fundamental incompatibility of expectations of privacy with the maintenance of a sound educational environment; and (2) the minimal interest of the child in bringing any items of personal property into the school. Both premises are severely flawed.

Although this Court may take notice of the difficulty of maintaining discipline in the public schools today, the situation is not so dire that students in the schools may claim no legitimate expectations of privacy. . . .

Nor does the State's suggestion that children have no legitimate need to bring personal property into the schools seem well anchored in reality. Students at a minimum must bring to school not only the supplies needed for their studies, but also keys, money, and the necessaries of personal hygiene and grooming. In addition, students may carry on their persons or in purses or wallets such nondisruptive yet highly personal items as photographs, letters, and diaries. Finally, students may have perfectly legitimate reasons to carry with them articles of property needed in connection with extracurricular or recreational activities. In short, schoolchildren may find it necessary to carry with them a variety of legitimate, noncontraband items, and there is no reason to conclude that they have necessarily waived all rights to privacy in such items merely by bringing them onto school grounds.

Against the child's interest in privacy must be set the substantial interest of teachers and administrators in maintaining discipline in the classroom and on school grounds. Maintaining order in the classroom has never been easy, but in recent years, school disorder has often taken particularly ugly forms: drug use and violent crime in the schools have become major social problems. . . . "Events calling for discipline are frequent occurrences and sometimes require immediate, effective action." Accordingly, we have recognized that maintaining security and order in the schools requires a certain degree of flexibility in school disciplinary procedures, and we have respected the value of preserving the informality of the student-teacher relationship.

How, then, should we strike the balance between the schoolchild's legitimate expectations of privacy and the school's equally legitimate need to maintain an environment in which learning can take place? It is evident that the school setting requires some easing of the restrictions to which searches by public authorities are ordinarily subject. The warrant requirement, in particular, is unsuited to the school environment: requiring a teacher to obtain a warrant before searching a child suspected of an infraction of school rules (or of the criminal law) would unduly interfere with the maintenance of the swift and informal disciplinary procedures needed in the schools. Just as we have in other cases dispensed with the warrant requirement when "the burden of obtaining a warrant is likely to frustrate the governmental purpose behind the search," we hold today that school officials need not obtain a warrant before searching a student who is under their authority.

The school setting also requires some modification of the level of suspicion of illicit activity needed to justify a search. Ordinarily, a search — even one that may permissibly be carried out without a warrant — must be based upon "probable cause" to believe that a violation of the law has occurred. However, "probable cause" is not an irreducible requirement of a valid search. The fundamental command of the Fourth Amendment is that searches and seizures be reasonable, and although "both the concept of probable cause and the requirement of a warrant bear on the reasonableness of a search, . . . in certain limited circumstances neither is required." Thus, we have in a number of cases recognized the legality of searches and seizures based on suspicions that, although "reasonable," do not rise to the level of probable cause. Where a careful balancing of governmental and private interests suggests that the public interest is best served by a Fourth Amendment standard of reasonableness that stops short of probable cause, we have not hesitated to adopt such a standard.

. . . [T]he legality of a search of a student should depend simply on the reasonableness, under all the circumstances, of the search. Determining the reasonableness of any search involves a twofold inquiry: first, one must consider "whether the . . . action was justified at its inception"; second, one must determine whether the search as actually conducted "was reasonably related in scope to the circumstances which justified the interference in the first place." Under ordinary circumstances, a search of a student by a teacher or other school official will be "justified at its inception" when there are reasonable grounds for suspecting that the search will turn up evidence that the student has violated or is violating either the law or the rules of the school. Such a search will be permissible in its scope when the measures adopted are reasonably related to the objectives of the search and not excessively intrusive in light of the age and sex of the student and the nature of the infraction.

This standard will, we trust, neither unduly burden the efforts of school authorities to maintain order in their schools nor authorize unrestrained intrusions upon the privacy of schoolchildren. By focusing attention on the question of reasonableness, the standard will spare teachers and school administrators the necessity of schooling themselves in the niceties of probable cause and permit them to regulate their conduct according to the dictates of reason and common sense. At the same time, the reasonableness standard should ensure that the interests of students will be invaded no more than is necessary to achieve the legitimate end of preserving order in the schools. . . .

There remains the question of the legality of the search in this case. . . . Our review of the facts surrounding the search leads us to conclude that the search was in no sense unreasonable for Fourth Amendment purposes. . . .

T.L.O. had been accused of smoking, and had denied the accusation in the strongest possible terms when she stated that she did not smoke at all. Surely it cannot be said that under these circumstances, T.L.O.'s possession of cigarettes would be irrelevant to the charges against her or to her response to those charges. T.L.O.'s possession of cigarettes, once it was discovered, would both corroborate the report that she had been smoking and undermine the credibility of her defense to the charge of smoking. . . . The relevance of T.L.O.'s possession of cigarettes to the question whether she had been smoking and to the credibility of her denial that she smoked supplied the necessary "nexus" between the item searched for and the infraction under investigation. Thus, if Mr. Choplick in fact had a reasonable suspicion that T.L.O. had cigarettes in her purse, the search was justified despite the fact that the cigarettes, if found, would constitute "mere evidence" of a violation. . . .

Mr. Choplick's suspicion that there were cigarettes in the purse was not an "inchoate and unparticularized suspicion or 'hunch'"; rather, it was the sort of "common-sense conclusio[n] about human behavior" upon which "practical people" — including government officials — are entitled to rely. . . .

STEVENS, J. joined by MARSHALL J. (and partially by BRENNAN, J.) concurring in part and dissenting in part. . . . Justice Brandeis was both a great student and a great teacher. It was he who wrote:

> Our Government is the potent, the omnipresent teacher. For good or for ill, it teaches the whole people by its example. Crime is contagious. If the Government becomes a lawbreaker, it breeds contempt for law; it invites every man to become a law unto himself; it invites anarchy. *Olmstead v. United States,* 277 U.S. 438, 485 (1928) (dissenting opinion).

Those of us who revere the flag and the ideals for which it stands believe in the power of symbols. We cannot ignore that rules of law also have a symbolic power that may vastly exceed their utility.

Schools are places where we inculcate the values essential to the meaningful exercise of rights and responsibilities by a self-governing citizenry. If the Nation's students can be convicted through the use of arbitrary methods destructive of personal liberty, they cannot help but feel that they have been dealt with unfairly. The application of the exclusionary rule in criminal proceedings arising from illegal school searches makes an important statement to young people that "our society attaches serious consequences to a violation of constitutional rights," and that this is a principle of "liberty and justice for all." . . .

. . . The majority holds that "a search of a student by a teacher or other school official will be 'justified at its inception' when there are reasonable grounds for suspecting that the search will turn up evidence that the student has violated or is violating either the law or the rules of the school." This standard will permit teachers and school administrators to search students when they suspect that the search will reveal evidence of even the most trivial school regulation or precatory guideline for student behavior. The Court's standard for deciding whether a search is justified "at its inception" treats all violations of the rules of the school as though they were fungible. For the Court, a search for curlers and sunglasses in order to enforce the school dress code is apparently just as important as a search for evidence of heroin addiction or violent gang activity. . . .

In this case, Mr. Choplick overreacted to what appeared to be nothing more than a minor infraction — a rule prohibiting smoking in the bathroom of the freshmen's and sophomores' building. . . . Because this conduct was neither unlawful nor significantly disruptive of school order or the educational process, the invasion of privacy associated with the forcible opening of T.L.O.'s purse was entirely unjustified at its inception. . . .

BRENNAN, J. joined by MARSHALL, J. concurring in part and dissenting in part. . . . I emphatically disagree with the Court's decision to cast aside the constitutional probable-cause standard when assessing the constitutional validity of a schoolhouse search. The Court's decision jettisons the probable-cause standard — the only standard that finds support in the text of the Fourth Amendment — on the basis of its Rohrschach-like "balancing test." Use of such a "balancing test" to determine the standard for evaluating the validity of a full-scale search represents a sizable innovation in Fourth Amendment analysis. This innovation finds support neither in precedent nor policy and portends a dangerous weakening of the purpose of the Fourth Amendment to protect the privacy and security of our citizens. Moreover, even if this Court's historic understanding of the Fourth Amendment were mistaken and a balancing test of some kind were appropriate, any such test that gave adequate weight to the privacy and security interests protected by the Fourth Amendment would not reach the preordained result the Court's conclusory analysis reaches today. Therefore, because I believe that the balancing test used by the Court today is flawed both in its inception and in its execution, I respectfully dissent.

NOTES & QUESTIONS

1. ***After Columbine: The Privacy Implications.*** On April 20, 1999, two high school students entered their school (Columbine High School) in Littleton, Colorado, armed with firearms and explosives. In a brutal rampage, they killed 12 students and 1 teacher and injured 23 others before killing themselves. As a result of the Columbine massacre and other shootings and violent threats in high schools across the country, school administrators began to adopt stricter safety measures to prevent violence. Such measures include the installation of metal detectors, surveillance cameras, routine backpack and locker searches by police officers, and requirements that students carry identification cards at all times while on school grounds. In one particularly controversial experiment in California, grade school children were to be required to wear RFID-enabled identity tags around their necks. After protests and national media attention, the school rescinded the proposed policy.

   What are the pros and cons of having students wear RFID identification tags? Some critics argue that adopting these measures will teach students that the only way to be secure is to live in a police state. Supporters contend that the loss of privacy is justified by additional security and protection. Under *T.L.O.*, are the new measures described above constitutional?

2. DRUG TESTING

VERNONIA SCHOOL DISTRICT V. ACTON

515 U.S. 646 (1995)

SCALIA, J. . . . Petitioner Vernonia School District 47J (District) operates one high school and three grade schools in the logging community of Vernonia, Oregon. As elsewhere in small-town America, school sports play a prominent role in the town's life, and student athletes are admired in their schools and in the community.

Drugs had not been a major problem in Vernonia schools. In the mid-to-late 1980's, however, teachers and administrators observed a sharp increase in drug use. Students began to speak out about their attraction to the drug culture, and to boast that there was nothing the school could do about it. Along with more drugs came more disciplinary problems. . . .

Not only were student athletes included among the drug users but, as the District Court found, athletes were the leaders of the drug culture. This caused the District's administrators particular concern, since drug use increases the risk of sports-related injury. Expert testimony at the trial confirmed the deleterious effects of drugs on motivation, memory, judgment, reaction, coordination, and performance. The high school football and wrestling coach witnessed a severe sternum injury suffered by a wrestler, and various omissions of safety procedures and misexecutions by football players, all attributable in his belief to the effects of drug use.

Initially, the District responded to the drug problem by offering special classes, speakers, and presentations designed to deter drug use. It even brought in a specially trained dog to detect drugs, but the drug problem persisted. . . .

At that point, District officials began considering a drug-testing program. They held a parent "input night" to discuss the proposed Student Athlete Drug Policy (Policy), and the parents in attendance gave their unanimous approval. The school board approved the Policy for implementation in the fall of 1989. Its expressed purpose is to prevent student athletes from using drugs, to protect their health and safety, and to provide drug users with assistance programs. . . .

The Policy applies to all students participating in interscholastic athletics. Students wishing to play sports must sign a form consenting to the testing and must obtain the written consent of their parents. Athletes are tested at the beginning of the season for their sport. In addition, once each week of the season the names of the athletes are placed in a "pool" from which a student, with the supervision of two adults, blindly draws the names of 10% of the athletes for random testing. Those selected are notified and tested that same day, if possible.

The student to be tested completes a specimen control form which bears an assigned number. Prescription medications that the student is taking must be identified by providing a copy of the prescription or a doctor's authorization. The student then enters an empty locker room accompanied by an adult monitor of the same sex. Each boy selected produces a sample at a urinal, remaining fully clothed with his back to the monitor, who stands approximately 12 to 15 feet behind the student. Monitors may (though do not always) watch the student while he produces the sample, and they listen for normal sounds of urination. Girls produce samples in an enclosed bathroom stall, so that they can be heard but not observed. After the sample is produced, it is given to the monitor, who checks it for temperature and tampering and then transfers it to a vial.

The samples are sent to an independent laboratory, which routinely tests them for amphetamines, cocaine, and marijuana. Other drugs, such as LSD, may be screened at the request of the District, but the identity of a particular student does not determine which drugs will be tested. The laboratory's procedures are 99.94% accurate. . . . Only the superintendent, principals, vice-principals, and athletic directors have access to test results, and the results are not kept for more than one year.

If a sample tests positive, a second test is administered as soon as possible to confirm the result. If the second test is negative, no further action is taken. If the second test is positive, the athlete's parents are notified, and the school principal convenes a meeting with the student and his parents, at which the student is given the option of (1) participating for six weeks in an assistance program that includes weekly urinalysis, or (2) suffering suspension from athletics for the remainder of the current season and the next athletic season. The student is then retested prior to the start of the next athletic season for which he or she is eligible. The Policy states that a second offense results in automatic imposition of option (2); a third offense in suspension for the remainder of the current season and the next two athletic seasons. . . .

In the fall of 1991, respondent James Acton, then a seventh grader, signed up to play football at one of the District's grade schools. He was denied participation, however, because he and his parents refused to sign the testing consent forms. The Actons filed suit, seeking declaratory and injunctive relief from enforcement of the Policy on the grounds that it violated the Fourth and Fourteenth Amendments to the United States Constitution and Article I, §9, of the Oregon Constitution. . . .

As the text of the Fourth Amendment indicates, the ultimate measure of the constitutionality of a governmental search is "reasonableness." . . . Where a search is undertaken by law enforcement officials to discover evidence of criminal wrongdoing, this Court has said that reasonableness generally requires the obtaining of a judicial warrant. Warrants cannot be issued, of course, without the showing of probable cause required by the Warrant Clause. But a warrant is not required to establish the reasonableness of *all* government searches; and when a warrant is not required (and the Warrant Clause therefore not applicable), probable cause is not invariably required either. A search unsupported by probable cause can be constitutional, we have said, "when special needs, beyond the normal need for law enforcement, make the warrant and probable-cause requirement impracticable."

We have found such "special needs" to exist in the public school context. There, the warrant requirement "would unduly interfere with the maintenance of the swift and informal disciplinary procedures [that are] needed," and "strict adherence to the requirement that searches be based upon probable cause" would undercut "the substantial need of teachers and administrators for freedom to maintain order in the schools." *T.L.O.,* 469 U.S., at 340. The school search we approved in *T.L.O.,* while not based on probable cause, *was* based on individualized *suspicion* of wrongdoing. . . .

The first factor to be considered is the nature of the privacy interest upon which the search here at issue intrudes. The Fourth Amendment does not protect all subjective expectations of privacy, but only those that society recognizes as "legitimate." What expectations are legitimate varies, of course, with context, depending, for example, upon whether the individual asserting the privacy interest is at home, at work, in a car, or in a public park. . . .

. . . [W]hile children assuredly do not "shed their constitutional rights . . . at the schoolhouse gate," the nature of those rights is what is appropriate for children in school.

Fourth Amendment rights, no less than First and Fourteenth Amendment rights, are different in public schools than elsewhere; the "reasonableness" inquiry cannot disregard the schools' custodial and tutelary responsibility for children. For their own good and that of their classmates, public school children are routinely required to submit to various physical examinations, and to be vaccinated against various diseases. . . . Particularly with regard to medical examinations and procedures, therefore, "students within the school environment have a lesser expectation of privacy than members of the population generally."

Legitimate privacy expectations are even less with regard to student athletes. School sports are not for the bashful. They require "suiting up" before each practice or event, and showering and changing afterwards. Public school locker rooms, the usual sites for these activities, are not notable for the privacy they afford. The locker rooms in Vernonia are typical: No individual dressing rooms are provided; shower heads are lined up along a wall, unseparated by any sort of partition or curtain; not even all the toilet stalls have doors. . . . [T]here is "an element of 'communal undress' inherent in athletic participation."

There is an additional respect in which school athletes have a reduced expectation of privacy. By choosing to "go out for the team," they voluntarily subject themselves to a degree of regulation even higher than that imposed on students generally. In Vernonia's public schools, they must submit to a preseason physical exam (James testified that his included the giving of a urine sample), they must acquire adequate insurance coverage or sign an insurance waiver, maintain a minimum grade point average, and comply with any "rules of conduct, dress, training hours and related matters as may be established for each sport by the head coach and athletic director with the principal's approval." Somewhat like adults who choose to participate in a "closely regulated industry," students who voluntarily participate in school athletics have reason to expect intrusions upon normal rights and privileges, including privacy. . . .

Having considered the scope of the legitimate expectation of privacy at issue here, we turn next to the character of the intrusion that is complained of. . . . Under the District's Policy, male students produce samples at a urinal along a wall. They remain fully clothed and are only observed from behind, if at all. Female students produce samples in an enclosed stall, with a female monitor standing outside listening only for sounds of tampering. These conditions are nearly identical to those typically encountered in public restrooms, which men, women, and especially schoolchildren use daily. Under such conditions, the privacy interests compromised by the process of obtaining the urine sample are in our view negligible.

The other privacy-invasive aspect of urinalysis is, of course, the information it discloses concerning the state of the subject's body, and the materials he has ingested. In this regard it is significant that the tests at issue here look only for drugs, and not for whether the student is, for example, epileptic, pregnant, or diabetic. Moreover, the drugs for which the samples are screened are standard, and do not vary according to the identity of the student. And finally, the results of the tests are disclosed only to a limited class of school personnel who have a need to know; and they are not turned over to law enforcement authorities or used for any internal disciplinary function.

Respondents argue, however, that the District's Policy is in fact more intrusive than this suggests, because it requires the students, if they are to avoid sanctions for a falsely positive test, to identify *in advance* prescription medications they are taking. We agree that this raises some cause for concern. . . . Nothing in the Policy [states that the school would not keep the information confidential], and when respondents choose, in effect, to challenge the Policy on its face, we will not assume the worst. Accordingly . . . the invasion of privacy was not significant. . . .

Finally, we turn to consider the nature and immediacy of the governmental concern at issue here, and the efficacy of this means for meeting it. . . . Is there a compelling state interest here? . . . .

That the nature of the concern is important — indeed, perhaps compelling — can hardly be doubted. Deterring drug use by our Nation's schoolchildren is at least as important as enhancing efficient enforcement of the Nation's laws against the importation of drugs. . . . [T]he effects of a drug-infested school are visited not just upon the users, but upon the entire student body and faculty, as the educational process is disrupted. . . .

As to the efficacy of this means for addressing the problem: It seems to us self-evident that a drug problem largely fueled by the "role model" effect of athletes' drug use, and of particular danger to athletes, is effectively addressed by making sure that athletes do not use drugs. Respondents argue that a "less intrusive means to the same end" was available, namely, "drug testing on suspicion of drug use." We have repeatedly refused to declare that only the "least intrusive" search practicable can be reasonable under the Fourth Amendment. Respondents' alternative entails substantial difficulties — if it is indeed practicable at all. It may be impracticable, for one thing, simply because the parents who are willing to accept random drug testing for athletes are not willing to accept accusatory drug testing for all students, which transforms the process into a badge of shame. Respondents' proposal brings the risk that teachers will impose testing arbitrarily upon troublesome but not drug-likely students. It generates the expense of defending lawsuits that charge such arbitrary imposition, or that simply demand greater process before accusatory drug testing is imposed. And not least of all, it adds to the ever-expanding diversionary duties of schoolteachers the new function of spotting and bringing to account drug abuse, a task for which they are ill prepared, and which is not readily compatible with their vocation. In many respects, we think, testing based on "suspicion" of drug use would not be better, but worse. . . .

Taking into account all the factors we have considered above — the decreased expectation of privacy, the relative unobtrusiveness of the search, and the severity of the need met by the search — we conclude Vernonia's Policy is reasonable and hence constitutional. . . .

O'CONNOR, J. joined by STEVENS and SOUTER, J.J. dissenting. . . . The population of our Nation's public schools, grades 7 through 12, numbers around 18 million. By the reasoning of today's decision, the millions of these students who participate in interscholastic sports, an overwhelming majority of whom have given school officials no reason whatsoever to suspect they use drugs at school, are open to an intrusive bodily search.

. . . Blanket searches, because they can involve "thousands or millions" of searches, "pos[e] a greater threat to liberty" than do suspicion-based ones, which "affec[t] one person at a time." Searches based on individualized suspicion also afford potential targets considerable control over whether they will, in fact, be searched because a person can avoid such a search by not acting in an objectively suspicious way. And given that the surest way to avoid acting suspiciously is to avoid the underlying wrongdoing, the costs of such a regime, one would think, are minimal.

But whether a blanket search is "better" than a regime based on individualized suspicion is not a debate in which we should engage. In my view, it is not open to judges or government officials to decide on policy grounds which is better and which is worse. For most of our constitutional history, mass, suspicionless searches have been generally considered *per se* unreasonable within the meaning of the Fourth Amendment. And we have allowed exceptions in recent years only where it has been clear that a suspicion-based regime would be ineffectual. Because that is not the case here, I dissent. . . .

[H]aving misconstrued the fundamental role of the individualized suspicion requirement in Fourth Amendment analysis, the Court never seriously engages the practicality of such a requirement in the instant case. And that failure is crucial because nowhere is it *less* clear that an individualized suspicion requirement would be ineffectual than in the school context. In most schools, the entire pool of potential search targets — students — is under constant supervision by teachers and administrators and coaches, be it in classrooms, hallways, or locker rooms.

The record here indicates that the Vernonia schools are no exception. The great irony of this case is that most (though not all) of the evidence the District introduced to justify its suspicionless drug testing program consisted of first- or second-hand stories of particular, identifiable students acting in ways that plainly gave rise to reasonable suspicion of in-school drug use — and thus that would have justified a drug-related search under our *T.L.O.* decision. Small groups of students, for example, were observed by a teacher "passing joints back and forth" across the street at a restaurant before school and during school hours. Another group was caught skipping school and using drugs at one of the students' houses. Several students actually *admitted* their drug use to school officials (some of them being caught with marijuana pipes). One student presented himself to his teacher as "clearly obviously inebriated" and had to be sent home. Still another was observed dancing and singing at the top of his voice in the back of the classroom; when the teacher asked what was going on, he replied, "Well, I'm just high on life." To take a final example, on a certain road trip, the school wrestling coach smelled marijuana smoke in a motel room occupied by four wrestlers, an observation that (after some questioning) would probably have given him reasonable suspicion to test one or all of them.

In light of all this evidence of drug use by particular students, there is a substantial basis for concluding that a vigorous regime of suspicion-based testing (for which the District appears already to have rules in place) would have gone a long way toward solving Vernonia's school drug problem while preserving the Fourth Amendment rights of James Acton and others like him. And were there any doubt about such a conclusion, it is removed by indications in the record that suspicion-based testing could have been supplemented by an equally vigorous campaign to have Vernonia's parents encourage their children to submit to the District's *voluntary* drug testing program. In these circumstances, the Fourth Amendment dictates that a mass, suspicionless search regime is categorically unreasonable.

. . . [I]ntrusive, blanket searches of schoolchildren, most of whom are innocent, for evidence of serious wrongdoing are not part of any traditional school function of which I am aware. Indeed, many schools, like many parents, prefer to trust their children unless given reason to do otherwise. As James Acton's father said on the witness stand, "[suspicionless testing] sends a message to children that are trying to be responsible citizens . . . that they have to prove that they're innocent . . . , and I think that kind of sets a bad tone for citizenship." . . .

BOARD OF EDUCATION V. EARLS

536 U.S. 822 (2002)

THOMAS, J. . . . The city of Tecumseh, Oklahoma, is a rural community located approximately 40 miles southeast of Oklahoma City. The School District administers all Tecumseh public schools. In the fall of 1998, the School District adopted the Student Activities Drug Testing Policy (Policy), which requires all middle and high school students to consent to drug testing in order to participate in any extracurricular activity. In practice, the Policy has been applied only to competitive extracurricular activities sanctioned by the Oklahoma Secondary Schools Activities Association, such as the Academic Team, Future Farmers of America, Future Homemakers of America, band, choir, pom pon, cheerleading, and athletics. Under the Policy, students are required to take a drug test before participating in an extracurricular activity, must submit to random drug testing while participating in that activity, and must agree to be tested at any time upon reasonable suspicion. The urinalysis tests are designed to detect only the use of illegal drugs, including amphetamines, marijuana, cocaine, opiates, and barbiturates, not medical conditions or the presence of authorized prescription medications. . . .

In *Vernonia,* this Court held that the suspicionless drug testing of athletes was constitutional. The Court, however, did not simply authorize all school drug testing, but rather conducted a fact-specific balancing of the intrusion on the children's Fourth Amendment rights against the promotion of legitimate governmental interests. Applying the principles of *Vernonia* to the somewhat different facts of this case, we conclude that Tecumseh's Policy is also constitutional. . .

We first consider the nature of the privacy interest allegedly compromised by the drug testing. . . . A student's privacy interest is limited in a public school environment where the State is responsible for maintaining discipline, health, and safety. Schoolchildren are routinely required to submit to physical examinations and vaccinations against disease. Securing order in the school environment sometimes requires that students be subjected to greater controls than those appropriate for adults.

Respondents argue that because children participating in nonathletic extracurricular activities are not subject to regular physicals and communal undress, they have a stronger expectation of privacy than the athletes tested in *Vernonia.* This distinction, however, was not essential to our decision in

Vernonia, which depended primarily upon the school's custodial responsibility and authority.

In any event, students who participate in competitive extracurricular activities voluntarily subject themselves to many of the same intrusions on their privacy as do athletes. Some of these clubs and activities require occasional off-campus travel and communal undress. All of them have their own rules and requirements for participating students that do not apply to the student body as a whole. . . . We therefore conclude that the students affected by this Policy have a limited expectation of privacy. . . .

Next, we consider the character of the intrusion imposed by the Policy. Urination is "an excretory function traditionally shielded by great privacy." . . .

Under the Policy, a faculty monitor waits outside the closed restroom stall for the student to produce a sample and must "listen for the normal sounds of urination in order to guard against tampered specimens and to insure an accurate chain of custody." The monitor then pours the sample into two bottles that are sealed and placed into a mailing pouch along with a consent form signed by the student. This procedure is virtually identical to that reviewed in *Vernonia,* except that it additionally protects privacy by allowing male students to produce their samples behind a closed stall. Given that we considered the method of collection in *Vernonia* a "negligible" intrusion, the method here is even less problematic.

In addition, the Policy clearly requires that the test results be kept in confidential files separate from a student's other educational records and released to school personnel only on a "need to know" basis. Respondents nonetheless contend that the intrusion on students' privacy is significant because the Policy fails to protect effectively against the disclosure of confidential information and, specifically, that the school "has been careless in protecting that information: for example, the Choir teacher looked at students' prescription drug lists and left them where other students could see them." But the choir teacher is someone with a "need to know," because during off-campus trips she needs to know what medications are taken by her students. Even before the Policy was enacted the choir teacher had access to this information. In any event, there is no allegation that any other student did see such information. This one example of alleged carelessness hardly increases the character of the intrusion.

Moreover, the test results are not turned over to any law enforcement authority. Nor do the test results here lead to the imposition of discipline or have any academic consequences. Rather, the only consequence of a failed drug test is to limit the student's privilege of participating in extracurricular activities. Indeed, a student may test positive for drugs twice and still be allowed to participate in extracurricular activities. After the first positive test, the school contacts the student's parent or guardian for a meeting. The student may continue to participate in the activity if within five days of the meeting the student shows proof of receiving drug counseling and submits to a second drug test in two weeks. For the second positive test, the student is suspended from participation in all extracurricular activities for 14 days, must complete four hours of substance abuse counseling, and must submit to monthly drug tests. Only after a third positive test will the student be suspended from participating in any extracurricular activity for the remainder of the school year, or 88 school days, whichever is longer.

Given the minimally intrusive nature of the sample collection and the limited uses to which the test results are put, we conclude that the invasion of students' privacy is not significant.

Finally, this Court must consider the nature and immediacy of the government's concerns and the efficacy of the Policy in meeting them. . . . The drug abuse problem among our Nation's youth has hardly abated since *Vernonia* was decided in 1995. In fact, evidence suggests that it has only grown worse. . . . The health and safety risks identified in *Vernonia* apply with equal force to Tecumseh's children. Indeed, the nationwide drug epidemic makes the war against drugs a pressing concern in every school.

Additionally, the School District in this case has presented specific evidence of drug use at Tecumseh schools. Teachers testified that they had seen students who appeared to be under the influence of drugs and that they had heard students speaking openly about using drugs. A drug dog found marijuana cigarettes near the school parking lot. Police officers once found drugs or drug paraphernalia in a car driven by a Future Farmers of America member. And the school board president reported that people in the community were calling the board to discuss the "drug situation.". . .

GINSBURG, J. joined by STEVENS, O'CONNOR, and SOUTER, J.J. dissenting. . . . The particular testing program upheld today is not reasonable, it is capricious, even perverse: Petitioners' policy targets for testing a student population least likely to be at risk from illicit drugs and their damaging effects. . . .

Vernonia cannot be read to endorse invasive and suspicionless drug testing of all students upon any evidence of drug use, solely because drugs jeopardize the life and health of those who use them. Many children, like many adults, engage in dangerous activities on their own time; that the children are enrolled in school scarcely allows government to monitor all such activities. If a student has a reasonable subjective expectation of privacy in the personal items she brings to school, see *T.L.O.,* surely she has a similar expectation regarding the chemical composition of her urine. Had the *Vernonia* Court agreed that public school attendance, in and of itself, permitted the State to test each student's blood or urine for drugs, the opinion in *Vernonia* could have saved many words.

The second commonality to which the Court points is the voluntary character of both interscholastic athletics and other competitive extracurricular activities. . .

The comparison is enlightening. While extracurricular activities are "voluntary" in the sense that they are not required for graduation, they are part of the school's educational program. . . . Participation in such activities is a key component of school life, essential in reality for students applying to college, and, for all participants, a significant contributor to the breadth and quality of the educational experience. Students "volunteer" for extracurricular pursuits in the same way they might volunteer for honors classes: They subject themselves to additional requirements, but they do so in order to take full advantage of the education offered them. . . .

Observing that students produce urine samples in a bathroom stall with a coach or teacher outside, *Vernonia* typed the privacy interests compromised by the process of obtaining samples "negligible.". . .

In this case, however, Lindsay Earls and her parents allege that the School District handled personal information collected under the policy carelessly, with little regard for its confidentiality. Information about students' prescription drug use, they assert, was routinely viewed by Lindsay's choir teacher, who left files containing the information unlocked and unsealed, where others, including students, could see them; and test results were given out to all activity sponsors whether or not they had a clear "need to know." . . .

The School District cites the dangers faced by members of the band, who must "perform extremely precise routines with heavy equipment and instruments in close proximity to other students," and by Future Farmers of America, who "are required to individually control and restrain animals as large as 1500 pounds." . . . Notwithstanding nightmarish images of out-of-control flatware, livestock run amok, and colliding tubas disturbing the peace and quiet of Tecumseh, the great majority of students the School District seeks to test in truth are engaged in activities that are not safety sensitive to an unusual degree. There is a difference between imperfect tailoring and no tailoring at all.

Even if students might be deterred from drug use in order to preserve their extracurricular eligibility, it is at least as likely that other students might forgo their extracurricular involvement in order to avoid detection of their drug use. Tecumseh's policy thus falls short doubly if deterrence is its aim: It invades the privacy of students who need deterrence least, and risks steering students at greatest risk for substance abuse away from extracurricular involvement that potentially may palliate drug problems.

NOTES & QUESTIONS

1. **Earls *vs.* Vernonia.** Do you agree with the Court's conclusion that the holding in this case flows logically from *Vernonia*? Why or why not?
2. ***Steroid Testing.*** Would a school be justified pursuant to *T.L.O., Vernonia,* and *Earls* to test for steroid abuse among student athletes? Among all students engaged in extracurricular activities?
3. ***Drug Testing for All Students?*** Suppose a school district decided to implement mandatory drug testing for *all* students. Based on the Supreme Court's reasoning, would this policy be constitutional? In other words, is the fact that the students tested are voluntarily engaged in extracurricular activities an essential element of the Court's holding?
4. ***Routine School Searches?*** Suppose, in response to concerns over violence and guns in school, a school district decides to engage in routine searches of the bags and backpacks of all students engaging in extracurricular activities. Based on *T.L.O., Vernonia,* and *Earls,* would this policy be constitutional?
5. ***Prescription Drugs.*** Note that the school in *Vernonia* collected from each student that it tested information about any prescription medication that the student was taking. Why did the school collect this information? Does such information add significantly to the privacy invasion in this case?

6. ***Searches and Symbolism.*** Consider the Supreme Court's holding in *Chandler v. Miller,* 520 U.S. 305 (1997), a case in which the Court struck down a drug testing requirement for candidates for public office. Writing for the Court, Justice Ginsburg said:

> What is left, after close review of Georgia's scheme, is the image the State seeks to project. By requiring candidates for public office to submit to drug testing, Georgia displays its commitment to the struggle against drug abuse. . . . But Georgia asserts no evidence of a drug problem among the State's elected officials, those officials typically do not perform high-risk, safety-sensitive tasks, and the required certification immediately aids no interdiction effort. The need revealed, in short, is symbolic, not "special," as that term draws meaning from our case law. . . .
>
> However well meant, the candidate drug test Georgia has devised diminishes personal privacy for a symbol's sake. The Fourth Amendment shields society against that state action.

At what point does drug testing of students become symbolic? Can *Earls* be reconciled with *Chandler*? We will consider *Chandler* in more detail in Part C of this chapter.

7. ***State Constitutional Law: The California Approach.*** Many states have their own versions of the Fourth Amendment in their constitutions. Accordingly, the constitutions of some states may provide more privacy protection to students than the federal Constitution. In addition to provisions that resemble the Fourth Amendment, some state constitutions contain an explicit right to privacy. One of these states is California, and its constitution states:

> All people are by nature free and independent and have inalienable rights. Among these are enjoying and defending life and liberty, acquiring, possessing, and protecting property, and pursuing and obtaining safety, happiness, and privacy. Cal. Const. Art I, §1.

In *Hill v. National Collegiate Athletic Ass'n,* 865 P.2d 633 (Cal. 1994), the National Collegiate Athletic Association (NCAA) randomly selected college athletes competing in postseason football games to provide urine samples to be tested for drugs. Student athletes attending Stanford University sued, contending that the NCAA drug testing violated their right to privacy. As we will discuss later in this chapter, the California Supreme Court found that this provision of the state constitution applied to the private sector. The California high court also rejected the challenge to the NCAA drug testing:

> By its nature, sports competition demands highly disciplined physical activity conducted in accordance with a special set of social norms. Unlike the general population, student athletes undergo frequent physical examinations, reveal their bodily and medical conditions to coaches and trainers, and often dress and undress in same-sex locker rooms. In so doing, they normally and reasonably forgo a measure of their privacy in exchange for the personal and professional benefits of extracurricular athletics.
>
> A student athlete's already diminished expectation of privacy is outweighed by the NCAA's legitimate regulatory objectives in conducting testing for proscribed drugs. As a sponsor and regulator of sporting events, the

NCAA has self-evident interests in ensuring fair and vigorous competition, as well as protecting the health and safety of student athletes. These interests justify a set of drug testing rules reasonably calculated to achieve drug-free athletic competition. The NCAA's rules contain elements designed to accomplish this purpose, including: (1) advance notice to athletes of testing procedures and written consent to testing; (2) random selection of athletes actually engaged in competition; (3) monitored collection of a sample of a selected athlete's urine in order to avoid substitution or contamination; and (4) chain of custody, limited disclosure, and other procedures designed to safeguard the confidentiality of the testing process and its outcome. As formulated, the NCAA's regulations do not offend the legitimate privacy interests of student athletes.

3. SCHOOL RECORDS

THE FAMILY EDUCATION RIGHTS AND PRIVACY ACT

The Family Educational Rights and Privacy Act (FERPA) of 1974, Pub. L. No. 93-380, 20 U.S.C. § 1232g, commonly known as the "Buckley Amendment," generally prohibits schools from releasing student "education records" without the authorization of the student and/or parent. Schools may release such "directory" information as names, addresses, dates of attendance, degrees earned, and activities unless the student and/or parent expressly indicates in writing that he or she wants it to remain confidential.

FERPA covers only records and information from education records, not information per se. Thus, school authorities' personal knowledge and observations that are not part of a record are not covered. *See Frasca v. Andrews*, 463 F. Supp. 1043, 1050 (E.D.N.Y. 1979) ("Congress could not have constitutionally prohibited comment on, or discussion of, facts about a student which were learned independently of his school records."). As a result, FERPA does not apply to "personal knowledge derived from direct, personal experience with a student."[4] For example, an employee of an educational institution, such as a faculty or staff member, can share information with others if she "personally observes a student engaging in erratic and threatening behavior."[5]

Education Records. "Education records" are "those records, files, documents, and other materials which contain information directly related to a student; and are maintained by an educational agency or institution." 20 U.S.C. § 1232g(a)(4)(A). "Law enforcement unit records" and certain medical treatment records maintained by school officials do not constitute education records, § 1232g(a)(4)(B), but virtually all other institutional records that are personally identifiable to one or more students are covered.

Notice. Schools must inform students and parents of their rights under FERPA. *See* 34 C.F.R. § 99.7.

---

[4] Nancy E. Tribbensee & Steven J. McDonald, *FERPA and Campus Safety*, 5 NACU Notes (No. 4, Aug. 6, 2007).

[5] *Id.*

Access and Ability to Correct Errors. Schools generally must provide students and/or parents with access to their education records — a chance to review their records upon request. § 1232g(a)(1)(A). Schools must provide the student with an opportunity for a hearing "to challenge the content of such student's education records, in order to insure that the records are not inaccurate, misleading, or otherwise in violation of the privacy or other rights of students, and to provide an opportunity for the correction or deletion of any inaccurate, misleading, or otherwise inappropriate data contained therein. . . ." § 1232g(a)(2).

Limits on Disclosure. Pursuant to § 1232g(b), schools cannot disclose a student's education records without written consent. Certain disclosures are exempted from this rule. For example, the school can disclose records to "school officials" with a "legitimate educational interest," to appropriate persons in order to protect health or safety of the student or others, as well as to a number of other entities and officials. § 1232g(b)(1). If the student does not opt out, a school may release to the public the student's name, address, telephone numbers, birth date, major, activities and sports, dates of attendance, degrees and awards received, and certain other such "directory" information. § 1232g(b)(5).

Enforcement. FERPA authorizes the Secretary of Education to end all federal funding if a school fails to comply with the statute. § 1232g(f). The Department of Education's Family Policy Compliance Office oversees the enforcement of FERPA. *See* 34 C.F.R. § 99.60(b). Before the Compliance Office takes action, an individual must file a complaint against a school. The Compliance Office then investigates and if the school is found in violation of FERPA, the Compliance Office recommends specific steps that the institution must take to comply. *See* 34 C.F.R. § 99.66. If the school fails to comply, then funding can be stopped.

The Law Enforcement Exception. Prior to a number of amendments in the 1990s, campus law enforcement records were covered by FERPA and therefore could not be disclosed to the public at large. In 1990, FERPA was amended to permit schools to inform violent crime victims of the results of school disciplinary proceedings. Pursuant to § 1232g(b)(6):

> Nothing in this section shall be construed to prohibit an institution of postsecondary education from disclosing, to an alleged victim of any crime of violence . . . the results of any disciplinary proceeding conducted by such institution against the alleged perpetrator of such crime with respect to such crime.[6]

---

[6] For more background on FERPA, see Nicholas Trott Long, *Privacy in the World of Education: What Hath James Buckley Wrought?*, 46 Rhode Island B.J. 9 (Feb. 1998); Maureen P. Rada, Note, *The Buckley Conspiracy: How Congress Authorized the Cover-up of Campus Crime and How It Can Be Undone*, 59 Ohio St. L.J. 1799 (1998); Sandra L. Macklin, *Students' Rights in Indiana: Wrongful Distribution of Student Records and Potential Remedies*, 74 Ind. L.J. 1321 (1999).

A subsequent amendment to FERPA, in 1992, excluded from the definition of "education records" certain records created by an institution's "law enforcement unit" at least in part for law enforcement purposes and maintained by that unit. § 1232g(a)(4)(B)(ii).

Other Disclosure Exceptions. Beyond the law enforcement exception, FERPA also contains other exceptions to its general prohibition against disclosure of education records. For example, it allows campus personnel to share information from records with other "school officials" who have "legitimate educational interests" in the information. According to the Family Policy Compliance Office of the Department of Education, a legitimate educational interest exists when "the official needs to review an educational record in order to fulfill his or her professional responsibilities for the University." In addition, FERPA contains an emergency exception for disclosure "to appropriate parties . . . if knowledge is necessary to protect the health or safety of the student or other individuals."

OWASSO INDEPENDENT SCHOOL DISTRICT V. FALVO

534 U.S. 426 (2002)

KENNEDY, J. Teachers sometimes ask students to score each other's tests, papers, and assignments as the teacher explains the correct answers to the entire class. Respondent contends this practice, which the parties refer to as peer grading, violates the Family Educational Rights and Privacy Act of 1974 (FERPA or Act), 88 Stat. 571, 20 U.S.C. § 1232g. We took this case to resolve the issue. . . .

Respondent claimed the peer grading embarrassed her children. She asked the school district to adopt a uniform policy banning peer grading and requiring teachers either to grade assignments themselves or at least to forbid students from grading papers other than their own. The school district declined to do so, and respondent brought a class action pursuant to 42 U.S.C. § 1983. Respondent alleged the school district's grading policy violated FERPA and other laws not relevant here. . . .

Petitioners, supported by the United States as amicus curiae, contend the definition covers only institutional records — namely, those materials retained in a permanent file as a matter of course. They argue that records "maintained by an educational agency or institution" generally would include final course grades, student grade point averages, standardized test scores, attendance records, counseling records, and records of disciplinary actions — but not student homework or classroom work. . . .

Two statutory indicators tell us that the Court of Appeals erred in concluding that an assignment satisfies the definition of education records as soon as it is graded by another student. First, the student papers are not, at that stage, "maintained" within the meaning of § 1232g(a)(4)(A). The ordinary meaning of the word "maintain" is "to keep in existence or continuance; preserve; retain." Random House Dictionary of the English Language 1160 (2d ed. 1987). Even assuming the teacher's grade book is an education record — a point the parties contest and one we do not decide here — the score on a student-graded assignment is not "contained therein," § 1232g(b)(1), until the teacher records it. The teacher does not maintain the grade while students correct their peers' assignments or call out their own marks. Nor do the student graders maintain the grades within the meaning of § 1232g(a)(4)(A). The word "maintain" suggests FERPA records will be kept in a filing cabinet in a records room at the school or on a permanent secure database, perhaps even after the student is no longer enrolled. The student graders only handle assignments for a few moments as the teacher calls out the answers. It is fanciful to say they maintain the papers in the same way the registrar maintains a student's folder in a permanent file. . . .

Respondent's construction of the term "education records" to cover student homework or classroom work would impose substantial burdens on teachers across the country. It would force all instructors to take time, which otherwise could be spent teaching and in preparation, to correct an assortment of daily student assignments. . . . At argument, counsel for respondent seemed to agree that if a teacher in any of the thousands of covered classrooms in the Nation puts a happy face, a gold star, or a disapproving remark on a classroom assignment, federal law does not allow other students to see it.

We doubt Congress meant to intervene in this drastic fashion with traditional state functions. Under the Court of Appeals' interpretation of FERPA, the federal power would exercise minute control over specific teaching methods and instructional dynamics in classrooms throughout the country. The Congress is not likely to have mandated this result, and we do not interpret the statute to require it. . . .

NOTES & QUESTIONS

1. ***The Enforcement of FERPA.*** In *Owasso,* the individual plaintiffs used 42 U.S.C. § 1983 to challenge the grading policy as an infringement of their FERPA rights. Section 1983 authorizes individuals to sue state officials for violations of federal law and the Constitution. Recall also that FERPA does not directly provide for a private cause of action; it is enforced by the Secretary of Education. The Court did not reach the issue of whether § 1983 was an appropriate vehicle for private parties to seek redress for violations of FERPA. Instead, the Court addressed the issue in a case decided later in the same term.

   In *Gonzaga University v. Doe,* 536 U.S. 273 (2002), a student at Gonzaga University was attempting to become a public elementary school teacher upon graduation. Gonzaga was currently investigating Doe for allegations of sexual misconduct. Gonzaga contacted the state agency for teacher certification and disclosed to the agency the allegations. The victim of the alleged sexual misconduct later denied the allegations and stated that Gonzaga officials were wrong in their assessment of her relationship with Doe. Doe sued Gonzaga under § 1983, alleging a violation of FERPA. Doe contended that FERPA conferred to him a right not to have his education records disclosed to unauthorized persons without his consent. A jury awarded him $1,155,000, including compensatory and punitive damages. The Court held that FERPA could not be enforced by a private right of action under § 1983: "[A] plaintiff must assert the violation of a federal *right,* not merely a violation of federal *law.*" A federal statute must provide for an "unambiguously conferred right to support a cause of action brought under § 1983." The court concluded:

> [I]f Congress wishes to create new rights enforceable under § 1983, it must do so in clear and unambiguous terms — no less and no more than what is required for Congress to create new rights enforceable under an implied private right of action. FERPA's nondisclosure provisions contain no rights-creating language, they have an aggregate, not individual, focus, and they serve primarily to direct the Secretary of Education's distribution of public funds to educational institutions. They therefore create no rights enforceable under § 1983.

Justices Stevens and Ginsburg dissented, contending that FERPA contains numerous references to rights, including the title of the statute: "The entire statutory scheme was designed to protect such rights."

Recall the other federal privacy statutes that do not explicitly create a private right of action, such as the Health Insurance Portability and Accountability Act (HIPAA) regulations and Children's Online Privacy Protection Act (COPPA). What are the implications of this case for private causes of action under § 1983 to enforce these other privacy laws?

2. ***FERPA and the Virginia Tech Shooter.*** On April 16, 2007, Seung Cho, a student at Virginia Tech, shot and killed 32 students and faculty, wounded many others, and then took his own life. In the immediate aftermath of the tragedy, the Governor of Virginia appointed a panel to review the events leading up to the shootings and the handling of the incidents. Among other topics, the report looked at FERPA and other privacy laws.

The Review Panel found that many people knew about Cho's mental instability yet did not share what they knew with others because of widespread (and often incorrect) beliefs that information privacy laws blocked such information sharing:

> While Cho was a student at Virginia Tech, his professors, fellow students, campus police, the Office of Judicial Affairs, the Care Team, and the Cook Counseling Center all had dealings with him that raised questions about his mental stability. There is no evidence that Cho's parents were ever told of these contacts, and they say they were unaware of his problems at school. Most significantly, there is no evidence that Cho's parents, his suitemates, and their parents were ever informed that he had been temporarily detained, put through a commitment hearing for involuntary admission, and found to be a danger to himself. Efforts to share this information were impeded by laws about privacy of information, according to several university officials and the campus police. Indeed, the university's attorney, during one of the panel's open hearings and in private meetings, told the panel that the university could not share this information due to privacy laws.
>
> The panel's review of information privacy laws governing mental health, law enforcement, and educational records and information revealed wide-spread lack of understanding, conflicting practice, and laws that were poorly designed to accomplish their goals. Information privacy laws are intended to strike a balance between protecting privacy and allowing information sharing

> that is necessary or desirable. Because of this difficult balance, the laws are often complex and hard to understand.
>
> The widespread perception is that information privacy laws make it difficult to respond effectively to troubled students. This perception is only partly correct. Privacy laws can block some attempts to share information, but even more often may cause holders of such information to default to the nondisclosure option — even when laws permit the option to disclose. Sometimes this is done out of ignorance of the law, and sometimes intentionally because it serves the purposes of the individual or organization to hide behind the privacy law. A narrow interpretation of the law is the least risky course, notwithstanding the harm that may be done to others if information is not shared.

Among other recommendations, the Report of the Review Panel suggested:

> The provisions [of privacy law] should insulate a person or organization from liability (or loss of funding) for making a disclosure with a good faith belief that the disclosure was necessary to protect the health, safety, or welfare of the person involved or members of the general public. Laws protecting good-faith disclosure for health, safety, and welfare can help combat any bias toward nondisclosure.[7]

What are the costs and benefits of this recommendation? Are there viable alternatives? How should officials share the mental health information of troubled students?

Regarding FERPA more specifically, the Report noted that "FERPA does not address the differences between medical records and ordinary educational records such as grade transcripts. It is not clear whether FERPA preempts state law regarding medical records and confidentiality of medical information or merely adds another requirement on top of these records." The Report recommended that "FERPA should make explicit an exception regarding treatment records. Disclosure of treatment records from university clinics should be available to any health care provider without the student's consent when the records are needed for medical treatment, as they would be if covered under HIPAA." Additionally, it recommended that FERPA's exception for release of records in an emergency should be interpreted more flexibly.

A federal task force also reported to the President after the Virginia Tech shooting. Among its key findings were the presence of "substantial obstacles" to information sharing; the panel stated: "Education officials, healthcare providers, law enforcement personnel, and others are not fully informed about when they can share critical information on persons who are likely to be a danger to self or others, and the resulting confusion may chill legitimate information sharing." It observed that it had repeatedly heard of "information silos" within educational institutions. It called for an increase in information sharing and collaboration among state and local communities, educators, mental health officers and law enforcement. It also requested that federal agencies provide additional guidance as to how information can be legally shared under HIPAA and FERPA.

---

[7] Virginia Tech Review Panel, *Mass Shootings at Virginia Tech* 63, 68 (Aug. 2007), http://www.governor.virginia.gov/TempContent/techPanelReport.cfm.

As a first step in providing such guidance, the U.S. Department of Education published a Notice of Proposed Rulemaking on March 24, 2008. The proposed regulations amend the regulations interpreting FERPA. Perhaps the most notable of these proposed amendments concerns the rules for emergency disclosures to parents of college students.

FAMILY EDUCATIONAL RIGHTS AND PRIVACY: PROPOSED RULE

73 Fed. Reg. 15574 (March 24, 2008)

Proposed Regulations: The proposed regulations in § 99.5 clarify that even after a student has become an eligible student, an educational agency or institution may disclose education records to the student's parents, without the consent of the eligible student, if the student is a dependent for Federal income tax purposes (§ 99.31(a)(8)); in connection with a health or safety emergency (§ 99.31(a)(10)); if the student is under the age of 21 and has violated an institutional rule or policy governing the use or possession of alcohol or a controlled substance (§ 99.31(a)(15)); and if the disclosure falls within any other exception to the consent requirement in § 99.31(a) of the regulations, such as the disclosure of directory information or in compliance with a court order or lawfully issued subpoena. The proposed regulations in § 99.36(a) would clarify that an eligible student's parents are appropriate parties to whom an educational agency or institution may disclose personally identifiable information from education records without consent in a health or safety emergency.

Reasons: The Secretary is concerned that some institutions are under the mistaken impression that FERPA prevents them from providing parents with any information about a college student. The proposed regulations are needed to clarify that FERPA contains exceptions to the written consent requirement that permit colleges and other educational agencies and institutions to disclose personally identifiable information from education records to parents of certain eligible students whether or not the student consents.

Section 99.31(a)(8) permits an educational agency or institution to disclose education records, without consent, to either parent if at least one of the parents has claimed the student as a dependent on the parent's most recent tax return. Because many college students (and 18-year-old high school students) are tax dependents of their parents, this provision allows these institutions to disclose information from education records to the students' parents without meeting the written consent requirements in § 99.30. (Institutions must first determine that a parent has claimed the student as a dependent on the parent's Federal income tax return. Institutions can determine that a parent claimed a student as a dependent by asking the parent to submit a copy of the parent's most recent Federal tax return. Institutions can also rely on a student's assertion that he or she is not a dependent unless the parent provides contrary evidence.)

The proposed regulations are also needed to clarify that colleges and other institutions may disclose information from education records to an eligible student's parents, without consent, under § 99.31(a)(15) if the institution has determined that the student has violated Federal, State, or local law or an institution's rules or policies governing alcohol or substance abuse (provided the student is under 21 years of age), and in connection with a health or safety emergency under §§ 99.31(a)(10) and 99.36 (regardless of the student's age) if the information is needed to protect the health or safety of the student or other individuals. These exceptions apply whether or not the student is a dependent of a parent for tax purposes. These proposed regulations would clarify the Department's policy with respect to an agency's or institution's disclosure of information from education records to parents under the health and safety emergency exception and do not represent a change in the Department's interpretation of who may qualify as an appropriate party under the health or safety emergency exception to the consent requirement. While institutions may choose to follow a policy of not disclosing education records to parents of eligible students in these circumstances, FERPA does not mandate such a policy.

Health and Safety Emergencies (§ 99.36)

Section 99.36(c) (Conditions That Apply to Disclosure of Information in Health and Safety Emergencies)

Statute: Under 20 U.S.C. 1232g(b)(1)(I), an educational agency or institution may disclose personally identifiable information from education records without prior written consent, subject to regulations by the Secretary, in connection with an emergency to appropriate persons if the knowledge of such information is necessary to protect the health or safety of the student or other persons.

Proposed Regulations: The Department proposes to revise § 99.36(c) to remove the language requiring strict construction of this exception and add a provision that in making a determination under § 99.36(a), an educational agency or institution may take into account the totality of the circumstances pertaining to a threat to the safety or health of a student or other individuals. If the educational agency or institution determines that there is an articulable and significant threat to the health or safety of a student or other individuals, it may disclose information from education records to any person whose knowledge of the information is necessary to protect the health and safety of the student or other individuals. If, based on the information available at the time of the determination, there is a rational basis for the determination, the Department will not substitute its judgment for that of the educational agency or institution in evaluating the circumstances and making its determination.

Reasons: . . . [I]n balancing the interests of safety, privacy, and treatment, the Secretary proposes to revise the regulation to specify legal standards, but to couple those standards with greater flexibility and deference to administrators so they can bring appropriate resources to bear on a circumstance that threatens the health or safety of individuals. . . .

Section 99.36 is amended by revising paragraphs (a) and (c) to read as follows:

34 CFR § 99.36

§ 99.36 What conditions apply to disclosure of information in health and safety emergencies?

(a) An educational agency or institution may disclose personally identifiable information from an education record to appropriate parties, including parents of an eligible student, in connection with an emergency if knowledge of the information is necessary to protect the health or safety of the student or other individuals. . . .

(c) In making a determination under paragraph (a) of this section, an educational agency or institution may take into account the totality of the circumstances pertaining to a threat to the safety or health of a student or other individuals. If the educational agency or institution determines that there is articulable and significant threat to the health or safety of a student or other individuals, it may disclose information from education records to any person whose knowledge of the information is necessary to protect the health and safety of the student or other individuals. If, based on the information available at the time of the determination, there is a rational basis for the determination, the Department will not substitute its judgment for that of the educational agency or institution in evaluating the circumstances and making its determination. . . .

NOTES & QUESTIONS

1. ***Telling Mom and Dad?*** Should FERPA and the appropriate regulation permit or even require schools to release information about students to their parents? Should the rule apply beyond minors to adult college students, such as Cho at Virginia Tech?
2. ***"A Rational Basis."*** The proposed regulations excerpted above set up a test with strong and weak elements concerning disclosure of information from an educational record during a health and safety emergency. To make use of this disclosure rule, the educational institution must determine that "knowledge of the information is necessary to protect the health or safety of the student or other individuals." At the same time, however, the Department of Education will "not substitute its judgment for that of the educational agency or institution" so long as there was a rational basis for the judgment at the time of the decision. Moreover, the educational institution is to take into account "the totality of the circumstances" in determining whether an "articulable and significant threat" exists. In the analysis of Steven McDonald, general counsel at the Rhode Island School of Design, the proposed language is meant to make it clear that a campus will not "get in trouble for a good faith decision made in the heat of the moment before all facts are known."[8] Does the resulting regulatory safety net extend too far?

[8] Doug Lederman, *U.S. Proposes New Rules on Student Privacy*, Inside Higher Ed, Mar. 24, 2008, at www.insidehighered.com/news/2008/03/24/ferpa.

C. PRIVACY AT WORK

1. INTRODUCTION

Privacy in the workplace is a difficult and complex issue that continues to grow in importance as technology enables new forms of testing and monitoring of workers. Employer monitoring of workers is not new. For decades, employers have sought to keep close tabs on their employees. For example, in the early twentieth century, Ford Motor Company had its "Sociological Department" scrutinize employees to determine whether they gambled, drank, or conducted other frowned-upon activities. The purpose of the examination was to determine whether employees deserved bonuses.

Today, modern technology has enabled vastly more sophisticated forms of surveillance of workers. Employers routinely engage in a number of forms of investigation and monitoring of employees, such as conducting drug tests, obtaining credit reports and medical records, hiring private investigators to scrutinize employees, conducting psychological tests, administering polygraph examinations, requiring employees to fill out questionnaires containing detailed information about their personal lives, listening to telephone calls and voice mail, reading e-mail, monitoring computer use, searching offices and other employee work spaces, monitoring the number of keystrokes that an employee types, installing video surveillance devices to monitor workers, and even using electronic devices to track the location of workers.

Workplace monitoring is all but omnipresent. According to a 2001 survey by the American Management Association (AMA), 77.7 percent of major United States firms "record and review employee communications and activities on the job, including their phone calls, e-mail, Internet connections, and computer files." This figure had doubled since 1997.[9] A 2007 AMA survey found that "[e]mployers are primarily concerned about inappropriate Web surfing, with 66% monitoring Internet connections."[10] Employers use software to block connections to websites considered inappropriate (65 percent); use URL blocks to stop employees from visiting external blogs (18 percent); track content, keystrokes, and time spent at the keyboard (45 percent); store and review employees' computer files (43 percent); and monitor social networking sites (10 percent) and the blogosphere (12 percent) to observe comments about the company.

This survey also found that a wide majority of companies informed employees that they were being monitored. For example, "83% inform workers that the company is monitoring content, keystrokes, and time spent at the keyboard." Only 27 percent of employers addressed monitoring as part of their formal employee training whereas 70 percent of employers used an employee handbook to tell workers of Internet and e-mail surveillance. Employers believe that they have good reason to engage in employee surveillance and testing. First, employers desire to hire competent workers who are not likely to cause

---

[9] American Management Association, *Workplace Monitoring & Surveillance: Policies and Practices* (2001), at http://www.amanet.org/research/pdfs/emsfu_short.pdf.

[10] AMA/ePolicy Institute Research, *2007 Electronic Monitoring & Surveillance Survey* (2008), at www.amanet.org/research/pdfs/electronic-monitoring-surveillance-survey08.pdf.

workplace disruptions or be careless and reckless on the job, possibly exposing the employer to liability. Employers want workers who are not likely to have problems in their personal life or health that will cause absences from work or will decrease productivity. In certain professions, if an employee's troubled past comes to light, it could place the employer in a bad light (e.g., the staff of a politician). In other professions, such as child care, there is strong pressure for employers to scrutinize their employees' pasts and other aspects of their private lives to minimize the risk that the employee will engage in misconduct. Employers can be directly liable for negligent hiring.

Second, employers desire to monitor workers to force increased productivity and to curtail employee misconduct. Liability for sexual harassment has made employers more likely to investigate and monitor their employees to ensure that the workplace is free from harassment. The legal trend is to make employers more responsible for training and monitoring their workers and for ensuring that their workers are competent to perform their jobs, especially when their jobs affect the safety of others (e.g., truck drivers, train operators, pilots, mechanics, and so on). Employers can be vicariously liable if their employees commit a tort on the job. Employers can also be directly liable for inadequate supervision.

Third, employers may desire to search workers to investigate particular incidents of misconduct in the workplace. If items are being stolen or important secrets or documents are being leaked, the employer may want to engage in searches and surveillance to catch the offenders.

Thus, there are several reasons why employers may want to monitor their workers. Yet privacy in the workplace is also an important value. Today, people are spending increasingly more time at work, often well over a third of the day and over half of their time while awake. Also, more workers are "telecommuting" from home.

A wide spectrum of law governs the privacy of employees. To understand how this law applies, it is important to distinguish between public and private sector employees.

Public Sector Employees. The federal government is the largest employer in the United States. There are approximately 2.75 million federal civilian employees and 1.4 million employed in the armed forces. State and local governments employ millions of employees as well. Public sector employees are protected by a number of laws. The Fourth Amendment applies not just to the police, but to all government officials, including government employers. Public sector employees are thus protected by the Fourth Amendment, although, as you will see, in a rather limited way. The constitutional right to information privacy can protect against employer disclosures of information. In *Whalen v. Roe,* 429 U.S. 589 (1977), the Supreme Court held that the right to privacy encompasses the "individual interest in avoiding disclosure of personal matters." In many states, state constitutions also protect the privacy of public employees. Federal wiretap law applies to government employers and restricts their ability to conduct certain forms of electronic surveillance. State wiretap law may provide additional protection. The Americans with Disabilities Act (ADA) prohibits employers from asking certain questions about employees. The federal Privacy Act protects against disclosures by government entities and could apply to disclosures of information about federal government employees in certain circumstances. Employees can also sue employers for privacy invasions under the privacy torts — particularly for intrusion upon seclusion, public disclosure of private facts, and false light.

Private Sector Employees. Private sector employees enjoy some of the same protections as public sector employees, although the Fourth Amendment and most state constitutions do not apply to these employees. As you will see later in this chapter, however, in some states, federal and state constitutions can serve as a source of public policy for suits for wrongful termination in violation of public policy. Federal wiretap law applies not only to government employers but to private sector actors as well, including private sector employers. Additionally, the ADA, breach of contract, and privacy torts serve to protect the privacy of private sector employees.[11]

Depending upon the type of employment contract, employees may have additional contractual remedies. Pursuant to some types of employment contracts, employees can only be terminated for certain reasons, such as inadequate performance, unprofessional conduct, or disciplinary violations. If an employee is terminated and the reason is invalid, the employee can sue for wrongful termination and breach of contract. In contrast, many employees are "at-will" employees and may be dismissed at the whim of the employer. Generally, an at-will employee cannot bring a wrongful termination action. However, in many jurisdictions, there is an exception to this rule when the employee was fired for a reason that violates public policy (e.g., when the reason is discriminatory or the employee is fired for refusing to commit a criminal act). Employees who are terminated because of a refusal to comply with privacy-invasive testing, questioning, or monitoring or who are terminated because of the facts revealed by such activities can sometimes sue for wrongful termination in violation of public policy.

2. WORKPLACE SEARCHES

O'CONNOR V. ORTEGA

480 U.S. 709 (1987)

O'CONNOR, J. (plurality opinion). This suit under 42 U.S.C. §1983 presents two issues concerning the Fourth Amendment rights of public employees. First, we must determine whether the respondent, a public employee, had a reasonable expectation of privacy in his office, desk, and file cabinets at his place of work. Second, we must address the appropriate Fourth Amendment standard for a search conducted by a public employer in areas in which a public employee is found to have a reasonable expectation of privacy. . . .

---

[11] For more background about privacy in the workplace, see Sharona Hoffman, *Preplacement Examinations and Job-Relatedness: How to Enhance Privacy and Diminish Discrimination in the Workplace*, 49 U. Kan. L. Rev. 517 (2001).

Dr. Magno Ortega, a physician and psychiatrist, held the position of Chief of Professional Education at Napa State Hospital (Hospital) for 17 years, until his dismissal from that position in 1981. As Chief of Professional Education, Dr. Ortega had primary responsibility for training young physicians in psychiatric residency programs.

In July 1981, Hospital officials, including Dr. Dennis O'Connor, the Executive Director of the Hospital, became concerned about possible improprieties in Dr. Ortega's management of the residency program. In particular, the Hospital officials were concerned with Dr. Ortega's acquisition of an Apple II computer for use in the residency program. The officials thought that Dr. Ortega may have misled Dr. O'Connor into believing that the computer had been donated, when in fact the computer had been financed by the possibly coerced contributions of residents. Additionally, the Hospital officials were concerned with charges that Dr. Ortega had sexually harassed two female Hospital employees, and had taken inappropriate disciplinary action against a resident.

On July 30, 1981, Dr. O'Connor requested that Dr. Ortega take paid administrative leave during an investigation of these charges. . . . Dr. Ortega remained on administrative leave until the Hospital terminated his employment on September 22, 1981.

Dr. O'Connor selected several Hospital personnel to conduct the investigation, including an accountant, a physician, and a Hospital security officer. Richard Friday, the Hospital Administrator, led this "investigative team." At some point during the investigation, Mr. Friday made the decision to enter Dr. Ortega's office. The specific reason for the entry into Dr. Ortega's office is unclear from the record. . . .

The resulting search of Dr. Ortega's office was quite thorough. The investigators entered the office a number of times and seized several items from Dr. Ortega's desk and file cabinets, including a Valentine's Day card, a photograph, and a book of poetry all sent to Dr. Ortega by a former resident physician. These items were later used in a proceeding before a hearing officer of the California State Personnel Board to impeach the credibility of the former resident, who testified on Dr. Ortega's behalf. The investigators also seized billing documentation of one of Dr. Ortega's private patients under the California Medicaid program. . . .

Dr. Ortega commenced this action against petitioners in Federal District Court under 42 U.S.C. §1983, alleging that the search of his office violated the Fourth Amendment. . . .

The strictures of the Fourth Amendment, applied to the States through the Fourteenth Amendment, have been applied to the conduct of governmental officials in various civil activities. *New Jersey v. T.L.O.,* 469 U.S. 325 (1985). Thus, we have held in the past that the Fourth Amendment governs the conduct of school officials, building inspectors, and Occupational Safety and Health Act inspectors. . . . Searches and seizures by government employers or supervisors of the private property of their employees, therefore, are subject to the restraints of the Fourth Amendment.

. . . Our cases establish that Dr. Ortega's Fourth Amendment rights are implicated only if the conduct of the Hospital officials at issue in this case infringed "an expectation of privacy that society is prepared to consider reasonable." We have no talisman that determines in all cases those privacy expectations that society is prepared to accept as reasonable. Instead, "the Court has given weight to such factors as the intention of the Framers of the Fourth Amendment, the uses to which the individual has put a location, and our societal understanding that certain areas deserve the most scrupulous protection from government invasion." *Oliver v. United States,* 466 U.S. 170, 178 (1984).

Because the reasonableness of an expectation of privacy, as well as the appropriate standard for a search, is understood to differ according to context, it is essential first to delineate the boundaries of the workplace context. The workplace includes those areas and items that are related to work and are generally within the employer's control. At a hospital, for example, the hallways, cafeteria, offices, desks, and file cabinets, among other areas, are all part of the workplace. These areas remain part of the workplace context even if the employee has placed personal items in them, such as a photograph placed in a desk or a letter posted on an employee bulletin board.

Not everything that passes through the confines of the business address can be considered part of the workplace context, however. An employee may bring closed luggage to the office prior to leaving on a trip, or a handbag or briefcase each workday. While whatever expectation of privacy the employee has in the existence and the outward appearance of the luggage is affected by its presence in the workplace, the employee's expectation of privacy in the *contents* of the luggage is not affected in the same way. The appropriate standard for a workplace search does not necessarily apply to a piece of closed personal luggage, a handbag or a briefcase that happens to be within the employer's business address.

Within the workplace context, this Court has recognized that employees may have a reasonable expectation of privacy against intrusions by police. . . .

Individuals do not lose Fourth Amendment rights merely because they work for the government instead of a private employer. The operational realities of the workplace, however, may make *some* employees' expectations of privacy unreasonable when an intrusion is by a supervisor rather than a law enforcement official. Public employees' expectations of privacy in their offices, desks, and file cabinets, like similar expectations of employees in the private sector, may be reduced by virtue of actual office practices and procedures, or by legitimate regulation. . . . The employee's expectation of privacy must be assessed in the context of the employment relation. An office is seldom a private enclave free from entry by supervisors, other employees, and business and personal invitees. Instead, in many cases offices are continually entered by fellow employees and other visitors during the workday for conferences, consultations, and other work-related visits. Simply put, it is the nature of government offices that others — such as fellow employees, supervisors, consensual visitors, and the general public — may have frequent access to an individual's office. . . . Given the great variety of work environments in the public sector, the question whether an employee has a reasonable expectation of privacy must be addressed on a case-by-case basis. . . .

. . . [W]e recognize that the undisputed evidence suggests that Dr. Ortega had a reasonable expectation of privacy in his desk and file cabinets. The undisputed evidence discloses that Dr. Ortega did not share his desk or file cabinets with any other employees. Dr. Ortega had occupied the office for 17 years and he kept materials in his office, which included personal correspondence, medical files, correspondence from private patients unconnected to the Hospital, personal financial records, teaching aids and notes, and personal gifts and mementos. The files on physicians in residency training were kept outside Dr. Ortega's office. . . .

. . . [A]s we have stated in *T.L.O.,* "[t]o hold that the Fourth Amendment applies to searches conducted by [public employers] is only to begin the inquiry into the standards governing such searches. . . . [W]hat is reasonable depends on the context within which a search takes place." Thus, we must determine the appropriate standard of reasonableness applicable to the search. A determination of the standard of reasonableness applicable to a particular class of searches requires "balanc[ing] the nature and quality of the intrusion on the individual's Fourth Amendment interests against the importance of the governmental interests alleged to justify the intrusion." In the case of searches conducted by a public employer, we must balance the invasion of the employees' legitimate expectations of privacy against the government's need for supervision, control, and the efficient operation of the workplace.

"[I]t is settled . . . that 'except in certain carefully defined classes of cases, a search of private property without proper consent is "unreasonable" unless it has been authorized by a valid search warrant.'" There are some circumstances, however, in which we have recognized that a warrant requirement is unsuitable. . . . [A]s Justice Blackmun stated in *T.L.O.,* "[o]nly in those exceptional circumstances in which special needs, beyond the normal need for law enforcement, make the warrant and probable-cause requirement impracticable." . . .

The legitimate privacy interests of public employees in the private objects they bring to the workplace may be substantial. Against these privacy interests, however, must be balanced the realities of the workplace, which strongly suggest that a warrant requirement would be unworkable. While police, and even administrative enforcement personnel, conduct searches for the primary purpose of obtaining evidence for use in criminal or other enforcement proceedings, employers most frequently need to enter the offices and desks of their employees for legitimate work-related reasons wholly unrelated to illegal conduct. Employers and supervisors are focused primarily on the need to complete the government agency's work in a prompt and efficient manner. An employer may have need for correspondence, or a file or report available only in an employee's office while the employee is away from the office. Or, as is alleged to have been the case here, employers may need to safeguard or identify state property or records in an office in connection with a pending investigation into suspected employee misfeasance.

In our view, requiring an employer to obtain a warrant whenever the employer wished to enter an employee's office, desk, or file cabinets for a work-related purpose would seriously disrupt the routine conduct of business and would be unduly burdensome. Imposing unwieldy warrant procedures in such cases upon supervisors, who would otherwise have no reason to be familiar with such procedures, is simply unreasonable. In contrast to other circumstances in which we have required warrants, supervisors in offices such as at the Hospital are hardly in the business of investigating the violation of criminal laws. Rather, work-related searches are merely incident to the primary business of the agency. Under these circumstances, the imposition of a warrant requirement would conflict with "the common-sense realization that government offices could not function if every employment decision became a constitutional matter."

Whether probable cause is an inappropriate standard for public employer searches of their employees' offices presents a more difficult issue. . . .

The governmental interest justifying work-related intrusions by public employers is the efficient and proper operation of the workplace. Government agencies provide myriad services to the public, and the work of these agencies would suffer if employers were required to have probable cause before they entered an employee's desk for the purpose of finding a file or piece of office correspondence. Indeed, it is difficult to give the concept of probable cause, rooted as it is in the criminal investigatory context, much meaning when the purpose of a search is to retrieve a file for work-related reasons. Similarly, the concept of probable cause has little meaning for a routine inventory conducted by public employers for the purpose of securing state property. To ensure the efficient and proper operation of the agency, therefore, public employers must be given wide latitude to enter employee offices for work-related, noninvestigatory reasons.

We come to a similar conclusion for searches conducted pursuant to an investigation of work-related employee misconduct. Even when employers conduct an investigation, they have an interest substantially different from "the normal need for law enforcement." Public employers have an interest in ensuring that their agencies operate in an effective and efficient manner, and the work of these agencies inevitably suffers from the inefficiency, incompetence, mismanagement, or other work-related misfeasance of its employees. Indeed, in many cases, public employees are entrusted with tremendous responsibility, and the consequences of their misconduct or incompetence to both the agency and the public interest can be severe. . . . In our view, therefore, a probable cause requirement for searches of the type at issue here would impose intolerable burdens on public employers. . . . It is simply unrealistic to expect supervisors in most government agencies to learn the subtleties of the probable cause standard. . . . [W]e conclude that a reasonableness standard will permit regulation of the employer's conduct "according to the dictates of reason and common sense." . . .

. . . We hold, therefore, that public employer intrusions on the constitutionally protected privacy interests of government employees for noninvestigatory, work-related purposes, as well as for investigations of work-related misconduct, should be judged by the standard of reasonableness under all the circumstances. . . .

On remand . . . the District Court must determine the justification for the search and seizure, and evaluate the reasonableness of both the inception of the search and its scope. . . .

BLACKMUN, joined by BRENNAN, MARSHALL, and STEVENS, J.J. dissenting. . . . [T]he reality of work in modern time, whether done by public or private employees, reveals why a public employee's expectation of privacy in the workplace should be carefully safeguarded and not lightly set aside. It is, unfortunately, all too true that the workplace has become another home for most working Americans. Many employees spend the better part of their days and much of their evenings at work. Consequently, an employee's private life must intersect with the workplace, for example, when the employee takes advantage of work or lunch breaks to make personal telephone calls, to attend to personal business, or to receive personal visitors in the office. As a result, the tidy distinctions (to which the plurality alludes) between the workplace and professional affairs, on the one hand, and personal possessions and private activities, on the other, do not exist in reality. Not all of an employee's private possessions will stay in his or her briefcase or handbag. . . .

Although the plurality mentions the "special need" step, it turns immediately to a balancing test to formulate its standard of reasonableness. This error is significant because, given the facts of this case, no "special need" exists here to justify dispensing with the warrant and probable-cause requirements. As observed above, the facts suggest that this was an investigatory search undertaken to obtain evidence of charges of mismanagement at a time when Dr. Ortega was on administrative leave and not permitted to enter the Hospital's grounds. There was no special practical need that might have justified dispensing with the warrant and probable-cause requirements. Without sacrificing their ultimate goal of maintaining an effective institution devoted to training and healing, to which the disciplining of Hospital employees contributed, petitioners could have taken any evidence of Dr. Ortega's alleged improprieties to a magistrate in order to obtain a warrant. . . .

Furthermore, this seems to be exactly the kind of situation where a neutral magistrate's involvement would have been helpful in curtailing the infringement upon Dr. Ortega's privacy. Petitioners would have been forced to articulate their exact reasons for the search and to specify the items in Dr. Ortega's office they sought, which would have prevented the general rummaging through the doctor's office, desk, and file cabinets. . . .

NOTES & QUESTIONS

1. ***Is the Workplace Different?*** Why does the Court conclude that people's expectation of privacy is diminished in the workplace? Recall in *Katz* that the Court declared that privacy "protects people, not places." Is this declaration still true after *O'Connor v. Ortega*?

   Consider the observation of John Craig on the Court's decisions on workplace privacy:

   > A common element in the Court's constitutional workplace jurisprudence is the view that employment is a separate and unique context in which the Constitution operates less rigorously to restrain the state. The Court has clearly been concerned that imposing strict constitutional limitations on

privacy-invasive practices will hamper the day-to-day operations of the public sector workplace, and thereby create inefficiencies.[12]

2. ***The Privacy-Maximizing Aspects of* Ortega.** William Stuntz contends that the result in *Ortega* was paradoxically protective of privacy:

> . . . [I]f the law were to forbid these ordinary work-related entries, employers would have a substantial incentive to restructure the work environment to recover their ability to retrieve information. There are a number of ways of doing this. File cabinets can be moved from closed offices to open secretarial pools to make access easy; more records can be kept in the accounting department and fewer in individual employees' files; computer space can be arranged so that private (and secure) recordkeeping by individual employees is difficult.
>
> In short, the employer . . . has a fair degree of substantive power to reshape the rules of the workplace, in order to accomplish indirectly what he cannot do directly. If information cannot be taken from offices, offices can be turned into places where little information is stored. . . .
>
> Given this kind of authority, it is easy to imagine that employees might prefer a regime that gives their superiors broad discretion to enter presumptively private work areas. Such authority reduces the likelihood that sanctions (such as the failure to get a desired promotion or job assignment) will be imposed based on unverifiable, and possibly false, suspicions. More importantly, broad search authority vastly reduces the cost to government employers of creating private spaces for their employees. The Fourth Amendment issue is thus turned upside down: the rule that probably maximizes privacy (and thus the rule that search targets would probably want) is the rule that permits searches of work areas for any authentically work-related reason. That is the rule *Ortega* adopts.[13]

Had the Court in *Ortega* adopted a warrant and probable cause requirement, would employers likely restructure their workplaces in the privacy-reducing ways Stuntz suggests?

3. ***Reasonable Expectations of Privacy in One's Desk.*** In *Sheppard v. Beerman,* 18 F.3d 147, 152 (2d Cir.1994), plaintiff Brian Sheppard served as a law clerk to Justice Leon Beerman of the Supreme Court of New York. In New York, the Supreme Court is a trial court. Sheppard alleged that Beerman, after speaking ex parte with the prosecutor in a murder case, requested that Sheppard draft a denial of the defendant's speedy trial motion. Sheppard voiced his objection to the judge that the denial was unfair to the defendant. The argument became heated, with Sheppard accusing the judge of engaging in other instances of misconduct and he called the judge "corrupt" and a "son of a bitch." Beerman subsequently fired Sheppard.

Sheppard subsequently sued, claiming, among other things a violation of his Fourth Amendment rights. The court held:

---

[12] John D.R. Craig, *Privacy and Employment Law* 64-65 (1999).

[13] William J. Stuntz, *Implicit Bargains, Government Power, and the Fourth Amendment*, 44 Stan. L. Rev. 553, 579 (1992).

> Sheppard alleges that after the dismissal, Beerman searched his office, desk, and file cabinets in violation of his Fourth Amendment rights. . . .
>
> An "employee's expectation of privacy must be assessed in the context of the employment relation[ship]." *Ortega.* The working relationship between a judge and her law clerk, as noted by the district court, is unique. Unlike a typical employment relationship where an employer may limit the information she wants to share with her employees, in order for a judicial chambers to function efficiently, an absolute free flow of information between the clerk and the judge is usually necessary. Accordingly, the clerk has access to all the documents pertaining to a case. More importantly, clerks regularly have access to the judge's confidential thoughts on a case. The judge may discuss her feelings with her clerk, or may allow the clerk access to her personal notes. In turn, the judge necessarily has access to the files and papers kept by the clerk, which will often include the clerk's notes from discussions with the judge. Because of this distinctive open access to documents characteristic of judicial chambers, we agree with the district court's determination that Sheppard had "no reasonable expectation of privacy in chambers' appurtenances, embracing desks, file cabinets or other work areas."

4. ***Waiver of Fourth Amendment Rights.*** Can government employers require that their employees undergo unreasonable searches under the Fourth Amendment as a condition of employment? In short, the answer is no. *See Pickering v. Board of Education,* 391 U.S. 563 (1968). But if an employee voluntarily consents to the search, then such searches can be conducted. *See McDonell v. Hunter,* 809 F.2d 1302 (8th Cir. 1987).

K-MART CORP. V. TROTTI

677 S.W.2d 632 (Tex. Ct. App. 1984)

BULLOCK, J. K-Mart Corporation appeals from a judgment awarding the appellee, Trotti, $8,000.00 in actual damages and $100,000.00 in exemplary damages for [intrusion upon seclusion]. . . .

The appellee was an employee in the hosiery department at the appellants' store number 7441. Her supervisors had never indicated any dissatisfaction with her work nor any suspicion of her honesty.

The appellants provided their employees with lockers for the storage of personal effects during working hours. There was no assignment of any given locker to any individual employee. . . . The appellee, with appellants' knowledge, used one of these lockers and provided her own combination lock.

On October 31, 1981, the appellee placed her purse in her locker when she arrived for work. She testified that she snapped the lock closed and then pulled on it to make sure it was locked. When she returned to her locker during her afternoon break, she discovered the lock hanging open. Searching through her locker, the appellee further discovered her personal items in her purse in considerable disorder. Nothing was missing from either the locker or the purse. The store manager testified that, in the company of three junior administrators at the store, he had that afternoon searched the lockers because of a suspicion raised by the appellants' security personnel that an unidentified employee, not the appellee, had stolen a watch. The manager and his assistants were also searching for missing price-marking guns. The appellee further testified that, as she left the employee's locker area after discovering her locker open, she heard the manager suggest to his assistants, "Let's get busy again." The manager testified that none of the parties searched through employees' personal effects. . . .

The manager testified that during the initial hiring interviews, all prospective employees received verbal notification from personnel supervisors that it was the appellants' policy to conduct ingress-egress searches of employees and also to conduct unannounced searches of lockers. A personnel supervisor and an assistant manager, however, testified that, although locker searches did regularly occur, the personnel supervisors did not apprise prospective employees of this policy. . . .

We hold that the weight of the evidence indicates that the appellants' employees came upon a locker with a lock provided by an employee, disregarded the appellee's demonstration of her expectation of privacy, opened and searched the locker, and probably opened and searched her purse as well; and, in so holding, we consider it is immaterial whether the appellee actually securely locked her locker or not. It is sufficient that an employee in this situation, by having placed a lock on the locker at the employee's own expense and with the appellants' consent, has demonstrated a legitimate expectation to a right of privacy in both the locker itself and those personal effects within it. . . .

NOTES & QUESTIONS

1. ***Public Disclosure and the Workplace.*** Employers can be liable for public disclosure of private facts for revealing confidential information about their employees. For example, in *Levias v. United Airlines,* 500 N.E.2d 370 (Ohio Ct. App. 1985), the court held that a flight attendant had a viable public disclosure action when her employer disclosed medical information from her gynecologist to her supervisors and her husband. The disclosure of personal information by public sector employers can give rise to a § 1983 action for a violation of the constitutional right to information privacy.

3. WORKPLACE SURVEILLANCE

THOMPSON V. JOHNSON COUNTY COMMUNITY COLLEGE

930 F. Supp. 501 (D. Kan. 1996)

[The plaintiffs, a group of community college security personnel, sued the college for conducting video surveillance of their locker area. Among other things, the plaintiffs alleged that the surveillance violated federal wiretap law and the Fourth Amendment.]

VAN BEBBER, J. . . . Plaintiffs first claim that defendants violated Title I by conducting video surveillance in the workplace. Under Title I, "any person whose wire or oral communications is intercepted, disclosed or used in violation of [the Act] may in a civil action recover from the person or entity which engage in that violation such relief as may be appropriate." 18 U.S.C. §2520. . . .

Virtually every circuit that has addressed the issue of silent video surveillance has held that Title I does not prohibit its use. . . .

On the other hand, the above cited cases implicitly imply that video surveillance that includes the capability to record audio conversations would violate Title I. In that situation, the video image captured by the surveillance camera is not what violates Title I. Rather, it is the interception of an oral communication that subjects the interceptor to liability.

In their current motion, defendants argue that they installed a silent video surveillance camera in the security personnel locker area. Defendants contend that, as a matter of law, they are entitled to summary judgment on this issue because silent video surveillance does not fall within the protection of Title I. The court agrees. . . .

In Count II, plaintiffs have brought a claim pursuant to 42 U.S.C. §1983. They contend that defendants' warrantless video surveillance searches of the security personnel locker area violated their Fourth Amendment rights. The court disagrees.

Domestic silent video surveillance is subject to Fourth Amendment prohibitions against unreasonable searches. However, this does not mean that defendants' use of video surveillance automatically violated plaintiffs' Fourth Amendment rights. Rather, the court first must determine whether plaintiffs had a reasonable expectation of privacy in their locker area. If plaintiffs had no reasonable expectation of privacy in this area, there is "no fourth amendment violation regardless of the nature of the search." . . .

. . . [D]efendants assert that the security personnel locker area is similar to hallway lockers in a school. The security personnel locker area was part of a storage room that also housed the College's heating and air-conditioning equipment. Additionally, the College did not limit access to this storage room. Security personnel and other college employees, including maintenance and service personnel, had unfettered access to this storage room. Consequently, defendants argue that the open, public nature of the security personnel locker area defeats any reasonable expectation of privacy in this area. The court agrees.

. . . [V]ideo surveillance "in public places, such as banks, does not violate the fourth amendment; the police may record what they normally may view with the naked eye." In the employment context, the Supreme Court has held that "some government offices may be so open to fellow employees or the public that no expectation of privacy is reasonable." *O'Connor v. Ortega,* 480 U.S. 709 (1987). . . .

In the instant action, viewing the facts in a light most favorable to plaintiffs, the court finds that they did not have a reasonable expectation of privacy in the security personnel locker area. This area was not enclosed. Plaintiffs' activities could be viewed by anyone walking into or through the storage room/security personnel locker area. Additionally, plaintiffs cannot maintain that the security personnel locker area was reserved for their exclusive use considering that other college personnel also had regular access to this area. The court concludes that plaintiffs' lack of a reasonable expectation of privacy in the security personnel locker area defeats their claim that defendants violated their Fourth Amendment right to privacy.

NOTES & QUESTIONS

1. ***Intrusion upon Seclusion and Surveillance in the Workplace.*** In *Speer v. Ohio Department of Rehabilitation & Correction,* 624 N.E.2d 251 (Ohio Ct. App. 1993), rumors reached Leroy Payton, the supervisor of plaintiff Theresa Speer (a prison official) that Speer was being "too friendly" with two inmates. Payton launched an investigation and surveillance of Speer. In one instance, Payton hid in the ceiling of a co-ed staff rest room for over seven hours to spy on Speer. The trial court held that Payton's surveillance was pursuant to a broad policy of decision making and refused to second-guess Payton's choice of surveillance tactic. The court of appeals reversed, concluding that Payton's tactics were unreasonable and not defensible as a policy matter.
2. ***Intrusion upon Seclusion and Surveillance Outside the Workplace.*** In *Saldana v. Kelsey-Hayes,* 443 N.W.2d 382 (Mich. Ct. App. 1981), the plaintiff injured his back and arm from falling off a bicycle on the property of his employer, defendant Kelsey-Hayes Company. The defendant's property was comprised of different buildings, and plaintiff used his bicycle to travel from building to building. The plaintiff's employer suspected that the plaintiff was malingering and hired a private investigating firm to determine the extent of the plaintiff's injuries. The investigator observed the plaintiff's home from a parked car near his house, telephoned the plaintiff to determine whether he was home, walked passed the plaintiff's house and observed the plaintiff through an open window, used a powerful zoom lens to observe the plaintiff through the windows to his house, and posed as a process server in order to gain entry to the plaintiff's home and look around. According to the investigator, the plaintiff was able to move around freely. The plaintiff brought an action against his employer for intrusion upon seclusion. The court, however, concluded that the plaintiff's action should be dismissed:

   > . . . [P]laintiff can show an intrusion. First, agents of defendants entered plaintiff's home under false pretenses. Also, agents of defendants observed plaintiff through the windows of his home by the naked eye and with a powerful camera lens. Other jurisdictions have held that "window-peeping" is actionable. Whether the intrusion is objectionable to a reasonable person is a factual question best determined by a jury. It may not be objectionable to peer through an open window where the curtains are not drawn, but the use of a powerful lens to observe the interior of a home or of a subterfuge to enter a home could be found objectionable to a reasonable person.
   >
   > However, even if we find that looking into plaintiff's window with the naked eye and with a powerful camera lens is an intrusion which would be objectionable to a reasonable person, plaintiff still cannot prevail. Plaintiff does not allege facts that show the intrusions were into matters which plaintiff had a right to keep private. . . . The defendants' duty to refrain from intrusion into another's private affairs is not absolute in nature, but rather is limited by those rights which arise from social conditions, *including the business*

> *relationship of the parties.* Defendants' surveillance of plaintiff at his home involved matters which defendants had a legitimate right to investigate. . . . Plaintiff's privacy was subject to the legitimate interest of his employer in investigating suspicions that plaintiff's work-related disability was a pretext. We conclude that plaintiff does not meet the second requirement of the intrusion into seclusion test. Defendant also has a right to investigate matters that are potential sources of legal liability.

The *Saldana* court apparently treated the surveillance of the plaintiff outside the workplace as equivalent to surveillance inside the workplace. Should an employer be permitted to spy on its employees when they are not at work?

3. ***Limits on Employee Consent.*** Some states have enacted laws prohibiting surveillance cameras in certain areas of the workplace, such as rest rooms. Some of these prohibitions have criminal penalties. For example, pursuant to Conn. Gen. Stat. § 31-48b(b):

> No employer or agent or representative of an employer shall operate any electronic surveillance device or system, including but not limited to the recording of sound or voice or a closed circuit television system, or any combination thereof, for the purpose of recording or monitoring the activities of his employees in areas designed for the health or personal comfort of the employees or for safeguarding of their possessions, such as rest rooms, locker rooms or lounges.

Violations are punishable by fines; repeat violations (third and subsequent violations) are punishable by imprisonment for 30 days.

Can employees consent to video surveillance in such areas? Why would they give such consent freely? Recall from the notes following *O'Connor v. Ortega* that employees can consent to searches that would ordinarily be unreasonable under the Fourth Amendment. But what about consenting to violations of criminal statutes? For an answer, see *Cramer v. Consolidated Freightways, Inc.* in the notes following *Baggs v. Eagle-Pitcher Industries, Inc.*

4. ***United States vs. European Workplace Privacy Rights.*** For Matthew Finkin, employee privacy law sits on a continental divide. In European civil law systems, employers may limit employee privacy rights only to realize "legitimate, even necessary, business objectives."[14] These civil rights rest on a perception of employees as persons "who bear inalienable rights, assertable against their employers, including a right to privacy." In contrast, the U.S. common law "accords the employer near plenary power to govern the workplace; in fact, to govern the worker." Finkin concludes that the conception of the "employee as a person — the law's Menschenbild — in the civil and common law differs and sharply." Finkin finds that in the United States, the workplace is often not viewed as a shared life "where property rights and individual liberties have any need to be reconciled." Finkin ends his article by demanding: "[A]re we so very confident . . . [t]hat employees can

---

[14] Matthew W. Finkin, *Menschenbild: The Conception of the Employee as a Person in Western Law*, 23 Comp. Lab. L. & Pol'y J. 577 (2002).

make no claim whatsoever to any private space at work?" Do you agree that employee privacy rights in the United States are so restricted to allow the "employer near plenary power to govern the workplace"? How should the law reconcile the employer's ability to carry out legitimate business objectives and employees' privacy rights?

4. DRUG TESTING

NATIONAL TREASURY EMPLOYEES UNION V. VON RAAB

489 U.S. 656 (1989)

KENNEDY, J. . . . The United States Customs Service, a bureau of the Department of the Treasury, is the federal agency responsible for processing persons, carriers, cargo, and mail into the United States, collecting revenue from imports, and enforcing customs and related laws. An important responsibility of the Service is the interdiction and seizure of contraband, including illegal drugs. . . . In the routine discharge of their duties, many Customs employees have direct contact with those who traffic in drugs for profit. Drug import operations, often directed by sophisticated criminal syndicates, may be effected by violence or its threat. As a necessary response, many Customs operatives carry and use firearms in connection with their official duties.

In December 1985, respondent, the Commissioner of Customs . . . announced his intention to require drug tests of employees who applied for, or occupied, certain positions within the Service. . . .

In May 1986, the Commissioner announced implementation of the drug-testing program. Drug tests were made a condition of placement or employment for positions that meet one or more of three criteria. The first is direct involvement in drug interdiction or enforcement of related laws, an activity the Commissioner deemed fraught with obvious dangers to the mission of the agency and the lives of Customs agents. The second criterion is a requirement that the incumbent carry firearms, as the Commissioner concluded that "[p]ublic safety demands that employees who carry deadly arms and are prepared to make instant life or death decisions be drug free." The third criterion is a requirement for the incumbent to handle "classified" material, which the Commissioner determined might fall into the hands of smugglers if accessible to employees who, by reason of their own illegal drug use, are susceptible to bribery or blackmail.

After an employee qualifies for a position covered by the Customs testing program, the Service advises him by letter that his final selection is contingent upon successful completion of drug screening. An independent contractor contacts the employee to fix the time and place for collecting the sample. On reporting for the test, the employee must produce photographic identification and remove any outer garments, such as a coat or a jacket, and personal belongings. The employee may produce the sample behind a partition, or in the privacy of a bathroom stall if he so chooses. To ensure against adulteration of the specimen, or substitution of a sample from another person, a monitor of the same sex as the employee remains close at hand to listen for the normal sounds of urination. Dye is added to the toilet water to prevent the employee from using the water to adulterate the sample. . . .

The laboratory tests the sample for the presence of marijuana, cocaine, opiates, amphetamines, and phencyclidine. . . .

Customs employees who test positive for drugs and who can offer no satisfactory explanation are subject to dismissal from the Service. Test results may not, however, be turned over to any other agency, including criminal prosecutors, without the employee's written consent. . . .

Petitioners, a union of federal employees and a union official, commenced this suit . . . on behalf of current Customs Service employees who seek covered positions. Petitioners alleged that the Custom Service drug-testing program violated, inter alia, the Fourth Amendment. . . .

It is clear that the Customs Service's drug-testing program is not designed to serve the ordinary needs of law enforcement. Test results may not be used in a criminal prosecution of the employee without the employee's consent. The purposes of the program are to deter drug use among those eligible for promotion to sensitive positions within the Service and to prevent the promotion of drug users to those positions. These substantial interests . . . present a special need that may justify departure from the ordinary warrant and probable-cause requirements. . . .

. . . [A] warrant would provide little or nothing in the way of additional protection of personal privacy. A warrant serves primarily to advise the citizen that an intrusion is authorized by law and limited in its permissible scope and to interpose a neutral magistrate between the citizen and the law enforcement officer "engaged in the often competitive enterprise of ferreting out crime." . . . A covered employee is simply not subject "to the discretion of the official in the field." The process becomes automatic when the employee elects to apply for, and thereafter pursue, a covered position. Because the Service does not make a discretionary determination to search based on a judgment that certain conditions are present, there are simply "no special facts for a neutral magistrate to evaluate." . . .

Even where it is reasonable to dispense with the warrant requirement in the particular circumstances, a search ordinarily must be based on probable cause. Our cases teach, however, that the probable-cause standard "'is peculiarly related to criminal investigations.'" In particular, the traditional probable-cause standard may be unhelpful in analyzing the reasonableness of routine administrative functions, especially where the Government seeks to prevent the development of hazardous conditions or to detect violations that rarely generate articulable grounds for searching any particular place or person. Our precedents have settled that, in certain limited circumstances, the Government's need to discover such latent or hidden conditions, or to prevent their development, is sufficiently compelling to justify the intrusion on privacy entailed by conducting such searches without any measure of individualized suspicion. We think the Government's need to conduct the suspicionless searches required by the Customs program outweighs the privacy interests of employees engaged directly in drug interdiction, and of those who otherwise are required to carry firearms. . . .

We think Customs employees who are directly involved in the interdiction of illegal drugs or who are required to carry firearms in the line of duty likewise have a diminished expectation of privacy in respect to the intrusions occasioned by a urine test. Unlike most private citizens or government employees in general, employees involved in drug interdiction reasonably should expect effective inquiry into their fitness and probity. Much the same is true of employees who are required to carry firearms. Because successful performance of their duties depends uniquely on their judgment and dexterity, these employees cannot reasonably expect to keep from the Service personal information that bears directly on their fitness. While reasonable tests designed to elicit this information doubtless infringe some privacy expectations, we do not believe these expectations outweigh the Government's compelling interests in safety and in the integrity of our borders.

. . . [P]etitioners argue that the program is unjustified because it is not based on a belief that testing will reveal any drug use by covered employees. In pressing this argument, petitioners point out that the Service's testing scheme was not implemented in response to any perceived drug problem among Customs employees, and that the program actually has not led to the discovery of a significant number of drug users. Counsel for petitioners informed us at oral argument that no more than 5 employees out of 3,600 have tested positive for drugs. Second, petitioners contend that the Service's scheme is not a "sufficiently productive mechanism to justify [its] intrusion upon Fourth Amendment interests," because illegal drug users can avoid detection with ease by temporary abstinence or by surreptitious adulteration of their urine specimens. These contentions are unpersuasive. . . .

We are unable, on the present record, to assess the reasonableness of the Government's testing program insofar as it covers employees who are required "to handle classified material." We readily agree that the Government has a compelling interest in protecting truly sensitive information from those who, "under compulsion of circumstances or for other reasons, . . . might compromise [such] information." We also agree that employees who seek promotions to positions where they would handle sensitive information can be required to submit to a urine test under the Service's screening program, especially if the positions covered under this category require background investigations, medical examinations, or other intrusions that may be expected to diminish their expectations of privacy in respect of a urinalysis test.

It is not clear, however, whether the category defined by the Service's testing directive encompasses only those Customs employees likely to gain access to sensitive information. Employees who are tested under the Service's scheme include those holding such diverse positions as "Accountant," "Accounting Technician," "Animal Caretaker," "Attorney (All)," "Baggage Clerk," "Co-op Student (All)," "Electric Equipment Repairer," "Mail Clerk/Assistant," and "Messenger." . . . [I]t is not evident that those occupying these positions are likely to gain access to sensitive information, and this apparent discrepancy raises in our minds the question whether the Service has defined this category of employees more broadly than is necessary to meet the purposes of the Commissioner's directive.

We cannot resolve this ambiguity on the basis of the record before us, and we think it is appropriate to remand the case to the Court of Appeals for such proceedings as may be necessary to clarify the scope of this category of employees subject to testing. Upon remand the Court of Appeals should examine the criteria used by the Service in determining what materials are classified and in deciding whom to test under this rubric. . . .

SCALIA, J. joined by STEVENS, J. dissenting. . . Until today this Court had upheld a bodily search separate from arrest and without individualized suspicion of wrongdoing only with respect to prison inmates, relying upon the uniquely dangerous nature of that environment. . . .

The Court's opinion in the present case . . . will be searched in vain for real evidence of a real problem that will be solved by urine testing of Customs Service employees. . . . The only pertinent points, it seems to me, are supported by nothing but speculation, and not very plausible speculation at that. It is not apparent to me that a Customs Service employee who uses drugs is significantly more likely to be bribed by a drug smuggler, any more than a Customs Service employee who wears diamonds is significantly more likely to be bribed by a diamond smuggler — unless, perhaps, the addiction to drugs is so severe, and requires so much money to maintain, that it would be detectable even without benefit of a urine test. Nor is it apparent to me that Customs officers who use drugs will be appreciably less "sympathetic" to their drug-interdiction mission, any more than police officers who exceed the speed limit in their private cars are appreciably less sympathetic to their mission of enforcing the traffic laws. . . . Nor, finally, is it apparent to me that urine tests will be even marginally more effective in preventing gun-carrying agents from risking "impaired perception and judgment" than is their current knowledge that, if impaired, they may be shot dead in unequal combat with unimpaired smugglers — unless, again, their addiction is so severe that no urine test is needed for detection.

What is absent in the Government's justifications — notably absent, revealingly absent, and as far as I am concerned dispositively absent — is the recitation of even a single instance in which any of the speculated horribles actually occurred: an instance, that is, in which the cause of bribe-taking, or of poor aim, or of unsympathetic law enforcement, or of compromise of classified information, was drug use. Although the Court points out that several employees have in the past been removed from the Service for accepting bribes and other integrity violations, and that at least nine officers have died in the line of duty since 1974, there is no indication whatever that these incidents were related to drug use by Service employees. . . .

Today's decision would be wrong, but at least of more limited effect, if its approval of drug testing were confined to that category of employees assigned specifically to drug interdiction duties. Relatively few public employees fit that description. But in extending approval of drug testing to that category consisting of employees who carry firearms, the Court exposes vast numbers of public employees to this needless indignity. Logically, of course, if those who carry guns can be treated in this fashion, so can all others whose work, if performed under the influence of drugs, may endanger others — automobile drivers, operators of other potentially dangerous equipment, construction workers, school crossing guards. A similarly broad scope attaches to the Court's approval of drug testing for those with access to "sensitive information." Since this category is not limited to Service employees with drug interdiction duties, nor to "sensitive information" specifically relating to drug traffic, today's holding apparently approves drug testing for all federal employees with security clearances — or, indeed, for all federal employees with valuable confidential information to impart. Since drug use is not a particular problem in the Customs Service, employees throughout the Government are no less likely to violate the public trust by taking bribes to feed their drug habit, or by yielding to blackmail. Moreover, there is no reason why this super-protection against harms arising from drug use must be limited to public employees; a law requiring similar testing of private citizens who use dangerous instruments such as guns or cars, or who have access to classified information, would also be constitutional. . . .

NOTES & QUESTIONS

1. **Von Raab *on Remand*.** The Supreme Court in *Von Raab* remanded the case "to clarify the scope of this category of employees subject to testing." In *National Treasury v. Hallett*, 756 F. Supp. 947 (E.D. La 1991), the district court decided the remaining issues in this case. It found that there was "no constitutional infirmity in Customs drug screening program for applicants for covered positions." The *Hallett* court rejected the plaintiffs' argument that it distinguish between "Customs employees holding top secret security clearances and those holding secret or confidential clearances." It found a compelling interest at stake, which it broadly defined as the risk that "an employee with access to sensitive information may disclose such information through off duty intoxication, blackmail, or bribery." Moreover, each applicant for a covered position is required to undergo a background check, which meant Customs already had substantial information regarding her personal life and finances. The court added that "[s]uch disclosures significantly reduce an applicant's privacy expectations."
2. ***Skinner v. Railway Labor Executives' Ass'n.*** In *Skinner v. Railway Labor Executives' Ass'n,* 489 U.S. 602 (1989), decided on the same day as *Von Raab,* the Court upheld regulations mandating blood and urine tests of railroad employees who were involved in certain train accidents:

   > The Government's interest in regulating the conduct of railroad employees to ensure safety, like its supervision of probationers or regulated industries, or its operation of a government office, school, or prison, "likewise presents 'special needs' beyond normal law enforcement that may justify departures from the usual warrant and probable-cause requirements." . . .
   >
   > . . . [T]he Government interest in testing without a showing of individualized suspicion is compelling. Employees subject to the tests discharge duties fraught with such risks of injury to others that even a momentary lapse of attention can have disastrous consequences. Much like persons who have routine access to dangerous nuclear power facilities, employees who are subject to testing under the FRA regulations can cause great human loss before any signs of impairment become noticeable to supervisors or others. . . .
   >
   > A requirement of particularized suspicion of drug or alcohol use would seriously impede an employer's ability to obtain this information, despite its

> obvious importance. Experience confirms the FRA's judgment that the scene of a serious rail accident is chaotic. Investigators who arrive at the scene shortly after a major accident has occurred may find it difficult to determine which members of a train crew contributed to its occurrence. Obtaining evidence that might give rise to the suspicion that a particular employee is impaired, a difficult endeavor in the best of circumstances, is most impracticable in the aftermath of a serious accident.

Justice Scalia was in the majority in *Skinner.* Is this consistent with his dissent in *Von Raab*? Consider Scalia's explanation:

> Today, in *Skinner,* we allow a less intrusive bodily search of railroad employees involved in train accidents. I joined the Court's opinion there because the demonstrated frequency of drug and alcohol use by the targeted class of employees, and the demonstrated connection between such use and grave harm, rendered the search a reasonable means of protecting society. I decline to join the Court's opinion in the present case because neither frequency of use nor connection to harm is demonstrated or even likely. In my view the Customs Service rules are a kind of immolation of privacy and human dignity in symbolic opposition to drug use.

3. **Vernonia *vs.* Von Raab.** Recall Justice Scalia's opinion for the majority in *Vernonia School District,* where the Court held that suspicionless drug testing of student athletes passed constitutional muster. Can his majority opinion in *Vernonia School District* be reconciled with his dissent in *Von Raab*?
4. ***Drug Testing.*** Drug tests often do not merely test for current drug impairment on the job; they can detect the presence of drug use in urine even if the person is not currently under the influence of drugs. Indeed, drugs can be detected in urine several weeks after use. As one court has observed: "[U]rine testing — unaided by blood or breath testing — is a blunt instrument. A single positive urine test is silent as to when and how much of the drug was taken, the pattern of the employee's drug use, or whether the employee was intoxicated when the test was given." *National Federation of Federal Employees v. Cheney,* 884 F.2d 603 (D.C. Cir. 1989) (sustaining U.S. Army's drug testing program based on *Von Raab* and *Skinner*). Imagine a worker who uses marijuana while at home and never on the job. What is the justification for forcing that worker to be tested for drugs? An assumption behind drug testing programs is that a drug user will more likely be impaired at work. Is this assumption warranted? For the purposes of ensuring workers are not likely to be impaired on the job, is there any difference between the recreational pot smoker and the social drinker?[15]

---

[15] For more background about drug testing in the workplace, see John Gilliom, *Surveillance, Privacy, and the Law: Employee Drug Testing and the Politics of Social Control* (1994); John B. Wefing, *Employer Drug Testing: Disparate Judicial and Legislative Responses,* 63 Albany L. Rev. 799 (2000); Stephen M. Fogel et al., *Survey of the Law on Employee Drug Testing,* 42 U. Miami L. Rev. 553 (1988); Edward M. Chen, Pauline T. Kim & John M. True, *Common Law Privacy: A Limit on an Employer's Power to Test for Drugs,* 12 Geo. Mason U. L. Rev. 651 (1990).

CHANDLER V. MILLER

520 U.S. 305 (1997)

GINSBURG, J. [The State of Georgia required candidates for certain state offices to take a drug test in order to qualify for election.]

Our precedents establish that the proffered special need for drug testing must be substantial — important enough to override the individual's acknowledged privacy interest, sufficiently vital to suppress the Fourth Amendment's normal requirement of individualized suspicion. Georgia has failed to show, in justification of §21-2-140, a special need of that kind.

Respondents' defense of the statute rests primarily on the incompatibility of unlawful drug use with holding high state office. The statute is justified, respondents contend, because the use of illegal drugs draws into question an official's judgment and integrity; jeopardizes the discharge of public functions, including antidrug law enforcement efforts; and undermines public confidence and trust in elected officials. The statute, according to respondents, serves to deter unlawful drug users from becoming candidates and thus stops them from attaining high state office. Notably lacking in respondents' presentation is any indication of a concrete danger demanding departure from the Fourth Amendment's main rule.

Nothing in the record hints that the hazards respondents broadly describe are real and not simply hypothetical for Georgia's polity. . . .

In contrast to the effective testing regimes upheld in *Skinner, Von Raab,* and *Vernonia,* Georgia's certification requirement is not well designed to identify candidates who violate antidrug laws. Nor is the scheme a credible means to deter illicit drug users from seeking election to state office. The test date — to be scheduled by the candidate anytime within 30 days prior to qualifying for a place on the ballot — is no secret. As counsel for respondents acknowledged at oral argument, users of illegal drugs, save for those prohibitively addicted, could abstain for a pretest period sufficient to avoid detection. . . . Moreover, respondents have offered no reason why ordinary law enforcement methods would not suffice to apprehend such addicted individuals, should they appear in the limelight of a public stage. Section 21-2-140, in short, is not needed and cannot work to ferret out lawbreakers, and respondents barely attempt to support the statute on that ground.

Respondents and the United States as *amicus curiae* rely most heavily on our decision in *Von Raab,* which sustained a drug-testing program for Customs Service officers prior to promotion or transfer to certain high-risk positions, despite the absence of any documented drug abuse problem among Service employees. . . .

Hardly a decision opening broad vistas for suspicionless searches, *Von Raab* must be read in its unique context. As the Customs Service reported in announcing the testing program: "Customs employees, more than any other Federal workers, are routinely exposed to the vast network of organized crime that is inextricably tied to illegal drug use." . . .

Respondents overlook a telling difference between *Von Raab* and Georgia's candidate drug-testing program. In *Von Raab* it was "not feasible to subject employees [required to carry firearms or concerned with interdiction of controlled substances] and their work product to the kind of day-to-day scrutiny that is the norm in more traditional office environments." Candidates for public office, in contrast, are subject to relentless scrutiny — by their peers, the public, and the press. Their day-to-day conduct attracts attention notably beyond the norm in ordinary work environments.

What is left, after close review of Georgia's scheme, is the image the State seeks to project. By requiring candidates for public office to submit to drug testing, Georgia displays its commitment to the struggle against drug abuse. . . . But Georgia asserts no evidence of a drug problem among the State's elected officials, those officials typically do not perform high-risk, safety-sensitive tasks, and the required certification immediately aids no interdiction effort. The need revealed, in short, is symbolic, not "special," as that term draws meaning from our case law. . . .

BORSE V. PIECE GOODS SHOP

963 F.2d 611 (3d Cir. 1992)

BECKER, C.J. Plaintiff Sarah Borse brought suit against her former employer, Piece Goods Shop, Inc., in the district court for the Eastern District of Pennsylvania. She claimed that, by dismissing her when she refused to submit to urinalysis screening and personal property searches (conducted by her employer at the workplace pursuant to its drug and alcohol policy), the Shop violated a public policy that precludes employers from engaging in activities that violate their employees' rights to privacy and to freedom from unreasonable searches. Pursuant to Federal Rule of Civil Procedure 12(b)(6), the district court dismissed her complaint for failure to state a claim on which relief could be granted. This appeal requires us to decide whether an at-will employee who is discharged for refusing to consent to urinalysis screening for drug use and to searches of her personal property states a claim for wrongful discharge under Pennsylvania law. . . .

Borse was employed as a sales clerk by the Piece Goods Shop for almost fifteen years. In January 1990, the Shop adopted a drug and alcohol policy which required its employees to sign a form giving their consent to urinalysis screening for drug use and to searches of their personal property located on the Shop's premises.

Borse refused to sign the consent form. On more than one occasion, she asserted that the drug and alcohol policy violated her right to privacy and her right to be free from unreasonable searches and seizures as guaranteed by the United States Constitution. The Shop continued to insist that she sign the form and threatened to discharge her unless she did. On February 9, 1990, the Shop terminated Borse's employment.

The complaint alleges that Borse was discharged in retaliation for her refusal to sign the consent form and for protesting the Shop's drug and alcohol policy. It asserts that her discharge violated a public policy, embodied in the First and Fourth Amendments to the United States Constitution, which precludes employers from engaging in activities that violate their employees' rights to privacy and to freedom from unreasonable searches of their persons and property. Plaintiff seeks compensatory damages for emotional distress, injury to reputation, loss of earnings, and diminished earning capacity. She also alleges that the discharge was willful and malicious and, accordingly, seeks punitive damages. . . .

Ordinarily, Pennsylvania law does not provide a common-law cause of action for the wrongful discharge of an at-will employee. Rather, an employer "may discharge an employee with or without cause, at pleasure, unless restrained by some contract."

In *Geary v. United States Steel Corp.*, 319 A.2d 174 (Pa. 1974), however, the Pennsylvania Supreme Court recognized the possibility that an action for wrongful discharge might lie when the firing of an at-will employee violates public policy. . . .

In order to evaluate Borse's claim, we must attempt to "discern whether any public policy is threatened" by her discharge. As evidence of a public policy that precludes employers from discharging employees who refuse to consent to the practices at issue, Borse primarily relies upon the First and Fourth Amendments to the United States Constitution and the right to privacy included in the Pennsylvania Constitution. As will be seen, we reject her reliance on these constitutional provisions, concluding instead that, to the extent that her discharge implicates public policy, the source of that policy lies in Pennsylvania common law. . . .

In light of the narrowness of the public policy exception and of the Pennsylvania courts' continuing insistence upon the state action requirement, we predict that if faced with the issue, the Pennsylvania Supreme Court would not look to the First and Fourth Amendments as sources of public policy when there is no state action. . . .

Although we have rejected Borse's reliance upon constitutional provisions as evidence of a public policy allegedly violated by the Piece Goods Shop's drug and alcohol program, our review of Pennsylvania law reveals other evidence of a public policy that may, under certain circumstances, give rise to a wrongful discharge action related to urinalysis or to personal property searches. Specifically, we refer to the Pennsylvania common law regarding tortious invasion of privacy.

Pennsylvania recognizes a cause of action for tortious "intrusion upon seclusion." *Marks v. Bell Telephone Co.*, 331 A.2d 424 (Pa. 1975). The Restatement defines the tort as follows:

> One who intentionally intrudes, physically or otherwise, upon the solitude or seclusion of another or his private affairs or concerns, is subject to liability to the other for invasion of his privacy, if the intrusion would be highly offensive to a reasonable person. Restatement (Second) of Torts § 652B. . . .

We can envision at least two ways in which an employer's urinalysis program might intrude upon an employee's seclusion. First, the particular manner in which the program is conducted might constitute an intrusion upon seclusion as defined by Pennsylvania law. The process of collecting the urine sample to be tested clearly implicates "expectations of privacy that society has long recognized as reasonable." In addition, many urinalysis programs monitor the collection of the urine specimen to ensure that the employee does not adulterate it or substitute a sample from another person. Monitoring collection of the urine sample appears to fall within the definition of an intrusion upon seclusion because it involves the use of one's senses to oversee the private activities of another.

As the United States Supreme Court has observed:

> There are few activities in our society more personal or private than the passing of urine. Most people describe it by euphemisms if they talk about it at all. It is a function traditionally performed without public observation; indeed, its performance in public is generally prohibited by law as well as social custom.

Skinner, 109 S. Ct. at 1413. If the method used to collect the urine sample fails to give due regard to the employees' privacy, it could constitute a substantial and highly offensive intrusion upon seclusion.

Second, urinalysis "can reveal a host of private medical facts about an employee, including whether she is epileptic, pregnant, or diabetic." *Skinner,* 109 S. Ct. at 1413. A reasonable person might well conclude that submitting urine samples to tests designed to ascertain these types of information constitutes a substantial and highly offensive intrusion upon seclusion.

The same principles apply to an employer's search of an employee's personal property. If the search is not conducted in a discreet manner or if it is done in such a way as to reveal personal matters unrelated to the workplace, the search might well constitute a tortious invasion of the employee's privacy. See, for example, *K-Mart Corp. v. Trotti,* 677 S.W.2d 632 (Tex. App. 1984) (search of employee's locker). . . .

. . . [W]e believe that when an employee alleges that his or her discharge was related to an employer's invasion of his or her privacy, the Pennsylvania Supreme Court would examine the facts and circumstances surrounding the alleged invasion of privacy. If the court determined that the discharge was related to a substantial and highly offensive invasion of the employee's privacy, we believe that it would conclude that the discharge violated public policy. . . .

In view of the foregoing analysis, we predict that the Pennsylvania Supreme Court would apply a balancing test to determine whether the Shop's drug and alcohol program (consisting of urinalysis and personal property searches) invaded Borse's privacy. . . . The test we believe that Pennsylvania would adopt balances the employee's privacy interest against the employer's interest in maintaining a drug-free workplace in order to determine whether a reasonable person would find the employer's program highly offensive. . . .

In sum, based on our prediction of Pennsylvania law, we hold that dismissing an employee who refused to consent to urinalysis testing and to personal property searches would violate public policy if the testing tortiously invaded the employee's privacy. . . .

NOTES & QUESTIONS

1. ***Sources of Public Policy.*** Do you agree with the reasoning of *Borse*'s distinction between constitutional law and tort law as sources of public policy in suits for wrongful termination in violation of public policy against private sector employers? For a contrasting view with regard to constitutional law, consider *Hennessey v. Coastal Eagle Point Oil Co.,* 609 A.2d 11 (N.J. 1992),

where the New Jersey Supreme Court held that state constitutional law could be a source of public policy as applied in wrongful termination suits against private sector employers (for random urine testing). The court concluded:

> . . . [P]ersuasive precedent supports finding a clear mandate of public policy in privacy rights from several sources. Although one of those sources is the State Constitution, we emphasize that we are *not* finding in this opinion a constitutional right to privacy that governs the conduct of private actors. Rather, we find only that existing constitutional privacy protections may form the basis for a clear mandate of public policy supporting a wrongful-discharge claim. . . .
>
> In ascertaining whether an employee's individual rights constitute a "clear mandate of public policy," we must balance the public interest against the employee's right. If the employee's duties are so fraught with hazard that his or her attempts to perform them while in a state of drug impairment would pose a threat to co-workers, to the workplace, or to the public at large, then the employer must prevail.

For other states that follow a similar approach to *Hennessey,* see *Palmateer v. International Harvester Co.,* 421 N.E.2d 876 (Ill. 1981); *Cort v. Bristol-Myers Co.,* 431 N.E.2d 908 (Mass. Ct. App. 1982); *Twigg v. Hercules Corp.,* 406 S.E.2d 52 (W. Va. Ct. App. 1990); *Luedtke v. Nabors Alaska Drilling, Inc.,* 768 P.2d 1123 (Alaska 1989).

Consider Pauline Kim's argument that the privacy torts should serve as a source of public policy:

> . . . [T]he public-policy exception is now widely recognized to apply in at least three types of situations: when an employee is discharged for refusing to commit an illegal act, for asserting an established job-related right (for example, by filing for workers' compensation benefits), or for fulfilling a public obligation (such as serving on jury duty). . . .
>
> The common law privacy tort, by prohibiting unreasonable intrusions on the private concerns of another, also imposes a socially defined duty independent of any contractual relationship between the parties. Like participation in the jury system, respect for personal privacy is high on the scale of values in this society. And, as in the case of workers' compensation benefits, an employee's common law right of privacy is socially established independent of the terms of the employment relationship and should not be subject to waiver under threat of discharge. Because the interests it protects are at least as fundamental as others already found to warrant an exception to the at-will rule, the common law tort of invasion of privacy should be recognized as a public policy limiting an employer's authority to discharge.[16]

What other forms of information privacy law might serve as sources of public policy?

2. ***Direct Constitutional Liability for Private Sector Employers.*** In most states, and under the federal Constitution, constitutional provisions do not apply directly to private sector employers. As you have seen, however, state and federal constitutional law can serve in some jurisdictions as the source of

---

[16] Pauline T. Kim, *Privacy Rights, Public Policy, and the Employment Relationship*, 57 Ohio St. L.J. 671, 722, 724 (1996).

public policy in a wrongful termination claim. Moreover, in California, as we have noted above, the California Constitution applies directly to private sector employers. The California Supreme Court has held that the right to privacy in Article I, § 1 of the California Constitution "creates a right of action against private as well as government entities." *Hill v. NCAA,* 865 P.2d 633 (Cal. 1994).

5. THE ISSUE OF CONSENT

BAGGS V. EAGLE-PICHER INDUSTRIES, INC.

750 F. Supp. 264 (W.D. Mich. 1990)

BELL, J. . . . This case arises out of surprise drug test conducted by defendant in August 1989. Defendant is an Ohio corporation with a division located in Kalkaska, Michigan. The Kalkaska plant is defendant's Trim Division which makes parts such as headliners and door panels for the automotive industry. Employees at defendant's plant work in teams in the assembly process. Some of the activities conducted by the teams are potentially hazardous such as hydraulic and electronic presses, forklifts and hot glue and adhesive.

Defendant employs approximately 230 people at its Kalkaska plant. [The employees were at-will employees and could be terminated without cause.]. . .

In 1988 and 1989, defendant's management became aware of a drug problem at its Kalkaska plant. . . . In response to this information, defendant posted a drug free workplace policy in April 1989. This policy prohibited employees from possessing, using or being under the influence of drugs while at work and provided that employees could be tested for drug use. Defendant also required all new applicants to submit to drug testing as a prerequisite to being hired.

In April 1989, defendant consulted with the Grand Traverse Narcotics Team and the Kalkaska County Sheriff and placed an undercover officer in the plant as an employee. . . . After the undercover officer finished his undercover work, he reported to defendant's management that he estimated that as many as 60% of defendant's employees used drugs at home, at work or both. . . .

On July 17, 1989 a new drug free workplace policy was posted. That policy stated:

> . . . In order to protect the well-being of our employees, our facilities and the community in which we live, each employee, as a condition of employment will be required, upon request of Company supervisory personnel, to submit to blood and/or urine tests for determining use of alcohol and/or illegal or illicit drugs. . .

On August 10 and 11, 1989, defendant announced that it was going to conduct drug testing on those days. Only three people in management knew about the tests ahead of time. The men and women employees were asked to go into the men and women's bathrooms respectively and produce urine samples. There was a nurse present in each bathroom (a male nurse in the men's bathroom and a female nurse in the women's). Employees were told that, if they did not want to take the test, they could leave the plant and they would be considered a voluntary quit. Some employees who are plaintiffs in this suit did leave and were considered as voluntary quits as of that date. . . . A number of the plaintiffs tested positive for marijuana, one tested positive for cocaine and one for propoxyphene. . . .

Count I of plaintiffs' third amended complaint alleges breach of contract for the failure of defendant to follow the progressive disciplinary stages set forth in the employee handbook in the drug testing and termination of employees. . . .

Defendant argues that Count I of plaintiffs' third amended complaint should be dismissed because defendant did not breach any contract with plaintiffs. Defendants argue that plaintiffs' employment was an at-will employment and that defendant was under no obligation to use the progressive disciplinary procedures set out in the handbook in this situation. . .

. . . [T]he employees in the present case signed employment applications which contained language making their employment at-will and the handbook did not contain any language stating that employment with defendant would terminate only upon a showing of just cause. [Therefore, the defendant's motion for summary judgment as to Count I is granted.] . . .

Count III of plaintiffs' third amended complaint alleges invasion of privacy under the United States and Michigan constitutions. Defendant argues that plaintiffs have no cause of action for a constitutional violation because defendant is a private not a government actor. . . .

The Fourth Amendment to the United States Constitution does not protect against a search or seizure by a private party on its own initiative, even if the search or seizure is an arbitrary action. The Court knows of no such protection under the Michigan Constitution and plaintiffs have provided no support for such protection. Plaintiffs are, therefore, left to their claims of the tort of [intrusion upon seclusion.] . . .

Plaintiffs in this case are divided into two classes. One class consists of plaintiffs who refused to participate in the testing and the other consists of those who tested positive for drugs. Those who did not participate cannot succeed on this count because there was no intrusion. Therefore, Count III will be dismissed as to those plaintiffs.

As to the remaining plaintiffs, the Court finds that the taking of urine samples is an intrusion in an area in which plaintiffs may have an expectation of privacy. However, in this case, the Court finds that plaintiffs had no expectation of privacy with regard to drug testing since they had been on notice since July 17, 1989 that they might be subjected to drug testing as a condition of employment. . . . [E]mployers have a right to investigate into areas which would normally be private if the investigation springs from the business relationship. In this case, the employer was concerned about the safety of its workers and the productivity of the plant. This was a justifiable concern since the work at defendant's plant included activity which could be hazardous to someone who was not in total control of his faculties. Defendant has stated that there were several activities at its plant which gave rise to concern. The combination of the notice and the business concerns leads this Court to find that plaintiffs did not have an expectation of privacy with regard to urinalysis under the law of Michigan.

The final element of the tort is that the intrusion be offensive to a reasonable person. The Court finds that plaintiffs cannot prove this third element. The testing was carried on in the bathroom with a nurse present and the nurse was of the appropriate gender. In addition, anyone who wanted the additional privacy of a stall in which to give the sample had just to ask. . . .

In conclusion, the Court finds that all of plaintiffs' claims are without merit and grants defendant's motion for summary judgment as to all counts of plaintiffs' third amended complaint. Plaintiffs' third amended complaint will be dismissed.

NOTES & QUESTIONS

1. ***The Effect of Consent on Employer Liability for Privacy Torts.*** In *Baggs,* do you agree that providing notice to employees that they will be subjected to drug testing eliminates their expectations of privacy? In a number of cases, courts have held that employers requiring employees to consent to drug testing (or to surveillance or monitoring) shield themselves from liability under the intrusion upon seclusion tort because the employees consented to the intrusion. For example, in *Jennings v. Minco Technology Labs,* 765 S.W.2d 497 (Tex. Ct. App. 1989), Minco Technology Labs initiated a random drug testing program requiring employees to consent before testing about 16 months after plaintiff Brenda Jennings had begun to work for the defendant. An at-will employee, Jennings was unwilling to accept the new terms of employment and sued for intrusion upon seclusion, arguing that she was permitted to continue her employment without agreeing to the drug tests. The Texas court concluded:

> Jennings's employer threatens no *unlawful* invasion of any employee's privacy interest; therefore it threatens no act contrary to the public policy underlying the common-law right of privacy. The company's plan contemplates, rather, that an employee's urine will be taken and tested only if he consents. The plan therefore assumes, respects, and depends upon the central element of the right of privacy and its attendant public policy: the individual's exclusive right to determine the occasion, extent, and conditions under which he will disclose his private affairs to others. This consensual predicate to any test reduces Jennings's argument to her remaining contention.
>
> Jennings contends finally that she is poor and needs her salary to maintain herself and her family. Consequently, any "consent" she may give, in submitting to urinalysis, will be illusory and not real. For that practical reason, she argues, the company's plan *does* threaten a non-consensual, and therefore unlawful, invasion of her privacy. We disagree with the theory. A competent person's legal rights and obligations, under the common law governing the making, interpretation, and enforcement of contracts, cannot vary according to his economic circumstances. There cannot be one law of contracts for the rich and another for the poor. We cannot imagine a theory more at war with the basic assumptions held by society and its law. Nothing would introduce greater disorder into both. Because Jennings may not be denied the legal rights others have under the common law of contracts, she may not be given greater rights than they. The law views her economic circumstances as neutral and irrelevant facts insofar as her contracts are concerned.

2. ***The Limits of Consent.*** What does "consent" mean? Given the disparate power relationship between employers and employees, are many employment conditions really consensual? If you view consent narrowly to exist only when power relationships are close to equal, then what is the effect on the ability for employers and employees to make contracts?

Consider *Feminist Women's Health Center v. Superior Court,* 61 Cal. Rptr. 2d 187 (Cal. Ct. App. 1997). The Feminist Women's Health Center hired the plaintiff for the position of "feminist health worker." One of the responsibilities in the job description was to demonstrate a cervical self-examination to other women. In front of a group of other women, the plaintiff was to insert a plastic speculum into her vagina. According to the Health Center, the reason for the demonstration "is to demystify and redefine the normal functions of a woman's body. Our unique and effective, although not strictly necessary tool to accomplish this is for women to visualize their own cervixes and vaginas, which are not usually seen with the naked eye without the use of a vaginal speculum." After being hired, the plaintiff refused to demonstrate the cervical self-examination, and she was terminated by the Health Center. She sued for wrongful termination in violation of public policy, as embodied in the California Constitution, art. I, § 1, which provides: "All people are by nature free and independent and have inalienable rights. Among these are enjoying and defending life and liberty, acquiring, possessing, and protecting property, and pursuing and obtaining safety, happiness, and privacy." The court held:

> . . . [W]e agree with plaintiff that the observation of the insertion of a speculum into plaintiff's vagina by fellow employees and female clients of the Center infringes a legally protected privacy interest. This invasion is at least as serious as observing urination, and we do not question plaintiff's assertions that it was contrary to her religious and cultural beliefs. . .
>
> The real issue is whether this type of cervical self-examination may reasonably be required of the Center's employees. In other words, the seriousness of the privacy invasion leads us to the third part of the *Hill* test: consideration of the Center's countervailing interests and the feasibility of the alternatives proposed by plaintiff.
>
> . . . [C]ervical self-examination is important in advancing the Center's fundamental goal of educating women about the function and health of their reproductive systems. . . .
>
> The Center also could reasonably conclude that the alternative methods of self-examination proposed by plaintiff would have stifled such candor. These alternatives, such as the use of mannequins, or the private use of the speculum followed by discussion, are pale imitations of uninhibited group cervical self-examination. . . .
>
> In balancing these competing interests, we return to plaintiff's consent to demonstrate cervical self-examination as part of her employment agreement with the Center. The Center was not obligated to hire plaintiff, and consent remains a viable defense even in cases of serious privacy invasions. Therefore, we believe the facts as disclosed in the trial court give rise to the following inferences only: the requirement that health workers perform cervical self-examinations in front of other females is a reasonable condition of employment and does not violate the health worker's right to privacy where

> the plaintiff's written employment agreement evidences her knowledge of this condition and agreement to be bound by it. Where the employee thereafter refuses to abide by the agreement, the employee's wrongful termination claim based on a violation of the right to privacy is rendered infirm. Such is the case under the facts presented, and the superior court should have granted summary adjudication of this claim.

Many laws restrict an employee's freedom to contract. For example, an employee may not agree to work for below minimum wage, be exposed to certain toxic materials, or commit an illegal act. Upon what basis should legislatures and courts distinguish between those things to which people can and cannot consent?

3. ***Consenting to Violations of Privacy Law and Collective Bargaining.*** Should labor law prohibit employers from bargaining with a union over certain privacy rights? Consider *Cramer v. Consolidated Freightways, Inc.,* 255 F.3d 683 (9th Cir. 2001) (en banc). Consolidated Freightways, a large trucking company, installed concealed video cameras and audio listening devices behind two-way mirrors in its rest rooms in order to discover and prevent drug use by its drivers. Employees discovered the cameras when a mirror fell off the rest room wall. Consolidated employees brought several suits seeking damages for invasion of privacy and infliction of emotional distress. They also sought an injunction to stop the surveillance. These cases were consolidated into one action.

   The employees' union had a collective bargaining agreement (CBA) with Consolidated. One of the central issues in the case turned on whether § 301 of the Labor Management Relations Act (LMRA), 29 U.S.C. § 185, preempted the plaintiffs' claims, an issue that turned on whether the CBA's provisions could be interpreted as addressing the issue of surreptitious videotaping. The court concluded that it did not. The court also concluded:

> Even if the CBA did expressly contemplate the use of two-way mirrors to facilitate detection of drug users, such a provision would be illegal under California law, and it is well established in California that illegal provisions of a contract are void and unenforceable. Section 653n of the California Penal Code makes the installation and maintenance of two-way mirrors permitting the observation of restrooms illegal without reference to the reasonable expectations of those so viewed. Determination of guilt under the statute is not dependent on context or subjective factors; use of the mirrors is a per se violation of the penal code, and an assumption that the mirrors will not be used is per se reasonable.
>
> Under settled Supreme Court precedent, "§ 301 does not grant the parties to a collective-bargaining agreement the ability to contract for what is illegal under state law." Consolidated was therefore required to abide by the provisions of California penal law, and its employees had a right to assume their employer would obey the law. This assumption is inherently reasonable. Indeed, any contrary assumption would be irrational, because illegal behavior is unreasonable. Even if the CBA purported to reduce or limit this expectation in some way, that reduction would be illegal and therefore unenforceable. Because installation of two-way mirrors is immutably illegal, and freedom from the illegality is a "nonnegotiable state-law right[ ]," a court reviewing

> plaintiffs' claims that their privacy rights were violated need not interpret the CBA to arrive at its conclusion. By definition, therefore, plaintiffs in this action were reasonable in expecting to be free of the two-way mirrors and hidden video cameras installed in the restrooms.

Under California Penal Code § 653n, "[a]ny person who installs or who maintains . . . any two-way mirror permitting observation of any restroom, toilet, bathroom, washroom, shower, locker room, fitting room, motel room, or hotel room, is guilty of a misdemeanor." Do you agree with the court that employers and the union cannot bargain around this law? Would your conclusion be different if the applicable provision were tort law rather than criminal law?

Under *Cramer,* even if the employees desired to sacrifice their privacy in return for higher wages or other benefits, they could not make this bargain under the reasoning of the court. Does this result prevent employees from having the freedom to contract? Would a default rule that such surveillance is improper, but nonetheless could be bargained around, be preferable? Or if the law could be bargained around, would employees be able to circumvent the law too easily by forcing employees to agree to the privacy invasion?

4. ***Is Notice and Consent Adequate to Protect Privacy in the Workplace?*** Many employers are now providing privacy policies to their employees informing them of the types of workplace monitoring. Does providing notice and obtaining consent adequately protect employee privacy in the workplace? Consider the following argument by Pauline Kim:

> Clearly, the right to fire at will is not absolute. It has come into conflict with fundamental public concerns before, and yielded. Almost all the states recognize an exception to the at-will rule based on public policy. Even the staunchest defenders of employment at will acknowledge some legitimate exceptions to the rule, as when the performance of a public duty or the protection of a public right is threatened. . . .
>
> . . . [E]mployment is not an all-encompassing relationship. Although some territorial boundaries are necessarily breached to make employment possible, this implicit waiver of territorial claims does not automatically extend to those areas recognized to be at the core of personal privacy. Because employer and employee enter into the relationship for a specific, limited purpose, any implied waiver only extends as far as necessary to achieve that purpose. To conclude otherwise would set the employment relationship apart among social relationships, for the individual who could expect — and enforce — limits on unjustified intrusions by the government or third parties on core areas of privacy would have no such expectation vis-à-vis her employer. Given that the interests at stake are the same regardless of the source of the intrusion, it would be anomalous to treat the employer's actions as uniquely privileged. When core areas of privacy — those central to the self — are threatened, employer intrusions should not be permitted unless essential to meet some business need. . . .[17]

---

[17] Pauline T. Kim, *Privacy Rights, Public Policy, and the Employment Relationship*, 57 Ohio St. L.J. 671, 682, 703 (1996).

Suppose an employer wanted to film its employees all hours of the day. Should employees be permitted to consent to such monitoring? Isn't this what the "Big Brother" television show did? This television show placed individuals in a house that had cameras in every room, including the bathrooms. The show was filmed in California. Suppose a contestant sued for intrusion upon seclusion. Under the reasoning of *Cramer,* would the contestant be able to sue for intrusion?

5. ***The Limits of Consenting to Privacy Protection.*** In *Giannecchini v. Hospital of St. Raphael,* 780 A.2d 1006 (Conn. Super. 2000), the plaintiff, a nurse, was fired by the defendant hospital (Hospital of St. Raphael) for making serious medication errors and demonstrating below average ability and industry. With the help of an attorney, the plaintiff negotiated an agreement with the hospital that all references in the nurse's file to an involuntary termination of employment would be expunged and that in response to any inquiries or reference requests by prospective employers, the hospital would not disclose any information except the plaintiff's dates of service, title, position, and salary information. The plaintiff later applied for a position as a registered nurse with another hospital, which sent St. Raphael a letter requesting information about the plaintiff. St. Raphael responded by stating that the nurse had been discharged, had below average ability and industry, and made several serious medication errors. Among other things, the plaintiff sued for breach of contract.

St. Raphael argued that the confidentiality agreement that it entered into with the nurse violated public policy because it did not account for the interest of third parties (namely, the safety of the patients in the hospital planning to hire the nurse). The court concluded that public policy was against disclosure, and therefore, the agreement was valid and that St. Raphael had breached it. Should public policy prohibit confidentiality agreements that restrict the disclosure of information that might be relevant to the health and safety of third parties?

6. TESTING, QUESTIONNAIRES, AND POLYGRAPHS

(a) Testing and Questionnaires

GREENAWALT V. INDIANA DEPARTMENT OF CORRECTIONS

397 F.3d 587 (7th Cir. 2005)

[Kristin Greenawalt, a research analyst at the Indiana Department of Corrections, was told that in order to retain her job, she would be required to undergo a psychological test. This occurred two years after she was hired. She underwent the test but then sued under 42 U.S.C. § 1983, alleging that the test was an unreasonable search under the Fourth Amendment. She requested damages as well as an injunction forcing the department to remove the results of the test from her file.]

POSNER, C.J. . . . Almost any quest for information that involves a physical touching, which a test does not, is nowadays deemed a "search" within the meaning of the Fourth Amendment, which the Fourteenth Amendment has been interpreted as making fully applicable to state action. Drawing a tiny amount of blood from an unconscious person to determine the level of alcohol in his blood is a search, and so even is administering a breathalyzer test, where physical contact is at its minimum — the subject's lips merely touch the breathalyzer. And so finally is a urine test, in which the subject is required merely to provide a urine sample, so that the test instrument does not touch the subject's body at all. The invasion of privacy caused by submitting to the kind of psychological test given to the plaintiff in this case may well have been more profound than the invasion caused by a blood test, a breathalyzer test, or a urine test, though we cannot say for sure; the test is not in the record — all we know is that, according to the complaint, "the battery of psychological tests examined Ms. Greenawalt's personality traits, psychological adjustments and health-related issues." It is true that she consented to take the test, but had she not done so she would have lost her job, which, if she had a constitutional right not to take the test, would place a heavy burden on the exercise of her constitutional rights. . . .

. . . [W]e do not think that the Fourth Amendment should be interpreted to reach the putting of questions to a person, even when the questions are skillfully designed to elicit what most people would regard as highly personal private information. The cases we have cited show, it is true, that a Fourth Amendment claim does not depend on the claimant's being able to establish an invasion of such interests that tort law traditionally protects as the interest in bodily integrity (protected by the tort of battery), in freedom of movement (protected by the tort of false imprisonment), and in property (protected by the torts of trespass and of conversion). But that is all they show, so far as bears on the issue in this case. The implications of extending the doctrine of those cases to one involving mere questioning would be strange. In a case involving sex or some other private matter, a government trial lawyer might be required to obtain a search warrant before being allowed to conduct a cross-examination — or the judge before being allowed to ask a question of the witness. Police might have to obtain search warrants or waivers before conducting routine inquiries, even of the complaining witness in a rape case, since they would be inquiring about the witness's sexual behavior. Questioning in a police inquiry or a background investigation or even a credit check would be in peril of being deemed a search of the person about whom the questions were asked. Psychological tests, widely used in a variety of sensitive employments, would be deemed forbidden by the Constitution if a judge thought them "unreasonable." . . .

Even though administering a lie-detector test involves placing sensors on the skin of the person being interrogated, the Supreme Court has suggested that because the objective is to obtain testimonial rather than physical evidence, the relevant constitutional amendment is not the Fourth but the Fifth. . . . The Fourth Amendment was not drafted, and has not been interpreted, with interrogations in mind. . . .

Our conclusion that the plaintiff has not stated a Fourth Amendment claim does not leave people in her position remediless — or indeed leave her remediless. States are free to protect privacy more comprehensively than the

Fourth Amendment commands; and Greenawalt is free to continue to press her state-law claims in state court, where they belong. In most states if prison officials were to publicize highly personal information obtained from someone in Greenawalt's position by the kind of test of which she complains, she would have a state-law claim for invasion of her tort right of privacy. Indiana, it is true, has thus far refused to recognize this branch of the tort law of privacy. *Felsher v. University of Evansville,* 755 N.E.2d 589 (Ind. 2001). But the Fourth Amendment does not expand accordion-like to fill what may be a gap in the privacy law of a particular state. And there are other strings to the plaintiff's state-law bow; it is possible, though perhaps unlikely in light of *Cullison v. Medley,* 570 N.E.2d 27 (Ind. 1991), that Indiana recognizes "intrusion into a person's emotional solace" as an actionable invasion of privacy. *Branham v. Celadon Trucking Services, Inc.,* 744 N.E.2d 514 (Ind. App. 2001). Greenawalt may also be able to obtain mileage from cases, none however in Indiana, that hold that requiring a public employee to take a lie-detector test without good cause is an invasion of privacy. *Texas State Employees Union v. Texas Dept. of Mental Health & Mental Retardation,* 746 S.W.2d 203 (Tex. 1987); *Long Beach City Employees Ass'n v. City of Long Beach,* 719 P.2d 660 (Cal. 1986). She may also be able to prove intentional infliction of emotional distress.

NOTES & QUESTIONS

1. ***Should Questioning Be a "Search" Under the Fourth Amendment?*** Judge Posner argues that if the Fourth Amendment deemed questioning a search, then a warrant might be required for a cross-examination or for the police to question a rape victim about her rape. Do these implications necessarily follow from a holding that the psychological test constitutes a Fourth Amendment search? Posner also argues that the plaintiff has other state law options for redress. Assess her likelihood of prevailing on these alternative grounds.
2. ***The Constitutional Right to Information Privacy.*** In *Norman-Bloodsaw v. Lawrence Berkeley Laboratory,* 135 F.3d 1260 (9th Cir. 1998), plaintiffs were offered employment at Lawrence Berkeley Laboratory, but their employment was conditioned on their undergoing a medical examination. In addition to a questionnaire, the blood and urine of the employees was tested for syphilis, sickle cell, and pregnancy. This was done without the plaintiffs' knowledge and consent. The court held that the plaintiffs had a viable case for violations of two constitutional rights. The first was the right to information privacy, which the Supreme Court first identified in *Whalen v. Roe,* 429 U.S. 589 (1977) (the right to privacy protects "the individual interest in avoiding disclosure of personal matters"). The second constitutional right implicated in *Norman-Bloodsaw* was the Fourth Amendment. The Ninth Circuit stated:

   > The constitutionally protected privacy interest in avoiding disclosure of personal matters clearly encompasses medical information and its confidentiality. Although cases defining the privacy interest in medical information have typically involved its disclosure to "third" parties, rather

than the collection of information by illicit means, it goes without saying that the *most basic* violation possible involves the performance of unauthorized tests — that is, the non-consensual retrieval of previously unrevealed medical information that may be unknown even to plaintiffs. These tests may also be viewed as searches in violation of Fourth Amendment rights that require Fourth Amendment scrutiny. The tests at issue in this case thus implicate rights protected under both the Fourth Amendment and the Due Process Clause of the Fifth or Fourteenth Amendments.

Because it would not make sense to examine the collection of medical information under two different approaches, we generally "analyze [ ] [medical tests and examinations] under the rubric of [the Fourth] Amendment." Accordingly, we must balance the government's interest in conducting these particular tests against the plaintiffs' expectations of privacy. Furthermore, "application of the balancing test requires not only considering the degree of intrusiveness and the state's interests in requiring that intrusion, but also 'the efficacy of this [the state's] means for meeting' its needs." . . .

One can think of few subject areas more personal and more likely to implicate privacy interests than that of one's health or genetic make-up. Furthermore, the facts revealed by the tests are highly sensitive, even relative to other medical information. With respect to the testing of plaintiffs for syphilis and pregnancy, it is well established in this circuit "that the Constitution prohibits unregulated, unrestrained employer inquiries into personal sexual matters that have no bearing on job performance." The fact that one has syphilis is an intimate matter that pertains to one's sexual history and may invite tremendous amounts of social stigma. Pregnancy is likewise, for many, an intensely private matter, which also may pertain to one's sexual history and often carries far-reaching societal implications. Finally, the carrying of sickle cell trait can pertain to sensitive information about family history and reproductive decisionmaking. Thus, the conditions tested for were aspects of one's health in which one enjoys the highest expectations of privacy.

Also consider *Nelson v. National Aeronautics and Space Administration,* 512 F.3d 1134 (9th Cir. 2008). A group of contract employees of the Jet Propulsion Laboratory sued the National Aeronautics and Space Administration (NASA) and other employers to enjoin a requirement that they fill out an extensive questionnaire and submit to a background investigation. These employees were "low risk" employees who did not work with classified documents. The questionnaire requested "residential, education, employment, and military histories," the names of three references, and "disclosure of any illegal drug use within the past year, along with any treatment or counseling received for such use." The background check then would proceed by checking the answers to the questionnaire against several government databases. The applicants' references, employers, and landlords would be asked about the applicants' honesty, violations of law, alcohol or drug use, mental stability, and other matters. Among other claims, the plaintiffs alleged that the background investigations violated their constitutional right to information privacy and the Fourth Amendment. They sought a preliminary injunction against having to complete the questionnaire and background investigation. The district court rejected both claims. On appeal, the Ninth Circuit agreed that the Fourth Amendment claims should be dismissed because "that Amendment has not generally been applied to direct questioning." The Fourth Amendment did not apply to questions asked of references, employers, and landlords because it does not apply to "information knowingly disclosed to the government by a third party."

Regarding the constitutional right to information privacy claims, the *Nelson* court concluded:

> We have repeatedly acknowledged that the Constitution protects an "individual interest in avoiding disclosure of personal matters." This interest covers a wide range of personal matters, including sexual activity, medical information, and financial matters. If the government's actions compel disclosure of private information, it "has the burden of showing that its use of the information would advance a legitimate state interest and that its actions are narrowly tailored to meet the legitimate interest."
>
> The district court correctly concluded that the requested information in this case is sufficiently private to implicate the right to informational privacy. [The questionnaire given directly to the applicant] requires the applicant to disclose any illegal drug use within the past year, along with any treatment or counseling received. The Supreme Court has made clear, in the Fourth Amendment context, that individuals' reasonable expectations of privacy in their medical history includes information about drug use, *Skinner v. R.R. Labor Executives' Ass'n,* 489 U.S. 602 (1989), and, by analogy, drug treatment or counseling.

The questionnaires to third parties and references also raised right to information privacy claims:

> Form 42 solicits "any adverse information" concerning "financial integrity," "abuse of alcohol and/or drugs," "mental or emotional stability," and "other matters." These open-ended questions are designed to elicit a wide range of adverse, private information that "is not generally disclosed by individuals to the public"; accordingly, they must be deemed to implicate the right to informational privacy.
>
> Considering the breadth of Form 42's questions, it is difficult to see how they could be narrowly tailored to meet any legitimate need, much less the specific interests that Federal Appellees have offered to justify the new requirement. Asking for "*any* adverse information about this person's employment, residence, or activities" may solicit some information relevant to "identity," "national security," or "protecting federal information systems," but there are absolutely no safeguards in place to limit the disclosures to information relevant to these interests. Instead, the form invites the recipient to reveal *any* negative information of which he or she is aware. There is nothing "narrowly tailored" about such a broad inquisition.

In *Nelson,* what is the nature of the disclosure? In *Whalen v. Roe,* the Supreme Court articulated the right as "the individual interest in avoiding disclosure of personal matters." It appeared to view the right as one protecting against disclosure of personal information that the government had already collected, not as a right that would prevent the government's gathering of personal information. Is *Nelson* an information gathering case or an information disclosure case? Can *Nelson* be reconciled with *Whalen*?

3. ***Employer Questionnaires.*** In *American Federation of Government Employees v. HUD,* 118 F.3d 786 (D.C. Cir. 1997), the Department of Housing and Urban Development required employees holding positions of public trust to fill out a questionnaire requesting personal information, such as prior drug use and financial history. The Department of Defense required employees to fill out a questionnaire for positions requiring a security clearance that requested information about drug and alcohol history, financial history, criminal history, and mental health history. These questionnaires were challenged as a violation of the constitutional right to information privacy. The court concluded:

> To begin with, we hold that the individual interest in protecting the privacy of the information sought by the government is significantly less important where the information is collected by the government but not disseminated publicly. In fact, the employees could cite no case in which a court has found a violation of the constitutional right to privacy where the government has collected, but not disseminated, the information. . . .
>
> Here, as [in *Whalen v. Roe*], there are measures designed to protect the confidentiality of the employees' responses to questionnaires. The Privacy Act, 5 U.S.C. § 552a(b), states that no agency shall disclose any record, except where it has written consent from the individual or under certain limited exceptions, none of which would permit public dissemination of the information obtained here. In addition, the records are maintained under secure conditions. Those charged with maintaining the records are, themselves, subject to background checks. These measures, designed to protect the confidentiality of the information, substantially reduce the employees' privacy interests. Security precautions are never fool-proof, but where the government has enacted reasonable devices to secure the confidentiality of records we cannot, without grounds, assume that the devices will prove insufficient.
>
> Given the employees' diminished interest in resisting disclosure in cases in which disclosure is not likely to lead to public dissemination, we conclude that the agencies have presented sufficiently important justifications for each item on the questionnaires. . . . [HUD] has presented evidence that an employee using illegal drugs is more likely to compromise the integrity of the computer database by making a negligent error. HUD has also determined that employees with a substance abuse history or a history of financial indiscretion are more likely to embezzle funds. . . . When presented with a reasonable determination we are reluctant to second-guess the agencies' conclusions regarding the dangers associated with drug use or financial trouble among employees in public trust positions. . . . We hold that HUD may constitutionally require employees to disclose prior drug use and financial history. . . .
>
> . . . The drug use and financial history questions posed by DOD are slightly more intrusive than those asked by HUD, but the questions are the same in their material particulars. The release form is substantially identical. As the questions could constitutionally be required to protect the integrity of a computer database they are, *a fortiori,* constitutional when used in the interests of national security. DOD employees also challenged questions regarding the employees' mental health and expunged criminal history. No constitutional right of privacy is violated even by the disclosure "of an official

> act such as an arrest." *Paul v. Davis,* 424 U.S. 693, 713 (1976). Questions concerning an employees' mental health, on the other hand, may solicit highly personal information. Nevertheless, we uphold the requirement consistent with our traditional reluctance to intrude on Executive decisionmaking in the area of national defense. . . .

In *Walls v. City of Petersburg,* 895 F.2d 188 (4th Cir. 1990), the plaintiff Walls was hired as the administrator of the city's program to provide alternative sentencing for nonviolent offenders. About six months after Walls was hired, the program was transferred to the city's Bureau of Police. Her supervisor requested that she fill out a questionnaire as part of the background check that all police department employees go through. Walls refused to answer four questions:

> Question 12: Has any member of your immediate family (father, mother, brother, sister, husband, wife, father-in-law, mother-in-law) ever been arrested and/or convicted of a felony, misdemeanor, or other violation other than a minor traffic violation?
>
> Question 30: List all marriages you have had and the present status thereof: If divorced, annulled or separated, give details of date, offending party as decreed by law, and the reason therefore [sic] on a separate sheet of paper. . . . List every child born to you.
>
> Question 40: Have you ever had sexual relations with a person of the same sex?
>
> Question 43: Debts: List all outstanding debts or judgments against you or your spouse or for which you are the co-maker?

When she refused to comply with answering the questions, Walls was fired. Among other things, Walls brought a § 1983 claim alleging a violation of the constitutional right to information privacy. The court held that her claim should be dismissed. With regard to Question 30 (marital history), the court concluded:

> . . . [T]o the extent that this information is freely available in public records, the police should be able to require Walls to disclose the information in this background questionnaire. However, any details that are not part of the public record concerning a divorce, separation, annulment, or the birth of children are private and thus protected. The City's interests in discovering possible alternative names used by employees and identifying potential conflicts of interests can be satisfied by the information in the public records.
>
> We interpret Question 30 to be asking only for information that is available from public records, and therefore hold that it also can be an appropriate part of a background check.

As for Question 12 (criminal history), the court held:

> The analysis here is exactly the same as for Question 30. Walls has no reasonable expectation of privacy in this information because it is already part of the public records. Because she would have access in her position to criminal records, this information would be relevant and could be requested in a questionnaire.

Regarding Question 43 (financial information), the court reasoned that awareness of "Walls' financial position" was necessary to guard against potential corruption, and this interest outweighed her privacy interests. With regard to Question 40 (homosexuality), the court reasoned:

> In *Bowers v. Hardwick,* 478 U.S. 186 (1986), the Supreme Court "register[ed] [its] disagreement . . . that the Court's prior cases have construed the Constitution to confer a right of privacy that extends to homosexual sodomy. . . ." The Court explicitly rejected "the proposition that any kind of private sexual conduct between consenting adults is constitutionally insulated from state proscription." The relevance of this type of question to Walls' employment is uncertain, but because the *Bowers* decision is controlling, we hold that Question 40 does not ask for information that Walls has a right to keep private.

Do you agree with the reasoning of the court on this question? Recall *Sterling v. Borough of Minersville* in Chapter 6 (in the notes after *Scheetz v. The Morning Call*). Compare the reasoning of the impact of *Bowers* in *Sterling* and *Walls.* Which case do you find more persuasive? In light of *Lawrence v. Texas,* 539 U.S. 558 (2003), which reversed *Bowers,* would the court in *Walls* reach a different conclusion?

In *Fraternal Order of Police, Lodge No. 5 v. City of Philadelphia,* 812 F.2d 105 (3d Cir. 1987), a police union challenged the constitutionality of a questionnaire used by the police department to select candidates for a special investigations unit. Among other things, the questionnaire contained questions dealing with physical and mental conditions, behavior, and financial information. The court held that the questions about physical and mental conditions were necessary to determine the officers' fitness for their positions in the special investigations unit. The financial information was relevant because of the assumption that officers with large debts would be more susceptible to the temptations of corruption in narcotics investigations. Likewise, the behavior information (gambling and alcohol use) was relevant for this purpose. However, the court held that the city's safeguards against unnecessary disclosure of the information were inadequate:

> Safeguards against disclosure of private material have been held to be adequate when there exists a statutory penalty for unauthorized disclosures; when there exist security provisions to prevent mishandling of files coupled with an express regulatory policy prohibiting disclosure; and in a unique situation when, even absent an explicit statutory or regulatory policy, the record supported the conclusion that those officials with private information would not disclose it.
>
> In contrast, we find a complete absence of comparable protection of the confidential information to be disclosed in response to the SIU questionnaire. There is no directive limiting access to the responses to specific persons or specifying the handling and storage of the responses. . . . Apparently, there is no statute or regulation that penalizes officials with confidential information from disclosing it. . . .

Finally, the court held that a question requiring each applicant to disclose all the positions she or a member of her family held in any entity or association was unconstitutional as a violation of freedom of association.[18]

4. *The Americans with Disabilities Act.* The Americans with Disabilities Act (ADA), 42 U.S.C. §§ 12112 *et seq.*, restricts the ability of employers to conduct medical examinations of job applicants. The ADA protects the rights of those with disabilities. A "disability" is defined as "a physical or mental impairment that substantially limits one or more of the major life activities of such individual." § 12102.

The ADA treats pre-employment and post-employment examinations and inquiries differently. Pursuant to § 12112(d):

> (2) Preemployment.
>
> (A) Prohibited examination or inquiry. Except as provided in paragraph (3), a covered entity shall not conduct a medical examination or make inquiries of a job applicant as to whether such applicant is an individual with a disability or as to the nature and severity of such disability.
>
> (B) Acceptable injury. A covered entity may make preemployment inquiries into the ability of an applicant to perform job-related functions.
>
> (3) Employment entrance examination. A covered entity may require a medical examination after an offer of employment has been made to a job applicant and prior to the commencement of the employment duties of such applicant, and may condition an offer of employment on the results of such examination, if—
>
> (A) all entering employees are subjected to such an examination regardless of disability. . . .

Employers are more restricted in testing and making inquiries of employees once they are hired. Pursuant to § 12112(d)(4):

> (4) Examination and inquiry
>
> (A) Prohibited examinations and inquiries. A covered entity shall not require a medical examination and shall not make inquiries of an employee as to whether such employee is an individual with a disability or as to the nature and severity of the disability, unless such examination or inquiry is shown to be job-related and consistent with business necessity.
>
> (B) Acceptable examinations and inquiries. A covered entity may conduct voluntary medical examinations, including voluntary medical histories, which are part of an employee health program available to employees at the work site. A covered entity may make inquiries into the ability of an employee to perform job-related functions.

---

[18] For more background on workplace testing and questionnaires, see Chai Feldblum, *Medical Examinations and Inquiries Under the Americans with Disabilities Act: A View from the Inside,* 64 Temp. L. Rev. 521 (1991); Mark A. Rothstein, *The Law of Medical and Genetic Privacy in the Workplace,* in *Genetic Secrets: Protecting Privacy and Confidentiality in the Genetic Era* 281-98 (Mark A. Rothstein ed., 1997).

Drug testing is not considered a "medical examination" under the ADA. § 12114(d).

5. ***State Statutory Law.*** Many states restrict certain forms of employment testing and questionnaires. For example, Wisconsin prohibits employers from requiring employees or applicants to undergo HIV testing:

> . . . [N]o employer or agent of an employer may directly or indirectly . . . [s]olicit or require as a condition of employment of any employee or prospective employee a test for the presence of HIV, antigen or nonantigenic products of HIV or an antibody to HIV. Wisc. Stat. Ann. §103.15(2).

Massachusetts prohibits employers from asking prospective employees about arrests not leading to conviction, misdemeanor convictions, or any prior commitment to medical treatment facilities. *See* Mass. Gen. Laws ch. 151B § 4(9). Maryland restricts questions about disability or handicap unless it bears a direct and material relationship to the applicant's fitness for the job. *See* Md. Lab. & Empl. Code § 3-701. A number of states restrict genetic testing. *See, e.g.,* Cal. Govt. Code § 12940(o); Conn. Gen. Stat. Ann. § 46a-60(11)(A); Del. Code Ann. tit. 19 § 711(e); N.Y. Exec. Law § 296.19 (a)(1).

(b) Polygraph Testing

The first lie detector was invented by William Marston around 1917. Marston claimed that his device could detect deception by measuring increases in systolic blood pressure. In *Frye v. United States,* 293 F. 1013 (D.C. Cir. 1923), a famous case in evidence law, a defendant wanted to offer evidence about his successful lie detector test, but the trial court refused to admit the evidence. The court of appeals concluded that "the systolic blood pressure deception test has not yet gained such standing and scientific recognition among physiological and psychological authorities as would justify the courts in admitting expert testimony deduced from the discovery, development, and experiments thus far made." In the 1930s, the prototype of the modern polygraph machine was developed. The modern polygraph device is a portable machine that uses moving paper and three styluses to record three physiological responses: galvanic skin response, relative blood pressure, and respiration. These responses are recorded by placing devices on the person's chest, abdomen, fingers, and arm.

The reliability of polygraphs is still subject to significant dispute. In his comprehensive history of the polygraph machine, Ken Adler argues:

> The proponents of lie detection have packaged their technique as a mechanical oracle that can read the body's hidden signs for evidence of deceit — while they sidestep the skeptical interpretative labor that scientists ordinarily demand of such claims. The lie detector and its progeny have been repeatedly denounced by respectable science — but since when has that stopped millions of Americans from believing in something, especially when the public media breathlessly extols its successes?[19]

[19] Ken Adler, *The Lie Detectors: The History of an American Obsession* 270-71 (2007).

According to Adler, the lie detector is "less a 'technology of truth' than a 'technology of truthiness.'"

Despite these concerns, polygraph use is at its highest level in two decades. Laurie Cohen argues that polygraph results should be considered as "good enough" in many settings. In particular, Cohen observes that the polygraph machine has become the "centerpiece in an expanding range of parole and probation programs that are designed to dissuade sex offenders and other felons from committing more crimes."[20] Adherents of the polygraph propose that the machine is useful even if its reliability levels are too low for many uses, because criminal offenders believe it works, which may deter them from committing new crimes.

Many courts continue to exclude polygraph evidence. A recent report from the National Research Council concluded that polygraph testing was too flawed for security screening. "Polygraph testing now rests on weak scientific underpinnings despite nearly a century of study," the report said. "And much of the available evidence for judging its validity lacks scientific rigor."[21]

Despite their questionable reliability, polygraphs are used by many employers when deciding whether to hire people or when investigating workplace misconduct. Polygraphs merely detect physiological responses to emotional arousal; they cannot detect thoughts or feelings directly. Are polygraphs more invasive to privacy than drug tests or written psychological exams?

In *Anderson v. City of Philadelphia,* 845 F.2d 1216 (3d Cir. 1988), a group of unsuccessful applicants for Philadelphia police and correctional officers claimed that the requirement of taking a polygraph test to obtain such jobs was unconstitutional. They argued that being forced to take a polygraph test violated their due process and equal protection rights. The court, however, concluded:

> In *Board of Regents v. Roth,* the Supreme Court made it clear that "[t]he requirements of procedural due process apply only to the deprivation of interests encompassed by the Fourteenth Amendment's protection of liberty and property." 408 U.S. 564, 569 (1972). . . .
>
> To demonstrate a property interest . . . these plaintiffs must show that under Pennsylvania law they had a legitimate claim of entitlement to employment as City police or prison officers.
>
> The plaintiffs here were never more than applicants for employment by the City. Although the plaintiffs occupied high positions on the civil service eligibility lists for the type of employment they sought, occupancy of these positions entitled the plaintiffs to nothing more than consideration for employment when openings occurred. . . .
>
> We therefore conclude that the plaintiffs' interest in the civil service positions they sought did not rise to the level of a property interest protected by the Constitution. . . .
>
> We next address the plaintiffs' argument that they have been denied equal protection of the law. . . . [We] will apply the "general rule . . . that legislation is presumed to be valid and will be sustained if the classification drawn by the

---

[20] Laurie P. Cohen, *The Polygraph Paradox*, Wall St. J., A1 (Mar. 22-23, 2008).

[21] National Research Council, *The Polygraph and Lie Detection* (2002), available at http://www.nap.edu/books/0309084369/html/.

> statute is rationally related to a legitimate state interest." *City of Cleburne v. Cleburne Living Center, Inc.,* 473 U.S. 432 (1985). The plaintiffs bear the burden of proof on this issue, and so must show that the requirements imposed by law or regulation "so lack rationality that they constitute a constitutionally impermissible denial of equal protection." . . .
>
> . . . [W]e think it rational for the departments to believe that the polygraph requirement results in fuller, more candid disclosures on the PDQ and thus provides additional information that is helpful in selecting qualified law enforcement officers. . . .
>
> Accordingly, we conclude that in the absence of a scientific consensus, reasonable law enforcement administrators may choose to include a polygraph requirement in their hiring process without offending the equal protection clause. . . .

In *States Employees Union v. Department of Mental Health,* 746 S.W.2d 203 (Tex. 1987), the Texas State Employees Union and several employees sued the Texas Department of Mental Health and Mental Retardation to invalidate the department's mandatory polygraph policy. Under the policy, employees were subject to "adverse personnel action" if they refused to submit to a polygraph examination to investigate patient abuse, theft, criminal activity, or health or safety threats. The court concluded:

> We hold that the Texas Constitution protects personal privacy from unreasonable intrusion. This right to privacy should yield only when the government can demonstrate that an intrusion is reasonably warranted for the achievement of a compelling governmental objective that can be achieved by no less intrusive, more reasonable means. . . .
>
> As justification for its polygraph policy, the Department asserts its interest in maintaining a safe environment for Department patients. This interest is in many respects compelling. The Department is not concerned solely with the smooth operation of its agency. It has been charged by the legislature with a unique responsibility towards its patients. . . . In its effort to achieve these goals, the Department must minimize incidents of employee misconduct. . . .
>
> . . . The Department's objectives, important as they are, are not adequately compelling to warrant an intrusion into the privacy rights of the employees.
>
> The polygraph policy itself undoubtedly implicates the privacy rights of the employees. The trial court found that "[the Department's] polygraph's intrusion is highly offensive to a regular person." Further, the trial court found that in light of its unreliability, a polygraph test was not a reasonable means of identifying miscreant employees.
>
> We do not doubt that the Department is entitled to require employees to answer questions that are narrowly and specifically related to the performance of their job duties. The use of a lie detector, however, presents a qualitatively different question. The Department's asserted interests are inadequate to overcome the privacy interests impinged upon by the polygraph testing. We hold that the Department's polygraph policies impermissibly violate privacy rights protected by the Texas Constitution.

Can a public sector employer force its employees to engage in a polygraph examination as part of an investigation of employee misconduct? Under the Fourth Amendment, is a polygraph examination a "reasonable" search based on *O'Connor v. Ortega*?

THE EMPLOYEE POLYGRAPH PROTECTION ACT

In 1988, Congress passed the Employee Polygraph Protection Act (EPPA), Pub. L. No. 100-618, codified at 29 U.S.C. §§ 2001–2009. The EPPA applies only to private sector employers. It specifically exempts "the United States Government, any State or local government, or any political subdivision of a State or local government." § 2006(a).

Limitations on Polygraph Testing. Pursuant to 29 U.S.C. § 2002, it is unlawful for private sector employers:

> (1) directly or indirectly, to require, request, suggest, or cause any employee or prospective employee to take or submit to any lie detector test;
>
> (2) to use, accept, refer to, or inquire concerning the results of any lie detector test of any employee or prospective employee;
>
> (3) to discharge, discipline, discriminate against in any manner, or deny employment or promotion to, or threaten to take any such action against
>
> > (A) any employee or prospective employee who refuses, declines, or fails to take or submit to any lie detector test, or
> >
> > (B) any employee or prospective employee on the basis of the results of any lie detector test. . . .

Exception for Ongoing Investigations. However, there are certain exceptions where employers may use polygraphs:

> (1) the test is administered in connection with an ongoing investigation involving economic loss or injury to the employer's business, such as theft, embezzlement, misappropriation, or an act of unlawful industrial espionage or sabotage;
>
> (2) the employee had access to the property that is the subject of the investigation;
>
> (3) the employer has a reasonable suspicion that the employee was involved in the incident or activity under investigation; and
>
> (4) the employer executes a statement, provided to the examinee before the test, that [among other things, describes the particular incident being investigated and describes the basis of the employer's reasonable suspicion of the employee's involvement in the incident]. § 2006(d).

Exception for Security Services. Certain employers who engage in security services (e.g., armored car services, security alarm services, security personnel) are exempt. These security services must protect government interests such as nuclear power, water supply facilities, toxic waste disposal, and public transportation; or the services must protect "currency, negotiable securities, precious commodities or instruments, or proprietary information." § 2006(e).

When polygraphs are used under these exceptions, the test or the refusal to take the test cannot be the sole basis of any adverse employment action. § 2007(a). Further, the EPPA provides certain procedures, responsibilities, and restrictions on the use of polygraphs. For example, polygraph examiners cannot ask questions concerning beliefs regarding religion, racial matters, politics, sexual behavior, or union activities. § 2007(b). The EPPA limits the disclosure of polygraph information to people authorized by the examinee, the employer, or pursuant to a court order. § 2008.

Enforcement. Violations will result in a civil penalty of up to $10,000. The Secretary of Labor may bring an action to obtain restraining orders and injunctions to require compliance with the EPPA. Employers who violate the EPPA are liable to employees or prospective employees for legal and equitable relief including reinstatement, promotion, and payment of lost wages and benefits. § 2005.

Preemption. The EPPA does not preempt state law. About half of the states regulate the use of polygraphs by statute.

Waiver. The EPPA prohibits the waiver of rights and procedures provided by the Act except in the case of a written settlement, signed by the parties to the pending action or complaint under the Act. § 2005(d).

7. TELEPHONE MONITORING

Recall that federal electronic surveillance law (Chapter 3) applies not only to government and law enforcement officials but also to private parties as well. Thus, employers are subject to the restrictions of federal electronic surveillance law. However, three notable exceptions to electronic surveillance law are relevant to the employment context.

First, the Wiretap Act does not apply when one party to a communication consents to the interception. *See* 18 U.S.C. § 2511(2)(d).

Second, the providers of wire or electronic communications services are exempt from the Stored Communications Act's restrictions on accessing stored communications. *See* 18 U.S.C. § 2701(c)(1). Under the Wiretap Act, providers of wire or electronic communication services whose facilities are used in the transmission of such communications are permitted to intercept, disclose, or use that communication as a necessary incident to render the service or to protect the rights or property of the service. *See* 18 U.S.C. § 2511(2). The service provider exception is relevant in the employment context because many employers serve as the providers of certain communications services, such as Internet connections.

Third, under the "ordinary course of business" exception, the Wiretap Act does not apply when an employer uses certain intercepting devices "in the ordinary course of [the employer's] business." § 2510(5). The device must be furnished to the employer by the provider of the wire or electronic communication service. § 2510(5)(a)(i).

WATKINS V. L.M. BERRY & CO.

704 F.2d 577 (11th Cir. 1983)

SMITH, J. In this case appellant Watkins sued her employer, L.M. Berry & Company, and others, alleging violation of the federal wiretapping statute, title

III of the Omnibus Crime Control and Safe Streets Act of 1968, 18 U.S.C. §§ 2510–2520. The district court granted summary judgment on the merits against Watkins, and she now appeals. . . .

. . . Carmie Watkins was employed as a sales representative by L.M. Berry & Company (Berry Co.). Watkins' immediate supervisor was Martha Little, and Little's supervisor was Diane Wright. Berry Co. was under contract with South Central Bell to solicit Yellow Pages advertising from South Central Bell's present and prospective Yellow Pages advertisers. Much of this solicitation was done by telephone and Watkins was hired and trained to make those calls.

Berry Co. has an established policy, of which all employees are informed, of monitoring solicitation calls as part of its regular training program. The monitored calls are reviewed with employees to improve sales techniques. This monitoring is accomplished with a standard extension telephone, located in the supervisor's office, which shares lines with the telephones in the employees' offices. Employees are permitted to make personal calls on company telephones, and they are told that personal calls will not be monitored except to the extent necessary to determine whether a particular call is of a personal or business nature.

In April or May 1980, during her lunch hour, Watkins received a call in her office from a friend. At or near the beginning of the call (there are conflicting indications), the friend asked Watkins about an employment interview Watkins had had with another company (Lipton) the evening before. Watkins responded that the interview had gone well and expressed a strong interest in taking the Lipton job. Unbeknownst to Watkins, Little was monitoring the call from her office and heard the discussion of the interview.

After hearing the conversation (how much is unclear), Little told Wright about it. Later that afternoon Watkins was called into Wright's office and was told that the company did not want her to leave. Watkins responded by asking whether she was being fired. Upon discovering that her supervisors' questions were prompted by Little's interception of her call, Watkins became upset and tempers flared. The upshot was that Wright did fire Watkins the next day. However, Watkins complained to Wright's supervisor and was reinstated with apologies from Wright and Little. Within a week Watkins left Berry Co. to work for Lipton. . . .

Title III forbids the interception, without judicial authorization, of the contents of telephone calls. . . .

It is not disputed that Little's conduct violates section 2511(1)(b) unless it comes within an exemption "specifically provided in" title III (18 U.S.C. § 2511(1)). Appellees claim the applicability of two such exemptions. The first is the consent exemption set out in section 2511(2)(d):

> It shall not be unlawful under this chapter for a person not acting under color of law to intercept a wire or oral communication . . . where one of the parties to the communication has given prior consent to such interception. . . .

Appellees argue that, by using Berry Co.'s telephones and knowing that monitoring was possible, Watkins consented to the monitoring. The second is the business extension exemption in section 2510(5)(a)(i):

> "electronic, mechanical, or other device" [in §2511(1)(b)] means any device or apparatus which can be used to intercept a wire or oral communication other than —
>
> > (a) any telephone or telegraph instrument, equipment or facility, or any component thereof, (i) furnished to the subscriber or user by a communications common carrier in the ordinary course of its business and being used by the subscriber or user *in the ordinary course of its business*. . . . [emphasis supplied].

"[E]quipment . . . furnished to the subscriber or user by a communications common carrier in the ordinary course of its business" means in this case simply a standard extension telephone. *See Briggs v. American Air Filter Co.,* 630 F.2d 414 (5th Cir. 1980). The issue is therefore whether the monitoring of this call was in the ordinary course of Berry Co.'s business. Appellees contend that it was and hence that the extension telephone was not a "device" within the statutory meaning (section 2511(1)(b)) of "interception."

Briggs v. American Air Filter Co., decided by the Fifth Circuit in 1980, provides the framework for interpreting these exemptions. The consent and business extension exemptions are analytically separate. Consent may be obtained for any interceptions, and the business or personal nature of the call is entirely irrelevant. Conversely, the business extension exemption operates without regard to consent. So long as the requisite business connection is demonstrated, the business extension exemption represents the "circumstances under which non-consensual interception" is not violative of section 2511(1)(b). Accordingly, in analyzing the present case we will first consider the scope of Watkins' consent to the monitoring of this call and then move to the question whether the interception was justified as being in the ordinary course of Berry Co.'s business, notwithstanding the absence of consent. . . .

Appellees argue that Watkins' acceptance of employment with Berry Co. with knowledge of the monitoring policy constituted her consent to the interception of this call. This is erroneous with respect to both Watkins' actual and implied consent.

It is clear, to start with, that Watkins did not actually consent to interception of *this* particular call. Furthermore, she did not consent to a *policy* of general monitoring. She consented to a policy of monitoring sales calls but not personal calls. This consent included the inadvertent interception of a personal call, but only for as long as necessary to determine the nature of the call. So, if Little's interception went beyond the point necessary to determine the nature of the call, it went beyond the scope of Watkins' actual consent.

Consent under title III is not to be cavalierly implied. Title III expresses a strong purpose to protect individual privacy by strictly limiting the occasions on which interception may lawfully take place. Stiff penalties are provided for its violation. It would thwart this policy if consent could routinely be implied from circumstances. Thus, knowledge of the *capability* of monitoring alone cannot be considered implied consent. . . .

If, as appears from the undisputed facts, there was no consent to interception of the call beyond what was initially required to determine its nature, appellees must rely on the business extension exemption to shield them from liability for any listening beyond that point. To prevail, they must show that the interception of the call beyond the initial period was in the ordinary course of business. It is not enough for Berry Co. to claim that its general policy is justifiable as part of the ordinary course of business. We have no doubt that it is. The question before us, rather, is whether the interception of *this* call was in the ordinary course of business.

Under *Briggs,* the general rule seems to be that if the intercepted call was a business call, then Berry Co.'s monitoring of it was in the ordinary course of business. If it was a personal call, the monitoring was probably, but not certainly, *not* in the ordinary course of business. The undisputed evidence strongly suggests that the intercepted call here was not a business call. Watkins received the call and so could not have been soliciting advertising; the caller was a personal friend; and the topics discussed were mainly social. To that extent this was certainly a personal call.

Appellees argue, however, that the signal topic was Watkins' interview with another employer. This was obviously of interest and concern to Berry Co., so, appellees argue, it was in the ordinary course of business to listen. . . .

The phrase "in the ordinary course of business" cannot be expanded to mean anything that interests a company. Such a broad reading "flouts the words of the statute and establishes an exemption that is without basis in the legislative history" of title III. Berry Co. might have been curious about Watkins' plans, but it had no legal interest in them. Watkins was at liberty to resign at will and so at liberty to interview with other companies. Her interview was thus a personal matter, neither in pursuit nor to the legal detriment of Berry Co.'s business. To expand the business extension exemption as broadly as appellees suggest would permit monitoring of obviously personal and very private calls on the ground, for example, that the company was interested in whether Watkins' friends were "nice" or not. We therefore conclude that the subject call was personal. . . .

We hold that a personal call may not be intercepted in the ordinary course of business under the exemption in section 2510(5)(a)(i), except to the extent necessary to guard against unauthorized use of the telephone or to determine whether a call is personal or not. In other words, a personal call may be intercepted in the ordinary course of business to determine its nature but never its contents. The limit of the exemption for Berry Co.'s business was the policy that Berry Co. in fact instituted. It thus appears that Little was justified in listening to that portion of the call which indicated that it was not a business call; beyond that, she was not. Determination of the relevant points in the call is for the trier of fact. . . .

A final issue remains with respect to both exemptions. *If* it turns out that Little was justified in listening to the beginning of the conversation, either to determine its nature or with consent, and *if* it turns out that during that portion of the conversation the interview was discussed, then we must decide whether Little was obliged to hang up or, having entered the conversation legally, could remain on the line indefinitely. We think that the conclusion is inescapable that these exemptions do not automatically justify interception of an entire call. The expectation of privacy in a conversation is not lost entirely because the privacy of part of it is violated. Under title III a law enforcement officer executing a wiretap order must minimize his intrusion to the extent possible. 18 U.S.C. § 2518(5). Therefore, Little was obliged to cease listening as soon as she had determined that the call was personal, regardless of the contents of the legitimately heard conversation.

The violation of section 2511(1)(b) is the intercepting itself, not the interception of particular material. It is not necessary to recovery of damages that the violator hear anything in particular; she need do no more than listen. Thus, the reinstatement of Watkins and her subsequent departure, while they may affect the amount of actual damages, do not moot or render *de minimis* her claim. Watkins' right to recover at least the minimum statutory damages flows from the interception, not from the actual damage caused. It is for the trier of fact to determine at what point the telephone should have been hung up. . . .

We hold that this case was not properly disposed of by summary judgment, as genuinely disputed issues of material fact remain. A detailed factual inquiry into the interception is necessary if the standards set forth above are to be adequately addressed. Among the factual questions that should be considered are: What was the monitoring policy to which Watkins consented? Did Little know that Watkins had received the call and if so did that necessarily indicate a personal call? How long was the call? When was the interview discussed? Were other subjects discussed? For how long did Little listen? How long does it take to discover that a call is personal, for example, is there an immediately recognizable pattern to a sales call? This list of questions is not exhaustive, but it is hoped that it points out the directions in which further inquiries should be pursued. . . .

DEAL V. SPEARS

980 F.2d 1153 (8th Cir. 1992)

BOWMAN, J. . . . Newell and Juanita Spears have owned and operated the White Oak Package Store near Camden, Arkansas, for about twenty years. The Spearses live in a mobile home adjacent to the store. The telephone in the store has an extension in the home, and is the only phone line into either location. The same phone line thus is used for both the residential and the business phones.

Sibbie Deal was an employee at the store from December 1988 until she was fired in August 1990. The store was burglarized in April 1990 and approximately $16,000 was stolen. The Spearses believed that it was an inside job and suspected that Deal was involved. Hoping to catch the suspect in an unguarded admission, Newell Spears purchased and installed a recording device on the extension phone in the mobile home. When turned on, the machine would automatically record all conversations made or received on either phone, with no indication to the parties using the phone that their conversation was being recorded. Before purchasing the recorder, Newell Spears told a sheriff's department investigator that he was considering this surreptitious monitoring and the investigator told Spears that he did not "see anything wrong with that."

Calls were taped from June 27, 1990, through August 13, 1990. During that period, Sibbie Deal, who was married to Mike Deal at the time, was having an extramarital affair with Calvin Lucas, then married to Pam Lucas. Deal and Lucas spoke on the telephone at the store frequently and for long periods of time while Deal was at work. (Lucas was on 100% disability so he was at home all day.) Based on the trial testimony, the District Court concluded that much of the conversation between the two was "sexually provocative." Deal also made or received numerous other personal telephone calls during her workday. Even before Newell Spears purchased the recorder, Deal was asked by her employers to cut down on her use of the phone for personal calls, and the Spearses told her they might resort to monitoring calls or installing a pay phone in order to curtail the abuse.

Newell Spears listened to virtually all twenty-two hours of the tapes he recorded, regardless of the nature of the calls or the content of the conversations, and Juanita Spears listened to some of them. Although there was nothing in the record to indicate that they learned anything about the burglary, they did learn, among other things, that Deal sold Lucas a keg of beer at cost, in violation of store policy. On August 13, 1990, when Deal came in to work the evening shift, Newell Spears played a few seconds of the incriminating tape for Deal and then fired her. Deal and Lucas filed this action on August 29, 1990 [alleging that the Spearses violated Federal Wiretap Law. The district court found the Spearses liable and assessed damages at a total of $40,000 — $10,000 to Deal and Lucas respectively assessed against Newell Spears and $10,000 to Deal and Lucas respectively assessed against Juanita Spears]. . . .

The Spearses challenge the court's finding of liability. They admit the taping but contend that the facts here bring their actions under two statutory exceptions to civil liability. Further, Juanita Spears alleges that she did not disclose information learned from the tapes, thus the statutory damages assessed against her on that ground were improper. For their part Deal and Lucas challenge the court's failure to award them punitive damages as permitted by statute.

The elements of a violation of the wire and electronic communications interception provisions (Title III) of the Omnibus Crime Control and Safe Streets Act of 1968 are set forth in the section that makes such interceptions a criminal offense. 18 U.S.C. § 2511 (1988). Under the relevant provisions of the statute, criminal liability attaches and a federal civil cause of action arises when a person intentionally intercepts a wire or electronic communication or intentionally discloses the contents of the interception. The successful civil plaintiff may recover actual damages plus any profits made by the violator. If statutory damages will result in a larger recovery than actual damages, the violator must pay the plaintiff "the greater of $100 a day for each day of violation or $10,000." Further, punitive damages, attorney fees, and "other litigation costs reasonably incurred" are allowed.

The Spearses first claim they are exempt from civil liability because Sibbie Deal consented to the interception of calls that she made from and received at the store. Under the statute, it is not unlawful "to intercept a wire, oral, or electronic communication . . . where one of the parties to the communication has given prior consent to such interception," 18 U.S.C. § 2511(2)(d), and thus no civil liability is incurred. The Spearses contend that Deal's consent may be implied because Newell Spears had mentioned that he might be forced to monitor calls or restrict telephone privileges if abuse of the store's telephone for personal calls continued. They further argue that the extension in their home gave actual notice to Deal that her calls could be overheard, and that this notice resulted in her implied consent to interception. We find these arguments unpersuasive. . . .

We do not believe that Deal's consent may be implied from the circumstances relied upon in the Spearses' arguments. The Spearses did not inform Deal that they were monitoring the phone, but only told her they might do so in order to cut down on personal calls. Moreover, it seems clear that the couple anticipated Deal would not suspect that they were intercepting her calls, since they hoped to catch her making an admission about the burglary, an outcome they would not expect if she knew her calls were being recorded. . . .

Given these circumstances, we hold as a matter of law that the Spearses have failed to show Deal's consent to the interception and recording of her conversations.

The Spearses also argue that they are immune from liability under what has become known as an exemption for business use of a telephone extension. The exception is actually a restrictive definition. Under Title III, a party becomes criminally and civilly liable when he or she "intercepts" wire communications. "'[I]ntercept' means the aural or other acquisition of the contents of any wire, electronic, or oral communication through the use of any electronic, mechanical, or other device[.]" Such a device is "any device or apparatus which can be used to intercept a wire, oral, or electronic communication" except when that device is a

> telephone . . . instrument, equipment or facility, or any component thereof, (i) furnished to the subscriber or user by a provider of wire or electronic communication service in the ordinary course of its business and being used by the subscriber or user in the ordinary course of its business or furnished by such subscriber or user for connection to the facilities of such service and used in the ordinary course of its business[.]

Thus there are two essential elements that must be proved before this becomes a viable defense: the intercepting equipment must be furnished to the user by the phone company or connected to the phone line, and it must be used in the ordinary course of business. The Spearses argue that the extension in their residence, to which the recorder was connected, meets the equipment requirement, and the listening-in was done in the ordinary course of business. We disagree. . . .

We hold that the recording device, and not the extension phone, intercepted the calls. But even if the extension phone intercepted the calls, we do not agree that the interception was in the ordinary course of business.

We do not quarrel with the contention that the Spearses had a legitimate business reason for listening in: they suspected Deal's involvement in a burglary of the store and hoped she would incriminate herself in a conversation on the phone. Moreover, Deal was abusing her privileges by using the phone for numerous personal calls even, by her own admission, when there were customers in the store. The Spearses might legitimately have monitored Deal's calls to the extent necessary to determine that the calls were personal and made or received in violation of store policy.

But the Spearses recorded twenty-two hours of calls, and Newell Spears listened to all of them without regard to their relation to his business interests. Granted, Deal might have mentioned the burglary at any time during the conversations, but we do not believe that the Spearses' suspicions justified the extent of the intrusion. We conclude that the scope of the interception in this case takes us well beyond the boundaries of the ordinary course of business. . . .

NOTES & QUESTIONS

1. ***Postscript.*** Following the court's decision, a number of other plaintiffs who were speaking with Deal while the conversations were being wiretapped filed suit. Each new plaintiff sought damages of $10,000 and attorneys' fees and costs. The court, however, declined to award damages, noting 18 U.S.C. § 2520(c)(2) provides that "the court *may* assess . . . statutory damages of . . . $10,000." Damages were thus at the discretion of the court, and the judge reasoned:

    > [T]he plaintiffs suffered no actual damages; the privacy intrusion as to these plaintiffs appears to have been relatively minor as compared to the intrusion into the affairs of Sibbie and Calvin Lucas; the Spears have already paid approximately $60,000.00 for their unlawful acts; the Spears, who are now retired and in their seventies, have no source of income other than their accumulated wealth; and Newell Spears used the recorder solely for the purpose of discovering who robbed his business. Though the court notes that the Spears' accumulated wealth is substantial and would allow them to pay a significant judgment, this factor is outweighed by the others listed above, all of which counsel against an award of damages.

    Reynolds v. Spears, 857 F. Supp. 1341 (W.D. Ark. 1994). The district court's judgment was affirmed in *Reynolds v. Spears,* 93 F.3d 428 (8th Cir. 1996).
2. ***Telephone Monitoring Policy.*** Suppose the Spearses had a policy that all calls, regardless of whether they were personal or business related, would be recorded and monitored. Would the Spearses still be liable under the Wiretap Act?
3. ***Other Means of Investigating.*** Would it be likely that Deal would speak about the burglary on a business-related call? If the Spearses could not listen to Deal's private calls, their investigation might be significantly limited. If you were the Spearses' attorney and they came to you, explained that they suspected Deal of the burglary, and wanted your advice about how they could legally investigate, how would you advise them?

8. COMPUTER MONITORING AND SEARCHES

(a) E-mail

E-mail presents an interesting privacy problem in the workplace. Unlike regular mail, e-mail is less secure from prying eyes. Because e-mail travels through numerous computers to reach its final destination, it can be intercepted and copied at many points. E-mail goes through the employer's computer network. It may be stored by the employer as part of the routine system backup. E-mail is often stored on the employee's computer even after it is received and read. Employers can easily scan e-mail for certain words. At the same time, encryption techniques may enable employees to send messages so that at least the content is not easily accessible to employers. Given the nature of e-mail — especially e-mail correspondence at the workplace — how should we assess whether individuals have a reasonable expectation of privacy in e-mail?[22]

The answer to this question depends in part on how we analogize e-mail. Some view e-mail as akin to a letter — just one in electronic form rather than on paper. Should e-mail deserve the same legal protection and privacy expectations as regular letters? Others argue that without any encryption, e-mail is quite insecure and is more akin to a postcard than a letter. Another analogy is that e-mail should be understood as similar to a telephone call. E-mail often travels across phone lines, and e-mail correspondence is often conducted fairly rapidly with frequent responses and replies. Should e-mail be given the same legal protection and privacy expectations as telephone conversations? One might argue that given how insecure e-mail is from being intercepted by unauthorized individuals, it is more akin to a radio communication. The following cases examine the privacy of e-mail in the workplace:

SMYTH V. PILLSBURY CO.

914 F. Supp. 97 (E.D. Pa. 1996)

WEINER, J. In this diversity action, plaintiff, an at-will employee, claims he was wrongfully discharged from his position as a regional operations manager by the defendant. Presently before the court is the motion of the defendant to dismiss pursuant to Rule 12(b)(6) of the Federal Rules of Civil Procedure. For the reasons which follow, the motion is granted.

A claim may be dismissed under Fed. R. Civ. P. 12(b)(6) only if the plaintiff can prove no set of facts in support of the claim that would entitle him to relief. The reviewing court must consider only those facts alleged in the Complaint and accept all of the allegations as true. Applying this standard, we find that plaintiff has failed to state a claim upon which relief can be granted.

Defendant maintained an electronic mail communication system ("e-mail") in order to promote internal corporate communications between its employees. Defendant repeatedly assured its employees, including plaintiff, that all e-mail communications would remain confidential and privileged. Defendant further assured its employees, including plaintiff, that e-mail communications could not be intercepted and used by defendant against its employees as grounds for termination or reprimand.

In October 1994, plaintiff received certain e-mail communications from his supervisor over defendant's e-mail system on his computer at home. In reliance on defendant's assurances regarding defendant's e-mail system, plaintiff responded and exchanged e-mails with his supervisor. At some later date,

---

[22] For more background about e-mail and the workplace, see Michael S. Leib, *E-Mail and the Wiretap Laws: Why Congress Should Add Electronic Communications to Title II's Statutory Exclusionary Rule and Expressly Reject a "Good Faith" Exception*, 34 Harv. J. Legis. 393 (1997); Kevin P. Kopp, *Electronic Communications in the Workplace: E-Mail Monitoring and the Right of Privacy*, 8 Seton Hall Const. L.J. 861 (1998); Scott A. Sundstrom, *You've Got Mail (and the Government Knows It): Applying the Fourth Amendment to Workplace E-Mail Monitoring*, 73 N.Y.U. L. Rev. 2064 (1998).

contrary to the assurances of confidentiality made by defendant, defendant, acting through its agents, servants and employees, intercepted plaintiff's private e-mail messages made in October 1994. On January 17, 1995, defendant notified plaintiff that it was terminating his employment effective February 1, 1995, for transmitting what it deemed to be inappropriate and unprofessional comments over defendant's e-mail system in October, 1994.

As a general rule, Pennsylvania law does not provide a common law cause of action for the wrongful discharge of an at-will employee such as plaintiff. . . . However, in the most limited of circumstances, exceptions have been recognized where discharge of an at-will employee threatens or violates a clear mandate of public policy. . . .

Plaintiff claims that his termination was in violation of "public policy which precludes an employer from terminating an employee in violation of the employee's right to privacy as embodied in Pennsylvania common law." . . . [O]ur Court of Appeals stated "our review of Pennsylvania law reveals other evidence of a public policy that may, under certain circumstances, give rise to a wrongful discharge action related to urinalysis or to personal property searches. Specifically, we refer to the Pennsylvania common law regarding tortious invasion of privacy."

The Court of Appeals . . . observed that one of the torts which Pennsylvania recognizes as encompassing an action for invasion of privacy is the tort of "intrusion upon seclusion." As noted by the Court of Appeals, the Restatement (Second) of Torts defines the tort as follows:

> One who intentionally intrudes, physically or otherwise, upon the solitude or seclusion of another or his private affairs or concerns, is subject to liability to the other for invasion of his privacy, if the intrusion would be highly offensive to a reasonable person.

Restatement (Second) of Torts §652B.

Applying the Restatement definition of the tort of intrusion upon seclusion to the facts and circumstances of the case sub judice, we find that plaintiff has failed to state a claim upon which relief can be granted. In the first instance, unlike urinalysis and personal property searches, we do not find a reasonable expectation of privacy in e-mail communications voluntarily made by an employee to his supervisor over the company e-mail system notwithstanding any assurances that such communications would not be intercepted by management. Once plaintiff communicated the alleged unprofessional comments to a second person (his supervisor) over an e-mail system which was apparently utilized by the entire company, any reasonable expectation of privacy was lost. Significantly, the defendant did not require plaintiff, as in the case of an urinalysis or personal property search to disclose any personal information about himself. Rather, plaintiff voluntarily communicated the alleged unprofessional comments over the company e-mail system. We find no privacy interests in such communications.

In the second instance, even if we found that an employee had a reasonable expectation of privacy in the contents of his e-mail communications over the company e-mail system, we do not find that a reasonable person would consider the defendant's interception of these communications to be a substantial and highly offensive invasion of his privacy. Again, we note that by intercepting such communications, the company is not, as in the case of urinalysis or personal property searches, requiring the employee to disclose any personal information about himself or invading the employee's person or personal effects. Moreover, the company's interest in preventing inappropriate and unprofessional comments or even illegal activity over its e-mail system outweighs any privacy interest the employee may have in those comments.

In sum, we find that the defendant's actions did not tortiously invade the plaintiff's privacy and, therefore, did not violate public policy. As a result, the motion to dismiss is granted.

NOTES & QUESTIONS

1. ***E-mail Monitoring by Employers: Weighing the Interests.*** Employers contend that e-mail monitoring is important because the use of e-mail (and the Internet) can bring in viruses that can harm the employer's computer system. Employers are liable for defamation, copyright violations, and sexual harassment, which can take place over e-mail. Chevron Corporation was sued for hostile work environment when some employees sent around via e-mail a joke list called "Why beer is better than women." The case settled out of court for $2.2 million. Should employers be permitted to monitor e-mail? How would you balance the employees' interest in privacy against the employers' interests in monitoring?[23]
2. ***The Rights of Third Parties.*** The employees' privacy rights are not the only rights implicated here. The rights of third parties who mail employees or chat with them over the Internet are also implicated. Would a third party who e-mailed a private document to an employee, which was subsequently opened and inspected by that employee's employer, have an action for intrusion upon seclusion? Are there other theories or remedies, including self-help, available in this situation?
3. ***E-mail Privacy Policies.*** One of the troubling aspects of *Pillsbury* is that the employer promised that the e-mail would remain confidential. Suppose you were counsel to a company that wanted to establish an e-mail privacy policy. What elements would you include in the policy and why?

   Suppose that the employer had an e-mail privacy policy that stated: "The employer's e-mail system is the property of the employer. The employer reserves the right to monitor all e-mail communications over its e-mail system." First, should the employer be permitted to have such a blanket policy without a legitimate reason? Under such a policy, would the employee have a reasonable expectation of privacy in a private e-mail?

---

[23] For a proposal of how to balance employer and employee interests, see Jay P. Kesan, *Cyber-Working or Cyber-Shirking?: A First Principles Examination of Electronic Privacy in the Workplace,* 54 Fla. L. Rev. 289 (2002). For a discussion of how sexual harassment law inappropriately threatens employee privacy, see Jeffrey Rosen, *The Unwanted Gaze: The Destruction of Privacy in America* (2000). For a critique of Rosen's view, see Anita L. Allen, *The Wanted Gaze: Accountability for Interpersonal Conduct at Work,* 89 Geo. L.J. 2013 (2001).

Suppose that the e-mail policy stated: "The employer's e-mail system shall be used exclusively for business-related purposes. The use of e-mail for an employee's own private purposes is prohibited." Would such a policy eliminate any reasonable expectation of privacy in e-mail?

4. ***Webmail.*** Employees now have the ability to e-mail others while at work without using the employer's e-mail system. They can establish a webmail account such as Hotmail, Yahoo E-mail, or Gmail. To what extent should employers have the ability to control the use of e-mailing from an employee's own private webmail account at work? Consider the following two situations: (1) an employee accesses her Hotmail account from her employer's computer; and (2) an employee accesses her Hotmail account from her own laptop, Blackberry, or other device with the wireless Internet service that the employee herself pays for. Should the employer have the ability to monitor in (1) or (2) or both of these situations?
5. ***Email, Text Messages, and Workplace Privacy Policies.*** In *Quon v. Arch Wireless Operating Co., Inc.,* 529 F.3d 892 (9th Cir. 2008), a city police department provided pages to several of its employees. The department contracted with Arch Wireless Operating Company, Inc. to provide the wireless service. The department "had no official policy directed to text-messaging by use of the pagers." Its general policy regarding computer, Internet, and email use was that they were not to be used for "personal benefit," that the city reserved the right to monitor all network activity, and that "[u]sers should have no expectation of privacy or confidentiality when using these resources." Jeff Quon exceeded his text messaging usage limits repeatedly, and the lieutenant billed him for the overages. Quon paid the city each time. Finally, after Quon exceeded his usage limits again, the city sought and obtained from Arch Wireless transcripts of Quon's texting. The transcripts revealed that many of his messages were personal and sexually explicit in nature.

   Quon and several others sued, claiming that the city and Arch Wireless violated the Stored Communications Act (SCA) and the Fourth Amendment. The court concluded that Arch Wireless violated the SCA when it disclosed the messages to the city. The court then analyzed whether the officers had Fourth Amendment protection in the messages. First, the court reasoned that text messages should be treated as content information (similar to letters and e-mail text) rather than as envelope information (similar to pen registers or e-mail headers). Second, the court declared that although the city had a general Internet and e-mail usage policy, it was not the "operational reality" with regard to the pagers. The lieutenant stated that he would not monitor the text messages if officers paid for overages. Quon had exceeded his text character limit on several occasions before without his messages being reviewed. Thus, the court concluded:

   > This demonstrated that the [police department] followed its "informal policy" and that Quon reasonably relied on it. Nevertheless, without warning, his text messages were audited by the Department. Under these circumstances, Quon

had a reasonable expectation of privacy in the text messages archived on Arch Wireless's server.

The court then held that the search was "reasonable" under the *O'Connor v. Ortega* approach:

> There were a host of simple ways to verify the efficacy of the 25,000 character limit (if that, indeed, was the intended purpose) without intruding on Appellants' Fourth Amendment rights. For example, the Department could have warned Quon that for the month of September he was forbidden from using his pager for personal communications, and that the contents of all of his messages would be reviewed to ensure the pager was used only for work-related purposes during that time frame. Alternatively, if the Department wanted to review past usage, it could have asked Quon to count the characters himself, or asked him to redact personal messages and grant permission to the Department to review the redacted transcript. Under this process, Quon would have an incentive to be truthful because he may have previously paid for work-related overages and presumably would want the limit increased to avoid paying for such overages in the future.

Is the court correct in its conclusion that Quon had a reasonable expectation of privacy in his text messages despite the department's general Internet and e-mail usage policy? If an employer with a monitoring policy does not monitor, does this create an expectation in employees that there is an informal policy of non-monitoring? Many employers have broad network monitoring policies yet might not routinely exercise their right to monitor or may tell employees that they generally won't be monitored. Can these informal statements and practices negate the employer's general policy?

6. ***Mail vs. E-mail.*** In *Vernars v. Young*, 539 F.2d 966 (3d Cir. 1976), a plaintiff sued her employer under the intrusion upon seclusion tort for opening and reading her mail that "was delivered to the corporation's office but was addressed to her and marked personal." The court concluded:

> Just as private individuals have a right to expect that their telephonic communications will not be monitored, they also have a reasonable expectation that their personal mail will not be opened and read by unauthorized persons. Recognition of a cause of action for violation of that expectation seems particularly fitting under the right of privacy doctrine.

Generally, private letters mailed to a workplace are monitored much less frequently than e-mail. Suppose an employer adopted a policy that all employees' mail will be opened and read. What legal recourse would employees objecting to this policy have?

7. ***Will the Market Establish the Proper Level of Workplace Privacy?*** Some might argue for a laissez-faire approach. Workers will choose to work for employers providing greater privacy. In this way, the market will decide the appropriate level of workplace privacy. Do you agree that the market is properly functioning to reach the appropriate level of workplace privacy? If not, for what reasons is the market failing?

8. ***Is There a Reasonable Expectation of Privacy in Workplace E-mail?*** Consider *United States v. Maxwell,* 45 M.J. 406 (U.S. Ct. App. Armed Forces 1996):

> E-mail transmissions are not unlike other forms of modern communication. We can draw parallels from these other mediums. For example, if a sender of first-class mail seals an envelope and addresses it to another person, the sender can reasonably expect the contents to remain private and free from the eyes of the police absent a search warrant founded upon probable cause. However, once the letter is received and opened, the destiny of the letter then lies in the control of the recipient of the letter, not the sender, absent some legal privilege.
>
> Similarly, the maker of a telephone call has a reasonable expectation that police officials will not intercept and listen to the conversation; however, the conversation itself is held with the risk that one of the participants may reveal what is said to others.
>
> Drawing from these parallels, we can say that the transmitter of an e-mail message enjoys a reasonable expectation that police officials will not intercept the transmission without probable cause and a search warrant. However, once the transmissions are received by another person, the transmitter no longer controls its destiny. In a sense, e-mail is like a letter. It is sent and lies sealed in the computer until the recipient opens his or her computer and retrieves the transmission. The sender enjoys a reasonable expectation that the initial transmission will not be intercepted by the police. The fact that an unauthorized "hacker" might intercept an e-mail message does not diminish the legitimate expectation of privacy in any way.
>
> There is, however, one major difference between an e-mail message which has been transmitted via a network such as AOL and a direct computer "real time" transmission. The former transmission is stored in a centralized computer until the recipient opens his or her network and retrieves the e-mail, while the latter is lost forever, unless one of the communicators chooses to download the conversation to a disk. This latter action would be much like clandestinely recording one's telephone conversation. Thus, while a user of an e-mail network may enjoy a reasonable expectation that his or her e-mail will not be revealed to police, there is the risk that an employee or other person with direct access to the network service will access the e-mail, despite any company promises to the contrary. One always bears the risk that a recipient of an e-mail message will redistribute the e-mail or an employee of the company will read e-mail against company policy. However, this is not the same as the police commanding an individual to intercept the message. . . .

Compare *Maxwell* to *Pillsbury.* How do the courts differ as to their view about whether there is a reasonable expectation of privacy in e-mail?

9. ***The Union Setting.*** In *The Guard Publishing Co. d/b/a The Register Guard*, 351 NLRB No. 70, 2007 WL 4540458 (N.L.R.B. 2007), the National Labor Relations Board (NLRB) found that a company could "lawfully bar employees' nonwork-related use of its e-mail system" unless it acted in a manner that discriminated against a worker's rights under Section 7 of the National Labor Relations Act. This section protects an employee's ability to engage in "concerted activities . . . for mutual aid or protection." It safeguards collective bargaining, and the right to form and join a union.

In a 3–2 decision, the NLRB upheld a company's Communications System Policy (CSP), which governed employee use of its communications systems, including e-mail. The CSP limited use of company communication systems to "assist in conducting" company business. The policy also stated: "Communication systems are not to be used to solicit or proselytize for commercial ventures, religious or political causes, outside organizations, or other non-job-related solicitations." The majority of the NLRB found that the employer had a basic property right to regulate employee use of company property, and that, absent discrimination, employees had no statutory right under the NLRA to "use an employer's equipment or media for Section 7 communications." Since the CSP did not "on its face" discriminate against Section 7 activity, the NLRB upheld it.

In dissent, Members Wilma Liebman and Dennis Walsh accused the majority of turning the NRLB into the "Rip Van Winkle of administrative agencies." In their view: "Only a Board that has been asleep for the past 20 years could fail to recognize that e-mail has revolutionized communication both inside and outside the workplace." As a result, "[w]here, as here, an employer has given employees access to email for regular routine use in their work, we would find that banning all non-work related 'solicitations' is presumptively unlawful absent special circumstances." Employees had an affirmative right to engage in Section 7 communications in the workplace, even though the employee's "property" was involved. The dissent also noted that the company had failed to demonstrate any special circumstances in this case, and that it had consistently permitted employees, with its knowledge and tacit approval, to use e-mail for nonwork-related matters, including "baby announcements, party invitations, a request for a dog walker, and offers of sports tickets." It drew the line only at union related e-mails.

10. ***The Service Provider Exception.*** Under federal electronic surveillance law, service providers (who provide e-mail service) are exempt under the Wiretap Act, 18 U.S.C. § 2511(2)(a)(i), "while engaged in any activity which is necessary to provide the service, or to protect the rights or property of the provider." *See Bohach v. City of Reno*, 932 F. Supp. 1232 (D. Nev. 1996). In many workplaces — such as government workplaces, universities, and large corporations — the employers are also the service providers. Therefore, they would be exempt from intercepting e-mail under the Wiretap Act. Additionally, employers can have employees sign consent forms to the monitoring, and consent is an exception to federal wiretap law.

(b) Internet Use

LEVENTHAL V. KNAPEK

266 F.3d 64 (2d Cir. 2001)

SOTOMAYOR, J. After receiving anonymous allegations that an employee reasonably suspected to be plaintiff-appellant Gary Leventhal was neglecting his duties in the Accounting Bureau of the New York State Department of

Transportation ("DOT"), DOT investigators, without Leventhal's consent, printed out a list of the file names found on Leventhal's office computer. The list of file names contained evidence that certain non-standard software was loaded on Leventhal's computer. This led to additional searches confirming that Leventhal had a personal tax preparation program on his office computer and to disciplinary charges against Leventhal for misconduct. After settling the disciplinary charges, Leventhal sued defendants-appellees, challenging the legality of the searches and of two employment actions taken against him. . . .

Leventhal began his career at the DOT in 1974. At the time of the searches in question, Leventhal had risen to the position of Principal Accountant in the Accounting Bureau of the DOT, a grade 27 position. In 1996, and for several previous years, Leventhal maintained a private tax practice while employed at the DOT. He received DOT approval to make up on weekends or after normal work hours any time he missed because of his outside employment. In order to receive approval for this arrangement, Leventhal declared that his outside employment would "not interfere with the complete and proper execution of my duties with the Department of Transportation."

The DOT had a written policy prohibiting theft. The policy broadly defined theft to include:

> improper use of State equipment, material or vehicles. Examples include but are not limited to: conducting personal business on State time; using State equipment, material or vehicles for personal business; improper use of the mail, copiers, fax machines, personal computers, lincs codes or telephones and time spent on non-State business related activities during the workday.

During the DOT's interrogation of Leventhal after the searches of his office computer, Leventhal acknowledged that using DOT equipment for private purposes was "a violation of [DOT] policies."

The DOT also had an unwritten rule that only "standard" DOT software could be loaded on DOT computers. Although this rule was never officially promulgated as a DOT policy, Leventhal remarked during his interrogation that "the stated policy" was that employees were not to have personal software on a DOT computer "without permission." Nevertheless, it was known that the staff of the Accounting Bureau had loaded unlicensed copies of "non-standard" software on DOT computers and used the software to perform work-related activities due, at least in part, to the DOT's inability to purchase needed software for its employees. The DOT also had an official policy restricting office Internet access to DOT business.

In July 1996, the DOT circulated a memo from Ann Snow, the Network Administrator for the Budget and Finance Division, which stated that only original, licensed copies of software could be installed on DOT computers. Following the distribution of this memo, however, Leventhal's supervisors discussed their difficulties in complying with the memo because of the department's dependance upon the use of unlicensed software. Leventhal's immediate supervisor at the time, John Chevalier, instructed his subordinates, including Leventhal, that they could continue to use non-standard software for departmental business. . . .

On October 15, 1996, the New York State Office of the Inspector General referred to the DOT an anonymous letter it had received complaining of abuses at the DOT Accounting Bureau. This letter described specific employees by reference to their salary grades, genders, and job titles, without providing names. The letter made certain allegations concerning a grade 27 employee. Leventhal was the only grade 27 employee in the office at that time and, therefore, the DOT investigators inferred that the grade 27 employee described in the letter was Leventhal. The relevant portion of the letter states:

> The abuse of time and power is so far out of line with the intended functions of the bureau that to cite all specifics would be an endless task. The day to day operation of this bureau is a slap in the face to all good state workers. You have to see this place to believe it. I will cite a few examples. A grade 27 who is late everyday. The majority of his time is spent on non-DOT business related phone calls or talking to other personnel about personal computers. He is only in the office half the time he is either sick or on vacation. . . . [Half the time of a grade 23] is spent playing computer games and talking on the phone to his family or talking sports to one his subordinates, the guy who sleeps at his desk. . . . A grade 18 with an apparent alcohol problem who is so incompetent that his supervisor allows him to sleep at his desk. The grade 27 is aware of this problem. When [the grade 18] is not sleeping he is playing computer games or drafting up letters which are typed by [another] grade 18, who is barely able to function at an entry level clerical position. . . . And the sad part is that management knows what is going on although they would deny it if you asked them. . . . I think its [sic] time for some new leadership in the bureau.

Lawrence Knapek, the Assistant Commissioner of the DOT for the Office of Budget and Finance, met with John Samaniuk, the acting director of the Office of Internal Audit and Investigations, and Gary Cuyler, the chief investigator for that office, to discuss how to respond to the allegations made in the letter. They decided that the Office of Internal Audit and Investigation would conduct an investigation employing "such techniques as reviewing telephone records, reviewing computer records, Internet logs, that kind of thing." A "computer review" was ordered for all of the employees who could be identified from the letter. This involved printing out a list of file names found on these DOT computers to determine whether any contained non-standard software. After business hours on October 25, 1996, the investigators entered Leventhal's office through an open door, turned on his DOT computer, and reviewed the directories of files on the computer's hard drive. There was no power-on password to gain access to Leventhal's computer, but once the machine was turned on, some of the menu selections that appeared were password-protected. In order to perform their search, the investigators may have used a "boot-disk," a disk which allows the computer to start up without encountering the menus normally found there.

Having located the computer directories, the investigators printed out a list of the file names to enable the later identification of the programs loaded on Leventhal's computer without having to open each program. This included a printout of the names of the "hidden" files on Leventhal's computer. These "hidden" directories, the investigators found, contained "Morph," a type of drawing program and "PPU," a program suspected of containing tax software because of file names such as "TAX.FNT," and "CUSTTAX.DBF." On the non-"hidden" directories, the investigators found other non-standard software, including the programs Prodigy, Quicken, and Lotus Suite (although one part of Lotus Suite was standard DOT software at the time). . . .

In February 1997, DOT management and investigators met to examine the results from these searches. Assistant DOT Commissioner Knapek attended the meeting and, aware of Leventhal's private tax practice, was particularly interested in confirming the investigators' suspicion that Leventhal had loaded tax software on his DOT office computer. They decided to conduct a further search of Leventhal's computer to determine with greater certainty whether the "PPU" directory they had discovered during the first search was part of a tax preparation program. Investigators reexamined the computer in Leventhal's office once in February 1997 and twice in April 1997. During these subsequent searches, they copied the "Morph" and "PPU" directories onto a laptop computer, obtained additional printouts of the file directories, and opened a few files to examine their contents. In the first April search, an investigator noticed that some items had been added to the PPU directory since the previous search, indicating recent activity. The PPU directory was later identified as belonging to "Pencil Pushers," a tax preparation program. . . .

In September 1997, the DOT brought disciplinary charges against Leventhal under N.Y. Civ. Serv. Law § 75 charging six grounds of misconduct or incompetence. . . . Three months later, on October 18, 1999, Leventhal settled with the DOT. As part of the settlement, the DOT agreed to withdraw all disciplinary charges except that of lateness, to which Leventhal pleaded guilty. As a result, Leventhal was penalized thirty work days leave without pay. . . .

Four days after he settled the DOT disciplinary charges, Leventhal filed this action in United States District Court for the Northern District of New York. In his complaint, Leventhal alleged, under 42 U.S.C. § 1983 . . . Fourth Amendment violations arising out of the computer searches. . . .

"[T]he Fourth Amendment protects individuals from unreasonable searches conducted by the Government, even when the Government acts as an employer." *Nat'l Treasury Employees Union v. Von Raab,* 489 U.S. 656 (1989). The "special needs" of public employers may, however, allow them to dispense with the probable cause and warrant requirements when conducting workplace searches related to investigations of work-related misconduct. *See O'Connor v. Ortega,* 480 U.S. 709 (1987) (plurality opinion). In these situations, the Fourth Amendment's protection against "unreasonable" searches is enforced by "a careful balancing of governmental and private interests." *New Jersey v. T.L.O.,* 469 U.S. 325 (1985). A public employer's search of an area in which an employee had a reasonable expectation of privacy is "reasonable" when "the measures adopted are reasonably related to the objectives of the search and not excessively intrusive in light of" its purpose. *O'Connor,* 480 U.S. at 726.

We begin by inquiring whether "the conduct . . . at issue . . . infringed an expectation of privacy that society is prepared to consider reasonable." Without a reasonable expectation of privacy, a workplace search by a public employer will not violate the Fourth Amendment, regardless of the search's nature and scope. The workplace conditions can be such that an employee's expectation of privacy in a certain area is diminished.

We hold, based on the particular facts of this case, that Leventhal had a reasonable expectation of privacy in the contents of his office computer. We make this assessment "in the context of the employment relation, after considering what access other employees or the public had to Leventhal's office.

Leventhal occupied a private office with a door. He had exclusive use of the desk, filing cabinet, and computer in his office. Leventhal did not share use of his computer with other employees in the Accounting Bureau nor was there evidence that visitors or the public had access to his computer.

We are aware that "[p]ublic employees' expectations of privacy in their offices, desks, and file cabinets, like similar expectations of employees in the private sector, may be reduced by virtue of actual office practices and procedures, or by legitimate regulation." Construing the evidence in favor of Leventhal, as we must in reviewing this grant of summary judgment against him, we do not find that the DOT either had a general practice of routinely conducting searches of office computers or had placed Leventhal on notice that he should have no expectation of privacy in the contents of his office computer.

Viewing the DOT anti-theft policy in the light most favorable to Leventhal, we find that it did not prohibit the mere storage of personal materials in his office computer. Rather, the anti-theft policy prohibited "using" state equipment "for personal business" without defining further these terms. John Samaniuk, acting director of the DOT's Office of Internal Audits and Investigations, testified at Leventhal's disciplinary hearing that an employee would not violate state policies by keeping a personal checkbook in an office drawer, even though it would take up space there. Under the circumstances presented here, we cannot say that the same anti-theft policy prohibited Leventhal from storing personal items in his office computer.

Although the DOT technical support staff had access to all computers in the DOT offices, their maintenance of these computers was normally announced and the one example in the record of an unannounced visit to Leventhal's computer was only to change the name of a server. DOT personnel might also need, at times, to search for a document in an unattended computer, but there was no evidence that these searches were frequent, widespread, or extensive enough to constitute an atmosphere "so open to fellow employees or the public that no expectation of privacy is reasonable." This type of infrequent and selective search for maintenance purposes or to retrieve a needed document, justified by reference to the "special needs" of employers to pursue legitimate work-related objectives, does not destroy any underlying expectation of privacy that an employee could otherwise possess in the contents of an office computer. . . .

Even though Leventhal had some expectation of privacy in the contents of his office computer, the investigatory searches by the DOT did not violate his Fourth Amendment rights. An investigatory search for evidence of suspected work-related employee misfeasance will be constitutionally "reasonable" if it is "justified at its inception" and of appropriate scope. . . .

The initial consideration of the search's justification examines whether "there are reasonable grounds for suspecting that the search will turn up evidence that the employee is guilty of work-related misconduct." Here, there were reasonable grounds to believe that the searches would uncover evidence of misconduct. The specific allegations against the grade 27 employee, who was reasonably assumed to be Leventhal, were that (1) he was "late everyday"; (2) he spent "[t]he majority of his time . . . on non-DOT business related phone calls or talking to other personnel about personal computers"; and that (3) "[h]e is only in the office half the time[; the other half] he is either sick or on vacation." Probable cause is not necessary to conduct a search in this context, a plurality of the Court has explained, because "public employers have a direct and overriding interest in ensuring that the work of the agency is conducted in a proper and efficient manner." The individualized suspicion of misconduct in this case justified the DOT's decision to instigate some type of search.

The scope of a search will be appropriate if "reasonably related to the objectives of the search and not excessively intrusive in light of the nature of the misconduct." We conclude that the DOT search to identify whether Leventhal was using non-standard DOT software was "reasonably related" to the DOT's investigation of the allegations of Leventhal's workplace misconduct. Although the anonymous letter did not allege that the grade 27 employee was misusing DOT office computers, it did allege that the grade 27 employee was not attentive to his duties and spent a significant amount of work time discussing personal computers with other employees. Furthermore, the letter's allegations assumed that the DOT prohibition against misusing office computers was not rigorously enforced in the Accounting Bureau, remarking that a grade 18 employee "play[ed] computer games," that a grade 23 employee spent a substantial part of the day "playing computer games" or in non-work related conversations, and that another grade 23 employee "amuses himself by learning about computer software which have nothing to do with work." In view of the allegations of the misuse of DOT computers among other employees in the Accounting Bureau, Leventhal's alleged penchant for discussing personal computers during work hours, and Leventhal's general inattention to his duties which included, we presume, supervision of the computer use of others, we find that the searches of his computer were "reasonably related" to the DOT investigation of allegations of Leventhal's workplace misconduct.

Leventhal argues that a search for non-standard software would be irrelevant to charges of misconduct because the DOT had, *de facto,* approved of the use of non-standard software needed to conduct DOT business. Even assuming that this were true, the investigation was more broadly aimed at uncovering evidence that Leventhal was using his office computer for non-DOT purposes. The searches accomplished this task by uncovering evidence that Leventhal had loaded a tax preparation program onto his office computer, a program that he later admitted he used to print out personal tax returns in his office. . . .

NOTES & QUESTIONS

1. ***Applying the "Special Needs" Doctrine.*** Did the anonymous letter focus enough on Leventhal's computer misuse to justify the search? Given the court's reasoning, would a search of Leventhal's desk drawers have been "reasonable"?
2. ***Reasonable Expectations of Privacy in Workplace Computers.*** In *United States v. Simons*, 206 F.3d 392 (4th Cir. 2000), Simons was employed at the

Foreign Bureau of Information Services (FBIS) within the CIA. The FBIS had an Internet use policy that provided that employees were to use the Internet only for official government business. Furthermore, the policy provided, the "FBIS will periodically audit, inspect, and/or monitor the user's Internet access as deemed appropriate." FBIC contracted with an outside company to manage its computer network. One day, a manager at the company was testing the firewall database by entering the keyword "sex," and he discovered a "a large number of Internet 'hits' originating from Simons's computer." The manager informed FBIS, and a person from FBIS along with employees of the company remotely examined Simons's computer. They discovered more than 1,000 pornographic images. Among the pictures were images of child pornography. Criminal investigators then became involved. A company official entered Simons's office and swapped his hard drive with a copy. FBI Agent John Mesisca found over 50 images of child pornography on Simons's hard drive. Simons was indicted on one count of knowingly receiving child pornography and one count of knowingly possessing material containing images of child pornography. Simons moved to suppress the evidence, arguing that the searches of his office and computer violated the Fourth Amendment. The district court denied his motion. Simons was convicted and sentenced to 18 months' imprisonment.

Simons contended that the search of his computer violated his Fourth Amendment rights. The court concluded that Simons lacked a reasonable expectation of privacy in his computer:

> We first consider Simons's challenge to the warrantless searches of his computer and office by FBIS. We conclude that the remote searches of Simons's computer did not violate his Fourth Amendment rights because, in light of the Internet policy, Simons lacked a legitimate expectation of privacy in the files downloaded from the Internet. Additionally, we conclude that Simons's Fourth Amendment rights were not violated by FBIS' retrieval of Simons's hard drive from his office.
>
> Simons did not have a legitimate expectation of privacy with regard to the record or fruits of his Internet use in light of the FBIS Internet policy. The policy clearly stated that FBIS would "audit, inspect, and/or monitor" employees' use of the Internet, including all file transfers, all websites visited, and all e-mail messages, "as deemed appropriate." This policy placed employees on notice that they could not reasonably expect that their Internet activity would be private. Therefore, regardless of whether Simons subjectively believed that the files he transferred from the Internet were private, such a belief was not objectively reasonable after FBIS notified him that it would be overseeing his Internet use. Accordingly, FBIS's actions in remotely searching and seizing the computer files Simons downloaded from the Internet did not violate the Fourth Amendment.

The court noted that the warrantless entry into Simons's office did trigger the Fourth Amendment, as he had a reasonable expectation of privacy in his office. However, the court concluded that the search was reasonable under the special needs doctrine:

> We have little trouble concluding that the warrantless entry of Simons's office was reasonable under the Fourth Amendment standard announced in *O'Connor.* At the inception of the search FBIS had "reasonable grounds for suspecting" that the hard drive would yield evidence of misconduct because FBIS was already aware that Simons had misused his Internet access to download over a thousand pornographic images, some of which involved minors. The search was also permissible in scope. The measure adopted, entering Simons's office, was reasonably related to the objective of the search, retrieval of the hard drive. And, the search was not excessively intrusive. Indeed, there has been no suggestion that Harper searched Simons's desk or any other items in the office; rather, Harper simply crossed the floor of Simons's office, switched hard drives, and exited.

Compare *Simons* with *Leventhal.* Why did Leventhal have a reasonable expectation of privacy in his computer but not Simons?

3. ***Telecommuting.*** Consider an employee working from home. What factors should be considered if a dispute arises concerning e-mail or use of the Internet? Would it matter if the computer or the e-mail service were provided by the employer? What if the computer is also for personal use?
4. ***Electronic Surveillance Law: Telephone Use vs. Internet Use.*** Consider Clifford Fishman:

> [W]hile the Wiretap Act presumes all phone conversations are protected and obliges the employer to demonstrate a legitimate business purpose to justify monitoring, the Stored Communications Act gives the employer/ISP the unrestricted right to make a post-transmission examination of employees' every e-mail and Web-surf. There is no logical reason for this dichotomy.[24]

5. ***Unauthorized Access to Password-Protected Websites.*** In *Konop v. Hawaiian Airlines, Inc.,* 302 F.3d 868 (9th Cir. 2002), Konop, a pilot for Hawaiian Airlines, maintained a website where he posted comments criticizing his employer. To access Konop's website, visitors had to log in with a user name and password. Moreover, users had to indicate that they accepted the website's terms and conditions of use, which prohibited any Hawaiian manager from viewing the website and restricted users in divulging the website's contents to others. Konop gave the password to a select group of people, primarily pilots and employees of the airline. Hawaiian Airlines vice president James Davis obtained the passwords of two pilots on Konop's list and accessed the website. The court held that there was no violation of the Wiretap Act because there was no interception. Relying on *Steve Jackson Games,* the court concluded that Konop's website postings were not acquired in transmission. Applying the Stored Communications Act, the court accepted the parties' stipulation that the content of the website was in "electronic storage" and subject to the Stored Communications Act. However, the Act states that a "user" can authorize a third party to access the communication. *See* 18 U.S.C. § 2701(c)(2). The court concluded that it was unclear from the

---

[24] Clifford S. Fishman, *Technology and the Internet: The Impending Destruction of Privacy by Betrayers, Grudgers, Snoops, Spammers, Corporations, and the Media*, 72 Geo. Wash. L. Rev. 1503, 1530 (2004).

record whether the two pilots were users because merely having the password was insufficient to establish the statutory definition of user, which requires that a user not only be authorized to use the communication service but also must actually use the service. Since there was no evidence that the pilots used Konop's website, the court refused to grant summary judgment to the defendants on this claim. Would Konop have a viable intrusion upon seclusion claim? Should an employer have any legal interest in finding out about statements workers are making about that employer outside the workplace?

UNITED STATES V. ZIEGLER

474 F.3d 1184 (9th Cir. 2007)

O'SCANNLAIN, J. . . . Frontline Processing ("Frontline"), a company that services Internet merchants by processing on-line electronic payments, is located in Bozeman, Montana. On January 30, 2001, Anthony Cochenour, the owner of Frontline's Internet-service provider and the fiancé of a Frontline employee, contacted Special Agent James A. Kennedy, Jr. of the FBI with a tip that a Frontline employee had accessed child-pornographic websites from a workplace computer.

Agent Kennedy pursued the report that day, first contacting Frontline's Internet Technology ("IT") Administrator, John Softich. One of Softich's duties at Frontline was to monitor employee use of the workplace computers including their Internet access. He informed Kennedy that the company had in place a firewall, which permitted constant monitoring of the employees' Internet activities.

During the interview, Softich confirmed Cochenour's report that a Frontline employee had accessed child pornography via the Internet. Softich also reported that he had personally viewed the sites and confirmed that they depicted "very, very young girls in various states of undress." Softich further informed Kennedy that, according to the Internet Protocol address and log-in information, the offending sites were accessed from a computer in the office of Appellant Jeffrey Brian Ziegler, who had been employed by Frontline as director of operations since August 2000. Softich also informed Kennedy that the IT department had already placed a monitor on Ziegler's computer to record its Internet traffic by copying its cache files.

Agent Kennedy next interviewed William Schneider, Softich's subordinate in Frontline's IT department. Schneider confirmed that the IT department had placed a device in Ziegler's computer that would record his Internet activity. He reported that he had "spot checked" Ziegler's cache files and uncovered several images of child pornography. A review of Ziegler's "search engine cache information" also disclosed that he had searched for "things like 'preteen girls' and 'underage girls.'" Furthermore, according to Schneider, Frontline owned and routinely monitored all workplace computers. The employees were aware of the IT department's monitoring capabilities.

The parties dispute what happened next. According to testimony that Softich and Schneider provided to a federal grand jury, Agent Kennedy instructed them to make a copy of Ziegler's hard drive because he feared it might be tampered with before the FBI could make an arrest. Agent Kennedy, however, denied that he directed the Frontline employees to do anything. According to his testimony, his understanding was that the IT department had already made a backup copy of Ziegler's hard drive. As the government points out, his notes from the Softich interview say, "IT Dept has backed up JZ's hard drive to protect info." Thinking that the copy had already been made, Kennedy testified that he instructed Softich only to ensure that no one could tamper with the backup copy.

Whatever Agent Kennedy's actual instructions, the Frontline IT employees' subjective understanding of that conversation seems evident from their actions during the late evening of January 30, 2001. Around 10:00 p.m., Softich and Schneider obtained a key to Ziegler's private office from Ronald Reavis, the chief financial officer of Frontline, entered Ziegler's office, opened his computer's outer casing, and made two copies of the hard drive.

Shortly thereafter, Michael Freeman, Frontline's corporate counsel, contacted Agent Kennedy and informed him that Frontline would cooperate fully in the investigation. Freeman indicated that the company would voluntarily turn over Ziegler's computer to the FBI and thus explicitly suggested that a search warrant would be unnecessary. On February 5, 2001, Reavis delivered to Agent Kennedy Ziegler's computer tower (containing the original hard drive) and one of the hard drive copies made by Schneider and Softich. Schneider delivered the second copy sometime later. Forensic examiners at the FBI discovered many images of child pornography.

On May 23, 2003, a federal grand jury handed down a three-count indictment charging Ziegler with receipt of child pornography, in violation of 18 U.S.C. § 2252A(a)(2); possession of child pornography, in violation of 18 U.S.C. § 2252A(a)(5)(B); and receipt of obscene material, in violation of 18 U.S.C. § 1462. . . .

Ziegler's sole contention on appeal is that the January 30, 2001, entry into his private office to search his workplace computer violated the Fourth Amendment and, as such, the evidence contained on the computer's hard drive must be suppressed.

Ziegler argues that "[t]he district court erred in its finding that Ziegler did not have a legitimate expectation of privacy in his office and computer." He likens the workplace computer to the desk drawer or file cabinet given Fourth Amendment protection in cases such as *O'Connor v. Ortega,* 480 U.S. 709 (1987). Ziegler further contends that the Fourth Circuit's *Simons* case is inapposite. Whereas in *Simons* "the person conducting the search was a network administrator whose purpose was to search for evidence of employee misconduct," in this case "the search was conducted at the behest of Agent Kennedy who was undeniably seeking evidence of a crime."

The government, of course, views the matter quite differently. It contends that the district court's ruling was correct — Ziegler did not have an objectively reasonable expectation of privacy in his workplace computer. . . .

As we know, the Fourth Amendment protects people, not places. Although it is often true that "for most people, their computers are their most private spaces," the validity of that expectation depends entirely on its context.

In that vein, a criminal defendant may invoke the protections of the Fourth Amendment only if he can show that he had a *legitimate* expectation of privacy in the place searched or the item seized. . . .

The government does not contest Ziegler's claim that he had a subjective expectation of privacy in his office and the computer. The use of a password on his computer and the lock on his private office door are sufficient evidence of such expectation.

But Ziegler's expectation of privacy in his office and workplace computer must also have been objectively reasonable. The seminal case addressing the reasonable expectations of private employees in the workplace is *Mancusi v. DeForte,* 392 U.S. 364 (1968). In *Mancusi,* the Supreme Court addressed whether a union employee had a legitimate expectation of privacy, and therefore Fourth Amendment standing, in the contents of records that he stored in an office that he shared with several other union officials. The Court held that DeForte had standing to object to the search and that the search was unreasonable, noting that it was clear that "if DeForte had occupied a 'private' office in the union headquarters, and union records had been seized from a desk or a filing cabinet in that office, he would have had standing." That was so because he could expect that he would not be disturbed except by business or personal invitees and that the records would not be taken except with the permission of his supervisors. The Court thought the fact that the office was shared with a few other individuals to be of no constitutional distinction.

Mancusi compels us to recognize that in the private employer context, employees retain at least some expectation of privacy in their offices.

Furthermore, Ziegler's expectation of privacy in his office was reasonable on the facts of this case. His office was not shared by co-workers, and kept locked.

Because Ziegler had a reasonable expectation of privacy in his office, any search of that space and the items located therein must comply with the Fourth Amendment.

The next step is to inquire whether there was a search or seizure by the government. We need not dwell upon this matter too long. Given the district court's factual findings, we treat Softich and Schneider as de facto government agents. While the two Frontline employees may not have scoured the desk drawers and cabinets for evidence, as the agents did in *Mancusi,* they undoubtedly "searched" Ziegler's office when they entered to make a copy of the hard drive of his computer. . . .

The remaining question is whether the search of Ziegler's office and the copying of his hard drive were "unreasonable" within the meaning of the Fourth Amendment. As in *Mancusi,* the government does not deny that the search and seizure were without a warrant, and "it is settled for purposes of the Amendment that 'except in certain carefully defined classes of cases, a search of private property without proper consent is 'unreasonable' unless it has been authorized by a valid search warrant.'"

One well-settled exception is where valid consent is obtained by the government. In proving voluntary consent, the government "is not limited to proof that consent was given by the defendant, but may show that permission to search was obtained from a third party who possessed common authority over or other sufficient relationship to the premises or effects sought to be inspected." *United States v. Matlock,* 415 U.S.164 (1974).

We first consider whether Frontline exercised common authority over the office and the workplace computer such that it could validly consent to a search. *Mancusi* is again instructive. In *Mancusi,* the Supreme Court recognized that in his office, DeForte retained an expectation "that records would not be taken [by the police] except with his permission or that of his union superiors." The Court continued: "It is, of course, irrelevant that the Union or some of its officials might validly have consented to a search of the area where the records were kept, regardless of DeForte's wishes, for it is not claimed that any such consent was given, either expressly or by implication." *Mancusi* thus establishes that even where a private employee retains an expectation that his private office will not be the subject of an unreasonable government search, such interest may be subject to the possibility of an employer's consent to a search of the premises which it owns.

We are also convinced that Frontline could give valid consent to a search of the contents of the hard drive of Ziegler's workplace computer because the computer is the type of workplace property that remains within the control of the employer "even if the employee has placed personal items in [it]." *O'Connor v. Ortega,* 480 U.S. 709 (1987). In *Ortega,* the Supreme Court offered an analogy that is helpful to our resolution of this question. The Court posited a situation where an employee brings a piece of personal luggage to work and places it within his office. The Court noted that "[w]hile . . . the outward appearance of the luggage is affected by its presence in the workplace, the employee's expectation of privacy in the *contents* of the luggage is not affected in the same way." The Court further explained that "[t]he appropriate standard for a workplace search does not necessarily apply to a piece of closed personal luggage, a handbag or a briefcase that happens to be within the employer's business address."

The workplace computer, however, is quite different from the piece of personal luggage which the Court described in *Ortega.* Although use of each Frontline computer was subject to an individual log-in, Schneider and other IT-department employees "had complete administrative access to anybody's machine." The company had also installed a firewall, which, according to Schneider, is "a program that monitors Internet traffic . . . from within the organization to make sure nobody is visiting any sites that might be unprofessional." Monitoring was routine, and the IT department reviewed the log created by the firewall "[o]n a regular basis," sometimes daily if Internet traffic was high enough to warrant it. Finally, upon their hiring, Frontline employees were apprised of the company's monitoring efforts through training and an employment manual, and they were told that the computers were company-owned and not to be used for activities of a personal nature.

In this context, Ziegler could not reasonably have expected that the computer was his personal property, free from any type of control by his employer. The contents of his hard drive, like the files in *Mancusi,* were work-related items that contained business information and which were provided to, or created by, the employee in the context of the business relationship. Ziegler's downloading of personal items to the computer did not destroy the employer's common authority. Thus, Frontline, as the employer, could consent to a search of the office and the computer that it provided to Ziegler for his work.

The remaining question is, given Frontline's *ability* to consent to a search, did it consent to a search of the office and the computer. We conclude that it did. The exact type of employer consent that was absent in *Mancusi* clearly exists in this case. While the district court found that Softich and Schneider acted at the direction of Agent Kennedy, the record shows that Softich and Schneider received consent to search the office and the keys to the office from the Chief Financial Officer of Frontline Ronald Reavis. . . .

Although Ziegler retained a legitimate expectation of privacy in his workplace office, Frontline retained the ability to consent to a search of Ziegler's office and his business computer. And because valid third party consent to search the office and computer located therein was given by his employer, the district court's order denying suppression of the evidence of child pornography existing on Ziegler's computer is affirmed.

NOTES & QUESTIONS

1. ***Public vs. Private Sector Employment.*** *Simons* involves a search of a public sector employee; *Ziegler* involves a search of a private sector employee. Does the Fourth Amendment apply differently in these settings? If so, how?
2. ***A Duty to Monitor Employees?*** In *Doe v. XYC Corp.*, 887 A.2d 1156 (N.J. Super. Ct. App. Div. 2005), XYC Corporation employed Jane Doe's husband as an accountant. The network administrator discovered that the employee was visiting porn sites. The employee's supervisors told him to stop, and the employee said he would. The employee, however, had been videotaping and photographing his ten-year-old stepdaughter, Jill Doe, in the nude and transmitted three pictures of Jill Doe from his workplace computer to gain access to a child porn website. Jane Doe sued XYC on behalf of Jill, alleging that it knew or should have known that her husband was using his computer to view child porn and that it had a duty to report the employee to the authorities. XYC moved for summary judgment, but the court sided with the plaintiff:

> We hold that an employer who is on notice that one of its employees is using a workplace computer to access pornography, possibly child pornography, has a duty to investigate the employee's activities and to take prompt and effective action to stop the unauthorized activity, lest it result in harm to innocent third parties. No privacy interest of the employee stands in the way of this duty on the part of the employer. . . .
>
> In this case, defendant had an e-mail policy which stated that "all messages composed, sent or received on the e-mail system are and remain the property of the [defendant]. They are not the private property of any employee." Further, defendant reserved the "right to review, audit, access and disclose all messages created, received or sent over the e-mail system as deemed necessary by and at the sole discretion of [defendant]." Concerning the

internet, the policy stated that employees were permitted to "access sites, which are of a business nature only" and provided that:

> Any employees who discover a violation of this policy shall notify personnel. Any employee who violates this policy or uses the electronic mail or Internet system for improper purposes shall be subject to discipline, up to and including discharge.

The written e-mail policy contained an acknowledgement page to be signed by each employee. While the record does not contain a copy of such acknowledgement signed by Employee, there is no suggestion that he was not aware of the company policy. In addition, as we have noted, Employee's office, as with others in the same area, did not have a door and his computer screen was visible from the hallway, unless he took affirmative action to block it. Under those circumstances, we readily conclude that Employee had no legitimate expectation of privacy that would prevent his employer from accessing his computer to determine if he was using it to view adult or child pornography. As a result, we turn to whether defendant had reason to investigate Employee's use of his computer. . . .

Viewed in a light favorable to plaintiff, defendant was on notice of Employee's pornographic related computer activity by early 2000. By late March 2001, defendant had knowledge, through its supervisory personnel, that Employee had visited a variety of "porn sites" including one that suggested child pornography. Yet, despite being reported to high level management, no action was taken. A reasonable fact-finder could conclude that an appropriate investigation at that time would have revealed the extent of Employee's activities and, presumably, would have led to action to shut down those activities. It is true, as defendant contends, that Employee could still have possibly utilized a computer elsewhere, such as at home or at a library, to transmit Jill's photos. But that possibility does not negate proximate cause as a matter of law; it simply presents a contested issue for a jury.

Doe v. XYC Corp. suggests that if an employer has a policy of monitoring its employees' computer use, then that employer is responsible for harm resulting from failing to monitor or from failing to discipline employees who violate the underlying rules regarding computer use at work. What incentives does this create for employers? Is this case likely to be followed in other jurisdictions?

CHAPTER 9

INTERNATIONAL PRIVACY LAW

The study of information privacy provides an opportunity to understand privacy law in different countries. This chapter explores the European Union Data Protection Directive, important European privacy case law, Canadian privacy law, and other international privacy materials. It focuses on international legal developments that will have an impact in the United States as well as on texts that offer a useful comparative perspective on the U.S. privacy regime.

U.S. and foreign privacy regimes differ in some respects. Consider the standard description of privacy legislation in Europe as "omnibus" and privacy law in the United States as "sectoral." In Europe, one statute typically regulates the processing of personal information in public and private sectors alike. In the absence of more specific legislation, the general information privacy law in Europe sets the terms for the processing, storage, and transfer of personal information. In the United States, in contrast, a series of narrower laws focus on specific sectors of the economy or certain technologies. Joel Reidenberg has observed:

> Despite the growth of the Information Society, the United States has resisted all calls for omnibus or comprehensive legal rules for fair information practice in the private sector. Legal rules have developed on an ad hoc, targeted basis, while industry has elaborated voluntary norms and practices for particular problems. Over the years, there has been an almost zealous adherence to this ideal of narrowly targeted standards. In other countries, the response to the Information Age has been quite different. Foreign nations have enacted broad, sweeping "data protection" laws to establish fair information practices in both public and private sectors.[1]

Outside of Europe, other countries from around the world are moving toward adopting comprehensive privacy legislation on the European model. According to David Banisar and Simon Davies:

> There are three major reasons for the movement towards comprehensive privacy and data protection laws. Many countries are adopting these laws for one or more of the following reasons:

---

[1] Joel R. Reidenberg, *Setting Standards for Fair Information Practice in the U.S. Private Sector,* 80 Iowa L. Rev. 497, 500 (1995).

> To remedy past injustices. Many countries, especially in Central Europe, South America and South Africa, are adopting laws to remedy privacy violations that occurred under previous authoritarian regimes.
>
> To promote electronic commerce. Many countries, especially in Asia, but also Canada, have developed or are currently developing laws in an effort to promote electronic commerce. These countries recognize consumers are uneasy with their personal information being sent worldwide. Privacy laws are being introduced as part of a package of laws intended to facilitate electronic commerce by setting up uniform rules.
>
> To ensure laws are consistent with Pan-European laws. Most countries in Central and Eastern Europe are adopting new laws based on the Council of Europe Convention and the European Union Data Protection Directive. Many of these countries hope to join the European Union in the near future. Countries in other regions, such as Canada, are adopting new laws to ensure that trade will not be affected by the requirements of the EU Directive.[2]

In Europe, privacy law is shaped by the traditional role of the Council of Europe and the emerging role of the European Union. It was Article 8 of the Council of Europe Convention of 1950 that firmly established privacy protection as a critical human rights claim in postwar Europe. The provision in Article 8 has been given effect both by the decisions of the European Court of Human Rights and also by the Convention on Data Protection established by the Council of Europe in 1980.

Despite the importance of Article 8, the related case law, and the Data Protection Convention, the central focus of European privacy law for almost a decade has been the Data Protection Directive of the European Union. The Data Protection Directive establishes a basic legislative framework for the processing of personal information in the European Union. The EU Data Directive has had a profound effect on the development of privacy law, not only in Europe but also around the world.

It is worth noting that the phrase "data protection" is frequently used to describe privacy protection in the European context. This term reflects the modern concept of privacy protection that emerged in the 1970s as computer systems were increasingly used to process information on citizens. At the same time, the concept of privacy, sometimes referred to as that of private life or the private domain, continues to play an important role in the European conception of information privacy.

Beyond Europe, important international and regional agreements have helped shape the structure of national privacy law and influenced the development of privacy as a legal claim in particular countries. The Privacy Guidelines of the Organization for Economic Cooperation and Development (OECD), adopted in 1980, represent a consensus position of countries from North America, Europe, and East Asia as to the basic structure of privacy law.

Other privacy laws follow from Article 12 of the Universal Declaration of Human Rights, adopted by the United Nations in 1948, which states that "[n]o one shall be subjected to arbitrary interference with his privacy, family, home or

---

[2] David Banisar & Simon Davies, *Global Trends in Privacy Protection: An International Survey of Privacy, Data Protection, and Surveillance Laws and Developments,* 18 J. Marshall J. Computer & Info. L. 1, 11-12 (1999).

correspondence, nor to attacks upon his honor and reputation. Everyone has the right to the protection of the law against such interference or attacks."

A. THE OECD PRIVACY GUIDELINES

On September 23, 1980, the Organization for Economic Cooperation and Development (OECD), a group of leading industrial countries concerned with global economic and democratic development, issued guidelines for privacy protection in the transfer of personal information across national borders. These are the Guidelines on the Protection of Privacy and Transborder Flows of Personal Data (the Guidelines), which establish eight key principles for the protection of personal information.

Scope. The Guidelines "apply to personal data, whether in the public or private sectors, which, because of the manner in which they are processed, or because of their nature or the context in which they are used, pose a danger to privacy and individual liberties." "Personal data" is defined as "any information relating to an identified or identifiable individual (data subject)." The Guidelines provide a floor of protection; member countries can adopt more stringent protections.

Principles. The OECD Privacy Guidelines establish eight principles regarding the processing of personal data:

1. *Collection Limitation Principle.* There should be limits to the collection of personal data and any such data should be obtained by lawful and fair means and, where appropriate, with the knowledge or consent of the data subject.
2. *Data Quality Principle.* Personal data should be relevant to the purposes for which they are to be used, and, to the extent necessary for those purposes, should be accurate, complete and kept up-to-date.
3. *Purpose Specification Principle.* The purposes for which personal data are collected should be specified not later than at the time of data collection and the subsequent use limited to the fulfillment of those purposes or such others as are not incompatible with those purposes and as are specified on each occasion of change of purpose.
4. *Use Limitation Principle.* Personal data should not be disclosed, made available or otherwise used for purposes other than those specified in accordance with [the purpose specification principle] except: a) with the consent of the data subject; or b) by the authority of law.
5. *Security Safeguards Principle.* Personal data should be protected by reasonable security safeguards against such risks as loss or unauthorised access, destruction, use, modification or disclosure of data.
6. *Openness Principle.* There should be a general policy of openness about developments, practices and policies with respect to personal data. Means should be readily available of establishing the existence and nature of personal data, and the main purposes of their use, as well as the identity and usual residence of the data controller.
7. *Individual Participation Principle.* An individual should have the right: (a) to obtain from a data controller, or otherwise, confirmation of whether or not the

data controller has data relating to him; (b) to have communicated to him, data relating to him (i) within a reasonable time; (ii) at a charge, if any, that is not excessive; (iii) in a reasonable manner; and (iv) in a form that is readily intelligible to him; (c) to be given reasons if a request made under subparagraphs (a) and (b) is denied, and to be able to challenge such denial; and (d) to challenge data relating to him and, if the challenge is successful to have the data erased, rectified, completed or amended.

8. *Accountability Principle.* A data controller should be accountable for complying with measures which give effect to the principles stated above. . . .

The Worldwide Influence of the OECD Privacy Guidelines. The OECD Privacy Guidelines are nonbinding on members of the OECD. Nonetheless, they have had a significant impact on the development of national law in North America, Europe, and East Asia.[3] For example, in the United States, the subscriber privacy provisions in the Cable Act of 1984 include many of the principles of the OECD Privacy Guidelines. In Australia, the Privacy Act of 1988 establishes 11 privacy principles based on the OECD Privacy Guidelines. New Zealand's 1993 Privacy Act, which regulates both the public and private sectors, adopts 12 principles based on the OECD Privacy Guidelines. South Korea's Act on the Protection of Personal Information Managed by Public Agencies of 1994 follows a number of the OECD Privacy Guidelines.

The OECD Privacy Guidelines and the Fair Information Practices. How do the OECD Privacy Guidelines compare with the articulation of Fair Information Practices in the Department of Housing, Education, and Welfare (HEW) Report of 1973 (Chapter 6)? Is either framework more comprehensive? More detailed? Which framework would be easier to comply with? To enforce?[4]

B. PRIVACY PROTECTION IN EUROPE

1. DIVERGENCE OR CONVERGENCE?

JAMES Q. WHITMAN, *THE TWO WESTERN CULTURES OF PRIVACY: DIGNITY VERSUS LIBERTY*

113 Yale L.J. 1151 (2004)

Continental law is avidly protective of many kinds of "privacy" in many realms of life, whether the issue is consumer data, credit reporting, workplace privacy, discovery in civil litigation, the dissemination of nude images on the Internet, or shielding criminal offenders from public exposure. To people accustomed to the continental way of doing things, American law seems to tolerate relentless and

---

[3] For an analysis of privacy laws around the world, see EPIC & Privacy International, *Privacy and Human Rights* (2006).

[4] For a comparison of U.S. privacy law to the OECD Privacy Guidelines, see Joel R. Reidenberg, *Restoring Americans' Privacy in Electronic Commerce,* 14 Berkeley J.L. & Tech. 771 (1999).

brutal violations of privacy in all these areas of law. I have seen Europeans grow visibly angry, for example, when they learn about routine American practices like credit reporting. How, they ask, can merchants be permitted access to the entire credit history of customers who have never defaulted on their debts? Is it not obvious that this is a violation of privacy and personhood, which must be prohibited by law?

[Differences about privacy in the United States and Europe] are clashes in attitude that go well beyond the occasional social misunderstanding. In fact, they have provoked some tense and costly transatlantic legal and trade battles over the last decade and a half. Thus, the European Union and the United States slid into a major trade conflict over the protection of consumer data in the 1990s, only problematically resolved by a 2000 "safe harbor" agreement. Europeans still constantly complain that Americans do not accept the importance of protecting consumer privacy. Those tensions have only grown in the aftermath of September 11. . . .

For sensitive Europeans, indeed, a tour through American law may be an experience something like a visit to the latrines of Ephesus. Correspondingly, it has become common for Europeans to maintain that they respect a "fundamental right to privacy" that is either weak or wholly absent in the "cultural context" of the United States. Here, Europeans point with pride to Article 8 of the European Convention on Human Rights, which protects "the right to respect for private and family life," and to the European Union's new Charter of Fundamental Rights, which demonstratively features articles on both "Respect for Private and Family Life" and "Protection of Personal Data." By the standards of those great documents, American privacy law seems, from the European point of view, simply to have "failed.". . .

What we must acknowledge, instead, is that there are, on the two sides of the Atlantic, two different cultures of privacy, which are home to different intuitive sensibilities, and which have produced two significantly different laws of privacy. . . .

So why do these sensibilities differ? Why is it that French people won't talk about their salaries, but will take off their bikini tops? Why is it that Americans comply with court discovery orders that open essentially all of their documents for inspection, but refuse to carry identity cards? Why is it that Europeans tolerate state meddling in their choice of baby names? Why is it that Americans submit to extensive credit reporting without rebelling? . . .

At its conceptual core, the American right to privacy still takes much the form that it took in the eighteenth century: It is the right to freedom from intrusions by the state, especially in one's own home. The prime danger, from the American point of view, is that "the sanctity of [our] home[s]," in the words of a leading nineteenth-century Supreme Court opinion on privacy, will be breached by government actors. American anxieties thus focus comparatively little on the media. Instead, they tend to be anxieties about maintaining a kind of private sovereignty within our own walls.

Such is the contrast that lies at the base of our divergent sensibilities about what counts as a "privacy" violation. On the one hand, we have an Old World in which it seems fundamentally important not to lose public face; on the other, a New World in which it seems fundamentally important to preserve the home as a citadel of individual sovereignty. . . . When Americans seem to continental Europeans to violate norms of privacy, it is because they seem to display an embarrassing lack of concern for public dignity — whether the issue is the public indignity inflicted upon Monica Lewinsky by the media, or the self-inflicted indignity of an American who boasts about his salary. Conversely, when continental Europeans seem to Americans to violate norms of privacy, it is because they seem to show a supine lack of resistance to invasions of the realm of private sovereignty whose main citadel is the home — whether the issue is wiretapping or baby names. . . .

Where do the peculiar continental anxieties about "privacy" come from? To understand the continental law of privacy, we must start by recognizing how deeply "dignity" and "honor" matter in continental law more broadly. Privacy is not the only area in which continental law aims to protect people from shame and humiliation, from loss of public dignity. The law of privacy, in these continental countries, is only one member of a much wider class of legal protections for interpersonal respect. The importance of the value of respect in continental law is most familiar to Americans from one body of law in particular: the continental law of hate speech, which protects minorities against disrespectful epithets. But the continental attachment to norms of respect goes well beyond hate speech. Minorities are not the only ones protected against disrespectful epithets on the Continent. Everybody is protected against disrespect, through the continental law of "insult," a very old body of law that protects the individual right to "personal honor." Nor does it end there. Continental law protects the right of workers to respectful treatment by their bosses and coworkers, through what is called the law of "mobbing" or "moral harassment." This is law that protects employees against being addressed disrespectfully, shunned, or even assigned humiliating tasks like xeroxing. Continental law also protects the right of women to respectful treatment through its version of the law of sexual harassment. It even tries to protect the right of prison inmates to respectful treatment . . . to a degree almost unimaginable for Americans. . . .

If I may use a cosmological metaphor: American privacy law is a body caught in the gravitational orbit of liberty values, while European law is caught in the orbit of dignity. . . . Continental Europeans are consistently more drawn to problems touching on public dignity, while Americans are consistently more drawn to problems touching on the depredations of the state. . . .

Why does continental law work so hard to guarantee norms of "respect," "dignity," and "personal honor" in so many walks of life? This is a question to which I believe we must give a different answer from the one Europeans themselves commonly give. Europeans generally give a dramatic explanation for why dignity figures so prominently in their law: They assert that contemporary continental dignity is the product of a reaction against fascism, and especially against Nazism. Having experienced the horrific indignities of the 1930s and 1940s, continental societies, Europeans say, have mended their ways. Europe has dignity today because Europe was traumatized seventy years ago. . . .

In fact, the history of the continental law of dignity begins long before the postwar period. It begins in the eighteenth, and even the seventeenth, centuries. The continental societies that we see today are the descendants of the sharply hierarchical societies that existed two or two-and-a-half centuries ago — of the aristocratic and monarchical societies of which the France of Louis XIV was the model. In point of fact, continental law has enforced norms of respect and dignity for a very long time. In earlier centuries, though, only persons of high social status could expect their right to respect to be protected in court. Indeed, well into the twentieth century, only high-status persons could expect to be treated respectfully in the daily life of Germany or France, and only high-status persons could expect their "personal honor" to be protected in continental courts. . . .

What we see in continental law today is the result of a centuries-long, slow-maturing revolt against that style of status privilege. Over time, it has come to seem unacceptable that only certain persons should enjoy legal protections for their "dignity." Indeed, the rise of norms of respect for everybody — even minorities, even prison inmates — represents a great social transformation on the Continent. Everybody is now supposed to be treated in ways that only highly placed and wealthy people were treated a couple of centuries ago. . . .

The uncomfortable paradox . . . is that much of this leveling up took place during the fascist period, for fascist politics involved precisely the promise that all members of the nation-state would be equal in "honor" — that all racial Germans, for example, would be "masters." For that very reason, some of the fundamental institutions of the continental law of dignity experienced significant development under the star of fascism. In fact, the fascist period, seen in proper sociological perspective, was one stage in a continuous history of the extension of honor throughout all echelons of continental society.

This long-term secular leveling-up tendency has shaped continental law in a very fundamental way. Contemporary continental hate speech protections, for example, can be traced back to dueling law: In the nineteenth century, continental courts protected the right to respect only of the dueling classes. Today they protect everybody's right to respect; indeed, the rules of dueling have had a striking influence in the Continent, sometimes being imported bodily into the law. . . . As for Americans: They have their own concepts of personhood, their own traditions, and their own values. And the consequence is that there will always be practices that intuitively seem to represent obvious violations to Americans. Most especially, state action will raise American hackles much more often than European ones.

This is indeed almost too obvious to need describing for American readers. Suspicion of the state has always stood at the foundation of American privacy thinking, and American scholarly writing. . . .

What matters in America, over the long run, is liberty against the state within the privacy of one's home. This does not mean that the American approach to "privacy" is narrowly limited to Fourth Amendment search and seizure problems, of course. Lawyers do ingenious things, and the conception of privacy as liberty within the sanctity of the home can be extended in important ways. This has been notably true, of course, in the famous series of "constitutional privacy" decisions that began with *Griswold v. Connecticut*. . . .

Nevertheless, the fundamental limit on American thinking always remains: American "privacy" law, however ingenious its elaborations, always tends to imagine the home as the primary defense, and the state as the primary enemy. This gives American privacy law a distinctive coloration. Where American law perceives a threat to privacy, it is typically precisely because the state has become involved in the transaction. . . .

In truth, there is little reason to suppose that Americans will be persuaded to think of their world of values in a European way any time soon; American law simply does not endorse the general norm of personal dignity found in Europe. Nor is there any greater hope that Europeans will embrace the American ideal; the law of Europe does not recognize many of the antistatist concerns that Americans seem to take for granted. Of course we are all free to plead for a different kind of law — in Europe or in the United States. But pleading for privacy as such is not the way to do it. There is no such thing as privacy as such. The battle, if it is to be fought, will have to be fought over more fundamental values than that.

NOTES & QUESTIONS

1. ***U.S. vs. EU Privacy Regulation of the Private Sector.*** Is Whitman correct that the United States has little concern about privacy with regard to private actors? As you read this chapter, consider whether there are areas where U.S. information privacy regulation might well exceed those of the Europeans.
2. ***Regional Variation in Privacy Norms.*** How well does Whitman's analysis apply to regional diversities for privacy culture within the United States or Europe? Are individuals in New York City more likely to share the views of those in Paris or London, or those in a small town in South Carolina?
3. ***Divergence or Convergence?*** Whitman describes a divergence between European and U.S. views toward privacy. In 1992, Colin Bennett, a Canadian political scientist, proposed that convergence was taking place between U.S. and European information privacy law. He argued:

> The process of policy making in the data protection area is clearly one where broad transnational forces for convergence have transcended variations in national characteristics. The background to the legislation is the rapid technological process that is commonly recognized to be restructuring individual, social, economic, and political relationships. . . .
>
> The technology, however, should not be regarded as an independent force that "causes" anything. The crucial variable is the common set of attitudes that developed about the technology. . .
>
> In this context, the salience of national factors as independent variables has been reduced. The partisan orientation of governments has been insignificant. . . . Fair information practice exposes the commonalities among the closely interlinked historical, cultural, and political developments of these societies.[5]

More recently, Bennett has modified this identification of convergence. In *The Governance of Privacy*, Bennett and Charles Raab identify a "decentering of privacy." In their view, "The governance of privacy is exercised through a variety of institutional forms — public and private, domestic and transnational, with the result that in certain contexts the government regulators are

---

[5] Colin J. Bennett, *Regulating Privacy: Data Protection and Public Policy in Europe and the United States* 150-53 (1992).

not necessarily the most important actors, and the laws they enact not necessarily the most important instruments." There is now a "fragmentation" with privacy regulation involving "a plurality of actors and a range of methods of operation and coordination." As a consequence, Bennett and Raab point to a lack of any single race to the bottom or top among different countries in different policy areas: "There are many races, many tops and many bottoms as a host of actors, public and private, use or resist the expanding repertoire of privacy instruments to encourage or obstruct the more responsible use of personal information within modern organizations."[6]

Compare Whitman's concluding paragraph to Bennett and Raab's argument that the many different policy areas and policy instruments throughout the world make any single comparison impossible. Is there an unbridgeable rift between the privacy laws in different countries based on different cultural values? Or is increasing globalization forcing countries to resolve these rifts?

4. ***Culture and Privacy Norms.*** As you go through the materials in this chapter, consider whether privacy claims vary in different parts of the world, and more generally, which factors contribute to the structuring of privacy norms. For example, is the concept of privacy determined by cultural traditions, trade requirements, legal developments, or technological influences?

5. ***Why Do the Privacy Law Regimes in the EU and the United States Differ?*** Francesca Bignami contends that "[w]hen individual privacy in the age of information technology first became a policy problem, American policymakers were every bit as active as their European counterparts. In fact, a case can be made that European privacy law was influenced by American law and policy." But then things changed. Why? Bignami offers a number of reasons, one of which is that the EU has different enforcement mechanisms than the United States:

> In the American case, the primary enforcers are individual litigants; in the European case, they are independent privacy agencies. This is consistent with broader patterns of regulation in the two legal systems: Americans litigate in court and Europeans negotiate with government agencies. The American choice, however, appears to have been particularly ill suited to the realities of information privacy in the work of government agencies. The injuries suffered by individuals — not to speak of the polity — when the government secretly undertakes a program like that for call records are generally not recognized by common law courts. . . . A government agency with the authority to investigate other agencies for privacy violations, to recommend changes if such violations are found, and, in the last resort, to impose an administrative sanction or to take an offending government official to court, is likely to be a better enforcer than private attorneys general.[7]

---

[6] Colin J. Bennett & Charles D. Raab, *The Governance of Privacy: Policy Instruments in Global Perspective* 294 (2006).

[7] Francesca Bignami, *European versus American Liberty: A Comparative Privacy Analysis of Antiterrorism Data Mining*, 48 B.C. L. Rev. 609, 682-88 (2007).

2. EUROPEAN CONVENTION ON HUMAN RIGHTS ARTICLE 8

(a) Introduction

The European Convention on Human Rights (ECHR), an international convention covering a wide range of civil and political rights, was adopted in 1950, shortly after the Universal Declaration of Human Rights of the United Nations. It was drafted under the auspices of the Council of Europe, an international organization composed today of over forty European states, which was formed in 1949 as a result of a strong political willingness to unify European countries, to consolidate and stabilize its democracies after World War II, to prevent any future violations of human rights such as those that had taken place during the Nazi regime, and to establish a bulwark against Communism. The European Convention was intended to bring violations of human rights to the attention of the international community. As some commentators have observed:

> In practice, this function of the ECHR, which imagines large-scale violations of human rights, has largely remained dormant. The ECHR has instead been used primarily to raise questions of isolated weaknesses in legal systems that basically conform to its requirements and which are representative of the "common heritage of political traditions, ideals, freedom and the rule of law" to which the Preamble to the ECHR refers.[8]

The Convention is enforced by the European Commission on Human Rights, the Council of Ministers, and the European Court on Human Rights. Individual applications first go to the European Commission of Human Rights at Strasbourg. The Commission examines the applications to see whether local remedies have been exhausted. The Commission will consider first whether the application alleges a violation of the Convention. If it does not, then the application will be dismissed. The Commission will next consider whether the application presents sufficient facts to establish that a right defined in the Convention has been breached. If not, the application will be rejected as "manifestly ill-founded." The Commission may also choose to reject an application if it is unsigned, is an abuse of the right to petition, is "substantially the same as a matter which has already been examined by the Commission or has already been submitted to another procedure of international investigation or settlement and it contains no relevant new information." The Commission's decision to reject an application is final.[9]

The Commission next establishes the facts and drafts a report expressing its opinion, which is not legally binding, on the existence of a breach of the Convention. The Commission then encourages parties to reach a friendly settlement. If these efforts fail, the Commission determines whether there has been a breach of the Convention. Its opinions are not per se legally binding on the parties. The case may subsequently be referred to the Court itself by either the Commission, a defendant state, a state bringing an application, or a contracting party whose nation is an alleged victim. In practice, most cases that

---

[8] S.H. Bailey, D.J. Harris, & B.L. Jones, *Civil Liberties — Cases and Materials* 749-50 (3d ed. 1991).

[9] *Id.* at 757-58.

reach the Court are referred to it by the Commission. No individual can bring a matter directly to the Court. Identified elements that might be influential in the Commission's referral decision include whether the case raises a point of interpretation that has not previously arisen, whether the Commission is divided as to whether there has been a violation, or whether a case is perceived to have particularly serious political implications.[10]

The Court's judgment, which is binding, is normally declaratory. If the Court finds that a breach of the Convention has occurred, it brings into operation the defendant state's obligation in international law to make reparation. However, the Court may always award "just satisfaction" to the injured if the internal law of the defendant state allows only partial reparation.

The whole procedure can take up to five years between the registration of the application and the Court's final ruling. Although this is a slow procedure, "the primary purpose of state and individual applications is not to offer an international remedy for individual victims of violations of the Convention but to bring to light violations of an inter-state guarantee."[11]

The role of the European Court is of particular importance for several reasons. First, the volume of cases brought to the Court has increased over the years and has raised more complex jurisprudential issues than those that came before the court in earlier years. Second, the Court is the longest standing international human rights court; it is considered the model against which other regional courts can be measured. Finally, the jurisprudence of the court has influenced the normative development of other parts of the international human rights system. The Convention itself has a fundamental role in the European legal system as it has gradually acquired the status of a "constitutional instrument of European public order in the field of human rights."[12]

The critical privacy provision in the European Convention on Human Rights is Article 8. The language in Article 8 of the ECHR is similar to Article 12 of the Universal Declaration of Human Rights.

ECHR ARTICLE 8

Article 8 — Right to Respect for Private and Family Life

1. Everyone has the right to respect for his private and family life, his home and his correspondence.

2. There shall be no interference by a public authority with the exercise of this right except such as is in accordance with the law and is necessary in a democratic society in the interests of national security, public safety or the economic well-being of the country, for the prevention of disorder or crime, for

---

[10] J.G. Merrills, *The Development of International Law by the European Court of Human Rights* 4 (2d ed. 1993).

[11] S.H. Bailey, D.J. Harris, & B.L. Jones, *Civil Liberties: Cases and Materials* 761 (3d ed. 1991).

[12] J. Polakiewicz & V. Jacob-Foltzer, *The European Human Rights Convention in Domestic Law,* 12 Hum. Rts. L.J. 65, 125 (1991).

the protection of health or morals, or for the protection of the rights and freedoms of others.

NOTES & QUESTIONS

1. ***"In Accordance with Law."*** As John Wadham describes it, a central requirement of Article 8 is "the rule of law":

> No matter how desirable the end to be achieved, no interference with a right protected under the Convention is permissible unless the citizen knows the basis for the interference because it is set out in an ascertainable law. In the absence of such detailed authorisation by the law, any interference, however justified, will violate the Convention. . . . No such interference can be permitted by executive rules alone.
>
> To be "prescribed by law" or "in accordance with law" means that there must be an ascertainable legal regime governing the interference in question. The Strasbourg court explained the concept in *Sunday Times v. United Kingdom* (1979) 2 EHRR 245 at paragraph 49: "Firstly, the law must be adequately accessible: the citizens must be able to have an indication that is adequate in the circumstances of the legal rules applicable to a given case. Secondly, a norm cannot be regarded as a 'law' unless it is formulated with sufficient precision to enable the citizen to regulate his conduct."
>
> The common law may be sufficiently clear for this purpose and statute law or regulation is not necessary. . . .
>
> It is not acceptable for an interference with a Convention right to occur without any legal regulation. . . .

Moreover, "any interference by a public authority with a Convention right must be directed towards an identified legitimate aim. . . . The sorts of aims which are legitimate are the interests of public safety, national security, the protection of health and morals and the economic well-being of the country or the protection of the rights and freedoms of others."[13]

2. ***"Necessary in a Democratic Society."*** Wadham notes:

> Although a few rights in the Convention are absolute, most are not. The Convention approach is to decide whether a particular limitation from a right is justified in the sense of being "proportionate to the legitimate aim pursued."
>
> This means that even if a policy which interferes with a Convention right might be aimed at securing a legitimate aim of social policy, for example, the prevention of crime, this will not in itself justify the violation if the means adopted to secure the aim are excessive in the circumstances. . . .
>
> Where the Convention allows restrictions on rights it requires them to be justified by a legitimate aim and proportional to the need at hand, that is, "necessary in a democratic society." The case law interprets this to mean that there must be a "pressing social need" for the interference. . . . [T]he state's desire to protect a legitimate aim does not allow it to restrict the right of the

---

[13] John Wadham, *Human Rights and Privacy — The Balance,* speech given at Cambridge (Mar. 2000), http://www.liberty-human-rights.org.uk/mhrp6j.html.

individual disproportionately — the state cannot use a sledgehammer to crack a nut.[14]

(b) Privacy and the Media

VON HANNOVER V. GERMANY

59320/00 [2004] ECHR 294 (24 June 2004)

---

1. The case originated in an application against the Federal Republic of Germany lodged with the Court under Article 34 of the Convention for the Protection of Human Rights and Fundamental Freedoms ("the Convention") by a national of Monaco, Caroline von Hannover ("the applicant"), on 6 June 2000.

2. The applicant alleged that the German court decisions in her case had infringed her right to respect for her private and family life as guaranteed by Article 8 of the Convention. . . .

THE FACTS

8. The applicant, who is the eldest daughter of Prince Rainier III of Monaco, was born in 1957. Her official residence is in Monaco but she lives in the Paris area most of the time. . . .

9. Since the early 1990s the applicant has been trying — often through the courts — in a number of European countries to prevent the publication of photos about her private life in the tabloid press.

10. The photos that were the subject of the proceedings described below were published by the publishing company Burda in the German magazines *Bunte* and *Freizeit Revue* and by the publishing company Heinrich Bauer in the German magazine *Neue Post*.

11. [Five photos in *Freizeit Revue* magazine] show her with the actor Vincent Lindon at the far end of a restaurant courtyard in Saint-Rémy-de-Provence. [Photos in the magazine *Bunte* show her riding on horseback, with her children Peter and Andrea, in a canoe with her daughter, in a restaurant, on a bicycle, shopping in a market, skiing, leaving her house, and playing tennis. Photos in *Neue Post* magazine show her at a beach club in a swimsuit. Photos in the *Neue Post* magazine shows her in a swimsuit and wrapped up in a bathing towel. In this sequence, she tripped over an obstacle and fell down. The photos, which were described as "quite blurred," were accompanied by an article entitled, "Prince Ernst August played fisticuffs and Princess Caroline fell flat on her face."] . . .

[The regional court denied her application under German law, reasoning that she did not have a right to protection against photos taken in public places. The case was appealed to the German Federal Court of Justice, and then to the German Federal Constitutional Court.] . . .

25. In a landmark judgment of 15 December 1999, delivered after a hearing, the Constitutional Court allowed the applicant's appeal in part on the ground that

---

[14] *Id.*

the three photos that had appeared in the 32nd and 34th editions of *Bunte* magazine, dated 5 August 1993 and 19 August 1993, featuring the applicant with her children had infringed her right to the protection of her personality rights guaranteed by sections 2(1) and 1(1) of the Basic Law, reinforced by her right to family protection under section 6 of the Basic Law. It referred the case to the Federal Court of Justice on that point. However, the Constitutional Court dismissed the applicant's appeal regarding the other photos.

The relevant extract of the judgment reads as follows:

> The fact that the press fulfils the function of forming public opinion does not exclude entertainment from the functional guarantee under the Basic Law. The formation of opinions and entertainment are not opposites. Entertainment also plays a role in the formation of opinions. It can sometimes even stimulate or influence the formation of opinions more than purely factual information. Moreover, there is a growing tendency in the media to do away with the distinction between information and entertainment both as regards press coverage generally and individual contributions, and to disseminate information in the form of entertainment or mix it with entertainment ("infotainment"). Consequently, many readers obtain information they consider to be important or interesting from entertaining coverage. . . .
>
> Nor can mere entertainment be denied any role in the formation of opinions. That would amount to unilaterally presuming that entertainment merely satisfies a desire for amusement, relaxation, escapism or diversion. Entertainment can also convey images of reality and propose subjects for debate that spark a process of discussion and assimilation relating to philosophies of life, values and behaviour models. In that respect it fulfils important social functions. . . . When measured against the aim of protecting press freedom, entertainment in the press is neither negligible nor entirely worthless and therefore falls within the scope of application of fundamental rights. . . .
>
> The same is true of information about people. Personalization is an important journalistic means of attracting attention. Very often it is this which first arouses interest in a problem and stimulates a desire for factual information. Similarly, interest in a particular event or situation is usually stimulated by personalised accounts. Additionally, celebrities embody certain moral values and lifestyles. Many people base their choice of lifestyle on their example. They become points of crystallisation for adoption or rejection and act as examples or counter-examples. This is what explains the public interest in the various ups and downs occurring in their lives. . . .
>
> The public has a legitimate interest in being allowed to judge whether the personal behaviour of the individuals in question, who are often regarded as idols or role models, convincingly tallies with their behaviour on their official engagements. . . . .
>
> The decision of the Federal Court of Justice cannot be criticised under constitutional law regarding the photos of the appellant at a market, doing her market shopping accompanied by her bodyguard or dining with a male companion at a well-attended restaurant. The first two cases concerned an open location frequented by the general public. The third case admittedly concerned a well circumscribed location, spatially speaking, but one in which the appellant was exposed to the other people present.
>
> It is for this reason, moreover, that the Federal Court of Justice deemed it legitimate to ban photos showing the applicant in a restaurant garden, which

were the subject of the decision being appealed but are not the subject of the constitutional appeal.

The presence of the applicant and her companion there presented all the features of seclusion. The fact that the photographs in question were evidently taken from a distance shows that the applicant could legitimately have assumed that she was not exposed to public view.

Nor can the decision being appealed be criticised regarding the photos of the applicant alone on horseback or riding a bicycle. In the Federal Court of Justice's view, the appellant had not been in a secluded place, but in a public one. That finding cannot attract criticism under constitutional law. The applicant herself describes the photos in question as belonging to the intimacy of her private sphere merely because they manifest her desire to be alone. In accordance with the criteria set out above, the mere desire of the person concerned is not relevant in any way.

The three photos of the applicant with her children require a fresh examination, however, in the light of the constitutional rules set out above. We cannot rule out the possibility that the review that needs to be carried out in the light of the relevant criteria will lead to a different result for one or other or all the photos. The decision must therefore be set aside in that respect and remitted to the Federal Court of Justice for a fresh decision. . . .

39. The relevant provisions of the Basic Law are worded as follows:

Section 1(1) — "The dignity of human beings is inviolable. All public authorities have a duty to respect and protect it."

Section 2(1) — "Everyone shall have the right to the free development of their personality provided that they do not interfere with the rights of others or violate the constitutional order or moral law (*Sittengesetz*)."

Section 5(1) — "(1) Everyone shall have the right freely to express and disseminate his or her opinions in speech, writing and pictures and freely to obtain information from generally accessible sources. Freedom of the press and freedom of reporting on the radio and in films shall be guaranteed. There shall be no censorship. (2) These rights shall be subject to the limitations laid down by the provisions of the general laws and by statutory provisions aimed at protecting young people and to the obligation to respect personal honour (*Recht der persönlichen Ehre*)."

Section 6(1) and (2) — "(1) Marriage and the family enjoy the special protection of the State. (2) The care and upbringing of children is the natural right of parents and a duty primarily incumbent on them. The State community shall oversee the performance of that duty."

40. Section 22(1) of the Copyright (Arts Domain) Act provides that images can only be disseminated with the express approval of the person concerned.

41. Section 23(1) no. 1 of that Act provides for exceptions to that rule, particularly where the images portray an aspect of contemporary society (*Bildnisse aus dem Bereich der Zeitgeschichte*) on condition that publication does not interfere with a legitimate interest (*berechtigtes Interesse*) of the person concerned (section 23(2)). . . .

THE LAW

43. The applicant submitted that the German court decisions had infringed her right to respect for her private and family life guaranteed by Article 8 of the Convention. . . .

44. The applicant stated that she had spent more than ten years in unsuccessful litigation in the German courts trying to establish her right to the protection of her private life. She alleged that as soon as she left her house she was constantly hounded by paparazzi who followed her every daily movement, be it crossing the road, fetching her children from school, doing her shopping, out walking, practising sport or going on holiday. In her submission, the protection afforded to the private life of a public figure like herself was minimal under German law because the concept of a "secluded place" as defined by the Federal Court of Justice and the Federal Constitutional Court was much too narrow in that respect. Furthermore, in order to benefit from that protection the onus was on her to establish every time that she had been in a secluded place. She was thus deprived of any privacy and could not move about freely without being a target for the paparazzi. She affirmed that in France her prior agreement was necessary for the publication of any photos not showing her at an official event. Such photos were regularly taken in France and then sold and published in Germany. The protection of private life from which she benefited in France was therefore systematically circumvented by virtue of the decisions of the German courts. On the subject of the freedom of the press the applicant stated that she was aware of the essential role played by the press in a democratic society in terms of informing and forming public opinion, but in her case it was just the entertainment press seeking to satisfy its readers' voyeuristic tendencies and make huge profits from generally anodyne photos showing her going about her daily business. Lastly, the applicant stressed that it was materially impossible to establish in respect of every photo whether or not she had been in a secluded place. As the judicial proceedings were generally held several months after publication of the photos, she was obliged to keep a permanent record of her every movement in order to protect herself from paparazzi who might photograph her. With regard to many of the photos that were the subject of this application it was impossible to determine the exact time and place at which they had been taken.

45. The Government submitted that German law, while taking account of the fundamental role of the freedom of the press in a democratic society, contained sufficient safeguards to prevent any abuse and ensure the effective protection of the private life of even public figures. In their submission, the German courts had in the instant case struck a fair balance between the applicant's rights to respect for her private life guaranteed by Article 8 and the freedom of the press guaranteed by Article 10, having regard to the margin of appreciation available to the State in this area. The courts had found in the first instance that the photos had not been taken in a secluded place and had, in the second instance, examined the limits on the protection of private life, particularly in the light of the freedom of the press and even where the publication of photos by the entertainment press were concerned. The protection of the private life of a figure of contemporary society "*par excellence*" did not require the publication of photos without his or

her authorisation to be limited to showing the person in question engaged in their official duties. The public had a legitimate interest in knowing how the person behaved generally in public. The Government submitted that this definition of the freedom of the press by the Federal Constitutional Court was compatible with Article 10 and the European Court's relevant case-law. Furthermore, the concept of a secluded place was only one factor, albeit an important one, of which the domestic courts took account when balancing the protection of private life against the freedom of the press. Accordingly, while private life was less well protected where a public figure was photographed in a public place other factors could also be taken into consideration, such as the nature of the photos, for example, which should not shock the public. Lastly, the Government reiterated that the decision of the Federal Court of Justice — which had held that the publication of photos of the applicant with the actor Vincent Lindon in a restaurant courtyard in Saint-Rémy-de-Provence were unlawful — showed that the applicant's private life was protected even outside her home. . . .

B. The Court's assessment

50. The Court reiterates that the concept of private life extends to aspects relating to personal identity, such as a person's name or a person's picture.

Furthermore, private life, in the Court's view, includes a person's physical and psychological integrity; the guarantee afforded by Article 8 of the Convention is primarily intended to ensure the development, without outside interference, of the personality of each individual in his relations with other human beings. . . .

52. As regards photos, with a view to defining the scope of the protection afforded by Article 8 against arbitrary interference by public authorities, the Commission had regard to whether the photographs related to private or public matters and whether the material thus obtained was envisaged for a limited use or was likely to be made available to the general public.

53. In the present case there is no doubt that the publication by various German magazines of photos of the applicant in her daily life either on her own or with other people falls within the scope of her private life.

54. The Court notes that, in its landmark judgment of 15 December 1999, the Federal Constitutional Court interpreted sections 22 and 23 of the Copyright (Arts Domain) Act (see paragraphs 40-41 above) by balancing the requirements of the freedom of the press against those of the protection of private life, that is, the public interest in being informed against the legitimate interests of the applicant. In doing so the Federal Constitutional Court took account of two criteria under German law, one functional and the other spatial. It considered that the applicant, as a figure of contemporary society "*par excellence*", enjoyed the protection of her private life even outside her home but only if she was in a secluded place out of the public eye "to which the person concerned retires with the objectively recognisable aim of being alone and where, confident of being alone, behaves in a manner in which he or she would not behave in public". In the light of those criteria the Federal Constitutional Court held that the Federal Court of Justice's judgment of 19 December 1995 regarding publication of the photos in question was compatible with the Basic Law. The court attached

decisive weight to the freedom of the press, even the entertainment press, and to the public interest in knowing how the applicant behaved outside her representative functions. . . .

56. In the present case the applicant did not complain of an action by the State, but rather of the lack of adequate State protection of her private life and her image.

57. The Court reiterates that although the object of Article 8 is essentially that of protecting the individual against arbitrary interference by the public authorities, it does not merely compel the State to abstain from such interference: in addition to this primarily negative undertaking, there may be positive obligations inherent in an effective respect for private or family life. These obligations may involve the adoption of measures designed to secure respect for private life even in the sphere of the relations of individuals between themselves. . . .

58. That protection of private life has to be balanced against the freedom of expression guaranteed by Article 10 of the Convention. In that context the Court reiterates that the freedom of expression constitutes one of the essential foundations of a democratic society. Subject to paragraph 2 of Article 10, it is applicable not only to "information" or "ideas" that are favourably received or regarded as inoffensive or as a matter of indifference, but also to those that offend, shock or disturb. Such are the demands of that pluralism, tolerance and broadmindedness without which there is no "democratic society."

In that connection the press plays an essential role in a democratic society. Although it must not overstep certain bounds, in particular in respect of the reputation and rights of others, its duty is nevertheless to impart — in a manner consistent with its obligations and responsibilities — information and ideas on all matters of public interest. . . .

59. Although freedom of expression also extends to the publication of photos, this is an area in which the protection of the rights and reputation of others takes on particular importance. The present case does not concern the dissemination of "ideas", but of images containing very personal or even intimate "information" about an individual. Furthermore, photos appearing in the tabloid press are often taken in a climate of continual harassment which induces in the person concerned a very strong sense of intrusion into their private life or even of persecution. . . .

61. The Court points out at the outset that in the present case the photos of the applicant in the various German magazines show her in scenes from her daily life, thus engaged in activities of a purely private nature such as practising sport, out walking, leaving a restaurant or on holiday. . . .

63. The Court considers that a fundamental distinction needs to be made between reporting facts — even controversial ones — capable of contributing to a debate in a democratic society relating to politicians in the exercise of their functions, for example, and reporting details of the private life of an individual who, moreover, as in this case, does not exercise official functions. While in the former case the press exercises its vital role of "watchdog" in a democracy by contributing to "impart[ing] information and ideas on matters of public interest, it does not do so in the latter case.

64. Similarly, although the public has a right to be informed, which is an essential right in a democratic society that, in certain special circumstances, can

even extend to aspects of the private life of public figures, particularly where politicians are concerned, this is not the case here. The situation here does not come within the sphere of any political or public debate because the published photos and accompanying commentaries relate exclusively to details of the applicant's private life.

65. As in other similar cases it has examined, the Court considers that the publication of the photos and articles in question, of which the sole purpose was to satisfy the curiosity of a particular readership regarding the details of the applicant's private life, cannot be deemed to contribute to any debate of general interest to society despite the applicant being known to the public. . . .

68. The Court finds another point to be of importance: even though, strictly speaking, the present application concerns only the publication of these photos and articles by various German magazines, the context in which these photos were taken — without the applicant's knowledge or consent — and the harassment endured by many public figures in their daily lives cannot be fully disregarded.

In the present case this point is illustrated in particularly striking fashion by the photos taken of the applicant at the Monte Carlo Beach Club tripping over an obstacle and falling down. . . .

69. The Court reiterates the fundamental importance of protecting private life from the point of view of the developments of every human being's personality. That protection . . . extends beyond the private family circle and also includes a social dimension. . . . [A]nyone, even if they are known to the general public, must be able to enjoy a "legitimate expectation" of protection of and respect for their private life.

74. The Court therefore considers that the criteria on which the domestic courts based their decisions were not sufficient to protect the applicant's private life effectively. As a figure of contemporary society "*par excellence*" she cannot — in the name of freedom of the press and the public interest — rely on protection of her private life unless she is in a secluded place out of the public eye and, moreover, succeeds in proving it (which can be difficult). Where that is not the case, she has to accept that she might be photographed at almost any time, systematically, and that the photos are then very widely disseminated even if, as was the case here, the photos and accompanying articles relate exclusively to details of her private life.

75. In the Court's view, the criterion of spatial isolation, although apposite in theory, is in reality too vague and difficult for the person concerned to determine in advance. In the present case merely classifying the applicant as a figure of contemporary society "*par excellence*" does not suffice to justify such an intrusion into her private life.

76. As the Court has stated above, it considers that the decisive factor in balancing the protection of private life against freedom of expression should lie in the contribution that the published photos and articles make to a debate of general interest. It is clear in the instant case that they made no such contribution since the applicant exercises no official function and the photos and articles related exclusively to details of her private life.

77. Furthermore, the Court considers that the public does not have a legitimate interest in knowing where the applicant is and how she behaves

generally in her private life even if she appears in places that cannot always be described as secluded and despite the fact that she is well known to the public.

Even if such a public interest exists, as does a commercial interest of the magazines in publishing these photos and these articles, in the instant case those interests must, in the Court's view, yield to the applicant's right to the effective protection of her private life.

78. Lastly, in the Court's opinion the criteria established by the domestic courts were not sufficient to ensure the effective protection of the applicant's private life and she should, in the circumstances of the case, have had a "legitimate expectation" of protection of her private life.

79. Having regard to all the foregoing factors, and despite the margin of appreciation afforded to the State in this area, the Court considers that the German courts did not strike a fair balance between the competing interests.

80. There has therefore been a breach of Article 8 of the Convention. . . .

85. The Court considers the question of the application of Article 41 [providing for "just satisfaction to the injured party," i.e., damages] is not ready for decision. Accordingly, it shall be reserved and the subsequent procedure fixed having regard to any agreement which might be reached between the Government and the applicant.

NOTES & QUESTIONS

1. **Von Hannover*'s Impact on German Law.*** *Von Hannover* represents what one law professor has termed the European Court of Human Rights' (ECHR) "censure" of the German Constitutional Court, the highest German court, and its case law regarding the press and privacy.[15] For Andreas Heldrich, the European Court of Human Rights in its decision "overruled nearly point for point" the German Court's arguments in its decisions. Heldrich points in particular to the German court's need to change, after *Von Hannover,* its existing jurisprudence, which had required "absolute persons of contemporary history" (*absolute Personen der Zeitgeschichte*) to accept being photographed anywhere outside of their homes as long as they did not retreat into a private place to be alone. In Heldrich's prediction, *Von Hannover* means that in the future, "we will be able to enjoy colorful pictures from the private life of our celebrities only with their permission. Nonetheless, we need not worry. There will be enough of them left over."

   In contrast, Stefan Engels and Uwe Jürgens describes a path by which German courts might integrate *Von Hannover* with existing case law. For them, the core of the ECHR's decision turns on whether there has been "constant annoyances that the affected party feels as a weighty invasion of her private life and even as a persecution."[16] Yet, not every such confrontation with the press will qualify under this proposed test. Engels and Jürgens argue

---

[15] Andreas Heldrich, *Persönlichkeitsschuz und Pressefreiheit nach der Europäischen Menschenrechtskonvention*, Neue Juristische Wochenschrift 2634 (2004).

[16] Stefan Engels & Uwe Jürgens, *Auswirkungen der EGMR-Rechtsprechung zum Privatsphärenschutz-Möglichkeiten und Grenzen der Umsetzung des "Caroline"-Urteils im deutschen Recht*, NJW 2517, 2521 (2007).

that "prominent persons of public life" who jog by a river in Hamburg or leave a famous nightclub in Munich cannot claim that they have retreated to the private sphere. In their view, the law must accept that there is also a "reverse side" to fame, namely, public attention. The plaintiff must demonstrate that an image has been taken in the context of a "weighty persecution" by the press of her, and the court must evaluate the image in the context of the journalist's report that accompanies it. Do Engels and Jürgens or Heldrich make the more convincing case about the extent of the impact of *Von Hannover* with existing German protection of the press?

2. ***Privacy in Public.*** How would *Von Hannover* be decided under the American privacy torts? Is the ECHR's protection of privacy in public too strong? For Nicholas Nohlen, "German courts had long given too much weight to the freedom of the press (even protecting 'news' that was merely entertaining), to the disadvantage of the individual's right to protection of private life."[17] In contrast, Nohlen states that the ECHR emphasized that "the decisive factor for balancing the right to private life and freedom of the press lies in the contribution of the delivered information to a debate of general interest." In other words, the focus should now be placed on the value of the information that the press delivers.

   How is a court, however, to assess the whether information is connected to a "debate of general interest" (the ECHR's test in *Von Hannover*)? Nohlen concedes:

   > The ECHR's criterion in *Von Hannover* remains unclear. The Court held that the decisive criterion in balancing the right to private life against freedom of the press is whether the published photos contribute to a debate of general interest. It did not then establish a criterion, however, for determining what is to be considered as contributing to such a debate.

   Nohlen generates these examples as possibly contributing to a debate of general interest: "published articles with photos showing a well-known musician, who was said to be a family man, secretly cheating on his wife, or of a young soccer star, who always appeared to be shy and reserved, involved in a street fight." As he notes, moreover, nothing in *Von Hannover* limits the test of a "debate of general interest" to merely political topics.

   Consider as well the reasoning of the German Constitutional Court, which noted that the "applicant herself describes the photos in question as belonging to the intimacy of her private sphere merely because they manifest her desire to be alone. . . . [T]he mere desire of the person concerned is not relevant in any way." Does the ECHR have a satisfactory answer to this objection—namely, that there must be more objective criteria to define what is private than merely an individual's desires? Does the ruling of the ECHR threaten to make privacy too subjective a matter by not relying as heavily upon the fact that at least some of the photographs of Princess Caroline were taken while she was in public places?

---

[17] Nicholas Hohlen, Case Note: Von Hannover v. Germany, 100 Am. J. Int'l L. 196, 198 (2006).

3. ***Article 8 vs. Article 10.*** Whereas Article 8 of the Convention protects privacy, Article 10 protects freedom of speech and press:

> 1. Everyone has the right to freedom of expression. This right shall include freedom to hold opinions and to receive and impart information and ideas without interference by public authority and regardless of frontiers. This article shall not prevent States from requiring the licensing of broadcasting, television or cinema enterprises.
>
> 2. The exercise of these freedoms, since it carries with it duties and responsibilities, may be subject to such formalities, conditions, restrictions or penalties as are prescribed by law and are necessary in a democratic society, in the interests of national security, territorial integrity or public safety, for the prevention of disorder or crime, for the protection of health or morals, for the protection of the reputation or rights of others, for preventing the disclosure of information received in confidence, or for maintaining the authority and impartiality of the judiciary.

How are Article 8 and Article 10 to be reconciled? In *Von Hannover,* how does the ECHR's balance between Articles 8 and 10 compare to the U.S. Supreme Court's analysis of privacy laws that conflict with the First Amendment right to freedom of speech and press? How does the ECHR differ from the German Constitutional Court on the scope of freedom of press?

Does *Von Hannover* strike the right balance between privacy and free speech? Consider Barbara McDonald:

> [E]ven in the case of public figures, the court's decision [in *Von Hannover*] indicates a greater respect for the notion that some aspects of their lives should remain private and free of intrusion even when they are in public. The applicable tests — whether the information came within their "legitimate expectation" of privacy so as to invoke a need to be balanced with the right to freedom of expression, and if so, whether it contributes to a debate of general interest — is a fairly high bar for the media to overcome.[18]

4. ***The English Breach of Confidence Tort.*** In England, courts have frequently considered and consistently rejected recognizing the Warren and Brandeis privacy torts. Instead, the tort of breach of confidence is the primary common law protection of privacy. The tort traces back to *Prince Albert v. Strange*, (1848) 41 Eng. Rep. 1171 (Ch.), the case that Warren and Brandeis relied heavily upon in arguing that a basis for the privacy torts existed in the common law. Later on, in *Coco v. Clark,* [1969], R.P.C. 41 (U.K.), three elements for the tort were established: (1) the information must have "the necessary quality of confidence about it"; (2) the information "must have been imparted in circumstances importing an obligation of confidence"; and (3) there must be an "unauthorised use of that information to the detriment of the party communicating it."

The English breach of confidence tort is quite broad. Unlike the American version of the tort, which applies to doctors, bankers, and other professionals, the English tort also applies to friends and family. *See Stephens v. Avery*,

---

[18] Barbara McDonald, *Privacy, Princesses, and Paparazzi,* 50 N.Y. L. Sch. L. Rev. 205, 223 (2005).

(1988) 1 Ch. 449 (U.K.) (breach of confidence tort applies to friends); *Argyll v. Argyll*, (1967) 1 Ch. 302 (U.K.) (breach of confidence applies to spouses). The tort even applies to lovers, such as in the case of *Barrymore v. News Group Newspapers, Ltd.*, [1997] F.S.R. 600 (Ch.) (U.K.), where the court declared: "when people kiss and later one of them tells, that second person is almost certainly breaking a confidential arrangement." In *A v. B*, [2003] Q.B. 195, 207 (U.K.), the court explained the full scope of the tort:

> A duty of confidence will arise whenever the party subject to the duty is in a situation where he either knows or ought to know that the other person can reasonably expect his privacy to be protected. The range of situations in which protection can be provided is therefore extensive. Obviously, the necessary relationship can be expressly created. More often its existence will have to be inferred from the facts. Whether a duty of confidence does exist which courts can protect, if it is right to do so, will depend on all the circumstances of the relationship between the parties at the time of the threatened or actual breach of the alleged duty of confidence.

Parties who induce breaches of confidence or receive information based on another's a breach of confidence can also be liable. Similar third-party liability exists with the American breach of confidentiality tort. Some commentators have noted that the English tort has become too broad. Consider Joshua Rozenberg:

> The need for a formal relationship between two parties has become attenuated almost to the point of non-existence. Where information has the necessary quality of confidence about it, the courts are more than willing to infer an obligation of confidence from the surrounding facts. . . . That means they will hold that someone who has received confidential information is bound by a duty of confidence. Put bluntly, if the judges think something ought to remain private then they will find a way of making it so.[19]

Although the English breach of confidence tort is quite broad, it does not cover some of the actions that the privacy torts protect against. For example, in *Kay v. Robertson,* [1991] F.S.R. 62 (C.A.) (U.K.), a famous actor suffered a severe head injury. In the hospital where he was recovering, notices were placed in several locations near his room and on the room's door that only permitted individuals would be allowed to visit him. A journalist and photographer snuck in, interviewed the actor, and took photographs of him and his room. He was eventually discovered by hospital security staff and ejected. The actor was not in a good condition to be interviewed and had no recollection of the events. The actor sought to stop the publication of an article about the interview and containing the photos. The court considered whether to recognize a common law protection of privacy but concluded that doing so would be a matter for Parliament:

> It is well-known that in English law there is no right to privacy, and accordingly there is no right of action for breach of a person's privacy. The facts of the present case are a graphic illustration of the desirability of

---

[19] Joshua Rozenberg, *Privacy and the Press* 15 (2004).

> Parliament considering whether and in what circumstances statutory provision can be made to protect the privacy of individuals. . . .

What Warren and Brandeis privacy tort(s) could apply in this case? Would the actor have a successful case under the tort(s)? The English breach of confidence tort was not among the causes of action considered in the case. Would it have provided protection? If so, under what theory would it have applied?

Neil Richards and Daniel Solove contrast the American privacy torts with the English breach of confidence tort and note several important differences. Many of the privacy torts contain a "highly offensive" requirement; the breach of confidence tort does not. The public disclosure tort requires "publicity" (widespread disclosure); the breach of confidence tort does not. The public disclosure tort also does not apply when the disclosure is newsworthy; the English tort contains no such restriction.

> In contrast to Warren and Brandeis's individualistic conception of privacy, the English law of confidentiality focuses on relationships rather than individuals. Far from a right to be let alone, confidentiality focuses on the norms of trust within relationships. Indeed, most of our personal information is known by other people, such as doctors, spouses, children, and friends, as well as institutions, such as ISPs, banks, merchants, insurance companies, phone companies, and other businesses. We need to share our secrets with select others, and when we tell others a secret, we still consider it to be a secret. We confide in others, we trust them with information that can make us vulnerable, and we expect them not to betray us. These norms are missing from the Warren and Brandeis conception of privacy.
>
> The key conceptual difference between the breach of confidence tort and public disclosure of private facts tort is the nature of what is protected. The public disclosure tort focuses on the nature of the information being made public. By contrast, the focus of the tort of breach of confidentiality is on the nature of the relationship.[20]

Under the Human Rights Act (HRA) of 1998, the United Kingdom now follows the European Convention on Human Rights. This means that courts must balance Article 8 with Article 10. The result has been a broader protection of privacy as well as of free speech. The HRA prompted English courts to once again consider whether to recognize the Warren and Brandeis privacy torts. Instead of doing so, the courts have thus far concluded that the breach of confidence tort can be stretched to include a wider range of privacy violations. As for incorporating Article 10, England does not have a First Amendment, so Article 10 purportedly increases protection for speech. Courts consider freedom of speech and the press as a factor in assessing whether a party ought to be liable under the breach of confidence tort.

5. ***Photos of J.K. Rowling's Son in Public.*** In *Murray v. Big Pictures Ltd.*, [2008] EWCA Civ 446, the England and Wales Court of Appeal concluded that David Murray (the son of J.K. Rowling, author of the Harry Potter book

[20] Neil M. Richards & Daniel J. Solove, *Privacy's Other Path: Recovering the Law of Confidentiality,* 96 Geo. L.J. 123, 174 (2007).

series) was entitled to privacy protection from being photographed in public. When David was less than two years old, a photographer secretly snapped a photograph of him with a zoom lens when he was out in public in Edinburgh with his parents. The photo captured nothing "embarrassing or untoward." The photo appeared in a magazine in 2005. David's parents sued on his behalf. The judge below dismissed "the claim based on breach of confidence or invasion of privacy . . . [because] on my understanding of the law including *Von Hannover* there remains an area of innocuous conduct in a public place which does not raise a reasonable expectation of privacy." The judge reasoned:

> It seems to me that a distinction can be drawn between a child (or an adult) engaged in family and sporting activities and something as simple as a walk down a street or a visit to the grocers to buy the milk. The first type of activity is clearly part of a person's private recreation time intended to be enjoyed in the company of family and friends. Publicity on the test deployed in *Von Hannover* is intrusive and can adversely affect the exercise of such social activities. But if the law is such as to give every adult or child a legitimate expectation of not being photographed without consent on any occasion on which they are not, so to speak, on public business then it will have created a right for most people to the protection of their image. If a simple walk down the street qualifies for protection then it is difficult to see what would not.

The appellate court, however, disagreed:

> It seems to us that, although the judges regarded the parents' concerns as overstated, the parents' wish, on behalf of their children, to protect the freedom of the children to live normal lives without the constant fear of media intrusion is (at least arguably) entirely reasonable and, other things being equal, should be protected by the law. It is true . . . that the photographs showed no more than could be seen by anyone in the street but, once published, they would be disseminated to a potentially large number of people on the basis that they were children of well-known parents, leading to the possibility of further intrusion in the future. . . .
>
> We do not share the predisposition . . . that routine acts such as a visit to a shop or a ride on a bus should not attract any reasonable expectation of privacy. All depends upon the circumstances. The position of an adult may be very different from that of a child. In this appeal we are concerned only with the question whether David, as a small child, had a reasonable expectation of privacy, not with the question whether his parents would have had such an expectation. Moreover, we are concerned with the context of this case, which was not for example a single photograph taken of David which was for some reason subsequently published.
>
> It seems to us that, subject to the facts of the particular case, the law should indeed protect children from intrusive media attention, at any rate to the extent of holding that a child has a reasonable expectation that he or she will not be targeted in order to obtain photographs in a public place for publication which the person who took or procured the taking of the photographs knew would be objected to on behalf of the child. That is the context in which the photographs of David were taken.

How broadly does the *Von Hannover* decision extend? Is there any way to avoid the slippery slope problem described by the judge below, that "[i]f a simple walk down the street qualifies for protection then it is difficult to see what would not"?

6. ***Use of CCTV Footage by the Media.*** In England, the government uses an extensive system of millions of public surveillance cameras that are monitored via closed circuit television, a system known as CCTV. The government frequently supplies the video to the media. Consider *Peck v. United Kingdom,* 44647/98 [2003] ECHR 44 (28 January 2003):

> The present applicant was in a public street but he was not there for the purposes of participating in any public event and he was not a public figure. It was late at night, he was deeply perturbed and in a state of distress. While he was walking in public wielding a knife, he was not later charged with any offence. The actual suicide attempt was neither recorded nor therefore disclosed. However, footage of the immediate aftermath was recorded and disclosed by the Council directly to the public in its CCTV News publication. In addition, the footage was disclosed to the media for further broadcasting and publication purposes. Those media included the audiovisual media: Anglia Television broadcast locally to approximately 350,000 people and the BBC broadcast nationally, and it is "commonly acknowledged that the audiovisual media have often a much more immediate and powerful effect than the print media." The Yellow Advertiser was distributed in the applicant's locality to approximately 24,000 readers. The applicant's identity was not adequately, or in some cases not at all, masked in the photographs and footage so published and broadcast. He was recognised by certain members of his family and by his friends, neighbours and colleagues.
>
> As a result, the relevant moment was viewed to an extent which far exceeded any exposure to a passer-by or to security observation . . . and to a degree surpassing that which the applicant could possibly have foreseen when he walked in Brentwood on 20 August 1995. . . .
>
> [T]he Court appreciates the strong interest of the State in detecting and preventing crime. It is not disputed that the CCTV system plays an important role in these respects and that that role is rendered more effective and successful through advertising the CCTV system and its benefits.
>
> However, the Court notes that the Council had other options available to it to allow it to achieve the same objectives. In the first place, it could have identified the applicant through enquiries with the police and thereby obtained his consent prior to disclosure. Alternatively, the Council could have masked the relevant images itself. A further alternative would have been to take the utmost care in ensuring that the media, to which the disclosure was made, masked those images. The Court notes that the Council did not explore the first and second options and considers that the steps taken by the Council in respect of the third were inadequate. . . .
>
> In sum, the Court does not find that, in the circumstances of this case, there were relevant or sufficient reasons which would justify the direct disclosure by the Council to the public of stills from the footage in its own CCTV News article without the Council obtaining the applicant's consent or masking his identity, or which would justify its disclosures to the media without the Council taking steps to ensure so far as possible that such masking would be effected by the media. The crime-prevention objective and context of the

> disclosures demanded particular scrutiny and care in these respects in the present case. . . .
>
> Accordingly, the Court considers that the disclosures by the Council of the CCTV material in the CCTV News and to the Yellow Advertiser, Anglia Television and the BBC were not accompanied by sufficient safeguards to prevent disclosure inconsistent with the guarantees of respect for the applicant' private life contained in Article 8. As such, the disclosure constituted a disproportionate and therefore unjustified interference with his private life and a violation of Article 8 of the Convention.

Could the English breach of confidentiality tort have provided an adequate remedy for the plaintiff?

(c) Privacy and Law Enforcement

P.G. & J.H. v. UNITED KINGDOM

E.C.H.R., 9/25/2001

Principal Facts

The applicants are both British nationals.

On 28 February 1995, D.I. Mann received information that an armed robbery of a Securicor cash collection van was going to be committed on or around 2 March 1995 by the first applicant and B. at one of several possible locations. Visual surveillance of B.'s home began the same day. No robbery took place.

By 3 March, however, the police had been informed the robbery was to take place "somewhere" on 9 March 1995. In order to obtain further details, D.I. Mann prepared a report applying for authorisation to install a covert listening device in B.'s flat. On 4 March 1995, the Chief Constable gave oral authorisation and a listening device was installed in a sofa in B.'s flat the same day; the Deputy Chief Constable gave retrospective written authorisation on 8 March 1995. On 14 March 1995, the police requested itemised billing for calls from the telephone in B.'s flat. On 15 March 1995, B. and others who were with him in his home discovered the listening device and abandoned the premises. The robbery did not take place.

The applicants were arrested on 16 March 1995 in a stolen car containing two black balaclavas, five black plastic cable ties, two pairs of leather gloves, and two army kitbags.

As they wished to obtain speech samples to compare with the tapes, the police applied for authorisation to use covert listening devices in the applicants' cells and to attach listening devices to the police officers who were to be present when the applicants were charged. Written authorisation was given by the Chief Constable and samples of the applicants' speech were recorded without their knowledge or permission. An expert concluded it was "likely" the first applicant's voice featured on the taped recordings and "very likely" the second applicant's voice featured on them.

B. and the applicants were charged with conspiracy to rob. During their trial, evidence derived from the use of the covert listening devices was deemed admissible . . . .

34. The applicants complained that covert listening devices were used by the police to monitor and record their conversations at a flat, that information was obtained by the police concerning the use of a telephone at the flat and that listening devices were used while they were at the police station to obtain voice samples. They invoked Article 8 of the Convention. . . .

B. Concerning Information Obtained About the Use of B.'s Telephone

42. It is not in dispute that the obtaining by the police of information relating to the numbers called on the telephone in B.'s flat interfered with the private lives or correspondence (in the sense of telephone communications) of the applicants who made use of the telephone in the flat or were telephoned from the flat. The Court notes however that metering, which does not *per se* offend against Article 8 if for example done by the telephone company for billing purposes, is by its very nature to be distinguished from the interception of communications which may be undesirable and illegitimate in a democratic society unless justified. . . .

"In Accordance with the Law"

44. The expression "in accordance with the law" requires, firstly, that the impugned measure should have some basis in domestic law; secondly, it refers to the quality of the law in question, requiring that it should be accessible to the person concerned, who must moreover be able to foresee its consequences for him, and that it is compatible with the rule of law.

45. Both parties agreed that the obtaining of the billing information was based on statutory authority, in particular, section 45 of the Telecommunications Act 1984 and section 28(3) of the Data Protection Act 1984. The first requirement therefore poses no difficulty. The applicants argued that the second requirement was not fulfilled in their case, as there were insufficient safeguards in place concerning the use, storage and destruction of the records.

46. . . . In this case, the information obtained concerned the telephone numbers called from B.'s flat between two specific dates. It did not include any information about the contents of those calls, or who made or received them. The data obtained, and the use that could be made of it, were therefore strictly limited.

47. . . . [T]he Court is not persuaded that the lack of such detailed formal regulation raises any risk of arbitrariness or misuse. Nor is it apparent that there was any lack of foreseeability. Disclosure to the police was permitted under the relevant statutory framework where necessary for the purposes of the detection and prevention of crime and the material was used at the applicants' trial on criminal charges to corroborate other evidence relevant to the timing of telephone calls. It is not apparent that the applicants did not have an adequate indication as to the circumstances in, and conditions on, which the public authorities were empowered to resort to such a measure.

48. The Court concludes that the measure in question was "in accordance with the law."

"Necessary in a Democratic Society"

[The Court did not have to analyze the issue of proportionality under Article 8 (2) as it was not raised by the applicants.] . . .

51. The Court concludes that there has been no violation of Article 8 of the Convention in respect of the applicants' complaints about the metering of the telephone in this case.

C. Concerning the Use of Listening Devices in the Police Station

1. The Parties' Submissions

52. The applicants complained that their voices were recorded secretly when they were being charged in the police station and when they were held in their cells. They submitted that it was irrelevant what was said, which ranged from the giving of personal details to a conversation about football instigated by a police officer. They considered that it was the circumstances in which the words were spoken which was significant and that there was a breach of privacy if the speaker believed that he was only speaking to the person addressed and had no reason to believe the conversation was being broadcast or recorded. The key issue in their view was whether the speaker knew or had any reason to suspect that the conversation was being recorded. In the present case, the police knew that the applicants had refused to provide voice samples voluntarily and sought to trick to them into speaking in an underhand procedure which was wholly unregulated, arbitrary and attended by bad faith. It was also irrelevant that the recording was used for forensic purposes rather than to obtain information about the speaker, as it was the covert recording itself, not the use made of it, which amounted to the breach of privacy.

53. The applicants further submitted that the use of the covert listening devices was not "in accordance with the law" as there was no domestic law regulating the use of such devices and no safeguards provided within the law to protect against abuse of such surveillance methods. They rejected any assertion that the police could rely on any general power to obtain and store evidence.

54. The Government submitted that the use of the listening devices in the cells and when the applicants were being charged did not disclose any interference, as these recordings were not made to obtain any private or substantive information. The aural quality of the applicants' voices was not part of private life but was rather a public, external feature. . . .

55. Assuming that there was an interference with any right under Article 8, the Government contended that it was justified under the second paragraph as necessary in a democratic society to protect public safety, prevent crime and/or protect the rights of others. . . .

2. The Court's Assessment The Existence of an Interference with Private Life

56. Private life is a broad term not susceptible to exhaustive definition. The Court has already held that elements such as gender identification, name and sexual orientation and sexual life are important elements of the personal sphere protected by Article 8. . . . Article 8 also protects a right to identity and personal development, and the right to establish and develop relationships with other human beings and the outside world. . . . There is therefore a zone of interaction of a person with others, even in a public context, which may fall within the scope of "private life."

57. There are a number of elements relevant to a consideration of whether a person's private life is concerned in measures effected outside a person's home or private premises. Since there are occasions when people knowingly or intentionally involve themselves in activities which are or may be recorded or reported in a public manner, a person's reasonable expectations as to privacy may be a significant, though not necessarily conclusive factor. A person who walks down the street will, inevitably, be visible to any member of the public who is also present. Monitoring by technological means of the same public scene (e.g. a security guard viewing through close circuit television) is of a similar character. Private life considerations may arise however once any systematic or permanent record comes into existence of such material from the public domain. It is for this reason that files gathered by security services on a particular individual fall within the scope of Article 8 even where the information has not been gathered by any intrusive or covert method. . . .

59. The Court's case-law has, on numerous occasions, found that the covert taping of telephone conversations falls within the scope of Article 8 in both aspects of the right guaranteed, namely, respect for private life and correspondence. While it is generally the case that the recordings were made for the purpose of using the content of the conversations in some way, the Court is not persuaded that recordings taken for use as voice samples can be regarded as falling outside the scope of the protection afforded by Article 8. A permanent record has nonetheless been made of the person's voice and it is subject to a process of analysis directly relevant to identifying that person in the context of other personal data. . . .

60. The Court concludes therefore that the recording of the applicants' voices when being charged and when in their police cell discloses an interference with their right to respect for private life within the meaning of Article 8 § 1 of the Convention.

Compliance with the Requirements of the Second Paragraph of Article 8

61. The Court has examined, firstly, whether the interference was "in accordance with the law." As noted above, this criterion imports two main requirements: that there be some basis in domestic law for the measure and that the quality of the law is such as to provide safeguards against arbitrariness.

62. It recalls that the Government relied as the legal basis for the measure on the general powers of the police to store and gather evidence. While it may be permissible to rely on the implied powers of police officers to note evidence and

collect and store exhibits for steps taken in the course of an investigation, it is trite law that specific statutory or other express legal authority is required for more invasive measures, whether searching private property or taking personal body samples. The Court has found that the lack of any express basis in law for the interception of telephone calls on public and private telephone systems and for using covert surveillance devices on private premises does not conform with the requirement of lawfulness. It considers that no material difference arises where the recording device is operated, without the knowledge or consent of the individual concerned, on police premises. The underlying principle that domestic law should provide protection against arbitrariness and abuse in the use of covert surveillance techniques, applies equally in that situation.

63. . . . [A]t the relevant time, there existed no statutory system to regulate the use of covert listening devices by the police on their own premises.

The interference was not therefore "in accordance with the law" as required by the second paragraph of Article 8 and there has been a violation of this provision. In these circumstances, an examination of the necessity of the interference is no longer required. . . .

NOTES & QUESTIONS

1. ***Reasonable Expectation of Privacy.*** Reread paragraph 57 of the decision. What does the ECHR mean? Compare the scope of the ECHR's conception of "reasonable expectation of privacy" with that set out by the U.S. Supreme Court.[21] Is one approach more protective of privacy than the other? How does the introduction of new technology for surveillance affect the analysis?
2. ***Identification.*** The ECHR, because it considers identification evidence as a processing of personal data (*see* paragraph 59), will necessarily conclude that such activities implicate the right to privacy. Once again, this approach may be contrasted with the approach in the United States.
3. ***Pen Registers.*** Consider paragraph 46 of the decision. Would the ECHR's decision have been different if the police had intercepted the contents of the phone calls or the identity of the persons who made or received them? Compare this case with the U.S. Supreme Court case *Smith v. Maryland* (Chapter 3). How do the outcomes differ? Would surveillance pursuant to the Pen Register Act provisions of the ECPA, Title III, 18 U.S.C. §§ 3121–3127 (Chapter 3) satisfy the requirements of Article 8?
4. ***The NSA Surveillance Program and EU Law.*** Recall the excerpt from James Whitman, arguing that European privacy law primarily protects dignity and American privacy law primarily protects liberty against the state. Compare Francesca Bignami, who argues:

> In Europe, a secret government data-mining program like the NSA's would be clearly illegal. Why? To summarize the rather complicated analysis that follows, such a data-mining program would violate two different types of

[21] For a further discussion of this issue, see H. Tomás Gómez-Arostegui, *Defining Private Life Under the European Convention on Human Rights by Referring to Reasonable Expectations*, 35 Cal. W. Int'l L.J. 153 (2005).

> privacy guarantees — procedural and substantive. Procedurally, government data mining, even for national security ends, would have to be authorized by a public law or regulation that specified the purposes of the personal data processing and the limits on that data processing, to minimize the government's interference with private life. Before the program could be enacted, an independent government body would have to be consulted and, while the program was in operation, that same government body would need to have oversight and enforcement powers. . . .
>
> Substantively, the reach of a European data-mining program would be narrower than that of the NSA call database. Although a spy agency might be allowed access to all call information held by national telecommunications providers, it would not be allowed to retain the personal data as long as the NSA has — over five years now. Furthermore, the type of analysis performed on the data, as well as the uses of the results of the analysis, would have to be carefully circumscribed. The government would be permitted to use only search terms, statistical models, mathematical algorithms, and other analytical processes designed to uncover serious threats. . . . A spy agency in Germany would be allowed to pass on to law enforcement the names of individuals obtained through such data-mining techniques only if those individuals were suspected of planning to commit, or having already committed, a serious offense, and only if sufficient reasons existed for entertaining that suspicion.
>
> Another substantive difference would be the right, under European law, of individuals to check on their information. This right of access enables individuals to ensure that their information is factually correct and is being handled in accordance with the guarantees of privacy law. Finally, to switch the focus briefly from the government to the private sector, the same amount of call data in the hands of telecommunications providers would not have been available to a European government. Under European law, telecommunications companies are prohibited from retaining personal data in the same quantities and for the same length of time as is routine — and legal — in the American business world.

Bignami later takes issue with Whitman:

> Whitman obscures an important aspect of European privacy law. True, European privacy law promotes interpersonal respect among individuals. But it also protects privacy against the state. And it is not always true, as Whitman argues, that "state action will raise American hackles much more often than European ones." . . . [I]n the context of antiterrorism data mining, European law protects liberty interests more than American law. At least European spy agencies tell their citizens when their personal data is being collected and combined and, depending on the results, sent to the police for further action, a lot more than can be said for American spy agencies.[22]

[22] Francesca Bignami, *European versus American Liberty: A Comparative Privacy Analysis of Antiterrorism Data Mining*, 48 B.C. L. Rev. 609, 635-36, 681 (2007).

(d) Privacy and Identification

B. v. France

ECHR, 03/25/1992 Series A no. 232-C

The applicant before the Court, a French citizen, was registered with the civil status registrar as of male sex, with the forenames Norbert Antoine. Miss B. (referred in the judgment in the feminine, in accordance with the sex claimed by her) "adopted female behavior from a very early age" and was "noticeably homosexual" until the time she decided to undergo a surgical operation in 1972 to modify the appearance of her external genital organs. Miss B., after deciding in 1978 to get married with a man, had to bring proceedings before a French court to have the Court hold that, "registered in the civil status register of [her] place of birth as of male sex, [she was] in reality of feminine constitution; . . . declare that [she was] of female sex; . . . order rectification of [her] birth certificate; . . . [and] declare that [she should] henceforth bear the forenames Lyne Antoinette." The French Court dismissed her action concluding that "the change of sex was intentionally brought about by artificial processes," that "the application of Norbert [B.] cannot be granted without attacking the principle of the inalienability of the status of individuals." Miss B. then appealed her case before the Bordeaux Court of Appeal and the French Court of Cassation (Supreme Court) which both dismissed Miss B.'s appeal.

A. Alleged Violation of Article 8

43. According to the applicant, the refusal to recognise her true sexual identity was a breach of Article 8. . . .

She argued that by failing to allow the indication of her sex to be corrected in the civil status register and on her official identity documents, the French authorities forced her to disclose intimate personal information to third parties; she also alleged that she faced great difficulties in her professional life. . . .

45. Miss B. argued that it was not correct to consider her application as substantially identical to those of Mr. Rees and Miss Cossey previously before the Court.

Firstly, it was based on new scientific, legal and social elements.

Secondly, there was a fundamental difference between France and England in this field, with regard to their legislation and the attitude of their public authorities.

Thus the application of the very criteria stated in the above-mentioned judgments of 17 October 1986 and 27 September 1990 would have led to a finding of a violation by France, as French law, unlike English law, did not even acknowledge the appearance lawfully assumed by a transsexual. . .

1. Scientific, Legal and Social Developments

. . . 48. The Court considers that it is undeniable that attitudes have changed, science has progressed and increasing importance is attached to the problem of transsexualism.

It notes, however, in the light of the relevant studies carried out and work done by experts in this field, that there still remains some uncertainty as to the essential nature of transsexualism and that the legitimacy of surgical intervention in such cases is sometimes questioned. The legal situations which result are moreover extremely complex: anatomical, biological, psychological and moral problems in connection with transsexualism and its definition; consent and other requirements to be complied with before any operation; the conditions under which a change of sexual identity can be authorised (validity, scientific presuppositions and legal effects of recourse to surgery, fitness for life with the new sexual identity); international aspects (place where the operation is performed); the legal consequences, retrospective or otherwise, of such a change (rectification of civil status documents); the opportunity to choose a different forename; the confidentiality of documents and information mentioning the change; effects of a family nature (right to marry, fate of an existing marriage, filiation), and so on. On these various points there is as yet no sufficiently broad consensus between the member States of the Council of Europe to persuade the Court to reach opposite conclusions to those in its *Rees* and *Cossey* judgments.

2. The Differences Between the French and English Systems

50. In the Government's opinion, . . . the Court could not depart in the case of France from the solution adopted in the *Rees* and *Cossey* judgments. The applicant might no doubt in the course of her daily life experience a number of embarrassing situations, but they were not serious enough to constitute a breach of Article 8. At no time had the French authorities denied transsexuals the right to lead their own lives as they wished. . . .

51. The Court finds, to begin with, that there are noticeable differences between France and England with reference to their law and practice on civil status, change of forenames, the use of identity documents, etc. . . .

(a) Civil Status

(i) Rectification of Civil Status Documents

52. The applicant considered the rejection of her request for rectification of her birth certificate to be all the more culpable since France could not claim, as the United Kingdom had done, that there were any major obstacles linked to the system in force.

The Court had found, in connection with the English civil status system, that the purpose of the registers was not to define the present identity of an individual but to record a historic fact, and their public character would make the protection of private life illusory if it were possible to make subsequent corrections or additions of this kind. This was not the case in France. Birth certificates were intended to be updated throughout the life of the person concerned, so that it would be perfectly possible to insert a reference to a judgment ordering the amendment of the original sex recorded. Moreover, the only persons who had direct access to them were public officials authorised to do so and persons who had obtained permission from the procureur de la République; their public character was ensured by the issuing of complete copies or extracts. France could therefore uphold the applicant's claim without amending the legislation; a change in the Court of Cassation's case-law would suffice.

53. In the Government's opinion, French case-law in this respect was not settled, and the law appeared to be in a transitional phase.

54. In the Commission's opinion, none of the Government's arguments suggested that the Court of Cassation would agree to a transsexual's change of sex being recorded in the civil status register. It had rejected the appeal in the present case on the grounds that the applicant's situation derived from a voluntary choice on her part and not from facts which had existed prior to the operation.

55. . . . It is true that the applicant underwent the surgical operation abroad, without the benefit of all the medical and psychological safeguards which are now required in France. The operation nevertheless involved the irreversible abandonment of the external marks of Miss B.'s original sex. The Court considers that in the circumstances of the case the applicant's manifest determination is a factor which is sufficiently significant to be taken into account, together with other factors, with reference to Article 8.

(ii) Change of Forenames

56. The applicant pointed out that the law of 6 Fructidor Year II prohibited any citizen from bearing a surname or forename other than those recorded on his or her birth certificate. In the eyes of the law, her forename was therefore Norbert; all her identity documents (identity card, passport, voting card, etc.), her cheque books and her official correspondence (telephone accounts, tax demands, etc.) described her by that name. Unlike in the United Kingdom, whether she could change her forename did not depend on her wishes only; Article 57 of the Civil Code made this subject to judicial permission and the demonstration of a "legitimate interest" capable of justifying it. . . . Miss B. knew of no decision which had regarded transsexualism as giving rise to such an interest. In any event, the Libourne tribunal de grande instance and the Bordeaux Court of Appeal had refused to allow her the forenames Lyne Antoinette. . . .

58. . . . To sum up, the Court considers that the refusal to allow the applicant the change of forename requested by her is also a relevant factor from the point of view of Article 8. . . .

(b) Documents

59. (a) The applicant stressed that an increasing number of official documents indicated sex: extracts of birth certificates, computerised identity cards, European Communities passports, etc. Transsexuals could consequently not cross a frontier, undergo an identity check or carry out one of the many transactions of daily life where proof of identity is necessary, without disclosing the discrepancy between their legal sex and their apparent sex.

(b) According to the applicant, sex was also indicated on all documents using the identification number issued to everyone by [the National Institute for Statistics and Economic Studies (INSEE)]. . . . This number was used as part of the system of dealings between social security institutions, employers and those insured; it therefore appeared on records of contributions paid and on payslips. A transsexual was consequently unable to hide his or her situation from a potential employer and the employer's administrative staff; the same applied to the many occasions in daily life where it was necessary to prove the existence and amount of one's income (taking a lease, opening a bank account, applying for credit, etc). This led to difficulties for the social and professional integration of transsexuals. . . .

60. The Commission agreed substantially with the applicant's arguments. In its opinion the applicant, as a result of the frequent necessity of disclosing information concerning her private life to third parties, suffered distress which was too serious to be justified on the ground of respect for the rights of others. . . .

(c) Conclusion

63. The Court thus reaches the conclusion, on the basis of the above-mentioned factors which distinguish the present case from the *Rees* and *Cossey* cases and without it being necessary to consider the applicant's other arguments, that she finds herself daily in a situation which, taken as a whole, is not compatible with the respect due to her private life. Consequently, even having regard to the State's margin of appreciation, the fair balance which has to be struck between the general interest and the interests of the individual has not been attained, and there has thus been a violation of Article 8. . . .

The respondent State has several means to choose from for remedying this state of affairs. It is not the Court's function to indicate which is the most appropriate.

PETTITI, J., dissenting. . . . The European Convention on Human Rights does not impose any obligation on the High Contracting Parties to legislate on the question of rectification of civil status in connection with transsexualism, even in application of the theory of positive obligations for States (case of *X v. the Netherlands*). Thus several member States have not enacted any legislation relating to transsexualism. The various national laws on the point show a great variety of criteria and mechanisms.

In any event, member States who wish to confront these problems have a choice between the legislative path and the case-law path, and in this sensitive area, dependent on very diverse social and moral situations, the margin of appreciation allowed to the State is a wide one.

Whichever path is chosen, legislative or by means of case-law, the State remains free to define the criteria for recognition of cases of intersexualism or true transsexualism, dependent upon undisputed scientific knowledge. A national court can take a decision on the basis of such criteria without violating the Convention. . . .

If there is a field where States should be allowed the maximum margin of appreciation, having regard to moral attitudes and traditions, it is certainly that of transsexualism, having regard also to developments in the opinions of the medical and scientific experts.

A solution by means of case-law may be a legitimate choice for the State to make. If the development of case-law makes it possible for domestic law to respond to undeniable cases, making it possible for rectification of civil status to take place, . . . it appears to be consistent with Article 8 to regard this case-law method as in accordance with the requirements of that Article.

. . . Even if the member State agrees to rectification, it remains free to restrict the conditions for it and its consequences in civil law, if it does not systematically refuse applications in all such cases. . . .

Conclusion: in the present state of French law and the status of the family, and taking into account the rights of others, it is apparent that the case-law path is the one which best respects Article 8 of the Convention, subject to the margin of appreciation allowed to the State.

NOTES & QUESTIONS

1. ***Gender on Identification Documents.*** The ECHR's holding is unclear as to how France violated Article 8. In addition, it leaves the respondent state free to choose the means for remedying the violation of privacy. How do you think France, or generally any nation, should change its current administrative practices regarding the history of gender on official documents? Allow transsexuals to rectify their civil status document? Change their first name? Have the statement or indication of sex deleted from the documents and identity papers for use in daily life? What would be the factors you would take into account? What are the factors taken into account by the dissenting opinion by Judge Pettiti?
2. ***Differences Between Nations vs. a Unified European Approach.*** Should the regulation of transsexualism remain within the competence of each country, taking into account the traditions and moral views of each nation? What would be the impact of this approach on transborder data flow?

(e) Privacy and Government Records and Databases

ROTARU V. ROMANIA

ECHR, 5/4/2000

Principal Facts

The applicant, Aurel Rotaru, a Romanian national, was born in 1921 and lives in Bârlad (Romania).

In 1992 the applicant, who in 1948 had been sentenced to a year's imprisonment for having expressed criticism of the communist regime established in 1946, brought an action in which he sought to be granted rights that Decree No. 118 of 1990 afforded persons who had been persecuted by the communist regime. In the proceedings which followed in the Bârlad Court of First Instance, one of the defendants, the Ministry of the Interior, submitted to the court a letter sent to it on 19 December 1990 by the Romanian Intelligence Service, which contained, among other things, information about the applicant's political activities between 1946 and 1948. According to the same letter, Mr.

Rotaru had been a member of the Christian Students' Association, an extreme right-wing "legionnaire" movement, in 1937.

The applicant considered that some of the information in question was false and defamatory — in particular, the allegation that he had been a member of the legionnaire movement — and brought proceedings against the Romanian Intelligence Service, claiming compensation for the non-pecuniary damage he had sustained and amendment or destruction of the file containing the untrue information. . . .

[The claim the applicant filed was rejected by the Romanian courts.] These . . . courts held that they had no power to order amendment or destruction of the information in the letter of 19 December 1990 as it had been gathered by the State's former security services, and the Romanian Intelligence Service had only been a depositary.

[The applicant lodged his complaint in 1995 with the European Commission of Human Rights.]

In . . . 1997 the Director of the Romanian Intelligence Service [recognized] that the information about being a member of the "legionnaire" movement referred not to the applicant but to another person of the same name.

In the light of that letter the applicant sought a review of the Bucharest Court of Appeal's [last] judgment of . . . 1994 and claimed damages. [T]he Bucharest Court of Appeal quashed the judgment of 15 December 1994 and declared the information about the applicant's past membership of the "legionnaire" movement null and void. . . .

The Facts

I. Relevant Domestic Law . . .

[G. Law no. 187 of 20 October 1999 provides:

> (1) All Romanian citizens, and all aliens who have obtained Romanian nationality since 1945, shall be entitled to inspect the files kept on them by the organs of the Securitate. . . . This right shall be exercisable on request and shall make it possible for the file itself to be inspected and copies to be made of any document in it or relating to its contents.
>
> (2) Additionally, any person who is the subject of a file from which it appears that he or she was kept under surveillance by the Securitate shall be entitled, on request, to know the identity of the Securitate agents and collaborators who contributed documents to the file.]

The Law . . .

II. Alleged Violation of Article 8 of the Convention

1. The applicant complained that the RIS [Romanian Intelligence Service] held and could at any moment make use of information about his private life, some of which was false and defamatory. He alleged a violation of Article 8 of the Convention. . . .

A. Applicability of Article 8

3. The Court reiterates that the storing of information relating to an individual's private life in a secret register and the release of such information comes within the scope of Article 8 § 1. . . .

The Court has already emphasised the correspondence of this broad interpretation with that of the Council of Europe's Convention of 28 January 1981 for the Protection of Individuals with regard to Automatic Processing of Personal Data, which came into force on 1 October 1985 and whose purpose is "to secure . . . for every individual . . . respect for his rights and fundamental freedoms, and in particular his right to privacy with regard to automatic processing of personal data relating to him" (Article 1), such personal data being defined in Article 2 as "any information relating to an identified or identifiable individual."

Moreover, public information can fall within the scope of private life where it is systematically collected and stored in files held by the authorities. That is all the truer where such information concerns a person's distant past.

4. In the instant case the Court notes that the RIS's letter of 19 December 1990 contained various pieces of information about the applicant's life, in particular his studies, his political activities and his criminal record, some of which had been gathered more than fifty years earlier. In the Court's opinion, such information, when systematically collected and stored in a file held by agents of the State, falls within the scope of "private life" for the purposes of Article 8 § 1 of the Convention. That is all the more so in the instant case as some of the information has been declared false and is likely to injure the applicant's reputation.

Article 8 consequently applies.

B. Compliance with Article 8

1. Whether There Was Interference

6. The Court points out that both the storing by a public authority of information relating to an individual's private life and the use of it and the refusal to allow an opportunity for it to be refuted amount to interference with the right to respect for private life secured in Article 8 § 1 of the Convention.

Both the storing of that information and the use of it, which were coupled with a refusal to allow the applicant an opportunity to refute it, amounted to interference with his right to respect for family life as guaranteed by Article 8 § 1.

2. Justification for the Interference

7. The cardinal issue that arises is whether the interference so found is justifiable under paragraph 2 of Article 8. That paragraph, since it provides for an exception to a right guaranteed by the Convention, is to be interpreted narrowly. While the Court recognises that intelligence services may legitimately exist in a democratic society, it reiterates that powers of secret surveillance of citizens are tolerable under the Convention only in so far as strictly necessary for safeguarding the democratic institutions.

8. If it is not to contravene Article 8, such interference must have been "in accordance with the law," pursue a legitimate aim under paragraph 2 and, furthermore, be necessary in a democratic society in order to achieve that aim. . . .

11. The Commission considered that domestic law did not define with sufficient precision the circumstances in which the RIS could archive, release and use information relating to the applicant's private life. . . .

The Court must . . . determine whether Law No. 14/1992 on the organisation and operation of the RIS, which was likewise relied on by the Government, can provide the legal basis for these measures. [Law No. 14/1992 grants broad authority to the Romanian Intelligence Services to gather information to protect the national security and made such information secret.] In this connection, it notes that the law in question authorises the RIS to gather, store and make use of information affecting national security. The Court has doubts as to the relevance to national security of the information held on the applicant. Nevertheless, it reiterates that it is primarily for the national authorities, notably the courts, to interpret and apply domestic law and notes that in its judgment of 25 November 1997 the Bucharest Court of Appeal confirmed that it was lawful for the RIS to hold this information as depositary of the archives of the former security services.

That being so, the Court may conclude that the storing of information about the applicant's private life had a basis in Romanian law. . . .

15. As regards the requirement of foreseeability, the Court reiterates that a rule is "foreseeable" if it is formulated with sufficient precision to enable any individual — if need be with appropriate advice — to regulate his conduct. The Court has stressed the importance of this concept with regard to secret surveillance in the following terms:

> The Court would reiterate its opinion that the phrase "in accordance with the law" does not merely refer back to domestic law but also relates to the quality of the "law," requiring it to be compatible with the rule of law, which is expressly mentioned in the preamble to the Convention. . . . The phrase thus implies — and this follows from the object and purpose of Article 8 — that there must be a measure of legal protection in domestic law against arbitrary interferences by public authorities with the rights safeguarded by paragraph 1. . . . Especially where a power of the executive is exercised in secret, the risks of arbitrariness are evident. . . .
>
> Since the implementation in practice of measures of secret surveillance of communications is not open to scrutiny by the individuals concerned or the public at large, it would be contrary to the rule of law for the legal discretion granted to the executive to be expressed in terms of an unfettered power. Consequently, the law must indicate the scope of any such discretion conferred on the competent authorities and the manner of its exercise with sufficient clarity, having regard to the legitimate aim of the measure in question, to give the individual adequate protection against arbitrary interference.

16. The "quality" of the legal rules relied on in this case must therefore be scrutinised, with a view, in particular, to ascertaining whether domestic law laid down with sufficient precision the circumstances in which the RIS could store and make use of information relating to the applicant's private life.

17. The Court notes in this connection that section 8 of Law No. 14/1992 provides that information affecting national security may be gathered, recorded and archived in secret files.

No provision of domestic law, however, lays down any limits on the exercise of those powers. Thus, for instance, domestic law does not define the kind of information that may be recorded, the categories of people against whom surveillance measures such as gathering and keeping information may be taken, the circumstances in which such measures may be taken or the procedure to be followed. Similarly, the Law does not lay down limits on the age of information held or the length of time for which it may be kept.

Section 45 empowers the RIS to take over for storage and use the archives that belonged to the former intelligence services operating on Romanian territory and allows inspection of RIS documents with the Director's consent.

The Court notes that this section contains no explicit, detailed provision concerning the persons authorised to consult the files, the nature of the files, the procedure to be followed or the use that may be made of the information thus obtained.

18. It also notes that although section 2 of the Law empowers the relevant authorities to permit interferences necessary to prevent and counteract threats to national security, the ground allowing such interferences is not laid down with sufficient precision.

19. The Court must also be satisfied that there exist adequate and effective safeguards against abuse, since a system of secret surveillance designed to protect national security entails the risk of undermining or even destroying democracy on the ground of defending it.

In order for systems of secret surveillance to be compatible with Article 8 of the Convention, they must contain safeguards established by law which apply to the supervision of the relevant services' activities. Supervision procedures must follow the values of a democratic society as faithfully as possible, in particular the rule of law, which is expressly referred to in the Preamble to the Convention. The rule of law implies, *inter alia,* that interference by the executive authorities with an individual's rights should be subject to effective supervision, which should normally be carried out by the judiciary, at least in the last resort, since judicial control affords the best guarantees of independence, impartiality and a proper procedure.

20. In the instant case the Court notes that the Romanian system for gathering and archiving information does not provide such safeguards, no supervision procedure being provided by Law No. 14/1992, whether while the measure ordered is in force or afterwards.

21. That being so, the Court considers that domestic law does not indicate with reasonable clarity the scope and manner of exercise of the relevant discretion conferred on the public authorities.

22. The Court concludes that the holding and use by the RIS of information on the applicant's private life was not "in accordance with the law," a fact that suffices to constitute a violation of Article 8. . . .

23. There has consequently been a violation of Article 8.

NOTES & QUESTIONS

1. ***Article 8 vs. FISA.*** Referring to paragraphs 17 and 19 of this decision and its requirements, consider how the national security surveillance claims are treated under Article 8 of the ECHR and under the U.S. Foreign Intelligence Surveillance Act (FISA), as amended by the USA PATRIOT Act (Chapter 3). Which legal regime provides a more effective means of oversight? Which other provisions in U.S. law regulate the collection of similar information by the police?

(f) Privacy and Place

NIEMIETZ V. GERMANY

ECHR, 12/16/1992

. . . As to the Facts

I. The Particular Circumstances of the Case

6. Mr. Niemietz lives in Freiburg im Breisgau, Germany, where he practises as a lawyer (*Rechtsanwalt*). . . .

10. In the context of [criminal] proceedings the Munich District Court issued, on 8 August 1986, a warrant to search the law office of the applicant and his colleague and the homes of Ms. D. and Ms. G. [The warrant was issued to find out who sent a letter, signed by a "Klaus Wegner," insulting a judge. One of the places to be searched was the law office of Gottfried Niemietz.] Those searching neither found the documents they were seeking nor seized any materials. . . .

12. The homes of Ms. D. and Ms. G. were also searched; documents were found that gave rise to a suspicion that the letter to Judge Miosga had been sent by Ms. D. under an assumed name. . . .

II. Relevant Domestic Law

18. Article 13 para. 1 of the Basic Law (*Grundgesetz*) guarantees the inviolability of the home (*Wohnung*); this provision has been consistently interpreted by the German courts in a wide sense, to include business premises. . . .

19. Article 103 of the Code of Criminal Procedure provides that the home and other premises (*Wohnung und andere Räume*) of a person who is not suspected of a criminal offence may be searched only in order to arrest a person charged with an offence, to investigate indications of an offence or to seize specific objects and provided always that there are facts to suggest that such a person, indications or objects is or are to be found on the premises to be searched.

21. . . . An unauthorised breach of secrecy by a lawyer is punishable by imprisonment for a maximum of one year or a fine (Article 203 para. 1(3) of the Criminal Code). A lawyer is entitled to refuse to give testimony concerning any

matter confided to him in a professional capacity (Article 53 para. 1(2) and (3) of the Code of Criminal Procedure). The last-mentioned provisions, in conjunction with Article 97, prohibit, with certain exceptions, the seizure of correspondence between lawyer and client. . . .

As to the Law

I. Alleged Violation of Article 8 of the Convention

26. Mr. Niemietz alleged that the search of his law office had given rise to a breach of Article 8 (art. 8) of the Convention. . . .

A. Was There an "Interference"?

27. In contesting the Commission's conclusion, the Government maintained that Article 8 did not afford protection against the search of a lawyer's office. In their view, the Convention drew a clear distinction between private life and home, on the one hand, and professional and business life and premises, on the other.

28. . . . The Court . . . [has doubts] as to whether this factor can serve as a workable criterion for the purposes of delimiting the scope of the protection afforded by Article 8 (art. 8). Virtually all professional and business activities may involve, to a greater or lesser degree, matters that are confidential, with the result that, if that criterion were adopted, disputes would frequently arise as to where the line should be drawn.

29. The Court does not consider it possible or necessary to attempt an exhaustive definition of the notion of "private life". However, it would be too restrictive to limit the notion to an "inner circle" in which the individual may live his own personal life as he chooses and to exclude there from entirely the outside world not encompassed within that circle. Respect for private life must also comprise to a certain degree the right to establish and develop relationships with other human beings.

There appears, furthermore, to be no reason of principle why this understanding of the notion of "private life" should be taken to exclude activities of a professional or business nature since it is, after all, in the course of their working lives that the majority of people have a significant, if not the greatest, opportunity of developing relationships with the outside world. This view is supported by the fact that . . . it is not always possible to distinguish clearly which of an individual's activities form part of his professional or business life and which do not. Thus, especially in the case of a person exercising a liberal profession, his work in that context may form part and parcel of his life to such a degree that it becomes impossible to know in what capacity he is acting at a given moment of time. . . .

30. As regards the word "home," appearing in the English text of Article 8, the Court observes that in certain Contracting States, notably Germany . . . , it has been accepted as extending to business premises. Such an interpretation is, moreover, fully consonant with the French text, since the word "domicile" has a broader connotation than the word "home" and may extend, for example, to a professional person's office.

In this context also, it may not always be possible to draw precise distinctions, since activities which are related to a profession or business may well be conducted from a person's private residence and activities which are not so related may well be carried on in an office or commercial premises. A narrow interpretation of the words "home" and "domicile" could therefore give rise to the same risk of inequality of treatment as a narrow interpretation of the notion of "private life" (see paragraph 29 above).

31. More generally, to interpret the words "private life" and "home" as including certain professional or business activities or premises would be consonant with the essential object and purpose of Article 8, namely to protect the individual against arbitrary interference by the public authorities. . . .

32. To the above-mentioned general considerations, which militate against the view that Article 8 is not applicable, must be added a further factor pertaining to the particular circumstances of the case. The warrant issued by the Munich District Court ordered a search for, and seizure of, "documents" — without qualification or limitation — revealing the identity of Klaus Wegner. . . .

33. Taken together, the foregoing reasons lead the Court to find that the search of the applicant's office constituted an interference with his rights under Article 8 (art. 8).

B. Was the Interference "in Accordance with the Law"?

. . . [The Court considered that the search was lawful in terms of Article 103 of the Code of Criminal Procedure (see paragraph 19 above).] . . .

C. Did the Interference Have a Legitimate Aim or Aims?

36. . . . [T]he Court finds that . . . the interference pursued aims that were legitimate under Article 8 (2), namely the prevention of crime and the protection of the rights of others, that is the honour of Judge Miosga.

D. Was the Interference "Necessary in a Democratic Society"?

. . . It is true that the offence in connection with which the search was effected, involving as it did not only an insult to but also an attempt to bring pressure on a judge, cannot be classified as no more than minor. On the other hand, the warrant was drawn in broad terms, in that it ordered a search for and seizure of "documents", without any limitation, revealing the identity of the author of the offensive letter; this point is of special significance where, as in Germany, the search of a lawyer's office is not accompanied by any special procedural safeguards, such as the presence of an independent observer. More importantly, having regard to the materials that were in fact inspected, the search impinged on professional secrecy to an extent that appears disproportionate in the circumstances; it has, in this connection, to be recalled that, where a lawyer is involved, an encroachment on professional secrecy may have repercussions on the proper administration of justice and hence on the rights guaranteed by Article 6 of the Convention. In addition, the attendant publicity must have been capable of affecting adversely the applicant's professional reputation, in the eyes both of his existing clients and of the public at large.

E. Conclusion

38. The Court thus concludes that there was a breach of Article 8. . . .

NOTES & QUESTIONS

1. ***"In Accordance with Law."*** The ECHR case law requires that a governmental measure be taken "in accordance with a law." Is this a significant limitation on the activities of government? Compare this with federal electronic surveillance law in the United States. Which approach is preferable?
2. ***Article 8 vs. the Reasonable Expectation of Privacy Test.*** Article 8 presents a multifactor approach to judicial review of privacy complaints. How does this approach compare with the "reasonable expectation of privacy" analysis generally followed by the courts in the United States? How are these factors derived? Could they be codified in a civil code system of law?

COPLAND V. UNITED KINGDOM

ECHR, 03/07/07

The Facts

6. The applicant was born in 1950 and lives in Llanelli, Wales.

7. In 1991 the applicant was employed by Carmarthenshire College ("the College"). The College is a statutory body administered by the State and possessing powers under sections 18 and 19 of the Further and Higher Education Act 1992 relating to the provision of further and higher education.

8. In 1995 the applicant became the personal assistant to the College Principal ("CP") and from the end of 1995 she was required to work closely with the newly appointed Deputy Principal ("DP").

9. In about July 1998, whilst on annual leave, the applicant visited another campus of the College with a male director. She subsequently became aware that the DP had contacted that campus to enquire about her visit and understood that he was suggesting an improper relationship between her and the director.

10. During her employment, the applicant's telephone, e-mail and internet usage were subjected to monitoring at the DP's instigation. According to the Government, this monitoring took place in order to ascertain whether the applicant was making excessive use of College facilities for personal purposes. The Government stated that the monitoring of telephone usage consisted of analysis of the college telephone bills showing telephone numbers called, the dates and times of the calls and their length and cost. The applicant also believed that there had been detailed and comprehensive logging of the length of calls, the number of calls received and made and the telephone numbers of individuals calling her. She stated that on at least one occasion the DP became aware of the name of an individual with whom she had exchanged incoming and outgoing telephone calls. The Government submitted that the monitoring of telephone usage took place for a few months up to about 22 November 1999. The applicant

contended that her telephone usage was monitored over a period of about 18 months until November 1999.

11. The applicant's internet usage was also monitored by the DP. The Government accepted that this monitoring took the form of analysing the web sites visited, the times and dates of the visits to the web sites and their duration and that this monitoring took place from October to November 1999. The applicant did not comment on the manner in which her internet usage was monitored but submitted that it took place over a much longer period of time than the Government admit.

12. In November 1999 the applicant became aware that enquiries were being made into her use of e-mail at work when her step-daughter was contacted by the College and asked to supply information about e-mails that she had sent to the College. The applicant wrote to the CP to ask whether there was a general investigation taking place or whether her e-mails only were being investigated. By an e-mail dated 24 November 1999 the CP advised the applicant that, whilst all e-mail activity was logged, the information department of the College was investigating only her e-mails, following a request by the DP.

13. The Government submitted that monitoring of e-mails took the form of analysis of e-mail addresses and dates and times at which e-mails were sent and that the monitoring occurred for a few months prior to 22 November 1999. According to the applicant the monitoring of e-mails occurred for at least six months from May 1999 to November 1999. She provided documentary evidence in the form of printouts detailing her e-mail usage from 14 May 1999 to 22 November 1999 which set out the date and time of e-mails sent from her e-mail account together with the recipients' e-mail addresses. . . .

15. There was no policy in force at the College at the material time regarding the monitoring of telephone, e-mail or internet use by employees. . . .

The Law

39. The Court notes the Government's acceptance that the College is a public body for whose acts it is responsible for the purposes of the Convention. Thus, it considers that in the present case the question to be analysed under Article 8 relates to the negative obligation on the State not to interfere with the private life and correspondence of the applicant and that no separate issue arises in relation to home or family life. . . .

41. According to the Court's case-law, telephone calls from business premises are *prima facie* covered by the notions of "private life" and "correspondence" for the purposes of Article 8 § 1. . . It follows logically that e-mails sent from work should be similarly protected under Article 8, as should information derived from the monitoring of personal internet usage.

42. The applicant in the present case had been given no warning that her calls would be liable to monitoring, therefore she had a reasonable expectation as to the privacy of calls made from her work telephone. The same expectation should apply in relation to the applicant's e-mail and internet usage.

43. The Court recalls that the use of information relating to the date and length of telephone conversations and in particular the numbers dialed can give rise to an issue under Article 8 as such information constitutes an "integral

element of the communications made by telephone" The mere fact that these data may have been legitimately obtained by the College, in the form of telephone bills, is no bar to finding an interference with rights guaranteed under Article 8. Moreover, storing of personal data relating to the private life of an individual also falls within the application of Article 8 § 1. Thus, it is irrelevant that the data held by the college were not disclosed or used against the applicant in disciplinary or other proceedings.

44. Accordingly, the Court considers that the collection and storage of personal information relating to the applicant's telephone, as well as to her e-mail and internet usage, without her knowledge, amounted to an interference with her right to respect for her private life and correspondence within the meaning of Article 8.

45. The Court recalls that it is well established in the case-law that the term "in accordance with the law" implies — and this follows from the object and purpose of Article 8 — that there must be a measure of legal protection in domestic law against arbitrary interferences by public authorities with the rights safeguarded by Article 8 § 1. This is all the more so in areas such as the monitoring in question, in view of the lack of public scrutiny and the risk of misuse of power.

46. This expression not only requires compliance with domestic law, but also relates to the quality of that law, requiring it to be compatible with the rule of law. In order to fulfil the requirement of foreseeability, the law must be sufficiently clear in its terms to give individuals an adequate indication as to the circumstances in which and the conditions on which the authorities are empowered to resort to any such measures.

47. The Court is not convinced by the Government's submission that the College was authorised under its statutory powers to do "anything necessary or expedient" for the purposes of providing higher and further education, and finds the argument unpersuasive. Moreover, the Government do not seek to argue that any provisions existed at the relevant time, either in general domestic law or in the governing instruments of the College, regulating the circumstances in which employers could monitor the use of telephone, e-mail and the internet by employees. Furthermore, it is clear that the Telecommunications (Lawful Business Practice) Regulations 2000 (adopted under the Regulation of Investigatory Powers Act 2000) which make such provision were not in force at the relevant time.

48. Accordingly, as there was no domestic law regulating monitoring at the relevant time, the interference in this case was not "in accordance with the law" as required by Article 8 § 2 of the Convention. The Court would not exclude that the monitoring of an employee's use of a telephone, e-mail or internet at the place of work may be considered "necessary in a democratic society" in certain situations in pursuit of a legitimate aim. However, having regard to its above conclusion, it is not necessary to pronounce on that matter in the instant case.

49. There has therefore been a violation of Article 8 in this regard. . . .

54. The Government submitted that the report presented by the applicant gave no indication that the stress complained of was caused by the facts giving rise to her complaint. Furthermore, as the Court had held in a number of cases relating to complaints involving the interception of the communications of

suspected criminals by the police, in their view, a finding of a violation should in itself constitute sufficient just satisfaction. Moreover, since the conduct alleged consisted of monitoring and not interception, the nature of such interference was of a significantly lower order of seriousness than the cases mentioned above.

55. The Court notes the above cases cited by the Government, but recalls also that, in *Halford,* which concerned the interception of an employee's private telephone calls by her employer, it awarded GBP 10,000 in respect of non-pecuniary damage. Making an assessment on an equitable basis in the present case, the Court awards the applicant EUR 3,000 in respect of non-pecuniary damage.[23]

58. . . . Taking into account all the circumstances, it awards the applicant EUR 6,000 for legal costs and expenses, in addition to any VAT that may be payable.

FOR THESE REASONS, THE COURT UNANIMOUSLY

1. *Holds* that there has been a violation of Article 8 of the Convention. . . .

3. *Holds* . . . that the respondent State is to pay the applicant, within three months from the date on which the judgment becomes final in accordance with Article 44 § 2 of the Convention, the following amounts, to be converted into pounds sterling at the rate applicable at the time of settlement: (i) EUR 3,000 (three thousand euros) in respect of non-pecuniary damage; (ii) EUR 6,000 (six thousand euros) in respect of costs and expenses; (iii) any tax that may be chargeable on the above amounts. . . .

NOTES & QUESTIONS

1. ***Content and Telecommunication Attributes.*** In *Copland v. United Kingdom*, the ECHR found that monitoring by employers did not have to collect the content of communications to be actionable under Article 8. In *Copland*, the employer had examined the data and length of telephone conversations, the numbers dialed, and websites visited. But how might employers engage in such monitoring consistent with Article 8? The ECHR indicates in *Copland* that it "would not exclude" that "the monitoring of an employee's use of a telephone, e-mail or internet at the place of work may be considered 'necessary in a democratic society' in certain situations in pursuit of a legitimate aim." In your judgment, what kind of workplace monitoring would be appropriate? Should it depend on the particular position that an employee holds in the workplace? Note as well that Copland had not been warned that her telephone calls and e-mails would be subject to monitoring. Moreover, at the time of the employer's surveillance, there was no law in the U.K. to govern such behavior. How could a European firm craft a workplace monitoring policy that would comport with *Copland*?
2. ***The EU vs. the United States?*** In an analysis of *Copland*, Fred Cate has argued that it "may further widen the gulf between U.S. and European data

[23] [Editors' Note: 3,000 Euros are worth approximately 2,400 British Pounds (GBP) and 4,800 (U.S. dollars).]

protection laws and create challenges for multinational businesses and other organizations operating in Europe."[24] In addition to *Copland*, Cate identifies other EU decisions that block employer monitoring of telephone and Internet usage — even monitoring to investigate suspected wrongdoing and carried out with proper notice and authorized by a specific law. Cate concludes that *Copland* is "a potent reminder of how far European law has moved in the direction of workplace privacy and how great a challenge this movement poses for U.S. and multinational entities."

3. THE EUROPEAN UNION DATA PROTECTION DIRECTIVE

(a) Introduction

The European Union Data Protection Directive of 1995 establishes common rules for data protection among Member States of the European Union. The Directive was created in the early 1990s and formally adopted in 1995. Although prior to the adoption of the Directive, many EU countries had broad national privacy legislation, the statutory protections diverged. The Directive's purpose, somewhat paradoxically, is to facilitate the free flow of personal data within the EU by setting an equally high privacy level in all EU Member States. An increased harmonization of the privacy laws of various European nations would enable the free flow of goods and services, labor, and capital.

The Directive imposes obligations on the processors of personal data. It requires technical security and the notification of individuals whose data are being collected, and outlines circumstances under which data transfer may occur. The Directive also gives individuals substantial rights to control the use of data about themselves. These rights include the right to be informed that their personal data are being transferred, the need to obtain "unambiguous" consent from the individual for the transfer of certain data, the opportunity to make corrections in the data, and the right to object to the transfer. Data regulatory authority, enforcement provisions, and sanctions are also key elements of the directive. Following passage of the Directive, the various national governments of the EU amended their own national data protection legislation to bring it into line with the Directive.

The Directive extends privacy safeguards to personal data that are transferred outside of the European Union. Article 25 of the Directive states that data can only be transferred to third countries that provide an "adequate level of data protection." As a result, implementation focuses on both the adoption of national law within the European Union and the adoption of adequate methods for privacy protection in third party countries.[25]

---

[24] Fred Cate, *European Court of Human Rights Expands Privacy Protections*, 11 Am. Soc'y Int'l L. Insight (Aug. 6, 2007).

[25] For perspectives on the EU Directive, see Peter P. Swire & Robert E. Litan, *None of Your Business: World Data Flows, Electronic Commerce, and the European Privacy Directive* (1998); Spiros Simitis, *From the Market to the Polis: The EU Directive on the Protection of Personal Data*, 80 Iowa L. Rev. 445 (1995); Symposium, *Data Protection Law and the European Union's Directive: The Challenge for the United States*, 80 Iowa L. Rev. 431 (1995).

Directives are a form of EU law that is binding for Member States, but only as to the result to be achieved. They allow the national authorities to choose the form and the methods of their implementation and generally fix a deadline for it. Therefore, the rules of law applicable in each Member State are the national laws implementing the directives and not the directive itself. However, the directive has a "direct effect" on individuals: it grants them rights that can be upheld by the national courts in their respective countries if their governments have not implemented the directive by the set deadline. A directive thus grants *rights* rather than creates obligations, and they are enforceable by *individuals* rather than by public authorities.

It is important to distinguish between vertical and horizontal effects. "Vertical effects" means that the rights established by a directive flow from the European Union to citizens of the EU. Where a violation occurs, citizens may petition EU institution and their national government that has adopted (or "transposed") a directive into national law. But this interest does not create a right for one citizen of the EU to bring an action against another citizen. For such an impact to occur ("horizontal effects") there must be national law or an EU regulation in place. Whereas the EU "regulations" or treaty provisions are able to confer rights on private individuals and impose obligations on them, directives can only confer rights on individuals against the State; they cannot impose on them obligations in favor of the State or other individuals. Directives are only capable of "vertical" direct effect, unlike treaty provisions and regulations, which are also capable of "horizontal" direct effect.

Directives are enacted in the context of the European Community (EC)'s competences, the EC being one of the legal entities that is part of the European Union. It means that their scope is limited to the area of competence of the EC. The EU Data Directive, as a result, does not cover activities, which fall outside the scope of EC law, such as the data processing operations concerning public security, defense, State security, and the activities of the State in areas of criminal law. *See, e.g.,* EU Data Directive, Article 3(2). In such cases, the only authorities that may promulgate enforceable legislation are the Member States. The European Union, however, can voice its concerns on privacy issues regarding policing and security through its "Justice and Home Affairs" branch. Under the direction of the EU Council,[26] the Justice and Home Affairs branch can take common positions defining the approach of the EU to a particular matter or even establish conventions, although each Member State can always oppose these decisions and not implement them into national law. The EU Council is the group of delegates of the Member States, each State being represented by a government minister who is authorized to commit his government.

Definitions. Article 2 defines a number of important terms used throughout the Directive:

> (a) "personal data" shall mean any information relating to an identified or identifiable natural person ("data subject"); an identifiable person is one who can be identified, directly or indirectly, in particular by reference to an

[26] The EU Council is the group of delegates of the Member States, each State being represented by a government minister who is authorized to commit his government.

identification number or to one or more factors specific to his physical, physiological, mental, economic, cultural or social identity;

(b) "processing of personal data" ("processing") shall mean any operation or set of operations which is performed upon personal data, whether or not by automatic means, such as collection, recording, organization, storage, adaptation or alteration, retrieval, consultation, use, disclosure by transmission, dissemination or otherwise making available, alignment or combination, blocking, erasure or destruction;

(c) "personal data filing system" ("filing system") shall mean any structured set of personal data which are accessible according to specific criteria, whether centralized, decentralized or dispersed on a functional or geographical basis;

(d) "controller" shall mean the natural or legal person, public authority, agency or any other body which alone or jointly with others determines the purposes and means of the processing of personal data; where the purposes and means of processing are determined by national or Community laws or regulations, the controller or the specific criteria for his nomination may be designated by national or Community law;

(e) "processor" shall mean a natural or legal person, public authority, agency or any other body which processes personal data on behalf of the controller;

(f) "third party" shall mean any natural or legal person, public authority, agency or any other body other than the data subject, the controller, the processor and the persons who, under the direct authority of the controller or the processor, are authorized to process the data;

(g) "recipient" shall mean a natural or legal person, public authority, agency or any other body to whom data are disclosed, whether a third party or not; however, authorities which may receive data in the framework of a particular inquiry shall not be regarded as recipients;

(h) "the data subject's consent" shall mean any freely given specific and informed indication of his wishes by which the data subject signifies his agreement to personal data relating to him being processed.

Scope. Pursuant to Article 3, the Directive applies "to the processing of personal data wholly or partly by automatic means." It also applies to nonautomatic processing that involves a "filing system."

The Directive does not apply to the processing of personal data "in the course of an activity which falls outside the scope of Community law." Further, it does not apply "in any case to processing operations concerning public security, defence, State security (including the economic well-being of the State when the processing operation relates to State security matters) and the activities of the State in areas of criminal law." Finally, the Directive does not apply to the processing of personal data "by a natural person in the course of a purely personal or household activity."

Implementation by Member States. The Directive provides general parameters for legislation by each Member State, which must pass its own laws and regulations to carry out the general dictates of the Directive. As Article 5 states: "Member States shall, within the limits of the provisions of this Chapter, determine more precisely the conditions under which the processing of personal data is lawful." Member States must "adopt suitable measures to ensure the full implementation of the provisions of this Directive." Article 24. Further, Member

States must establish sanctions for the infringement of provisions adopted pursuant to the Directive.

Right of Access. Article 12(a) provides that every data subject be guaranteed the right to obtain from the data controller "at reasonable intervals and without excessive delay or expense" the following: (1) "confirmation as to whether or not data relating to him are being processed and information at least as to the purposes of the processing, the categories of data concerned, and the recipients or categories of recipients to whom the data are disclosed"; (2) "communication to him in an intelligible form of the data undergoing processing and of any available information as to their source"; (3) "knowledge of the logic involved in any automatic processing of data concerning him at least in the case of the automated decisions referred to in Article 15 (1)."

Right to Correct Inaccurate Information. If data is incomplete or inaccurate, the data subject shall have the right to rectify, erase, or block the processing of the data. *See* Article 12(b). Further, any third parties to whom the data were disclosed shall be notified of the errors and restricted in the same manner from processing of the data. *See* Article 12(c).

Exemptions and Restrictions. Article 13 provides that Member State may restrict the scope of the obligations and rights under the Directive when it is necessary to protect:

(a) national security;
(b) defence;
(c) public security;
(d) the prevention, investigation, detection and prosecution of criminal offences, or of breaches of ethics for regulated professions;
(e) an important economic or financial interest of a Member State or of the European Union, including monetary, budgetary and taxation matters;
(f) a monitoring, inspection or regulatory function connected, even occasionally, with the exercise of official authority in cases referred to in (c), (d) and (e);
(g) the protection of the data subject or of the rights and freedoms of others.

When data is processed for the purpose of scientific or statistical research, is not used to make decisions about the data subject, and "where there is clearly no risk of breaching the privacy of the data subject," member states may restrict by way of a legislative measure the rights provided for in Article 12.

Right to Object. Pursuant to Article 14, the data subject shall be granted the right to "object at any time on compelling legitimate grounds relating to his particular situation" in cases referred to in Article 7(e) (processing for tasks carried out in the public interest) and Article 7(f) (processing for legitimate interests pursued by the controller or third parties). If the objection is justified, the processing of the data subject's data must cease. *See* Article 14(a).

Additionally, the data subject can object to

> the processing of personal data relating to him which the controller anticipates being processed for the purposes of direct marketing, or to be informed before personal data are disclosed for the first time to third parties or used on their behalf for the purposes of direct marketing, and to be expressly offered the right to object free of charge to such disclosures or uses. Article 14(b).

Member States must take measures to ensure that data subjects know about their rights to object.

Right Not to Be Subject to Certain Automated Decisions. An automated decision is one made based not on personal judgment but upon an automated processing technique using an individual's personal data. Article 15 of the Directive restricts the instances in which automated decisions can be made about data subjects:

> Member States shall grant the right to every person not to be subject to a decision which produces legal effects concerning him or significantly affects him and which is based solely on automated processing of data intended to evaluate certain personal aspects relating to him, such as his performance at work, creditworthiness, reliability, conduct, etc. Article 15(1).

There are some exceptions: (1) if the automated decision is made pursuant to a contractual arrangement with the data subject; (2) if "there are suitable measures to safeguard his legitimate interests, such as arrangements allowing him to defend his point of view"; or (3) if it "is authorized by a law which also lays down measures to safeguard the data subject's legitimate interests."

NOTES & QUESTIONS

1. ***Dynamic IP Addresses and Graffiti Registers.*** The EU Data Directive's definition of "personal data" (Art. 2(a)) is one of the keys to understanding the scope and application of the Directive as it only applies to the processing of personal data. Although a more precise definition might simplify the application of data protection across the EU, this formulation reflects the diversity in Member States' laws. To help interpret the concept, the Directive's Recital 26 recommends that "account should be taken of all the means likely reasonably to be used either by the controller or by any other person to identify the said person." It also advises that the data protection rules should not be applicable to "data rendered anonymous in such a way that the data subject is no longer identifiable." As a result, the determination of the scope of "personal data" constitutes a crucial issue when enforcing data protection rules, particularly in the online context.

   In 2007, the Article 29 Working Group, the independent advisory body made up of data protection commissioners from EU Member States, issued an opinion concerning "the concept of personal data."[27] As the opinion states, "Working on a common definition of the notion of personal data is

[27] Article 29 Data Protection Working Party, Opinion 2/2007 on the concept of personal data (June 20, 2007).

tantamount to defining what falls inside or outside the scope of data protection rules." For the Article 29 Group, dynamic IP addresses can be considered as personal data:

> [e]specially in those cases where the processing of IP addresses is carried out with the purpose of identifying the users of the computer (for instance, by Copyright holders in order to prosecute computer users for violation of intellectual property rights), the controller anticipates that the "means likely reasonably to be used" to identify the persons will be available e.g. through the courts appealed to (otherwise the collection of the information makes no sense). . . .

This view has been controversial. Some experts have argued that ISPs are generally unable to identify a specific user associated with an IP, but only tie an IP address with an account holder for it.

Another interesting hypothetical from this opinion concerns graffiti, and a transportation company choosing to create a register with information about the circumstances of damage to its passenger vehicles "as well as the images of the damaged items and of the 'tags' or 'signatures' of the author." When the register is created, the creator of the graffiti is unknown and may never be known. Nonetheless, "the purpose of the processing is precisely to identify individuals to whom the information relates as the authors of the damage, so as to be able to exercise legal claims against them." Hence, the processing is to be made "subject to data protection rules, which allow such processing as legitimate under certain circumstances and subject to certain safeguards."

Compare these notions of "personal data" with the notion of "personally identifiable information" found in U.S. privacy laws. Are they identical?

2. ***The Underlying Philosophy of the EU Data Directive.*** Consider the following argument by Joel Reidenberg:

> The background and underlying philosophy of the European Directive differs in important ways from that of the United States. While there is a consensus among democratic states that information privacy is a critical element of civil society, the United States has, in recent years, left the protection of privacy to markets rather than law. In contrast, Europe treats privacy as a political imperative anchored in fundamental human rights. European democracies approach information privacy from the perspective of social protection. In European democracies, public liberty derives from the community of individuals, and law is the fundamental basis to pursue norms of social and citizen protection. This vision of governance generally regards the state as the necessary player to frame the social community in which individuals develop and in which information practices must serve individual identity. Citizen autonomy, in this view, effectively depends on a backdrop of legal rights. Law thus enshrines prophylactic protection through comprehensive rights and responsibilities. Indeed, citizens trust government more than the private sector with personal information.[28]

As you examine the various provisions of the EU Data Directive and the OECD Privacy Guidelines throughout this chapter, consider how the overall

[28] Joel R. Reidenberg, *E-Commerce and Trans-Atlantic Privacy,* 38 Hous. L. Rev. 717, 730-31 (2001).

approach of European democracies toward protecting differs from that of the United States. Are there ways in which the approaches are similar? To the extent that the approaches are different, think about why such differences exist.

3. ***Electronic Communication and the Processing of Personal Data.*** Personal data processed in connection with electronic communications are the subject of a specific directive (Directive 2002/58/EC concerning the processing of personal data and the protection of privacy in the electronic communications sector). This directive, the Directive on Privacy and Electronic Communications, establishes specific protections covering electronic mail, telephone communications, traffic data, calling line identification, and unsolicited communications. Member states were required to transpose the Directive before October 31, 2002.

Like the EU Data Protection Directive, the EU Directive on Privacy and Electronic Communications is intended to harmonize national law in Europe. Article 5 of the Directive sets out a strong presumption in favor of communications privacy:

> Member States shall ensure the confidentiality of communications and the related traffic data by means of a public communications network and publicly available electronic communications services, through national legislation. In particular, they shall prohibit listening, tapping, storage or other kinds of interception or surveillance of communications and the related traffic data by persons other than users, without the consent of the users concerned, except when legally authorised to do so in accordance with Article 15(1). This paragraph shall not prevent technical storage which is necessary for the conveyance of a communication without prejudice to the principle of confidentiality.

But there has already been some dispute concerning the Article 15(1) provision that may allow for access to electronic communications. That provision states:

> Member States may adopt legislative measures to restrict the scope of the rights and obligations provided for in Article 5, Article 6, Article 8(1), (2), (3) and (4), and Article 9 of this Directive when such restriction constitutes a necessary, appropriate and proportionate measure within a democratic society to safeguard national security (i.e. State security), defence, public security, and the prevention, investigation, detection and prosecution of criminal offences or of unauthorised use of the electronic communication system, as referred to in Article 13(1) of Directive 95/46/EC. To this end, Member States may, *inter alia*, adopt legislative measures providing for the retention of data for a limited period justified on the grounds laid down in this paragraph. All the measures referred to in this paragraph shall be in accordance with the general principles of Community law, including those referred to in Article 6(1) and (2) of the Treaty on European Union.

Recall the approach taken in the United States under the Electronic Communications Privacy Act for interception (Chapter 3). How does that compare with the approach in the EU Directive? What about Article 8 of the European Convention on Human Rights?

CRIMINAL PROCEEDINGS AGAINST BODIL LINDQVIST

European Court of Justice, 11/6/2003

---

1. By order of 23 February 2001, received at the Court on 1 March 2001, the Gota hovratt (Gota Court of Appeal) referred to the Court for a preliminary ruling under Article 234 EC seven questions concerning *inter alia* the interpretation of Directive 95/46/EC of the European Parliament and of the Council of 24 October 1995 on the protection of individuals with regard to the processing of personal data and on the free movement of such data.

2. Those questions were raised in criminal proceedings before that court against Mrs. Lindqvist, who was charged with breach of the Swedish legislation on the protection of personal data for publishing on her internet site personal data on a number of people working with her on a voluntary basis in a parish of the Swedish Protestant Church. . . .

12. In addition to her job as a maintenance worker, Mrs. Lindqvist worked as a catechist in the parish of Alseda (Sweden). She followed a data processing course on which she had *inter alia* to set up a home page on the internet. At the end of 1998, Mrs. Lindqvist set up internet pages at home on her personal computer in order to allow parishioners preparing for their confirmation to obtain information they might need. At her request, the administrator of the Swedish Church's website set up a link between those pages and that site.

13. The pages in question contained information about Mrs. Lindqvist and 18 colleagues in the parish, sometimes including their full names and in other cases only their first names. Mrs. Lindqvist also described, in a mildly humorous manner, the jobs held by her colleagues and their hobbies. In many cases family circumstances and telephone numbers and other matters were mentioned. She also stated that one colleague had injured her foot and was on half-time on medical grounds.

14. Mrs. Lindqvist had not informed her colleagues of the existence of those pages or obtained their consent, nor did she notify the Datainspektionen (supervisory authority for the protection of electronically transmitted data) of her activity. She removed the pages in question as soon as she became aware that they were not appreciated by some of her colleagues.

15. The public prosecutor brought a prosecution against Mrs. Lindqvist charging her with breach of the PUL [Personuppgiftslag, Swedish law on personal data] on the grounds that she had:

- processed personal data by automatic means without giving prior written notification to the Datainspektionen (Paragraph 36 of the PUL);
- processed sensitive personal data (injured foot and half-time on medical grounds) without authorisation (Paragraph 13 of the PUL);
- transferred processed personal data to a third country without authorisation (Paragraph 33 of the PUL).

16. Mrs. Lindqvist accepted the facts but disputed that she was guilty of an offence. Mrs. Lindqvist was fined by the Eksjo tingsratt (District Court) (Sweden) and appealed against that sentence to the referring court.

17. The amount of the fine was SEK 4000,[29] which was arrived at by multiplying the sum of SEK 100, representing Mrs. Lindqvist's financial position, by a factor of 40, reflecting the severity of the offence. Mrs. Lindqvist was also sentenced to pay SEK 300[30] to a Swedish fund to assist victims of crimes. . . .

19. . . . [T]he referring court asks whether the act of referring, on an internet page, to various persons and identifying them by name or by other means, for instance by giving their telephone number or information regarding their working conditions and hobbies, constitutes the processing of personal data wholly or partly by automatic means within the meaning of Article 3(1) of Directive 95/46. . . .

24. The term personal data used in Article 3(1) of Directive 95/46 covers, according to the definition in Article 2(a) thereof, any information relating to an identified or identifiable natural person. The term undoubtedly covers the name of a person in conjunction with his telephone coordinates or information about his working conditions or hobbies.

25. According to the definition in Article 2(b) of Directive 95/46, the term processing of such data used in Article 3(1) covers any operation or set of operations which is performed upon personal data, whether or not by automatic means. That provision gives several examples of such operations, including disclosure by transmission, dissemination or otherwise making data available. It follows that the operation of loading personal data on an internet page must be considered to be such processing.

27. . . . [T]he act of referring, on an internet page, to various persons and identifying them by name or by other means, for instance by giving their telephone number or information regarding their working conditions and hobbies, constitutes the processing of personal data wholly or partly by automatic means within the meaning of Article 3(1) of Directive 95/46. . . .

[The court concludes that neither the exception for the processing of personal data or for charitable and religious organizations in Article 3(2) apply in this case. Hence, the court affirmed the convictions for illegal processing of information and illegal disclosure of health information.]

37. Article 3(2) of Directive 95/46 provides for two exceptions to its scope.

38. The first exception concerns the processing of personal data in the course of an activity which falls outside the scope of Community law, such as those provided for by Titles V and VI of the Treaty on European Union, and in any case processing operations concerning public security, defence, State security (including the economic well-being of the State when the processing operation relates to State security matters) and the activities of the State in areas of criminal law.

39. As the activities of Mrs Lindqvist which are at issue in the main proceedings are essentially not economic but charitable and religious, it is necessary to consider whether they constitute the processing of personal data in the course of an activity which falls outside the scope of Community law within the meaning of the first indent of Article 3(2) of Directive 95/46. . . .

---

[29] [Editor's Note — This sum is approximately $670.]

[30] [Editor's Note — This sum is approximately $50.]

43. The activities mentioned by way of example in the first indent of Article 3(2) of Directive 95/46 (in other words, the activities provided for by Titles V and VI of the Treaty on European Union and processing operations concerning public security, defence, State security and activities in areas of criminal law) are, in any event, activities of the State or of State authorities and unrelated to the fields of activity of individuals.

44. It must therefore be considered that the activities mentioned by way of example in the first indent of Article 3(2) of Directive 95/46 are intended to define the scope of the exception provided for there, with the result that that exception applies only to the activities which are expressly listed there or which can be classified in the same category (*ejusdem generis*).

45. Charitable or religious activities such as those carried out by Mrs Lindqvist cannot be considered equivalent to the activities listed in the first indent of Article 3(2) of Directive 95/46 and are thus not covered by that exception.

46. As regards the exception provided for in the second indent of Article 3(2) of Directive 95/46, the 12th recital in the preamble to that directive, which concerns that exception, cites, as examples of the processing of data carried out by a natural person in the exercise of activities which are exclusively personal or domestic, correspondence and the holding of records of addresses.

47. That exception must therefore be interpreted as relating only to activities which are carried out in the course of private or family life of individuals, which is clearly not the case with the processing of personal data consisting in publication on the internet so that those data are made accessible to an indefinite number of people.

48. The answer to the third question must therefore be that processing of personal data such as that described in the reply to the first question is not covered by any of the exceptions in Article 3(2) of Directive 95/46.

49. By its fourth question, the referring court seeks to know whether reference to the fact that an individual has injured her foot and is on half-time on medical grounds constitutes personal data concerning health within the meaning of Article 8(1) of Directive 95/46.

50. In the light of the purpose of the directive, the expression data concerning health used in Article 8(1) thereof must be given a wide interpretation so as to include information concerning all aspects, both physical and mental, of the health of an individual.

51. The answer to the fourth question must therefore be that reference to the fact that an individual has injured her foot and is on half-time on medical grounds constitutes personal data concerning health within the meaning of Article 8(1) of Directive 95/46.

65. For its part, Article 25 of Directive 95/46 imposes a series of obligations on Member States and on the Commission for the purposes of monitoring transfers of personal data to third countries in the light of the level of protection afforded to such data in each of those countries. . . .

69. If Article 25 of Directive 95/46 were interpreted to mean that there is transfer [of data] to a third country every time that personal data are loaded onto an internet page, that transfer would necessarily be a transfer to all the third countries where there are the technical means needed to access the internet. The

special regime provided for by Chapter IV of the directive would thus necessarily become a regime of general application, as regards operations on the internet. Thus, if the Commission found, pursuant to Article 25(4) of Directive 95/46, that even one third country did not ensure adequate protection, the Member States would be obliged to prevent any personal data being placed on the internet.

70. Accordingly, it must be concluded that Article 25 of Directive 95/46 is to be interpreted as meaning that operations such as those carried out by Mrs. Lindqvist do not as such constitute a transfer [of data] to a third country. It is thus unnecessary to investigate whether an individual from a third country has accessed the internet page concerned or whether the server of that hosting service is physically in a third country. . . .

[The referring court had also asked whether the provisions of Directive 95/46 conflicted with the general principles of freedom of expression or other freedoms and rights, protected by Article 10 of the ECHR and other EU law. The *Lindqvist* court found that the Directive did not conflict with general principles of freedom of expression or other freedoms and rights, which are applicable within the European Union and enshrined inter alia in Article 10 of the ECHR. But the court also found that "national authorities and courts responsible for applying the national legislation implementing Directive 95/46" would have an important responsibility in ensuring "a fair balance between the rights and interests in question, including the fundamental rights protected by the Community legal order."]

91. By its seventh question, the referring court essentially seeks to know whether it is permissible for the Member States to provide for greater protection for personal data or a wider scope than are required under Directive 95/46.

95. Directive 95/46 is intended, as appears from the eighth recital in the preamble thereto, to ensure that the level of protection of the rights and freedoms of individuals with regard to the processing of personal data is equivalent in all Member States. The tenth recital adds that the approximation of the national laws applicable in this area must not result in any lessening of the protection they afford but must, on the contrary, seek to ensure a high level of protection in the Community.

96. The harmonisation of those national laws is therefore not limited to minimal harmonisation but amounts to harmonisation which is generally complete. It is upon that view that Directive 95/46 is intended to ensure free movement of personal data while guaranteeing a high level of protection for the rights and interests of the individuals to whom such data relate.

97. It is true that Directive 95/46 allows the Member States a margin for manoeuvre in certain areas and authorises them to maintain or introduce particular rules for specific situations as a large number of its provisions demonstrate. However, such possibilities must be made use of in the manner provided for by Directive 95/46 and in accordance with its objective of maintaining a balance between the free movement of personal data and the protection of private life.

98. On the other hand, nothing prevents a Member State from extending the scope of the national legislation implementing the provisions of Directive 95/46 to areas not included within the scope thereof, provided that no other provision of Community law precludes it.

99. In the light of those considerations, the answer to the seventh question must be that measures taken by the Member States to ensure the protection of personal data must be consistent both with the provisions of Directive 95/46 and with its objective of maintaining a balance between freedom of movement of personal data and the protection of private life. However, nothing prevents a Member State from extending the scope of the national legislation implementing the provisions of Directive 95/46 to areas not included in the scope thereof provided that no other provision of Community law precludes it.

THE COURT, in answer to the questions referred to it by the Gota hovratt by order of 23 February 2001, hereby rules:

1. The act of referring, on an internet page, to various persons and identifying them by name or by other means, for instance by giving their telephone number or information regarding their working conditions and hobbies, constitutes the processing of personal data. . . .

4. There is no transfer [of data] to a third country within the meaning of Article 25 of Directive 95/46 where an individual in a Member State loads personal data onto an internet page which is stored on an internet site on which the page can be consulted and which is hosted by a natural or legal person who is established in that State or in another Member State, thereby making those data accessible to anyone who connects to the internet, including people in a third country. . . .

NOTES & QUESTIONS

1. ***A Sweeping Decision.*** The *Lindqvist* court found that Mrs. Lindqvist's posting of her website on the Internet constituted the processing of data. It found that she had illegally processed personal information as well as health information. It read the Directive's provisions about personal data about health to extend even to a mention of a foot injury. Without the data subject's permission, such personal information could not be subject to processing. The court also found that Member States could enact data privacy protections beyond the areas specified within the Directive. It stated that "nothing prevents a Member State from extending the scope of the national legislation implementing the provisions of Directive 95/46 to areas not included within the scope thereof, provided that no other provision of Community law precludes it."

   In a negative reaction to this case, a student note in the United States argues: "The possibility of having each and every citizen claim that his or her privacy has been compromised by a use of information about him or her somewhere on the Internet is a monumental bureaucratic disaster, one which is difficult to imagine was the imagined intent of the drafters of the European Union's Data Protection Directive."[31] Do you agree that the decision is "draconian and abusive"?

[31] Flora J. Garcia, *Bodil Lindqvist: A Swedish Churchgoer's Violation of the European Union's Data Protection Directive Should Be a Warning to U.S. Legislators*, 15 Fordham Intell. Prop. Media & Ent. L.J. 1206, 1232 (2005).

2. ***Lindqvist in the United States?*** Imagine that Mrs. Lindqvist worked at the Lutheran Church in Lake Wobegon, Minnesota, and created a website similar to the one at stake in the above decision. Imagine you are an attorney and that an offended member of the church visits your office and seeks legal action against the Minnesota Mrs. Lindqvist. What are the available legal claims under U.S. law? Are they likely to be successful?
3. ***No Transfer of Information.*** The *Lindqvist* court also decided that she had not transferred the information on the site to a third country. Why did it reach this conclusion? Under what circumstances might a European court decide, to the contrary, that a website was transferring information to a third country? Would this decision have been decided differently if technology existed that could restrict access to a website based on the location of the viewer?

(b) Article 8 and Harmonization

Article 8. Article 8 of the Data Directive provides for a special treatment for data that are particularly sensitive for data subjects. It restricts the processing of certain categories of personal data — "personal data revealing racial or ethnic origin, political opinions, religious or philosophical beliefs, trade-union membership, and the processing of data concerning health or sex life."

There are a number of exceptions. Such data may be processed if (a) the data subject explicitly consents; (b) "processing is necessary for the purposes of carrying out the obligations and specific rights of the controller in the field of employment law in so far as it is authorized by national law providing for adequate safeguards"; (c) processing is necessary to safeguard the data subject's "vital interests"; (d) subject to certain limits, by an organization with a political, philosophical, religious, or trade union aim; (e) processing of data made public by the data subject or necessary to exercise or defend legal claims. Further, the Article 8 restrictions do not apply when the data are necessary "for the purposes of preventive medicine, medical diagnosis, the provision of care or treatment or the management of health-care services" and where the processing is by a health professional subject by national laws to maintain patient confidentiality.

Member States may, for reasons of "substantial public interest," make further exceptions to the ones included in Article 8. The Commission must be notified of all derogations.

Think about the data that are considered "sensitive" by the Directive. Do you consider this information to be sensitive? Would you have added more? Why are financial data not in the list? How does the EU Data Directive regulate children's personal data?

Harmonization and Article 8. Consider the following argument by Peter Swire:

> Although the Directive has led to significant convergence in data protection laws, harmonization is far from complete. Actual enforcement does not take place under the Directive itself. Instead, national laws are being enacted to implement the Directive. These laws will differ in both large and small ways from each other. The level of enforcement effort will also undoubtedly vary by

country, due both to differences in views about proper policy and differing levels of enforcement resources and experience. . . .

(c) Supervisory Authority and Individual Remedies

Article 28. Article 28 of the Directive requires that each Member State shall establish one or more public authorities to monitor the application of the laws and regulations adopted pursuant to the Directive. It states, "These authorities shall act with complete independence in exercising the functions entrusted to them." Article 28(1). Member States are to consult with the supervisory authorities when creating the rules and regulations for the protection of individuals' rights with regard to data processing. Article 28(2). The supervisory authority is to have the following powers: (1) investigative powers; (2) "effective powers of intervention" — the ability to express opinions before the carrying out of processing operations, the ability to order the blocking, erasure, or destruction of data, the ability to warn or admonish the controller, and the ability to refer the matter to national parliaments or other political institutions; and (3) powers to engage in legal proceedings when rules and regulations adopted pursuant to the Directive are violated. If an objection is raised to the supervisory authority's decision, it may be appealed in the courts. Article 28(3).

The supervisory authority hears individual claims concerning the protection of her rights regarding the processing of personal data. Article 28(4). Further, the supervisory authority hears "claims for checks on the lawfulness of data processing lodged by any person when the national provisions adopted pursuant to Article 13 of this Directive apply." Article 28(4). The supervisory authority is to issue public reports on its activities at regular intervals. Article 28(5).

Members and staff of the supervisory authority are subject to a "duty of processional secrecy with regard to confidential information to which they have access." This duty applies even after their employment has terminated. Article 28(7).

Obligation to Notify the Supervisory Authority. Under Article 18, the "controller" (the entity determining the purposes of the data processing) must notify the "supervisory authority" before carrying out any partly or wholly automatic processing operation. If certain conditions are met, Member States may enact rules exempting controllers from notifying the supervisory authority (or simplifying the notification). Such conditions include (1) where processing operations are unlikely to "affect adversely the rights and freedoms of data subjects" and Member States have specified detailed information concerning the processing; and (2) where the controller appoints a "personal data protection official" who is responsible for "ensuring in an independent manner the internal application of the national provisions taken pursuant to this Directive" and "for keeping the register of processing operations carried out by the controller, containing the items of information referred to in Article 21(2)."

Contents of the Notification to the Supervisory Authority. Article 19 describes the contents of the notification to the supervisory authority as required by Article 18. The notification must include

(a) the name and address of the controller and of his representative, if any;
(b) the purpose or purposes of the processing;
(c) a description of the category or categories of data subject and of the data or categories of data relating to them;
(d) the recipients or categories of recipient to whom the data might be disclosed;
(e) proposed transfers of data to third countries;
(f) a general description allowing a preliminary assessment to be made of the appropriateness of the measures taken pursuant to Article 17 to ensure security of processing.

Individual Remedies. Pursuant to Article 22, "Member States shall provide for the right of every person to a judicial remedy for any breach of the rights guaranteed him by the national law applicable to the processing in question."

Further, Article 23 requires that Member States "shall provide that any person who has suffered damage as a result of an unlawful processing operation or of any act incompatible with the national provisions adopted pursuant to this Directive is entitled to receive compensation from the controller for the damage suffered."

A U.S. Data Protection Authority? Would you support the creation of a federal data protection authority in the United States? What are the benefits and drawbacks of such an authority? What alternatives to a privacy agency exist and how would you measure their effectiveness?[32]

The FTC as a Data Protection Authority? Steven Hetcher argues that the Federal Trade Commission is evolving into a federal data protection authority:

> In the short history of the Internet, there has been a major shift — a norm cascade — toward norms that are more respectful of privacy. The transition has been from a Wild West world in which Web sites acted with near impunity in collecting whatever personal data they could, to a world in which a significant percentage of Web sites are explicitly addressing privacy concerns. . . .
>
> Reacting to this sub-optimal social situation, the FTC promoted the fair information practice principles. The FTC then used threats to induce Web sites to adopt these principles. The FTC created a large-scale collective action problem for the Web site industry, where none had existed before. It did this by creating a collective good that the industry would be interested to promote, the avoidance of congressional legislation. The agency threatened to push for legislation unless the industry demonstrated greater respect for privacy. Some of the large sites in turn threatened to withhold advertising from smaller sites with whom they do business, if these sites were not more respectful of consumer privacy. The result of this network of threats by the FTC and large Web sites is a new situation in which there is no longer a uniform norm of disrespect for privacy. . . . On the whole, this represents a significant increase in the degree to which Web sites are subject to governmental regulation with regard to their

---

[32] For the background on the proposal to create a federal privacy agency in the United States, see Marc Rotenberg, *In Support of a Data Protection Board in the United States,* 8 Gov't Info. Q. 79-94 (Spring 1991).

data-collection practices. Accordingly, the FTC is fairly viewed as a nascent, de facto federal privacy commission.[33]

Recall the cases you read in Chapter 7 involving the FTC's enforcement efforts of privacy policies. Has the FTC performed well in its current role? How would you compare the FTC's authority to investigate unfair or deceptive trade practices with authority granted by the EU Data Protection Directive to enforce its substantive provisions?

One example of the limitations in the FTC's jurisdiction is the issue of workplace privacy. Jack Karns argues that a special agency should be created to address issues involving privacy in the workplace. Karns argues: "With the evolution of privacy rights under common law concepts, it has been a difficult transition to bring within the reach of traditional legal theories modern methods of conducting business transactions and handling personal matters." Karns further contends that the FTC is not the appropriate agency to handle these problems:

> As for current agencies, such as the Federal Trade Commission ("FTC"), this body is charged with regulating unfair and deceptive trade, and this creates the question as to whether privacy protection falls within this agency's enabling legislation. The business community, in general, supports the delegation of work related privacy issues to the FTC given its well established involvement in business regulation. But is this position self serving, and would it really protect the worker adequately? . . . [T]he FTC is not well situated to take on this aspect of the regulatory task and that a comparable consumer and worker oriented agency with separate and distinct enabling legislation is needed to protect fundamental constitutional rights in this area.[34]

Effective Privacy Regimes. A complicated interplay exists between rights of private enforcement and authority granted to public agencies. It is possible to construct privacy regimes that make private enforcement impractical and agency oversight ineffective. What lessons might be learned from the experience in the United States, Europe, and elsewhere about the development of effective privacy regimes?

Privacy Commissioners in Other Countries. In addition to EU countries, a number of other countries have privacy commissioners. For example, similar to the United States, Canada has a Privacy Act to regulate personal information in government records. The Canadian Privacy Act adopts many of the Fair Information Practices. In contrast to the U.S. Privacy Act, the Canadian version is supervised by a privacy commissioner, who can investigate complaints and initiate judicial review. Canada also has privacy commissioners for each of its provinces. New Zealand's Privacy Act establishes a privacy commissioner with independent oversight powers. Switzerland's 1992 Federal Act of Data

---

[33] Steven Hetcher, *The De Facto Federal Privacy Commission,* 19 J. Marshall J. Computer & Info. L. 109, 130-31 (2000).

[34] Jack Karns, *Protecting Individual Online Privacy Rights: Making the Case for a Separately Dedicated, Independent Regulatory Agency*, 19 J. Marshall J. Computer & Info. L. 93, 95-96 (2000).

Protection establishes a Federal Data Protection Commission. Hong Kong's Personal Data (Privacy) Ordinance, which became effective in 1996, created the Office of the Privacy Commissioner. The Privacy Commissioner has significant powers; the Hong Kong Commissioner can initiate investigations, require the users of personal data to publicize how their data is processed, and issue codes to facilitate compliance with the Ordinance.[35]

C. PRIVACY PROTECTION IN NORTH AMERICA

1. CANADA

In 2001, a sweeping new privacy law became effective in Canada. This statute, the Personal Information Protection and Electronic Documents Act (PIPEDA), S.C. 2000 ch. 5 (Can.), governs all entities that collect personal information on Canadians.

PIPEDA extends to all "personal information" used in connection with any commercial activity. *Id.* § 4(1)–(2). The Act applies to all personal information collected prior to the enactment of PIPEDA, and it does not exempt non-Canadian entities. PIPEDA is based on the OECD Privacy Guidelines and, even more directly, the Canadian Standards Association (CSA) Model Code for the Protection of Personal Information, which articulate ten privacy principles.

PIPEDA requires that the individual must consent prior the collection, use, or disclosure of personal data. *See id.* sched. 1, § 4.3. It also incorporates the OECD purpose specification principle, security safeguard principle, openness principle, accountability principle, and data quality principle, among others. As Mark Hayes has stated, "PIPEDA is unusual and perhaps unique in its structure."[36] Its core is found in its Schedule 1, which reprints most of the CSA Model Code. Hayes notes, "This statutory structure is even more unusual when one considers that the CSA Code was meant to be a flexible guide for business behaviour, not a general regulatory code." As a result, PIPEDA's statutory text sometimes contradicts its Schedule 1, which creates an interpretive challenge for courts and the Privacy Commissioner. More follows about the role of the Privacy Commissioner below.

On December 20, 2001, the EU Commission issued a Decision that PIPEDA provides an adequate level of protection:

> The Canadian Act covers all the basic principles necessary for an adequate level of protection for natural persons, even if exceptions and limitations are also provided for in order to safeguard important public interests and to recognize certain information which exists in the public domain. The application of these standards is guaranteed by judicial remedy and by independent supervision carried out by the authorities, such as the Federal Privacy Commissioner invested with powers of investigation and intervention. Furthermore, the

---

[35] For more information about Hong Kong's privacy commissioner, see http://www.pco.org.hk.

[36] Mark S. Hayes, *Privacy Law in Canada* in Proskauer on Privacy (Christopher Wolf, ed. 2006).

> provisions of Canadian law regarding civil liability apply in the event of unlawful processing which is prejudicial to the persons concerned.[37]

PIPEDA may have substantial effects on transborder flows between Canada and the United States. According to some commentators:

> Although Canada's privacy laws certainly apply to covered organizations located in Canada, a more difficult question is raised when trying to determine their effects on companies located solely within the United States that happen to collect, use, or disclose the personal information of Canadians. . . . PIPEDA will certainly affect American companies. This is because of PIPEDA's secondary data transfer requirements which force Canadian companies to incorporate the Act's privacy requirements into all contracts which contemplate the transfer of Canadians' personal information to U.S. or other foreign companies. But to date Canadian law provides mixed guidance on how it will address the extraterritorial effects of the Act.[38]

Under PIPEDA, the Privacy Commissioner of Canada has the power to investigate citizen complaints and to conduct audits. The Commissioner can also publish information about personal information processing in the public and private sectors, and promote awareness and understanding of privacy issues. It also has an important ombudsman role in resolving complaints. Individuals are given a right under PIPEDA § 11(1) to file a complaint with the Privacy Commissioner. The Privacy Commissioner can also initiate a complaint, summon witnesses, and compel production of evidence. The Commissioner lacks power to make binding orders or impose penalties for violations of PIPEDA. The results of a complaint investigation by the Commissioner can be appealed to federal court, which under PIPEDA does have the power to order an organization to correct its practices, and to award damages.

ENGLANDER V. TELUS COMMUNICATIONS, INC.

2004 FCA 387 (Federal Court of Appeal, 2004)

[Matthew Englander was a residential subscriber for telephone service from Telus Communications, a telecommunications corporation. In order to have his phone unlisted, Telus Communications charged him an initial set-up fee as well as a monthly fee. Englander objected and charged a violation of PIPEDA, because he had not provided consent for the collection, use, and disclosure of his customer personal information and because he was to be charged him if he wished to have a nonpublished number. The Federal Court of Appeal found that Telus Corporation infringed § 5 of Act in not informing its first-time customers,

---

[37] Commission Decision of 20 December 2001 Pursuant to Directive 95/46/EC of the European Parliament and of the Council on the Adequate Protection of Personal Data Provided by the Canadian Personal Information Protection and Electronic Documents Act, C(2001) 4539, available at http://www.europa.eu.int/comm/internal_market/en/dataprot/adequacy/index.htm.

[38] Juliana M. Spaeth, Mark J. Plotkin, & Sandra C. Sheets, *Privacy, Eh!: The Impact of Canada's Personal Information Protection and Electronic Documents Act on Transnational Business*, 4 Vand. J. Ent. L. & Prac. 29 (2002). For a detailed analysis of PIPEDA, see Stephanie Perrin, Heather H. Black, David H. Flaherty & T. Murray Rankin, *The Personal Information Protection and Electronic Documents Act: An Annotated Guide* (2001).

at time of enrollment, of the primary and secondary purposes for which personal information was collected and in not informing them at that time of availability of nonpublished number service. It found the tariff, or charge, to have an unlisted phone number to be permissible.]

DÉCARY J. . . .

22. The Non-Published Number Service (NPNS) is a telecommunications service regulated by the CRTC [Canadian Radio-television and Telecommunications Commission]. The tariff applicable in British Columbia is CRTC 1005, General Tariff Item 145. The monthly service charge for NPNS is $2.00 and there is a one-time set up fee of $9.50 (A.B. vol. 1, pp. 87, 88). . . .

39. The PIPED Act is a compromise both as to substance and as to form.

40. With respect to the compromise on substance, Michael Geist, in *Internet Law in Canada*, 3rd ed., Captus Press, 2002, at 303, puts it as follows:

> The subject of intense negotiation between business, consumer groups, and government in the early and mid-1990s, the Code represents a compromise between the need to protect individual privacy and the desire of organizations to collect personal data for marketing and other commercial purposes. This compromise remains intact in the new law, and is reflected in its purpose clause, which explicitly refers to the balance between the competing interests of individuals and business. (An early version of the bill referred only to personal privacy.)

41. Five of the ten principles set out in Schedule 1 [of PIPEDA] (accountability, accuracy, safeguards, individual access and challenging compliance) impose on organizations obligations pertaining essentially to their internal handling of personal information once it is in their possession. One principle (openness) relates to the public relations policy of organizations with respect to their management of personal information. The four other principles (identifying purposes, consent, limiting collection and limiting use, disclosure and retention) are of a more substantial nature, in the sense that they purport to ensure that individuals do not reveal their personal information unless they know for what specific purposes it will be used or disclosed, unless these purposes are legitimate and unless they consent to the use and disclosure that is intended to be made of that information. These are the four principles that are in play in these proceedings.

42. It appears from a reading of principles 4.2 (identifying purposes), 4.3 (consent), 4.4 (limiting collection) and 4.5 (limiting use, disclosure and retention), that the focus of Schedule 1 is not so much on the prevention of collection, use and disclosure of personal information, which are almost taken for granted, as on the purposes for which the information is collected, used or disclosed. These purposes must be appropriate and legitimate, and reasonable efforts must have been made to ensure that the individual is advised of and understands them. Once these purposes are identified and once informed consent is expressly or implicitly obtained, the individual's information can be collected, used or disclosed. . . .

45. [With many provisions of PIPEDA, the] Court is sometimes left with little, if any guidance at all. Clause 4.3, for example, requires knowledge and

consent "except where inappropriate." Clause 4.3.4 sets up a standard of "sensitivity of the information," only to add that "any information can be sensitive, depending on the context." Clause 4.3.5 then goes on to say that "[i]n obtaining consent, the reasonable expectations of the individual are also relevant."

46. All of this to say that, even though Part 1 and Schedule 1 of the Act purport to protect the right of privacy, they also purport to facilitate the collection, use and disclosure of personal information by the private sector. In interpreting this legislation, the Court must strike a balance between two competing interests. Furthermore, because of its non-legal drafting, Schedule 1 does not lend itself to typical rigorous construction, In these circumstances, flexibility, common sense and pragmatism will best guide the Court. . . .

56. Principles 2, "Identifying Purposes," and 3, "Consent," are at the heart of this appeal. Principle 3, I hasten to add, despite its name, "requires 'knowledge and consent'" (clause 4.3.2). In other words, Principle 3 requires informed consent.

57. Principle 2 requires an organization to identify the purposes for which personal information is collected *at or before* the time the information is collected (clause 4.2). It also requires the organization to specify the identified purposes to the individual *at or before* the time of the collection (clause 4.2.3) and, where personal information that has been collected is to be used for a purpose not previously identified, the new purpose shall be identified prior to use and the consent of the individual is required *before* information can be used for that purpose (clause 4.2.4) (my emphasis). . . .

59. Principle 3 requires "the knowledge and consent of the individual . . . for the collection, use or disclosure of personal information, except where inappropriate." Inappropriateness is not defined and I suspect that it may refer at least to section 7 of the Act which authorizes collection without knowledge or consent in some circumstances. . . .

60. Organizations shall make a *reasonable effort to ensure* that the individual is advised of the purposes for which the information *will* be used (clause 4.3.2). Consent, and therefore knowledge, are required *for* the collection of personal information and the *subsequent* use or disclosure of this information and, typically, an organization will seek consent *for* the use or disclosure of the information *at the time of collection* (clause 4.3.1). The *form of the consent sought* by the organization, and the *way* in which the organization seeks consent, may vary, depending upon the circumstances and the type of information (clauses 4.3.4 and 4.3.6). In obtaining consent, the reasonable expectations of the individual are relevant (clause 4.3.5). Implied consent would generally be appropriate when the information is less sensitive (clause 4.3.6). Examples of *ways* in which individuals can give consent are: on application forms, on checkoff boxes, over the telephone, at the time of use, all of which imply that the consent is given at the time of collection and before use (my emphasis).

61. Timing, therefore, as was the case with respect to Principle 2, is also of the essence with respect to Principle 3. In most instances, the requirement of knowledge and consent has to be met by the organization at the time of collection and prior to use. . . .

63. Telus' practice with respect to seeking the consent of its first-time customers was summarized as follows by the judge:

> [44] In his affidavit, Jim Brooks, *Telus* Vice-President, Business Transformation, informs us of the procedure that is followed when a customer subscribes to a new telephone line. *Telus* customer service representatives are instructed to indicate to customers that the telephone line includes a listing in *Telus* directories; customers are asked how they would like their personal information to appear in the directories; and the representatives discuss privacy concerns and listing options with the customer if the customer expresses an interest in not being published. New customers also receive a welcoming letter with an accompanying brochure entitled "Our Privacy Commitment to You". The brochure sets out, *inter alia*, the purposes for which *Telus* collects, uses, and discloses customers' personal information. It also advises customers of their right to be de-listed.
>
> [45] The White Pages specifically detail how *Telus* uses personal information and the various privacy oriented service options provided by *Telus*. . . .
>
> [46] Furthermore, *Telus* maintains a toll free number which is dedicated to providing information to customers who wish to discuss privacy issues. *Telus* also maintains a website where customers can obtain information about its privacy practices. In addition to those services, *Telus* employs a full-time Privacy Officer who is accountable for privacy policies and practices.

65. I find, in the circumstances, that proper consent was not, and could not have been given, by Telus first-time customers with respect to the use by Telus of the personal information in its Internet directory assistance service, in its Directory File Service and Basic Listing Interchange File Service and its CD-ROM service [which provided telephone listing information and was sold as a retail product]. These services were not identified at the time of enrolment and there is no evidence that they were so connected with the primary purposes of telephone directories that a new customer would reasonably consider them as appropriate. There is no evidence that TELUS made any "effort," let alone a "reasonable" one, within the meaning of clause 4.3.2, to ensure that its first-time customers are advised of the secondary purposes at the time of collection. . . .

67. . . . A consent is not informed if the person allegedly giving it is not aware at the time of giving it that he or she had the possibility to opt out. First-time customers have the right to know before their personal information becomes "publicly available" within the meaning of section 7 of the Act, with all the consequences that might flow from such publicity, that they can exercise their right to privacy and choose not to be listed. This, it seems to me, is a fair compromise between one's right to privacy and the industry's needs. . . .

81. The appellant does not argue that fees can never be charged for the exercise of one's statutory right. He argues, rather, that a fee can only be charged if a statute provides for it.

82. I take issue with the appellant's proposition that no statute or regulations allow imposition of a fee in the case at bar. Quite to the contrary, it appears from the clear wording of the *Telecommunications Act* that, when approving rates and services, the CRTC must take into consideration the objectives of the Canadian telecommunications policy, including that of contributing to the protection of the privacy of persons. Services may therefore be provided for the protection of

privacy and rates may be imposed for the provision of those services. There could not be clearer indications that Parliament contemplated the imposition of fees for providing privacy services. . . .

85. [T]he CRTC, in its Report on Directory Subscriber Listings and on Unlisted Number Service, expressed the view that "it is increasingly important that unlisted number service not be priced beyond the financial reach of subscribers." A rate that does not exceed $2 per month for residence subscribers was approved. . . .

89. I would find that TELUS has infringed section 5 of the *Personal Information Protection and Electronic Documents Act* in not informing its first-time customers, at the time of enrollment, of the primary and secondary purposes for which their personal information was collected and in not informing them at that time of the availability of the Non-Published Number Service. . . .

NOTES & QUESTIONS

1. ***Opt in vs. Opt out.*** After *Englander*, how are Canadian telecommunication companies required to obtain consent for use of customer information? Would you term this system opt out or opt in?
2. ***The PIPEDA Approach to Privacy Protection.*** PIPEDA seeks to regulate privacy through fairly broad principles, many of which are very flexible in order to establish a balance between privacy and business interests. Is PIPEDA too vague and broad? What are the pros and cons of a generalized principle-based approach to protecting privacy as opposed to a more detailed set of specific regulations? How does PIPEDA compare with the U.S. approach to regulating the private sector? Does it seem closer to the U.S. or European approach to information privacy?

2. MEXICO

The constitution of Mexico has a bill of rights that guarantees a broad series of fundamental rights and freedoms. These constitutional guarantees include a right to due process, and a right not to be disturbed in one's person, domicile, or documents without written order by competent authority. Since 1996, the Mexican constitution contains an explicit guarantee of the privacy of private communications.

Mexico also has a law that regulates credit bureaus and a Freedom of Information Act. It lacks any general information privacy law; legislators have, however, introduced data privacy bills in the last few years. According to one account: "Mexican lawyers regularly tell anyone who asks that their law imposes no significant limits on businesses processing personal data."[39] On a more positive note, however, Jorge Vargas argues that constitutional rights in Mexico have great potential to be "used to provide a more modern protection in that emerging area known as privacy rights."[40]

---

[39] Donald C. Dowling Jr. & Jeremy M. Mittman, *International Privacy Law*, in Proskauer on Privacy (Christopher Wolf, ed. 2006).

[40] Jorge A. Vargas, *Privacy Rights Under Mexican Law*, 27 Hous. J. Int'l L. 73, 136 (2004).

D. PRIVACY PROTECTION IN SOUTH AMERICA

1. ARGENTINA

In 2000, Argentina became the first country in South America to adopt a comprehensive data protection law. The Law for the Protection of Personal Data is based on the European Union Data Protection Directive, several provisions of the Argentine constitution, and earlier national laws. It contains provisions relating to general data protection principles, the rights of data subjects, the obligations of data controllers and data users, the supervisory authority, sanctions, and rules of procedure in seeking "habeas data" as a judicial remedy. Habeas data is a special, simplified, and quick judicial remedy for the protection of personal data. Enshrined in the constitution, the habeas rule permits any person to know the content and purpose of the data pertaining to her in public records, or in certain private records. The Argentina data protection law also prohibits international transfers of personal information to countries without adequate protection.

The Commission of the European Community decided in 2003 that Argentina provided an adequate level of protection for personal data.[41] It thereby meets the standards of the EU Data Protection Directive. The adequacy finding means that all transborder data flows between Argentina and the European Union are presumptively in compliance with the EU Data Directive. Argentina is the first and thus far only country in Latin American to obtain a finding of adequacy.

2. BRAZIL

The constitution of Brazil explicitly protects privacy in its Article 5. Like Mexico, it also contains a constitutional right to habeas data. Two experts in international privacy law consider it "more watered-down" than Argentina's similar right.[42] Also like Mexico, Brazil lacks a general information privacy statute. It does, however, contain some sectoral privacy laws. These include a consumer protection law from 1990 that sets out regulations for personal data recordkeeping and a federal law from 1996 that regulates wiretapping.

E. PRIVACY PROTECTION IN AFRICA AND THE MIDDLE EAST

1. AFRICA

In its Constitution, Zimbabwe provides a right to be free from "arbitrary search or entry." This right is subject to significant exceptions when a law allows a search in the interests of public safety and public order, among other grounds, and when there are reasonable grounds for investigating a criminal offense. In

---

41 Commission Decision of 30/06/2003, Brussels C(2003) 1731 final.

42 Dowling & Mittman, *International Privacy Law*, at 14-43.

2002, Zimbabwe adopted a controversial Access to Information and Protection of Privacy Act. This statute largely does not have to do with access to information or privacy. Rather, this statute severely limits the freedom of the press. It allocates regulatory powers over the media and journalists to a Media and Information Commission, and requires media outlets to obtain a certification of registration from this organization.

The 1996 Constitution of South Africa grants a right to privacy, which includes protections for the person, home, and communications. The South African's Constitutional Court's "interpretation of the right is a mixture of U.S. and European jurisprudence."[43] The court emphasizes both human dignity and the need to protect reasonable expectations of privacy.

2. THE MIDDLE EAST

The constitutions of several Arab countries mention privacy. For example, Article 10 of Jordan's constitution provides: "Dwelling houses shall be inviolable and shall not be entered except in the circumstances and in the manner prescribed by law." Saudi Arabia's constitution, Article 37, declares: "The home is sacrosanct and shall not be entered without the permission of the owner or be searched except in cases specified by statutes." Article 44 of Egypt's constitution protects the privacy of the home, and Article 45 contains a broader protection of privacy:

> The law shall protect the inviolability of the private life of citizens. Correspondence, wires, telephone calls an other means of communication shall have their own sanctity and secrecy and may not be confiscated or monitored except by a causal judicial warrant and for a definite period according to the provisions of the law.

In 2002, Dubai's Electronic Transactions and Commerce Law, No. 2/2002, restricted ISPs from disclosing customer data.

According to Jacqueline Klosek:

> Privacy rights were not very well developed in the Middle East even before September 11. Generally, the region is well known for being a territory in which the government exercises great level of control over the conduct, including, without limitation, the Internet-related activity of their users. Cultural issues may also play a role in the stagnant development of privacy rights in the region. Indeed, Arabic law has no equivalent to the English word "privacy" — some may say that the closest is the term *khususi* meaning "personal." According to one author, in the Arab world, the connotation of privacy does not relate to "personal" or "secret," as it does in other cultures. Rather, it concerns two specific spheres: women and the family. Another author goes even further, claiming: "There is no concept of privacy among Arabs. In translation, the Arabic world that comes closest to 'privacy' means loneliness!"[44]

[43] EPIC & Privacy International, *Privacy and Human Rights* 865 (2006).

[44] Jacqueline Klosek, *The War on Privacy* 62 (2007).

Israel provides stronger protections of privacy than many other Middle Eastern countries. It lacks a formal constitution, but its Basic Law, Article 7, provides for a right to privacy:

> (a) All persons have the right to privacy and to intimacy.
> (b) There shall be no entry into the private premises of a person who has not consented thereto.
> (c) No search shall be conducted on the private premises of a person, nor in the body or personal effects.
> (d) There shall be no violation of the confidentiality of conversation, or of the writings or records of a person.

F. PRIVACY PROTECTION IN ASIA-PACIFIC

1. THE APEC PRIVACY FRAMEWORK

Asia-Pacific Economic Cooperation (APEC) is a cooperative of economies located along the Pacific Ocean. It includes the United States, China, Japan, the Russian Federation, China, Australia, New Zealand, Peru, Indonesia, Mexico, Singapore, Thailand, and Vietnam. Ministers of these countries adopted a privacy framework, based on the OECD Privacy Guidelines, on November 24, 2004 at a meeting in Santiago, Chile. Then U.S. Secretary of State Colin Powell stated, "The APEC Privacy Framework will establish a consistent approach to privacy across APEC member economies, while also avoiding the creation of unnecessary barriers to information flows." The APEC privacy framework seeks to enable multinational businesses to implement uniform approaches to the use of personal data. It contains nine principles. These are: (1) preventing harm; (2) notice; (3) collection limitation; (4) use of personal information; (5) choice; (6) integrity; (7) security safeguards; (8) access and correction; and (9) accountability. *See* APEC, Privacy Framework (Nov. 2004).

APEC's Cross Border Privacy Rules Working Party, led by Australia, is now working on a system to implement the APEC Privacy Framework on an international basis. The Cross Border Privacy Rules (CBPR) will permit a business to fill out an application before engaging in an international data transfer to demonstrate that its privacy practices matched APEC privacy principles. The CBPR would permit resolving violations of CBPR's through government enforcement agencies as well as private bodies for achieving accountability.

2. AUSTRALIA

The primary protection of privacy in Australia is the Privacy Act of 1988, which establishes eleven Information Privacy Principles based on the OECD Privacy Guidelines. The 1988 statute only applied to the public sector. In 2000, the Privacy Amendment Act created ten new privacy principles that extend to private sector entities. These principles are known as the National Privacy Principles (NPPs).

The 2000 law also established a "co-regulatory" scheme. Companies can apply to the Privacy Commissioner to substitute their own privacy practice standards if they are an "overall equivalent" to the NPPs. It also exempts "small businesses" entirely from its privacy rules. A further exemption exists for employment records.

Following a request by the Attorney General, the Australian Law Reform Commission (ALRC) has reviewed the nation's privacy laws and made recommendations for their improvement. In its Discussion Paper 72, the ALRC made a number of important reform suggestions.[45] First, it called for an end for the exemption or small businesses. It flatly stated, "The ALRC has not heard any compelling reason to continue to exempt small businesses in Australia from the Privacy Act. No comparable jurisdiction exempts small businesses from privacy laws." Second, it proposed an end to the employee record exemption.

Third, it called for a strengthening of the power of the Australian Privacy Commissioner. In the ALRC's view, the Privacy Commissioner should be permitted to require an agency or organization "to prepare a privacy impact assessment for a new project or development that may have a significant impact on the handling of personal information." In addition to its existing power to audit government agencies, the ALRC proposed that the Privacy Commissioner be granted the power to audit private sector organization's for their compliance with privacy laws. Finally, and perhaps most importantly, the Privacy Commissioner is given the power "to request the development of a [privacy] code, and to develop and impose a code that applies to particular agencies and organizations." At present, organizations are free to develop privacy codes — or not.

3. JAPAN

The Japanese Diet enacted the Personal Data Protection Act in May 2003.[46] The law came into effect on April 1, 2005. According to an ordinance-cabinet order issued under the statute, the law covers all businesses with databases containing information on more than 5,000 individuals. It specifically excludes a number of entities, including broadcast and other reporting media, "individuals who are writers by trade," scholarly research, religious organizations, and political organizations.

The Japanese Personal Data Protection Act requires strong Fair Information Practices. Before collecting personal information, a business must articulate a "purpose of use." No business can process personal information beyond its stated purpose of use. A business that collects personal information must inform an individual of the planned purpose of use.

Businesses are forbidden from sharing personal information with any third party without the individual's consent unless pursuant to a law or ordinance, or necessary to protect human life, or subject to certain other exceptions.

---

[45] Australian Law Reform Commission, *Review of Australian Privacy Law: An Overview of Discussion Paper* 72 (2007).

[46] For an English translation of the law, see Japan's Personal Information Protection Act, 2003 Law No. 57, http://www.privacyexchange.org/japan/japanindex.html.

Subject to certain exceptions, an individual has a right to ask a business to disclose his stored personal information to him. An individual has a right to correct, supplement, or delete his stored personal information if it is incorrect. Certain government ministers, termed "competent ministers," are responsible for supervision and enforcement under the Act.

A special issue of the *Privacy and American Business* newsletter notes that the law allows the Japanese "a degree of control over their own information virtually unknown to American consumers." The newsletter also observed that the Personal Data Protection Act "does not appear to provide aggrieved individuals with any formal mechanism through which they may pursue a complaint against a business that may have breached the law." Instead, the law provides that businesses are to use "best efforts" to resolve any complaints regarding the handling of personal data. In addition, "[t]he decision to admonish a business that harms an individual is entirely within the discretion of the competent Minister."[47]

4. CHINA AND HONG KONG

The Chinese constitution has several protections for privacy, including a protection against defamation, against intrusions into the home, and against monitoring of correspondence. However, the Chinese government engages in extensive surveillance and searches of its citizens:

> China has had a long-standing policy — dating back to the 4th Century B.C. — of keeping close track of its citizens. . . .
>
> China's law states that the "freedom of privacy of correspondence of citizens are protected by law." Furthermore, warrants are required before law enforcement officials can search premises. However, this requirement is frequently ignored; moreover, the Public Security Bureau and prosecutors can issue search warrants on their own authority without judicial consent, review, or consideration.[48]

According to Lü Yao-Huai, Chinese law and culture have long eschewed privacy, but are gradually moving toward an increased recognition of its value:

> Though many common Chinese still link privacy with *Yinsi* (shameful secret) — to a large extent, at least in the relevant discussion of many contemporary Chinese scholars, the concept of privacy is no longer limited to the earlier, narrower sense of [*Yinsi*], but now includes all personal information (i.e., whether shameful or not) that people do not want others to know. Such a concept is gradually exerting influence on the average Chinese. This expanding scope of "privacy" is apparently based, at least in part, on the expansion of physical personal space in contemporary China. . . .
>
> [S]ince China entered the World Trade Organization, the problem of data privacy has caused more extensive concern. On the one hand, more and more foreign enterprises enter China to produce and market goods and services, which

---

[47] Special Issue on Consumer Privacy in Japan and the New National Privacy Law, 10 *Privacy and American Business* (Nov. 2003), http://www.privacyexchange. org/japan/japanindex.html.

[48] Electronic Privacy Information Center & Privacy International, *Privacy and Human Rights* 338 (2006).

> further inspires the Chinese consumer's request for protection for data privacy; on the other hand, more and more Chinese enterprises will go abroad, which requires that they must adopt the privacy rules for members of the WTO. The supra-regional and international character of the Internet and WTO make contemporary Chinese ideas of privacy break through the earlier limits of native culture, and to some degree, Chinese ideas are probably coming to more closely resemble common foreign ideas of privacy. . . .
>
> Up until now, there has been no general data protection law in China, with the exception of some local laws involving data protection. Therefore, the protection of data privacy is a very urgent problem. . . .
>
> [T]he protection of privacy in contemporary China, compared with its past, has relatively increased consideration of personal benefits, but still takes social benefits as the center of gravity, and the protection of personal privacy is obviously limited by the social benefits and national interest. Compared with Western countries, the protection of a right to privacy in China is still limited.[49]

In contrast, Hong Kong enacted an information privacy statute in 1996. It has been termed an "Asian Privacy Pioneer."[50] Its Personal Data Ordinance regulates entities in both the public and private sector through a series of Fair Information Practices. This statute also establishes an Office of the Privacy Commissioner. The Privacy Commissioner explains the Ordinance in these terms:

> The Ordinance gives rights to data subjects. They have the right to confirm with data users whether their personal data are held, to obtain a copy of such data, and to have personal data corrected. Any charge for providing a copy of personal data to a data subject may not be excessive. They may complain to the Privacy Commissioner for Personal Data about a suspected breach of the Ordinance's requirements and claim compensation for damage caused to them as a result of a contravention of the Ordinance through civil proceedings.

The Privacy Commissioner has wide-ranging authority under the law, including direct enforcement powers. These powers include providing guidance on compliance with the Ordinance, investigating violations of the Ordinance, and examining requests from data users who desire to conduct automated matching of personal information.

5. INDIA

India lacks any information privacy law. It does have a constitutional right to privacy, however, which the Indian Supreme Court identified as part of the constitution's protection in its Article 21 of individual liberty. This right of privacy applies only to the public sector.[51]

This lack of statutory privacy protection in India is particularly significant since it is emerging as an important country for outsourcing of personal information processing. According to one prediction:

---

49 Lü Yao-Huai, *Privacy and Data Privacy Issues in Contemporary China*, 7 Ethics & Info. Tech. 15, (2005).

50 Warren B. Chik, *The Lion, the Dragon and the Wardrobe Guarding the Doorway to Information and Communications Privacy on the Internet*, 14 Int'l J.L. & Info. Tech. 47, 91 (2005).

51 Dowling & Mittman, *International Privacy Law*, in *Proskauer on Privacy*, 14-47 (Christopher Wolf, ed. 2006).

> India's government is currently working on new legislation to quell growing privacy concerns. The government plans to study laws both in the European Union and the United States to ascertain how to best structure India's own laws. Any proposal ultimately adopted by the Indian parliament will likely reflect the European Union's requirements on data privacy which served as India's original impetus to review its own laws. Nevertheless, U.S. business concerns will likely play a role too by inducing India to refrain from setting standards that are too stringent and costly.[52]

G. INTERNATIONAL TRANSFERS OF DATA

We live today in a global economy that is becoming increasingly dependent upon information. The Internet has enabled a dramatic increase in international communication and commerce. As a result, personal information increasingly flows across the borders of different nations around the world. International data transfers can also occur pursuant to discovery requests in litigation in the United States that involves foreign parties.

Each nation has its own set of privacy laws and regulations. These differences raise at least two difficulties. First, differing levels of protection might interfere with the smooth and efficient flow of personal information between countries. There is thus a need for harmonization or convergence of approaches to regulating the processing of personal data. Second, countries seeking to protect the privacy of their citizens must depend upon the protections accorded by other countries since a vast amount of personal data flows out of its borders to these other countries.

1. INTERNATIONAL DATA TRANSFERS IN LITIGATION

VOLKSWAGEN, A.G. v. VALDEZ

909 S.W.2d 900 (Tex. 1995)

This mandamus action involves a conflict between Texas' discovery rules and Germany's privacy laws. We conclude that the trial court abused its discretion in failing to balance the competing interests of the parties and disregarding German law in its entirety. After balancing the respective parties' interests, we further conclude that the information sought should not be produced. Accordingly, we conditionally grant the writ of mandamus. . .

The real parties in interest sued both Volkswagen of America and its German parent company, Volkswagen A.G. (VWAG), in products liability for personal injuries resulting from an accident involving their 1970 model Volkswagen. The real parties sought production of VWAG's current corporate telephone book to identify individuals who might have relevant information concerning defects in the automobile's door latches. This book contains the names, job titles, position

---

[52] Bryan Bertram, *Building Fortress India*, 29 B.C. Int'l & Comp. L. Rev. 245, 259 (2006).

within the company, and direct dial work numbers of more than 20,000 employees as well as the private home numbers of individuals in management positions. VWAG objected to this request on the basis of the German Federal Data Protection Act, which prohibits the dissemination of private information without the consent of the individuals. *Bundesdatenschutzgesetz*, BGBl, I, 2954 (1990) (FRG) (BDSG). The trial court overruled VWAG's objection and ordered it to produce the phone book.

When information sought for production is located in a foreign country, guidance is provided by the Restatement (Third) of Foreign Relations Law § 442 (1987). Section 442(1)(a) states:

> A court or agency in the United States, when authorized by statute or rule of court, may order a person subject to its jurisdiction to produce documents, objects, or other information relevant to an action or investigation, even if the information or the person in possession of the information is outside the United States.

However, when the laws of the foreign sovereign protect relevant information from discovery, the interests of the domestic court or agency must be balanced with those of the foreign sovereign. The Restatement suggests:

> In deciding whether to issue an order directing production of information located abroad, and in framing such an order, a court or agency in the United States should take into account the importance to the investigation or litigation of the documents or other information requested; the degree of specificity of the request; whether the information originated in the United States; the availability of alternative means of securing the information; and the extent to which noncompliance with the request would undermine important interests of the United States, or compliance with the request would undermine important interests of the state [or country] where the information is located.

Restatement (Third) of Foreign Relations Law § 442(1)(c) (1987). Accordingly, only after a careful balancing of these interests should the trial court rule on a party's request for production.

Before the Restatement's balancing test may be applied, we must determine whether German and U.S. laws actually conflict. That a conflict exists is readily apparent after examination. Texas discovery rules allow an opposing party to discover evidence relevant to the subject matter in the pending action. Tex. R. Civ. P. 166b(2)(a). Germany's privacy laws protect from dissemination "personal data," which is defined as "information concerning the personal or material circumstances of an identified or identifiable individual." BDSG § 3(1). VWAG produced a plethora of authorities confirming its allegation that information contained in its current corporate phone book is, in fact, personal data. The affidavit of Horst-Gunther Bens explicitly acknowledges that VWAG's production of the book would violate the BDSG, while also explaining that privacy rights under German law are "equal in rank to the right of freedom of speech." Likewise, Paul Schwartz, a professor at the University of Arkansas School of Law and expert on German data protection law, opined that production of the book would be violative. This fact is also confirmed by Dr. Gerard Dronsch, the state commissioner for data protection for Lower Saxony, and the

German Federal Ministry of Labor and Social Order. Additionally, the country of Germany submitted an amicus curiae brief, explicitly stating that production of the book would violate the BDSG. In the face of such overwhelming evidence, we have little doubt that German privacy laws conflict with the discovery laws of Texas.

As mentioned, the Restatement balancing test involves five factors. Two of the five factors are undisputed. First, as to the degree of specificity of the request, we note that the real parties' request is specific. All they seek is production of the one easily identifiable current corporate directory. Second, regarding where the document originated, VWAG is a German company and the book contains the names and other information of its German employees employed at its Wolfsburg plant and its facilities located in Brunswick, Emden, Kassel and Salzgitter, all within the country of Germany. The real parties do not contest that this book originated in Germany.

The remaining three factors deserve careful consideration. One, we must look to alternative discovery sources that are available. There are numerous alternative means that the real parties can and have used to obtain information which is the substantial equivalent of VWAG's current corporate phone book. VWAG produced its 1969 corporate phone book, and its United States subsidiary, Volkswagen of America, produced its current corporate phone book. Additionally, Erich Unterreiner, a current engineer for VWAG who also worked there in 1969, identified 29 past and present employees knowledgeable in the design of the 1970 model Volkswagen. He also provided a great deal of information about VWAG's organizational structure and identified Ernst Nockemann as "the man who did most of the design and development work in door latches." Therefore, there are adequate alternatives the real parties may use to discover the names of VWAG employees knowledgeable about the design of the subject vehicle.

Two, as to whether important interests of either this country or Germany are undermined, we conclude that, as asserted by Germany in its amicus curiae brief, its interests would be undermined if VWAG complied with the real parties' request for production. As we discussed, production of the book would violate German privacy laws. And, there is no evidence in the record suggesting that VWAG's failure to produce this phone book would undermine any important interest of this country, particularly when the record shows that alternative methods for obtaining the information exist.

Finally, VWAG's current corporate phone book bears little importance to the present litigation. The real parties already possess VWAG's 1969 corporate phone book that contains the names of the people who worked on the 1970 model Volkswagen. They have Volkswagen of America's current corporate phone book. And, they have the names of many VWAG employees directly responsible for the design and construction of the 1970 model Volkswagen. The plaintiffs simply desire to have the telephone book produced so they might double check the information provided in previous requests.

The trial court failed to balance the interests of the foreign sovereign with those of the real parties in any respect. In fact, the trial court rejected any consideration of German law. This was an abuse of discretion. Further, based on the record, we conclude that the trial court abused its discretion in ordering production of the book in question. VWAG's current corporate phone book should not be produced in contravention of German law. . . .

NOTES & QUESTIONS

1. ***The Effects of Foreign Data Protection Law on the United States.*** The *Valdez* case shows another way in which foreign data protection law can affect the United States. Prior to this opinion, a Texas trial court had ordered Volkwagen A.G. to turn over information located in Germany. In *Valdez*, the Texas Supreme Court reversed this lower court because its order would violate the legal obligation under U.S. Foreign Relations law to balance the interest of a foreign sovereign with those of the U.S. court. How well do you think the Texas High Court balanced the different interests involved? Why was the information in the corporate phone book considered to be personal data?
2. ***Privacy Logs.*** In *In re Vitamins Antitrust Litigation*, 2001 WL 1049433 (D.D.C. 2001), a U.S. district court allowed German defendants to maintain a "privacy log detailing exactly what requested information would be covered by the German privacy laws." This court felt that the protective order in the case provided some privacy protection, and also believed that the German defendants should "not be allowed to withhold information based upon minor inequivalencies between the Protective Order in this case and the [Federal Data Protection statute of Germany]." But the court also noted that the German defendants appeared "to have some legitimate privacy law concerns and that the Protective Order in this case may not be sufficiently detailed to shield them for criminal liability in their own country." Hence, to gain a better understanding of the information that was at stake and how necessary it would be to plaintiffs' claims, the court decided to allow the use of a privacy log, which would allow a determination of the importance of the information that was sought and "whether there was a way to amend the Protective Order to safeguard defendants from liability in the production of this information."

2. ADEQUATE LEVEL OF PROTECTION UNDER THE EU DIRECTIVE

Transborder Data Flows. Article 25 governs when Member States may permit the flow of personal data to other countries. This provision has particular relevance for the United States, because it governs the level of privacy protections other countries must have in place for data transfers to occur:

> 1. The Member States shall provide that the transfer to a third country of personal data which are undergoing processing or are intended for processing after transfer may take place only if, without prejudice to compliance with the national provisions adopted pursuant to the other provisions of this Directive, the third country in question ensures an adequate level of protection.
>
> 2. The adequacy of the level of protection afforded by a third country shall be assessed in the light of all the circumstances surrounding a data transfer

> operation or set of data transfer operations; particular consideration shall be given to the nature of the data, the purpose and duration of the proposed processing operation or operations, the country of origin and country of final destination, the rules of law, both general and sectoral, in force in the third country in question and the professional rules and security measures which are complied with in that country.

Article 25 enables the European Union to block the transfer of personal information on European citizens processed in third-party countries that fails to meet the requirements of "adequacy." What do you think the reason is behind this requirement? Is this an example of an "extraterritorial" application of European law? To what extent do the United States and other countries regulate the practices of companies based elsewhere, but providing goods and services in domestic markets?

Derogations. Article 26(1) provides for certain derogations, or exceptions, to Article 25. Transfers of personal data to a third-party country that does not ensure an adequate level of protection under Article 25(2) may still take place on condition that the data subject has unambiguously consented, the transfer of data is "necessary in order to protect the vital interests of the data subject," or the transfer serves "important public interest grounds." There are several additional exceptions.

A Member State may also authorize transfers of personal data to third countries without an adequate level of protection where protection of the privacy and individual freedoms "result from appropriate contractual clauses." Article 26(2).

Working Party. Article 29 provides for the creation of a "Working Party on the Protection of Individuals with regard to the Processing of Personal Data." The Article 29 Working Party "shall have advisory status and act independently." It is composed of a representative of the supervisory authorities in each Member State and a representative of the Commission. Decisions made by the Working Party are made by a simple majority of the representatives. The Working Party elects a chairman who serves for two years.

Article 30 describes the tasks of the Article 29 Working Party. The Working Party, among other things, (1) examines questions concerning the uniform application of national measures adopted under the Directive, (2) provides an opinion to the Commission on the level of protection in the Community and in third countries, and (3) advises the Committee on any additional measures to safeguard the rights of individuals with regard to data processing. The Working Party should inform the Commission of any "divergences likely to affect the equivalence of protection for persons with regard to the processing of personal data in the Community." The Commission must inform the Working Party of the action it takes in response to the Working Party's recommendations in a public report. The Working Party also must draw up an annual public report regarding the protections regarding processing of personal data in the Community and in third countries.

Adequate Level of Protection. Adequate protection does not necessarily mean "equivalent" protection. The Article 29 Working Party has provided some clarifications on the meaning of "adequate" protection:

> For its part, the Committee regards it as necessary to be even-handed in implementing the provisions of the Directive that deal with third countries. The Committee expresses its commitment to the principle of non-discrimination and recall that the general principle of equality, of which the prohibition of discrimination on grounds of nationality is a specific enunciation, is one of the fundamental principles of Community law. This principle requires that similar situations shall not be treated differently unless differentiation is objectively justified. The Committee also recalls obligations emanating from other international instruments, in particular the European Convention of Human Rights. Article 14 of the ECHR requires that the rights and freedoms set forth in the Convention (which include the right to respect for privacy — Article 8) be secured without discrimination on any ground, including *inter alia* national origin.
>
> The Committee also regards it as important to be able to judge different situations on their merits and not to regard the equal treatment principle as imposing a single model on third countries. Such an interpretation of the principle would fly in the face of the deliberately flexible wording of Article 25 (which requires "adequate" protection in third countries and which allows circumstances to be judged on a case by case basis) and of the need to take into account different countries' varied approaches to achieving effective data protection. This approach means that adequacy findings may sometimes be made despite certain weaknesses in a particular system, provided of course that such a system can be assessed as adequate overall, for example because of compensating strengths in other areas. The principle of equal treatment does not mean that allowances made to take account of the particular traditions of one country, as described above, are automatically applicable to or acceptable in the cases of other third countries. It does mean that assessments of adequacy should be made broadly by reference to the same standard. . . .[53]

How is the "adequacy" determination made; that is, what factors are considered?

The Effects of the EU Data Directive on Other Countries. Consider the following observation by Peter Swire:

> The Directive undoubtedly increases the level of harmonization within the European Union by requiring every Member State to create a data protection agency and implement detailed statutes. In some significant, but difficult to measure way, passage of the Directive has also put pressure on other countries to adopt similar legislation. A wide range of countries with extensive trade relations with the European Union might be found to lack adequate protection of privacy and thus might encounter limits on the transfers of personal information. The last few years have seen data protection laws enacted or seriously considered in European countries outside of the European Union and in far-flung countries such as Argentina, Brazil, Canada, and New Zealand. In conversations with persons knowledgeable about these developments, it is clear

[53] Text on Non-Discrimination adopted by the Article 31 Committee (May 31, 2000).

that the Directive has played a prominent role in encouraging such legislation. The possible finding of inadequate protection has also been used as an argument for enacting new privacy legislation in the United States.[54]

How did the United States respond to the EU Data Directive? Consider the materials in the next section.

3. THE SAFE HARBOR ARRANGEMENT

(a) Conflicting Privacy Approaches in the EU and United States

There are substantial differences in the privacy protections set out in the EU Directive and the approach in the United States. Pursuant to Article 25 of the EU Directive, transfers of personal data about European citizens can be blocked if third party countries (such as the United States) do not provide "an adequate level of protection." As Joel Reidenberg observes:

> The European Directive exerts significant pressure on U.S. information rights, practices and policies. The Directive facilitates a single information market place within Europe through a harmonized set of rules, but also forces scrutiny of U.S. data privacy. In this context, the lack of legal protection for privacy in the United States threatens the flow of personal information from Europe to the United States. At the same time, the EU Directive is having an important influence on privacy protection around the world and leaves Americans with legal protections as second class citizens in the global marketplace. . . .
>
> The European Directive requires the national supervisory authorities in each of the Member States and the European Commission to make comparisons between European data protection principles and foreign standards of fair information practice. The European Directive further requires that foreign standards of fair information practice be "adequate" in order to permit transfers of personal information to the foreign destination.
>
> For the United States, this means that both national supervisory authorities and the European Commission must assess the level of protection offered in the United States to data of European origin. Because the United States lacks directly comparable, comprehensive data protection legislation, the assessment of "adequacy" is necessarily complex. The European Commission and national supervisory authorities recognize that the context of information processing must be considered to make any determination of "adequacy."
>
> Under the European Directive, the national data protection supervisory authorities and the European Commission must report to each other the non-European countries that do not provide adequate protection. This bifurcated assessment of foreign standards means that intra-European politics can play a significant role in the evaluation of U.S. data practices. While a European level decision is supposed to apply in each Member State, the national supervisory authorities are independent agencies and will still have a degree of interpretive power over any individual case.
>
> The end result for the United States and for American companies is that U.S. corporate information practices are under scrutiny in Europe and under threat of disruption when fair information processing standards are not applied to protect

[54] Peter P. Swire, *Of Elephants, Mice, and Privacy: International Choice of Law and the Internet,* 32 Int'l. L. 991, 1002 (1998).

> European data. Some commentators have predicted that any European export prohibition might spark a trade war that Europe could lose before the new World Trade Organization. While, in theory, such a situation is possible, an adverse WTO ruling is unlikely.
>
> Even with the difficulties of the European approach, countries elsewhere are looking at the European Directive as the basic model for information privacy, and significant legislative movements toward European-style data protection exist in Canada, South America, and Eastern Europe. . . . In effect, Europe through the European Directive has displaced the role that the United States held since the famous Warren and Brandeis article in setting the global privacy agenda. . . .[55]

While Reidenberg prefers the approach of the EU Data Directive and welcomes it as a great incentive to improve U.S. privacy law as well as privacy regulation around the world, Peter Swire and Robert Litan are less sanguine about the Data Directive. According to Swire and Litan, "there is also the possibility that strict data protection rules in Europe, coupled with less strict rules in other countries, will pose a competitive disadvantage for Europe. The risk is that Europe will fall behind in creating the information society." One possible solution would be for the United States to adopt comprehensive privacy legislation. Swire and Litan observe that "[t]o American sensibilities . . . [adopting omnibus privacy legislation] might easily seem an unnecessary regulatory intrusion into how an organization should manage its own information." As a result, the authors note, the EU will be forced to compromise: "As it has become more clear to the Europeans that the United States and other countries will not pass comprehensive privacy laws, European officials have become more willing to find workable contract and other [self-regulatory] solutions."[56]

In response to Swire and Litan, Robert Gellman argues that self-regulatory solutions will be inadequate:

> The United States is now awash in overlapping privacy self-regulatory mechanisms that were developed at great expense and with great effort. Yet not one of them meets all of the fair information practices included in the Directive. It is unclear whether market forces alone can produce an adequate form of self-regulation or can induce anyone but major international players to comply. Contracts may be even more expensive and more complicated. Multinational companies like IBM and EDS may require thousands of contracts and an army of lawyers to satisfy EU regulators.[57]

Reidenberg contends that although the EU must make compromises, the United States must also make some as well:

---

[55] Joel Reidenberg, *The EU Data Protection Directive: Implications for the U.S. Privacy Debate* (2001), http://energycommerce.house.gov/107/hearings/03082001Hearing49/Reidenberg104.htm.

[56] Peter P. Swire & Robert E. Litan, *None of Your Business: World Data Flows, Electronic Commerce, and the European Privacy Directive* 151, 178, 173 (1998).

[57] Robert Gellman, *Book Review,* 32 Geo. Wash. J. Intl. L. & Econ. 179, 186 (1999) (reviewing Swire & Litan, *None of Your Business*).

For the European side, the United States posed a major problem. American law did not provide comparable protections to European standards, and fair information practices in the United States were rather spotty. Yet, European regulators did not want to cause a disruption in international data flows. The prospect of change in U.S. law seemed remote, and the European Commission would have serious political difficulty insisting on an enforcement action against data processing in the United States prior to the full implementation of the European Directive within the European Union. Similarly, while transposition remained incomplete, an aggressive enforcement strategy by a national supervisory authority could have hampered the national legislative debates on transposition. Safe Harbor offered a mechanism to delay facing tough decisions about international privacy and, in the meantime, hopefully advance U.S. privacy protections for European data.

On the U.S. side, the Department of Commerce faced strong pressure from the American business community to block the European Directive. The United States was not prepared to respond to the Directive with new privacy rights and wanted to prevent interruptions in transborder data flows. Safe Harbor became a mechanism to avoid a showdown judgment on the status of American law and defer action against any American companies.[58]

(b) The Safe Harbor Arrangement

In 1998, the U.S. Department of Commerce began negotiations with the EU Commission to formulate a "safe harbor" agreement to ensure that the United States met the EU Data Directive's "adequacy" requirement in Article 25. In July 2000, the negotiations yielded the Safe Harbor Arrangement as well as other supportive documents elaborating on the principles, such as letters and a list of Frequently Asked Questions.

The process for EU approval of the Safe Harbor agreement began with the EU Parliament, which commented on the efficacy of the agreement by issuing a nonbinding resolution. The EU Parliament rejected the Safe Harbor agreement by a vote of 279 to 259 because of concerns over the adequacy of U.S. protections and numerous loopholes.[59] An excerpt of the EU Parliament's resolution is included in section (c) below.

The ultimate decision on whether the EU would approve the Safe Harbor agreement rested in the EU Commission. The EU Parliament's resolution was nonbinding on the Commission, and on July 26, 2000, the Commission approved the Safe Harbor agreement.

SAFE HARBOR PRIVACY PRINCIPLES

U.S. Department of Commerce (July 21, 2000)

Decisions by organizations to qualify for the safe harbor are entirely voluntary, and organizations may qualify for the safe harbor in different ways.

---

[58] Joel R. Reidenberg, *E-Commerce and Trans-Atlantic Privacy,* 38 Hous. L. Rev. 717, 739-40 (2001).

[59] Steven R. Salbu, *The European Union Data Privacy Directive and International Relations,* 35 Vand. J. Transnat'l L. 655, 678-79 (2002). There were 22 abstentions.

Organizations that decide to adhere to the Principles must comply with the Principles in order to obtain and retain the benefits of the safe harbor and publicly declare that they do so. For example, if an organization joins a self-regulatory privacy program that adheres to the Principles, it qualifies for the safe harbor. Organizations may also qualify by developing their own self-regulatory privacy policies provided that they conform with the Principles. Where in complying with the Principles, an organization relies in whole or in part on self-regulation, its failure to comply with such self-regulation must also be actionable under Section 5 of the Federal Trade Commission Act prohibiting unfair and deceptive acts or another law or regulation prohibiting such acts. . . . In addition, organizations subject to a statutory, regulatory, administrative or other body of law (or of rules) that effectively protects personal privacy may also qualify for safe harbor benefits. In all instances, safe harbor benefits are assured from the date on which each organization wishing to qualify for the safe harbor self-certifies to the Department of Commerce (or its designee) its adherence to the Principles in accordance with the guidance set forth in the Frequently Asked Question on Self-Certification.

Adherence to these Principles may be limited: (a) to the extent necessary to meet national security, public interest, or law enforcement requirements; (b) by statute, government regulation, or case law that create conflicting obligations or explicit authorizations, provided that, in exercising any such authorization, an organization can demonstrate that its non-compliance with the Principles is limited to the extent necessary to meet the overriding legitimate interests furthered by such authorization; or (c) if the effect of the Directive or Member State law is to allow exceptions or derogations, provided such exceptions or derogations are applied in comparable contexts. Consistent with the goal of enhancing privacy protection, organizations should strive to implement these Principles fully and transparently, including indicating in their privacy policies where exceptions to the Principles permitted by (b) above will apply on a regular basis. For the same reason, where the option is allowable under the Principles and/or U.S. law, organizations are expected to opt for the higher protection where possible. . . .

"Personal data" and "personal information" are data about an identified or identifiable individual that are within the scope of the Directive, received by a U.S. organization from the European Union, and recorded in any form.

NOTICE: An organization must inform individuals about the purposes for which it collects and uses information about them, how to contact the organization with any inquiries or complaints, the types of third parties to which it discloses the information, and the choices and means the organization offers individuals for limiting its use and disclosure. This notice must be provided in clear and conspicuous language when individuals are first asked to provide personal information to the organization or as soon thereafter as is practicable, but in any event before the organization uses such information for a purpose other than that for which it was originally collected or processed by the transferring organization or discloses it for the first time to a third party.[60]

CHOICE: An organization must offer individuals the opportunity to choose (opt out) whether their personal information is (a) to be disclosed to a third party or (b) to be used for a purpose that is incompatible with the purpose(s) for which it was originally collected or subsequently authorized by the individual. Individuals must be provided with clear and conspicuous, readily available, and affordable mechanisms to exercise choice.

For sensitive information (i.e. personal information specifying medical or health conditions, racial or ethnic origin, political opinions, religious or philosophical beliefs, trade union membership or information specifying the sex life of the individual), they must be given affirmative or explicit (opt in) choice if the information is to be disclosed to a third party or used for a purpose other than those for which it was originally collected or subsequently authorized by the individual through the exercise of opt in choice. In any case, an organization should treat as sensitive any information received from a third party where the third party treats and identifies it as sensitive.

ONWARD TRANSFER: To disclose information to a third party, organizations must apply the Notice and Choice Principles. Where an organization wishes to transfer information to a third party that is acting as an agent, as described in the endnote, it may do so if it first either ascertains that the third party subscribes to the Principles or is subject to the Directive or another adequacy finding or enters into a written agreement with such third party requiring that the third party provide at least the same level of privacy protection as is required by the relevant Principles. If the organization complies with these requirements, it shall not be held responsible (unless the organization agrees otherwise) when a third party to which it transfers such information processes it in a way contrary to any restrictions or representations, unless the organization knew or should have known the third party would process it in such a contrary way and the organization has not taken reasonable steps to prevent or stop such processing.

SECURITY: Organizations creating, maintaining, using or disseminating personal information must take reasonable precautions to protect it from loss, misuse and unauthorized access, disclosure, alteration and destruction.

DATA INTEGRITY: Consistent with the Principles, personal information must be relevant for the purposes for which it is to be used. An organization may not process personal information in a way that is incompatible with the purposes for which it has been collected or subsequently authorized by the individual. To the extent necessary for those purposes, an organization should take reasonable steps to ensure that data is reliable for its intended use, accurate, complete, and current.

ACCESS: Individuals must have access to personal information about them that an organization holds and be able to correct, amend, or delete that information where it is inaccurate, except where the burden or expense of

---

[60] It is not necessary to provide notice or choice when disclosure is made to a third party that is acting as an agent to perform task(s) on behalf of and under the instructions of the organization. The Onward Transfer Principle, on the other hand, does apply to such disclosures.

providing access would be disproportionate to the risks to the individual's privacy in the case in question, or where the rights of persons other than the individual would be violated.

ENFORCEMENT: Effective privacy protection must include mechanisms for assuring compliance with the Principles, recourse for individuals to whom the data relate affected by non-compliance with the Principles, and consequences for the organization when the Principles are not followed. At a minimum, such mechanisms must include (a) readily available and affordable independent recourse mechanisms by which each individual's complaints and disputes are investigated and resolved by reference to the Principles and damages awarded where the applicable law or private sector initiatives so provide; (b) follow up procedures for verifying that the attestations and assertions businesses make about their privacy practices are true and that privacy practices have been implemented as presented; and (c) obligations to remedy problems arising out of failure to comply with the Principles by organizations announcing their adherence to them and consequences for such organizations. Sanctions must be sufficiently rigorous to ensure compliance by organizations.

THE COMMISSION DECISION ON SAFE HARBOR

On July 26, 2000, the Commission found the Safe Harbor to provide an adequate level of protection. *See* Commission Decision Finding the Safe Harbor to Provide Adequate Protection, C (2000) 2441 (July 26, 2000).

Adequate Level of Protection. Pursuant to the Commission's Decision:

> The adequate level of protection for the transfer of data from the Community to the United States recognised by this Decision, should be attained if organisations comply with the Safe Harbor Privacy Principles for the protection of personal data transferred from a Member State to the United States (hereinafter "the Principles") and the Frequently Asked Questions (hereinafter "the FAQs") providing guidance for the implementation of the Principles issued by the Government of the United States on 21.07.2000. Furthermore the organisations should publicly disclose their privacy policies and be subject to the jurisdiction of the Federal Trade Commission (FTC) under Section 5 of the Federal Trade Commission Act which prohibits unfair or deceptive acts or practices in or affecting commerce, or that of another statutory body that will effectively ensure compliance with the Principles implemented in accordance with the FAQs.

The Commission's Decision states that two government bodies in the United States are "empowered to investigate complaints and to obtain relief against unfair or deceptive practices as well as redress for individuals" in instances of noncompliance with the Safe Harbor Principles. These bodies are (1) the FTC and (2) the U.S. Department of Transportation. The Decision notes that the FTC's jurisdiction is limited in a number of respects:

> The Federal Trade Commission acts on the basis of its authority under Section 5 of the Federal Trade Commission Act. The jurisdiction of the Federal Trade Commission under Section 5 is excluded with respect to: banks, saving and loans and credit unions; telecommunications and interstate transportation common carriers, air carriers and packers and stockyard operators. Although the

> insurance industry is not specifically included in the list of exceptions in Section 5, the McCarran-Ferguson Act leaves the regulation of the business of insurance to the individual states. However, the provisions of the FTC Act apply to the insurance industry to the extent that such business is not regulated by State law. The FTC retains residual authority over unfair or deceptive practices by insurance companies when they are not engaged in the business of insurance. EU Commission Decision, Annex VII.

The U.S. Department of Transportation "institutes cases based on its own investigations as well as formal and informal complaints received from individuals, travel agents, airlines, U.S. and foreign government agencies." EU Commission Decision, Annex VII.

According to the Decision:

> Sectors and/or data processing not subject to the jurisdiction of any of the government bodies in the United States listed in Annex VII to this Decision should fall outside the scope of this Decision.

List of Participating Organizations. According to the Commission, organizations adhering to the Safe Harbor principles and FAQs must be able to be known to data subjects, data exporters, and data protection authorities. The U.S. Department of Commerce must issue a "public list of organisations self-certifying their adherence to the Principles implemented in accordance with the FAQs."

Relevant Documents for the Safe Harbor Principles. In addition to the Safe Harbor Principles, the Commission concluded that a number of other documents establish that there is an "adequate level of protection" in the United States. These documents include a letter from the FTC, a letter from the U.S. Department of Transportation, and a memorandum on damages for breaches of privacy and explicit authorizations in U.S. law. *See* EU Commission Decision, Article 1(1).

Conditions Relating to the Transfer of Data. Article 1(2) of the EU Commission decision sets forth the following conditions that must be met in relation to each transfer of data:

> (a) the organisation receiving the data has unambiguously and publicly disclosed its commitment to comply with the Principles implemented in accordance with the FAQs, and
>
> (b) the organisation is subject to the statutory powers of a government body in the United States listed in Annex VII to this Decision which is empowered to investigate complaints and to obtain relief against unfair or deceptive practices as well as redress for individuals, irrespective of their country of residence or nationality, in case of non-compliance with the Principles implemented in accordance with the FAQs.

These conditions "are considered to be met for each organisation that self-certifies its adherence to the Principles implemented in accordance with the FAQs." Article 3. The organization must inform the U.S. Department of Commerce of its public disclosure pursuant to Article 2(a) above and must identify the government body that will investigate complaints and provide redress for violations pursuant to Article 2(b) above.

Suspension of Data Flows with Participating Organizations. Under Article 3 of the Commission's decision:

> 1. Without prejudice to their powers to take action to ensure compliance with national provisions adopted pursuant to provisions other than Article 25 of Directive 95/46/EC, the competent authorities in Member States may exercise their existing powers to suspend data flows to an organisation that has self-certified its adherence to the Principles implemented in accordance with the FAQs in order to protect individuals with regard to the processing of their personal data in cases where:
>
> (a) the government body in the United States referred to in Annex VII to this Decision or an independent recourse mechanism within the meaning of letter a) of the Enforcement Principle set out in Annex I to this Decision has determined that the organisation is violating the Principles implemented in accordance with the FAQs; or
>
> (b) there is a substantial likelihood that the Principles are being violated, there is a reasonable basis for believing that the enforcement mechanism concerned is not taking or will not take adequate and timely steps to settle the case at issue, the continuing transfer would create an imminent risk of grave harm to data subjects, and the competent authorities in the Member State have made reasonable efforts under the circumstances to provide the organisation with notice and an opportunity to respond.
>
> The suspension shall cease as soon as compliance with the Principles implemented in accordance with the FAQs is assured and the competent authorities concerned in the Community are notified thereof.

Member States must immediately inform the Commission of measures adopted pursuant to the above provisions. If there is evidence that the U.S. governmental body responsible for ensuring compliance with the Safe Harbor Principles is not "effectively fulfilling its role," then the Commission will inform the U.S. Department of Commerce and may draft measures to suspend the Commission's decision or limit its scope. Article 3(4).

Evaluation of Implementation of the Commission's Decision. Pursuant to Article 4, the Commission will evaluate the implementation of the Commission's decision within three years.

NOTES & QUESTIONS

1. ***The Efficiencies of the EU Data Directive for U.S. Businesses.*** There has been some criticism of the costs for U.S. businesses created by having to comply with the EU Data Directive. However, consider the following argument by Robert Gellman:

> For all the consternation about the Directive, everyone — including the United States — will benefit because it exists. The Directive will solve the same problem for third countries that it solves for Europe: how to function in

a multi-jurisdictional environment characterized by differing local privacy rules. If there were no Directive then it would be necessary for U.S. companies seeking business in Europe to independently address the same privacy issues fifteen times in EU member states rather than once. If there were no Directive U.S. businesses would demand that one be developed to open EU markets to foreign information processors. The absence of an EU directive harmonizing data protection laws would be a greater barrier to trade.[61]

2. ***Financial Data.*** Why does financial data fall outside the scope of the Safe Harbor Arrangement? What is so specific about this kind of data that justifies such temporary exemption? How would you frame safe harbor guidelines for such data? What are the interests at stake? Which U.S. authority should regulate the protection of financial data? The same question could be asked concerning the insurance industry or the telecommunications industry, aspects of whose regulation is left to the individual states.
3. ***Convergence.*** Recall Colin Bennett's argument at the beginning of this chapter on policy convergence in the privacy realm. The Safe Harbor Arrangement appears to provide support for Bennett's hypothesis. What are we to make now of "American exceptionalism"?

EUROPEAN PARLIAMENT RESOLUTION ON THE DRAFT COMMISSION DECISION ON THE ADEQUACY OF THE PROTECTION PROVIDED BY THE SAFE HARBOUR PRIVACY PRINCIPLES

European Parliament (July 5, 2000)

C. [W]hereas in the United States:

(a) there is not at present any generally applicable legal data protection in the private sector and virtually all data are currently processed without specific guarantees of judicial protection;

(b) there are, however, numerous legislative proposals pending before Congress and the President of the United States himself recently referred to the need for further legislative measures, while the Federal Trade Commission expressed the same opinion in its third report to Congress on the functioning of the system of self-regulation in the electronic marketplace;

(c) the guidelines approved by the OECD (signed by the USA in 1980 and ratified at the Ottawa OECD Conference in September 1998) must in any case be applied in the area of personal data protection. . . .

D. [W]hereas, rather than encouraging a legislative approach, the U.S. Department of Commerce intends to propose to companies "safe harbour privacy principles" (and the Frequently Asked Questions (FAQs) arising from such principles), which:

(a) will apply only to personal data of EU origin, with the status of the voluntary "standard" suggested to the businesses intending to receive data from the

---

[61] Robert Gellman, *Book Review,* 32 Geo. Wash. J. Intl. L. & Econ. 179, 186 (1999) (reviewing Swire & Litan, *None of Your Business*).

EU, but are binding on those businesses that opt to adhere to them and are enforceable by private dispute resolution bodies and government bodies with powers to obtain relief against unfair or deceptive practices;

(b) relate only to firms which fall within the competence of the Federal Trade Commission and the Department of Transportation (so that, for example, firms in the banking and telecommunications sectors are excluded);

(c) are subject to exceptions as regards public record and publicly available data (e.g. land register, telephones, tax declarations, electoral rolls), which are protected by Community legislation;

(d) use ambiguous terms such as "organisation" (which may refer both to businesses and business conglomerates) and "explicit authorisations" (which allow exemptions to the principles);

(e) do not provide a right of effective, personal appeal to a public body;

(f) do not allow it to be concluded with certainty that it will be possible to obtain compensation for individual damage suffered as a result of possible violations of the safe harbour principles. . . .

NOTES & QUESTIONS

1. *Dissatisfaction with the Safe Harbor Principles.* Consider the following comment by Steven Salbu:

> As some domestic observers question whether the United States has given up too much, the concern of the EU Parliament is that the United States has given away too little. Driven by fears that the Safe Harbor Principles lack meaningful enforcement mechanisms, the EU Parliament's fears seem to have some merit, given the slow pace at which U.S. companies have responded to the provisions. As of a March 2001 report, a mere two dozen or so U.S. companies had registered as Safe Harbor compliant. By August 2001, the number had risen to about seventy, a miniscule portion of all U.S. firms. Perhaps partially in response to concerns that meaningful data flow controls under the Privacy Directive may fizzle, the European Union is pressing implementation forward.62

According to Yves Poullet:

> Although the American system does represent innovative and courageous solutions for ensuring an effective protection of the European personal data, we think that certain serious reservations ought to be expressed in connection with the adequacy of the protection that could be afforded by Safe Harbor and the declaration by a public or private body that these are being complied with. These reservations are justified as follows:
>
> 1. The scope remains vague and is subject to interpretation.
>
> 2. The "Safe Harbor" principles concern only data covered by the directive and not all data processed by American organisations. As a consequence, for European data they introduce a system of exception which risks being little known and poorly respected in reality.

---

[62] Steven R. Salbu, *The European Union Data Privacy Directive and International Relations*, 35 Vand. J. Transnat'l L. 655, 684 (2002).

> 3. The "Safe Harbor" principles disregard the principle of determined legitimate purpose. This introduces risks regarding the conditions for application of the other principles.
>
> 4. The "Safe Harbor" principles give too relative a scope to the right of access and as a result leave organisations the opportunity to shirk their duty with regard to transparency too easily.
>
> 5. Application of the "Safe Harbor" principles rests on case law or on the intervention of numerous self-regulation bodies, the uniformity of interpretation of which is not guaranteed by any official authority. In particular, the competence of the FTC in the matter is too indirect to guarantee it. . . .
>
> 7. Generally, the American approach is based on the intervention of private Alternative Dispute Resolution institutions which, one can only note, are in the early stages of their existence, with the result that their operation makes little impression, and finally that their investigative powers are inadequately defined.[63]

2. ***The "Ratcheting Up" Effect.*** Gregory Schaffer has observed a "ratcheting up" effect in the relationship between the United States and Europe in the area of privacy policy.[64] As a consequence of laws in Europe that safeguard privacy, it is more likely today that similar laws will be adopted in the United States or at least that U.S. firms will improve their privacy protection. This observation goes against a popular view of the global economy as involving a "race to the bottom," that is, the tendency for trade to lead to a reduction in regulatory authority. Why do you think the "race to the bottom" often does not occur in the privacy realm?
3. ***Remedying the EU Parliament's Concerns.*** The European Parliament's major concerns regarding the Safe Harbor Principles are the absence of an individual right of judicial appeal and the failure to have an agreement to oblige companies to pay compensation for unlawfully processed data. How could a system of judicial remedies be implemented in the United States?

JOEL R. REIDENBERG, *E-COMMERCE AND TRANS-ATLANTIC PRIVACY*

38 Hous. L. Rev. 717, 744-46 (2001)

For the national supervisory authorities in Europe, Safe Harbor poses a weakening of European standards. . . .

. . . Safe Harbor weakens European standards for redress of data privacy violations. Under the European Directive, victims must be able to seek legal recourse and have a damage remedy. The U.S. Department of Commerce assured the European Commission that Safe Harbor and the U.S. legal system provided remedies for individual European victims of Safe Harbor violations. The European Commission expressly relied on representations made by the U.S. Department of Commerce concerning available damages in American law. The

---

[63] Yves Poullet, *The Safe Harbor Principles: An Adequate Protection?*, IFCLA International Colloquium, Paris, France (June 2000).

[64] *See* Gregory Shaffer, *Globalization and Social Protection: The Impact of EU and International Rules in the Ratcheting Up of U.S. Privacy Standards*, 25 Yale J. Int'l L. 1 (2000).

memorandum presented by the U.S. Department of Commerce to the European Commission, however, made misleading statements of U.S. law. For example, the memorandum provides a lengthy discussion of the privacy torts and indicates that the torts would be available. The memorandum failed to note that the applicability of these tort actions to data processing and information privacy has never been established by U.S. courts and is, at present, purely theoretical. Indeed, the memorandum cites the tort for misappropriation of a name or likeness as a viable damage remedy, but all three of the state courts that have addressed this tort in the context of data privacy have rejected it. Safe Harbor is also predicated on dispute resolution through seal organizations such as TRUSTe. Yet, only one seal organization, the ESRB, proposes any direct remedy to the victim of a breach of a privacy policy, and other organizations' membership lists look like a "Who's Who" of privacy scandal-plagued companies.

Lastly, the enforcement provisions of Safe Harbor rely on the FTC. Even if the FTC has jurisdiction to enforce Safe Harbor, the assertion that the FTC will give priority to European enforcement actions is hard to believe. First, although the FTC has become active in privacy issues recently, the agency's record of enforcing the Fair Credit Reporting Act, one of the country's most important fair information practices statutes, is less than aggressive. Second, were the FTC to devote its limited resources to the protection of Europeans' privacy, Americans should and would be offended that a U.S. government agency — charged with protecting American consumers — chose to commit its energies and U.S. taxpayer money to the protection of European privacy in the United States against U.S. businesses at a higher level than the FTC asserts for the protection of Americans' privacy.

Sadly, though, for many American companies even these weakened European standards impose substantially greater obligations than U.S. law. In particular, the notice, choice, access, and correction requirements are only sporadically found in U.S. law. As a result, pitifully few American companies have subscribed to Safe Harbor; indeed, as of June 21, 2001, fewer than fifty-five companies had signed up.

The upshot of these sui generis standards, the unenthusiastic reception by American companies, and enforcement weaknesses is a likelihood that the national supervisory agencies will be dissatisfied with Safe Harbor and the Member States will face great political pressure to suspend Safe Harbor once transposition is completed. Thus, for e-commerce, the utility of Safe Harbor is rather dubious. . . .

NOTES & QUESTIONS

1. ***Is the Safe Harbor Arrangement in Breach of the EC Treaty?*** The issue of the enforceability of the Safe Harbor Arrangement might arise as the exchange of letters between the Commission and the U.S. Department of Commerce on the implementation of the Safe Harbor Arrangement might be interpreted by European and/or United States judicial authorities as having the substance of an international agreement adopted in breach of Article 300 of the Treaty establishing the European Community and the requirement to seek

Parliament's assent. How would you rule on this issue if you were the judge of a U.S. jurisdiction?

2. ***DRM and International Privacy Protection.*** The development of new tools for Digital Rights Management (DRM), which provide publishers with technological controls over the use of digital works, is likely to raise new privacy concerns as individual user information is recorded and monitored to determine whether consumers are complying with the terms of a new digital product. Consider a hypothetical company, DigitoMusico, that provides online music to consumers all around the world for a very modest rate. DigitoMusico takes advantage of a new technique that monitors over the Internet every single use of every song that it provides to its customers. It is able to determine with virtual certainty whether the device that plays a song is owned by the person who purchased the song and also whether the song is playing on two devices owned by the same person simultaneously. What issues does this raise under the EU Data Directive or the OECD Privacy Guidelines? What about the Safe Harbor Arrangement? If DigitoMusico is based in Spain, does it matter for privacy purposes whether its customers are in Europe, the United States, or Canada?
3. ***Article 8 of the European Charter of Fundamental Rights.*** In December 2000, the leaders of the institutions of the European Union gathered in Nice to sign the European Union Charter of Fundamental Rights.[65] The Charter of Fundamental Rights sets out in a single text, for the first time in the European Union's history, the whole range of civil, political, economic, and social rights of European citizens and all persons living in the European Union. Article 8 of the Charter, concerning Protection of Personal Data, states:

> 1. Everyone has the right to the protection of personal data concerning him or her.
> 2. Such data must be processed fairly for specified purposes and on the basis of the consent of the person concerned or some other legitimate basis laid down by law. Everyone has the right of access to data which has been collected concerning him or her, and the right to have it rectified.
> 3. Compliance with these rules shall be subject to control by an independent authority.

As the Charter explains:

> This Article is based on Article 286 of the Treaty establishing the European Community and Directive 95/46/EC of the European Parliament and of the Council on the protection of individuals with regard to the processing of personal data and on the free movement of such data (OJ L 281, 23.11.1995) as well as on Article 8 of the ECHR and on the Council of Europe Convention of 28 January 1981 for the Protection of Individuals with regard to Automatic Processing of Personal Data, which has been ratified by all the Member Sates. The right to protection of personal data is to be exercised under the conditions laid down in the above Directive, and may be limited under the conditions set out by Article 52 of the Charter.

---

[65] Available at http://www.europarl.eu.int/charter/default_en.htm.

Compare the text of Article 8 of the Charter with Article 12 of the Universal Declaration of Human Rights ("No one shall be subjected to arbitrary interference with his privacy, family, home or correspondence, nor to attacks upon his honour and reputation. Everyone has the right to the protection of the law against such interference or attacks."). Can you identify the developments in information privacy law over the second half of the twentieth century that contributed to this new articulation? How does this definition for the "Protection of Personal Information" compare with the description of privacy provided by Brandeis and Warren?

4. ***Binding Corporate Rules.*** In addition to Model Contract Clauses, the EU permits the use of Binding Corporate Rules (BCRs) as a means to meet the Directive's "adequacy test." BCRs can be used only when international data transfers occur within a single company or a group of affiliated companies. In June 2003, the Article 29 Working Party proposed BCRs were an acceptable way to permit international data transfer within a corporate entity or group. The BCRs must be uniform throughout the corporate group, and be enforceable by the individual whose data is being transferred. In addition, each local EU data protection authority (DPA) must approve the BCR. A company with EU entities intending to transfer personal information internationally from France, Spain, Germany, and Poland would need approval of the BCR from DPA's in each of these countries.

   In January 2007, the Article 29 Working Group released a recommendation on BCRs. As part of its recommendation, the Article 29 Group developed a standard application, a single form, intended to streamline the process of obtaining the DPA's approval. Only a single copy of the form need to be filled out and submitted to a so-called "lead DPA." The recommendation also proposes a multi-factor test for deciding which Member Nation's DPA should be the lead one. The Article 29 Group adds, "The DPAs are not obligated to accept the choice that you make if they believe another DPA is more suitable to be lead DPA."[66] Companies using BCR's include General Electric, Phillips, Daimler Chrysler, and Shell.[67]

4. OUTSOURCING DATA PROCESSING

Many companies have shifted a variety of information services to firms overseas. The entry of personal data into computers is increasingly being handled abroad. Call centers that handle customer inquiries are also frequently located in other countries. The privacy implications of these practices are now receiving increasing attention.

In one case that received wide coverage, the University of California at San Francisco (UCSF) Medical Center outsourced transcription services to a

---

[66] Article 29 Data Protection Working Party, *Recommendation 1/2007 on the Standard Application for Approval of Binding Corporate Rules for the Transfer of Personal Data*, Adopted on 10 January 2007.

[67] Francoise Gilbert, *Binding Corporate Rules* 451, 463-64 in I *Eighth Annual Institute on Privacy and Security Law* (Francoise Gilbert et al., eds., 2007).

Sausalito firm. The Sausalito firm had its own subcontractors, one of whom further subcontracted work to another party, who further subcontracted work to a woman in Pakistan. When her bills were not paid, the woman in Pakistan directly threatened via an e-mail to the UCSF Medical Center to expose patient records on the Internet. To prove that her threat was real, the person attached two authentic patient records to the threatening e-mail. The subcontractor in the United States then paid the sub-sub-subcontractor in Pakistan, who e-mailed the USCF Medical Center to rescind her threat.

Outsourcing remains a growing threat to privacy. As one news article reports:

> Companies increasingly are outsourcing more than just programming jobs to places like India. They are using foreign accountants to prepare U.S. tax returns, foreign radiologists to examine X-rays and even foreign clerks to transcribe dictation of sensitive medical data from American doctors. In these cases, most Americans have no idea that someone outside the United States handled private information about them. More worrisome, Americans might not be able to sue or collect damages from foreigners who misuse the information.[68]

Lawmakers are also beginning to respond to the privacy implications of outsourcing. Senator Diane Feinstein has written the chief executives of bank and credit companies that engage in international outsourcing and warned them of their obligation to protect the privacy of their customer information. Senator Feinstein also said that she might introduce federal legislation if these companies did not establish privacy safeguards and assume responsibility for the data. Two other lawmakers, Senator Hillary Clinton and Congressman Ed Markey, introduced a bill, the SAFE-ID Act, that would permit consumers "to object" to the disclosure of financial or medical data to a "foreign branch, affiliate, subcontractor, or unaffiliated third party." The language that permits consumers to "object to" the disclosure appears intended to create an individual interest in nondisclosure. Senator John Kerry also has proposed a "Call Center Consumer's Right to Know Act," which would require foreign call centers used within the United States to identify the country in which they were located.[69]

Finally, the Federal Deposit Insurance Corporation has issued a report on the implications of outsourcing by financial institutions. As you read excerpts from this report below, consider whether U.S. law adequately regulates the privacy risks that this practice creates.

---

[68] Kim Zetter, *Outsourcing: Danger to Privacy*, Wired.com, Feb. 20, 2004 at http://www.wired.com/news/ business/0,1367,62356,00.html.

[69] Call Center Consumer's Right to Know Act of 2003, S. 1873. For Senator Kerry's statement on introducing the Bill, see Congressional Record, s14966 (Nov. 17, 2003).

FEDERAL DEPOSIT INSURANCE CORPORATION, OFFSHORE OUTSOURCING OF DATA SERVICES BY INSURED INSTITUTIONS AND ASSOCIATED CONSUMER PRIVACY RISKS

(June 2004)

Traditional outsourcing to domestic third-party service providers or domestic affiliates has been done by financial institutions in the United States for many years. However, the use of offshore contractors has grown dramatically in the past few years due to the flexibility offered by new information technology (IT) and the prospect of lower costs. At the same time, consumers have become more concerned about privacy, and the abuse of personal data has increased as instances of fraud, such as identity theft, have become commonplace. . . .

The rapid increase in offshoring by many U.S. financial institutions and their data vendors is due in large part to the potential cost savings that are achievable as low-wage labor pools are tapped in foreign countries. . . .

Domestic outsourcing and offshoring share most risk characteristics. However, the more complicated chain of control incurred when offshoring financial services and related data may create new risks when compared to domestic outsourcing. Offshoring also introduces an element of country risk to the outsourcing process. In particular, geographic distance from the function and timing lags in reporting heighten the potential risk exposures. Significant offshoring risk areas include:

- Country Risk: political, socio-economic, or other factors may amplify any of the traditional outsourcing risks, including those listed below.
- Operations/Transaction Risk: weak controls may affect customer privacy.
- Compliance Risk: offshore vendors may not have adequate privacy regulations.
- Strategic Risk: different country laws may not protect "trade secrets."
- Credit Risk: a vendor may not be able to fulfill its contract due to financial losses.

For each form of offshoring (captive, joint venture, direct third party, and indirect third party) nothing precludes the offshore transfer of customer data by a financial institution or one of its service providers. Financial institution customers may not opt out of these information transfers to nonaffiliated service providers if the transfer is for a purpose described in section 502(e) of the Gramm-Leach-Bliley Act (GLBA). For example, the opportunity to opt out does not apply where the information transfer is to:

- service or process a financial product or service that the customer requested or authorized; or
- maintain or service the customer's account.

Even relatively lower-risk activities such as source-coding or software development may pose operations risks and threats to privacy of data should offshore, contract programmers operate with malicious intent.

However, GLBA does provide important protections that cover both domestic and offshore outsourcing. GLBA establishes affirmative and continuing obligations for financial institutions to respect customer privacy and protect customer personal information against reasonably foreseeable internal or external threats to its security, confidentiality, and integrity. The Federal Banking Agencies (FBAs) have extended these obligations to include the monitoring of the activities of those service providers to which financial institutions transfer customer information.

The FBAs issued . . . Guidelines [that] provide that each financial institution shall: (1) exercise appropriate due diligence in selecting service providers; (2) require them by contract to implement appropriate measures designed to meet the objectives of the Guidelines; and (3) where indicated based upon the institution's risk assessment, monitor the service providers to confirm that they implement the procedures required by the Guidelines.

NOTES & QUESTIONS

1. ***Policy Proposals.*** What regulation, if any, should be imposed on the outsourcing of personal data services to other countries? The FDIC Report recommends that outsourcing of personal data by financial institutions be reported in "one shared, central repository of institution notices of outsourcing arrangements for use in analysis, monitoring, and tracking by the Federal Financial Institutions Examination Council." The proposed SAFE-ID Bill, in contrast, would provide information about foreign outsourcing to consumers and allow them "to object to it." What are the pros and cons of these different approaches?
2. ***Outsourcing Personal Data to the United States.*** In 2004, the Privacy Commissioner for British Columbia issued a report regarding the outsourcing of personal data on Canadians to U.S. companies for processing. The report noted:

> There is ongoing tension between the U.S. and Europe regarding the adequacy of U.S. privacy laws. Canada's privacy laws are much more in tune with Europe. . . .
>
> Canadian personal information flowing across the border into the U.S. does not always enjoy the same standards for protection that we have come to expect here. . . .
>
> [I]f information is located outside British Columbia, it will be subject to the law that applies where it is found, regardless of the terms of the outsourcing contract.

The report recommended that British Columbia amend its Freedom of Information and Protection of Privacy Act (FOIPPA) to "prohibit personal information in the custody or under the control of a public body from being temporarily or permanently sent outside Canada for management, storage, or safekeeping and from being accessed outside Canada."[70]

---

[70] Information and Privacy Commissioner for British Columbia, *Privacy and the USA Patriot Act: Implications for British Columbia Public Sector Outsourcing* 13, 132, 134-35 (Oct. 2004).

TABLE OF CASES

Principal cases are in italics.

TABLE OF AUTHORITIES

Cate, Fred, *European Court of Human Rights Expands Privacy Protections*, 11 American Society of International Law Insight (August 6, 2007), 1042, 1043

_____, *Principles of Internet Privacy*, 32 Conn. L. Rev. 877 (2000), 66, 68

_____, Privacy in Perspective 26 (2001), 787

_____, Privacy in the Information Age (1997), 787

_____, *The Privacy Problem: A Broader View of Information Privacy and the Costs and Consequences of Protecting It,* 4 First Reports 1 (2003), 65

Cate, Fred H. & Michael E. Staten, *Another Notice Isn't an Answer*, USA Today, Feb. 27, 2005, at 14A, 827

_____, *The Impact of Opt-In Privacy Rules on Retail Credit Markets: A Case Study of MBNA,* 52 Duke L.J. 745 (2003), 768, 771, 852, 853

Chemerinsky, Erwin, In Defense of Truth, 41 Case W. Res. L. Rev. 745 (1991), 159

_____, *Protect the Press: A First Amendment Standard for Safeguarding Aggressive Newsgathering*, 33 U. Rich. L. Rev. 1143 (2000), 101, 102

Chen, Edward M., Pauline T. Kim, & John M. True, *Common Law Privacy: A Limit on an Employer's Power to Test for Drugs,* 12 Geo. Mason U. L. Rev. 651 (1990), 941

Chik, Warren B., *The Lion, the Dragon and the Wardrobe Guarding the Doorway to Information and Communications Privacy on the Internet*, 14 Int'l J.L. & Info Tech. 47, 91 (2005), 1070

Church Committee, *Intelligence Activities and the Rights of Americans* (Vol. 2) (Apr. 26, 1976), 354, 355, 378

Citron, Danielle Keats, *Reservoirs of Danger: The Evolution of Public and Private Law at the Dawn of the Information Age,* 80 S. Cal. L. Rev. 241, 243-44, 263-67 (2007), 833, 834

Clancy, Thomas K., *The Fourth Amendment Aspects of Computer Searches and Seizures: A Perspective and a Primer*, 75 Miss. L.J. 193, 196 (2005), 315

Clarke, Roger, *Human Identification and Identity Authentication* (1998), http://www.anu.edu.au/people/Roger.Clarke/DV/SCTISK3.html, 578

_____, *Human Identification in Information Systems: Management Challenges and Public Policy Issues*, 7 Information Tech. & People 6 (1994), http://www.anu.edu.au/people/Roger.Clarke/DV/ HumanID.html, 579

Cohen, Jean L., *Is Privacy a Legal Duty?*, in *Public and Private: Legal, Political, and Philosophical Perspectives* (Maurizio Passerin d'Entreves & Ursula Vogel, eds., 2000), 124

Cohen, Julie E., *A Right to Read Anonymously: A Closer Look at "Copyright Management" in Cyberspace*, 28 Conn. L. Rev. 981 (1996), 569, 570, 576

_____, *DRM and Privacy,* 18 Berkeley Tech. L.J. 575 (2003), 574, 575, 576

_____, *Examined Lives: Informational Privacy and the Subject as Object,* 52 Stan. L. Rev. 1373 (2000), 46, 48, 49, 852

Cohen, Laurie P., *The Polygraph Paradox*, Wall St. J., A1 (March 22-23, 2008), 963

Colb, Sherry F., *The Qualitative Dimension of Fourth Amendment "Reasonableness,"* 98 Colum. L. Rev. 1642 (1998), 237

Comment, *An Actionable Right to Privacy?*, 12 Yale L.J. 34 (1902), 26

Commission Decision of 30/06/2003, Brussels C(2003) 1731 final, 1065

Commission Decision of 20 December 2001 Pursuant to Directive 95/46/EC of theEuropean Parliament and of the Council on the Adequate Protection of Personal Data Provided by the Canadian Personal Information Protection and Electronic Documents Act, C(2001) 4539, available at http://www.europa.eu.int/comm/internal_market/en/dataprot/adequacy/index.htm, 1060

Congressional Research Service, *Presidential Authority to Conduct Warrantless Electronic Surveillance to Gather Foreign Intelligence Information* (Jan. 5, 2006), 396

Cooley, Thomas C., Law of Torts (2d ed. 1888), 14, 24, 26, 447

Coombe, Rosemary J., The Cultural Life of Intellectual Properties: Authorship, Appropriation, and the Law (1998), 213

Craig, John D.R., Privacy and Employment Law (1999), 929, 930

Dann, Michael, *The Fifth Amendment Privilege Against Self-Incrimination: Extorting Evidence from a Suspect*, 43 S. Cal. L. Rev. 597 (1970), 235

Dash, Samuel, Richard Schwartz & Robert Knowlton, The Eavesdroppers (1959), 295

Dash, Samuel, *The Intruders: Unreasonable Searches and Seizures from King John to John Ashcroft* 74-78 (2004), 246

Davidson, Martin, D.L. Rosenhan, Terri Wolff Teitelbaum, & Kathi Weiss Teitelbaum, *Warning Third Parties: The Ripple Effects of Tarasoff*, 24 Pac. L.J. 1165 (1993), 420

Davies, Simon & David Banisar, *Global Trends in Privacy Protection: An International Survey of Privacy, Data Protection, and Surveillance Laws and Developments,* 18 J. Marshall J. Computer & Info. L. 1 (1999), 995, 996

De Armond, Elizabeth D., *Frothy Chaos: Modern Data Warehousing and Old-Fashioned Defamation*, 41 Val. U. L. Rev. 1061, 1099-1102, 1108 (2007), 732, 733, 737

DeCew, Judith W., In Pursuit of Privacy: Law, Ethics, and the Rise of Technology (1997), 59, 76

DeLaTorre, Phillip E., *Resurrecting a Sunken Ship: An Analysis of Current Judicial Attitudes Toward Public Disclosure Claims*, 38 Sw. L.J. 1151 (1985), 155

Dendy, Geoff, Note, *The Newsworthiness Defense to the Public Disclosure Tort*, 85 Ky. L.J. 147 (1997), 106, 124

DeRosa, Mary, *Data Mining and Data Analysis for Counterterrorism* (2004), 691

DeWaal, Ian C. Smith, *Successfully Prosecuting Health Insurance Portability and Accountability Act Medical Privacy Violations Against Noncovered Entities*, 55 U.S. Att'ys Bull., 10, 15, (July 2007), 440

Dickens, Charles, American Notes (1842), 11

_____, The Life and Adventures of Martin Chuzzlewit (1844), 11

Dienes, C. Thomas, *Protecting Investigative Journalism,* 67 Geo. Wash. L. Rev. 1139 (1999), 89, 102

Diffie, Whitfield & Susan Landau, Privacy on the Line: The Politics of Wiretapping and Encryption (1998), 241, 311, 312, 321, 322

Directive of the European Parliament and the Council of Europe on the Protection of Individuals with Regard to the Processing of Personal Data and on the Free Movement of Such Data (1996), 38, 1050, 1089

Donlinko, David, *Is There a Rationale for the Privilege Against Self-Incrimination?*, 33 UCLA L. Rev. 1063 (1986), 235

Donnelly, Sally B., *You Say Yusuf, I Say Youssouf . .* , Time.com, Sept. 25, 2004, www.time.com/time/nation/article/0,8599,702062,00.html, 687

Dowling Jr., Donald C. & Jeremy M. Mittman, *International Privacy Law*, in Proskauer on Privacy (Christopher Wolf, ed. 2006), 1064, 1065, 1070

Dripps, Donald A., *Self-Incrimination and Self-Preservation: A Skeptical View*, 1991 U. Ill. L. Rev. 329, 235

Duby, Georges, Foreword, in A History of the Private Life I: From Pagan Rome to Byzantium (Paul Veyne, ed. & Arthur Goldhammer, trans., 1987), 39

Earl-Hubbard, Michele L., Comment, *The Child Sex Offender Registration Laws: The Punishment, Liberty Deprivation, and Unintended Results Associated with the Scarlet Letter Laws of the 1990s*, 90 Nw. U. L. Rev. 788 (1996), 652, 653

Easterbrook, Frank, *Abstraction and Authority*, 59 U. Chi. L. Rev. 349 (1992), 462

Edelman, Peter B., *Free Press v. Privacy: Haunted by the Ghost of Justice Black*, 68 Tex. L. Rev. 1195 (1990), 142, 155, 156

Elder, David A., Privacy Torts (2002), 360

Electronic Privacy Information Center & Privacy International, *Privacy and Human Rights 2006,* 1066, 1069

Ellis, Jr., Dorsey D., *Damages and the Privacy Tort: Sketching a "Legal Profile,"* 64 Iowa L. Rev. 1111 (1979), 106

Elwood, John P., Note, *Outing, Privacy, and the First Amendment*, 102 Yale L.J. 747 (1992), 123

Ely, John H., *The Wages of Crying Wolf: A Comment on* Roe v. Wade, 82 Yale L.J. 920, 930 (1973), 454

Emerson, Thomas I., *The Right of Privacy and Freedom of Press*, 14 Harv. CR-CL L. Rev. 329 (1979), 142

_____, The System of Freedom of Expression (1970), 157, 169

Enforcement of Privacy Rule Stresses Voluntary Compliance, HHS Official Says, 7 Privacy & Security Law 479 (Mar. 31, 2008), 440

Epstein, Richard A., *The Legal Regulation of Genetic Discrimination: Old Responses to New Technology,* 74 B.U. L. Rev. 1 (1994), 508, 509, 511

Ernst, Morris L. & Alan U. Schwartz, Privacy: The Right to Be Let Alone (1962), 12

Etzioni, Amitai, The Limits of Privacy (1999), 59, 60, 61, 594, 653

Federal Bureau of Investigation, Frequently Asked Questions, http://www.fbi.gov/aboutus/faqs/faqsone.html (Dec. 4, 2003), 375

Federal Data Banks, Computers and the Bill of Rights: Hearings Before the Subcomm. on Constitutional Rights of the House Comm. on the Judiciary, 92d Cong., 1st Sess. Part I (1971), 679

Federal Deposit Insurance Corporation, Offshore Outsourcing of Data Services by Insured Institutions and Associated Consumer Privacy Risks (2004), 1092

Felcher, Peter L. & Edward L. Rubin, *Privacy, Publicity, and the Portrayal of Real People by the Media,* 88 Yale L.J. 1577 (1979), 106

Feldblum, Chai, *Medical Examinations and Inquiries Under the Americans with Disabilities Act: A View from the Inside,* 64 Temp. L. Rev. 521 (1991), 961

Feldman, Daniel L., *The "Scarlet Letter Laws" of the 1990s: A Response to Critics*, 60 Alb. L. Rev. 1081 (1997), 652

Feuer, Alan & Jason George, *Internet Fame Is Cruel Mistress for Dancer of the Numa Numa,* N.Y. Times, Feb. 26, 2005, 9

Finkin, Matthew W., *Menschenbild: The Conception of the Employee as a Person in Western Law*, 23 Comp. Lab. L. & Pol'y J. 577 (2002), 935

Firestone, Marvin & Fillmore Buckner, *"Where the Public Peril Begins" 25 Years After* Tarasoff, 21 J. Legal Med. 187 (2000), 420

Fisher, Linda E., *Guilt by Expressive Association: Political Profiling, Surveillance and the Privacy of Groups*, 46 Ariz. L. Rev. 621 (2004), 467

Fishman, Clifford S., *Technology and the Internet: The Impending Destruction of Privacy by Betrayers, Grudgers, Snoops, Spammers, Corporations, and the Media,* 72 Geo. Wash. L. Rev. 1503 (2004), 987

Flaherty, David H., Protecting Privacy in Surveillance Societies (1989), 38, 668

_____, Stephanie Perrin, Heather H. Black, & T. Murray Rankin, The Personal Information Protection and Electronic Documents Act: An Annotated Guide (2001), 1060

Fogel, Stephen M., Gerri L. Kornblut, & Newton P. Porter, *Survey of the Law on Employee Drug Testing,* 42 U. Miami L. Rev. 553 (1988), 941

Franklin, Marc A., *A Constitutional Problem in Privacy Protection: Legal Inhibitions on Reporting of Fact*, 16 Stan. L. Rev. 107 (1963), 142

Franzen, Jonathan, *How to Be Alone: Essays* 42, 45-46 (2003), 69

Freiwald, Susan, *Online Surveillance: Remembering the Lessons of the Wiretap Act,* 56 Ala. L. Rev. 9 (2004), 267, 268, 296, 343, 344

_____, *Uncertain Privacy: Communication Attributes After the Digital Telephony Act,* 69 S. Cal. L. Rev. 949 (1996), 302, 303, 309

Fried, Charles, *Privacy*, 77 Yale L.J. 475 (1968), 44, 45

Friedman, Lawrence M., *Guarding Life's Dark Secrets: Legal and Social Controls over Reputation, Propriety, and Privacy* 66-68, 216-18 (2007), 147, 468, 469

Friendly, Fred W., *Gays, Privacy and a Free Press*, Wash. Post, April 8, 1990, 124

Froomkin, A. Michael, *Flood Control on the Information Ocean: Living with Anonymity, Digital Cash, and Distributed Databases*, 15 J.L. & Comm. 395 (1996), 526, 557

_____, *The Constitution and Encryption Regulation: Do We Need a "New Privacy"?,* 3 N.Y.U. J. Legis. & Pub. Pol'y 25 (1999), 321

_____, *The Metaphor Is the Key: Cryptography, the Clipper Chip, and the Constitution,* 143 U. Pa. L. Rev. 709 (1995), 321

Funk, T. Markus, *The Dangers of Hiding Criminal Pasts*, 66 Tenn. L. Rev. 287 (1998), 148

Gandy, Jr., Oscar H., *Exploring Identity and Identification in Cyberspace,* 14 Notre Dame J.L. Ethics & Pub. Pol'y (2000), 525

Garcia, Flora J., *Bodil Lindqvist: A Swedish Churchgoer's Violation of the European Union's Data Protection Directive Should Be a Warning to U.S. Legislators*, 15 Fordham Intell. Prop. Media & Ent. L.J. 1206, 1232 (2005), 1054

Garfinkel, Simson, Database Nation: The Death of Privacy in the 21st Century (2000), 587

Garment, Leonard, *Crazy Rhythm: From Brooklyn and Jazz to Nixon's White House, Watergate, and Beyond* (1997), 201

Garrow, David J., The FBI and Martin Luther King, Jr. (1980), 295

Gavison, Ruth, *Feminism and the Public/Private Distinction,* 45 Stan. L. Rev. 21 (1992), 73

_____, *Privacy and the Limits of Law*, 89 Yale L.J. 421 (1980), 45, 76

Gellman, Robert M., *Book Review,* 32 Geo. Wash J. Intl. L. & Econ. 179 (1999), 1078, 1085

_____, *Does Privacy Law Work?* in Technology and Privacy: The New Landscape (Philip E. Agre & Marc Rotenberg, eds., 1997), 668, 675, 676

_____, *Prescribing Privacy: The Uncertain Role of the Physician in the Protection of Patient Privacy,* 62 N.C. L. Rev. 255 (1984), 427, 428

_____, *Privacy, Consumers, and Costs: How the Lack of Privacy Costs Consumers and Why Business Studies of Privacy Costs Are Biased and Incomplete* (March 2002), at http://www.epic.org/reports/dmfprivacy.html, 853

Gentry, Curt, J. Edgar Hoover: The Man and the Secrets (1991), 375

George, Jason & Alan Feuer, *Internet Fame Is Cruel Mistress for Dancer of the Numa Numa,* N.Y. Times, Feb. 26, 2005, 9

Gerety, Tom, *Redefining Privacy*, 12 Harv. C.R.-C.L. L. Rev. 233 (1977), 46

Gerstein, Robert S., *Intimacy and Privacy*, in Philosophical Dimensions of Privacy: An Anthology (Ferdinand David Schoeman, ed., 1984), 45

Gewirtz, Paul, *Privacy and Speech,* 2001 Sup. Ct. Rev. 139 (2001), 168, 169

Gilbert, Francoise, *Binding Corporate Rules* 451, 463-64 in I *Eighth Annual Institute on Privacy and Security Law* (Francoise Gilbert et al, eds., 2007), 1090

Gilles, Susan M., *All Truths Are Equal, But Are Some Truths More Equal Than Others?*, 41 Case W. Res. L. Rev. 725 (1991), 159

_____, *Promises Betrayed: Breach of Confidence as a Remedy for Invasions of Privacy,* 43 Buffalo L. Rev. 1 20-25 (1995), 139, 411

Gilliom, John, Overseers of the Poor: Surveillance, Resistance, and the Limits of Privacy (2001), 685

_____, Surveillance, Privacy, and the Law: Employee Drug Testing and the Politics of Social Control (1994), 941

Ginsburg, Douglas H., *Genetics and Privacy,* 4 Tex. Rev. L. & Pol. 17 (1999), 506

Giordano, Philip, *Invoking Law as a Basis for Identity in Cyberspace,* 1998 Stan. Tech. L. Rev. 1, 554

Glancy, Dorothy J., *The Invention of the Right to Privacy*, 21 Ariz. L. Rev. 1 (1979), 11, 12

Glensy, Rex D., *Which Countries Count?:* Lawrence v. Texas *and the Selection of Foreign Persuasive Authority*, 45 Va. J. Int'l L. 347 (2005), 470

Godkin, E.L., *The Right to Privacy*, The Nation (Dec. 25, 1890), 12

_____, *The Rights of the Citizen: IV. To His Own Reputation*, Scribner's Magazine (1890), 11, 12

Goldman, Eric, *A Cosean Analysis of Marketing*, 2006 Wisc. L. Rev. 1151, 1154-55, 1202, 1211-12, 820

_____, *The Privacy Hoax,* Forbes (Oct. 14, 2002), available at http://www.ericgoldman.org/Articles/privacyhoax.htm, 787, 788

Hertzel, Dorothy A., Note, *Don't Talk to Strangers: An Analysis of Government and Industry Efforts to Protect a Child's Privacy Online*, 52 Fed. Comm. L.J. 429 (2000), 803

Hess, Jennifer A. & Dan L. Burk, *Genetic Privacy: Constitutional Considerations in Forensic DNA Testing*, 5 Geo. Mason U. Civ. Rts. L.J. 1 (1994), 512

Hetcher, Steven A., *Changing the Social Meaning of Privacy in Cyberspace*, 15 Harv. J. L. & Tech. 149 (2001), 785

_____, *Norm Proselytizers Create a Privacy Entitlement in Cyberspace*, 16 Berkeley Tech. L.J. 877 (2001), 785

_____, Norms in a Wired World (2004), 785

_____, *The De Facto Federal Privacy Commission,* 19 J. Marshall J. Computer & Info. L. 109 (2000), 1057, 1058

_____, *The FTC as Internet Privacy Norm Entrepreneur*, 53 Vand. L. Rev. 2041 (2000), 785, 787

Hill, Alfred, *Defamation and Privacy Under the First Amendment*, 76 Colum. L. Rev. 1205 (1976), 142

Hirsch, Dennis D., *Protecting the Inner Environment: What Privacy Regulation Can Learn from Environmental Law*, 41 Ga. L. Rev. 1, 8-10 (2006), 789, 790

Hodge, Jr., James G. & Lawrence O. Gostin, *Personal Privacy and Common Goods: A Framework for Balancing Under the National Health Information Privacy Rule*, 86 Minn. L. Rev. 1439 (2002), 432

_____, Piercing the Veil of Secrecy in HIV/AIDS and Other Sexually Transmitted Diseases: Theories of Privacy and Disclosure in Partner Notification, 5 Duke J. of Gender L. & Pol'y 9 (1998), 412, 428

Hoffman, Charlotte A. & Tamela J. White, *The Privacy Standards Under the Health Insurance Portability and Accountability Act*, 106 W. Va. L. Rev. 709 (2004), 432

Hoffman, Sharona, *Preplacement Examinations and Job-Relatedness: How to Enhance Privacy and Diminish Discrimination in the Workplace,* 49 U. Kan. L. Rev. 517 (2001), 924

Hohlen, Nicholas, Case Note: Von Hannover v. Germany, 100 Am. J. Int'l Law 196, 198 (2006), 1015

Hoofnagle, Chris Jay, *Big Brother's Little Helpers: How ChoicePoint and Other Commercial Data Brokers Collect and Package Your Data for Law Enforcement,* 29 N.C. J Int'l L. & Commercial Reg. 595, (2004), 678, 824

_____, *Identity Theft: Making the Known Unknowns Known*, 21 Harv. J. Law & Tech. 97 (2007)

Howell, Beryl A., *Seven Weeks: The Making of the USA Patriot Act,* 72 Geo. Wash. L. Rev. 1145 (2004), 743, 744

H.R. Rep. 104-795 (104th Cong. 2d Sess) (1996), 603

Hudson, Zoe, Joy Pritts, Janlori Goldman, Aimee Berenson, & Elizabeth Hadley, *The State of Health Privacy: An Uneven Terrain (A Comprehensive Survey of State Health Privacy Statutes)* (1999), http://www.georgetown.edu/research/ihcrp/privacy/ statereport.pdf, 429, 505

Information and Privacy Commissioner for British Columbia, *Privacy and the USA Patriot Act: Implications for British Columbia Public Sector Outsourcing* (Oct. 2004), 1093

Inness, Julie C., Privacy, Intimacy, and Isolation (1992), 45

Jacob-Foltzer, V. & J. Polakiewicz, *The European Human Rights Convention in Domestic Law,* 12 Hum. Rts. L.J. 65 (1991), 1005

Jacobson, Peter D., *Medical Records and HIPAA: Is It Too Late to Protect Privacy?*, 86 Minn. L. Rev. 1497 (2002), 432

Janger, Edward J., *Muddy Property: Generating and Protecting Information Privacy Norms in Bankruptcy*, 44 William & Mary L. Rev. 1801 (2002), 783, 784

Janger, Ted & Paul M. Schwartz, *Notification of Data Security Breaches*, 105 Mich. L. Rev. 913, 924-25 (2007), 826, 827

_____, *The Gramm-Leach-Bliley Act, Information Privacy, and the Limits of Default Rules*, 86 Minn. L. Rev. 1219 (2002), 739, 740

Jensen, Joan M., Army Surveillance in America 1775-1980 (1991), 540
Joh, Elizabeth E., *Reclaiming "Abandoned" DNA*, 100 Nw. U. L. Rev. 857, 860, 881 (2006), 523
Jones, B.L., S.H. Bailey, D.J. Harris, Civil Liberties — Cases and Materials (3d ed. 1991), 1004, 1005
Jones, William K., Insult to Injury: Libel, Slander, and Invasions of Privacy (2003), 142
Jourard, Sidney M., *Some Psychological Aspects of Privacy*, 31 L. & Contemp. Probs. 307 (1966), 45
Jurata, Jr., John A., Comment, *The Tort That Refuses to Go Away: The Subtle Reemergence of Public Disclosure of Private Facts*, 36 San Diego L. Rev. 489 (1999), 155

Kahn, Jonathan, *Bringing Dignity Back to Light: Publicity Rights and the Eclipse of the Tort of Appropriation of Identity,* 17 Cardozo Arts & Ent. L.J. 213 (1999), 207
_____, *What's in a Name? Law's Identity Under the Tort of Appropriation,* 74 Temp. L. Rev. 263 (2001), 207
Kalven, Jr., Harry, *Privacy in Tort Law — Were Warren and Brandeis Wrong?*, 31 L. & Contemp. Probs. 326 (1966), 10, 142, 157, 169
Kang, Jerry, *Information Privacy in Cyberspace Transactions*, 50 Stan. L. Rev. 1193 (1998), 32, 760, 788, 789
Karas, Stan, *Privacy, Identity, Databases,* 52 Am. U. L. Rev. 393 (2002), 760
Karns, Jack, *Protecting Individual Online Privacy Rights: Making the Case for a Separately Dedicated, Independent Regulatory Agency,* 19 J. Marshall J. Computer & Info. L. 93 (2000), 1058
Karst, Kenneth L., *"The Files": Legal Controls over the Accuracy and Accessibility of Stored Personal Data*, 31 L. & Contemp. Probs. 342 (1966), 35
Katyal, Neal & Richard Caplan, *The Surprisingly Strong Case for the Legality of the NSA Surveillance Program: The FDR Precedent*, 60 Stan. L. Rev. 1023 (2008), 393, 394
Katyal, Sonia K., *The New Surveillance*, 54 Case W. Res. L. Rev. 297 (2003), 577
Keefe, Patrick Radden, *Annals of Surveillance: State Secrets*, New Yorker, April 28, 2008, 390
Kennedy, Charles H. & Peter P. Swire, *State Wiretaps and Electronic Surveillance After September 11,* 54 Hastings L.J. 971 (2003), 308
Kerr, Orin S., *Are We Overprotecting Code? Thoughts on First-Generation Internet Law*, 57 Wash. & Lee L. Rev. 1287 (2000), 323
_____, *A User's Guide to the Stored Communications Act, and a Legislator's Guide to Amending It,* 72 Geo. Wash. L. Rev. 1208 (2004), 300, 342
_____, *Cybercrime's Scope: Interpreting "Access" and "Authorization" in Computer Misuse Statutes*, 78 N.Y.U. L. Rev. 1596 (2003), 812
_____, *Internet Surveillance Law After the USA PATRIOT Act: The Big Brother That Isn't*, 97 Nw. U. L. Rev. 607 (2003), 341
_____, *Lifting the "Fog" of Internet Surveillance: How a Suppression Remedy Would Change Computer Crime Law*, 54 Hastings L.J. 805 (2003), 344, 809, 810
_____, *Searches and Seizures in a Digital World*, 119 Harv. L. Rev. 531, 556 (2005), 315
_____, *The Fourth Amendment and New Technologies: Constitutional Myths and the Case for Caution*, 102 Mich. L. Rev. 801 (2004), 292, 293
_____, *The Fourth Amendment in Cyberspace: Can Encryption Create a "Reasonable Expectation of Privacy?,"* 33 Conn. L. Rev. 503 (2001), 323, 324
_____, *The Problem of Perspective in Internet Law,* 91 Geo. L.J. 357 (2003), 327
_____, *Updating the Foreign Intelligence Surveillance Act,* 75 U. Chicago L. Rev. 238 (2008), 395
_____, *Virtual Analogies, Physical Searches, and the Fourth Amendment,* Volokh Conspiracy, Apr. 26, 2007, http://www.volokh.com/posts/1177562355.shtml, 321
Kesan, Jay P., *Cyber-Working or Cyber-Shirking?: A First Principles Examination of Electronic Privacy in the Workplace,* 54 Fla. L. Rev. 289 (2002), 976
Kessler, Ronald, The Bureau: The Secret History of the FBI (2002), 375
Killingsworth, Scott, *Minding Your Own Business: Privacy Policies in Principle and in Practice*, 7 J. Intell. Prop. L. 57 (1999), 771, 772

Kim, Pauline T., Edward M. Chen, & John M. True, *Common Law Privacy: A Limit on an Employer's Power to Test for Drugs,* 12 Geo. Mason U. L. Rev. 651 (1990), 941

_____, *Genetic Discrimination, Genetic Privacy: Rethinking Employee Protections for a Brave New Workplace*, 96 Nw. U. L. Rev. 1497 (2002), 506, 512

_____, *Privacy Rights, Public Policy, and the Employment Relationship,* 57 Ohio St. L.J. 671 (1996), 946, 952

Klosek, Jacqueline, *The War on Privacy* 62 (2007), 1066

Knowlton, Robert, Samuel Dash, & Richard Schwartz, The Eavesdroppers (1959), 295

Komuves, Flavio L., *We've Got Your Number: An Overview of Legislation and Decisions to Control the Use of Social Security Numbers as Personal Identifiers*, 16 J. Marshall J. Computer & Info. L. 529 (1998), 588

Kopp, Kevin P., *Electronic Communications in the Workplace: E-Mail Monitoring and the Right of Privacy,* 8 Seton Hall Const. L.J. 861 (1998), 974

Kornblut, Gerri L., Stephen M. Fogel, & Newton P. Porter, *Survey of the Law on Employee Drug Testing,* 42 U. Miami L. Rev. 553 (1988), 941

Kramer, Irwin R., *The Birth of Privacy Law: A Century Since Warren and Brandeis*, 39 Cath. U. L. Rev. 703 (1990), 12

Kronman, Anthony T., *The Privacy Exemption to the Freedom of Information Act*, 9 J. Legal Stud. 727 (1980), 605

Ku, Raymond Shih Ray, *Think Twice Before You Type*, 163 N.J.L.J. 747 (Feb. 19, 2001), 348

Landau, Susan & Whitfield Diffie, Privacy on the Line: The Politics of Wiretapping and Encryption (1998), 241, 311, 312, 321, 322

Lasswell, Bryan R., *In Defense of False Light: Why False Light Must Remain a Viable Cause of Action*, 34 S. Tex. L. Rev. 149 (1993), 197, 198

Lederman, Doug, U.S. Proposes New Rules on Student Privacy, Inside Higher Ed, March 24, 2008, at www.insidehighered.com/news/2008/03/24/ferpa, 921

Lee, Ronald D. & Paul M. Schwartz, *Beyond the "War on Terrorism": Towards the New Intelligence Network*, 103 Mich. L. Rev. 1446 (2005), 378

Leib, Michael S., *E-Mail and the Wiretap Laws: Why Congress Should Add Electronic Communications to Title II's Statutory Exclusionary Rule and Expressly Reject a "Good Faith" Exception,* 34 Harv. J. Legis. 393 (1997), 974

Lenz, Timothy O., *"Rights Talk" About Privacy in State Courts*, 60 Alb. L. Rev. 1613 (1997), 34

Lessig, Lawrence, Code and Other Laws of Cyberspace (1999), 32, 791

_____, *Privacy and Attention Span*, 89 Geo. L. J. 2063 (2001), 46

Levy, Steven, Crypto: How the Code Rebels Beat the Government-Saving Privacy in the Digital Age (2002), 321

Lewis, Anthony, Make No Law: The Sullivan Case and the First Amendment (1991), 189

Lewis, Caroline Louise, *The Jacob Wetterling Crimes Against Children and Sexually Violent Offender Registration Act: An Unconstitutional Deprivation of the Right to Privacy and Substantive Due Process*, 31 Harv. C.R.-C.L. L. Rev. 89 (1996), 651

Lidsky, Lyrissa Barnett, *Silencing John Doe: Defamation and Discourse in Cyberspace*, 49 Duke L.J. 855 (2000), 554

Lilienfeld, Robert & Joseph Bensman, Between Public and Private: Lost Boundaries of the Self (1979), 56

Lindgren, James, *Unraveling the Paradox of Blackmail,* 84 Colum. L. Rev. 670, 670-71 (1984), 469, 470

Litan, Robert E. & Peter P. Swire, None of Your Business: World Data Flows, Electronic Commerce, and the European Privacy Directive (1998), 38, 1043, 1078, 1085

Litman, Jessica, *Information Privacy/Information Property*, 52 Stan. L Rev. 1283 (2000), 759

Loewy, Arnold H., *The Fourth Amendment as a Device for Protecting the Innocent*, 81 Mich. L. Rev. 1229 (1983), 241

Long, Nicholas Trott, *Privacy in the World of Education: What Hath James Buckley Wrought?,* 46 Rhode Island B.J. 9 (Feb. 1998), 914

Myers, Ken S., *Wikimmunity: Fitting the Communications Decency Act to Wikipedia,* 20 Harv. J.L. & Tech. 163, 188-190 (2006), 185, 186

National Research Council, The Polygraph and Lie Detection (2002), http://www.nap.edu/books/0309084369/html/, 963

Nehf, James P., *Incomparability and the Passive Virtues of Ad Hoc Privacy Policy*, 76 U. Colo. L. Rev. 1, 29-36, 42 (2005), 854, 855

Neier, Aryeh, The Secret Files They Keep on You (1975), 35

Nguyen, Xuan-Thao N., *Collateralizing Privacy,* 78 Tul. L. Rev. 553 (2004), 785

Nieves, Evelyn, *A Festival with Nudity Sues a Sex Web Site,* N.Y. Times, July 5, 2002, 105

Nimmer, Melville B., *The Right of Publicity*, 19 Law & Contemp. Probs. 203 (1954), 206

_____, *The Right to Speak from Times to Time: First Amendment Theory Applied to Libel and Misapplied to Privacy*, 56 Calif. L. Rev. 935 (1968), 142

9/11 Commission, The 9/11 Commission Report (2004), 363, 366, 367, 377, 686, 687

Nissenbaum, Helen, *Privacy as Contextual Integrity,* 79 Wash. L. Rev. 119 (2004), 51

_____, *Protecting Privacy in an Information Age: The Problem of Privacy in Public*, 17 Law & Philosophy 559 (1998), 104, 286

Nock, Steven L., *The Costs of Privacy: Surveillance and Reputation in America* (1993), 702

Nomos XII: Privacy (J. Ronald Pennock & J.W. Chapman, eds., 1971), 64, 517

Norris, Clive & Gary Armstrong, The Maximum Surveillance Society: The Rise of CCTV (1999), 280

Note, *The Right to Privacy in Nineteenth Century America,* 94 Harv. L. Rev. 1892 (1981), 881

Nunziato, Dawn C., *Freedom of Expression, Democratic Norms, and Internet Governance,* 52 Emory L.J. 187 (2003), 557, 558

O'Brien, David, Privacy, Law, and Public Policy (1979), 45

O'Brien, Denis, *The Right to Privacy*, 2 Colum. L. Rev. 486 (1902), 26

Office of the Inspector General, *A Review of the Federal Bureau of Investigation's Use of National Security Letters* x-xiv (March 2007), 876

O'Harrow, Jr., Robert, No Place to Hide (2005), 824, 825

Ohm, Paul K., *Parallel-Effect Statutes and E-mail "Warrants": Reframing the Internet Surveillance Debate,* 72 Geo. Wash. L. Rev. 1599 (2004), 296

Olsen, Frances, *Constitutional Law: Feminist Critiques of the Public/Private Distinction*, 10 Const. Commentary 327 (1993), 76

_____, *The Family and the Market: A Study of Ideology and Legal Reform*, 96 Harv. L. Rev. 1497 (1983), 76

O'Neil, Robert M., The First Amendment and Civil Liability (2001), 142

O'Reilly, James T., *Expanding the Purpose of Federal Records Access: New Private Entitlement or New Threat to Privacy?*, 50 Admin. L. Rev. 371 (1998), 605

Orwell, George, Nineteen Eighty-Four (1949), 233, 234, 280, 516, 760

Packard, Vance, The Naked Society (1964), 35

Papandrea, Mary-Rose, *Under Attack: The Public's Right to Know and the War on Terror,* 25 B.C. Third World L.J.35 (2005), 618

Parker, Laura, *Medical Privacy Law Creates Wide Confusion,* USA Today, Oct. 16, 2003, 437, 438

Peek, Marcy E., Information *Privacy and Corporate Power: Towards a Re-Imagination of Information Privacy Law*, 37 Seton Hall L. Rev. 127, 147-49, 137 (2006), 740

Pember, Donald R., Privacy and the Press (1972), 25

Perrin, Stephanie, Heather H. Black, David H. Flaherty, & T. Murray Rankin, The Personal Information Protection and Electronic Documents Act: An Annotated Guide (2001), 1060

Pew Internet & American Life Project, *Exposed Online: Why the New Federal Health Privacy Regulation Doesn't Offer Much Protection to Internet Users* (Nov. 2001), 433, 441

_____, *The Online Health Care Revolution: How the Web Helps Americans Take Better Care of Themselves* (Nov. 2000), 441

Pierre, Mitchelle C., Note, *New Technology, Old Issues: The All-Digital Hospital and Medical Information Privacy*, 56 Rutgers L. Rev. 541 (2004), 399

Plotkin, Mark J., Juliana M. Spaeth, & Sandra C. Sheets, *Privacy, Eh!: The Impact of Canada's Personal Information Protection and Electronic Documents Act on Transnational Business*, 4 Vand. J. Ent. L. & Prac. 29 (2002), 1060

Plucknett, Theodore F.T., A Concise History of the Common Law (5th ed. 1956), 173

Polakiewicz, J. & V. Jacob-Foltzer, *The European Human Rights Convention in Domestic Law,* 12 Hum. Rts. L.J. 65 (1991), 1005

Porter, Newton P., Stephen M. Fogel, & Gerri L. Kornblut, *Survey of the Law on Employee Drug Testing,* 42 U. Miami L. Rev. 553 (1988), 941

Posner, Eric A. & Adrian Vermeule, *Terror in the Balance: Security, Liberty, and the Courts* 4, 5, 18 (2006), 355

Posner, Richard A., An Economic Theory of Privacy, Regulations (1978), 64

_____, Law, Pragmatism, and Democracy (2003), 354

_____, Not a Suicide Pact: The Constitution in a Time of National Emergency (2006), 355

_____, Overcoming Law (1995), 64

_____, *Privacy, Surveillance, and Law,* 75 U. Chicago L. Rev. — (forthcoming 2008), 711

_____, The Economics of Justice (1981), 32, 63, 64, 149

_____, *The Right of Privacy,* 12 Ga. L. Rev. 393 (1978), 61

_____, *Uncertain Shield* 101-02 (2006), 361

Post, Robert C., *Encryption Source Code and the First Amendment,* 15 Berkeley Tech. L.J. 713 (2000), 321

_____, *Foreword: Fashioning the Legal Constitution: Culture, Courts and Law*, 117 Harv. L. Rev. 4 (2003), 470

_____, *Rereading Warren and Brandeis: Privacy, Property, and Appropriation*, 41 Case W. Res. L. Rev. 647 (1991), 214

_____, *The Social Foundations of Defamation Law: Reputation and the Constitution*, 74 Cal. L. Rev. 691 (1986), 173

_____, *The Social Foundations of Privacy: Community and Self in the Common Law Tort,* 77 Cal. L. Rev. 957 (1989), 27, 106, 119

_____, *Three Concepts of Privacy*, 89 Geo. L.J. 2087 (2001), 41

Poullet, Yves, *The Safe Harbor Principles: an Adequate Protection?* IFCLA International Colloquium, Paris, France (June 2000), 1086, 1087

Pritts, Joy, Janlori Goldman, Zoe Hudson, Aimee Berenson, & Elizabeth Hadley, *The State of Health Privacy: An Uneven Terrain (A Comprehensive Survey of State Health Privacy Statutes)* (1999), http://www.georgetown.edu/research/ihcrp/privacy/ statereport.pdf, 429, 505

Privacy International & Electronic Privacy Information Center, *Privacy and Human Rights* 338, 865 (2006), 1066, 1069

Privacy Rights Clearinghouse, *North Dakota Votes for "Opt-In" Financial Privacy*, June 21, 2002, http://www.privacyrights.org/ar/nd_optin.htm, 742

Prosser, William, *Privacy*, 48 Cal. L. Rev. 383 (1960), 26, 51

Rachels, James, *Why Privacy Is Important,* in *Philosophical Dimensions of Privacy: An Anthology* (Ferdinand David Schoeman, ed., 1984), 45

Rada, Maureen P., Note, *The Buckley Conspiracy: How Congress Authorized the Cover-Up of Campus Crime and How It Can Be Undone,* 59 Ohio St. L.J. 1799 (1998), 914

Radin, Margaret Jane, Contested Commodities (1996), 791

Ramasastry, Anita, *Lost in Translation? Data Mining, National Security, and the "Adverse Inference" Problem*, 22 Santa Clara Computer & High Tech. L.J. 757, 773 (2006), 700, 706

Ranking, T. Murray, Stepahie Perrin, Heather H. Black, & David H. Flaherty, The Personal Information Protection and Electronic Documents Act: An Annotated Guide (2001), 1060

Rao, Radhika, *Property, Privacy, and the Human Body*, 80 B.U. L. Rev. 359 (2000), 504

Ravishankar, Poornima L., Comment, *Planned Parenthood Is Not a Bank: Closing the Clinic Doors to the Fourth Amendment Third Party Doctrine,* 34 Seton Hall L. Rev. 1093 (2004), 488

Ray, Nathan E., *Let There Be False Light: Resisting the Growing Trend Against an Important Tort,* 84 Minn. L. Rev. 713 (2000), 197, 198

Regan, Priscilla M., Legislating Privacy: Technology, Social Values, and Public Policy (1995), 35, 60, 61, 241, 597, 684, 685, 821

Reidenberg, Joel R. & Paul M. Schwartz, Data Privacy Law (1996), 38

_____, *Online Services and Data Protection Law: Regulatory Responses* (EUR-OP:1998), http://europa.eu.int/comm/internal_market/en/dataprot/studies/regul.htm, 913

Reidenberg, Joel R., *E-Commerce and Trans-Atlantic Privacy,* 38 Hous. L. Rev. 717 (2001), 1048, 1079, 1087

_____, *Lex Informatica: The Formulation of Information Policy Rules Through Technology*, 76 Tex. L. Rev. 553 (1998), 790

_____, *Privacy in the Information Economy: A Fortress or Frontier for Individual Rights?*, 44 Fed. Comm. L.J. 195 (1992), 822

_____, *Privacy Wrongs in Search of Remedies,* 54 Hastings L.J. 877 (2003), 786, 787

_____, *Resolving Conflicting International Data Privacy Rules in Cyberspace,* 52 Stan. L. Rev. 1315 (2000), 59

_____, *Restoring Americans' Privacy in Electronic Commerce,* 14 Berkeley J.L. & Tech. 771 (1999), 998

_____, *Setting Standards for Fair Information Practice in the U.S. Private Sector*, 80 Iowa L. Rev. 497 (1995), 761, 995

_____, *The EU Data Protection Directive: Implications for the U.S. Privacy Debate* (2001), http://energycommerce.house.gov/107/hearings/03082001Hearing49/Reidenberg104.htm, 1077, 1078

Reiman, Jeffrey H., *Privacy, Intimacy, and Personhood*, in *Philosophical Dimensions of Privacy: An Anthology* (Ferdinand David Schoeman, ed., 1984), 55, 56

Richards, Neil M., *Reconciling Data Privacy and the First Amendment,* 52 UCLA L. Rev. 1149 (2005), 859, 860

_____, *The Information Privacy Law Project,* 94 Geo. L.J. 1087, 1107-1112 (2006), 451, 452

Richards, Neil M. & Daniel J. Solove, *Privacy's Other Path: Recovering the Law of Confidentiality,* 96 Geo. L.J. 123 (2007), 139, 411, 412, 1018

Risen, James & Eric Lichtblau, *Bush Lets U.S. Spy on Callers Without Courts*, N.Y. Times, Dec. 16. 2005, at A1, 378

Rolfs, Jacqueline K., The Florida Star v. B.J.F.: *The Beginning of the End for the Tort of Public Disclosure*, 1990 Wis. L. Rev. 1107, 155

Rosen, Jeffrey, *A Cautionary Tale for a New Age of Surveillance*, N.Y. Times Magazine (Oct. 7, 2001), 280

_____, *The Naked Crowd: Reclaiming Security and Freedom in an Anxious Age* (2004), 281

_____, *The Unwanted Gaze: The Destruction of Privacy in America* (2000), 46, 976

Rosenhan, D.L., Terri Wolff Teitelbaum, Kathi Weiss Teitelbaum, & Martin Davidson, *Warning Third Parties: The Ripple Effects of Tarasoff,* 24 Pac. L.J. 1165 (1993), 420

Rosenzweig, Paul, *Civil Liberty and the Response to Terrorism,* 42 Duq. L. Rev. 663 (2004), 354, 372

Ross, Jacqueline E., *The Place of Covert Surveillance in Democratic Societies: A Comparative Study of the United States and Germany*, 55 Am. J. Comp. l. 493 (2007), 261

Rotenberg, Marc & Philip E. Agre, eds., Technology and Privacy: The New Landscape (1997), 668, 676, 790

Rotenberg, Marc, ed., *Fair Information Practices and the Architecture of Privacy (What Larry Doesn't Get)*, 2001 Stan. Tech. L. Rev. 1, 36, 556, 657, 822, 823

_____, *In Support of a Data Protection Board in the United States*, 8 Gov't Info. Q. 79-94 (1991), 1057

_____, Letter FTC Commissioner Christine Varney, Dec. 14, 1995, 776

_____, *Privacy and Secrecy After September 11*, 86 Minn. L. Rev. 1115 (2002), 677, 678

_____, Testimony and Statement for the Record on The WIPO Copyright Treaties Implementation Act and Privacy Issues Before the Subcommittee on Telecommunications, Trade, and Consumer Protection, Committee on Commerce, U.S. House of Representatives (June 5, 1998), 576, 577

Rothstein, Mark A., The Law of Medical and Genetic Privacy in the Workplace, in Genetic Secrets: Protecting Privacy and Confidentiality in the Genetic Era (Mark A. Rothstein, ed., 1997), 494, 961

Rozenberg, Joshua, *Privacy and the Press* 15 (2004), 1017

Rubenfeld, Jed, *The Right to Privacy*, 102 Harv. L. Rev. 737, 784 (1989), 454

Rubin, Edward L. & Peter L. Felcher, *Privacy, Publicity, and the Portrayal of Real People by the Media,* 88 Yale L.J. 1577 (1979), 106

Rubinstein, Ira, Ronald D. Lee, & Paul M. Schwartz, *Data Mining and Internet Profiling*, 75 U. Chicago L. Rev. 261 (2008), 689, 711

Salbu, Steven R., *The European Union Data Privacy Directive and International Relations,* 35 Vand. J. Transnat'l L. 655 (2002), 1079, 1086

Samuelson, Pamela, *Privacy as Intellectual Property?*, 52 Stan. L. Rev. 1125 (2000), 791, 792

Sánchez Abril, Patricia, *Recasting Privacy Torts in a Spaceless World,* 21 Harv. J.L. & Tech. 1 (2007), 139

Sanford, Bruce W., Don't Shoot the Messenger: How Our Growing Hatred of the Media Threatens Free Speech for All of Us (1999), 142

_____, Libel and Privacy (2d ed. 1991), 83

Schauer, Frederick, Profiles, Probabilities, and Stereotypes (2003), 700, 701

_____, *Reflections on the Value of Truth*, 41 Case W. Res. L. Rev. 699 (1991), 159

Scheppele, Kim Lane, Legal Secrets: Equality and Efficiency in the Common Law (1988), 65

Schneier, Bruce, Beyond Fear (2003), 687, 688

_____, *REAL ID: Costs and Benefits*, Schneier on Security (Jan. 30, 2007, http://www.schneier.com/blog/archives/2007/01/realid_costs_an.html, 595

Schoeman, Ferdinand D., ed., Philosophical Dimensions of Privacy (1984), 45, 46, 56, 59

Schuck, Peter H. & Daniel J. Givelber, Tarasoff v. Regents of the University of California, Torts Stories 99 (Robert L. Rabin & Stephen D. Sugarman, 2003), 419, 420

Schulhofer, Stephen J., *Some Kind Words for the Privilege Against Self-Incrimination*, 26 Val. U. L. Rev. 311 (1991), 235

Schumacher, Joseph E. & Christopher Slobogin, *Reasonable Expectations of Privacy and Autonomy in Fourth Amendment Cases: An Empirical Look at "Understandings Recognized and Permitted by Society,"* 42 Duke L.J. 727 (1993), 255, 282, 283

Schwartz, Alan U. & Morris L. Ernst, Privacy: The Right to Be Let Alone (1962), 12

Schwartz, Gary T., *Explaining and Justifying a Limited Tort of False Light Invasion of Privacy*, 41 Case W. Res. L. Rev. 885 (1991), 198

Schwartz, Paul M., *Evaluating Telecommunications Surveillance in Germany,* 72 George Washington L. Rev. 1244 (2004), 305

_____, *Free Speech vs. Information Privacy: Eugene Volokh's First Amendment Jurisprudence,* 52 Stan. L. Rev. 1559 (2000), 857, 858

_____, *German and U.S. Telecommunications Privacy Law: Legal Regulation of Domestic Law Enforcement Surveillance,* 54 Hastings L.J. 751 (2003), 305, 308

_____, *Internet Privacy and the State*, 32 Conn L.Rev. 815 (2000), 61, 633

_____, *Privacy and Democracy in Cyberspace*, 52 Vand. L. Rev. 1609 (1999), 54, 761, 821, 822

_____, *Privacy and Participation: Personal Information and Public Sector Regulation in the United States,* 80 Iowa L. Rev. 553 (1995), 38, 474, 668, 675

_____, *Privacy and the Economics of Health Care Information,* 76 Tex. L. Rev. 1 (1997), 400, 508, 509

_____, *Property, Privacy and Personal Data*, 117 Harv. L. Rev. 2055 (2004), 8, 406, 792, 793, 816, 817, 819, 820

Schwartz, Paul M. & Edward Janger, *Notification of Data Security Breaches*, 105 Mich. L. Rev. 913, 924-25 (2007), 826, 827

Schwartz, Paul M., Ira S. Rubinstein & Ronald D. Lee, *Data Mining and Internet Profiling*, 75 U. Chi. L. Rev. 261, 265 (2008), 689, 711

Schwartz, Paul M. & Joel R. Reidenberg, Data Privacy Law (1996), 38

Schwartz, Paul M. & Ronald D. Lee, *Beyond the "War on Terrorism": Towards the New Intelligence Network,* 103 Mich. L. Rev. 1446 (2005), 378

Schwartz, Paul M. & Ted Janger, *The Gramm-Leach-Bliley Act, Information Privacy, and the Limits of Default Rules*, 86 Minn. L. Rev. 1219 (2002), 739, 740

Schwartz, Richard, Samuel Dash, & Robert Knowlton, The Eavesdroppers (1959), 295

Schwarz, Jr., Frederick A.O. & Aziz Z. Huq, *Unchecked and Unbalanced: Presidential Power in a Time of Terror* 23 (2007), 295, 378

Scott, Gini Graham, Mind Your Own Business: The Battle for Personal Privacy (1995), 11

Seidman, Louis Michael & Silas J. Wasserstrom, *The Fourth Amendment as Constitutional Theory*, 77 Geo. L.J. 19 (1988), 237

Seigenthaler, John, *A False Wikipedia "Biography,"* USA Today, Nov. 29, 2005, 185

Shaffer, Gregory, *Globalization and Social Protection: The Impact of EU and International Rules in the Ratcheting Up of U.S. Privacy Standards,* 25 Yale J. Intl. L. 1 (2000), 1087

S.H. Bailey, D.J. Harris, B.L. Jones, Civil Liberties — Cases and Materials (3d ed. 1991), 1004, 1005

Sheets, Sandra C., Juliana M. Spaeth, & Mark J. Plotkin, Privacy, *Eh!: The Impact of Canada's Personal Information Protection and Electronic Documents Act on Transnational Business*, 4 Vand. J. Ent. L. & Prac. 29 (2002), 1060

Shils, Edward, *Privacy: Its Constitution and Vicissitudes*, 31 L. & Contemp. Probs. 281(1966), 39, 45

Sidel, Mark, More Secure, Less Free?: Antiterrorism Policy and Civil Liberties After September 11 (2004), 875

Siegel, Reva B., *"The Rule of Love": Wife Beating as Prerogative and Privacy*, 105 Yale L.J. 2117 (1996), 72, 76

Silverman, Gregory M., *Rise of the Machines: Justice Information Systems and the Question of Public Access to Court Records over the Internet*, 79 Wash. L. Rev. 175 (2004), 602

Silverstein, Mark, Note, *Privacy Rights in State Constitutions: Models for Illinois?*, 1989 U. Ill. L. Rev. 215, 34

Simitis, Spiros, *From the Market to the Polis: The EU Directive on the Protection of Personal Data,* 80 Iowa L. Rev. 445 (1995), 1043

_____, *Reviewing Privacy in an Information Society*, 135 U. Pa. L. Rev. 707 (1987), 56-58

Singh, Simon, The Code: The Evolution of Secrecy from Mary, Queen of Scots to Quantum Cryptography (1999), 321

Singleton, Solveig, *Privacy Versus the First Amendment: A Skeptical Approach,* 11 Fordham Intell. Prop. Media & Ent. L.J. 97 (2000), 157, 169, 853

Sklansky, David A., *Katz v. United States*, in *Criminal Procedure Stories* (Carol S. Steiker, ed., 2006), 255, 257, 258

Slobogin, Christopher & Joseph E. Schumacher, *Reasonable Expectations of Privacy and Autonomy in Fourth Amendment Cases: An Empirical Look at "Understandings Recognized and Permitted by Society,"* 42 Duke L.J. 727 (1993), 255, 282, 283

Slobogin, Christopher, *Public Privacy: Camera Surveillance of Public Places and the Right to Anonymity,* 72 Miss. L.J. 213 (2002), 281, 541, 542

_____, *Subpoenas and Privacy,* 53 DePaul L. Rev. 805 (2005), 862

_____, *Technologically-Assisted Physician Surveillance: The American Bar Association's Tentative Draft Standards*, 10 Harv. J.L. & Tech. 383 (1997), 292

_____, *The World Without a Fourth Amendment*, 39 UCLA L. Rev. 1 (1991), 237

_____, *Why Liberals Should Chuck the Exclusionary Rule*, 1999 U. Ill. L. Rev. 363 (1999), 241

Small, Jane A., *Who Are the People in Your Neighborhood? Due Process, Public Protection, and Sex Offender Notification Laws*, 74 N.Y.U. L. Rev. 1451 (1999), 652

Smith, H. Jeff, *Managing Privacy* (1994), 866

Steinbock, Daniel J., *Data Matching, Data Mining, and Due Process,* 40 Ga. L. Rev. 1, 82-83 (2005), 706, 707

Steinfeld, Lauren B. & Peter P. Swire, *Security and Privacy After September 11: The Health Care Example*, 86 Minn. L. Rev. 1515 (2002), 432

Strahilevitz, Lior Jacob, *A Social Networks Theory of Privacy,* 72 U. Chi. L. Rev. 919 (2005), 114, 115

_____, *Consent, Aesthetics, and the Boundaries of Sexual Privacy after* Lawrence v. Texas, 54 DePaul L. Rev. 671, 678 n.35 (2005), 468

_____, *"How's* My *Driving?" For Everyone (and Everything?)* 81 N.Y.U. L. Rev. 1699, 1706 (2006), 140

Strum, Philippa, Brandeis: Beyond Progressivism (1993), 12

Stuntz, William J., *Implicit Bargains, Government Power, and the Fourth Amendment,* 44 Stan. L. Rev. 553 (1992), 930

_____, *Privacy's Problem and the Law of Criminal Procedure*, 93 Mich. L. Rev. 1016 (1995), 237

_____, *Self-Incrimination and Excuse*, 99 Colum. L. Rev. 1227 (1988), 235

Sullivan, Bob, Your Evil Twin: Behind the Identity Theft Epidemic (2004), 742, 742

Sundby, Scott E., "Everyman's" Fourth Amendment: Privacy or Mutual Trust Between Government and Citizen?, 94 Colum. L. Rev. 1751 (1994), 237

Sundstrom, Scott A., *You've Got Mail (and the Government Knows It): Applying the Fourth Amendment to Workplace E-Mail Monitoring,* 73 N.Y.U. L. Rev. 2064 (1998), 974

Suter, Sonia M., *Disentangling Privacy from Property: Toward a Deeper Understanding of Genetic Privacy,* 72 Geo. Wash. L. Rev. 737 (2004), 504, 505

Swidey, Neil, *A Nation of Voyeurs: How the Internet Search Engine Google Is Changing What We Can Find Out About Each Other and Raising Questions About Whether We Should,* Boston Globe Mag., Feb. 2, 2003, 9

Swire, Peter P., *Financial Privacy and the Theory of High-Tech Government Surveillance,* 77 Wash. U. L.Q. 461 (1999), 716

_____, *Justice Department Opinion Undermines Protection of Medical Privacy* (Jun 7, 2005), http://www.americanprogress.org/site/pp.asp?c =biJRJ8OVF&b =743281, 439, 440

_____, *Katz Is Dead.. Long Live Katz.,* 102 Mich. L. Rev. 904 (2004), 293, 294

_____, *Of Elephants, Mice, and Privacy: International Choice of Law and the Internet,* 32 Int'l L. 991 (1998), 1076, 1077

_____, *The Surprising Virtues of the New Financial Privacy Law*, 86 Minn. L. Rev.1263 (2002), 740, 741

_____, *The System of Foreign Intelligence Surveillance Law,* 72 Geo. Wash. L. Rev. 1306 (2004), 372, 373

_____, *Trustwrap: the Importance of Legal Rules to Electronic Commerce and Internet Privacy*, 54 Hastings L.J. 847 (2003), 788

Swire, Peter P. & Charles H. Kennedy, *State Wiretaps and Electronic Surveillance After September 11,* 54 Hastings L.J. 971 (2003), 308

Swire, Peter P. & Lauren B. Steinfeld, *Security and Privacy After September 11: The Health Care Example*, 86 Minn. L. Rev. 1515 (2002), 432

Swire, Peter P. & Robert E. Litan, None of Your Business: World Data Flows, Electronic Commerce, and the European Privacy Directive (1998), 38, 1043, 1078

Sykes, Charles J., The End of Privacy: Personal Rights in the Surveillance Society (1999), 712, 881

Symposium, Computers, Data Banks, and Individual Privacy, 53 Minn. L. Rev. (1968), 35

_____, *Critical Perspectives on Megan's Law: Protection vs. Privacy*, 13 N.Y.L. Sch. J. Hum. Rts. 1 (1996), 651

_____, *Cyberspace and Privacy — A New Legal Paradigm?*, 52 Stan. L. Rev. 987 (2000), 625

_____, *Data Protection Law and the European Union's Directive: The Challenge for the United States,* 80 Iowa L. Rev. 431 (1995), 1043

_____, *Privacy*, 31 L. & Contemp. Probs. (1966), 35

_____, *The Future of Internet Surveillance Law*, 72 Geo. Wash. L. Rev. (2004), 296

_____, *The Right to Privacy One Hundred Years Later*, 41 Case W. Res. L. Rev. (1991), 12

Synovate, Federal Trade Commission — 2006 Identity Theft Survey Report (Nov. 2007), 743

_____, *Thinking Outside the Box: Considering Transparency, Anonymity, and Pseudonymity as Overall Solutions to the Problems of Information Privacy in the Internet Society,* 58 U. Miami L. Rev. 991 (2004), 565

Zekan Makdisi, June Mary, *Commercial Use of Protected Health Information Under HIPAA's Privacy Rule: Reasonable Disclosure or Disguised Marketing?*, 82 Neb. L. Rev. 741 (2004), 435

Zimmerman, Diane Leehneer, *False Light Invasion of Privacy: The Light That Failed*, 64 N.Y.U. L. Rev. 364 (1989), 198

_____, *Real People in Fiction: Cautionary Words About Troublesome Old Torts Poured into New Jugs*, 51 Brook. L. Rev. 355 (1985), 142

_____, *Requiem for a Heavyweight: A Farewell to Warren and Brandeis's Privacy Tort*, 68 Cornell L. Rev. 291 (1983), 157, 158, 159, 170

INDEX